T0180021

Lecture Notes in Computer Science 600
Edited by G. Goos and J. Hartmanis

J. W. de Bakker C. Huizing
W. P. de Roever G. Rozenberg (Eds.)

Real-Time: Theory in Practice

REX Workshop
Mook, The Netherlands, June 3-7, 1991
Proceedings

Springer-Verlag
Berlin Heidelberg New York
London Paris Tokyo
Hong Kong Barcelona
Budapest

Series Editors

Gerhard Goos
Universität Karlsruhe
Postfach 69 80
Vincenz-Priessnitz-Straße 1
W-7500 Karlsruhe, FRG

Juris Hartmanis
Department of Computer Science
Cornell University
5149 Upson Hall
Ithaca, NY 14853, USA

Volume Editors

J. W. de Bakker
Centre for Mathematics and Computer Science
P. O. Box 4079, 1009 AB Amsterdam, The Netherlands

C. Huizing
Dept. of Mathematics and Computer Science, Technical University of Eindhoven
Den Dolech 2, P. O. Box 513, 5600 MB Eindhoven, The Netherlands

W. P. de Roever
Institute of Computer Science and Practical Mathematics II
Christian-Albrechts-Universität zu Kiel, Preußerstraße 1-9, W-2300 Kiel, FRG

G. Rozenberg
Department of Computer Science, Leiden University
P. O. Box 9512, 2300 RA Leiden, The Netherlands

CR Subject Classification (1991): C.2-3, C.5, D, F.1, F.3-4, G.2

ISBN 3-540-55564-1 Springer-Verlag Berlin Heidelberg New York
ISBN 0-387-55564-1 Springer-Verlag New York Berlin Heidelberg

Printed in Germany

Typesetting: Camera ready by author/editor
Printing and binding: Druckhaus Beltz, Hemsbach/Bergstr.
45/3140-543210 - Printed on acid-free paper

To everything there is a season and a time to every purpose under heaven: (...) a time to cast away stones and a time to gather stones together. *Ecclesiastes* 3:1,5[a]

Preface

In the past decade, the formal theory of specification, verification, and development of real-time programs has grown from work of a few specialised groups to a real "bandwagon". Many eminent research groups have shifted their interests into this direction. Consequently, the research in real-time is now entering established research areas in formal methods, such as process algebra, temporal logic, and model checking. Many dragons that we believed were slain long ago have risen from their ashes in the real-time world. Real-time specification and programming is more detailed and complex and usually more demanding, hence good methodologies and theories with powerful possibilities for abstraction are very much needed. Real-time is pre-eminently the touchstone of your theory. The scope of this research now includes:

Models of time: Time models possess characteristics which may range broadly from partial to total ordering, from referencing to points to intervals, from dense or even continuous to discrete domains, they may differ in the set of allowed operations (on the time domain), and finally time may be linear or branching.

Execution models: The introduction of time gives rise to many specific models, with familiar distinctions such as interleaving versus true concurrency, synchrony versus asynchrony, communication mechanisms, and new aspects such as local versus global clocks and the relation between actions and time (e.g., zero duration actions). Attempts are made to abstract from these specific models and treat them as features within one framework.

Logics: Many different approaches exist to quantify temporal logic, e.g., by means of an explicit clock reference (GCTL, RTTL, XCTL, TPTL) or by introducing bounded operators (METRIC TL).

Languages: We mention OCCAM, Estelle, Esterel as imperative languages, Lustre and Signal as declarative, and Statecharts as a graphical language.

Theories: Proof systems for programming languages have been developed (Timed CSP, OCCAM), but also process algebras have entered the field of real-time theories (Timed CCS, ATP, ACPS).

Analysing the model: Problems ranging from simulation through executable temporal logics to model checking against temporal formulas are investigated.

Applications Digital watches, fighter planes, process control, discrete control of continuous systems are some of the more standard examples.

Apparently, the time was ripe to organise a workshop dedicated solely to the theory of real-time with the purpose of stepping back and viewing the results achieved as well as of considering the directions of the ongoing research. This volume contains the proceedings of such a workshop. We believe that it gives a representative picture of what is going on in this field worldwide, presented by eminent, active researchers. Considering the number of authors from the United States and the quality of their contributions we conclude with pleasure that the theory of real-time is catching on there and that the area is also breaking new ground in the new world. The material presented in this volume was prepared by the lecturers, their co-authors, and some of the observers after the workshop took place - in this way the results of the discussions during the workshop could be reflected in the proceedings. We are very grateful to the lecturers and the other participants for making the workshop a scientific and social success. We wish to thank R. Gerth and R. Koymans for their help in suggesting speakers. We gratefully acknowledge the financial support from our funding agency, the Netherlands National Facility for Informatics (NFI). We thank the Eindhoven University of Technology for the technical organisation of the workshop and its financial support, in particular A. Heijligers for his kind and flexible cooperation. We thank Jozef Hooman, Ron Koymans, and Marieke Munter for their help in the preparation and the local organisation.

The REX project

The REX — **R**esearch and **E**ducation in **C**oncurrent **S**ystems — project investigates syntactic, semantic and proof-theoretic aspects of concurrency. In addition, its objectives are the education of young researchers and, in general, the dissemination of scientific results relating to these themes. REX is a collaborative effort of the Leiden University (G. Rozenberg), the Centre for Mathematics and Computer Science in Amsterdam (J.W. de Bakker), and the Eindhoven University of Technology (W.P. de Roever), representing the areas of syntax, semantics and proof theory, respectively. The project is supported by the Netherlands National Facility for Informatics (NFI); its duration is approximately four years starting in 1988. The educational activities of REX include regular "concurrency days", consisting of tutorial introductions, presentations of research results, and lecture series of visiting professors. The research activities of the REX project include, more specifically:

a) Three subprojects devoted to the themes: syntax of concurrent systems, process theory and the semantics of parallel logic programming languages, high-level specification and refinement of real-time distributed systems.

b) Collaboration with visiting professors and post-doctoral researchers.

c)Workshops and Schools. In 1988 a school/workshop on "Linear Time, Branching Time and Partial Order in Logics and Models for Concurrency" was organised; in 1989 a workshop followed on "Stepwise Refinement of Distributed Systems" and in 1990 one on "Foundations of Object-oriented Languages"(FOOL). The proceedings of these workshops appeared in the LNCS series of the Springer Publishing Company. The workshop "Real-Time: Theory in Practice" continues this series in 1991. In 1992, a workshop is organised on "Semantics: Theory and Applications". The project closes in 1993 with the symposium "A Decade of Concurrency: Highlights and Perspectives", where the accomplishments of the project will be surveyed and a look into the future will be attempted as to (un)expected developments in the theory of concurrency.

April, 1992

J.W. de Bakker
C. Huizing
W.P. de Roever
G. Rozenberg

Contents

An Old-Fashioned Recipe for Real Time

Martín Abadi and Leslie Lamport

Digital Equipment Corporation
130 Lytton Avenue
Palo Alto, California 94301, USA

Abstract. Traditional methods for specifying and reasoning about concurrent systems work for real-time systems. However, two problems arise: the real-time programming version of Zeno's paradox, and circularity in composing real-time assumption/guarantee specifications. Their solutions rest on properties of machine closure and realizability. TLA (the temporal logic of actions) provides a formal framework for the exposition.

1 Introduction

A new class of systems is often viewed as an opportunity to invent a new semantics. A number of years ago, the new class was distributed systems. More recently, it has been real-time systems. The proliferation of new semantics may be fun for semanticists, but developing a practical method for reasoning about systems is a lot of work. It would be unfortunate if every new class of systems required inventing new semantics, along with proof rules, languages, and tools.

Fortunately, no fundamental change to the old methods for specifying and reasoning about systems has been needed for these new classes. It has long been known that the methods originally developed for shared-memory multiprocessing apply equally well to distributed systems [7, 9]. The first application we have seen of a clearly "off-the-shelf" method to a real-time algorithm was in 1983 [13], but there were probably earlier ones. Indeed, the "extension" of an existing temporal logic to real-time programs by Bernstein and Harter in 1981 [6] can be viewed as an application of that logic.

The old-fashioned methods handle real time by introducing a variable, which we call *now*, to represent time. This idea is so simple and obvious that it seems hardly worth writing about, except that few people appear to be aware that it works in practice. We therefore present a brief description of how to apply conventional methods to real-time systems. We also discuss two problems with this approach that seem to have received little attention, and we present new solutions.

The first problem is the real-time programming version of Zeno's paradox. If time becomes an ordinary program variable, then one can inadvertently write programs in which time behaves improperly. An obvious danger is deadlock, where time stops. A more insidious possibility is that time keeps advancing but is bounded, approaching closer and closer to some limit. One way to avoid such "Zeno" behaviors is to place an a priori lower bound on the duration of any action, but this can complicate the representation of some systems. We provide a more general and, we feel, a more natural solution.

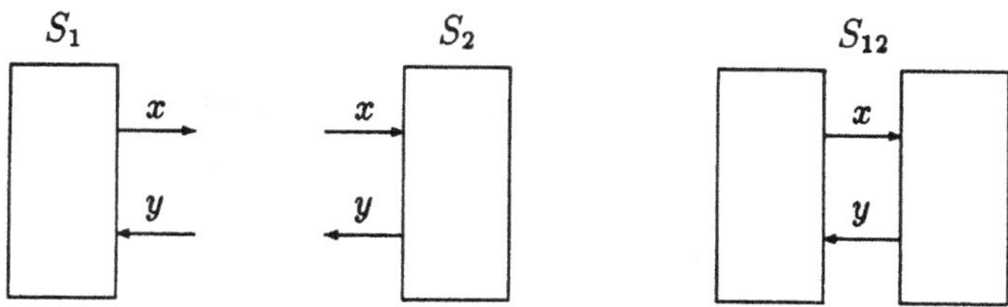

Figure 1: The composition of two systems.

The second problem arises in open system specifications, in which a system is required to operate correctly only under some assumptions on its environment. A modular specification method requires a rule asserting that, if each component behaves correctly in isolation, then it behaves correctly in concert with other components. Consider the two components S_1 and S_2 of Figure 1. Suppose that S_1 guarantees to produce a sequence of outputs on x satisfying P_x assuming it receives a sequence of inputs on y satisfying P_y, and S_2 guarantees to produce a sequence of outputs on y satisfying P_y assuming it receives a sequence of inputs on x satisfying P_x. If P_x and P_y are safety properties, then existing composition principles permit the conclusion that, in the composite system S_{12}, the sequence of values on x and y satisfy P_x and P_y [1]. Now, suppose P_x and P_y both assert that the value 0 is sent by noon. These are safety properties, asserting that the undesirable event of noon passing without a 0 having been sent does not occur. Hence, the composition principle apparently asserts that S_{12} sends 0's along both x and y by noon. However, specifications S_1 and S_2 are satisfied by systems that wait for a 0 to be input, whereupon they immediately output a 0. The composition of those two systems does nothing.

This paradox depends on the ability of a system to respond instantaneously to an input. It is tempting to rule out such systems—perhaps even to outlaw specifications like S_1 and S_2. We show that this Draconian measure is unnecessary. Indeed, if S_2 is replaced by the specification that a 0 must unconditionally be sent over y by noon, then there is no paradox, and the composition does guarantee that a 0 is sent on each wire by noon. All paradoxes disappear when one carefully examines how the specifications must be written.

Our results are relevant for any method whose semantics is based on sequences of states or actions. However, we will describe them only for TLA—the temporal logic of actions [11].

2 Closed Systems

We briefly review here how to represent closed systems in TLA. A closed system is one that is self-contained and does not communicate with an environment. No one intentionally designs autistic systems; in a closed system, the environment is represented as part of the system. Open systems, in which the environment and system are separated, are discussed in Section 4.

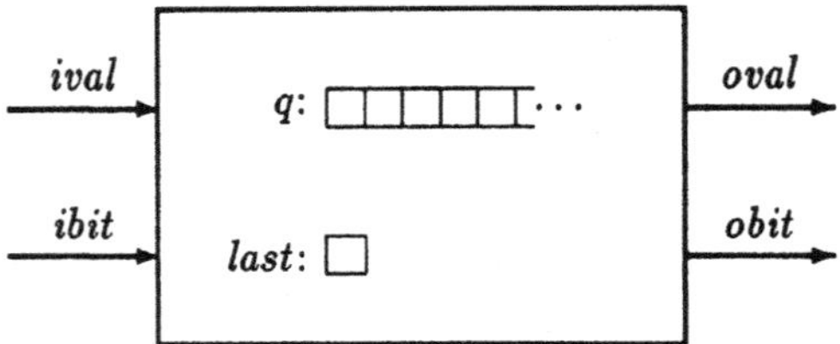

Figure 2: A simple queue.

We begin our review of TLA with an example. Section 2.2 summarizes the formal definitions—a more leisurely exposition can be found in [11]. Section 2.3 reviews the concepts of safety [4] and machine closure [2] (also known as feasibility [5]) and relates them to TLA, and Section 2.4 defines a useful class of history variables [2].

2.1 The Lossy-Queue Example

We introduce TLA with the example of the lossy queue shown in Figure 2. The interface consists of two pairs of "wires", each pair consisting of a *val* wire that holds a message and a boolean-valued *bit* wire. A message m is sent over a pair of wires by setting the *val* wire to m and complementing the *bit* wire. Input to the queue arrives on the wire pair $(ival, ibit)$, and output is sent on the wire pair $(oval, obit)$. There is no acknowledgment protocol, so inputs are lost if they arrive faster than the queue processes them. The property guaranteed by this lossy queue is that the sequence of output messages is a subsequence of the sequence of input messages. In Section 3.1, we add timing constraints to rule out the possibility of lost messages.

The specification of the lossy queue is a TLA formula describing the set of allowed *behaviors* of the queue, where a behavior is the sequence of states produced by an execution. The specification mentions the four variables *ibit*, *obit*, *ival*, and *oval*, as well as two internal variables: q, which equals the sequence of messages received but not yet output; and *last*, which equals the value of *ibit* for the last received message. (The variable *last* is used to prevent the same message from being received twice.) These six variables are *flexible variables*; their values can change during a behavior. We also introduce a *rigid variable* Msg denoting the set of possible messages; it has the same value throughout a behavior. We usually refer to flexible variables simply as variables, and to rigid variables as *constants*.

The TLA specification is shown in Figure 3, using the following notation. A list of formulas prefaced by $\wedge$'s denotes the conjunction of the formulas, and indentation is used to eliminate parentheses. The expression $\langle\langle\,\rangle\rangle$ denotes the empty sequence, $\langle\langle m\rangle\rangle$ denotes the singleton sequence having m as its one element, "$\circ$" denotes concatenation, $Head(\sigma)$ denotes the first element of σ, and $Tail(\sigma)$ denotes the sequence obtained by removing the first element of σ. The symbol "$\triangleq$" means *is defined to equal.*

The first definition is of the *predicate* $Init_Q$, which describes the initial state. This predicate asserts that the values of variables *ibit* and *obit* are arbitrary booleans, the values of *ival* and *oval* are elements of Msg, the values of *last* and *ibit* are equal, and the

$$
\begin{array}{lcl}
Init_Q & \triangleq & \land\ ibit, obit \in \{\mathsf{true}, \mathsf{false}\} \\
 & & \land\ ival, oval \in \mathsf{Msg} \\
 & & \land\ last = ibit \\
 & & \land\ q = \langle\langle\rangle\rangle \\
Inp & \triangleq & \land\ ibit' = \neg ibit \\
 & & \land\ ival' \in \mathsf{Msg} \\
 & & \land\ (obit, oval, q, last)' = (obit, oval, q, last) \\
EnQ & \triangleq & \land\ last \neq ibit \\
 & & \land\ q' = q \circ \langle\langle ival \rangle\rangle \\
 & & \land\ last' = ibit \\
 & & \land\ (ibit, obit, ival, oval)' = (ibit, obit, ival, oval) \\
DeQ & \triangleq & \land\ q \neq \langle\langle\rangle\rangle \\
 & & \land\ oval' = Head(q) \\
 & & \land\ q' = Tail(q) \\
 & & \land\ obit' = \neg obit \\
 & & \land\ (ibit, ival, last)' = (ibit, ival, last) \\
\mathcal{N}_Q & \triangleq & Inp \lor EnQ \lor DeQ \\
v & \triangleq & (ibit, obit, ival, oval, q, last) \\
\Pi_Q & \triangleq & Init_Q \land \Box[\mathcal{N}_Q]_v \\
\Phi_Q & \triangleq & \exists q, last : \Pi_Q
\end{array}
$$

Figure 3: The TLA specification of a lossy queue.

value of q is the empty sequence.

Next is defined the *action* Inp, which describes all state changes that represent the sending of an input message. (Since this is the specification of a closed system, it includes the environment's Inp action.) The first conjunct, $ibit' = \neg ibit$, asserts that the new value of $ibit$ equals the complement of its old value. The second conjunct asserts that the new value of $ival$ is an element of Msg. The third conjunct asserts that the value of the four-tuple $(obit, oval, q, last)$ is unchanged; it is equivalent to the assertion that the value of each of the four variables $obit$, $oval$, q, and $last$ is unchanged. The action Inp is always *enabled*, meaning that, in any state, a new input message can be sent.

Action EnQ represents the receipt of a message by the system. The first conjunct asserts that $last$ is not equal to $ibit$, so the message on the input wire has not yet been received. The second conjunct asserts that the new value of q equals the sequence obtained by concatenating the old value of $ival$ to the end of q's old value. The third conjunct asserts that the new value of $last$ equals the old value of $ibit$. The final conjunct asserts that the values of $ibit$, $obit$, $ival$, and $oval$ are unchanged. Action EnQ is enabled in a state iff (if and only if) the values of $last$ and $ibit$ in that state are unequal.

The action DeQ represents the operation of removing a message from the head of q and sending it on the output wire. It is enabled iff the value of q is not the empty sequence.

The action $\mathcal{N}_Q$ is the specification's *next-state relation*. It describes all allowed changes to the queue system's variables. Since the only allowed changes are the ones described by the actions *Inp*, *EnQ*, and *DeQ*, action $\mathcal{N}_Q$ is the disjunction of those three actions.

In TLA specifications, it is convenient to give a name to the tuple of all relevant variables. Here, we call it v.

Formula Π_Q is the internal specification of the lossy queue—the formula specifying all sequences of values that may be assumed by the queue's six variables, including the internal variables q and *last*. Its first conjunct asserts that $Init_Q$ is true in the initial state. Its second conjunct, $\Box[\mathcal{N}_Q]_v$, asserts that every step is either an $\mathcal{N}_Q$ step (a state change allowed by $\mathcal{N}_Q$) or else leaves v unchanged, meaning that it leaves all six variables unchanged.

Formula Φ_Q is the actual specification, in which the internal variables q and *last* have been hidden. A behavior satisfies Φ_Q iff there is some way to assign sequences of values to q and *last* such that Π_Q is satisfied. The free variables of Φ_Q are *ibit*, *obit*, *ival*, and *oval*, so Φ_Q specifies what sequences of values these four variables can assume. All the preceding definitions just represent one possible way of structuring the definition of Φ_Q; there are infinitely many ways to write formulas that are equivalent to Φ_Q and are therefore equivalent specifications.

TLA is an untyped logic; a variable may assume any value. Type correctness is expressed by the formula $\Box T$, where T is the predicate asserting that all relevant variables have values of the expected "types". For the internal queue specification, the type-correctness predicate is

$$T_Q \triangleq \begin{array}{l} \land\ ibit, obit, last \in \{\mathsf{true}, \mathsf{false}\} \\ \land\ ival, oval \in \mathsf{Msg} \\ \land\ q \in \mathsf{Msg}^* \end{array} \qquad (1)$$

where Msg^* is the set of finite sequences of messages. Type correctness of Π_Q is asserted by the formula $\Pi_Q \Rightarrow \Box T_Q$, which is easily proved [11]. Type correctness of Φ_Q follows from $\Pi_Q \Rightarrow \Box T_Q$ by the usual rules for reasoning about quantifiers.

Formulas Π_Q and Φ_Q are *safety properties*, meaning that they are satisfied by an infinite behavior iff they are satisfied by every finite initial portion of the behavior. Safety properties allow behaviors in which a system performs properly for a while and then the values of all variables are frozen, never to change again. In asynchronous systems, such undesirable behaviors are ruled out by adding *fairness* properties. We could strengthen our lossy-queue specification by conjoining the *weak fairness* property $\mathrm{WF}_v(DeQ)$ and the *strong fairness* property $\mathrm{SF}_v(EnQ)$ to Π_Q, obtaining

$$\exists\, q, last : (Init_Q \land \Box[\mathcal{N}_Q]_v \land \mathrm{WF}_v(DeQ) \land \mathrm{SF}_v(EnQ)) \qquad (2)$$

Property $\mathrm{WF}_v(DeQ)$ asserts that if action *DeQ* is enabled forever, then infinitely many *DeQ* steps must occur. This property implies that every message reaching the queue is eventually output. Property $\mathrm{SF}_v(EnQ)$ asserts that if action *EnQ* is enabled infinitely often, then infinitely many *EnQ* steps must occur. It implies that if infinitely many inputs are sent, then the queue must receive infinitely many of them. The formula (2) implies the *liveness property* [4] that an infinite number of inputs produces an infinite number of outputs. This formula also implies the same safety properties as Φ_Q. A formula such as (2), which is the conjunction of an initial predicate, a term of the form $\Box[\mathcal{A}]_f$, and a fairness property, is said to be in *canonical form*.

2.2 The Semantics of TLA

We begin with some definitions. We assume a set of constant *values*, and we let $[\![F]\!]$ denote the semantic meaning of a formula F.

state A mapping from variables to values. We let $s.x$ denote the value that state s assigns to variable x.

state function An expression formed from variables, constants, and operators. The meaning of a state function is a mapping from states to values. For example, $x + 1$ is a state function such that $[\![x + 1]\!](s)$ equals $s.x + 1$, for any state s.

predicate A boolean-valued state function, such as $x > y + 1$.

transition function An expression formed from variables, primed variables, constants, and operators. The meaning of a transition function is a mapping from pairs of states to values. For example, $x + y' + 1$ is a transition function and $[\![x + y' + 1]\!](s, t)$ equals the value $s.x + t.y + 1$, for any pair of states s, t.

action A boolean-valued transition function, such as $x > (y' + 1)$.

step A pair of states s, t. It is called an $\mathcal{A}$ *step* iff $[\![\mathcal{A}]\!](s, t)$ equals **true**, for an action $\mathcal{A}$. It is called a *stuttering* step iff $s = t$.

f' The transition function obtained from the state function f by priming all the free variables of f, so $[\![f']\!](s, t) = [\![f]\!](t)$ for any states s and t.

$[\mathcal{A}]_f$ The action $\mathcal{A} \vee (f' = f)$, for any action $\mathcal{A}$ and state function f.

$\langle \mathcal{A} \rangle_f$ The action $\mathcal{A} \wedge (f' \neq f)$, for any action $\mathcal{A}$ and state function f.

Enabled $\mathcal{A}$ For any action $\mathcal{A}$, the predicate such that $[\![\mathit{Enabled}\ \mathcal{A}]\!](s)$ equals $\exists t : [\![\mathcal{A}]\!](s, t)$, for any state s.

Informally, we often confuse a formula and its meaning. For example we say that a predicate P is true in state s instead of $[\![P]\!](s) = \mathbf{true}$.

An RTLA (raw TLA) formula is an expression built from actions, classical operators (boolean operators and quantification over rigid variables), and the unary temporal operator $\Box$. The meaning of an RTLA formula is a boolean-valued function on *behaviors*, where a behavior is an infinite sequence of states. The meaning of the operator $\Box$ is defined by

$$[\![\Box F]\!](s_0, s_1, s_2, \ldots) \;\triangleq\; \forall n \geq 0 : [\![F]\!](s_n, s_{n+1}, s_{n+2}, \ldots)$$

Intuitively, $\Box F$ asserts that F is "always" true. The meaning of an action as an RTLA formula is defined in terms of its meaning as an action by letting $[\![\mathcal{A}]\!](s_0, s_1, s_2, \ldots)$ equal $[\![\mathcal{A}]\!](s_0, s_1)$. A predicate P is an action; P is true for a behavior iff it is true for the first state of the behavior, and $\Box P$ is true iff P is true in all states. For any action $\mathcal{A}$ and state function f, the formula $\Box[\mathcal{A}]_f$ is true for a behavior iff each step is an $\mathcal{A}$ step or else leaves f unchanged. The classical operators have their usual meanings.

A TLA formula is one that can be constructed from predicates and formulas $\Box[\mathcal{A}]_f$ using classical operators, $\Box$, and existential quantification over flexible variables. The semantics of actions, classical operators, and $\Box$ are defined as before. The approximate meaning of quantification over a flexible variable is that $\exists x : F$ is true for a behavior iff there is some sequence of values that can be assigned to x that makes F true. The precise definition is in [11]. As usual, we write $\exists\, x_1, \ldots, x_n : F$ instead of $\exists\, x_1 : \ldots, \exists\, x_n : F$.

A *property* is a set of behaviors that is *invariant under stuttering*, meaning that it contains a behavior σ iff it contains every behavior obtained from σ by adding and/or removing stuttering steps. The set of all behaviors satisfying a TLA formula is a property, which we often identify with the formula.

For any TLA formula F, action $\mathcal{A}$, and state function f:

$$\begin{array}{lcl} \Diamond F & \triangleq & \neg\Box\neg F \\ \mathrm{WF}_f(\mathcal{A}) & \triangleq & \Box\Diamond\neg(\mathit{Enabled}\ \langle\mathcal{A}\rangle_f) \ \vee\ \Box\Diamond\langle\mathcal{A}\rangle_f \\ \mathrm{SF}_f(\mathcal{A}) & \triangleq & \Diamond\Box\neg(\mathit{Enabled}\ \langle\mathcal{A}\rangle_f) \ \vee\ \Box\Diamond\langle\mathcal{A}\rangle_f \end{array}$$

These are TLA formulas, since $\Diamond\langle\mathcal{A}\rangle_f$ equals $\neg\Box[\neg\mathcal{A}]_f$.

2.3 Safety and Fairness

A *finite behavior* is a finite sequence of states. We identify the finite behavior $s_0, \ldots, s_n$ with the behavior $s_0, \ldots, s_n, s_n, s_n, \ldots$. A property F is a *safety property* [4] iff the following condition holds: F contains a behavior iff it contains every finite prefix of the behavior. Intuitively, a safety property asserts that something "bad" does not happen. Predicates and formulas of the form $\Box[\mathcal{A}]_f$ are safety properties.

Safety properties form closed sets for a topology on the set of all behaviors. Hence, if two TLA formulas F and G are safety properties, then $F \wedge G$ is also a safety property. The *closure* $\mathcal{C}(F)$ of a property F is the smallest safety property containing F. It can be shown that $\mathcal{C}(F)$ is expressible in TLA, for any TLA formula F.

If Π is a safety property and L an arbitrary property, then the pair (Π, L) is *machine closed* iff every finite behavior satisfying Π can be extended to an infinite behavior satisfying $\Pi \wedge L$. If Π is the set of behaviors allowed by the initial condition and next-state relation of a program, then machine closure of (Π, L) corresponds to the intuitive concept that L is a fairness property of the program. The *canonical form* for a TLA formula is

$$\exists\, x : (\mathit{Init} \ \wedge\ \Box[\mathcal{N}]_v \ \wedge\ L) \tag{3}$$

where $(\mathit{Init} \wedge \Box[\mathcal{N}]_v, L)$ is machine closed and x is a tuple of variables called the *internal variables* of the formula. The state function v will usually be the tuple of all variables appearing free in *Init*, $\mathcal{N}$, and L (including the variables of x). A behavior satisfies (3) iff there is some way of choosing values for x such that (a) *Init* is true in the initial state, (b) every step is either an $\mathcal{N}$ step or leaves all the variables in v unchanged, and (c) the entire behavior satisfies L.

An action $\mathcal{A}$ is said to be a *subaction* of a safety property Π iff for every finite behavior $s_0, \ldots, s_n$ in Π with *Enabled* $\mathcal{A}$ true in state s_n, there exists a state s_{n+1} such that (s_n, s_{n+1}) is an $\mathcal{A}$ step and $s_0, \ldots, s_{n+1}$ is in Π. By this definition, $\mathcal{A}$ is a subaction of $\mathit{Init} \wedge \Box[\mathcal{N}]_v$ iff[1]

$$\mathit{Init} \wedge \Box[\mathcal{N}]_v \ \Rightarrow\ \Box(\mathit{Enabled}\ \mathcal{A} \Rightarrow \mathit{Enabled}\ (\mathcal{A} \wedge [\mathcal{N}]_v))$$

[1] We let $\Rightarrow$ have lower precedence than the other boolean operators.

Two actions $\mathcal{A}$ and $\mathcal{B}$ are *disjoint for* a safety property Π iff no behavior satisfying Π contains an $\mathcal{A} \wedge \mathcal{B}$ step. By this definition, $\mathcal{A}$ and $\mathcal{B}$ are disjoint for $Init \wedge \Box[\mathcal{N}]_v$ iff

$$Init \wedge \Box[\mathcal{N}]_v \;\Rightarrow\; \Box\neg Enabled\;(\mathcal{A} \wedge \mathcal{B} \wedge [\mathcal{N}]_v)$$

The following result shows that the conjunction of WF and SF formulas is a fairness property.

Proposition 1 *If* Π *is a safety property and* L *is the conjunction of a finite or countably infinite number of formulas of the form* $\mathrm{WF}_w(\mathcal{A})$ *and/or* $\mathrm{SF}_w(\mathcal{A})$ *such that each* $\langle\mathcal{A}\rangle_w$ *is a subaction of* Π, *then* (Π, L) *is machine closed.*

In practice, each w will usually be a tuple of variables changed by the corresponding action $\mathcal{A}$, so $\langle\mathcal{A}\rangle_w$ will equal $\mathcal{A}$.[2] In the informal exposition, we often omit the subscript and talk about $\mathcal{A}$ when we really mean $\langle\mathcal{A}\rangle_w$.

Machine closure for more general classes of properties can be proved with the following two propositions. To apply the first, one must prove that $\exists x : \Pi$ is a safety property. By Proposition 2 of [2, page 265], it suffices to prove that Π has finite internal nondeterminism (fin), with x as its internal state component. Here, fin means roughly that there are only a finite number of sequences of values for x that can make a finite behavior satisfy Π.

Proposition 2 *If* (Π, L) *is machine closed,* x *is a tuple of variables that do not occur free in* L, *and* $\exists x : \Pi$ *is a safety property, then* $((\exists x : \Pi), L)$ *is machine closed.*

Proposition 3 *If* (Π, L_1) *is machine closed and* $\Pi \wedge L_1$ *implies* L_2, *then* (Π, L_2) *is machine closed.*

2.4 History-Determined Variables

A *history-determined* variable is one whose current value can be inferred from the current and past values of other variables. For the precise definition, let

$$Hist(h, f, g, v) \;\triangleq\; (h = f) \;\wedge\; \Box[(h' = g) \wedge (v' \neq v)]_{\langle h, v\rangle} \tag{4}$$

where f and v are state functions and g is a transition function. A variable h is a history-determined variable for a formula Π iff Π implies $Hist(h, f, g, v)$, for some f, g, and v such that h does not occur free in f and v, and h' does not occur free in g.

If f and v do not depend on h and g does not depend on h', then $\exists h : Hist(h, f, g, v)$ is identically true. Therefore, if h does not occur free in formula Φ, then $\exists h : (\Phi \wedge Hist(h, f, g, v))$ is equivalent to Φ. In other words, conjoining $Hist(h, f, g, v)$ to Φ does not change the behavior of its variables, so it makes h a "dummy variable" for Φ—in fact, it is a special kind of history variable [2, page 270].

As an example, we add to the lossy queue's specification Φ_Q a history variable hin that records the sequence of values transmitted on the input wire. Let

$$\begin{aligned} H_{in} \;\triangleq\; & \wedge\; hin = \langle\!\langle\,\rangle\!\rangle \\ & \wedge\; \Box[\;\wedge\; hin' = hin \circ \langle\!\langle ival' \rangle\!\rangle \\ & \qquad\;\; \wedge\; (ival, ibit)' \neq (ival, ibit)\;]_{\langle hin, ival, ibit\rangle} \end{aligned} \tag{5}$$

[2]More precisely, $T \wedge \mathcal{A}$ will imply $w' \neq w$, where T is the type-correctness invariant.

H_{in} equals $Hist(hin, \langle\langle\,\rangle\rangle, hin \circ \langle\langle ival' \rangle\rangle, (ival, ibit))$, so hin is a history-determined variable for $\Phi_Q \wedge H_{in}$, and $\exists\, hin : (\Phi_Q \wedge H_{in})$ equals Φ_Q.

If h is a history-determined variable for a property Π, then Π is fin, with h as its internal state component. Hence, if Π is a safety property, then $\exists h : \Pi$ is also a safety property.

3 Real-Time Closed Systems

3.1 Time and Timers

In real-time TLA specifications, real time is represented by the variable *now*. Although it has a special interpretation, *now* is just an ordinary variable of the logic. The value of *now* is always a real number, and it never decreases—conditions expressed by the TLA formula

$$RT \;\triangleq\; (now \in \mathbf{R}) \wedge \Box[now' \in (now, \infty)]_{now}$$

where $\mathbf{R}$ is the set of real numbers and (r, ∞) is $\{t \in \mathbf{R} : t > r\}$.

It is convenient to make time-advancing steps distinct from ordinary program steps. This is done by strengthening the formula RT to

$$RT_v \;\triangleq\; (now \in \mathbf{R}) \;\wedge\; \Box[(now' \in (now, \infty)) \;\wedge\; (v' = v)]_{now}$$

This property differs from RT only in asserting that v does not change when *now* advances. Thus, RT_v is equivalent to $RT \wedge \Box[now' = now]_v$, and

$$Init \wedge \Box[\mathcal{N}]_v \wedge RT_v \;=\; Init \wedge \Box[\mathcal{N} \wedge (now' = now)]_v \wedge RT$$

Real-time constraints are imposed by using *timers* to restrict the increase of *now*. A *timer for* Π is a state function t such that Π implies $\Box(t \in \mathbf{R} \cup \{\pm\infty\})$. Timer t is used as an upper-bound timer by conjoining the formula

$$MaxTime(t) \;\triangleq\; (now \leq t) \wedge \Box[now' \leq t']_{now}$$

to a specification. This formula asserts that *now* is never advanced past t. Timer t is used as a lower-bound timer for an action $\mathcal{A}$ by conjoining the formula

$$MinTime(t, \mathcal{A}, v) \;\triangleq\; \Box[\mathcal{A} \Rightarrow (t \leq now)]_v$$

to a specification. This formula asserts that an $\langle \mathcal{A} \rangle_v$ step cannot occur when *now* is less than t.[3]

A common type of timing constraint asserts that an $\mathcal{A}$ step must occur within δ seconds of when the action $\mathcal{A}$ becomes enabled, for some constant δ. After an $\mathcal{A}$ step, the next $\mathcal{A}$ step must occur within δ seconds of when action $\mathcal{A}$ is re-enabled. There are at least two reasonable interpretations of this requirement.

---

[3]Unlike the usual timers in computer systems that represent an increment of time, our timers represent an absolute time. To allow the type of strict time bound that would be expressed by replacing $\leq$ with $<$ in the definition of *MaxTime* or *MinTime*, we could introduce, as additional possible values for timers, the set of all "infinitesimally shifted" real numbers r^-, where $t \leq r^-$ iff $t < r$, for any reals t and r.

The first interpretation is that the $\mathcal{A}$ step must occur if $\mathcal{A}$ has been continuously enabled for δ seconds. This is expressed by $MaxTime(t)$ when t is a state function satisfying

$$
\begin{array}{rcl}
VTimer(t, A, \delta, v) & \triangleq & \wedge\ t = \textbf{if } Enabled\ \langle \mathcal{A} \rangle_v \textbf{ then } now + \delta \\
& & \qquad\qquad\qquad\qquad\quad \textbf{else } \infty \\
& & \wedge\ \Box[\wedge\ t' = \textbf{if } (Enabled\ \langle \mathcal{A} \rangle_v)' \\
& & \qquad\qquad \textbf{then if } \langle \mathcal{A} \rangle_v \vee \neg Enabled\ \langle \mathcal{A} \rangle_v \\
& & \qquad\qquad\qquad \textbf{then } now + \delta \\
& & \qquad\qquad\qquad \textbf{else } t \\
& & \qquad\qquad \textbf{else } \infty \\
& & \quad \wedge\ v' \neq v\ ]_{(t,v)}
\end{array}
$$

Such a t is called a *volatile δ-timer.*

Another interpretation of the timing requirement is that an $\mathcal{A}$ step must occur if $\mathcal{A}$ has been enabled for a total of δ seconds, though not necessarily continuously enabled. This is expressed by $MaxTime(t)$ when t satisfies

$$
\begin{array}{rcl}
PTimer(t, A, \delta, v) & \triangleq & \wedge\ t = now + \delta \\
& & \wedge\ \Box[\wedge\ t' = \textbf{if } Enabled\ \langle \mathcal{A} \rangle_v \\
& & \qquad\qquad \textbf{then if } \langle \mathcal{A} \rangle_v \textbf{ then } now + \delta \\
& & \qquad\qquad\qquad\qquad\quad \textbf{else } t \\
& & \qquad\qquad \textbf{else } t + (now' - now) \\
& & \quad \wedge\ (v, now)' \neq (v, now)\ ]_{(t,v,now)}
\end{array}
$$

Such a t is called a *persistent δ-timer.* We can use δ-timers as lower-bound timers as well as upper-bound timers.

Observe that $VTimer(t, \mathcal{A}, \delta, v)$ has the form $Hist(t, f, g, v)$ and $PTimer(t, \mathcal{A}, \delta, v)$ has the form $Hist(t, f, g, (v, now))$, where $Hist$ is defined by (4). Thus, if formula Π implies that a variable t satisfies either of these formulas, then t is a history-determined variable for Π.

As an example of the use of timers, we make the lossy queue of Section 2.1 nonlossy by adding the following timing constraints.

- Values must be put on a wire at most once every δ_{snd} seconds. There are two conditions—one on the input wire and one on the output wire. They are expressed by using δ_{snd}-timers t_{Inp} and t_{DeQ}, for the actions Inp and DeQ, as lower-bound timers.

- A value must be added to the queue at most Δ_{rcv} seconds after it appears on the input wire. This is expressed by using a Δ_{rcv}-timer T_{EnQ}, for the enqueue action, as an upper-bound timer.

- A value must be sent on the output wire within Δ_{snd} seconds of when it reaches the head of the queue. This is expressed by using a Δ_{snd}-timer T_{DeQ}, for the dequeue action, as an upper-bound timer.

The timed queue will be nonlossy if $\Delta_{rcv} < \delta_{snd}$. In this case, we expect the Inp, EnQ, and DeQ actions to remain enabled until they are "executed", so it doesn't matter whether we use volatile or persistent timers. We use volatile timers because they are a little easier to reason about.

The timed version Π^t_Q of the queue's internal specification Π_Q is obtained by conjoining the timing constraints to Π_Q:

$$\begin{aligned}\Pi^t_Q \;\triangleq\; & \land\, \Pi_Q \,\land\, RT_v \\ & \land\, VTimer(t_{Inp}, Inp, \delta_{snd}, v) \,\land\, MinTime(t_{Inp}, Inp, v) \\ & \land\, VTimer(t_{DeQ}, DeQ, \delta_{snd}, v) \,\land\, MinTime(t_{DeQ}, DeQ, v) \\ & \land\, VTimer(T_{EnQ}, EnQ, \Delta_{rcv}, v) \,\land\, MaxTime(T_{EnQ}) \\ & \land\, VTimer(T_{DeQ}, DeQ, \Delta_{snd}, v) \,\land\, MaxTime(T_{DeQ})\end{aligned} \tag{6}$$

The external specification Φ^t_Q of the timed queue is obtained by existentially quantifying first the timers and then the variables q and $last$.

Formula Π^t_Q of (6) is not in the canonical form for a TLA formula. A straightforward calculation, using the type-correctness invariant (1) and the equivalence of $(\Box F) \land (\Box G)$ and $\Box(F \land G)$, converts the expression (6) for Π^t_Q to the canonical form given in Figure 4.[4] Observe how each subaction $\mathcal{A}$ of the original formula has a corresponding timed version $\mathcal{A}^t$. Action $\mathcal{A}^t$ is obtained by conjoining $\mathcal{A}$ with the appropriate relations between the old and new values of the timers. If $\mathcal{A}$ has a lower-bound timer, then $\mathcal{A}^t$ also has a conjunct asserting that it is not enabled when now is less than this timer. (The lower-bound timer t_{Inp} for Inp does not affect the enabling of other subactions because Inp is disjoint from all other subactions; a similar remark applies to the lower-bound timer t_{DeQ}.) There is also a new action, $QTick$, that advances now.

Formula Π^t_Q is the TLA specification of a program that satisfies each maximum-delay constraint by preventing now from advancing before the constraint has been satisfied. Thus, the program "implements" timing constraints by stopping time, an apparent absurdity. However, the absurdity results from thinking of a TLA formula, or the abstract program that it represents, as a *prescription of how* something is accomplished. A TLA formula is really a *description of what* is supposed to happen. Formula Π^t_Q says only that an action occurs before now reaches a certain value. It is just our familiarity with ordinary programs that makes us jump to the conclusion that now is being changed by the system.

3.2 Reasoning About Time

Formula Π^t_Q is a safety property; it is satisfied by a behavior in which no variables change values. In particular, it allows behaviors in which time stops. We can rule out such behaviors by conjoining to Π^t_Q the liveness property

$$NZ \;\triangleq\; \forall t \in \mathbf{R} : \Diamond(now > t)$$

which asserts that now gets arbitrarily large. However, when reasoning only about real-time properties, this is not necessary. For example, suppose we want to show that our timed queue satisfies a real-time property expressed by formula Ψ^t, which is also a safety

[4] Further simplification of this formula is possible, but it requires an invariant. In particular, the fourth conjunct of DeQ^t can be replaced by $T'_{EnQ} = T_{EnQ}$.

$$
\begin{array}{lcl}
Init_Q^t & \triangleq & \land\ Init_Q \\
 & & \land\ now \in \mathbf{R} \\
 & & \land\ t_{Inp} = now + \delta_{snd} \\
 & & \land\ t_{DeQ} = T_{EnQ} = T_{DeQ} = \infty \\
Inp^t & \triangleq & \land\ Inp \\
 & & \land\ t_{Inp} \leq now \\
 & & \land\ t'_{Inp} = now' + \delta_{snd} \\
 & & \land\ T'_{EnQ} = \textbf{if } last' \neq ibit' \textbf{ then } now' + \Delta_{rcv} \textbf{ else } \infty \\
 & & \land\ (t_{DeQ}, T_{DeQ})' = \textbf{if } q = \langle\!\langle\,\rangle\!\rangle \textbf{ then } (\infty, \infty) \textbf{ else } (t_{DeQ}, T_{DeQ}) \\
 & & \land\ now' = now \\
EnQ^t & \triangleq & \land\ EnQ \\
 & & \land\ T'_{EnQ} = \infty \\
 & & \land\ (t_{DeQ}, T_{DeQ})' = \textbf{if } q = \langle\!\langle\,\rangle\!\rangle \textbf{ then } (now + \delta_{snd},\ now + \Delta_{snd}) \\
 & & \qquad\qquad\qquad\qquad\qquad\qquad\quad \textbf{else } \ (t_{DeQ}, T_{DeQ}) \\
 & & \land\ (t_{Inp}, now)' = (t_{Inp}, now) \\
DeQ^t & \triangleq & \land\ DeQ \\
 & & \land\ t_{DeQ} \leq now \\
 & & \land\ (t_{DeQ}, T_{DeQ})' = \textbf{if } q' = \langle\!\langle\,\rangle\!\rangle \textbf{ then } (\infty, \infty) \\
 & & \qquad\qquad\qquad\qquad\qquad\qquad\quad \textbf{else } \ (now + \delta_{snd},\ now + \Delta_{snd}) \\
 & & \land\ T'_{EnQ} = \textbf{if } last' = ibit' \textbf{ then } \infty \textbf{ else } T_{EnQ} \\
 & & \land\ (t_{Inp}, now)' = (t_{Inp}, now) \\
QTick & \triangleq & \land\ now' \in (now, \min(T_{DeQ}, T_{EnQ})] \\
 & & \land\ (v, t_{Inp}, t_{DeQ}, T_{DeQ}, T_{EnQ})' = (v, t_{Inp}, t_{DeQ}, T_{DeQ}, T_{EnQ}) \\
vt & \triangleq & (v, now, t_{Inp}, t_{DeQ}, T_{DeQ}, T_{EnQ}) \\
\Pi_Q^t & \triangleq & \land\ Init_Q^t \\
 & & \land\ \Box[Inp^t \lor EnQ^t \lor DeQ^t \lor QTick]_{vt}
\end{array}
$$

Figure 4: The canonical form for Π_Q^t, where $(r, s]$ denotes the set of reals u such that $r < u \leq s$.

property. If Π_Q^t implies Ψ^t, then $\Pi_Q^t \wedge NZ$ implies $\Psi^t \wedge NZ$. Conversely, we don't expect conjoining a liveness property to add safety properties; if $\Pi_Q^t \wedge NZ$ implies Ψ^t, then Π_Q^t by itself should imply Ψ^t—a point discussed in Section 3.3 below. Hence, there is no need to introduce the liveness property NZ.

A safety property we might want to prove for the timed queue is that it does not lose any inputs. To express this property, let *hin* be the history variable, determined by H_{in} of (5), that records the sequence of input values; and let *hout* and H_{out} be the analogous history variable and property for the outputs. The assertion that the timed queue loses no inputs is expressed by

$$\Pi_Q^t \wedge H_{in} \wedge H_{out} \;\Rightarrow\; \Box(hout \preceq hinp)$$

where $\alpha \preceq \beta$ iff α is an initial prefix of β. This is a standard invariance property. The usual method for proving such properties leads to the following invariant

$$\begin{array}{l}
\wedge\; T_Q \;\wedge\; (t_{Inp}, now \in \mathbf{R}) \;\wedge\; (T_{EnQ}, t_{DeQ}, T_{DeQ} \in \mathbf{R} \cup \{\infty\}) \\
\wedge\; now \leq \min(T_{EnQ}, T_{DeQ}) \\
\wedge\; (last = ibit) \;\Rightarrow\; (T_{EnQ} = \infty) \;\wedge\; (hinp = hout \circ q) \\
\wedge\; (last \neq ibit) \;\Rightarrow\; (T_{EnQ} < t_{Inp}) \;\wedge\; (hinp = hout \circ q \circ \langle\!\langle ival \rangle\!\rangle) \\
\wedge\; (q = \langle\!\langle\,\rangle\!\rangle) \;\equiv\; (T_{DeQ} = \infty)
\end{array}$$

and to the necessary assumption $\Delta_{rcv} < \delta_{snd}$. (Recall that T_Q is the type-correctness predicate (1) for Π_Q.)

Property NZ is needed to prove that real-time properties imply liveness properties. The desired liveness property for the timed queue is that the sequence of input messages up to any point eventually appears as the sequence of output messages. It is expressed in TLA by

$$\Pi_Q^t \wedge NZ \;\Rightarrow\; \forall \sigma : \Box((hinp = \sigma) \Rightarrow \Diamond(hout = \sigma))$$

This formula is proved by first showing

$$\Pi_Q^t \wedge NZ \;\Rightarrow\; \mathrm{WF}_v(EnQ) \wedge \mathrm{WF}_v(DeQ) \tag{7}$$

and then using a standard TLA liveness argument to prove

$$\Pi_Q^t \wedge \mathrm{WF}_v(EnQ) \wedge \mathrm{WF}_v(DeQ) \;\Rightarrow\; \forall \sigma : \Box((hinp = \sigma) \Rightarrow \Diamond(hout = \sigma))$$

The proof that $\Pi_Q^t \wedge NZ$ implies $\mathrm{WF}_v(EnQ)$ is by contradiction. Assume EnQ is forever enabled but never occurs. An invariance argument then shows that Π_Q^t implies that T_{EnQ} forever equals its current value, preventing *now* from advancing past that value; and this contradicts NZ. The proof that $\Pi_Q^t \wedge NZ$ implies $\mathrm{WF}_v(DeQ)$ is similar.

3.3 The NonZeno Condition

The timed queue specification Π_Q^t asserts that a DeQ action must occur between δ_{snd} and Δ_{snd} seconds of when it becomes enabled. What if $\Delta_{snd} < \delta_{snd}$? If an input occurs, it eventually is put in the queue, enabling DeQ. At that point, the value of *now* can never become more than Δ_{snd} greater than its current value, so the program eventually reaches a "time-blocked state". In a time-blocked state, only the *QTick* action can be enabled, and it cannot advance *now* past some fixed time. In other words, eventually a state is reached in which every variable other than *now* remains the same, and *now* either remains the same or keeps advancing closer and closer to some upper bound.

We can attempt to correct such pathological specifications by requiring that *now* increase without bound. This is easily done by conjoining the liveness property *NZ* to the safety property Π^t_Q, but that doesn't accomplish anything. Since $\Pi^t_Q \wedge NZ$ rules out behaviors in which *now* is bounded, it allows only behaviors in which there is no input, if $\Delta_{snd} < \delta_{snd}$. Such a specification is no better than the original specification Π^t_Q. The fact that the safety property allows the possibility of reaching a time-blocked state indicates an error in the specification. One does not add timing constraints on output actions with the intention of forbidding input.

We call a safety property *Zeno* if it allows the system to reach a state from which *now* must remain bounded. More precisely, a safety property Π is *nonZeno* iff every finite behavior satisfying Π can be completed to an infinite behavior satisfying Π in which *now* increases without bound. In other words, Π is nonZeno iff the pair (Π, NZ) is machine closed. NonZenoness means that the liveness property *NZ* cannot help in proving safety properties.[5] The following result is used to prove that a real-time specification written in terms of δ-timers is nonZeno.

Theorem 1 *Let*

- Π *be a safety property.*
- t_i *and* T_j *be timers for* Π *and let* $\mathcal{A}_k$ *be an action, for all* $i \in I$, $j \in J$, *and* $k \in I \cup J$, *where* I *and* J *are sets, with* J *finite.*
- $\Pi^t \triangleq \Pi \wedge RT_v \wedge \forall i \in I : MinTime(t_i, \mathcal{A}_i, v) \wedge \forall j \in J : MaxTime(T_j)$

If 1. $\langle \mathcal{A}_i \rangle_v$ *and* $\langle \mathcal{A}_j \rangle_v$ *are disjoint for* Π, *for all* $i \in I$ *and* $j \in J$ *with* $i \neq j$.

2. (a) *now does not occur free in* v.

   (b) $(now' = r) \wedge (v' = v)$ *is a subaction of* Π, *for all* $r \in \mathbf{R}$.

3. *For all* $j \in J$:

   (a) $\langle \mathcal{A}_j \rangle_v \wedge (now' = now)$ *is a subaction of* Π.

   (b) $\Pi \Rightarrow VTimer(T_j, \mathcal{A}_j, \Delta_j, v)$ *or*
   $\Pi \Rightarrow PTimer(T_j, \mathcal{A}_j, \Delta_j, v)$, *where* $\Delta_j \in (0, \infty)$.

   (c) $\Pi^t \Rightarrow \Box(Enabled\ \langle \mathcal{A}_j \rangle_v = Enabled\ (\langle \mathcal{A}_j \rangle_v \wedge (now' = now)))$

4. $\Pi^t \Rightarrow \Box(t_k \leq T_k)$, *for all* $k \in I \cap J$.

then (Π^t, NZ) *is machine closed*

[5] An arbitrary property Π is nonZeno iff $(\mathcal{C}(\Pi), \Pi \wedge NZ)$ is machine closed. We restrict our attention to real-time constraints for safety specifications.

We can apply the theorem to prove that the specification Π_Q^t is nonZeno if $\delta_{snd} \leq \Delta_{snd}$ by substituting

$$\begin{aligned}\Pi_Q \ \wedge\ &VTimer(t_{Inp}, Inp, \delta_{snd}, v) \ \wedge\ VTimer(t_{DeQ}, DeQ, \delta_{snd}, v)\\ &\wedge\ VTimer(T_{EnQ}, EnQ, \Delta_{rcv}, v) \ \wedge\ VTimer(T_{DeQ}, DeQ, \Delta_{snd}, v)\end{aligned}$$

for Π, so Π^t equals Π_Q^t. The hypotheses of the theorem are checked as follows.

1. The actions $\langle Inp\rangle_v$, $\langle DeQ\rangle_v$, and $\langle EnQ\rangle_v$ are pairwise disjoint, so they are pairwise disjoint for Π_Q^t. (Two actions are said to be disjoint if their conjunction equals **false**.)
2. (a) Trivially satisfied.

   (b) Intuitively, this asserts that Π allows an arbitrary change to *now* when v remains unchanged, which holds because neither Π_Q nor the *VTimer* formulas constrain *now*. Formally, the hypothesis asserts that *Enabled* $((now' = r) \wedge (v' = v))$ implies *Enabled* $(\mathcal{M} \wedge (now' = r) \wedge (v' = v))$, for any $r \in \mathbf{R}$, where $\mathcal{M}$ is the conjunction of $[\mathcal{N}_Q]_v$ and the *VTimer* actions. The definitions of $\mathcal{N}_Q$ and *VTimer* imply that now' does not occur in $\mathcal{M}$, from which it follows that both *Enabled* predicates equal **true**. (The hypothesis would also hold if persistent instead of volatile Δ-timers had been used, but a rigorous proof is a bit more complicated.)
3. (a) Actions $\langle Inp\rangle_v$, $\langle DeQ\rangle_v$, and $\langle EnQ\rangle_v$ imply $\mathcal{N}_Q$, so they are subactions of Π_Q. Since these three actions have no primed variables in common with the *VTimer* formulas, they are subactions of Π. The hypothesis then follows because now' does not occur in the *VTimer* formulas. (Again, the hypothesis is true for persistent timers, but the proof is more involved.)

   (b) Immediate from the definition of Π.

   (c) Holds because now' does not occur in the actions *Inp*, *DeQ*, and *EnQ*.
4. Follows from the general result that $\delta \leq \Delta$ implies

   $$RT_v \ \wedge\ VTimer(t, \mathcal{A}, \delta, v) \ \wedge\ VTimer(T, \mathcal{A}, \Delta, v) \ \Rightarrow\ \Box(t \leq T)$$

   which is proved by a simple invariance argument. (The analogous result holds for persistent timers.)

Theorem 1 can be generalized in two ways. First, J can be infinite—if Π^t implies that only a finite number of actions $\mathcal{A}_j$ with $j \in J$ are enabled before time r, for any $r \in \mathbf{R}$. For example, by letting $\mathcal{A}_j$ be the action that sends message number j, we can apply the theorem to a program that sends messages number 1 through n at time n, for every integer n. This program is nonZeno even though the number of actions per second that it performs is unbounded. Second, we can extend the theorem to the more general class of timers obtained by letting the Δ_j be arbitrary real-valued state functions, rather than just constants—if all the Δ_j are bounded from below by a positive constant Δ.

Theorem 1 is proved using Propositions 1 and 3 and ordinary TLA reasoning. By these propositions, it suffices to display a formula L that is the conjunction of fairness conditions on subactions of Π^t such that $\Pi^t \wedge L$ implies NZ. A suitable L is defined by

$$\begin{array}{lcl}
\mathcal{A}_j^t & \triangleq & (now' = now) \wedge (\textbf{if } j \in I \textbf{ then } \mathcal{A}_j \wedge (now \geq t_j) \textbf{ else } \mathcal{A}_j) \\
J_E & \triangleq & \{j \in J : \mathit{Enabled}\ \langle \mathcal{A} \rangle_j\} \\
T & \triangleq & \min(now + \min_{j \in J} \Delta_j,\ \min_{j \in J_E} T_j) \\
\mathcal{B} & \triangleq & ((now = T) \wedge \mathcal{A}_j^t) \vee ((now \neq T) \wedge (now' = T) \wedge (v' = v)) \\
L & \triangleq & \mathrm{WF}_{(now, v)}(\mathcal{B})
\end{array}$$

We omit the proof.

Most nonaxiomatic approaches, including both real-time process algebras and more traditional programming languages with timing constraints, essentially use δ-timers for actions. Hence, our theorem implies that they automatically yield nonZeno specifications.

Theorem 1 does not cover all situations of interest. For example, one can require of our timed queue that the first value appear on the output line within ϵ seconds of when it is placed on the input line. This effectively places an upper bound on the sum of the times needed for performing the EnQ and DeQ actions; it cannot be expressed with δ-timers on individual actions. For these general timing constraints, nonZenoness must be proved for the individual specification. The method of proof is the same as we used to prove Theorem 1: we add to the timed program Π^t a liveness property L that is the conjunction of any fairness properties we like, including fairness of the action that advances now, and prove that $\Pi^t \wedge L$ implies NZ. NonZenoness then follows from Propositions 1 and 3.

There is another possible approach to proving nonZenoness. One can make granularity assumptions—lower bounds both on the amount by which now is incremented and on the minimum delay for each action. Under these assumptions, nonZenoness is equivalent to the absence of deadlock, which can be proved by existing methods. Granularity assumptions are probably adequate—after all, what harm can come from pretending that nothing happens in less than 10^{-100} nanoseconds? However, they can be unnatural and cumbersome. For example, distributed algorithms often assume that only message delays are significant, so the time required for local actions is ignored. The specification of such an algorithm should place no lower bound on the time required for a local action, but that would violate any granularity assumptions. We believe that any proof of deadlock freedom based on granularity can be translated into a proof of nonZenoness using the method outlined above.

So far, we have been discussing nonZenoness of the internal specification, where both the timers and the system's internal variables are visible. Timers are defined by adding history-determined variables, so existentially quantifying over them preserves nonZenoness by Proposition 2. We expect most specifications to be fin [2, page 263], so nonZenoness will also be preserved by existentially quantifying over the system's internal variables. This is the case for the timed queue.

3.4 An Example: Fischer's Protocol

As another example of real-time closed systems, we treat a simplified version of a real-time mutual exclusion protocol proposed by Michael Fischer [10, page 2]. The example was

$$
\begin{array}{lcl}
Init_F & \triangleq & \forall i \in \mathsf{Proc} : pc[i] = \text{“a”} \\
Go(i, u, v) & \triangleq & \begin{array}{l} \land\ pc[i] = u \\ \land\ pc'[i] = v \\ \land\ \forall j \in \mathsf{Proc} : (j \neq i) \Rightarrow (pc'[j] = pc[j]) \end{array} \\
\mathcal{A}_i & \triangleq & Go(i, \text{“a”}, \text{“b”}) \land (x = x' = 0) \\
\mathcal{B}_i & \triangleq & Go(i, \text{“b”}, \text{“c”}) \land (x' = i) \\
\mathcal{C}_i & \triangleq & Go(i, \text{“c”}, \text{“cs”}) \land (x = x' = i) \\
\mathcal{N}_F & \triangleq & \exists i \in \mathsf{Proc} : (\mathcal{A}_i \lor \mathcal{B}_i \lor \mathcal{C}_i) \\
\Pi_F & \triangleq & Init_F \land \Box[\mathcal{N}_F]_{(x,pc)} \\
\Pi_F^t & \triangleq & \begin{array}{l} \land\ \Pi_F \land RT_{(x,pc)} \\ \land\ \forall i \in \mathsf{Proc} : \begin{array}{l} \land\ VTimer(T_b[i], \mathcal{B}_i, \Delta_b, (x, pc)) \\ \land\ MaxTime(T_b[i]) \end{array} \\ \land\ \forall i \in \mathsf{Proc} : \begin{array}{l} \land\ VTimer(t_c[i], Go(i, \text{“c”}, \text{“cs”}), \delta_c, (x, pc)) \\ \land\ MinTime(t_c[i], \mathcal{C}_i, (x, pc)) \end{array} \end{array} \\
\Phi_F^t & \triangleq & \exists T_b, t_c : \Pi_F^t
\end{array}
$$

Figure 5: The TLA specification of Fischer's real-time mutual exclusion protocol.

suggested by Fred Schneider [14]. The protocol consists of each process i executing the following code, where angle brackets denote instantaneous atomic actions:

$$
\begin{array}{rl}
a: & \textbf{await}\ \langle x = 0 \rangle; \\
b: & \langle x := i \rangle; \\
c: & \textbf{await}\ \langle x = i \rangle; \\
cs: & \text{critical section}
\end{array}
$$

There is a maximum delay Δ_b between the execution of the test in statement a and the assignment in statement b, and a minimum delay δ_c between the assignment in statement b and the test in statement c. The problem is to prove that, with suitable conditions on Δ_b and δ_c, this protocol guarantees mutual exclusion (at most one process can enter its critical section).

As written, Fischer's protocol permits only one process to enter its critical section one time. The protocol can be converted to an actual mutual exclusion algorithm. The correctness proof of the protocol is easily extended to a proof of such an algorithm.

The TLA specification of the protocol is given in Figure 5. The formula Π_F describing the untimed version is standard TLA. We assume a finite set Proc of processes. Variable x represents the program variable x, and variable pc represents the control state. The value of pc will be an array indexed by Proc, where $pc[i]$ equals one of the strings “a”, “b”, “c”, “cs” when control in process i is at the corresponding statement. The initial predicate $Init_F$ asserts that $pc[i]$ equals “a” for each process i, so the processes start with control at statement a. No assumption on the initial value of x is needed to prove mutual exclusion.

Next come the definitions of the three actions corresponding to program statements

a, b, and c. They are defined using the formula Go, where $Go(i, u, v)$ asserts that control in process i changes from u to v, while control remains unchanged in the other processes. Action $\mathcal{A}_i$ represents the execution of statement a by process i; actions $\mathcal{B}_i$ and $\mathcal{C}_i$ have the analogous interpretation. In this simple protocol, a process stops when it gets to its critical section, so there are no other actions. The program's next-state action $\mathcal{N}_F$ is the disjunction of all these actions. Formula Π_F asserts that all processes start at statement a, and every step consists of executing the next statement of some process.

Action $\mathcal{B}_i$ is enabled by the execution of action $\mathcal{A}_i$. Therefore, the maximum delay of Δ_b between the execution of statements a and b can be expressed by an upper-bound constraint on a volatile Δ_b-timer for action $\mathcal{B}_i$. The variable T_b is an array of such timers, where $T_b[i]$ is the timer for action $\mathcal{B}_i$.

The constant δ_c is the minimum delay between when control reaches statement c and when that statement is executed. Therefore, we need an array t_c of lower-bound timers for the actions $\mathcal{C}_i$. The delay is measured from the time control reaches statement c, so we want $t_c[i]$ to be a δ_c-timer on an action that becomes enabled when process i reaches statement c and is not executed until $\mathcal{C}_i$ is. A suitable choice for this action is $Go(i, \text{“c”}, \text{“cs”})$.

Adding these timers and timing constraints to the untimed formula Π_F yields formula Π_F^t of Figure 5, the TLA specification of the real-time protocol with the timers visible. The final specification, Φ_F^t, is obtained by quantifying over the timer variables T_b and t_c. Since $\mathcal{B}_j$ is a subaction of Π_F and $pc[i] = \text{“c”}$ is disjoint from $\mathcal{B}_j$, for all i and j in Proc, Theorem 1 implies that Π_F^t is nonZeno if Δ_b is positive. Proposition 2 can then be applied to prove that Φ_F^t is nonZeno.

Mutual exclusion asserts that two processes cannot be in their critical sections at the same time. It is expressed by the predicate

$$Mutex \;\triangleq\; \forall i, j \in \mathsf{Proc} : (pc[i] = pc[j] = \text{“cs”}) \Rightarrow (i = j)$$

The property to be proved is

$$Assump \wedge \Phi_F^t \;\Rightarrow\; \Box Mutex \tag{8}$$

where $Assump$ expresses the assumptions about the constants Proc, Δ_b, and δ_c needed for correctness. Since the timer variables do not occur in $Mutex$ or $Assump$, (8) is equivalent to

$$Assump \wedge \Pi_F^t \;\Rightarrow\; \Box Mutex$$

The standard method for proving this kind of invariance property leads to the invariant

$$\begin{array}{l}
\wedge\ now \in \mathbf{R} \\
\wedge\ \forall i \in \mathsf{Proc} : \\
\qquad \wedge\ T_b[i], t_c[i] \in \mathbf{R} \cup \{\infty\} \\
\qquad \wedge\ pc[i] \in \{\text{“a”}, \text{“b”}, \text{“c”}, \text{“cs”}\} \\
\qquad \wedge\ (pc[i] = \text{“cs”}) \Rightarrow \wedge\ x = i \\
\qquad \qquad \qquad \qquad \qquad \quad \wedge\ \forall j \in \mathsf{Proc} : pc[j] \neq \text{“b”} \\
\qquad \wedge\ (pc[i] = \text{“c”}) \Rightarrow \wedge\ x \neq 0 \\
\qquad \qquad \qquad \qquad \qquad \quad \wedge\ \forall j \in \mathsf{Proc} : (pc[j] = \text{“b”}) \Rightarrow (t_c[i] > T_b[j]) \\
\qquad \wedge\ (pc[i] = \text{“b”}) \Rightarrow (T_b[i] < now + \delta_c) \\
\qquad \wedge\ now \leq T_b[i]
\end{array}$$

and the assumption

$$Assump \triangleq (0 \notin \mathsf{Proc}) \land (\Delta_b, \delta_c \in \mathbf{R}) \land (\Delta_b < \delta_c)$$

4 Open Systems

4.1 Realizability

We begin by recasting the definitions of [1] into TLA. In the semantic model of [1], a behavior is a sequence of alternating states and agents of the form

$$s_0 \xrightarrow{\alpha_1} s_1 \xrightarrow{\alpha_2} s_2 \xrightarrow{\alpha_3} \ldots \tag{9}$$

To translate from this semantic model into that of TLA, we identify agents with state transitions. Agents are pairs of states, and a behavior $s_0, s_1, \ldots$ in TLA's model is identified with the behavior (9) in which α_i equals (s_{i-1}, s_i). An action μ is identified with the set of all agents that are μ steps. All the important definitions and results in [1] that do not concern agent-abstractness continue to hold—except that some results require the assumption that μ does not allow stuttering steps. (An action μ does not allow stuttering steps iff μ implies $v' \neq v$, where v is the tuple of all variables occurring in μ.)

If μ is an action and Π a safety property, then Π *does not constrain* μ iff for any finite behavior $s_0, \ldots, s_n$ and state s_{n+1}, if $s_0, \ldots, s_n$ satisfies Π and (s_n, s_{n+1}) is a μ step, then $s_0, \ldots, s_{n+1}$ satisfies Π. Property Π *constrains at most* μ iff Π does not constrain $\neg\mu$ and every behavior consisting of a single state satisfies Π. Any safety property Π can be written as the conjunction of a property Π_1 that does not constrain μ and a property Π_2 that constrains at most μ. If Π equals $Init \land \Box[\mathcal{N}]_v$, then we can take Π_1 to be $Init \land \Box[\mathcal{N} \lor \mu]_v$ and Π_2 to be $\Box[\mathcal{N} \lor \neg\mu]_v$.

A predicate P is said to be a μ *invariant* of a property Π iff no μ step of a behavior satisfying Π can make P false. More precisely, P is a μ invariant of Π iff

$$\Pi \Rightarrow \Box[\mu \land P \Rightarrow P']_P$$

For an action μ and property Π, the *μ-realizable part* $\mathcal{R}_\mu(\Pi)$ is the set of behaviors that can be achieved by an implementation of Π that performs only μ steps—the environment being able to perform any $\neg\mu$ step. The reader is referred to [1] for the precise definition.[6] (The concept of receptiveness is due to Dill [8].) Property Π is said to be *μ-receptive* iff it equals $\mathcal{R}_\mu(\Pi)$. The realizable part $\mathcal{R}_\mu(\Pi)$ of any TLA formula Π can be written as a TLA formula.

The generalization of machine closure to open systems is *machine realizability.* Intuitively, (Π, L) is μ-machine realizable iff an implementation that performs only μ steps can ensure that any finite behavior satisfying Π is completed to an infinite behavior satisfying $\Pi \land L$. Formally, (Π, L) is defined to be μ-machine realizable iff (Π, L) is machine closed and $\Pi \land L$ is μ-receptive. For μ equal to true, machine realizability reduces to machine closure. Corresponding to Propositions 1, 2 and 3 are:

---

[6] $\mathcal{R}_\mu(\Pi)$ was not defined in [1] if μ equals true or false. The appropriate definitions are $\mathcal{R}_{\mathsf{true}}(\Pi) \triangleq \Pi$ and $\mathcal{R}_{\mathsf{false}}(\Pi) \triangleq \mathsf{false}$.

Proposition 4 *If* Π *is a safety property that constrains at most* μ*, and* L *is the conjunction of a finite or countably infinite number of formulas of the form* $\mathrm{WF}_w(\mathcal{A})$ *and/or* $\mathrm{SF}_w(\mathcal{A})$*, where (a) each* $\langle\mathcal{A}\rangle_w$ *is a subaction of* Π *and (b) Enabled* $\langle\mathcal{A}\rangle_w$ *is a* $\neg\mu$ *invariant of* Π *for each* $\mathcal{A}$ *appearing in a formula* $\mathrm{SF}_w(\mathcal{A})$*, then* (Π, L) *is* μ*-machine realizable.*

Proposition 5 ([1], Proposition 10) *If* μ *does not allow stuttering steps,* x *is a tuple of variables that do not occur free in* μ *or* L*, and*

(a) $\exists x : \mathit{Init}$ *holds.*

(b) $(\Box[\mathcal{N} \vee \neg\mu]_v, \mathit{Init} \wedge \Box[\mu \vee (x' = x)]_x \Rightarrow L)$ *is* μ*-machine realizable.*

(c) $\exists x : (\mathit{Init} \wedge \Box[\mu \vee (x' = x)]_x \wedge \Box[\mathcal{N} \vee \neg\mu]_v)$ *is a safety property.*

then $(\exists x : (\mathit{Init} \wedge \Box[\mu \vee (x' = x)]_x \wedge \Box[\mathcal{N} \vee \neg\mu]_v), L)$ *is* μ*-machine realizable.*

Proposition 6 *If* (Π, L_1) *is* μ*-machine realizable and* $\Pi \wedge L_1$ *implies* L_2*, then* (Π, L_2) *is* μ*-machine realizable.*

For properties Φ and Π, we define $\Phi \multimap \Pi$ to be the property satisfied by a behavior σ iff σ satisfies $\Phi \Rightarrow \Pi$ and every finite prefix of σ satisfies $\mathcal{C}(\Phi) \Rightarrow \mathcal{C}(\Pi)$.[7] If Φ and Π are safety properties, then $\Phi \multimap \Pi$ is the safety property asserting that Π remains true at least as long as Φ does. The property $\Phi \multimap \Pi$ is sometimes written Π *while* Φ; it is expressible in TLA, for any TLA formulas Φ and Π.

The operator $\multimap$ is the implication operator for an intuitionistic logic of safety properties [3]. Most valid propositional formulas without negation remain valid when $\Rightarrow$ is replaced by $\multimap$, if all the formulas that appear on the left of a $\multimap$ are safety properties. For example, the following formulas are valid if Φ and Π are safety properties.

$$
\begin{array}{c}
\Phi \multimap (\Pi \multimap \Psi) \;\equiv\; (\Phi \wedge \Pi) \multimap \Psi \\
(\Phi \multimap \Psi) \wedge (\Pi \multimap \Psi) \;\equiv\; (\Phi \vee \Pi) \multimap \Psi
\end{array} \tag{10}
$$

Valid formulas can also be obtained by certain partial replacements of $\Rightarrow$ by $\multimap$ in valid formulas. For example, the following equivalence is valid if P is a safety property.

$$
\begin{array}{rl}
(E \Rightarrow (P \multimap M_1)) \;\Rightarrow\; (E \Rightarrow (P \multimap M_2)) & \\
\equiv\; (E \wedge P \wedge M_1) \;\Rightarrow\; (E \wedge P \wedge M_2) &
\end{array} \tag{11}
$$

A precise relation between $\multimap$ and $\Rightarrow$ is established by:

Proposition 7 ([1], Proposition 8) *If* μ *is an action that does not permit stuttering steps,* Φ *and* Π *are safety properties,* Φ *does not constrain* μ*, and* Π *constrains at most* μ*, then* $\mathcal{R}_\mu(\Phi \Rightarrow \Pi)$ *equals* $\Phi \multimap \Pi$*.*

Substituting **true** for Φ in Proposition 7 proves that a safety property is μ-receptive if it constrains at most μ.

The following variant of Proposition 6 is useful. Note that if $(\mathbf{true}, L)$ is μ-machine realizable, then L is a liveness property.

---

[7] This definition is slightly different from the one in [1]; but the two definitions agree when Φ and Π are safety properties.

Proposition 8 *If μ is an action that does not allow stuttering steps, Φ and Π are safety properties, $(\Phi \twoheadrightarrow \Pi, L_1)$ and (true, L_2) are μ-machine realizable, and $\Phi \wedge \Pi \wedge L_1$ implies L_2, then $(\Phi \twoheadrightarrow \Pi, L_2)$ is μ-machine realizable.*

By using Propositions 4 and 8 instead of Propositions 1 and 3, the proof of Theorem 1 generalizes to the proof of the following result. If Π has the form $Init \wedge \Box[\mathcal{N}]_v$, we write Π_0 to denote $Init$ and $\Pi_\Box$ to denote $\Box[\mathcal{N}]_v$.

Theorem 2 *With the notation and hypotheses of Theorem 1, if E and M are safety properties such that $\Pi = E \wedge M$, μ is an action that does not allow stuttering steps, and*

5. *M constrains at most μ.*
6. *(a) $\langle \mathcal{A}_k \rangle_v \Rightarrow \mu$, for all $k \in I \cup J$.*
   (b) $(now' \neq now) \Rightarrow \mu$

then $(E^t \twoheadrightarrow M^t,\ NZ)$ is μ-machine realizable, where

$$\begin{aligned} E^t &\triangleq E \wedge (RT_v)_0 \wedge \forall j \in J : MaxTime(T_j)_0 \\ M^t &\triangleq M \wedge (RT_v)_\Box \wedge \forall i \in I : MinTime(t_i, \mathcal{A}_i, v) \wedge \forall j \in J : MaxTime(T_j)_\Box \end{aligned}$$

Observe how the initial predicates of RT_v and $MaxTime(T_j)$ appear in the environment assumption E^t. (Formula $MinTime(t_i, \mathcal{A}_i, v)$ has no initial predicate.) If P is a predicate, then $P \twoheadrightarrow \Pi$ is equivalent to $P \Rightarrow \Pi$, and $(P \wedge \Pi, L)$ is machine closed if $(P \Rightarrow \Pi, L)$ is. Since machine realizability implies machine closure, Theorem 1 can be obtained from Theorem 2 by letting E and μ equal true and M equal Π.

4.2 Open Systems as Implications

An open system specification is one in which the system guarantees a property M only if the environment satisfies an assumption E. The set of allowed behaviors is described by the formula $E \Rightarrow M$. The specification also includes an action μ that defines which steps are under the control of (or blamed on) the system. For a reasonable specification, $\mathcal{C}(E)$ must not constrain μ, and $\mathcal{C}(M)$ must constrain at most μ.[8] The following result shows that, under reasonable hypotheses, E can be taken to be a safety property.

Proposition 9 ([1], Theorem 1) *If I is a predicate, E_S and M_S are safety properties, and $(E_S, E_S \wedge E_L)$ is $\neg\mu$-machine realizable, then*

$$\mathcal{R}_\mu(I \wedge E_S \wedge E_L \Rightarrow M_S \wedge M_L) = \mathcal{R}_\mu(I \wedge E_S \Rightarrow M_S \wedge (E_L \Rightarrow M_L))$$

An open system specification can then be written as $E \Rightarrow M$, with

$$\begin{aligned} E &\triangleq Init \wedge \exists e : (Init_e \wedge \Box[(\mu \wedge (e' = e)) \vee \mathcal{N}_E]_{(e,v)}) \\ M &\triangleq \exists m : (Init_m \wedge \Box[(\neg\mu \wedge (m' = m)) \vee \mathcal{N}_M]_{(m,v)} \wedge (L_E \Rightarrow L_M)) \end{aligned}$$

[8] The slight asymmetry in these conditions results from the arbitrary choice that initial conditions appear in E and not in M.

where e and m denote the internal variables of the environment and module, which are each disjoint from all variables appearing in the scope of the other's "$\exists$"; L_E and L_M are conjunctions of suitable fairness properties; $\exists e : Init_e$ and $\exists m : Init_m$ are identically true; the system's next-state action $\mathcal{N}_M$ implies μ, and the environment's next-state action $\mathcal{N}_E$ implies $\neg\mu$. Under these assumptions, it can be shown that $\mathcal{C}(E)$ does not constrain μ, and $\mathcal{C}(M)$ constrains at most μ. It is easy to show that $E \wedge M$, the TLA formula describing the closed system formed by the open system and its environment, equals

$$\exists\, e, m : (Init \wedge Init_E \wedge Init_M \wedge \Box[\mathcal{N}_E \vee \mathcal{N}_M]_{(e,m,v)} \wedge (L_E \Rightarrow L_M)) \qquad (12)$$

Thus, $E \wedge M$ has precisely the form we expect for a closed system comprising two components with next-state actions $\mathcal{N}_E$ and $\mathcal{N}_M$.

Implementation means implication. A system with guarantee M implements a system with guarantee $\widehat{M}$, under environment assumption E, iff $E \Rightarrow M$ implies $E \Rightarrow \widehat{M}$. But this is logically equivalent to $E \wedge M$ implying $E \wedge \widehat{M}$. In other words, proving that one open system implements another is equivalent to proving the implementation relation for the corresponding closed systems. Hence, implementation for open systems reduces to implementation for closed systems.[9]

4.3 Composition

The distinguishing feature of open systems is that they can be composed. The proof that the composition of two specifications implements a third specification is based on the following result, which is a slight generalization of Theorem 2 of [1].

Theorem 3 *If P, E, E_1, and E_2 are safety properties, M_1 and M_2 are arbitrary properties, and μ_1 and μ_2 are actions such that*

1. *(a) E_1 does not constrain μ_1, (b) E_2 does not constrain μ_2, and (c) E does not constrain $\mu_1 \vee \mu_2$,*
2. *$\mathcal{C}(M_1)$ constrains at most μ_1, and $\mathcal{C}(M_2)$ constrains at most μ_2,*
3. *$\mu_1 \vee \mu_2$ does not allow stuttering steps,*

then the following proof rule is valid.

$$\frac{P \wedge E \wedge \mathcal{C}(M_1) \wedge \mathcal{C}(M_2) \;\Rightarrow\; E_1 \wedge E_2}{\mathcal{R}_{\mu_1}(E_1 \Rightarrow M_1) \wedge \mathcal{R}_{\mu_2}(E_2 \Rightarrow M_2) \;\Rightarrow\; (E \Rightarrow (P \mathrel{-\!\!\triangleright} M_1) \wedge (P \mathrel{-\!\!\triangleright} M_2))}$$

This theorem differs from Theorem 2 of [1] in two significant ways:

- The assumption $\mu_1 \wedge \mu_2 = \emptyset$ is missing, and the conclusion of the proof rule has been weakened by removing the $\mathcal{R}_{\mu_1 \vee \mu_2}$. An examination of the proof of the theorem in [1] reveals that the assumption is not needed for this weaker conclusion.
- The hypothesis has been weakened to include the conjunct P and the conclusion weakened by adding the "$P \mathrel{-\!\!\triangleright}$"s. The original theorem is obtained by letting P be **true**. A simple modification to the argument in [1] proves the generalization.

[9] A similar argument shows that we can replace $L_E \Rightarrow L_M$ by $L_E \wedge L_M$ in (12) when proving that $E \wedge M$ implements $E \wedge \widehat{M}$.

5 Real-Time Open Systems

5.1 The Paradox Revisited

We now consider the paradoxical example of the introduction, illustrated in Figure 1. For simplicity, let the possible output actions be the setting of x and y to 0. The untimed version of S_1 then asserts that, if the environment does nothing but set y to 0, then the system does nothing but set x to 0. This is expressed in TLA by letting

$$\begin{array}{lll} \mathcal{M}_x \triangleq (x'=0) \land (y'=y) & \quad & \nu_1 \triangleq x' \neq x \\ \mathcal{M}_y \triangleq (y'=0) \land (x'=x) & & \end{array}$$

and defining the untimed version of specification S_1 to be

$$\Box[\nu_1 \lor \mathcal{M}_y]_{(x,y)} \Rightarrow \Box[\neg\nu_1 \lor \mathcal{M}_x]_{(x,y)} \tag{13}$$

To add timing constraints, we must first decide whether the system or the environment should change *now*. Since the advancing of *now* is a mythical action that does not have to be performed by any device, either decision is possible. Somewhat surprisingly, it turns out to be more convenient to let the system advance time. Remembering that initial conditions must appear in the environment assumption, we define

$$\begin{array}{lll} \mathcal{N}_x \triangleq \mathcal{M}_x \land (now' = now) & \quad & MT_x \triangleq MaxTime(T_x) \\ \mathcal{N}_y \triangleq \mathcal{M}_y \land (now' = now) & & MT_y \triangleq MaxTime(T_y) \\ T_x \triangleq \textbf{if } x \neq 0 \textbf{ then } 12 \textbf{ else } \infty & & \mu_1 \triangleq \nu_1 \lor (now' \neq now) \\ T_y \triangleq \textbf{if } y \neq 0 \textbf{ then } 12 \textbf{ else } \infty & & \end{array}$$

$$E_1 \triangleq (now = 0) \land (MT_x)_0 \land \Box[\mu_1 \lor \mathcal{N}_y]_{(x,y,now)}$$
$$M_1 \triangleq \Box[\neg\mu_1 \lor \mathcal{N}_x]_{(x,y,now)} \land (RT_{(x,y)})_\Box \land (MT_x)_\Box$$

Adding timing constraints to (13) the same way we did for closed systems then leads to the following timed version of specification S_1.

$$E_1 \land MT_y \Rightarrow M_1 \tag{14}$$

However, this does not have the right form for an open system specification because MT_y constrains the advance of *now*, so the environment assumption constrains μ_1. The conjunct MT_y must be moved from the environment assumption to the system guarantee. This is easily done by rewriting (14) in the equivalent form

$$E_1 \Rightarrow (MT_y \Rightarrow M_1)$$

so the system guarantee becomes $MT_y \Rightarrow M_1$.[10] However, this guarantee is not a safety property. To make it one, we must replace $\Rightarrow$ by $\mathrel{-\!\!\triangleright}$, obtaining

$$S_1 \triangleq E_1 \Rightarrow (MT_y \mathrel{-\!\!\triangleright} M_1)$$

[10]Because MT_y appears on the left of an implication, there is no need to put its initial condition in the environment assumption.

The specification S_2 of the second component in Figure 1 is similar, where μ_2, E_2, M_2, and S_2 are obtained from μ_1, E_1, M_1, and S_1 by substituting 2 for 1, x for y, and y for x.

We now compose specifications S_1 and S_2. The definitions and the observation that $P \twoheadrightarrow Q$ implies $P \Rightarrow Q$ yield

$$(MT_x \vee MT_y) \wedge E \wedge (MT_y \twoheadrightarrow M_1) \wedge (MT_x \twoheadrightarrow M_2) \;\Rightarrow\; E_1 \wedge E_2$$

where

$$E \;\triangleq\; (now = 0) \;\wedge\; (MT_x)_0 \;\wedge\; (MT_y)_0 \;\wedge\; \Box[\mu_1 \vee \mu_2]_{(x,y,now)}$$

We can therefore apply Theorem 3, substituting $MT_x \vee MT_y$ for P, $MT_y \twoheadrightarrow M_1$ for M_1, and $MT_x \twoheadrightarrow M_2$ for M_2, to deduce

$$\begin{aligned}\mathcal{R}_{\mu_1}(S_1) \wedge \mathcal{R}_{\mu_2}(S_2) \;\Rightarrow\; (E \;\Rightarrow\; &\wedge (MT_x \vee MT_y) \twoheadrightarrow (MT_y \twoheadrightarrow M_1)\\ &\wedge (MT_x \vee MT_y) \twoheadrightarrow (MT_x \twoheadrightarrow M_2))\end{aligned}$$

Using the implication-like properties of $\twoheadrightarrow$, this simplifies to

$$\mathcal{R}_{\mu_1}(S_1) \;\wedge\; \mathcal{R}_{\mu_2}(S_2) \;\Rightarrow\; (E \;\Rightarrow\; (MT_y \twoheadrightarrow M_1) \;\wedge\; (MT_x \twoheadrightarrow M_2)) \tag{15}$$

All one can conclude about the composition from (15) is: either x and y are both 0 when *now* reaches 12, or neither of them is 0 when *now* reaches 12. There is no paradox.

As another example, we replace S_2 by the specification $E_2 \Rightarrow M_2$. This specification, which we call S_3, asserts that the system sets y to 0 by noon, regardless of whether the environment sets x to 0. The definitions imply

$$MT_y \wedge E \wedge (MT_y \twoheadrightarrow M_1) \wedge M_2 \;\Rightarrow\; E_1 \wedge E_2$$

and Theorem 3 yields

$$\mathcal{R}_{\mu_1}(S_1) \;\wedge\; \mathcal{R}_{\mu_2}(S_3) \;\Rightarrow\; (E \;\Rightarrow\; (MT_x \twoheadrightarrow M_1) \;\wedge\; M_2)$$

Since M_2 implies MT_x, this simplifies to

$$\mathcal{R}_{\mu_1}(S_1) \;\wedge\; \mathcal{R}_{\mu_2}(S_3) \;\Rightarrow\; (E \;\Rightarrow\; M_1 \;\wedge\; M_2)$$

The composition of S_1 and S_3 does guarantee that both x and y equal 0 by noon.

5.2 Timing Constraints in General

Our no-longer-paradoxical example suggests that the form of a real-time open system specification should be

$$E \Rightarrow (P \twoheadrightarrow M) \tag{16}$$

where M describes the system's timing constraints and the advancing of *now*, and P describes the upper-bound timing constraints for the environment. Since the environment's lower-bound timing constraints do not constrain the advance of *now*, they can remain in E. By (11), proving that one specification in this form implements another reduces to the proof for the corresponding closed systems.

For the specification (16) to be reasonable, its closed-system version, $E \wedge P \wedge M$, should be nonZeno. However, this is not sufficient. Consider a specification guaranteeing that the system produces a sequence of outputs until the environment sends a *stop* message, where the nth output must occur by time $(n-1)/n$. There is no timing assumption on the environment; it need never send a *stop* message. This is an unreasonable specification because *now* can't reach 1 until the environment sends its *stop* message, so the advance of time is contingent on an optional action of the environment. However, the corresponding closed system specification is nonZeno, since time can always be made to advance without bound by having the environment send a *stop* message.

If advancing *now* is a μ action, then a system that controls μ actions can guarantee time to be unbounded while satisfying a safety specification S iff the pair (S, NZ) is μ-machine realizable. This condition cannot be satisfied if S contains unrealizable behaviors. By Proposition 7, we can eliminate unrealizable behaviors by changing "$\Rightarrow$" to "$\twoheadrightarrow$" in (16). Using (10), we then see that the appropriate definition of nonZenoness for an open system specification of the form (16), with M a safety property, is that $((E \wedge P) \twoheadrightarrow M,\ NZ)$ be μ-machine realizable. This condition is proved using Theorem 2. To apply the theorem, one must show that M constrains at most μ. Any property of the form $\Box[\mathcal{N} \vee \mu]_v$ constrains at most μ. To prove that a formula with internal variables (existential quantification) constrains at most μ, one applies Proposition 5 with **true** substituted for L, since M constrains at most μ iff (M, true) is μ-machine realizable.

6 Conclusion

6.1 What We Did

We started with a simple idea—specifying and reasoning about real-time systems by representing time as an ordinary variable. This idea led to an exposition that most readers probably found quite difficult. What happened to the simplicity?

About half of the exposition is a review of concepts unrelated to real time. We chose to formulate these concepts in TLA. Like any language, TLA seems complicated on first encounter. We believe that a true measure of simplicity of a formal language is the simplicity of its formal description. The complete syntax and formal semantics of TLA are given in about 1-1/2 pages of figures in [11].

All the fundamental concepts described in Sections 2 and 4, including machine closure, machine realizability, and the $\twoheadrightarrow$ operator, have appeared before [1, 2]. However, they are expressed here for the first time in terms of TLA. These concepts are subtle, but they are important for understanding any concurrent system; they were not invented for real-time systems.

We never claimed that specifying and reasoning about concurrent systems is easy. Verifying concurrent systems is difficult and error prone. Our assertions that one formula follows from another, made so casually in the exposition, must be backed up by detailed calculations. The proofs for our examples, propositions, and theorems occupy some sixty pages.

We did claim that existing methods for specifying and reasoning about concurrent systems could be applied to real-time systems. Now, we can examine how hard they were to apply.

We found few obstacles in the realm of closed systems. The second author has more than fifteen years of experience in the formal verification of concurrent algorithms, and we knew that old-fashioned methods could be applied to real-time systems. However, TLA is relatively new, and we were pleased by how well it worked. The formal specification of Fischer's protocol in Figure 5, obtained by conjoining timing constraints to the untimed protocol, is as simple and direct as we could have hoped for. Moreover, the formal correctness proofs of this protocol and of the queue example, using the method of reasoning described in [11], were straightforward. Perhaps the most profound discovery was the relation between nonZenoness and machine closure.

Open systems made up for any lack of difficulty with closed systems. State-based approaches to open systems are a fairly recent development, and we have little practical experience with them. The simple idea of putting the environment's timing assumptions to the left of a $\dashv\!\!\triangleright$ in the system's guarantee came only after numerous failed efforts. We still have much to learn before reasoning about open systems becomes routine. However, the basic intellectual tools we needed to handle real-time open systems were all in place, and we have confidence in our basic approach to open-system verification.

6.2 Beyond Real Time

Real-time systems introduce a fundamentally new problem: adding physical continuity to discrete systems. Our solution is based on the observation that, when reasoning about a discrete system, we can represent continuous processes by discrete actions. If we can pretend that the system progresses by discrete atomic actions, we can pretend that those actions occur at a single instant of time, and that the continuous change to time also occurs in discrete steps. If there is no system action between noon and $\sqrt{2}$ seconds past noon, we can pretend that time advances by those $\sqrt{2}$ seconds in a single action.

Physical continuity arises not just in real-time systems, but in "real-pressure" and "real-temperature" process-control systems. Such systems can be described in the same way as real-time systems: pressure and temperature as well as time are represented by ordinary variables. The continuous changes to pressure and temperature that occur between system actions are represented by discrete changes to the variables. The fundamental assumption is that the real, physical system is accurately represented by a model in which the system makes discrete, instantaneous changes to the physical parameters it affects.

The observation that continuous parameters other than time can be modeled by program variables has probably been known for years. However, the only published work we know of that uses this idea is by Marzullo, Schneider, and Budhiraja [12].

References

[1] Martín Abadi and Leslie Lamport. Composing specifications. In J. W. de Bakker, W.-P. de Roever, and G. Rozenberg, editors, *Stepwise Refinement of Distributed Systems*, volume 430 of *Lecture Notes in Computer Science*, pages 1–41. Springer-Verlag, May/June 1989.

[2] Martín Abadi and Leslie Lamport. The existence of refinement mappings. *Theoretical Computer Science*, 82(2):253–284, May 1991.

[3] Martín Abadi and Gordon Plotkin. A logical view of composition and refinement. In *Proceedings of the Eighteenth Annual ACM Symposium on Principles of Programming Languages*, pages 323–332, January 1991.

[4] Bowen Alpern and Fred B. Schneider. Defining liveness. *Information Processing Letters*, 21(4):181–185, October 1985.

[5] Krzysztof R. Apt, Nissim Francez, and Shmuel Katz. Appraising fairness in languages for distributed programming. *Distributed Computing*, 2:226–241, 1988.

[6] Arthur Bernstein and Paul K. Harter, Jr. Proving real time properties of programs with temporal logic. In *Proceedings of the Eighth Symposium on Operating Systems Principles*, pages 1–11, New York, 1981. ACM. *Operating Systems Review 15*, 5.

[7] K. Mani Chandy and Jayadev Misra. *Parallel Program Design*. Addison-Wesley, Reading, Massachusetts, 1988.

[8] David L. Dill. *Trace Theory for Automatic Hierarchical Verification of Speed-Independent Circuits*. PhD thesis, Carnegie Mellon University, February 1988.

[9] Leslie Lamport. An assertional correctness proof of a distributed algorithm. *Science of Computer Programming*, 2(3):175–206, December 1982.

[10] Leslie Lamport. A fast mutual exclusion algorithm. *ACM Transactions on Computer Systems*, 5(1):1–11, February 1987.

[11] Leslie Lamport. The temporal logic of actions. Technical Report 79, Digital Equipment Corporation, Systems Research Center, 1991. To appear.

[12] Keith Marzullo, Fred B. Schneider, and Navin Budhiraja. Derivation of sequential, real-time process-control programs. In Andreé M. van Tilborg and Gary M. Koob, editors, *Foundations of Real-Time Computing: Formal Specifications and Methods*, chapter 2, pages 39–54. Kluwer Academic Publishers, Boston, Dordrecht, and London, 1991.

[13] Peter G. Neumann and Leslie Lamport. Highly dependable distributed systems. Technical report, SRI International, June 1983. Contract Number DAEA18-81-G-0062, SRI Project 4180.

[14] Fred B. Schneider, Bard Bloom, and Keith Marzullo. Putting time into proof outlines. This volume.

Verifying Automata Specifications of Probabilistic Real-time Systems

Rajeev Alur
AT&T Bell Laboratories
Murray Hill, NJ 07974, USA.

Costas Courcoubetis [1]
Computer Science Department, University of Crete, and
Institute of Computer Science, FORTH, Heraklion, Crete 71110, Greece.

David Dill [2]
Department of Computer Science
Stanford University, Stanford, CA 94305, USA.

Abstract. We present a model-checking algorithm for a system presented as a generalized semi-Markov process and a specification given as a deterministic timed automaton. This leads to a method for automatic verification of timing properties of finite-state probabilistic real-time systems.

Keywords: Real-time, Probabilistic systems, Automatic verification.

1 Introduction

There is increasing awareness that unexpected behavior from interacting processes can cause serious problems. This observation applies not only to programs and digital systems, but also to physical processes, such as robots, automobiles, manufacturing processes, and so on. Indeed, as digital systems become smaller and cheaper, their use to control and interact with physical processes will inevitably increase.

Formal verification of these systems seeks mathematical methods for reasoning about their behavior. Automatic formal verification is particularly promising, because it requires far less labor than the manual techniques. There has been a great deal of research on automatic verification methods for concurrent systems whose behavior is *timing independent.* However, physical processes work in *real-time* — their correctness depends crucially on the actual timing of events; furthermore, physical processes are *probabilistic.* Automatic verification techniques have been developed for several different models of real-time

[1] Supported by ESPRIT BRA project SPEC.
[2] Supported by the NSF under grant MIP-8858807.

[AH89, Ko90, ACD90, AD90, Le90], and for discrete Markov chains [LS82, Va85, PZ86, CY88, HJ89]. We aim to develop automatic verification techniques that can deal with probabilistic real-time processes.

We add probabilities to our model of state-transition graphs with timing constraints by associating fixed distributions with the delays. This extension makes our processes *generalized semi-markov processes*, which have been studied by researchers in the field of stochastic modeling [Sh87, Wh80]. In previous work [ACD91], we developed an algorithm for checking whether such a system satisfied a formula in TCTL [ACD90], an extension of the branching-time temporal logic CTL [EC82] that allowed the inclusion of explicit constant upper and lower time bounds in formulas. Here, we describe a different model-checking algorithm that uses *deterministic timed automata* [AD90] to specify properties to be checked. These automata can express certain types of linear behavior that cannot be described using TCTL. An example of such a requirement is the "convergent bounded response property": events a and b occur in alternation and *eventually always* b occurs within 2 seconds of the previous a" (note that this property allows an arbitrary delay between an a and the next b for any finite time, as long as the bounded response eventually holds). Furthermore, in [ACD91] we required all delays to have continuous distributions with bounded interval support. Now, in addition, we also allow discrete probability functions (this allows fixed delays) and exponential distributions.

The model-checking problem is to determine whether, with probability 1, every trajectory of the probabilistic real-time system is accepted by the timed automaton specification. We present an algorithm that combines model-checking for real-time non-probabilistic systems [AD90] with model-checking for finite-state discrete-time Markov chains [Va85, CY88]. The correctness of the algorithm is not obvious, because it analyzes the projection of a Markov process onto a finite state space. The projection process is not Markov, so our most significant result is that the model-checking algorithm works.

The paper is organized as follows: The model for probabilistic real-time system is described in section 2. Section 3 considers the specification language of timed automata. Section 4 develops the model-checking algorithm and proves its correctness. The concluding section discusses some directions in which this work can be extended.

2 The process model

In probabilistic verification, a program is usually modeled by a Markov chain over a finite state space. We want to introduce the notion of time in this model of probabilistic systems. A typical property we want to model is the following: "the delay between the request and the response is distributed according to a given probability distribution". To this end, whenever the request event happens the response event will be scheduled with an associated clock. The value of the clock will be some negative number chosen in accordance with the desired probability distribution. The reading of the clock changes with the elapsing of time, and the response event gets triggered when the clock reaches 0. We assume that all the system delays have probability distributions of one of the following two forms:

- Exponential distributions.

- Distributions with finite interval support; that is, distributions that satisfy the following constraint: there exist bounded intervals $I_1, I_2, \ldots I_n$ with integer boundaries such that the probability density function is positive in each I_i and zero everywhere else.

The latter category includes a large number of distributions such as bounded uniform distributions, and discrete probability functions which choose the values from a finite set of integers. To keep the presentation simple, we assume that for every (nonexponential) density function f there exists a single bounded interval I such that for every $t \in \mathbf{R}$, $f(t)$ is positive iff $t \in I$. The model-checking algorithm needs only a trivial modification when the distributions have support of more than one interval.

To model concurrent delays we need to introduce several clocks running concurrently. Our notation is based upon the literature on generalized semi-Markov processes [Wh80, Sh87].

A (finite-state) *real-time probabilistic process* $\mathcal{M}$ has the following components:

- *States:* A finite set S of states.

- *Events:* Associated with each state s is a finite set of events $E(s)$. $E(s)$ gives the set of events that are scheduled to occur when the process is in state s. Let E be the set of all events ($\bigcup_{s \in S} E(s)$), $\Sigma(s)$ be the set of all nonempty subsets of $E(s)$, and Σ be the set of all nonempty subsets of E.

- *Initial distribution:* An initial probability distribution function f_0 such that $\Sigma_{s \in S} f_0(s)$ equals 1.

- *Transitions:* A probabilistic transition function $next : S \times \Sigma \times S \mapsto [0,1]$. $next(s, a, s')$ is the probability that the next state is s' when the event set $a \in \Sigma(s)$ occurs in state s. For every state s and every $a \in \Sigma(s)$, we require that the sum $\Sigma_{s' \in S}\, next(s, a, s')$ equals 1.

- *Delay distributions:* The set of events is partitioned into two sets: E_e are the events with exponential distribution, and E_b are the events with bounded distribution. The functions $l : E_b \mapsto \mathbf{N}$, and $u : E_b \mapsto \mathbf{N}$, giving the lower and upper bounds on the times at which bounded events get scheduled. A bounded event x is called a *fixed-delay* event if $l_x = u_x$, and a *variable-delay* event if $l_x < u_x$. Associated with each variable-delay event x is a probability density function $f_x(r)$ such that $\int_{l_x}^{u_x} f_x(r)dr$ equals 1.

The process starts in some state s such that $f_0(s)$ positive. The set of initially scheduled events is $E(s)$. A (real-valued) clock is associated with each event, and it shows the time remaining till the occurrence of the event. The initial values for the clocks are chosen as follows: for each event x, a random value d_x is chosen independently using the associated probability distribution, and the clock is set to the negative value $-d_x$. Thus all the clock values are negative, and all the clocks count up at the same rate as the real-time [3]. A

[3]In an equivalent, and more conventional, formulation the clocks get set to positive values, and count down triggering the events on reaching 0. Our formulation was motivated by the existing definitions for timed automata which have clocks counting up.

state-transition is triggered when the clocks associated with some events become 0. A *generalized state* of the system is described by giving its state and a vector giving the readings of clocks corresponding to all the currently scheduled events. A generalized state is then represented by $\langle s, \nu \rangle$, where ν is a vector of real numbers of length $|\mathrm{E}(s)|$ assigning values to the clocks. Note that, in our presentation, we use the same symbol to denote an event and the clock associated with it.

If the current generalized state is $\langle s, \nu \rangle$ then after a delay of ϵ such that $\nu(x) + \epsilon < 0$ for all $x \in \mathrm{E}(s)$, the generalized state is $\langle s, \nu + \epsilon \rangle$. A state transition will be triggered when some element of the clock vector becomes 0. Note that two (or more) clocks can reach 0 value simultaneously; this is because we allow fixed-delay events. Let a be the set of events that trigger the state-transition. The process moves to some state s' such that $next(s, a, s')$ is positive. With this transition some events get descheduled, whereas some events get newly scheduled. We partition the set $\mathrm{E}(s')$ into two sets:

1. the set $old(s, a, s') = \mathrm{E}(s') \cap [\mathrm{E}(s) - a]$ is the set of events that were scheduled previously, and

2. the set $new(s, a, s') = \mathrm{E}(s') - old(s, a, s')$ is the set of events that are newly scheduled.

The clock readings in the new state are determined as follows: The clocks in $old(s, a, s')$ keep counting without being affected by the state-transition. For each newly scheduled event x, a random value d_x is chosen independently using the associated probability distribution, and the clock is set to the negative value $-d_x$. Notice that for a fixed-delay event x, this value is predetermined; for a variable-delay event x, the value d_x lies in the interval (l_x, u_x); and for an exponential event x, this value can be arbitrary.

The generalized state has enough information to decide the future behavior of the process, hence, what we have defined is a continuous-time Markov process $X(t)$ over the space of all generalized states. As far as the correctness of the system is concerned, we are mainly interested in the sequence of events the process participates in. Note that, with probability 1, the process makes a finite number of transitions in a bounded interval of time. Hence a particular behavior of the process can be described by an ω-sequence of event sets paired with their occurrence times. Such a sequence is called a *timed word*. To be precise, a timed word $\rho = (\sigma, \tau)$ consists of

- an infinite word σ over the alphabet Σ of event sets, and

- an infinite, strictly increasing sequence τ of positive real numbers satisfying the *progress* property that "for every $t \in \mathbf{R}$ there is some τ_j greater than t".

The probabilistic structure of the process gives a probability measure on the space of all timed words.

3 Timed automata

The correctness of the system is usually specified by ω-automata or temporal logics. In this paper we use deterministic timed automata [AD90] as a specification formalism. The formalism of timed automata is a generalization of finite-state machines over infinite strings (see [Th90] for an exposition to ω-automata). While ω-automata accept infinite words, timed automata are additionally constrained by timing requirements and accept timed words (see the article *The Theory of Timed Automata* in this issue for a detailed discussion).

A timed automaton operates with finite control — a finite set of locations and a finite set of real-valued clocks. All clocks proceed at the same rate and measure the amount of time that has elapsed since they were started (or reset). Each transition of the automaton has an associated constraint on the values of the clocks: the transition may be taken only if the current values of the clocks satisfy this constraint. A transition, in addition to changing the location of the automaton, may reset some of the clocks.

Formally, a timed automaton $\mathcal{A}$ consists of

- a finite set of locations Q,
- a start location $q_{init} \in Q$,
- a finite set of clocks C, and
- a finite set of transitions $\mathcal{E}$. An edge $\langle q, q', a, \lambda, \delta \rangle$ represents a transition from location q to location q' on input symbol $a \in \Sigma$. The set $\lambda \subseteq C$ gives the clocks to be reset with this transition, and δ is the associated clock constraint. A clock constraint is a boolean combination of atomic conditions of the form $x \leq c$ and $c \leq x$, where x is a clock and c is an integer constant.

Given a time word (σ, τ), the timed automaton $\mathcal{A}$ starts in its start location q_{init} at time 0 with all its clocks initialized to 0. As time advances, the values of all clocks change reflecting the elapsed time. At time τ_i, $\mathcal{A}$ changes location from q_{i-1} to q_i using some transition of the form $\langle q_{i-1}, q_i, \sigma_i, \lambda_i, \delta_i \rangle$ reading the input σ_i, provided the current values of clocks satisfy δ_i. With this transition the clocks in λ_i get reset to 0, and thus start counting time with respect to it. This behavior is captured by defining *runs* of timed automata. A run records the location and the values of all the clocks at the transition points. Specifically, a run r, denoted by $(\overline{q}, \overline{\nu})$, of a timed automaton $\mathcal{A}$ over a timed word (σ, τ) is an infinite sequence of the form

$$r:\ \langle q_0, \nu_0 \rangle \xrightarrow[\tau_1]{\sigma_1} \langle q_1, \nu_1 \rangle \xrightarrow[\tau_2]{\sigma_2} \langle q_2, \nu_2 \rangle \xrightarrow[\tau_3]{\sigma_3} \cdots$$

where each $q_i \in Q$ and ν_i is an assignment from C to $\mathbf{R}$. In addition, the following conditions are satisfied:

- *Initiation:* $q_0 = q_{init}$, and $\nu_0(x) = 0$ for all $x \in C$.
- *Consecution:* for all $i \geq 1$, there is an edge in $\mathcal{E}$ of the form $\langle q_{i-1}, q_i, \sigma_i, \lambda_i, \delta_i \rangle$ such that the clock vector $(\nu_{i-1} + \tau_i - \tau_{i-1})$ satisfies δ_i, and $\nu_i(x) = 0$ if $x \in \lambda_i$, and $\nu_i(x) = \nu_{i-1}(x) + \tau_i - \tau_{i-1}$ otherwise.

As an example of a timed automaton, consider the automaton of Figure 1. The automaton starts in location q_0, and loops between the locations q_0, q_1, q_2, and q_3. It has two clocks x and y. The clock x gets set to 0 each time it moves from q_0 to q_1 reading a. The check $(x < 1)$? associated with the c-transition from q_2 to q_3 ensures that c happens

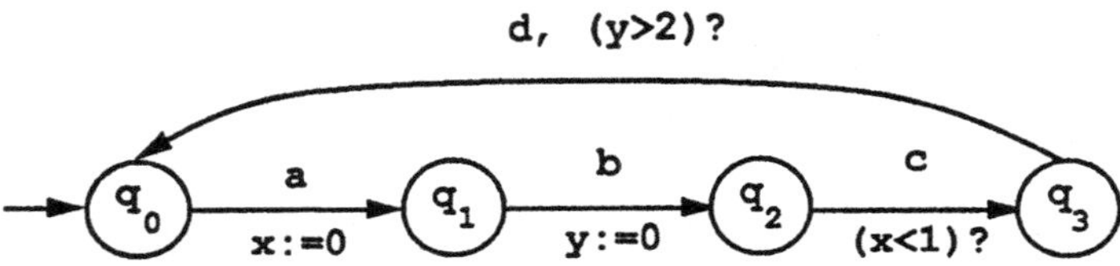

Figure 1: Timed automaton

within time 1 of the preceding a. A similar mechanism of resetting another independent clock y while reading b and checking its value while reading d, ensures that the delay between b and the following d is always at least 2. Thus the automaton has a run over (σ, τ) iff (1) $\sigma = (abcd)^\omega$, and (2) for each $j \geq 0$, $\tau_{4j+3} < \tau_{4j+1} + 1$, and $\tau_{4j+4} > \tau_{4j+2} + 2$.

We can couple acceptance criteria with timed automata, and use them to define languages of timed words. A *timed Muller automaton* $\mathcal{A}$ is a timed automaton with a Muller acceptance family $\mathcal{F} \subseteq 2^Q$. A run $r = (\overline{q}, \overline{\nu})$ of the automaton $\mathcal{A}$ over a timed word (σ, τ) is called an *accepting run* iff the set of locations appearing infinitely often along r is in $\mathcal{F}$. The language $L(\mathcal{A})$ of timed words accepted by $\mathcal{A}$ is defined to be the set of timed words $\{(\sigma, \tau) \mid \mathcal{A}$ has an accepting run over $(\sigma, \tau)\}$.

When used as a specification formalism, the language of a timed automaton describes the desired property of timed words. A real-time probabilistic process $\mathcal{M}$ satisfies a specification presented as a timed automaton $\mathcal{A}$ iff the probability that $\mathcal{A}$ accepts the timed word generated by $\mathcal{M}$ equals 1. In other words, the set $L(\mathcal{A})$ has probability 1 according to the probability measure induced by $\mathcal{M}$ on the space of timed words. The probabilistic verification problem is to decide whether or not $\mathcal{M}$ satisfies $\mathcal{A}$. In general, the specification automaton $\mathcal{A}$ can be nondeterministic, and we donot know how to solve the probabilistic verification problem. However, the problem is solvable for a special class of timed automata, namely, *deterministic* automata.

For the conventional finite-state automata, the property of determinism requires that, for each location, given the next input symbol, the next location is uniquely determined. We want a similar criterion for determinism for the timed automata: given a location along with the clock values, and the next input symbol along with its time of occurrence, the location and the clock values after the next transition should be uniquely determined. So we allow multiple transitions starting at the same location with the same label, but require their clock constraints to be mutually exclusive so that at any time only one of these transitions is enabled. Formally, a timed automaton $\mathcal{A}$ is called *deterministic* iff for all $q \in Q$, for all $a \in \Sigma$, for every pair of edges of the form $\langle q, -, a, -, \delta_1 \rangle$ and $\langle q, -, a, -, \delta_2 \rangle$, the clock constraints δ_1 and δ_2 are mutually exclusive (i.e., $\delta_1 \wedge \delta_2$ is unsatisfiable). The property of determinism ensures that a deterministic timed automaton has at most one run over a given timed word.

Deterministic timed Muller automata (DTMA) can specify many interesting properties of real-time systems. As an example, consider the automaton of Figure 2. The automaton starts in location q_0, and uses a single clock x. The clock is reset every time the automaton

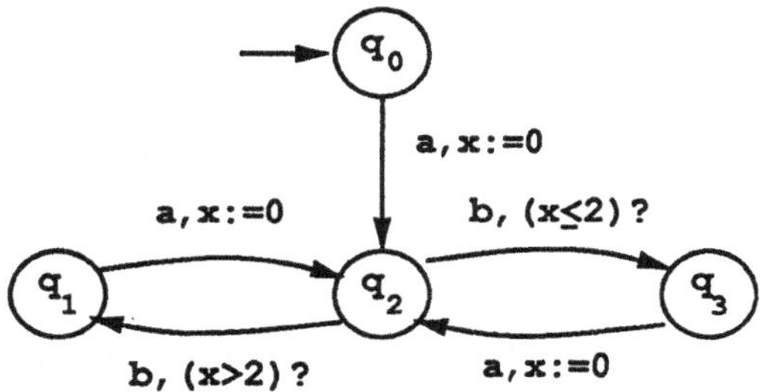

Figure 2: Deterministic timed Muller automaton

moves to location q_2 reading the symbol a. The location q_2 has two mutually exclusive outgoing transitions on b. The automaton moves to location q_3 if b appears within 2 time units after the previous a, and to location q_1 otherwise. The Muller acceptance condition is given by $\{\{q_2, q_3\}\}$. So any accepting run should loop between locations q_1 and q_2 only finitely many times, and between locations q_2 and q_3 infinitely many times. Interpreting the symbol b as a response to a request denoted by the symbol a, the automaton models the requirement of *convergent response time*: the response time should "eventually" be always less than 2 time units. The language of the automaton can be described as

$$L_{crt} = \{((ab)^\omega, \tau) \mid \exists i. \forall j \geq i. (\tau_{2j} < \tau_{2j-1} + 2)\}.$$

4 Verification algorithm

In this section, we show how to solve the probabilistic verification problem for specifications given as deterministic timed automata.

Let $\mathcal{M}$ be a probabilistic real-time process, and let $\mathcal{A}$ be a deterministic timed Muller automaton. We assume that $\mathcal{A}$ has precisely one run over any timed word. In general, a DTMA may not satisfy this property: it may not have any run over some timed words. However, this property can be attained by a simple transformation. First we add a dummy location q to the automaton. From each location q', for each symbol a, we add an a-labeled edge from q' to q. The clock constraint for this edge is the negation of the disjunction of the clock constraints of all the a-labeled edges starting at q'. We leave the acceptance condition unchanged. This construction preserves determinism as well as the set of accepted timed words. The new automaton has the property that for each location q' and each input symbol a, the disjunction of the clock constraints of the a-labeled edges starting at q' is a valid formula.

Before we present the algorithm, let us define an extension $\mathcal{M}^*$ of the process $\mathcal{M}$. The state of $\mathcal{M}^*$ records, in addition to the state of $\mathcal{M}$, the location and the clock values of the automaton $\mathcal{A}$ also. The $\mathcal{A}$-component of the state of $\mathcal{M}^*$ is updated so as to simulate the behavior of $\mathcal{A}$ while reading the timed word generated by $\mathcal{M}$. Observe that since $\mathcal{A}$ is deterministic, this update is completely determined by the choices made by $\mathcal{M}$. A generalized state of $\mathcal{M}^*$ is of the form $\langle s, q, \nu \rangle$, where s is a state of $\mathcal{M}$, q is a location of $\mathcal{A}$, and ν is a vector of real numbers of length $|\mathrm{E}(s) \cup \mathrm{C}|$. The interpretation ν gives values for the clocks corresponding to the scheduled events of $\mathcal{M}$ and the clocks of $\mathcal{A}$. For a state s of $\mathcal{M}$, the set of all active clocks is $\mathrm{E}^*(s) = \mathrm{E}(s) \cup \mathrm{C}$; the set of all nonexponential clocks is $\mathrm{E}_b^*(s) = \mathrm{E}_b(s) \cup \mathrm{C}$; All the clocks count the elapsed time, and thereby increasing the values in ν. The state of $\mathcal{M}$ changes when some of the clocks reach 0; the location of $\mathcal{A}$ is also updated accordingly. Let $a \in \Sigma(s)$ be the set of events causing the transition, and let $\langle q, q', a, \lambda, \delta \rangle$ be the unique edge of $\mathcal{A}$ such that the clock vector at the time of the state-transition satisfies δ. The state of $\mathcal{M}^*$ after the transition is $\langle s', q', \nu' \rangle$ such that $next(s, a, s')$ is positive. For each newly scheduled event x the value of $\nu'(x)$ is chosen according to its probability distribution, each clock y in λ is reset to 0, and all the remaining clocks keep counting without being affected by the state-transition.

This gives us a continuous-time Markov process $X^*(t)$ over the space of all generalized states of $\mathcal{M}^*$. A sample path ρ of the process is a map from $\mathbf{R}$ to the set of its generalized states. It can be constructed as described above by choosing the next state and specific values for the clocks corresponding to the newly scheduled events at all the transition points. The probability functions of $\mathcal{M}$ give a probability measure over the space of all sample paths.

The next step in this construction is to group the uncountably many generalized states of $\mathcal{M}^*$ into a finite number of equivalence classes. Informally, $\langle s, q, \nu \rangle$ is equivalent to $\langle s, q, \nu' \rangle$ iff ν and ν' agree on the integral parts of all the clock values and the integral parts of the differences between clock values. A *projected state* of $\mathcal{M}^*$ corresponds to an equivalence class of its generalized states. It keeps track of the integer parts of the clock values and the ordering of the fractional parts. The integer parts are needed to determine which clock constraints are currently satisfied, and which clocks have reached the value 0. The ordering of the fractional parts is needed to update the integral parts of different clocks in a consistent manner. This information is not required in two cases. For an exponential event x we need not keep track of its actual value. This is due to the "memoryless" property of the exponential distributions. Secondly, for a clock $y \in \mathrm{C}$, if y is never compared with a constant greater than d in the clock constraints of $\mathcal{A}$ then the value of y, once it crosses d, is of no importance. This observation is used to keep the number of projected states finite.

Let us make this precise. Let $\lfloor t \rfloor$ denote the greatest integer not exceeding t, for $t \in \mathbf{R}$. Given two real numbers t and t', we say that they *agree on the integral parts* iff (1) $\lfloor t \rfloor = \lfloor t' \rfloor$, and (2) either both t and t' are integers, or neither is an integer. For a clock $x \in \mathrm{C}$, let d_x be the largest constant d such that either $x \leq d$ or $d \leq x$ appears in some clock constraint in the transitions of $\mathcal{A}$. For a clock vector ν, a clock $x \in \mathrm{C}$ is *relevant* if $\nu(x) \leq d_x$.

Formally, define $\langle s, q, \nu \rangle \sim \langle s, q, \nu' \rangle$ iff

1. for each $x \in \mathrm{E}_b^*(s)$, either $\nu(x)$ and $\nu'(x)$ agree on the integral parts or x is not relevant for both ν and ν', and

2. for every pair x and x' in $\mathrm{E}_b^*(s)$ and relevant for ν, $[\nu(x) - \nu(x')]$ and $[\nu'(x) - \nu'(x')]$ agree on the integral parts.

We use $[s, q, \nu]$ to denote the equivalence class to which $\langle s, q, \nu \rangle$ belongs. We will call such a class a *projected state*. As an example, consider a system in state s with

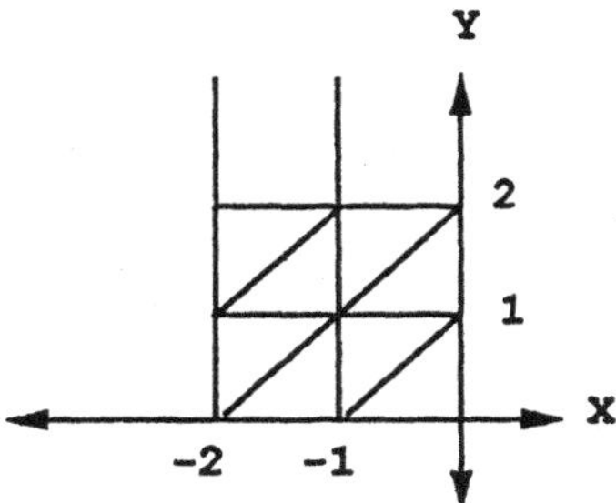

Figure 3: Equivalence classes

$E(s) = \{x\}$. Let $u_x = 2$. Suppose the automaton is in location q, and it has a single clock y with $d_y = 2$. The equivalence relation on the clock vectors is depicted in Figure 3. For instance, the clock vector $[x = -0.8, y = 0.6]$ belongs to the projected state

$$\{\langle s, q, \nu\rangle : \nu(x) \in (-1, 0) \wedge \nu(y) \in (0, 1) \wedge \nu(y) > \nu(x) + 1\}.$$

We will denote it by $[s, q, -1 < x < 0, x + 1 < y < 1]$.

Let V denote the set of all projected states. There are only a finite number of projected states; the following bound can be proved by a simple combinatorial argument:

$$|V| < |Q| \cdot \Pi_{x \in C}\, d_x \cdot \Sigma_{s \in S}[\,|E_b(s) \cup C|! \cdot \Pi_{x \in E_b(s)}\, u_x\,].$$

Thus the number of projected states is linear in the number of states of $\mathcal{M}$, linear in the number of locations of $\mathcal{A}$, exponential in the number of simultaneously scheduled events in $\mathcal{M}$, exponential in the number of clocks of $\mathcal{A}$, and proportional to the constants involved. Each projected state can be represented in length linear in the size of the input.

Let $X_p(t)$ be the process over the state space V obtained from $\mathcal{M}^*$ by projecting each generalized state onto its equivalence class. Note that though $X_p(t)$ has a finite state space, it is not Markovian: the projected state does not have enough information to determine the future behavior of the system completely. Let ρ_p be a sample path of the projection process $X_p(t)$. Note that ρ_p is piecewise constant and right-continuous. It can be characterized by an ω-sequence over V, denoted by $\gamma(\rho_p)$, which records all the projected states appearing along ρ_p. In other words, we can find a sequence of times $t_0, t_1, t_2 \ldots$ and a sequence of projected states $\gamma_0\gamma_1\gamma_2 \ldots$ such that for each i, $\rho_p(t_i) = \gamma_i$ and for any $t_i < t < t_{i+1}$, $\rho_p(t)$ is either γ_i or γ_{i+1}. For a sample path ρ_p of the projected process, let $inf(\rho_p)$ denote the set of projected states appearing infinitely often along $\gamma(\rho_p)$, and let $inf_Q(\rho_p)$ denote the projection of $inf(\rho_p)$ on Q. The following lemma relates the ergodic behavior of $\mathcal{M}^*$ to the probabilistic verification problem; its proof follows from the definitions.

Lemma [1]. The process $\mathcal{M}$ satisfies the specification $\mathcal{A}$ iff for every $Q' \subseteq Q$, the set of sample paths ρ of $\mathcal{M}^*$ such that $inf_Q(\rho_p) = Q'$ has positive probability only if $Q' \in \mathcal{F}$. ∎

The first step of the model-checking algorithm is to define a graph G whose vertex set is V such that $X_p(t)$ moves along the paths in G. The state of $X_p(t)$ may change either because of a state transition of $\mathcal{M}$ or because of the change in the equivalence class of clock values due to the passage of time. For example, consider the system of Figure 3, and suppose the current state is $\langle s, q, [-0.8, 0.6]\rangle$. The projected state does not change for next 0.4 time units. However, at $t = 0.4$, the clock vector is $[-0.4, 1.0]$, which belongs to a different equivalence class. This projected state is only transient: at time $0.4 + \epsilon$, for any small positive ϵ, the generalized state belongs to a different equivalence class described by $[s, q, -1 < x < 0, 1 < y < x + 2]$. The projected state changes again at time 0.8 because the clock for x reaches 0, and a state-transition is triggered. Notice that the projected states that the process visits, are obtained by drawing a line from the point $[-0.8, 0.6]$ in the diagonally upward direction (parallel to the line $x = y$).

We call a projected state $[s, q, \nu]$ *transient* iff some clock x relevant to ν has zero fractional part. For such a state, the generalized state after a time delay of ϵ, however small, belongs to a different equivalence class. In Figure 3, the equivalence classes that lie on horizontal or vertical lines correspond to transient states.

The set of initial vertices V_0 consists of projected states of the form $[s, q_{init}, \nu]$ such that

(1) $f_0(s)$ is positive, and
(2) for every fixed-delay event $x \in E_b(s)$, $\nu(x) = -l_x$, and
(3) for every variable-delay event $x \in E_b(s)$, $\nu(x) \in (l_x, u_x)$, and
(4) for every exponential event $x \in E_e(s)$, $-\infty < \nu(x) < 0$, and
(5) if x is a variable-delay event or an exponential event, $\nu(x)$ is not an integer and for any x', $\nu(x') - \nu(x)$ is not an integer, and
(6) for every clock $x \in C$, $\nu(x) = 0$.

Now we define an edge relation over the vertex set V to get a graph G. There are four different types of edges:

1. Consider a transient projected state $[s, q, \nu]$, and suppose for every $x \in E(s)$, $\nu(x) \neq 0$. In this case, the change in the projected state is due to the passage of time. Let $\epsilon > 0$ be such that for each $0 < \epsilon' < \epsilon$, $[s, q, \nu + \epsilon']$ and $[s, q, \nu + \epsilon]$ are equivalent. There is exactly one edge out of $[s, q, \nu]$ to $[s, q, \nu + \epsilon]$. For example, the vertex $[s, q, -1 < x < 0, y = 1]$ has a single edge to $[s, q, -1 < x < 0, 1 < y < x + 2]$.

2. Consider a transient vertex $[s, q, \nu]$ such that the set a consisting of events $x \in E(s)$ with $\nu(x) = 0$, is nonempty. In this case, the event set a triggers a state-transition of $\mathcal{M}$. Let $\langle q, q', a, \lambda, \delta\rangle$ be the unique edge such that ν satisfies δ. We have an edge to every vertex $[s', q', \nu']$ satisfying

   (1) $next(s, a, s')$ is positive,
   (2) for every $x \in \lambda$, $\nu'(x) = 0$,
   (3) for every $x \in old(s, e, s')$ or $x \in C - \lambda$, $\nu'(x) = \nu(x)$, and
   (4) for every $x \in new(s, a, s')$,

      (a) if x is a variable-delay event then $\nu'(x) \in (l_x, u_x)$, and
      (b) if x is an exponential event then $-\infty < \nu'(x) < 0$, and
      (c) if x is a fixed-delay event then $\nu'(x) = -l_x$, and

(d) if x is a variable-delay or an exponential event, $\nu'(x)$ is not an integer and for any x', $\nu'(x') - \nu'(x)$ is not an integer,

For example, consider the vertex $[s, q, x = 0 < y < 1]$. Consider the change in the projected state triggered by the occurrence of x. Suppose $next(s, \{x\}, s')$ is positive, and $E(s') = \{z\}$ with $l_z = 1$ and $u_z = 2$. Suppose $\mathcal{A}$ has a transition from $\langle q, q', \{x\}, \emptyset, true\rangle$. There are two possible edges corresponding to the state-transition from s to s' on x: $[s', q', -2 < z < -1, 0 < y < z + 2]$ and $[s', q', 0 < y < 1, -2 < z < y - 2]$, depending upon whether the fractional part of z is less than or greater than that of y. Note that the condition $4(d)$ disallows the choice $z + 2 = y$.

3. Consider the case when $[s, q, \nu]$ is a nontransient state, and suppose there is some nonexponential clock relevant to ν. As time progresses, some of the clocks in ν reach integer values changing the projected state. Let a be the set of clocks x relevant for ν such that for every relevant x', the fractional part of x is at least as much as the fractional part of x'. There is an edge corresponding to the clocks in a reaching an integral value; the new projected state is $[s, q, \nu']$ where $\nu'(x) = \lfloor \nu(x) \rfloor + 1$ if $x \in a$, and $\nu'(x) = \nu(x)$ otherwise. For instance, the projected state $[s, q, -2 < x < -1, x + 2 < y < 1]$ has an edge to $[s, q, -2 < x < -1, y = 1]$ corresponding to the event of the clock y reaching the value 1.

4. In addition, for a nontransient state $[s, q, \nu]$, for every exponential event $x \in E_e(s)$, there is an edge to the projected state $[s, q, \nu']$ where $\nu'(x) = 0$ and $\nu'(x') = \nu(x')$ for $x' \neq x$. For instance, suppose in our example there was an additional exponential event z scheduled in state s, then the projected state $[s, q, -1 < x < 0, x + 1 < y < 1, -\infty < z < 0]$ has an edge to $[s, q, -1 < x < 0, x + 1 < y < 1, z = 0]$. This captures the fact that z may happen at any instant.

We will now relate properties of $\mathcal{M}^*$ to the graph G. The following lemma asserts that the process X_p faithfully follows the finite paths in G.

Lemma [2]. For every vertex $v \in V$, the set of sample paths ρ such that v appears on ρ_p is positive iff there is a path in G from some initial vertex $v_0 \in V_0$ to v.

Proof. The definition of G ensures the following: If there is no edge from u to u' in G, and if the current projected state is u, then the probability of the next projected state being u' is zero. The "only if" direction follows from this observation.

For the other direction, it suffices to show that for every edge from u to u' in G, if the process $X^*(t)$ is in some generalized state in u, then there is a positive probability that the next projected state will be u'. This follows from the definitions if the edge from u to u' is according to the clause 1 or 2. Suppose the edge from u to u' is according to the clause 3. The state u is a nontransient state, and consider the process $X^*(t)$ in some generalized state $\langle s, q, \nu\rangle$ in u. Let a be the set of nonexponential clocks reaching the integral values corresponding to this edge. Let ϵ be the time at which the clocks in a reach integral values according to ν. If all the exponential events have clock values smaller than $-\epsilon$ in ν, which has positive probability by the definition of the exponential distribution, then the next projected state is u'. The argument for the edges according to the clause 4 is similar. ∎

Now we need to relate the set of Q-states that X_p visits infinitely often to the strongly connected components of G. Given a set V' of projected states, we need to find a necessary and sufficient condition on V' so that the probability of $inf(\rho_p) = V'$ is positive. The algorithms for probabilistic model-checking for discrete Markov chains [CY88, Va85] rely on the following "probabilistic" property: if the process visits a vertex v infinitely often then each successor v' of v is also visited infinitely often. This property follows trivially from the fact that the probability of a transition from v to v', for discrete Markov chains, is a fixed positive number. We wish to prove a similar property for the projection process. But unlike the discrete case, $X_p(t)$ is not Markovian. Furthermore, the probability of a transition along an edge in G is not bounded from below, in general. Let us see how this could pose difficulties. Suppose the automaton has two clocks y and z, and there is one event x which has uniform distribution with $l_x = 0$ and $u_x = 1$. Consider a projected state $u = [s, q, x = 0 < y < z < 1]$. Consider an edge to $u' = [s', q', 0 < y < z < 1, y - 1 < x < z - 1]$. This corresponds to a state transition triggered by the event x; it gets rescheduled in state s', the new clock value is between -1 and 0, and its fractional part lies between those of y and z. If the current generalized state is $\langle s, q, \nu \rangle \in u$, the probability of the next projected state being u' is proportional to the difference $[\nu(z) - \nu(y)]$. Assume that the projection process visits u infinitely many times. If the sequence of the value of $[\nu(z) - \nu(y)]$ upon entry to u converges to 0, then the probability of transitioning from u to u' also converges to 0. This prevents us from concluding that X_p visits u' also infinitely often. The following lemma shows that this case cannot happen.

A set $W \subseteq V$ is a *bottom strongly connected component* (BSCC) of G iff (1) it is a strongly connected component, and (2) for every $v \in W$, if there is an edge from v to v' then v' is also in W.

Lemma [3]. Let $W \subseteq$ V be a set of projected states, and assume that the process starts in some $\langle s, q, \nu \rangle \in v$, for some $v \in W$. The set of sample paths ρ such that $inf(\rho_p) = W$ has positive measure iff W is a bottom strongly connected component of G.

Proof. By the previous lemma the process follows only the edges in G. Hence, if W is a BSCC, if started in V, the process stays in W with probability 1.

Now let us consider the other direction. To demonstrate better the ideas in the proof we start with a simpler case first, and then we consider the more general cases.

Case 1: We start with the case in which there are no clocks in the timed automaton and hence all the clocks correspond to events. We also assume that for each event x, x is a variable-delay event. We need first a definition which is key to our proof. We say that a visit of X_p to a projected state v is δ-separated iff upon entry all the fractional parts of the clock values differ by at least δ. Consider an edge from v to v' in G. First we observe the following fact.

Fact 1: For any sufficiently small $\delta > 0$, there is a positive ε and a positive δ' such that for any δ-separated visit to v, the probability of the next projected state to be a δ'-separated visit to v', is bounded below by ε.

Consequently, if X_p has infinitely many δ-separated visits to v, then with probability 1 it must have infinitely many δ'-separated visits to v'.

Now we identify another property of the process. Let $n = 3|\mathrm{E}^*|$, and $\delta_0 = 1/n$. Divide the interval $(0, 1)$ into n disjoint intervals $I_1, I_2, \ldots I_n$, each of length δ_0. Whenever a new clock value x is chosen, there exists an interval I_j such that if the fractional part of x lies in I_j then it is at least δ_0-separated from all the old clocks. Hence, for each event

x, each time it gets scheduled, there is a positive probability p_x that the clock for x is chosen at least δ_0-separated from all the other clocks. Note that p_x depends only upon the distribution f_x and the separation δ_0. Let $T = \max\{u_x : x \in E^*\}$. We will show the following.

Fact 2: Consider the process in some arbitrary state $\langle s, q, \nu \rangle$. Then the probability that after time T the clocks of the process will be δ_0-separated is bounded below by some constant.

We prove this as follows. By time T all the active clocks in $\langle s, q, \nu \rangle$ will have reached 0 at least once. For each event x, let P_x denote the property that at time T either x is not scheduled, or that the last time x was scheduled before T, its clock was chosen at least δ_0-separated from the other clocks. One can easily see that independently of the other choices, the probability of P_x is bounded below by p_x since it corresponds to the probability that the fractional part of x will be chosen in some "free" interval I_j (containing no other clock). Let p_m be the smallest such constant for all events $x \in E^*$. From the above discussion it follows that the probability of all properties P_x holding at time T is at least ${p_m}^{|E^*(s)|} > {p_m}^{|E^*|} > 0$.

We now complete the proof of the lemma as follows. Let $W \subset V$ be a subset such that the probability that the process stays in W and visits exactly all the states in W infinitely often, is positive. That is, the set of sample paths ρ such that ρ_p has only vertices from W and $inf(\rho_p) = W$, has positive measure. One can easily see that Fact 2 implies that conditioned on this event, each trajectory of the process X_p makes almost surely infinitely many δ_0-separated visits to at least one vertex u in W (possibly different for each trajectory). Now Fact 1 implies that all successors of u will appear on this trajectory with probability one infinitely often and being δ'-separated. By induction, all the vertices reachable from u must appear infinitely often with probability one. This implies that W must be a bottom strongly connected component.

Case 2: We now allow the timed automaton to have its own clocks. The proof will follow basically the same argument as the proof of Case 1. Now while defining δ-separation for a clock vector ν we require that all the scheduled events and all the relevant and distinct clocks of $\mathcal{A}$ have fractional parts δ-apart. Thus we allow the possibility of two clocks of the automaton to have the same value; that is, two automaton clocks x and y with $\nu(x) = \nu(y)$ are considered as a single clock for what concerns δ-separation; and we donot worry about the clocks not relevant to ν. We need to modify slightly Fact 2 as follows.

Fact 2′: If some generalized state $\langle s, q, \nu \rangle$ appears infinitely often in a trajectory then, with probability 1, it will infinitely often be the case that $\langle s, q, \nu \rangle$ is δ_0-separated (on the same trajectory).

We prove this as follows. Observe that every relevant clock x in ν has been reset by the expiration of some event $y(x) \in E$ (possibly different each time ν appears in the trajectory). Hence the value of x is a continuation of the value of $y(x)$ (think of $y(x)$ as being "incarnated" into x). This implies that the fractional part of x will also be δ_0-separated from the same events and clocks from which the fractional part of $y(x)$ was δ_0-separated, when $y(x)$ was scheduled. Since $\langle s, q, \nu \rangle$ appears infinitely often there must exist a subsequence of times t_i, $i = 1, 2, \ldots$, at which $\langle s, q, \nu \rangle$ appears, such that during the interval from t_i to t_{i+1} all active events in ν and all events resetting relevant clocks in ν have been scheduled at least once. This is true if one chooses the above time sequence such that $t_{i+1} - t_i > T + d$ where d is the maximum constant d_x for all clocks x. Then ν

will be δ_0-separated at time t_{i+1} if for each event which is either in ν or resets a relevant clock in ν, at the last time it was scheduled it was δ_0-separated from the rest of the clocks. By using a similar argument as in the proof of Case 1, the probability of this happening is bounded below by ${p_m}^{|E^*|} > 0$ independently of the history up to time t_{i+1}. The proof of Case 2 of the lemma can now be completed as in Case 1.

Case 3: Now we consider the case when the events are of both fixed-delay and variable-delay types. The reader should notice that if there are no fixed-delay events, then the graph G contains no reachable vertices with ν containing events with equal fractional parts since the probability of such transitions is zero (by the definition of the distribution function for the variable-delay events).

The idea in the proof is the following. All the events and clocks which have equal fractional parts must have some common "ancestor" event which is of the variable-delay type and has scheduled them by sequences of fixed-delay events (it is defined as the "initial" event expiring at time 0 if such an ancestor does not exist). An ancestor event of a singleton group is the event itself if this event is a variable-delay event, or the first variable-delay event by tracing back the "family" history of the event; a similar definition holds for clocks. Let us group the events and relevant clocks of a vertex $\langle s, q, \nu \rangle$ in groups where the events and clocks in each group have equal fractional parts and assume that the ancestor event of each group is a variable-delay event. Then the probability that when this vertex appears the fractional parts of the groups will be δ_0-separated is bounded from below by the probability that all ancestor events be δ_0-separated when scheduled, which is bounded below by ${p_m}^{|E^*|}$.

In order to follow the steps of the proof in the previous case, we would like to show that if $\langle s, q, \nu \rangle$ appears infinitely often, then there are infinitely many time values $t_1, t_2, \ldots$ such that the probability that $\langle s, q, \nu \rangle$ appears at each time t_i with ν δ_0-separated, is bounded from below by some constant, independently of the history of the system. Unfortunately, this does not hold for the following reason. Two events could always be separated by less than δ, for any δ, in $\langle s, q, \nu \rangle$ with positive probability. Consider the following example: at time zero two variable delay events x_1 and x_2 with uniform distribution on $(0,1)$ are scheduled. When each x_i expires, it schedules an event x'_i with fixed delay of 1; the events x'_i reschedule themselves when they expire. One can easily see that the separation between the x'_is will always be the same, equal to the initial separation of x_1 and x_2 which can be arbitrarily small. This example suggests the following idea. If some of the events in $\langle s, q, \nu \rangle$ eventually "synchronize", they will always have some constant separation from then on. If the minimum of the separation over all such events (after all synchronizations have occurred) is δ', we can show that with probability one, after all "synchronizations" have occurred, $\langle s, q, \nu \rangle$ will appear infinitely often being δ'_0-separated, where δ'_0 is the minimum of δ_0 and δ'. Then we can use similar steps as in the previous cases to prove the lemma.

For completeness we add some steps of the proof. Consider a trajectory which repeats $\langle s, q, \nu \rangle$ infinitely often. Let $x_1, \ldots, x_n$ denote the ancestor events in ν (possibly different each time $\langle s, q, \nu \rangle$ appears). Let E_s be the ancestor events which eventually remain the same after some finite time t, and let δ' be the minimum of the separation of the fractional parts of the events in E_s. From the definition of E_s it follows that after some finite time $\langle s, q, \nu \rangle$ will appear infinitely often with (a) its events in E_s being δ' separated, and (b) the remaining of the events in ν, which do not have ancestors in E_s, will have ancestor

events which are scheduled infinitely often; denote this set of events by E_c. Observe that we can find a sequence $t < t_1 < t_2 \ldots$ such that the trajectory is in state $\langle s, q, \nu \rangle$ at each time t_i, and all the ancestors of the events in E_c are scheduled at least once between each t_i and t_{i+1}. By repeating the steps in the previous proofs, it follows that at the end of the each interval the probability that the events in E_c are δ_0-separated is bounded below by a constant, hence with probability one, $\langle s, q, \nu \rangle$ will appear infinitely often being δ_0'-separated. Since for each trajectory which repeats $\langle s, q, \nu \rangle$ infinitely often such a $\delta_0' > 0$ exists, by repeating the arguments we used in the previous cases the proof follows.
Case 4: Same as in Case 3, with the additional events with exponential distributions. The proof is an easy extension of the proof of Case 3 as follows. Consider the state of the system projected on the bounded events. Then with probability one if $\langle s, q, \nu \rangle$ appears infinitely often, it will also appear infinitely often with its bounded events and relevant clocks being δ_0'-separated for some positive δ_0'. One can easily see that each time $\langle s, q, \nu \rangle$ appears and is δ_0'-separated, then all events are at least δ_0' away from 0. By the memoryless property of the exponential distributions, the probability that each exponential event lies in the interval $(-\delta_0', 0)$ is bounded from below. This implies that infinitely often when $\langle s, q, \nu \rangle$ is visited, a transition corresponding to the expiration of an exponential clock will be taken. ∎

Now putting together all the lemmas we get the following:

Theorem [1]. The process $\mathcal{M}$ satisfies its specification $\mathcal{A}$ iff for every bottom strongly connected component W of G such that W is reachable from some initial vertex in V_0, the projection of V' on Q belongs to $\mathcal{F}$. ∎

This gives a decision procedure for model-checking. After constructing the graph G, we only need to compute its bottom strongly connected components that are accessible from the initial vertices, and check if the set of Q-states corresponding to each such component is an accepting set for $\mathcal{A}$. The size of the graph G is exponential in the size of the input (particularly, the number of events and clocks, and the length of the constants involved). However, the graph need not be constructed explicitly. Since each vertex can be represented in length linear in the size of the input, the following theorem follows:

Theorem [2]. The verification problem for a finite-state probabilistic real-time process $\mathcal{M}$ and a deterministic timed automaton specification $\mathcal{A}$ can be solved in PSPACE. ∎

5 Conclusions

In this paper, we have presented a way of reasoning about finite-state real-time systems. The process model is quite general, and accounts for both the real-time and the probabilistic aspects of the system behavior.

In this presentation, we have required all distributions to be either bounded, discrete, or exponential. One can easily extend the proofs in the paper for arbitrary unbounded distributions with increasing hazard rate, or mixtures of arbitrary distributions one of which has increasing hazard rate. We conjecture that the algorithm is correct even for more general continuous distributions, however, proving the correctness may be nontrivial.

The other question of interest is whether the basic technique of the algorithm, which involves constructing the projection process, can be used to check other types of specifications. We do not yet know how to check properties specified using nondeterministic timed automata or using linear real-time logics.

The algorithm outlined here is expensive. To make it more practical, some heuristic techniques need to be devised. Observe that the verification problems are typically PSPACE, even in the absence of real-time and probabilities. We feel hopeful that the techniques emerging from the ongoing research on how to cope with the state-explosion problem [BCMDH90], [GW90] will be useful in implementing the algorithm presented here.

Acknowledgements: We thank Gerald Shedler for pointing us to the existing literature on modeling systems as generalized semi-Markov processes. We also thank Joseph Halpern and Moshe Vardi for useful discussions.

References

[ACD90] R. Alur, C. Courcoubetis, D.L. Dill, "Model-checking for real-time systems," In *Proceedings of the Fifth IEEE Symposium on Logic in Computer Science*, pages 414-425, 1990.

[ACD91] R. Alur, C. Courcoubetis, D.L. Dill, "Model-checking for probabilistic real-time systems," In *Automata, Languages, and Programming: Proceedings of the 18th ICALP*, Lecture Notes in Computer Science 510, 1991.

[AD90] R. Alur, D.L. Dill, "Automata for modeling real-time systems," In *Automata, Languages, and Programming: Proceedings of the 17th ICALP*, Lecture Notes in Computer Science 443, pages 322-335, 1990.

[AH89] R. Alur, T.A. Henzinger, "A really temporal logic," In *Proceedings of the 30th IEEE Symposium on Foundations of Computer Science*, pages 164-169, 1989.

[BCMDH90] J.R. Burch, E.M. Clarke, K.L. McMillan, D.L. Dill, L.J. Hwang, "Symbolic model-checking: 10^{20} states and beyond," In *Proceedings of the Fifth IEEE Symposium on Logic in Computer Science*, pages 428-439, 1990.

[CY88] C. Courcoubetis, M. Yannakakis, "Verifying temporal properties of finite-state probabilistic programs," In *Proceedings of the 29th IEEE Symposium on Foundations of Computer Science*, pages 338-345, 1988.

[EC82] E.A. Emerson, E.M. Clarke, "Using branching-time temporal logic to synthesize synchronization skeletons," *Science of Computer Programming* **2**, pages 241-266, 1982.

[GW91] P. Godefroid, P. Wolper, "A partial approach to model-checking," In *Proceedings of the Sixth IEEE Symposium on Logic in Computer Science*, pages 406-415, 1991.

[HJ89] H. Hansson, B. Jonsson, "A framework for reasoning about time and reliability," In *Proceedings of the Tenth IEEE Real-Time Systems Symposium*, pages 102-111, 1989.

[Ko90] R. Koymans, "Specifying real-time properties with Metric Temporal Logic," *Journal of Real-Time Systems*, **2**, pages 255-299, 1990.

[Le90] H.R. Lewis, "A logic of concrete time intervals," In *Proceedings of the Fifth IEEE Symposium on Logic in Computer Science*, pages 380-389, 1990.

[LS82] D. Lehman, S. Shelah, "Reasoning with time and chance," *Information and Control* **53**, 1982.

[PZ86] A. Pnueli, L. Zuck, "Probabilistic verification by tableaux," In *Proceedings of the First IEEE Symposium on Logic in Computer Science*, 1986.

[Sh87] G.S. Shedler, *Regeneration and Networks of Queues*, Springer-Verlag, 1987.

[Th90] W. Thomas, "Automata on infinite objects," *Handbook of Theoretical Computer Science,* volume B, pages 133-191, 1990.

[Wh80] W. Whitt, "Continuity of generalized semi-Markov processes," *Math. Oper. Res.* **5**,1980.

[Va85] M. Vardi, "Automatic verification of probabilistic concurrent finite-state programs," In *Proceedings of the 26th IEEE Symposium on Foundations of Computer Science*, pages 327-338, 1985.

The Theory of Timed Automata

Rajeev Alur
AT&T Bell Laboratories
Murray Hill, NJ 07974, USA.

David Dill [1]
Department of Computer Science
Stanford University, Stanford, CA 94305, USA.

Abstract. We propose *timed automata* to model the behavior of real-time systems over time. Our definition provides a simple, and yet powerful, way to annotate state-transition graphs with timing constraints using finitely many real-valued *clocks*. A timed automaton accepts *timed words* — strings in which a real-valued time of occurrence is associated with each symbol. We study timed automata from the perspective of formal language theory: we consider closure properties, decision problems, and subclasses. We discuss the application of this theory to automatic verification of real-time requirements of finite-state systems.

Keywords: Real-time systems, Automatic verification, Formal languages and Automata theory.

1 Introduction

Modal logics and ω-automata for *qualitative* temporal reasoning about concurrent systems have been studied in great detail (selected references: [Pnu77, MP81, EC82, Lam83, WVS83, Var87, Pnu86, CES86]) These formalisms abstract away from time, retaining only the sequencing of events. In the *linear time model,* it is assumed that an execution can be completely modeled as a linear sequence of states or system events, called an *execution trace* (or just *trace*). The *behavior* of the system is a set of execution sequences. Since a set of sequences is a formal language, this leads naturally to the use of automata for the specification and verification of systems. When the systems are finite-state, as many are, we can use finite automata, leading to effective constructions and decision procedures for automatically manipulating and analyzing system behavior. Even when automata are not used directly, they are never far away; for example, automata theory proves useful in developing the basic decision procedures for propositional linear temporal logic.

[1] Supported by the NSF under grant MIP-8858807.

Although the decision to abstract away from quantitative time has had many advantages, it is ultimately counterproductive when reasoning about systems that must interact with physical processes; the correct functioning of the control system of airplanes and toasters depends crucially upon *real time* considerations. We would like to be able to specify and verify models of real-time systems as easily as qualitative models. Our goal is to modify finite automata for this task.

For simplicity, we discuss models that consider executions to be infinite sequences of events, not states (the theory with state-based models differs only in details). Within this framework, it is possible to add timing to an execution trace by pairing it with a sequence of times, where the i'th element of the time sequence gives the time of occurrence of the i'th event. At this point, however, a fundamental question arises: what is the nature of time?

One alternative, which leads to the *discrete-time* model, requires the time sequence to be a monotonically increasing sequence of integers. This model is appropriate for certain kinds of synchronous digital circuits, where signal changes are considered to have changed exactly when a clock signal arrives. One of the advantages of this model is that it can be transformed easily into an ordinary formal language. Each timed trace can be expanded into a trace where the times increase by exactly one at each step, by inserting a special *silent* event as many times as necessary between events in the original trace. Once this transformation has been performed, the time of each event is the same as its position, so the time sequence can be discarded, leaving an ordinary string. Hence, discrete time behaviors can be manipulated using ordinary finite automata. Of course, in physical processes events do not always happen at integer-valued times. The discrete-time model requires that continuous time be approximated by choosing some fixed quantum *a priori*, which limits the accuracy with which physical systems can be modeled.

The *fictitious-clock model* is similar to the discrete time model, except that it only requires the sequence of integer times to be non-decreasing. The interpretation of a timed execution trace in this model is that events occur in the specified order at real-valued times, but only the (integer) readings of the actual times with respect to a digital clock are recorded in the trace. This model is also easily transformed into a conventional formal language. First, add to the set of events a new one, called *tick*. The untimed trace corresponding to a timed trace will include all of the events from the timed trace, in the same order, but with $t_{i+1} - t_i$ number of *ticks* inserted between the i'th and the $(i+1)$'th events (note that this number may be 0). Once again, it is conceptually simple to manipulate these behaviors using finite automata, but the compensating disadvantage is that it represents time only in an approximate sense.

We prefer a *dense-time* model, in which time is a dense set, because it is more realistic physically. In this model, the times of events are real numbers, which increase monotonically without bound. Dealing with dense time in a finite-automata framework is more difficult than the other two cases, because it is not obvious how to transform a set of dense-time traces into an ordinary formal language. Instead, we have developed a theory of *timed* formal languages and *timed automata* to support automated reasoning about such systems.

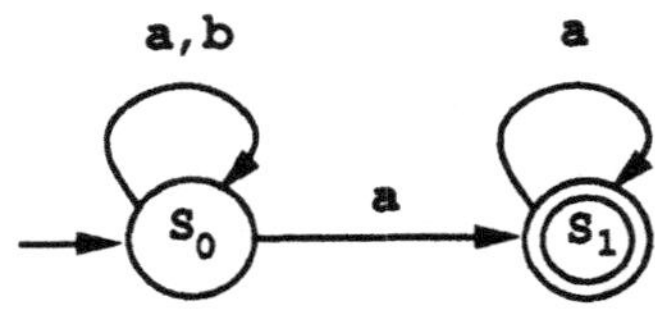

Figure 1: Büchi automaton accepting $(a+b)^*a^\omega$

2 ω-automata

In this section we will briefly review the relevant aspects of the theory of *ω-regular languages.*

The more familiar definition of a formal language is as a set of finite words over some given alphabet (see, for example, [HU79]). As opposed to this, an ω-language consists of infinite words. Thus an ω-language over an alphabet Σ is a subset of Σ^ω — the set of all infinite words over Σ. ω-automata provide a finite representation for certain types of ω-languages. An ω-automaton is essentially the same as a nondeterministic finite-state automaton, but with the acceptance condition modified suitably so as to handle infinite input words. Various types of ω-automata have been studied in the literature [Büc62, McN66, Cho74, Tho90]. We will mainly consider two types of ω-automata: Büchi automata and Muller automata.

A *transition table* $\mathcal{A}$ is a tuple $\langle \Sigma, \mathrm{S}, \mathrm{S}_0, \mathrm{E}\rangle$, where Σ is an input alphabet, S is a finite set of automaton states, $\mathrm{S}_0 \subseteq \mathrm{S}$ is a set of start states, and $\mathrm{E} \subseteq \mathrm{S}\times\mathrm{S}\times\Sigma$ is a set of edges. The automaton starts in an initial state, and if $\langle s, s', a\rangle \in \mathrm{E}$ then the automaton can change its state from s to s' reading the input symbol a.

For $\sigma \in \Sigma^\omega$, we say that

$$r\ :\ s_0 \xrightarrow{\sigma_1} s_1 \xrightarrow{\sigma_2} s_2 \xrightarrow{\sigma_3} \cdots$$

is a *run* of $\mathcal{A}$ over σ, provided $s_0 \in \mathrm{S}_0$, and $\langle s_{i-1}, s_i, \sigma_i\rangle \in \mathrm{E}$ for all $i \geq 1$. For such a run, the set $inf(r)$ consists of the states $s \in \mathrm{S}$ such that $s = s_i$ for infinitely many $i \geq 0$.

Different types of ω-automata are defined by adding an acceptance condition to the definition of the transition tables. A *Büchi automaton* $\mathcal{A}$ is a transition table $\langle \Sigma, \mathrm{S}, \mathrm{S}_0, \mathrm{E}\rangle$ with an additional set $\mathrm{F} \subseteq \mathrm{S}$ of accepting states. A run r of $\mathcal{A}$ over a word $\sigma \in \Sigma^\omega$ is an *accepting run* iff $inf(r) \cap \mathrm{F} \neq \emptyset$. In other words, a run r is accepting iff some state from the set F repeats infinitely often along r. The language $L(\mathcal{A})$ accepted by $\mathcal{A}$ consists of the words $\sigma \in \Sigma^\omega$ such that $\mathcal{A}$ has an accepting run over σ.

Example 2.1 Consider the 2-state automaton of Figure 1 over the alphabet $\{a, b\}$. The state s_0 is the start state and s_1 is the accepting state. Every accepting run of the automaton has the form

$$r\ :\ s_0 \xrightarrow{\sigma_1} s_0 \xrightarrow{\sigma_2} \cdots \xrightarrow{\sigma_n} s_0 \xrightarrow{a} s_1 \xrightarrow{a} s_1 \xrightarrow{a} \cdots$$

The automaton accepts all words with only a finite number of b's; that is, the language $L_0 = (a+b)^*a^\omega$. ■

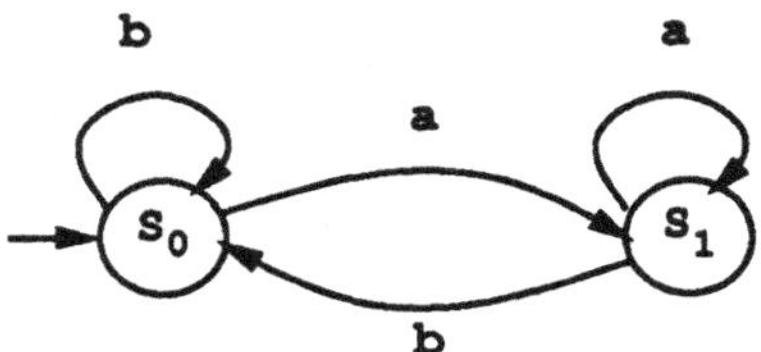

Figure 2: Deterministic Muller automaton accepting $(a+b)^*a^\omega$

An ω-language is called *ω-regular* iff it is accepted by some Büchi automaton. Thus the language L_0 of Example 2.1 is an ω-regular language.

The class of ω-regular languages is closed under all the Boolean operations. Language intersection is implemented by a product construction for Büchi automata [Cho74, WVS83]. There are known constructions for complementing Büchi automata [SVW87, Saf88].

When Büchi automata are used for modeling finite-state concurrent processes, the verification problem reduces to that of language inclusion. The inclusion problem for ω-regular languages is decidable. To test whether the language of one automaton is contained in the other, we check for emptiness of the intersection of the first automaton with the complement of the second. Testing for emptiness is easy; we only need to search for a cycle that is reachable from a start state and includes at least one accepting state. In general, complementing a Büchi automaton involves an exponential blow-up in the number of states, and the language inclusion problem is known to be PSPACE-complete [SVW87]. However, checking whether the language of one automaton is contained in the language of a *deterministic* automaton can be done in polynomial time [Kur87].

A transition table $\mathcal{A} = \langle \Sigma, \mathrm{S}, \mathrm{S}_0, \mathrm{E} \rangle$ is *deterministic* iff (i) there is a single start state, that is, $|\mathrm{S}_0| = 1$, and (ii) the number of a-labeled edges starting at s is at most one for all states $s \in \mathrm{S}$ and for all symbols $a \in \Sigma$. Thus, for a deterministic transition table, the current state and the next input symbol determine the next state uniquely. Consequently, a deterministic automaton has at most one run over a given word. Unlike the automata on finite words, the class of languages accepted by deterministic Büchi automata is strictly smaller than the class of ω-regular languages. For instance, there is no deterministic Büchi automaton which accepts the language L_0 of Example 2.1. Muller automata (defined below) avoid this problem at the cost of a more powerful acceptance condition.

A *Muller automaton* $\mathcal{A}$ is a transition table $\langle \Sigma, \mathrm{S}, \mathrm{S}_0, \mathrm{E} \rangle$ with an *acceptance family* $\mathcal{F} \subseteq 2^{\mathrm{S}}$. A run r of $\mathcal{A}$ over a word $\sigma \in \Sigma^\omega$ is an *accepting run* iff $\mathit{inf}(r) \in \mathcal{F}$. That is, a run r is accepting iff the set of states repeating infinitely often along r equals some set in $\mathcal{F}$. The language accepted by $\mathcal{A}$ is defined as in case of Büchi automata.

The class of languages accepted by Muller automata is the same as that accepted by Büchi automata, and, more importantly, also equals that accepted by deterministic Muller automata.

Example 2.2 The deterministic Muller automaton of Figure 2 accepts the language L_0 consisting of all words over $\{a, b\}$ with only a finite number of b's. The Muller acceptance family is $\{\{s_1\}\}$. Thus every accepting run can visit the state s_0 only finitely often. ∎

Thus deterministic Muller automata form a strong candidate for representing ω-regular languages: they are as expressive as their nondeterministic counterpart, and they can be complemented in polynomial time. Algorithms for constructing the intersection of two Muller automata and for checking the language inclusion are known [CDK89].

3 Timed automata

In this section we define timed words by coupling a real-valued time with each symbol in a word. Then we augment the definition of ω-automata so that they accept timed words, and use them to develop a theory of timed regular languages analogous to the theory of ω-regular languages.

3.1 Timed languages

We define timed words so that a behavior of a real-time system corresponds to a timed word over the alphabet of events. As in the case of the dense-time model, the set of nonnegative real numbers, R, is chosen as the time domain. A word σ is coupled with a time sequence τ as defined below:

Definition 3.1 A *time sequence* $\tau = \tau_1\tau_2\cdots$ is an infinite sequence of time values $\tau_i \in \mathsf{R}$ with $\tau_i > 0$, satisfying the following constraints:

1. *Monotonicity:* τ increases strictly monotonically; that is, $\tau_i < \tau_{i+1}$ for all $i \geq 1$.
2. *Progress:* For every $t \in \mathsf{R}$, there is some $i \geq 1$ such that $\tau_i > t$.

A *timed word* over an alphabet Σ is a pair (σ, τ) where $\sigma = \sigma_1\sigma_2\ldots$ is an infinite word over Σ and τ is a time sequence. A *timed language* over Σ is a set of timed words over Σ. ∎

If a timed word (σ, τ) is viewed as an input to an automaton, it presents the symbol σ_i at time τ_i. If each symbol σ_i is interpreted to denote an event occurrence then the corresponding component τ_i is interpreted as the time of occurrence of σ_i. Let us consider some examples of timed languages.

Example 3.2 Let the alphabet be $\{a, b\}$. Define a timed language L_1 to consist of all timed words (σ, τ) such that there is no b after time 5.6. Thus the language L_1 is given by

$$L_1 \;=\; \{(\sigma,\tau) \mid \forall i.\,((\tau_i > 5.6) \rightarrow (\sigma_i = a))\}.$$

Another example is the language L_2 consisting of timed words in which a and b alternate, and the time difference between the successive pairs of a and b keeps increasing. L_2 is given as

$$L_2 \;=\; \{((ab)^\omega,\tau) \mid \forall i.\,((\tau_{2i} - \tau_{2i-1}) < (\tau_{2i+2} - \tau_{2i+1}))\}.$$

∎

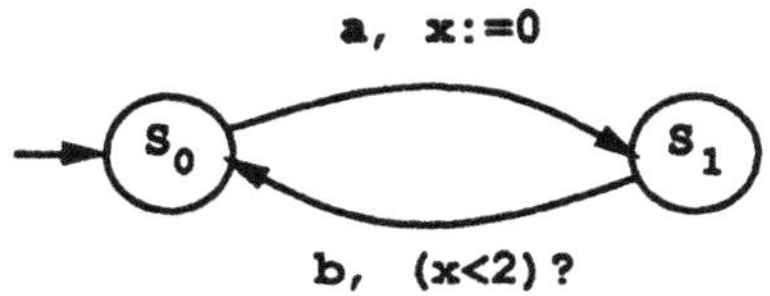

Figure 3: Example of a timed transition table

The language-theoretic operations such as intersection, union, complementation are defined for timed languages as usual. In addition we define the *Untime* operation which discards the time values associated with the symbols, that is, it considers the projection of a timed trace (σ, τ) on the first component.

Definition 3.3 For a timed language L over Σ, *Untime*(L) is the ω-language consisting of $\sigma \in \Sigma^\omega$ such that $(\sigma, \tau) \in L$ for some time sequence τ. ∎

For instance, referring to Example 3.2, *Untime*(L_1) is the ω-language $(a+b)^*a^\omega$, and *Untime*(L_2) consists of a single word $(ab)^\omega$.

3.2 Transition tables with timing constraints

Now we extend transition tables to *timed transition tables* so that they can read timed words. When an automaton makes a state-transition, the choice of the next state depends upon the input symbol read. In case of a timed transition table, we want this choice to depend also upon the time of the input symbol relative to the times of the previously read symbols. For this purpose, we associate a finite set of (real-valued) *clocks* with each transition table. A clock can be set to zero simultaneously with any transition. At any instant, the reading of a clock equals the time elapsed since the last time it was reset. With each transition we associate a clock constraint, and require that the transition may be taken only if the current values of the clocks satisfy this constraint. Before we define the timed transition tables formally, let us consider some examples.

Example 3.4 Consider the timed transition table of Figure 3. The start state is s_0. There is a single clock x. An annotation of the form $x := 0$ on an edge corresponds to the action of resetting the clock x when the edge is traversed. Similarly an annotation of the form $(x < 2)$? on an edge gives the clock constraint associated with the edge.

The automaton starts in state s_0, and moves to state s_1 reading the input symbol a. The clock x gets set to 0 along with this transition. While in state s_1, the value of the clock x shows the time elapsed since the occurrence of the last a symbol. The transition from state s_1 to s_0 is enabled only if this value is less than 2. The whole cycle repeats when the automaton moves back to state s_0. Thus the timing constraint expressed by this transition table is that the delay between a and the following b is always less than 2; more formally, the language is

$$\{((ab)^\omega, \tau) \mid \forall i. (\tau_{2i} < \tau_{2i-1} + 2)\}.$$

∎

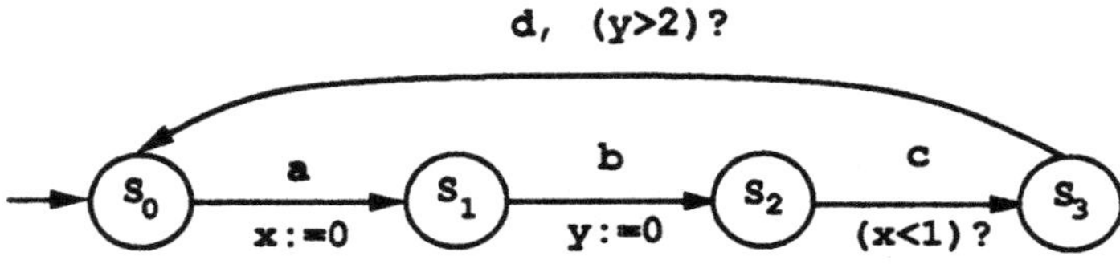

Figure 4: Timed transition table with 2 clocks

Thus to constrain the delay between two transitions e_1 and e_2, we require a particular clock to be reset on e_1, and associate an appropriate clock constraint with e_2. Note that clocks can be set asynchronously of each other. This means that different clocks can be restarted at different times, and there is no lower bound on the difference between their readings. Having multiple clocks allows multiple concurrent delays, as in the next example.

Example 3.5 The timed transition table of Figure 4 uses two clocks x and y, and accepts the language

$$L_3 = \{((abcd)^\omega, \tau) \mid \forall j. ((\tau_{4j+3} < \tau_{4j+1} + 1) \wedge (\tau_{4j+4} > \tau_{4j+2} + 2))\}.$$

The automaton loops between the states s_0, s_1, s_2 and s_3. The clock x gets set to 0 each time it moves from s_0 to s_1 reading a. The check $(x < 1)?$ associated with the c-transition from s_2 to s_3 ensures that c happens within time 1 of the preceding a. A similar mechanism of resetting another independent clock y while reading b and checking its value while reading d, ensures that the delay between b and the following d is always greater than 2. ∎

Notice that in the above example, to constrain the delay between a and c and between b and d the automaton does not put any bounds on the time difference between a and the following b, or c and the following d. This is an important advantage of having access to multiple clocks which can be set independently of each other. The above language L_3 is the intersection of the two languages L_3^1 and L_3^2 defined as

$$L_3^1 = \{((abcd)^\omega, \tau) \mid \forall j. (\tau_{4j+3} < \tau_{4j+1} + 1)\},$$
$$L_3^2 = \{((abcd)^\omega, \tau) \mid \forall j. (\tau_{4j+4} > \tau_{4j+2} + 2)\}.$$

Each of the languages L_3^1 and L_3^2 can be expressed by an automaton which uses just one clock; however to express their intersection we need two clocks.

We remark that the clocks of the automaton do not correspond to the local clocks of different components in a distributed system. All the clocks increase at the uniform rate counting time with respect to a fixed global time frame. They are fictitious clocks invented to express the timing properties of the system. Alternatively, we can view the automaton to be equipped with a finite number of stop-watches which can be started and checked independently of one another, but all stop-watches refer to the same clock.

3.3 Clock constraints and clock interpretations

To define timed automata formally, we need to say what type of clock constraints are allowed on the edges. The simplest form of a constraint compares a clock value with a time constant. We allow only the Boolean combinations of such simple constraints. Any value from Q, the set of nonnegative rationals, can be used as a time constant. Allowing more complex constraints, such as those involving addition of clock values, makes any sort of analysis impossible, for instance, the emptiness problem becomes undecidable.

Definition 3.6 For a set X of clocks, the set $\Phi(X)$ of *clock constraints* δ is defined inductively by

$$\delta := x \leq c \mid c \leq x \mid \neg\delta \mid \delta_1 \wedge \delta_2,$$

where x is a clock in X and c is a constant in Q. ∎

Observe that constraints such as **true**, $(x = c)$, $x \in [2,5)$ can be defined as abbreviations.

A *clock interpretation* ν for a set X of clocks assigns a real value to each clock; that is, it is a mapping from X to R. We say that a clock interpretation ν for X satisfies a clock constraint δ over X iff δ evaluates to true using the values given by ν.

For $t \in$ R, $\nu + t$ denotes the clock interpretation which maps every clock x to the value $\nu(x) + t$, and the clock interpretation $t \cdot \nu$ assigns to each clock x the value $t \cdot \nu(x)$. For $Y \subseteq X$, $[Y \mapsto t]\nu$ denotes the clock interpretation for X which assigns t to each $x \in Y$, and agrees with ν over the rest of the clocks.

3.4 Timed transition tables

Now we give the precise definition of timed transition tables.

Definition 3.7 A *timed transition table* is a tuple $\langle \Sigma, S, S_0, C, E \rangle$, where

- Σ is a finite alphabet,
- S is a finite set of states,
- $S_0 \subseteq S$ is a set of start states,
- C is a finite set of clocks, and
- $E \subseteq S \times S \times \Sigma \times 2^C \times \Phi(C)$ gives the set of transitions. An edge $\langle s, s', a, \lambda, \delta \rangle$ represents a transition from state s to state s' on input symbol a. The set $\lambda \subseteq C$ gives the clocks to be reset with this transition, and δ is a clock constraint over C.

∎

Given a timed word (σ, τ), the timed transition table $\mathcal{A}$ starts in one of its start states at time 0 with all its clocks initialized to 0. As time advances the values of all clocks change, reflecting the elapsed time. At time τ_i, $\mathcal{A}$ changes state from s to s' using some transition of the form $\langle s, s', \sigma_i, \lambda, \delta \rangle$ reading the input σ_i, if the current values of clocks satisfy δ. With this transition the clocks in λ are reset to 0, and thus start counting time with respect to it. This behavior is captured by defining *runs* of timed transition tables. A run records the state and the values of all the clocks at the transition points. For a time sequence $\tau = \tau_1\tau_2\ldots$ we define $\tau_0 = 0$.

Definition 3.8 A run r, denoted by $(\overline{s}, \overline{\nu})$, of a timed transition table $\langle \Sigma, S, S_0, C, E \rangle$ over a timed word (σ, τ) is an infinite sequence of the form

$$r : \langle s_0, \nu_0 \rangle \xrightarrow[\tau_1]{\sigma_1} \langle s_1, \nu_1 \rangle \xrightarrow[\tau_2]{\sigma_2} \langle s_2, \nu_2 \rangle \xrightarrow[\tau_3]{\sigma_3} \cdots$$

with $s_i \in S$ and $\nu_i \in [C \to R]$, for all $i \geq 0$, satisfying the following requirements:

- *Initiation:* $s_0 \in S_0$, and $\nu_0(x) = 0$ for all $x \in C$.
- *Consecution:* for all $i \geq 1$, there is an edge in E of the form $\langle s_{i-1}, s_i, \sigma_i, \lambda_i, \delta_i \rangle$ such that $(\nu_{i-1} + \tau_i - \tau_{i-1})$ satisfies δ_i and ν_i equals $[\lambda_i \mapsto 0](\nu_{i-1} + \tau_i - \tau_{i-1})$.

The set $inf(r)$ consists of $s \in S$ such that $s = s_i$ for infinitely many $i \geq 0$. ∎

Example 3.9 Consider the timed transition table of Example 3.5. Consider a timed word

$$(a, 2) \to (b, 2.7) \to (c, 2.8) \to (d, 5) \to \cdots$$

Below we give the initial segment of the run. A clock interpretation is represented by listing the values $[x, y]$.

$$\langle s_0, [0,0] \rangle \xrightarrow[2]{a} \langle s_1, [0,2] \rangle \xrightarrow[2.7]{b} \langle s_2, [0.7, 0] \rangle \xrightarrow[2.8]{c} \langle s_3, [0.8, 0.1] \rangle \xrightarrow[5]{d} \langle s_0, [3, 2.3] \rangle \cdots$$

∎

Along a run $r = (\overline{s}, \overline{\nu})$ over (σ, τ), the values of the clocks at time t between τ_i and τ_{i+1} are given by the interpretation $(\nu_i + t - \tau_i)$. When the transition from state s_i to s_{i+1} occurs, we use the value $(\nu_i + \tau_{i+1} - \tau_i)$ to check the clock constraint; however, at time τ_{i+1}, the value of a clock that gets reset is defined to be 0.

Note that a transition table $\mathcal{A} = \langle \Sigma, S, S_0, E \rangle$ can be considered to be a timed transition table $\mathcal{A}'$. We choose the set of clocks to be the empty set, and replace every edge $\langle s, s', a \rangle$ by $\langle s, s', a, \emptyset, \mathbf{true} \rangle$. The runs of $\mathcal{A}'$ are in an obvious correspondence with the runs of $\mathcal{A}$.

3.5 Timed regular languages

We can couple acceptance criteria with timed transition tables, and use them to define timed languages.

Definition 3.10 A *timed Büchi automaton* (in short TBA) is a tuple $\langle \Sigma, S, S_0, C, E, F \rangle$, where $\langle \Sigma, S, S_0, C, E \rangle$ is a timed transition table, and $F \subseteq S$ is a set of *accepting* states.

A run $r = (\overline{s}, \overline{\nu})$ of a TBA over a timed word (σ, τ) is called an *accepting run* iff $inf(r) \cap F \neq \emptyset$.

For a TBA $\mathcal{A}$, the language $L(\mathcal{A})$ of timed words it accepts is defined to be the set $\{(\sigma, \tau) \mid \mathcal{A} \text{ has an accepting run over } (\sigma, \tau)\}$. ∎

In analogy with the class of languages accepted by Büchi automata, we call the class of timed languages accepted by TBAs timed regular languages.

Definition 3.11 A timed language L is a *timed regular language* iff $L = L(\mathcal{A})$ for some TBA $\mathcal{A}$. ∎

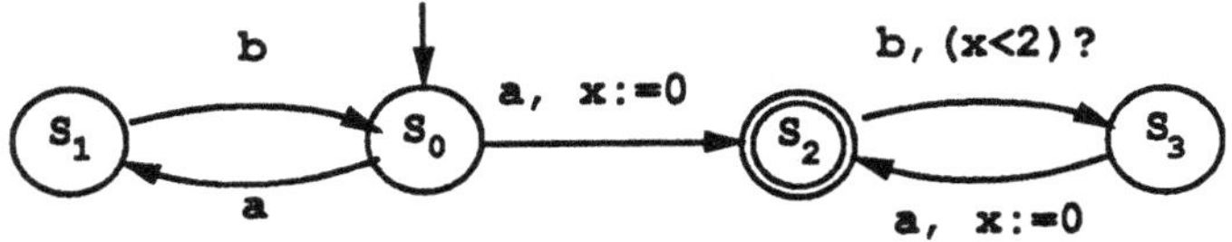

Figure 5: Timed Büchi automaton accepting L_{crt}

Example 3.12 The language L_3 of Example 3.5 is a timed regular language. The timed transition table of Figure 4 is coupled with the acceptance set consisting of all the states.

For every ω-regular language L over Σ, the timed language $\{(\sigma, \tau) \mid \sigma \in L\}$ is regular.

A typical example of a nonregular timed language is the language L_2 of Example 3.2. It requires that the time difference between the successive pairs of a and b form an increasing sequence.

Another nonregular language is $\{(a^\omega, \tau) \mid \forall i. (\tau_i = 2^i)\}$. ∎

The automaton of Example 3.13 combines the Büchi acceptance condition with the timing constraints to specify an interesting convergent response property:

Example 3.13 The automaton of Figure 5 accepts the timed language L_{crt} over the alphabet $\{a, b\}$.

$$L_{crt} = \{((ab)^\omega, \tau) \mid \exists i. \forall j \geq i. (\tau_{2j} < \tau_{2j-1} + 2)\}.$$

The start state is s_0, the accepting state is s_2, and there is a single clock x. The automaton starts in state s_0, and loops between the states s_0 and s_1 for a while. Then, nondeterministically, it moves to state s_2 setting its clock x to 0. While in the loop between the states s_2 and s_3, the automaton resets its clock while reading a, and ensures that the next b is within 2 time units. Interpreting the symbol b as a response to a request denoted by the symbol a, the automaton models a system with a *convergent response time*; the response time is "eventually" always less than 2 time units. ∎

The next example shows that timed automata can specify periodic behavior also.

Example 3.14 The automaton of Figure 6 accepts the following language over the alphabet $\{a, b\}$.

$$\{(\sigma, \tau) \mid \forall i. \exists j. (\tau_j = 3i \wedge \sigma_j = a)\}$$

The automaton has a single state s_0, and a single clock x. The clock gets reset at regular intervals of period 3 time units. The automaton requires that whenever the clock equals 3 there is an a symbol. Thus it expresses the property that a happens at all time values that are multiples of 3. ∎

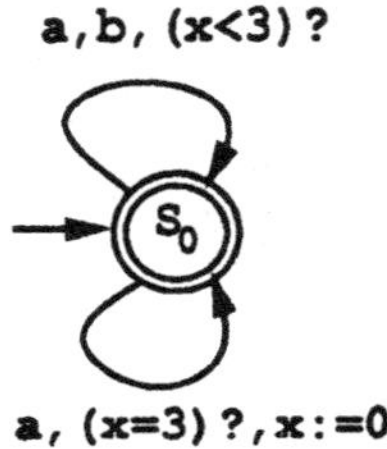

Figure 6: Timed automaton specifying periodic behavior

3.6 Properties of timed regular languages

The study of formal languages has been greatly enriched by the consideration of closure properties and decision problems. Here, we summarize the answers to some of the basic questions of these types, especially those that are relevant to verification.

The next theorem considers some closure properties of timed regular languages.

Theorem 3.15 The class of timed regular languages is closed under (finite) union and intersection. ∎

The construction for union is trivial, since we are considering nondeterministic automata. The construction for intersection is a straightforward product of automata. While constructing the product of n TBAs $\mathcal{A}_i = \langle \Sigma, \mathrm{S}_i, \mathrm{S}_{0_i}, \mathrm{C}_i, \mathrm{E}_i, \mathrm{F}_i \rangle$, $i = 1, 2 \ldots n$, the number of states of the resulting automaton is $n \cdot \Pi_i |\mathrm{S}_i|$. The number of clocks is $\Sigma_i |\mathrm{C}_i|$, and the size of the edge set is $n \cdot \Pi_i |\mathrm{E}_i|$. Note that $|\mathrm{E}|$ includes the length of the clock constraints assuming binary encoding for the constants.

The main result on timed automata is an algorithm for checking the emptiness of the language. The existence of an infinite accepting path in the underlying transition table is clearly a necessary condition for the language of an automaton to be nonempty. However, the timing constraints of the automaton rule out certain additional behaviors. We show that a Büchi automaton can be constructed that accepts exactly the set of untimed words that are consistent with the timed words accepted by a timed automaton (see [Alu91] for a detailed description of this construction).

Theorem 3.16 Given a TBA $\mathcal{A} = \langle \Sigma, \mathrm{S}, \mathrm{S}_0, \mathrm{C}, \mathrm{E}, \mathrm{F} \rangle$, there exists a Büchi automaton over Σ which accepts $Untime[L(\mathcal{A})]$. ∎

Theorem 3.16 says that the timing information in a timed automaton is "regular" in character; its consistency can be checked by a finite-state automaton. An equivalent formulation of the theorem is

If a timed language L is timed regular then $Untime(L)$ is ω-regular.

The untiming construction is interesting by itself, but also gives an immediate solution to the problem of testing a timed automaton for emptiness, since the timed language is empty iff the untimed language is empty. For a timed automaton $\mathcal{A} = \langle \Sigma, \mathrm{S}, \mathrm{S}_0, \mathrm{C}, \mathrm{E}, \mathrm{F} \rangle$, the Büchi automaton constructed by Theorem 3.16 has size $O[(|S| + |E|) \cdot 2^{\delta(\mathcal{A})}]$, where $\delta(\mathcal{A})$ denotes the length of the timing constraints labeling the edges of $\mathcal{A}$ (assuming binary encoding for the constants). Consequently, the complexity of the algorithm for deciding emptiness of a TBA is exponential in the number of clocks and the length of the constants in the timing constraints. One need not construct the untimed automaton explicitly, and the emptiness test can be implemented in polynomial space. This blow-up in complexity seems unavoidable; we reduce the acceptance problem for linear bounded automata, a known PSPACE-complete problem [HU79], to the emptiness question for TBAs to prove the PSPACE lower bound for the emptiness problem. This gives the following theorem.

Theorem 3.17 The problem of deciding the emptiness of the language of a given timed automaton $\mathcal{A}$, is PSPACE-complete. ■

Note that the source of this complexity is not the choice of R to model time. The PSPACE-hardness result can be proved if we leave the syntax of timed automata unchanged, but use the discrete domain N to model time. Also this complexity is insensitive to the encoding of the constants; the problem is PSPACE-complete even if we encode all constants in unary.

Surprisingly, several problems that are decidable for finite automata are undecidable for timed automata. The most basic of these is the *universality problem:* Does the language of a given automaton over Σ comprise of all the timed words over Σ? Equivalently: Is the complement of the language of the automaton empty? The next theorem gives this undecidability result.

Theorem 3.18 Given a timed automaton over an alphabet Σ the problem of deciding whether it accepts all timed words over Σ is Π_1^1-hard. ■

The above theorem is proved by reducing a Π_1^1-hard problem of 2-counter machines to the universality question. The class Π_1^1 consists of highly undecidable problems, including some nonarithmetical sets (for an exposition of the analytical hierarchy consult, for instance, [Rog67]). Part of the surprise value of this result is the continuous versions of many other problems are *easier* to solve than the discrete versions: for example, number theory is undecidable but the theory of the reals is decidable, and linear programming can be solved in polynomial time, but integer programming is NP-complete[2].

Recall that the language inclusion problem for Büchi automata can be solved in PSPACE. However, it follows from Theorem 3.18 that there is no decision procedure to check whether the language of one TBA is a subset of the other. This result is an obstacle in using timed automata as a specification language for automatic verification of finite-state real-time systems.

Corollary 3.19 Given two TBAs $\mathcal{A}_1$ and $\mathcal{A}_2$ over an alphabet Σ, the problem of checking $L(\mathcal{A}_1) \subseteq L(\mathcal{A}_2)$ is Π_1^1-hard. ■

It is equally difficult to decide whether the languages of two timed automata are the same. It can be proved by using these decidability results that, unlike regular languages, timed regular languages are not closed under complementation. The (non-constructive) proof depends on the Π_1^1-hardness of the inclusion problem.

[2]Thanks to Moshe Vardi for this observation

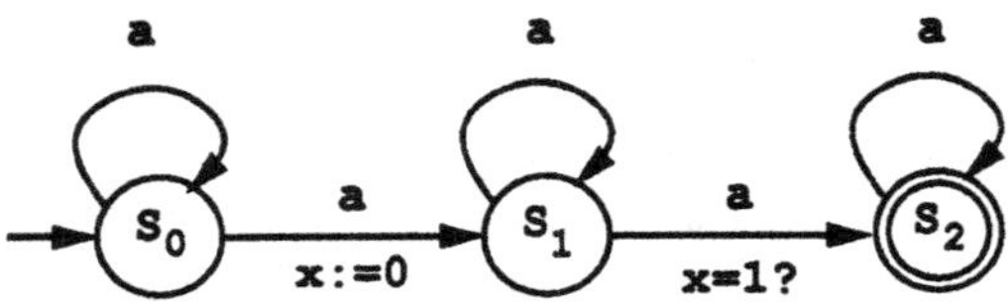

Figure 7: Noncomplementable automaton

Corollary 3.20 The class of timed regular languages is not closed under complementation. ∎

The following example provides some insight regarding the nonclosure under complementation.

Example 3.21 The language accepted by the automaton of Figure 7 over $\{a\}$ is

$$\{(a^\omega, \tau) \mid \exists i \geq 1.\, \exists j > i.\, (\tau_j = \tau_i + 1)\}.$$

The complement of this language cannot be characterized using a TBA. The complement needs to make sure that no pair of a's is separated by distance 1. Since there is no bound on the number of a's that can happen in a time period of length 1, keeping track of the times of all the a's within past 1 time unit, would require an unbounded number of clocks. ∎

3.7 Comparison of dense and discrete time

For the timed regular languages arbitrarily many symbols can occur in a finite interval of time. Furthermore, the symbols can be arbitrarily close to each other. The following example shows that there is a timed regular language L such that for every $(\sigma, \tau) \in L$, there exists some $\epsilon \geq 0$ such that the sequence of time differences $(\tau_{i+1} - \tau_i)$ converges to the limit ϵ.

Example 3.22 The language accepted by the automaton in Figure 8 is

$$L_{converge} = \{((ab)^\omega, \tau) \mid \forall i.\, (\tau_{2i-1} = i \wedge (\tau_{2i} - \tau_{2i-1} > \tau_{2i+2} - \tau_{2i+1}))\}.$$

Every word accepted by this automaton has the property that the sequence of time differences between a and the following b converges. A sample word accepted by the automaton is

$$(a,1) \rightarrow (b,1.5) \rightarrow (a,2) \rightarrow (b,2.25) \rightarrow (a,3) \rightarrow (b,3.125) \rightarrow \cdots$$

∎

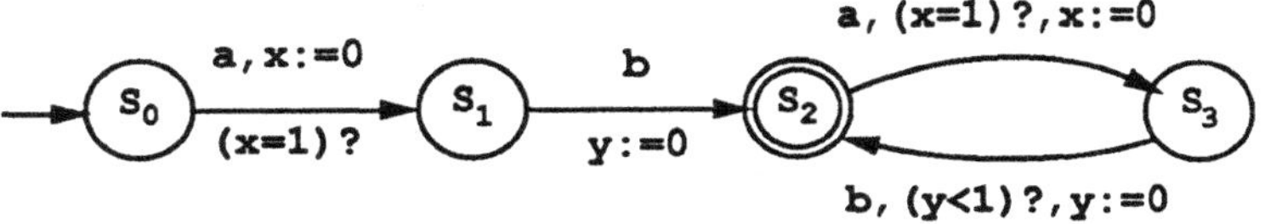

Figure 8: Timed automaton accepting $L_{converge}$

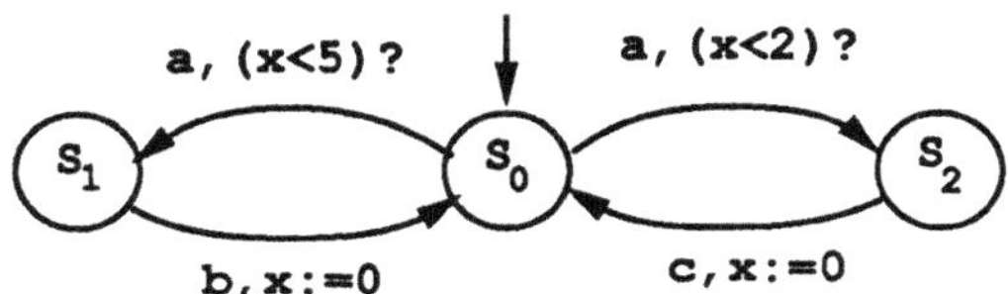

Figure 9: Timed Muller automaton

This example illustrates that the model of reals is indeed different from the discrete-time model. If we require all the time values τ_i to be multiples of some fixed constant ϵ, however small, the language accepted by the automaton of Figure 8 will be empty.

On the other hand, timed automata do not distinguish between the set of reals R and the set of rationals Q. Only the denseness of the underlying domain plays a crucial role. In particular, Theorem 3.23 shows that if we require all the time values in time sequences to be rational numbers, the untimed language $Untime[L(\mathcal{A})]$ of a timed automaton $\mathcal{A}$ stays unchanged.

Theorem 3.23 Let L be a timed regular language. For every word σ, $\sigma \in Untime(L)$ iff there exists a time sequence τ such that $\tau_i \in \mathrm{Q}$ for all $i \geq 1$, and $(\sigma, \tau) \in L$. ∎

3.8 Timed Muller automata

We can define timed automata with Muller acceptance conditions also.

Definition 3.24 A *timed Muller automaton* (TMA) is a tuple $\langle \Sigma, \mathrm{S}, \mathrm{S}_0, \mathrm{C}, \mathrm{E}, \mathcal{F} \rangle$, where $\langle \Sigma, \mathrm{S}, \mathrm{S}_0, \mathrm{C}, \mathrm{E} \rangle$ is a timed transition table, and $\mathcal{F} \subseteq 2^{\mathrm{S}}$ specifies an acceptance family.

A run $r = (\bar{s}, \bar{\nu})$ of the automaton over a timed word (σ, τ) is an accepting run iff $inf(r) \in \mathcal{F}$.

For a TMA $\mathcal{A}$, the language $L(\mathcal{A})$ of timed words it accepts is defined to be the set $\{(\sigma, \tau) \mid \mathcal{A}$ has an accepting run over $(\sigma, \tau)\}$. ∎

Example 3.25 Consider the automaton of Figure 9 over the alphabet $\{a, b, c\}$. The start state is s_0, and the Muller acceptance family consists of a single set $\{s_0, s_2\}$. So any accepting run should loop between states s_0 and s_1 only finitely many times, and between states s_0 and s_2 infinitely many times. Every word (σ, τ) accepted by the automaton satisfies: (1) $\sigma \in (a(b+c))^*(ac)^\omega$, and (2) for all $i \geq 1$, the difference $(\tau_{2i-1} - \tau_{2i-2})$ is less than 2 if the $(2i)$-th symbol is c, and less than 5 otherwise. ■

Recall that Büchi automata and Muller automata have the same expressive power. The following theorem states that the same holds true for TBAs and TMAs. Thus the class of timed languages accepted by TMAs is the same as the class of timed regular languages. The proof of the following theorem closely follows the standard argument that an ω-regular language is accepted by a Büchi automaton iff it is accepted by some Muller automaton.

Theorem 3.26 A timed language is accepted by some timed Büchi automaton iff it is accepted by some timed Muller automaton. ■

4 Deterministic timed automata

The results of Section 3 show that the class of timed automata is not closed under complement, and one cannot automatically compare the languages of two automata. In this section we define deterministic timed automata, and show that the class of deterministic timed Muller automata (DTMA) is closed under all the Boolean operations.

4.1 Definition

Recall that in the untimed case a deterministic transition table has a single start state, and from each state, given the next input symbol, the next state is uniquely determined. We want a similar criterion for determinism for the timed automata: given a state, the values for all the clocks, and the next input symbol *along with its time of occurrence*, the next transition should be uniquely determined. So we allow multiple transitions starting at the same state with the same label, but require their clock constraints to be *mutually exclusive* so that at any time only one of these transitions is enabled.

Definition 4.1 A timed transition table $\langle \Sigma, S, S_0, C, E \rangle$ is called *deterministic* iff

1. it has only one start state, $|S_0| = 1$, and
2. for all $s \in S$, for all $a \in \Sigma$, for every pair of edges of the form $\langle s, -, a, -, \delta_1 \rangle$ and $\langle s, -, a, -, \delta_2 \rangle$, the clock constraints δ_1 and δ_2 are mutually exclusive (i.e., $\delta_1 \wedge \delta_2$ is unsatisfiable).

A timed automaton is deterministic iff its timed transition table is deterministic. ■

Note that in absence of clocks the above definition matches with the definition of determinism for transition tables. Thus every deterministic transition table is also a deterministic timed transition table. Let us consider an example of a DTMA.

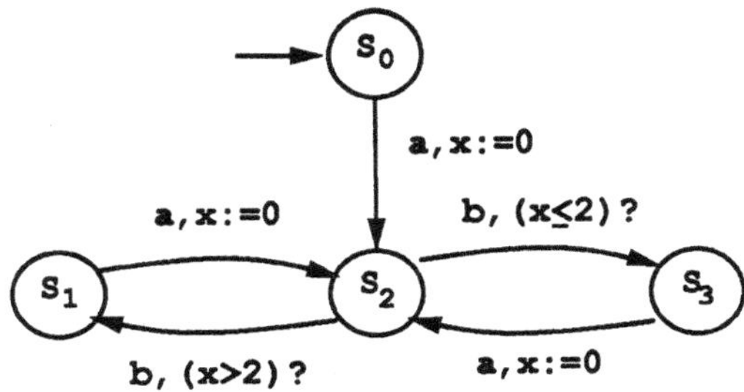

Figure 10: Deterministic timed Muller automaton

Example 4.2 The DTMA of Figure 10 accepts the language L_{crt} of Example 3.13

$$L_{crt} = \{((ab)^\omega, \tau) \mid \exists i. \forall j \geq i. (\tau_{2j+2} \leq \tau_{2j+1} + 2)\}$$

The Muller acceptance family is given by $\{\{s_2, s_3\}\}$. The state s_2 has two mutually exclusive outgoing transitions on b. The acceptance condition requires that the transition with the clock constraint $(x > 2)$ is taken only finitely often. ■

Observe that a deterministic timed transition table has at most one run over a given timed word. Consequently, deterministic timed automata can be easily complemented.

4.2 Closure properties

Now we consider the closure properties for deterministic timed automata. Like deterministic Muller automata, DTMAs are also closed under all Boolean operations.

Theorem 4.3 The class of timed languages accepted by deterministic timed Muller automata is closed under union, intersection, and complementation. ■

Now let us consider the closure properties of deterministic timed Büchi automata (DTBA). Recall that deterministic Büchi automata (DBA) are not closed under complement. The property that "there are infinitely many a's" is specifiable by a DBA, however, the complement property, "there are only finitely many a's" cannot be expressed by a DBA. Consequently we do not expect the class of DTBAs to be closed under complementation. However, since every DTBA is also a DTMA, the complement of a DTBA-language is accepted by a DTMA. The next theorem states the closure properties.

Theorem 4.4 The class of timed languages accepted by DTBAs is closed under union and intersection, but not closed under complement. The complement of a DTBA language is accepted by some DTMA. ■

4.3 Decision problems

In this section we examine the complexity of the emptiness problem and the language inclusion problem for deterministic timed automata.

The emptiness of a timed automaton does not depend on the symbols labeling its edges. Consequently, checking emptiness of deterministic automata is no simpler; it is PSPACE-complete.

Since deterministic automata can be complemented, checking for language inclusion is decidable. In fact, while checking $L(\mathcal{A}_1) \subseteq L(\mathcal{A}_2)$, only $\mathcal{A}_2$ need be deterministic, $\mathcal{A}_1$ can be nondeterministic. The problem can be solved in PSPACE:

Theorem 4.5 For a timed automaton $\mathcal{A}_1$ and a deterministic timed automaton $\mathcal{A}_2$, the problem of deciding whether $L(\mathcal{A}_1)$ is contained in $L(\mathcal{A}_2)$ is PSPACE-complete. ■

4.4 Expressiveness

In this section we compare the expressive power of the various types of timed automata.

Every DTBA can be expressed as a DTMA simply by rewriting its acceptance condition. However the converse does not hold. First observe that every ω-regular language is expressible as a DMA, and hence as a DTMA. On the other hand, since deterministic Büchi automata are strictly less expressive than deterministic Muller automata, certain ω-regular languages are not specifiable by DBAs. The next lemma shows that such languages cannot be expressed using DTBAs either. It follows that DTBAs are strictly less expressive than DTMAs. In fact, DTMAs are closed under complement, whereas DTBAs are not.

Lemma 4.6 For an ω-language L, the timed language $\{(\sigma, \tau) \mid \sigma \in L\}$ is accepted by some DTBA iff L is accepted by some DBA. ■

From the above discussion one may conjecture that a DTMA language L is a DTBA language if *Untime*(L) is a DBA language. To answer this let us consider the convergent response property L_{crt} specifiable using a DTMA (see Example 4.2). This language involves a combination of liveness and timing. We conjecture that no DTBA can specify this property.

Along the lines of the above proof we can also show that for an ω-language L, the timed language $\{(\sigma, \tau) \mid \sigma \in L\}$ is accepted by some DTMA (or TMA, or TBA) iff L is accepted by some DMA (or MA, or BA, respectively).

Since DTMAs are closed under complement, whereas TMAs are not, it follows that the class of languages accepted by DTMAs is strictly smaller than that accepted by TMAs. In particular, the language of Example 3.21, ("some pair of a's is distance 1 apart") is not representable as a DTMA; it relies on nondeterminism in a crucial way.

We summarize the discussion on various types of automata in the table of Figure 11 which shows the inclusions between various classes and the closure properties of various classes. Compare this with the corresponding results for the various classes of ω-automata shown in Figure 12.

Class of timed languages	Operations closed under
TMA = TBA	union, intersection
$\cup$	
DTMA	union, intersection, complement
$\cup$	
DTBA	union, intersection

Figure 11: Classes of timed automata

Class of ω-languages	Operations closed under
MA = BA = DMA	union, intersection, complement
$\cup$	
DBA	union, intersection

Figure 12: Classes of ω-automata

5 Verification

In this section we discuss how to use the theory of timed automata to prove correctness of finite-state real-time systems. We start by introducing time in linear trace semantics for concurrent processes.

5.1 Trace semantics

In trace semantics, we associate a set of observable *events* with each process, and model the process by the set of all its *traces*. A trace is a (linear) sequence of events that may be observed when the process runs. For example, an event may denote an assignment of a value to a variable, or pressing a button on the control panel, or arrival of a message. All events are assumed to occur instantaneously. Actions with duration are modeled using events marking the beginning and the end of the action. Hoare originally proposed such a model for CSP [Hoa78]. In our model, we allow several events to happen simultaneously. Also we consider only infinite sequences, which model nonterminating interaction of reactive systems with their environments.

Formally, given a set A of events, a *trace* $\sigma = \sigma_1\sigma_2\ldots$ is an infinite word over $\mathcal{P}^+(A)$ — the set of nonempty subsets of A. An *untimed process* is a pair (A, X) comprising of the set A of its observable events and the set X of its possible traces.

Example 5.1 Consider a channel P connecting two components. Let a represent the arrival of a message at one end of P, and let b stand for the delivery of the message at the other end of the channel. The channel cannot receive a new message until the previous one has reached the other end. Consequently the two events a and b alternate. Assuming that the messages keep arriving, the only possible trace is

$$\sigma_P \;:\; \{a\} \rightarrow \{b\} \rightarrow \{a\} \rightarrow \{b\} \rightarrow \cdots.$$

Often we will denote the singleton set $\{a\}$ by the symbol a. The process P is represented by $(\{a,b\},(ab)^\omega)$. ■

Various operations can be defined on processes; these are useful for describing complex systems using the simpler ones. We will consider only the most important of these operations, namely, parallel composition. The parallel composition of a set of processes describes the joint behavior of all the processes running concurrently.

The parallel composition operator can be conveniently defined using the projection operation. The *projection* of $\sigma \in \mathcal{P}^+(A)^\omega$ onto $B \subseteq A$ (written $\sigma\lceil B$) is formed by intersecting each event set in σ with B and deleting all the empty sets from the sequence. For instance, in Example 5.1 $\sigma_P\lceil\{a\}$ is the trace a^ω. Notice that the projection operation may result in a finite sequence; but we will consider the projection of a trace σ onto B only when $\sigma_i \cap B$ is nonempty for infinitely many i.

For a set of processes $\{P_i = (A_i, X_i) \mid i = 1,2,\ldots n\}$, their *parallel composition* $\|_i\, P_i$ is a process with the event set $\cup_i A_i$ and the trace set

$$\{\sigma \in \mathcal{P}^+(\cup_i A_i)^\omega \mid \wedge_i \;\sigma\lceil A_i \in X_i\}.$$

Thus σ is a trace of $\|_i\, P_i$ iff $\sigma\lceil A_i$ is a trace of P_i for each $i = 1,\ldots n$. When there are no common events the above definition corresponds to the unconstrained interleavings of all the traces. On the other hand, if all event sets are identical then the trace set of the composition process is simply the set-theoretic intersection of all the component trace sets.

Example 5.2 Consider another channel Q connected to the channel P of Example 5.1. The event of message arrival for Q is same as the event b. Let c denote the delivery of the message at the other end of Q. The process Q is given by $(\{b,c\},(bc)^\omega)$.

When P and Q are composed we require them to synchronize on the common event b, and between every pair of b's we allow the possibility of the event a happening before the event c, the event c happening before a, and both occurring simultaneously. Thus $[P \parallel Q]$ has the event set $\{a,b,c\}$, and has an infinite number of traces. ■

In this framework, the verification question is presented as an inclusion problem. Both the implementation and the specification are given as untimed processes. The implementation process is typically a composition of several smaller component processes. We say that an implementation (A, X_I) is *correct* with respect to a specification (A, X_S) iff $X_I \subseteq X_S$.

Example 5.3 Consider the channels of Example 5.2. The implementation process is $[P \parallel Q]$. The specification is given as the process $S = (\{a,b,c\},(abc)^\omega)$. Thus the specification requires the message to reach the other end of Q before the next message arrives at P. In this case, $[P \parallel Q]$ does not meet the specification S, for it has too many other traces, specifically, the trace $ab(acb)^\omega$. ■

5.2 Adding timing to traces

An untimed process models the sequencing of events but not the actual times at which the events occur. Thus the description of the channel in Example 5.1 gives only the sequencing of the events a and b, and not the delays between them. Timing can be added to a trace by coupling it with a sequence of time values. We choose the set of reals to model time.

Recall that a *time sequence* $\tau = \tau_1\tau_2\ldots$ is an infinite sequence of time values $\tau_i \in \mathsf{R}$ satisfying the monotonicity and progress constraints. A *timed trace* over a set of events A is a pair (σ, τ) where σ is a trace over A, and τ is a time sequence.

In a timed trace (σ, τ), each τ_i gives the time at which the events in σ_i occur. In particular, τ_1 gives the time of the first observable event; we always assume $\tau_1 > 0$, and define $\tau_0 = 0$. Observe that the progress condition implies that only a finite number of events can happen in a bounded interval of time. In particular, it rules out convergent time sequences such as $1/2, 3/4, 7/8, \ldots$ representing the possibility that the system participates in infinitely many events before time 1.

A *timed process* is a pair (A, L) where A is a finite set of events, and L is a set of timed traces over A.

Example 5.4 Consider the channel P of Example 5.1 again. Assume that the first message arrives at time 1, and the subsequent messages arrive at fixed intervals of length 3 time units. Furthermore, it takes 1 time unit for every message to traverse the channel. The process has a single timed trace

$$\rho_P \;=\; (a,1) \;\rightarrow\; (b,2) \;\rightarrow\; (a,4) \;\rightarrow\; (b,5) \;\rightarrow\; \cdots$$

and it is represented as a timed process $P^T = (\{a,b\}, \{\rho_P\})$. ■

The operations on untimed processes are extended in the obvious way to timed processes. To get the projection of (σ, τ) onto $B \subseteq A$, we first intersect each event set in σ with B and then delete all the empty sets along with the associated time values. The definition of parallel composition remains unchanged, except that it uses the projection for timed traces. Thus in parallel composition of two processes, we require that both the processes should participate in the common events at the same time. This rules out the possibility of interleaving: parallel composition of two timed traces is either a single timed trace or is empty.

Example 5.5 As in Example 5.2 consider another channel Q connected to P. For Q, as before, the only possible trace is $\sigma_Q = (bc)^\omega$. In addition, the timing specification of Q says that the time taken by a message for traversing the channel, that is, the delay between b and the following c, is some real value between 1 and 2. The timed process Q^T has infinitely many timed traces, and it is given by

$$[\,\{b,c\},\;\{(\sigma_Q,\tau) \mid \forall i.\,(\tau_{2i-1}+1 < \tau_{2i} < \tau_{2i-1}+2)\}\,].$$

The description of $[\,P^T \parallel Q^T\,]$ is obtained by composing ρ_P with each timed trace of Q^T. The composition process has uncountably many timed traces. An example trace is

$$(a,1) \;\rightarrow\; (b,2) \;\rightarrow\; (c,3.8) \;\rightarrow\; (a,4) \;\rightarrow\; (b,5) \;\rightarrow\; (c,6.02) \;\rightarrow\; \cdots$$

■

The time values associated with the events can be discarded by the *Untime* operation. For a timed process $P = (A, L)$, $Untime[(A, L)]$ is the untimed process with the event set A and the trace set consisting of traces σ such that $(\sigma, \tau) \in L$ for some time sequence τ.

Note that
$$Untime(P_1 \parallel P_2) \subseteq Untime(P_1) \parallel Untime(P_2).$$

However, as Example 5.6 shows, the two sides are not necessarily equal. In other words, the timing information retained in the timed traces constrains the set of possible traces when two processes are composed.

Example 5.6 Consider the channels of Example 5.5. Observe that $Untime(P^T) = P$ and $Untime(Q^T) = Q$. $[\,P^T \parallel Q^T\,]$ has a unique untimed trace $(abc)^\omega$. On the other hand, $[\,P \parallel Q\,]$ has infinitely many traces; between every pair of b events all possible orderings of an event a and an event c are admissible. ∎

The verification problem is again posed as an inclusion problem. Now the implementation is given as a composition of several timed processes, and the specification is also given as a timed process.

Example 5.7 Consider the verification problem of Example 5.3 again. If we model the implementation as the timed process $[\,P^T \parallel Q^T\,]$ then it meets the specification S. The specification S is now a timed process $(\{a, b, c\}, \{((abc)^\omega, \tau)\})$. Observe that, though the specification S constrains only the sequencing of events, the correctness of $[\,P^T \parallel Q^T\,]$ with respect to S crucially depends on the timing constraints of the two channels. ∎

5.3 ω-automata and verification

We start with an overview of the application of Büchi automata to verify untimed processes [VW86, Var87]. Observe that for an untimed process $A, X)$, X is an ω-language over the alphabet $\mathcal{P}^+(A)$. If it is a regular language it can be represented by a Büchi automaton.

We model a finite-state (untimed) process P with event set A using a Büchi automaton $\mathcal{A}_P$ over the alphabet $\mathcal{P}^+(A)$. The states of the automaton correspond to the internal states of the process. The automaton $\mathcal{A}_P$ has a transition $\langle s, s', a\rangle$, with $a \subseteq A$, if the process can change its state from s to s' participating in the events from a. The acceptance conditions of the automaton correspond to the fairness constraints on the process. The automaton $\mathcal{A}_P$ accepts (or generates) precisely the traces of P; that is, the process P is given by $(A, L(\mathcal{A}_P))$. Such a process P is called an *ω-regular process*.

The user describes a system consisting of various components by specifying each individual component as a Büchi automaton. In particular, consider a system I comprising of n components, where each component is modeled as an ω-regular process $P_i = (A_i, L(\mathcal{A}_i))$. The implementation process is $[\|_i\, P_i]$. We can automatically construct the automaton for I using the construction for language intersection for Büchi automata. Since the event sets of various components may be different, before we apply the product construction, we need to make the alphabets of various automata identical. Let $A = \cup_i A_i$. From each $\mathcal{A}_i$, we construct an automaton $\mathcal{A}_i'$ over the alphabet $\mathcal{P}^+(A)$

such that $L(\mathcal{A}'_i) = \{\sigma \in \mathcal{P}^+(A)^\omega \mid \sigma\lceil A_i \in L(\mathcal{A}_i)\}$. Now the desired automaton $\mathcal{A}_I$ is the product of the automata $\mathcal{A}'_i$.

The specification is given as an ω-regular language S over $\mathcal{P}^+(A)$. The implementation meets the specification iff $L(\mathcal{A}_I) \subseteq S$. The property S can presented as a Büchi automaton $\mathcal{A}_S$. In this case, the verification problem reduces to checking emptiness of $L(\mathcal{A}_I) \cap L(\mathcal{A}_S)^c$.

The verification problem is PSPACE-complete. The size of $\mathcal{A}_I$ is exponential in the description of its individual components. If $\mathcal{A}_S$ is nondeterministic, taking the complement involves an exponential blow-up, and thus the complexity of verification problem is exponential in the size of the specification also. However, if $\mathcal{A}_S$ is deterministic, then the complexity is only polynomial in the size of the specification.

Even if the size of the specification and the sizes of the automata for the individual components are small, the number of components in most systems of interest is large, and in the above method the complexity is exponential in this number. Thus the product automaton $\mathcal{A}_I$ has prohibitively large number of states, and this limits the applicability of this approach. Alternative methods which avoid enumeration of all the states in $\mathcal{A}_I$ have been proposed, and shown to be applicable to verification of some moderately sized systems [BCD+90, GW91].

5.4 Verification using timed automata

For a timed process (A, L), L is a timed language over $\mathcal{P}^+(A)$. A *timed regular process* is the one for which the set L is a timed regular language, and can be represented by a timed automaton.

Finite-state systems are modeled by TBAs. The underlying transition table gives the state-transition graph of the system. We have already seen how the clocks can be used to represent the timing delays of various physical components. As before, the acceptance conditions correspond to the fairness conditions. Notice that the progress requirement imposes certain fairness requirements implicitly. Thus, with a finite-state process P, we associate a TBA $\mathcal{A}_P$ such that $L(\mathcal{A}_P)$ consists of precisely the timed traces of P.

Typically, an implementation is described as a composition of several components. Each component should be modeled as a timed regular process $P_i = (A_i, L(\mathcal{A}_i))$. The first step in the verification process is to construct a TBA $\mathcal{A}_I$ which represents the composite process $[\|_i\ P_i]$. To implement this, first we need to make the alphabets of various automata identical, and then take the intersection. Combining the two steps, however, reduces the size of the implementation automaton.

Theorem 5.8 Given timed processes $P_i = (A_i, L(\mathcal{A}_i))$, $i = 1, \ldots n$, represented by timed automata $\mathcal{A}_i$, there is a TBA $\mathcal{A}$ over the alphabet $\mathcal{P}^+(\cup_i A_i)$ which represents the timed process $[\|_i\ P_i]$. ∎

The number of states in $\mathcal{A}_I$ is $[(n+1) \cdot \Pi_i |S_i|]$. The number of clocks for $\mathcal{A}_I$ is $\Sigma_i |C_i|$, and for all clocks x, the value of c_x, the largest constant it gets compared with, remains the same.

The specification of the system is given as another timed regular language S over the alphabet $\mathcal{P}^+(A)$. The system is *correct* iff $L(\mathcal{A}_I) \subset S$. If S is given as a TBA, then in general, it is undecidable to test for correctness. However, if S is given as a DTMA $\mathcal{A}_S$, then we can solve this as outlined in Section 4.3.

Putting together all the pieces, we conclude:

Theorem 5.9 Given timed regular processes $P_i = (A_i, L(\mathcal{A}_i))$, $i = 1, \ldots n$, modeled by timed automata $\mathcal{A}_i$, and a specification as a deterministic timed automaton $\mathcal{A}_S$, the inclusion of the trace set of $[\|_i P_i]$ in $L(\mathcal{A}_S)$ can be checked in PSPACE. ■

The verification algorithm checks for a cycle with several desired properties in the untimed graph of the product of all the automata. The number of vertices in this graph is $O[|\mathcal{A}_S| \cdot \Pi_i |\mathcal{A}_i| \cdot 2^{|\delta(\mathcal{A}_S)|+\Sigma_i |\delta(\mathcal{A}_i)|}]$.

There are mainly three sources of exponential blow-up:

1. The complexity is proportional to the number of states in the global timed automaton describing the implementation $[\|_i P_i]$. This is exponential in the number of components.

2. The complexity is proportional to the product of the constants c_x, the largest constant x is compared with, over all the clocks x involved.

3. The complexity is proportional to the number of permutations over the set of all clocks.

The first factor is present in the simplest of verification problems, even in the untimed case. Since the number of components is typically large, this exponential factor has been a major obstacle in implementing model-checking algorithms.

The second factor is typical of any formalism to reason about quantitative time. The blow-up by actual constants is observed even for simpler, discrete models. Note that if the bounds on the delays of different components are relatively prime then this factor leads to a major blow-up in the complexity.

Lastly, in the untiming construction, we need to account for all the possible orderings of the fractional parts of different clocks, and this is the source of the third factor. We remark that switching to a simpler, say discrete-time, model will avoid this blow-up in complexity. However since the total number of clocks is linear in the number of independent components, this blow-up is same as contributed by the first factor, namely, exponential in the number of components.

5.5 Verification example

We consider an example of a gate controller at a railroad crossing. The system is composed of three components: TRAIN, GATE and CONTROLLER.

The automaton modeling the train is shown in Figure 13. The event set is {*approach, exit, in, out*, id_T}. The train starts in state s_0. The event id_T represents its idling event; the train is not required to enter the gate. The train communicates with the controller with two events *approach* and *exit*. The events *in* and *out* mark the events of entry and exit of the train from the railroad crossing. The train is required to send the signal *approach* at least 2 minutes before it enters the crossing. Thus the minimum delay between *approach* and *in* is 2 minutes. Furthermore, we know that the maximum delay between the signals *approach* and *exit* is 5 minutes. This is a liveness requirement on the train. Both the timing requirements are expressed using a single clock x.

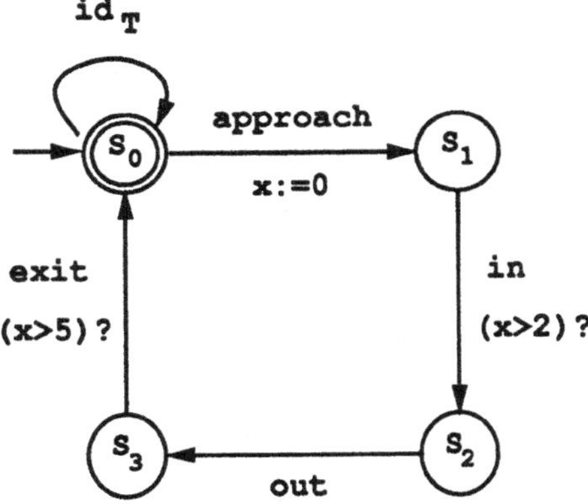

Figure 13: TRAIN

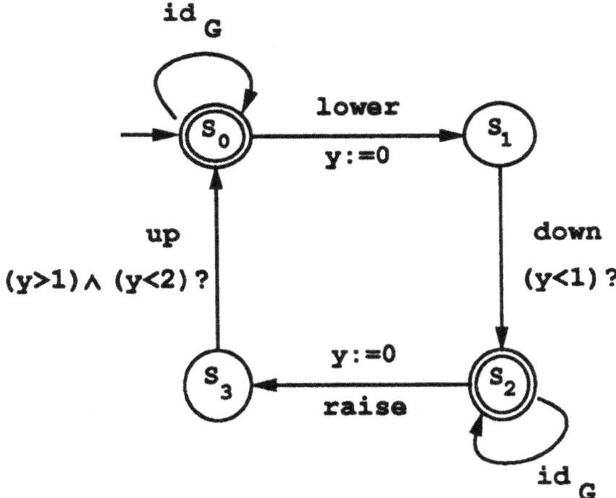

Figure 14: GATE

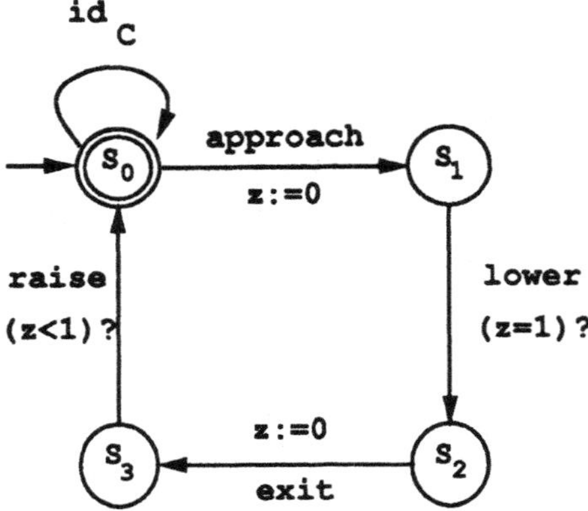

Figure 15: CONTROLLER

The automaton modeling the gate component is shown in Figure 14. The event set is {*raise, lower, up, down*, id_G}. The gate is open in state s_0 and closed in state s_2. It communicates with the controller through the signals *lower* and *raise*. The events *up* and *down* denote the opening and the closing of the gate. The gate responds to the signal *lower* by closing within 1 minute, and responds to the signal *raise* within 1 to 2 minutes. The gate can take its idling transition id_G in states s_0 or s_2 forever.

Finally, Figure 15 shows the automaton modeling the controller. The event set is {*approach, exit, raise, lower*, id_C}. The controller idle state is s_0. Whenever it receives the signal *approach* from the train, it responds by sending the signal *lower* to the gate. The response time is 1 minute. Whenever it receives the signal *exit*, it responds with a signal *raise* to the gate within 1 minute.

The entire system is then

$$[\text{TRAIN} \parallel \text{GATE} \parallel \text{CONTROLLER}].$$

The event set is the union of the event sets of all the three components. In this example, all the automata are particularly simple; they are deterministic, and do not have any fairness constraints (every run is an accepting run). The timed automaton $\mathcal{A}_I$ specifying the entire system is obtained by composing the above three automata.

The correctness requirements for the system are the following:

1. *Safety:* Whenever the train is inside the gate, the gate should be closed.

2. *Real-time Liveness:* The gate is never closed at a stretch for more than 10 minutes.

The specification refers to only the events *in, out, up, down*. The safety property is specified by the automaton of Figure 16. An edge label *in* stands for any event set containing *in*, and an edge label "*in*, $\sim$ *out*" means any event set not containing *out*, but containing *in*. The automaton disallows *in* before *down*, and *up* before *out*. All the states are accepting states.

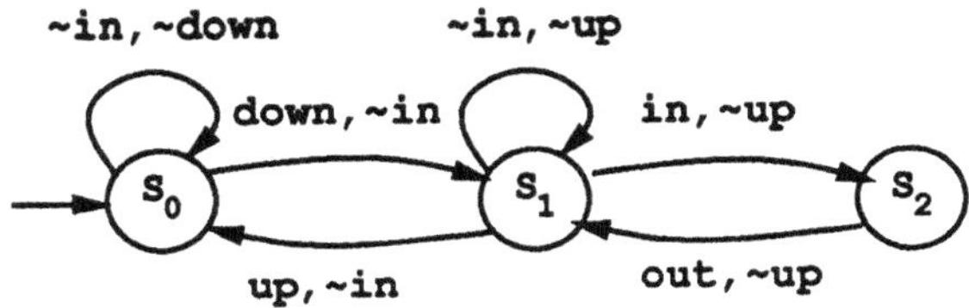

Figure 16: Safety property

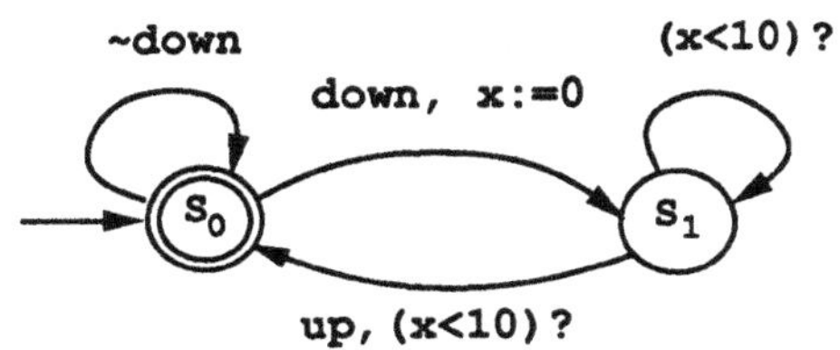

Figure 17: Real-time liveness property

The real-time liveness property is specified by the timed automaton of Figure 17. The automaton requires that every *down* be followed by *up* within 10 minutes.

Note that the automaton is deterministic, and hence can be complemented. Furthermore, observe that the acceptance condition is not necessary; we can include state s_1 also in the acceptance set. This is because the progress of time ensures that the self-loop on state s_1 with the clock constraint $(x < 10)$ cannot be taken indefinitely, and the automaton will eventually visit state s_0.

The correctness of $\mathcal{A}_I$ against the two specifications can be checked separately as outlined in Section 5. Observe that though the safety property is purely a qualitative property, it does not hold if we discard the timing requirements.

6 Related results

Timed automata provide a natural way of expressing timing delays of a real-time system. In this presentation, we have studied them from the perspective of formal language theory. Now we briefly review other results about timed automata. We warn the reader that the precise formulation of timed automata is different in different papers, but the underlying idea remains the same.

Timed automata are useful for developing a decision procedure for the logic MITL, a real-time extension of the linear temporal logic PTL [AFH91]. The decision procedure constructs a timed automaton $\mathcal{A}_\phi$ from a given MITL-formula ϕ, such that $\mathcal{A}_\phi$ accepts precisely the satisfying models of ϕ; thereby reducing the satisfiability question for ϕ to the emptiness question for $\mathcal{A}_\phi$. This construction can also be used to check the correctness of a system modeled as a product of timed automata against MITL-specification.

Alternatively, specifications can be written in branching-time temporal logics also. In [ACD90], we develop a model-checking algorithm for specifications written in TCTL — a real-time extension of the branching-time temporal logic CTL of [EC82].

Timed automata is a fairly low-level representation, and automatic translations from more structured representations such as process algebras, timed Petri nets, or high-level real-time programming languages, should exist. Recently, Sifakis et.al. have shown how to translate a term of the real-time process algebra ATP to a timed automaton (see the article *From ATP to Timed Graphs and Hybrid Systems* in this issue).

One promising direction of extending the process model discussed here is to incorporate probabilistic information. This is particularly relevant for systems that control and interact with physical processes. We add probabilities to timed automata by associating fixed distributions with the delays. This extension makes our processes *generalized semi-Markov processes*. Surprisingly, the untiming construction used to test for emptiness of a timed automaton can be used to analyze the behavior of GSMPs also. In [ACD91], we present an algorithm that combines model-checking for TCTL with model-checking for discrete-time Markov chains. The method can also be adopted to check properties specified using deterministic timed automata (see the article *Verifying Automata Specifications of Probabilistic Real-Time Systems* in this issue).

Questions other than verification can also be studied using timed automata. For example, Wong-Toi and Hoffmann study the problem of supervisory control of discrete event systems when the plant and specification behaviors are represented by timed automata [WH91]. The problem of synthesizing schedulers from timed automata specifications is addressed in [DW90]. Courcoubetis and Yannakakis use timed automata to solve certain minimum and maximum delay problems for real-time systems [CY91]. For instance, they show how to compute the earliest and the latest time a target state can appear along the runs of an automaton from a given initial state.

References

[ACD90] Rajeev Alur, Costas Courcoubetis, and David Dill. Model-checking for real-time systems. In *Proceedings of the Fifth IEEE Symposium on Logic in Computer Science*, pages 414–425, 1990.

[ACD91] Rajeev Alur, Costas Courcoubetis, and David Dill. Model-checking for probabilistic real-time systems. In *Automata, Languages and Programming: Proceedings of the 18th ICALP*, Lecture Notes in Computer Science 510, 1991.

[AFH91] Rajeev Alur, Tomás Feder, and Thomas Henzinger. The benefits of relaxing punctuality. In *Proceedings of the Tenth ACM Symposium on Principles of Distributed Computing*, pages 139–152, 1991.

[Alu91] Rajeev Alur. *Techniques for Automatic Verification of Real-Time Systems.* PhD thesis, Stanford University, 1991.

[BCD+90] J.R. Burch, E.M. Clarke, D.L. Dill, L.J. Hwang, and K. L. McMillan. Symbolic model checking: 10^{20} states and beyond. In *Proceedings of the Fifth IEEE Symposium on Logic in Computer Science*, pages 428–439, 1990.

[Büc62] Richard Büchi. On a decision method in restricted second-order arithmetic. In *Proceedings of the International Congress on Logic, Methodology, and Philosophy of Science 1960*, pages 1–12. Stanford University Press, 1962.

[CDK89] E.M. Clarke, I.A. Draghicescu, and R.P. Kurshan. A unified approach for showing language containment and equivalence between various types of ω-automata. Technical report, Carnegie Mellon University, 1989.

[CES86] Edmund Clarke, E. Allen Emerson, and A. Prasad Sistla. Automatic verification of finite-state concurrent systems using temporal-logic specifications. *ACM Transactions on Programming Languages and Systems*, 8(2):244–263, 1986.

[Cho74] Yaacov Choueka. Theories of automata on ω-tapes: a simplified approach. *Journal of Computer and System Sciences*, 8:117–141, 1974.

[CY91] Costas Courcoubetis and Mihalis Yannakakis. Minimum and maximum delay problems in real-time systems. In *Proceedings of the Third Workshop on Computer-Aided Verification, Aalborg University, Denmark*, 1991.

[DW90] David Dill and Howard Wong-Toi. Synthesizing processes and schedulers from temporal specifications. In *Proceedings of the Second Workshop on Computer-Aided Verification, Rutgers University*, 1990.

[EC82] E. Allen Emerson and Edmund M. Clarke. Using branching-time temporal logic to synthesize synchronization skeletons. *Science of Computer Programming*, 2:241–266, 1982.

[GW91] Patrice Godefroid and Pierre Wolper. A partial approach to model-checking. In *Proceedings of the Sixth IEEE Symposium on Logic in Computer Science*, pages 406–415, 1991.

[Hoa78] C.A.R. Hoare. Communicating sequential processes. *Communications of the ACM*, 21(8):666–677, 1978.

[HU79] John Hopcroft and Jeff Ullman. *Introduction to Automata Theory, Languages, and Computation.* Addison-Wesley, 1979.

[Kur87] Robert Kurshan. Complementing deterministic Büchi automata in polynomial time. *Journal of Computer and System Sciences*, 35:59–71, 1987.

[Lam83] Leslie Lamport. What good is temporal logic? In R.E.A. Mason, editor, *Information Processing 83: Proceedings of the Ninth IFIP World Computer Congress*, pages 657–668. Elsevier Science Publishers, 1983.

[McN66] Robert McNaughton. Testing and generating infinite sequences by a finite automaton. *Information and Control*, 9:521–530, 1966.

[MP81] Zohar Manna and Amir Pnueli. The temporal framework for concurrent programs. In R.S. Boyer and J.S. Moore, editors, *The correctness problem in Computer science*, pages 215–274. Academic Press, 1981.

[Pnu77] Amir Pnueli. The temporal logic of programs. In *Proceedings of the 18th IEEE Symposium on Foundations of Computer Science*, pages 46–77, 1977.

[Pnu86] Amir Pnueli. Applications of temporal logic to the specification and verification of reactive systems: a survey of current trends. In *Current Trends in Concurrency*, Lecture Notes in Computer Science 224, pages 510–584. Springer-Verlag, 1986.

[Rog67] Hartley Rogers. *Theory of Recursive Functions and Effective Computability.* McGraw-Hill, 1967.

[Saf88] Shmuel Safra. On the complexity of ω-automata. In *Proceedings of the 29th IEEE Symposium on Foundations of Computer Science*, pages 319–327, 1988.

[SVW87] A. Prasad Sistla, Moshe Vardi, and Pierre Wolper. The complementation problem for Büchi automata with applications to temporal logic. *Theoretical Computer Science*, 49, 1987.

[Tho90] Wolfgang Thomas. Automata on infinite objects. In J. van Leeuwen, editor, *Handbook of Theoretical Computer Science*, volume B, pages 133–191. Elsevier Science Publishers, 1990.

[Var87] Moshe Vardi. Verification of concurrent programs – the automata-theoretic framework. In *Proceedings of the Second IEEE Symposium on Logic in Computer Science*, pages 167–176, 1987.

[VW86] Moshe Vardi and Pierre Wolper. An automata-theoretic approach to automatic program verification. In *Proceedings of the First IEEE Symposium on Logic in Computer Science*, pages 332–344, 1986.

[WH91] Howard Wong-Toi and Girard Hoffmann. The control of dense real-time discrete event systems. 1991.

[WVS83] Pierre Wolper, Moshe Vardi, and A. Prasad Sistla. Reasoning about infinite computation paths. In *Proceedings of the 24th IEEE Symposium on Foundations of Computer Science*, pages 185–194, 1983.

Logics and Models of Real Time: A Survey

Rajeev Alur
AT&T Bell Laboratories
Murray Hill, NJ 07974, U.S.A.

Thomas A. Henzinger
Computer Science Department, Cornell University
Ithaca, NY 14853, U.S.A.

Abstract. We survey logic-based and automata-based languages and techniques for the specification and verification of real-time systems. In particular, we discuss three syntactic extensions of temporal logic: time-bounded operators, freeze quantification, and time variables. We also discuss the extension of finite-state machines with clocks and the extension of transition systems with time bounds on the transitions. All of the resulting notations can be interpreted over a variety of different models of time and computation, including linear and branching time, interleaving and true concurrency, discrete and continuous time. For each choice of syntax and semantics, we summarize the results that are known about expressive power, algorithmic finite-state verification, and deductive verification.

Keywords: Temporal logic, finite-state machines, transition systems, semantics, verification, real time.

1 Introduction

The number of formalisms that purportedly facilitate the modeling, specifying, and proving of timing properties for reactive systems has exploded over the past few years. The authors, who confess to have added to the confusion by advancing a variety of different syntactic and semantic proposals, feel that it would be beneficial to pause for a second — to pause and look back to sort out what has been accomplished and what needs to be done. This paper attempts such a meditation by surveying logic-based and automata-based real-time formalisms and putting them into perspective.

As many of the formalisms that have been promoted in the literature not only suggest different notations, but make radically different assumptions when modeling time and computation, the task of comparing them is often a nontrivial one. We attempt such a comparison by putting, first, all languages on a common semantical ground. Second, we offer a number of common semantical abstractions, and for each abstract semantics, we survey what is known about each language. This two-dimensional analysis of real-time formalisms as syntax-semantics pairs allows us to discuss in the same context different models of computation, such as linear and branching models, as well as different models of time, such as discrete and continuous models. The two-dimensional analysis also reveals that many meaningful coordinate points have not been addressed in the literature. For some of these, known results can be easily extrapolated (and we do so whenever possible); for others, we pose questions of expressiveness, complexity, and axiomatizability as open problems.

The remainder of the paper is organized in five sections. Section 2 attempts to give a unified semantical framework for real-time systems. The subsequent two sections present syntax. Real-time extensions of temporal logic are summarized in Section 3; real-time extensions of state-transition formalisms, in Section 4. The final two sections survey technical results about these languages. First, in Section 5, we collect all results regarding the impossibility, possibility, and complexity of verifying timing requirements of reactive systems. Second, in Section 6, we review what is known about the absolute and relative expressive power of real-time specification methods.

2 Real-time Semantics

We attempt to define a general semantics for real-time systems. Many previous suggestions are special cases of our definition.

2.1 Concrete semantics

We define a real-time system to be a set of timed state sequences, each of which represents a possible behavior of the system. As time domain, we choose the set of nonnegative real numbers, denoted by R. In a timed state sequence, we use intervals of the real line to specify the duration of system states.

Interval sequences

An interval is a convex subset of R. Intervals may be open, halfopen, or closed; bounded or unbounded. More precisely, every interval is of the form $[a,b]$, $[a,b)$, $[a,\infty)$, $(a,b]$, (a,b), or (a,∞), where $a \leq b$ and $a, b \in$ R for the left end-point a and the right end-point b. The left end-point of an interval I is denoted by $l(I)$ and the right end-point, for bounded I, is denoted by $r(I)$. An interval I is *singular* iff it is of the form $[a,a]$; that is, I is closed and $l(I) = r(I)$. Two intervals I and I' are *adjacent* iff (1) either I is right-open and I' is left-closed, or I is right-closed and I' is left-open, and (2) $r(I) = l(I')$. For instance, the intervals $(1,2]$ and $(2,2.5)$ are adjacent.

An *interval sequence* $\overline{I} = I_0 I_1 I_2 \ldots$ is a finite or infinite sequence of intervals that partitions the real line:

1. Any two neighboring intervals I_i and I_{i+1} are adjacent.

2. For all $t \in$ R, there is some interval I_i with $t \in I_i$.

In particular, I_0 is left-closed and $l(I_0) = 0$. The last interval of any finite interval sequence is unbounded.

Real-time systems

A *real-time system* $S = (\mathcal{S}, \mathcal{P}, \mu, \mathcal{T})$ consists of four components:

- A set $\mathcal{S}$ of system *states*.
- A set $\mathcal{P}$ of *observables*. The set $\mathcal{P}$ typically contains either observable events or observable propositions about the system state. Each element in the powerset $2^{\mathcal{P}}$ is a possible *observation*.
- A *labeling function* μ from $\mathcal{S}$ to $2^{\mathcal{P}}$ that determines the observable component of each system state. If $\mathcal{P}$ consists of events, then every state $s \in \mathcal{S}$ is labeled with the (possibly empty) set $\mu(s) \subseteq \mathcal{P}$ of events that are observed when the system is in state s. If $\mathcal{P}$ consists of propositions, then s is labeled with the set $\mu(s)$ of observable propositions that are true in state s.
- A fusion-closed set $\mathcal{T}$ of *timed state sequences.*

  Each timed state sequence $\tau \in \mathcal{T}$ represents a system behavior by identifying a unique system state $\tau(t) \in \mathcal{S}$ with every time instant $t \in \mathrm{R}$. Formally, a timed state sequence τ is a function from R to $\mathcal{S}$ that satisfies the *finite-variability* condition:

  > There exists an interval sequence $\overline{I} = I_0 I_1 I_2 \ldots$ such that throughout each interval I_i, the observable component of the system state does not change; that is, $\mu(\tau(t)) = \mu(\tau(t'))$ for all $t, t' \in I_i$. The interval sequence $\overline{I}$ is called *compatible* with the timed state sequence τ.

  Instantaneous events correspond to singular intervals. The finite-variability assumption asserts that in any bounded interval of time, there can be only finitely many observable events or state changes.

  A set $\mathcal{T}$ of timed state sequences is *fusion-closed* if each system state contains all information necessary to determine the future evolution of the system:

  > For all timed state sequences $\tau_1, \tau_2 \in \mathcal{T}$ and time instants $t_1, t_2 \in \mathrm{R}$, if $\tau_1(t_1) = \tau_2(t_2)$, then $\tau \in \mathcal{T}$ for the timed state sequence τ with $\tau(t) = \tau_1(t)$ for $t \leq t_1$ and $\tau(t) = \tau_2(t + t_2 - t_1)$ for $t > t_1$.

As a concrete example, let us consider a controller that responds to an environment stimulus. Whenever the stimulus p occurs, the controller reaches, within one time unit, an internal decision to either perform the response q two time units after the stimulus or not to respond at all. If a new stimulus occurs before the previous one has been served, by a response or by the decision not to respond, it is ignored. Suppose that S is the real-time system consisting of the environment and the controller. The only observables $\mathcal{P} = \{p, q\}$ are the environment stimulus p and the system response q. We assume that both events, p and q, are instantaneous. A state of the system must contain enough information to determine the future evolution of the system. Thus, we may characterize the states $\mathcal{S}$ of S as triples of the form (s_0, s_1, s_2):

- The boolean parameter s_0 indicates if there is a current stimulus.

- The ternary parameter $s_1 \in \{none, respond, ignore\}$ indicates which decision has been reached concerning the most recent stimulus that has not been ignored.
- The real parameter $s_2 \in [0,2] \cup \{\infty\}$ indicates the time that has elapsed since the most recent stimulus that has not been ignored. In particular, $s_2 = \infty$ if more than 2 time units have elapsed.

The labeling function μ is defined as follows:

$p \in \mu(s_0, s_1, s_2)$ iff $s_0 = true$;
$q \in \mu(s_0, s_1, s_2)$ iff $s_1 = respond$ and $s_2 = 2$.

The following timed state sequence $\hat{\tau}$ describes one possible behavior of the system S:

$\hat{\tau}(t) = (false, none, \infty)$ for $t \in [0,1)$,
$\hat{\tau}(1) = (true, none, 0)$,
$\hat{\tau}(t) = (false, none, t-1)$ for $t \in (1, 1.5)$,
$\hat{\tau}(t) = (false, respond, t-1)$ for $t \in [1.5, 3]$,
$\hat{\tau}(t) = (false, respond, \infty)$ for $t > 3$.

According to this behavior, a single stimulus occurs, at time 1. At time 1.5 the system decides to respond and does so at time 3.

Observation sequences

An *observation sequence* $\overline{\sigma} = \sigma_0\sigma_1\sigma_2\ldots$ is a finite or infinite sequence of observations $\sigma_i \subseteq 2^{\mathcal{P}}$. A *timed observation sequence* $\rho = (\overline{\sigma}, \overline{I})$, also written as a sequence

$$(\sigma_0, I_0) \rightarrow (\sigma_1, I_1) \rightarrow (\sigma_2, I_2) \rightarrow \cdots$$

of observation-interval pairs, consists of an observation sequence $\overline{\sigma}$ and an interval sequence $\overline{I}$ of equal length. The timed observation sequence ρ is *stutter-free* iff any two neighboring observations σ_i and σ_{i+1} are distinct. A set of timed observation sequences is closed under *stuttering* iff whenever the set contains a timed observation sequence of the form

$$\cdots \rightarrow (\sigma_i, I_i) \rightarrow \cdots$$

and $I_i = I_i' \cup I_i''$ for adjacent intervals I_i' and I_i'', then it contains also the timed observation sequence

$$\cdots \rightarrow (\sigma_i, I_i') \rightarrow (\sigma_i, I_i'') \rightarrow \cdots.$$

The stuttering closure of a timed observation sequence ρ is the smallest set of timed observation sequences that contains ρ and is closed under stuttering.

From a timed state sequence τ, we can extract a set $\mu(\tau)$ of timed observation sequences that represent the observations made when the system exhibits the behavior described by τ. Formally, a timed observation sequence $(\overline{\sigma}, \overline{I})$ is contained in $\mu(\tau)$ iff the interval sequence $\overline{I}$ is compatible with τ and $\sigma_i = \mu(\tau(t))$ for $t \in I_i$. It is easy to check that the set $\mu(\tau)$ is the stuttering closure of a single stutter-free timed observation sequence. For instance, the timed state sequence $\hat{\tau}$ of the example given above yields the stuttering closure $\mu(\hat{\tau})$ of the timed observation sequence

$$(\{\}, [0,1)) \rightarrow (\{p\}, [1,1]) \rightarrow (\{\}, (1,3)) \rightarrow (\{q\}, [3,3]) \rightarrow (\{\}, (3,\infty)).$$

Special cases of real-time systems

If we restrict ourselves to the analysis of certain systems, we may assume that all interval sequences are of a particular form. Here we present some common assumptions about real-time systems that lead to one or both of the following simplifications of interval sequences:

1. If the interval types in a sequence follow a particular pattern, interval sequences can be represented as sequences of time instants. Suppose, for instance, that we observe only instantaneous events. Then we may restrict ourselves to timed observation sequences containing singular intervals, associated with events, that alternate with open intervals, indicating the distance between events. In this case, it suffices only to record the time instants at which events occur. In our example, the observable component of the timed state sequence $\hat{\tau}$ is completely specified by the sequence

$$(\{p\},1) \rightarrow (\{q\},3).$$

   Similarly, suppose that we observe only propositions about the system states that have a duration in time, and suppose that whenever there is a change in the observation from state s to state s', the observation at the transition point is $\mu(s')$. Then we may limit ourselves to timed observation sequences all of whose intervals are left-closed and right-open. In this case, it suffices to record the left end-points of all intervals. For instance, the sequence $0, 3, 3.5$ of real numbers could stand for the interval sequence $[0,3), [3,3.5), [3.5,\infty)$. In the symmetric case, we may restrict ourselves to timed observation sequences all of whose intervals are left-open and right-closed.

2. If all events or state changes occur with the ticks of a global clock, the nonnegative integers N suffice as time domain. We call such systems *synchronous*.

2.2 Abstract semantics

Given our concrete semantics of a real-time system as a set of timed state sequences, one may choose several abstractions to model systems by simpler objects than sets of timed state sequences. The system aspects in which we are interested determine the abstraction mechanisms we can employ. We discuss three common abstractions, which are independent of each other — first, the restriction only to observable linear behaviors; second, the linearization of simultaneous activities; and, third, the digitization of time. The paradigm of digitization, which is obviously related to timing considerations, is the only one of these three abstraction mechanisms that is particular to the modeling of real-time systems.

A Trace semantics

Trace semantics sacrifices information about the internal structure of a system. If we are content to analyze the observable traces of a system, we may ignore all nonobservable state components. Thus, trace semantics identifies a real-time system with the set of timed observation sequences that are obtained from the timed state sequences representing possible system behaviors. The trace semantics of the system $S = (\mathcal{S}, \mathcal{P}, \mu, \mathcal{T})$ is the pair $(\mathcal{P}, \mathcal{R})$, where the set $\mathcal{R}$ of timed observation sequences is the union of all sets $\mu(\tau)$ for $\tau \in \mathcal{T}$. For instance, the trace semantics of our stimulus-response example contains all timed observation sequences in which (1) the difference between any two system responses q is at least two time units and (2) every response q is preceded by an environment stimulus p two time units earlier.

B Interleaving semantics

Interleaving semantics sacrifices information about the simultaneity of activities. Independent simultaneous events are often nondeterministically sequentialized so that at most one action of a distributed system has to be analyzed at any point in a timed state sequence (or a timed observation sequence). To allow the interleaving of simultaneous activities in our framework, we need to generalize our definitions concerning interval sequences:

- Two intervals I and I' are *almost* adjacent iff $r(I) = l(I')$; that is, they have at most one point in common. If we relax the requirement of adjacency of neighboring intervals in an interval sequence to almost adjacency, we obtain the notion of *weakly-monotonic* interval sequences. An example of a weakly-monotonic interval sequence is the sequence
$$[0,1.3],[1.3,1.3],[1.3,4],[4,5],[5,\infty).$$
- A *weakly*-timed observation sequence consists, then, of an observation sequence and a corresponding weakly-monotonic interval sequence.
- A weakly-timed state sequence maps every time instant $t \in \mathrm{R}$ to a finite sequence of system states. The number of states in this sequence is called the multiplicity m_t of t. Formally, a *weakly*-timed state sequence τ associates a multiplicity m_t with every time instant $t \in \mathrm{R}$ and maps every pair (t,i), for $t \in \mathrm{R}$ and $1 \leq i \leq m_t$, to a system state $\tau(t,i) \in \mathcal{S}$. In addition, the mapping τ is finitely variable; that is, there exists a weakly-timed observation sequence $(\overline{\sigma}, \overline{I})$ and a monotone onto mapping from lexicographic pairs (t,i) to indexes $j \geq 0$ such that (1) $t \in I_j$ and (2) $\mu(\tau(t,i)) = \sigma_j$. The lexicographically ordered pairs (t,i) can be viewed as specifying a metric "macro-time" $t \in \mathrm{R}$ and a linearly ordered discrete "micro-time" $1 \leq i \leq m_t$.

Using this generalized notion of timed state sequences, any number of simultaneous events can be modeled as a sequence of events at the same time instant. Consider, for example, the timed observation sequence

$$(\{\},[0,3)) \rightarrow (\{p,q\},[3,3]) \rightarrow (\{\},(3,\infty)),$$

in which the two events p and q occur at time 3. An interleaving semantics may model this behavior, instead, by the two weakly-timed observation sequences

$$(\{\},[0,3)) \rightarrow (\{p\},[3,3]) \rightarrow (\{q\},[3,3]) \rightarrow (\{\},(3,\infty)),$$

$$(\{\},[0,3)) \rightarrow (\{q\},[3,3]) \rightarrow (\{p\},[3,3]) \rightarrow (\{\},(3,\infty)).$$

Indeed, an interleaving semantics typically abstracts further by assuming that all observation intervals are either closed or unbounded. The behavior of a system is viewed as a two-phase activity [HMP90]: macro-phases, during which time (i.e., macro-time) advances, alternate with micro-phases, during which the observable part of the system state changes finitely often. The micro-phases result from the interleaving of independent instantaneous events and correspond to finite repetitions of singular intervals. Under these assumptions, weakly-monotonic interval sequences may be represented by sequences of weakly monotonically increasing real numbers. For instance, the behavior of our example is often modeled by the two sequences

$$(\{\},0) \rightarrow (\{\},3) \rightarrow (\{p\},3) \rightarrow (\{q\},3) \rightarrow (\{\},3),$$

$$(\{\},0) \rightarrow (\{\},3) \rightarrow (\{q\},3) \rightarrow (\{p\},3) \rightarrow (\{\},3),$$

each of which contains one micro-phase, at time 3, between two macro-phases during the intervals $[0,3]$ and $[3,\infty)$, respectively.

C Fictitious-clock semantics

Fictitious-clock semantics sacrifices information about the precise times of activities. The introduction of a global fictitious clock, which records the times of events with finite precision only, allows the use of the nonnegative integers as time domain, thereby simplifying the reasoning about time. If several events fall between two clock ticks, then the fictitious clock can distinguish them only by temporal ordering, not by time.

To allow the digitization of times, we have to consider, once again, weakly-monotonic interval sequences. Using the notion of weakly-timed state sequences, any number of events that occur between two ticks of the fictitious clock can be modeled as a sequence of events at the "same" integer time. Consider, for example, the timed observation sequence

$$(\{p\},[0,1.3)) \rightarrow (\{q\},[1.3,1.3]) \rightarrow (\{p\},(1.3,1.8]) \rightarrow (\{q\},(1.8,\infty))$$

of a system that satisfies the proposition q at time 1.3 and after time 1.8, and otherwise it satisfies the proposition p. We assume that a fictitious clock ticks at all integer times. The fictitious-clock semantics may model this behavior, then, by the weakly-timed observation sequence

$$(\{p\},[0,1]) \rightarrow (\{q\},[1,1]) \rightarrow (\{p\},[1,1]) \rightarrow (\{q\},[1,\infty)),$$

which results from ignoring the fractional parts of all interval end-points.

Summary

Any combination of system restrictions and choices of abstractions we presented leads to one of sixteen possible formal semantics of real-time systems:

1. *State sequences or observation sequences.* Observation sequences suffice for the study of the observable traces of a system.

2. *Time intervals or time points.* Time points suffice in a variety of cases, such as the study of instantaneous events and under the assumption of two-phase interleaving.

3. *Strictly monotonic or weakly monotonic time.* Time is weakly monotonic if adjacent time intervals may overlap in a common point, or if adjacent time instants may be identical. Weakly monotonic time is necessary for employing one or both of two independent abstractions — the modeling of simultaneous activities by interleaving and the recording of times by a fictitious clock.

4. *Real-numbered time or integer time.* Integer time suffices for the study of synchronous systems and in the presence of a fictitious clock.

In previous papers, we investigated the following combinations of semantical options:

- an observation-oriented point-based weakly-monotonic integer-time semantics [AH89, AH90, Hen90, HMP91];
- an observation-oriented point-based weakly-monotonic real-time semantics [Hen91b];
- an observation-oriented point-based strictly-monotonic real-time semantics [AD90];
- an observation-oriented interval-based strictly-monotonic real-time semantics [AFH91, AH91];
- a state-oriented point-based strictly-monotonic real-time semantics [ACD90];
- a state-oriented interval-based strictly-monotonic real-time semantics [Alu91].

In this paper, we review our results and identify the semantical assumptions that were necessary to obtain them. This allows us to generalize many results to a broader spectrum of semantical choices than was previously known.

3 Real-time Logics

We discuss three ways of extending the syntax of temporal logic for specifying real-time systems. The main point of this section is to demonstrate that these extensions apply equally to any particular choice of temporal logic.

3.1 Choosing the temporal logic

Temporal logic (or tense logic, the term sometimes preferred by philosophers) is the class designation for modal logics whose modal operators are interpreted in a temporal manner: the basic operator $\Box$ is interpreted as "always" and, consequently, its dual $\Diamond$ means "eventually." The use of temporal logic as a formalism for specifying the behavior of reactive systems over time was first proposed by Pnueli [Pnu77] and has been studied extensively since then. Temporal logic provides a succinct and natural way of expressing the desired *qualitative* temporal requirements of speed-independent systems, including invariance, precedence, and responsiveness (cf. [Pnu86]). The traditional temporal operators, however, cannot refer to metric time and, hence, are insufficient for the specification of *quantitative* temporal requirements, or so-called *hard* real-time constraints, which put timing deadlines on the behavior of reactive systems.

Having emphasized that the term temporal logic covers a variety of particular logical formalisms, with syntactic as well as semantic differences, we refer the reader to [Eme90] for a comprehensive overview of individual temporal logics that have been used for specifying and verifying reactive systems. Any of these logics can be, and some have been, extended by the constructs we will present for expressing timing constraints. Before proceeding to the issue of real time, however, let us briefly review some of the design decisions involved in choosing a particular underlying logic for qualitative temporal reasoning.

First, depending on the nature of the problems we wish to formalize, we use either a first-order temporal logic or the propositional fragment. This choice is determined by the data domains over which the reactive systems under investigation operate, and interests us little, as we treat the issue of time independent of other system parameters. We are mostly concerned with propositional fragments, because those allow us to study issues of expressiveness and complexity without interference by data considerations.

Second, many of the temporal logics that are used in computer science can be classified into linear-time and branching-time logics. This distinction is important, because it determines if we can choose a trace semantics for real-time systems. Throughout this section, we assume a given real-time system $\mathrm{S} = (\mathcal{S}, \mathcal{P}, \mu, \mathcal{T})$ with the trace semantics $(\mathcal{P}, \mathcal{R})$. The set $\mathcal{P}$ of observables constitutes the set of atomic propositions for the logics we discuss. Hence, the truth value of any atomic proposition is fully determined by the observable component of a system state ($s \models p$ iff $p \in \mu(s)$).

1. *Linear-time* logics are interpreted over linear structures of states. Every state sequence represents an execution sequence of a reactive system. A classical example of a linear-time logic is PTL [GPSS80]. In PTL, the typical response property that "every environment stimulus p must be followed by a system response q" is defined by the formula
$$\Box(p \rightarrow \Diamond q),$$
which requires that in any possible behavior, if the system is in a state in which p is observed, then it will, at some later point, be in a state in which q is observed. Real-time extensions of PTL introduce a way of defining timing requirements such as the time-bounded response property that "every stimulus p is followed by a response q within 3 time units."

   Formally, the real-time system S satisfies a linear-time formula ϕ iff every timed state sequence in $\mathcal{T}$ satisfies ϕ. Since the truth value of ϕ over a timed state sequence τ is completely determined by the observable component of τ, it suffices to consider the trace semantics of S and interpret ϕ over timed observation sequences: S satisfies ϕ iff $\rho \models \phi$ for every timed observation sequence $\rho \in \mathcal{R}$.

2. *Branching-time* temporal logics, on the other hand, are interpreted over tree structures of states. Every tree represents a reactive system, whose possible execution sequences correspond to the paths in the tree. Classical examples of branching-time logics include $\mathcal{UB}$ [BMP81], CTL [EC82], and CTL* [CES86]. In CTL, the property that "every stimulus p is possibly followed by a response q" is defined by the formula
$$\forall\Box(p \rightarrow \exists\Diamond q),$$
which asserts that in any possible behavior, if the system is in a state in which p is observed, then there is a possible continuation along which the system will, at some

later point, be in a state in which q is observed. Real-time extensions of CTL allow to put a time bound on the distance between the stimulus p and the response q.

Since we require that each state $s \in \mathcal{S}$ contains all the information necessary to decide the future behavior of the real-time system S, the set $\mathcal{T}$ of timed state sequences contains all the branching information for constructing a unique tree, with root s, whose paths represent the possible behaviors of S if started in state s. This is because the formal requirement of fusion closure for $\mathcal{T}$ captures the intuitive notion of a tree; it ensures that the reachability relation over $\mathcal{S}$ induced by $\mathcal{T}$ is transitive. Thus, the truth value $s \models \phi$ of a branching-time formula ϕ can be determined for each state $s \in \mathcal{S}$. The real-time system S satisfies ϕ iff $s \models \phi$ for all $s \in \mathcal{S}$.

It follows that linear-time logics employ an observation-oriented semantics, and branching-time logics employ a state-oriented semantics.

Third, there is the choice of temporal operators. The temporal operator most typically employed is the *until* operator $\mathcal{U}$, which can be used to define the *always* operator $\Box$ and provides a generally desired level of expressiveness [GPSS80]. Many temporal logics exclude the *next* operator to ensure that the models of a formula are closed under stuttering [Lam83]. Some logics include past temporal operators such as *since*, the dual of *until* [LPZ85]. Branching-time formulas are built from linear-time formulas using path quantifiers. The logic CTL constrains the linear-time formulas that can be used to a very simple form by coupling the path quantifiers with the temporal operators. The logic CTL* allows arbitrary linear-time formulas.

3.2 Writing the timing constraints

The fourth question raised when defining the syntax of a real-time extension for a temporal logic is how to incorporate timing requirements in a formula. We consider three possible solutions.

A Bounded temporal operators

A common way of introducing real time in the syntax replaces the unrestricted temporal operators by time-bounded versions. For example, the bounded operator $\Diamond_{[2,4]}$ is interpreted as "eventually within 2 to 4 time units." This approach to the specification of timing properties has been advocated by Koymans, Vytopil, and de Roever [KVdR83, KdR85, Koy90], although an early proposal by Bernstein and Harter can be viewed as a precursor [BH81]. More applications of the bounded-operator method for expressing timing constraints can be found in [SPE84, Har88, PH88, HW89, Lew90]. Bounded operators have been analyzed for their expressiveness and complexity in [EMSS89, ACD90, AH90, AFH91].

To be concrete, let us define a propositional linear-time logic that employs time-bounded temporal operators. The formulas of this bounded-operator logic are built from atomic propositions by boolean connectives and time-bounded versions of the *until* operator. The *until* operator may be bounded (i.e., subscripted) by any interval with rational end-points. Hence, the bounded-operator formulas are inductively defined as follows:

$$\phi := p \mid \neg\phi \mid \phi_1 \wedge \phi_2 \mid \phi_1 \mathcal{U}_I \, \phi_2,$$

where $p \in \mathcal{P}$ and the end-points of the interval I are rational numbers.

We interpret the formulas of this linear-time logic over timed observation sequences, which provide a unique interpretation for the atomic propositions at every time instant. Informally, the formula $\phi_1 \mathcal{U}_I \phi_2$ holds at time t in a timed observation sequence iff there is a later time instant $t' \in t + I$ such that ϕ_2 holds at time t' and ϕ_1 holds throughout the interval (t, t'). Formally, given a bounded-operator formula ϕ, a timed observation sequence $\rho = (\overline{\sigma}, \overline{I})$, and a time instant $t \in \mathrm{R}$, the satisfaction relation $(\rho, t) \models \phi$ is defined inductively as follows:

$(\rho, t) \models p$ iff $p \in \sigma_i$, where $t \in I_i$;
$(\rho, t) \models \neg\phi$ iff $(\rho, t) \not\models \phi$;
$(\rho, t) \models (\phi_1 \wedge \phi_2)$ iff $(\rho, t) \models \phi_1$ and $(\rho, t) \models \phi_2$;
$(\rho, t) \models \phi_1 \mathcal{U}_I \phi_2$ iff $(\rho, t') \models \phi_2$ for some $t' \in t + I$, and $(\rho, t'') \models \phi_1$ for all $t < t'' < t'$.

The timed observation sequence ρ satisfies the formula ϕ iff $(\rho, 0) \models \phi$.

Now we can introduce some standard abbreviations for additional temporal operators. The defined operators $\Diamond_I \phi$ (time-bounded *eventually*) and $\Box_I \phi$ (time-bounded *always*) stand for $true\, \mathcal{U}_I \phi$ and $\neg\Diamond_I \neg\phi$, respectively. It follows that the formula $\Box_I \phi$ (or $\Diamond_I \phi$) holds at time $t \in \mathrm{R}$ of a timed observation sequence iff ϕ holds at all times (at some time, respectively) within the interval $t + I$. The typical time-bounded response property that "every stimulus p is followed by a response q within 3 time units" may then be defined by the bounded-operator formula

$$\Box(p \rightarrow \Diamond_{[0,3]}\, q),$$

which is usually written as

$$\Box(p \rightarrow \Diamond_{\leq 3}\, q). \qquad (\dagger)$$

We have chosen an interval-based strictly-monotonic real-time semantics for our sample bounded-operator logic. It is not difficult to interpret the same set of formulas over alternative semantics. For instance, we may adopt an interleaving semantics and interpret bounded-operator formulas over weakly-timed observation sequences [Hen91b].

B Freeze quantification

The bounded-operator notation can relate only adjacent temporal contexts. Consider, for instance, the property that "every stimulus p is followed by a response q and, then, by another response r such that r is within 5 time units of the stimulus p." There is no direct way of expressing this "nonlocal" timing requirement using time-bounded operators. This shortcoming of bounded temporal operators can be remedied by extending temporal logic with explicit references to the times of temporal contexts. We discuss two such methods. In this subsection, we access the time of a state through a quantifier, which binds ("freezes") a variable to the corresponding time; in the next subsection, we access the time of a state through a (dynamic) state variable.

The idea of *freeze* quantification was introduced and has been analyzed by the authors [AH89, Hen90, Alu91, Hen91b]. We present it here by considering again the propositional linear-time case. The freeze quantifier "$x.$" binds the associated variable x to the time of the current temporal context: the formula $x.\phi(x)$ holds at time t iff $\phi(t)$ does. Thus, in the formula $\Diamond y.\phi$, the time variable y is bound to the time of the state at which ϕ is "eventually" true. By admitting atomic formulas that relate the times of different states, we can write the time-bounded response property (†) as

$$\Box x.(p \rightarrow \Diamond y.(q \wedge y \leq x+3)).$$

We read the this formula as "in every state with time x, if p holds, then there is a later state with time y such that q holds and y is at most $x+3$." The nonlocal property that "every stimulus p is followed by a response q and, then, by another response r within 5 time units of the stimulus p" may be specified by the formula

$$\Box x.(p \rightarrow \Diamond(q \wedge \Diamond z.(r \wedge z \leq x+5))). \qquad (\ddagger)$$

Freeze quantification allows only references to times that are associated with states. Consequently, the freeze quantifier $x.$ behaves differently from standard first-order quantifiers over time; it is, for example, its own dual:

$$\neg(x.\phi) \leftrightarrow x.(\neg\phi).$$

Since the expressive power of a modal logic with freeze quantification lies, in general, between the expressive power of the corresponding propositional and first-order modal logics, we refer to a logic with freeze quantification as *half-order* [Hen90].

Let us now be more precise and define a half-order linear-time logic. Given a set V of time variables and a set $\Pi(V)$ of atomic timing constraints with free variables from V, the half-order formulas are inductively defined as follows:

$$\phi := p \mid \pi \mid \neg\phi \mid \phi_1 \wedge \phi_2 \mid \phi_1 \mathcal{U} \phi_2 \mid x.\phi$$

for $x \in V$, $p \in \mathcal{P}$, and $\pi \in \Pi(V)$. Additional temporal operators such as $\Diamond$ (*eventually*) and $\Box$ (*always*) can be defined in terms of the *until* operator as usual. The atomic timing constraints (e.g., $y \leq x+3$) typically involve comparisons between terms containing variables, constants, and primitive operations on time such as addition.

We interpret the half-order formulas again over timed observation sequences (other semantical choices are, of course, possible). The timed observation sequence $\rho = (\overline{\sigma}, \overline{I})$ satisfies the formula ϕ iff $(\rho, 0) \models_{\mathcal{E}} \phi$ for every environment $\mathcal{E} : V \rightarrow \mathrm{R}$, where the satisfaction predicate $\models$ is inductively defined as follows:

$(\rho, t) \models_{\mathcal{E}} p$ iff $p \in \sigma_i$, where $t \in I_i$;
$(\rho, t) \models_{\mathcal{E}} \pi$ iff $\mathcal{E} \models \pi$;
$(\rho, t) \models_{\mathcal{E}} \neg\phi$ iff $(\rho, t) \not\models_{\mathcal{E}} \phi$;
$(\rho, t) \models_{\mathcal{E}} \phi_1 \wedge \phi_2$ iff $(\rho, t) \models_{\mathcal{E}} \phi_1$ and $(\rho, t) \models_{\mathcal{E}} \phi_2$;
$(\rho, t) \models_{\mathcal{E}} \phi_1 \mathcal{U} \phi_2$ iff $(\rho, t') \models_{\mathcal{E}} \phi_2$ for some $t' \in t + I$, and $(\rho, t'') \models_{\mathcal{E}} \phi_1$ for all $t < t'' < t'$;
$(\rho, t) \models_{\mathcal{E}} x.\phi$ iff $(\rho, t) \models_{\mathcal{E}[x:=t]} \phi$.

Here $\mathcal{E}[x := t]$ denotes the environment that agrees with the environment $\mathcal{E}$ on all variables except x, which is mapped to $t \in \mathrm{R}$.

If the atomic timing constraints in $\Pi(V)$ permit at least comparisons and addition of constants, then the bounded-operator notation is a fragment of the freeze-quantifier notation: the bounded-operator formula $\phi_1 \mathcal{U}_I \phi_2$ is equivalent to the half-order formula

$$x.(\phi_1 \mathcal{U} y.(y \in x + I \wedge \phi_2)).$$

C Explicit clock variable

A third way of writing real-time requirements is based on standard first-order temporal logic. The syntax uses a dynamic state variable T — the *clock* variable — and first-order quantification for global (rigid) variables over the time domain. The clock variable T assumes, in each state, the value of the corresponding time. For instance, the time-bounded response property (†) can be specified by the formula

$$\forall x. \Box((p \wedge T = x) \rightarrow \Diamond(q \wedge T \leq x + 3)).$$

Here, the global variable x is bound to the time of every state in which p is observed. We refer to the use of a clock variable as the "explicit-clock" notation. Examples of this method for expressing timing constraints can be found in [PdR82, Ron84, Har88, PH88, Ost90, LA]; it has been studied for its expressiveness and complexity in [AH90, HLP90].

Let us once again define a propositional linear-time logic with an interval-based strictly-monotonic real-time semantics. As before, let V be a set of (global) time variables, and let $\Pi(V \cup \{T\})$ be a set of timing constraints over the variables in $V \cup \{T\}$. The explicit-clock formulas are inductively defined as follows:

$$\phi := p \mid \pi \mid \neg\phi \mid \phi_1 \wedge \phi_2 \mid \phi_1 \mathcal{U} \phi_2 \mid \exists x. \phi$$

for $x \in V$, $p \in \mathcal{P}$, and $\pi \in \Pi(V \cup \{T\})$. The timed observation sequence $\rho = (\overline{\sigma}, \overline{I})$ satisfies the formula ϕ iff $(\rho, 0) \models_{\mathcal{E}} \phi$ for every environment $\mathcal{E} : V \rightarrow \mathbb{R}$. Only the following two clauses in the definition of the satisfaction predicate $\models$ differ from the evaluation of half-order formulas:

$(\rho, t) \models_{\mathcal{E}} \pi$ iff $\mathcal{E}[T := t] \models \pi$;
$(\rho, t) \models_{\mathcal{E}} \exists x. \phi$ iff $(\rho, t) \models_{\mathcal{E}[x:=t']} \phi$ for some $t' \in \mathbb{R}$.

Assuming the same set of atomic timing constraints, the half-order notation is a fragment of the explicit-clock notation: the half-order formula $x. \phi$ is equivalent to the first-order formula

$$\exists x. (T = x \wedge \phi)$$

(or, alternatively, to the formula $\forall x. (T = x \rightarrow \phi)$).

3.3 Examples of real-time logics

After considering the various choices available for defining a real-time temporal logic, let us examine the decisions that have been made for some logics proposed in the literature. To summarize the discussion so far, we list the questions that need to be answered when designing a real-time temporal logic:

1. Is it propositional or first-order?

2. Is it linear-time or branching-time?

3. Which temporal operators are used?

4. Which semantic abstractions such as interleaving or a fictitious clock are assumed?

5. Of the three possible choices for writing timing constraints — bounded operators, freeze quantification, or a clock variable — which one is used?

6. What are the primitive operations of the assertion language for timing constraints?

We emphasize that all of the above choices are independent.

Linear-time logics

The logics MTL (*metric* temporal logic) [AH90], TPTL (*timed* temporal logic) [AH89], RTTL (*real-time* temporal logic) [Ost90], and XCTL (for *explicit-clock* temporal logic) [HLP90] are linear-time logics that assume both the interleaving and fictitious-clock abstractions; that is, they are defined over a point-based weakly-monotonic integer-time semantics:

- MTL is a propositional bounded-operator logic; its temporal operators include time-bounded versions of the *until*, *next*, *since*, and *previous* (the past dual of *next*) operators.

- TPTL is a propositional half-order logic that uses only the future temporal operators *until* and *next*; its atomic timing constraints include the primitives $\leq$ (comparison), $\equiv_c$ (congruence modulo a constant), and $+c$ (addition by an integer constant).

- RTTL is a first-order explicit-clock logic. Although RTTL was defined without restrictions on the assertion language for atomic timing constraints, we shall refer by the name RTTL to the propositional fragment with the primitives of TPTL for timing constraints.

- XCTL is a propositional explicit-clock logic, whose assertion language for atomic timing constraints allows the primitives of comparisons and addition. Thus, the timing constraints of XCTL are richer than those of the previous logics, which prohibit the addition of time variables. XCTL, on the other hand, forbids explicit quantification over the time variables; that is, all global time variables are assumed to be implicitly universally quantified on the outside of any given formula.

While all of the above logics assume integer time, the logic MITL (*metric interval* temporal logic) [AFH91] employs the nonnegative reals as time domain. MITL is a propositional linear-time logic with an interval-based strictly-monotonic real-time semantics; that is, it is interpreted over timed observation sequences, just like our three sample logics. MITL uses the bounded-operator syntax with the restriction that the temporal operators must not be bounded (subscripted) by singular intervals. For example, the formula

$$\Box(p \rightarrow \Diamond_{[3,3]}\, q)$$

is disallowed; that is, MITL rules out a form of equality constraints.

Branching-time logics

The logic RTCTL (for *real-time* computation tree logic) [EMSS89] is a propositional branching-time logic for synchronous systems; it is a bounded-operator extension of CTL with a point-based strictly-monotonic integer-time semantics.

The logic TCTL (*timed* computation tree logic) [ACD90] is a propositional branching-time logic with a less restrictive semantics; it is a bounded-operator extension of CTL with a point-based strictly-monotonic real-time semantics. A later version of the logic uses an interval-based semantics and half-order syntax with the primitives of comparisons and addition by constants [Alu91].

4 Automata-based Real-time Formalisms

We discuss an extension of finite automata and an extension of transition systems to specify real-time systems.

4.1 Timed automata

Timed automata were proposed as an abstract model for real-time systems [Dil89, AD90] (see also the article *The Theory of Timed Automata* in this volume). The formalism of timed automata generalizes finite-state machines over infinite strings. While ω-automata generate (or accept) infinite sequences of states (cf. [Tho90]), timed automata are additionally constrained by timing requirements and produce timed state sequences. While timed automata were originally given a point-based strictly-monotonic real-time semantics, we present an interval-based variant [AFH91]. It is also not difficult to interpret timed automata under the semantic assumptions of interleaving, a fictitious clock, and/or synchronicity.

A timed automaton operates with finite control — a finite set of locations and a finite set of real-valued clocks. All clocks proceed at the same rate and measure the amount of time that has elapsed since they were started (or reset). Each edge of the automaton may reset some of the clocks; each location of the automaton puts certain constraints on the values of the atomic propositions as well as on the values of the clocks: the control of the automaton can reside in a particular location only if the values of the propositions and clocks satisfy the corresponding constraints.

Formally, a *timed automaton* $\mathrm{A} = (\mathcal{P}, Q, Q_0, C, \mu, \nu, E, F)$ consists of eight components:

- A set $\mathcal{P}$ of *propositions.*
- A finite set Q of *locations.*
- A subset $Q_0 \subseteq Q$ of *initial locations.*
- A finite set C of *clocks.*
- A labeling function μ that assigns to each location in Q a boolean formula over the set $\mathcal{P}$ of propositions. For $\ell \in Q$, the formula $\mu(\ell)$ is called a *propositional constraint.*

- A labeling function ν that assigns to each location in Q a *timing constraint* over the variables in C. Each timing constraint is a boolean combination of atomic timing constraints from a set $\Pi(C)$, which typically contains comparisons between terms involving clock variables and primitive operations such as addition by constants. For $\ell \in Q$, the timing constraint $\mu(\ell)$ constrains the values of the clocks.

- A set $E \subseteq Q^2 \times 2^C$ of *edges*. Each edge (ℓ, ℓ', λ) identifies a source location ℓ, a target location ℓ', and a set $\lambda \subseteq C$ of clocks to be reset. The target location ℓ' is called an E-successor of the source location ℓ.

- A family $F \subseteq 2^Q$ of *acceptance sets* of locations. The (Muller) acceptance condition requires that the set of locations that is visited infinitely often during any run of the automaton A belongs to the acceptance family F.

The runs of a timed automaton define timed state sequences. At any time instant during a run, the configuration of the automaton is completely determined by the location in which the control resides and the values of all propositions and all clocks. The values of the clocks are given by a *clock interpretation* γ, which is a map from C to R: for any clock $x \in C$, the value of x under the interpretation γ is the nonnegative real number $\gamma(x)$. A *state* of the timed automaton A is a triple (ℓ, σ, γ), where $\ell \in Q$ is a location and

1. $\sigma \subseteq \mathcal{P}$ is an observation that satisfies the propositional constraint $\mu(\ell)$;

2. γ is a clock interpretation that satisfies the timing constraint $\nu(\ell)$.

Before defining the runs of A formally, let us give some intuition. Assume that, at time $t \in$ R, a timed automaton is in state (ℓ, σ, γ). Suppose that the location ℓ of the automaton and the observation σ remain unchanged during the time interval I with $l(I) = t$. All clocks proceed at the same rate as time elapses; at any time $t' \in I$ the value of any clock x is $\gamma(x) + t' - t$. During all this time, the clock values satisfy the timing constraint that is associated with ℓ:

$$(\gamma + t' - t) \models \nu(\ell).$$

Now suppose that the automaton changes its location at time $r(I) = t''$ via the edge (ℓ, ℓ', λ). This location change happens in one of two ways. If the interval I is right-closed, then the state at time t'' is $(\ell, \sigma, \gamma + t'' - t)$; otherwise, the state at time t'' is $(\ell', \sigma', \gamma')$, where σ' is an observation consistent with $\mu(\ell')$ and the clock interpretation γ' is defined by (1) $\gamma'(x) = 0$ for all clocks $x \in \lambda$, which are reset, and (2) $\gamma'(x) = \gamma(x) + t'' - t$ for all other clocks.

Let us formalize this intuition. A *run* of the automaton $\mathrm{A} = (\mathcal{P}, Q, Q_0, C, \mu, \nu, E, F)$ is a finite or infinite sequence

$$r: \quad \xrightarrow[\gamma_0]{} (\ell_0, \sigma_0, I_0) \xrightarrow[\gamma_1]{\lambda_1} (\ell_1, \sigma_1, I_1) \xrightarrow[\gamma_2]{\lambda_2} (\ell_2, \sigma_2, I_2) \xrightarrow[\gamma_3]{\lambda_3} \cdots$$

of locations $\ell_i \in Q$, observations $\sigma_i \subseteq \mathcal{P}$, intervals I_i, clock sets $\lambda_i \subseteq C$, and clock interpretations $\gamma_i : C \to$ R such that

1. $\ell_0 \in Q_0$;

2. $(s_i, s_{i+1}, \lambda_i) \in E$ for all $i \geq 0$;

3. σ_i satisfies $\mu(\ell_i)$ for all $i \geq 0$;

4. $\overline{I} = I_0 I_1 I_2 \ldots$ is an interval sequence;

5. for all $x \in C$ and $i \geq 0$, $\gamma_{i+1}(x) = 0$ if $x \in \lambda_{i+1}$, and $\gamma_{i+1}(x) = \gamma_i(x) + r(I_i) - l(I_i)$ otherwise;

6. $\gamma_i + t - l(I_i)$ satisfies $\nu(\ell_i)$ for all $i \geq 0$ and $t \in I_i$;

7. either $\overline{I} = I_0 I_1 \ldots I_n$ is finite and $\{\ell_n\} \in F$, or r is infinite and $\{\ell \mid \ell = \ell_i$ for infinitely many $i \geq 0\} \in F$.

Every run r of the timed automaton A uniquely determines a timed state sequence τ_r: let $\tau_r(t) = (\ell_i, \sigma_i, \gamma_i + t - l(I_i))$ for all $t \in I_i$. By $\mathcal{T}_A$ we denote the set of all timed state sequences τ_r that correspond to runs of the automaton A. The timed automaton A defines, then, the real-time system $S_A = (\mathcal{S}, \mathcal{P}, \mu', \mathcal{T}_A)$, where $\mathcal{S}$ is the set of states of the automaton A and and the labeling function μ' is defined as the projection $\mu'(\ell, \sigma, \gamma) = \sigma$. It is easy to check that the set $\mathcal{T}_A$ satisfies the requirement of fusion closure.

The set $\mu'(\tau_r)$ of timed observation sequences that are associated with the timed state sequence τ_r describes the observed behavior during the run r of the timed automaton A. Notice that the same stutter-free timed observation sequence may correspond to two different runs of A. This makes timed automata nondeterministic. The timed automaton A is called *deterministic* iff the following conditions hold for every location $\ell \in Q$:

1. For every pair $\ell_1, \ell_2 \in Q$ of E-successors of ℓ, either the propositional constraints $\mu(\ell_1)$ and $\mu(\ell_2)$ are mutually exclusive (i.e., contradictory), or the clock constraints $\nu(\ell_1)$ and $\nu(\ell_2)$ are mutually exclusive.

2. For every E-successor ℓ' of ℓ, either $\mu(\ell)$ and $\mu(\ell')$ are mutually exclusive, or $\nu(\ell)$ and $\nu(\ell')$ are mutually exclusive.

It is easy to check that for any deterministic timed automaton, there is a unique run to generate (or accept) a given timed observation sequence.

As an example, consider the following timed automaton A, which defines the real-time system we described informally in Section 2:

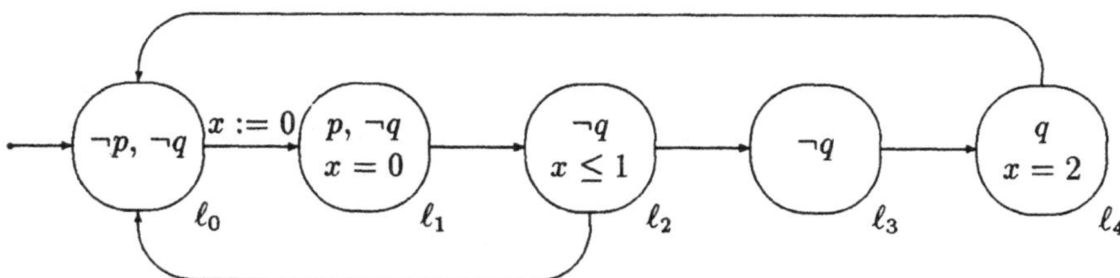

The automaton A has five locations and one clock, x; it starts in location ℓ_0 and every subset of locations containing the initial location ℓ_0 is an acceptance set. As soon as an external stimulus p occurs, the automaton A moves through location ℓ_1 to location ℓ_2.

The clock x is used to measure the time that elapses from the time of the stimulus. Within one time unit after the stimulus, the automaton decides, nondeterministically, either to respond and proceed to location ℓ_3, or not to respond and return to location ℓ_0. If the decision is to respond, the automaton does so by issuing the instantaneous response q in location ℓ_4 two time units after the stimulus (note that all new stimuli that may have occurred in the meantime were ignored). Then the automaton returns to its start location ℓ_0, ready for the next stimulus, for which the clock x will be reused.

4.2 Timed transition systems

A different approach to the definition of real-time systems generalizes the formalism of transition systems [Kel76, Pnu77] by imposing timing constraints on the transitions [Ost90, Har88, LA90, HMP91] (see also the article *Timed Transition Systems* in this volume). A *transition system* $\mathrm{T}_0 = (\mathcal{P}, \mathcal{I}, \mathcal{E})$ consists of three components:

1. A set $\mathcal{P}$ of *propositions*. The subsets of $\mathcal{P}$, to which we refer as observations, are often called the "states" of the transition system. We refrain from this terminology to avoid confusion with our usage of the term "state."

2. A set $\mathcal{I} \subseteq 2^{\mathcal{P}}$ of *initial observations*.

3. A finite set $\mathcal{E}$ of *transitions*. Every transition $e \in \mathcal{E}$ is a binary relation on the set $2^{\mathcal{P}}$ of observations; that is, it defines for every observation $\sigma \subseteq \mathcal{P}$ a (possibly empty) set of e-successors $e(\sigma) \subseteq 2^{\mathcal{P}}$. A transition e is *enabled* on the observation σ iff $e(\sigma) \neq \emptyset$.

Time is incorporated into the transition system model, under the assumption that all transitions happen instantaneously, by restricting the times at which transitions may occur. The timing constraints on transitions are classified into two categories: lower-bound and upper-bound requirements. They ensure that transitions occur neither too early nor too late, respectively. Consequently, a *timed transition system* $\mathrm{T} = (\mathcal{P}, \mathcal{I}, \mathcal{E}, l, u)$ consists of an underlying transition system $\mathrm{T}_0 = (\mathcal{P}, \mathcal{I}, \mathcal{E})$ as well as

4. A *minimal delay* (lower bound) $l_e \in \mathrm{N}$ for each transition $e \in \mathcal{E}$.

5. A *maximal delay* (upper bound) $u_e \geq l_e$, with $u_e \in \mathrm{N} \cup \{\infty\}$, for each transition $e \in \mathcal{E}$.

Informally, the lower-bound requirement for a transition e asserts that e cannot be taken unless it has been continuously enabled for l_e time units. In the case that the maximal delay u_e is finite, the upper-bound requirement for the transition e asserts that e cannot be continuously enabled for more than u_e time units without being taken. An infinite maximal delay (i.e., $u_e = \infty$) puts a fairness condition on the transition e: it cannot be enabled perpetually without being taken. Formally, the timed transition system T defines the real-time system $\mathrm{S}_\mathrm{T} = (\mathcal{S}, \mathcal{P}, \mu, \mathcal{T})$:

- Every state $s \in \mathcal{S}$ consists of an observation $\mu(s) \subseteq \mathcal{P}$ and a delay $\delta_e(s) \in \mathrm{R}$ for each transition $e \in \mathcal{E}$:

$$\mathcal{S} = 2^{\mathcal{P}} \times \mathrm{R}^{\mathcal{E}}.$$

The delay $\delta_e(s)$ indicates the time that has elapsed since the transition e became enabled.

- A timed state sequence τ belongs to $\mathcal{T}$ iff $\mu(\tau(0)) \in \mathcal{I}$ and there exists an interval sequence $\overline{I} = I_0 I_1 I_2 \ldots$ of right-closed (or unbounded) intervals that is compatible with τ and satisfies the following conditions:

  1. (*observation consecution*) For all $t \in I_i$ and $t' \in I_{i+1}$, there is a transition $e \in \mathcal{E}$ such that $\mu(\tau(t')) \in e(\mu(\tau(t)))$. The transition e is *taken* at time $r(I_i)$.
  2. (*delay consecution*) For all $t \in I_i$, if the transition $e \in \mathcal{E}$ is enabled on $\mu(\tau(t))$ and not taken at time $l(I_i)$, then $\delta_e(\tau(t)) = \delta_e(\tau(l(I_i))) + t - l(I_i)$; if e is enabled on $\mu(\tau(t))$ and taken at time $l(I_i)$, then $\delta_e(\tau(t)) = t - l(I_i)$; otherwise, $\delta_e(\tau(t)) = 0$.
  3. (*timing*) If the transition $e \in \mathcal{E}$ is taken at time $t \in \mathrm{R}$, then $l_e \leq \delta_e(\tau(t)) \leq u_e$. In other words, once enabled, e is delayed for at least l_e time units and at most u_e time units (if $u_e \in \mathrm{N}$).
  4. (*fairness*) If the transition $e \in \mathcal{E}$ with $u_e = \infty$ is not taken after time $t \in \mathrm{R}$, then e is not enabled on $\mu(\tau(t'))$ for some later time $t' \geq t$.
  5. (*termination*) If $\overline{I} = I_0 I_1 \ldots I_n$ is finite and $t \in I_n$, then no transition $e \in \mathcal{E}$ is enabled on $\mu(\tau(t))$.

It is not difficult to check that the set $\mathcal{T}$ of timed state sequences is fusion-closed.

nslation to timed automata

e set $\mathcal{P}$ of propositions is finite, then the real-time system $\mathrm{S_T}$ can, alternatively, efined by a timed automaton $\mathrm{A_T}$. For simplicity, let us assume that all transitions become disabled once they are taken; that is, $(\sigma, \sigma') \in e$ implies $e(\sigma') = \emptyset$. The d automaton $\mathrm{A_T} = (\mathcal{P}, Q, Q_0, C, \mu, \nu, E, F)$ contains a location for each observation-sition pair and a clock for each transition of the timed transition system T:

$$Q = 2^{\mathcal{P}} \times \mathcal{E};$$
$$Q_0 = \mathcal{I} \times \mathcal{E};$$
$$C = \{x_e \mid e \in \mathcal{E}\};$$
$$\mu(\sigma, e) = \textstyle\bigwedge_{p \in \sigma} p \wedge \bigwedge_{p \notin \sigma} \neg p \quad \text{for all locations } (\sigma, e) \in Q.$$

cation (σ, e) of the timed automaton $\mathrm{A_T}$ records the current observation σ and the sition e that was taken most recently. The automaton $\mathrm{A_T}$ contains an edge from location (σ, e) to the location (σ', e') iff $\sigma' \in e'(\sigma)$; that is, if the transition e' leads the observation σ to the observation σ'. Along this edge, all clocks $x_{e''}$ whose esponding transitions e'' are disabled on σ but enabled on σ' are reset. Thus, for currently enabled transition e, the clock x_e shows the time that has elapsed since e me enabled. Now it is not hard to enforce all minimal and maximal delays:

- Each location $(\sigma, e) \in Q$ is labeled with the timing constraint $x_e > l_e$; this ensures the lower-bound requirements.

- In addition, each location $(\sigma, e) \in Q$ is labeled with the timing constraint $x_{e'} \leq u_{e'}$ for every transition e' that is enabled on σ (if $u_{e'} \in \mathrm{N}$); this enforces the finite upper-bound requirements.

- Finally, the acceptance family F of the timed automaton A_T contains all subsets $F_i \subseteq Q$ such that for every transition $e \in \mathcal{E}$ with an infinite maximal delay, there is a location $(\sigma, e') \in F_i$ and either e is not enabled on σ or $e = e'$. This construction takes care of the infinite upper-bound requirement that the transition e is either disabled infinitely often or taken infinitely often.

Interleaving semantics

We presented an interval-based strictly-monotonic real-time semantics for timed transition systems. The alternatives include, as usual, interleaving (i.e., weakly-monotonic), fictitious-clock, and synchronous semantics. Indeed, timed transition systems are generally given an interleaving semantics, which allows finitely many transitions to be taken at the same time.

The advantage of an interleaving semantics for transition systems becomes apparent when we attempt to compose two systems in parallel. In the untimed case, the size of the product system explodes without interleaving, because it must contain a new transition for every pair of transitions that may be taken simultaneously. In the timed case, the product cannot even be defined in this manner, because a single minimal delay and a single maximal delay would have to be assigned to the joint transitions. By employing an interleaving semantics, on the other hand, the transition set of the product system is simply the union of the transition sets for the component systems. If desired, one may define additional joint transitions for a few pairs of transitions that must be taken simultaneously, such as synchronization transitions. For concrete examples of how timed transition systems (with an interleaving semantics) can be used to model real-time systems, we refer to the article *Timed Transition Systems* in this volume.

5 Verification Results

We presented several automata-based and logic-based languages for the description of real-time systems and timing requirements. We now survey the results concerning the verification of systems that are defined in these formalisms. The verification problem assumes two descriptions of real-time behavior, I and S, and asks if I conforms with (satisfies, refines, implements) S. Typically, the implementation I describes a real-time system and the specification S describes timing requirements of I. We distinguish between homogeneous verification methods, which assume that both the implementation and the specification are given in the same language, and heterogeneous methods, for the case that that the system and its requirements are defined in different formalisms.

5.1 Homogeneous verification 1: Logics

If both the implementation and the specification are given as formulas ϕ_I and ϕ_S, respectively, of a logic $\mathcal{L}$, then the system I meets the specification S iff the implication

$$\phi_I \rightarrow \phi_S$$

is valid; or, equivalently, iff the conjunction

$$\phi_I \wedge \neg\phi_S$$

is unsatisfiable. Consequently, we may use (1) decision procedures for $\mathcal{L}$ to solve the verification problem algorithmically, and (2) proof systems for $\mathcal{L}$ to solve the verification problem deductively.

Decidability of real-time logics

Only propositional versions of temporal logics are decidable (cf. [Aba87]). With regard to real-time extensions of propositional temporal logics, there are two parameters that determine the decidability of a language — the domain *Dom* of time and the operations *Ops* on time. Let $\mathcal{L}_{Dom,Ops}$ be an extension of a propositional linear-time or branching-time logic employing any of the three notations for writing timing constraints:

- The time domain *Dom* is a semantic parameter that defines the models of $\mathcal{L}_{Dom,Ops}$. We distinguish between dense time domains *Dom* = *Dense*, such as the nonnegative reals, and discrete time domains *Dom* = *Discrete*, such as the nonnegative integers.

- The set *Ops* of operations on time is a syntactic parameter that defines the formulas of $\mathcal{L}_{Dom,Ops}$; it contains the primitive predicates and functions that occur in the atomic timing constraints of $\mathcal{L}_{Dom,Ops}$. The order predicate $\leq$ and addition $+c$ by integer constants are necessary to specify constant lower and upper bounds on the time distance between events. Thus, the minimal set of real-time operators we consider is the set *Ops* = *Succ*, which contains these primitives. Addition by constants is a binary notation for iterated successor operations; we will use the standard assumption of binary encoding of time constants for classifying the complexity of problems and algorithms. Bounded-operator logics fall into the class $\mathcal{L}_{Dom,Succ}$, because every bounded-operator formula (with constant time bounds on the temporal operators) can be rewritten with freeze quantifiers or a clock variable and timing constraints over the operations from *Succ*.

  More complicated timing constraints can be expressed using the set *Plus* = $\{\leq, +, 0, 1\}$ of real-time operators. Addition on time is needed, for example, to specify the property that the distance between successive events remains constant.

There is an intrinsic characterization of the timing requirements whose satisfiability can be decided. This characterization is independent of the details of any particular real-time logic as long as the logic is sufficiently expressive to define punctuality properties of the form

$$\Box(p \rightarrow \Diamond_{=n}\, q),$$

which requires that every event p is followed by an event q after *precisely* n time units, for some constant n. Punctuality is definable in all logics we presented, with the exception of MITL.

Let $\mathcal{L}$ be a language that (1) is closed under all boolean operations and (2) can express punctuality. Then the satisfiability problem is undecidable for both $\mathcal{L}_{Dense,Succ}$ and $\mathcal{L}_{Discrete,Plus}$. In fact, if infinite recurrence (i.e., $\Box\Diamond p$) is definable in $\mathcal{L}$, then the complexity of the satisfiability problem is located deep in the hierarchy of undecidable problems — Σ^1_1-complete, to be precise (cf. [Rog67]). This result was first obtained for linear temporal logic with freeze quantification [AH89] and immediately applies to both explicit-clock and branching-time logics. The undecidability of time-bounded operators over a dense time domain was proved along the same lines [AH90].

Complexity of discrete-time logics

The satisfiability problem is, on the other hand, decidable for $\mathcal{L}_{Discrete,Succ}$, for all logics $\mathcal{L}$ we presented. For linear-time logics, the exact complexity of the satisfiability problems is known and independent of interval-based or point-based, synchronous (i.e., strictly-monotonic) or asynchronous (i.e., weakly-monotonic) interpretation: EXPSPACE-complete for TPTL [AH89] and MTL [AH90]; nonelementary for RTTL [AH90]. These results show the freeze quantification of TPTL to be superior to the classical quantification of RTTL. The extra exponential on top of the untimed linear temporal logic PTL, which can be decided in PSPACE, is inherent to real-time reasoning with binary encoding of time constants. The set *Ops* of primitive operations on time for the logics TPTL, MTL, and RTTL also includes congruence modulo constants ($\Box_{\equiv_0 2}$ means "in all states with an even time difference from the current state"); introducing this primitive does not affect the complexity of the logics.

The papers cited above give doubly-exponential-time decision procedures for both TPTL and MTL and compare both logics. The verification algorithm for MTL is somewhat less expensive than the algorithm for TPTL, as the first one depends exponentially on the value of the largest time constant involved and the latter depends exponentially on the value of the product of all time constants. In addition, while MTL includes past temporal operators, which do not affect its complexity, the addition of past operators renders the satisfiability problem for TPTL nonelementary [AH90]. On the other hand, even though we will see (in Section 6) that the same timing requirements are definable in both TPTL and MTL, we observed that TPTL specifies nonlocal timing constraints more succinctly. Thus, we conclude that, for a given specification and verification task, either one of TPTL and MTL may be more suitable.

For completeness, we include two related results. First, the satisfiability problem for the quantifier-free explicit-clock logic XCTL is PSPACE-complete, despite the admission of addition over time [HLP90]. XCTL, however, is a language that is not closed under negation and, hence, cannot be used to solve the homogeneous verification problem. Second, the satisfiability problem for the branching-time bounded-operator logic RTCTL is doubly-exponential-time-complete [EMSS89]. Little else is known about the precise complexity of branching-time logics for timed reasoning.

Towards dense-time logics

The proof of the undecidability of real-time logics over a dense time domain makes crucial use of punctuality properties. The bounded-operator logic MITL originated in an effort to define a nontrivial real-time logic that cannot express punctuality requirements and, indeed, the satisfiability problem for MITL was recently shown to be EXPSPACE-complete [AFH91]. The doubly-exponential-time verification algorithm for MITL, which is the first such algorithm for a linear-time logic over a dense time domain, is considerably more complex than discrete-time algorithms and it is not yet fully understood precisely which real-time properties (which superset of MITL) can be verified by this method.

Axiomatization of real-time logics

The Σ_1^1-hardness results mentioned above imply that there cannot be complete proof systems for many logics over a dense time domain as well as logics with addition on time. In the case of discrete time, a complete finite axiomatization is known for TPTL [Hen90]. That axiom system characterizes the freeze quantifier as a construct of modal logic independent of the notion of time. For time-bounded operators, several axioms have been suggested without claim of completeness [Koy90]. The authors suspect that MTL has a clean, complete, finite axiomatization, which is yet to be found.

5.2 Homogeneous verification 2: Automata

Assuming a trace semantics, the implementation I defines a set L_I of generated timed observation sequences and the specification S defines a set L_S of admitted timed observation sequences. In this case, the verification problem reduces to the problem of checking the containment

$$L_I \subseteq L_S$$

between sets of timed observation sequences. Linear-time logics, timed automata, and timed transition systems all define sets of timed observation sequences. In the previous subsection, we discussed the case that both L_I and L_S are given by formulas of a linear-time logic. In this subsection, we discuss trace verification for the case that both the implementation and the specification are given by timed automata.

A real-time system I often is defined naturally by a finite set $\{\mathrm{A}_I^1, \ldots \mathrm{A}_I^m\}$ of timed automata, each of which represents a parallel process of I. The generated timed observation sequences correspond, then, to the runs of the product automaton

$$\mathrm{A}_I = \mathrm{A}_I^1 \times \cdots \times \mathrm{A}_I^m.$$

A specification S that is given as another timed automaton, A_S, is violated by any timed observation sequence that corresponds to a run of the complementary automaton $\neg\mathrm{A}_S$. Thus, the implementation I meets the specification S iff the product automaton

$$\mathrm{A}_I \times \neg\mathrm{A}_S$$

has no run. Consequently, the verification problem can be solved by algorithms for (1) constructing the product of timed automata, (2) complementing a timed automaton, and (3) checking if a timed automaton defines the empty language.

Algorithms for constructing the product of timed automata and for checking emptiness of timed automata were given for a point-based strictly-monotonic real-time interpretation [AD90] and can easily be modified for other semantical assumptions such as time intervals, interleaving, or discrete time:

- As in the untimed case, the number of locations of the product automaton is proportional to the product of the number of locations for the component automata. Hence, the size of the implementation automaton is exponential in the description of the individual processes. This blow-up is known as the state explosion problem.

- The problem of checking if a timed automaton A defines the empty language is PSPACE-complete, provided that the timing constraints of A contain only operations from *Succ*. Assuming binary encoding of time constants, the running time of the algorithm for checking the emptiness of A depends exponentially on the length of the timing constraints for A. Similar to the satisfiability problem for real-time logics, checking emptiness is undecidable for timed automata with addition of clock variables, even in the case of discrete time [Alu91].

This leaves the task of complementing timed automata. Unfortunately, over a dense time domain, timed (Muller) automata are not closed under complement [AD90]. There are three options for circumventing this problem:

1. We may choose the fictitious-clock abstraction of a discrete time domain, which allows the determinization and complementation of timed (Muller) automata just as in the untimed case.

2. We may restrict ourselves to specifications that are given by deterministic timed automata, which are trivially complementable. In this case, the overall time complexity of checking the containment $L_I \subseteq L_S$ is exponential in both the descriptions of L_I and L_S.

3. We may define the set L_S of admitted timed observation sequences by the temporal logic MITL. This option will be discussed in the following subsection.

In each of the three cases, the implementation language L_I can, alternatively, be defined by a timed transition system.

5.3 Heterogeneous verification

Finally, we discuss the case that the implementation is given by a product of timed automata or by a timed transition system, and the specification is given by a logical formula. The corresponding verification problem can be solved either algorithmically, by so-called model checking procedures, or deductively.

Model checking

In the case of linear-time logics, the model checking problem is equally difficult as checking satisfiability; that is, it is undecidable for dense-time logics capable of expressing punctuality and EXPSPACE-complete for the discrete-time logics TPTL [AH89] and MTL [AH90] and the dense-time logic MITL [AFH91]. Given a specification S by a formula ϕ_S, the decision procedures for TPTL, MTL, and MITL construct from the negated formula $\neg\phi_S$ a timed automaton $A_{\neg\phi_S}$ whose runs correspond precisely to the timed observation sequences that violate the specification S. We can then proceed as in the homogeneous case and check if the product automaton

$$A_I \times A_{\neg\phi_S}$$

has a run. It follows that the running time of the model checking algorithms depends singly exponentially on the size of the implementation and doubly exponentially on the size of the specification formula. For the logic XCTL, a different procedure allows the model checking of timing properties that contain addition, in PSPACE [HLP90].

Perhaps surprisingly, in the case of branching-time logics, model checking of punctuality properties is possible even over a dense time domain. The model checking problem is PSPACE-complete for the branching-time logic TCTL of the type $\mathcal{L}_{Dense,Succ}$ for a bounded-operator as well as a half-order syntax [ACD90, Alu91]. The running time of the verification algorithm depends exponentially on the length of the timing constraints in both the implementation and the specification. The complexity of branching-time model checking remains the same under a synchronous discrete-time interpretation, as was observed earlier [EMSS89]. Recently, a model-checking algorithm has been designed for expressions of a dense-time process algebra over timed automata [NSY].

Temporal proof rules

Two important classes of timing requirements are *bounded-response* properties, such as

$$\Box(p \rightarrow \Diamond_{\leq 3}\, q), \qquad (\dagger)$$

and *bounded-invariance* properties, such as

$$\Box(p \rightarrow \Box_{<3}\, \neg q).$$

Bounded-response properties assert that "something good" will happen within a specified amount of time; bounded-invariance properties assert that "nothing bad" will happen for a certain amount of time. In other words, bounded-response and bounded-invariance properties define upper and lower bounds, respectively, on the time distance between events (such as the events p and q of our sample formulas).

Bounded-response and bounded-invariance properties of timed transition systems can be proved in two different ways. First, it is a well-known observation that both classes of properties are safety properties under the assumption that time progresses [LA90, Hen91a, Lam91]. For example, the bounded-response property ($\dagger$) that was expressed by a "liveness-like" bounded-operator formula (employing a time-bounded version of the liveness operator $\Diamond$) can alternatively be specified by an explicit-clock formula that uses the safety operator U (*unless*; cf. [MP83]):

$$\forall x.\, \Box((p \wedge T = x) \rightarrow (T < x + 3)\, \mathrm{U}\, q).$$

This formula asserts that if a stimulus p happens at time x, then from this point on the time will not reach $x + 3$ either forever (which is impossible because time must progress) or until the response q happens. Consequently, q must occur within at most 3 time units from p. This translation shows that no new proof rules are necessary for the *explicit-clock* style of timed verification, which proves safety formulas containing the clock variable T by assertional reasoning [Haa81, SL87, HMP91, Hoo91]. All time-bounded properties of timed transition systems can, in principle, be verified using a standard, uniform set of untimed temporal-logic rules (e.g., [MP89]).

In the bounded-operator notation, on the other hand, upper-bound properties bear a close resemblance to liveness properties and lower-bound properties closely resemble safety properties. This similarity may be cultivated using separate bounded-operator proof principles for the classes of bounded-response and bounded-invariance properties: the standard temporal-logic rules for the untimed response and invariance classes can be decorated with time bounds on the temporal operators [HMP91]. Relative completeness (with respect to state reasoning, which need not be propositional) of this *bounded-operator* style of timed verification was shown for a restricted class of timed transition systems [Hen91b]. Deductive bounded-operator reasoning has not been explored yet for more complicated real-time properties than bounded response and bounded invariance.

6 Expressiveness Results

We now compare the expressive power of the real-time specification languages presented in this paper. The questions regarding the expressiveness of linear-time formalisms versus branching-time formalisms have been studied in the untimed case (cf. [Eme90]). As the introduction of real-time considerations does not seem to raise any new questions in this context, we restrict our attention to the linear-time case.

Given a semantics SEM, an expression ϕ of a linear-time specification language LAN defines a set L_ϕ of timed observation sequences (or weakly-monotonic timed observation sequences, in the interleaving case). The set L_ϕ is called a *real-time property* or, more specifically, a SEM-property. The expressive power of the language LAN under the semantic assumption SEM is measured as the set

$$\mathbf{LAN}_{\mathrm{SEM}} = \{L_\phi \mid \phi \in \mathrm{LAN}\}$$

of SEM-properties that are definable in LAN.

As syntactic options, we consider the languages of the logics MTL, TPTL, RTTL, XCTL, and MITL, as well as timed automata (TA) and deterministic timed automata (DTA) whose assertion language for timing constraints is that of TPTL (and RTTL). Since we are interested primarily in questions concerning time, we concentrate on the fictitious-clock abstraction. Accordingly, we consider the two semantic options of real-numbered time and integer time. A set of timed observation sequences over the time domain R is a *dense-time* property; a set of timed observation sequences over N, a *discrete-time* property. For example, we write $\mathbf{MITL}_{\mathrm{R}}$ for the set of dense-time properties that can be defined by MITL-formulas. Similarly, $\mathbf{DTA}_{\mathrm{N}}$ stands for the set of discrete-time properties that are definable by deterministic timed automata.

We first compare all languages assuming a common semantics. Then we compare the expressive power of similar languages with different semantics, with the goal of characterizing the loss of expressiveness introduced by the semantic abstraction of a fictitious clock.

6.1 Comparison of syntax

We presented various ways of writing timing constraints; they include the bounded-operator, half-order, and explicit-clock notations for temporal logics, and timed automata. All of these notations can be interpreted over integer time and over real-numbered time.

Integer time

To compare the different notations, it is best to study the underlying logical theory of timed observation sequences over the time domain N. The theory of the natural numbers with linear order and monadic predicates underlies linear temporal logic (cf. [GPSS80]). We combine this theory of observation sequences with a theory of integer time, via a monotonic function that maps every observation to its time. The timing constraints are restricted to use only the ordering, successor, and congruence operations on time. The resulting second-order theory $\mathbf{T}^2_{\mathrm{N}}$ (with quantification over the monadic predicates) — the *theory of discrete timed observation sequences* — is decidable; its expressive power can be characterized by ω-regular sets employing auxiliary propositions that record some finite information about the time differences between neighboring observations [AH90]. Using the theory $\mathbf{T}^2_{\mathrm{N}}$ as point of reference, we have the following results.

1. All the three logical notations are equally expressive as the first-order fragment $\mathbf{T}_{\mathrm{N}}$ of the theory $\mathbf{T}^2_{\mathrm{N}}$ of discrete timed observation sequences:

   $$\mathbf{T}_{\mathrm{N}} = \mathbf{MTL}_{\mathrm{N}} = \mathbf{TPTL}_{\mathrm{N}} = \mathbf{RTTL}_{\mathrm{N}}.$$

   Since the decision problem for $\mathbf{T}_{\mathrm{N}}$ is nonelementary, both MTL and TPTL (but not RTTL) characterize comparatively tractable and expressively complete fragments of $\mathbf{T}_{\mathrm{N}}$. As in the untimed case, the expressive power of the second-order theory $\mathbf{T}^2_{\mathrm{N}}$ can be attained by introducing quantification over propositions or the grammar operators of the extended temporal logic of [Wol83]. These expressiveness results were obtained under a point-based weakly-monotonic semantics [AH90], but they apply equally to the interval-based and the synchronous case.

2. It is not hard to show that timed automata, too, identify an expressively complete fragment of the second-order theory of discrete timed observation sequences:

   $$\mathbf{T}^2_{\mathrm{N}} = \mathbf{DTA}_{\mathrm{N}} = \mathbf{TA}_{\mathrm{N}}.$$

Since the class $\mathbf{T}^2_{\mathrm{N}}$ is so robust, closed under all boolean operations, and emptiness is elementarily decidable for reasonable definition languages, it provides a clean notion of finite-state property for integer time: a discrete-time property L is *finite-state* iff $L \in \mathbf{T}^2_{\mathrm{N}}$. Overall, the untimed theoretical properties of observation sequences generalize conservatively to timed observation sequences over a discrete time domain.

The expressive power of the logic XCTL, the quantifier-free fragment of RTTL with addition over time, is incomparable to the class $\mathbf{T}_{\mathrm{N}}$ [HLP90]. On one hand, XCTL forbids quantification over the time variables; on the other hand, it permits stronger timing constraints that involve the use of addition.

Real-numbered time

Much less is known about the relative expressive power of the various languages if they are interpreted over timed observation sequences with real-numbered time. Since the satisfiability problem is undecidable for MTL over dense time and the class $\mathbf{TA_R}$ is not closed under complementation, the authors looked for less expressive languages:

$$\mathbf{MITL_R} \subset \mathbf{MTL_R} \quad \text{and} \quad \mathbf{DTA_R} \subset \mathbf{TA_R}$$

[AFH91, AD90] (by $\subset$, we denote strict containment). Since also

$$\mathbf{MITL_R} \subset \mathbf{TA_R},$$

both classes $\mathbf{MITL_R}$ and $\mathbf{DTA_R}$ do have all desired closure and decidability properties; unfortunately, neither one is a subset of the other: since MITL prohibits timing constraints that involve equality (i.e., singular intervals), the two classes $\mathbf{MITL_R}$ and $\mathbf{DTA_R}$ are incomparable. Furthermore, both classes seem quite nonrobust, with heavy dependence on syntactic idiosyncrasies. Thus, the main question the authors would like to see answered [AH91] remains open:

> *Is there an agreeable notion of finite-state property for real-numbered time?* The set of such properties ought to be closed under all boolean operations, have a characterization with an elementarily decidable emptiness problem, and be, in a suitable sense, "maximal."

Another interesting question asks how the bounded-operator notation compares with the half-order notation. We know that they are equally expressive in the case of integer time, but the proof makes crucial use of the discreteness of time. Hence, the authors conjecture that freeze quantifiers are more expressive than bounded operators in the case of real-numbered time:

$$\mathbf{MTL_R} \overset{?}{\subset} \mathbf{TPTL_R}.$$

In particular, the nonlocal timing property (‡) of Subsection 3.2 is suspected to be inexpressible by the bounded-operator notation of MTL.

6.2 Comparison of semantics

Motivated by the result that the verification of punctuality properties is undecidable over a dense time domain, we presented two solutions for obtaining decidable dense-time logics. First, we weakened the expressiveness of languages, such as MTL, by adopting the *semantic* abstraction of a fictitious clock. Second, we weakened the expressiveness of MTL by adopting the *syntactic* concession of prohibiting singular intervals in MITL. Both the semantic abstraction of digitizing models as well as the syntactic restriction of excluding equality in timing constraints limit the real-time properties that are definable in a similar way: they rule out the notion of absolute punctuality and replace it by a looser concept of *almost*-on-time behavior. This sacrifice is viable because, by choosing the clock tick of the fictitious clock small enough, we can still achieve arbitrary precision in either approach. Moreover, the corresponding costs for achieving the desired accuracy are the same. This raises the question if one technique is superior to the other in expressive power. In other words, how do the two classes $\mathbf{MTL}_\mathbf{N}$ and $\mathbf{MITL}_\mathbf{R}$ compare?

To relate the expressiveness of two languages under different semantical assumptions, we have to put them on common ground. A semantical abstraction, such as a fictitious clock, is an equivalence relation on the set of timed observation sequences over the time domain R; it does not discriminate between timed observation sequences within the same equivalence class. For instance, the fictitious clock that ticks every 0.5 time units (beginning at time 0) cannot distinguish between the two timed observation sequences

$$(\{p\}, 0.2) \to (\{q\}, 1) \to (\{p\}, 5.9),$$

$$(\{p\}, 0.4) \to (\{q\}, 1) \to (\{p\}, 5.8).$$

The dense-time property defined by an expression ϕ of a language LAN under a semantic abstraction SEM is, then, the union of the SEM-equivalence classes of the models of ϕ. This approach determines the ***absolute*** expressive power of the syntax-semantics pair (LAN, SEM) in terms of which dense-time properties are definable.

The authors know of only one result that relates the expressive power of different models. MITL is, in the above sense, strictly more expressive than MTL with respect to a fictitious clock of any stepwidth; that is, the dense-time properties that can be defined in MITL are a proper superset of those definable with equality under a fictitious-clock interpretation [AFH91]. Also, many of the practically interesting forms of punctuality are still expressible in MITL, such as the requirement that every event p is separated from the *closest* subsequent event q by precisely 3 time units. These observations suggest a more thorough study of real-numbered time in the directions taken by MITL and timed automata, rather than a surrender to fictitious-clock models.

References

[Aba87] M. Abadi. *Temporal-Logic Theorem Proving.* PhD thesis, Stanford University, 1987.

[ACD90] R. Alur, C. Courcoubetis, and D.L. Dill. Model checking for real-time systems. In *Proceedings of the Fifth Annual Symposium on Logic in Computer Science*, pages 414–425. IEEE Computer Society Press, 1990.

[AD90] R. Alur and D.L. Dill. Automata for modeling real-time systems. In M.S. Paterson, editor, *ICALP 90: Automata, Languages, and Programming*, Lecture Notes in Computer Science 443, pages 322–335. Springer-Verlag, 1990.

[AFH91] R. Alur, T. Feder, and T.A. Henzinger. The benefits of relaxing punctuality. In *Proceedings of the Tenth Annual Symposium on Principles of Distributed Computing*, pages 139–152. ACM Press, 1991.

[AH89] R. Alur and T.A. Henzinger. A really temporal logic. In *Proceedings of the 30th Annual Symposium on Foundations of Computer Science*, pages 164–169. IEEE Computer Society Press, 1989.

[AH90] R. Alur and T.A. Henzinger. Real-time logics: complexity and expressiveness. In *Proceedings of the Fifth Annual Symposium on Logic in Computer Science*, pages 390–401. IEEE Computer Society Press, 1990.

[AH91] R. Alur and T.A. Henzinger. Time for logic. *SIGACT News*, 22(3):6–12, 1991.

[Alu91] R. Alur. *Techniques for Automatic Verification of Real-time Systems.* PhD thesis, Stanford University, 1991.

[BH81] A. Bernstein and P.K. Harter, Jr. Proving real-time properties of programs with temporal logic. In *Proceedings of the Eighth Annual Symposium on Operating System Principles*, pages 1–11. ACM Press, 1981.

[BMP81] M. Ben-Ari, Z. Manna, and A. Pnueli. The temporal logic of branching time. In *Proceedings of the Eighth Annual Symposium on Principles of Programming Languages*, pages 164–176. ACM Press, 1981.

[CES86] E.M. Clarke, E.A. Emerson, and A.P. Sistla. Automatic verification of finite-state concurrent systems using temporal-logic specifications. *ACM Transactions on Programming Languages and Systems*, 8(2):244–263, 1986.

[Dil89] D.L. Dill. Timing assumptions and verification of finite-state concurrent systems. In J. Sifakis, editor, *CAV 89: Automatic Verification Methods for Finite-state Systems*, Lecture Notes in Computer Science 407, pages 197–212. Springer-Verlag, 1989.

[EC82] E.A. Emerson and E.M. Clarke. Using branching-time temporal logic to synthesize synchronization skeletons. *Science of Computer Programming*, 2(3):241–266, 1982.

[Eme90] E.A. Emerson. Temporal and modal logic. In J. van Leeuwen, editor, *Handbook of Theoretical Computer Science*, volume B, pages 995–1072. Elsevier Science Publishers (North-Holland), 1990.

[EMSS89] E.A. Emerson, A.K. Mok, A.P. Sistla, and J. Srinivasan. Quantitative temporal reasoning. Presented at the First Annual Workshop on Computer-aided Verification, Grenoble, France, 1989.

[GPSS80] D. Gabbay, A. Pnueli, S. Shelah, and J. Stavi. On the temporal analysis of fairness. In *Proceedings of the Seventh Annual Symposium on Principles of Programming Languages*, pages 163–173. ACM Press, 1980.

[Haa81] V.H. Haase. Real-time behavior of programs. *IEEE Transactions on Software Engineering*, SE-7(5):494–501, 1981.

[Har88] E. Harel. Temporal analysis of real-time systems. Master's thesis, The Weizmann Institute of Science, Rehovot, Israel, 1988.

[Hen90] T.A. Henzinger. Half-order modal logic: how to prove real-time properties. In *Proceedings of the Ninth Annual Symposium on Principles of Distributed Computing*, pages 281–296. ACM Press, 1990.

[Hen91a] T.A. Henzinger. Sooner is safer than later. Technical report, Stanford University, 1991.

[Hen91b] T.A. Henzinger. *The Temporal Specification and Verification of Real-time Systems.* PhD thesis, Stanford University, 1991.

[HLP90] E. Harel, O. Lichtenstein, and A. Pnueli. Explicit-clock temporal logic. In *Proceedings of the Fifth Annual Symposium on Logic in Computer Science*, pages 402–413. IEEE Computer Society Press, 1990.

[HMP90] T.A. Henzinger, Z. Manna, and A. Pnueli. An interleaving model for real time. In *Proceedings of the Fifth Jerusalem Conference on Information Technology*, pages 717–730. IEEE Computer Society Press, 1990.

[HMP91] T.A. Henzinger, Z. Manna, and A. Pnueli. Temporal proof methodologies for real-time systems. In *Proceedings of the 18th Annual Symposium on Principles of Programming Languages*, pages 353–366. ACM Press, 1991.

[Hoo91] J. Hooman. *Specification and Compositional Verification of Real-time Systems.* PhD thesis, Technische Universiteit Eindhoven, The Netherlands, 1991.

[HW89] J. Hooman and J. Widom. A temporal-logic-based compositional proof system for real-time message passing. In E. Odijk, M. Rem, and J.-C. Syre, editors, *PARLE 89: Parallel Architectures and Languages Europe*, vol. II, Lecture Notes in Computer Science 366, pages 424–441. Springer-Verlag, 1989.

[KdR85] R. Koymans and W.-P. de Roever. Examples of a real-time temporal specification. In B.D. Denvir, W.T. Harwood, M.I. Jackson, and M.J. Wray, editors, *The Analysis of Concurrent Systems*, Lecture Notes in Computer Science 207, pages 231–252. Springer-Verlag, 1985.

[Kel76] R.M. Keller. Formal verification of parallel programs. *Communications of the ACM*, 19(7):371–384, 1976.

[Koy90] R. Koymans. Specifying real-time properties with metric temporal logic. *Real-time Systems*, 2(4):255–299, 1990.

[KVdR83] R. Koymans, J. Vytopil, and W.-P. de Roever. Real-time programming and asynchronous message passing. In *Proceedings of the Second Annual Symposium on Principles of Distributed Computing*, pages 187–197. ACM Press, 1983.

[LA] L. Lamport and M. Abadi. Refining and composing real-time specifications. This volume.

[LA90] N.A. Lynch and H. Attiya. Using mappings to prove timing properties. In *Proceedings of the Ninth Annual Symposium on Principles of Distributed Computing*, pages 265–280. ACM Press, 1990.

[Lam83] L. Lamport. What good is temporal logic? In R.E.A. Mason, editor, *Information Processing 83: Proceedings of the Ninth IFIP World Computer Congress*, pages 657–668. Elsevier Science Publishers (North-Holland), 1983.

[Lam91] L. Lamport. The temporal logic of actions. Technical report, DEC Systems Research Center, Palo Alto, California, 1991.

[Lew90] H.R. Lewis. A logic of concrete time intervals. In *Proceedings of the Fifth Annual Symposium on Logic in Computer Science*, pages 380–389. IEEE Computer Society Press, 1990.

[LPZ85] O. Lichtenstein, A. Pnueli, and L.D. Zuck. The glory of the past. In R. Parikh, editor, *Logics of Programs*, Lecture Notes in Computer Science 193, pages 196–218. Springer-Verlag, 1985.

[MP83] Z. Manna and A. Pnueli. Proving precedence properties: the temporal way. In J. Diaz, editor, *ICALP 83: Automata, Languages, and Programming*, Lecture Notes in Computer Science 154, pages 491–512. Springer-Verlag, 1983.

[MP89] Z. Manna and A. Pnueli. The anchored version of the temporal framework. In J.W. de Bakker, W.-P. de Roever, and G. Rozenberg, editors, *Linear Time, Branching Time, and Partial Order in Logics and Models for Concurrency*, Lecture Notes in Computer Science 354, pages 201–284. Springer-Verlag, 1989.

[NSY] X. Nicollin, J. Sifakis, and S. Yovine. From ATP to timed graphs and hybrid systems. This volume.

[Ost90] J.S. Ostroff. *Temporal Logic of Real-time Systems.* Research Studies Press, 1990.

[PdR82] A. Pnueli and W.-P. de Roever. Rendez-vous with Ada: a proof-theoretical view. In *Proceedings of the SIGPLAN AdaTEC Conference on Ada*, pages 129–137. ACM Press, 1982.

[PH88] A. Pnueli and E. Harel. Applications of temporal logic to the specification of real-time systems. In M. Joseph, editor, *Formal Techniques in Real-time and Fault-tolerant Systems*, Lecture Notes in Computer Science 331, pages 84–98. Springer-Verlag, 1988.

[Pnu77] A. Pnueli. The temporal logic of programs. In *Proceedings of the 18th Annual Symposium on Foundations of Computer Science*, pages 46–57. IEEE Computer Society Press, 1977.

[Pnu86] A. Pnueli. Applications of temporal logic to the specification and verification of reactive systems: a survey of current trends. In J.W. de Bakker, W.-P. de Roever, and G. Rozenberg, editors, *Current Trends in Concurrency*, Lecture Notes in Computer Science 224, pages 510–584. Springer-Verlag, 1986.

[Rog67] H. Rogers, Jr. *Theory of Recursive Functions and Effective Computability.* McGraw-Hill Book Company, 1967.

[Ron84] D. Ron. Temporal verification of communication protocols. Master's thesis, The Weizmann Institute of Science, Rehovot, Israel, 1984.

[SL87] A.U. Shankar and S. Lam. Time-dependent distributed systems: proving safety, liveness, and timing properties. *Distributed Computing*, 2(2):61–79, 1987.

[SPE84] D.E. Shasha, A. Pnueli, and W. Ewald. Temporal verification of carrier-sense local area network protocols. In *Proceedings of the 11th Annual Symposium on Principles of Programming Languages*, pages 54–65. ACM Press, 1984.

[Tho90] W. Thomas. Automata on infinite objects. In J. van Leeuwen, editor, *Handbook of Theoretical Computer Science*, volume B, pages 133–191. Elsevier Science Publishers (North-Holland), 1990.

[Wol83] P. Wolper. Temporal logic can be more expressive. *Information and Control*, 56(1/2):72–99, 1983.

The State Operator in Real Time Process Algebra

J.C.M. Baeten
Department of Software Technology, CWI,
P.O.Box 4079, 1009 AB Amsterdam, The Netherlands
and
Programming Research Group, University of Amsterdam,
P.O.Box 41882, 1009 DB Amsterdam, The Netherlands

J.A. Bergstra
Programming Research Group, University of Amsterdam,
P.O.Box 41882, 1009 DB Amsterdam, The Netherlands
and
Department of Philosophy, Utrecht University,
Heidelberglaan 2, 3584 CS Utrecht, The Netherlands

Abstract: We extend the real time process algebra of [BB91a] with the state operator of [BB88]. We show the usefulness of this extension in several examples. We use concepts from (classical) real space process algebra of [BB91b] in order to deal with different locations.

Key words & Phrases: process algebra, real time, state operator, locations.
Note: Partial support received by ESPRIT basic research action 3006, CONCUR, and by RACE contract 1046, SPECS. This document does not necessarily reflect the views of the SPECS consortium.

Contents:

1. INTRODUCTION

We provide an extension of real time process algebra of [BB91a] with a state operator. For this purpose it is plausible to use a version of real time process algebra with located actions. Departing from a finite set A of action names and a finite set L of location names, a version of the real space process algebra of [BB91b] is developed. As in [BB91a], timed deadlocks are used instead of the untimed deadlock of [BB91b]. Further, an operational semantics is given in the style of KLUSENER [K91], which is a modification of the operational semantics of [BB91a].

The work on extensions of process algebra that encorporate notions of time started with the work of REED & ROSCOE (e.g. [RR88]), who discuss an extension of CSP (of [H85]). In 1989, we presented our extension of ACP (see [BB91a]). Extensions of CCS (of [M80, M89]) followed, see e.g. MOLLER & TOFTS [MT90], JEFFREY [J91a]. The real time process algebra as presented in [BB91a] uses a dense time domain, affixes timestamps to all atomic actions, and uses an integral operator to express that an action occurs within a certain time interval.

In [BB91b], we extended our previous work to take space coordinates into account. This leads to a relativistic calculus where events are not totally ordered by time any longer. This idea is also taken up in JEFFREY [J91b], MURPHY [MU91]. In the present paper, we limit the use of space to a finite set of *locations*.

This extension of real time process algebra is not as straightforward as one might expect because the effect of actions with components at various locations (multi-actions) on a state has to be evaluated in some predefined order. This reflects the fact that it is difficult to have a notion of a global state in a distributed system. In order to solve the problem, we assume an ordering on the locations and require that multi-actions are evaluated in increasing order (if possible). One might expect it to be more natural to require that actions can be effectuated in arbitrary order, resulting in the same state, but that will exclude many useful applications of the state operator.

Nevertheless we consider our combination of a state operator and classical real space process algebra to be satisfactory. We notice that adding the state operator to the relativistic real space process algebra of [BB91b] is difficult if not impossible.

Finally, we remark that we only consider *concrete* process algebra here: there is no concept of a silent or empty step.

2. REAL TIME PROCESS ALGEBRA

We start with a review of real time process algebra as introduced in [BB91a], but instead of the operational semantics given there, we use the variant of KLUSENER [K91].

2.1 BASIC PROCESS ALGEBRA

Process algebra (see [BK84, BK86, BW90]) starts from a given *action alphabet* A (usually finite). Elements a,b,c of A are called *atomic actions*, and are constants of the sort P of *processes*. The theory Basic Process Algebra (BPA) has two binary operators $+,\cdot: P \times P \to P$; + stands for alternative composition and $\cdot$ for sequential composition. BPA has the axioms from table 1.

$X + Y = Y + X$	A1
$(X + Y) + Z = X + (Y + Z)$	A2
$X + X = X$	A3
$(X + Y) \cdot Z = X \cdot Z + Y \cdot Z$	A4
$(X \cdot Y) \cdot Z = X \cdot (Y \cdot Z)$	A5

Table 1. BPA.

If we add to BPA a special constant δ in P (not in A) standing for *inaction*, comparable to NIL or 0 of CCS (see MILNER [M80, 89] or HENNESSY [HE88]) or STOP of CSP (see HOARE [H85]), we obtain the theory BPAδ. The two axioms for δ are in table 2.

$X + \delta = X$	A6
$\delta \cdot X = \delta$	A7

Table 2. BPAδ = BPA + A6, A7.

When we add real time to this setting, our basic actions are not from the set $A_\delta = A \cup \{\delta\}$, but from the set

$$AT = \{a(t) \mid a \in A_\delta, t \in \mathbb{R}^{\geq 0}\} \cup \{\delta\}.$$

Here, $\mathbb{R}^{\geq 0} = \{r \in \mathbb{R} \mid r \geq 0\}$. The process $a(t)$ performs action a at time t, and then terminates. The process $\delta(t)$ deadlocks at time t. The process δ cannot do anything, in particular it cannot wait. Again, these actions can be combined by $+,\cdot$. We have the identification $\delta(0) = \delta$.

The letter A in the names of the following axioms refers to *absolute time* (versions with relative time were also considered in [BB91a], but are not treated here).

As in [BB91a], we have the additional operation $\gg$, the *(absolute) time shift*. $t \gg X$ denotes the process X starting at time t. This means that all actions that have to be performed at or before time t are turned into deadlocks because their execution has been delayed too long.

In table 3, we have $a \in A_\delta$.

$a(0) = \delta(0)$	ATA1
$\delta(t) \cdot X = \delta(t)$	ATA2
$t < r \Rightarrow \delta(t) + \delta(r) = \delta(r)$	ATA3
$a(t) + \delta(t) = a(t)$	ATA4
$a(t) \cdot X = a(t) \cdot (t \gg X)$	ATA5
$t < r \Rightarrow t \gg a(r) = a(r)$	ATB1
$t \geq r \Rightarrow t \gg a(r) = \delta(t)$	ATB2
$t \gg (X + Y) = (t \gg X) + (t \gg Y)$	ATB3
$t \gg (X \cdot Y) = (t \gg X) \cdot Y$	ATB4

Table 3. BPAρδ.

A *closed process expression* (CPE) over the signature of BPAρδ with atoms A is an expression that does not contain variables for atoms, processes or real numbers. We allow every real number as a constant, which means there are uncountably many such closed process expressions. For finite closed process expressions an initial algebra can be defined. This is the initial algebra model of BPAρδ. This structure identifies two closed expressions whenever these can be shown identical by means of application of the axioms. This definition of closed process expressions and an initial model can be extended to all extensions of BPA that are described below.

We will look at an operational model next. We denote the set of actions over A without variables by IA (the set of instantiated actions), and write $IA\delta$ when we use the set A_δ.

2.2 OPERATIONAL SEMANTICS.

We describe an operational semantics for BPAρδ following KLUSENER [K91]. His operational semantics is a simplification of the one in [BB91a]. In fact the operational semantics of [K91] is more abstract than the one given in [BB91a]. We have two relations

$$\text{step} \subseteq CPE \times IA \times CPE$$
$$\text{terminate} \subseteq CPE \times IA\delta.$$

The extension of the relations for atomic actions (so excluding δ-termination) is found as the least fixed point of a simultaneous inductive definition. We write

$x \xrightarrow{a(r)} x'$ for step(x, a(r), x'), and

$x \xrightarrow{a(r)} \surd$ for terminate(x, a(r)).

Notice that in the first case $a \in A$ and in the second case $a \in A_\delta$.

The inductive rules for the operational semantics are similar to those used in structural operational semantics. We list the rules for atomic actions. In table 4, we have $a \in \mathrm{IA}$, $r,s > 0$ (we never allow timestamp 0!), $x,x',y \in \mathrm{CPE}$.

$$r > 0 \Rightarrow a(r) \xrightarrow{a(r)} \surd$$

$$\frac{x \xrightarrow{a(r)} x'}{x+y \xrightarrow{a(r)} x',\ y+x \xrightarrow{a(r)} x'}$$

$$\frac{x \xrightarrow{a(r)} \surd}{x+y \xrightarrow{a(r)} \surd,\ y+x \xrightarrow{a(r)} \surd}$$

$$\frac{x \xrightarrow{a(r)} x'}{x \cdot y \xrightarrow{a(r)} x' \cdot y} \qquad \frac{x \xrightarrow{a(r)} \surd}{x \cdot y \xrightarrow{a(r)} r \gg y}$$

$$\frac{x \xrightarrow{a(r)} x',\ r>s}{s \gg x \xrightarrow{a(r)} x'} \qquad \frac{x \xrightarrow{a(r)} \surd,\ r>s}{s \gg x \xrightarrow{a(r)} \surd}$$

Table 4. Action rules for atomic actions for BPAρδ.

2.3 Ultimate Delay

In order to state the rule for deadlock actions, we need an auxiliary notion: U(x) is the *ultimate delay* of x. This notion is defined as follows (table 5, $a \in A$).

The ultimate delay operator U takes a process expression X in CPE, and returns an element of $\mathbb{R}^{\geq 0}$. The intended meaning is that X can idle before U(X), but X can never reach time U(X) or a later time by just idling.

$U(a(t)) = t$	ATU1
$U(\delta(t)) = t$	ATU2
$U(X + Y) = \max\{U(X), U(Y)\}$	ATU3
$U(X \cdot Y) = U(X)$	ATU4
$U(t \gg X) = \max\{t, U(X)\}$	ATU5

Table 5. Ultimate delay operator.

Now we construct a transition system for a term as follows: first generate all transitions involving atomic actions using the inductive rules of table 4. Then, for every node (term) p in this transition system we do the following: first determine its ultimate delay $U(p) = u$ by means of table 5. Then, if the ultimate delay is larger than the supremum of the time stamps of all outgoing transitions, we add a transition

$$p \xrightarrow{\delta(u)} \surd.$$

Otherwise, we do nothing (add no transitions).

2.4 BISIMULATIONS

Again we consider the class CPE of closed process expressions over BPAρδ. A *bisimulation* on CPE is a binary relation R such that

i. for each p and q with $R(p, q)$: if there is a step $a(s)$ possible from p to p', then there is a CPE q' such that $R(p', q')$ and there is a step $a(s)$ possible from q to q'.

ii. for each p and q with $R(p, q)$: if there is a step $a(s)$ possible from q to q', then there is a CPE p' such that $R(p', q')$ and there is a step $a(s)$ possible from p to p'.

iii. for each p and q with $R(p, q)$: a termination step $a(s)$ or $\delta(s)$ is possible from p iff it is possible from q.

We say expressions p and q are *bisimilar*, denoted $p \leftrightarrow q$, if there exists a bisimulation on CPE with $R(p,q)$. In [K91] it is shown that bisimulation is a congruence relation on CPE, and that CPE/$\leftrightarrow$ is a model for BPAρδ. Indeed, this model is isomorphic to the initial algebra. The advantage of this operational semantics is, that it allows extensions to models containing recursively defined processes.

Next, we extend the system BPAρδ with an operator for parallel composition.

2.5 OPERATIONAL SEMANTICS FOR PARALLEL COMPOSITION.

$$\frac{x \xrightarrow{a(r)} x',\ r < U(y)}{x \| y \xrightarrow{a(r)} x' \| (r \gg y),\ y \| x \xrightarrow{a(r)} (r \gg y) \| x'}$$

$$\frac{x \xrightarrow{a(r)} \surd,\ r < U(y)}{x \| y \xrightarrow{a(r)} r \gg y,\ y \| x \xrightarrow{a(r)} r \gg y}$$

$$\frac{x \xrightarrow{a(r)} x',\ y \xrightarrow{b(r)} y',\ a \mid b = c \neq \delta}{x \| y \xrightarrow{c(r)} x' \| y'}$$

$$\frac{x \xrightarrow{a(r)} x',\ y \xrightarrow{b(r)} \surd,\ a \mid b = c \neq \delta}{x \| y \xrightarrow{c(r)} x',\ y \| x \xrightarrow{c(r)} x'}$$

$$\frac{x \xrightarrow{a(r)} \surd,\ y \xrightarrow{b(r)} \surd,\ a \mid b = c \neq \delta}{x \| y \xrightarrow{c(r)} \surd}$$

Table 6. Action rules for parallel composition.

Now we extend the system BPAρδ with the parallel composition operator $\|$ (merge). We assume we have given a communication function $| : A_\delta \times A_\delta \to A_\delta$. $|$ is commutative, associative and δ is a zero element for it. The operational semantics for atomic actions is given in table 6. With the additional rules of table 6, a transition system is generated. We then add δ-rules as before.

We see that the action rules for parallel composition make use of the ultimate delay operator. This operator was introduced in 2.3. We add rules so that the ultimate delay can be syntactically determined for every term.

$U(X \| Y) = \min\{U(X), U(Y)\}$	ATU6
$U(X \mathbin{⌊\!⌊} Y) = \min\{U(X), U(Y)\}$	ATU7
$U(X \mid Y) = \min\{U(X), U(Y)\}$	ATU8
$U(X \gg t) = \min\{t, U(X)\}$	ATU9
$U(\partial_H(X)) = U(X)$	ATU10

Table 7. Ultimate delay with parallel composition.

In table 7, we also find a number of auxiliary operators that are needed to give a axiomatic characterization of parallel composition (cf. [BB91a]).

2.6 Bounded Initialization

The bounded initialization operator is also denoted by $\gg$, and is the counterpart of the operator with the same name that we saw in the axiomatization of BPAρδ. With $X \gg t$ we denote the process X with its behaviour restricted to the extent that its first action must be performed at a time before $t \in \mathbb{R}^{\geq 0}$. Axioms defining $\gg$ are in table 8, where we have $a \in A_\delta$.

$r \geq t \;\Rightarrow\; a(r) \gg t = \delta(t)$	ATB5
$r < t \;\Rightarrow\; a(r) \gg t = a(r)$	ATB6
$(X + Y) \gg t = (X \gg t) + (Y \gg t)$	ATB7
$(X \cdot Y) \gg t = (X \gg t) \cdot Y$	ATB8

Table 7. Bounded initialization operator.

2.7 Algebra of Communicating Processes.

Apart from the ultimate delay and bounded initialization operators, an axiomatization of parallel composition also uses the left merge operator $\mathbin{⌊\!⌊}$ and communication merge operator $|$ of [BK84]. Let H be some subset of A, and let a,b,c be elements of A_δ.

$a \mid b = b \mid a$	C1
$a \mid (b \mid c) = (a \mid b) \mid c$	C2
$\delta \mid a = \delta$	C3
$t \neq r \Rightarrow a(t) \mid b(r) = \delta(\min(t,r))$	ATC1
$a(t) \mid b(t) = (a \mid b)(t)$	ATC2
$X \parallel Y = X \mathbin{\lfloor\!\lfloor} Y + Y \mathbin{\lfloor\!\lfloor} X + X \mid Y$	CM1
$a(t) \mathbin{\lfloor\!\lfloor} X = (a(t) \gg U(X)) \cdot X$	ATCM2
$(a(t) \cdot X) \mathbin{\lfloor\!\lfloor} Y = (a(t) \gg U(Y)) \cdot (X \parallel Y)$	ATCM3
$(X + Y) \mathbin{\lfloor\!\lfloor} Z = X \mathbin{\lfloor\!\lfloor} Z + Y \mathbin{\lfloor\!\lfloor} Z$	CM4
$(a(t) \cdot X) \mid b(r) = (a(t) \mid b(r)) \cdot X$	CM5'
$a(t) \mid (b(r) \cdot X) = (a(t) \mid b(r)) \cdot X$	CM6'
$(a(t) \cdot X) \mid (b(r) \cdot Y) = (a(t) \mid b(r)) \cdot (X \parallel Y)$	CM7'
$(X + Y) \mid Z = X \mid Z + Y \mid Z$	CM8
$X \mid (Y + Z) = X \mid Y + X \mid Z$	CM9
$\partial_H(a) = a$ if $a \notin H$	D1
$\partial_H(a) = \delta$ if $a \in H$	D2
$\partial_H(a(t)) = (\partial_H(a))(t)$	ATD
$\partial_H(X + Y) = \partial_H(X) + \partial_H(Y)$	D3
$\partial_H(X \cdot Y) = \partial_H(X) \cdot \partial_H(Y)$	D4

Table 8. ACPρ = BPAρδ + ATU1-4 + ATB5-8 + C1-3 + + ATC1,2 + CM1,4,8,9 + CM5',6',7' + ATCM2,3 + D1-4 + ATD.

2.8 OPERATIONAL SEMANTICS

We can also give action rules for the auxiliary operators. The rules are straightforward.

$$\frac{x \xrightarrow{a(r)} x',\ r < t}{x \gg t \xrightarrow{a(r)} x'} \qquad \frac{x \xrightarrow{a(r)} \surd,\ r < t}{x \gg t \xrightarrow{a(r)} \surd}$$

$$\frac{x \xrightarrow{a(r)} x',\ r < U(y)}{x \,⫫\, y \xrightarrow{a(r)} x' \| (r \gg y)} \qquad \frac{x \xrightarrow{a(r)} \surd,\ r < U(y)}{x \,⫫\, y \xrightarrow{a(r)} r \gg y}$$

$$\frac{x \xrightarrow{a(r)} x',\ y \xrightarrow{b(r)} y',\ a|b=c\neq\delta}{x \mid y \xrightarrow{c(r)} x' \| y'}$$

$$\frac{x \xrightarrow{a(r)} x',\ y \xrightarrow{b(r)} \surd,\ a|b=c\neq\delta}{x \mid y \xrightarrow{c(r)} x',\ y \mid x \xrightarrow{c(r)} x'}$$

$$\frac{x \xrightarrow{a(r)} \surd,\ y \xrightarrow{b(r)} \surd,\ a|b=c\neq\delta}{x \mid y \xrightarrow{c(r)} \surd}$$

$$\frac{x \xrightarrow{a(r)} x',\ a \notin H}{\partial_H(x) \xrightarrow{a(r)} \partial_H(x')} \qquad \frac{x \xrightarrow{a(r)} \surd,\ a \notin H}{\partial_H(x) \xrightarrow{a(r)} \surd}$$

Table 9. Action relations for auxiliary operators of ACPρ.

2.9 INTEGRATION

An extension of ACPρ (called ACPρI) that is very useful in applications is the extension with the integral operator, denoting a choice over a continuum of alternatives. I.e., if V is a subset of $\mathbb{R}^{\geq 0}$, and v is a variable over $\mathbb{R}^{\geq 0}$, then $\int_{v \in V} P$ denotes the alternative composition of alternatives $P[t/v]$ for $t \in V$ (expression P with nonnegative real t substituted for variable v). For more information, we refer the reader to [BB91a] and [K91]. The operational semantics is straightforward (table 10).

$$\frac{x(t) \xrightarrow{a(r)} x',\ t \in V}{\int_{v \in V} x(v) \xrightarrow{a(r)} x'} \qquad \frac{x(t) \xrightarrow{a(r)} \surd,\ t \in V}{\int_{v \in V} x(v) \xrightarrow{a(r)} \surd}$$

Table 10. Action relations for integration.

We will not provide axioms for the integral operator here (and refer the reader to [BB91a] and [K91]), except for the axiom for the ultimate delay operator:

$$U(\int_{v \in V} P) = \sup\{U(P[t/v]) : t \in V\} \qquad \text{ATU11.}$$

2. 10 GRAPH MODEL

It is possible to construct a graph model for ACPρI. However, we obtain a number of simplifications if we only consider the domain of process *trees*. Therefore, we will limit our domain to trees.

Process trees are directed rooted trees with edges labeled by timed atomic or delta actions, satisfying the condition that for each pair of consecutive transitions $s_1 \xrightarrow{a(r)} s_2 \xrightarrow{b(t)} s_3$ it is required that $r < t$ (however, in case $b \equiv \delta$, we also allow $r = t$). Moreover, we require that the endnode of a δ-transition has no outgoing edges, and that the timestamp of a δ-transition is larger than the supremum of the timestamps of its brother edges (edges starting from the same node).

Now $+, \cdot, \|, \lfloor\!\lfloor, \mid, \partial_H, \gg, U, \gg$ and $\int$ can be defined on these trees in a straightforward manner:

- For +, take the disjoint union of the trees and identify the roots. If one of the roots has an outgoing δ-edge, remove this edge if its timestamp is less than or equal than the supremum of the timestamps of the outgoing edges of the other root (but keep one of the two δ-edges, if both roots have a δ-edge with the same timestamp).
- $t \gg g$ is obtained by removing every edge from the root with label $a(r)$ with $r \leq t$. If this removes all edges starting from the root, add a $\delta(t)$-edge to an endpoint.
- $g \cdot h$ is constructed as follows: identify each non-δ endpoint s of g (endpoint with no incoming δ-edge) with the root of a copy of $t \gg h$, where t is the time of the edge leading to s.
- $U(g) = \sup\{r \in \mathbb{R}^{\geq 0} \mid root(g) \xrightarrow{a(r)} s$ for $a \in A_\delta$ and certain $s \in g\}$. If g is the trivial one-node graph, put $U(g) = \infty$.
- Let for $s \in g$, $(g)_s$ denote the subgraph of g with root s. Then $g \| h$ is defined as follows:
  - the set of states is the cartesian product of the state sets of g and h, the root the pair of roots.
  - transitions: if $s \xrightarrow{a(r)} s'$, $a \neq \delta$ and $r < U((h)_t)$ then $\langle s,t \rangle \xrightarrow{a(r)} \langle s',t \rangle$;
    if $t \xrightarrow{a(r)} t'$, $a \neq \delta$ and $r < U((g)_s)$ then $\langle s,t \rangle \xrightarrow{a(r)} \langle s,t' \rangle$;
    if $s \xrightarrow{a(r)} s'$ and $t \xrightarrow{b(r)} t'$ and $a \mid b = c \neq \delta$ then $\langle s,t \rangle \xrightarrow{c(r)} \langle s',t' \rangle$.

  Lastly, if a node $\langle s,t \rangle$ with s and t not both endnodes in g resp. h does not have an outgoing edge with timestamp equal to $t = \min\{U((g)_s, (h)_t\}$, we add a transition $\langle s,t \rangle \xrightarrow{\delta(t)}$ to an endpoint.

It is an exercise to show that this construction always yields a tree again.

- the construction of $g \lfloor\!\lfloor h$, $g \mid h$ and $\partial_H(g)$ is now straightforward.
- Finally, the graph of $\int_{v \in V} P$ is constructed by first identifying the roots of the graphs $P[t/v]$ for $t \in V$. Next, remove all δ-edges that do not satisfy the condition above (i.e. its timestamp is not larger than the supremum of the timestamps of its brother edges). Add again a δ-edge with timestamp t, if the ultimate delay t of the first graph is larger than the supremum of the timestamps of the remaining edges.

As an example, notice that the graph of $\int_{v \in (0,1)} \delta(v)$ only has one edge, with label $\delta(1)$.

Bisimulation on these graphs is defined as e.g. in BERGSTRA & KLOP [BK84]. One may prove in a standard fashion that bisimulation is a congruence for all operators of ACPρI.

3. LOCATIONS

We get a straightforward extension of the theory in section 2, if we add a location coordinate to all atomic actions except δ. We use a *finite* set of locations L (the use of an infinite set of locations was discussed in [BB91b]; here, we do not need that). The set of timed located atomic actions, ALT is now generated by

$\{a(\ell;t) \mid a \in A, \ell \in L, t \in \mathbb{R}^{\geq 0}\} \cup \{\delta(t) \mid t \geq 0\}$.

It will be useful to consider also the set of *untimed* located actions, i.e. the set AL generated by

$\{a(\ell) \mid a \in A, \ell \in L\} \cup \{\delta\}$.

We can draw the following picture of the algebraic signature (fig. 1).

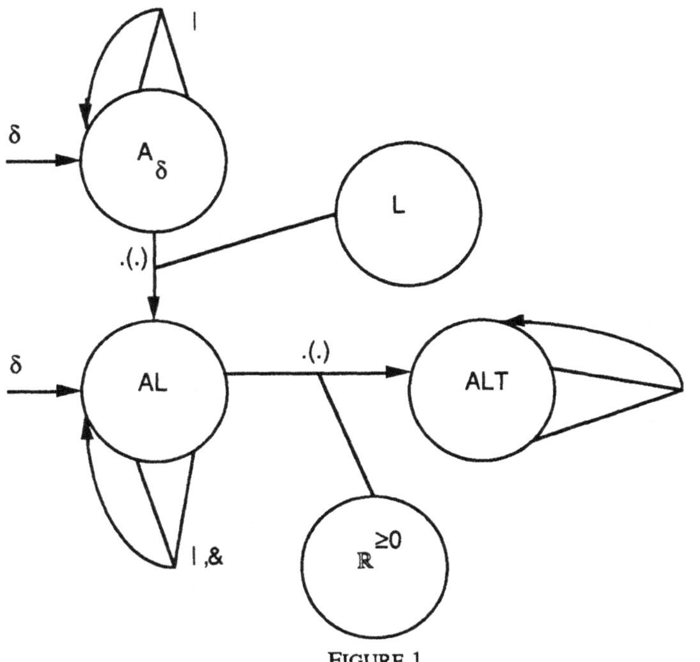

FIGURE 1.

We use $a(\ell)(t)$ as an alternative notation for $a(\ell;t)$.

3.1 MULTI-ACTIONS

Multi-actions are process terms generated by located actions and the *synchronisation function* &. Multi-actions contain actions that occur synchronously at different locations. For α,β,γ elements of AL, we have the following conditions on the synchronisation function (table 11). Further, $\ell \in L$, $a,b \in A$.

$\alpha \,\&\, \beta = \beta \,\&\, \alpha$	LO1
$\alpha \,\&\, (\beta \,\&\, \gamma) = (\alpha \,\&\, \beta) \,\&\, \gamma$	LO2
$\delta \,\&\, \alpha = \delta$	LO3
$a(\ell) \,\&\, b(\ell) = \delta$	LO4
$\delta(\ell) = \delta$	LO5

Table 11. Synchronisation function for located actions.

Using the axioms of table 11, each multi-action can be reduced to one of the following two forms:

- δ,

- $a_1(\ell_1)$ & ... & $a_n(\ell_n)$, with all locations ℓ_i different, all $a_i \in A$.

Next, we have the *communication function* $\mid$. As usual, and as required by axioms C1-3 in table 8, we assume that a communication function is given on atomic actions, that is commutative, associative, and has δ as a neutral element. We have the following axioms. In table 12, $a,b,c \in A$, $\alpha,\beta,\gamma \in AL$. In order to state axiom CL7, we need an auxiliary function locs, that determines the set of locations of a multi-action.

$a \mid b = b \mid a$	C1
$a \mid (b \mid c) = (a \mid b) \mid c$	C2
$\delta \mid a = \delta$	C3
$\alpha \mid \beta = \beta \mid \alpha$	CL1
$\alpha \mid (\beta \mid \gamma) = (\alpha \mid \beta) \mid \gamma$	CL2
$\delta \mid \alpha = \delta$	CL3
$a(\ell) \mid b(\ell) = (a \mid b)(\ell)$	CL4
$a(\ell) \mid (b(\ell) \& \beta) = (a \mid b)(\ell) \& \beta$	CL5
$(a(\ell) \& \alpha) \mid (b(\ell) \& \beta) = (a \mid b)(\ell) \& (\alpha \mid \beta)$	CL6
$locs(\alpha) \cap locs(\beta) = \varnothing \Rightarrow \alpha \mid \beta = \alpha \& \beta$	CL7
$locs(\delta) = \varnothing$	LOC1
$locs(a(\ell)) = \{\ell\}$	LOC2
$\ell \notin locs(\alpha), locs(\alpha) \neq \varnothing \Rightarrow$	
$locs(a(\ell) \& \alpha) = locs(\alpha) \cup \{\ell\}$	LOC3

Table 12. Communication function for located actions.

3.2 TIMED MULTI-ACTIONS

It is now straightforward to extend the definition of the synchronisation and communication functions to timed multi-actions. In table 13, $\alpha,\beta \in AL$.

$t \neq s \Rightarrow \alpha(t) \mid \beta(s) = \delta(min(t,s))$	CL8
$\alpha(t) \mid \beta(t) = (\alpha \mid \beta)(t)$	CL9

Table 13. Communication function on timed multi-actions.

3.3 REAL TIME PROCESS ALGEBRA WITH LOCATIONS

Real time process algebra with locations now has exactly the same axioms as real time process algebra, only the letters a,b now do not range over A respectively A_δ, but over multi-actions from AL as above.

The axioms for ultimate delay are again ATU1-11 (with in ATU1 a ranging over the larger set). Parallel composition is dealt with likewise, obtaining the axiom system ACPρl by adding axioms CM1,4-9, ATCM2,3, D1-4, ATD.

The operational semantics is just like in the temporal case, in section 2. Transitions are labeled with multi-actions, and these play exactly the same role as the timed actions in the case of ACPρ. Similarly we may define a graph model for ACPρl. In both cases bisimulation can be defined in the same way.

4. STATE OPERATOR

The state operator was introduced in BAETEN & BERGSTRA [BB88]. It keeps track of the global state of a system, and is used to describe actions that have a side effect on a state space. The state operator has showed itself useful in a range of applications, e.g. in the translation of programming or specification languages into process algebra (see VAANDRAGER [V90] or SPECS [S90]).

The state operator comes equiped with two functions: given a certain state and an action to be executed from that state, the function action gives the resulting action and the function effect the resulting state. Now, when we apply these functions to a located action, we have the obvious axioms

$$\mathsf{action}(a(\ell), s) = \mathsf{action}(a, s)(\ell) \qquad \mathsf{effect}(a(\ell), s) = \mathsf{effect}(a, s).$$

Things become more difficult if we go to multi-actions: in order to calculate the resulting global state, we need to apply the effect function to the component actions in a certain order. How is this order determined? We will assume that there is a partial order $<$ on locations, and that we can apply the effect function *only* on multi-actions that determine a totally ordered set of locations. We make this precise in the following definition.

4.1 DEFINITION

Let A be a set of atomic actions, let S be a set of states. Assume we have functions

$$\mathsf{action}: A_\delta \times S \to A_\delta \qquad \mathsf{effect}: A_\delta \times S \to S$$

such that $\mathsf{action}(\delta, s) = \delta$ and $\mathsf{effect}(\delta, s) = s$ for all $s \in S$ (we say: δ is inert).
Let L be a set of locations, and let $<$ be a partial order on L. If M is a set of locations, write $TO(M)$ if M is totally ordered by $<$, and write $\ell < M$ if $\ell < m$ for all $m \in M$. Then we define the extension of the functions action and effect to multi-actions as follows ($\alpha \in AL$).

$\mathsf{action}(a(\ell), s) = \mathsf{action}(a, s)(\ell)$
$\mathsf{effect}(a(\ell), s) = \mathsf{effect}(a, s)$
$\neg TO(\mathsf{locs}(\alpha)) \Rightarrow \mathsf{action}(\alpha, s) = \delta$
$\neg TO(\mathsf{locs}(\alpha)) \Rightarrow \mathsf{effect}(\alpha, s) = s$
$TO(\mathsf{locs}(\alpha))\ \&\ \ell < \mathsf{locs}(\alpha) \Rightarrow$
$\mathsf{action}(a(\ell)\ \&\ \alpha, s) = \mathsf{action}(a, \mathsf{effect}(\alpha,s))(\ell)\ \&\ \mathsf{action}(\alpha,s)$
$TO(\mathsf{locs}(\alpha))\ \&\ \ell < \mathsf{locs}(\alpha) \Rightarrow$
$\mathsf{effect}(a(\ell)\ \&\ \alpha, s) = \mathsf{effect}(a, \mathsf{effect}(\alpha, s))$

Table 14. Action and effect on multi-actions.

4.2 DEFINITION

The defining equations for the state operator are now straightforward (cf. [BB88]). If S is a set of states, then for each $s \in S$ we have an operator $\lambda_s: P \to P$. In table 15, $s \in S$, $\alpha \in AL$, $t \geq 0$, x,y processes.

$\lambda_s(\alpha(t)) = \mathsf{action}(\alpha, s)(t)$	SO1
$\lambda_s(\alpha(t) \cdot x) = \mathsf{action}(\alpha, s)(t) \cdot \lambda_{\mathsf{effect}(\alpha, s)}(x)$	SO2
$\lambda_s(x + y) = \lambda_s(x) + \lambda_s(y)$	SO3

Table 15. State operator.

In case we deal with integrals, the last equation SO3 has to be extended to the following:

$$\lambda_s(\int_{v\in V} P) = \int_{v\in V} \lambda_s(P) \qquad \text{SO4.}$$

It is equally straightforward to give action rules for the operational semantics ($\alpha \in AL$, $\alpha \neq \delta$).

$\dfrac{x \xrightarrow{\alpha(r)} x',\ action(\alpha,s)=\beta\neq\delta}{\lambda_s(x) \xrightarrow{\beta(r)} \lambda_{effect(\alpha,s)}(x')}$	$\dfrac{x \xrightarrow{\alpha(r)} \surd,\ action(\alpha,s)=\beta\neq\delta}{\lambda_s(x) \xrightarrow{\beta(r)} \surd}$

Table 16. Action relations for the state operator.

In order to deal with δ-transitions, we add the axiom

$$U(\lambda_s(x)) = U(x) \qquad \text{ATU12.}$$

Then, we determine the existence of δ-transitions as before (in 2.3).

4.3 EXAMPLES

1. A clock. Suppose we have a fixed location ℓ. Define, for each $s \in \mathbb{N}$,

 $effect(tick, s) = s+1$

 $action(tick, s) = tick.$

Then a clock is given by the process $\lambda_0(P(0))$, where $P(t) = tick(\ell; t+1)\cdot P(t+1)$.

2. Listing when action a occurs at location m (measured in discrete time). The state space is $\mathbb{N} \times \mathbb{L}$, where $\mathbb{L}$ denotes the set of lists over $\mathbb{N}$. Look at the process $\lambda_{0,\varnothing}(Q \parallel P(0))$, where $P(t)$ is as in example 1 and Q is given by $Q = \int_{t\geq 0} a(m; t)\cdot Q$.

We have the following definitions:

 $effect(tick, \langle n, \sigma\rangle) = \langle n+1, \sigma\rangle$

 $action(tick, \langle n, \sigma\rangle) = tick$

 $effect(a, \langle n, \sigma\rangle) = \langle n, \sigma * n\rangle$

 $action(a, \langle n, \sigma\rangle) = a.$

Moreover we have $m < \ell$. As a consequence, we have e.g.

 $effect(a(m)\ \&\ tick(\ell), \langle n, \sigma\rangle) = \langle n+1, \sigma*(n+1)\rangle.$

3. Serial switch. We can draw the following picture of a serial switch (fig. 2).

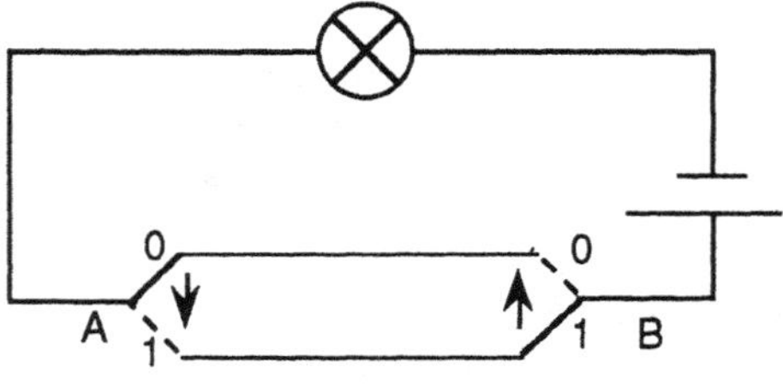

FIGURE 2.

The switches A and B are given by the equations

$$A = \int_{t \geq 0} switch(left; t) \cdot A$$

$$B = \int_{t \geq 0} switch(right; t) \cdot B$$

(here, we have locations left, right corresponding to the positions of the switches). We have state space S = {on, off}. E.g. in figure 2, the lamp is in state off. We define the action and effect functions as follows.

action(switch, off) = turnon
action(switch, on) = turnoff
effect(switch, on) = off
effect(switch, off) = on

Starting in state off (as in the figure) we have the process

$$P = \lambda_{off}(A \parallel B).$$

(We assume no communication occurs.)

An interesting situation occurs if both switches are turned at the same time. Suppose we have the ordering right < left. Let t_0 be a fixed time. Then we have

$$\lambda_{off}(switch(left; t_0) \cdot A \parallel switch(right; t_0) \cdot B) = (turnon(left) \,\&\, turnoff(right))(t_0) \cdot \lambda_{off}(A \parallel B),$$

$$\lambda_{on}(switch(left; t_0) \cdot A \parallel switch(right; t_0) \cdot B) = (turnoff(left) \,\&\, turnon(right))(t_0) \cdot \lambda_{on}(A \parallel B).$$

4.4 EXAMPLE

As a larger example, we present a version of the Concurrent Alternating Bit Protocol. We base our description on the specification in VAN GLABBEEK & VAANDRAGER [GV89]. Other descriptions can be found in KOYMANS & MULDER [KM90], LARSEN & MILNER [LM87].

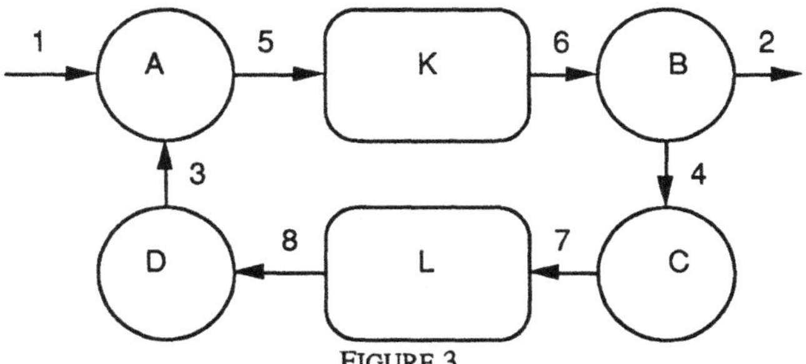

FIGURE 3.

In figure 3, elements of a finite data set D are sent from location 1 to location 2. From A to B, frames consisting of a data element and an alternating bit are sent, from C to D, independently, acknowledgements. K and L are unbounded faulty queues, that can lose data. It was shown in [GV89] that we can assume that loss of data only occurs at the top of the queue. We will model the queues by means of a state operator. We present the specification first, and then define the state operator.

In the specification, there are two parameters: w_0 is the amount of time that a sender allows to pass before a message is sent into the queue again, and w_1 is the amount of time after which a receiver checks the queue again after an unsuccessful attempt. Put another way, $\frac{1}{w_0}$ is the retransmission frequency, and $\frac{1}{w_1}$ is the polling frequency. These parameters can be filled in arbitrarily, and do not affect the correctness of the protocol. Moreover, in the specification, we use a system delay constant 1.

The specification of the senders and receivers now looks as follows:

$A = A(0)$

$A(b) = \int_{t \geq 0} \sum_{d \in D} r(d)(1; t) \cdot enq(db)(5; t+1) \cdot A(d, b, t+2)$ for each $b \in \{0, 1\}$

$A(d, b, t) = enq(db)(5; t+w_0) \cdot A(d, b, t+w_0) + \int_{v \in (t, t+w_0]} r(next)(3; v) \cdot A(1-b)$

for each $b \in \{0,1\}, d \in D, t \geq 0$.

$B = B(0, 0)$

$B(b, t) = \big(deq(\perp)(6; t+w_1) + \sum_{d \in D} deq(d(1-b))(6; t+w_1)\big) \cdot B(b, t+w_1) +$

$+ \sum_{d \in D} deq(db)(6; t+w_1) \cdot B(d, b, t+w_1)$ for each $b \in \{0,1\}, t \geq 0$.

$B(d, b, t) = s(d)(2; t+1) \cdot s(next)(4; t+2) \cdot B(1-b, t+2)$ for each $b \in \{0,1\}, d \in D, t \geq 0$.

$C = C(1, 0)$

$C(b, t) = enq(b)(7; t+w_0) \cdot C(b, t+w_0) + \int_{v \in (t, t+w_0]} r(next)(4; v) \cdot enq(7; v+1) \cdot C(1-b, v+2)$

for each $b \in \{0,1\}, t \geq 0$.

$D = D(0, 0)$

$D(b, t) = \big(deq(\perp)(8, t+w_1) + deq(1-b)(8; t+w_1)\big) \cdot D(b, t+w_1) +$

$+ deq(b)(8; t+w_1) \cdot s(next)(3; t+w_1+1) \cdot D(1-b, t+w_1+1)$ for each $b \in \{0, 1\}, t \geq 0$.

$E = \int_{t \geq 0} error(6; t) \cdot E$ $\qquad$ $F = \int_{t \geq 0} error(8; t) \cdot F$

Now the Concurrent Alternating Bit Protocol is defined by:

$CABP = \partial_H(\lambda_\varnothing(A \parallel E \parallel B) \parallel \lambda_\varnothing(C \parallel F \parallel D))$.

Here, the encapsulation set is

$H = \{r(next)(k), s(next)(k) : k \in \{2, 3\}\}$.

In the process CABP, we are actually dealing with two state operators: the state operator for processes A, E, B has a state space consisting of lists of frames, the state operator for C, F, D has a state space consisting of lists of booleans. We have the following ordering on locations: 6 > 5 and 8 > 7. This makes it impossible to add an element to an empty queue and read it out at the same instant of time: an element needs a positive amount of time to propagate through the queue.

In order to save space, we define the action and effect function for both state operators at the same time (so in the following, either $x \in D \times B$ or $x \in B$, and either $\sigma \in (D \times B)^*$ or $\sigma \in B^*$):

$action(enq(x), \sigma) = c(x)$

$effect(enq(x), \sigma) = \sigma^* x$

$action(deq(\perp), \sigma) = i$ $\qquad$ if $\sigma = \varnothing$

$action(deq(\perp), \sigma) = \delta$ $\qquad$ if $\sigma \neq \varnothing$

$action(deq(x), \sigma) = \delta$ $\qquad$ if $\sigma = \varnothing$ or $top(\sigma) \neq x$

$action(deq(x), \sigma) = c(x)$ $\qquad$ if $top(\sigma) = x$

$effect(deq(x), \sigma) = \sigma$ $\qquad$ if $\sigma = \varnothing$ or $top(\sigma) \neq x$

effect(deq(x), σ) = tail(σ) if top(σ) = x
action(error, $\varnothing$) = δ
action(error, σ) = i if $\sigma \neq \varnothing$
effect(error, $\varnothing$) = $\varnothing$
effect(error, σ) = tail(σ) if $\sigma \neq \varnothing$.

Now we believe that this specification constitutes a correct protocol, if the queues behave fairly (i.e. data do not get lost infinitely many times in a row). At this point, we will not state explicitly what this statement means (leaving this for further research), so we will not give a specification that process CABP satisfies after abstraction of internal actions (the internal actions are the c(x) actions and i).

Note that multi-actions can occur in this protocol also: we can add to a non-empty queue and read from it at the same time.

5. CONCLUSION

We conclude that it is possible to add a state operator to real time process algebra, and that we can specify interesting examples by means of it. We claim that the state operator will be useful to describe communication between a sender and a moving receiver.

REFERENCES

[BB88] J.C.M. BAETEN & J.A. BERGSTRA, *Global renaming operators in concrete process algebra,* Information & Computation 78 (3), 1988, pp. 205-245.

[BB91a] J.C.M. BAETEN & J.A. BERGSTRA, *Real time process algebra,* Formal Aspects of Computing 3 (2), 1991, pp. 142-188. (Report version appeared as report P8916, University of Amsterdam 1989.)

[BB91b] J.C.M. BAETEN & J.A. BERGSTRA, *Real space process algebra,* in Proc. CONCUR'91, Amsterdam (J.C.M. Baeten & J.F. Groote, eds.), Springer LNCS 527, 1991, pp. 96-110. To appear in Formal Aspects of Computing.

[BW90] J.C.M. BAETEN & W.P. WEIJLAND, *Process algebra,* Cambridge Tract in TCS 18, Cambridge University Press 1990.

[BK84] J.A. BERGSTRA & J.W. KLOP, *Process algebra for synchronous communication,* Inf. & Control 60, 1984, pp. 109-137.

[BK86] J.A. BERGSTRA & J.W. KLOP, *Process algebra: specification and verification in bisimulation semantics,* in: Math. & Comp. Sci. II (M. Hazewinkel, J.K. Lenstra & L.G.L.T. Meertens, eds.), CWI Monograph 4, North-Holland, Amsterdam 1986, pp. 61-94.

[GV89] R.J. VAN GLABBEEK & F.W. VAANDRAGER, *Modular specifications in process algebra (with curious queues,* in: Algebraic Methods: Theory, Tools & Applications, Passau 1987 (M. Wirsing & J.A. Bergstra, eds.), Springer LNCS 394, 1989, pp. 465-506.

[HE88] M. HENNESSY, *Algebraic theory of processes,* MIT Press 1988.

[H85] C.A.R. HOARE, *Sequential communicating processes,* Prentice Hall, 1985.

[J91a] A. JEFFREY, *A linear time process algebra,* in Proc. 3rd CAV, (K.G. Larsen & A. Skou, eds.), Aalborg 1991, report IR-91-4/5, Aalborg University, pp. 501-512.

[J91b] A. JEFFREY, *Abstract timed observation and process algebra,* in Proc. CONCUR'91, Amsterdam (J.C.M. Baeten & J.F. Groote, eds.), Springer LNCS, 1991, pp. 332-345.

[K91] A.S. KLUSENER, *Completeness in real time process algebra,* in Proc. CONCUR'91, Amsterdam (J.C.M. Baeten & J.F. Groote, eds.), Springer LNCS, 1991, pp. 376-392.

[KM90] C.P.J. KOYMANS & J.C. MULDER, *A modular approach to protocol verification using process algebra,* in: Applications of Process Algebra (J.C.M. Baeten, ed.), Cambridge Tracts in TCS 17, Cambridge University Press 1990, pp. 261-306.

[LM87] K.G. LARSEN & R. MILNER, *A complete protocol verification using relativized bisilulation,* in: Proc. 14th ICALP, Karlsruhe (Th. Ottmann, ed.), Springer LNCS 267, 1987, pp. 126-135.

[M80] R. MILNER, *A calculus of communicating systems,* Springer LNCS 92, 1980.

[M89] R. MILNER, *Communication and concurrency,* Prentice Hall, 1989.

[MT90] F. MOLLER & C. TOFTS, *A temporal calculus of communicating systems,* in: Proc. CONCUR'90, Amsterdam (J.C.M. Baeten & J.W. Klop, eds.), Springer LNCS 458, 1990, pp. 401-415.

[MU91] D.V.J. MURPHY, *Testing, betting and timed true concurrency,* in Proc. CONCUR'91, Amsterdam (J.C.M. Baeten & J.F. Groote, eds.), Springer LNCS, 1991, pp. 439-454.

[RR88] G.M. REED & A.W. ROSCOE, *A timed model for communicating sequential processes,* TCS 58, 1988, pp. 249-261.

[S90] SPECS CONSORTIUM, *Definition of MR and CRL version 2.1,* 1990.

[V90] F.W. VAANDRAGER, *Process algebra semantics of POOL,* in: Applications of Process Algebra (J.C.M. Baeten, ed.), Cambridge Tracts in TCS 17, Cambridge University Press 1990, pp. 173-236.

Timed process algebras with urgent interactions and a unique powerful binary operator

Tommaso Bolognesi
CNUCE / C.N.R. - 36, Via S. Maria - 56100 Pisa - Italy (bolog@fdt.cnuce.cnr.it)

Ferdinando Lucidi
Fondazione U. Bordoni - 59, Via B. Castiglione, 00142 Roma - Italy

Abstract. A timed process algebra called ρ1 is introduced, which offers operators for specifying time-dependent behaviours and, in particular, the urgency of a given (inter-)action involving one or more processes. The formal semantics of the language is given in a style similar to the one adopted by Tofts and Moller for TCCS: two independent sets of inference rules are provided, which handle, respectively, the occurrence of actions and the passing of time. The language, partly inspired to LOTOS, can specify in a natural way the "wait-until-timeout" scenario, and we prove that, due to its two time-related operators, it can simulate Turing machines. The formalism appears as a most natural transposition in the realm of process algebras of an expressivity-preserving subset of the well known Time Petri Nets of Merlin and Farber. An enhanced timed process algebra called ρ2, which includes only five operators, and preserves the expressivity of ρ1, is then proposed: it combines mutual disabling, choice, parallel composition with synchronization, and pure interleaving, into a unique, general-purpose, parametric binary operator.

Keywords. timed process algebra, timed Petri Net.

Contents

1. Introduction

We present here a simple timed process algebra, and an enrichment of it, both meant to describe the time dependent behaviour of sets of interacting processes. In formulating our algebras we have been essentially inspired by three models:

- the LOTOS (Language of Temporal Ordering Specification) standard specification language for concurrent systems [B89, BB87],
- the Time Petri Net model of Merlin and Farber [MF76], and
- TCCS (Timed Calculus of Communicating Systems), by Moller and Tofts [MT90].

Indeed, one of the early motivations of our work has been to select a very basic subset of LOTOS (including just the fundamental operators of action prefix, choice, parallel composition with multi-way synchronization, process instantiation) and to enrich it by adding a minimum number of elementary operators for expressing time-related features. A concrete motivation for such an exercise is found in one of the primary application areas of LOTOS, that of communication protocols, where, at a sufficiently low level of abstraction, it becomes crucial to be able to express time parameters such as message transmission delays or timeout periods. (For an account on time in communication protocols, see [R85].) Standard LOTOS cannot express time parameters and time dependent behaviours.

Another initial requirement was to *imitate* as closely as possible the timed enhancement of Petri Nets proposed by Merlin and Farber (called Time Petri Nets hereafter), since it appeared to us as a most simple and natural approach and, at the same time, it provably offers enhanced expressive capabilities with respect to (untimed) place-transition Petri Nets. Indeed [JLL77] proves that Time Petri Nets can simulate Turing machines, while it is known that standard Petri Nets can not do so.

Finally, an important requirement was to provide our proposed timed algebras with a concise, clear and elegant formal semantics. The degree of success in achieving this goal, which, in our opinion is quite satisfactory, is largely due to the adoption of an approach already used in TCCS by Tofts and Moller [MT90], where the time and action dimensions are handled separately from each other.

A first timed process algebra, called ρ1, is introduced informally in Section 2, where its analogy with Time Petri Nets is also illustrated. Its formal semantics is given in Section 3. The main time-related feature of this language is represented by a unary, prefix, parametric operator called *urgency*, denoted by 'ρ(a)', used to express the fact that a given action *or interaction a* is to be performed urgently, as soon as *all* the involved partners are ready for it. Ultimately, the effect of such operator is to prevent the passing of time as an alternative to the occurrence of an *a*-event. A typical application of the operator is found in the specification of timeouts. The expressive power of the language is shown in Section 4, where a ρ1 specification of a generic Two-Counter Machine is provided. The relations between the ρ1 language and other process algebras are discussed in Section 5, where we also list some strong-bisimulation equivalence laws.

In Section 6 we consider what might be called 'hierarchical timeout' scenarios; their specification in ρ1 seems possible, but is cumbersome. Then we show that mutual disabling, choice, parallel composition with synchronization, and pure interleaving, that is, all the binary operators in which we are interested, can be combined into a unique, general-purpose, parametric binary operator. A compact timed process algebra called ρ2, which preserves the expressive power of ρ1, and enhances its expressive flexibility, is thus obtained.

A preliminary proposal for a Timed-Interaction LOTOS was presented by us in [BLT90]. Although the current proposals are consistent with several ideas expressed in that paper, many substantial differences exist between the two approaches, both at the syntactic and at the semantic levels (see Section 5).

We warn the reader that, although we locate our proposal in the (rapidly growing) family of process *algebras*, the emphasis of this paper is not on the axiomatization of the language, or on complete axiomatizations of some subsets of little practical interest; only a few algebraic laws are presented in Section 5. Rather, we emphasise on the relations with Timed Petri Nets, on expressive power and flexibility, and on clarity of semantic definition.

2. Informal presentation of the ρ1 language

The purposes of this section are to introduce the syntax of the ρ1 language and the informal meanings of its constructs, and to illustrate the analogies between the language and the Time Petri Nets proposed in [MF76].

We assume that time be discrete, and represent it by natural numbers. At integer time instants, an action, or even an action sequence, can be executed in zero time: actions are instantaneous. These assumptions are common to other process algebras, such as TCCS [MT90] and ATP[NS90].

Syntax and informal semantics

The syntax of ρ1 is described by the following grammar, where *B*, *B1* and *B2* denote behaviour expressions, *P* is a process identifier, *a* is an action identifier, *S* is a possibly empty set of gate identifiers, and *U* is a nonempty set of gate identifiers, *t* is a positive time value (natural number). Following the LOTOS terminology, we think of *actions* as occurring at *gates*; an action is identified just by the identifier of the gate where it occurs. Thus, we shall use the terms *action-identifier* and *gate-identifier* interchangeably.

```
B       ::=

(* basic operators: *)

|       a.B            (* action prefix *)
|       (1).B          (* tick prefix *)
|       B1+ B2         (* choice *)
|       B1 |S| B2      (* parallel composit. over the gates of set S (synchronization gates) *)
|       ρ(U)B          (* urgency of (inter-)actions at the gates of set U (urgent gates) *)
|       P              (* process instantiation *)

(* shorthands / derived operators: *)

|       (t).B          (* time prefix: shorthand for t occurrences of tick prefix) *)
|       1              (* time passing process *)
|       0              (* time deadlock process *)
|       B1 ||| B2      (* interleaving: shorthand for 'B1 |Ø| B2' *)
```

A process definition has the form: *P* := *Bp*, where *P* is a process-identifier and *Bp* is the *defining behaviour expression* of *P*. A *specification* in ρ1 has the form:

B [where P1 := B1, ..., Pn := Bn]

where *B* is a behaviour expression, 'where' is a keyword introducing a list of process definitions, called the (process definition) *environment* of *B*, the *Pi's* are process identifiers, and the *Bi's* are behaviour expressions (the part in square brackets is optional). Indeed, we shall sometimes omit to provide the environment of a behaviour expression, for notational conciseness.

Action prefix expression *a.B* denotes a process that can perform an a-action at any time, and then transform into process *B*. Tick prefix expression *(1).B* denotes a process that transforms into process *B* after one time unit (tick). The choice expression *B1* + *B2* denotes a process for which time passes until one of the two alternative behaviours, *B1* or *B2*, performs an action, thus eliminating the other. The parallel expression *B1 |[S]| B2* denotes a process where two components proceed in time independently from each other, except for actions at the synchronization gates in *S*, which must occur simultaneously.

The urgency expression *ρ(U)B* denotes a process that behaves like *B*, except that as soon as an action (at some gate) in the set *U* is ready for execution, it is immediately executed. If *P := B* is a process definition, where *P* is a process identifier and *B* is a behaviour expression, then the process instantiation expression *P* denotes a process that behaves like *B*.

Time prefix expression *(t).B* denotes a process that transforms into process *B* after *t* time units. It is a shorthand for *t* occurrences of the tick-prefix. Symbol **1** denotes the (instantiation of) the *time passing process*, which is unable to perform any action and can only age. Process **1** is defined as follows: **1** := (1). **1**. Finally, we can also define a process **0**, called *time deadlock*, for which any action or time delay is impossible. This is achieved by imposing a synchronization, at gate *a*, between a process urgently needing to perform action *a* and another process unable to participate in the interaction: **0** := (ρ(a) a. **1**) |[a]| **1**.

The binding power of the ρ1 operators is as follows: the unary prefix operators action prefix, tick prefix and urgency bind more tightly than the choice operator, which in turn binds more tightly than the parallel operator. The two binary operators (choice and parallel) are assumed to be right associative.

Analogies with Merlin and Faber's Time Petri Nets

Our ρ1 language exhibits analogies with the Time Petri Nets of [MF76]. We are not interested here in providing a formal, compositional mapping between the two languages. (Indeed, we conjecture that such a complex goal can only be approximated, not achieved in its entirety.) Our more realistic objective is to show that our language borrows from that specific type of timed Petri Nets the essence of its time-related constructions.

The Time Petri Nets of [MF76] are standard Petri Nets where transitions are labelled both by an action identifier and by a time interval (t1, t2), where t1, t2 ≥ 0. The rule is that, as soon as a (t1, t2)-labelled transition is *enabled* by the tokens, an implicit timer is started: the transition is actually *fireable* when t1 ≤ timer ≤ t2. In view of the analogy with our language, we assume t1 and t2 to be natural numbers. An example of such a net, describing a *symmetric timeout* scenario, is shown in Figure 2.1.

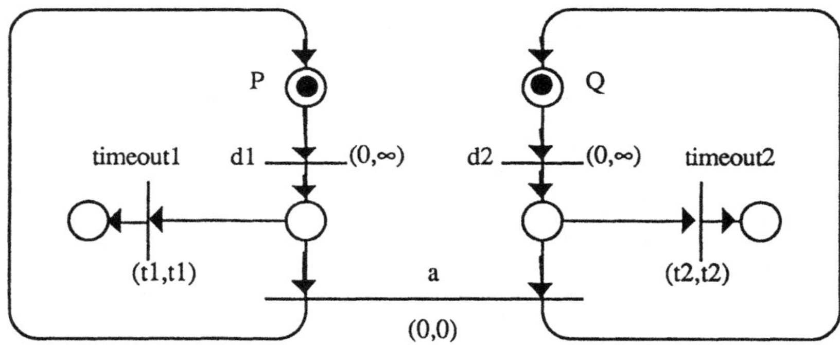

Figure 2.1 - Time Petri Net for a symmetric timeout system

The system can be conceived as the composition of two agents *P* and *Q* that, at any time, and independently from each other, can perform, respectively, actions *d1* and *d2*, thus becoming ready for synchronization *a*. Such synchronization occurs as soon as both agents are ready for it. Timeout actions prevent each process to wait indefinitely for the other.

We shall say that a transition is *local* when it has exactly one input arc; those with two or more input arcs shall be called *synchronization*-transitions. It should be noted that in the net of Figure 2.1 we are using a subset of the model: local transitions are labelled by (0, ∞) time intervals, or by zero-width intervals (such as (t1, t1)), while synchronization transitions are labelled (0, 0). That is, we are able to model our system by just using the capability to specify that:

- a local transition can occur at any time (*unconstrained* local transition),
- or a precisely specified number *t* of time units after it has become available (*fixed-time* local transition, which can be an *urgent* local transition if t = 0);
- a synchronization transition occurs as soon as possible (*urgent* synchronization transition).

Our ρ1 language supports such concepts quite directly, as follows:

- an unconstrained local transition *x* is expressed by the *action prefix*: operator 'x. ...';
- a fixed-time local transition *x* that must occur *t* time units after it has become available is expressed by a combination of the *time prefix* and *urgency* operators: '(t).ρ(x) x. ...';
- an urgent transition *x*, be it local or not, is expressed by the urgency operator: 'ρ(x)...'.

The complete specification in ρ1 of the symmetric timeout system is given in Figure 2.2 below:

S := ρ(a, timeout1, timeout2)
(P |[a]| Q)

where

P := d1. (a.P + (t1).timeout1.**1**)
Q := d2. (a.Q + (t2).timeout2.**1**)

Figure 2.2 - Specification in ρ1 of the symmetric timeout system of Fig. 2.1

Observe that the urgency of actions *timeout1* and *timeout2* could have been expressed also within the definitions of processes P and Q, while this is not possible for the synchronization action *a*.

Indeed, there exists an even smaller expressivity-conservative subset of Time Petri Nets, where also unconstrained local transitions are eliminated: urgent synchronization transitions and fixed-time local transitions are enough (by this, we precisely mean that such sub-model is sufficient for simulating Turing Machines, see [JLL77]). However, we did not explore the possibility to reduce, correspondingly, the set of ρ1 operators.

A two-fold break in the analogy between Time Petri Nets and the ρ1 language can be observed. Consider expression '(a.P1+ a.P2 + a.P3) |[a]| (a.Q1+ a.Q2 + a.Q3)'. We have three action prefixes for each operand of the composition, and just one parallel operator. The described behaviour offers 3*3 = 9 different synchronization possibilities. We can model such a scenario as a Petri net, but we would need to specify explicitly in the net, by synchronization transitions, all these nine possibilities. Thus, a first difference is that action capability (action prefix) and interaction (parallel composition) are decoupled in ρ1 (as well as in many process algebras), with benefits in terms of expressive flexibility and conciseness, while they are coupled in Petri nets.

A second difference, which appears as an important consequence of the first one, is that ρ1 can describe both *action-deadlock*, by the time-passing process **1**, and *time-deadlock*, by process **0**, while Time Petri Nets can only model the former: an irreversibly inactive Time Petri net grows old undefinitely. Indeed, the definition of time-deadlock, **0** := (ρ(a) a. **1**) |[a]| **1**, is possible just because the local action (urgent, in this case) can be distinguished from the potential synchronization (which, in this case, is impossible).

Different timing policies are adopted in different timed Petri Net models. The *timed-transition* (or *urgent-transition*) policy of the Time Petri Nets discussed above provides an increased expressivity w.r.t. the untimed model, as shown in [JLL77]. Such an approach can be contrasted with the *timed-arc* policy of, for example, [W83] (or with the coupled-time-graphs of [BR85]), where time labels are associated to the arcs connecting a place to a transition. [BC89] proves that such timed-arc policy fails to increase the expressivity of untimed Petri Nets.

In the timed enhancements of LOTOS proposed in [QF87] and [QAF89], time labels are associated to the action prefix construct, thus following what we may call a *timed-action-prefix policy*. An analogy can be established between the expressively weak timed-arc policy for Petri Nets, and the timed-action-prefix policy for process algebras. In both cases the time interval has a completely *local* significance, that is, the implicit timer is started at the occurrence of a local event: in the Petri Net case, the event is that of a token entering a place; in the timed algebra, it is the instantiation of a timed-action-prefix expression. For these reasons, we have chosen to inspire our proposal on a timed-transition (as opposed to timed-arc) Petri Net model, thus obtaining a *timed-interaction* (as opposed to timed-action-prefix) language. Further discussion on these alternative timing policies is found in [BLT90].

3. Formal semantics

The formal semantics of the ρ1 language is essentially given in the SOS (Structured Operational Semantics) style of [P81], and consists of three elements:

- a set of inference rules for deriving *action transitions*;
- a set of inference rules for deriving *tick (time passing) transitions*;
- an auxiliary function which decides on the immediate executability of an action.

By applying the inference rules of action and time passing transitions to a given ρ1 specification, one can grow *time/action trees* (Figure 3.1).

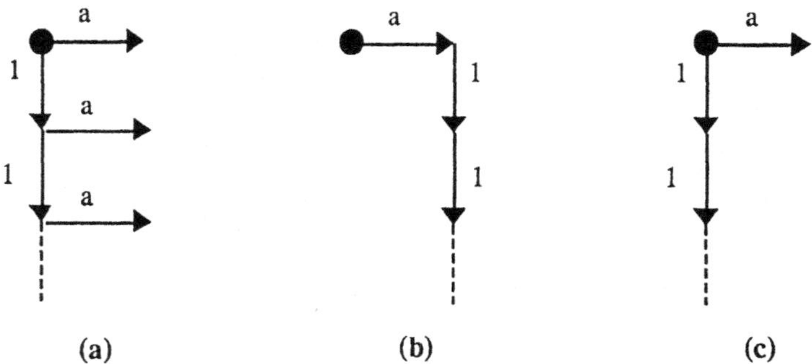

Figure 3.1 - Time/action trees

In such trees, by convention we associate the time dimension to the vertical axis, so that tick transitions are represented by vertical arrows, labelled by '1', while action transitions are depicted as horizontal arrows, labelled by action identifiers. The orthogonality of actions and time steps is meant to pictorially suggest that actions are instantaneous, since their projection on the time axis is null. In Figure 3.1. Tree (a) expresses the fact that action *a* can occur at any non-negative integer time. In case (b), action *a must* occur immediately, since no tick is possible before it. In case (c), action *a may* occur immediately, or time can pass, in which case *a* is no longer possible. We anticipate that only the first two trees can be expressed by ρ1.

The two sets of rules for action and tick transitions are provided in Table 3.1, and illustrated below.

Table 3.1 - Inference rules for action and aging transitions of ρ1

<table>
<tr><th>Syntax</th><th>Action transitions</th><th>Tick transitions</th></tr>
<tr><td>action prefix
a. B</td><td>a1) a.B--a-->B</td><td>t1) a.B==1==>a.B</td></tr>
<tr><td>tick prefix
(1). B</td><td></td><td>t2) (1).B==1==>B</td></tr>
<tr><td>choice
B1 + B2</td><td>a2) B1--a-->B1'
B1+B2--a-->B1'
a3) symmetric of rule above</td><td>t3) B1==1==>B1' and B2==1==>B2'
B1+B2==1==>B1'+B2'</td></tr>
<tr><td>parallel
B1 |S| B2</td><td>a4) B1--a-->B1' and B2--a-->B2' and a in S
B1|S|B2--a-->B1'|S|B2'
a5) B1--a-->B1' and a not in S
B1|S|B2--a-->B1'|S|B2
a6) symmetric of rule above</td><td>t4) B1==1==>B1' and B2==1==>B2'
B1|S|B2==1==>B1'|S|B2'</td></tr>
<tr><td>urgency
ρ(U) in B</td><td>a7) B--a-->B'
ρ(U)B --a-->ρ(U)B'</td><td>t5) B==1==>B' and ∀a ∈ U. not αa(B)
ρ(U)B ==1==> ρ(U)B'</td></tr>
<tr><td>proc. inst.
P</td><td>a8) B--a-->B' and P:=B is a proc.def.
P--a-->B'</td><td>t6) B==1==>B' and P:=B is a proc.def.
P=1==>B'</td></tr>
</table>

Inference rules for action transitions

These rules define the transition relation B1---a--->B2, where B1 and B2 are behaviour expressions and *a* is an action identifier. A consequence of separating action transition and tick transition rules is that when we write B1---a--->B2, we mean that B1 performs action *a* immediately (and instantaneously). At the semantic level, any time delay that precedes such an action should be represented explicitly. Another nice consequence of the separation is that the action transition rules of ρ1 turn out to be *identical* to those of basic LOTOS [BB87] (note that in the latter the ρ operator is not present, the choice operator is denoted by the box symbol '[]' instead of '+', and in *action prefix* a semicolon is used in place of the dot).

In an *action prefix expression,* the action can occur immediately (rule a1). In a *choice expression* the possible immediate actions are those of its components (rules a2 and a3). With the *parallel operator*, the two parallel components can proceed independently from each other with actions that are not in the set of synchronization actions (gates) S, while they must proceed together on the actions in S (rules a5, a6, and rule a4).

The *urgency operator,* ρ, is a 'passthrough' operator with respect to actions: the actions of expression $\rho(U)B$ are exactly those of expression *B* (rule a7). Note that the operator does *not* impose any priority of urgent actions over non urgent ones. For example, in the context of a 'wait-ack-until-timeout' scenario, if the ack-arrival and timeout events are possible at the same time, the choice is nondeterministic. The rule for *process instantiation* indicates that the actions of a process instantiation are those of the behaviour expression of its associated process definition (rule a8).

Inference rules for tick transitions

These rules define the transition relation B1===1===>B2, where *B1* and *B2* are behaviour expressions and *1* is the time unit, or 'tick'. Thus, these rules define whether and how a behaviour can be aged.

An *action prefix expression* can age by one time unit without transforming into a different expression (rule t1). This implies that the same expression can age unboundedly. Rule t2 indicates that a *tick prefix* is consumed by a tick transition. The *choice* and *parallel expressions* can age provided that the two arguments of the operator be able to do so (rules t3 and t4).

The *urgency operator,* ρ, is meant to allow the passing of time only if no urgent action is immediately possible. That is, the operator imposes a priority of urgent action transitions over tick transitions. This is expressed by rule t5, the only one that makes use of the function α_a defined below. The urgency operator has a special dynamic nature, in the sense that, at the semantic level, it operates at the time when the first occurrence of action *a* becomes possible: its effect is the pruning of the time axis at that point in time. Rule t6 for process instantiation, combined with the similar rule a8, indicates that we can always replace a process identifier with the behaviour expression of its associated process definition. As an immediate consequence of the inference rules for tick transitions and of the definition of the time passing process **'1'**, we have that **1==1==>1.**

Auxiliary function α_a and consistency of definitions

Definition 3.1 (Function α_a)

Function α_a: Processes ---> {true, false}, parametric in action *a*, is a boolean function meant to indicate whether or not process B can immediately perform an a-action.

α_a (a.B)	=	true	
α_a(b.B)	=	false	if $b \neq a$
α_a((1).B)	=	false	
α_a(B1 + B2)	=	α_a(B1) or α_a(B2)	
α_a(B1 |S| B2)	=	α_a(B1) and α_a(B2)	if a is in S
	=	α_a(B1) or α_a(B2)	if a is not in S
α_a(ρ(U)B)	=	α_a(B)	
α_a(P)	=	α_a(B)	if P := B is a process definition. •

Proposition 3.1 (consistency of relation '--a-->' and function α_a)
If "B where P1 := B1, ..., Pn := Bn" is a guarded ρ1 specification, then B--a-->B', for some B', iff $\alpha_a(B)$ = true.
Proof See Appendix A, which also includes the definition of guarded specification.•

Tick transitions vs. time transitions

We discuss here an alternative formulation of the semantics in which *tick transitions* of type B==1==>B' are replaced by the more general class of *time transitions* of type B==t==>B', where t ranges in an integer time domain. The case of a dense (e.g. real) time domain is also shortly addressed. Let us initially assume an integer time domain. If time transitions are handled at the semantic level, it seems natural to consider the time prefix

(t). B

as a primitive operator. Every inference rule for tick transitions of Table 3.1 could be generalized in a straightforward way into a rule for time transitions. For example, rule t1 would become

rule t'1) a. B ==t==> a. B (t > 0).

The only exception is represented by rule t2 for tick prefix, whose direct generalization into the rule for time prefix

rule t'2.1) (t). B ==t==> B (t > 0)

would not suffice. Such rule expresses the total consumption of the time prefix in a single step. Clearly, for properly handling expressions such as

(t1). a. **1** ||| (t1+t2). b. **1**

where t1, t2 > 0, we should be able to split the transition '==(t1+t2)==>' into two steps. This would be made possible by the following

rule t'2.2) (t1+t2). B ==t1==> (t2). B (t1, t2 > 0).

Rules t'2.1 and t'2.2 are present also in TCCS [MT90].

Opposite to performing a time transition into two steps (splitting), one might consider performing two of them in a single step (merging). In principle, such merging is easily achieved by the rule (also present in TCCS):

rule t'2.3) B ==t2==> B' implies (t1). B ==(t1+t2)==> B'

However, such rule can *not* be included in our language, because it would annihilate the effect of the urgency operator. For example, given expression:

ρ(a)
((t1). a. **1** |[a]| (t1+t2). a. **1**),

due to such rule, the time transition '==(t1+t2+t3)==>' would be possible, with t1, t2, t3 > 0, while the intention was to force an execution of interaction *a* at time (t1+t2). In other words, if we do not want to overlook urgent synchronizations, we must proceed carefully in time: we can not consume in a single transition more time than what is expressed in a single time prefix. A somewhat bizarre consequence of this fact is that the two expressions

(t1+t2). B   and   (t1).(t2). B

would not be equivalent: only the first one can perform transition '==(t1+t2)==>'.

In conclusion, in the context of integer time we only see disadvantages, both at an intuitive and at a technical level, in adopting a time transition semantics (notably rules t'2.1 and t'2.2), as opposed to a tick transition semantics. In integer time, the time unit is to be considered as a fundamental building block of the language, and there is no point in expliciting all the ways in which a time interval is split (as done by rule t'2.2) when we can say, at a more fundamental level, that it can be consumed in steps on unit length. And, even when a *primitive* time prefix operator '(t). B' is desired, we can easily replace rules t'2.1 and t'2.2 by:

rule t"2.1)   (1). B ==1==> B
rule t"2.2)   (t). B ==1==> (t-1). B   (t > 0).

Furthermore, any technical problem introduced by the consideration of time transitions of unbounded length vanishes by definition when we stick to a tick transition semantics. For example, the two time prefix expressions introduced above are in such case equivalent.

On the contrary, rules t'2.1 and t'2.2 are very appropriate in the context of dense time, where no indivisible time unit is available. Indeed, rule t'2.2 can be considered, in a sense, as *the definition* of time density. However, in a dense time version of our semantics, the reasons for omitting rule t'2.3 would still be valid, and the difficulty of coping with the bizarre inequivalence of the two time prefix expressions would return.

Persistency of action possibility

In the Time Petri Net model of [MF76] an enabled transition cannot be disabled by a pure time delay, but exclusively by the firing of another transition. In line with the analogy between these timed nets and the $\rho 1$ language, a similar property holds for the latter, as captured by the proposition below.

Proposition 3.2 (persistency of action possibility)
If "B where P1 := B1, ..., Pn := Bn" is a guarded $\rho 1$ specification, such that B--a-->, for some action *a*, and B==1==>B', for some behaviour expression B', then B'--a-->.

Proof See Appendix A, which also includes the definition of guarded specification .

4. Expressivity

Two points of view are possible for discussing the *expressivity* of a language or formalism. On one hand one may use informal but convincing arguments and examples (e.g. Figures 2.1 and 2.2) for showing that the language under consideration is indeed able to express a given set of desired concepts or constructs in a concise and intuitive way. In such case, we could also use the term *expressive flexibility*. As a second possibility, one may take the formal, well-established, language-theoretic approach, and show that the formalism under study is capable of expressing the widest possible class of formal languages, that is, it is capable of simulating Turing Machines. We can pose such problem with respect to $\rho 1$ since, by abstracting away the tick-transitions of the time/action trees that the language ultimately expresses, we can indeed view the paths on such trees as words of a language.

We show here that ρ1 can simulate Turing Machines by proving that it can simulate Two-Counter machines, which, in turn, can simulate Turing Machines [M61]. In deriving such result we shall take advantage of the analogy between our language and the Merlin-Farber's Time Petri Nets: Two-Counter machines can be simulated by such Petri Nets, as shown in [JLL77], and, although no formal mapping between Time Petri Nets and ρ1 is available, the analogy between the two models has been helpful in deriving the construction introduced below from the one of [JLL77].

Two-counter machines

An input-free two-counter machine is a 6-tuple <States, S_0, S_{fin}, I, C1, C2> where:

States	is a finite set of states; we shall let P, Q and R range in this set;
S_0	is the initial state;
S_{fin}	is the final state;
I	is a finite set of instructions;
C1 and C2	are counters, each of which can store a nonnegative integer.

The counters are initially set to 0. The types of instructions and their meanings are listed in Table 4.1 below. P, Q , and R are states.

Table 4.1 - Types of instructions for two counter machines (and ρ1 actions)

Instruction		Meaning	ρ1 actions
(P, incr-i, Q)	i = 1, 2	in state P, increment Ci by one and go to state Q.	p-incr-i
(P, decr-i, Q)	i = 1, 2	in state P, decrement Ci by one and go to state Q.	p-decr-i
(P, test-i, Q, R)	i = 1, 2	in state P, test counter Ci: go to Q if Ci = 0, otherwise go to R.	p-test-i p-timeout-i

The machine is deterministic, so that there is at most one instruction for each state P. Computations that attempt to decrement any empty counter are undefined.

Specification in ρ1 of a generic two-counter machine

For every instruction of the two-counter machine we shall have one or two actions in the ρ1 specification, according to Table 4.1. In such table, *p* and *i* are, respectively, a variable prefix and a variable suffix of action identifiers (*p* ranges in States, *i* ranges in {1, 2}). We shall group the actions above in sets, as follows:

$$\text{Incr-i} = \{\text{p-incr-i} \mid (P, \text{incr-i}, Q) \text{ is an instruction}\} \qquad (i = 1, 2)$$

$$\text{Incr} = \text{Incr-1} \cup \text{Incr-2}$$

The sets Decr-i, Test-i, Timeout-i, and Decr, Test, Timeout are similarly defined. The basic idea of the specification is to have a ρ1 process P for each state P of the machine, and two processes C1 and C2 for the two counters.

```
Two-counter-machine :=      ρ(Test)      (      S0
                                                | Incr ∪ Decr ∪ Test |
                                                (C1 ||| C2)
                                         )
where

P  := p-incr-i.  Q          (* if (P, incr-i, Q) is an instruction (i = 1,2) *)
P  := p-decr-i.  Q          (* if (P, decr-i, Q) is an instruction (i = 1,2) *)

P  :=     (1). p-timeout-i. Q
       +  p-test-i. R       (* if (P, test-i, Q, R) is an instruction (i = 1,2)*)

P  := 1                     (* if P only appears as a target state in the instructions *)


Ci    := Σ{incr. (Ci ||| CCi)  | incr ∈ Incr-i}                       (* i = 1, 2 *)
CCi   := Σ{test.CCi + decr. 1  | test ∈ Test-i, decr ∈ Decr-i}        (* i = 1, 2 *)
```

We use the symbol 'Σ' for multiple applications of the choice operator '+', and we let Σ{ }=**1**. Observe that all the operators of the language are represented in the specification.

Example

Consider the two-counter machine M = <States, S_0, S_{fin}, I, C1, C2> where:

States	= {S_0, P, Q, R, S, S_{fin}}
S_0	is the initial state;
S_{fin}	is the final state;
I	= {(S_0, incr-1, P), (P, decr-1, Q), (Q, test-1, R, S), (R, test-2, S, S_{fin})};
C1 and C2	are the two counters, initially set to 0.

The ρ1 specification of such machine is:

```
Two-counter-machine :=      ρ (q-test-1, r-test-2)
                                (       S0
                                        |[ s0-incr-1, p-decr-1, q-test-1, r-test-2 ]|
                                        (C1 ||| C2)
                                )
where
S0     :=    s0-incr-1.  P
P      :=    p-decr-1.  Q
Q      :=    (1). q-timeout-1. R  +  q-test-1. S
R      :=    (1). r-timeout-2. S  +  r-test-2. Sfin
Sfin   :=    1

C1     :=    s0-incr-1.  (C1 ||| CC1)
CC1    :=    q-test-1. CC1  +  p-decr-1.  1
C2     :=    1
CC2    :=    r-test-2. CC2
```

The specification above can be better understood by considering the Time Petri Net of Figure 4.1.

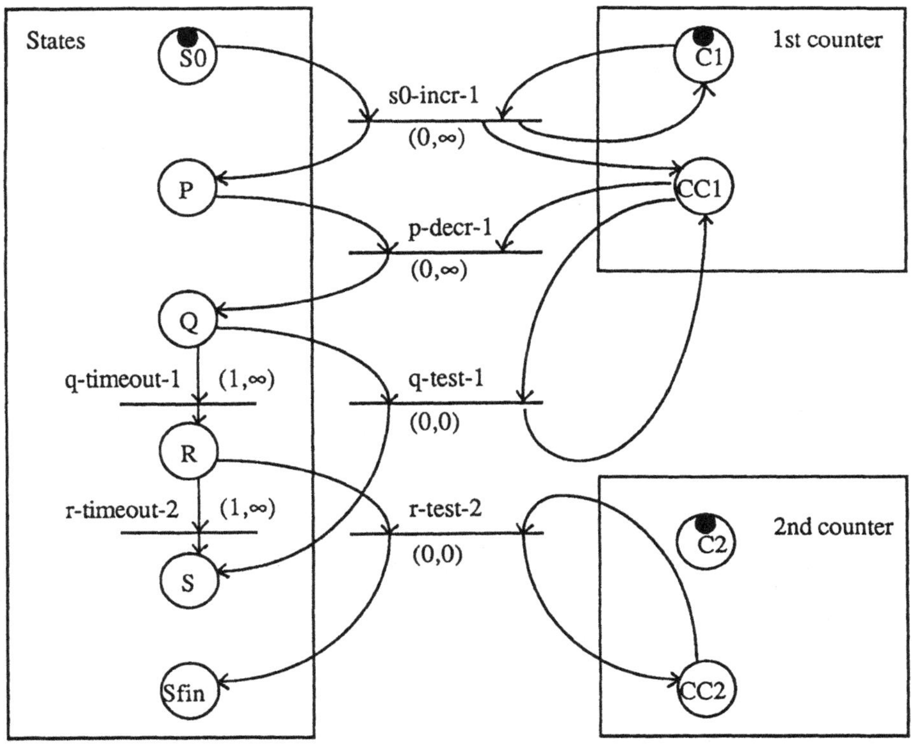

Figure 4.1 - A Time Petri Net for the ρ1 specification of a two-counter machine

5. Related models and laws

We examine now some related work. We have already mentioned in Section 2 timed extensions to LOTOS based on a timed-action prefix policy ([QF87] and [QAF89]), and the fact that, driven by the lesson of Petri nets, we have chosen instead a timed-interaction policy. Our first attempt to enhance the LOTOS language with timed-interactions is presented in [BLT90]. The key feature of that proposal is the 'timer' operator:

timer a(t1, t2) in B

where (t1, t2) is a time interval and B is a behaviour expression. The idea is that any action or interaction *a* which becomes enabled during the evolution of *B*, say, at time t, can only occur within time window (t+t1, t+t2). Clearly, the operator was inspired by the timed transitions of Time Petri Nets. The ρ1 language proposed here improves [BLT90] in two ways. First, we have replaced the unique 'timer' operator by two more fundamental operators, namely time-prefix and urgency. By decoupling these two time related constructs, and by adopting an action prefix operator where the action is offered at any time, ρ1 reflects quite directly the three types of transitions (namely unconstrained local, fixed-time local, and urgent synchronization transitions) that characterize a fully expressive subset of Time Petri Nets, as discussed in Section 2. Second, by decoupling the time and action dimensions, as suggested for instance by TCCS, and adopting time/action trees (Figure 3.1), as opposed to timed-action trees (where arcs are labelled by actions with absolute or relative time stamps), we have completely changed the shape of the Structured Operational Semantics of the language, which consists now of three clear and concise pieces (Section 3). The formal semantics provided in [BLT90] was certainly more complex, and suffered from some weak points, that are discussed in [BLT90a].

While the 'timer' operator of [BLT90] is not an operator of ρ1, we can still define a derived operator that associates a time interval to an *action prefix.* The *timed-action-prefix* operator is defined in terms of the primitive tick-prefix and action-prefix, as follows:

$$a(t1, t2).\ B \quad = \quad (t1).\ a.\ B\ +\ (t2).\ \mathbf{0}$$

Another timed extension of LOTOS is presented in [VHTZ89]; more than a basic calculus, this Clock-Extended LOTOS has the flavour of an implementation-oriented enhancement of the language that offers constructs for explicitly starting, reading and resetting timers upon the occurrence of events. The formal semantics is correspondingly complex, but the comparison with timed process algebras is probably inappropriate. (An unpleasant feature of this language is that a time deadlock is never possible: thus, action necessity cannot be expressed.) Some ideas on the explicit manipulation of timers in LOTOS are discussed also in [B88].

The literature on timed process algebras is rapidly growing, and an exhaustive survey of the area is out of the scope of this paper (see [NS90], Section 7). Here, we shall mainly concentrate on two approaches, namely TCCS, the Timed Calculus of Communicating Systems [MT90] and ATP, Algebra for Timed Processes [NRSV90] (an algebra closest to the latter is presented in [G90]), since their comparison with ρ1 provides a sufficient basis for covering the fundamental aspects and possible choices connected with time-related constructs.

Some differences among these three languages are independent of their time related features, and are due to the facts that TCCS is a timed extension of CCS [M80], ATP borrows some features of ACP [BK84], and our algebras are based on LOTOS. Thus the communication features of these timed algebras reflect those of their untimed counterparts: TCCS only supports two-way synchronization, while multi-way synchronization is possible for ATP and ρ1, although in the latter the action set has less structure than in ATP. The discussion becomes more interesting when we concentrate on the time-related features of these languages. In this respect, the following commonalities and differences can be observed:

1. At the semantic level, all these languages distinguish between the time passing event and all the other actions, which take no time to execute. Thus, the underlying model is what we have called time/action trees. In ATP the tick event is called χ, while in ρ1 tick transitions are labelled by '1': in both cases time is discrete. In TCCS, the inference rules for time passing transitions handle directly time delays of any length , and can be interpreted also in the context of a dense time domain. We have already discussed tick-transitions vs. time-transitions in Section 3, and have already argued that, in the context of discrete time, the former approach seems more appropriate.

2. At the syntax level, a time delay prefix operator *(t).B* is available as a primitive operator in TCCS, and as a derived operator in ρ1 and ATP.

3. In TCCS and in ATP, an action prefix *a.B* expresses the fact that *a* must occur immediately; however, by using a delay prefix operator *δ. B* (which is a primitive operator in TCCS, and a derived operator in ATP and in SCCS [M83]), one can delay the (first) actions of *B* by an undefined amount of time. In ρ1 we take a somewhat dual approach: the arbitrary delay of the action in an action prefix *a.B* is built in the language (similarly to Milner's ASCCS [M83]), while the urgency of an action (which may or may not be currently available) can be expressed by applying the ρ operator.
In our opinion, the combination of a *delayed* action prefix with an *urgency* operator offers an advantage over the combination of an *urgent* action prefix with a *delay* operator: once

the urgency operator is explicitly available, it can be applied not only locally, to an action prefix, but also at a more global level, to a synchronization event in a parallel composition. Such usage of the operator was crucial in the construction of Section 4. The ideas above are summarized in Table 5.1 (the symbol ρ was indeed chosen for its similarity with a reversed δ) .

Table 5.1 - Urgency in TCCS and in ρ1

	TCCS	ρ1 language
action prefix	a. B urgent	a. B not urgent
time-related operator	δ. B for relaxing urgency	ρ(a) B for enforcing urgency of *a*

4. In all three languages, rules are provided for expressing the fact that time transitions in the components of a parallel composition or of a choice (a 'strong' choice, see below) occur synchronously, so that, as long as all the components are active, time progress is the same in all of them.

5. All three languages offer what TCCS calls a 'strong' choice operator, denoted by '+' in TCCS and in ρ1, and by '⊕' in ATP: the choice can only be made by an action, not by a time event. However, TCCS offers also a 'weak' choice, denoted by '⊕' (the coincidence is unfortunate), which can be driven by time transitions too. As a consequence, a time transition can disable an action transition. A similar capability is offered by the *unit delay* binary operator of ATP: expression ⌊P⌋(Q) denotes the process that behaves as P (the *body*), if P starts immediately, or that performs a tick transition and then behaves like Q (the *exception*). For example, TCCS expression 'a.P ⊕ (1).Q' (which includes a tick-prefix) and ATP expression '⌊a.P⌋(Q)' are equivalent, and correspond to the time/action tree of Figure 5.1 below:

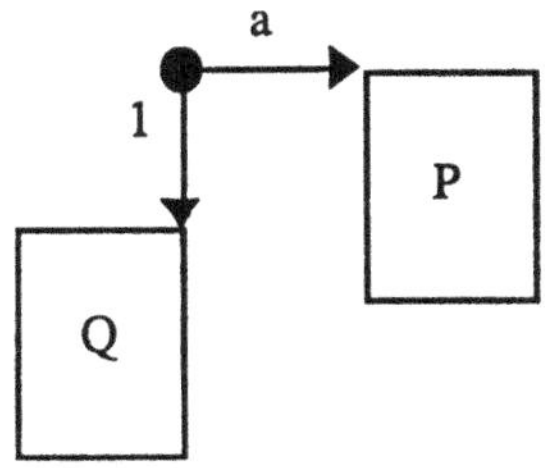

Figure 5.1 - A choice driven by a tick-transition

Conversely, in analogy with Time Peri Nets, where an enabled transition cannot be disabled by a pure time delay, the ρ1 language *cannot* express such a scenario. This is due to the persistency of action possibility (Section 3). The weak choice or unit-delay binary operator can be typically used for describing a timeout situation where a boundary tick-transition separates the 'still in time' and the 'too late' phases. However, a timeout scenario can still be adequately described in the ρ1 language, as we have done in Figure

2.2: the only difference is that, at the very moment when the timeout is executable, the action waited for (message arrival) is still possible, the choice being nondeterministic.

Other proposals for timed CCS are found in [HR90] and [Y90]. In both proposals only internal actions, which may result from synchronization, are urgent, while the actions expressed in action prefix are not. In the second one, time is continuous. Timed extensions of the ACP algebra [BK84] are found in the already mentioned [G90] and in [BB89]. (See [NS90] for a concise survey on these algebras.)

Another extension of CCS with time and also probabilities is presented in [HJ90], where a binary timeout operator is proposed which resembles the unit-delay operator of ATP.

In Timed CSP [RR86], urgency is built into the *hiding* operator. Based on the idea that internal actions, including synchronization, do not need participation from the external environment, they can take place as soon as they are possible. We have not included internal actions and hiding in ρ1, and urgency is provided by our language via the explicit ρ operator.

The formal semantics presented in [RR86] is given in a denotational style completely different from the one adopted here for ρ1 (SOS - Structured Operational Semantics). However a SOS semantics for Timed CSP has been given very recently [S91], where the time and action dimensions are treated separately, as in (e.g.) TCCS, ATP and ρ1. In particular, the time transition P==(t)==>P' is represented by the *evolution* relation E(P, P', t). A peculiar feature of Timed CSP, meant to achieve realism, is that, after performing an action, a process takes some non zero time δ to recover, before offering the next action.

We provide now some simple strong bisimulation equivalence laws for ρ1 expressions, mainly involving the time-related operators and processes **0** and **1**.

ρ(a) (b. B)	~	b. ρ(a) B	(a ≠ b)
ρ(a) ((1). B)	~	(1). ρ(a) B	
ρ(a) (B1 + B2)	~	ρ(a)B1 + ρ(a)B2	
ρ(a) (B1 |S| B2)	~	ρ(a)B1 |S| ρ(a)B2	(when a ∉ S)
ρ(a) (a. B)	~	a. B + **0**	(when a is not an action of B)
(1).B + **0**	~	**0**	
(1).B |S| **0**	~	**0**	
B + **1**	~	B	
B ||| **1**	~	B	
(1).(B1 + B2)	~	(1).B1 + (1).B2	
(1).(B1 |S| B2)	~	(1).B1 |S| (1).B2	

Finally, we give some special combinations of the operators, and their meanings:

B + **0**	Makes the possible first actions of B urgent.
B ||| **0**	Only what B can do immediately.
B + (t). **0**	Forces B to be active at most at time t.
B ||| (t). **0**	The behaviour of B up to at most at time t.
B |AllGates| **1**	A time delay equal to the maximum inactivity time of B.

6. The ρ2 language and its general-purpose binary operator

The Time Petri Nets of [MF76] were explicitly introduced for expressing timeouts in communication protocols. We have shown how our ρ1 language, inspired to those nets, is indeed capable of satisfactorily expressing a timeout behaviour (Figure 2.2). The essence of a timeout scenario is captured by the ρ1 expression:

(6.1) a.P + (t). ρ(timeout) timeout.Q

When action *a* occurs in the first argument of the choice, the second argument is eliminated, and when the *timeout* action occurs in the second argument, it is the first one to be eliminated. However, a frequently occurring timeout scenario is one were the possibility of a timeout event is not pre-emptied by the first event of the behaviour controlled by the (implicit) timer. In such case, expression

(6.2) a. b. c. P + (t). ρ(timeout) timeout.Q

would not capture what we want, because the timer does not survive the *a* event. The binary operator which lets its components survive each other's actions is interleaving ('|||'). However, expression

(6.3) a. b. c. P ||| (t). ρ(timeout) timeout.Q

would still be inappropriate, because the left argument would survive even the timeout event. We could then consider a combination of the choice and the interleaving operators, that behaves as the former w.r.t. the left argument, and as the latter w.r.t. the right argument, and denote it by the symbol '|||+"; the inference rules for it would be copies of rules (a3), (a5) and (t3) of Table 3.1). Then, we could try to specify our timeout scenario by the expression:

(6.4) a. b. c. P |||+ (t). ρ(timeout) timeout.Q

However, the new operator is not yet satisfactory in one respect: the timer can indeed survive the sequence of actions a, b, and c, but is not disabled by anyone of them. This is unfortunate, because in the previous expression (6.1) we were actually able to say that the precise occurrence of action *a* has such an effect. A step in this direction has been taken by LOTOS, via the disabling operator. In expression B1[>B2 (which reads "B1 is disabled by B2"), any first action of B2 disables B1, but the occurrence of the *successful termination action* (δ) in B1 disables, in turn, B2. A completely similar effect is achieved, in the context of the binary delay operators of ATP [NS90], by a special *cancel* action, denoted ξ.

A direct generalization of these ideas has suggested us to define a parametric binary operator which, again, combines the features of '+' and '|||', and offers at the same time more flexibility. We shall denote it by '+G1|||G2+', or (for improving readability) '<G1|||G2>', where G1 and G2 are gate sets. The behaviour B1 <G1|||G2> B2 consists of the interleaving of the two behaviours B1 and B2, with the exception that any action of B1 (resp. B2) in gate set G1 (resp. G2) disables behaviour B2 (resp. B1).

Indeed, by considering that interleaving is a special case of parallel composition where the set S of synchronization gates is empty, we can further generalize our binary operator, thus obtaining:

B1 <G1|S|G2> B2

We impose that both G1 and G2 be disjoint with S: no argument is eliminated by a synchronization action. The formal semantics of this powerful binary operator is provided in

Table 6.1 below, which indeed presents all the operators of a new language, called ρ2. We have simply imported the action- and tick-prefix operators, urgency, and process instantiation from ρ1; choice and parallel composition are not needed, being special cases of the newly introduced operator. Since this is the only binary operator needed, it needs no other name than 'binary operator'.

Table 6.1 - Inference rules for action and aging transitions of ρ2

<table>
<tr><th>Syntax</th><th>Action transitions</th><th>Tick transitions</th></tr>
<tr><td>action prefix
a. B</td><td>a1) a.B--a-->B</td><td>t1) a.B==1==>a.B</td></tr>
<tr><td>tick prefix
(1). B</td><td>-</td><td>t2) (1).B==1==>B</td></tr>
<tr><td>binary operator
$B1\langle G1 \mid S \mid G2\rangle B2$</td><td>a2) $\dfrac{B1\text{--a-->}B1',\ a \text{ in } G1}{B1\langle G1 \mid S \mid G2\rangle B2\text{--a-->}B1'}$

a3) symmetric of rule above

a4) $\dfrac{B1\text{--a-->}B1',\ a \text{ not in } G1,\ a \text{ not in } S}{B1\langle G1 \mid S \mid G2\rangle B2\text{--a-->}B1'\langle G1 \mid S \mid G2\rangle B2}$

a5) symmetric of rule above

a6) $\dfrac{B1\text{--a-->}B1',\ B2\text{--a-->}B2',\ a \text{ in } S}{B1\langle G1 \mid S \mid G2\rangle B2\text{--a-->}B1'\langle G1 \mid S \mid G2\rangle B2'}$</td><td>t3) $\dfrac{B1\text{==1==>}B1' \text{ and } B2\text{==1==>}B2'}{B1\langle G1 \mid S \mid G2\rangle B2\text{==1==>}B1'\langle G1 \mid S \mid G2\rangle B2'}$</td></tr>
<tr><td>urgency
ρ(U) in B</td><td>a7) $\dfrac{B\text{--a-->}B'}{\rho(U)B \text{ --a-->}\rho(U)B'}$</td><td>t5) $\dfrac{B\text{==1==>}B' \text{ and } \forall a \in U.\ \text{not } \alpha a(B)}{\rho(U)B \text{ ==1==> } \rho(U)B'}$</td></tr>
<tr><td>proc. inst.
P</td><td>a8) $\dfrac{B\text{--a-->}B' \text{ and } P{:=}B \text{ is a proc.def.}}{P\text{--a-->}B'}$</td><td>t6) $\dfrac{B\text{==1==>}B' \text{ and } P{:=}B \text{ is a proc.def.}}{P\text{=1==>}B'}$</td></tr>
</table>

Definition 6.1 (Function α_a - Compare with Def. 3.1)

α_a (a.B)	=	true	
α_a(b.B)	=	false	if $b \neq a$
α_a((1).B)	=	false	
α_a(B1 <G1|S|G2> B2)	=	α_a(B1) and α_a(B2)	if $a \in S$
	=	α_a(B1) or α_a(B2)	if $a \notin S$
$\alpha_a(\rho(U)B)$	=	α_a(B)	
α_a(P)	=	α_a(B)	if P:=B is a proc. def. •

The set of derived operators and shorthands can be summarized as follows:

<table>
<tr><td>1</td><td>time passing process</td><td>1 := (1). 1</td></tr>
<tr><td>0</td><td>time deadlock process</td><td>0 := (ρ(a) a. 1) |[a]| 1</td></tr>
<tr><td>(t). B</td><td>time prefix</td><td>(1).(1). ... (1). B
(t occurrences of the tick-prefix).</td></tr>
<tr><td>a(t1, t2). B</td><td>timed action prefix</td><td>((t1). a. B + (t2). 0)</td></tr>
<tr><td>B1 + B2</td><td>choice</td><td>B1 <AllGates|Ø|AllGates> B2</td></tr>
<tr><td>B1 ||| B2</td><td>interleaving</td><td>B1 <Ø|Ø|Ø> B2</td></tr>
<tr><td>B1 |S| B2</td><td>general parallel composition</td><td>B1 <Ø|S|Ø> B2</td></tr>
<tr><td>B1 |||+ B2</td><td>disabling</td><td>B1 <Ø|Ø|AllGates> B2</td></tr>
<tr><td>(B1 [> B2</td><td>LOTOS-like disabling</td><td>B1 <δ|Ø|AllGates> B2)</td></tr>
</table>

We conclude this section by giving two examples. The first one is a Login Procedure, taken from [NS90] (the informal description below is also borrowed from that source).

> To start the procedure, the system sends a login *prompt*. Then the user must enter a *valid* login response within *t* time units. In this case the login procedure is terminated, and the system enters a *Session* phase. If the login response is *invalid* , or if it is not provided before *t* units of time, the system rejects the current login request and starts a new one. However, we want to control the overall duration of the login procedure by imposing the execution of an *Exception* if a valid response has not been entered within *d* time units.

[NS90] presents a quite compact specification in ATP of the Login Procedure. In Figure 6.1 we present our Time Petri Net formalization of the procedure.

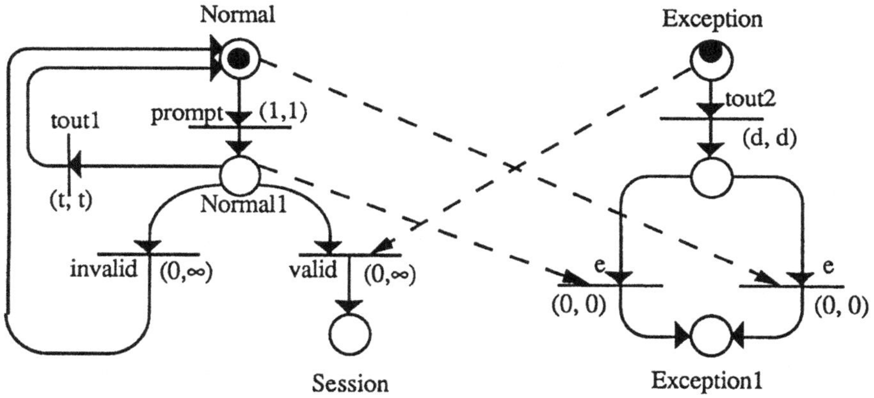

Figure 6.1 - A Time Petri Net for the Login Procedure

In Figure 6.2 we formalize the login procedure in the ρ1 language. Note that the processes Session and Exception1 are left unspecified (both here and in the subsequent example). The structural similarity of such specification with the Petri Net above is quite evident.

LoginProcedure := ρ(e)
(Normal |[valid, e]| Exception)
where

Normal := (1). ρ(prompt)(prompt. Normal1)
+ e. **1**

Normal1 := invalid. Normal + valid. Session + (t).ρ(tout1) (tout1. Normal)
+ e. **1**

Exception := (d). ρ(tout2) (tout2. e. Exception1)
+ valid. **1**

Figure 6.2 - A specification in ρ1 of the Login Procedure

The second example is an improved version of the Login Procedure, meant to illustrate the enhanced expressive flexibility of the newly introduced parametric binary operator. The example is called 'Login Procedure with Counter', because the user repeatedly attempting to login can be interrupted either when the 'external' timer expires (after *d* time units) or when the number of failures (wrong passwords) has reached a pre-defined upper bound, whichever comes first.

LoginProcedureWithCounter :=

Normal <valid | invalid | tout2, toomany> Exception
where

Normal := (1). ρ(prompt)(prompt. Normal1)

Normal1 := invalid. Normal + valid. Session + (t).ρ(tout1) (tout1. Normal)

Exception := Timer <tout2 |Ø| toomany > $Counter_n$

Timer := (d). ρ(tout2) (tout2. Exception1)

$Counter_n$:= invalid. $Counter_{n-1}$

......

$Counter_0$:= ρ(toomany) (toomany. Exception1)

Figure 6.3 - A specification in ρ2 of the Login Procedure with Counter

We find that the inclusion of gate lists in the binary operator improves the readability of the specification: by reading the topmost expression of the specification above, we immediately get the information that a *valid* event in process *Normal* disables process *Exception*, that a *tout2* or *toomany* event in process *Exception* disables process *Normal*, and that the *invalid* event must involve both processes.

7. Conclusions

The ρ1 language is the result of an effort to transpose in the realm of process algebras the main ideas and features of the Time Petri Net model of [MF76]. The language can be seen as a timed enhancement of (a subset of) LOTOS: indeed the inference rules for action transitions, relative to the operators shared by the two languages, turn out to be identical. We claim that the formal semantics of the language, as presented here, is quite clear and concise, due to the choice of separating the time and the action dimensions, which we have borrowed from the elegant definition of TCCS by Tofts and Moller [MT90].

Emphasis has been put in this paper on the *expressive power* and *expressive flexibility* of the proposed languages. An important clarification is necessary here. We have argued that the timed-interaction policy, essentially represented by the urgency operator, is preferable to a timed-action-prefix policy. In saying this, we refer both to expressive power and to expressive flexibility, in the following sense. The weak *expressive flexibility* of the timed-action-prefix approach is revealed, for instance, by trying to specify the symmetric timeout example of Figure 2.1. With timed-action-prefixes only, there is no way to structure the system as a parallel composition of two processes, as desirable (P and Q might be more complex than depicted by the example...). The only solution to express the urgency of synchronization *a* would be to express explicitly the interleaving of the delay actions d1 and d2 (essentially: 'd1(0, ∞); d2(0, ∞); a(0, 0) ... + d2(0, ∞); d1(0, ∞); a(0, 0) ...').

As far as the theoretic expressive power is concerned, the comparison between the two approaches should not be oversimplified. Clearly, the complete set of Basic LOTOS operators, enhanced just by the inclusion of timed-action-prefix (in the spirit of the proposals of [QF87] and [QAF89]) *can* simulate Turing Machines, since the pure Basic LOTOS itself, as well as CCS and all reasonable, untimed process algebras can. Our aim, in designing the ρ1 language, has been, rather, to deliberately select a small, fundamental yet *not* Turing powerful, set of operators (simply *action prefix, choice, parallel composition, recursion*), and to provide it with such expressive power by just adding elementary time-related operators (tick-prefix and urgency). As already mentioned, a similar step in expressive power can be observed in passing from untimed Petri Nets to the Timed Nets of [MF76].

The ρ2 language absorbs the two binary operators of ρ1 into a unique, powerful, parametric, binary operator that offers the additional functionality of a flexible two-way disabling operator. The expressive power of ρ2 is the same as for ρ1; its expressive flexibility has been illustrated by an example.

A topic for further resarch is the (possibly partial) formalization of the mapping between Time Petri Nets and ρ1 or ρ2. In particular, variants of Time Petri Nets that match the disabling functionality of ρ2 could be investigated. The possibility to translate some perhaps restricted version of ρ2 into some form of timed Petri nets should be favoured by the fact that the former does not include a hiding, nor any gate relabelling operator.

Acknowledgement
We would like to express our gratitude to Sebastiano Trigila and Xavier Nicollin for discussions on various aspects of the work presented here, to an anonymous referee for having suggested the definition of the time deadlock process, and to Paola Quaglia for her careful reading of the manuscript.

References

[B88] E. Brinksma, "On the Design of Extended LOTOS", Ph.D. Thesis, University of Twente, 1988.

[B89] E. Brinksma (ed.) - ISO - Information Processing Systems - Open Systems Interconnection - "LOTOS - A Formal Description Technique Based on the Temporal Ordering of Observational Behaviour", IS 8807, 1989.

[BB87] T. Bolognesi, E. Brinksma, "Introduction to the ISO Specification Language LOTOS", *Computer Networks and ISDN Systems*, Vol. 14, No 1, 1987.

[BB89] J.C.M. Baeten, J.A. Bergstra, 'Real Time Process Algebra', Technical Report, Centre for Mathematics and Computer Science, Amsterdam, 1989.

[BC89] T. Bolognesi, P. Cremonese, "The Weakness of Some Timed Models for Concurrent Systems", Technical Report CNUCE C89-29, CNUCE - C.N.R., Pisa, October 1989.

[BK84] J. A. Bergstra, J. W. Klop, "Process Algebra for Synchronous Communication", *Information and Control*, 60 (1-3), 1984.

[BLT90] T. Bolognesi, F. Lucidi, S. Trigila, "From Timed Petri Nets to Timed LOTOS", *Proceedings of the Tenth International IFIP WG6.1 Symposium on Protocol Specification, Testing, and Verification*, L. Logrippo, R. L. Probert, H. Ural editors, North-Holland 1990.

[BLT90a] T. Bolognesi, F. Lucidi, S. Trigila, "New Proposals for Timed-Interaction LOTOS", Technical Rep. 5-B-55-90 , Fondazione U. Bordoni, Roma, Italy, 1990.

[BR85] T. Bolognesi, H. Rudin, "On the Analysis of Time-Dependent Protocols by Network Flow Algorithms", *Proceedings of the IFIP WG6.1 Fourth International Workshop on Protocol Specification, Testing, and Verification*, Y. Yemini, R. Strom, S. Yemini editors, North-Holland 1985, pp.491-514.

[G90] J. F. Groote, "Specification and Verification of Real Time Systems in ACP", *Proceedings of the Tenth International IFIP WG6.1 Symposium on Protocol Specification, Testing, and Verification*, L. Logrippo, R. L. Probert, H. Ural editors, North-Holland 1990.

[HJ90] H. Hansson, B. Jonsson, 'A Calculus for Communicating Systems with Time and Probabilities', *Proceedings of the 11th Real-Time Systems Symposium*, IEEE Computer Society, 1990, pp. 278-287

[HR90] M. Hennessy, T. Regan, 'A Temporal Process Algebra', Tech. Rep. 2/90, University of Sussex, April 1990.

[JLL77] N. D. Jones, L. H. Landweber, Y. E. Lien, "Complexity of some problems in Petri Nets", *Theoretical Computer Science* 4, 1977, pp. 277-299.

[M61] M. Minsky, "Recursive unsolvability of Post's problem", *Ann. of Math.* 74, 1961, pp. 437-454.

[M80] R. Milner, A Calculus of Communicating Systems, *Lecture Notes in Computer Science*, Vol.92, Springer-Verlag, 1980.

[M83] R. Milner, "Calculi for Synchrony and Asynchrony", *Theor. Computer Science*, 25, 1983.

[MF76] P. Merlin, D. J. Farber, "Recoverability of Communication Protocols - Implications of a Theoretical Study", *IEEE Trans. Commun.*, Vol. COM-24, Sept. 1976, pp. 1036-1043.

[MT90] F. Moller, C. Tofts, "A Temporal Calculus of Communicating Systems", *Proceed. of CONCUR'90*, LNCS N. 458, North-Holland, 1990.

[NRSV90] X. Nicollin, J.-L. Richier, J. Sifakis, J. Voiron, "ATP: An Algebra for Timed Processes" Project SPECTRE, Groupe Spécification et Analyse des Systemes, Laboratoire de Génie Informatique de Grenoble, Technical Report RT-C16, Jan. 1990.

[NS90] X. Nicollin, J. Sifakis "The Algebra of Timed Processes ATP: Theory and Applications " Project SPECTRE, Groupe Spécification et Analyse des Systemes, Laboratoire de Génie Informatique de Grenoble, Technical Report RT-C26, Dec. 1990.

[P81] G. D. Plotkin, "A structural approach to operational semantics", Tech. Rep. DAIMI FN-19, Aarhus Univ., Computer Science Dept., Denmark, 1981.

[QAF89] J. Quemada, A. Azcorra, D.Frutos "A Timed Calculus for LOTOS", *Proceedings of FORTE '89 Second International Conference on Formal Description Techniques for Distributed Systems and Communications Protocols*, Vancouver,Canada, December 1989.

[QF87] J. Quemada, A. Fernandez, "Introduction of Quantitative Relative Time into LOTOS", *Proceedings of IFIP WG 6.1 Seventh International Conference on Protocol Specification, Testing, and Verification*, H.Rudin, C. H. West Editors, North-Holland, 1987, pp. 105-121.

[R85] H. Rudin, "Time in Formal Protocol Specifications", *Proceedings of the GI/NTG Conference on Communication in Distrib. Systems*, Karlsruhe, West Germany, March 11-15, 1985, Springer-Verlag Informatic Series N. 95, pp. 575-587.

[RR86] G. M. Reed and A. W. Roscoe, "A Timed Model for Communicating Sequential Processes", *Proceedings of ICALP'86, Lecture Notes in Computer Science* n. 226, Springer-Verlag, 1986, pp. 314-323.

[S91] S. Schneider, 'An Operational Semantics for Timed CSP', unpublished manuscript, Oxford University, Programming Research Group, may 1991.

[VHTZ89] W. H. P. van Hulzen, P. A. J. Tilanus, H. Zuidweg, "LOTOS Extended with Clocks", *proceedings of FORTE '89, Second International Conference on Formal Description Techniques for Distributed Systems and Communication Protocols*, S. T. Vuong editor, North-Holland 1990.

[W83] B. Walter, "Timed Petri-Nets for Modelling and Analyzing Protocols with Real-Time Characteristics", *Proceedings of 3rd IFIP Workshop on Protocol Specification, Testing, and Verification*, (H.Rudin, C. H. West Editors), North-Holland, 1983, pp. 149-159.

[Y90] W. Yi, 'Real-time behaviour of asynchronous agents', in J. C. M. Baeten and J. W. Klop, editors, LNCS 458, *Proceedings of Concur '90*, Amsterdam, The Netherlands, Springer-Verlag , Aug. 1990, pp. 502-520.

Appendix A

Definition A.1 (guarded ρ1 expression)
A *guarded* ρ1 *expression* is any expression derived from the root symbol E of the grammar below, which is built on top of the grammar for ρ1 expressions whose root is B. (Some instances of the nonterminals E and B are numbered for ease of reference.)

E ::= x.B | (t).B | E1+ E2 | E1 |S| E2 | ρ(U) E.

B ::= x.B | (t).B | B1+ B2 | B1 |S| B2 | ρ(U) B | P. •

x is an action identifier, t is non-negative integer time value, S is a set of gate identifiers, U is a nonempty set of gate identifiers, and P is a process identifier.

Proposition A.2
A guarded ρ1 expression is a ρ1 expression.

Proof
By structural induction on the set of guarded expressions, with a partial order '>' where 'x.B' and '(t).B' are the bottom elements (also of class B, trivially), and E1+ E2 > E1, E1+ E2 > E2, E1|S| E2 > E1, E1|S| E2 > E2, ρ(U) E > E. •

Clearly, a guarded expression has the property that any process identifier in it can only appear in the context of a prefix sub-expression (*a.B* or *(t).B*) of it.

Proposition A.3 (consistency of relation '--a-->' and function α_a for guarded expressions)
If E is a guarded expression, then E--a--> iff α_a(E) = true.

Proof
By structural induction on the set of guarded expressions, with a partial order '>' defined as in the proof of Proposition A.2 (where 'x.B' and '(t).B' are the bottom elements). We shall refer to the inference rules of Table 1.
Basis
If E = x.B, then: E--a--> iff x = a (by rule a1) iff α_a(x.B) = true (by definition of α_a). If E = (t).B, then E--a--> is false (since no action transition rules exist for time prefix) and α_a(E) = false (by definition of α_a), thus the double implication vacuously holds.
Step
If E = E1 + E2, then: E--a--> iff E1--a--> or E2--a--> (by rules a2 and a3), iff α_a(E1) = true or α_a(E2) = true (by the inductive hypothesis), iff α_a(E) = true (by definition of α_a).
Similarly, if E = E1 |S| E2, then E--a--> means that either rule a4 was applied, or rule a5 was applied (the case of rule a6 is symmetric). In the first case: E--a--> iff E1--a--> and E2--a-->, with a in S, iff α_a(E1) = true and α_a(E2) = true, iff α_a(E) = true. In the second case: E--a--> iff E1--a-->, with a not in S , iff α_a(E1) = true, iff α_a(E) = true. If E = ρ(U) E1, then: E--a--> iff E1--a-->, iff α_a(E1) = true, iff α_a(E) = true. •

Definition A.4 (guarded ρ1 specification)
The ρ1 specification *'B where P1 := B1, ..., Pn := Bn'* is ***guarded*** if, by recursively substituting for a finite number of times the expressions Bi's for the process identifiers Pi's occurring in B and in the Bi's themselves, it is possible to obtain an *expanded* ρ1 specification *'E where P1 := E1, ..., Pn := En'*, where E and the Ei's are guarded expressions. •

Clearly the two transition systems associated respectively with a ρ1 specification and with any of its expansions are identical, as implied by the substitution rules a8 and t6. Furthermore it is easy to realize that a guarded ρ1 specification can only transform, after an action or tick transition, into another guarded ρ1 specification.

Proposition 3.1 (consistency of relation '--a-->' and function α_a for guarded specifications) If *'B where P1 := B1, ..., Pn := Bn'* is a guarded ρ1 specification, then B--a-->B', for some B', iff α_a(B) = true.

Proof
Without loss of generality, we consider the expanded version E where P1 := E1, ..., Pn := En of the given, guarded specification, so that E and the Ei's are guarded expressions. The proof is done by structural induction on the set of guarded expressions, with a partial order '>' where the bottom elements are the process identifiers Pi's, including the special process identifiers **0** and **1**, and the partial order is defined by: x.B > B, (t).B > B, E1+E2 > E1, E1+E2 > E2, E1|S| E2 > E1, E1|S| E2 > E2, ρ(U) E > E. We shall refer to the inference rules of Table 3.1.
Basis
Let P be a process identifier. We have: P--a--> iff the process definition P := Ep, where Ep is a guarded expression, is such that Ep--a--> (by rule a8), iff α_a(Ep) = true (by Proposition A.3), iff α_a(P) = true (by definition of α_a). •
Step
The cases E = x.B and E = (t).B are handled as done in the 'basis' part of the proof of Proposition A.3 (the inductive hypothesis in not needed here). The remaining cases of the choice, parallel and urgency operators are handled as done in the 'step' part of that proof. •

Proposition A.5 (persistency of action possibility for guarded expressions)
If E is a guarded expression, then E--a--> and E=1=>E' implies E'--a-->.

Proof
By structural induction on the set of guarded expressions, with a partial order '>' defined as in the proof of Proposition A.2 (where 'x.B' and '(t).B' are the bottom elements). We shall refer to the inference rules of Table 1.
Basis If E = x.B, then: E--a--> implies x = a (by rule a1), which, together with E=t=>E', implies E' = a. B; thus, by rule t1, E--a-->. If E = (t).B, then E--a--> is false and the implication vacuously holds. •
Step Routine. As an example, we show the case of E = ρ(U) E1. In such case, E--a--> implies E1--a--> (by rule a7), while E=1=>E' implies E1=1=>E1', and a∉U, and E' = ρ(U)E1 (by rule t5). Now, E1--a--> and E1=1=>E1' imply E1'--a--> (by the inductive hypothesis), which, together with a∉U, implies E'--a--> (by rule t5). •

Proposition 3.2 (persistency of action possibility for guarded specifications)
If "B where P1 := B1, ..., Pn := Bn" is a guarded ρ1 specification, such that B--a-->, for some action *a*, and B==1==>B', for some behaviour expression B', then B'--a-->.

Proof
By structural induction, analogous to the proof of Proposition 3.1, and based on the same partial order of expressions. The basis deals just with process instantiation (bottom), and makes use of Proposition A.5. •

TIME
IN STATE BASED FORMAL DESCRIPTION TECHNIQUES FOR DISTRIBUTED SYSTEMS

JP. COURTIAT, M. DIAZ

LABORATOIRE d'AUTOMATIQUE et d'Analyse des Systèmes du Centre National de la Recherche Scientifique
7, avenue du Colonel Roche
31077 TOULOUSE Cedex - FRANCE
Tel: (33)61336200 - Fax: (33)61336411
E-mail: courtiat@laas.laas.fr, diaz@laas.laas.fr

Abstract. Formal Approaches have been recognized to be of high importance for designing communication and cooperation protocols. They provide unambiguous descriptions, support validation analyses and allow assessment of the conformance of implementations against specifications. This paper presents how some mature and important techniques based on extensions of state machines are able to handle in an integrated way functional and time requirements. It is in particular shown how Time Petri net models can be combined together with the Estelle Formal Description Technique to define Estelle*, a very powerful language for describing highly dynamic and time dependent hierarchies of communicating architectures.

Keywords: Distributed Systems, Specification, FDTs Formal Description Techniques, Verification, Manipulating Explicit Time values, Time Petri nets, Estelle, Integrating Time Petri nets and Estelle

I. INTRODUCTION

Many formal approaches have been developed for describing protocols in distributed systems, based on: extended state machines [BOC], Petri nets [DIA], CCS [MIL], specific languages [SMI] [ANS] [AYA]. Two of them, the Formal Description Techniques (FDTs) Estelle [ISO1] [BUD] [DIA1] and LOTOS [ISO2] [VAN], developed in particular by the European ESPRIT/SEDOS Project, have reached the status of ISO International Standards. Estelle is based on extended state machines communicating through FIFOs queues while LOTOS is based on temporal orderings of events.

One may consider that formal models have been developed with respect two different main points of view:

1- a selective point of view, where emphasis is put only on specific aspects, independently of others; this point of view may be illustrated, for instance, by the development of functional languages for high level programming and of queuing theory for performance evaluation;

2- a systemic point of view, intended to express and handle all aspects which are relevant when designing a complex system. This point of view is the one followed in this paper where the results presented rely on a set of extensions performed on state and Petri net models. Enrichment towards a powerful language came from adding typed data, hierarchies of modules, and explicit time constraints, as time is becoming more and more important for the design of new (high speed) systems.

It is the purpose of this paper to show that a selected set of state based approaches (discussed here) allows one to easily specify complex behaviours, functionally validate them, evaluate their potential performances, describe an implementation solution and automatically generate the actual running code. For an easy reading, the paper is organized in three main sections: the first section presents an integrated view of state based designs; the second section details the semantics of Time Petri nets; finally, in a third section, after a brief survey of the Estelle Formal Description Technique, a dialect of Estelle, called Estelle*, is introduced showing how it is possible to combine the nice features of both Estelle and Time Petri nets.

II. STATE BASED DESIGN

The first formal descriptions of protocols were given by tables representing extended state machines. The extensions were mainly related to the introduction of variables and of predicates. Others recent extensions introduced hierarchies of modules and explicit representation of time. Then, these descriptions, after being integrated, are shown to provide a coherent formal basis for all system design phases.

II.1. STATE BASED MODELS AND FORMAL DESCRIPTION TECHNIQUES

II.1.1. Untimed Extended Petri nets

Coloured nets allow the distinction between tokens as each token can be given an identity or a colour. The identity of the tokens is not always sufficient to model complex systems because some relationships between tokens must be clearly expressed, leading to Predicate-Transition nets [GEN].

Other extended Petri nets have been developed, consisting of a control part and of a data part: the control part consists of a Petri net, where places represent the control states, and transitions represent all changes between states; the data part, concerning data and their modifications, is defined by attaching to each transition t an expression of the form "when $Predicate_t$ (x) do x' = F_t(x)", where $Predicate_t$ is a predicate, and F_t an action, both on the vector x of program variables [KEL]. For a transition to fire, it must be enabled in the Petri net sense and its predicate must be true. When the transition fires, its associated action is atomically executed and a new marking is produced.

II.1.2. Time in Petri nets

Two basic extensions of Petri net based models have been proposed, namely Timed Petri nets [RAM] and Time Petri nets [MER, MER1].

Timed Petri nets [RAM] have been introduced for performance evaluation purposes. They are derived from Petri nets by associating a (finite) firing duration with each transition of the net. The classical firing rule of Petri nets must then be modified: 1) to account for the time it takes to fire a transition and 2) to express the fact that a transition must fire as soon as it is enabled.

Time Petri Nets (or TPNs for short) [MER, MER1] have been introduced for expressing and validating communication protocols. They were informally defined as Petri nets with time labels: two values of time, a and b, with $a \leq b$, are associated with each transition. Assuming that any transition, e. g. t_i, is being continuously enabled after it has been enabled, then

- a is the minimal time that must elapse, starting from the time at which transition t_i is enabled, until this transition can fire, and
- b denotes the maximum time during which transition t_i may remain enabled without being fired.

Times a and b, for transition t_i, are related to the moment at which transition t_i has become enabled. Using these nets, Merlin discussed some recoverability problems in communication protocols.

Time Petri nets are more general than Timed Petri nets: a Timed Petri net can be modelled by using a TPN, but the converse is not true. TPNs have been proven very convenient for expressing most of the temporal constraints, while some of these constraints are difficult to express only with durations.

The informal behaviour of TPNs can be stated as follows: when some transition, say t_i, is enabled, then a virtual clock, associated to that transition, is started: t_i being continuously enabled, a is the minimal time that must elapse before firing t_i, starting from the time τ at which transition t_i became enabled. So, t_i cannot fire before time τ+a. b is the maximum time during which transition t_i may be continuously enabled without being fired: transition t_i will be fired at the latest at time τ+b, if it has been continuously enabled.

Other models have been proposed [HOL] [RAZ] but they can be represented by Time Petri nets.

II.1.3. Estelle

The previous models do not allow one to describe dynamic systems, i. e. dynamic processes and dynamic links among processes. Estelle [BUD] [COU] [DIA1] [ISO1] provides a solution for these two problems.

A system in Estelle is a set of communicating tasks where each task has input/output interaction points. The internal behaviour of a task is described by a nondeterministic communicating state automaton (a transition system) whose transition actions are given in the form of Pascal compound statements. The tasks may exchange messages, called interactions. A task can send an interaction to another task through a previously established communication link connecting two interaction points of two different tasks. An interaction received by a task at one of its interaction point is appended to an unbounded FIFO queue associated to this receiving interaction point.

The tasks may be nested, dynamically created and released; four Estelle statements exist to "attach", "detach", "connect" , "disconnect" links between interaction points, providing a solution to the needed dynamic problems.

II.1.4. Estelle* : Estelle and Time Extended Petri nets

As Estelle semantics is based on communicating state machines, Petri nets features may be used for extending the Estelle Formal Description Technique. In particular, a coloured time Petri net based semantics has been developed in [COU1], leading to the definition of Estelle*: this extension, which encompasses the properties of predicate coloured, time Petri nets, has led to a very clean and powerful language.

Estelle* in particular provides the definition of a rendez-vous mechanism (as a transition merging) which is not supported by the Estelle International Standard; of course, rendez-vous properties have been derived from Petri net properties, and Estelle* also uses the semantics of Time Petri nets, for consistency purposes.

As a consequence, it is possible to express, using Estelle*, specifications describing sets of dynamic time Petri nets where furthermore the mergings of the transitions themselves are dynamic; this shows the power of the proposed approach.

II.1.5. Stochastic requirements

Another advantage of Petri net based models is that they are able to represent and handle probabilities, by using Stochastic Petri nets (SPNs) for performance analysis and dependability evaluation [MOL]. In SPNs, Petri nets are extended by assigning a random variable to each transition, this variable representing a possible random firing. SPN specifications can be used to solve conflicts between firings or express stochastic firings. The former case is related to non deterministic and probabilistic choices between the firing of transitions in conflict. The latter may, for instance, be related to occurrences of equipment failures: the transition is fired with a exponential distribution corresponding to the failure rate of the equipment. Different

SPNs have been proposed [DUG] [MAR].

More recently, Time Petri nets have also been extended with stochastic distributions [ROU] [MAR1]. The interest is that timed behaviours are still enforced, but the timed behaviours can further be defined by adding stochastic constraints [JUA] [JUA1]. Of course, the distribution is located inside the time interval, and is 0 outside. Note that SPNs become the model in which the time interval is not restricted, i. e. is 0-infinity.

Of course, Estelle* could also easily be extended to support stochastic parameters and so to handle stochastic properties.

II.1.6. Analyses of state based models

Petri net and state based based models allow powerful verification analyses [YUA]. Relevant properties can be checked, for instance on the Forward Marking Graph (FMG), the set of all reachable markings; transition firings permit a very easy computation of the FMG. Analyzing Time Petri nets is more difficult as time is assumed to be dense. A finite representation, to be addressed in the sequel, for representing infinite behaviours has been proposed [BER] [BER1]: FMGs can be constructed for TPNs and time based descriptions can be formally verified. Note that adding stochastic parameters may reduce the complexity of the FMG [ROU].

Two classes of properties are considered:

A) general properties, which are to be satisfied whatever the net, such as: boundedness, liveness, etc. A Petri net is bounded by an integer n for an initial marking M0 iff, for all markings of the FMG and for all places p, M(p) is less or equal than n. It is live for an initial marking M0 iff for all Mj belonging to FMG, for all t, there exists a sequence σ such that (Mj --σ--> and σ contains t).

B) specific properties, depending on the functional characteristics of the system. They are generally expressed by using invariants which are assertions that must be true for a given system.

Verification. Different approaches have been proposed, such as:

- the induction principle [KEL]. Invariants include net places and data variables. The resulting approach is complex, but can be made easier if some invariants are derived from the underlying (unlabelled) net [LAU].
- temporal analyses [PNU] [RIC] [AZE]. Invariants can be expressed as formulas of modal or temporal logic; this is because the FMG can be considered as a modal structure where the worlds are the global states and the accessibility relation is the next state relation. Verification is then performed by evaluating the temporal formulas on the states of the FMG.
- observational equivalence [MIL]. Two representations, even if they are different, can in fact represent the same behaviour with respect to an external observer. They are observationally equivalent and algorithms exist to check this equivalence and

other related equivalences [NIC].

Simulation. As usual, when the FMG becomes too large, exhaustive verification is no more possible and simulation has to be conducted instead. In this view, where simulation is a subset of verification, any model can be handled as far as it uses a next state relation. Simulators exist for all approaches. In particular, an Estelle* Simulator ESTIM [COU3][DES] has been written in Standard ML, and it is freely available on SUN Sparcstations. ESTIM is an interpreter which allows to simulate Estelle* specifications. The selection of transitions can be made by the user or randomly by ESTIM. ESTIM also provides an interactive access for displaying components of the global state and modifying them when adequate.

Note that ESTIM also provides, whenever possible, the construction of the Estelle* derived FMG, which may later be verified by abstraction (i.e. looking for a simplified quotient automaton - with respect to the observational equivalence - exhibiting the same observational behaviour as the complete FMG) [COU3].

Stochastic Performance and Reliability Evaluation. Stochastic nets have a quite important property: there exists an isomorphism between a Markov chain and a SPN. Any SPN can generate, using the reachability graph of the underlying Petri net a Markov chain that represents the random state transitions. The corresponding performance analyses and/or dependability evaluations can be performed using the Markov model deduced from the SPN: it allows the computation of pertinent probabilities, for instance the probabilities to be in given markings, and so performance and reliability figures [MOL]. The interests are that SPNs provide compact models for large Markov chains and they can easily express tightly synchronized concurrent behaviours [AKY].

As a FMG can be built for TPNs and SPNs, this FMG can be interpreted by associating with each of the transitions linking two states the time interval during which it is allowed to fire. It follows that cycles existing in the FMG give performance figures for firing sequences.

II.1.7. Implementation

The ultimate goal of most descriptions is implementation. Such implementations can be easily produced using state based descriptions. In fact, deriving efficient implementations was the main objective that guided the development of Estelle. As a consequence, Estelle compilers do exist, such as the one developed within the SEDOS/Estelle/Demonstrator project [AYA] [DIA3]. The aim is to describe protocols in Estelle and then to generate automatically C-code implementations from Estelle descriptions.

II.2. METHODOLOGY AND DESIGN APPROACHES

The set of the previously presented techniques and their relationships are shown in Figure 1, in which some technique T1 is an extension of some other technique T2 if there is an arrow from T1 to T2.

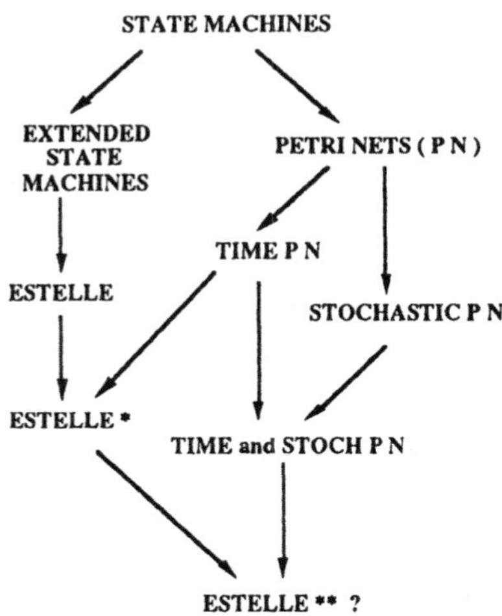

Figure 1: Relationships among Formal Techniques

As a a designer can start from two rather different points of view, two approaches may be followed for applying these techniques:

- *from simple to complex*: the designer will first develop a model of the system using a Petri net formalism; the resulting description, that already expresses timed behaviours, will be first validated using Petri net based algorithms, and then extended by translating it into Estelle* and/or Estelle; the complete description will then be simulated and/or compiled using the Estelle support tools.

- *from complex to simple*: a complete Estelle or Estelle* description will be produced first; then its more critical parts will be simplified, translated into the right Petri net based model, and validated; it is assumed here that the fact of starting from the complete description will ensure that the user will make no error when simplifying the description and so that the validated models imply a good validation of the complete description.

Among the techniques discussed, it should appear that two of them are of particular importance, namely Time Petri nets and Estelle*. Time Petri nets allow the verification of timed behaviours and Estelle* allows the expression of sophisticated dynamic systems. For this reason, these two techniques will be presented in detail in the next two sections.

III. TIME PETRI NETS

III.1. SEMANTICS OF TIME PETRI NETS

A Time Petri net is a tuple (P, T, B, F, Mo, SI) where (P, T, B, F, Mo) defines a classical Petri net [BER]. Thus:

- P is a finite, non empty, set of Places p_i;
- T is a finite, non empty, ordered set of Transitions $\{ t_1 , t_2 , ... \ t_i , ... \}$;
- B is the Backward Incidence function $B : P \times T \longrightarrow N$
  where N is the set of non negative integers;
- F is the Forward Incidence function $F : P \times T \longrightarrow N$
- Mo is the Initial Marking function $Mo : P \longrightarrow N$
- SI is the static time mapping called Static Interval $SI : T \longrightarrow Q^* \times (Q^* \cup \infty)$
  where Q^* is the set of positive rational numbers,
  and $SI(t_i) = [a_i^s, b_i^s]$, with $0 \leq a_i^s < \infty$, $0 \leq b_i^s \leq \infty$, $a_i^s \leq b_i^s$.
- $[a_i^s, b_i^s]$ is the Static Firing Interval of transition t_i , a_i^s is the Static Earliest Firing Time (Static EFT), b_i^s the Static Latest Firing Time (Static LFT). Values of firing intervals, during behaviours, become different from the Static Firing Intervals; let a_i be its EFT lower bound and b_i its LFT upper bound.

Note that as no restriction is stated, time will be considered to be dense. As time elapses during the net behaviour, an assumption must be made to relate firing and time. It will be assumed here that, as usual in Petri nets, firing is a state change, indivisible AND instantaneous: firing takes no time, i. e. takes zero time. Of course, 0-cycle, i. e. cycle where a=0 and b=0 may be described. The intuition behind the approach given here is that these 0-cycle must be such that it is possible to report their existence to the user. The user will be in charge of handling the underlying perhaps complex implicit semantics.

In order to simplify the presentation, let us assume first that TPNs cannot become enabled more than once "simultaneously": any marking M is such that any t_i cannot be fireable twice.

Let us consider the simple TPN given in Figure 2-a. The FMG of this net is given in Figure 2-b. Let us now consider TPNs derived from Figure 2-a. Three of them appear in Figure 3. Let us consider first Figure 3-a. The intuitive behaviour of this TPN should give the FMG given in Figure 4-a: in the initial situation, a common time is assumed, from which the two transitions are enabled, and the two transition clocks start. Then, either t1 or t2 can be fired, at the same time, $\tau=1$. So, two situations can occur, one after firing t1, and one after firing t2. When transition t1 (or t2) is fired, time equals 1 ($\tau=1$), and t2 must be fired immediately; this is represented by situations C2 and C3, in which the unfired transition must be fired immediately: see, for instance, C2 where $t2 \in [0,0]$. Note that when a transition has been fired, it seems intuitively necessary to disable it and then to enable it again indivisibly, i. e. to assign to it, after being fired, its static EFT and LFT.

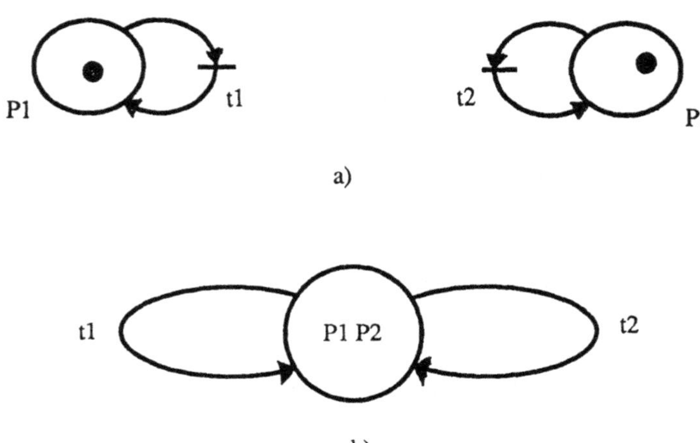

Figure 2 - a simple Petri net and its FMG

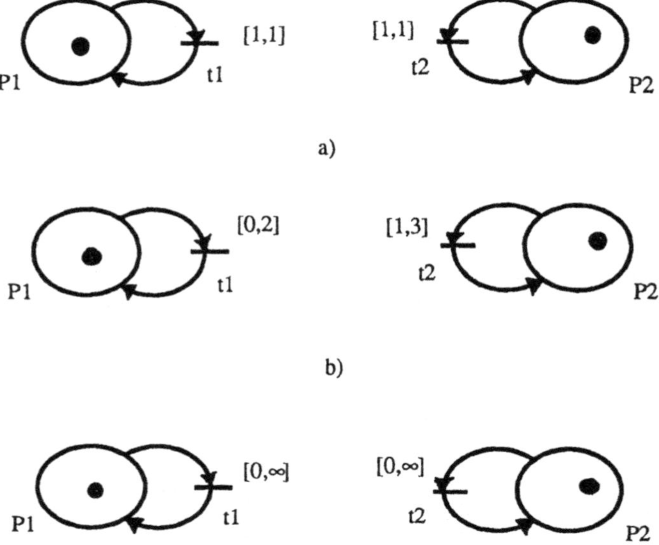

Figure 3 - simple TPNs with different time intervals

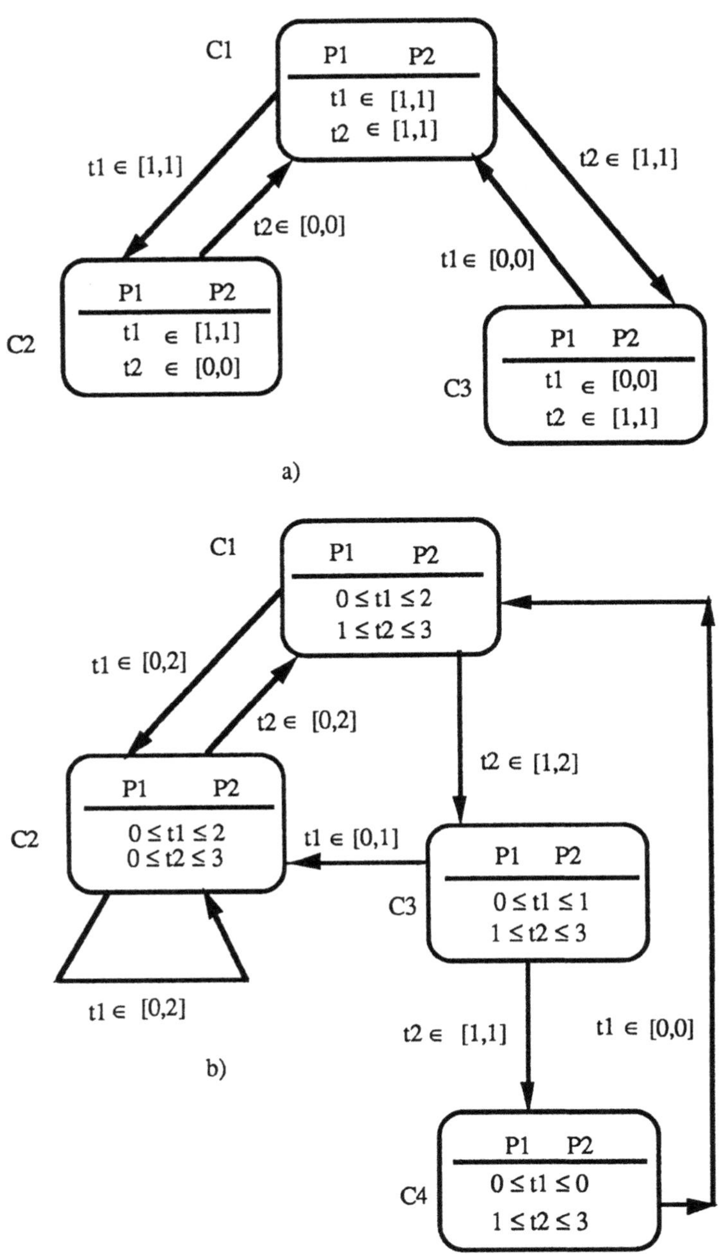

Figure 4 - FMGs of Figure 3

The FMG of the TPN in Figure 3-b turns to become a bit more complex; it is given in Figure 4-b. Now, the firing time is located inside a given interval, in which an infinite number of firing times can be selected. What is important is that all these firing times can be represented in a finite way by using the inequalities related to the considered transitions. For instance, in C1, t1 can be fired between 0 and 2, as its static FT values, but t2 cannot be fired between its FT values. This is because, in any case, by definition, t1 will fire at time 2; it follows that t2 can be fired within the allowed interval corresponding to this situation, so between 0 and 2. Note again that firing a transition, t1 for instance from C1 leads to a situation C2 where t1 is included in the interval [0,2]. This is because t1 is considered to be disabled and enabled again by the firing and so receives its static values. Also, this firing can occur between 0 and 2: it follows for t2 that, in C2, t2 can be fired at 0 at the earliest, the (0 or positive) value EFT(t2)-LFT(t1), and at 3 at the latest, the value of LFT(t2)-EFT(t1), each corresponding respectively to the firing of t1 at 2 and 0. Using these simple rules leads to the FMG given in Figure 4-b.

The difficulties come when considering behaviours where more than two transitions are enabled concurrently and that these transitions stay enabled after a firing. This is because these transitions had time relationships before the firing and those relationships must always hold after the firing. It has been shown in [BER] that some of these relationships can be modified if the simple computation given for Figure 4-b is used. A more sophisticated approach is needed, which is based on the concept of State Classes, as presented in [BER].

III.1.1. State classes

Informally speaking, State Classes are the union of states corresponding to all firing values which are possible from another State Class: a state Class, C = (M,D), is a pair : a marking M and a domain D.

• M is a marking, the marking of the Class: all states in the Class have the same marking. The marking is the usual marking in Petri nets

• D is the firing domain of the Class; the domain D is defined as the solutions of inequalities, these inequalities capturing the global timed behaviour of the TPN. It is defined as the union of the firing domains of all the states in the Class. D is the solution set of a system of inequalities in which variables are 1 to 1 associated with the transitions enabled by marking M: $D = \{ t \mid A.\, t \geq b \}$, where A is a matrix, b and t are vectors of constants and variables, respectively.

With such a semantics, classical Place-Transition Petri nets are nets where all labels are: [$a_i^s = 0$, $b_i^s = \infty$]. As a consequence, the inequalities for all enabled transitions are of the form: $ti \geq 0$ and $ti \leq \infty$; the systems of inequalities are always trivially satisfied, the system is redundant and the markings suffice to define the situations the Place-Transition Petri nets may reach: TPNs include Petri nets.

III.1.2. Fireability of transitions from Classes

Assuming that transition t (i) is the ith transition enabled by marking M, t (i) is fireable from Class C = (M,D) iff two conditions hold:

(i) t (i) is enabled by marking M and :

$(\forall p) \quad (M(p) \geq B (t(i), p))$ -the usual firing condition-,

(ii) the firing interval of t (i) must satisfy the following augmented systems:

$A \,.\, t \geq b$

$t(i) \leq t(j)$ for all $j, j \neq i$

where t (j) also denotes the firing interval related to the jth component of vector t: this enforces that firing t (i) must occur before the min of all enabled transition LFTs.

III.1.3. Firing rule for Time Petri nets

Let us now assume that transition t (f) is fired from a Class C = (M,D) where $D = \{ t \mid A \,.\, t \geq b \}$. Its firing leads to Class C' = (M',D').

The firing of t (f) is defined as follows:

1) As in Petri nets, the new marking is defined by:

$(\forall p) \quad (M'(p) = M(p) - B(t(f),p) + F(t(f),p))$

2) Domain D' is computed from domain D by a three steps procedure:

a) Add to the system A . t ≥ b, that defines domain D, the fireability conditions for transition t (f); this leads to the augmented system :

$A \,.\, t \geq b$

$t(f) \leq t(j)$ for all $j, j \neq f$.

Make the following change of variables: express all times related to variables t(j), with j ≠ f, as the sum of the time of fired transition t (f) and of a new variable t"(j) with: $t(j) = t(f) + t''(j)$, for all $j, j \neq f$, and eliminate from the system the variable t (f), by deriving the new firing intervals and the needed constraint relationships.

The resulting system may be written:

$A'' \,.\, t'' \geq b''$

$0 \leq t''$

with A", b" computed from A, b, the equations that define the new variables, and using Fourier's method for eliminating variable t (f).

b) As for t (f) , in a similar way, eliminate from the system obtained after step a), accounting for the relationships they imply, all variables corresponding to the transitions disabled when t (f) is fired: these transitions are those enabled by M and not enabled by M(.) - B (t(f), .) .

c) Extend the system obtained after step b) with new variables, one associated with each transition newly enabled, and define these variables to belong to their Static

Firing Intervals. The newly enabled transitions are those not enabled by M - B(t(f),.) and enabled by M'.

That this new system of inequalities may be written as [BER] : $A' . t' \geq b'$; it has as many variables as there are transitions enabled by marking M' and its solution set defines D'.

III.1.4. State Classes and Reachability

Using the firing rule, a tree of Classes can be built. Its root is the initial Class (the initial marking and the initial set of inequalities) . There is an arc labelled with t_i from Class C to Class C' if t_i is fireable from Class C and if its firing leads to Class C'. Note that each Class has at most one successor for each transition enabled by the marking of the Class.

When the tree of Classes of a TPN will have a bounded number of distinct nodes, a finite graph, a FMG, will be associated to the net, obtained by grouping equal Classes into the same Class.

Two state Classes C1 and C2 are defined to be equal iff both their markings and their firing domain solutions are equal, i. e. iff M1 = M2 and D1 = D2.

The number of state Classes, with Static EFTs and LFTs for transitions chosen among rational numbers, has been shown to be bounded iff the TPN is bounded in the sense of ordinary Petri net theory, i. e. iff the number of tokens in any place, and for any reachable marking, is bounded.

III.2. VERIFICATION OF TPN BEHAVIORS

The boundedness problem is whether or not all markings in the FMG R(Mo) are bounded, i.e. : $(\exists\, k \in N)\ (\forall\, M \in R(Mo))\ (\forall\, p \in P)\ (M(p) \leq k)$. The boundedness and reachability problems are undecidable for TPNs [JON].

If the values of the EFTs or of the LFTs are real numbers, then the number of reachable state classes is not bounded because the number of domains may not be bounded [BER]. Now, if these values are rational numbers, then a TPN has a bounded number of state Classes if and only if it is bounded. In particular, it is important to emphasize that, as the number of domains is bounded, then an unbounded TPN has an unbounded number of markings.

So, any sufficient condition for the boundedness property provides a sufficient condition for the finiteness of the set of Classes. Sufficient conditions of interests have been provided, as:

A TPN is bounded if no pair of state Classes C = (M,D) and C' = (M',D') , reachable from the initial state Class, fulfils the following conditions:

(i) C' is reachable from C

(ii) $M'(p) \geq M(p)$

(iii) $D' = D$

(iv) $\forall p \in \{\, p \in P \mid M'(P) > M(P) \,\}$ and $(M(p) > \max B(t_i,p))$

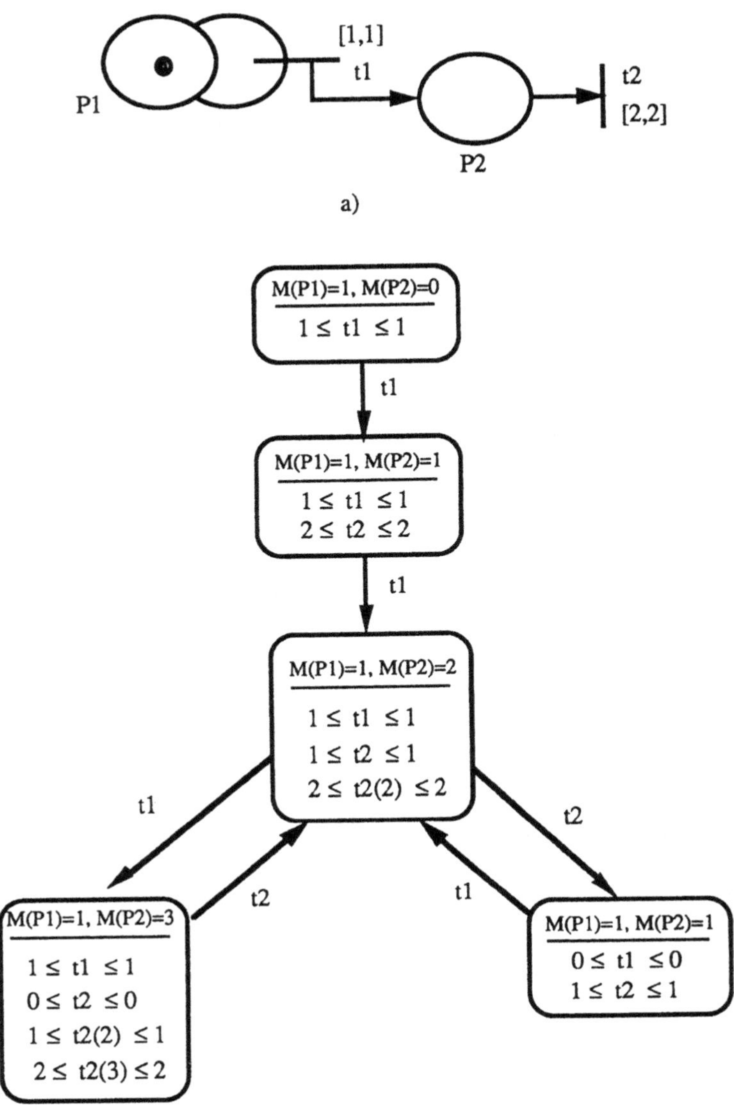

Figure 5 - Multiple enabledness of transitions

where M' $\geq$ M means:

$$(\forall p \in P)\ (M'(p) \geq M(p)) \text{ and } (\exists p \in P)\ (M'(p) > M(p))$$

Finally, when TPNs are bounded, it becomes possible, using the graph of Classes, to prove properties that characterize their correct behaviours. Furthermore, liveness properties, similar to those defined for Petri nets, can be defined for TPNs and, for bounded TPNs, proven using the graph of state Classes. The state Class graph can also be used as an usual state transition system for verification, for instance by checking temporal logic assertions on it or by using reduction techniques based on observational equivalence.

This technique has been proven to be adequate for all applications treated so far. The state Class graph allows the users to verify the correctness of explicit time values in dense time dependent systems.

Let us now consider transitions that are enabled more than once simultaneously. For instance, let us first assume that transition t_i , with firing interval $[a_i , b_i]$, is enabled by the current marking and that a different transition t_i' is fired at time q (with $a_i \leq q \leq b_i$) ; this is possible because another transition can fire independently of t_i . After step (2) of the firing of t_i ', the current firing interval of t_i is $[\max(0, a_i-q), b_i-q]$.

Let us now assume that firing transition t_i ' makes transition t_i twice enabled, i. e. that firing t_i ' adds one or more tokens to the input places of transition t_i in such a way that the new marking M' enables again t_i, in such a way that t_i becomes only twice (but not three times) enabled, with

$$(\forall p)\ (\ 2.B(t_i,p) \leq M'(p)\ ) \text{ and } (\ \exists\ p)\ (\ M'(p) < 3.B(t_i,p)\ ).$$

Transition t_i , twice enabled, is related to two intervals:

- $[\ \max(0, a_i - q), b_i - q\ ]$ for the first time it was enabled, timeinterval1;
- $[a_i^s , b_i^s]$ for the second time it is enabled, timeinterval2.

One of these intervals must be considered for t_i to be fired when time elapses: anyone randomly? the oldest? etc.

If transitions enabled several times simultaneously are considered to be independent occurrences of the same transition, the choice has been to fire the occurrence related to the oldest interval.

This assumption is illustrated by Figure 5 where the TPN of Figure 5-a gives the FMG of Figure 5-b, in which t2 is enabled more than once simultaneously.

IV. RELATIONSHIPS BETWEEN ESTELLE AND PETRI NETS

IV.1. THE ESTELLE FDT [BUD] [DIA1]

IV.1.1. Module instances

An Estelle specification describes a hierarchically structured system of nondeterministic extended state machine based components (module instances) interchanging messages (called interactions) through bidirectional links between their ports (called interaction points). Both the hierarchy of modules and the structure of their links may change over time, making thereby the system a dynamic one.

A module is defined by a module_header_definition and a (or a set of) module_body_definition associated with this header. Several instances of a module may be created during the execution of an Estelle specification. Each one of them has the same external visibility as its the module_header_definition and the same internal behaviour defined by one module_body_definition.

IV.1.2.External visibility of a module instance

A module instance is a "black box". Access in and out of that box is made with finite sets of interaction points (ips) (elsewhere called external interaction points, to distinguish them from internal interaction points, not considered here) and exported variables. These are the means a module instance communicates with its enclosing environment defined by its parent module instance:

• Each ip of a module instance x has an associated unbounded FIFO queue to receive and store interactions sent to x through that interaction point. This FIFO queue may be either a dedicated queue of an ip ("individual queue" discipline) or it may be shared by several interaction points of the module instance ("common queue" discipline). An instance of a module sends interactions to other instances through its own ips, i. e. by naming one of the ips defined in its header. The sets of interactions (together with their parameters) that can be received and sent through a specific ip are restricted by a channel definition associated with the ip declaration;

• Exported variables are also declared in the module_header_definition. External access (read/write) of exported variables is restricted exclusively to the parent module instance (i.e. the one which created the considered instance).

• Finally, parameters may also be declared in a module_header definition; the value of these parameters is assigned at the instance creation ("init" statement).

IV.1.3.Internal behaviour of a module instance

The visible results of a module behaviour, interactions and exported variables, are the effects of the module activity, described by a module_body_definition. The internal behaviour of a module instance may be characterized by a nondeterministic extended state machine. Informally, each local state of a module instance has a complex structure characterized by the following components:

- a control part, a value that characterizes the control state (also called major state) of a module instance;

- an input_environment part: the contents of all the input queues associated with the module instance interaction points;

- a data part: the values of the variables declared in the module_body definition and the module_header_definition;

- a "delay" part: the values of the dynamic firing time intervals associated with the (enabled) delay transitions;

The declaration_part of a module body includes the declaration of constants, the definition of data types, channel types, Pascal procedures and functions, and the declaration of major states and local variables.

The init_part of a module_body definition specifies an initial control state, the way variables are initialized, an initial hierarchy and interconnection structure of descendant module instances (if any).

The next_state relation of a module instance is specified within the transition part of a module_body_definition by transitions. Each transition is made up of a guard and an action which may be characterized as follows :

• the guard may contain the clauses "from", "when", "provided", "delay" and "priority" where :

– the clauses "from", "when" and "provided" determine the enabling condition of a transition by testing, respectively, the major state of a module instance, the existence of an interaction in head of the FIFO associated with an interaction point, and by evaluating a Pascal predicate. A transition is said to be enabled iff all the previous clauses are satisfied;

– the clauses "delay" and "priority" characterize the firing condition of an enabled transition; in particular, the clause "delay(tmin,tmax)" defines the minimum time tmin (respectively the maximum time tmax) during which an enabled transition must (respectively may) be delayed; the clause "priority" defines a priority relationship among fireable transitions of the same module instance.

• the action is made up of the clause "to" and of a transition_block where :

– the clause "to" specifies the next value of the control state;

– the transition_block defines an action to be performed by the transition; the transition_block is given by a Pascal-like compound statement with some extensions, i. e. specific Estelle statements like "init" (for creating a new module instance), "release" (for releasing a module instance), "connect" (for creating a link between two interaction points of two distinct module instances), "disconnect" (for releasing a link between two interaction points), "attach" (for relabeling an interaction point), "detach" (for releasing an attachment), "output" for sending interactions, ...); executing a transition_block may therefore change the module instance state, modify the configuration of its descendant module instances and of course output interactions to the environment.

As in state machines, handling a transition is considered to be *an indivisible* operation. Once a transition execution is started, it cannot be interrupted, and, conceptually, one cannot view intermediate results regardless of how "large" a transition is (i.e, how many statements its transition_block is defined with).

IV.1.4. Parallelism expression among module instances

The declaration_part of a module_body_definition may nest other module definitions which may in turn include other module definitions, and so on. Existing module instances of a specification behave with respect to each other according to: 1- the textual nesting of the module definitions; 2- the way their headers are qualified by the attributes: "systemprocess", "systemactivity", "process", "activity"; and 3- the execution priority of any transition of a parent instance over all transitions of its children.

An module instance may dynamically create, release, and modify the connection configuration of its children instances; this implies that an active instance acts as a supervising-like manager of its children instances. Estelle nesting principles state that system modules (attributed by either "systemactivity" or "systemprocess") are not included inside each other, and they behave therefore fully asynchronously with respect to each other.

The behaviour within one system (i.e. among instances of descendant modules of a system module) is regulated by the "parent/child" priority and by the "process/activity" attributes that must be assigned to each module definition nested within a system module. Using the attribute "process" or "activity" for a module (and its instances) distinguishes the two following possible forms of behaviour:

- a synchronous behaviour in the case of the "process" attribute;
- a non deterministic behaviour in the case of the "activity" attribute.

IV.2. SOME COMMENTS ABOUT ESTELLE

IV.2.1. Assessment of the Estelle nesting principles

The global behaviour of an Estelle specification is characterized by the set of the valid transition firing sequences. These firing sequences are obtained in the general case (i.e. the case of a specification structured into several system modules) from the reachability graph of the global situations [ISO1][BUD]. A global situation characterizes the global state of the specification as well as the set of the transitions which are preselected in each system in order to be fired later on; thus nothing can prevent a preselected transition to be fired, which is a direct consequence that systems behave fully asynchronously.

A "systemprocess" instance in an Estelle specification defines a permanent and implicit synchronization without value passing among all transitions belonging to the different module instances of the considered system instance. This global synchronization for the whole "systemprocess" instance is, from the authors' point of view, both unrealistic (note that such a synchronization mechanism is very difficult to implement on a multiprocessors) and not very useful for protocol descriptions. This implicit synchronization mechanism further prevents from introducing, within the "systemprocess" instance, an explicit synchronization mechanism which appears to be very useful for representing the abstract interactions between a service provider and service users. These rationales led us to not further considering the "systemprocess" concept, as well as, in consequence, the "process" concept.

The way of structuring a distributed system into asynchronous Estelle system instances ("systemactivity" or "systemprocess") depends on the particular software and/or hardware implementation of the system. This choice is completely justified if the purpose of the Estelle specification is to produce an implementation, but leads to unnecessary overspecifications if the purpose is to produce a more formal description of an OSI architecture.

Let us consider a specification SPEX where several system instance configurations are possible with respect to the Estelle nesting principles. Without modifying Estelle, one way for avoiding this overspecification is to impose a few restrictions (hopefully light) to the use of Estelle features: attribute the global specification SPEX by "systemactivity". Then, *the non deterministic firing of the transitions does represent an asynchronous parallelism among the module instances which are not in a "ascendant/descendant" relationship*; this non deterministic behaviour for the whole specification expresses the behaviour of any "systemactivity" instance configuration valid for SPEX. These restrictions may be expressed by means of two sufficient condition, which have to be satisfied by Estelle specifications [COU2] :

- there is no "priority" clause associated with any transition defined with a "when" clause;
- once initialized ("init" statement) and attached ("attach" statement), the module instances are autonomous with respect to their parent module instance; in particular, any decision of "detach" or "release" is local to a module instances and depends on the interactions it receives from the lower layer service (PDUs from the peer entity or interactions generated by the service).

These sufficient conditions are realistic, as they take into account a dynamic module instance configuration and enforce a description style corresponding to the user requirements when substructuring a protocol entity into elementary components; in particular, most of the Estelle specifications produced within the ESPRIT/SEDOS project satisfy this condition directly [DIA1], e.g. the specification of the ISO Presentation service, the CCITT T70 Transport protocol, a significant subset of the ISO FTAM protocol and the ISO Session protocol.

IV.2.2. Assessment of the Estelle FIFO queue mechanism

The FIFO queue mechanism is the basic communication mechanism in Estelle, as it supports connected ips to exchange interactions. This mechanism may be not satisfactory when applied to the communication between adjacent protocol entities. As service access points represent internal interfaces between adjacent protocol layers within some OSI system, the exchange of service primitives must be defined in a most abstract way. The current version of Estelle enforces particular implementation schemes using FIFO queues, whereas other valid schemes could also be implemented (procedure call for instance). Moreover, representing a service primitive interaction between a service user and a service provider in a non atomic way (message appended to a queue) introduces some problems which have to be explicitly dealt with, in a case by case basis, by the Estelle specification. Three kinds of problems have been so far identified: service primitive collisions, connection endpoint allocation conflicts and backpressure flow control [COU2].

IV.2.3. Assessment of the Estelle "Delay" clause semantics

In Estelle, a "delay" clause may be associated with a transition. This "delay" clause is useful for modeling time-outs, which have to be specified in most protocols. Two time values are specified in a "delay" clause.

As stated in paragraph 5.3.5 of the Estelle IS [ISO1] "The computational model for Estelle is intentionally formulated in time-independent terms; one of the principal assumptions of this model is that nothing is known about the execution time of a transition in a module instance. Knowledge of execution speed is considered implementation dependent". A consequence of this is that an Estelle specification with "delay" clauses is not self contained as it requires the specification of an external "time process".

IV.3. ESTELLE*

Let us now solve the previously identified problems by defining Estelle*, which extends Estelle as follows.

First, the "systemprocess" concept is not supported for the previously invoked reasons. So, only a non deterministic firing rule has to be considered among the transitions of the specification module instances. The valid firing sequences expressing the global behaviour of the specification may then be directly obtained from the reachability graph of the specification global states. This approach is consistent with the semantics of parallelism considered in the Petri net field [GEN][DIA1] and in the models, based on communicating state machines, commonly used for protocol modeling and verification.

Also, Estelle has been extended with a Rendez-Vous mechanism [COU1]. The Rendez-Vous introduces new clauses (called synchronization clauses) which make it possible to express explicit synchronizations with value passing between two transitions of two distinct module instances (informal semantics corresponds to transition mergings). This mechanism has been formalized in [COU2][DES1] and its usefulness demonstrated on several complex OSI protocols (like the Session and Transport protocols).

A full semantics of the "delay" clause has been selected, relying on the semantics of Time Petri nets. The starting point of this semantics is the assumption that the firing time of a transition is very short with respect to the time values expressed in the "delay" clause; it is then possible to consider that the firing time is equal to zero. This approach, consistent with the assumptions dealing with time progression in Estelle, makes it possible to update the time evolution at the global model, which is needed to model protocol time-outs; furthermore, as in TPNs, the time evolution does not directly depend on the number of transitions which have been fired, nor on the speed of the processors involved in the implementation.

Let us call Estelle* the version of the Estelle FDT introduced so far [COU2]. Estelle* may be seen as the same time as a slightly simplified version of Estelle (only nondeterministic transition firing rules are considered), on the top of which some important features (essentially a Rendez-Vous mechanism) are introduced to produce OSI protocol specifications with a significant higher level of abstraction. The main rationales for the features added to (or removed from) Estelle have been detailed in the previous section. Estelle*, the result of our experience in applying Estelle to several OSI protocols, gives also the possibility to bridge the gap between Estelle and models used in the Petri net community (Petri nets, Predicate/Transition nets, Predicate/Action nets, ...), mainly by introducing an explicit merging mechanism between transitions, the Rendez-Vous, and by using Petri net based semantics. Figure 6 presents how Estelle* non FIFO interaction points (declared with the no-queue attribute) can be dynamically merged by using the Estelle statements. Starting from a situation were the transitions are not connected, two examples are given. They successively show how the module that is the father of M1, M2 and M3: in b), uses the two connect statements to link the transitions corresponding to ip1 and ip3, and to ip2 and ip4; in c) cut these two links and creates another link between ip1 and ip4.

IV.4. COMMON FORMAL SEMANTICS FOR ESTELLE(*)

A Petri Net based formalization of the Estelle semantics has been proposed in the framework of SEDOS Project [DIA1]; it combines both an operational and a denotational approach as follows [COU2]:

• On the one hand, the operational approach has permitted to establish a relation between Estelle specifications and Petri Nets derived models. The global model associated to an Estelle specification is fully consistent with Estelle semantics. It takes into account all the specific features of Estelle, and particularly those dealing with the dynamic architecture of module and ip instances. The intuition behind is that all module instances having the same generic behaviour are represented by the same Coloured Extended State Machine, each particular instance being identified during its lifetime by a coloured token; finally, the global model may be obtained by composition of the Coloured Extended State Machines;

• On the other hand, expressing in a lambda-calculus based model the denotations of Estelle declarations, statements and expressions has led to define unambiguously the transition enabling conditions as well as the different transition firing policies

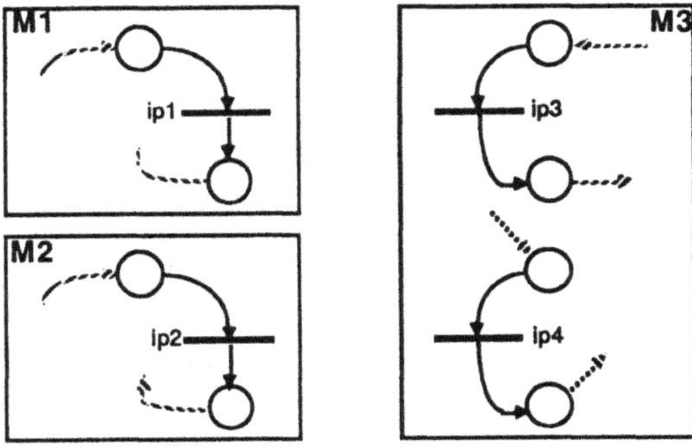

a) initial configuration of modules and transitions

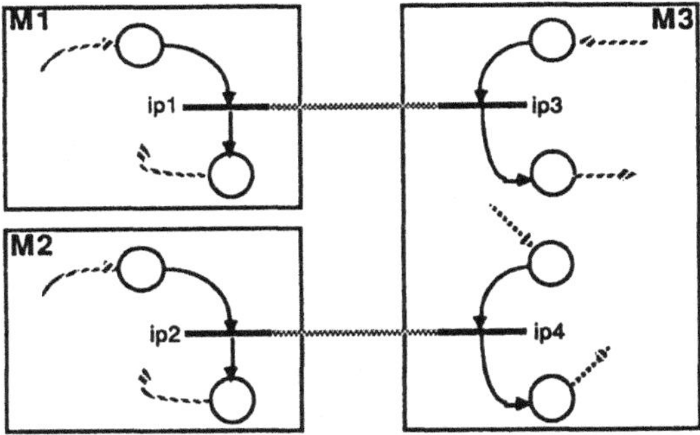

b) after: connect M1.ip1 to M3.ip3; connect M2.ip2 to M3.ip4

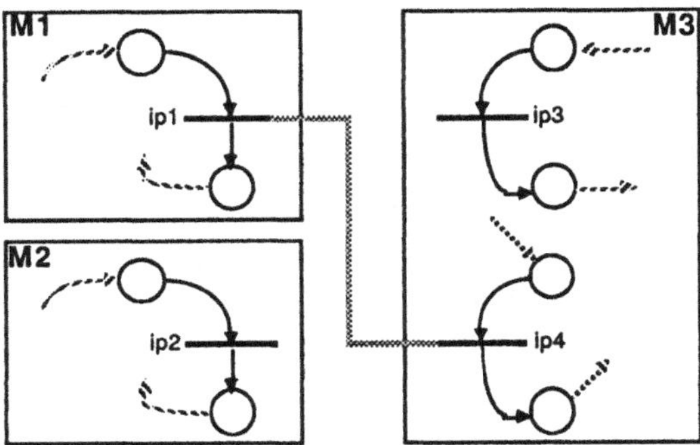

c) from b), after: disconnect M1.ip1; disconnect M2.ip2;

connect M1.ip1 to M3.ip4

Figure 6 - Dynamic transition merging in Estelle*

available with Estelle.

• Furthermore, a particular semantics has been proposed, as previously mentioned, for the "delay" clause; this semantics, which satisfies Estelle requirements for time progression, is derived from TPNs. The considered semantics handles both the time progression and the firing interval computation, which is, from the authors' point of view, an essential condition for a fully adequate model.

The major contribution of this semantics deals with the characterization of the global state S of an Estelle* specification as a subset of the Cartesian product:

$$[\mathrm{M} \times \mathrm{PARENT} \times \mathrm{CONNECTED} \times \mathrm{ATTACHED} \times \mathrm{MARKING} \times \mathrm{ENV} \times \mathrm{STORE} \times \mathrm{DFTI}]$$

where :

- the space M represents all the possible module instance configurations

(M = [X → [[BODY × HEADER] + {unused}]]), where X denotes the primitive set of all the potential module references which may be considered in the specification, and where BODY (respectively HEADER) denotes the set of the module body (respectively header) identifiers; let μ be a typical member of M : (μ x) <> unused denotes the type of module instance x (i.e. the pair (bi,hj)), (μ x) = unused indicates that currently reference x does not identify any module instance;

- the space PARENT represents all the possible module instance architectures

(PARENT = [X → [X + {⊥}]]); let p be a typical member of PARENT: (p x) identifies the current parent module instance of module instance x, if any (⊥ denotes undefined);

- the space CONNECTED represents all the possible interaction point instance "connection" configuration:

(CONNECTED = [IPI → [IPI + {⊥}]]), where IPI = [IP × X] denotes the set of all the potential interaction point instances (an interaction point instance ipi = (ip,x) denotes interaction ip under the particular context of module instance x); let c be a typical member of CONNECTED): (c ipi) identifies the interaction point instance to which ipi is currently connected, if any;

- the space ATTACHED represents all the possible interaction point instance "attachment" configuration

(ATTACHED = [IPI → [IPI + {⊥}]]); let a be a typical member of ATTACHED: (a ipi) identifies the lower level interaction point instance to which ipi is currently attached, if any;

- the space MARKING represents all the possible "marking" functions

(MARKING = [X → [P + {⊥}]]), where P denotes the set of all the major states of the specification; let m be a typical member of MARKING: (m x) identifies the current major state of module instance x, if any;

- the space ENV represents all the possible "environment" functions

(ENV = [IDI → [LOC + {unbound}]]), where IDI denotes the set of all the potential identifier instances of the specification (an identifier represents either a variable identifier or an interaction point identifier declared in the specification) and where LOC denotes the primitive set of all the available memory locations; let e be a typical member of ENV: (e (id,x)) identifies the current memory location associated with identifier id of module instance x, if any;

- the space STORE represents all the possible "store" functions (STORE $= [LOC \rightarrow [SV + \{unused\}]]$); let s be a typical member of STORE): (s l) identifies the current value of l, if memory location l is currently allocated to a module instance ((s l) = unused in the opposite case);

- the space DFTI represents all the possible "dynamic firing time interval" functions (DFTI $= [[T \times X] \rightarrow [[N \times [N + \{\mu\}]] + \{\perp\}]]$), where T denotes the set of all the transitions of the specification; let t be a typical member of DFTI: (t (t,x)) represents the current dynamic firing time interval associated with transition t, if t is enabled under the context of module instance x.

The global state s of an Estelle specification, and therefore the one of an Estelle* specification, may then be expressed as the 8-tuple of functions s = (μ,p,c,a,m,e,s,t) where functions μ and p characterize the dynamic module instance configuration (μ defines the module instances existing in the current global state whereas p defines the module instances tree); functions c and a characterize the dynamic configuration of the links between interaction point instances (respectively the connections and the attachments); function m characterizes the local marking (i.e. the control states of the module instances); function e characterizes the environment (i.e. the memory locations associated with the identifiers of the module instances); function s characterizes the store (i.e. the values of the memory locations of the module instances); finally, function t characterizes the dynamic firing time intervals associated with the transitions of the module instances.

Starting from that definition of the global state s = (μ,p,c,a,m,e,s,t) of an Estelle specification, it is possible to define the semantics of all the Estelle* constructs as well as the transition enabling and firing conditions associated with the transition firing rules; the corresponding functions have directly been implemented in the ESTIM tool.

V. CONCLUSION

This paper has dealt with some results about Petri net based models, including timed behaviours, the Estelle FDT and its Petri net based extension, Estelle*.

This paper presents an approach which permits first to model timed systems by TPNs, and then to analyse TPNs, providing a solution to check the properties of systems in which values of time must be explicit, as in communication protocols, real time designs and high performance architectures. Although no necessary and sufficient condition can be stated for checking the boundedness property, an appropriate sufficient condition has been given. Also, more specific checks could be developed in order to be able to stop the enumeration as early as possible if the behaviour of the net is not the expected one.

A complete and fully coherent extension of TPNs is then presented in order to actually design complex dynamic systems. This technique, Estelle*, can also be understood as a Petri net extension of Estelle, and can be used in order to describe pre-implementable descriptions of protocols. At last, this description may quite easily be translated into an Estelle text which will be automatically compiled by existing tools. In particular, Estelle and Estelle* have been used for designing the driving system of a flexible assembly cell, starting from its modular specification in Estelle* until its automatic implementation in Estelle [MAZ]. Such an approach allows the users to handle all main steps required in the design of complex systems by using a fully coherent hierarchy of description techniques and related support tools.

VI. REFERENCES

[AKY] I. F. AKYILDIZ, G. CHIOLA, D. KOFMAN, H. KOEREZLIOKLU, "Stochastic Petri net Modeling of the FDDI Network Protocol", Int Symp on Protocol Specification, Verification and Testing, IFIP PSTV XI, Stockholm, June 1991, North-Holland, B. Pershon et al Editors.

[BUD] S. BUDKOWSKI, P. DEMBINSKI, "An introduction to Estelle: a specification language for distributed systems", Computer Networks and ISDN Systems, 14, 1987, pp 3-23

[COU2] J.-P. COURTIAT, "Estelle and Petri Nets : A Petri Net based Semantics for Estelle - Introducing a Rendez-Vous mechanism in Estelle: Estelle*" in [Diaz 89].

[COU3] J.-P. COURTIAT, P. de SAQUI-SANNES, "ESTIM: an integrated environment for the simulation and verification of OSI protocols specified in Estelle*", Special Issue of the Journal of Computer Networks and ISDN Systems on Tools for Protocol Engineering, to appear, end of 1991.

[DES] P. DE SAQUI-SANNES, J.P. COURTIAT, "From the Simulation to the Verification of Estelle Specifications", 2nd International Conference on Formal Description Techniques (FORTE 89), S.T. Vuong Editor, North-Holland, 1990.

[DES1] P. DE SAQUI-SANNES, J.P. COURTIAT, "An extension of the Multi-way synchronization mechanism concealed by Estelle", Int Symp on Protocol Specification, Verification and Testing, IFIP PSTV XI, Stockholm, June 1991, North-Holland.

[DIA] M. DIAZ, "Modeling and analysis of communication and cooperation protocols using Petri net based models", Tutorial paper, Computer Networks, vol.6, n° 6, December 1982.

[DIA1] M. DIAZ, J.P. ANSART, J.P. COURTIAT, P. AZEMA, V. CHARI, Editors,

"The Formal description techniques Estelle", North-Holland, 1989.
[DIA2] M. DIAZ, C.A. VISSERS, "SEDOS, Software environment for the design of open distributed systems", IEEE Software Magazine, November 1989.
[DIA3] M. DIAZ, J. DUFAU, R. GROZ, Experiences using Estelle within SEDOS-Estelle-Demonstrator, 2nd Int Conf on Formal Description Techniques, FORTE 89, Vancouver, December 1989, North Holland.
[DEM] P. DEMBINSKI, S. BUDKOWSKI, "Simulating Estelle Specifications with Time Parameters", Int. Symp. on Protocol Specification, Testing and Verification, IFIP PSTV VII, Zurich, May 1987, North-Holland.
[DUG] J. DUGAN, K. TRIVEDI, R. GEIST, V. NICOLA, “Extended stochastic Petri nets applications and analysis”, Performance 84, December 1984.
[GEN] H.J GENRICH, K. LAUTENBACH, "The Analysis of Distributed Systems by means of Predicate/ Transition Nets" in Lecture Notes on Computer Science, Springer Verlag, 1979.
[HOL] M.A. HOLLIDAY, M.K. VERNON, "A generalized timed Petri net model for performance analysis", IEEE Trans. on Software Engineering, vol.SE-13, n°12, December 1987, pp.1297-1310.
[ISO1] ISO-IS9074,ISO/TC97/SC21/WG1-FDT/SC-B, "Estelle, a formal description technique based on an extended state transition model",1989.
[ISO2] ISO-IS9074,ISO/TC97/SC21/WG1-FDT/SC-C, "LOTOS, a formal description technique based on an extended state transition model", 1989.
[JON] N.D. JONES, L.H. LANDWEBER, Y.E. LIEN, "Complexity of some problems in Petri nets", Theoretical Computer Science 4, 1977.
[JUA1] G. JUANOLE, J. L. ROUX, "On the Pertinence of Extended Time Petri Net Model for Analyzing Communication Activities", IEEE 3rd Int Workshop on Petri Nets and Performance Models", Kyoto, December 1989.
[JUA2] G. JUANOLE, Y. ATAMNA, "Dealing with arbitrary time distributions with the Stochastic Timed Petri net model - Application to Queuing systems", Int Conf on Petri Nets and Performance Models, Melbourne, 1991.
[KEL] R. M. KELLER, "Formal Verification of Parallel Programs", Comm. of the ACM, July 1986.
[LAU] K. LAUTENBACH, H. A. SCHMID, "Use of Petri Nets for proving Correctness of Concurrent process systems", Proc. of the IFIP Congress, North Holland, 1974.
[MAR] M. A. MARSAN, G. BALBO, G. CONTE, "A Class of Generalized Stochastic Petri Nets for the Performance Evaluation of Multiprocessor System", ACM Trans. on Comp. Syst., May 1984, pp. 93-122.
[MAR1] M. A. MARSAN, G. BALBO, A. BOBBIO, G. CHIOLA, G. CONTE, A. CUMANI, "On Petri nets with stochastic timing", Int. Workshop on Timed Petri Nets, Torino, July 1985.
[MAZ] V.B. MAZZOLA , J-P. COURTIAT, M. DIAZ, A-M. DRUILHE, J-F.

LENOTRE, P. MICHAUD, "Flexible Assembly Cell: an implementation using the Estelle FDT", 6th CIM-Europe Conf., Lisboa, Portugal, May 1990.

[MER] P. M. MERLIN, "A methodology for design and implementation of protocols", IEEE Tr on Communications, June 1976.

[MER1] P. M. MERLIN, D.J. FARBER, "Recoverability of communications protocols", IEEE Trans. on Communications, September 1976.

[MIL] R. MILNER, "Communication and Concurrency", Prentice-Hall,1989.

[MOL] M. K. MOLLOY, "Performance Analyses using Stochastic Petri Nets", IEEE Tr on Computers, September 1982.

[NIC] R. de NICOLA, "Extensional equivalences for transition systems", Acta Informatica, Vol. 24, 1987.

[PNU] A. PNUELI, "Applications of Temporal Logic to Reactive Systems: a Survey of Current Trends", LNCS, V 224, 1986.

[11] C. RAMCHANDANI, "Analysis of asynchronous concurrent systems by timed Petri nets", Project MAC, TR 120, Massachussets Institute of Technology, Feb. 1974.

[25] R.R. RAZOUK, C.V. PHELPS, "Performance analysis using time Petri nets", 4th IFIP Protocol Specification, Testing and Verification, North-Holland, 1985, Y. Yemini Ed.

[REE1] G. M. REED and A. W. ROSCOE, A timed Model for Communicating Sequential Processes, volume 58, pages 249-261. North-Holland, 1988.

[RIC] J. L. RICHIER, C. RODRIGUEZ, J. SIFAKIS, J. VOIRON, Verification in XESAR of the sliding window protocol, Int. Symp. on Protocol Specification, Testing and Verification, IFIP PSTV VII, North-Holland, 1987.

[ROU] J. L. ROUX, G. JUANOLE, "Functional and Performance Analyses using Extended Petri Nets", Int . Work. on Petri Nets and Performance Models, Madison-WI, August 1987.

[SMI] F.D. SMITH, C.H. WEST, "Technologies for network architecture and implementation", IBM J. of Res. and Develop., vol.27, n°1, January 1983.

[VAN1] P. VAN EIJK, C. VISSERS, M. DIAZ Editors, The Formal description technique LOTOS, North-Holland, 1989.

[YUA] M.C. YUANG, "Survey of Protocol Verification Techniques Based on Finite State Models", Proc. of the IEEE Computer Networking Symposium, Washington, April 1988.

Real-Time and the Mu-Calculus*
(Preliminary Report)

E. Allen Emerson
Computer Sciences Department
University of Texas at Austin
Austin, Texas 78712
USA

Abstract

We argue that the Mu-Calculus provides a conceptually advantageous framework for specifying and reasoning about Real-Time Systems. We show that mechanical reasoning can be done efficiently in a quantitative formulation of the Mu-Calculus. Our work also suggests a new complexity theory for reactive systems.

1 Introduction

We argue that the Mu-Calculus, a formalism for characterizing correctness properties of concurrent programs as extreme fixpoint solutions of predicate transformer equations, provides a conceptually advantageous framework for specifying and reasoning about Real-Time systems. The Mu-Calculus can be seen as generalizing both "classical" Temporal Logic, a system for qualitative reasoning about concurrent program correctness, and Real-Time Temporal Logics corresponding to metric tense logics, which have been studied for real-time system applications. We show that model checking and satisfiability testing can be done efficiently for a quantitative formulation of the Mu-Calculus. We also discuss how our work suggests a new complexity theory for reactive systems.

The remainder of the paper is organized as follows. The framework of classical qualitative reasoning is discussed in Section 2, while Section 3 describes the refinement of this framework to quantitative temporal reasoning. The Mu-Calculus is reviewed in its classical qualitative formulation in Section 4. Section 5 introduces the quantitative Mu-Calculus and presents mechanical reasoning algorithms for it. Some concluding remarks are given in Section 6.

2 Qualitative Temporal Reasoning

There has been an ever-growing interest in formal methods for specifying and reasoning about *reactive systems*. These correspond to continuously operating concurrent programs such as computer operating systems, network communication protocols, and air-traffic control systems. For such systems, the appropriate abstraction is that their operation is nonterminating and described in terms of infinite computation sequences or trees recording the sequence of state configurations the system

*This work was supported in part by NSF grant DCR-8511354 and ONR Contract N00014-89-J-1913.

proceeds through. These reactive systems typically maintain an ongoing interaction with their environment, acting upon it, and reacting to it. Another characteristic is that they are usually highly nondeterministic, the nondeterminism arising from interactions with an unpredictable environment, inherent nondeterminism at low levels of hardware to resolve race conditions, and in our framework from the usual nondeterministic interleaving of fine grained steps of individual processes used to model concurrency.

In the landmark paper of Pnueli [Pn77], Temporal Logic was proposed as a formalism particularly well-suited to describing the ongoing behavior of reactive systems. Temporal Logic was originally developed by philosophers as a specialization of Modal Logic suited to describing how the truth values of assertions vary with time. Typical temporal modalities include Gp (always p), Fp (sometime p), and Xp (nexttime p). Important safety properties asserting that "nothing bad happens" can easily be specified in Temporal Logic using a formula of the form $G(\neg bad)$. Fundamental liveness properties, such as responsiveness, $G(request \Rightarrow Fgrant)$, are also readily expressible.

There is now a broad consensus among theoreticians and practitioners that Temporal Logic, in some form, is probably the best way to formally specify and reason about reactive systems. However, there are a number of different systems of Temporal Logic and there is no consensus as to which specific system or type of system is best. We have been discussing linear time Temporal Logic where the formulas are technically defined as true or false of individual computation sequences. When a linear temporal formula is interpreted over a program, there is an implicit universal quantification over all possible computations of the program. However, it is frequently important to be able to assert that there exists a computation of the program with a certain temporal property. For this reason, we have branching time Temporal Logic, which supplies the additional temporal operators A (for all computations) and E (for some computations). This makes it possible to distinguish between properties like AFp (inevitability of p along all futures) and EFp (potentiality of p along some future). We find it convenient to henceforth consider only branching time logic. Technically, formulas of branching time logic are defined over (branching, tree-like) structures, as described below.

Much work has been devoted to the development of proof rules, systems, and methodologies for establishing that a reactive system meets a Temporal Logic specification. In our view, this is valuable work that can be applied, with effort, to critical, small-scale systems. However, we are skeptical regarding the widespread application of these techniques. They generally require that one manually construct an intricate and detailed proof, using formal axioms and inference rules, that the program meets its specification. Such proofs are notably tedious and can require considerable ingenuity to organize in an intellectually manageable fashion. The opportunities for errors, either constructing an incorrect proof or failing to construct a proof even when the specification is valid, are considerable.

We therefore believe that it is important to focus on mechanical reasoning about program correctness using temporal logic and related formalisms. There are at least three approaches to explore:

0. Mechanical *assistance* for verification of programs using a *validity* tester applied to assertions of the form $p_1 \wedge \ldots \wedge p_k \Rightarrow q$. Intuitively, $p_1, \ldots, p_k$ are assertions already proved to hold for the program and q is a new assertion to be established for the program.

1. Mechanical *verification* that a given finite state program M meets a specification p formulated in temporal logic, using a *model checking* algorithm (cf. [CE81, CES83]).

2. Mechanical *synthesis* of a program M meeting a temporal specification p using a decision procedure for testing *satisfiability* (cf. [EC82, MW84, PR89]).

We note that approach 0, while less ambitious than approach 2, relies on the technical machinery of approach 2, a decision procedure for satisfiability/validity. In the sequel, we shall thus focus on model checking algorithms and decision procedures for satisfiability.

Temporal Logic is designed for qualitative reasoning. For example, we can assert that a program eventually reaches a goal state by writing $Fgoal$. But this provides no indication of when or how soon the goal is achieved. This suppression of detailed information regarding the time at which the goal is achieved is an appropriate separation of concerns. Correctness is more basic than complexity, and we should be able to reason abstractly about qualitative correctness while ignoring details concerning performance and efficiency of implementation. Thus Temporal Logic is just the appropriate tool, essentially forcing us to reason abstractly at the qualitative level.

We now give the technical framework we shall use, focusing on the qualitative logic CTL (cf. [EC82, EH82]).

Syntax

Let Σ be an underlying alphabet of atomic propositions P, Q, etc. The set of CTL (Computation Tree Logic) formulae is generated by the following rules:

S1. Each atomic proposition P is a formula.

S2. If p, q are formulae, then so are $p \wedge q$ and $\neg p$.

S3. If p, q are formulae, then so are $A(p\ U\ q), E(p\ U\ q)$, and EXp.

The other propositional connectives are defined as abbreviations in the usual way: $\vee$ for disjunction, $\Rightarrow$ for implication, and $\equiv$ for logical equivalence. Other basic modalities of CTL are also defined as abbreviations: AFq abbreviates $A(true\ U\ q)$, EFq abbreviates $E(true\ U\ q)$, AGq abbreviates $\neg EF\neg q$, EGq abbreviates $\neg AF\neg q$, and AXq abbreviates $\neg EX\neg q$.

Semantics

A formula of CTL is interpreted with respect to a *structure* $M = (S, R, L)$ where S is a set of *states*, R is a binary *relation* on S that is total (so each state has at least one successor), and L is a *labelling* which assigns to each state a set of atomic propositions, those intended to be true at the state. The *size* of M, denoted $|M|$, $= |S| + |R|$, the size of S plus the size of R. Intuitively, the states of a structure could be thought of as corresponding to the states of a concurrent program, the state transitions of which are specified by the binary relation R. A *fullpath* $x = s_0, s_1, s_2, \ldots$ in M is an infinite sequence of states such that $(s_i, s_{i+1}) \in R$ for each i; intuitively, a fullpath captures the notion of an execution sequence. We write $M, s \models p$ to mean that "formula p is true at state s in structure M". When M is understood we write only $s \models p$. We define $\models$ by induction on formula structure:

S1. $s_0 \models P$ iff P is an element of $L(s_0)$

S2. $s_0 \models p \wedge q$ iff $s_0 \models p$ and $s_0 \models q$
$s_0 \models \neg p$ iff it is not the case that $s_0 \models p$

S3. $s_0 \models A(p\,U\,q)$ iff for all fullpaths $s_0, s_1, s_2, \ldots$ in M, $\exists i \geq 0$ such that $s_i \models q$ and $\forall j, 0 \leq j < i, s_j \models p$

$s_0 \models E(p\,U\,q)$ iff for some fullpath $s_0, s_1, s_2, \ldots$ in M, $\exists i \geq 0$ such that $s_i \models q$ and $\forall j, 0 \leq j < i, s_j \models p$

$s_0 \models EXp$ iff there exists an R-successor t of s_0 such that $t \models p$

Example Specifications

Mutual Exclusion (a safety property):

$AG(\neg(C_1 \wedge C_2))$

where C_1, C_2 indicates that process 1 (process 2, respectively) is in its critical section.

Absence of Starvation (a liveness property):

$AG(T_1 \Rightarrow AFC_1)$

where T_1 indicates that process 1 is in its trying region while
C_1 indicates that process 1 is in its critical region.

Self-Stabilization:

$AG(P \Rightarrow AGP) \wedge$
$AG(true \Rightarrow AFP)$

where P indicates the set of "stable" states.

3 Quantitative Temporal Reasoning

It is important to get a formalism for specifying and reasoning about quantitative correctness or complexity issues, as "classical" Temporal Logic does not cater for this. As discussed above, Temporal Logic provides operators for qualitative specification and reasoning such as

$Fgoal$ – $\exists$ time i $goal$ is true at time i.

Such qualitative modalities provide no information on how soon the time i, when the goal is reached, occurs. A natural extension is therefore to permit qualitative, time bounded modalities such as

$F^{\leq k}goal$ – $\exists$ time $i \leq k$ $goal$ is true at time i.

This extension was studied by philosophers under the name of "metric tense logic" (cf. [Bu84]), and in the linear time framework for distributed computing systems in [KVD83, Koy90].

In [EMSS89] such a quantitative branching time temporal logic based on CTL, RTCTL (Real Time Computation Tree Logic) was proposed. We shall review results from [EMSS89] on RTCTL. We will subsequently argue that they can be elegantly generalized and most naturally understood in terms of the Mu-Calculus.

The basic idea is simply to augment CTL modalities with time bounds, e.g.,

$AF^{\leq k}p$ – bounded inevitability of p
$EF^{\leq k}p$ – bounded potentiality of p
$AG^{\leq k}p$ – bounded invariance of p

to permit expression of real-time properties.

The formal definition of RTCTL is as follows.

Syntax

The set of RTCTL (Real-Time Computation Tree Logic) formulae is generated by the rules S1–S3 for CTL above together with the rule:

S4. If p, q are formulae and k is any natural number, then $A(p\,U^{\leq k}q)$ and $E(p\,U^{\leq k}q)$ are formulae.

Other basic modalities of RTCTL are defined as abbreviations: $AF^{\leq k}q$ abbreviates $A(true\,U^{\leq k}q)$ and $EF^{\leq k}q$ abbreviates $E(true\,U^{\leq k}q)$. We also define the modality $G^{\leq k}$ as the dual of $F^{\leq k}$, i.e., $AG^{\leq k}p$ abbreviates $\neg EF^{\leq k}\neg p$, and $EG^{\leq k}p$ abbreviates $\neg AF^{\leq k}\neg p$.

Semantics

The structures over which RTCTL formulae are interpreted are the same as CTL structures. The semantics of the new RTCTL modalities are given by:

S4. $s_0 \models A(p\,U^{\leq k}q)$ iff for all fullpaths $s_0, s_1, s_2, \ldots$ in M, $\exists i, 0 \leq i \leq k$, such that $s_i \models q$ and $\forall j, 0 \leq j < i, s_j \models p$

$s_0 \models E(p\,U^{\leq k}q)$ iff for some fullpath $s_0, s_1, s_2, \ldots$ in M, $\exists i, 0 \leq i \leq k$, such that $s_i \models q$ and $\forall j, 0 \leq j < i, s_j \models p$

Intuitively, k corresponds to the maximum time along a path of a structure before the eventuality $p\ U\ q$ is fulfilled by q holding.

Remark 1 For simplicity, we have assumed the cost of a transition is 1 time unit. It is easy to generalize the notion of a model to permit any positive real costs. The algorithms for model checking perform in the same bound. The reason is that the cost of a path is the sum of the costs of the individual transitions. We can just as easily add up a sequence of nonunit costs as a sequence of unit costs.

Remark 2 The interleaving semantics for concurrency are realistic for many real time applications, e.g. on-board flight control systems with one (logical) hardware processor multiprogramming multiple software processes. (We refer to a logical hardware processor because in such situations there may be, say, three physical processors providing redundancy and fault tolerance in the implementation of a single logical processor, which in normal operation is represented in all three physical processors. In case of discrepancy among the processors, the two that agree prevail and define the logical processor.)

Example Specifications

Bounded Temporal Implication or Leads-To (Prompt Responsiveness):

$$AG(request \Rightarrow AF^{\leq k}\ grant)$$

where *request, grant* indicate that a request for service is made, granted respectively.

Bounded Self-Stabilization (Stability attained within k time units):

$$AG(P \Rightarrow AGP)\wedge$$
$$AG(\neg P \Rightarrow AF^{\leq k}P)$$

where P indicates the set of stable states.

Temporary Stability (when P becomes true, it remains true for at least k time units):

$$AG(\neg P \Rightarrow AX(P \Rightarrow AG^{\leq k}P)$$

where, again, P indicates the set of stable states. Note the crucial word "becomes" in the English characterization of this property. Were it replaced by "is", the most naturally rendering into the formalism would be simply $AG(P \Rightarrow AG^{\leq k}P)$. However, in that case, we would have $AG(P \Rightarrow AGP)$ as a consequence, corresponding to "permanent" stability. To ensure P *becomes* true after having been false, we write the formula shown.[1, 2]

Discussion

The first thing to note is that RTCTL can actually be translated into CTL on account of the nexttime operator (X), which can be iterated an appropriate bounded number of times. For example,

$$AF^{\leq 3}P \equiv P \vee AX(P \vee AX(P \vee AXfalse))$$

The drawback, of course, is that this translation causes an exponential blowup in formula size since it amounts to translating the bound k in a bounded modality such as $AF^{\leq k}P$ from binary to unary. Thus, while RTCTL offers no literal gain in raw expressive power, it does offer an exponential succinctness advantage, providing a notation that is far more convenient and usable in practice. (It is also worth noting that CTL without the nexttime operator is indeed strictly less expressive than CTL and RTCTL.)

Next we have the following as direct consequences of the linear time model checking algorithm (cf. [CES83]) and exponential time decision procedure (cf. [EH82]) for CTL:

Proposition RTCTL model checking is doable in exponential time.

Proposition RTCTL satisfiability is decidable in double exponential time.

Owing to the exponential succinctness advantage of RTCTL over CTL, we might think that these complexities are the best we can do. Fortunately, we can, in both cases, improve the complexity by an exponential factor back down to match that for CTL.

Theorem [EMSS89] RTCTL model checking is doable in time linear in the structure and formula size.

Theorem [EMSS89] RTCTL satisfiability is decidable in exponential time.

We can briefly and informally explain here why the former theorem is true. For the proofs, we refer the reader to [EMSS89].

Basically, model checking for RTCTL is in polynomial time because the original polynomial (but not linear) time CTL model checking algorithm of [CE81] works by computing the "ranks" or "bounds" on the eventualities. For example, to calculate the set of states where AFp holds, it successively calculates $AF^{\leq 0}p\ (= p), AF^{\leq 1}p, \ldots AF^{\leq |S|}p$ in structure $M = (S, R, L)$. The explicit ranks are not used in the [CE81] algorithm but they are in essence calculated and can be used to solve

[1]This notion of temporary stability makes sense over structures that are trees. When there is a branching past its meaning is less clear.

[2]We thank Leslie Lamport for pointing out the problem with the naive formulation.

the RTCTL model checking problem also. It is possible as shown in [EMSS89] to eliminate some redundant computation, essentially calculating, for example, $AF^{\leq 0}p, AF^{\leq 1}p \backslash AF^{\leq 0}p, \ldots$, thereby improving the complexity to be linear in the size of the structure and formula.

However, the model checking algorithm is best explained in terms of the Mu-Calculus as discussed below.

Remark One can legitimately ask if there is really a need for real-time considerations. In particular, if the hardware is "sufficiently" fast, the problem of meeting promptness requirements would seem to vanish. If the critical constant time bounds imposed by the external environment are many orders of magnitude larger than the time to execute the required instructions on extremely fast hardware, then there is indeed no need to concerns ourselves with real-time issues. But, as a practical matter, we are not usually fortunate enough to have such circumstances: the hardware is in fact quite limited, while the necessary promptness requirements are quite stringent. As a theoretical framework, it is also quite unsatisfactory to assume that our real-time problems will be solved by the existence of "arbitrarily" fast hardware or even "infinitely" fast hardware. The former would mean that any total recursive function could be computed in unit time, leading to the collapse of classical complexity theory. The latter would mean that the halting problem is solvable in unit time, and even classical computability theory would collapse. Thus, we believe that the problems of real-time can not be obviated by appeals to "sufficiently" fast hardware.[3]

4 Mu-Calculus

In this section we describe another way of extending CTL. We can view CTL as a sublanguage of the *propositional Mu-Calculus* $L\mu$ (cf. [Ko83, Pr81, EC80, deB80, deR76, SdeB69]). The propositional Mu-Calculus provides a *least fixpoint* operator (μ) and a *greatest fixpoint* operator (ν) which make it possible to give *fixpoint characterizations* of the branching time modalities. Intuitively, the Mu-Calculus makes it possible to characterize the modalities in terms of recursively defined tree-like patterns. For example, the CTL assertion EFp (along some computation path p will become true eventually) can be characterized as $\mu Z.p \vee EXZ$, the least fixpoint of the functional $p \vee EXZ$ where Z is an atomic proposition variable (intuitively ranging over sets of states) and EX denotes the existential nexttime operator.

We first give the formal definition of the Mu-Calculus.

Syntax

The formulae of the propositional Mu-Calculus $L\mu$ are those generated by rules (1)-(6):

(1) Atomic proposition constants P, Q

(2) Atomic proposition variables $Y, Z, \ldots$

(3) EXp, where p is any formula.

(4) $\neg p$, the negation of formula p.

(5) $p \wedge q$, the conjunction of formulae p, q.

[3]These considerations were inspired by remarks of and discussions with E. W. Dijkstra.

(6) $\mu Y.p(Y)$, where $p(Y)$ is any formula syntactically monotone in the propositional variable Y, i.e., all "free" occurrences of Y in $p(Y)$ fall under an even number of negations.

The set of formulae generated by the above rules forms the language $L\mu$. The other connectives are introduced as abbreviations in the usual way: $p \wedge q$ abbreviates $\neg(\neg p \wedge \neg q)$, AXp abbreviates $\neg EX\neg p$, $\nu Y.p(Y)$ abbreviates $\neg\mu Y.\neg p(\neg X)$, etc. Intuitively, $\mu Y.p(Y)$ ($\nu Y.p(Y)$) stands for the least (greatest, resp.) fixpoint of $p(Y)$, EXp (AXp) means p is true at some (every) successor state reachable from the current state, $\wedge$ means "and", etc. We use $|p|$ to denote the *length* (i.e., number of symbols) of p.[4]

We say that a formula q is a *subformula* of a formula p provided that q, when viewed as a sequence of symbols, is a substring of p. A subformula q of p is said to be *proper* provided that q is not p itself. A *top-level* (or *immediate*) subformula is a maximal proper subformula. We use $SF(p)$ to denote the set of subformulae of p.

The fixpoint operators μ and ν are somewhat analogous to the quantifiers $\exists$ and $\forall$. Each occurrence of a propositional variable Y in a subformula $\mu Y.p(Y)$ (or $\nu Y.p(Y)$) of a formula is said to be *bound*. All other occurrence are *free*. By renaming variables if necessary we can assume that the expression $\mu Y.p(Y)$ (or $\nu Y.p(Y)$) occurs at most once for each Y.

A *sentence* (or *closed* formula) is a formula that contains no free propositional variables, i.e., every variable is bound by either μ or ν. A formula is said to be in *positive normal form* (PNF) provided that no variable is quantified twice and all the negations are applied to atomic propositions only. Note that every formula can be put in PNF by driving the negations in as deep as possible using DeMorgan's Laws and the dualities $\neg\mu Y.p(Y) = \nu Y.\neg p(\neg Y), \neg\nu Y.p(Y) = \mu Y.\neg p(\neg Y)$. (This can at most double the length of the formula). *Subsentences* and *proper subsentences* are defined in the same way as subformulae and proper subformulae.

Let σ denote either μ or ν. If Y is a bound variable of formula p, there is a unique μ or ν subformula $\sigma Y.p(Y)$ of p in which Y is quantified. Denote this subformula by σY. Y is called a *μ-variable* if $\sigma Y = \mu Y$; otherwise, Y is called a *ν-variable*. A *σ-subformula* (*σ-subsentence*, resp.) is a subformula (subsentence) whose main connective is either μ or ν. We say that q is a *top-level* σ-subformula of p provided q is a proper σ-subformula of p but not a proper σ-subformula of any other σ-subformula of p. Finally, a *basic modality* is a σ-sentence that has no proper σ-subsentences.

Semantics

We are given a set Σ of atomic proposition constants and a set Γ of atomic proposition variables. We let AP denote $\Sigma \cup \Gamma$.Sentences of the propositional Mu-Calculus $L\mu$ are interpreted with respect to a structure $M = (S, R, L)$ as before.

The power set of S, 2^S, may be viewed as the complete lattice $(2^S, S, \emptyset, \subseteq, \cup, \cap)$. Intuitively, we identify a predicate with the set of states which make it true. Thus, *false* which corresponds to the empty set is the bottom element, *true* which corresponds to S is the top element, and implication $(\forall s \in S[P(s) \Rightarrow Q(s)])$ which corresponds to simple set-theoretic containment $(P \subseteq Q)$ provides the partial ordering on the lattice.

Let $\tau : 2^S \rightarrow 2^S$ be given; then we say that τ is *monotonic* provided that $P \subseteq Q$ implies $\tau(P) \subseteq \tau(Q)$. A monotonic functional τ always has both a least fixpoint, $\mu X.\tau(X)$, and a greatest fixpoint $\nu X.\tau(X)$:

[4]Alternatively, we can define $|p|$ as the size of the syntax diagram for p.

Theorem [Tarski-Knaster]. Let $\tau : 2^S \to 2^S$ be a given monotonic functional. Then

(a) $\mu Y.\tau(Y) = \cap \{Y : \tau(Y) = Y\} = \cap \{Y : \tau(Y) \subseteq Y\}$,

(b) $\nu Y.\tau(Y) = \cup \{Y : \tau(Y) = Y\} = \cup \{Y : \tau(Y) \supseteq Y\}$,

(c) $\mu Y.\tau(Y) = \cup_i \tau^i(\mathit{false})$ where i ranges over all ordinals of cardinality at most that of the state space S, so that when S is finite i ranges over $[0{:}|S|]$, and

(d) $\nu Y.\tau(Y) = \cap_i \tau^i(\mathit{true})$ where i ranges over all ordinals of cardinality at most that of the state space S, so that when S is finite i ranges over $[0{:}|S|]$.

A formula p with free variables $Y_1, \ldots, Y_n$ is thus interpreted as a mapping p^M from $(2^S)^n$ to 2^S, i.e., it is interpreted as a predicate transformer. We write $p(Y_1, \ldots, Y_n)$ to denote that all free variables of p are among $Y_1, \ldots, Y_n$. A valuation $\mathcal{V}$, denoted $(V_1, \ldots, V_n)$, is an assignment of the subsets of S, $V_1, \ldots, V_n$ to free variables $Y_1, \ldots, Y_n$, respectively. We use $p^M(\mathcal{V})$ to denote the value of p on the (actual) arguments $V_1, \ldots, V_n$ (cf. [EC80, Pr81, Ko83]). The operator p^M is defined inductively as follows:

(1) $P^M(\mathcal{V}) = \{s : s \in S \text{ and } P \in L(s)\}$ for any atomic propositional constant $P \in AP$

(2) $Y_i^M(\mathcal{V}) = V_i$

(3) $(p \wedge q)^M(\mathcal{V}) = p^M(\mathcal{V}) \cap q^M(\mathcal{V})$

(4) $(\neg p)^M(\mathcal{V}) = S \backslash (p^M(\mathcal{V}))$

(5) $(EXp)^M(\mathcal{V}) = \{s : \exists t \in p^M(\mathcal{V}), (s,t) \in R\}$

(6) $\mu Y_1.p(Y_1)^M(\mathcal{V}) = \cap\{S' \subseteq S : p(Y_1)^M(S', V_2, \ldots, V_n) \subseteq S'\}$

Note that our syntactic restrictions on monotonicity ensure that least and greatest fixpoints are well-defined.

Usually we write $M, s \models p$ ($M, s \models p(\mathcal{V})$, resp.) instead of $s \in p^M$ ($s \in p^M(\mathcal{V})$) to mean that sentence (formula) p is true in structure M at state s (under valuation $\mathcal{V}$). When M is understood, we write simply $s \models p$.

Discussion

We can get some additional understanding of the Mu-Calculus by noting the following extreme fixpoint characterizations for CTL properties.

$EFp \equiv \mu Z.P \vee EXZ$
$AGp \equiv \nu Z.P \wedge AXZ$
$AFp \equiv \mu Z.P \vee AXZ$
$EGp \equiv \nu Z.P \wedge EXZ$
$A(p\ U\ q) \equiv \mu Z.P \vee AXZ$ (strong until)
$A(p\ U_w q) \equiv \nu Z.P \vee AXZ$ (weak until)

Now the Tarski-Knaster theorem provides a systematic basis for model checking with the Mu-Calculus. To calculate the states where $\mu Z.\tau(Z)$ holds we successively calculate $\tau(false) \subseteq \tau^2(false) \subseteq \ldots \subseteq \tau^k(false)$, for the least $k \leq |S|$ such that $\tau^k(false) = \tau^{k+1}(false)$, in structure $M = (S, R, L)$. In the particular case where $\tau(Z) \equiv P \vee AXZ$, since $AFP \equiv \mu Z.\tau(Z)$, we would calculate $P \equiv AF^{\leq 0}P \equiv \tau(false) \subseteq AF^{\leq 1}P \equiv \tau^2(false) \subseteq \ldots \subseteq AF^{\leq k}P \equiv \tau^{k+1}(false)$. This idea provides a (naive) Mu-Calculus model checking algorithm subsuming that for CTL as shown in Figure 1. Its complexity is $O((|M||P|)^{k+1})$ for input structure M and input formula p with μ, ν formulas nested k deep.

The complexity of the model checking algorithm for the Mu-Calculus can be improved based on the *alternation depth* of the formula. Intuitively, the alternation depth refers to the depth of nesting of alternating μ's and ν's. The alternation must be "significant", entailing a subformula of the form

$$(*)\ \mu Y.p(\nu Z.q(Y, Z)) \text{ or } \nu Y.p(\mu Z.q(Y, Z)).$$

All the basic modalities AFq, AGq, EFq, etc. of CTL can be expressed in the Mu-Calculus with alternation depth 1. So can all CTL formula. For example, $EFAGq$ has the Mu-Calculus characterization $\mu Y(EXY \vee \nu Z(P \wedge AX\, Z))$, which is still of alternation depth 1 since while νZ appears inside μY, the "alternation" does not have Y inside νZ and does not match the above form (*). A property such as $E(P^*Q)^*R$, meaning there exists a path matching the regular expression $(P^*Q)^*R$, can be expressed by $\mu Y.\mu Z(P \wedge EXZ \vee (Q \wedge EXY) \vee R$, which is still of alternation depth 1.

However, this formula, $\mu Y.\mu Z(P \wedge EXZ \vee (Q \wedge EXY) \vee R$, is of *mu-depth* 2 since it involves 2 nested subformulas. Mu-depth refers to the depth of nesting of succesive μ's without intervening ν's which interact entailing a subformula of the form

$$(**)\ \mu Y.p(\mu Z.q(Y, Z)) \text{ where } p \text{ and } q \text{ are free of } \sigma\text{-subformula.}$$

Similarly we have the notion of nu-depth defined in terms of nested ν's, but since the dual of a formula of nu-depth k is a formula of mu-depth k, we shall simply refer to mu-depth. Note that all the basic modalites and, indeed, all formulas of CTL are therefore of alternation depth 1 and mu-depth 1.

On the other hand, properties associated with fairness require alternation depth 2. For example, $EGFP$ (along some path P occurs infinitely often) can be characterized by $\nu Y.\mu Z.EX(P \wedge Y \vee Z)$. It can be shown that $EGFP$ is not expressible by any alternation depth 1 formula.

Let $L\mu_k$ denote the Mu-Calculus $L\mu$ restricted to formulas of alternation depth at most k. It turns out that most all modal or temporal logics of programs can be translated into $L\mu_1$ or $L\mu_2$, often succinctly (cf. [EL86]). By the following theorem, many modal and temoral logics of programs can therefore be model checked in small polynomial time.

Theorem [EL86] Model checking for $L\mu_k$ can be done time $O((|M||p|)^{k+1})$ for input formula p and structure M.

In the case of $L\mu_1$ we can do still better:

Theorem [EL87] Model checking for $L\mu_1$ can be done in time $O(|M||p|)$ for input formula p and structure M.

The basic idea behind the model checking algorithms is to calculate the fixpoints by successive approximation using the Tarski-Knaster theorem as discussed above. Various optimizations can be applied to speed up the algorithms for certain classes of formulas, eliminating redundant computation.

Algorithm for model checking a μ-calculus sentence
Input: given a structure $M = (S, R, L)$, and a sentence p_0 which contains variables $Y_1, Y_2, \ldots Y_n$
Output: determine whether M is a model for p_0

Step 1. Convert p_0 to its equivalent PNF p_0'.
Step 2. $S' = eval(p_0')$; /* Compute the set of states at which p_0' holds */
Step 3. If $S' \neq \emptyset$ then M is a model for p_0 else M is not a model for p_0

```
Recursive function eval(f); var S', S'';
      /* return the set of states which satisfy f */
begin
      case f of the form
            P (atomic prop.): S' = {s ∈ S : P ∈ L(s)};
            Y_i (σ-variable): S' = S_i;
            ¬p : S' = S\eval(p);
            p ∧ q : S' = eval(p) ∩ eval(q);
            p ∨ q : S' = eval(p) ∪ eval(q);
            EXp : S'' = eval(p); S' = {s ∈ S : ∃t ∈ S''[(s,t) ∈ R]};
            AXp : S'' = eval(p); S' = {s ∈ S : ∀t ∈ S[(s,t) ∈ R ⇒ t ∈ S'']};
            μY_i.p_i:
                  begin
                        S_i = ∅;
                        repeat S' = S_i; S_i = eval(p_i) until S' = S_i;
                  end;
            νY_i.p_i:
                  begin
                        S_i = S;
                        repeat S' = S_i; S_i = eval(p_i) until S' = S_i;
                  end;
      end;
      return(S');
end.
```

Figure 1: Model Checker for Mu-Calculus

5 Quantitative Mu-Calculus

We now describe a quantitative formulation of the Mu-Calculus well-suited to specifying and reasoning about quantitative as well as qualitative correctness properties. The basic idea is simple and elegant; it is suggested by the Tarski-Knaster theorem:

$$\mu Z.p(Z) \equiv \bigcup_{i \geq 0} p^i(false)$$

The superscript i in $p^i(false)$ corresponds to the time bound so that the "bottom" goal $p(false)$ will be attained in $< i$ steps. Many model checking algorithms for qualitative logics are implicitly based on the Tarski-Knaster theorem and, in effect, calculate the ranks i implicitly anyway, but do not use or explicitly record them.[5]

What is needed is a nice notation to signify $p^i(false)$ and dually $p^i(true)$ to permit both bounded least fixpoints and bounded greatest fixpoints (cf. [Ko83]). Thus we shall write

$\mu i Z.p(Z)$ for $p^i(false)$,
$\nu i Z.p(Z)$ for $p^i(true)$.

Let $\leq \omega$-$L\mu$ denote the logic with formulas of $L\mu$ plus fixpoint formulas annotated with natural number ordinal ranks. We write $\leq \omega$-$L\mu_k$ to denote $\leq \omega$-$L\mu$ restricted to formulas of alternation depth at most k, and we write $\leq \omega$-$L\mu_{kl}$ to denote $\leq \omega$-$L\mu_k$ restricted to mu-depth at most l.

We now give the formal definition of the quantitative Mu-calculus $\leq \omega$-$L\mu$.

Syntax

The formulas of $\leq \omega$-$L\mu$ are generated by rules (1)-(6) for $L\mu$ plus

(7) $\mu kY.p(Y)$, where k is a natural number and $p(Y)$ is any formula syntactically monotone in the propositional variable Y.

We have the dual bounded greatest fixpoint formula $\nu kY.p(Y)$ defined as an abreviation for $\neg\mu kY.\neg p(\neg Y)$.

Semantics

Formulas of $\leq \omega$-$L\mu$ are interpreted over structures $M = (S, R, L)$ as before. The semantics of the new formula $\mu kY.p(Y)$ is defined inductively:

(7a) $s \models \mu 0Y.p(Y)$ iff $s \models false$

(7b) $s \models \mu(k+1)Y.p(Y)$ iff $s \models p(\mu kY.p(Y))$

[5]There are some exceptions, such as algorithms based on Depth First Search (cf. [CES83]).

Example Specifications

We can now specify in a uniform fashion many real-time correctness properties including bounded eventualities, bounded invariances, and all properties expressible in RTCTL. For example, the following RTCTL bounded eventualities may be rendered as shown:

$AF^{\leq k}q \equiv \mu(k+1)Z.q \vee AXZ$ (bounded inevitability)
$EF^{\leq k}q \equiv \mu(k+1)Z.q \vee EXZ$ (bounded potentiality)

Bounded invariance properties can also be captured since we permit bounded greatest fixpoints:

$AG^{\leq k}p \equiv \nu(k+1)Z.p \wedge AXZ$
$EG^{\leq k}p \equiv \nu(k+Z)Z.p \wedge EXZ$

Of course, we can express much more. In particular, we can now count modulo k, $k \geq 2$. For example,

$\nu Z.p \wedge AXAXZ$

captures the property that, along all futures, at every even time point, p occurs (cf. [Wo83]).

We can also express notions of bounded fairness, such as:

$EGF^{\leq k}Q \equiv$
$\nu Y.\mu(k-1)Z.EX((Q \wedge Y) \vee Z)$

which asserts that along some path Q always recurs within k time units.

Discussion

We now have the following results.

Theorem 5.1 Satisfiability for $\leq \omega\text{-}L\mu$ can be decided in single exponential time.

Theorem 5.2 Model checking for $\leq \omega\text{-}L\mu$ can be done in time $O((|M| \cdot exp(|p|)))$ which is linear in the size of the input structure M and exponential in the size of the input formula p.

However, for $\leq \omega\text{-}L\mu_{1,1}$ we can do much better:

Theorem 5.3 Model checking for $\leq \omega\text{-}L\mu_{11}$ can be done in time $O((|M||p|))$ for input structure M and input formula p.

The proof Theorem 5.1 follows by combining the techniques of [SE84] for the qualitative $L\mu$ and of [EMSS89] for the quantitative RTCTL. Theorem 5.2 follows by a cross product construction combining the structure M with the tableau for p as in [LP85] (cf. [SC82]).

We now indicate the ideas behind the proof of Theorem 5.3, by giving the model checking algorithm for $\leq \omega\text{-}L\mu_{1,1}$. It runs in time linear in in the size of the input structure $M = (S, R, L)$ and the size of the input formula p_0, and is a generalization of the algorithm for $L\mu_1$ of [EL87]. It is sufficient to consider only basic modalities of $\leq \omega\text{-}L\mu_{1,1}$ since subsentences can be evaluated by recursive descent.

Each basic modality is of one of four forms

```
ecursive procedure calc(f);(* return in WHOLE(f) the set of states which satisfy f *)
  case f of the form
    μkY.p : r := 0;
          repeat
             calc(p); r := r + 1;
             while NEW(p) ≠ ∅ do
                   transfer some s from NEW(p) to OLD(p);
                   add s to NEW(μYk.p), NEW(Y);
             end;
          until NEW(μkY.p) = ∅;
    p ∨ q : calc(p); calc(q);
          while NEW(p) ≠ ∅ do
             transfer some s from NEW(p) to OLD(p);
             if s ∉ WHOLE(p ∨ q) then add s to NEW(p ∨ q);
          end;
          while NEW(q) ≠ ∅ do
             transfer some s from NEW(q) to OLD(q);
             if s ∉ WHOLE(p ∨ q) then add s to NEW(p ∨ q);
          end;
    p ∧ q : calc(p); calc(q);
          while NEW(p) ≠ ∅ do
             transfer some s from NEW(p) to OLD(p);
             if s ∈ WHOLE(q) and s ∉ WHOLE(p ∧ q) then
                   add s to NEW(p ∧ q);
          end;
    EXp : calc(p);
          while NEW(p) ≠ ∅ do
             transfer some s from NEW(p) to OLD(p);
             for each R-predecessor t of s where t ∉ WHOLE(EXp) do
                   add t to NEW(EXp);
             end;
          end;
    AXp : calc(p);
          while NEW(p) ≠ ∅ do
             transfer some s from NEW(p) to OLD(p);
             for each R-predecessor t of s do
                   C(t, AXp) := C(t, AXp) + 1;
                   if C(t, AXp) = degree(t) then add t to NEW(AXp);
             end;
          end;
    P (atomic proposition): skip;
    Y (σ-variable): skip;
    ¬P (negated atomic proposition): skip;
  end
```

Figure 2: Model Checking algorithm for $\leq \omega\text{-}L\mu_{1,1}$ basic modality $f = \mu kY.p$

$$\mu kY.p(Y),\ \mu Y.p(Y),\ \nu kY.p(Y),\ \text{or}\ \nu Y.p(Y)$$

where $p(Y)$ does not contain any σ-subformulae. It suffices to consider only the case $\mu k'Y.p(Y)$ where $k' = \min(k,|S|)$, since, over M:

$$\mu kY.p(Y) \equiv \mu k'Y.p(Y),$$
$$\mu Y.p(Y) \equiv \mu |S| Y.p(Y),$$
$$\nu kY.p(Y) \equiv \neg\mu k'Y.\neg p(\neg Y),\ \text{and}$$
$$\nu Y.p(Y) \equiv \neg\mu |S| Y.\neg p(\neg Y).$$

In Figure 2 we give the algorithm for the basic modality $f = \mu kY.p = \mu kY.p(Y)$ where $k \leq |S|$. We assume, without loss of generality, that f is in Positive Normal Form with all negations driven inward so that only atomic propositions appear negated.

We associate with each subformula p $\in SF(f)$ three sets of states:

$NEW(p)$ – the set of states newly discovered to satisfy p.
$OLD(p)$ – the set of states satsifying p that were previously removed from $NEW(p)$.
$WHOLE(p) = NEW(p) \cup OLD(p)$.

For each state $s \in S$ and universal nexttime formula $AXq \in SF(f)$ we keep a counter $C(s, AXq)$, initially set to 0, which will be used to keep track of how many successor states of s have been determined to satisfy q.

We initialize $NEW(p) := OLD(p) := \emptyset$ for all $p \in SF(f)$. For the atomic propositons P and their negations $\neg P$ we then set $NEW(P) := \{s : P \in L(s)\}$ and $NEW(\neg P) := \{s : P \notin L(s)\}$.

Assuming this initialization, when the algorithm terminates we have that $WHOLE(\mu kY.p) = \{s \in S : M, s \models \mu kY.p\}$. Because each state $s \in S$ is removed from $NEW(p)$ for each subformula $p \in SF(f)$ at most once, and each arc $(s,t) \in R$ is examined at most once for each subformula of the form AXq or EXq, it follows that the complexity is $O(|M||f|)$.

6 Reactive Complexity

These ideas suggest to us that there is an as yet undeveloped theory of the complexity of reactive systems.

Let us first consider transformational programs. The "classical" qualitative correctness of a transformational program M may be captured by a total correctness assertion $< p > M < q >$ (or in Dijkstra's weakest precondition calculus as $p \Rightarrow wp(M, q)$) meaning that if program M is started in a state satisfying precondition predicate p, it eventually terminates in a state satisfying postcondition predicate q. We can render this in the temporal framework by an assertion of the form

$$AG((\text{START} \wedge p) \Rightarrow AF(\text{HALT} \wedge q))$$

where START, HALT indicate the set of initial, final states, respectively, of M.

In "classical" complexity, we are concerned with the worst-case time bound $T(n)$ such that the program M halts in at most $T(n)$ time units when started on any input of size n. We can then think of expressing $T(n)$-time bounded total correctness by an assertion of the form

$$AG((\text{START} \wedge p) \Rightarrow AF^{\leq T(n)}(\text{HALT} \wedge q))$$

where n is the "size" of the initial input state, perhaps the size of the significant input variables.

The quantitative Mu-Calculus we have proposed allows constant time bounds $\mu i Z.p(Z)$ where i is a natural number constant. However, we could also define a quantitative Mu-Calculus where a time bound $T(n)$ is a function of n, the size of the (initial) state (in which the Mu-Calculus formula is evaluated):

$$\mu T(n) Z.p(Z)$$

Thus,

$$AF^{\leq T(n)} q \equiv \mu T(n) Z.q \vee AXZ$$

and we can account for "classical" complexity for transformational programs in the framework of the Mu-Calculus.

Turning our attention now to reactive systems, we first note that basic qualitative correctness properties such as responsiveness

$$AG(request \Rightarrow AF\ grant)$$

can easily be rendered in "classical" temporal logic as shown.

There is now great interest in Real-Time correctness properties such as boundness responsiveness

$$AG(request \Rightarrow AF^{\leq k}\ grant)$$

which can be captured in quantitative temporal logic as shown. Note that the bound is given as a natural number constant k. Thus we might better term this property *constant bounded responsiveness.* While constant bounds make sense and are even desirable in many contexts (particularly when the constant is small), they are rather restrictive and unrealistic for certain applications.

It is worthwhile to consider a more general notion of Reactive Complexity comprising such properties as $T(n)$-bounded responsiveness which we can express using a formula of the form

$$AG(request \Rightarrow AF^{\leq T(|request|)}\ grant)$$

where $n = |request| =$ the size of the request.

This is reasonable because the time to grant, i.e., process, a request may in general be proportional to its size. For example, the request may be to sort and store a list of sensor readings, while the granting of the request amounts to actually performing the sorting and committing to storage.

We believe that the area of reactive complexity itself as well as formal tools for reasoning about it are well worthy of further study and seem likely to turn out to be important.

7 Conclusion

We have argued that the Mu-Calculus provides a conceptually advantageous framework for specifying and reasoning about Real-Time Systems. We showed that mechanical reasoning can be done efficiently in a quantitative formulation of the Mu-Calculus. Our work has also suggested a new complexity theory for reactive systems.

References

[Ab80] Abrahamson, K. Decidability and Expressiveness of Logics of Processes, Ph.D. Thesis, Univ. of Washington, 1980.

[Al91] Alur, R., Techniques for Automatic Verification of Real-Time Systems, PhD Thesis, Computer Science Department, Stanford University, August 1991, Technical Report STAN-CS-91-1378.

[ACD90] Alur, R., Courcoubetis, C., and Dill, D., Model-checking for Real-Time Systems, Proc. of the Fifth IEEE Symp. on Logic in Computer Science (LICS), pp. 414-425, 1990.

[AC88] Arnold, A., and Crubille, P., A Linear Time Algorithm to Solve Fixed Point Equations of Transitions Systems, Information Processing Letters, vol. 29, pp. 57-66, Sept., 1988.

[Br86] Browne, M.C., An Improved Algorithm for the Automatic Verification of Finite State Systems Using Temporal Logic, *Proc. Symp. on Logic in Computer Science*, Cambridge, pp. 260–266, 1986.

[Bu84] Burgess, J., Basic Tense Logic, in *Handbook of Philosophical Logic*, D. Gabbay and F. Guenthner, eds., D. Reidel Pub. Co, 1984.

[CKS81] Chandra, A., Kozen, D., and Stockmeyer, L., Alternation, JACM, vol. 28, no. 1, pp. 114-133, 1981.

[CE81] Clarke, E.M., E.A. Emerson, Design and Synthesis of Synchronization Skeletons Using Branching Time Temporal Logic, *Proc. of the Workshop on Logics of Programs*, Yorktown Heights, D. Kozen, editor, LNCS#131, Springer–Verlag, pp. 52–71, 1981.

[CES83] Clarke, E.M., E.A. Emerson, A.P. Sistla, Automatic Verification of Finite State Concurrent Systems Using Temporal Logic Specifications: A Practical Approach, *Proc. 10th Annual ACM Symp. on Principles of Programming Languages*, Austin, pp. 117–126, 1983; *also appeared in ACM Transactions on Programming Languages and Systems*, vol. 8, no. 2, pp. 244–263, 1986.

[CG87] Clarke, E., and Grumber, O., Research on Automatic Verification of Finite State Concurrent Systems, Ann. Rev. Comp. Sci., vol. 2, pp. 269-290, 1987.

[CBBG87] E. Clarke, S. Bose, M. Browne, O. Grumberg, The Design and Verification of Finite State Hardware Controllers, Technical Report CMU-CS-87-145, Carnegie-Mellon Univ., July 1987.

[CS91] Cleaveland, R., and Steffen, B., A Linear Time Model Checking Algorithm for the Alternation Free Modal Mu-Calculus, Proc. of the Third Workshop on Computer Aided Verification (Participant's Version), ed. K. Larsen and A. Skou, Math. and CS Dept, Univ. of Aalbourg, Denmark, July 1-4, 1991.

[deB80] de Bakker, J. W., Mathematical Theory of Program Correctness, Prentice-Hall, Englewood Cliffs, NJ, 1980.

[deR76] de Roever, W.P., *Recursive Program Schemes: Semantics and Proof Theory*, Mathematical Centre Tracts 70, Mathematisch Centrum, Amsterdam, 1976.

[deR91] de Roever, W.-P., editor, Real-Time: Theory in Practice, Springer LNCS, to appear.

[Di76] Dijkstra, E.W., *A Discipline of Programming*, Prentice–Hall, 1976.

[Em90] Emerson, E.A., Temporal and Modal Logic, in *Handbook of Theoretical Computer Science, vol. B.*, J. van Leeuwen, editor, North–Holland, pp. 995-1072

[EC80] Emerson, E.A., E.M. Clarke, Characterizing Correctness Properties of Parallel Programs Using Fixpoints, *Proc. 7th Annual International Colloquium on Automata, Languages and Programming*, LNCS#85, Springer–Verlag, pp. 169–181, 1980.

[EC82] Emerson, E.A., E.M. Clarke, Using Branching Time Logic to Synthesize Synchronization Skeletons, *Science of Computer Programming*, vol. 2, pp. 241–266, 1982.

[EH82] Emerson, E.A., J.Y. Halpern, Decision Procedures and Expressiveness in the Temporal Logic of Branching Time, *Proc. of the 14th Annual ACM Symp. on Theory of Computing*, San Francisco, pp. 169–180, 1982; *also appeared in Journal of Computer and System Sciences*, vol 30, no. 1, pp. 1–24, 1985.

[EL85] Emerson, E.A., C.L. Lei, Modalities for Model Checking: Branching Time Logic Strikes Back, *Proc. 12th Annual ACM Symp. on Principles of Programming Languages*, New Orleans, pp. 84–96, 1985; *also appeared in Science of Computer Programming*, **vol.** 8, pp. 275–306, 1987.

[EL86] Emerson, E. A., and Lei, C.-L., Efficient Model Checking in Fragments of the Mu-Calculus, IEEE Symp. on Logic in Computer Science, 1986.

[EL87] Emerson, E.A., C.L. Lei, New Results on Model-Checking in the Propositional Mu-Calculus, presented at the *Colloquium on Temporal Logic and Specification*, Altrincham, England, 1987.

[EMSS89] Emerson, E. A., Mok, A. K., Sistla, A. P., and Srinivasan, J., Quantitative Temporal Reasoning, Proceedings of the Workshop on Automatic Verification Methods for Finite State Systems (Participants Version), C-cube, the French National Concurrency Project, June 12-14, 1989.

[FL79] Fischer, M., and Ladner, R., Propositional Dynamic Logic of Regular Programs, JCSS, vol. 18, no. 2, pp. 194-211, 1979.

[GB87] Gerth, R., and Boucher, A., A Timed Failures Model for Extending Communicating Processes, In Proc. of the 14th Ann. ICALP, pp. 95-114, Springer LNCS no. 267, 1987.

[He91] Henzinger, T., The Temporal Specification and Verification of Real Time Systems, PhD Thesis, Computer Science Department, Stanford University, August 1991, Technical Report STAN-CS-91-1380.

[Ho91] Hooman, J. Specification and Compositional Verification of Real Time Systems, PhD Thesis, Eindhoven University of Technology, 1991.

[JM86] Jahanian, F., and A. K. Mok, Safety Analysis of Timing Properties in Real Time Systems, IEEE Trans. Software Eng., SE-12(9), pp. 890-904, 1986.

[JM87] Jahanian, F., A.K. Mok, A Graph-Theoretic Approach for Timing Analysis and its Implementation, *IEEE Transactions on Computers*, **vol.** C–36, no. 8, pp. 961–975, 1987.

[JS88] Jahanian, F., and Mok, A., A Method for Verifying Properties of Modechart Specifications, Proc. of the Ninth IEEE Real-Time Systems Symposium, pp. 12-21, 1988.

[Koy89] Koymans, R., Specifying Message Passing and Time Critical Systems with Temporal Logic, PhD Thesis, Eindhoven University of Technology, 1989.

[Koy90] Koymans, R. Specifying Real Time Properties with Metric Temporal Logic, *Real Time Systems*, vol. 2, no. 4., pp. 255-299, 1990.

[KVD83] Koymans, R., Vytopil, J., and de Roever, W.-P., Real Time Programming and Asynchronous Message Passing, Proceedings of the Second Annual ACM Symp. on Principles of Distributed Computing (PODC), pp. 187-197, 1983.

[Ko83] Kozen, D., Results on the Propositional μ-Calculus, *Proc. 9th Annual International Colloquium on Automata, Languages and Programming*, LNCS#140, Springer–Verlag, pp. 348–359, 1982; *also appeared in Theoretical Computer Science*, **vol.** 27, no. 3, pp. 333–354, 1983.

[Le90] Lewis, H. R., A Logic of Concrete Time Intervals, Proceedings of the Fifth Annual Symposium on Logic in Computer Science (LICS), IEEE Press, pp. 380-399, 1990.

[LP85] Lichtenstein, O., A. Pnueli, Checking That Finite State Concurrent Programs Satisfy Their Linear Specification, *Proc. 12th Annual ACM Symp. on Principles of Programming Languages*, New Orleans, pp. 97–107, 1985.

[LPZ85] Lichtenstein, O., A. Pnueli, L. Zuck, The Glory of The Past, *Proc. Conf. on Logics of Programs*, Brooklyn, R. Parikh, editor, LNCS#193, Springer–Verlag, pp. 196–218, 1985.

[MW84] Manna, Z., P. Wolper, Synthesis of Communicating Processes from Temporal Logic Specifications, *ACM Transactions on Programming Languages and Systems*, vol. 6, no. 1, pp. 68–93, 1984.

[Os90] Ostroff, J., Temporal Logic of Real-Time Systems, Research Studies Press, 1990.

[Pn77] Pnueli, A., The Temporal Logic of Programs, *18th Annual Symp. on Foundations of Computer Science*, Providence, pp. 46–57, 1977.

[PH88] Pnueli, A., and Harel, E., Application of Temporal Logic to the Specification of Real-Time Systems, in Formal Techniques in Real-Time and Fault Tolerant Systems, M. Joseph (ed.), Springer LNCS #331, 1988.

[PR89] Pnueli, A., R. Rosner, On the Synthesis of a Reactive Module, *Proc. 16th Annual ACM Symp. on Principles of Programming Languages*, Austin, pp. 179–190, 1989.

[QS81] Queille, J.P., J. Sifakis, Specification and Verification of Concurrent Systems in CESAR, *Proc. of the 5th International Symposium on Programming*, LNCS#137, Springer–Verlag, pp. 337–350, 1981.

[Pr81] Pratt, V., A Decidable Mu-Calculus, 22nd FOCS, pp. 421-427, 1981.

[SdeB69] Scott, D., and de Bakker, J., A Theory of Programs, unpublished notes, IBM seminar, Vienna, 1969.

[SC82] Sistla, A.P., E.M. Clarke, The Complexity of Propositional Linear Temporal Logics, *Proc. of the 14th Annual ACM Symp. on Theory of Computing*, San Francisco, pp. 159–168, 1982; *also appeared in Journal ACM*, vol. 32, no. 3, pp. 733–749, 1985.

[SE84] Streett, R., Emerson, E. A., An Automata-Theoretic Decision Procedure for the Propositional Mu-calculus, ICALP84, also appears in Information and Computation, vol. 81, no. 3, June 1989., pp. 249-264.

[vB83] van Benthem, J., The Logic of Time, D. Reidel Pub. Co., 1983.

[Wo83] Wolper, P., Temporal Logic can be More Expressive, Information and Control, 1983.

[YR90] Yodaiken, V., and Ramamritham, K., Specifying and Verifiying a Real-Time Priority Queue with Modal Algebra, Proc. 11th IEEE Symp on Real-Time Systems, pp. 300-311, Dec. 5-7, 1990.

Implementing reactive programs on circuits
A hardware implementation of LUSTRE

Frédéric Rocheteau
DEC / Paris Research Laboratory

Nicolas Halbwachs
IMAG / LGI - Grenoble

Abstract. Synchronous languages constitute effective tools for programming real-time systems as far as they can be efficiently implemented. Implementing them by hardware is of course a good way for increasing their performances. Moreover, configurable hardware is now available which makes practical such an implementation. This paper describes an implementation of the synchronous declarative language LUSTRE on a "programmable active memory".

Keywords: Reactive systems, synchronous languages, silicon compilation

Contents

1 Introduction

Synchronous programming [BCG87] has been proposed as a paradigm for designing reactive systems. It is an abstract point of view about real-time, which consists of assuming that a program *instantly* reacts to external events (synchrony hypothesis). It allows providing programs with precise, deterministic and machine-independent semantics. Several programming languages have been designed according to this point of view, e.g., STATECHARTS [Har84], ESTEREL [BG85], SML [BC85], SIGNAL [BL90] and LUSTRE [CPHP87].

In practice, an implementation on a given machine satisfies the synchrony hypothesis if the reaction time is always shorter than the minimum delay separating two successive external events. So, the only real-time problem with a synchronous program is to minimize and measure its reaction time. A specific compiling technique has been proposed [BG85] for synchronous languages, which synthesizes the control structure of the program as a finite automaton. This technique has been applied to ESTEREL and LUSTRE and has been shown to produce very efficient sequential code.

In this paper, we consider an other, more radical way for minimizing the reaction time of a synchronous program, which consists of translating it directly into a circuit. Synchronous languages are especially good candidates for such a translation, because usual circuits behave synchronously, from some reasonable level of abstraction (SML was designed as a hardware description language). And among synchronous languages, LUSTRE is perhaps the one for which this translation is the most natural: LUSTRE is a data-flow language, and one goal we had when designing it, was to be able to describe hardware. As a matter of fact, one solution considered for translating ESTEREL into circuits [Ber91] was to translate ESTEREL into LUSTRE.

One can wonder whether the hardware implementation of reactive systems is of general and practical interest, considering the cost of circuit manufacturing. A first answer is that many reactive systems — for instance low level communication protocols — are actually implemented by special purpose circuits. An other answer is provided by *configurable hardware.* The prototype compiler described in this paper configures a *Programmable Active Memory* (PAM [BRV89]), designed in the Paris Research Laboratory of Digital Equipment. By loading a bitstream — an operation performed in about 20 milliseconds — the PAM can be configured into any digital circuit.

The paper is organized as follows: In section 2 we explain the notion of time in synchronous languages, in order to show the importance of minimizing program reaction times. Section 3 recalls the main aspects of LUSTRE and the PAM is briefly presented in Section 4. In Section 5, we show how a boolean LUSTRE program can be translated into a circuit description which is accepted as input by standard CAD tools. Then, we describe some extensions to LUSTRE which are needed for using it as a programming language for the PAM (Section 6). These extensions concern arrays and only affect the surface level of the language.

Throughout the paper, we shall consider a very simple example of real-time program implementing a watchdog.

2 Time in synchronous languages

Let us first recall how synchronous languages pretend to express real-time constraints without making reference to a global physical notion of time. In the synchronous world, the notion of physical metric time is replaced by a simple notion of order and simultaneity between events. The physical time (measured in *seconds*, e.g.) will be considered as an input event, among others, and will not play any privileged role. We say that time is *multiform*. For instance, consider the two following constraints:

> "The train must stop within 10 seconds"
> "The train must stop within 100 meters"

There is no conceptual difference between them, and there is no reason to express them by means of different primitives, as it would be the case in languages where the metric time has a special status. In a synchronous language, they will be expressed by analogous precedence constraints:

> "The event `STOP` must precede the 10th (100th) next occurrence of the event `SECOND` (`METER`)"

A synchronous program is supposed to receive external events, which can be either simultaneous or ordered. In response to these events, and *simultaneously* with them, it emits output events. When no input event occur, nothing happens in the program. We shall only consider *logical instants*, which are instants when one or several input events occur. Here is an example of behavior of a speed counter; it receives two kinds of events, `SECOND` and `METER`, and emit the value of the `SPEED` synchronously with any occurrence of `METER`:

Logical instant	1	2	3	4	5	6
Input events	`METER`	`METER`	`METER`	`SECOND`	`METER`	`METER, SECOND`
Output events				`SPEED(3)`		`SPEED(2)`

This simple and abstract point of view appeared to be very fruitful for programming real-time systems and for providing languages with clean, machine-independent semantics. Of course, it raises two practical problems:

- How does the interface of a synchronous program proceed, for deciding whether events are simultaneous or ordered?
- How can an actual machine instantly react to unpredictable input events?

Study of the former problem is ongoing; we consider it to be a bit apart from the main research about synchronous languages. In this paper, we shall focus on the later problem. The basic idea is that if the implementation on a given machine behaves "as if" the reactions be instantaneous, the synchrony hypothesis is a valuable and acceptable abstraction. It will be the case, in particular, if the system reacts to any input event before the next event occurs. Notice that, in that sense, the correctness of an implementation is "monotonic": if a program behaves well on a given machine, it will also behave well on a faster machine. Any other assumption than "zero time" about the reaction time of the machine would violate this property.

So, our problem is to minimize and measure the program reaction time, on a given machine. The first attempt to achieve this goal was to generate efficient, linear (i.e., without loop nor recursion) sequential code for program reactions. It has been achieved in the compilers of the languages ESTEREL [BG85] and LUSTRE [CPHP87,HRR91], by static synthesis of the control structure of the code as a finite automaton. A reaction of the program corresponds to a transition of the automaton. More recently [Ber91], a more radical solution has been investigated, which consists of implementing programs by hardware. This is the solution presented here for LUSTRE.

3 Overview of LUSTRE

We don't give here a detailed presentation of the language LUSTRE, which can be found elsewhere [CPHP87]. We only recall the elements which are necessary for understanding the paper.

A LUSTRE program specifies a relation between input and outputs variables. A variable is intended to be a function of time. Time is assimilated to the set of natural numbers. Variables are defined by means of equations: An equation `X=E` , where `E` is a LUSTRE expression, specifies that the variable `X` is always equal to `E`.

Expressions are made of variable identifiers, constants (considered as constant functions), usual arithmetic, boolean and conditional operators (considered as pointwisely applying to functions) and only two specific operators: the "previous" operator and the "followed-by" operator:

- If `E` is an expression denoting the function $\lambda n.e(n)$, then `pre(E)` is an expression denoting the function
$$\lambda n.\begin{cases} nil & \text{if } n = 0 \\ e(n-1) & \text{if } n > 0 \end{cases}$$
where *nil* is an undefined value.

- If `E` and `F` are two expressions of the same type, respectively denoting the functions $\lambda n.e(n)$ and $\lambda n.f(n)$, then `E -> F` is an expression denoting the function
$$\lambda n.\begin{cases} e(n) & \text{if } n = 0 \\ f(n) & \text{if } n > 0 \end{cases}$$

A LUSTRE program is structured into *nodes*: a node is a subprogram specifying a relation between its input and output parameters. This relation is expressed by an unordered set of equations, possibly involving local variables. Once declared, a node may be functionally instantiated in any expression, as a basic operator.
As an illustration, Figure 1 shows a node describing a "watchdog": it receives

- two boolean inputs, `on` and `off`, which control its state: the watchdog is initially inactive, it becomes active whenever the input `on` is true, and becomes inactive whenever the input `off` is true.

- a boolean input `millisecond`, and an integer `delay`.

It returns a boolean output `alarm` which must be true whenever the watchdog remained active during `delay` milliseconds, i.e., during a delay in which `millisecond` has been `delay` times true. Notice that, while it is active, the watchdog can be set again with a new delay.

Figure 2 illustrates the behavior of the program: it shows the sequence of values of the expressions of the program, in response to particular sequences for input parameters. Vertical reading of this table gives the value of each expression at each execution cycle of the program.

LUSTRE programs can be viewed as data-flow operator nets: each variable is a "wire" in the net, and nodes are compound operators. Figure 3 shows the net associated with the program `WATCHDOG`. This point of view will be the basis of the translation to hardware.

4 Programmable Active Memories

Let us recall the concept of Programmable Active Memory, as defined in [BRV89]:

```
node WATCHDOG (on, off, millisecond:  bool; delay:  int)
   returns (alarm:  bool);
var active:  bool; remaining:  int;
let
   alarm = active and (remaining = 0);
   active = if on then true
            else if off then false
            else (false -> pre(active));
   remaining = if on then delay
               else if active and millisecond
               then pre(remaining) - 1
               else pre(remaining);
tel;
```

Figure 1: Example of LUSTRE program: A watchdog

cycle nr.	0	1	2	3	4	5	6	7	8	9	10	11	12
`on`	*ff*	*tt*	*ff*	*ff*	*ff*	*tt*	*ff*	*tt*	*ff*	*ff*	*ff*	*ff*	*ff*
`off`	*ff*	*ff*	*ff*	*tt*	*ff*	*ff*	*ff*	*ff*	*ff*	*ff*	*ff*	*ff*	*tt*
`delay`	4	4	4	4	4	2	2	3	3	3	3	3	3
`millisecond`	*ff*	*ff*	*tt*	*ff*	*tt*	*ff*	*tt*	*ff*	*tt*	*ff*	*tt*	*tt*	*ff*
`active`	*ff*	*tt*	*tt*	*ff*	*ff*	*tt*	*tt*	*tt*	*tt*	*tt*	*tt*	*tt*	*ff*
`pre(active)`	*nil*	*ff*	*tt*	*tt*	*ff*	*ff*	*tt*	*tt*	*tt*	*tt*	*tt*	*tt*	*tt*
`remaining`	*nil*	4	3	3	3	2	1	3	2	2	1	0	0
`pre(remaining)-1`	*nil*	*nil*	3	2	2	2	1	0	2	1	1	0	-1
`alarm`	*ff*	*ff*	*ff*	*ff*	*ff*	*ff*	*ff*	*ff*	*ff*	*ff*	*ff*	*tt*	*ff*

Figure 2: Behavior of the Watchdog program

A PAM *is a uniform array of identical cells all connected in the same repetitive fashion. Each cell, called a* PAB *for programmable active bit, must be general enough so that the following holds true: Any synchronous digital circuit can be realized (through suitable programming) on a large enough* PAM *for a slow enough clock.*

To support intuition, we shall consider a particular architecture, represented in Fig. 4. This particular PAM is a matrix of identical PABs, each of which having (see Fig. 4.a):

- 4 bits of input $< i_0, i_1, i_2, i_3 >$
- 1 bit of output O
- A 1-bit register (flip-flop) with input R and output r, synchronized on the PAM's global clock

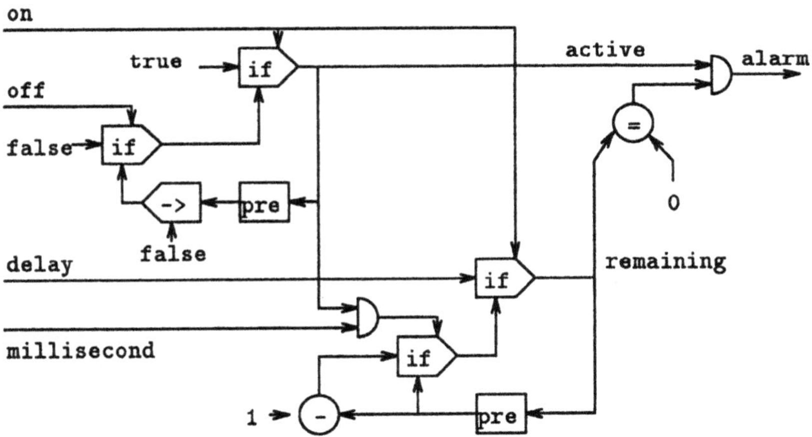

Figure 3: The operator net of the watchdog

- A universal combinatorial gate, with inputs $< i_0, i_1, i_2, i_3, r >$ and outputs $< O, R >$. This gate can be configured into any boolean function with 5 inputs and 2 outputs, by means of $2 \times 2^5 = 64$ control bits, which specify the truth table of the function.

Between the rows and the columns of cells, there are communication lines (see Fig 4.b) to which the pins of the cells can be connected. These connections and the connections between horizontal and vertical lines can also be configured by means of additional control bits.

Such a PAM, with n active bits, can be configured by downloading a sequence of control bits for configuring the PABs and their connections.

We shall keep this simple model as intuitive support, although the actual target machine of our prototype compiler is slightly more complicated. The target machine is the *Perle* family, studied and built in DEC-PRL, and based on Logic Cell Arrays designed by Xilinx Inc. [Xil88]. The presently available *Perle-0* version is a matrix of 40×80 (double) PABs, and the next version will be about 4 times larger.

Building the control bitstream corresponding to a given circuit configuration is of course a non trivial problem, in spite of available tools. In the case of *Perle*, the standard tools provided by Xilinx, together with the tools developed in DEC-PRL, take as input a logical description of each PAB, together with optional placement indications. They finish the placement, perform automatic routing, and produce the bitstream. Our goal is to translate a LUSTRE program into a description being usable as input of these tools.

5 Implementing boolean LUSTRE on the PAM

We briefly describe the translation of a boolean LUSTRE program into a layout for the PAM (see [Roc89] for more details). It requires

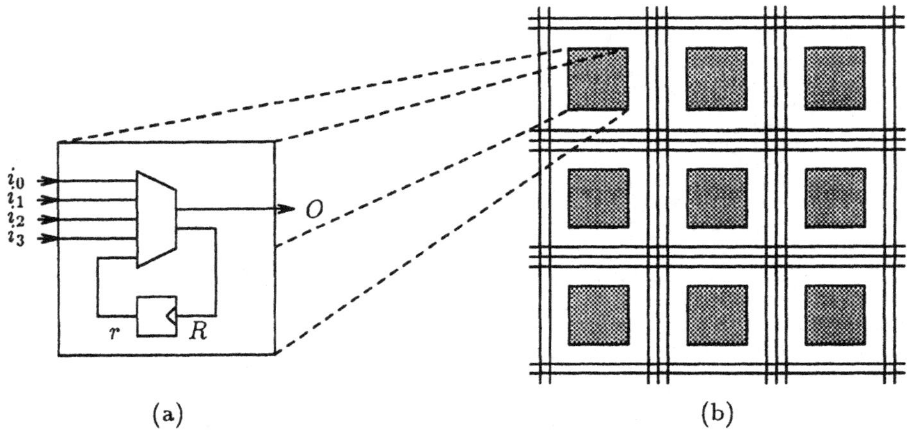

Figure 4: A simple Programmable Active Memory

- translating LUSTRE operators in terms of hardware operators (gates, flip-flops)
- implementing the resulting operator net by means of connected PABs

Translation of LUSTRE operators

The first step of the compilation of a boolean program consists of translating its corresponding operator net into a net of gates and flip-flops.

The operator net corresponding to a boolean LUSTRE program contains boolean operators (`or`, `and`, `not`, `=`), conditional (`if_then_else`), and temporal (`pre`, `->`) operators.

Notice that what we call "boolean operators" in LUSTRE are not strictly boolean because of the undefined value *nil*. However, although most of the LUSTRE operators are strict with respect to *nil*, in a legal LUSTRE program, the apparition of a *nil* value may not influence the outputs of the program. This property is checked by the compiler. So, in a legal program we can replace the undefined value by any boolean value without changing the outputs of the program. As a consequence, LUSTRE boolean operators can be straightforwardly translated into gates. The conditional operator can also be translated into a set of gates, using the boolean identity:

```
if A then B else C = (B and A) or (C and not A)
```

The "previous" operator will be obviously implemented by means of a flip-flop. In the technology used, the initial value of flip-flops is 0, so *nil* is considered to be 0. The "followed-by" operator is implemented by means of the *reset* input of the circuit:

```
A -> B = if RESET then A else B = (A and RESET) or (B and not RESET)
```

Example: The definition of the variable `active` of the watchdog

```
active = false -> if on then true
                  else if off then false
                  else pre(active)
```

will be translated into

```
active = (false and RESET) or
              (not RESET and ((true and on) or (not on and
              ((false and off) or (not off and FLIP_FLOP(active))))))
```

which, of course, can be simplified into

```
active = not RESET and (on or (not off and FLIP_FLOP(active)))
```

"Packing" operators into PABs

The next task concerns the expression of the resulting net of gates and flip-flops by means of PABs. The simplest way for performing this task consists of using one PAB for each operator in the net. Of course this solution is very unefficient, but we shall use it as a starting point. It is then improved by applying a set of packing rules. Fig. 5.b shows some of these rules, using the notations of Fig. 5.a. The rules are applied according to some simple heuristics. For instance, the net computing the variable `active` (see Fig. 6) may be packed into one PAB.

6 Extending LUSTRE for programming the PAM

We have shown that the implementation of boolean LUSTRE on the PAM is quite straightforward. If we want to deal with a greatest subset of the language, we have to implement integer variables by vectors of bits. On the other hand, LUSTRE is a good candidate as a high level language for programming the PAM, but lacks some features, concerning regular structures (arrays) and net geometry. In this section, we propose some extensions to the language, which permit

- to deal with a greatest subset of LUSTRE than the purely boolean part. In particular, integers will be considered as vectors of bits.
- to make easier its use for describing circuits. Arrays will be available for describing regular structures. They will also carry placement informations.

6.1 Arrays in LUSTRE

Although they were considered in the very first design of the language, arrays have not yet been introduced in LUSTRE, since their translation to sequential code raises difficult problems, concerning the order of computations. These problems disappear when a fully parallel implementation is considered. We propose here a notion of array, compatible with the principles of the language. Introducing arrays will allow integer values to be considered as boolean arrays, with arithmetic operators operating on arrays. Considering a number

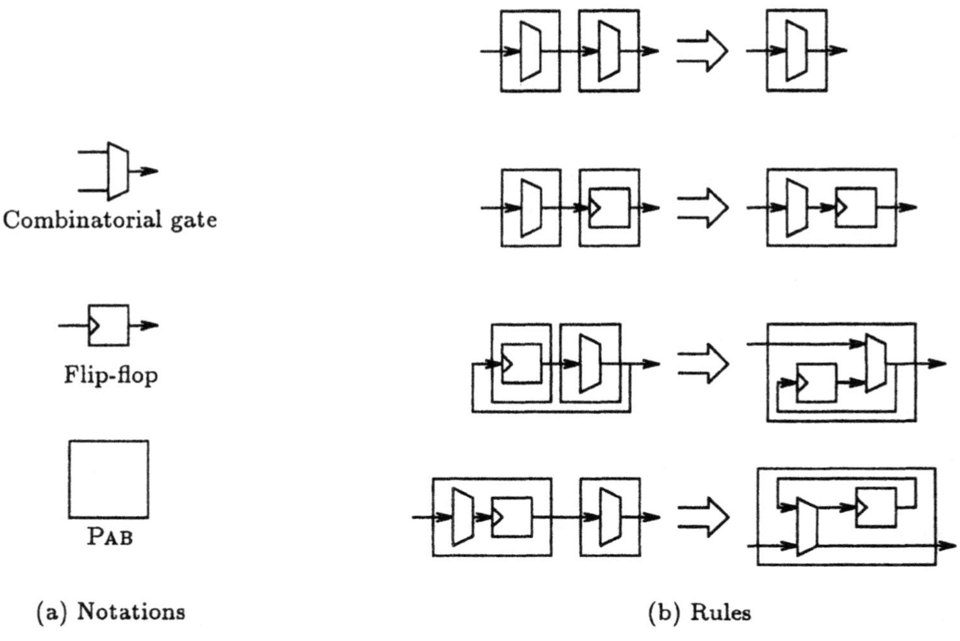

Figure 5: Some rules for packing operators into PABs

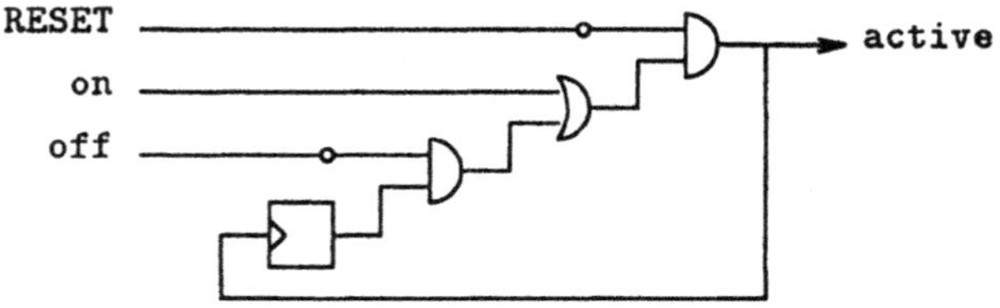

Figure 6: The net computing the variable "**active**"

as e.g., a 32-bit array instead of 32 unrelated boolean variables, is also interesting for placement on the PAM: it strongly suggests to implement it as a register.

LUSTRE contains three predefined data types: boolean, integer and real, and allows abstract data types to be imported from an host language. There is only one way for building compound types, by tupling: if τ_0, τ_1, ..., τ_n are types, so is $[\tau_0, \tau_1, \ldots, \tau_n]$, which is the type of tuples $[X_0, X_1, \ldots, X_n]$ of LUSTRE variables, where X_i is of type τ_i. If `X` is an expression of type tuple and `i` is an integer constant, `X[i]` denotes the $(i+1)$-th component of `X` (tuple components are numbered from 0).

The notion of array we propose is a special case of tuple: Let us define an *index* to be a non negative integer constant, known at compile time. If τ is a type, and n is an index, then τ`^n` is the type of arrays of n elements of type τ, numbered from 0 to `n-1` (this notation refers to Cartesian power of τ). An array is a tuple, all components of which have the same type. As a consequence, if `X` is an array of type τ`^n` and `i` is an index, `X[i]` denotes the i-th component of `X` (provided $0 \leq i < n$). One can also access a slice of an array: If `X` is as above and `i` and `j` are indexes smaller than n, then `X[i..j]` is the array

- `[X[i],X[i+1],...,X[j]]` of type τ`^(j-i+1)` , if $i \leq j$
- `[X[i],X[i-1],...,X[j]]` of type τ`^(i-j+1)` , otherwise.

If E_1, E_2, ..., E_n are expressions of the same type τ, $[E_1, E_2, \ldots, E_n]$ denotes the array whose i-th component is E_i. By extension, `E^n` denotes the array `[E,E,...,E]`.

Of course, polymorphic LUSTRE operators can be applied to arrays. We introduce also the following notion of polymorphism: any operator op of sort

$$\tau_1 \times \tau_2 \times \ldots \tau_i \;\rightarrow\; \tau_1' \times \tau_2' \times \ldots \tau_j'$$

(i.e., taking i parameters of respective types $\tau_1, \tau_2, \ldots, \tau_i$ and returning j results of respective types $\tau_1', \tau_2', \ldots, \tau_j'$) is implicitly overloaded to have the sort

$$\tau_1\texttt{\^{}n} \times \tau_2\texttt{\^{}n} \times \ldots \tau_i\texttt{\^{}n} \;\rightarrow\; \tau_1'\texttt{\^{}n} \times \tau_2'\texttt{\^{}n} \times \ldots \tau_j'\texttt{\^{}n}$$

for any index n. For instance, the operator and, of sort `bool` $\times$ `bool` $\rightarrow$ `bool` may be applied to two arrays `A` and `B` of type `bool^n`, returning the array `C` such that `C[i] = (A[i] and B[i])`, for any $i = 0 \ldots n-1$.

6.2 Examples

We shall translate our watchdog program into a boolean program. First, we have to express arithmetic operators as operating on boolean vectors. Let us give a comparator to zero and a combinatorial decrementer:

Zero comparator : It takes a vector of booleans, representing an integer, together with its size, and returns *true* if and only if the represented integer is zero (see the resulting net on Fig. 7):

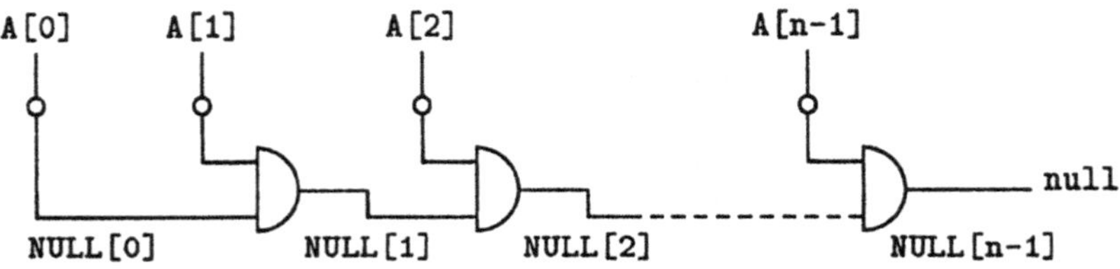

Figure 7: The net of the Zero comparator

```
node NULL(const n:  int; A: bool^n) returns(null:  bool);
var NULL: bool^n;
let
   null = NULL[n-1];
   NULL[1..n-1] = NULL[0..n-2] and not A[1..n-1];
   NULL[0] = not A[0];
tel;
```

Combinatorial decrementer: It is made of a general adder:

```
node DECR(const n:  int; A: bool^n) returns (D: bool^n);
var carry_out:  bool;
let
   (S,carry_out) = ADD(n,A,true^n);
tel;
```

The n-bits adder is standard; it is made of n 1-bit adders:

```
node ADD(const n:int;A,B:bool^n) returns (S:bool^n; carry_out:bool);
var CARRY: bool^n+1;
let
   CARRY[0] = false;
   (S,CARRY[1..n]) = AD1(A,B,CARRY[0..n-1]);
   carry_out = CARRY[n];
tel;

node AD1(a,b,carry_in:  bool) returns (s, carry_out:  bool);
let
   s = XOR(a, XOR(b,carry_in));
   carry_out = (a and b) or (b and carry_in) or (carry_in and a);
tel;
```

Full watchdog: Using these boolean implementations of arithmetic operators, the watchdog program can be translated into a boolean program. Here we choose a 8-bits representation of integers:

```
const size = 8;
type Int = bool^size;
node WATCHDOG (on, off, millisecond:  bool; delay:  Int)
   returns (alarm:  bool);
var active:  bool; remaining:  Int;
let
   alarm = active and NULL(size,remaining);
   active = if on then true
            else if off then false else (false->pre(active));
   remaining = if on^size then delay
               else if (active and millisecond)^size
               then DECR(size, pre(remaining))
               else pre(remaining);
tel;
```

The automatic translation of the initial program into this one is not yet implemented. However, our prototype compiler, called POLLUX, translates the above program into the layout (for *Perle-0*) shown in Fig. 8, described in a format that can be provided to standard CAD tools. This layout must be interpreted as follows:

- Cell (a) computes the 4th bit of `remaining-1`, according to the equation

```
D[3] = PR[3] xor 1 xor C[2]
```

- Cells (b) and (c) respectively compute the 3rd and 2nd bits of `remaining-1` and the corresponding carry, according to the equations

```
D[2] = PR[2] xor 1 xor C[1]
C[2] = PR[2] or C[1]
D[1] = PR[1] xor 1 xor C[0]
C[1] = PR[1] or C[0]
```

- Cell (d) computes its first bit and the first carry

```
D[0] = not PR[0]
C[0] = PR[0]
```

- Cells (e), (f), (g), (h) compute the 4 bits of `remaining` and `pre(remaining)`, according to the equations:

```
PR[i] = Flop(remaining[i])
remaining[i] = (on and delay[i]) or (decr and D[i]) or PR[i]
```

- Cell (i) computes

```
alarm = active and not(remaining[0] or
            remaining[1] or remaining[2] or remaining[3])
```

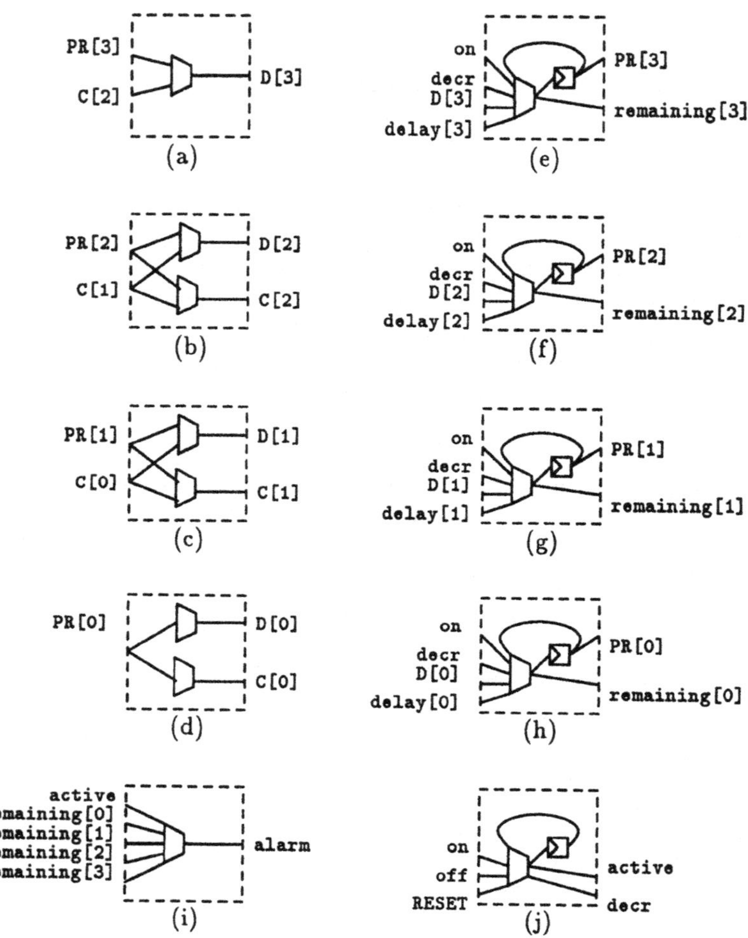

Figure 8: Layout of the Watchdog on Perle-0

- Cell (j) computes

```
active = on or (not off and not RESET and Flop(active))
decr = active and millisecond
```

Its critical path is of about 60ns (much less than the time needed by a MC-68000 to perform a "load register" statement!).

References

[BC85] M. C. Browne and E. M. Clarke. SML — *a high-level language for the design and verification of finite state machines.* Research Report CMU-CS-85-179, Carnegie Mellon University, 1985.

[BCG87] G. Berry, P. Couronné, and G. Gonthier. *Synchronous programming of reactive systems, an introduction to* ESTEREL. Technical Report 647, INRIA, 1987.

[Ber91] G. Berry. A hardware implementation of pure ESTEREL. In *ACM Workshop on Formal Methods in VLSI Design*, january 1991.

[BG85] G. Berry and G. Gonthier. *The synchronous programming language* ESTEREL, *design, semantics, implementation.* Technical Report 327, INRIA, 1985. to appear in Science of Computer Programming.

[BL90] A. Benveniste and P. LeGuernic. Hybrid dynamical systems theory and the SIGNAL language. *IEEE Transactions on Automatic Control*, 35(5):535–546, may 1990.

[BRV89] P. Bertin, D. Roncin, and J. Vuillemin. *Introduction to programmable active memories.* Technical Report, Digital Paris Research Laboratory, june 1989.

[CPHP87] P. Caspi, D. Pilaud, N. Halbwachs, and J. Plaice. LUSTRE: a declarative language for programming synchronous systems. In *14th ACM Symposium on Principles of Programming Languages*, january 1987.

[Har84] D. Harel. Statecharts: a visual approach to complex systems. In *Advanced NATO Institute on Logics and Models for Verification and Specification of Concurrent Systems*, 1984.

[HRR91] N. Halbwachs, P. Raymond, and C. Ratel. Generating efficient code from dataflow programs. In *Third International Symposium on Programming Language Implementation and Logic Programming*, Passau, august 1991.

[Roc89] F. Rocheteau. *Programmation d'un circuit massivement parallèle à l'aide d'un langage déclaratif synchrone.* Technical Report SPECTRE L10, IMAG, Grenoble, june 1989.

[Xil88] Xilinx, Inc. The programmable gate array data book. 1988. Product Specification.

Semantics and Completeness of Duration Calculus*†

Michael R. Hansen‡ and Zhou Chaochen‡§¶

Abstract: Duration Calculus was introduced in [1] as a notation to specify real-time systems, and as a calculus to verify theorems about such systems. Its distinctive feature is reasoning about *durations* of states within any time interval, without explicit mention of absolute time. Duration Calculus, which is an extension of Interval Temporal Logic, was originally designed to reason about real-time requirements for control systems; but it has been used at other levels of abstraction also: for example to give real-time semantics to communicating processes executed on a shared processor configuration and to reason about the correctness of a circuit transformation. The purpose of this paper is to introduce a formal syntax and semantics for Duration Calculus, and to prove its completeness — relative to the completeness of Interval Temporal Logic.

Keywords: Duration Calculus, Interval Temporal Logic, proof system, real-time systems, relative completeness, specifications, specification languages, verification.

Contents

---

*This work is partially funded by **ProCoS** ESPRIT BRA 3104.

†This work is partially funded by the Danish Technical Research Counsil under project **RapID**.

‡Department of Computer Science, Technical University of Denmark.

§Also visiting Programming Research Group, Oxford University, England.

¶On leave of absence from Institute of Software, Academia Sinica, Beijing, China.

1 Introduction

The purpose of this section is to motivate Duration Calculus by an example taken from [1]. This example will also be used later to illustrate syntax, semantics, and proof system of Duration Calculus.

A central step in the development of software for real-time systems is to formalize and reason about real-time requirements. Let for instance *Leak* denote an undesirable but unavoidable state of a gas burner system, which is present when there is a flow of unlit gas from the nozzle of the gas burner. Such a state can be represented as a function from time (represented by reals) to $\{0, 1\}$, where 1 denotes that the system is in the state, and 0 denotes that the system is not in the state.

A safety engineer may calculate that the ventilation required for normal combustion would prevent dangerous accumulation of gas, provided that the proportion of time spent in the leak state is not more than a twentieth of the elapsed time. The time interval over which the system is observed should be at least one minute long — otherwise the requirement would be violated immediately on the start of a leak.

This requirement is formalized by:

Req-1

$$(e - b) \geq 60\ sec. \ \Rightarrow\ 20 \int_b^e Leak(t)dt \leq (e - b)$$

for any time interval $[b, e]$, $b \leq e$.

Notice that $\int_b^e Leak(t)dt$ is a measure for the *duration* of leak in the time interval $[b, e]$.

Turning next to the task of design, certain decisions must be taken about how the agreed requirements are to be met. For example, a leak should be detectable and stoppable within one second; and then it is acceptable to wait thirty seconds before risking another leak by switching on the gas again. Using c and f to denote the end points of an arbitrary sub-interval of $[b, e]$ above, these two decisions can be formalized by:

Des-1

$$\int_c^f Leak(t)dt = (f - c) \ \Rightarrow\ (f - c) \leq 1\ sec.$$

Des-2

$$Leak(c) \wedge Leak(f) \wedge (\exists t \bullet c < t < f \wedge \neg Leak(t)) \ \Rightarrow\ 30\ sec. \leq (f - c)$$

The conjunction of these two formulae implies the original requirement, a fact which should be proved and certified by the designing engineer before implementation proceeds. The objective of Duration Calculus is to provide a simple notation for expressing such theorems, and a simple calculus for proving them. Since a time interval is a more basic notion in this example than an instant of time, the calculus is an extension of Interval Temporal Logic where one can reason about integrals of states.

In the next section Interval Temporal Logic [13] is defined on a continuous time domain, and section 3 defines syntax and semantics of Duration Calculus. The proof system for the calculus with (a sketch of) its soundness proof is given in section 4, and in section 5 the completeness of Duration Calculus is proven (relative to Interval Temporal Logic). Section 6, the conclusion, contains a summary of some of the work on Duration Calculus done so far.

2 Interval Temporal Logic

The Interval Temporal Logic of [13] is based on discrete time. In this section we give a definition of semantics for continuous time represented by reals.

2.1 Syntax

Interval temporal logic is a modal logic with alphabet of symbols:

- Some (possibly infinitely many) temporal variables $v_i, i \geq 0$
- The special symbol ℓ, which stands for the length of an interval
- Some (possibly infinitely many) global variables $x, y, z, \ldots$
- Some (possibly infinitely many) n-ary function letters $f_i^n, i, n \geq 0$
- Some (possibly infinitely many) n-ary predicate letters $A_i^n, i, n \geq 0$
- The special symbols *true* and *false*
- The connectives $\vee$ and $\neg$
- The quantifier $\forall$ and the modality $\frown$

Later we interpret a temporal variable v as a real valued function on intervals of time, a global variable x as a real, f_i^n as an n-ary function on reals, and A_i^n as an n-ary relation on reals.

Terms: the set of terms is generated by

1. temporal variables v, ℓ, and global variables x are terms
2. if $r_1, \ldots, r_n$ are terms and f_i^n is an n-ary function letter, then $f_i^n(r_1, \ldots, r_n)$ is a term
3. the set of terms are generated as in 1. and 2.

From now on we omit clauses such as 3. above in inductive definitions.

Atomic interval formulae: if A_i^n is a n-ary predicate letter and $r_1, \ldots, r_n$ are terms, then $A_i^n(r_1, \ldots, r_n)$ is an atomic interval formula.

Interval Formulae: the set of interval formulae is generated by

1. *true*, *false*, and atomic interval formulae are interval formulae
2. if $\mathcal{F}_1$ and $\mathcal{F}_2$ are interval formulae, so are $(\neg\mathcal{F}_1)$, $(\mathcal{F}_1 \vee \mathcal{F}_2)$, $(\mathcal{F}_1 \frown \mathcal{F}_2)$, and $(\forall x)\mathcal{F}_1$, where x is any global variable

We will use the abbreviations $\wedge, \Rightarrow, \Leftrightarrow, \Diamond$, and $\Box$ in interval formulae, where $\Diamond\mathcal{F}$ stands for $(true \frown (\mathcal{F} \frown true))$ and $\Box\mathcal{F}$ for $(\neg\Diamond(\neg\mathcal{F}))$. The interval formula $\Diamond\mathcal{F}$ is read: there is a sub-interval where $\mathcal{F}$ holds, and $\Box\mathcal{F}$ is read: for every sub-interval $\mathcal{F}$ holds.

2.2 Semantics

In the following we interpret function and predicate letters as functions on real numbers R, and respectively relations over real numbers.

We assume fixed meanings associated with function letters and predicate letters, i.e. there is a total function $\underline{f}_i^n : R^n \rightarrow R$ associated with each n-ary function letter f_i^n, and a total function $\underline{A}_i^n : R^n \rightarrow \{tt, ff\}$ associated with each n-ary predicate letter A_i^n.

We want to interpret temporal variables as real-valued functions on time intervals. We model continuous *time* as the set of reals R. Let a *bounded and closed interval* $[b, e]$ be $\{t \in R \mid b \leq t \leq e\}$, for $b \leq e$, and let *Intv* denote the set of all bounded and closed intervals. From now on we just say interval for bounded and closed interval.

An *interpretation* $\mathcal{I}$ associates a function $\underline{v} : Intv \rightarrow R$ with each temporal variable v. A *valuation* in $\mathcal{I}$ is a pair $(\mathcal{V}, [b, e])$ where $\mathcal{V}$ associates a real value $\underline{x} \in R$ with each global variable x.

We call two valuations $(\mathcal{V}, [b, e])$ and $(\mathcal{V}', [b, e])$ in $\mathcal{I}$ for *x-equivalent* if they associate the same value with any global variable y different from x.

Terms are interpreted over intervals of time. The value of a term r given a valuation $(\mathcal{V}, [b, e])$ in $\mathcal{I}$ is defined by:

$$\begin{array}{lcl} \mathcal{V}_{[b,e]}[\![v]\!] & = & \underline{v}(b, e) \\ \mathcal{V}_{[b,e]}[\![x]\!] & = & \underline{x} \\ \mathcal{V}_{[b,e]}[\![\ell]\!] & = & e - b \\ \mathcal{V}_{[b,e]}[\![f_i^n(r_1, \ldots, r_n)]\!] & = & \underline{f}_i^n(\mathcal{V}_{[b,e]}[\![r_1]\!], \ldots, \mathcal{V}_{[b,e]}[\![r_n]\!]) \end{array}$$

Interval formulae: the definition that a valuation $(\mathcal{V}, [b, e])$ in $\mathcal{I}$ *satisfies* an interval formula $\mathcal{F}$ is:

$\mathcal{V}_{[b,e]}[\![true]\!] = tt$

$\mathcal{V}_{[b,e]}[\![false]\!] = ff$

$\mathcal{V}_{[b,e]}[\![A_i^n(r_1, \ldots, r_n)]\!] = tt$ iff $\underline{A}_i^n(\mathcal{V}_{[b,e]}[\![r_1]\!], \ldots, \mathcal{V}_{[b,e]}[\![r_n]\!]) = tt$

$$\mathcal{V}_{[b,e]}[\![(\neg\mathcal{F})]\!] = tt \quad \text{iff } \mathcal{V}_{[b,e]}[\![\mathcal{F}]\!] = \mathit{ff}$$

$$\mathcal{V}_{[b,e]}[\![(\mathcal{F}_1 \vee \mathcal{F}_2)]\!] = tt \quad \text{iff } \mathcal{V}_{[b,e]}[\![\mathcal{F}_1]\!] = tt \text{ or } \mathcal{V}_{[b,e]}[\![\mathcal{F}_2]\!] = tt$$

$$\mathcal{V}_{[b,e]}[\![(\mathcal{F}_1 \frown \mathcal{F}_2)]\!] = tt \quad \text{iff } \mathcal{V}_{[b,m]}[\![\mathcal{F}_1]\!] = tt \text{ and } \mathcal{V}_{[m,e]}[\![\mathcal{F}_2]\!] = tt, \text{ for some } m \in [b,e]$$

$$\mathcal{V}_{[b,e]}[\![(\forall x)\mathcal{F})]\!] = tt \quad \text{iff } \mathcal{V}'_{[b,e]}[\![\mathcal{F}]\!] = tt, \text{ for all } (\mathcal{V}', [b,e]) \text{ } x\text{-equivalent with } (\mathcal{V}, [b,e])$$

An interval formula $\mathcal{F}$ is *true* in the interpretation $\mathcal{I}$ (written $\mathcal{I} \models \mathcal{F}$) iff $\mathcal{V}_{[b,e]}[\![\mathcal{F}]\!] = tt$, for any valuation $(\mathcal{V}, [b,e])$ in $\mathcal{I}$. Furthermore, $\mathcal{F}$ is *valid* (written $\models \mathcal{F}$) iff $\mathcal{I} \models \mathcal{F}$, for any interpretation $\mathcal{I}$.

3 Duration Calculus

We want to extend Interval Temporal Logic by adding structure to temporal variables in the following way:

State variables (such as *Leak* in section 1) are introduced as total functions from time to $\{0,1\}$. A *state*, being a propositional combination of state variables, also denotes a function from time to $\{0,1\}$. Temporal variables of Interval Temporal Logic are replaced by *durations* of states, i.e. functions from *Intv* to non-negative reals which given an interval is a measure for the time within the interval for which the state has the value 1.

The syntax and semantics of Duration Calculus is now defined.

3.1 Syntax

The alphabet of symbols for Duration Calculus is obtained from the alphabet of symbols of Interval Temporal Logic by deleting the temporal variables and by adding:

- Some (possibly infinitely many) state variables $X, Y, Z, \ldots$
- The special symbols 0 and 1

States: the set of states is generated by

1. $0, 1$, and every state variable are states
2. if P and Q are states, so are $(\neg P)$ and $(P \vee Q)$, where $\neg$ and $\vee$ are boolean operators on states and semantically different from the connectives on formulae

Durations: for any state P: $\int P$ is a duration.

Terms: the set of terms is generated by

1. ℓ, durations $\int P$, and global variables x are terms

2. if $r_1, \ldots, r_n$ are terms and f_i^n is an n-ary function letter, then $f_i^n(r_1, \ldots, r_n)$ is a term

Atomic duration formulae: if A_i^n is a n-ary predicate letter and $r_1, \ldots, r_n$ are terms, then $A_i^n(r_1, \ldots, r_n)$ is an atomic duration formula.

Duration formulae: the set of duration formulae is generated by

1. *true*, *false*, and atomic duration formulae are duration formulae

2. if $\mathcal{D}_1$ and $\mathcal{D}_2$ are duration formulae, so are $(\neg\mathcal{D}_1)$, $(\mathcal{D}_1 \vee \mathcal{D}_2)$, $(\mathcal{D}_1 \frown \mathcal{D}_2)$, and $(\forall x)\mathcal{D}_1$, where x is any global variable

We will use the standard abbreviations for $\wedge, \Rightarrow$, and $\Leftrightarrow$ for both states and duration formulae. In duration formulae $\Diamond\mathcal{D}$ stands for $(\mathit{true} \frown (\mathcal{D} \frown \mathit{true}))$ and $\Box\mathcal{D}$ for $(\neg\Diamond(\neg\mathcal{D}))$.

3.2 Semantics

We assume there is associated a total function $\underline{f}_i^n : R^n \rightarrow R$ with each n-ary function letter f_i^n, and a total function $\underline{A}_i^n : R^n \rightarrow \{tt, ff\}$ with each n-ary predicate letter A_i^n.

We want to interpret state variables as two valued functions on time. Global variables are interpreted as reals.

An *interpretation* $\mathcal{I}_\mathcal{D}$ associates a total function $\underline{X} : R \rightarrow \{0, 1\}$ with each state variable X. We require that each $\underline{X}$ has only a finite number of discontinuity points in any interval.

A *valuation* in $\mathcal{I}_\mathcal{D}$ is a pair $(\mathcal{V}_D, [b, e])$ where $\mathcal{V}_D$ associates a real value $\underline{x} \in R$ with each global variable x.

We call two valuations $(\mathcal{V}_D, [b, e])$ and $(\mathcal{V}'_D, [b, e])$ in $\mathcal{I}_\mathcal{D}$ for *x-equivalent* if they associate the same value with any global variable y different from x.

States: the value of a state P at time t in interpretation $\mathcal{I}_\mathcal{D}$ is defined by

$$
\begin{array}{lcl}
\mathcal{I}_\mathcal{D}[\![0]\!](t) & = & 0 \\
\mathcal{I}_\mathcal{D}[\![1]\!](t) & = & 1 \\
\mathcal{I}_\mathcal{D}[\![X]\!](t) & = & \underline{X}(t) \\
\mathcal{I}_\mathcal{D}[\![(\neg P)]\!](t) & = & 1 - \mathcal{I}_\mathcal{D}[\![P]\!](t) \\
\mathcal{I}_\mathcal{D}[\![(P \vee Q)]\!](t) & = & \left\{ \begin{array}{ll} 0 & \text{if } \mathcal{I}_\mathcal{D}[\![P]\!](t) = 0 \text{ and } \mathcal{I}_\mathcal{D}[\![Q]\!](t) = 0 \\ 1 & \text{otherwise} \end{array} \right.
\end{array}
$$

Durations, terms, and duration formulae are interpreted over intervals of time.

Terms: the value of a term r given a valuation $(\mathcal{V}_D, [b,e])$ in $\mathcal{I_D}$ is defined by:

$$
\begin{array}{lcl}
\mathcal{V}_{D\ [b,e]}[\![\ell]\!] & = & e-b \\
\mathcal{V}_{D\ [b,e]}[\![\textstyle\int P]\!] & = & \int_b^e \mathcal{I_D}[\![P]\!](t)dt \\
\mathcal{V}_{D\ [b,e]}[\![x]\!] & = & \underline{x} \\
\mathcal{V}_{D\ [b,e]}[\![f_i^n(r_1,\ldots,r_n)]\!] & = & \underline{f}_i^n(\mathcal{V}_{D\ [b,e]}[\![r_1]\!],\ldots,\mathcal{V}_{D\ [b,e]}[\![r_n]\!])
\end{array}
$$

Duration formulae: the definition that a valuation $(\mathcal{V}_D, [b,e])$ in $\mathcal{I_D}$ *satisfies* a duration formula $\mathcal{D}$ is:

$\mathcal{V}_{D\ [b,e]}[\![true]\!] = tt$

$\mathcal{V}_{D\ [b,e]}[\![false]\!] = f\!f$

$\mathcal{V}_{D\ [b,e]}[\![A_i^n(r_1,\ldots,r_n)]\!] = tt$ iff $\underline{A}_i^n(\mathcal{V}_{D\ [b,e]}[\![r_1]\!],\ldots,\mathcal{V}_{D\ [b,e]}[\![r_n]\!]) = tt$

$\mathcal{V}_{D\ [b,e]}[\![(\neg\mathcal{D})]\!] = tt$ iff $\mathcal{V}_{D\ [b,e]}[\![\mathcal{D}]\!] = f\!f$

$\mathcal{V}_{D\ [b,e]}[\![(\mathcal{D}_1 \vee \mathcal{D}_2)]\!] = tt$ iff $\mathcal{V}_{D\ [b,e]}[\![\mathcal{D}_1]\!] = tt$ or $\mathcal{V}_{D\ [b,e]}[\![\mathcal{D}_2]\!] = tt$

$\mathcal{V}_{D\ [b,e]}[\![(\mathcal{D}_1 \frown \mathcal{D}_2)]\!] = tt$ iff $\mathcal{V}_{D\ [b,m]}[\![\mathcal{D}_1]\!] = tt$ and $\mathcal{V}_{D\ [m,e]}[\![\mathcal{D}_2]\!] = tt$,
for some $m \in [b,e]$

$\mathcal{V}_{D\ [b,e]}[\![(\forall x)\mathcal{D})]\!] = tt$ iff $\mathcal{V}'_{D\ [b,e]}[\![\mathcal{D}]\!] = tt$,
for all $(\mathcal{V}'_D, [b,e])$ x-equivalent with $(\mathcal{V}_D, [b,e])$

A duration formula $\mathcal{D}$ is *true* in the interpretation $\mathcal{I_D}$ (written $\mathcal{I_D} \models_{\mathrm{D}} \mathcal{D}$) iff $\mathcal{V}_{D\ [b,e]}[\![\mathcal{D}]\!] = tt$, for any valuation $(\mathcal{V}_D, [b,e])$ in $\mathcal{I_D}$. Furthermore, $\mathcal{D}$ is *valid* (written $\models_{\mathrm{D}} \mathcal{D}$) iff $\mathcal{I_D} \models \mathcal{D}$, for any interpretation $\mathcal{I_D}$.

We use the following abbreviations:

$$
\begin{array}{lcl}
\lceil P \rceil & \triangleq & (\textstyle\int P = \ell) \wedge (\ell > 0) \\
\lceil\,\rceil & \triangleq & \ell = 0
\end{array}
$$

The standard infix notation for functions and relations of real arithmetics is used above and in the following sections.

Thus $\lceil P \rceil$ means that the state P is true everywhere (almost) in a given non-point interval. $\lceil\,\rceil$ is true only for point intervals.

The requirement and design of the gas burner of section 1 can be represented in Duration Calculus:

Req-1 $\quad \ell \geq 60 \;\Rightarrow\; 20 \textstyle\int Leak \leq \ell$

Des-1 $\quad \Box(\lceil Leak \rceil \;\Rightarrow\; \ell \leq 1)$

Des-2 $\quad \Box(((\Diamond\lceil Leak \rceil)\frown(\Diamond\lceil \neg Leak \rceil)\frown(\Diamond\lceil Leak \rceil)) \;\Rightarrow\; \ell \geq 30)$

4 Proof System for Duration Calculus

From now on we consider an arbitrary Duration Calculus with alphabet which includes function letters for zero "0" and addition "+" and predicate letters equal "=" and less or equal to "≤". We assume standard meanings given to these functions and relations.

We give axioms for which the validity of duration formulae can be proved. The notation $\vdash \mathcal{D}$ means that $\mathcal{D}$ is *provable*, i.e. that $\mathcal{D}$ is a theorem of Duration Calculus.

As Duration Calculus is an extension of Interval Temporal Logic, which is an extension of modal logic, which again is an extension of predicate logic of reals, we adopt all axioms and inference rules from these calculi.

Duration Calculus has the following axiom schemas:

$$
\begin{array}{ll}
(1) & \int 0 = 0 \\
(2) & \int 1 = \ell \\
(3) & \int P \geq 0 \\
(4) & \int P + \int Q = \int(P \vee Q) + \int(P \wedge Q) \\
(5) & ((\int P = x)^\frown(\int P = y)) \Leftrightarrow (\int P = x + y)
\end{array}
$$

In addition to these axiom schemas there are two induction rules:

Induction rule 1: Let $\mathcal{R}(\mathcal{X})$ be a duration formula containing the formula letter $\mathcal{X}$, and let P be any state.

$$
\begin{array}{ll}
\text{If} & \vdash \mathcal{R}(\lceil\,\rceil) \text{ and } \mathcal{R}(\mathcal{X}) \vdash \mathcal{R}(\mathcal{X} \vee (\lceil P \rceil^\frown \mathcal{X}) \vee (\lceil \neg P \rceil^\frown \mathcal{X})) \\
\text{then} & \mathcal{R}(\mathit{true})
\end{array}
$$

The duration formula $\mathcal{R}(\mathcal{D})$ is obtained from $\mathcal{R}(\mathcal{X})$ by replacing every occurrence of $\mathcal{X}$ with the duration formula $\mathcal{D}$. $\mathcal{D}_1 \vdash \mathcal{D}$ means that $\mathcal{D}$ is provable from the assumption $\mathcal{D}_1$.

Induction rule 2: Let $\mathcal{R}(\mathcal{X})$ be a duration formula containing the formula letter $\mathcal{X}$, and let P be any state.

$$
\begin{array}{ll}
\text{If} & \vdash \mathcal{R}(\lceil\,\rceil) \text{ and } \mathcal{R}(\mathcal{X}) \vdash \mathcal{R}(\mathcal{X} \vee (\mathcal{X}^\frown \lceil P \rceil) \vee (\mathcal{X}^\frown \lceil \neg P \rceil)) \\
\text{then} & \mathcal{R}(\mathit{true})
\end{array}
$$

In the following axiom schema for states we deliberately continue numbering with (8):

(8) If $P \Leftrightarrow Q$ is a theorem of propositional logic, then $\int P = \int Q$ is an axiom.

In [1] this proof system is used to prove **Des-1** $\wedge$ **Des-2** $\Rightarrow$ **Req-1** for the gas burner.

Furthermore, it can be proved that for any state P:

$$
\begin{array}{ll}
(6) & \lceil\,\rceil \vee (\mathit{true}^\frown \lceil P \rceil) \vee (\mathit{true}^\frown \lceil \neg P \rceil) \\
(7) & \lceil\,\rceil \vee (\lceil P \rceil^\frown \mathit{true}) \vee (\lceil \neg P \rceil^\frown \mathit{true})
\end{array}
$$

The proof of (6) uses $\mathcal{R}(\mathcal{X}) \triangleq (\mathcal{X} \Rightarrow (\lceil\rceil \vee (true \frown \lceil P \rceil) \vee (true \frown \lceil \neg P \rceil)))$ as induction hypothesis. Similarily for the proof of (7).

In the completeness proof given in the next section we refer to (6) and (7).

Theorem 1 (Soundness).

$$\text{If } \vdash \mathcal{D} \text{ then } \models_{\mathrm{D}} \mathcal{D}$$

The proof of soundness is by induction on the proof rules. Most cases are simple, so we sketch only the soundness proof for Induction rule 1, for which the following definitions and lemmas are convenient:

Definition (Equivalence). Given an interval $[b, e]$ and an interpretation $\mathcal{I}_{\mathcal{D}}$. We call two duration formulae $\mathcal{D}_1$ and $\mathcal{D}_2$ for *equivalent in* $[b, e]$ *of* $\mathcal{I}_{\mathcal{D}}$ iff

$$\mathcal{V}_{D\ [c,d]}[\![\mathcal{D}_1]\!] = \mathcal{V}_{D\ [c,d]}[\![\mathcal{D}_2]\!]$$

for any valuation $(\mathcal{V}_{\mathcal{D}}, [c, d])$ in $\mathcal{I}_{\mathcal{D}}$ where $[c, d] \subseteq [b, e]$.

Definition (Finite alternation). Given a state P. The duration formula $FA^i(P), i \geq 0$, describes less than i alternations of P:

$$\begin{array}{lcl} FA^0(P) & \triangleq & \lceil\rceil \\ FA^{i+1}(P) & \triangleq & FA^i(P) \vee (\lceil P \rceil \frown FA^i(P)) \vee (\lceil \neg P \rceil \frown FA^i(P)) \end{array}$$

Lemma (Equivalence). For given state P, interval $[b, e]$, and interpretation $\mathcal{I}_{\mathcal{D}}$, there is a natural number n such that *true* and $FA^n(P)$ are equivalent in $[b, e]$ of $\mathcal{I}_{\mathcal{D}}$.

Proof: Follows since $\mathcal{I}_{\mathcal{D}}[\![P]\!]$ has a finite number of discontinuity points in $[b, e]$.

Lemma (Substitution). Let $\mathcal{R}(\mathcal{X})$ be a duration formula with formula letter $\mathcal{X}$, $[b, e]$ an interval, and $\mathcal{I}_{\mathcal{D}}$ an interpretation. Then for any duration formulae $\mathcal{D}_1$ and $\mathcal{D}_2$:

If $\mathcal{D}_1$ and $\mathcal{D}_2$ are equivalent in $[b, e]$ of $\mathcal{I}_{\mathcal{D}}$
then $\mathcal{R}(\mathcal{D}_1)$ and $\mathcal{R}(\mathcal{D}_2)$ are equivalent in $[b, e]$ of $\mathcal{I}_{\mathcal{D}}$

Proof: By structural induction on $\mathcal{R}(\mathcal{X})$.

We sketch the proof of soundness for Induction rule 1:

Suppose

$$\begin{array}{rcll} & \vdash & R(\lceil\rceil) & (A1) \\ \text{and} \quad R(X) & \vdash & R(X \vee (\lceil P \rceil \frown X) \vee (\lceil \neg P \rceil \frown X)) & (A2) \end{array}$$

Consider an arbitrary valuation $(\mathcal{V}_D, [b, e])$ in $\mathcal{I}_{\mathcal{D}}$ (for any $\mathcal{I}_{\mathcal{D}}$). We must show that $\mathcal{V}_{D\ [b,e]}[\![R(true)]\!] = tt$.

By the equivalence lemma there is a natural number n such that *true* and $FA^n(P)$ are equivalent in $[b, e]$ of $\mathcal{I}_{\mathcal{D}}$, and by the substitution lemma $\mathcal{R}(true)$ and $\mathcal{R}(FA^n(P))$ are equivalent in $[b, e]$ of $\mathcal{I}_{\mathcal{D}}$ also.

From $(A1)$ and repeated application of $(A2)$ we get $\vdash \mathcal{R}(FA^n(P))$, and hence by the induction hypothesis of the soundness proof $\models \mathcal{R}(FA^n(P))$.

Thus $\mathcal{V}_{D\ [b,e]}[\![\mathcal{R}(true)]\!] = \mathcal{V}_{D\ [b,e]}[\![\mathcal{R}(FA^n(P))]\!] = tt$ as required.

5 Completeness of Duration Calculus

The key part of this proof is that for every duration formula $\mathcal{D}$ we can find an interval formula $\mathcal{F}_D$ such that $\models_D \mathcal{D}$ iff $\models \mathcal{F}_D$.

Let an arbitrary duration formula $\mathcal{D}$ be given. We now construct $\mathcal{F}_D$.

Let $X_1, \ldots, X_l$ be the state variables occurring in $\mathcal{D}$. Let S be the set of states which can be generated from these l state variables.

For $P \in S$ let $[P] = \{P' \in S \mid P \Leftrightarrow P' \textit{ in propositional logic }\}$, and let $S_\equiv$ be the set of equivalence classes: $\{[P] \mid P \in S\}$. The size k of $S_\equiv$ is the number of boolean functions in l variables, i.e. $k = 2^{2^l}$.

Select k temporal variables $v_1, \ldots, v_k$ and put them in one-to-one correspondence with the equivalence classes. Thus we can index the selected temporal variables with equivalence classes.

For each of the axiom schemas (1) to (5), and for the two schemas (6) and (7) we construct a finite set of interval formulae:

$H_1 \triangleq \{v_{[0]} = 0\}$

$H_2 \triangleq \{v_{[1]} = \ell\}$

$H_3 \triangleq \{v_{[P]} \geq 0 \mid [P] \in S_\equiv\}$

$H_4 \triangleq \{v_{[P]} + v_{[Q]} = v_{[P\vee Q]} + v_{[P\wedge Q]} \mid [P],[Q] \in S_\equiv\}$

$H_5 \triangleq \{(\forall x)(\forall y)(((v_{[P]} = x)^\frown(v_{[P]} = y)) \Leftrightarrow (v_{[P]} = x + y)) \mid [P] \in S_\equiv\}$

$H_6 \triangleq \{\lceil\,\rceil \vee (true^\frown\lceil v_{[P]}\rceil) \vee (true^\frown\lceil v_{[\neg P]}\rceil) \mid [P] \in S_\equiv\}$

$H_7 \triangleq \{\lceil\,\rceil \vee (\lceil v_{[P]}\rceil^\frown true) \vee (\lceil v_{[\neg P]}\rceil^\frown true) \mid [P] \in S_\equiv\}$

where we define $\lceil v_{[Q]}\rceil$ by $v_{[Q]} = v_{[1]} \wedge v_{[1]} > 0$.

Define $\mathcal{H}$ to be the conjunction of all the formulae in H_1 to H_7, and let $\mathcal{F}$ be the interval formula obtained from $\mathcal{D}$ by replacing each duration $\int P$ by $v_{[P]}$. Define $\mathcal{F}_D$ as $(\Box\mathcal{H}) \Rightarrow \mathcal{F}$.

The below definition and lemmas are convenient for the completeness proof.

Definition: We call a valuation $(\mathcal{V}, [b, e])$ in $\mathcal{I}$ for an $\mathcal{H}$*-pair* in $\mathcal{I}$ when $\mathcal{V}_{[b,e]}[\![\Box\mathcal{H}]\!] = tt$; i.e. for any sub-interval $[c, d]$ of $[b, e]$: $\mathcal{V}_{[c,d]}[\![\mathcal{H}]\!] = tt$.

Lemma 1. Given an $\mathcal{H}$-pair $(\mathcal{V}, [b, e])$ in $\mathcal{I}$. Then

$$\begin{array}{ll} (i) & 0 \leq \underline{v}_{[P]}(c, d) \leq d - c \\ (ii) & \underline{v}_{[P]}(c, d) = (d - c) - \underline{v}_{[\neg P]}(c, d) \\ (iii) & \underline{v}_{[P]}(c, d) \leq \underline{v}_{[P \vee Q]}(c, d) \end{array}$$

for any $P, Q \in S$ and any sub-interval $[c, d]$ of $[b, e]$.

Proof. (i) and (ii) are trivial.

Since $\neg P \vee (P \vee Q)$ is a tautology, we have from H_2 that

$$\underline{v}_{[1]}(c, d) = (d - c) = \underline{v}_{[\neg P \vee (P \vee Q)]}(c, d)$$

From H_4 we have

$$\underline{v}_{[\neg P]}(c, d) + \underline{v}_{[(P \vee Q)]}(c, d) = \underline{v}_{[\neg P \vee (P \vee Q)]}(c, d) + \underline{v}_{[\neg P \wedge (P \vee Q)]}(c, d)$$

i.e. using (ii) we get

$$(d - c) - \underline{v}_{[P]}(c, d) + \underline{v}_{[(P \vee Q)]}(c, d) = (d - c) + \underline{v}_{[\neg P \wedge (P \vee Q)]}(c, d)$$

which gives $\underline{v}_{[P]}(c, d) \leq \underline{v}_{[P \vee Q]}(c, d)$ (since $\underline{v}_{[\neg P \wedge (P \vee Q)]}(c, d) \geq 0$ by H_3).

Lemma 2. Given an $\mathcal{H}$-pair $(\mathcal{V}, [b, e])$ in $\mathcal{I}$, where $b < e$. For any $P \in S$, there is a finite partition $b = t_0 < t_1 < \ldots < t_n = e$ of $[b, e]$ such that: either

$$\mathcal{V}_{[t_{i-1}, t_i]}[\![\lceil v_{[P]} \rceil]\!] = tt \quad \text{or} \quad \mathcal{V}_{[t_{i-1}, t_i]}[\![\lceil v_{[\neg P]} \rceil]\!] = tt, \text{ for } i = 1, \ldots n.$$

Proof. For any $t : b < t < e$, there are (by H_6 and H_7) t' and t'' such that $b \leq t' < t < t'' \leq e$ and

$$\left.\begin{array}{c} \mathcal{V}_{[t', t]}[\![\lceil v_{[P]} \rceil]\!] = tt \ \text{ or } \ \mathcal{V}_{[t', t]}[\![\lceil v_{[\neg P]} \rceil]\!] = tt \\ \text{and} \\ \mathcal{V}_{[t, t'']}[\![\lceil v_{[P]} \rceil]\!] = tt \ \text{ or } \ \mathcal{V}_{[t, t'']}[\![\lceil v_{[\neg P]} \rceil]\!] = tt \end{array}\right\} \qquad (\dagger)$$

Thus there is an open interval (t', t'') covering t (but not b nor e) such that the closed interval $[t', t'']$ has the above property $(\dagger)$.

For the left end point b, there is by H_7 a t'' such that $b < t'' \leq e$ and

$$\mathcal{V}_{[b, t'']}[\![\lceil v_{[P]} \rceil]\!] = tt \quad \text{or} \quad \mathcal{V}_{[b, t'']}[\![\lceil v_{[\neg P]} \rceil]\!] = tt \qquad (\dagger_b)$$

Thus there is an open interval (t', t'') covering b such that the closed interval $[b, t'']$ has the above property $(\dagger_b)$. (Select arbitrary $t' < b$.)

Similarily for e, there is by H_6 a t' such that $b \leq t' < e$ and

$$\mathcal{V}_{[t', e]}[\![\lceil v_{[P]} \rceil]\!] = tt \quad \text{or} \quad \mathcal{V}_{[t', e]}[\![\lceil v_{[\neg P]} \rceil]\!] = tt \qquad (\dagger_e)$$

Thus there is an open interval (t', t'') covering e such that the closed interval $[t', e]$ has the above property $(\dagger_e)$. (Select arbitrary $t'' > e$.)

So we have an infinite collection of open intervals covering the closed and bounded interval $[b, e]$. Then by Heine-Borels theorem there is a finite sub-collection $\mathcal{C} = \{I_1, \ldots I_m\}$ of the open intervals covering $[b, e]$.

STEP 1: Select the open interval $I_i = (a_i, b_i)$ from $\mathcal{C}$ covering b. Then the closed interval $[b, b_i]$ satisfies by $(\dagger_b)$: $\mathcal{V}_{[b,b_i]}[\![\lceil v_{[P]}\rceil]\!] = tt$ or $\mathcal{V}_{[b,b_i]}[\![\lceil v_{[\neg P]}\rceil]\!] = tt$.

STEP 2: If $b_i = e$ we have proved the lemma.

Otherwise $b_i < e$. Select an open interval $I_j = (a_j, b_j)$ from $\mathcal{C}$ covering b_i.

If $e < b_j$, then by $(\dagger_e)$ the closed interval $[b_i, e]$ satisfies: $\mathcal{V}_{[b_i,e]}[\![\lceil v_{[P]}\rceil]\!] = tt$ or $\mathcal{V}_{[b_i,e]}[\![\lceil v_{[\neg P]}\rceil]\!] = tt$ and the lemma is proved.

If $b_j \leq e$, then the closed interval $[b_i, b_j]$ will by $(\dagger)$ satisfy one of

$$\begin{array}{ll}
1: & \mathcal{V}_{[b_i,b_j]}[\![\lceil v_{[P]}\rceil]\!] = tt \\
2: & \mathcal{V}_{[b_i,b_j]}[\![\lceil v_{[\neg P]}\rceil]\!] = tt \\
3: & \mathcal{V}_{[b_i,m]}[\![\lceil v_{[P]}\rceil]\!] = tt \text{ and } \mathcal{V}_{[m,b_j]}[\![\lceil v_{[\neg P]}\rceil]\!] = tt, \text{ for some } m : b_i < m < b_j \\
4: & \mathcal{V}_{[b_i,m]}[\![\lceil v_{[\neg P]}\rceil]\!] = tt \text{ and } \mathcal{V}_{[m,b_j]}[\![\lceil v_{[P]}\rceil]\!] = tt, \text{ for some } m : b_i < m < b_j
\end{array}$$

Repeat now *STEP 2*, until the required partition of $[b, e]$ is achieved. This terminates since there is a finite number m of open intervals in $\mathcal{C}$.

Lemma 3. Given an $\mathcal{H}$-pair $(\mathcal{V}, [b, e])$ in $\mathcal{I}$, where $b < e$. There is an interpretation $\mathcal{I}_{\mathcal{D}}$ such that for any $P \in S$, there is a finite partition $b = t_0 < t_1 < \ldots < t_n = e$ of $[b, e]$ which satisfies

$$\mathcal{V}_{[t_{i-1},t_i]}[\![\lceil v_{[P]}\rceil]\!] = tt \quad \text{or} \quad \mathcal{V}_{[t_{i-1},t_i]}[\![\lceil v_{[\neg P]}\rceil]\!] = tt, \quad \text{for } i = 1, \ldots, n,$$

and, for any $t : b \leq t < e$, there is an $i \in \{1, \ldots, n\}$ such that $t_{i-1} \leq t < t_i$ and

$$\mathcal{I}_{\mathcal{D}}[\![P]\!](t) = \begin{cases} 1, \text{ if } \mathcal{V}_{[t_{i-1},t_i]}[\![\lceil v_{[P]}\rceil]\!] = tt \\ 0, \text{ if } \mathcal{V}_{[t_{i-1},t_i]}[\![\lceil v_{[\neg P]}\rceil]\!] = tt \end{cases}$$

Proof. Define an interpretation $\mathcal{I}_{\mathcal{D}}$ as follows: For any state variable $Y \notin S$ let $\underline{Y}(t) = 0$ for $t \in R$. For any state variable $X \in S$, there is by lemma 2 a finite partition $b = t_0 < t_1 < \ldots < t_n = e$ of $[b, e]$ such that:

$$\mathcal{V}_{[t_{i-1},t_i]}[\![\lceil v_{[X]}\rceil]\!] = tt \quad \text{or} \quad \mathcal{V}_{[t_{i-1},t_i]}[\![\lceil v_{[\neg X]}\rceil]\!] = tt$$

for $i = 1, \ldots n$. Let

$$\underline{X}(t) = \begin{cases} 1, \text{ if } t_{i-1} \leq t < t_i \text{ and } \mathcal{V}_{[t_{i-1},t_i]}[\![\lceil v_{[X]}\rceil]\!] = tt, \text{ for some } i \in \{1, \ldots, n\} \\ 0, \text{ otherwise} \end{cases}$$

Each such function has only a finite number of discontinuity points in any interval, so $\mathcal{I}_{\mathcal{D}}$ is an interpretation.

We prove the remaining parts of the lemma by structural induction on P. If $P \notin S$ there is nothing to prove, so assume below that $P \in S$. The cases where P is $0, 1$, or X are trivial, so consider the

CASE: P has the form $\neg Q$.

By the induction hypothesis we get a finite partition $b = t_0 < t_1 < \ldots < t_n = e$ of $[b, e]$ for Q such that:

$$\mathcal{V}_{[t_{i-1},t_i]}[\![\lceil v_{[Q]} \rceil]\!] = tt \quad \text{or} \quad \mathcal{V}_{[t_{i-1},t_i]}[\![\lceil v_{[\neg Q]} \rceil]\!] = tt \text{ for } i = 1, \ldots, n.$$

This is the required partition for $\neg Q$ also, as $\neg\neg Q \Leftrightarrow Q$.

Consider an arbitrary $t, b \leq t < e$. I.e. $t_{i-1} \leq t < t_i$ for some $i \in \{1, \ldots, n\}$ and by definition $\mathcal{I}_\mathcal{D}[\![\neg Q]\!](t) = 1 - \mathcal{I}_\mathcal{D}[\![Q]\!](t)$.

If $\mathcal{V}_{[t_{i-1},t_i]}[\![\lceil v_{[\neg\neg Q]} \rceil]\!] = tt$, then $\mathcal{I}_\mathcal{D}[\![\neg Q]\!](t) = 0$ as we have $\mathcal{I}_\mathcal{D}[\![Q]\!](t) = 1$ from the induction hypothesis.

If $\mathcal{V}_{[t_{i-1},t_i]}[\![\lceil v_{[\neg Q]} \rceil]\!] = tt$, then $\mathcal{I}_\mathcal{D}[\![Q]\!](t) = 0$ (induction hypothesis). But then $\mathcal{I}_\mathcal{D}[\![\neg Q]\!](t) = 1$ as required.

CASE: P has the form $Q \vee R$.

By combination of the induction hypotheses for Q and R, we get a finite partition $b = t_0 < t_1 < \ldots < t_n = e$, such that one of the cases apply in each $[t_{i-1}, t_i]$:

(i) $\mathcal{V}_{[t_{i-1},t_i]}[\![\lceil v_{[Q]} \rceil]\!] = tt, \mathcal{V}_{[t_{i-1},t_i]}[\![\lceil v_{[R]} \rceil]\!] = tt$, and
$\mathcal{I}_\mathcal{D}[\![Q]\!](t) = \mathcal{I}_\mathcal{D}[\![R]\!](t) = 1$, i.e. $\mathcal{I}_\mathcal{D}[\![Q \vee R]\!](t) = 1$, for $t_{i-1} \leq t < t_i$.

(ii) $\mathcal{V}_{[t_{i-1},t_i]}[\![\lceil v_{[\neg Q]} \rceil]\!] = tt, \mathcal{V}_{[t_{i-1},t_i]}[\![\lceil v_{[\neg R]} \rceil]\!] = tt$, and
$\mathcal{I}_\mathcal{D}[\![Q]\!](t) = \mathcal{I}_\mathcal{D}[\![R]\!](t) = 0$, i.e. $\mathcal{I}_\mathcal{D}[\![Q \vee R]\!](t) = 0$, for $t_{i-1} \leq t < t_i$.

(iii) $\mathcal{V}_{[t_{i-1},t_i]}[\![\lceil v_{[Q]} \rceil]\!] = tt, \mathcal{V}_{[t_{i-1},t_i]}[\![\lceil v_{[\neg R]} \rceil]\!] = tt$, and
$\mathcal{I}_\mathcal{D}[\![Q]\!](t) = 1$ and $\mathcal{I}_\mathcal{D}[\![R]\!](t) = 0$, i.e. $\mathcal{I}_\mathcal{D}[\![Q \vee R]\!](t) = 1$, for $t_{i-1} \leq t < t_i$.

(iv) $\mathcal{V}_{[t_{i-1},t_i]}[\![\lceil v_{[\neg Q]} \rceil]\!] = tt, \mathcal{V}_{[t_{i-1},t_i]}[\![\lceil v_{[R]} \rceil]\!] = tt$, and
$\mathcal{I}_\mathcal{D}[\![Q]\!](t) = 0$ and $\mathcal{I}_\mathcal{D}[\![R]\!](t) = 1$, i.e. $\mathcal{I}_\mathcal{D}[\![Q \vee R]\!](t) = 1$, for $t_{i-1} \leq t < t_i$.

(i). From lemma 1:

$$0 \leq \underline{v}_{[Q \vee R]}(t_{i-1}, t_i) \leq t_i - t_{i-1} \quad \text{and} \quad 0 \leq v_{[Q \wedge R]}(t_{i-1}, t_i) \leq t_i - t_{i-1}$$

so it follows from H_4 that $\underline{v}_{[Q \vee R]}(t_{i-1}, t_i) = \underline{v}_{[Q \wedge R]}(t_{i-1}, t_i) = t_i - t_{i-1}$. I.e. $\mathcal{V}_{[t_{i-1},t_i]}[\![\lceil v_{[Q \vee R]} \rceil]\!] = tt$.

(ii). Since we have (from H_3)

$$\underline{v}_{[Q \vee R]}(t_{i-1}, t_i) \geq 0 \quad \text{and} \quad \underline{v}_{[Q \wedge R]}(t_{i-1}, t_i) \geq 0$$

it follows from H_4 that $\underline{v}_{[Q \vee R]}(t_{i-1}, t_i) = 0$. Then by lemma 1 we get that $\underline{v}_{[\neg(Q \vee R)]}(t_{i-1}, t_i) = t_i - t_{i-1}$ and hence $\mathcal{V}_{[t_{i-1},t_i]}[\![\lceil v_{[\neg(Q \vee R)]} \rceil]\!] = tt$.

(iii). Since by H_3 and lemma 1

$$\underline{v}_{[Q]}(t_{i-1}, t_i) \leq \underline{v}_{[Q \vee R]}(t_{i-1}, t_i) \leq t_i - t_{i-1}$$

it follows that $\underline{v}_{[Q\vee R]}(t_{i-1},t_i) = t_i - t_{i-1}$. I.e. $\mathcal{V}_{[t_{i-1},t_i]}[\![\lceil v_{[Q\vee R]}\rceil]\!] = tt$.

(*iv*). Similar to (*iii*). Lemma 3 is now proved.

Theorem 2. For a given $\mathcal{H}$-pair $(\mathcal{V},[b,e])$ in $\mathcal{I}$ let $\mathcal{I}_{\mathcal{D}}$ be the interpretation given by lemma 3. Then any valuation $(\mathcal{V}_D,[c,d])$ in $\mathcal{I}_{\mathcal{D}}$ satisfies

$$\mathcal{V}_{D\ [c,d]}[\![\textstyle\int P]\!] = \underline{v}_{[P]}(c,d)$$

whenever $P \in S$ and $[c,d]$ is a sub-interval of $[b,e]$.

Proof. Suppose $c = d$. Then $\mathcal{V}_{D\ [c,d]}[\![\int P]\!] = 0$. From lemma 1 we have $0 \leq \underline{v}_{[P]}(c,d) \leq d-c$, i.e. the desired $\underline{v}_{[P]}(c,d) = 0$.

So suppose that $c < d$. Since $(\mathcal{V},[b,e])$ is an $\mathcal{H}$-pair in $\mathcal{I}$, so is $(\mathcal{V},[c,d])$. By lemma 3, there is a finite partition $c = t_0 < t_1 < \ldots < t_n = d$ of $[c,d]$ such that:

$$\mathcal{V}_{[t_{i-1},t_i]}[\![\lceil v_{[P]}\rceil]\!] = tt \ \text{ or } \ \mathcal{V}_{[t_{i-1},t_i]}[\![\lceil v_{[\neg P]}\rceil]\!] = tt, \ \text{ for } i = 1,\ldots n,$$

and, for any $t : b \leq t < e$ there is an $i \in \{1,\ldots,n\}$ such that $t_{i-1} \leq t < t_i$ and

$$\mathcal{I}_{\mathcal{D}}[\![P]\!](t) = \begin{cases} 1, \text{ if } \mathcal{V}_{[t_{i-1},t_i]}[\![\lceil v_{[P]}\rceil]\!] = tt \\ 0, \text{ if } \mathcal{V}_{[t_{i-1},t_i]}[\![\lceil v_{[\neg P]}\rceil]\!] = tt \end{cases}$$

Thus $\int_{t_{i-1}}^{t_i} \mathcal{I}_{\mathcal{D}}[\![P]\!](t)dt = \underline{v}_{[P]}(t_{i-1},t_i)$, for $i = 1,\ldots,n$, and by H_5:

$$\mathcal{V}_{D\ [c,d]}[\![\textstyle\int P]\!] = \sum_{i=1}^{n} \underline{v}_{[P]}(t_{i-1},t_i) = \underline{v}_{[P]}(c,d)$$

Theorem 2 is now proved.

Theorem 3.

$$\models_{\mathrm{D}} \mathcal{D} \ \text{ iff } \ \models (\Box\mathcal{H}) \Rightarrow \mathcal{F}$$

Proof. We first prove that $\models_{\mathrm{D}} \mathcal{D}$ implies $\models (\Box\mathcal{H}) \Rightarrow \mathcal{F}$. Suppose $\not\models (\Box\mathcal{H}) \Rightarrow \mathcal{F}$, i.e. there is an interpretation $\mathcal{I}$ and an $\mathcal{H}$-pair $(\mathcal{V},[b,e])$ in $\mathcal{I}$ such that $\mathcal{V}_{[b,e]}[\![\mathcal{F}]\!] = ff$. By theorem 2 there is an interpretation $\mathcal{I}_{\mathcal{D}}$ and a valuation $(\mathcal{V}_D,[b,e])$ in $\mathcal{I}_{\mathcal{D}}$ such that for any $P \in S$:

$$\mathcal{V}_{D\ [c,d]}[\![\textstyle\int P]\!] = \underline{v}_{[P]}(c,d), \text{ for any sub-interval } [c,d] \text{ of } [b,e]$$

Since $\mathcal{V}_{[b,e]}[\![\mathcal{F}]\!] = ff$ we have that $\mathcal{V}_{D\ [b,e]}[\![\mathcal{D}]\!] = ff$ and hence $\not\models_{\mathrm{D}} \mathcal{D}$.

We now prove that $\models (\Box\mathcal{H}) \Rightarrow \mathcal{F}$ implies $\models_{\mathrm{D}} \mathcal{D}$. Suppose $\not\models_{\mathrm{D}} \mathcal{D}$, i.e. there is an interpretation $\mathcal{I}_{\mathcal{D}}$ and a valuation $(\mathcal{V}_D,[b,e])$ in $\mathcal{I}_{\mathcal{D}}$ such that $\mathcal{V}_{D\ [b,e]}[\![\mathcal{D}]\!] = ff$.

Construct an interpretation $\mathcal{I}$ such that $\underline{v}_{[P]}(c,d) = \mathcal{V}_{D\ [c,d]}[\![\int P]\!]$ for all $P \in S$ and intervals $[c,d]$. (By axiom (8) this is well-defined.) By construction, the valuation $(\mathcal{V}_D,[b,e])$ in $\mathcal{I}$ cannot satisfy $\mathcal{F}$ and from theorem 1 (soundness) $\mathcal{V}_{[b,e]}[\![\Box\mathcal{H}]\!] = tt$. So $\not\models (\Box\mathcal{H}) \Rightarrow \mathcal{F}$, which ends the proof of theorem 3.

The following completeness theorem we name *relative completeness* since we assume that valid interval formulae of the form $(\Box\mathcal{H}) \Rightarrow \mathcal{F}$ are provable[1]. That is, we assume a new rule for the calculus:

(9) If $\mathcal{F}$ is a valid interval formula, in which only the temporal variables: $v_1, \ldots, v_n$ occur. Then

$$\mathcal{D}$$

is an axiom, where $\mathcal{D}$ is obtained from $\mathcal{F}$ by replacing each temporal variable v_i with a duration $\int P_i$.

Theorem 4 (Relative completeness).

$$\models_{\mathrm{D}} \mathcal{D} \text{ implies } \vdash \mathcal{D}$$

Proof. Suppose $\models_{\mathrm{D}} \mathcal{D}$. By theorem 3 we get $\models (\Box\mathcal{H}) \Rightarrow \mathcal{F}$. Let $\mathcal{H}'$ be obtained from $\mathcal{H}$ by replacing each $v_{[P]}$ by $\int P$. Thus $\mathcal{H}'$ is a conjunction of Duration Calculus axioms. By $\Box$-generalization of modal logic, we have $\vdash \Box\mathcal{H}'$ and by axiom (9) we get $\vdash (\Box\mathcal{H}') \Rightarrow \mathcal{D}$. Therefore by modus ponens $\vdash \mathcal{D}$.

Acknowledgements: We greatly appreciate comments and discussions with A.P. Ravn and Liu Zhiming.

6 Conclusion

The Duration Calculus was introduced in [1] as a notation with a corresponding calculus to specify requirements and designs for real-time systems and to reason about such specifications. This paper adds to that work by giving a formal syntax and semantics for Duration Calculus and by proving the calculus to be complete (relative to the completeness of Interval Temporal Logic).

We refer to [1] for a discussion which relates other specification languages for real-time systems to Duration Calculus through the gas burner example of section 1. The other approaches discussed there are timed CSP, e.g. [17,16], Real Time Logic [10], temporal logic with an explicit variable for the current time [14], and metric temporal logic [11,8,9].

Duration Calculus has now been applied to various design levels of real-time systems. The top level is specification of requirements for control systems [5,15,18]. The requirements are refined in several steps to a stage including a specification of a program component (described in Duration Calculus also). The correctness of each refinement step is verified by proof in Duration Calculus.

In [7,2] Duration Calculus is used to give a real-time semantics to communicating sequential processes, and in [2] there is also given various specifications of schedulers for shared

[1]From the way $(\Box\mathcal{H}) \Rightarrow \mathcal{F}$ is constructed from $\mathcal{D}$, we may consider Duration Calculus a finite extension of Interval Temporal Logic, and we have the stronger result of relative decidability as well.

processors. Furthermore, Duration Calculus has, in [6], been used to give semantics to circuits, to prove the correctness of a circuit transformation, and to give an elegant definition of delay-insensitive circuits. Current work is going on to extend Duration Calculus to a version with probabilities [12].

References

[1] Zhou Chaochen, C.A.R. Hoare, and A.P. Ravn: A Calculus of Durations. In *Information Processing Letters* 40(5), 1992, pp. 269-276.

[2] Zhou Chaochen, Michael R. Hansen, A.P. Ravn, and Hans Rischel: Duration Specifications for Shared Processors. In proc. of *Symposium on Formal Techniques in Real-Time and Fault Tolerant Systems*, Nijmegen, Januar 6-10, 1992. (To appear in the LNCS series.)

[3] Roger Hale: Temporal Logic Programming. In *Temporal Logics and their applications*, (edited by Antony Galton), Academic Press, 1987, pp. 91-119.

[4] J. Halpern, B. Moskowski, and Z. Manna: A Hardware Semantics based on Temporal Intervals, In proc. *ICALP'83*, LNCS 154, Springer-Verlag 1983, pp. 278-291.

[5] K.M. Hansen, A.P. Ravn, and H. Rischel: Specifying and Verifying Requirements of Real-Time Systems. In proc. of the ACM SIGSOFT'91 Conference on Software for Critical Systems, New Orleans, December 4-6, 1991, *ACM Software Engineering Notes*, vol. 15, no. 5, 1991, pp. 44-54.

[6] M.R. Hansen, Zhou Chaochen, and Jørgen Staunstrup: *A Real-Time Duration Semantics for Circuits.* ProCoS Rep. ID/DTH MRH 7/1, September 1991. (To appear in proc. of *TAU'92: 1992 Workshop on Timing Issues in the Specification and Synthesis of Digital Systems*, Princeton Univ., NJ, March 1992.)

[7] Jifeng He: *A Predicative Semantics for a Divergence-Free Programming Language Based on Temporal Intervals.* ProCoS Techn. Rep. PRG/OU HJF 8/1, ESPRIT BRA 3104, 1991.

[8] J. Hooman and J Widom: A temporal-logic based compositional proof system for real-time message passing. In proc. *PARLE'89*, vol. II, LNCS 366, Springer-Verlag 1989, pp. 424-441.

[9] J. Hooman: *Specification and Compositional Verification of Real-Time Systems.* PhD Thesis 1991, Technical University of Eindhoven.

[10] F. Jahanian and A.K-L. Mok: Safety Analysis of Timing Properties in Real-Time Systems. In *IEEE Trans. SE*-12(9), 1986, pp. 890-904.

[11] R. Koymans: Specifying real-time properties with metric temporal logic, *Journal of Real-time Systems, 2*, 1990.

[12] Zhiming Liu: *A Probabilistic Duration Calculus.* Working Paper, Department of Computer Science, Technical University of Denmark, December 1991.

[13] Ben Moszkowski: A Temporal Logic for Multilevel Reasoning about Hardware, *IEEE Computer*, vol. 18, no. 2, 1985, pp. 10-19.

[14] A. Pnueli and E. Harel: Applications of temporal logic to the specification of real-time systems. In proc. *Symp. Formal Techn. in Real-Time and Fault-Tolerant Systems*, LNCS 311, (M. Joseph ed.), 1988, pp. 84-98.

[15] A.P. Ravn and H. Rischel: Requirements Capture for Embedded Real-Time Systems. In proc. *IMACS-IFAC Symposium MCTS, Lille, France*, vol. 2, 1991, pp. 147-152.

[16] G.M. Reed and A.W. Roscoe: Metric spaces as models for real-time concurrency. In proc. *Mathematical Foundations of Programming*, LNCS 298, 1987, pp. 331-343.

[17] S. Schneider: *Correctness and Communication of Real-Time Systems.* PhD Thesis 1989, Techn. Monograph PRG-84, Oxford Univ. Comp. Lab., March 1990.

[18] Jens U. Skakkebæk: *Development of a provably correct system.* Master's thesis, Department of Computer Science, Technical University of Denmark, August 1991.

Timed Transition Systems[1]

Thomas A. Henzinger
Computer Science Department, Cornell University
Ithaca, NY 14853, U.S.A.

Zohar Manna
Computer Science Department, Stanford University
Stanford, CA 94305, U.S.A.
and
Department of Applied Mathematics, Weizmann Institute of Science
Rehovot 76100, Israel

Amir Pnueli
Department of Applied Mathematics, Weizmann Institute of Science
Rehovot 76100, Israel

Abstract. We incorporate time into an interleaving model of concurrency. In timed transition systems, the qualitative fairness requirements of traditional transition system are replaced (and superseded) by quantitative lower-bound and upper-bound timing constraints on transitions. The purpose of this paper is to explore the scope of applicability for the abstract model of timed transition systems. We demonstrate that the model can represent a wide variety of phenomena that routinely occur in conjunction with the timed execution of concurrent processes. Our treatment covers both processes that are executed in parallel on separate processors and communicate either through shared variables or by message passing, and processes that time-share a limited number of processors under a given scheduling policy. Often it is this scheduling policy that determines if a system meets its real-time requirements. Thus we explicitly address such questions as time-outs, interrupts, static and dynamic priorities.

Keywords: Transition systems, concurrency, real time.

---

[1]This research was supported in part by an IBM graduate fellowship, by the National Science Foundation grants CCR-89-11512 and CCR-89-13641, by the Defense Advanced Research Projects Agency under contract N00039-84-C-0211, by the United States Air Force Office of Scientific Research under contract AFOSR-90-0057, and by the European Community ESPRIT Basic Research Action project 3096 (SPEC).

1 Introduction

In [HMP91], we extended the specification language of temporal logic and the corresponding verification framework to prove timing properties of reactive systems. To model the timed execution of reactive systems, we generalized the computational model of transition systems conservatively by imposing timing requirements on the transitions. We claimed that a wide variety of real-time phenomena that are encountered in practice can be represented and analyzed within the model of timed transition systems. In this paper, we substantiate that claim. We use timed transition systems to model the timed execution of both multiprocessing and multiprogramming systems. Specifically, we address issues that routinely occur in real-time process communication, such as time-outs, and issues of real-time process control, including typical time-sharing strategies. By doing so, we enlargen the scope of applicability of the temporal proof methodologies for verifying timing properties of reactive systems that were presented in [HMP91].

In our model, we assume a global, fictitious, real-valued clock, whose actions advance time by nonuniform amounts. The clock actions are interleaved with the system actions, which have no duration in time. In some other work aimed at the formal analysis of real-time systems, it has been claimed that while this *interleaving* model of computation may be adequate for the qualitative analysis of reactive systems, it is inappropriate for the real-time analysis of programs, and a more realistic model, such as *maximal parallelism*, is needed [KSdR+88]. One of the points that we demonstrate in this paper is a refutation of that claim. We show that by a careful incorporation of time into the interleaving model, we can still model adequately most of the phenomena that occur in the timed execution of programs. Yet we retain the important economic advantage of interleaving models, namely, that at any point only one transition can occur and has to be analyzed.

We define the formal semantics of a real-time system as a set of timed execution sequences. This is done in two steps. First, in Section 2, we review the *abstract* computational model of timed transition systems and identify the possible timed execution sequences (computations) of any such system. Then, we consider *concrete* real-time systems and show how the concrete constructs can be interpreted within the abstract model. We begin, in Section 3, with the representation of real-time processes that are executed in parallel and communicate either through a shared memory or by message passing. Although the timeless interleaving of concurrent activities identifies true parallelism with (sequential) nondeterminism, when time is of the essence, we can no longer ignore the difference between *multiprocessing*, where each parallel task is executed on a separate machine, and *multiprogramming*, where several tasks reside on the same machine. This is because questions of priorities, interrupts, and scheduling of tasks may strongly influence the ability of a system to meet its timing constraints. These issues in modeling time-sharing systems are discussed in Section 4.

2 Timing Constraints for Transition Systems

Timed transition systems generalize the basic computational model of transition systems [Kel76, Pnu77] by associating minimal and maximal time delays with the transitions. We use the real line as time domain and adapt the definition of timed transition systems that was given for a discrete time domain in [HMP91]. Similar notions of transition systems with timing constraints have been defined, for integer time, in [Har88, PH88, HMP90, Ost90].

A *transition system* $S = \langle V, \Sigma, \Theta, \mathcal{T} \rangle$ consists of four components:

1. a finite set V of *variables*.
2. a set Σ of *states*. Every state $\sigma \in \Sigma$ is an interpretation of V; that is, it assigns to every variable $x \in V$ a value $\sigma(x)$ in its domain.
3. a subset $\Theta \subseteq \Sigma$ of *initial states*.
4. a finite set $\mathcal{T}$ of *transitions*, including the idle transition τ_I. Every transition $\tau \in \mathcal{T}$ is a binary relation on Σ; that is, it defines for every state $\sigma \in \Sigma$ a (possibly empty) set of τ-successors $\tau(\sigma) \subseteq \Sigma$. We say that the transition τ is *enabled* on a state σ iff $\tau(\sigma) \neq \emptyset$. In particular, the *idle* (stutter) transition
$$\tau_I \;=\; \{(\sigma, \sigma) \mid \sigma \in \Sigma\}$$
is enabled on every state.

An infinite sequence $\sigma = \sigma_0\sigma_1\ldots$ of states is a *computation* (execution sequence, run) of the transition system $S = \langle V, \Sigma, \Theta, \mathcal{T} \rangle$ iff it satisfies the following two requirements:

Initiality $\sigma_0 \in \Theta$.

Consecution For all $i \geq 0$, there is a transition $\tau \in \mathcal{T}$ such that $\sigma_{i+1} \in \tau(\sigma_i)$ (which is also denoted by $\sigma_i \xrightarrow{\tau} \sigma_{i+1}$). We say that the transition τ is *taken* at position i of the computation σ.

We incorporate time into the transition system model by assuming that all transitions happen "instantaneously," while real-time constraints restrict the times at which transitions may occur. The timing constraints are classified into two categories: *lower-bound* and *upper-bound* requirements. They ensure that transitions occur neither too early nor too late, respectively. All of our time bounds are nonnegative integers $\mathbb{N}$. The absence of a lower-bound requirement is modeled by a lower bound of 0; the absence of an upper-bound requirement, by an upper bound of ∞. For notational convenience, we assume that $\infty \geq n$ for all $n \in \mathbb{N}$.

A *timed transition system* $S = \langle V, \Sigma, \Theta, \mathcal{T}, l, u \rangle$ consists of an underlying transition system $S^- = \langle V, \Sigma, \Theta, \mathcal{T} \rangle$ as well as

5. a *minimal delay* $l_\tau \in \mathbb{N}$ for every transition $\tau \in \mathcal{T}$. We require that $l_{\tau_I} = 0$.
6. a *maximal delay* $u_\tau \in \mathbb{N} \cup \{\infty\}$ for every transition $\tau \in \mathcal{T}$. We require that $u_\tau \geq l_\tau$ for all $\tau \in \mathcal{T}$, and that $u_\tau = \infty$ if τ is enabled on any initial state in Θ. In particular, $u_{\tau_I} = \infty$.

Let $\mathcal{T}_0 \subseteq \mathcal{T}$ be the set of transitions with the maximal delay 0. To allow time to progress, we put a restriction on these transitions. We require that there is no sequence

$$\sigma_0 \xrightarrow{\tau_0} \sigma_1 \xrightarrow{\tau_1} \cdots \xrightarrow{\tau_{n-1}} \sigma_n$$

of states and transitions such that $n > |\mathcal{T}_0|$ and $\tau_i \in \mathcal{T}_0$ for all $0 \leq i < n$. This condition ensures the operationality (machine-closure) of timed transition systems [Hen91a].

Timed state sequences

We model time by the real numbers R. A *timed state sequence* $\rho = (\sigma, \mathsf{T})$ consists of an infinite sequence σ of states $\sigma_i \in \Sigma$, where $i \geq 0$, and an infinite sequence T of corresponding times $\mathsf{T}_i \in \mathsf{R}$ that satisfy the following two conditions:

Monotonicity For all $i \geq 0$,

either $\mathsf{T}_{i+1} = \mathsf{T}_i$,
or $\mathsf{T}_{i+1} > \mathsf{T}_i$ and $\sigma_{i+1} = \sigma_i$;

that is, time never decreases. It may increase, by any amount, only between two consecutive states that are identical. The case that the time stays the same between two identical states is referred to as a *stutter step*; the case that the time increases is called a *time step*.

Progress For all $t \in \mathsf{R}$, there is some $i \geq 0$ such that $\mathsf{T}_i \geq t$; that is, time never converges. Since the time domain R contains no maximal element, there are infinitely many time steps in every timed state sequence.

It follows that a timed state sequence alternates *state* activities with *time* activities. Throughout state activities, time does not advance; throughout time activities, the state does not change. Since all state activities are represented by finite subsequences, timed state sequences observe the condition of *finite variability*, namely, that the state changes only finitely often throughout any finite interval of time [BKP86].

A set Π of timed state sequences is *closed under stuttering* iff (1) the sequence

$$\cdots \longrightarrow (\sigma_i, \mathsf{T}_i) \longrightarrow \cdots$$

is in Π precisely when the sequence

$$\cdots \longrightarrow (\sigma_i, \mathsf{T}_i) \longrightarrow (\sigma_i, \mathsf{T}_i) \longrightarrow \cdots$$

is in Π, and (2) the sequence

$$\cdots \longrightarrow (\sigma_i, \mathsf{T}_i) \longrightarrow (\sigma_i, \mathsf{T}_{i+1}) \longrightarrow \cdots$$

is in Π precisely when the sequence

$$\cdots \longrightarrow (\sigma_i, \mathsf{T}_i) \longrightarrow (\sigma_i, t) \longrightarrow (\sigma_i, \mathsf{T}_{i+1}) \longrightarrow \cdots$$

is in Π for $\mathsf{T}_i \leq t \leq \mathsf{T}_{i+1}$. To close a set of timed state sequences under stuttering, then, we must (1) add and delete finitely many stutter steps, and (2) split and merge finitely many time steps.

Timed execution sequences

Just as the execution sequences of transition systems are infinite state sequences, we model the execution sequences of timed transition systems by timed state sequences. The timed state sequence $\rho = (\sigma, \mathsf{T})$ is a *computation* of the timed transition system $S = \langle V, \Sigma, \Theta, \mathcal{T}, l, u \rangle$ iff the state sequence σ is a computation of the underlying transition system S^- and

Lower bound For every transition $\tau \in \mathcal{T}$ and all positions $i \geq 0$ and $j \geq i$ with $\mathsf{T}_j < \mathsf{T}_i + l_\tau$,

if τ is taken at position j of σ,
then τ is enabled on σ_i.

In other words, once enabled, τ is delayed for at least l_τ time units; it can be taken only after being continuously enabled for l_τ time units. Any transition that is enabled initially, on the first state of a timed state sequence, can be taken immediately (as if it has been enabled forever).

Upper bound For every transition $\tau \in \mathcal{T}$ and position $i \geq 0$, there is some position $j \geq i$ with $\mathsf{T}_j \leq \mathsf{T}_i + u_\tau$ such that

either τ is not enabled on σ_j,
or τ is taken at position j of σ.

In other words, once enabled, τ is delayed for at most u_τ time units; it cannot be continuously enabled for more than u_τ time units without being taken. Since the maximal delay of every transition that is enabled initially must be ∞, the first state change of a computation may occur at any time.

Note that at both stutter steps and time steps, the idle transition τ_I is taken. The idle transition marks phases of time activity throughout a computation; the other transitions are interleaved during phases of state activity. We consider all computations of a timed transition system to be infinite. Finite (terminating as well as deadlocking) computations are represented by infinite extensions that add only idle transitions; that is, a final, infinite phase of time activity.

It is not difficult to check that the computations of any timed transition system S are closed (1) under *stuttering* and (2) under *shifting the origin of time*. The former property ensures that timed transition systems can be refined [Hen91b]; the latter property means that timed transition systems cannot refer to absolute time. Specifically, the addition of a real constant to all times of a timed state sequence does not alter the property of being a computation of S. Thus we will often assume, without loss of generality, that the time of the first state change of a computation is 0.

Since the state component of any computation of S is a computation of the underlying untimed transition system S^-, ordinary timeless reasoning is sound for timed transition systems: every untimed property of infinite state sequences that is satisfied by all computations of S^-, is also satisfied by all computations of S. The converse, however, is generally not true. The timing constraints of S can be viewed as filters that prohibit certain possible behaviors of the untimed transition system S^-. Special cases are a minimal delay 0 and a maximal delay ∞ for a transition τ. While the former does not rule out any computations of S^-, the latter adds to S^- a *weak-fairness* (justice) assumption in the sense of [MP89]: τ cannot be continuously enabled without being taken.

The choice of the real numbers as time domain is taken for the sake of concreteness. Indeed, any total ordering with an appropriate definition of addition by a unit (i.e., $t \leq t+1$, and $t \leq t'$ implies $t+1 \leq t'+1$) can be chosen as a time domain. In the case that the time domain is any one-element set, timed transition systems are easily seen to coincide with ordinary fair transition systems (with a weak-fairness requirement for every transition).

3 Modeling Time-critical Multiprocessing Systems

The concrete real-time systems we consider first consist of a fixed number of sequential real-time programs that are executed in parallel, on separate processors, and communicate through a shared memory. We show how time-outs and real-time response can be programmed in this language. Then we add message passing primitives for process synchronization and communication.

3.1 Syntax: Timed transition diagrams

A *shared-variables multiprocessing system* P has the form

$$\{\theta\}[P_1 \| \ldots \| P_m].$$

Each *process* P_i, for $1 \leq i \leq m$, is a sequential nondeterministic real-time program over the finite set U_i of *private* (local) *data variables* and the finite set U_s of *shared data variables.* The formula θ, called the *data precondition* of P, restricts the initial values of the variables in

$$U \;=\; U_s \cup \bigcup_{1 \leq i \leq m} U_i.$$

The real-time programs P_i can be alternatively presented in a textual programming language or as transition diagrams. We shall use the latter, graphical, representation. For this purpose, we extend the untimed transition diagram language by labeling transitions with minimal and maximal time delays.

A *timed transition diagram* for the process P_i is a finite directed graph whose vertices $L_i = \{\ell_0^i, \ldots \ell_{n_i}^i\}$ are called *locations.* The *entry* location — usually ℓ_0^i — is indicated as follows:

The intended meaning of the entry location ℓ_0^i is that the control of the process P_i starts at the location ℓ_0^i. The component processes of a system are not required to start synchronously (i.e., at the same time). Each edge in the graph is labeled by a guarded instruction, a *minimal delay* $l \in \mathsf{N}$ and a *maximal delay* $u \in \mathsf{N} \cup \{\infty\}$ such that $u \geq l$:

$$\ell^i_j \xrightarrow[{[l,u]}]{c \;\rightarrow\; \bar{x} := \bar{e}} \ell^i_k$$

where the guard c is a boolean expression, $\bar{x}$ is a vector of variables, and $\bar{e}$ an equally typed vector of expressions (the guard *true* and the delay interval $[0, \infty]$ are usually suppressed; for the empty vector *nil*, the instruction $c \rightarrow nil := nil$ is abbreviated to $c?$). We require that every cycle in the graph consists of no fewer than two edges, at least one of which is labeled by a positive (nonzero) maximal delay.

The intended operational meaning of the given edge is as follows. The minimal delay l guarantees that whenever the control of the process P_i has resided at the location ℓ^i_j for at least l time units during which the guard c has been continuously true, then P_i *may* proceed to the location ℓ^i_k. The maximal delay u ensures that whenever the control of the process P_i has resided at ℓ^i_j for u time units during which the guard c has been continuously true, then P_i *must* proceed to ℓ^i_k (or, more precisely, time cannot advance before either the guard c becomes false, which may be caused by process parallel to P_i, or the process P_i proceeds). In doing so, the control of P_i moves to the location ℓ^i_k "instantaneously," and the current values of $\bar{e}$ are assigned to the variables $\bar{x}$. In general, a process may have to proceed via several edges all of whose guards have been continuously true for their corresponding maximal delays. In this case, any such edge is chosen nondeterministically.

It follows that the control of a process P_i may remain at a location ℓ^i_j forever only in one of two situations: if ℓ^i_j has no outgoing edges, we say that P_i has *terminated*; if each of the guards that are associated with the outgoing edges of the location ℓ^i_j is false infinitely often, we say that P_i has *deadlocked*. The second condition is necessary (although not sufficient) for stagnation, because if one guard is true forever, then the corresponding maximal delay $u \leq \infty$ guarantees the progress of P_i.

3.2 Semantics: Timed transition systems

The operational view of timed transition diagrams can be captured by a simple translation into the abstract model of timed transition systems. With the given shared-variables multiprocessing system

$$P: \quad \{\theta\}[P_1 \| \ldots \| P_m],$$

we associate the following timed transition system $S_P = \langle V, \Sigma, \Theta, \mathcal{T}, l, u \rangle$:

1. $V = U \cup \{\pi_1, \ldots \pi_m\}$. Each *control variable* π_i, where $1 \leq i \leq m$, ranges over the set $L_i \cup \{\bot\}$. The value of π_i indicates the location of the control for the process P_i; it is $\bot$ (undefined) before the process P_i starts.

2. Σ contains all interpretations of V.

3. Θ is the set of all states $\sigma \in \Sigma$ such that θ is true in σ and $\sigma(\pi_i) = \bot$ for all $1 \leq i \leq m$.

4. $\mathcal{T}$ contains, in addition to the idle transition τ_I, an *entry transition* τ^i_0 for every process P_i, where $1 \leq i \leq m$, as well as a transition τ_E for every edge E in the timed transition diagrams for $P_1, \ldots P_m$. In particular, $\sigma' \in \tau^i_0(\sigma)$ iff

$\sigma(\pi_i) = \bot$ and $\sigma'(\pi_i) = \ell_0^i$,
$\sigma'(y) = \sigma(y)$ for all $y \in V - \{\pi_i\}$.

If E connects the source location ℓ_j^i to the target location ℓ_k^i and is labeled by the instruction $c \rightarrow \bar{x} := \bar{e}$, then $\sigma' \in \tau_E(\sigma)$ iff

$\sigma(\pi_i) = \ell_j^i$ and $\sigma'(\pi_i) = \ell_k^i$,
c is true in σ and $\sigma'(\bar{x}) = \sigma(\bar{e})$,
$\sigma'(y) = \sigma(y)$ for all $y \in V - \{\pi_i, \bar{x}\}$.

5. If τ is an entry transition, then $l_\tau = 0$. For every edge E labeled by the minimal delay l, let $l_{\tau_E} = l$.

6. If τ is an entry transition, then $u_\tau = \infty$. For every edge E labeled by the maximal delay u, let $u_{\tau_E} = u$.

This translation defines the set of possible computations of the real-time system P as a set of timed state sequences. For instance, the computations of the trivial system P that consists of a single process with the timed transition diagram

$$P: \longrightarrow (\ell_0) \xrightarrow{[0,1]} (\ell_1)$$

are exactly the timed state sequences that result from closing all sequences of the form

$$(\bot, 0) \longrightarrow (\ell_0, 0) \longrightarrow (\ell_0, t) \longrightarrow (\ell_1, t) \longrightarrow (\ell_1, 1) \longrightarrow (\ell_1, 2) \longrightarrow \cdots$$

where $0 \leq t \leq 1$, under stuttering and shifting the origin of time. The condition on timed transition diagrams that every cycle contains at least one positive (nonzero) maximal delay ensures that the timed transition system S_P is operational. (The condition that every cycle contains at least two edges guarantees that once a transition is taken, it cannot stay enabled, which simplifies the reasoning about timed transition systems [HMP91].)

We remark that our semantics of shared-variables multiprocessing systems is conservative over the untimed case. Suppose that the system P contains no delay labels (recall that, in this case, all minimal delays are 0 and all maximal delays are ∞). Then the state components of the computations of S_P are precisely the legal execution sequences of P, as defined in the interleaving model of concurrency, that are weakly fair with respect to every transition [MP89]: no process can stop when one of its transitions is continuously enabled. Weak fairness for every individual transition and, consequently, progress for every process is guaranteed by the maximal delays ∞.

3.3 Examples: Time-out and timely response

We now model two typical real-time constructs as shared-variables multiprocessing systems to demonstrate the scope of the timed transition diagram language. In the first example (*time-out*), a process checks if an external event happens within a certain amount of time. In the second example (*traffic light*), a process reacts to an external event and is required to do so within a certain amount of time. A third example combines several processes.

Time-out

To see how a time-out situation can be programmed, consider the process P with the following timed transition diagram:

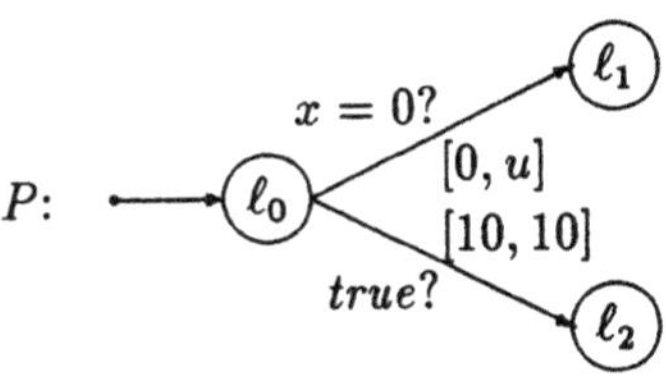

We assume that the variable x may be altered by some other process that is executed in parallel to P. When at the location ℓ_0, the process P attempts, for 10 time units, to proceed to the location ℓ_1 by checking the value of x. If the value of x is not found to be 0, then P does not succeed and proceeds to the alternative location ℓ_2 after 10 time units. The choice of the maximal delay u determines how often P checks the value of x. For example, if $u \geq 10$, then P may not check the value of x at all before timing out after 10 time units. If $0 < u < 10$, then P has to check the value of x at least once every u time units. Consequently, if the value of x is 0 for more than u time units, it will be detected. On the other hand, the value of x being 0 may go undetected if it fluctuates too frequently, even in the case of $u = 0$.

Traffic light

To give another typical real-time application of embedded systems, let us design a traffic light controller that turns a pedestrian light green within 5 time units after a button is pushed. The environment is given by the following process E. Whenever the request button is pushed, the shared boolean variable *request* is set to *true*:

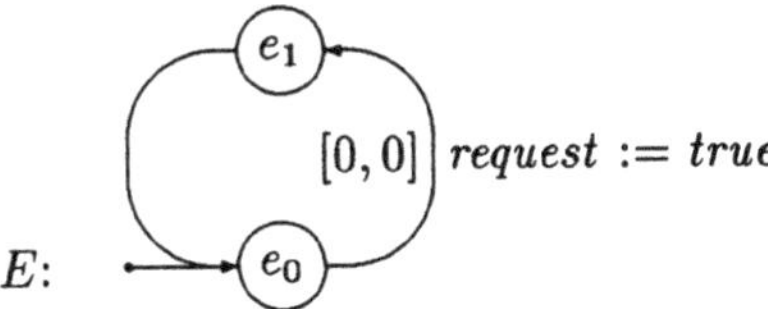

Recall that the edge labels *true*? and $[0, \infty]$ are suppressed; thus we have no knowledge about the frequency of requests.

We wish to design a traffic light controller Q that controls the status of the traffic light through the variable *light*, whose value is either *green* or *red*. As unit of time we take the amount of time it takes to switch the light; for simplicity, we also assume that the time needed for local operations within Q is negligible. Now let us specify the desired process Q. The controller Q should behave in such a way that the combined system

$$P: \quad \{request = false,\ light = red\}\ [E \| Q]$$

satisfies the following two correctness conditions:

(A) Whenever *request* is *true*, then *light* is *green* within 5 time units for at least 5 time units.

(B) Whenever *request* has been *false* for 25 time units, then *light* is *red*.

The first condition, (A), ensures that no pedestrian has to wait for more than 5 time units to cross the road and is given another 5 time units to do so. The second condition, (B), prevents the light from being green indefinitely (under the assumption that any controller Q resets the variable *request* to *false* whenever it is read and found to be *true*).

It is not hard to convince ourselves that, once it is started, the following process Q satisfies the specification:

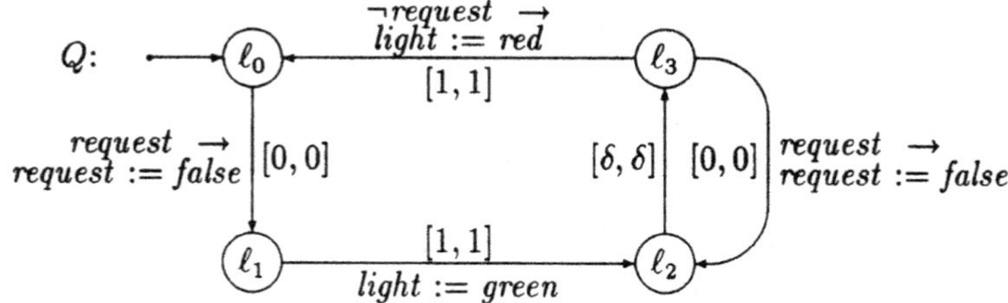

for any delay $4 \leq \delta \leq 23$. This implementation of the traffic light controller turns the light green as soon as possible after a request is received and then waits for δ time units before turning the light red again. If the request button has been pushed in the meantime, the light stays green for another δ time units.

Multiple traffic lights

We now generalize the *traffic light* example and design a system that reacts to several external events. We wish to do so by composing, in parallel, processes that are similar to Q. At this point it is convenient to accept some additional assumptions about the frequencies of the external events. In our example, we suppose that the distance between any two requests is at least 15 time units; that is,

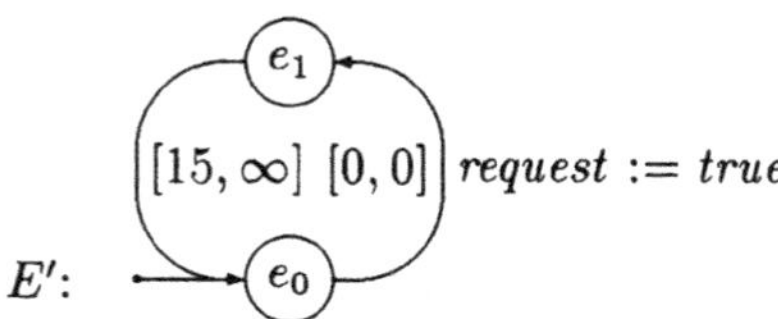

Under this assumption, we can simplify the traffic light controller to

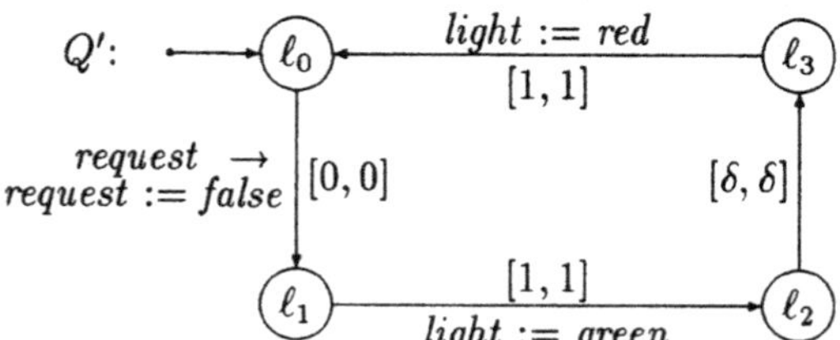

for any delay $4 \le \delta \le 17$. The combined system

$$P': \quad \{request = false,\ light = red\}\ [E' \| Q']$$

still satisfies both correctness requirements (A) and (B).

Now consider a more complex traffic light configuration, with two lights and two request buttons. In particular, we assume that the second light is designed for the special convenience of pedestrians in a hurry: it is required to turn green within 3 time units of a request but, on the other hand, has to stay green for only 3 time units. While pedestrians arrive at the first light with a frequency of at most one pedestrian every 15 time units, we assume that the more urgent requests are less frequent — at most one every 30 time units:

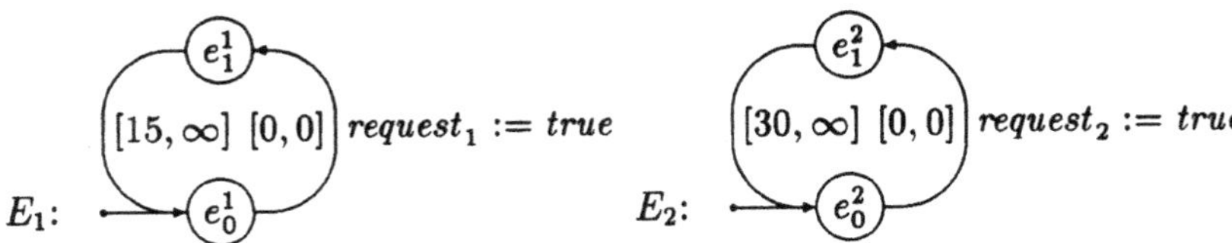

The controller for both lights executes the following two processes:

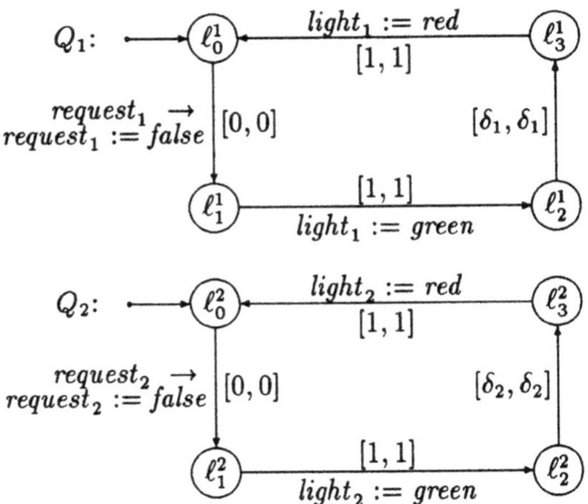

If the combined traffic light controller makes use of *two* processors and the processes Q_1 and Q_2 are executed in a truly concurrent fashion, then the correctness of the entire system

$$P_{\|}: \quad \{request_1 = request_2 = false,\ light_1 = light_2 = red\}\ [E_1 \| E_2 \| Q_1 \| Q_2]$$

follows from the correctness of its parts. Specifically, if $4 \le \delta_1 \le 17$ and $2 \le \delta_2 \le 23$, then all runs of $P_{\|}$ satisfy the following conditions:

(A_1) Whenever $request_1$ is *true*, then $light_1$ is *green* within 5 time units for 5 time units.

(A_2) Whenever $request_2$ is *true*, then $light_2$ is *green* within 3 time units for 3 time units.

(B_1) Whenever $request_1$ has been *false* for 25 time units, then $light_1$ is *red*.

(B_2) Whenever $request_2$ has been *false* for 25 time units, then $light_2$ is *red*.

A more interesting case is obtained if only a single processor is available to control both lights and the two processes Q_1 and Q_2 have to share it. Using the *interleaving* (shuffle) operator of [Hoa85], we denote the resulting system by the expression

$$P_{|||}: \quad \{request_1 = request_2 = false,\ light_1 = light_2 = red\}\ [E_1 \| E_2 \| (Q_1 ||| Q_2)].$$

Note that the behavior of the environment $E_1 \| E_2$ is still truly concurrent to the behavior of the traffic light controller $Q_1 ||| Q_2$, which executes both processes Q_1 and Q_2 on a single processor in an interleaved fashion.

Let us assume that $\delta_1 = 10$ and $\delta_2 = 2$, a case in which the multiprocessing $P_{\|}$ is correct. However, if we have no knowledge about the strategy by which the processes Q_1 and Q_2 are scheduled on the processor they share, other than that it is fair (i.e., the turn of each process will come eventually), then the time-sharing system $P_{|||}$ does not satisfy the specification consisting of the requirements (A_1), (A_2), (B_1), and (B_2). This is easy to see. Suppose that the process Q_1 is, for some time, given priority over the process Q_2, and the traffic light controller receives a request for the second light only 1 time unit after it has received a request for the first light. Then it will serve the first request by turning $light_1$ green and (busy) waiting for 10 time units, thus violating (A_2). On the other hand, if the process Q_2 that serves the more urgent yet less frequent requests is always given priority over the process Q_1, then the system $P_{|||}$ is correct. This is because of the low frequency of requests for the second light only one such request can interrupt the service of a request for the first light.

Before we discuss the modeling of time-sharing, priorities, and interrupts in greater detail, let us first stay with truly concurrent processes and introduce message-passing operations.

3.4 Message passing

Asynchronous message passing can be modeled by shared variables that represent message channels. In this subsection, we extend our timed transition diagram language by a primitive for *synchronous* (CSP-style) message passing, which can be used for the synchronization and communication of parallel processes.

Syntax

A (*message-passing*) *multiprocessing system* P has the form

$$\{\theta\}[P_1 \| \dots \| P_m],$$

where θ is a data precondition and each process P_i, for $1 \leq i \leq m$, is a sequential nondeterministic real-time program over the finite set $U_i \cup U_s$ of data variables (in the case of pure message-passing systems, $U_s = \emptyset$). We employ again timed transition diagrams to represent processes, but enrich the repertoire of instructions by guarded send and receive operations. The *send* operation $\alpha!e$ outputs the value of the expression e on the channel α. The *receive* operation $\alpha?x$ reads an input value from the channel α and assigns it to the variable x. A send instruction and a receive instruction *match* iff they belong to different processes and address the same channel:

$$P_i:\quad (\ell^i_j) \xrightarrow[{[l,u]}]{c \;\rightarrow\; \alpha!e} (\ell^i_k)$$

$$P_{i'}:\quad (\ell^{i'}_{j'}) \xrightarrow[{[l',u']}]{c' \;\rightarrow\; \alpha?x} (\ell^{i'}_{k'})$$

For any two matching communication instructions with the delay intervals $[l,u]$ and $[l',u']$, respectively, we require that $max(l,l') \leq min(u,u')$.

Since we use the paradigm of synchronous message passing, a send operation can be executed only jointly with a matching receive operation. Thus the intended operational meaning of the given two edges is as follows. Suppose that, for $max(l,l')$ time units, the control of the process P_i has resided at the location ℓ^i_j and the control of the process $P_{i'}$ has resided at the location $\ell^{i'}_{j'}$ and the guards c and c' have been continuously true. Then P_i and $P_{i'}$ *may* proceed, synchronously, to the locations ℓ^i_k and $\ell^{i'}_{k'}$, respectively. On the other hand, if P_i has resided at ℓ^i_j and $P_{i'}$ has resided at $\ell^{i'}_{j'}$ and the guards c and c' have been continuously true for $min(u,u')$ time units, then both processes *must* proceed. In doing so, the current value of e is assigned to x.

Semantics

Synchronous message passing can be modeled formally by timed transition systems. We define the timed transition system $S_P = \langle V, \Sigma, \Theta, \mathcal{T}, l, u \rangle$ that is associated with the given message-passing multiprocessing system P as in the shared-variables case, only that $\mathcal{T}$ contains an additional transition for every matching pair of communication instructions. Suppose that the two edges E (from ℓ^i_j to ℓ^i_k) and E' (from $\ell^{i'}_{j'}$ to $\ell^{i'}_{k'}$) in the timed transition diagrams for P_i and $P_{i'}$ are labeled by the matching instructions $c \rightarrow e!\alpha$ and $c' \rightarrow \alpha?x$, respectively. Then

- $\mathcal{T}$ contains, for the matching edges E and E', a transition $\tau_{E,E'}$ such that $\sigma' \in \tau_{E,E'}(\sigma)$ iff

  $\sigma(\pi_i) = \ell^i_j$ and $\sigma'(\pi_i) = \ell^i_k$,
  $\sigma(\pi_{i'}) = \ell^{i'}_{j'}$ and $\sigma'(\pi_{i'}) = \ell^{i'}_{k'}$,
  c and c' are true in σ and $\sigma'(x) = \sigma(e)$,
  $\sigma'(y) = \sigma(y)$ for all $y \in V - \{\pi_i, \pi_{i'}, x\}$.

- If the matching edges E and E' are labeled by the minimal delays l and l', respectively, let $l_{\tau_{E,E'}} = max(l,l')$.

- If the matching edges E and E' are labeled by the maximal delays u and u', respectively, let $u_{\tau_{E,E'}} = min(u,u')$.

This translation defines the set of possible computations of any distributed real-time system P whose processes communicate either through shared variables or by message passing.

Process synchronization

Recall that the component processes of the multiprocessing system $P_1 \| P_2$ may start at arbitrary, even vastly different, times. An important application of synchronous message passing is the synchronization of parallel processes. Let P_1 and P_2 be two real-time processes whose timed transition diagrams have the entry locations ℓ_0^1 and ℓ_0^2, respectively, and let α be a channel. Now consider the two processes $\hat{P}_1$ and $\hat{P}_2$ whose timed transition diagrams are obtained from the transition diagrams for P_1 and P_2 by adding new entry locations:

$$\hat{P}_1: \quad \longrightarrow (\hat{\ell}_0^1) \xrightarrow[{[0,0]}]{\alpha!} (\ell_0^1)$$

$$\hat{P}_2: \quad \longrightarrow (\hat{\ell}_0^2) \xrightarrow[{[0,0]}]{\alpha?} (\ell_0^2)$$

The added message-passing operations have the effect of synchronizing the start of the two processes P_1 and P_2 (whenever message passing is used for the purpose of process synchronization only, the data that is passed between processes is immaterial and the data components of the send and receive instructions are usually suppressed). It follows that the component processes of the multiprocessing system $\hat{P}_1 \| \hat{P}_2$ start synchronously, at the exact same (arbitrary) time.

From now on, we shall write $P_1 \|_s P_2$ for the system P whose component processes P_1 and P_2 start synchronously; that is, the notation $P_1 \|_s P_2$ is an abbreviation for the message-passing system $\hat{P}_1 \| \hat{P}_2$. Equivalently, we can directly define the formal semantics S_P of the *synchronous* multiprocessing system $P_1 \|_s P_2$ as containing a single entry transition $\tau_0^{1,2}$ for both processes P_1 and P_2; namely, $\sigma' \in \tau_0^{1,2}(\sigma)$ iff

$$\begin{aligned}
&\sigma(\pi_1) = \sigma(\pi_2) = \perp, \\
&\sigma'(\pi_1) = \ell_0^1 \text{ and } \sigma'(\pi_2) = \ell_0^2, \\
&\sigma'(y) = \sigma(y) \text{ for all } y \in V - \{\pi_1, \pi_2\}.
\end{aligned}$$

It is not hard to generalize our notion of synchronous message passing to synchronous broadcasting, which allows arbitrarily many parallel processes to synchronize simultaneously on joint transitions.

4 Modeling Time-critical Multiprogramming Systems

While the interleaving model for concurrency identifies true parallelism (multiprocessing) with nondeterminism (multiprogramming), the *traffic light* example of the previous section suggests that the ability of a system to meet its real-time constraints depends crucially on the number of processors that are available and on the process allocation algorithm. This dependence is already vividly demonstrated by the following trivial system consisting of the two processes P_1 and P_2:

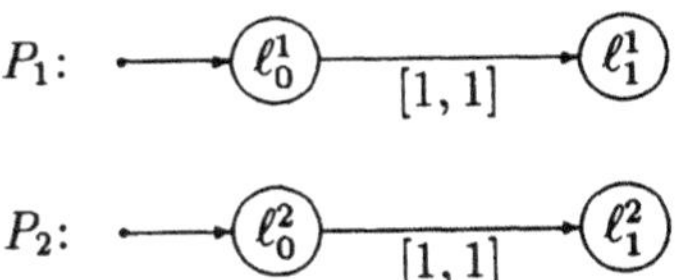

If both processes are executed in parallel on two processors, we denote the resulting system by $P_1 \| P_2$ (or $P_1 \|_s P_2$, if the processes are started at the same time); if they share a single processor and are executed one transition at a time according to some scheduling strategy, the composite system is denoted by $P_1 ||| P_2$.

In the untimed case, it is the very essence of the interleaving semantics to identify both systems with the same set of possible (interleaved) execution sequences — the stuttering closure of the two state sequences

$$(\ell_0^1, \ell_0^2) \xrightarrow{P_1} (\ell_1^1, \ell_0^2) \xrightarrow{P_2} (\ell_1^1, \ell_1^2) \longrightarrow \cdots,$$

$$(\ell_0^1, \ell_0^2) \xrightarrow{P_2} (\ell_0^1, \ell_1^2) \xrightarrow{P_1} (\ell_1^1, \ell_1^2) \longrightarrow \cdots$$

(a state is an interpretation of the two control variables π_1 and π_2). Real time, however, can distinguish between true concurrency and sequential nondeterminism: if both processes start synchronously, then the parallel execution of P_1 and P_2 terminates within 1 time unit; on the other hand, any interleaved sequential execution of P_1 and P_2 takes 2 time units. This distinction must be captured by our model:

1. In the two-processor case $P_1 \|_s P_2$, we obtain as computations the timed state sequences that result from closing the two sequences

   $$(\bot, \bot, 0) \longrightarrow (\ell_0^1, \ell_0^2, 0) \longrightarrow (\ell_0^1, \ell_0^2, 1) \xrightarrow{P_1} (\ell_1^1, \ell_0^2, 1) \xrightarrow{P_2} (\ell_1^1, \ell_1^2, 1) \longrightarrow (\ell_1^1, \ell_1^2, 2) \longrightarrow \cdots,$$

   $$(\bot, \bot, 0) \longrightarrow (\ell_0^1, \ell_0^2, 0) \longrightarrow (\ell_0^1, \ell_0^2, 1) \xrightarrow{P_2} (\ell_0^1, \ell_1^2, 1) \xrightarrow{P_1} (\ell_1^1, \ell_1^2, 1) \longrightarrow (\ell_1^1, \ell_1^2, 2) \longrightarrow \cdots$$

   under stuttering and shifting the origin of time (the third component of every triple denotes the time). The system $P_1 \| P_2$ has more computations, because the time difference between the start of P_1 and the start of P_2 can be arbitrarily large.

2. In the time-sharing case $P_1 ||| P_2$, the set of computations will be defined to be essentially the closure of the two timed state sequences

   $$(\bot, 0) \longrightarrow (\ell_0^1, \ell_0^2, 0) \longrightarrow (\ell_0^1, \ell_0^2, 1) \xrightarrow{P_1} (\ell_1^1, \ell_0^2, 1) \longrightarrow (\ell_1^1, \ell_0^2, 2) \xrightarrow{P_2} (\ell_1^1, \ell_1^2, 2) \longrightarrow \cdots,$$

   $$(\bot, 0) \longrightarrow (\ell_0^1, \ell_0^2, 0) \longrightarrow (\ell_0^1, \ell_0^2, 1) \xrightarrow{P_2} (\ell_0^1, \ell_1^2, 1) \longrightarrow (\ell_0^1, \ell_1^2, 2) \xrightarrow{P_1} (\ell_1^1, \ell_1^2, 2) \longrightarrow \cdots$$

   under stuttering and shifting the origin of time. We write "essentially," because we will augment the states by information about the status of the two processes (either active or suspended). Also, observe that we have silently assumed that the swapping of processes is instantaneous and that neither process has priority over the other process. All of these issues will be discussed in detail.

Thus, for modeling time-critical applications, we can no longer ignore the difference between multiprocessing and multiprogramming. In this section, we first show how our model extends to concrete real-time systems that consist of a fixed number of sequential programs that are executed, by time-sharing, on a single processor. Then we use our framework to represent general, distributed multiprogramming systems, in which several processes share a pool of processors statically or dynamically.

4.1 Syntax and semantics

A *multiprogramming system* P has the form

$$\{\theta\}[P_1|||\dots|||P_m].$$

Each process P_i, for $1 \leq i \leq m$, is again a sequential nondeterministic real-time program over the finite set U of data variables, whose initial values satisfy the data precondition θ. We represent the real-time programs P_i by timed transition diagrams as before. Note, however, that in the multiprogramming case the control of the (single) processor resides at one particular location of one particular process. Thus the intended operational meaning of the edge

$$\ell^i_j \xrightarrow[{[l,u]}]{c \,\rightarrow\, x := e} \ell^i_k$$

is as follows. The minimal delay l guarantees that whenever the control (of the single processor) has resided at the location ℓ^i_j for at least l time units and the guard c is true, then the control *may* proceed to the location ℓ^i_k. The maximal delay u ensures that whenever the control has resided at ℓ^i_j for u time units and the guard c is true, then it *must* proceed to ℓ^i_k. This is because, in the single-processor case, no other process can interfere with the active process and change the value of c.

The operational view of the concrete model is again captured formally by a translation into timed transition systems. With the given multiprogramming system P, we associate the following timed transition system $S_P = \langle V, \Sigma, \Theta, \mathcal{T}, l, u\rangle$:

1. $V = U \cup \{\mu, \pi_1, \dots \pi_m\}$. There are two kinds of control variables: the *processor control variable* μ ranges over the set $\{1, \dots m, \bot\}$; each *process control variable* π_i, for $1 \leq i \leq m$, ranges over the set L_i of locations of the process P_i. The value of the processor control variable μ is $\bot$ (undefined) before the (single) processor starts executing processes. Thereafter the control of the processor resides at the location π_μ of the process P_μ. We say that the process P_μ is *active*, while all other processes P_i, for $i \neq \mu$, are *suspended* (if the value of μ is undefined, then all processes are suspended). The process control variable π_i of a suspended process indicates the location at which the execution of P_i will resume when P_i (re)gains control of the processor.

2. Σ contains all interpretations of V.

3. Θ is the set of all states $\sigma \in \Sigma$ such that θ is true in σ, and $\sigma(\mu) = \bot$, and $\sigma(\pi_i) = \ell^i_0$ for all $1 \leq i \leq m$.

4. $\mathcal{T}$ contains, in addition to the idle transition τ_I, an *action* transition τ_E for every edge E in the timed transition diagrams for $P_1, \ldots P_m$. If E connects the source location ℓ^i_j to the target location ℓ^i_k and is labeled by the instruction $c \rightarrow \bar{x} := \bar{e}$, then $\sigma' \in \tau_E(\sigma)$ iff

   $\sigma(\mu) = i$,
   $\sigma(\pi_i) = \ell^i_j$ and $\sigma'(\pi_i) = \ell^i_k$,
   c is true in σ and $\sigma'(\bar{x}) = \sigma(\bar{e})$,
   $\sigma'(y) = \sigma(y)$ for all $y \in V - \{\pi_i, \bar{x}\}$.

   Furthermore, there are *scheduling* transitions $\tau \in \mathcal{T}$ that change the status of the processes by resuming a suspended process: $\sigma' \in \tau(\sigma)$ implies that

   $\sigma'(y) = \sigma(y)$ for all $y \in U$.

   The scheduling policy determines the set of scheduling transitions. A scheduling transition τ is called an *entry* transition iff it is enabled on some initial states. We restrict ourselves to scheduling policies with a single entry transition, τ_0, that is enabled on all initial states. Moreover, we require that $\sigma' \in \tau_0(\sigma)$ implies that

   $\sigma(\mu) = \perp$,
   $\sigma'(y) = \sigma(y)$ for all $y \in V - \{\mu\}$;

   that is, the entry transition τ_0 is enabled precisely on the initial states and activates, perhaps nondeterministically, one of the competing processes.

5. For every edge E labeled by the minimal delay l, let $l_{\tau_E} = l$. Furthermore, $l_{\tau_0} = 0$.

6. For every edge E labeled by the maximal delay u, let $u_{\tau_E} = u$. Furthermore, $u_{\tau_0} = \infty$.

The computations of S_P clearly depend on the scheduling transitions and their delays. In the untimed case, the scheduling issue can be reduced to fairness assumptions about the scheduling policy: correctness of an untimed multiprogramming system is generally shown for all fair scheduling strategies. It makes, however, little sense to to desire that a multiprogramming system satisfies a real-time requirement under all (fair) scheduling strategies, because the scheduling algorithm usually determines if a system meets its timing constraints. In fact, fair scheduling strategies admit *thrashing*: by switching control too often between processes, no action transition may be enabled long enough so that it has to be taken and only scheduling transitions will be performed. Thus the system may make no real progress at all and may certainly not meet any real-time deadlines. Consequently, we study the correctness of real-time multiprogramming systems always with respect to a particular given scheduling policy.

4.2 Scheduling strategies

Our selection of scheduling strategies is neither intended to be categorical nor comprehensive; we simply try to examine what we think is a representative variety of different scheduling mechanisms and, in the process, hope to convince ourselves of the utility of the timed transition system model. Throughout this subsection, we assume a fixed multiprogramming system

$$P: \quad \{\theta\}[P_1 ||| \ldots ||| P_m]$$

and define the scheduling transitions of the associated timed transition system S_P for various scheduling algorithms.

Greedy scheduling

The simplest reasonable scheduling strategy, as well as our default strategy, is *greedy.* According to this policy, the process that is currently in control of the processor remains active until all its transitions are disabled. At this point an arbitrary other process with an enabled transition takes over. Formally, the set $\mathcal{T}$ of transitions for the timed transition system S_P contains, in addition to the entry transition τ_0, a single scheduling transition, τ_G, with $\sigma' \in \tau_G(\sigma)$ iff

$\sigma(\mu) \neq \bot$,
$\sigma'(y) = \sigma(y)$ for all $y \in V - \{\mu\}$,
$\tau_E(\sigma) = \emptyset$ for all action transitions τ_E,
$\tau_E(\sigma') \neq \emptyset$ for some action transition τ_E.

If there is no cost associated with swapping processes, then $l_{\tau_G} = u_{\tau_G} = 0$. If switching processes is not instantaneous, then the minimal and maximal delays of τ_G should be adjusted accordingly.

Scheduling instructions

More flexible scheduling strategies can be implemented with explicit scheduling operations. For this purpose, we enrich our programming language by the instruction *resume*(s), where $s \subseteq \{1, \ldots m\}$ determines a subset of processes. The scheduling operation *resume*(s) suspends the currently active process, say, P_i and activates, nondeterministically, one of the processes $P_{i'}$ with $i' \in s$:

$$(\ell_j^i) \xrightarrow[{[l,u]}]{c \;\rightarrow\; resume(s)} (\ell_k^i)$$

We write *resume*(i') for *resume*$(\{i'\})$ and *suspend* for *resume*$(\{1 \leq i' \leq m \mid i' \neq i\})$; that is, the instruction *suspend* delegates the control from the currently active process to any one of the competing processes.

Formally, the set $\mathcal{T}$ of transitions of S_P contains, in addition to the entry transition τ_0, a scheduling transition τ_E for every *resume* edge E in the timed transition diagrams for $P_1, \ldots P_m$. If E connects the source location ℓ_j^i to the target location ℓ_k^i and is labeled by the instruction $c \rightarrow$ *resume*(s), then $\sigma' \in \tau_E(\sigma)$ iff

$\sigma(\mu) = i$ and $\sigma'(\mu) \in s$,
$\sigma(\pi_i) = \ell_j^i$ and $\sigma'(\pi_i) = \ell_k^i$,
c is true in σ,
$\sigma'(y) = \sigma(y)$ for all $y \in V - \{\mu, \pi_i\}$.

Furthermore, for every scheduling edge E labeled by the minimal delay l and the maximal delay u, let $l_{\tau_E} = l$ and $u_{\tau_E} = u$.

Delays and timers

Note that the instruction

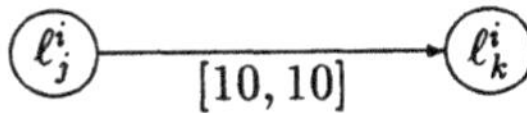

models a busy wait; the process P_i occupies the processor for 10 time units while waiting. To implement a nonbusy wait, in which P_i releases the processor to a competing process for 10 time units before resuming execution, we use a *timer* (alarm clock) $T_{[10,10]}$ as a parallel process:

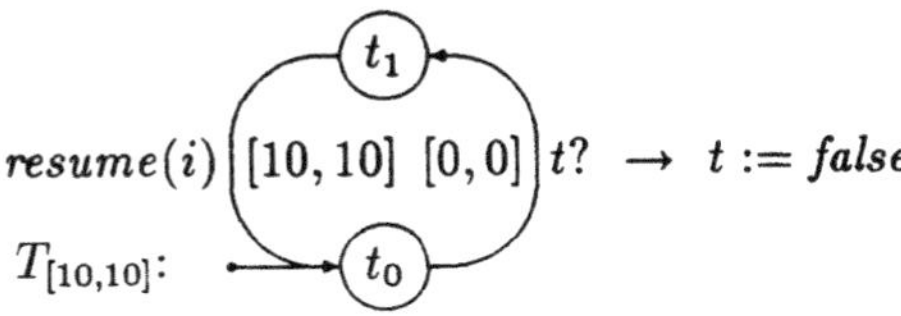

We make sure that the timer $T_{[10,10]}$ is started (i.e., waiting for activation) when the process P_i becomes active, with the precondition $\{t = \mathit{false}\}$. Then the timer is activated by the process P_i with the sequence

ℓ^i_j —— $t := \mathit{true}$ / [0, 0] ——→ ℓ^i_k —— *resume*(s) / [0, 0] ——→ ℓ^i_n

which releases the control of the processor to one of the processes in the set s. After exactly 10 time units, the timer process, which operates in parallel, will return the control of the processor to the process P_i.

In general, a timer process $T_{[l,u]}$ marks nondeterministically a time period between l and u time units and is executed in parallel to the other processes of a system:

$$\{\theta\}[(P_1|||\ldots|||P_m)||_s T_{[l,u]}].$$

The activation of the timer $T_{[l,u]}$ is abbreviated by the *delay* instruction

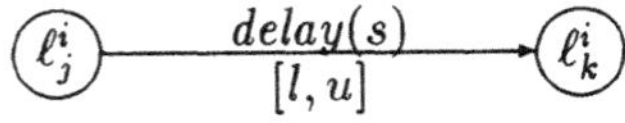

The *delay* instruction allows us to program nonbusy delays without explicitly mentioning timers; we simply assume that there exists, implicitly, a unique timer process for every *delay* instruction in a timed transition diagram. The parameter s of the instruction *delay*(s) determines the set of processes from which a process is selected when the active process is delayed.

Round-robin scheduling

A construction that is similar to the timer example allows us to implement a ***round-robin*** scheduling strategy for two processes P_1 and P_2 that share a single processor. In the system $(P_1|||P_2)||_s S$, the scheduler

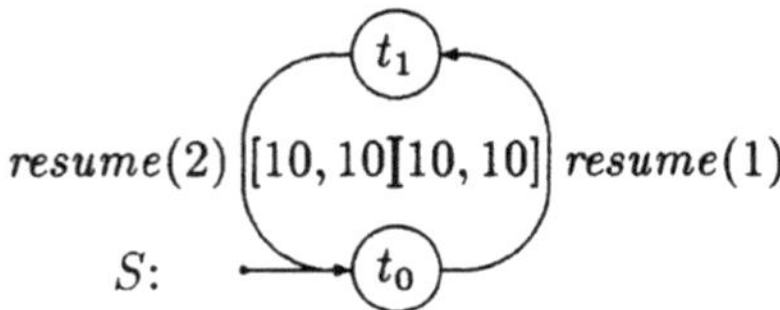

gives each of the two processes P_1 and P_2 in turn 10 time units of processor time. Needless to say, the explicit scheduling instructions give us the ability to design more sophisticated schedulers as well.

4.3 Processor allocation

Both the multiprogramming system with a timer and the multiprogramming system with a central scheduler are, in fact, combinations of multiprocessing and multiprogramming systems in which several tasks compete for some of the processors. For these systems, the question of *scheduling*, which determines the processor time that is granted to individual processes, is preceded by the question of *processor allocation*, which determines the assignment of processes to processors. This assignment can be either static, if every process is assigned to a fixed processor, or dynamic, if a set of processes competes for a pool of processors and processes may reside, over time, at different processors. We only hint how this very general notion of real-time system fits into our framework and can be modeled by timed transition systems.

A *static* (shared-variables or message-passing) system P with k processors is of the form

$$\{\theta\}[(P_{1,1}|||\cdots|||P_{1,m_1})||\cdots||(P_{k,1}|||\cdots|||P_{k,m_k})];$$

that is, m_i processes compete for the i-th processor. The definition of the associated timed transition system S_P is straightforward: every processor has its own process control variable μ_i, for $1 \leq i \leq k$, which ranges over the set of competing processes $\{1, \ldots m_i, \perp\}$ and designates the active process. Furthermore, every processor operates according to a local scheduling policy with a single entry transition τ_0^i for $1 \leq i \leq k$.

To model systems in which a process competes for more than one processor, we write

$$\{\theta\}[P_1, \ldots, P_m]_k$$

for the *dynamic* system in which m processes compete for k processors according to some global processor allocation and scheduling policy. To define dynamic systems, it is useful to have a more general scheduling instruction, $resume(s, x)$, which interrupts the process that is currently active on processor x and activates, on processor x, one of the processes from the set s.

4.4 Priorities and interrupts

While the scheduling instruction *resume* gives us the flexibility to design a scheduler, we often wish to adopt a simple, static scheduling strategy without having to explicitly construct a scheduler. In this subsection, we offer this possibility by generalizing the *greedy* strategy. We assign a priority to every transition, and at any point in a computation, choose only among the transitions with the highest priority. If the transition with the highest priority belongs to a suspended process, then the currently active process is interrupted and the execution of the suspended process is resumed.

A *priority* system P is a (shared-variables or message-passing, static or dynamic) system in which a priority is associated with every instruction; that is, with every edge in the timed transition diagrams for P. We use nonnegative integers as priorities (0 being the *highest* priority) and annotate an edge with a priority $p \in \mathbf{N}$ as follows:

$$\ell^i_j \xrightarrow[\;[l,u]\;]{p:\; c \;\rightarrow\; x := e} \ell^i_k$$

We formalize the priority semantics only for simple multiprogramming systems; the generalization to systems with several processors is straightforward. With a given priority system

$$P: \quad \{\theta\}[P_1 ||| \dots ||| P_m],$$

we associate the following timed transition system $S_P = \langle V, \Sigma, \Theta, \mathcal{T}, l, u \rangle$:

- V, Σ, and Θ are as before.
- $\mathcal{T}$ contains, in addition to τ_I, an action transition τ_E for every assignment edge E in the transition diagrams for $P_1, \dots P_m$. If E connects the source location ℓ^i_j to the target location ℓ^i_k and is labeled by the instruction p: $c \rightarrow \bar{x} := \bar{e}$, then the transition τ_E competes in state σ and would lead to state σ' (which is denoted by $\sigma \rightarrow_E \sigma'$) iff

  $\sigma(\pi_i) = \ell^i_j$ and $\sigma'(\pi_i) = \ell^i_k$,
  c is true in σ and $\sigma'(\bar{x}) = \sigma(\bar{e})$,
  $\sigma'(y) = \sigma(y)$ for all $y \in V - \{\mu, \pi_i, \bar{x}\}$.

  Then $\sigma' \in \tau_E(\sigma)$ iff

  $\sigma \rightarrow_E \sigma'$ and $\sigma(\mu) = \sigma'(\mu) = i$ and
  there is no edge E' that is labeled by a higher priority $p' < p$ such that
  $\sigma \rightarrow_{E'} \sigma''$ for some σ''.

  For any matching pair of communication edges E and E' that are labeled by the priorities p and p', respectively, we take the higher priority $min(p, p')$ for the combined transition $\tau_{E,E'}$ (although this choice is arbitrary and may be reversed, if the need arises).

  Furthermore, there is, in addition to the entry transition τ_0, a scheduling transition τ_P such that $\sigma' \in \tau_P(\sigma)$ iff

$\sigma(\mu) \neq \bot$,
$\sigma'(y) = \sigma(y)$ for all $y \in V - \{\mu\}$,
$\tau_E(\sigma) = \emptyset$ for all action transitions τ_E,
$\tau_E(\sigma') \neq \emptyset$ for some action transition τ_E.

- Let l_{τ_E} and u_{τ_E} be as before, and choose l_{τ_P} and u_{τ_P} to represent the cost of swapping processes.

Note that if all transitions have equal priority, then the scheduling strategy is greedy (that is, $\tau_G = \tau_P$). Thus priorities generalize our previous discussion conservatively: all systems can be viewed as priority systems whose instructions have the same default priority, unless they are annotated with explicit priorities.

Dynamic priorities

Priorities can be combined with explicit scheduling operations in the obvious way. It is, however, often more convenient to model dynamic scheduling strategies, which change over time, by *dynamic* priorities, which can be modified by any process during execution. Dynamic priorities offer exciting possibilities, such as the ability of a process to increase or decrease its own priority. Moreover, they are easily incorporated into our framework. We simply use data variables that range over the nonnegative integers **N** as priorities. Instead of giving the formal semantics of dynamic priorities, which is constructed straightforwardly from the semantics of constant (static) priorities, we present an interesting real-time application of dynamic priorities.

We have not yet pointed out that our interpretation of message passing is not entirely conservative over the untimed case: there the set of legal execution sequences usually is restricted by strong-fairness assumptions for communication transitions [MP89]. This is convenient for the study of time-independent properties of a system, where simple fairness assumptions about "nondeterministic" branching points abstract complex implementation details. Consider, for example, the multiprocessing system $P_1\|P_2\|Q$ that consists of the following three processes P_1, P_2, and Q:

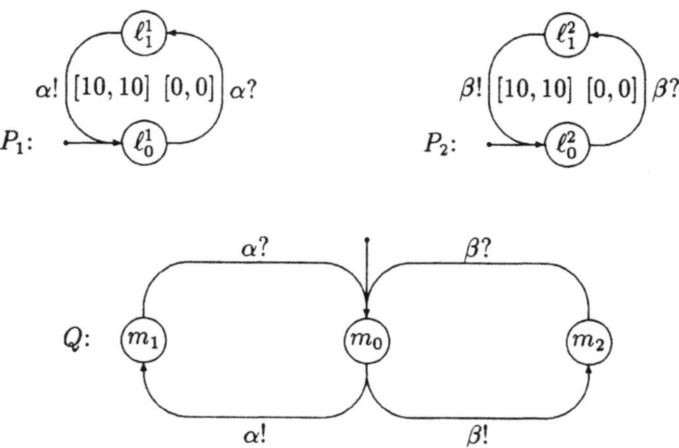

(Recall that we may omit the data components of message-passing operations, if they are immaterial.) The arbiter Q mediates between the two processes P_1 and P_2 and uses synchronous communication on the two channels α and β to ensure mutual exclusion: P_1 and P_2 can never be simultaneously in their critical sections ℓ_1^1 and ℓ_1^2, respectively.

Strong-fairness assumptions on the communication transitions are used to guarantee that, in addition to mutual exclusion, neither of the two processes P_1 and P_2 is shut out from its critical section forever: the arbiter cannot always prefer one process over the other. Any such infinitary fairness assumption, however, is clearly without bearing on the satisfaction of a real-time requirement such as the demand that a process has to wait at most 10 time units before being able to enter its critical section. As has been the case with scheduling, we encounter again a situation in which the infinitary notion of "fairness" is adequate for proving untimed properties, yet entirely inadequate for proving timing constraints. To verify compliance with real-time requirements, we can no longer forgo an explicit description of how the arbiter Q decides between the two processes P_1 and P_2 when both are waiting to enter their critical sections. For instance, the following refinement Q' of Q never makes the same "nondeterministic" choice twice in a row:

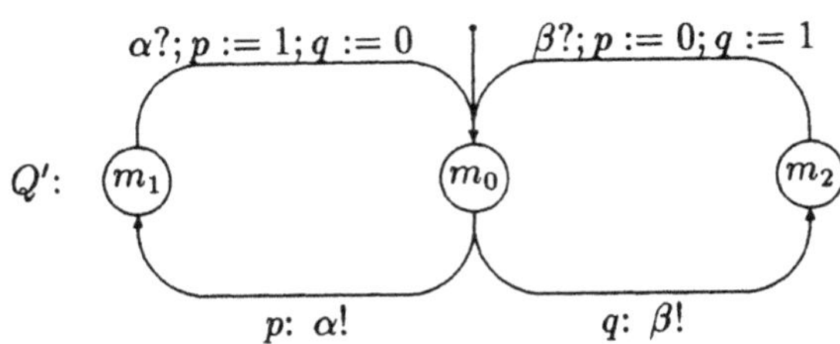

(We use semicolons to group several instructions to an atomic transition, which is defined in the obvious fashion. The default value of priorities is assumed to be 1.) The arbiter Q' modifies the priorities p and q of its nondeterministic alternatives to ensure that the system

$$\{p = q = 1\}[P_1 \| P_2 \| Q']$$

satisfies the requirement that each process has to wait at most 10 time units before being able to enter its critical section. Note that none of the two nondeterministic alternatives is ever disabled, but, at any time, one of them is "preferred."

Finitary branching fairness

Since infinitary fairness assumptions, such as weak fairness for scheduling and strong fairness for synchronization, are insufficient to guarantee the satisfaction of real-time deadlines, one may choose to add finitary branching conditions to timed transition systems. Such a finitary notion of fairness would restrict the nondeterminism of a system. We may want to require, for example, that no competitor of a transition τ can be taken more than n times without τ itself being taken (a similar concept has been called *bounded fairness* in [Jay88]). We prefer, both for scheduling and synchronization, an explicit description of the selection process to such implicit assumptions. Since all selection processes that we have found useful can be described within our language, we see no need to introduce additional concepts that would only complicate any verification methodology.

5 Conclusion

With timed transition systems, we presented an abstract model for real-time systems. We then explored its scope and demonstrated its practicality by modeling many important constructs of real-time computing. We conclude by pointing out that any abstract description of a real-time system ought to meet certain theoretical requirements as well. In [Hen91b], we suggested that system descriptions be (1) refinable, (2) digitizable, and (3) operational, and we showed that timed transition systems satisfy all three criteria:

1. We associated a fixed set of global states with every real-time system. This static view prohibits the study of large systems for managerial reasons. With each step in the hierarchical specification, design, and verification of a complex system, the state space must be refinable through expansion of its visible portion [Lam83]. The vertical decomposition of systems can be formalized by refinement mappings between increasingly detailed system descriptions [AL88]. Since expanding the visible portion of the state space may increase the frequency at which state changes occur, the timed state sequence semantics of a system description needs to be closed under our notion of stuttering to guarantee the existence of refinement mappings. The *refinability* of timed transition systems is further discussed in [Hen91b].

2. For verification, it is often convenient, and sometimes necessary, to assume a fictitious digital clock, which records the times of state changes with finitary precision only [AH89]. The integers suffice as time domain for such a digital-clock model. For the direct use of a digital-clock model, a system description must be independent of the time domain, in the sense that digitizing all execution sequences of a system can be achieved by simply changing the time domain from the reals to the integers. Sets of timed state sequences that enjoy this property are called digitizable. The *digitizability* of timed transition systems and the ensuing amenability to discrete-time verification methods is discussed in [Hen91b].

3. We want a system description to be executable. For untimed systems, this is the case if the liveness component of a system description does not preclude any safe prefixes of execution sequences; that is, a stepwise interpreter cannot "paint itself into a corner" from which no continuation is possible [AFK88]. The issue is more subtle in the timed case because of the implicit liveness requirement that time must progress eventually. In other words, we wish to rule out system descriptions that prevent time from progressing. Such system descriptions are called operational [Hen91a] (or machine-closed [LA]). The *operationality* of timed transition systems is discussed in [Hen91b].

No study of an abstract model for real-time systems is complete without progress on the verification front. Let P be a real-time system whose set of possible timed executions is the set $[\![P]\!]$ of timed state sequences and let ϕ be a specification that is satisfied by the timed state sequences in the set $[\![\phi]\!]$. Verification of P with respect to ϕ amounts, then, to checking the containment

$$[\![P]\!] \stackrel{?}{\subseteq} [\![\phi]\!]$$

of sets of timed state sequences. Systems are given as expressions of an implementation language; specifications as expressions of a specification language. We presented the implementation language of timed transition diagrams and defined the set $[\![P]\!]$ of timed executions for systems that are given in the timed transition diagram language as the set of computations for the timed transition system S_P. Verification methods of timed transition systems have been developed for various logical specification languages. The methods include both algorithmic techniques for finite-state systems [AH89, AH90, HLP90, Ost90, Hen91b] and deductive techniques based on proof systems [Hen90, Ost90, HMP91, Hen91b]. For an overview of the verification methods for timed transition systems, we refer to the article *Logics and Models of Real Time* in this volume.

Acknowledgment. The authors thank Rajeev Alur and Eddie Chang for many helpful comments.

References

[AFK88] K.R. Apt, N. Francez, and S. Katz. Appraising fairness in languages for distributed programming. *Distributed Computing*, 2(4):226–241, 1988.

[AH89] R. Alur and T.A. Henzinger. A really temporal logic. In *Proceedings of the 30th Annual Symposium on Foundations of Computer Science*, pages 164–169. IEEE Computer Society Press, 1989.

[AH90] R. Alur and T.A. Henzinger. Real-time logics: complexity and expressiveness. In *Proceedings of the Fifth Annual Symposium on Logic in Computer Science*, pages 390–401. IEEE Computer Society Press, 1990.

[AL88] M. Abadi and L. Lamport. The existence of refinement mappings. In *Proceedings of the Third Annual Symposium on Logic in Computer Science*, pages 165–175. IEEE Computer Society Press, 1988.

[BKP86] H. Barringer, R. Kuiper, and A. Pnueli. A really abstract concurrent model and its temporal logic. In *Proceedings of the 13th Annual Symposium on Principles of Programming Languages*, pages 173–183. ACM Press, 1986.

[Har88] E. Harel. Temporal analysis of real-time systems. Master's thesis, The Weizmann Institute of Science, Rehovot, Israel, 1988.

[Hen90] T.A. Henzinger. Half-order modal logic: how to prove real-time properties. In *Proceedings of the Ninth Annual Symposium on Principles of Distributed Computing*, pages 281–296. ACM Press, 1990.

[Hen91a] T.A. Henzinger. Sooner is safer than later. Technical report, Stanford University, 1991.

[Hen91b] T.A. Henzinger. *The Temporal Specification and Verification of Real-time Systems*. PhD thesis, Stanford University, 1991.

[HLP90] E. Harel, O. Lichtenstein, and A. Pnueli. Explicit-clock temporal logic. In *Proceedings of the Fifth Annual Symposium on Logic in Computer Science*, pages 402–413. IEEE Computer Society Press, 1990.

[HMP90] T.A. Henzinger, Z. Manna, and A. Pnueli. An interleaving model for real time. In *Proceedings of the Fifth Jerusalem Conference on Information Technology*, pages 717–730. IEEE Computer Society Press, 1990.

[HMP91] T.A. Henzinger, Z. Manna, and A. Pnueli. Temporal proof methodologies for real-time systems. In *Proceedings of the 18th Annual Symposium on Principles of Programming Languages*, pages 353–366. ACM Press, 1991.

[Hoa85] C.A.R. Hoare. *Communicating Sequential Processes.* Prentice-Hall, 1985.

[Jay88] D.N. Jayasimha. *Communication and Synchronization in Parallel Computation.* PhD thesis, University of Illinois at Urbana-Champaign, 1988.

[Kel76] R.M. Keller. Formal verification of parallel programs. *Communications of the ACM*, 19(7):371–384, 1976.

[KSdR+88] R. Koymans, R.K. Shyamasundar, W.-P. de Roever, R. Gerth, and S. Arun-Kumar. Compositional semantics for real-time distributed computing. *Information and Computation*, 79(3):210–256, 1988.

[LA] L. Lamport and M. Abadi. Refining and composing real-time specifications. This volume.

[Lam83] L. Lamport. What good is temporal logic? In R.E.A. Mason, editor, *Information Processing 83: Proceedings of the Ninth IFIP World Computer Congress*, pages 657–668. Elsevier Science Publishers (North-Holland), 1983.

[MP89] Z. Manna and A. Pnueli. The anchored version of the temporal framework. In J.W. de Bakker, W.-P. de Roever, and G. Rozenberg, editors, *Linear Time, Branching Time, and Partial Order in Logics and Models for Concurrency*, Lecture Notes in Computer Science 354, pages 201–284. Springer-Verlag, 1989.

[Ost90] J.S. Ostroff. *Temporal Logic of Real-time Systems.* Research Studies Press, 1990.

[PH88] A. Pnueli and E. Harel. Applications of temporal logic to the specification of real-time systems. In M. Joseph, editor, *Formal Techniques in Real-time and Fault-tolerant Systems*, Lecture Notes in Computer Science 331, pages 84–98. Springer-Verlag, 1988.

[Pnu77] A. Pnueli. The temporal logic of programs. In *Proceedings of the 18th Annual Symposium on Foundations of Computer Science*, pages 46–57. IEEE Computer Society Press, 1977.

Compositional Verification of Real-Time Systems using Extended Hoare Triples

Jozef Hooman*

Dept. of Mathematics and Computing Science
Eindhoven University of Technology
P.O. Box 513, 5600 MB Eindhoven, The Netherlands
e-mail: wsinjh@win.tue.nl

Abstract. To specify and verify the real-time behaviour of programs, a formalism based on Hoare triples (precondition, program, postcondition) is introduced. Programs are written in an Occam-like programming language with synchronous message passing along unidirectional channels. Real-time is incorporated by delay-statements and time-outs. To deal with reactive systems, a Hoare triple is extended with a third assertion, called commitment, which expresses the real-time communication interface of the program. We formulate a compositional axiomatization for these extended Hoare triples, first using the maximal parallelism assumption which represents the situation in which each process has its own processor. Next this framework is generalized to multiprogramming where several processes may share a single processor and scheduling is based on priorities of statements.

Keywords: Real-time, Specification, Verification, Compositionality, Hoare triples.

Contents

*Partially supported by ESPRIT-BRA project 3096 (SPEC).

1 Introduction

This paper concerns the formal verification of real-time embedded systems. We concentrate on open systems that are implemented in a real-time concurrent programming language with synchronous message passing along channels. Since the language includes delay-statements and time-outs, the functional behaviour of a program might be affected by the timing of actions such as the time at which input is available. On the other hand, the real-time behaviour of a program will, in general, be influenced by the initial values of variables and the values it receives from the environment on its input channels. Observing the close relation between the functional behaviour of a system and its real-time properties, we aim at a framework in which both aspects are integrated. Thus it should be possible to verify functional and timing properties simultaneously in a single formalism. This combined verification might be complicated, and hence the method should be flexible enough to allow separate analysis of both aspects when possible. Moreover, to be able to split up correctness proofs and to support top-down program design, our goal is a proof system which is compositional, i.e. allows reasoning by means of the specifications of components rather than their implementation.

To achieve our goal we extend classical Hoare triples, which are convenient for the compositional verification of functional properties, to real-time. In the remainder of this introduction we sketch the main characteristics of our programming language and the verification method.

1.1 Programs

We consider a concurrent programming language which is akin to Occam [Occ88b]. Parallel processes communicate via message passing along unidirectional channels that connect two processes. Communication is synchronous, i.e., either the sender or the receiver has to wait until a communication partner is available. For instance, the process $in?x$; $comp$; $out!y$ first waits to receive a value along channel in. When its environment is ready to send a value, a communication along in takes place and the value is assigned to x. After computation $comp$ the process tries to send the value of y on channel out. Since communication is synchronous, also this output statement has to wait until a corresponding input statement is ready to receive the value. The language contains guarded commands with input guards, such as,

$$[\, x > 1; in_1?x \rightarrow comp_1 \;;\; out_1!y \;[]\; y = 0; in_2?x \rightarrow comp_2 \;;\; out_2!y \,].$$

The boolean expressions $x > 1$ and $y = 0$ determine when the guard is open. For instance, when $x > 1$ and $y = 0$ both evaluate to true then this statement waits until a communication along one of the channels in_1 and in_2 is possible. To be able to program real-time systems, the language contains delay-statements which are allowed in the guard of a guarded command. This enables us to program a time-out, that is, to restrict the waiting period for a communication and to execute an alternative statement if no communication is possible within a certain number of time units. Consider the program

$[\, in_1?x \rightarrow comp_1 \,;\, out_1!y \;[]\; in_2?x \rightarrow comp_2 \,;\, out_2!y \;[]\; \textbf{delay}\ 15 \rightarrow comp_3 \,;\, out_3!y \,]$.

If no communication along in_1 or in_2 is possible within 15 time units then $comp_3$ is performed. We also allow a program such as

$in?x \,;\, [\, in?y \rightarrow comp_1 \,;\, out!y \,[]\, \textbf{delay}\ (x+5) \rightarrow comp_2 \,]$

where the deadline of the time-out depends on a value which is received from the environment. The execution of a guarded command can be repeated by placing a "$\star$" in front of it. For example, $\star[\, y > 0; in?x \rightarrow comp \,;\, out!y \,]$ repeats the guarded command as long as $y > 0$. It terminates if $y \leq 0$.

In our proof method it should be possible to verify the usual functional properties of programs such as the relation between input and output. Consider, for instance, the program P which consists of two parallel iterations:

$\star[\, in?x_1 \rightarrow y_1 := f_1(x_1) \,;\, link!y_1 \,] \;\|\; \star[\, link?x_2 \rightarrow y_2 := f_2(x_2) \,;\, out!y_2 \,]$.

Program P should satisfy the specification:

if value v is received along in then $f_2(f_1(v))$ is communicated along out.

Additionally, the aim is to verify real-time properties of programs, such as the termination time and the time at which communications take place. Note that, since there is synchronous communication, the timing of communications depends on the environment. Hence we usually specify when a process is ready to communicate, or we make explicit assumptions about when the environment is ready to communicate. For instance, for program P we can specify that, for some deadline D,

if value v is received along in at time t
then the program is ready to send $f_2(f_1(v))$ on out before time $t + D$.

By making assumptions about the environment, e.g., when it is ready to receive along out, we can specify the maximal time between successive inputs on in:

if the environment is always ready to receive along channel out
and if there is a communication on in at t,
then the program is ready for a next input on in within D time units after t.

To prove that a program satisfies such a specification, certain assumptions have to be made concerning the execution time of atomic statements. Further, assumptions have to be made about the execution mechanism of parallel composition. Clearly, the timed behaviour of a concurrent program depends on the number of available processors. First we consider the maximal parallelism model which represents the situation that each process has its own processor. As an example we compare in section 4 properties of concurrent program P and the following sequential program

$\star[in?x_1 \rightarrow y_1 := f_1(x_1)\ ;\ x_2 := y_1\ ;\ y_2 := f_2(x_2)\ ;\ out!y_2]$.

The maximal parallelism assumption, however, is not always realistic, since in many applications parallel processes share a single processor. Therefore we generalize this model by introducing brackets $\ll \cdots \gg$ to indicate that the processes inside these brackets are executed on a single processor. Execution of the processes

$P_1 \equiv \star[in_1?x_1 \rightarrow comp_1\ ;\ out_1!y_1]$ and $P_2 \equiv \star[in_2?x_2 \rightarrow comp_2\ ;\ out_2!y_2]$

under the maximal parallelism assumption is then expressed as $\ll P_1 \gg \| \ll P_2 \gg$, whereas $\ll P_1 \| P_2 \gg$ denotes that both processes are scheduled on one processor. To allow the programmer to influence the scheduling of statements, the programming language includes statements of the form $\mathbf{prio}\,p(S)$ which assign priority p to statement S. Consider $\ll P_1 \| P_2 \gg$ and assume the environment is always ready to receive messages on out_1 and out_2. Suppose that the computation of $comp_1$ in P_1 takes 10 time units and that after a communication on channel in_1 the process must be ready to receive a next input within 130 time units. For P_2 we assume that $comp_2$ takes 50 time units and that it should be ready for a next input in less than 70 time units. Thus P_2 has much stronger timing requirements than P_1. Hence we give P_2 a higher priority than P_1 (a higher number corresponds to a higher priority):

$\ll \mathbf{prio}\ 1\ (P_1)\ \|\ \mathbf{prio}\ 2\ (P_2) \gg$.

The question is whether this program satisfies the requirements mentioned above. First we discuss in section 5 the meaning of such programs. Especially the combination of priorities and synchronous communication gives rise to many questions about the precise semantics of programs. Then in section 6 we investigate the program above in detail and derive general conditions on the deadlines and the basic timing assumptions.

1.2 Verification

To verify (real-time) properties of programs, we aim at a proof system in which it is possible to consider parts of a program as a black box and use its specification only. For instance, to prove properties of $\star[in?x \rightarrow comp\ ;\ out!y]$ we would like to use the specification of *comp*, without knowing its implementation. Furthermore, the proof system should support hierarchical top-down program derivation. Therefore we aim at a proof system which is *compositional*, that is, for each compound programming language construct (such as sequential composition and parallel composition) there is a rule in which the specification of the construct can be deduced from specifications of its constituent parts without any further information about the internal structure of these parts. By means of a compositional proof system the design steps can be verified during the process of top-down program construction.

Our specifications are based on classical Hoare triples (precondition, program, post-condition) [Hoa69], which are extended with a third assertion, called commitment, to specify progress properties of terminating and non-terminating computations. The choice for this Hoare-style formalism is motivated by its nice compositional rules for sequential composition and iteration. We investigate how this framework can be adapted to deal with real-time properties. In classical Hoare logic for partial correctness, properties of an iteration construct (such as a while-loop) can be derived by means of a loop-invariant which should hold before and after each execution of the body of the iteration. In our extended real-time formalism also liveness properties of an iteration construct can be proved by using an invariant. As an example, consider the proof of termination of the iteration construct $\star[\ x > 0 \rightarrow x := x - 1\ ]$. Instead of proving the liveness property (termination) directly, we prove a stronger real-time safety property, namely that the program terminates within a certain time bound (this bound depends on the initial value of x and the execution time of the body of the loop). In our proof system this bound on the termination time can then be proved by means of an invariant. Details can be found in section 4.

Similarly, other liveness properties can be proved in our Hoare-style framework. First a liveness property is reduced to a real-time safety property which implies the desired property. For instance, to prove that eventually property P holds we show that P is achieved within a certain time bound. For the iteration construct this real-time safety property can be proved by means of an invariant.

1.3 Overview

In section 2 we give the syntax and informal semantics of a real-time programming language. Section 3 introduces our extended Hoare triples and an appropriate assertion language for the maximal parallelism model. A compositional proof system for this formalism is formulated in section 4. In section 5 we describe an extension of the programming language in which we can express that several processes share a single processor and assign priorities to statements. A compositional proof system for this extended framework is given in section 6.

In this paper we do not give a denotational semantics for the programming language and a formal interpretation of the specifications. Further we do not prove soundness nor aim at completeness of the proof systems. More information about these aspects can be found in [Hoo91b].

2 Programming Language

We consider an Occam-like programming language with synchronous communication along unidirectional channels that connect two processes. In section 2.1 we give the syntax of this language and the informal meaning of statements. Our notion of time and the basic timing assumptions, which are used to reason about real-time properties of programs, are described in section 2.2.

2.1 Syntax and Informal Meaning

Let *CHAN* be a nonempty set of channel names, *VAR* be a nonempty set of program variables, and *VAL* be a denumerable domain of values. $\mathbb{N}$ denotes the set of natural numbers (including 0). The syntax of our programming language is given in Table 1, with $n \in \mathbb{N}$, $n \geq 1$, $c, c_1, \ldots, c_n \in CHAN$, $x, x_1, \ldots, x_n \in VAR$, and $\vartheta \in VAL$.

Table 1: Syntax of the Programming Language

Expression	$e ::=$	$\vartheta \mid x \mid e_1 + e_2 \mid e_1 - e_2 \mid e_1 \times e_2$
Boolean Expression	$b ::=$	$e_1 = e_2 \mid e_1 < e_2 \mid \neg b \mid b_1 \vee b_2$
Statement	$S ::=$	**skip** $\mid x := e \mid$ **delay** $e \mid c!e \mid c?x \mid$
		$S_1; S_2 \mid G \mid \star G \mid S_1 \| S_2$
Guarded Command	$G ::=$	$[\,[]_{i=1}^{n} b_i \rightarrow S_i] \mid [\,[]_{i=1}^{n} b_i; c_i?x_i \rightarrow S_i \,[]\, b_0;$ **delay** $e \rightarrow S_0]$

Informally, the statements of our programming language have the following meaning:
Atomic statements

- **skip** terminates immediately.
- Assignment $x := e$ assigns the value of expression e to the variable x.
- **delay** e suspends execution for (the value of) e time units. If e yields a negative value then **delay** e is equivalent to **skip**.
- Output statement $c!e$ is used to send the value of expression e on channel c as soon as a corresponding input command is available. Since we assume synchronous communication, such an output statement is suspended until a parallel process executes an input statement $c?x$.
- Input statement $c?x$ is used to receive a value via channel c and assign this value to the variable x. As for the output command, such an input statement has to wait for a corresponding partner before a (synchronous) communication can take place.

Compound statements

- $S_1; S_2$ indicates sequential composition: first execute S_1, and continue with the execution of S_2 if and when S_1 terminates.
- Guarded command $[\|_{i=1}^{n} b_i \rightarrow S_i]$. If none of the b_i evaluate to true then this guarded command terminates after evaluation of the booleans. Otherwise, non-deterministically select one of the b_i that evaluates to true and execute the corresponding statement S_i.
- Guarded command $[\|_{i=1}^{n} b_i; c_i?x_i \rightarrow S_i \| b_0; \textbf{delay } e \rightarrow S_0]$. A guard is *open* if the boolean part evaluates to true. If none of the guards is open, the guarded command terminates after evaluation of the booleans. Otherwise, wait until an input statement of the open input-guards can be executed and continue with the corresponding S_i. If the delay guard is open (b_0 evaluates to true) and no input-guard can be taken within e time units (after the evaluation of the booleans), then S_0 is executed. If b_0 evaluates to true and e yields 0 or a negative value then S_0 is executed immediately after the evaluation of the booleans.
- Iteration $*G$ indicates repeated execution of guarded command G as long as at least one of the guards is open. When none of the guards is open $*G$ terminates.
- $S_1 \| S_2$ indicates parallel execution of the statements S_1 and S_2. We require that S_1 and S_2 do not have shared variables. The components S_1 and S_2 of a parallel composition are often called *processes*.

Henceforth we use $\equiv$ to denote syntactic equality. Conventional abbreviations are used, such as $true \equiv 0 = 0$, $false \equiv \neg true$, $b_1 \wedge b_2 \equiv \neg(\neg b_1 \vee \neg b_2)$, etc. For a guarded command G we define $b_G \equiv \begin{cases} b_1 \vee \ldots \vee b_n & \text{if } G \equiv [\|_{i=1}^{n} b_i \rightarrow S_i] \\ b_1 \vee \ldots \vee b_n \vee b_0 & \text{if } G \equiv [\|_{i=1}^{n} b_i; c_i?x_i \rightarrow S_i \| b_0; \textbf{delay } e \rightarrow S_0] \end{cases}$

Note that G terminates if b_G evaluates to false.
For a guarded command $[\|_{i=1}^{n} b_i; c_i?x_i \rightarrow S_i \| b_0; \textbf{delay } e \rightarrow S_0]$ we write $[\|_{i=1}^{n} b_i; c_i?x_i \rightarrow S_i]$ if $b_0 \equiv false$. An input-guard $b_i; c_i?x_i$ is written as $c_i?x_i$ if $b_i \equiv true$, and, similarly, a delay-guard $b_0; \textbf{delay } e$ is abbreviated as $\textbf{delay } e$ if $b_0 \equiv true$.

Let $var(S)$ be the set of program variables occurring in statement S. Recall that for $S_1 \| S_2$ we require $var(S_1) \cap var(S_2) = \emptyset$. Let $DCHAN$ be the set of channels extended with directional channels; $DCHAN = CHAN \cup \{c! \mid c \in CHAN\} \cup \{c? \mid c \in CHAN\}$.

Definition 2.1 (Channels Occurring in Statement) The set of (directional) channels occurring in a statement S, notation $dch(S)$, is defined as the smallest subset of $DCHAN$ such that if c is an output channel of S then $\{c, c!\} \subseteq dch(S)$, and if c is an input channel of S then $\{c, c?\} \subseteq dch(S)$.

For example, $dch(a?; b! \| b?; c!) = \{a, a?, b, b!, b?, c, c!\}$.

2.2 Basic Timing Assumptions

We express the timing behaviour of a program from the viewpoint of an external observer with his own clock. Thus, although parallel components of a system might have their own, physical, local clock, the observable behaviour of a system is described in terms of a single, conceptual, global clock. Since this global notion of time is not incorporated in the distributed system itself, it does not impose any synchronization upon processes.

In this paper we use a time domain which is dense, i.e., between every two points of time there exists an intermediate point. With such a dense time domain a communication can be represented by an interval of communication records, and we can easily model communications that overlap in time or that are arbitrarily close to each other in time. When combining the real-time specifications of independently designed components, it is convenient to have a dense time domain to avoid problems such as finding a common unit of time. Having dense time is also suitable for the description of reactive systems that interact with a time-continuous environment (see, e.g., [Koy90]). Furthermore, a dense time domain allows the refinement of a single action into a sequence of sub-actions.

In our proof system the correctness of a program with respect to a specification, which may include timing constraints, is verified relative to assumptions about:

- The execution time of atomic statements. In general, time bounds on the execution time will be given. In this paper we assume that there is a fixed constant which gives the execution time, but the framework can be easily adapted to the more general case. Thus assume that
  - there exists a constant $T_{assign} > 0$ such that each assignment takes T_{assign} time units;
  - **delay** e takes exactly e time units if e is positive and 0 time units otherwise;
  - there exists a constant $T_{comm} > 0$ such that each communication takes T_{comm} time units. Note that the execution of an input or output statement includes a waiting period when no communication partner is available. Since this waiting period depends on the environment of the communication statement, no assumptions can be made about its length.
- The overhead time required for compound programming constructs. Here we assume that there exists a constant $T_{exec} > 0$ such that the evaluation of guards in a guarded command takes T_{exec} time units. Note that in this way we avoid an infinite loop in zero time. There is no overhead for other compound statements.
- How long a process is allowed to wait with the execution of enabled statements. That is, we have to make assumptions about the progress of actions. We use in this paper the maximal progress model in which an enabled action will be executed as

soon as possible. First, in sections 3 and 4, we consider the *maximal parallelism model* to represent the situation that each parallel process has its own processor. Hence, a process never waits with the execution of a local, non-communication, command. An input or output command can cause a process to wait, but only when no communication partner is available; as soon as a partner is available the communication must take place. Thus maximal parallelism implies minimal waiting. In sections 5 and 6 the framework is generalized to multiprogramming where several processes may share a single processor.

3 Specifications

Our formalism is based on classical Hoare triples [Hoa69], that is, formulae of the form $\{p\}\ S\ \{q\}$ where S is a program and p and q are assertions expressed in a first-order logic. Informally, a triple $\{p\}\ S\ \{q\}$ has the following meaning: if S is executed in a state satisfying precondition p and if S terminates then the final state satisfies postcondition q. To extend a Hoare triple $\{p\}\ S\ \{q\}$ to real-time, a special variable *time* is introduced. Consider, for instance, the formula $\{time = 3\}$ **delay** $2\ \{time = 5\}$. In the precondition the variable *time* specifies the starting time of the program, whereas in the postcondition *time* denotes the termination time. Thus the formula

$$\{time = 2\}\ S\ \{17 < time < 23\}$$

expresses that if the execution of S is started at time 2 and if S terminates, then it terminates after time 17 and before time 23. Similarly, if $3 < T_{assign} < 5$, then

$$\{y = 5 \wedge time = 2\}\ \ x := y + 1\ \{y = 5 \wedge x = 6 \wedge 5 < time < 7\}.$$

These examples indicate that our assertion language should include:

- Program variables, such as $x, y \in VAR$, ranging over VAL.
- A special variable *time* which refers to our global notion of time. As motivated in section 2.2, *time* ranges over a dense time domain $TIME$. Here we use $TIME = \{\tau \in \mathbb{Q} \mid \tau \geq 0\}$, where $\mathbb{Q}$ is the set of rational numbers. An occurrence of *time* in the precondition represents the starting time of the statement whereas in the postcondition it denotes the termination time.

In a Hoare-style formalism usually *logical variables* (also called rigid variables) are used to relate pre- and postcondition. In contrast with program variables, these logical variables are not affected by program execution. Consider, for instance, the formula

$$\{x = v\}\ x := x + 1\ \{x = v + 1\},$$

where v is a logical variable ranging over VAL. Similarly, we introduce logical variables ranging over $TIME \cup \{\infty\}$. Let $VVAR$ and $TVAR$ be sets of logical variables ranging over, respectively, VAL and $TIME \cup \{\infty\}$. E.g., using $v \in VVAR$ and $t \in TVAR$, we have

$\{x = v \wedge time = t\}\ x := x + 3\ \{x = v + 3 \wedge time = t + T_{assign}\}$.

Quantification is only allowed over logical variables.

Since our aim is to specify and verify timing properties of open systems that communicate with their environment by synchronous message passing along channels, the logic contains the following primitives to express this communication behaviour:

- *comm* (c, exp_1) *at* exp_2 with $c \in CHAN$, exp_1 and exp_2 expressions yielding a value in, respectively, VAL and $TIME \cup \{\infty\}$. This predicate expresses that value exp_1 is communicated along channel c at time exp_2.

Recall that our maximal progress assumption implies minimal waiting for communications. To express this assumption in our compositional framework, we include the following primitives in the logic:

- *wait* $c!$ *at exp* and *wait* $c?$ *at exp* to express that a process is waiting to send, resp. waiting to receive, a message along channel c at time *exp*.

Our choice for a Hoare-style formalism is motivated by the following compositional rules for sequential composition and iteration:

$$\frac{\{p\}\ S_1\ \{r\},\ \ \{r\}\ S_2\ \{q\}}{\{p\}\ S_1; S_2\ \{q\}} \qquad\qquad \frac{\{p \wedge b_G\}\ G\ \{p\}}{\{p\}\ \star G\ \{p \wedge \neg b_G\}}$$

Consider, as a simple example, the proof of

$$\{y = 3 \wedge time = 5\}\ c?x; d!(x+y)$$
$$\{\exists t_1 \geq 5 : comm\ (c,x)\ at\ t_1 \wedge \exists t_2 \geq t_1 : comm\ (d, x+3)\ at\ t_2\}.$$

This can be proved with the rule for sequential composition, provided we can derive

$$\{y = 3 \wedge time = 5\}\ c?x\ \{\exists t_1 \geq 5 : comm\ (c,x)\ at\ t_1 \wedge time \geq t_1 \wedge y = 3\}$$

and

$$\{\exists t_1 \geq 5 : comm\ (c,x)\ at\ t_1 \wedge time \geq t_1 \wedge y = 3\}\ d!(x+y)$$
$$\{\exists t_1 \geq 5 : comm\ (c,x)\ at\ t_1 \wedge \exists t_2 \geq t_1 : comm\ (d, x+3)\ at\ t_2\}.$$

Thus the precondition of a statement not only expresses the initial state of program variables and the starting time, but it also describes the timed communication behaviour of the program before the execution of the statement. Similarly, the postcondition of a statement might include, besides the final state and the communication behaviour of the statement, also the communication history before the execution of the statement.

With Hoare triples we can only express *partial correctness* of programs, i.e., properties that hold if the program terminates. Hence a specification $\{p\}\ S\ \{q\}$ is trivially satisfied by non-terminating programs. This, however, is not appropriate for real-time embedded programs which are usually non-terminating, having an intensive interaction with their

environment. Therefore we extend a Hoare triple with a third assertion, called *commitment*, which should be satisfied by both terminating and non-terminating computations. This leads to formulae of the form $C : \{p\}\ S\ \{q\}$, where commitment C expresses the real-time communication interface of program S. Since in our programming language parallel processes communicate only by message passing (i.e., there are no shared variables), this commitment should not contain program variables. Similar to the postcondition, the commitment might also include (part of) the communication history before the start of program execution. E.g., using the commitment
$C \equiv comm\ (d,5)\ at\ 2 \wedge [(\forall t_1 \geq 6 : wait\ c!\ at\ t_1) \vee (\exists t_2 \geq 6 : comm\ (c,8)\ at\ t_2)]$ we have
$C : \{comm\ (d,5)\ at\ 2 \wedge time = 6\}\ c!8\ \{comm\ (d,5)\ at\ 2 \wedge \exists t_2 \geq 6 : comm\ (c,8)\ at\ t_2\}$.
In general, commitment C reflects the real-time communication interface between parallel components, whereas the pre- and postconditions facilitate the reasoning at sequential composition.

Finally, we argue that termination should be expressible in commitments. Consider, e.g., the statements $S_1 \equiv c!0$ and $S_2 \equiv [c!0 \rightarrow$ **skip** $[]\, c!0 \rightarrow \star[$**delay** $1 \rightarrow$ **skip**$]]$. Then the programs $S_1; d!1$ and $S_2; d!1$ cannot be distinguished with classical Hoare triples, but in our extended framework we can use the commitment

$\forall t_0 : (comm\ (c,0)\ at\ t_0 \rightarrow \exists t_1 \geq t_0 : [wait\ d!\ at\ t_1 \vee comm\ d\ at\ t_1])$

(which is satisfied by $S_1; d!1$ but not by $S_2; d!1$). Since we aim at a compositional proof system, the difference between $S_1; d!1$ and $S_2; d!1$ implies that S_1 and S_2 must also be distinguishable. This means that we have to express termination in the commitment. This can be done conveniently, without introducing new primitives, by allowing the special variable *time* to occur in commitments. Observe that the commitment can be seen as an extension of the postcondition to non-terminating computations. Hence, by interpreting *time* similar as in postconditions, *time* in commitments expresses the termination time of terminating computations. For non-terminating computations we use the special variable ∞ and such computations satisfy the commitment $time = \infty$. In the example above, S_1 and S_2 can be distinguished by using the commitment $\forall t_0 : (comm\ c\ at\ t_0 \rightarrow time < \infty)$.

The syntax of the assertion language is given in Table 2, with $\tau \in TIME \cup \{\infty\}$, $\vartheta \in VAL$, $t \in TVAR$, $v \in VVAR$, $c \in CHAN$, and $x \in VAR$.

Let $var(p)$ denote the set of program variables occurring in assertion p. $dch(p)$ denotes the set of (directed) channels occurring in assertion p. E.g., $dch(comm\ (c, exp_1)\ at\ exp_2) = \{c\}$ and $dch(wait\ c!\ at\ exp) = \{c!\}$.

The conventional abbreviations are used, such as $p_1 \wedge p_2 \equiv \neg(\neg p_1 \vee \neg p_2)$, $p_1 \rightarrow p_2 \equiv \neg p_1 \vee p_2$, and $\forall t : p \equiv \neg \exists t : \neg p$. Relativized quantifiers are defined as usual, for instance,

- $\forall t, t_0 \leq t < time : p \equiv \forall t : (t_0 \leq t < time \rightarrow p)$

Table 2: Syntax of the Assertion Language

Expression	$exp ::=$	$\tau \mid \vartheta \mid t \mid v \mid time \mid x \mid$ $exp_1 + exp_2 \mid exp_1 - exp_2 \mid exp_1 \times exp_2$
Assertion	$p ::=$	$comm\ (c, exp_1)\ at\ exp_2 \mid wait\ c!\ at\ exp \mid wait\ c?\ at\ exp \mid$ $exp_1 = exp_2 \mid exp_1 < exp_2 \mid exp \in \mathbb{N} \mid$ $\neg p \mid p_1 \vee p_2 \mid \exists t : p$

- $\exists t, t_0 \leq t < time : p \equiv \exists t : (t_0 \leq t < time \wedge p)$.

Furthermore, the following abbreviations are frequently used:

- $comm\ (c, v)\ during\ [t_0, t_1\rangle \equiv \forall t_2, t_0 \leq t_2 < t_1 : comm\ (c, v)\ at\ t_2$
- $comm\ c\ at\ exp \equiv \exists v : comm\ (c, v)\ at\ exp$
- $end\ comm\ (c, v)\ at\ t \equiv comm\ (c, v)\ during\ [t - T_{comm}, t\rangle$
- $end\ comm\ c\ at\ t \equiv \exists v : end\ comm\ (c, v)\ at\ t$
- $wait\ c!\ during\ [t_0, t_1\rangle \equiv \forall t_2, t_0 \leq t_2 < t_1 : wait\ c!\ at\ t_2$
- $no\ comm\ c\ during\ [t_0, t_1\rangle \equiv \forall t_2, t_0 \leq t_2 < t_1 : \neg\ comm\ c\ at\ t_2$
- $wait\ c!\ at\ t_0\ until\ comm\ (c, exp)\ at\ t_1 \equiv$
  $wait\ c!\ during\ [t_0, t_1\rangle \wedge\ comm\ (c, exp)\ during\ [t_1, t_1 + T_{comm}\rangle$
- $await\ (c!, exp)\ at\ t_0 \equiv \exists t_1 \geq t_0 : wait\ c!\ at\ t_0\ until\ comm\ (c, exp)\ at\ t_1$
- $await\ c!\ at\ t_0 \equiv \exists v : await\ (c!, v)\ at\ t_0$

Let *cset* be a finite subset of *DCHAN*. Then

- $no\ cset\ during\ [t_0, t_1\rangle \equiv \forall t, t_0 \leq t < t_1 : \bigwedge_{c! \in cset} \neg\ wait\ c!\ at\ t \wedge$
  $\bigwedge_{c? \in cset} \neg\ wait\ c?\ at\ t \wedge \bigwedge_{c \in cset} \neg\ comm\ c\ at\ t$

The abbreviations above are also used with $c?$ instead of $c!$, and with other intervals such as $\langle t_0, t_1\rangle$ and $\langle t_0, \infty\rangle$ instead of the interval $[t_0, t_1\rangle$. It is easy to extend these definitions to general expressions instead of t_0 or t_1.

Finally we describe the informal meaning of our correctness formulae. A formula $C : \{p\}\ S\ \{q\}$ is valid if

1. $var(C) = \emptyset$, and
2. if p holds in the initial state and the communication history in which S starts its execution then
   (a) C holds in the initial communication history extended with the communication behaviour of S, and
   (b) if the computation terminates then q holds in the final state and the initial communication history extended with the communication behaviour of S.

Examples

First a few general safety properties:

- Program S does not terminate.
  $true \; : \; \{true\} \; S \; \{false\}$.
  (S will also satisfy the formula $time = \infty \; : \; \{true\} \; S \; \{false\}$.)
- S does not perform any communication along channel c.
  $(\forall t \geq 0 : \neg comm \; c \; at \; t) \; : \; \{time = 0\} \; S \; \{true\}$.

Next a number of real-time safety properties:

- If S starts its execution in a state where variable x has the value 3 and if S terminates, then S terminates within 2 time units in a state where x has the value 4.
  $true \; : \; \{x = 3 \wedge time = t\} \; S \; \{x = 4 \wedge time < t + 2\}$.
- S terminates in less than 12 time units, incrementing x by 5.
  $time < 12 \; : \; \{x = v \wedge time = 0\} \; S \; \{x = v + 5\}$.
  (Instead of starting at time 0 we could also use a general starting time t_0:
  $time < t_0 + 12 \; : \; \{x = v \wedge time = t_0\} \; S \; \{x = v + 5\}$.)
- S communicates along channel c within 25 time units.
  $(\exists t < 25 : comm \; c \; at \; t) \; : \; \{time = 0\} \; S \; \{true\}$.
- If S receives value v via channel c then it will try to send the value $v + 7$ along channel d in less than 10 time units.
  $comm \; (c, v) \; at \; t_0 \rightarrow \exists t_1, t_0 < t_1 < t_0 + 10 : await \; (d!, v + 7) \; at \; t_1 :$
  $\{time = 0\} \; S \; \{false\}$

Some liveness properties:

- S terminates.
  $time < \infty \; : \; \{true\} \; S \; \{true\}$.
- S eventually communicates along channel c.
  $(\exists t : comm \; c \; at \; t) : \{time = 0\} \; S \; \{true\}$.
- Program S either communicates infinitely often via channel c, or it eventually waits forever to receive along c.
  $(\forall t_0 < \infty \; \exists t_1 > t_0 : comm \; c \; at \; t_1) \vee (\exists t_0 < \infty \; \forall t_1 > t_0 : wait \; c? \; at \; t_1) \; :$
  $\{time = 0\} \; S \; \{false\}$.
  Note that the program $\star[c?x \rightarrow$ **skip**$]$ satisfies this liveness specification.

Finally, a few examples of programs satisfying a certain specification:

- $await \; (c!, 8) \; at \; 5 : \{time = 3\}$ **delay** $2 \, ; \; c!8 \; \{true\}$.

- $(v < 5 \rightarrow time = \infty) \wedge (v \geq 5 \rightarrow time < \infty)$:

  $\{x = v\} \star [x > 5 \rightarrow x := x - 1 [] x < 5 \rightarrow \mathbf{skip}]\{x = 5\}$.

  This formula describes how the termination of the program depends on the initial value of x.

- $comm\ (c, 9)\ at\ 3 \wedge await\ (d!, 6)\ at\ 7$:

  $\{comm\ (c, 9)\ at\ 3 \wedge time = 5 \wedge x = 4\}$ **delay** $2\ ;\ d!(x + 2)$

  $\{comm\ (c, 9)\ at\ 3 \wedge await\ (d!, 6)\ at\ 7 \wedge time < \infty\}$

  Observe that the communication history before the starting time, i.e. $comm\ (c, 9)\ at\ 3$ in the precondition, is included in the commitment and the postcondition.

4 Proof System for Maximal Parallelism Model

We formulate a compositional proof system for our extended Hoare triples. First we formulate rules and axioms that are generally applicable to any statement. Next we axiomatize the programming language by formulating rules and axioms for all atomic statements and compound programming constructs.

A general requirement for all rules and axioms is that the commitment should not contain program variables. Further, we assume that all logical variables which are introduced in the rules are fresh. We use $p[exp/var]$ to denote the substitution of each free occurrence of variable var by expression exp.

We start with an axiom expressing general well-formedness properties of a computation. Define $WF_c \equiv \forall t < time : MW_c(t) \wedge Excl_c(t) \wedge Comm_c(t)$, with

$MW_c(t) \equiv \neg(wait\ c?\ at\ t \wedge wait\ c!\ at\ t)$

(*Minimal waiting*: It is not possible to be simultaneously waiting to send and waiting to receive on a particular channel.)

$Excl_c(t) \equiv \neg(wait\ c!\ at\ t \wedge comm\ c\ at\ t) \wedge \neg(wait\ c?\ at\ t \wedge comm\ c\ at\ t)$

(*Exclusion*: It is not possible to be simultaneously communicating and waiting to communicate on a given channel.)

$Comm_c(t) \equiv comm\ (c, exp_1)\ at\ t \wedge comm\ (c, exp_2)\ at\ t \rightarrow exp_1 = exp_2$

(*Communication*: at any time at most one value is transmitted on a particular channel.) Then, for every channel c we have the following axiom.

Axiom 4.1 (Well-Formedness) $WF_c\ :\ \{true\}\ S\ \{WF_c\}$

In examples we will use the following lemma which allows us to deduce the timing of a communication from the readiness to communicate of both partners.

Lemma 4.2 *await c! at* $t_1 \wedge$ *await c? at* $t_2 \wedge$ *no comm c during* $[min(t_1,t_2), max(t_1,t_2)\rangle \wedge$ $WF_c \rightarrow$ *end comm c at* $max(t_1,t_2) + T_{comm}$

Next we give two axioms to deduce invariance properties. The first axiom expresses that a precondition which satisfies certain restrictions remains valid during the execution of a program.

Axiom 4.3 (Initial Invariance) $C : \{p \wedge C\}\ S\ \{p\}$

provided *time* does not occur in p or C, and $var(S) \cap var(p) = \emptyset$.

The channel invariance axiom below expresses that during the execution of a program S no activity takes place on channels not occurring in S. Let *cset* be a finite subset of *DCHAN*.

Axiom 4.4 (Channel Invariance)

$$no\ cset\ during\ [t_0, time\rangle\ :\ \{time = t_0\}\ S\ \{no\ cset\ during\ [t_0, time\rangle\}$$

provided $cset \cap dch(S) = \emptyset$.

The proof system contains a consequence rule which is an extension of the classical consequence rule for Hoare triples. There is a disjunction rule which makes it possible to split a precondition in several cases (see the rules for guarded commands below). Further, the proof system contains the rules for conjunction and substitution.

Rule 4.5 (Consequence)
$$\frac{C_0\ :\ \{p_0\}\ S\ \{q_0\},\ p \rightarrow p_0,\ C_0 \rightarrow C,\ q_0 \rightarrow q}{C\ :\ \{p\}\ S\ \{q\}}$$

Rule 4.6 (Disjunction)
$$\frac{C_1\ :\ \{p_1\}\ S\ \{q_1\},\ C_2\ :\ \{p_2\}\ S\ \{q_2\}}{C_1 \vee C_2\ :\ \{p_1 \vee p_2\}\ S\ \{q_1 \vee q_2\}}$$

Rule 4.7 (Conjunction)
$$\frac{C_1\ :\ \{p_1\}\ S\ \{q_1\},\ C_2\ :\ \{p_2\}\ S\ \{q_2\}}{C_1 \wedge C_2\ :\ \{p_1 \wedge p_2\}\ S\ \{q_1 \wedge q_2\}}$$

Rule 4.8 (Substitution)
$$\frac{C\ :\ \{p\}\ S\ \{q\}}{C[exp/u]\ :\ \{p[exp/u]\}\ S\ \{q[exp/u]\}}$$

for any logical variable u, provided *time* does not occur in expression *exp*.

Axiom 4.9 (Skip) $C\ :\ \{p \wedge C\}$ **skip** $\{p\}$

Rule 4.10 (Assignment) $C\ :\ \{(q \wedge C)[time + T_{assign}/time, e/x]\}\ x := e\ \{q\}$

Note that by this rule, and the consequence rule, we can derive

$time = t_0 + T_{assign} : \{time = t_0 \wedge e = v\}\ x := e\ \{time = t_0 + T_{assign} \wedge x = v\}$,

since $time = t_0 \wedge e = v \rightarrow (time = t_0 + T_{assign} \wedge x = v)[time + T_{assign}/time, e/x]$.

Axiom 4.11 (Delay) $C\ :\ \{(q \wedge C)[time + max(0,e)/time]\}$ **delay** $e\ \ \{q\}$

Example 4.1 With the delay axiom we can derive the formula

$time = 5 : \{x = 3 \wedge time = 2\}$ **delay** $x\ \{x = 3 \wedge time = 5\}$,

because $(x = 3 \wedge time = 5)[time + max(0,x)/time] \equiv (x = 3 \wedge time + max(0,x) = 5)$ is equivalent to $x = 3 \wedge time = 2$. Similarly we can derive

$time = t_0 + max(0,e)\ :\ \{time = t_0\}$ **delay** $e\ \ \{time = t_0 + max(0,e)\}$. □

To obtain a compositional proof system we do not make any assumption about the environment of a statement. Thus in the rule for an output statement no assumption is made about when a communication partner is available, and hence this rule includes any arbitrary waiting period (including an infinite one). In the rule for $c!e$ this is achieved by using $\exists t \geq t_0 : wait\ c!\ at\ t_0\ until\ comm\ (c,e)\ at\ t$ where t_0 is the starting time. Observe that logical variables from $TVAR$, such as t, range over $TIME \cup \{\infty\}$, and thus

$\exists t \geq t_0 : wait\ c!\ at\ t_0\ until\ comm\ (c,e)\ at\ t$

is equivalent to

$wait\ c!\ at\ t_0\ until\ comm\ (c,e)\ at\ \infty \vee$

$\exists t, t_0 \leq t < \infty : wait\ c!\ at\ t_0\ until\ comm\ (c,e)\ at\ t$,

which is equivalent to

$wait\ c!\ during\ [t_0, \infty\rangle \vee$

$(\exists t, t_0 \leq t < \infty : wait\ c!\ during\ [t_0, t\rangle \wedge comm\ (c,e)\ during\ [t, t + T_{comm}\rangle)$,

since $comm\ (c,e)\ during\ [\infty, \infty + T_{comm}\rangle \leftrightarrow true$, and thus

$wait\ c!\ at\ t_0\ until\ comm\ (c,e) \leftrightarrow wait\ c!\ during\ [t_0, \infty\rangle$.

Hence the commitment can express a non-terminating computation in which the output statement waits forever to communicate. When a communication partner is available the actual communication takes place during an interval of length T_{comm}. This leads to the following rule.

Rule 4.12 (Output)

$$\frac{p[t_0/time] \wedge \exists t \geq t_0 : wait\ c!\ at\ t_0\ until\ comm\ (c,e)\ at\ t \wedge time = t + T_{comm} \rightarrow q \wedge C}{C\ :\ \{p\}\ c!e\ \{q \wedge time < \infty\}}$$

Example 4.2 With the output rule we can derive

$await\ (c!, 5)\ at\ 1 : \{time = 1 \wedge x = 3\}\ c!(x+2)\ \{end\ comm\ (c,5)\ at\ time \wedge time < \infty\}$

since, for the commitment,

$t_0 = 1 \wedge x = 3 \wedge \exists t \geq t_0 : \textit{wait } c! \textit{ at } t_0 \textit{ until comm } (c, x+2) \textit{ at } t \wedge \textit{time} = t + T_{comm}$ $\rightarrow \textit{await } (c!, 5) \textit{ at } 1$ and for the postcondition we have $t_0 = 1 \wedge x = 3 \wedge \exists t \geq t_0 : \textit{wait } c! \textit{ at } t_0 \textit{ until comm } (c, x+2) \textit{ at } t \wedge \textit{time} = t + T_{comm} \rightarrow$ $\exists t \geq t_0 : \textit{comm } (c, 5) \textit{ during } [t, t+T_{comm}\rangle \wedge \textit{time} = t + T_{comm}$, and thus we obtain the postcondition $\textit{end comm } (c, 5) \textit{ at time} \wedge \textit{time} < \infty$. □

In the input rule we allow any arbitrary input value, since no assumption should be imposed upon the environment, and hence any value can be received.

Rule 4.13 (Input)

$$\frac{p[t_0/\textit{time}] \wedge \exists t \geq t_0 : \textit{wait } c? \textit{ at } t_0 \textit{ until comm } (c, v) \textit{ at } t \wedge \textit{time} = t + T_{comm} \rightarrow q[v/x] \wedge C}{C \,:\, \{p\}\ c?x\ \{q \wedge \textit{time} < \infty\}}$$

Example 4.3 With the input rule we can derive

$\textit{comm } (d, 0) \textit{ at } 2 \wedge \exists v_1 : \textit{await } (c?, v_1) \textit{ at } 4 \,:$

$\{\textit{comm } (d, 0) \textit{ at } 2 \wedge \textit{time} = 4\}\ c?x\ \{\textit{comm } (d, 0) \textit{ at } 2 \wedge \textit{end comm } (c, x) \textit{ at time}\}$

since, for the commitment,

$\textit{comm } (d, 0) \textit{ at } 2 \wedge t_0 = 4 \wedge \exists t \geq t_0 : \textit{wait } c? \textit{ at } t_0 \textit{ until comm } (c, v) \textit{ at } t \wedge \textit{time} = t + T_{comm}$ $\rightarrow \textit{comm } (d, 0) \textit{ at } 2 \wedge \exists v_1 : \textit{await } (c?, v_1) \textit{ at } 4$. For the postcondition we have $\textit{comm } (d, 0) \textit{ at } 2 \wedge t_0 = 4 \wedge \exists t \geq t_0 : \textit{wait } c? \textit{ at } t_0 \textit{ until comm } (c, v) \textit{ at } t \wedge \textit{time} = t + T_{comm}$ $\rightarrow \textit{comm } (d, 0) \textit{ at } 2 \wedge \textit{end comm } (c, v) \textit{ at time} \equiv$ $(\textit{comm } (d, 0) \textit{ at } 2 \wedge \textit{end comm } (c, x) \textit{ at time})[v/x]$. □

The inference rule for sequential composition is an extension of the classical rule for Hoare triples. To explain the commitment of $S_1; S_2$, observe that a computation of $S_1; S_2$ is either a non-terminating computation of S_1 or a terminated computation of S_1 extended with a computation of S_2. The commitment of $S_1; S_2$ expresses the non-terminating computations of S_1 by using the commitment of S_1 with $\textit{time} = \infty$. Terminating computations of S_1 are characterized in the postcondition of S_1 which is also the precondition of S_2. Then these computations are extended by S_2 and described in the commitment of S_2.

Rule 4.14 (Sequential Composition)

$$\frac{C_1 \,:\, \{p\}\ S_1\ \{r\},\ C_2 \,:\, \{r\}\ S_2\ \{q\}}{(C_1 \wedge \textit{time} = \infty) \vee C_2 \,:\, \{p\}\ S_1; S_2\ \{q\}}$$

Example 4.4 Consider the program $c?x; d!(x+1)$. We prove

$(\textit{wait } c? \textit{ during } [0, \infty\rangle \wedge \textit{time} = \infty) \vee$

$(\exists t_1 < \infty\ \exists v : \textit{end comm } (c, v) \textit{ at } t_1 \wedge \textit{await } (d!, v+1) \textit{ at } t_1) \,:$

$\{\textit{time} = 0\}\ c?x\ ;\ d!(x+1)$

$$\{\exists t_1 < \infty\, \exists t_2, t_1 < t_2 < \infty : end\ comm\ (c,x)\ at\ t_1 \wedge\ end\ comm\ (d, x+1)\ at\ t_2\}.$$

Define $C^1_{nonterm} \equiv wait\ c?\ during\ [0,\infty\rangle$, $C^1_{term} \equiv end\ comm\ (c,v)\ at\ t_1$, and $q \equiv \exists t_1 < \infty\, \exists t_2, t_1 < t_2 < \infty : end\ comm\ (c,x)\ at\ t_1 \wedge\ end\ comm\ (d,x+1)\ at\ t_2$. Then $(time = \infty \rightarrow C^1_{nonterm})\ :\ \{time = 0\}\ c?x\ \{\exists t_1 < \infty\, \exists v : C^1_{term} \wedge time = t_1 \wedge x = v\}$.

For $d!(x+1)$, define $C_2 \equiv await\ (d!, v+1)\ at\ t_1$, then we can derive

$$(\exists t_1 < \infty\, \exists v : C^1_{term} \wedge C_2)\ :$$
$$\{\exists t_1 < \infty\, \exists v : C^1_{term} \wedge time = t_1 \wedge x = v\}\ d!(x+1)$$
$$\{\exists t_1 < \infty\, \exists v\, \exists t_2, t_1 < t_2 < \infty : C^1_{term} \wedge end\ comm\ (d, v+1)\ at\ t_2 \wedge x = v\}.$$

Observe that the terminating behaviour of $c?x$ is characterized by its postcondition, thus by the precondition of $d!(x+1)$, and hence can be included in the commitment of $d!(x+1)$. Since the postcondition of $d!(x+1)$ implies q, we obtain by the sequential composition rule and the consequence rule:
$(C^1_{nonterm} \wedge time = \infty) \vee (\exists t_1 < \infty\, \exists v : C^1_{term} \wedge C_2)\ :\ \{time = 0\}\ c?x\ ;\ d!(x+1)\ \{q\}$. □

For guarded commands, we start with a simple rule for the case that none of the guards is open, i.e. b_G evaluates to false. Recall that the evaluation of b_G takes T_{exec} time units.

Rule 4.15 (Guarded Command Termination)

$$\frac{C\ :\ \{p \wedge \neg b_G\}\ \textbf{delay}\ T_{exec}\ \{q\}}{C\ :\ \{p \wedge \neg b_G\}\ G\ \{q\}}$$

Next consider $G \equiv [\,[]_{i=1}^n\ b_i \rightarrow S_i]$.

Rule 4.16 (Guarded Command with Purely Boolean Guards)

$$\frac{C_i\ :\ \{p \wedge b_i\}\ \textbf{delay}\ T_{exec}\ ;\ S_i\ \{q_i\},\ \text{for all}\ i \in \{1,\ldots,n\}}{\bigvee_{i=1}^n C_i\ :\ \{p \wedge b_G\}\ [\,[]_{i=1}^n\ b_i \rightarrow S_i]\ \{\bigvee_{i=1}^n q_i\}}$$

Now let $G \equiv [\,[]_{i=1}^n\ b_i; c_i?x_i \rightarrow S_i\,[]\,b_0; \textbf{delay}\ e\ \rightarrow S_0]$. Define

- $wait\ in\ G\ during\ [t_0,t_1\rangle \ \equiv\ \bigwedge_{i=1}^n (b_i \leftrightarrow wait\ c_i?\ during\ [t_0,t_1\rangle) \wedge$ $no\ (dch(G) - \{c_1?,\ldots,c_n?\})\ during\ [t_0,t_1\rangle$, and
- $await\ comm\ G\ at\ t_0\ \equiv\ \exists t \geq t_0 : wait\ in\ G\ during\ [t_0,t\rangle \wedge (b_0 \rightarrow t < max(0,e)) \wedge$ $\exists i \in \{1,\ldots,n\} : b_i \wedge comm\ c_i\ during\ [t, t+T_{comm}\rangle \wedge$ $no\ (dch(G) - \{c_i\})\ during\ [t,t+T_{comm}\rangle \wedge time = t + T_{comm}$.

Then we can formulate the rule for a guarded command as follows.

Rule 4.17 (Guarded Command with Input Guards)

$$\frac{\begin{array}{l} true\ :\ \{p \wedge b_G\}\ \textbf{delay}\ T_{exec}\ \{\hat{p}\} \\ \hat{p}[t_0/time] \wedge wait\ in\ G\ during\ [t_0,\infty) \wedge time=\infty \rightarrow C_{nonterm} \\ \hat{p}[t_0/time] \wedge await\ comm\ G\ at\ t_0 \wedge end\ comm\ (c_i,v)\ at\ time \rightarrow p_i[v/x_i],\ \text{for } i=1,\ldots,n \\ \hat{p}[t_0/time] \wedge b_0 \wedge wait\ in\ G\ during\ [t_0,t_0+max(0,e)) \wedge time=t_0+max(0,e) \rightarrow p_0 \\ C_i\ :\ \{p_i\}\ S_i\ \{q_i\},\ \text{for } i=0,1\ldots,n \end{array}}{C_{nonterm} \vee \bigvee_{i=0}^{n} C_i\ :\ \{p \wedge b_G\}\ [\,[\!]_{i=1}^{n}\ b_i; c_i?x_i \rightarrow S_i\,[\!]\,b_0; \textbf{delay}\ e\ \rightarrow S_0]\ \{\bigvee_{i=0}^{n} q_i\}}$$

The rule for the iteration construct does not contain any explicit well-foundedness argument, although we deal with liveness properties. The main principle is that liveness properties can be derived from real-time safety properties, and these properties can be proved by means of an invariant.

Rule 4.18 (Iteration)

$$\frac{\begin{array}{l} C\ :\ \{p \wedge b_G\}\ G\ \{p\} \\ C_{term}\ :\ \{p \wedge \neg b_G\}\ G\ \{q\} \\ (\forall t_1 < \infty\ \exists t_2 > t_1 : C[t_2/time]) \rightarrow C_{nonterm} \end{array}}{(C_{nonterm} \wedge time=\infty) \vee C_{term}\ :\ \{p\}\ \star G\ \{q\}}$$

The soundness of this rule is shown as follows:
For a computation of $\star G$, starting in a state satisfying p, there are three possibilities:

- It is a terminating computation, obtained from a finite number of terminating computations from G. For all these computations of G, except for the last one, b_G is true initially. From the first condition of the rule we can then prove by induction also that p is true in the initial state of these computations. Since for the last computation $\neg b_G$ must be true, the second condition of the rule then leads to C_{term} and q for this computation.
- It is a non-terminating computation obtained from a non-terminating computation of G. Then, as in the previous point, we have $p \wedge b_G$ in the initial state of this computation. Thus, using the first condition and the fact that it is a non-terminating computation, $C \wedge time = \infty$ holds for this computation. Hence, $\forall t_1 < \infty\ \exists t_2 > t_1 :$ $C[t_2/time]$, and then the third condition leads to $C_{nonterm}$.
- It is a non-terminating computation obtained from an infinite sequence of terminating computations of G. Then, similar to the first point, the first condition leads by induction to C for all these computations. Since each computation of G takes at least T_{exec} time units, we obtain C after any point of time. Thus, $\forall t_1 < \infty\ \exists t_2 > t_1 : C[t_2/time]$, and then by the third condition we obtain $C_{nonterm}$.

Example 4.5 Termination of program $\star[x > 0 \to x := x-1]$ can be expressed as follows:

$time < \infty \;:\; \{x \in I\!N\} \;\star[x > 0 \to x := x - 1]\; \{true\}$.

We indicate how this formula is proved by means of an invariant. First this liveness property is strengthened to a real-time safety property. Let $K \equiv T_{exec} + T_{assign}$. We prove

$time = v \times K + T_{exec} \;:\; \{time = 0 \wedge x = v \wedge v \in I\!N\} \;\star[x > 0 \to x := x - 1]\; \{true\}$.

Define $C_{term} \equiv time = v \times K + T_{exec}$, $p_0 \equiv time = 0 \wedge x = v \wedge v \in I\!N$, and $q \equiv true$. Then we have to prove $C_{term} \;:\; \{p_0\} \;\star[x > 0 \to x := x - 1]\; \{q\}$. We apply the iteration rule with $p \equiv time = (v-x) \times K < \infty \wedge x \in I\!N$, $C \equiv time \leq v \times K$, and $C_{nonterm} \equiv false$. Observe that the three conditions of the rule are fulfilled:

1. $C \;:\; \{p \wedge x > 0\}\; [x > 0 \to x := x - 1]\; \{p\}$ can be proved as follows.
   Let $r \equiv time = (v - x) \times K + T_{exec} < \infty \wedge x \in I\!N \wedge x > 0$.
   By the delay axiom we obtain $time < \infty \;:\; \{p \wedge x > 0\}$ **delay** $T_{exec}\; \{r\}$,
   and from the assignment axiom, $time \leq v \times K \;:\; \{r\}\; x := x - 1\; \{p\}$.
   Then the sequential composition rule leads to
   $(time < \infty \wedge time = \infty) \vee (time \leq v \times K) \;:\; \{p \wedge x > 0\}$ **delay** $T_{exec}; x := x - 1\; \{p\}$,
   and thus $time \leq v \times K \;:\; \{p \wedge x > 0\}$ **delay** $T_{exec}; x := x - 1\; \{p\}$.
   Hence by rule 4.16 we obtain $C \;:\; \{p \wedge x > 0\}\; [x > 0 \to x := x - 1]\; \{p\}$.
2. $C_{term} \;:\; \{p \wedge x \leq 0\}\; [x > 0 \to x := x - 1]\; \{q\}$, can be derived from rule 4.15; observe that $C_{term} \;:\; \{p \wedge x \leq 0\}$ **delay** $T_{exec}\; \{q\}$ follows from the delay axiom since $(p \wedge x \leq 0) \to (time = v \times K)$.
3. $\forall t_1 < \infty\; \exists t_2 > t_1 : C[t_2/time] \equiv \forall t_1 < \infty\; \exists t_2 > t_1 : t_2 \leq v \times K$ implies $false$, i.e., $C_{nonterm}$.

Then by the iteration rule we obtain

$(C_{nonterm} \wedge time = \infty) \vee C_{term} \;:\; \{p\} \;\star[x > 0 \to x := x - 1]\; \{q\}$.

Since $C_{nonterm} \wedge time = \infty \to false$ and $p_0 \to p$, the consequence rule leads to

$C_{term} \;:\; \{p_0\} \;\star[x > 0 \to x := x - 1]\; \{q\}$.

Using $C_{term} \to time < \infty$, we obtain

$time < \infty \;:\; \{time = 0 \wedge x = v \wedge v \in I\!N\} \;\star[x > 0 \to x := x - 1]\; \{true\}$.

By the substitution rule, replacing v by x, we can derive

$time < \infty \;:\; \{time = 0 \wedge x \in I\!N\} \;\star[x > 0 \to x := x - 1]\; \{true\}$.

To obtain precondition $x \in I\!N$ one should replace $time = 0$ by $time = t_0$ and prove

$$time = t_0 + v \times K + T_{exec} < \infty \;:\; \{time = t_0 < \infty \wedge x = v \wedge v \in I\!N\} \;\star[x > 0 \to x := x - 1]\; \{true\}.$$

As a last step in the proof we can then replace t_0 by $time$, using the substitution rule. □

Example 4.6 Consider $\star[in?x \to comp; out!y]$. Assume

$time = t + T \;:\; \{time = t \wedge x = v\}\; comp\; \{y = f(v)\}$.

Then we prove

$C_0 \wedge C_1 \ : \ \{time = 0\} \ \star [in?x \rightarrow comp; out!y] \ \{false\}$

with $C_0 \equiv$ *await in? at* T_{exec}, and

$C_1 \equiv (end\ comm\ (in, v)\ at\ t_0 \rightarrow await\ (out!, f(v))\ at\ t_0 + T) \wedge$
$(end\ comm\ out\ at\ t_0 \rightarrow await\ in?\ at\ t_0 + T_{exec})$.

We use the iteration rule with $G \equiv [in?x \rightarrow comp; out!y]$, $C \equiv C_0 \wedge \forall t_0 < time : C_1$, $p \equiv (time \neq 0 \rightarrow C_0 \wedge end\ comm\ out\ at\ time) \wedge \forall t_0 < time : C_1$, and $C_{nonterm} \equiv C_0 \wedge C_1$. Since $b_G \equiv true$, we can take $C_{term} \equiv q \equiv false$. Hence $C_{term} \ : \ \{p \wedge \neg b_G\} \ G \ \{q\}$.

It remains to prove:

1. $C \ : \ \{p\} \ G \ \{p\}$. Therefore we use the rule for a guarded command with input guards, with $C_{nonterm} \equiv C_1 \equiv C$, $q_1 \equiv p$,
   $\hat{p} \equiv (time \neq T_{exec} \rightarrow C_0 \wedge end\ comm\ out\ at\ time - T_{exec}) \wedge (\forall t_0 < time - T_{exec} : C_1)$
   $no\ \{in, out\}\ during\ [time - T_{exec}, time\rangle$, and
   $p_1 \equiv C_0 \wedge \forall t_0 < time : C_1 \wedge \exists v_1 : x = v_1 \wedge end\ comm\ (in, v_1)\ at\ time.$
   Since there is no delay-guard, we have to prove
   (a) $true \ : \ \{p \wedge b_G\}$ **delay** T_{exec} $\{\hat{p}\}$. This can be derived easily in the proof system, using the delay axiom and the channel invariance axiom.
   (b) $\hat{p}[t_1/time] \wedge wait\ in\ G\ during\ [t_1, \infty\rangle \wedge time = \infty \rightarrow C_{nonterm}$.
   From the hypothesis of this implication we obtain
   $(t_1 \neq T_{exec} \rightarrow C_0 \wedge end\ comm\ out\ at\ t_1 - T_{exec}) \wedge (\forall t_0 < t_1 - T_{exec} : C_1) \wedge$
   $no\ \{in, out\}\ during\ [t_1 - T_{exec}, t_1\rangle \wedge\ wait\ in?\ during\ [t_1, \infty\rangle \wedge$
   $no\ \{in, out\}\ during\ [t_1, \infty\rangle$, and thus
   $(t_1 \neq T_{exec} \rightarrow C_0 \wedge end\ comm\ out\ at\ t_1 - T_{exec}) \wedge (\forall t_0 < t_1 - T_{exec} : C_1) \wedge$
   $no\ \{in, out\}\ during\ [t_1 - T_{exec}, \infty\rangle \wedge\ await\ in?\ at\ t_1$.
   Observe that, for all t_3, t_4, $no\ \{in, out\}\ during\ [t_3, t_4\rangle \rightarrow \forall t_0, t_3 < t_0 < t_4 : C_1$.
   Then
   $(t_1 \neq T_{exec} \rightarrow C_0 \wedge end\ comm\ out\ at\ t_1 - T_{exec}) \wedge (\forall t_0 < t_1 - T_{exec} : C_1) \wedge$
   $(\forall t_0 > t_1 - T_{exec} : C_1) \wedge\ await\ in?\ at\ t_1$.
   If $t_1 \neq T_{exec}$ this leads to $C_0 \wedge (\forall t_0 \neq t_1 - T_{exec} : C_1) \wedge\ end\ comm\ out\ at\ t_1 - T_{exec} \wedge$ $await\ in?\ at\ t_1$ and thus $C_0 \wedge (\forall t_0 \neq t_1 - T_{exec} : C_1) \wedge C_1[t_1 - T_{exec}/t_0]$ which is equivalent to $C_0 \wedge \forall t_0 : C_1$.
   If $t_1 = T_{exec}$ then we have $await\ in?\ at\ T_{exec} \wedge$ $(\forall t_0 > 0 : C_1)$. Since $C_1[0/t_0]$ holds, we obtain $C_0 \wedge \forall t_0 : C_1$.
   (c) $\hat{p}[t_1/time] \wedge await\ comm\ G\ at\ t_1 \wedge end\ comm\ (in, v)\ at\ time \rightarrow p_1[v/x]$.
   From the antecedent of the implication we obtain
   $(t_1 \neq T_{exec} \rightarrow C_0 \wedge end\ comm\ out\ at\ t_1 - T_{exec}) \wedge (\forall t_0 < t_1 - T_{exec} : C_1) \wedge$
   $no\ \{in, out\}\ during\ [t_1 - T_{exec}, t_1\rangle \wedge\ await\ in?\ at\ t_1 \wedge$

$\exists v_1 : v = v_1 \wedge$ *end comm* (in, v_1) *at time*$\wedge$ *no* $\{out\}$ *during* $[t_1, time\rangle$.
Thus if $t_1 \neq 0$ we obtain $C_0 \wedge (\forall t_0 < t_1 : C_1) \wedge C_1[t_1/t_0] \wedge (\forall t_0 \in \langle t_1, time\rangle : C_1) \wedge$ $\exists v_1 : v = v_1 \wedge$ *end comm* (in, v_1) *at time*, that is, $p_1[v/x]$. Similarly, if $t_1 = 0$.

(d) $C_1 : \{p_1\}$ *comp*; *out*!*y* $\{q_1\}$, that is, $C : \{p_1\}$ *comp*; *out*!*y* $\{p\}$.
This can be derived by the sequential composition rule from
$time < \infty : \{p_1\}$ *comp* $\{r\}$ and $C : \{r\}$ *out*!*y* $\{p\}$ with
$r \equiv C_0 \wedge (\forall t_0 < time : C_1) \wedge \exists v_1 :$ *end comm* (in, v_1) *at* $(time - T) \wedge y = f(v_1)$.
Note that to prove postcondition r for *comp* we have to require that *comp* does not communicate on the channels *in* and *out*, i.e., $dch(comp) \cap \{in, out\} = \emptyset$.

2. $(\forall t_1 < \infty\, \exists t_2 > t_1 : C[t_2/time]) \rightarrow C_{nonterm}$, since
$\forall t_1 < \infty\, \exists t_2 > t_1 : C[t_2/time] \equiv \forall t_1 < \infty\, \exists t_2 > t_1 : (C_0 \wedge \forall t_0 < t_2 : C_1)$ implies $C_0 \wedge \forall t_0 : C_1$, and thus $C_0 \wedge C_1$ (free variables are implicitly universally quantified).

Then the iteration rule leads to $(C_{nonterm} \wedge time = \infty) \vee C_{term} : \{p\} \star G \{q\}$, and thus $C_1 : \{p\} \star G \{false\}$. Since $time = 0 \rightarrow p$ this leads to $C_1 : \{time = 0\} \star G \{false\}$. □

Consider the parallel composition $S_1 \| S_2$. If *time* does not occur in commitments and postconditions of the components S_1 and S_2, then we have the following simple rule:

Rule 4.19 (Simple Parallel Composition)

$$\frac{C_1 : \{p_1\}\ S_1\ \{q_1\}, \quad C_2 : \{p_2\}\ S_2\ \{q_2\}}{C_1 \wedge C_2 : \{p_1 \wedge p_2\}\ S_1 \| S_2\ \{q_1 \wedge q_2\}}$$

provided $dch(C_i, q_i) \subseteq dch(S_i)$, $var(q_i) \subseteq var(S_i)$, for $i \in \{1, 2\}$, and *time* does not occur in C_1, C_2, q_1, and q_2.

Example 4.7 To illustrate the problem with the termination times at parallel composition, consider the following two (valid) formulae:
$time = 5 : \{time = 0\}$ **delay** 5 $\{time = 5\}$, and
$time = 7 : \{time = 0\}$ **delay** 7 $\{time = 7\}$.
Then for **delay** 5 $\|$ **delay** 7 we cannot take the conjunction of commitments and postconditions, since this would imply *false*. □

The problem is that, in general, the termination times of S_1 and S_2 will be different. Therefore we substitute a logical variable t_i for *time* in q_i, $i = 1, 2$. Then the termination time of $S_1 \| S_2$, expressed by *time* in its postcondition, is the maximum of t_1 and t_2. A similar construction is used for the commitments. This leads to the following rule:

Rule 4.20 (Parallel Composition)

$$\frac{\begin{array}{l} C_i \ : \ \{p_i\} \ S_i \ \{q_i\}, \ i = 1,2 \\ \bigwedge_{i=1}^{2} C_i[t_i/time] \wedge time = max(t_1, t_2) \rightarrow C \\ \bigwedge_{i=1}^{2} q_i[t_i/time] \wedge time = max(t_1, t_2) \rightarrow q \end{array}}{C \ : \ \{p_1 \wedge p_2\} \ S_1 \| S_2 \ \{q\}}$$

provided $dch(C_i, q_i) \subseteq dch(S_i)$, and $var(q_i) \subseteq var(S_i)$, for $i = 1,2$.
(To obtain a complete system one should add *no* $dch(S_i)$ *during* $[t_i, time\rangle$ to the conjunction before the implications in the rule.)

In example 4.7 we can now obtain the commitment and postcondition $time = 7$ because $(\exists t_1, t_2 : time = max(t_1, t_2) \wedge t_1 = 5 \wedge t_2 = 7) \rightarrow time = 7$.

Example 4.8 The aim is to design a program which, with precondition $time = 0$ and for some deadline D, satisfies the following commitment:

$$\begin{array}{l} await \ in? \ at \ T_{exec} \wedge \\ (end \ comm \ (in, v) \ at \ t_0 \rightarrow \exists t_1, t_0 < t_1 \leq t_0 + D : await \ (out!, f_2(f_1(v))) \ at \ t_1) \end{array}$$

Assume given, for $i = 1,2$, a program that computes the function f_i in T_i time units:

$time = t + T_i \ : \ \{time = t \wedge x_i = v\} \ comp_i \ \{y_i = f_i(v)\}$,

and $dch(comp_i) \cap \{in, link, out\} = \emptyset$.

We compare two possible implementations: a sequential program

$P_1 \equiv \star[in?x_1 \rightarrow comp_1; x_2 := y_1; comp_2; out!y_2]$

and a concurrent program

$P_2 \equiv \star[in?x_1 \rightarrow comp_1; link!y_1] \| \star [link?x_2 \rightarrow comp_2; out!y_2]$.

Since the correctness of the output value can be proved easily in a non-real-time framework, we concentrate on the proof of the responsiveness property. Further, assume the environment is always willing to receive on channel *out*, that is, the process never has to wait when it tries to send on this channel. Formally, define

$A \equiv \forall t : \neg wait \ out! \ at \ t$.

Then the aim is to find for each program P_i, $i = 1,2$, a constant D_i such that P_i satisfies the following commitment:

$$\begin{array}{l} A \rightarrow await \ in? \ at \ T_{exec} \wedge \\ \qquad (end \ comm \ in \ at \ t_0 \rightarrow \exists t_1, t_0 < t_1 \leq t_0 + D_i : await \ in? \ at \ t_1) \end{array}$$

For P_1 we can prove, similar to example 4.6, the commitment

$$\begin{array}{l} C_1 \equiv await \ in? \ at \ T_{exec} \wedge \\ \qquad (end \ comm \ (in, v) \ at \ t_0 \rightarrow await \ (out!, f_2(f_1(v))) \ at \ t_0 + T_1 + T_{assign} + T_2) \wedge \\ \qquad (end \ comm \ out \ at \ t_0 \rightarrow await \ in? \ at \ t_0 + T_{exec}). \end{array}$$

If *end comm in at* t_0 then, by C_1, *await* $(out!, f_2(f_1(v)))$ *at* $t_0 + T_1 + T_{assign} + T_2$.

Together with A this implies *end comm out at* $t_0 + T_1 + T_{assign} + T_2 + T_{comm}$.
Using C_1 this leads to *await in? at* $t_0 + T_1 + T_{assign} + T_2 + T_{comm} + T_{exec}$.
Hence for P_1 we have the following commitment:

$$A \rightarrow \textit{await in? at } T_{exec} \wedge \\ (\textit{end comm in at } t_0 \rightarrow \textit{await in? at } t_0 + T_1 + T_{assign} + T_2 + T_{comm} + T_{exec})$$

Next we look at $P_2 \equiv S_1 \| S_2$, with $S_1 \equiv \star[in?x_1 \rightarrow comp_1; link!y_1]$ and $S_2 \equiv \star[link?x_2 \rightarrow comp_2; out!y_2]$. For S_1 we can prove the commitment

$$C_1 \equiv \textit{no comm link during } [0, T_{exec}\rangle \wedge \textit{ await in? at } T_{exec} \wedge \\ (\textit{end comm in at } t_0 \rightarrow \textit{no comm link during } [t_0 - T_{comm} - T_{exec}, t_0 + T_1\rangle \wedge \\ \textit{await link! at } t_0 + T_1) \wedge \\ (\textit{end comm link at } t_1 \rightarrow \textit{await in? at } t_1 + T_{exec}),$$

and for S_2 we have

$$C_2 \equiv A \rightarrow \textit{await link? at } T_{exec} \wedge \\ (\textit{end comm link at } t_2 \rightarrow \\ \textit{no comm link during } [t_2, t_2 + T_2 + T_{comm} + T_{exec}\rangle \wedge \\ \textit{await link? at } t_2 + T_2 + T_{comm} + T_{exec}).$$

With the simple rule for parallel composition we obtain commitment $C_1 \wedge C_2$ for $S_1 \| S_2$. Using the well-formedness axiom and the conjunction rule we add WF_{link}. Now we show that, for certain values of deadline D_2, $C_1 \wedge C_2 \wedge WF_{link}$ implies the desired commitment $A \rightarrow (\textit{await in? at } T_{exec} \wedge (\textit{end comm in at } t_0 \rightarrow \exists t_1, t_0 < t_1 \leq t_0 + D_2 : \textit{await in? at } t_1))$.
First observe that from C_1 we obtain directly *await in? at* T_{exec}.
Next assume A and *end comm in at* t_0. By C_1 we obtain *no comm link during* $[t_0 - T_{comm} - T_{exec}, t_0 + T_1\rangle \wedge$ *await link! at* $t_0 + T_1$.
Now consider two cases:

- Either there is no $t_3 < t_0 - T_{comm} - T_{exec}$ such that *end comm link at* t_3. Then *no comm link during* $[0, t_0 + T_1\rangle$. By C_1 we have *no comm link during* $[0, T_{exec}\rangle$. From C_2 we obtain *await link? at* T_{exec}. Together with *await link! at* $t_0 + T_1$ and WF_{link} this implies, by lemma 4.2, *end comm link at* $max(t_0 + T_1, T_{exec}) + T_{comm}$. Hence, using C_1, *await in? at* $max(t_0 + T_1, T_{exec}) + T_{comm} + T_{exec}$. Then D_2 must be such that $max(t_0 + T_1, T_{exec}) + T_{comm} + T_{exec} \leq t_0 + D_2$. Thus we require $D_2 \geq max(T_1, T_{exec} - t_0) + T_{comm} + T_{exec}$, for all t_0. Since $t_0 \geq 0$, it is sufficient that $D_2 \geq max(T_1, T_{exec}) + T_{comm} + T_{exec}$.
- Or there exists a $t_3 < t_0 - T_{comm} - T_{exec}$ such that *end comm link at* t_3. Consider the last communication along *link* before t_0, that is,

  $$\exists t_3 < t_0 - T_{comm} - T_{exec} : \textit{no comm link during } [t_3, t_0 - T_{comm} - T_{exec}\rangle \wedge \\ \textit{end comm link at } t_3.$$

  Then, by C_2, we obtain

$$\exists t_3 < t_0 - T_{comm} - T_{exec} : no\ comm\ link\ during\ [t_3, t_3 + T_2 + T_{comm} + T_{exec}) \wedge$$
$$await\ link?\ at\ t_3 + T_2 + T_{comm} + T_{exec}.$$

From *end comm in at* t_0 we obtain, by C_1,
no comm link during $[t_0 - T_{comm} - T_{exec}, t_0 + T_1) \wedge$ *await link! at* $t_0 + T_1$.
Thus we have *await link? at* $t_3 + T_2 + T_{comm} + T_{exec}$, *await link! at* $t_0 + T_1$,
no comm link during $[t_3, t_0 + T_1)$, and
no comm link during $[t_3, t_3 + T_2 + T_{comm} + T_{exec})$.
Hence *no comm link during* $[t_3, max(t_3 + T_2 + T_{comm} + T_{exec}, t_0 + T_1))$.
Since $t_3 < t_0 - T_{comm} - T_{exec}$ we obtain $t_3 < t_0 + T_1$, and thus *no comm link during* $[min(t_3 + T_2 + T_{comm} + T_{exec}, t_0 + T_1), max(t_3 + T_2 + T_{comm} + T_{exec}, t_0 + T_1))$.
Using WF_{link}, lemma 4.2 leads to
end comm link at $max(t_0 + T_1, t_3 + T_2 + T_{comm} + T_{exec}) + T_{comm}$.
By C_1 this implies
await in? at $max(t_0 + T_1, t_3 + T_2 + T_{comm} + T_{exec}) + T_{comm} + T_{exec}$.
Hence we must have $D_2 \geq max(t_0 + T_1, t_3 + T_2 + T_{comm} + T_{exec}) + T_{comm} + T_{exec} - t_0$, for any $t_3 < t_0 - T_{comm} - T_{exec}$. Thus, using the upper bound of t_3,
$D_2 \geq max(t_0 + T_1, t_0 - T_{comm} - T_{exec} + T_2 + T_{comm} + T_{exec}) + T_{comm} + T_{exec} - t_0$, that is, $D_2 \geq max(T_1, T_2) + T_{comm} + T_{exec}$.

Combining both cases we see that P_2 satisfies the specification for $D_2 = max(T_1, T_2) + T_{comm} + T_{exec}$, provided $max(T_1, T_2) \geq T_{exec}$ which is a reasonable assumption. Clearly, the concurrent program gives a better response that the sequential program for which we have derived the bound $D_1 = T_1 + T_2 + T_{assign} + T_{comm} + T_{exec}$. □

5 Programming Language for Multiprogramming

As a first study of uniprocessor implementations, we consider in this section a programming language with a construct to express that (part of) a program, possibly containing parallel processes, is executed on a single processor. Using the syntax of the previous sections, the program $S_1 \| S_2 \| S_3$ expresses that each of the processes S_1, S_2 and S_3 has its own processor. In this section we introduce the brackets $\ll$ and $\gg$ in the syntax to express that (parallel) statements inside these brackets are executed on a single processor. Thus the program above is now written as $\ll S_1 \gg \| \ll S_2 \gg \| \ll S_3 \gg$. But we can also assign several processes to a single processor. Consider, for instance, $\ll S_{11} \| S_{12} \gg \| \ll S_{21} \| S_{22} \| S_{23} \gg \| \ll S_3 \gg$ where the processes S_{11} and S_{12} are executed on one processor and also S_{21}, S_{22} and S_{23} share a processor. Execution on a single processor is, in principle, an interleaving of the atomic actions of the processes assigned to it. This interleaving can be restricted by the programmer by assigning priorities to statements. The execution model is such that a processor only starts the execution of a statement when no other statement with a higher priority is ready to execute. The informal meaning of programs is discussed, leading to a number of open questions about the precise execution model. To answer these questions, we describe an operational model for the language.

5.1 Syntax and Informal Meaning

Let e be an expression, and b, b_i, for $i = 1, \ldots, n$, be boolean expressions, according to the syntax of Table 1. Then the syntax of our extended programming language is given in Table 3, with $d \in \mathit{TIME}$, $n \in \mathbb{N}$, $n \geq 1$, $c, c_1, \ldots c_n \in \mathit{CHAN}$, and $x, x_1, \ldots x_n \in \mathit{VAR}$.

Table 3: Syntax of the Programming Language for Multiprogramming

Statement	$S ::=$	**skip** $\mid$ **atomic** (d) $\mid$ $x := e$ $\mid$ **delay** e $\mid$ $c!e$ $\mid$ $c?x$ $\mid$
		$S_1; S_2$ $\mid$ G $\mid$ $\star G$ $\mid$ **prio** $e\,(S)$ $\mid$ $S_1 \parallel S_2$
Guarded Command	$G ::=$	$[\,[]_{i=1}^{n} b_i \rightarrow S_i]$ $\mid$ $[\,[]_{i=1}^{n} b_i; c_i?x_i \rightarrow S_i\,[]\, b_0;$ **delay** $e \rightarrow S_0]$
Network	$N ::=$	$\ll S \gg$ $\mid$ $N_1 \| N_2$
Program	$P ::=$	S $\mid$ N

There are three new statements, with the following informal meaning:

- **atomic** (d) represents an atomic action which executes non-interruptable during d time units.
- **prio** $e\,(S)$ assigns priority e to statement S. Statements without such an explicit priority assignment obtain priority 0. A higher number corresponds to a higher priority.
- $\ll$ **S** $\gg$ is called processor closure; it expresses that program S has its own processor and no process outside S executes on this processor.

Observe that we only have one symbol for parallel composition. If $P_1 \parallel P_2$ occurs inside the brackets $\ll$ and $\gg$ of processor closure, then it expresses uniprocessor parallelism and the statements P_1 and P_2 are executed on the same processor. Otherwise, the networks P_1 and P_2 are executed concurrently on disjoint sets of processors. Observe the difference between $\ll x := 5 \parallel y := 6 \gg$, expressing an interleaved execution of the two assignments, and $\ll x := 5 \gg \parallel \ll y := 6 \gg$, expressing true concurrency.

To achieve a uniform framework, parallel processes that are executed on a single processor only communicate by synchronous message passing. Any underlying implementation of this communication mechanism could, however, make use of shared variables. In addition to syntactic restrictions to guarantee that a channel connects at most two processes and parallel processes do not share variables, we require for **prio** $e\,(S)$ that S does not contain any parallel composition operator. Observe that there is a fixed assignment of processes to processors; it is not possible to change the allocation of a process during the execution. Priorities need not be static, but are evaluated dynamically. For instance, in $c?x;$ **prio** $x\ (S)$ the priority of S depends on a value which is received along channel c.

5.2 Operational Model

Although we have given an informal explanation of programs, there are still a number of questions about the precise meaning of programs. For instance:

- When and how are statements interrupted to allow the execution of statements with a higher priority?
- Is there any distinction between internal communications (within a single processor) and external communications that connect two processors?
- What is the priority of internal communications?

  Example 5.1 Consider $\ll$ **prio** $1\,(c!0) \parallel$ **prio** $2\,(x := 2) \parallel$ **prio** $3\,(c?y) \gg$.
  Should the priority of the c-communication be the maximum of the priorities of the two partners, or should it be the minimum—first executing the assignment? □

- What is the priority of external communications? What is the relation between priorities on different processors?

  Example 5.2 Consider the program

  $\ll$ **prio** $1\,(c!0) \parallel$ **prio** $5\,(d?x) \gg \parallel \ll$ **prio** $4\,(c?y) \parallel$ **prio** $3\,(d!1) \gg$.

  In which order are the two communications executed, or are they performed concurrently? Or maybe this program leads to deadlock? Is it significant that the maximum of the priorities of the statements for the d-communication is higher than the priorities of the statements for the c-communication? Compare this with:

  $\ll$ **prio** $1\,(c!0) \parallel$ **prio** $2\,(d?x) \gg \parallel \ll$ **prio** $2\,(c?y) \parallel$ **prio** $1\,(d!1) \gg$.

  Is there any difference between the execution of the two programs above? Consider also the program

  $\ll$ **prio** $1\,(c!0) \parallel$ **prio** $2\,(x := 4) \gg \parallel \ll$ **prio** $3\,(c?y) \parallel$ **prio** $2\,(z := 5) \gg$.

  Is the c-communication performed before or after the assignments? □

To answer these questions about the informal meaning of programs, we use an operational model which is inspired by the implementation of Occam on transputers (see, for instance, [Occ88a]). A transputer is a processor with internal memory and (four) *communication links* for connection with other transputers. Each link implements two channels (in opposite direction). Communication links are connected to the main processor via *link interfaces*. These interfaces can, independently, manage the communications of the link, including direct access to memory. As a result of this architecture, a transputer can simultaneously communicate on all links (in both directions) and execute an internal statement.

On transputers there is a clear distinction between the implementation of internal channels, which are within a single transputer, and external ones that must be mapped onto links. In our model, however, we do not distinguish between internal and external channels, and use the implementation model of external channels (with link interfaces) for all channels. This means that when a process tries to communicate on a channel its execution becomes suspended and the responsibility for the communication is delegated to the autonomous link interface. If the interfaces of sender and receiver are ready to communicate, the message is transferred and both processes involved become executable.

Priorities are only taken into account at the start and termination of the execution of basic statements; a statement can only start its execution if there are no other statements with a higher priority on the same processor which request processor-time at that moment. The execution of an atomic statement, an assignment, a delay-statement, or a communication statement cannot be interrupted. After the execution of an input or output statement there are two possibilities: either it waits for a partner or it starts the communication if a partner is available. In both cases other statements can be executed simultaneously. Concerning the meaning of the programs discussed previously we can now be more precise:

- The priority of an internal communication is the minimum of the priorities of both communication statements, since both partners must have been executed before the communication takes place.

  Example 5.3 Consider again $\ll \textbf{prio}\ 1\ (c!0) \parallel \textbf{prio}\ 2\ (x := 2) \parallel \textbf{prio}\ 3\ (c?y) \gg$. First the input statement is executed because it has the highest priority, and its link interface starts waiting for a partner. Next the assignment has the highest priority and is executed. Finally, the output statement is the only requesting statement and after its execution the communication along channel c takes place. □

- In case of equal priorities a nondeterministic choice is made (to abstract from specific scheduling policies). So with equal priorities we obtain all possible interleavings. No fairness assumptions are made.
- The priorities of statements on different processors are incomparable. Only the relative ordering of priorities on a single processor determines the execution order on that processor.

Example 5.4 Consider

$\ll$ **prio** 1 $(c!0)$ $\|$ **prio** 5 $(d?x) \gg \| \ll$ **prio** 4 $(c?y)$ $\|$ **prio** 3 $(d!1) \gg$.

Then first the two input statements are executed on each processor. Next the two output statements are executed and, assuming that the execution times of statements on both processors are equal, the two communications are performed simultaneously. The program above has exactly the same behaviour as:

$\ll$ **prio** 1 $(c!0)$ $\|$ **prio** 2 $(d?x) \gg \| \ll$ **prio** 2 $(c?y)$ $\|$ **prio** 1 $(d!1) \gg$.

Compare this with

$\ll$ **prio** 1 $(c!0)$ $\|$ **prio** 2 $(x := 4) \gg \| \ll$ **prio** 3 $(c?y)$ $\|$ **prio** 2 $(z := 5) \gg$

where first the assignment to x is performed concurrently with the execution of the input statement. As soon as the assignment to x has terminated the output statement is executed, and then—when the input statement has terminated—the communication takes place. Note that, depending on the execution times, the c-communication might overlap in time with the assignment to z. □

An algorithm which describes the operational execution of programs and a formal denotational semantics of the language can be found in [Hoo91a]. In [GL90] a priority-based process algebra is presented for a related programming language.

5.3 Basic Timing Assumptions

We assume that **skip** and priority assignments do not take any execution time. Any other statement has to wait until a processor becomes available and it can be executed. Then the execution of **atomic** (d) takes exactly d time units. Further, assume given positive constants T_{exec}, T_{assign}, and T_{comm}. The execution of a **delay** e statement takes T_{exec} time units and then it releases the processor for $max(0, e)$ time units. The execution of communication statements requires T_{exec} time units, and the actual communication (i.e., without waiting) takes T_{comm} time units. A guarded command executes during T_{exec} time units to evaluate the booleans.

Moreover, bounds must be given on how long a process is allowed to wait with the execution of a primitive statement when a processor is available, and with the execution of an input or output statement when a communication partner is available. As before, we assume *maximal progress* which means that a process never waits unnecessarily; if execution can proceed it will do so immediately. Note that there are now two possible reasons for a process to wait:

- Wait to execute an input or output statement because no communication partner is available. Since we assume that for each channel special link interfaces are available, we have maximal progress for communications. Hence two statements $c!$ and $c?$ are not allowed to wait simultaneously. As soon as both partners are available the communication must take place. Thus maximal progress implies minimal waiting for communications.

- Wait to execute an atomic statement because the processor is not available. The maximal progress constraint implies that if a processor is idle (that is, no statement is executing) then also no statement on that processor requests execution time. Hence we also have minimal waiting for processor-time.

6 Extension of the Proof System

To reason compositionally about the real-time behaviour of processes that share a processor, we have to extend the assertion language from section 3. Since statements are scheduled on the basis of their priorities, we add primitives to denote the priorities of the statements that are requesting to be executed and the priority of the executing statement. By means of these primitives we formulate a compositional Hoare-style axiomatization of our extended programming language in section 6.2. In this proof system there is a general requirement that the priority of an executing statement is greater than or equal to the priority of every requesting statement. We obtain this property by using priority ∞ during the execution of an atomic, uninterruptable, statement.

6.1 Extension Assertion Language

The assertion language is extended by primitives $req(exp)$ and $exec(exp)$ to express sets of priorities of, respectively, requesting and executing statements at time exp.

- $req(exp)$ denotes the set of priorities of all statements requesting to be executed at time exp.
- $exec(exp)$ denotes the set containing the priority of the statement executing at time exp. For this set there are three possibilities:
  - $exec(t) = \emptyset$ if no statement is executing at time t,
  - $exec(t) = \{p\}$ if a statement with priority p starts its execution at t, and
  - $exec(t) = \{\infty\}$ if an atomic statement is executed in an uninterruptable mode at t.

We use $pset_1 \leq pset_2$, for sets of priorities $pset_1$ and $pset_2$, to denote that every priority in $pset_1$ is less than or equal to any priority in $pset_2$:

- $pset_1 \leq pset_2$ iff for all $p_1 \in pset_1$, $p_2 \in pset_2$: $p_1 \leq p_2$.

Note that we can consider *req* and *exec* as functions from *TIME* to sets of priorities. For an easy formulation of proof rules it is convenient to have logical variables with the same functionality. Hence, in addition to *VVAR* and *TVAR*, we have a set *PVAR*, with typical elements $R, R_1, E, E_1, \ldots$, ranging over functions from *TIME* to sets of priorities.

In addition to the previously defined abbreviations, the *req* and *exec* functions are extended to intervals of time points (we list the abbreviations for left-closed right-open interval $[t_1, t_2\rangle$; similar abbreviations are used for open intervals and expressions instead of t_1 and t_2).

- $req[t_1, t_2\rangle = pset \;\equiv\; \forall t, t_1 \le t < t_2 : req(t) = pset$
- $exec[t_1, t_2\rangle = pset \;\equiv\; \forall t, t_1 \le t < t_2 : exec(t) = pset$
- $no\ ReqExec\ during\ [t_1, t_2\rangle \;\equiv\; req[t_1, t_2\rangle = \emptyset \wedge exec[t_1, t_2\rangle = \emptyset$

6.2 Proof System

We show how the proof system of section 4 can be adapted to multiprogramming. For any program P we can use the consequence rule, the initial invariance axiom, the channel invariance axiom, the conjunction rule, and the substitution rule from section 4. In the well-formedness axiom we add a predicate to express that the priority of a requesting statement is never higher than the priority of an execution statement. Let *cset* be a finite subset of *DCHAN*.

Axiom 6.1 (Well-Formedness) $\quad WF_c \;:\; \{true\}\ P\ \{WF_c\}$

where $WF_c \equiv \forall t < time : MW_c(t) \wedge Excl_c(t) \wedge Comm_c(t) \wedge Prio(t)$,
with $MW_c(t)$, $Excl_c(t)$ and $Comm_c(t)$ defined as in section 4 and

$$Prio(t) \equiv req(t) \le exec(t).$$

(The priority of a requesting statement is less than or equal to the priority of an executing statement.)

We include the skip axiom, the sequential composition rule and the iteration rule from section 4. In the rule for **atomic** (d) we express that first there is a period during which the statement is requesting execution time and if this period is finite then it will execute during d time units. Since no priority has been assigned to the statement, we use priority 0 (this priority can be overwritten by an explicit priority assignment, see rule 6.7). In the rule we use the following abbreviations:

- $request\ during\ [t_1, t_2\rangle \;\equiv\; req[t_1, t_2\rangle = \{0\} \wedge exec[t_1, t_2\rangle = \emptyset$
- $execute\ during\ [t_1, t_2\rangle \;\equiv$
$$(t_1 < \infty \rightarrow exec(t_1) = \{0\}) \wedge exec\langle t_1, t_2\rangle = \{\infty\} \wedge req[t_1, t_2\rangle = \emptyset$$

Observe that at the start of an execution period *exec* equals the set $\{0\}$ which represents a claim of the statement that there is no statement requesting to be executed with a higher priority at that moment. After this starting point an atomic statement executes uninterruptable with priority ∞.

Rule 6.2 (Atomic)

$$\frac{p[t_0/time] \wedge \exists t \geq t_0 : request\ during\ [t_0, t) \wedge execute\ during\ [t, t+d) \wedge time = t + d \rightarrow C \wedge q}{C \ : \ \{p\}\ \textbf{atomic}\ (d)\ \{q \wedge time < \infty\}}$$

Note that, to obtain a compositional proof system, the rule allows any arbitrary waiting period, including an infinite one (for $t = \infty$).

In the rule for an assignment we view this statement as an action **atomic** (T_{assign}), which requests to be executed and, if possible, executes during T_{assign} time units, followed by the actual assignment of e to x.

Rule 6.3 (Assignment)

$$\frac{C_0 \ : \ \{p\}\ \textbf{atomic}\ (T_{assign})\ \{\hat{p}\} \qquad \hat{p} \rightarrow C_1 \wedge q[e/x]}{(C_0 \wedge time = \infty) \vee C_1 \ : \ \{p\}\ x := e\ \{q\}}$$

Note that the statement **atomic** (T_{assign}) need not terminate. If the processor is never available, because its priority is too low, then it requests processor time forever. This is represented in the rule by $C_0 \wedge time = \infty$.

The rule for the **delay** e statement is very similar to the rule above. After the execution of the statement during T_{exec} time units, there is an additional delay-period during which the processor is released. Observe that we explicitly express that during this period the statement does not request execution time nor executes.

Rule 6.4 (Delay)

$$\frac{\begin{array}{l} C_0 \ : \ \{p\}\ \textbf{atomic}\ (T_{exec})\ \{\hat{p}\} \\ \hat{p}[t_0/time] \wedge no\ ReqExec\ during\ [t_0, t_0 + max(0,e)) \wedge time = t_0 + max(0,e) \rightarrow C_1 \wedge q \end{array}}{(C_0 \wedge time = \infty) \vee C_1 \ : \ \{p\}\ \textbf{delay}\ e\ \{q \wedge time < \infty\}}$$

Note that a delay-statement in this multiprogramming language can be considered as the sequential composition of **atomic** (T_{exec}) and a delay statement from the language of section 3 and 4.

For a send or receive statement we also have atomic execution during T_{exec} time units. Furthermore, the rule expresses that the statement does not request execution time or executes during the waiting or communication period.

Rule 6.5 (Output)

$$\frac{\begin{array}{l} C_0 \;:\; \{p\}\ \textbf{atomic}\ (T_{exec})\ \{\hat{p}\} \\ \hat{p}[t_0/time] \wedge \exists t \geq t_0 : \textit{wait } c! \textit{ at } t_0 \textit{ until comm } (c,e) \textit{ at } t \wedge \\ \qquad \textit{no ReqExec during } [t_0, t+T_{comm}\rangle \wedge time = t + T_{comm} \\ \qquad\quad \rightarrow C_1 \wedge q \end{array}}{(C_0 \wedge time = \infty) \vee C_1 \;:\; \{p\}\ c!e\ \{q \wedge time < \infty\}}$$

Similar to the output rule, we have the following rule for a receive statement.

Rule 6.6 (Input)

$$\frac{\begin{array}{l} C_0 \;:\; \{p\}\ \textbf{atomic}\ (T_{exec})\ \{\hat{p}\} \\ \hat{p}[t_0/time] \wedge \exists t \geq t_0 : \textit{wait } c? \textit{ at } t_0 \textit{ until comm } (c,v) \textit{ at } t \wedge \\ \qquad \textit{no ReqExec during } [t_0, t+T_{comm}\rangle \wedge time = t + T_{comm} \\ \qquad\quad \rightarrow C_1 \wedge q[v/x] \end{array}}{(C_0 \wedge time = \infty) \vee C_1 \;:\; \{p\}\ c?x\ \{q \wedge time < \infty\}}$$

The rules for guarded commands can be obtained from the rules 4.15 and 4.16 by replacing **delay** T_{exec} by **atomic** (T_{exec}). For $G \equiv [[]_{i=1}^{n} b_i; c_i?x_i \rightarrow S_i [] b_0; \textbf{delay}\ e \rightarrow S_0]$ we modify rule 4.17 similarly, and we use the following, extended, abbreviations:

- $\textit{wait in } G \textit{ during } [t_0, t_1\rangle \equiv \bigwedge_{i=1}^{n}(b_i \leftrightarrow \textit{wait } c_i? \textit{ during } [t_0, t_1\rangle) \wedge$
  $\textit{no } (dch(G) - \{c_1?, \ldots, c_n?\}) \textit{ during } [t_0, t_1\rangle \wedge$
  $\textit{no ReqExec during } [t_0, t_1\rangle$, and
- $\textit{await comm } G \textit{ at } t_0 \equiv \exists t \geq t_0 : \textit{wait in } G \textit{ during } [t_0, t\rangle \wedge (b_0 \rightarrow t < max(0, e)) \wedge$
  $\exists i \in \{1, \ldots, n\} : b_i \wedge \textit{comm } c_i \textit{ during } [t, t + T_{comm}\rangle \wedge$
  $\textit{no } (dch(G) - \{c_i\}) \textit{ during } [t, t + T_{comm}\rangle \wedge$
  $\textit{no ReqExec during } [t_0, t + T_{comm}\rangle \wedge time = t + T_{comm}$.

To formulate a rule for $\textbf{prio}\, e(S)$, we define the following predicate which replaces priority 0 by e in the *req* and *exec* functions of S which are represented by R and E.

$$\begin{array}{l} ReplacePrio(t_0, e, R, E) \equiv \forall t, t_0 \leq t < time : \\ \qquad (R(t) = \{0\} \rightarrow req(t) = \{e\}) \wedge (R(t) \neq \{0\} \rightarrow req(t) = R(t)) \wedge \\ \qquad (E(t) = \{0\} \rightarrow exec(t) = \{e\}) \wedge (E(t) \neq \{0\} \rightarrow exec(t) = E(t)). \end{array}$$

This is used in the following rule:

Rule 6.7 (Priority Assignment)

$$\frac{\begin{array}{l} C \;:\; \{p\}\ S\ \{q\} \\ C[R/req, E/exec] \wedge ReplacePrio(t_0, e, R, E) \rightarrow C_1 \\ q[R/req, E/exec] \wedge ReplacePrio(t_0, e, R, E) \rightarrow q_1 \end{array}}{C_1 \;:\; \{p \wedge time = t_0\}\ \textbf{prio}\ e\ (S)\ \{q_1\}}$$

In the rule for parallel composition we require, in addition to the rule of section 4, that at most one process is executing. Furthermore, we take the union of the *req* and *exec* sets.

$$Par_{t_0}(C_1,C_2) \equiv \bigwedge_{i=1}^{2} C_i[t_i/time, R_i/req, E_i/exec] \wedge time = max(t_1,t_2) \wedge$$
$$\forall t, t_0 \leq t < time : (E_1(t) = \emptyset \vee E_2(t) = \emptyset) \wedge$$
$$(req(t) = R_1(t) \cup R_2(t)) \wedge$$
$$(exec(t) = E_1(t) \cup E_2(t))$$

Rule 6.8 (Parallel Composition)

$$\frac{C_i \ : \ \{p_i\}\ P_i\ \{q_i\},\ i=1,2 \qquad Par_{t_0}(C_1,C_2) \rightarrow C, \quad Par_{t_0}(q_1,q_2) \rightarrow q}{C \ : \ \{p_1 \wedge p_2 \wedge time = t_0\}\ P_1 \| P_2\ \{q\}}$$

provided $dch(C_i, q_i) \subseteq dch(P_i)$ and $var(q_i) \subseteq var(P_i)$, for $i \in \{1,2\}$.

In the rule for processor closure we require that no process is requesting execution time if the processor is idle, i.e., if no process is executing. Define
$NoIdle_{t_0} \equiv \forall t, t_0 \leq t < time : exec(t) = \emptyset \rightarrow req(t) = \emptyset$.

Rule 6.9 (Processor Closure)

$$\frac{C \ : \ \{p\}\ S\ \{q\} \qquad C \wedge NoIdle_{t_0} \rightarrow C_1, \quad q \wedge NoIdle_{t_0} \rightarrow q_1}{C_1 \ : \ \{p \wedge time = t_0\}\ \ll S \gg\ \{q_1\}}$$

provided *req* and *exec* do not occur in C_1 and q_1.

Example 6.1 Consider $P \equiv \ll S_1 \| S_2 \gg$, with $S_1 \equiv$ **prio** $1\ (\star[in_1?x_1 \rightarrow comp_1\ ;\ out_1!y_1])$ and $S_2 \equiv$ **prio** $2\ (\star[in_2?x_2 \rightarrow comp_2\ ;\ out_2!y_2])$. Define $A_i \equiv \forall t : \neg wait\ out_i!\ at\ t$, for $i = 1,2$. The aim is to find constants D_1 and D_2 such that program P with precondition $time = 0$ satisfies the following commitment

$$\forall i \in \{1,2\} : A_i \rightarrow await\ in_i?\ at\ (3-i) \times T_{exec} \wedge$$
$$(end\ comm\ in_i\ at\ t_0 \rightarrow \exists t_1, t_0 < t_1 \leq t_0 + D_i : await\ in_i?\ at\ t_1)$$

Assume, for $i = 1,2$, $dch(comp_i) \cap \{in_i, out_i\} = \emptyset$ and

$time = t + T_i \ : \ \{time = t \wedge x_i = v\}\ comp_i\ \{y_i = f_i(v)\}$.

Next we give specifications for S_1 and S_2 which turn out to be strong enough to derive the required conditions on D_1 and D_2. The main observation is that between two successive communications on in_1 the process S_1 has three points at which it can only continue if S_2 does not (request to) execute. Thus the waiting time at these points depends on S_2 and we have to know how much time S_2 will use in three successive execution periods. This is expressed in assertion C_{24} below. On the other hand, between two successive communications on in_2, S_2 has two points at which it might have to wait because S_1 is executing uninterruptable, namely directly after the in_2 and out_2 communications. Note that S_2 does not have to wait between $comp_2$ and out_2 because it has the highest priority. Consequently, in assertion C_{15} below we express how long S_1 is executing uninterruptable in two successive execution periods.

For S_1, with precondition $time = 0$, we can prove the commitment $C_1 \equiv C_{10} \wedge C_{11} \wedge C_{12} \wedge C_{13} \wedge C_{14} \wedge C_{15}$ with

$$C_{10} \equiv time = \infty$$

$$C_{11} \equiv \exists t_1 : req[0, t_1\rangle = \{1\} \wedge\ exec[t_1, t_1 + T_{exec}\rangle \neq \emptyset \wedge \text{await } in_1? \text{ at } t_1 + T_{exec}$$

$$\begin{aligned} C_{12} \equiv\ & A_1 \wedge end\ comm\ in_1\ at\ t_0 \rightarrow \\ & \exists t_1 \geq t_0 : req[t_0, t_1\rangle = \{1\} \wedge\ exec[t_1, t_1 + T_1\rangle \neq \emptyset \wedge \\ & \exists t_2 \geq t_1 + T_1 : req[t_1 + T_1, t_2\rangle = \{1\} \wedge\ exec[t_2, t_2 + T_{exec}\rangle \neq \emptyset \wedge \\ & \exists t_3 \geq t_2 + T_{exec} + T_{comm} : req[t_2 + T_{exec} + T_{comm}, t_3\rangle = \{1\} \wedge \\ & \qquad await\ in_1?\ at\ t_3 + T_{exec} \end{aligned}$$

$$C_{13} \equiv \forall t : (req(t) \subseteq \{1\}) \wedge (exec(t) \subset \{1, \infty\}) \wedge (req(t) \neq \emptyset \rightarrow exec(t) = \emptyset)$$

$$C_{14} \equiv \forall t_1, t_2, t_3, t_1 < t_2 \leq t_3 : (exec[t_1, t_2\rangle = \emptyset \vee t_2 = 0) \wedge exec[t_2, t_3\rangle = \{\infty\} \rightarrow t_2 = t_3$$

$$\begin{aligned} C_{15} \equiv\ & \forall t_1, t_2, t_3, t_4, t_1 \leq t_2 \leq t_3, t_3 + T_{comm} \leq t_4 : \\ & exec[t_1, t_2\rangle = \{\infty\} \wedge exec[t_2, t_3\rangle = \emptyset \wedge exec[t_3 + T_{comm}, t_4\rangle = \{\infty\} \rightarrow \\ & \qquad (t_2 - t_1) + (t_4 - t_3 - T_{comm}) \leq T_1 + T_{exec} \end{aligned}$$

C_{12} denotes the request and execute behaviour between two successive communications on channel in_1. C_{14} expresses that an execution period never starts with priority ∞. Observe that this is a general property of programs.

For S_2 we have commitment $C_2 \equiv C_{20} \wedge C_{21} \wedge C_{22} \wedge C_{23} \wedge C_{24}$ with

$$C_{20} \equiv time = \infty$$

$$\begin{aligned} C_{21} \equiv\ & \exists t_1 : req[0, t_1\rangle = \{2\} \wedge\ exec[t_1, t_1 + T_{exec}\rangle \neq \emptyset \wedge \\ & \quad \text{await } in_2? \text{ at } t_1 + T_{exec} \wedge exec(t_1 + T_{exec}) = \emptyset \end{aligned}$$

$$\begin{aligned} C_{22} \equiv\ & A_2 \wedge end\ comm\ in_2\ at\ t_0 \rightarrow \\ & \exists t_1 \geq t_0 : req[t_0, t_1\rangle = \{2\} \wedge\ exec[t_1, t_1 + T_2\rangle \neq \emptyset \wedge \\ & \exists t_2 \geq t_1 + T_2 : req[t_1 + T_2, t_2\rangle = \{2\} \wedge\ exec[t_2, t_2 + T_{exec}\rangle \neq \emptyset \wedge \\ & \exists t_3 \geq t_2 + T_{exec} + T_{comm} : req[t_2 + T_{exec} + T_{comm}, t_3\rangle = \{2\} \wedge \\ & \qquad await\ in_2?\ at\ t_3 + T_{exec} \end{aligned}$$

$$C_{23} \equiv \forall t : (req(t) \subseteq \{2\}) \wedge (exec(t) \subset \{2, \infty\}) \wedge (req(t) \neq \emptyset \rightarrow exec(t) = \emptyset)$$

$$\begin{aligned} C_{24} \equiv\ & \forall t_1, t_2, t_3, t_4, t_5, t_6, t_1 \leq t_2 \leq t_3 \leq t_4 \leq t_5, t_5 + T_{comm} \leq t_6 : \\ & exec[t_1, t_2\rangle \neq \emptyset \wedge exec[t_2, t_3\rangle = \emptyset \wedge\ exec[t_3, t_4\rangle \neq \emptyset \wedge \\ & exec[t_4, t_5\rangle = \emptyset \wedge\ exec[t_5 + T_{comm}, t_6\rangle \neq \emptyset \rightarrow \\ & \qquad (t_2 - t_1) + (t_4 - t_3) + (t_6 - t_5 - T_{comm}) \leq 2 \times T_2 + 3 \times T_{exec} \end{aligned}$$

Combining these two specifications with the rules for parallel composition and processor closure (observe that $time = \infty$ by C_{11} and C_{21}), we obtain the commitment
$C \equiv C_1[R_1/req, E_1/exec] \wedge C_2[R_2/req, E_2/exec] \wedge \forall t : (E_1(t) = \emptyset \vee E_2(t) = \emptyset) \wedge$
$(req(t) = R_1(t) \cup R_2(t)) \wedge (exec(t) = E_1(t) \cup E_2(t)) \wedge (exec(t) = \emptyset \rightarrow req(t) = \emptyset)$.
Further, we add by the well-formedness axiom and the conjunction rule:
$\forall t : Prio(t)$, that is, $\forall t : req(t) \leq exec(t)$. Let $\hat{C}_{ij}$ denote $C_{ij}[R_i/req, E_i/exec]$.

Lemma 6.10 $C \rightarrow \forall t : R_1(t) \leq E_2(t) \wedge R_2(t) \leq E_1(t)$

Proof: This lemma follows directly from $Prio(t)$, $req(t) = R_1(t) \cup R_2(t)$ and $exec(t) = E_1(t) \cup E_2(t)$. □

Lemma 6.11 $C \rightarrow (\forall t : R_2(t) = \{2\} \rightarrow E_1(t) = \{\infty\})$

Proof: Assume $C \wedge R_2(t) = \{2\}$. Then from $req(t) = R_1(t) \cup R_2(t)$ we obtain $req(t) \neq \emptyset$, and by $exec(t) = \emptyset \rightarrow req(t) = \emptyset$ this leads to $exec(t) \neq \emptyset$. By $R_2(t) = \{2\}$ and $\hat{C}_{23}$ we have $E_2(t) = \emptyset$. Hence, using $exec(t) = E_1(t) \cup E_2(t)$, we obtain $E_1(t) \neq \emptyset$. From $R_2(t) = \{2\}$ and $Prio(t)$ we derive $E_1(t) \geq \{2\}$. Since, by $\hat{C}_{13}$, $E_1(t) \subset \{1, \infty\}$, this leads to $E_1(t) = \{\infty\}$. □
Similarly we can prove:

Lemma 6.12 $C \rightarrow (\forall t : R_1(t) = \{1\} \rightarrow E_2(t) \neq \emptyset)$

First we prove *await* in_1? *at* $2 \times T_{exec} \wedge$ *await* in_2? *at* T_{exec}.
By $\hat{C}_{21}$ we obtain
$\exists t_1 : R_2[0, t_1\rangle = \{2\} \wedge E_2[t_1, t_1 + T_{exec}\rangle \neq \emptyset \wedge$
await in_2? at $t_1 + T_{exec} \wedge E_2(t_1 + T_{exec}) = \emptyset$.
Using lemma 6.11 this leads to
$\exists t_1 : E_1[0, t_1\rangle = \{\infty\} \wedge E_2[t_1, t_1 + T_{exec}\rangle \neq \emptyset \wedge$
await in_2? at $t_1 + T_{exec} \wedge E_2(t_1 + T_{exec}) = \emptyset$.
By $\hat{C}_{14}$, $E_1[0, t_1\rangle = \{\infty\}$ implies $t_1 = 0$, and thus await in_2? at T_{exec}.
Moreover, $E_2[0, T_{exec}\rangle \neq \emptyset \wedge E_2(T_{exec}) = \emptyset$. Thus $E_1[0, T_{exec}\rangle = \emptyset \wedge E_2(T_{exec}) = \emptyset$.
By $\hat{C}_{11}$, $\exists t_1 : R_1[0, t_1\rangle = \{1\} \wedge E_1[t_1, t_1 + T_{exec}\rangle \neq \emptyset \wedge$ await in_1? at $t_1 + T_{exec}$.
Using lemma 6.12 and $\hat{C}_{13}$, $\exists t_1 : E_2[0, t_1\rangle \neq \emptyset \wedge E_1(t_1) \neq \emptyset \wedge$ await in_1? at $t_1 + T_{exec}$.
By $E_1[0, T_{exec}\rangle = \emptyset$ and $E_1(t_1) \neq \emptyset$ we have $T_{exec} \leq t_1$. From $E_2(T_{exec}) = \emptyset$ and $E_2[0, t_1\rangle \neq \emptyset$, we obtain $t_1 \leq T_{exec}$, and hence $t_1 = T_{exec}$. Thus await in_1? at $2 \times T_{exec}$.

Next we prove:

$$A_2 \rightarrow (end\ comm\ in_2\ at\ t_0 \rightarrow \exists t_1, t_0 < t_1 \leq t_0 + D_2 : await\ in_2?\ at\ t_1)$$

Assume A_2 and *end comm* in_2 *at* t_0. From $\hat{C}_{22}$ we obtain

$\exists t_1 \geq t_0 : R_2[t_0, t_1\rangle = \{2\} \wedge\ E_2[t_1, t_1 + T_2\rangle \neq \emptyset \wedge$
$\exists t_2 \geq t_1 + T_2 : R_2[t_1 + T_2, t_2\rangle = \{2\} \wedge\ E_2[t_2, t_2 + T_{exec}\rangle \neq \emptyset \wedge$
$\exists t_3 \geq t_2 + T_{exec} + T_{comm} : R_2[t_2 + T_{exec} + T_{comm}, t_3\rangle = \{2\} \wedge$
$\textit{await } in_2? \textit{ at } t_3 + T_{exec}$

Consider $E_2[t_1, t_1 + T_2\rangle = \{\infty\} \wedge R_2[t_1 + T_2, t_2\rangle = \{2\}$. By $E_1(t) = \emptyset \vee E_2(t) = \emptyset$ and lemma 6.11 this leads to $E_1[t_1, t_1 + T_2\rangle = \emptyset \wedge E_1[t_1 + T_2, t_2\rangle = \{\infty\}$. By $\hat{C}_{14}$ this implies $t_2 = t_1 + T_2$. Hence, we have

$\exists t_1 \geq t_0 : R_2[t_0, t_1\rangle = \{2\} \wedge\ E_2[t_1, t_1 + T_2 + T_{exec}\rangle \neq \emptyset \wedge$
$\exists t_3 \geq t_1 + T_2 + T_{exec} + T_{comm} : R_2[t_1 + T_2 + T_{exec} + T_{comm}, t_3\rangle = \{2\} \wedge$
$\textit{await } in_2? \textit{ at } t_3 + T_{exec}$

By $E_2(t) \neq \emptyset \rightarrow E_1(t) = \emptyset$ and lemma 6.11 this leads to

$\exists t_1 \geq t_0 : E_1[t_0, t_1\rangle = \{\infty\} \wedge\ E_1[t_1, t_1 + T_2 + T_{exec}\rangle = \emptyset \wedge$
$\exists t_3 \geq t_1 + T_2 + T_{exec} + T_{comm} : E_1[t_1 + T_2 + T_{exec} + T_{comm}, t_3\rangle = \{\infty\} \wedge$
$\textit{await } in_2? \textit{ at } t_3 + T_{exec}$

Then, by $\hat{C}_{15}$, we have $(t_1 - t_0) + (t_3 - (t_1 + T_2 + T_{exec} + T_{comm})) \leq T_1 + T_{exec}$, that is, $t_3 \leq t_0 + T_2 + T_{exec} + T_{comm} + T_1 + T_{exec}$. Hence $t_3 + T_{exec} \leq t_0 + T_1 + T_2 + T_{comm} + 3 \times T_{exec}$. Thus take $D_2 = T_1 + T_2 + T_{comm} + 3 \times T_{exec}$.

Finally we prove

$$A_1 \rightarrow (\textit{end comm } in_1 \textit{ at } t_0 \rightarrow \exists t_1, t_0 < t_1 \leq t_0 + D_1 : \textit{await } in_1? \textit{ at } t_1)$$

Assume A_1 and *end comm* in_1 *at* t_0. From $\hat{C}_{12}$ we obtain

$\exists t_1 \geq t_0 : R_1[t_0, t_1\rangle = \{1\} \wedge\ E_1[t_1, t_1 + T_1\rangle \neq \emptyset \wedge$
$\exists t_2 \geq t_1 + T_1 : R_1[t_1 + T_1, t_2\rangle = \{1\} \wedge\ E_1[t_2, t_2 + T_{exec}\rangle \neq \emptyset \wedge$
$\exists t_3 \geq t_2 + T_{exec} + T_{comm} : R_1[t_2 + T_{exec} + T_{comm}, t_3\rangle = \{1\} \wedge\ \textit{await } in_1? \textit{ at } t_3 + T_{exec}$

Using $E_1(t) \neq \emptyset \rightarrow E_2(t) = \emptyset$ and lemma 6.12 this leads to

$\exists t_1 \geq t_0 : E_2[t_0, t_1\rangle \neq \emptyset \wedge\ E_2[t_1, t_1 + T_1\rangle = \emptyset \wedge$
$\exists t_2 \geq t_1 + T_1 : E_2[t_1 + T_1, t_2\rangle \neq \emptyset \wedge\ E_2[t_2, t_2 + T_{exec}\rangle = \emptyset \wedge$
$\exists t_3 \geq t_2 + T_{exec} + T_{comm} : E_2[t_2 + T_{exec} + T_{comm}, t_3\rangle \neq \emptyset \wedge\ \textit{await } in_1? \textit{ at } t_3 + T_{exec}$

By $\hat{C}_{24}$, $(t_1 - t_0) + (t_2 - t_1 - T_1) + (t_3 - t_2 - T_{exec} - T_{comm}) \leq 2 \times T_2 + 3 \times T_{exec}$, and thus $t_3 \leq t_0 + T_1 + 2 \times T_2 + T_{comm} + 4 \times T_{exec}$. Hence $t_3 + T_{exec} \leq t_0 + T_1 + 2 \times T_2 + T_{comm} + 5 \times T_{exec}$, and we can take $D_1 = T_1 + 2 \times T_2 + T_{comm} + 5 \times T_{exec}$.

Now consider the example from the introduction where $T_1 = 10$, $T_2 = 50$, and S_1 and S_2 have deadlines of, respectively, 130 and 70. Then we must have that
$D_1 = T_1 + 2 \times T_2 + T_{comm} + 5 \times T_{exec} = 110 + T_{comm} + 5 \times T_{exec} \leq 130$ and
$D_2 = T_1 + T_2 + T_{comm} + 3 \times T_{exec} = 60 + T_{comm} + 3 \times T_{exec} \leq 70$.
Then this program satisfies the specification provided our basic timing assumptions satisfy

the following constraints: $T_{comm} + 5 \times T_{exec} \leq 20$ and $T_{comm} + 3 \times T_{exec} \leq 10$. Finally observe that if $T_{comm} + 3 \times T_{exec} \leq 10$ then $T_{comm} \leq 10 - 3 \times T_{exec}$ and, since all constants are nonnegative, $2 \times T_{exec} \leq 10$. Then $T_{comm} + 5 \times T_{exec} \leq 10 - 3 \times T_{exec} + 5 \times T_{exec} = 10 + 2 \times T_{exec} \leq 20$. Hence we obtain a correct implementation if $T_{comm} + 3 \times T_{exec} \leq 10$. □

7 Conclusion

To verify real-time properties of concurrent programs that communicate via synchronous message passing, we have formulated a compositional proof system for extended Hoare triples. In this framework safety as well as liveness properties can be specified and verified. Related to our approach is an early paper by Haase [Haa81] in which real-time is introduced as a variable in the data space of the program and assertions are derived by Dijkstra's weakest precondition calculus. Recently, in [SBM92] a non-compositional method based on proof outlines with control predicates has been extended to reason about timing properties of concurrent programs that communicate via shared variables.

Our proof method is inspired by the, non-real-time, compositional proof systems of Zwiers [Zwi89]. To compare different approaches we give in [Hoo91b] a compositional axiomatization of our real-time language using a real-time version of temporal logic, called Metric Temporal Logic [Koy90]. An alternative approach can be found in [Ost89] where Explicit Clock Temporal Logic [HLP90] has been used to extend the non-compositional method of [MP82] to real-time. In [HMP91] two proof methodologies have been formulated corresponding to the two real-time versions of temporal logic.

References

[GL90] R. Gerber and I. Lee. CCSR: a calculus for communicating shared resources. In *CONCUR '90*, pages 263–277. LNCS 458, Springer-Verlag, 1990.

[Haa81] V.H. Haase. Real-time behaviour of programs. *IEEE Transactions on Software Engineering*, SE-7(5):494–501, 1981.

[HLP90] E. Harel, O. Lichtenstein, and A. Pnueli. Explicit clock temporal logic. In *Proceedings Symposium on Logic in Computer Science*, pages 402–413, 1990.

[HMP91] T. Henzinger, Z. Manna, and A. Pnueli. Temporal proof methodologies for real-time systems. In *Proceedings 18th ACM Symposium on Principles of Programming Languages*, pages 353–366, 1991.

[Hoa69] C.A.R. Hoare. An axiomatic basis for computer programming. *Communications of the ACM*, 12(10):576–580,583, 1969.

[Hoo91a] J. Hooman. A denotational real-time semantics for shared processors. In *Parallel Architectures and Languages Europe*, volume II, pages 184–201. LNCS 506, Springer-Verlag, 1991.

[Hoo91b] J. Hooman. *Specification and Compositional Verification of Real-Time Systems.* LNCS 558, Springer-Verlag, 1991.

[Koy90] R. Koymans. Specifying real-time properties with metric temporal logic. *Real-Time Systems*, 2(4):255–299, 1990.

[MP82] Z. Manna and A. Pnueli. Verification of concurrent programs: a temporal proof system. In *Foundations of Computer Science IV, Distributed Systems: Part 2*, volume 159 of *Mathematical Centre Tracts*, pages 163–255, 1982.

[Occ88a] INMOS Limited. *Communicating process architecture*, 1988.

[Occ88b] INMOS Limited. OCCAM *2 Reference Manual*, 1988.

[Ost89] J. Ostroff. *Temporal Logic for Real-Time Systems.* Advanced Software Development Series. Research Studies Press, 1989.

[SBM92] F. Schneider, B. Bloom, and K. Marzullo. Putting time into proof outlines. In *REX Workshop on Real-Time: Theory in Practice.* LNCS (this volume), Springer-Verlag, 1992.

[Zwi89] J. Zwiers. *Compositionality, Concurrency and Partial Correctness.* LNCS 321, Springer-Verlag, 1989.

Semantics of Reactive Systems in Abstract Time *

C. Huizing R. Gerth

Eindhoven University of Technology †

Abstract. We explain that real-time reactive systems pose specific problems in defining languages to specify and program them. Three criteria are formulated, responsiveness, modularity, and causality, that are important to have for a high-level specification language for these systems. We prove that these properties can not be combined in one semantics. Since these properties are mandatory for a structured development of real-time reactive systems, we introduce a two-levelled semantics in which the three properties hold on different levels of the semantics: global events are treated more abstractly with respect to time than local events.

Keywords: Real-time, semantics, specification, Statecharts, reactive systems.

Contents

---

*This research is partially supported by ESPRIT projects 937 (DESCARTES) and 3096.

†Department of Mathematics and Computing Science, Eindhoven University of Technology, P.O.Box 513, 5600 MB Eindhoven, The Netherlands. Electronic mail: keesh@win.tue.nl

1 Introduction

There is a fundamental dichotomy in the analysis of computing systems. This dichotomy crosses all borderlines between sequential and parallel systems, central and distributed systems, and between functional and imperative systems. This is the dichotomy between *transformational* and *reactive systems* [HP85]. Transformational systems are well described by a relation between input and output value. They read some input value, then produce, perhaps non-deterministically, an output value and terminate. A reactive system, however, maintains a continuous interaction with its environment. Typically, the environment reacts upon the output of the system and in many cases the system is not expected to terminate.

Reactive systems can be found anywhere: they include digital watches, interactive software systems, integrated circuits, real-time embedded systems. Design, programming and verification of reactive systems is an important challenge, since existing techniques for transformational systems are not satisfactory for this purpose [HP85].

Recently, several formalism for the development of reactive systems have been proposed. We mention Esterel [BG88, BC85], Lustre [BCH85b], and Statecharts [Har87]. In the development of these formalisms, serious problems have been encountered. Apparently, it is not so simple to design a high-level language for reactive systems. The central problem is that all these languages try to combine the following three properties, or criteria, in one formalism. These properties are for the first time formally defined in this paper.

The first property is *responsiveness*, meaning that a system's output comes simultaneously with the input that causes it. This requires an abstract notion of time, since there is always some physical time needed to compute a reaction, ultimately. This property is important for high-level specification where one does not want to bother –yet– with implementation details on the one hand, but on the other hand does want to specify in an accurate, non-fuzzy way. Furthermore, it allows for step-wise refinement, without having to redo the timing over and over again.

The second property, *modularity*, means that all parts of the system should be treated symmetrically. The interface between the environment and the system should be the same as the interface between the parts of the system itself. Furthermore, every part of the system should have the same view of the events occurring in the total system *at any moment.* Consequently, in all the formalisms mentioned above, the communication mechanism between the subsystems is the immediate, asynchronous *broadcast*[1].

The third property, *causality*, means that for any event generated at a particular moment there must be a causal chain of events leading to the action that generated this

[1]If the travelling time of signals is too high, e.g. widely distributed systems, one has to introduce an explicit delay between the moment that an event can be generated and the moment it will actually be sensed by the other components. This can be done in the current framework.

event. No causal loops may occur and no events may be generated "spontaneously", i.e., without an input event that directly or indirectly caused it. This allows for an intuitive, operational understanding of the system's behaviour.

Unfortunately, these three properties can not be united in one semantics, as we prove in the paper. To prepare the way for this result we classify the semantics of reactive systems currently available — for Esterel [BC85, BG88], for Lustre [BCH85b], for Signal [LBBG85], for Statecharts [HPPSS87a, *i-Logix Inc*89, PS88, HGdR88] — in basically 5 types of semantics, each one trying to improve upon the others, but no one succeeding in a semantics which is satisfactory from the point of view of structured program development. To this end a bare-bones language for reactive systems is introduced, which can be identified with subsets of any of these languages for the purpose of our criteria. To define and enable comparison of our various semantics for this language, a simple formalism is introduced for transition systems with edges labelled by event/action pairs. As already stated, we prove that our criteria cannot be met by any uniform semantics[2].

We know a way out, however. Although very useful, the properties of modularity and causality are applied at different levels of development. Modularity is useful at a relative high level, where too much detailed knowledge of the execution of the subsystems would obstruct a good overview of the system. Causality, however, is useful at the level of operational reasoning, where a local part of the system can be completely understood. Therefore, we introduce the concept of *modules* into the language. A module is a relatively independent part of the system, in essence a reactive system in its own right. ***Between*** modules, the principle of modularity holds, thus helping to keep a global understanding of the system. *Within* modules, however, the principle of causality holds, making it possible to develop a smaller subsystem in an intuitive, operational way. This leads to a hybrid semantics: local events, which are used only inside a module, interact in a way satisfying the causality principle, whereas global events, which are used between modules, possibly in the whole system, are treated in a modular fashion.

2 Framework

Let some alphabet of primitive events, Π, be given. Primitive events can be generated by the environment as an input to the system, or by the processes in the system either as an output to the environment or for interaction with other processes of the system. These are instantaneous signals that cannot be interrupted or undone.

We model the behaviour of a reactive system as an infinite sequence of pairs (I, O), where $I, O \subseteq \Pi$. I is the set of input events, possibly containing timing information such as clock ticks. O is the set of output events, containing all events generated by the system. I and O are not necessarily disjunct. The events in I and O are considered to occur at the same time. Hence, the output events are timed by the events. The amount of detail that is desired can be achieved by providing an regular input event of which the timing is known (e.g., the tick of an external clock). The semantics of a reactive system is the

[2]This is serious, and it is worth to reflect a moment on its implications, for it concerns a veritable principle of (reactive) distributed computing. After all, structured program development, together with mechanization, promises the only hope for improving future software quality; and the important producers of critical software, s.a Boeing, McDonald-Douglas, Hughes etc., all use specification systems to which our result applies.

set of all possible behaviours.

We use infinite sequences, since many reactive systems are not expected to terminate. Termination can be modelled by emitting a special output event and after that producing only empty output sets.

If S is a reactive system and S produces output O at the moment that input I is provided, we write

$$S \overset{O}{\underset{I}{\Longrightarrow}} S'$$

In general, the state of the system has changed after the transition; the system with its new state is denoted by S'.

In case of singletons, we sometimes omit the curly braces: $S \overset{e}{\underset{f}{\Longrightarrow}} S'$

Leaving out something in this notation means existential quantification, e.g., $S \underset{I}{\Longrightarrow}$ means $\exists O, S' : S \overset{O}{\underset{I}{\Longrightarrow}} S'$.

We define the semantics $\mathcal{O}(P_0)$ of a reactive system P_0 as the set of all behaviours of the form $(I_1, G_1)(I_2, G_2) \ldots (I_n, G_n) \ldots$ such that there exist systems $P_1, P_2, \ldots, P_n, \ldots$ and for all $i > 0$

$$P_{i-1} \overset{G_i}{\underset{I_i}{\Longrightarrow}} P_i$$

holds.

Here, we give the language in which we express reactive systems and various proposals for the semantics as they have been circulating.

2.1 The language

We consider a very simple derivative of Statecharts in which every reactive system is a composition of flat statecharts, i.e. statecharts without hierarchy of states. Such a flat statechart can be viewed as a transition system where labels associated to transitions have the form "event-expression/action". When the machine is in the source state of such a transition and the event-expression is enabled, the transition will be taken (and if there is no non-determinism present enabling another transition it must be taken) and the action will be performed. This action is the generation of some primitive events. The event-expression is a propositional combination of primitive events, e.g.,

$$(\neg a \wedge b) \vee c\ .$$

A transition labelled with this event-expression becomes enabled either when primitive event c occurs, or when b occurs and a does not occur, or both. Exactly when the action is performed, and exactly what "event a does not occur" means, is different in the various versions of the semantics. A composition of transition systems is executed synchronously: all machines that can perform a transition at some moment, do this simultaneously.

Definition 1 *The set of labels L contains all expressions of the form e/a, where e is a proposition with the events from Π as atomic propositions and $a \subseteq \Pi$.*

A Transition Machine is a triple (S, s, T), where S is a set of states, $s \in S$ is the initial state, $T \subseteq S \times L \times S$ is the set of transitions.

A *Transition Machine*, or simply machine in the context of this paper, differs from the classical Finite State Machine in as much that it has no final state and that its purpose is not to accept words over its event-alphabet, but to serve as part of a formalism to describe reactive systems, since general reactive systems are combinations of synchronously executing transition machines.

Definition 2 *A* machine expression *has the syntax*

$$\langle machine\, exp \rangle \;\;\Rightarrow\;\; [\, \langle label \rangle ; \,]\; [\, \langle state \rangle \,]\; \langle machine \rangle$$

where $\langle machine \rangle$ is an Enhanced Finite State Machine, as defined above, and $\langle state \rangle$ is one of its states. sM stands for M with initial state s, so $s'(S, s, T) = (S, s', T)$. $l; M$ stands for M prefixed with a transition labelled l, so $l; (S, s, T) = (S \cup \{s'\}, s', T \cup \{(s', l, s)\})$, where $s' \notin S$.

A reactive system *is the composition of one or more machine expressions:*

$$\langle reactive\, system \rangle \;\;\Rightarrow\;\; \langle machine\, exp \rangle \,\|\, \ldots \,\|\, \langle machine\, exp \rangle$$

If two reactive systems S_1 and S_2 make a step together we write $S_1 \,\|\, S_2 \overset{O}{\underset{I}{\Longrightarrow}} S_1' \,\|\, S_2'$. If this step is the combination of two local steps $S_1 \overset{O_1}{\underset{I_1}{\Longrightarrow}} S_1'$ and $S_2 \overset{O_1}{\underset{I_1}{\Longrightarrow}} S_2'$, we say that these local steps combine *into the global step.*

Notation If there exists an S' such that $S \overset{O}{\underset{I}{\Longrightarrow}} S'$, we write $S \overset{O}{\underset{I}{\Longrightarrow}}$. If such an S' does not exist, we write $S \overset{O}{\underset{I}{\not\Longrightarrow}}$.

3 Criteria

3.1 Responsiveness

We can now define the criteria on which we judge the semantics.

As we have seen, in a reactive system it is important to know how much time elapses between an input and the resulting output.

One approach is to specify for each situation a concrete amount of time. This is cumbersome and not in accordance to the level of abstraction we are aiming at. It forces us to quantify time right from the beginning. At this stage one is in most cases only interested in the relative order and the coincidence of events.

Another approach is fixing the reaction time to, say, one time unit (assume we have a discrete time domain). This is simpler, but still not abstract, since specifications using this principle are difficult to refine without changing their high level meaning.

This approach has another disadvantage. In practice, a fixed amount of reaction time will be some kind of upperbound upon the execution times of different statements in different situations in the actual implementation. So the implementation will have to be artificially delayed in order to meet its specification. In many cases, however, we want the reaction to be as quick as possible. The delay of 1 time unit was only introduced for uniformity and the implementation is slower than necessary.

A third approach is to leave things open: only say that execution of a reaction takes some positive amount of time and see at a later stage (closer to the actual implementation) how much time things did take. This is also awkward, however, since it introduces a lot of non-determinism, which will make it difficult or even impossible to prove interesting things at an early stage of the development.

In our framework it is possible to specify that a certain reaction to an input comes simultaneously with that input. Although there is always some physical time needed to do the computing, in many cases this time is much shorter than the rate of the incoming events. In other words, the time scale of the computations is much shorter than the time scale of the environment. Therefore, it makes sense to adopt the *abstraction* that the reactions are immediate on the time scale of the environment. Naturally, it depends on the application and the implementation whether this abstraction is reasonable or not.

This abstraction gives us several important advantages:

(i). The reaction time is accurately known (i.e., 0), even at early stages of the development. This is important, since the relative timing of input and output events is important in reactive systems, as we have seen.

(ii). The reaction time does not depend on the actual implementation.

(iii). The reaction time is as short as possible (namely, 0). No artificial delays have to be introduced at an early stage of development to enforce synchronisation. Later on, when the implementation is better known, these delays could turn out unnecessary.

(iv). The timing behaviour is abstract, allowing further refinement without having to redo the timing. E.g., if a certain reaction is refined to include several sub-reactions, the timing behaviour is not changed, since $0 + 0 = 0$.

This approach, which is essentially a strategy of separation of concerns, is advocated by Berry under the name of *synchrony hypothesis*[BC85] and others [HP87]. We call a semantics in which it is possible to perform instantaneous reactions *responsive*.

In our framework this notion can be formalised as follows.

Definition 3 *A system S is* **responsive** *if there exist input sets I_1 and I_2 and output set O such that*

$$S \overset{O}{\underset{I_1}{\Longrightarrow}} \text{ and } S \overset{O}{\underset{I_2}{\not\Longrightarrow}}$$

Responsiveness of a system does not tell you much. It only says that there exist two input sets to which the system reacts differently in the current moment, *i.e. immediately*. A more general property is the following.

Notation:
If a reactive system consists of subsystems $S_1, \ldots, S_n$, we denote this by $S_1 \| \ldots \| S_n$.

Definition 4 *A semantics is* **responsive** *if for any two distinct input sets I_1 and I_2 and non-empty output set O with $O \cap (I_1 \cup I_2) = \emptyset$, there exists a system S such that*

$$S \overset{O}{\underset{I_1}{\Longrightarrow}} \text{ and } S \overset{O}{\underset{I_2}{\not\Longrightarrow}}$$

In other words, any two different inputs can be distinguished and *immediately so*.

3.2 Modularity

The first aspect of modularity is the symmetry of interface. The way the system interacts with, e.g., a human being as part of the environment, should be not different from the way it interacts with another reactive system. In other words, if we put two reactive systems together to form a new, bigger one, they see each other's behaviours as sequences of pairs (I, O), exactly as the environment sees them. In particular, the composition of two reactive systems is defined on basis of their observable behaviours: no inner details of the execution can be seen by the other system.

The second aspect of modularity is the uniformity of the view every subsystem has of what is going on. When an event is generated, it is broadcast all around the system and it is immediately available to everyone. Hence, every part of the system has the same view *at any moment*. This simplifies analysis and design considerably. Of course, this is not realistic for widely distributed systems in which it takes a considerable time for a signal to travel between parts of the system. In this case, one has to introduce an explicit delay between the moment that an event can be generated and the moment it will actually be sensed by the other components. We stress, however, that our framework is designed for tightly coupled systems in which a synchronous execution is realistic.

Definition 5 *A semantics is* **modular** *if for any two systems S_1 and S_2 the following two statements are equivalent:*

(i). $S_1 \parallel S_2 \overset{O}{\underset{I}{\Longrightarrow}} S_1' \parallel S_2'$

(ii). $S_i \overset{O_i}{\underset{I \cup O_{3-i}}{\Longrightarrow}} S_i'$ *for* $i = 1, 2$

where $O = O_1 \cup O_2$ and the first step is the combination of the last two.

In this definition we can see the two aspects of modularity. First, the interface between the subsystems is the same as the interface between a system and its environment, i.e., only the sets I and O are taken into account. Second, the output of one system is immediately available as input to the other one.

3.3 Causality

The combination of the principles modularity and responsiveness is what Gérard Berry calls the *synchrony hypothesis* [BG88]. This combination leads to several semantic problems. First, one can specify systems for which it is unclear what the semantics of their combination should be. The modular combination of these system can create cycles of reactions in which the reaction nullifies the action that caused it In Esterel [BC85],[BG88],[Gon88] and Lustre [BCH85a] combinations like these are simply forbidden. A check at compile time is performed to rule out programs that (might) give problems. In Statecharts [HPPSS87b] the principle of modularity is sacrificed to achieve a semantics in which every program combination is legal. In the next section we discuss all these semantic versions.

Although not modular, these versions have the advantage that they are *causal*: for every event that is generated there is a causal chain of events that leads to this event. In the modular-responsive semantics, however, events can occur "out of the blue"[3].

[3]Unless programs in which this may occur are ruled out, as is done in Esterel and Lustre.

Definition 6 *We call a semantics* **causal** *if we can add to every step $S \overset{O}{\underset{I}{\Longrightarrow}} S'$ a partial order $\preceq$ on $I \cup O$, such that:*

(i). if $S \overset{O}{\underset{I}{\Longrightarrow}}$ and $S \overset{O}{\underset{I'}{\not\Longrightarrow}}$, and $I, O \neq \emptyset$, then there is at least one dependency between I and O, i.e., $\exists a \in I, b \in O$ with $a \preceq b$

(ii). this ordering respects the composition of systems, i.e., if $S_1 \| S_2 \overset{O}{\underset{I}{\Longrightarrow}} S_1' \| S_2'$ with causal order $\preceq$, then there should exist a partitioning into systems $T_1, \ldots, T_n$ with $n \geq 2$, and causal orders $\preceq_1, \ldots, \preceq_n$ such that

- *$\preceq \restriction (I_i \cup O_i) = \preceq_i$ and*
- *$T_1 \| \ldots \| T_n = S_1 \| S_2$, and*
- *for each i, there exists a T_i', such that $T_i \overset{O_i}{\underset{I_i}{\Longrightarrow}} T_i'$ and these steps combine into the step of $S_1 \| S_2$.*

Here, $\restriction$ denotes the restriction of a relation.

Theorem 1 *No semantics of reactive systems can be responsive, modular and causal at the same time.*

Proof:
Suppose the contrary. Take events a, b with $a \neq b$. Then, by responsiveness, there must be S_1 and S_2 with

$S_1 \overset{b}{\underset{a}{\Longrightarrow}} S_1'$ and $S_1 \overset{b}{\underset{\emptyset}{\not\Longrightarrow}}$ and

$S_2 \overset{a}{\underset{b}{\Longrightarrow}} S_2'$ and $S_2 \overset{a}{\underset{\emptyset}{\not\Longrightarrow}}$.

If causality holds, there must be partial orders $\preceq_1$ and $\preceq_2$, such that $a \preceq_1 b$ and $b \preceq_2 a$, since there is a dependency between $\{a\}$ and $\{b\}$, resp. $\{b\}$ and $\{a\}$.

By modularity, we must have

$$S_1 \| S_2 \overset{\{a,b\}}{\underset{\emptyset}{\Longrightarrow}} S_1' \| S_2'$$

and for this step no causal order exists that respects $\preceq_1$ and $\preceq_2$, since $a \neq b$. □

4 Semantics

We now describe five versions of semantics for reactive systems in the framework described above.

A The events generated as a reaction to some input can only be sensed in the step following the input. The main drawback of this solution is that it is not possible to express simultaneity of action and reaction. Specifying a chain of reactions and independently the reaction time becomes cumbersome, because every element in the chain adds one step to the reaction time. This semantics is not *responsive.*

B In order to make the semantics responsive, the notion of *micro-step* was introduced. Every observable step is divided into an arbitrary number of micro-steps. Action and reaction strictly follow each other in micro-steps, but observably take place simultaneously. A detailed treatment of this semantics, applied to full Statecharts, can be found in [HPPSS87b] (operational model) and [HG89] (fully abstract model). The problem with this semantics is that it introduces a lot of non-determinism: if you take the micro-steps in a different order, you may get a different observable result. This semantics turned out to be too subtle and non-deterministic to be of practical use.

C Semantics C overcomes this problem by demanding global consistency of every micro-step. This means that a reaction of the system should not only be enabled by the events generated in previous micro-steps, but also be enabled by the set of events generated in the full macro-step. A full description of this semantics can be found in [PS88]; [HR88] gives an axiomatisation of Statecharts based on this semantics. Semantics C does not fully solve the problem of *modularity*, i.e., the behaviour of a process cannot be explained only in terms of macro-steps. This implies that a modular development of the system is cumbersome, since every developer has to know the detailed micro-behaviour of the other processes.

D In semantics D all events that are generated during some macro-step are considered as if they were present right from the start of the step, no matter at which particular micro-step they were generated. As a consequence, the macro-behaviour of a process suffices to describe its interaction with other processes. The advantage of semantics C over D, however, is that the first respects *causality*: each reaction can be traced back to the input from the environment via chain of reactions each causing the next one. In semantics D, however, it is possible that reactions trigger themselves. The languages Esterel, Lustre, and Argos [Mar89, Mar90] follow this approach. The appendix gives the relationship between Esterel and this semantics in detail.

E The current implementation of Statecharts models this fifth version of the semantics. This is an "acceleration" of semantics A. Events are generated at the next step, but before the reaction of the system has completely died out, no input from the environment is possible. This semantics is heavily non-modular, since one macro-step may contain several steps of the type of semantics A. Events remain active only for the duration of such a step, hence, in one macro-step an event can be activated and de-activated several times, thus leading to a much more complex interface between subsystems than between the system and the environment.

The following picture shows how each version of the semantics is an attempt to improve on another one.

4.1 Micro-semantics

The second transition relation is a labelled transition relation in the style of Plotkin [Plo81] reflecting the transformation of a configuration in one micro-step. A configuration is a pair $\langle P, v \rangle$, where

P is the system in its current state

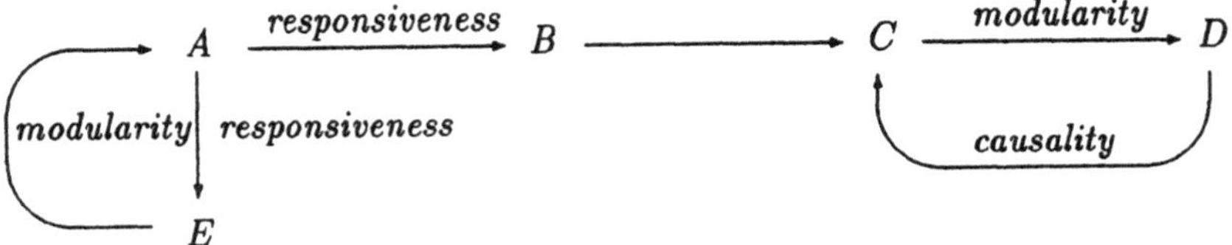

v is the set of machines (processes) that have already finished the current macro-step

We write $\langle S, v\rangle transition O[I]\langle S', v'\rangle$ to denote that the system S transforms in one *micro-step* to system S', generating output O, provided that I is currently as input. If $v' \neq v$, this means that one or more parts of the system have reached the end of the macro-step and can not perform any action until the next macro-step begins.

We denote that machine M has finished its macro-step by $\bar{M}$. E.g., we may write $M_1 \parallel \bar{M_2} \parallel M_3$ instead of $\langle M_1 \parallel M_2 \parallel M_3, \{M_2\}\rangle$ and $M_1 \parallel M_2 \parallel M_3$ instead of $\langle M_1 \parallel M_2 \parallel M_3, \emptyset\rangle$. We need this information, since in general a machine can only perform a limited amount of computation in one macro step; in many cases this is exactly one transition. Hence, we have to know whether a machine is still allowed to perform transitions, or whether it has completed its current macro-step.

4.2 Further definitions

Event-expressions are propositional formulae with primitive events as atomic propositions. The following definition tells us when a set of primitive events enables an event-expression.

Definition 7 . *Let* $e \in \Pi$ *and* $I \subseteq \Pi$. *Then*

$I \models e$ *iff* $e \in I$

$I \models e_1 \wedge e_2$ *iff* $I \models e_1$ *and* $I \models e_2$

$I \models e_1 \vee e_2$ *iff* $I \models e_1$ *or* $I \models e_2$

$I \models \neg e$ *iff* $I \not\models e$.

We define $gen(a)$ as the set of events generated by the action a. So

$gen(e) = \{e\}$ iff $e \in \Pi$

$gen(e1, e2) = gen(e1) \cup gen(e2)$.

The *null machine* **N** is the Transition Machine with only one node and no transitions. $P \not\rightarrow$ means: there exist no P', I and O such that $P \xrightarrow{O} [I]P'$.

4.3 Structure of the step relation

The definition of the step relation[4] has the following structure.

[4]Although, traditionally, this relation is called a *transition relation*, we want to reserve this term for the relation defining the computation steps in the Finite State Machines.

(i). There are one or more **transition axioms**, that define how a transition in one of the machines is taken.

(ii). There is one universal rule for parallel composition of machines. This is the following rule:

$$\textbf{PAR}\quad \frac{C_1 \xrightarrow{O} [I]C_1'}{C_1 \parallel C_2 \xrightarrow{O} [I]C_1' \parallel C_2 \quad C_2 \parallel C_1 \xrightarrow{O} [I]C_2 \parallel C_1'}$$

(iii). There is a **macro-step rule** with which one derives an observable step from a sequence of micro-steps.

If a global step uses the same micro-steps as several local steps, then these local steps combine into the global step.

4.4 Semantics A

The transition relations for A are defined by the following axioms and rules.

A1.1 $s \ldots M \xrightarrow[I]{\emptyset} /a; s'\bar{M}$ if $(s, e/a, s')$ is a transition in M and $I \models e$;

A1.2 $/a; \ldots M \xrightarrow{O} [I] \ldots M$ where $O = gen(a)$;

$$\textbf{A2}\quad \frac{\ldots S_0, \emptyset \xrightarrow{O_1} [I \cup O]S_1, v_1 \xrightarrow{O_2} [I \cup O] \ldots \xrightarrow{O_n} [I \cup O]S_n, v_n \not\longrightarrow [I \cup O]}{S_0 \xRightarrow[I]{O} S_n}, \text{ where } O = O_1 \cup$$

$\ldots \cup O_n$.

In semantics A, the events generated as a result of taking a transition become available only in the next macro-step. This means that after execution of a transition label *event/action*, control is left just before the */action*-part, which remains for the next macro-step. Axiom 1.2 deals with performing this action. After applying this axiom the machine has not completed its macro-step yet: it may still take a transition.

Rule 2 gives the completion of a macro-step and relates the two transition relations. A macro-step can be made of any maximal sequence of micro-steps.

Although the micro-step relation seems to be not effective, since the output of later steps is used as input set for a step, this is not the case. The sequence of micro-steps can be rearranged in such a way that all output generating steps are at the beginning. Since these steps are not dependent on the input, no "lookahead" is needed and the computation is effective. After these steps, no output is generated and the set $I \cup O$ is fixed.

Lemma 1 *Semantics A is order-independent, i.e., if*

$$S_0, \emptyset \xrightarrow[I]{O_1} \ldots \xrightarrow[I]{O_n} S_n, v_n \not\xrightarrow[I]{}$$

and π *is a permutation of* $[1, \ldots, n]$*, then there are* $S_1', v_1', \ldots, S_{n-1}', v_{n-1}'$ *with*

$$S_0, \emptyset \xrightarrow[I]{O_{\pi(1)}} \ldots \xrightarrow[I]{O_{\pi(n)}} S_n', v_n' \not\xrightarrow[I]{}$$

Proof. Let i range over $1 \dots m$ and let

$$\|_i M_i, v \xrightarrow[I]{O'} \|_i M_i', v' \xrightarrow[I]{O''} \|_i M_i'', v''$$

be two consecutive steps in the derivation of S_0. Then, by the nature of the transition system, there must be machines M_j and M_k that did the actual step in the two steps above: $M_i = M_i'$ for all $i \neq j$ and $M_j \xrightarrow[I]{O'} M_j'$ and for M_k likewise: $M_i' = M_i''$ for $i \neq k$ and $M_k' \xrightarrow[I]{O''} M_k''$. These steps must have been derived either from axiom A1.1 or from A1.2. Now, by repetitive application of rule **PAR**, we can derive (assume $j < k$)

$$\|_i M_i, v \xrightarrow[I]{O''} M_1' \| \dots \| M_{k-1}' \| M_k'' \| M_{k+1}' \| \dots \| M_n', v'' \setminus (v' \setminus v)$$

and

$$M_1' \| \dots \| M_{k-1}' \| M_k'' \| M_{k+1}' \| \dots \| M_n', v'' \setminus (v' \setminus v) \xrightarrow[I]{O'} \|_i M_i'', v''$$

Hence, by repetitively exchanging neighbours in the micro-step sequence, we can achieve the desired permutation. □

A consequence of this lemma is that the output of a macro-step does not depend on the input, since all output generating steps, which are input independent, can be put at the beginning of the sequence of micro-steps.

Corollary 1 *Semantics A is not responsive.*

Lemma 2 *Semantics A is modular.*

Proof

(ii) ⇒ (i)

Let $S \xRightarrow[I \cup O_2]{O_1} S'$ and $T \xRightarrow[I \cup O_1]{O_2} T'$. Since rule A2 must have been applied to achieve these relations, there exist an n and $S_1, \dots, S_{n-1}, v_1, \dots, v_n, O_1^1, \dots, O_1^{n-1}$ such that

$$S, \emptyset \xrightarrow[I \cup O_2 \cup O_1]{O_1^1} \dots \xrightarrow[I \cup O_2 \cup O_1]{O_1^{n-1}} S', v_n \not\xrightarrow[I \cup O_2 \cup O_1]{}$$

Likewise for T there exist an m and $T_1, \dots, T_{m-1}, v_1, \dots, v_m, O_2^1, \dots, O_2^{m-1}$ such that

$$T, \emptyset \xrightarrow[I \cup O_1 \cup O_2]{O_2^1} \dots \xrightarrow[I \cup O_1 \cup O_2]{O_2^{m-1}} T', v_m \not\xrightarrow[I \cup O_1 \cup O_2]{}$$

By repetitive application of rule **PAR**, these two sequences can be merged:

$$S \| T, \emptyset \xrightarrow[I \cup O_2 \cup O_1]{O_1^1} \dots \xrightarrow[I \cup O_2 \cup O_1]{O_1^{n-1}} S' \| T, v_n \xrightarrow[I \cup O_1 \cup O_2]{O_2^1} \dots \xrightarrow[I \cup O_1 \cup O_2]{O_2^{m-1}} S' \| T', v_m \not\xrightarrow[I \cup O_1 \cup O_2]{}$$

and hence, by rule A2,

$$S \| T Transition O_1 \cup O_2 [I] S' \| T'$$

(i) ⇒ (ii)

Suppose $S \parallel T \overset{O}{\underset{I}{\Longrightarrow}} S' \parallel T'$. Then there exist n and $S_0, \ldots, S_n, v_1, \ldots, v_n, T_0, \ldots, T_n$, $O^1, \ldots, O^n$ with $S_0 = S, T_0 = T, S_n = S', T_n = T', v_0 = \emptyset, O^1 \cup \ldots \cup O^n = O$, and

$$S_0 \parallel T_0, v_0 \xrightarrow[I \cup O_1 \cup O_2]{O^1} \cdots \xrightarrow[I \cup O_1 \cup O_2]{O^n} S_n \parallel T_n, v_n \not\xrightarrow[I \cup O_1 \cup O_2]{}$$

By the nature of the transition relation, we know that in all these micro-steps either S_i or T_i took the real step, i.e., appeared in the premise of rule **PAR**. So there is a partition of $\{1, \ldots, n\}$ into J_1 and J_2 such that the steps of S have index in J_1 and the steps of T have index in J_2. So,

$$i \in J_1 \Rightarrow S_{i-1}, v'_{i-1} \xrightarrow[I \cup O_1 \cup O_2]{O^i} S_i, v'_i \wedge T_{i-1} = T_i$$

(where v'_j is the restriction of v_j to the processes of S).

Furthermore, $S_{\max(J_1)} = S_{\max(J_1)+1} = \ldots = S_n$, since S makes no move after the one indexed with the last element in J_1. And since $S_n \parallel T_n, v_n \not\xrightarrow[I \cup O_1 \cup O_2]{}$, we also have $S_{\max(J_1)}, v_{\max(J_1)} \not\xrightarrow[I \cup O_1 \cup O_2]{}$ and thus we have established the premise of rule A2 and we can conclude

$$S \overset{O_1}{\Longrightarrow} S'$$

where $O_1 = \bigcup_{i \in J_1} O^i$ and likewise for T with $O_2 = \bigcup_{i \in J_2} O^i$. Hence, $O_1 \cup O_2 = O$. □

One can easily see that semantics A is causal: since the output generating steps are not dependent on the input, one can use the identity relation as the causality relation for any step.

4.5 Semantics B

In semantics B, events are sensed in the same macro-step in which the transition takes place that generates them, but only from the next micro-step onwards.

B1 $s \ldots M \xrightarrow{O} [I]s'\bar{M}$ if $(s, e/a, s')$ is a transition in M and $O = gen(a)$.

B2 $\dfrac{\ldots S_0, v_0 \xrightarrow{O_1} [I]S_1, v_1 \xrightarrow{O_2} [I \cup \bar{O}_1] \ldots \xrightarrow{O_n} [I \cup \bar{O}_{n-1}]S_n, v_n \not\longrightarrow [I \cup \bar{O}_n]}{S_0 \overset{\bar{O}_n}{\underset{I}{\Longrightarrow}} S_n}$, where $\bar{O}_i = O_1 \cup \ldots \cup O_i$.

Note that the sequence of input sets is an ascending chain: $I \cup \bar{O}_i \subseteq I \cup \bar{O}_{i+1}$ for any $i < n$.

It is easy to see that semantics B is responsive. Let I_1 and I_2 be given and $I_1 \neq I_2$. Suppose $e \in I_1 \setminus I_2$ (assume without loss of generality that $I_1 \setminus I_2 \neq \emptyset$), and let $a \notin I_1 \cup I_2$. Then $e/aM \xrightarrow[I_1]{a} \bar{M}$, whereas $e/aM \not\xrightarrow[I_2]{}$. Consequently, $e/aM \overset{a}{\underset{I_1}{\Longrightarrow}} M$ and $e/aM \overset{\emptyset}{\underset{I_2}{\Longrightarrow}} M$.

It is easy to find a counterexample for the modularity of semantics B. Take a/bM_1 and b/aM_2. Then $a/bM_1 \overset{b}{\underset{a}{\Longrightarrow}} M_1$ and $b/aM_2 \overset{a}{\underset{b}{\Longrightarrow}} M_2$. In contradiction to modularity, however, $a/bM_1 \parallel b/aM_2 \overset{\{a,b\}}{\underset{\emptyset}{\Longrightarrow}}$ does not hold. One can only derive $a/bM_1 \parallel b/aM_2 \overset{\{a,b\}}{\underset{a}{\Longrightarrow}}$ or $a/bM_1 \parallel b/aM_2 \overset{\{a,b\}}{\underset{b}{\Longrightarrow}}$.

Lemma 3 *Semantics B satisfies causality.*

Proof: If $S_0 \overset{O}{\underset{I}{\Longrightarrow}} S_n$ is a valid step, and $S_0, \emptyset \xrightarrow[I]{O_1} \cdots \xrightarrow[I \cup \bar{O}_{n-1}]{O_n} S_n, v_n$ is the sequence of micro-steps from the premise of rule 2, define the causal order $\preceq$ for this step as follows:

$$a \preceq b \text{ if there is a micro-step } i \text{ in which } a \in I \cup \bar{O}_{i-1} \text{ and } b \in O_i \setminus (I \cup \bar{O}_{i-1}).$$

and take the reflexive closure. We now show that this relation is a partial order. Let in the following I_i be the input set of micro-step i, i.e., $I \cup \bar{O}_{i-1}$.

(i). $\preceq$ is transitive. Suppose $a \preceq b$ and $b \preceq c$. Then there are micro-steps i and j with

$$\begin{array}{lcl} a \in I_i & \text{and} & b \in O_i \setminus I_i \\ b \in I_j & \text{and} & c \in O_j \setminus I_j \end{array}$$

Now, $i \leq j$, since otherwise $I_j \subseteq I_{i-1} \subseteq I_i$ and hence, $b \in I_i$, which is not the case. Hence, $I_i \subseteq I_j$ and $a \in I_j$, which implies $a \preceq c$.

(ii). $\preceq$ is anti-symmetric. Suppose $a \preceq b$ and $b \preceq a$. Assume $a \neq b$, then there must be micro-steps i and j with

$$\begin{array}{lcl} a \in I_i & \text{and} & b \in O_i \setminus I_i \\ b \in I_j & \text{and} & a \in O_j \setminus I_j \end{array}$$

Now, if $i \leq j$, then $I_i \subseteq I_j$ and $a \in I_j$, so $a \notin O_j \setminus I_j$, which is not the case. A symmetric argument for b applies if $j \leq i$. In both cases we derived a contradiction, hence $a = b$.

We now have to check that $\preceq$ satisfies the properties of a causal ordering relation.

(i). Suppose $S \overset{O}{\underset{I_1}{\Longrightarrow}} S'$ and $S \overset{O}{\underset{I_2}{\not\Longrightarrow}}$ and $I_1, O \neq \emptyset$ and assume a sequence of micro-steps $S, \emptyset \xrightarrow[I_1]{O_1} \cdots \xrightarrow[I_1 \cup \bar{O}_{n-1}]{O_n} S_n, v_n$ that led to this macro-step. Suppose a is one of the elements of I_1 and b is one of the elements of O. Then there must exist a micro-step $S_{i-1}, v_{i-1} \xrightarrow[I \cup \bar{O}_{i-1}]{O_i} S_i, v_i$ in this sequence in which b appeared for the first time in the output set, hence $b \in O_i$ and $b \notin O_{i-1}$. Hence, $a \preceq b$.

(ii). Suppose $S_1 \,\|\, S_2 \xrightarrow{O} [I] S_1' \,\|\, S_2'$ with causal order $\preceq$. Choose the maximal decomposition, i.e., $M_1 \,\|\, \ldots \,\|\, M_n$ with associated causal orderings $\preceq_1, \ldots, \preceq_n$. By the nature of the micro-step relation, there can be at most one micro-step in the sequence that led to the macro-step in which M_i makes a step.

Assume that M_i made a step at j. So, $M_i \xrightarrow[I \cup \bar{O}_{j-1}]{O_j} \bar{M}_i'$ and hence, $M_i \overset{O_j}{\underset{I \cup \bar{O}_{j-1}}{\Longrightarrow}} M_i'$. Now, if $a \preceq b$ on behalf of this step, we also have $a \preceq_i b$ and vice versa.

If M_i did not make a step, we have $M_i \underset{I \cup O}{\not\longrightarrow}$ and hence, $M_i \underset{I \cup O}{\not\Longrightarrow}$ and no ordering relations are induced from this.

4.6 Semantics C

Like in semantics B, events are available in the same macro-step as the transition, but an additional consistency constraint is made: every transition must be enabled by the complete set of events that is available after all output has been generated; i.e., consistency must be maintained.

C1 = **B1**

$$\textbf{C2}\quad \frac{\begin{array}{c}\ldots S_0, \xrightarrow{O_1} [I]S_1, v_1 \xrightarrow{O_2} [I \cup \bar{O}_1] \ldots \xrightarrow{O_n} [I \cup \bar{O}_{n-1}]S_n, v_n \not\longrightarrow [I \cup \bar{O}_n] \\ \ldots S_0, \emptyset \xrightarrow{O_1} [I \cup \bar{O}_n]S_1, v_1 \xrightarrow{O_2} [I \cup \bar{O}_n] \ldots \xrightarrow{O_n} [I \cup \bar{O}_n]S_n, v_n \not\longrightarrow [I \cup \bar{O}_n]\end{array}}{S_0 \xRightarrow[I]{\bar{O}_n} S_n}, \text{ where } \bar{O}_i = O_1 \cup \ldots \cup O_i.$$

Semantics C is responsive. The same construction as is used for semantics B can be applied here.

Semantics C is causal, since in the derivation of an arbitrary macro-step, the premise of rule C2 implies the premise of rule B2 and the same argument can be used here.

By theorem 1, semantics C is not modular, since it is responsive and causal.

4.7 Semantics D

Like in semantics B and C, events are generated in the same step as the transition, but, here, all transitions are triggered by the same set of events, viz. the complete set of events after the generation of all output.

D1 = **B1**

$$\textbf{D2}\quad \frac{\ldots S_0, \emptyset \xrightarrow{O_1} [I \cup O]S_1, v_1 \xrightarrow{O_2} [I \cup O] \ldots \xrightarrow{O_n} [I \cup O]S_n, v_n \not\longrightarrow [I \cup O]}{S_0 \xRightarrow[I]{O} S_n}, \text{ where } O = O_1 \cup \ldots \cup O_n.$$

The difference between C and D is that in semantics D, transitions can cause their own trigger. For example,

$$a/aM \xRightarrow[\emptyset]{\{a\}} M \quad \text{or} \quad a/bM_1 \parallel b/aN_2 \xRightarrow[\emptyset]{\{a,b\}} M_1 \parallel N_2$$

In semantics C, this is not possible. Although triggers are evaluated in a global set of events, there is an additional constraint that the events generated so far must also enable the transition. This leads to two premises in rule 2: both the complete set, $I \cup \bar{O}_n$, and the events that are currently available, $I \cup \bar{O}_i$, must be capable of triggering step i.

Semantics D is responsive. Use the same construction as for semantics B.

Semantics D is modular. The proof of modularity of semantics A uses only rule 2 and rule **PAR**. Since these rules are the same for semantics A and D, the same proof can be used here.

Because semantics D is already responsive and causal, it cannot satisfy modularity, due to Theorem 1.

In both semantics C and D, it is not always the case that there exists a macro-step for a given input. Take for instance $\neg a/aM$. Then

$$\neg a/aM \xrightarrow[I]{a} \bar{M} \text{ for any } I \not\ni a$$
$$\neg a/aM \not\xrightarrow[I]{} \text{ for any } I \ni a$$

Consequently, a premise of rule C2 and D2 that would yield the step $\neg a/aM \overset{I}{\underset{O}{\Longrightarrow}} S$ for some O and S does not exist.

Another example is $\neg a/bM_1 \parallel b/aM_2$. This example also shows that two well-behaved systems can lead to problems when put together.

4.8 Semantics E

This semantics is basically semantics A, but now a sequence of macro-steps that cannot be extended without new input from the environment is squeezed into one macro-step. The correspondence to semantics B is that events are generated in the micro-step following the step in which the transition is taken, but they remain only for the sequence of micro-steps that are immediately caused by the transition.

E1 = **B1**

E2 $$\frac{\ldots P_0, \emptyset \xrightarrow[I]{O_1}{}^{*} P_1, v_1 \not\xrightarrow[I]{} \quad \ldots \quad \ldots P_{n-1}, \emptyset \xrightarrow[I \cup O_{n-1}]{O_n}{}^{*} P_n, v_n \not\xrightarrow[I \cup O_{n-1}]{} \quad P_n, \emptyset \not\xrightarrow[I \cup O_n]{}}{P_0 \overset{O_1 \cup \ldots \cup O_n}{\underset{I}{\Longrightarrow}} P_n}$$

Here, $P, v \xrightarrow[I]{O}{}^{*} P', v'$ abbreviates

$$\exists P_1 \ldots P_{n-1}\, O_1 \ldots O_n : P, v \xrightarrow[I]{O_1} P_1, v_1 \xrightarrow[I]{O_1} \ldots \xrightarrow[I]{O_n} P', v' \text{ and } O = O_1 \cup \ldots \cup O_n$$

With the same construction as used for the other semantics, we can prove that semantics E is responsive. Here, we take the null machine, prefixed with a transition, to avoid unwanted transitions. First we have $e/a\mathbf{N} \xrightarrow[I_1]{a} /a\bar{\mathbf{N}}$. Because the step is finished, we have $/a\bar{\mathbf{N}} \not\xrightarrow[I_1]{}$. Then we have $/a\mathbf{N} \xrightarrow[I_1]{a} \mathbf{N}$. Since $\mathbf{N}$ is the null machine, we can not move any further: $\mathbf{N} \not\xrightarrow[I_1]{}$ and applying rule E2 with $n = 2$ we get $e/a\mathbf{N} \overset{a}{\underset{I_1}{\Longrightarrow}} \mathbf{N}$. On the other hand, $e/a\mathbf{N} \not\xrightarrow[I_2]{}$ and so $e/a\mathbf{N} \not\longrightarrow [I_2]$ (apply rule E2 with $n = 1$).

Semantics E is not modular, since it is possible to have an event that is several times "on" and "off" during one macro-step. Consider for instance $M_1 \parallel M_2$ where

$$M_1 = a/bM_1'$$
$$M_1' = c/bM_1''$$
$$M_2 = b/cM_2'$$

and $M_2' \not\xrightarrow{a}$. Then

$$M_1 \parallel M_2 \xrightarrow[a]{b} \bar{M}_1' \parallel M_2 \not\xrightarrow[a]{} .$$
$$M_1' \parallel M_2 \xrightarrow[a,b]{c} M_1' \parallel \bar{M}_2' \not\xrightarrow[a,b]{} .$$
$$M_1' \parallel M_2' \xrightarrow[a,c]{b} \bar{M}_1'' \parallel M_2' \not\xrightarrow[a,c]{} .$$
$$M_1'' \parallel M_2' \not\xrightarrow[a,b]{} .$$

Hence

$$M_1 \parallel M_2 Transitiona, b, c[a] M_1'' \parallel M_2',$$

but gives not enough information for modularity: Event b is sometimes enabled and sometimes not.

Like in semantics C and D, there are systems in semantics E that can not react properly to some inputs. A loop can lead to an infinite sequence of micro-steps, which cannot result in a macro-step. Take for instance

$$M = (\{s\}, s, \{(s, a/a, s\})$$

Then

$$M \xrightarrow[a]{\emptyset} /a\bar{M} \not\xrightarrow[a]{} .$$
$$/aM \xrightarrow[a]{a} M \xrightarrow[a]{\emptyset} /a\bar{M} \not\xrightarrow[a]{} .$$
$$\vdots$$

Theorem 2 *The following table gives an overview of the properties of the various semantics.*

semantics	responsiveness	modularity	causality
A	no	yes	yes
B	yes	no	yes
C	yes	no	yes
D	yes	yes	no
E	yes	no	no

5 Hybrid semantics

From theorem 2 we see that none of the five semantics satisfy all the criteria. Therefore, we propose a new version of the semantics in which modularity and causality are applied at different levels. We introduce the notion of *modules* and local events into the language. Modules are clusters of one or more subsystems that are closely connected. The idea is that they can easily be surveyed and hence the criterion of causality is applicable on the events that are local to a module. The events that are visible *between* modules, however, are treated in a modular fashion, since the interface between modules should be simple and transparent.

We change the syntax as follows.

$$\langle \textit{reactive system} \rangle \implies \langle \textit{module} \rangle \; [\; \parallel \langle \textit{reactive system} \rangle \;]$$
$$\langle \textit{module} \rangle \implies \textbf{mod} \; \langle \textit{locals} \rangle \; \textbf{in} \; \langle \textit{machine exp} \rangle \parallel \ldots \parallel \langle \textit{machine exp} \rangle$$

where $\langle locals \rangle$ denotes a subset of Π.

We have to change the micro-semantics in such a way that the label now records the output of the micro-step. This does not change the relation $\longrightarrow$ as restricted to configurations, since the label E is not used in the definition of semantics B. This leads to the following definitions.

M1 $s\bar{M} \xrightarrow{O} [I]s' \ldots M$ if $(s, e/a, s')$ is a transition in M, $I \models e$, and $O = gen(a)$.

$$\textbf{M2}\quad \frac{P_0, \emptyset \xrightarrow[I \cup O^M]{O_1} P_1, v_1 \xrightarrow[I \cup O^M \cup \bar{O}_1]{O_2} \cdots \xrightarrow[I \cup O^M \cup \bar{O}_{n-1}]{O_n} P_n, v_n \not\xrightarrow[I \cup O^M \cup \bar{O}_n]{}}{P_0 \overset{O^M}{\underset{I}{\Longrightarrow}}{}^* P_n},$$

where $O^M = (O_1 \cup \ldots \cup O_n) \setminus H$.

The events that are local to the module (denoted by the set H), are removed from the input of the micro-steps and from the output of the macro-step. Any event that is left must be global and must be treated as if it was available right from the start of the macro-step, in order to satisfy modularity. Therefore, the output of the micro-steps is added to the initial input.

Acknowledgement

We wish to thank Rob Nederpelt for his careful reading and commenting of a previous version of this paper.

References

[BC85] B. Berry and L. Cosserat. The synchronous programming language Esterel and its mathematical semantics. In *Proceedings CMU Seminar on Concurrency*, pages 389–449. LNCS 197, Springer-Verlag, 1985.

[BCH85a] J.-L. Bergerand, P. Caspi, and N. Halbwachs. Outline of a real-time data flow language. In *Proceedings IEEE Real-Time Systems Symposium*, 1985.

[BCH85b] J.-L. Bergerand, P. Caspi, and N. Halbwachs. Outline of a real-time dataflow language. In *Proc. IEEE-CS Real-Time systems Symposium, San Diego*, 1985.

[BG88] G. Berry and G. Gonthier. The ESTEREL synchronous programming language: Design, semantics, implementation. Technical report, Ecole Nationale Supérieure des Mines de Paris, 1988.

[Gon88] G. Gonthier. *Sémantiques et modèles d'exécution des langages réactifs synchrones; Application à ESTEREL.* PhD thesis, University of Orsay, 1988.

[Har87] D. Harel. Statecharts: A visual formalism for complex systems. *Science of Computer Programming*, 8(3):231–274, 1987.

[HG89] C. Huizing and R. Gerth. On the semantics of reactive systems. Deliverable in ESPRIT 3096 "SPEC", Eindhoven University of Technology, 1989.

[HGdR88] C. Huizing, R. Gerth, and W.P. de Roever. Modelling statecharts behaviour in a fully abstract way. In *Proc. 13th CAAP*, LNCS 299, pages 271–294, 1988.

[HP85] D. Harel and A. Pnueli. On the development of reactive systems. In K.R. Apt, editor, *Logics and Models of Concurrent Systems*, pages 477–498. NATO, ASI-13, Springer-Verlag, 1985.

[HP87] Derek J. Hatley and Imtiaz A. Pirbhai. *Strategies for real-time system specification.* Dorset House, New York, 1987.

[HPPSS87a] D. Harel, A. Pnueli, J. Pruzan-Schmidt, and R. Sherman. On the formal semantics of Statecharts. In *Proceedings Symposium on Logic in Computer Science*, pages 54–64, 1987.

[HPPSS87b] D. Harel, A. Pnueli, J. Pruzan-Schmidt, and R. Sherman. On the formal semantics of Statecharts. In *Proceedings Symposium on Logic in Computer Science*, pages 54–64, 1987.

[HR88] J. Hooman and S. Ramesh. Statecharts assertional framework. Computing Science Note CSN 88/14, Department of Mathematics and Computing Science Eindhoven University of Technology, The Netherlands, May 1988.

[*i-Logix Inc*89] *i-Logix Inc*, Burlington, Mass. *The Semantics of* STATECHARTS, 1989. *In* Documentation for the STATEMATE System.

[LBBG85] Guernic P. Le, A. Benveniste, P. Bournai, and T. Gonthier. Signal: A data flow oriented language for signal processing. Technical Report IRISA Report 246, IRISA, Rennes, France, 1985.

[Mar89] F. Maraninchi. Argonaute: Graphical description, semantics and verification of reactive systems by using a process algebra. In *Workshop on Automatic Verification methods for Finite State Systems, Grenoble 12-14 June 1989.* Springer-Verlag, 1989.

[Mar90] F. Maraninchi. *Statecharts: sémantique et application à la spécification de systèmes.* PhD thesis, INP Grenoble, 1990.

[Plo81] G.D. Plotkin. A structural approach to operational semantics. Technical report, 1981. Lecture Notes.

[PS88] A. Pnueli and M. Shalev. What is in a step. Technical report, Department of Applied Mathematics and Computer Science, The Weizmann Institute of Science, Rehovot, Israel, 1988. Draft.

A Relation between Esterel and the semantic framework

A.1 Short description of ESTEREL

Esterel is the oldest member of the so-called *synchronous languages*, which also include LUSTRE, SIGNAL, and STATECHARTS.

We now give a short description of the subset of ESTEREL that is relevant to our comparison to the semantic framework of this paper.

Esterel has a conventional imperative style, with standard imperative primitives such as assignment, sequencing, conditional, loop, trap-exit (comparable to exception-block constructions). Furthermore, there are temporal primitives that deal with triggers, watchdogs, etc. and primitives that handle the signals: the basic concept in Esterel by which communication, interaction with the environment, and time is modelled. Of these we mention:

- **`nothing`**
  the statement that does nothing (it doesn't even take time)

- **`halt`**
  finishes the current step and *does not terminate*; the only way to get rid of it is to terminate an enclosing construction, either by exiting a trap, or by a **`watching`** interrupt (see below);

- **`emit`** `S(`*exp*`)`
  emits signal `S` with the value of expression *exp*; if two processes emit a signal at the same time, a signal dependent *synchronous product* of the two values is computed and this is the value that is actually emitted;

- **`present`** `S` **`then`** $stat_1$ **`else`** $stat_2$ **`end`**
  tests for presence of the signal `S` (disregarding its value) at the current moment;

- **`do`** *stat* **`watching`** `S`
  executes the body *stat* until signal `S` occurs; this is the basic temporal operator;

- $stat_1 \parallel stat_2$
  executes both statements in parallel; it terminates when both statements are terminated;

- **`signal`** `S :` *type* **`in`** *stat* **`end`**
  declares `S` as a local signal in the body *stat*; at this point, the occurrences and absences of `S` can be computed.

On basis of these statements, more complex constructions are built, using heavily the **`trap-exit`** construction. Since we are only making a basic semantic comparison, we will not describe this construct here. It is interesting to remark that it is non-preemptive, unlike the **`watching`**-statement: when one of two parallel processes encounters an **`exit`**-statement that leaves the parallel construct, the other one finishes its computation of the current step before the construct is terminated. Statecharts does not have such a non-preemptive interrupt.

A.2 Semantics of Esterel

The formal semantics of Esterel is called the *behavioural semantics*, as opposed to the execution semantics, which is more effective, but also more complex. Two step-relations are used, one for complete programs, and defining *macro-steps* in our terminology, and one for arbitrary statements, and defining *micro-steps*. The first is denoted

$$P_0 \overset{O}{\underset{\hat{I}}{\longmapsto}} P_1$$

and means that P_0 transforms to P_1 in one time step with input I and output O. $\hat{I}$ means the completion if set I, a technical necessity due to the valued signals.

The second step-relation is notated

$$\langle \text{stat}, \rho \rangle \xrightarrow[\hat{E}]{E', b, T} \langle \text{stat}', \rho' \rangle$$

where ρ and ρ' are the *memories*, or states of the program, $\hat{E}$ the complete signal environment (input as well as output), E' the set of signals output by this statement, b a boolean denoting whether the statement has terminated (completed the current time-step) or not, and T a set of *trap labels*, trap constructions that have to be exited.

A.3 Relationship

We base ourselves for the description of Esterel on [BG88]. Since our framework is very basic, we have to restrict the Esterel language. Valued signals are not supported by our framework, so we have to leave them out; the same holds for variables. Parallel composition is not just another syntactic operator, but plays an essential role in our framework, we consider only parallelism at the top level of the program.

Note The terminology of Statecharts and Esterel differ in an essential point. The basic active notion of the semantics, the atomic action, is called *event* in Statecharts and *signal* in Esterel. In Esterel, the term *event* is used for anything that happens at a particular moment, i.e., a set of signals with the corresponding values. If there could be confusion, we will use the term *Esterel-event* in the latter case. We believe that the term signal in this context comes from the field of electronic engineering, whereas the term event fits better in the terminology of computer science.

To model non-valued events in Esterel, we use the trivial commutative monoid with the single element 1. Then, the synchronous product $E_1 * E_2$ boils down to set union. This follows from the definition of $E_1 * E_2$:

$S(1) \in E_1 * E_2$ iff either:
$S(1) \in E_1$ and $S(1) \notin E_2$ or:
$S(1) \in E_2$ and $S(1) \notin E_1$ or:
$S(1) \in E_1$ and $S(1) \in E_2$
which is indeed equivalent to
$S(1) \in E_1 \cup E_2$.
Hence, in the sequel, we will consider Esterel-events as sets of signals.

There are two ways to relate Esterel to our semantic framework. One way is to relate the transition relation of the Esterel behavioural semantics to the micro-step relation in our model, the other way is to define directly the semantics of the Esterel constructs in our framework. The advantage of the latter method is that it gives more insight in the Esterel language, the disadvantage is that not all constructs can be translated. In particular the "`trap`" construct can not be handled by our framework, nor, of course, parallelism nested in other constructs We will use the first method here.

Relating the relations

Let $\rightarrow_e$denote the $\rightarrow$ from the Esterel behavioural semantics. Then we define if $\hat{E}-E \subseteq I$:

$S \xrightarrow[\hat{E}]{E,ff,T}_e S'$ if and only if $S \xrightarrow[I]{E} \bar{S}'$

Note that the trap component T is not of any matter, since we will use only parallel composition to compose S further.

On the second level we define if $\hat{E} - E \subseteq I$:

$P \xmapsto[\hat{E}]{E} P'$ if and only if $P \xRightarrow[I]{E} P'$

What we have to check is whether the two definitions of parallel composition respect each other.

In Esterel we have the rule

$$\frac{S_1 \xrightarrow[E]{E_1, b_1}_e S_1' \quad S_2 \xrightarrow[E]{E_2, b_2}_e S_2'}{S_1 \parallel S_2 \xrightarrow[E]{E_1 * E_2, b_1 \wedge b_2}_e S_1' \parallel S_2'}$$

If we apply this rule to the cases where $b_1 = b_2 = ff$, we get

$$S_1 \parallel S_2 \xRightarrow[E]{E_1 * E_2} S_1' \parallel S_2'$$

In the other system we get via two applications of **PAR**:

$$S_1 \parallel S_2 \xrightarrow[E]{E_1} \bar{S_1}' \parallel S_2 \xrightarrow[E]{E_2} \bar{S_1}' \parallel \bar{S_2}'$$

and hence, in semantics D,

$$S_1 \parallel S_2 \xRightarrow[E]{E_1 \cup E_2} S_1' \parallel S_2'$$

which is what we have to prove, since we can read $E_1 \cup E_2$ for $E_1 * E_2$.

Using only premises where both the termination components equal false is not much of a restriction, since the Esterel transition relation $\rightarrow_e$is Church-Rosser, which means that we can postpone the application of the rule for parallel as long as possible, that is, until none of the components can make further computations during this time step.

Relating the language

The other approach is to model Esterel on the level of the language. We have to leave out the `trap`-construct.

Following the Esterel syntax we get the following axioms and rules.

6.5.1 $\texttt{nothing} \xrightarrow[E]{\emptyset} \texttt{nothing}$

6.5.2 $\texttt{halt} \xrightarrow[E]{\emptyset} \overline{\texttt{halt}}$

6.5.3,4 Assignment and procedure call are left out of the language, since we can not model states.

6.5.5 $\texttt{emit e} \xrightarrow[E]{\{e\}} \texttt{nothing}$

6.5.6

$$\frac{S_1 \xrightarrow[E]{E_1} \bar{S}'_1}{S_1; S_2 \xrightarrow[E]{E_1} \bar{S}'_1; S_2}$$

$$\frac{S_1 \xrightarrow[E]{E_1} S'_1 \quad S_2 \xrightarrow[E]{E_2} S'_2}{S_1; S_2 \xrightarrow[E]{E_1 \cup E_2} S'_1; S_2}$$

6.5.6' A simpler variant of the second rule is:

$$\frac{S_1 \xrightarrow[E]{E_1} \bar{S}'_1}{S_1; S_2 \xrightarrow[E]{E_1} S_2}$$

6.5.7,8 Loop and if-then-else are omitted, because they are not very interesting without traps and variables.

6.5.9

$$\frac{e \in E \quad S_1 \xrightarrow[E]{E_1} S'_1}{\texttt{present e then } S_1 \texttt{ else } S_2 \texttt{ end} \xrightarrow[E]{E_1} S'_1}$$

$$\frac{e \notin E \quad S_2 \xrightarrow[E]{E_2} S'_2}{\texttt{present e then } S_1 \texttt{ else } S_2 \texttt{ end} \xrightarrow[E]{E_2} S'_2}$$

6.5.10

$$\frac{S \xrightarrow[E']{E} S'}{\texttt{do } S \texttt{ watching e} \xrightarrow[E']{E} \texttt{present e else do } S' \texttt{ watching e end}}$$

6.5.11 Can be replaced by **PAR**.

6.5.12,13 Traps are omitted.

6.5.14 Variables are omitted, so no local variable declaration.

6.5.15

$$\frac{e \notin E' \quad S \xrightarrow[E \cup \{e\}]{E' \cup \{e\}} S'}{\texttt{signal e in } S \texttt{ end} \xrightarrow[E]{E'} \texttt{signal e in } S' \texttt{ end}}$$

$$\frac{e \in E' \quad S \xrightarrow[E]{E'} S'}{\texttt{signal e in } S \texttt{ end} \xrightarrow[E]{E'} \texttt{signal e in } S' \texttt{ end}}$$

A.4 Conclusion

We showed that the semantic framework presented in this paper is general enough to model Esterel. We presented a translation from Esterel to semantics D from the semantic framework. We had to leave out the values of signals, since the framework does not support these, and the `trap-exit` construct. The latter restriction is only for simplification: we are not only interested in how the processes work together and how the relation between micro- and macro-steps is made. The only real restriction is that a composition of parallel processes cannot be part of another construction anymore, but this is a restriction that is also in the semantic framework.

Hence, Esterel is modular and responsive, and not causal. The Esterel compiler rejects non-causal programs, however, and thus makes it possible to reason about programs in a simpler way.

Problems, promises and performance: some questions for real-time system specification

Mathai Joseph[*]
University of Warwick

Abstract. This paper considers how different views of real-time program specification and verification arise from different assumptions about the representation of time external to the program, the representation of time in the program and the verification of the timing properties on an implementation. Three different views are compared: real-time programming without time, the synchrony hypothesis and asynchronous real-time programs. Questions about the representation of time are then related to different models of time and their roles at different levels of analysis. The relationship between the development of a program from a specification and its timing characteristics in an implementation is discussed and it is suggested that the formal verification of timing properties can be extended towards the implementation. The need for fault-tolerance in a real-time system is then considered and ways examined of incorporating a formal proof of fault-tolerance along with proof of its timing properties.

Keywords: real-time specification, synchronous real-time, asynchronous real-time, fault-tolerance.

1 Introduction

In 1977, Wirth [28] pointed out the need for a distinction between program correctness and the satisfaction of timing properties. A few years later, Bernstein and Harter [2] introduced time into temporal logic by defining a 'temporal implication' operator with time bounds.

$$P \overset{\leq n}{\leadsto} Q$$

At about the same time, Lamport [15] suggested that reasoning about the safety properties of programs could be based on combining reasoning about time and program states. His *Timesets* had the form $[P \rightarrow Q)$ which is the union of all time intervals $[p, r]$ for which property P is true at time p and property Q is false throughout $[p, r]$.

Since that time, interest in the mathematical representation of time in relation to a program's execution has been high and today there are few models of concurrency that do not incorporate some theory of time. But there are many unanswered questions and many

[*]**Department of Computer Science, University of Warwick, Coventry CV4 7AL, U.K.** **(supported by Research Grants GR/D/73881 & GR/F 57960 from the Science and Engineering Research Council).**

problems that will only be solved when we know how to define them satisfactorily. On one hand there are well-argued suggestions that the introduction of time into a program must be viewed with suspicion [26]; and that the usual methods of establishing the correctness of programs should be used to reason about program timing [9], avoiding calculating the timing behaviour of a program as this is likely to be an unrewarding task. On the other, it is claimed that solutions to the problems of the reliability of complex embedded real-time systems will require no less than foundational research in computer science [24]. There are other positions that are either less extreme or less well-thought-out.

So is the real-time behaviour of a program a problem to be solved by specification and verification, or is it only of 'engineering' concern ? In this paper we consider how different sets of assumptions about the nature of a real-time program can lead to different solutions to the verification of correctness. We start with a definition of the characteristics of a real-time system and then describe the problems addressed by three different specification methods. We then show how program fault-tolerance can be treated in a specification/verification framework and how the real-time properties of fault-tolerant programs can be specified.

2 The *RT* Problem

If the *specification* of a real-time program needs bear no relation to a program in any real programming language, to implementability or to efficiency, many interesting programs can be specified (including the so-called *Zeno* programs which perform infinite computations in finite time). But more usually a real-time program is required to execute under a number of constraints which are characterised in the following definition[1].

The *RT* problem is to specify and verify a program which

1. Interacts with an environment with time-varying properties,
2. Exhibits predictable time-dependent behaviour, and
3. Executes on a system with limited resources.

Clearly such requirements exist and practical real-time systems are built to meet them. But the solutions can be based on very different assumptions about the problem. As these assumptions become stronger, the problem becomes easier to define and the solutions easier to obtain: how far you go depends on the needs of your application. In order to match the *RT* problem to a method of analysis, the assumptions can be used to define a model which eliminates some of the problems but which can then be used to solve the remaining problems. In the following sections we describe some common sets of assumptions.

[1]There are of course other definitions of a real-time system, such as the one given by Le Lann [16]: "A computing system where initiation and termination of activities must meet specified timing constraints. Time dependent activities are associated with activity terminations. System behaviour is determined by algorithms designed to maximise a global time-dependent value function."

3 Real-time without time

The need for simplicity and the dangers of overspecification both suggest making as little use as possible of explicit values of time in a real-time program specification. Turski [26] has argued that time may be an issue for an implementation but should never appear in a specification; observable time in a program's execution can differ to an arbitrary extent from universal or absolute time so the correctness of a program is more easily proved if its actions are based on observable events, rather than apparent values of time. Hehner [9] incorporates time in the semantics of programs as an auxiliary variable (using an explicit time variable) and shows how values of time can be used in assertions and reasoning about simple programming constructs; even with this, he recommends that where there are timing constraints, it is always better to construct a program with the required timing properties than to try and compute the timing properties of an arbitrary program.

Assumption Set 1

1a. External reckonings of time bear no fixed relation to explicit values of time observed during a program's execution.

1b. Computation of the set of possible execution times for a program can be avoided.

1c. Explicit timing is of no use in a distributed system.

Where such assumptions hold, there seems little reason to make any more complicated assumptions. Thus for programs that can be implemented with fixed schedules on a single processor, or those with restricted timing requirements which can be efficiently met by relatively simple programming constructs, Assumption Set 1 provides a good basis for reasoning about real-time programs without reasoning about time.

4 Synchronous real-time

Some of the most interesting recent work in real-time programming has been done using the *synchrony hypothesis*: external events are ordered in time and the program responds to each event as if instantaneously. The synchrony hypothesis has been used in the *ESTEREL*[3], *LUSTRE* and *SIGNAL*[7] family of languages, and in *Statecharts*[8]; it is finding increasing use in timed process algebras and similar notations in which time progresses by explicit manipulation.

The synchrony hypothesis is elegant and very effective, where it is applicable. The 'instantaneous-ness' of a response is of course an idealisation and can be approximated by any time of response which is smaller than the minimum time between external events. Moreover, this external instantaneous-ness does not need to be mirrored internally, so the expected computational properties of order and causality are preserved.

Assumption Set 2

2a. External time is modelled by a finite (non-dense) representation and internal actions are instantaneous with respect to external actions.

2b. Internal actions are deterministic and ordered and can be converted into the actions of an automaton.

2c. The 'natural' implementation is for a single processor; a distributed or multiple processor implementation must emulate this.

If an application can make either highly variable computing demands, or demand any of a large variety of responses, the synchronous hypothesis is difficult to sustain because it would require unreasonably powerful processing capacity. Also, if the nature of the application requires a distributed implementation and the time constants are sufficiently small, it becomes difficult for a single processor implementation to be emulated.

5 Asynchronous real-time

The real world is densely populated with real-time systems that are designed as asynchronous systems. From a simple real-time system with a single processor and a set of devices seeking its attention at intervals using interrupts, to a complex distributed system with varied control, processing and fault-tolerance requirements, the assumption of asynchrony has been a starting point. Communication has also been studied in terms of asynchrony because this allows an interpretation of communication phenomena that is close to what can be observed and implemented.

Popular reasons for introducing asynchrony are to combine good average case responsiveness with effective bounded response to infrequent (but perhaps critical) external events, to allow less restricted implementation on multiple processor or distributed systems, or even because of a belief that "that's how the world works". Combinatoric analysis and scheduling theory are commonly used for the analysis of asynchronous systems to allow a higher degree of optimisation in the use of computing resources. In contrast, the dedicated commitment of computing resources needed to support the synchrony hypothesis can make it hard to satisfy restrictions placed on the cost, weight or power consumption of a practical real-time system.

Assumption Set 3

3a. External events are 'timed' by external clocks and internal events must closely follow external timing.

3b. Finite state representations of internal actions are hard to obtain so other methods must be used for analysis.

3c. Possible implementations of the system may be constrained by external requirements.

With its popularity and widespread adoption, it is not surprising that there are many areas where the limitations of the methods of analysis mean that further restrictions must be imposed (or further assumptions made) if the timing properties of a system are to be fully determined. Among these restrictions are the use of discrete rather than continuous time, the imposition of determinism, and approximating cyclic behaviour and aperiodicity by periodic behaviours. Few of these restrictions are really compatible with the asynchrony hypothesis: they must be justified because without them the analysis of the timing behaviour is not possible.

6 Models of time

Questions of time have intrigued philosophers and mathematicians for thousands of years. The best known of these must be Zeno of Elea (5C B.C) whose paradoxes of time and space (cf. [27]) play games with our intuitive notions of temporal and spatial continuity and atomicity. The paradox of Achilles and the tortoise provides a basis for the so-called Zeno machine: a machine which performs infinitely many computations in finite time.

There is a mathematical justification for considering time as a dense domain, and a physical justification for choosing the real domain. In computational terms, there are three dominating arguments:

1. Independent events in a distributed computation may appear arbitrarily close together in time, and so time must be represented in some dense domain.

2. Physical processes are modelled with time in a continuous (real) domain, so programs that interact with physical processes must represent time in a similar way.

3. There is a lower bound to the execution time of every instruction, and by scaling with this a discrete time domain can represent any timing property of a program.

If a dense domain of time is chosen, computations may take arbitrarily small times and we have the kind of Zeno machine studied in 1967 by Bjorn Kirkerud [14] who showed that Zeno-computable is hyperarithmetical. To this must be added the argument first made by Best in 1978 (cf. the later paper [4]) that without a finiteness axiom, a Zeno machine can solve the Halting Problem. The first proof system in which such an axiom appeared was for Hewitt's Actors [11], and it next made an appearance in the compositional temporal logic of Barringer, Kuiper and Pnueli [1] and in most real-time semantic models from that of Reed and Roscoe [23] onwards.

There is at least one practical reason in favour of using a dense domain, which is that the execution time of an instruction typically lies in a real interval rather than having a fixed value. But there are technical reasons as well, for example as shown in the denotational semantics of Roncken and Gerth [25]. Thus both in terms of theory and practice, specification of time in some dense domain can be justified, though the reasons for choosing between different dense domains (e.g. the reals or the rationals) are less compelling.

Unfortunately, the analysis of implementations with timing properties expressed using a dense domain is difficult, and without further restrictions it seems at present not possible to determine whether an implementation satisfies such a specification. There is work in progress which suggests that the simplifications needed for a tractable method of analysis may be less severe than expected: for example, a wide range of timing properties may be expressed and proved using only the upper and lower bounds of real intervals, rather than all possible values in the interval[20]. And the recent work of Henzinger, Manna and

Pnueli[10] provides another solution by suggesting how a specification based on a model with discrete snapshots of a computation timed with a continuous model of time can be made amenable to model-checking.

7 Implementability

The specification and refinement of a real-time program will lead to a text in some programming language; additional timing constraints may need to be expressed in terms of constraints over the execution of the program, defining properties such as deadlines, periodicity and minimum separation. But having reached this far, it is usually assumed to be an engineering problem to ensure that the implementation of the program on a real system will satisfy the timing requirements.

This 'engineering' problem is usually addressed by scheduling theory (e.g. [18] [22]) using methods of establishing the *feasibility* of the implementation of a program. Unfortunately, the program models analyzable by scheduling theory are considerably more restricted than those that will typically satisfy a specification. Equally unfortunately, the timing characteristics of programs with multiprocessor or distributed implementations are difficult to express and *verify* in most specification notations. Thus there is a wide gap between the outcome of the specification/verification method – which may be a program with some time constraints – and the program models that are amenable to scheduling theory (this issue was first explored by Mok [21]).

There are many reasons why the gap between verification methods and performance analysis appears to be unbridgeable.

1. There is a wide variety of architectures on which a real-time program may be implemented and it is impossible to represent their timing characteristics in any sufficiently abstract way for it to be of use in a verification method.

2. The timing characteristics of programs are so varied that unless they are vastly simplified, it is difficult to predict their timing behaviour when executed on a particular system.

3. Effective use of the hardware requires efficient scheduling of the use of resources by the program; if this is functionally transparent to the programmer, no resource dependencies will be encoded into the program and the performance of the scheduler can be predicted.

It is fairly obvious from this that both in terms of levels of abstraction and objects of abstraction there is no meeting ground. Scheduling theory is unable to make any constructive use of the control and dependency structure of the program and verification methods fall far short of the ability to analyse the precise timing effects of program executions on particular systems with particular scheduling policies. And even when a scheduling policy is comparatively simple, as in the Transputer, the formal definition of its actions can be remarkably complex.

But the situation is not without hope. First, the development of programs from specifications need not stop with producing the text of the program but can proceed to consider, at least at an abstract level, the allocation of the program to the main resources of the architecture (some initial work in this direction has very recently been done by Davis [6] and Hooman [12]): thus the partitioning of processes between physical processors and the assignment of interprocess communication pathways to physical channels can be done without an unreasonable addition of complexity to the task of computing the timing characteristics [19].

Second, and this is harder, there is need for some abstraction of scheduling policies so that they are characterised by bounded time performance guarantees which can be used to determine the timing properties of programs. This is possible provided the scheduling margins are sufficiently generous to allow variations in scheduling tactics without violating the broad timing characteristics.

8 Global and local time

Specification notations for real-time programs are usually based on the uses of a global time, e.g. as seen by an external observer. However, in a distributed system it is only possible to approximate such an assumption and the extent of approximation may be significant; message propogation delays are often difficult to estimate accurately, and the kind of faults that may occur and their frequency may severely affect these estimates.

Bounds must be placed on timings made under a global time assumption in order for them to be effectively transformed into time values that are consistent with the specification and which can be observed and measured at the nodes of a distributed system.

9 Fault-tolerance

The problem of constructing fault-tolerant programs can be considered as one of transforming a program written for execution on a *fault-free* system into a *fault-tolerant* program for execution on a system which is susceptible to failures. For this to be possible, the fault environment must be represented by a specification F. Interference by the fault environment F on the execution of a program P can then be described as a *fault-transformation* $\mathcal{F}$ which transforms P into a program $\mathcal{F}(P)$. It can be shown[17] that this is equivalent to the program $P[]P_{\mathbf{F}}$, where $P_{\mathbf{F}}$ is derived from P and F, and $[]$ defines the union of the sets of actions of P and $F_{\mathbf{P}}$. A recovery transformation $\mathcal{R}$ transforms P into a program $\mathcal{R}(P) = P[]P_{\mathbf{R}}$ by adding a set of *recovery actions* $P_{\mathbf{R}}$, called a *recovery program*. If the system is *fail-stop* and faults do not affect recovery actions, we have

$$\mathcal{F}(\mathcal{R}(P)) = \mathcal{F}(P)[]P_{\mathbf{R}} = P[]P_{\mathbf{F}}[]P_{\mathbf{R}}$$

In practice, fault-tolerant systems usually have real-time constraints. So it is important that the timing properties of a program are refined along with the fault-tolerant and functional properties defined in a program specification. If we extend the model used in the transformational framework by adding timing properties with respect to some *time domain* [13], the recovery transformation and refinement can be defined with timing constraints. The specification and refinement of a fault-tolerant program can then be required to satisfy the condition that after a fault occurs, the system is restored to a consistent state within a time bound which includes the delay caused by the execution of a the recovery action.

This formal treatment of fault-tolerance assumes that faults are *detected* by some underlying mechanism and establishes the required fault-tolerant properties for detected faults only. It has been argued[5] that if time is added to the specification, then it can also be used explicitly to detect both transient and permanent faults. However, if this is done as part of the program specification, it is also necessary to make recovery actions (such as the taking of checkpoints and state restoration) explicit and this can have the consequence of making the attractive properties of compositionality, mentioned above, more difficult to obtain.

10 Conclusions

Real-time programs are designed for a number of different applications and the assumptions that can be made for each application determines the kind of specification method that can be used. Naturally, the simplest assumptions lead to the simplest systems but there are sometimes practical requirements for systems with more complex characteristics.

One part of the problem of designing a correct real-time program is that of specifying and verifying its properties; another is to prove that the implementation of the program satisfies these properties. If the system architecture is complex (and this may be necessary due to the nature of the application), the second part of this task is non-trivial and there is at present no single method which encompasses both tasks. So it seems essential that a mathematically sound 'interface' is provided and that the most appropriate methods are used for each task.

When the specification and verification of a real-time program also requires proof of its fault-tolerance, it too must be partitioned so that the fault environment can be specified independently of the program and recovery actions chosen so that they ensure that the system continues to have predictable behaviour.

References

[1] H. Barringer, R. Kuiper, and A. Pnueli. Now you may compose temporal logic specifications. In *Proceedings of the 16th ACM Symposium on the Theory of Computing*, pages 51–63, Washington D.C., 1984.

[2] A. Bernstein and P.K. Harter, Jr. Proving real-time properties of programs with temporal logic. In *Proceedings of the 8th Annual ACM Symposium on Operating Systems Principles*, pages 1–11, 1981.

[3] G. Berry and L. Cosserat. The ESTEREL synchronous programming language and its mathematical semantics. In *Lecture Notes in Computer Science 197*, pages 389–449. Springer-Verlag, Heidelberg, 1985.

[4] E. Best. A theorem on the characteristics of non-sequential processes. *Fundamenta Informaticae III.1*, pages 77–94, 1980.

[5] F. Cristian. Understanding fault-tolerant distributed systems. IBM Research Report RJ 6980, April 1990.

[6] J. Davis. *Specification and Proof in Real-time Systems.* PhD thesis, Programming Research Group, Oxford University Computing Laboratory, Oxford, 1991.

[7] P. le Guernic and A. Benveniste. Real-Time, Synchronous, Data-Flow Programming: The Language SIGNAL and its Mathematical Semantics. Technical Report 620, INRIA Rennes, 1986.

[8] D. Harel. Statecharts: A visual formalism for complex systems. *Science of Computer Programming*, 8(3):231–274, 1987.

[9] E.C.R. Hehner. Real-time programming. *Information Processing Letters*, 30:51–56, 1989.

[10] T. Henzinger and Z. Manna and A. Pnueli. What good are digital clocks? . Technical Report, Stanford University, 1991.

[11] C. Hewitt and H. Baker. Actors and continuous functionals. In E.J. Neuhold, editor, *Formal Description of Programming Concepts*, pages 367–390. North-Holland, Amsterdam, 1978.

[12] J. Hooman. *Specification and Compositional Verification of Real-time Systems.* PhD thesis, Department of Mathematics and Computing Science, Eindhoven University of Technology, Eindhoven, 1991.

[13] M. Joseph and A.K. Goswami. What's real about real-time systems? *Proc. RTSS88*, Huntsville, Alabama, pages 78-85, 1988.

[14] B. Kirkerud. *Hyperarithmetical Turing-machines.* PhD thesis, Department of Mathematics, University of Oslo, Oslo, 1967.

[15] L. Lamport. TIMESETS: a new method for temporal reasoning about programs. In *Lecture Notes in Computer Science 131*, pages 177–196. Springer-Verlag, Heidelberg, 1981.

[16] G. le Lann. Critical issues for the development of distributed real-time computing systems. Technical Report 1274, INRIA, Rocquencourt, 1990.

[17] Z. Liu and M. Joseph. Transformation of programs for fault-tolerance. *Formal Aspects of Computing*, (to appear).

[18] C.L. Liu and J.W. Layland. Scheduling algorithms for multiprocessing in a hard real-time environment. *Journal of the ACM*, 20:46–61, 1973.

[19] A. Moitra and M. Joseph. Implementing real-time systems by transformation. In H. Zedan, editor, *Real-time Systems: Theory and Applications*, pages 143–157. North-Holland, 1990.

[20] A. Moitra and M. Joseph. Determining timing properties of infinite real-time programs. Technical Report RR172, University of Warwick, Department of Computer Science, 1991.

[21] A.K. Mok. Fundamental design problems of distributed systems for the hard real-time environment. Technical Report MIT/LCS/TR-297, Massachusetts Institute of Technology, 1983.

[22] K. Ramamritham and J.A. Stankovic and P.F. Shiah. Efficient scheduling algorithms for real-time multiprocessor systems. *IEEE Transactions on Parallel and Distributed Systems*, 1(2):184–194, 1990.

[23] G.M. Reed and A.W. Roscoe. Metric spaces as models for real-time concurrency. In *Lecture Notes in Computer Science 298*, pages 331–343. Springer-Verlag, Heidelberg, 1988.

[24] W.-P. de Roever. Foundations of computer science: Leaving the ivory tower. Technical Report 9105, Institut für Informatik und Praktische Mathematik, Christian-Albrechts-Universität zu Kiel, Kiel, 1991.

[25] M. Roncken and R. Gerth. A denotational semantics for synchronous and asynchronous behaviour with multiform time. In *Proceedings of the International BCS-FACS Workshop on Semantics for Concurrency*, pages 21–37. Springer-Verlag, London, 1990.

[26] W.M. Turski. Time considered irrelevant for real-time systems. *BIT*, 28:473–486, 1988.

[27] G.J. Whitrow. *The Natural Philosophy of Time*. Clarendon Press, Oxford, 1980.

[28] N. Wirth. Towards a discipline of real-time programming. *Communications of the ACM*, 20(8):577–583, 1977.

Abstraction in Real Time Process Algebra

A.S. Klusener

CWI

P.O. Box 4079, 1009 AB Amsterdam, The Netherlands

e-mail: stevenk@cwi.nl

Abstract. In this paper we extend Real Time Process Algebra by the silent step τ. We start by giving the operational semantics and we find a characterizing law of which the soundness and the completeness is proven. By adding the integral construct we can interpret symbolic (untimed) process terms as timed processes. We investigate the resulting τ-equivalence and come to a delay bisimulation with a stronger root condition. Finally we test the applicability of this notion of real time abstraction by proving the PAR protocol (Positive Acknowledgement with Retransmission) correct.

1985 Mathematics Subject Classification: 68Q60.
1982 CR Categories: D.3.1, F.3.1, J.7.
Key Words & Phrases: Real Time, Process Algebra, ACP, Abstraction, Protocol Verification.
Note: This work is in part sponsored by ESPRIT Basic Research Action 3006, CONCUR. Some proofs have been omitted in this paper, they can be found in the full version which has appeared as CWI report CS9144 under the same title.

1 Introduction

In recent years much effort is paid to develop techniques for proving software systems correct w.r.t. to their specification. A motivation and an overview of these techniques can be found in [dR89]. In this paper we restrict ourselves to ACP ([BW90]), which is a Proces Algebra like CCS ([Mil89]) and CSP ([Hoa85]). The idea of protocol verification by using Process Algebra is that one has a specification and an implementation both formulated in the same language. One can abstract from the implementation details by renaming certain "internal" actions to the silent action τ. Then, one can apply the axioms of the algebra for proving the equality between the specification and the implementation. For examples of protocol verification in (untimed) Process Algebra we refer to [Bae90].

The most common notion of abstraction, weak bisimulation, is due to Milner [Mil80]. Van Glabbeek and Weijland introduced in [GW89] delay bisimulation and branching bisimulation, which are slightly different notions of abstraction.

In timed Process Algebra abstraction is not yet well developed. Only Wang studied abstraction in a timed Process Algebra (timed CCS) ([Wan90]), although his weak bisimulation is not a congruence. In another timed extension of a Process Algebra, Timed CSP ([RR88],[Ree89]), there is a special action $WAIT\ t$ which idles for t time units. In this way an internal activity can be expressed. Similar constructs can be found in [MT90], [HR90]. It may be the case that the introduction of a τ action to Real Time ACP makes it more easy to compare Real Time ACP with other calculi.

In this paper a notion of abstraction in Real Time Process Algebra is proposed. As starting point we take the work of Baeten and Bergstra, they presented in [BB91] their Real Time Process Algebra BPA$\rho\delta$. In that paper they suggested already to interpret a timed τ as an explicit idling. We will investigate this idea more thoroughly.

We take BPA$\rho\delta$ (without integrals) and add the timed action $\tau(t)$. The operational semantics is given and we give a complete axiomatization. The addition of the integral construct allows us to interpret symbolic process terms as a special class of timed process terms. It comes out that the resulting subtheory can be considered as being a delay bisimulation with a strongly rooted condition. By generalizing the laws of earlier sections we obtain axioms for process terms with integrals. Finally, we show the use of this theory by giving a protocol verification which depends on time.

This paper is based on "absolute" time, thus the timestamps of the actions are interpreted from the starting point. This is not a serious point since all results can be formulated in "relative" time as well.

2 Adding the Silent Step to the Original Semantics

2.1 The Syntax

In this Section we give some intuition for timed processes by introducing the operational semantics of [BB91] for process expressions over Basic Real Time Process Algebra (BPA$\rho\delta$). We do not yet consider integration in this section. Let $A_{\delta\tau}$ be the set of actions, containing the constants δ (for inaction) and τ (for internal activity). The alphabet of the theory BPA$\rho\delta\tau$ is

$$A_{\delta\tau}^{time} = \{a(t) | a \in A_{\delta\tau}, t \in \mathbb{R}^{\geq 0}\}$$

Similarly we use A_{τ}^{time}, as the set of timed actions without timed δ's. In the sequel we refer to actions from $A_{\delta\tau}$ as symbolic actions and we refer to actions from $A_{\delta\tau}^{time}$ as timed actions. Moreover, process expressions are simply called terms. The set $\mathcal{T}$ of (closed) terms over BPA$\rho\delta\tau$ is generated by the alphabet A_{δ}^{time} and the binary operators $+$ for alternative composition and $\cdot$ for sequential composition and the operator $\gg$, called the *(absolute) time shift.*

The *(absolute) time shift*, $\gg$, takes a nonnegative real number and a process term; $t \gg X$ denotes that part of X which starts after t. The set $\mathcal{T}$ with typical elements p, p_1, p_2 is defined in the following way, where $a \in A_{\delta\tau}$ and $r \in \mathbb{R}^{\geq 0}$:

$$p \in \mathcal{T} \quad p := a(r) \mid p_1 + p_2 \mid p_1 \cdot p_2 \mid r \gg p$$

Syntactical equivalence is denoted by $\equiv$, syntactical equivalence modulo associativity and commutativity of the $+$ is denoted by $\simeq$. Equivalence within a theory $\mathcal{TH}$ is denoted by $\mathcal{TH} \vdash p = q$ or simply $p = q$ when the theory is clear from the context. $\delta(0)$ is abbreviated by δ.

There are three functions defined by induction. $U(p)$ is the *ultimate delay* of p and $S(p)$ is the *earliest start time* of p and $L(p)$ is the *latest start time.* We need an auxiliary function *inittime*; *inittime*(p) contains all time stamps at which p can perform an initial action

These functions already occur in [Klu91]. a is taken from A_τ

$$
\begin{array}{lll lll}
U(a(t)) & = & t & inittime(a(t)) & = & \{t\} \\
U(\delta(t)) & = & t & inittime(\delta(t)) & = & \emptyset \\
U(p\cdot q) & = & U(p) & inittime(p\cdot q) & = & inittime(p) \\
U(p+q) & = & max(U(p),U(q)) & inittime(p+q) & = & inittime(p)\cup inittime(q) \\
U(r\gg p) & = & max(r,U(p)) & inittime(r\gg p) & = & inittime(p)\cap <r,\omega>
\end{array}
$$

We take $max(\emptyset) = min(\emptyset) = 0$ and we define $S(p) = min(inittime(p))$ and $L(p) = max(inittime(p))$.

2.2 The Original Semantics

The semantics of Baeten and Bergstra ([BB91]) assigns to every term (in $\mathcal{T}$) a transition system in which each state is a pair consisting of a term and a point in time and in which each transition is labeled by a timed (non δ) action.

For example the process $a(1)$ starts in state $<a(1),0>$, denoting that each process starts at 0. From $<a(1),0>$ an *idle* transition is possible to a state of the form $<a(1),t>$ with $0<t<1$. An *idle* transition is a transition in which only the time component is increased without executing any action. In general, from each state $<a(1),t>$ an *idle* transition is possible to $<a(1),t'>$, whenever $t<t'<1$. Furthermore, from each state $<a(1),t>$ a terminating $a(1)$-transition to $<\surd,1>$ is possible whenever $t<1$.

For technical reasons we add in this paper a boolean value to each state, which is initialized on F. So, the process $a(1)$ starts in $<a(1),0,F>$. An *idle* transition does not change the boolean value. As soon as an action is executed the value is set to T. Once the value is set to T it remains T throughout the execution of the proces.

For the moment it suffices to say that we need the boolean value to distinguish root states from internal states. A root state is a state with time 0 or a state which can be reached from a state with time 0 by idling only.

Within this semantics the transition system concerns three relations

$$
\begin{array}{lllllll}
Step & \subseteq & (\mathcal{T}\times \mathbb{R}^{\geq 0}\times\{T,F\}) & \times & A^{time} & \times & (\mathcal{T}\times \mathbb{R}^{\geq 0}\times\{T,F\}) \\
Idle & \subseteq & (\mathcal{T}\times \mathbb{R}^{\geq 0}\times\{T,F\}) & \times & (\mathcal{T}\times \mathbb{R}^{\geq 0}\times\{T,F\}) & & \\
Terminate & \subseteq & (\mathcal{T}\times \mathbb{R}^{\geq 0}\times\{T,F\}) & \times & A^{time} & \times & \mathbb{R}^{\geq 0}
\end{array}
$$

These three relations are defined as the least relations satisfying the action rules given in Table 1. The definition of an operational semantics by giving action rules is due to Plotkin ([Plo81]). We write

$$
\begin{array}{lll}
<x,t,b> \xrightarrow{a(r)} <x',t',b'> & \text{for} & (<x,t,b>,a(r),<x',t',b'>) \in Step \\
<x,t,b> \longrightarrow <x',t',b'> & \text{for} & (<x,t,b>,<x',t',b'>) \in Idle \\
<x,t,b> \xrightarrow{a(r)} <\surd,t'> & \text{for} & (<x,t,b>,a(r),t') \in Terminate
\end{array}
$$

The transition relation will be defined such that it is guaranteed that

$$
\begin{array}{lll}
<x,t,b> \xrightarrow{a(r)} <x',t',b'> & \Longrightarrow & t<r \wedge t'=r \wedge b'=T \\
<x,t,b> \longrightarrow <x',t',b'> & \Longrightarrow & t<t' \wedge b=b' \\
<x,t,b> \xrightarrow{a(r)} <\surd,t'> & \Longrightarrow & t<r \wedge t'=r
\end{array}
$$

As notion of equivalence we have strong bisimulation; every *step* or *idle* transition on the left hand side has to be matched with an associated *step* or *idle* transition on the right hand side. A bisimulation relation on $(\mathcal{T} \times \mathbb{R}^{\geq 0} \times \{F, T\}) \times (\mathcal{T} \times \mathbb{R}^{\geq 0} \times \{F, T\})$ is defined in the obvious way. Two terms p, q are bisimilar, denoted by $p \leftrightarrow_{orig} q$, if there is a bisimulation relation containing $(< p, 0, F >, < q, 0, F >)$. The action rules are given in Table 1.

From the atomic rules for $\tau(r)$ we see that executing the silent step τ is modeled by an *idle* step which changes the process term in the state. Therefore we have to cover now as well cases where idling may change the process term in the state.

2.3 Some Process Diagrams

The transition system of the term $a(1)$ can be represented by the left-hand process diagram given in Figure 1. A process diagram is simply a pictorial representation of a transition system. It is not possible to make a picture of the transition system itself, since it has uncountably many transitions. The intuition behind such a process diagram is that the process starts in the top-point. It can idle by going to a lower point without crossing any line, whereas the execution of an action a at time r is reflected by going to a dashed line at level r labeled with a. Only dashed lines may be crossed, after landing on them.

A very particular set of atomic actions is the set of $\delta(r)$-terms. $\delta(1)$ can do nothing more then idling until 1. Thus the root node is $< \delta(1), 0 >$ and from each state $< \delta(1), t >$ an *idle* transition to $< \delta(1), t' >$ is possible, whenever $t < t' < 1$.

The transition system of $p + q$ is defined in terms of the transition systems of p and q. The behaviour of $p + q$ can be considered as the "union" of the behaviour of p and that of q.

A state μ (in Figure 1) is of the form $< a(1) + b(2), t >$ with $0 < t < 1$. From μ both a terminating $a(1)$-transition to $< \surd, 1 >$ and a terminating $b(2)$-transition to $< \surd, 2 >$ are possible. However, from a state like ν of the form $< a(1) + b(2), t >$ with $1 \leq t < 2$ only a terminating $b(2)$-transition to $< \surd, 2 >$ is possible. Hence, by idling from $< a(1) + b(2), t_0 >$ to $< a(1) + b(2), t_1 >$ with $0 < t_0 < 1 \leq t_1 < 2$ we have lost the option of executing the $a(1)$-summand. Thus one could say that a choice has been made at time 1; after the choice has been made for $b(2)$ the summand $a(1)$ has become redundant.

The transition system of $a(1) + \delta(1)$ consists of exactly the same relations as the transition system of $a(1)$. The summand $\delta(1)$ contributes only *idle* steps which are con-

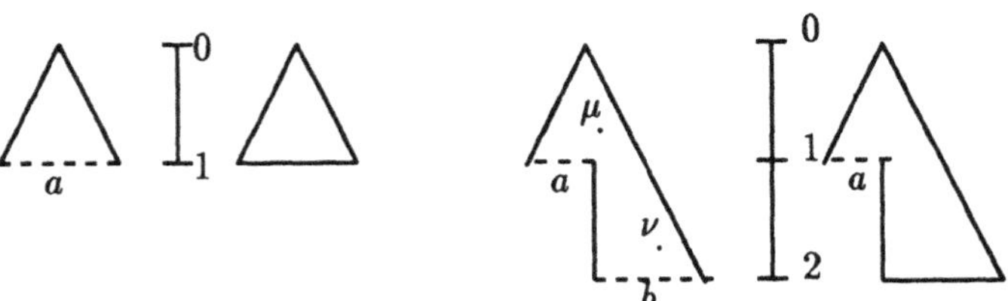

Figure 1: Process Diagrams of the terms $a(1)$,$\delta(1)$, $a(1) + b(2)$ and $a(1) + \delta(2)$

$$\frac{t < s < r}{< a(r), t, b > \longrightarrow < a(r), s, b >} \qquad \frac{t < r}{< a(r), t, b > \xrightarrow{a(r)} < \surd, r >}$$

$$\frac{t < s < r}{< \tau(r), t, b > \longrightarrow < \tau(r), s, b >} \qquad \frac{t < r}{< \tau(r), t, b > \longrightarrow < \surd, r >}$$

$$\frac{t < s < r}{< \delta(r), t, b > \longrightarrow < \delta(r), s, b >}$$

$$\frac{< p, t, F > \longrightarrow < p, r, F >}{< p + q, t, b > \longrightarrow < p + q, r, b >}$$

$$\frac{< p, t, b > \xrightarrow{a(r)} < \surd, r >}{< p + q, t, b > \xrightarrow{a(r)} < \surd, r >} \qquad \frac{< p, t, b > \xrightarrow{a(r)} < p', r, b' >}{< p + q, t, b > \xrightarrow{a(r)} < p', r, b' >}$$

$$\frac{< p, t, b > \longrightarrow < \surd, r >}{< p + q, t, b > \longrightarrow < \surd, r >} \qquad \frac{< p, t, F > \longrightarrow < p', r, T >}{< p + q, t, b > \longrightarrow < p', r, T >}$$

And similar rules for $q + p$

$$\frac{< p, t, b > \xrightarrow{a(r)} < \surd, r >}{< p \cdot q, t, b > \xrightarrow{a(r)} < q, r, T >} \qquad \frac{< p, t, b > \xrightarrow{a(r)} < p', r, b' >}{< p \cdot q, t, b > \xrightarrow{a(r)} < p' \cdot q, r, b' >}$$

$$\frac{< p, t, b > \longrightarrow < \surd, r >}{< p \cdot q, t, b > \longrightarrow < q, r, T >} \qquad \frac{< p, t, b > \longrightarrow < p', r, b' >}{< p \cdot q, t, b > \longrightarrow < p' \cdot q, r, b' >}$$

$$\frac{t < r < s}{< s \gg p, t, b > \longrightarrow < s \gg p, r, b >}$$

$$\frac{r > s \quad < p, t, b > \xrightarrow{a(r)} < \surd, r >}{< s \gg p, t, b > \xrightarrow{a(r)} < \surd, r >} \qquad \frac{r > s \quad < p, t, b > \xrightarrow{a(r)} < p', r, b' >}{< s \gg p, t, b > \xrightarrow{a(r)} < p', r, b' >}$$

$$\frac{r > s \quad < p, t, b > \longrightarrow < \surd, r >}{< s \gg p, t, b > \longrightarrow < \surd, r >} \qquad \frac{r > s \quad < p, t, b > \longrightarrow < p', r, b' >}{< s \gg p, t, b > \longrightarrow < p', r, b' >}$$

Table 1: The Original Transition System of BPA$\rho\delta\tau$, ($a \in A,\ r, s > 0$)

tributed by the summand $a(1)$ as well, hence we may consider the $\delta(1)$ summand as being redundant.

However if we consider $a(1)+\delta(2)$, the $\delta(2)$ summand contributes *idle* transitions which are not contributed by $a(1)$, since $\delta(2)$ has *idle* transitions to points in time between 1 and 2. The transition system of $a(1) + \delta(2)$ can be represented by the process diagram on the right-hand side in Figure 1.

The last operator we introduce is the *(absolute) time shift* denoted by $\gg$, which takes a real number s and a process X and delivers that part of X which starts after s. Hence, before s it can only *idle* or do a transition to a state after s.

2.4 The Closure Rules

In the original transition system of Baeten and Bergstra, thus the one without silent actions and without a boolean value in the state, the following property was guaranteed:

$$<p,t> \longrightarrow <p,s> \;\wedge\; <p,s> \xrightarrow{a(r)} <p',r> \quad \Longrightarrow \quad <p,t> \xrightarrow{a(r)} <p',r>$$

Since we require this property also in the context with silent steps (where idling may change the process term), we need the following *closure* rules. In the sequel we will discuss why these closure rules may only be applied on internal states.

$$\frac{<p,t,T> \longrightarrow <p',t',T> \quad <p',t',T> \xrightarrow{a(r)} <\surd,r>}{<p,t,T> \xrightarrow{a(r)} <\surd,r>} \qquad \frac{<p,t,T> \longrightarrow <p',t',T> \quad <p',t',T> \longrightarrow <\surd,r>}{<p,t,T> \longrightarrow <\surd,r>}$$

$$\frac{<p,t,T> \longrightarrow <p',t',T> \quad <p',t',T> \xrightarrow{a(r)} <p'',r,T>}{<p,t,T> \xrightarrow{a(r)} <p'',r,T>} \qquad \frac{<p,t,T> \longrightarrow <p',t',T> \quad <p',t',T> \longrightarrow <p'',r,T>}{<p,t,T> \longrightarrow <p'',r,T>}$$

Table 2: The Closure Rules, $(a \in A,\ r, s > 0)$

In Figure 2 we see process diagrams corresponding to the terms $a(1)\cdot(\tau(2)\cdot b(3)+c(3))$ and $a(1)\cdot(b(3)+\tau(2)\cdot c(3))$. On the left hand side the process diagrams without closure rules are given; without closure rules the terms are certainly not bisimilar. On the right hand side the process diagrams with closure rules are given; the two terms have become bisimilar.

Since in both terms the two summands are in a context $a(1)\cdot(...)$ we know that there are no other summands involved, hence the $\tau(2)$ action determines a moment of choice, namely at time 2. But it is not relevant whether the $\tau(2)$ is on the left hand side of the $+$ or on the right hand side. Consider $\tau(2)\cdot b(3)+c(3)$, thus without context $a(1)\cdot(...)$, then we can not say that the choice for the $c(3)$ is made at 2. This becomes clear when we would add $d(3)$. In the next Section we discuss this in more detail.

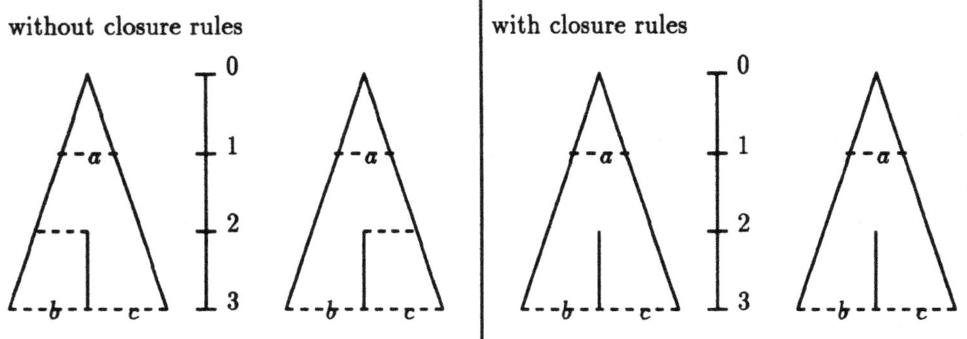

Figure 2: Process Diagrams for $a(1) \cdot (\tau(2) \cdot b(3) + c(3))$ and $a(1) \cdot (b(3) + \tau(2) \cdot c(3))$

In the sequel we refer to *idle* steps which are generated by the closure rules as *implicit (idle) steps*. Similarly we have *explicit (idle) steps.*

2.5 Closure Rules and Internal States

Now we can discuss the need for distinguishing root states from internal states. Assume that we would not make this distinction, so forget about the boolean values. And assume that we would apply the closure rules on the root level as well. Then we would have

$$a(1) + \tau(1) \cdot b(2) \quad \leftrightarrow \quad a(1) + b(2)$$

But if we add $c(2)$ then

$$a(1) + \tau(1) \cdot b(2) + c(2) \quad \not\leftrightarrow \quad a(1) + b(2) + c(2)$$

Since in the left hand process the choice for the $b(2)$-summand is made at time 1, while in the right hand side the corresponding choice is made at time 2. Thus in case of $a(1)+b(2)$ it is not right to say that the choice for the $b(2)$ is made at 1, since other summands, such as $c(2)$, may be there in the context.

If we put both terms in a sequential composition after $d(1)$ then

$$d(1) \cdot (a(1) + \tau(1) \cdot b(2)) \quad \not\leftrightarrow \quad d(1) \cdot (a(1) + b(2))$$

because only the right hand process has an option of doing the b at time 2.

So, when the closure rules are applied from the root level as well bisimulation equivalence is not a congruence. By making the distinction between root states and internal states we can apply the closure rules only for internal states and bisimulation equivalence is a congruence. For example:

$$a(1) + \tau(1) \cdot b(2) \quad \not\leftrightarrow \quad a(1) + b(2)$$

3 An Alternative Operational Semantics

3.1 Encoding the Course of Time in the Process Terms

In the previous Section the operational semantics is presented according to [BB91]. Each state consisted of three components. In this Section we give a transition relation, in which the course of time is encoded in the prefix by an occurrence of the $\gg$ operator. In [Klu91] a similar operational semantics is given. Since no abstraction was considered in that paper it was not necessary to model the *idle* steps there. Hence, the transition relation became finite for (recursion free) terms without integration. Now, we encorporate the silent step into this semantics; *idle* steps which determine a moment of choice are modeled by τ-steps. Moreover, we define a notion of equivalence, called *timed weak* bisimulation, which coincides with $\underline{\leftrightarrow}_{orig}$.

In the semantics for ACP, as presented in [Gla87], we have the following transitions

$$a \xrightarrow{a} \surd \quad \text{and} \quad a \cdot p \xrightarrow{a} p$$

In a real time setting we have to take the time stamps into account. In $a(r) \cdot p$, after doing the $a(r)$ action, only that part of p can be done which starts after r, which is denoted by $r \gg p$. Hence, after the addition of time we have the following transitions (we have also added the boolean values).

$$< a(r), b > \xrightarrow{a(r)} \surd \quad \text{and} \quad < a(r) \cdot p, b > \xrightarrow{a(r)} < r \gg p, T >$$

If p can perform an action $b(t)$ then $s \gg p$ can perform this action only if $t > s$.

3.2 The Transition System Specification

In table 3 an alternative operational semantics is given. Only the *implicit* τ-rule is new here, the other ones are taken from [Klu91]. This *implicit* τ-rule models a moment of choice by a τ-step. The alternative operational semantics given in this Section concerns two relations:

$$\begin{array}{llllll} Step & \subseteq (\mathcal{T} \times \{F,T\}) & \times & A_{\delta\tau}^{time} & \times & (\mathcal{T} \times \{F,T\}) \\ Terminate & \subseteq (\mathcal{T} \times \{F,T\}) & \times & A_{\delta\tau}^{time} & & \end{array}$$

These relations are defined as the least relations satisfying the action rules of Table 3. We write:

$$\begin{array}{lll} < p, b > \xrightarrow{a(r)} < p', b' > & \text{for} & ((p,b), a(r), (p',b')) \in Step \\ < p, b > \xrightarrow{a(r)} \surd & \text{for} & ((p,b), a(r)) \in Terminate \end{array}$$

Again it is guaranteed that $b' = T$ if $< p, b > \xrightarrow{a(r)} < p', b' >$. This can be shown by induction on the length of the derivation. It is also guaranteed that

$$a \in A_\tau \; : < p, T > \xrightarrow{a(r)} < p', T > \quad \Longrightarrow \quad r = S(p)$$

All initial actions of p with a time stamp greater than $S(p)$ are postponed till a later state, as is shown in Figure 3. Two terms p and q are bisimilar, denoted by $p \underline{\leftrightarrow}_{tw} q$, if there

$$< a(r), b > \xrightarrow{a(r)} \surd$$

$$\frac{< p, F > \xrightarrow{a(r)} \surd}{< p+q, F > \xrightarrow{a(r)} \surd} \qquad \frac{< p, F > \xrightarrow{a(r)} < p', T >}{< p+q, F > \xrightarrow{a(r)} < p', T >}$$

$$\frac{r \leq S(q) \quad < p, T > \xrightarrow{a(r)} \surd}{< p+q, T > \xrightarrow{a(r)} \surd} \qquad \frac{r \leq S(q) \quad < p, T > \xrightarrow{a(r)} < p', T >}{< p+q, T > \xrightarrow{a(r)} < p', T >}$$

And similar rules for $q + p$

$$\frac{< p, b > \xrightarrow{a(r)} \surd}{< p \cdot q, b > \xrightarrow{a(r)} < r \gg q, T >} \qquad \frac{< p, b > \xrightarrow{a(r)} < p', T >}{< p \cdot q, b > \xrightarrow{a(r)} < p' \cdot q, T >}$$

$$\frac{s < r \quad < p, b > \xrightarrow{a(r)} \surd}{< s \gg p, b > \xrightarrow{a(r)} \surd} \qquad \frac{s < r \quad < p, b > \xrightarrow{a(r)} < p', T >}{< s \gg p, b > \xrightarrow{a(r)} < p', T >}$$

δ-rule

$$\frac{U(p) > L(p)}{< p, b > \xrightarrow{\delta(U(p))} \surd}$$

implicit τ-rule

$$\frac{s = S(r \gg p) < U(s \gg p)}{< r \gg p, T > \xrightarrow{\tau(s)} < s \gg p, T >}$$

Table 3: An Alternative Operational Semantics, ($a \in A_\tau,\ r, s > 0$)

is a *timed weak* bisimulation relation containing $(< p, F >, < q, F >)$. In the following definition $< p, T > \stackrel{a(r)}{\Longrightarrow} < p', T >$ abbreviates $< p, T > \xrightarrow{\tau(t_1)} < p_1, T > \ldots < p_k, T > \xrightarrow{a(r)} < p', T >$ for some $k \geq 0$, moreover a is take from $A_{\delta\tau}$ and a' is taken from A_δ.

Definition 3.2.1 *$R \subset (\mathcal{T} \times \{T, F\}) \times (\mathcal{T} \times \{T, F\})$ is a timed weak bisimulation relation iff it is symmetric and $(< p, b >, < q, b >) \in R$ implies that*

- *if $b = F$ and $< p, F > \xrightarrow{a(r)} < p', T >$ then there is a q' such that $< q, F > \xrightarrow{a(r)} < q', T >$ and $(< p', T >, < q', T >) \in R$.*
- *if $b = F$ and $< p, F > \xrightarrow{a(r)} \surd$ then $< q, F > \xrightarrow{a(r)} \surd$.*
- *if $b = T$ and $< p, T > \xrightarrow{a'(r)} < p', T >$ then there is a q' such that $< q, T > \stackrel{a'(r)}{\Longrightarrow} < q', T >$ and $(< p', T >, < q', T >) \in R$.*

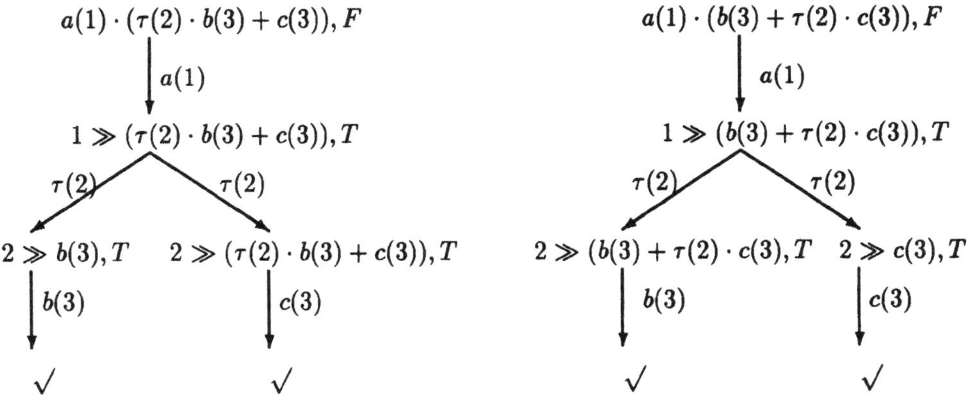

Figure 3: Transition Systems for $a(1) \cdot (\tau(2) \cdot b(3) + c(3))$ and $a(1) \cdot (b(3) + \tau(2) \cdot c(3))$

- *if* $b = T$ *and* $< p, T > \xrightarrow{\tau(r)} < p', T >$ *then either* $(< p', T >, < q, T >) \in R$ *or there is a* q' *such that* $< q, T > \overset{\tau(r)}{\Longrightarrow} < q', T >$ *and* $(< p', T >, < q', T >) \in R$
- *if* $b = T$ *and* $< p, T > \xrightarrow{a(r)} \surd$ *then* $< q, T > \overset{a(r)}{\Longrightarrow} \surd$.

The δ-rule generates transitions labeled with $\delta(t)$, for example if $t < 2$ then

$$< t \gg (a(1) + \delta(2)), b > \xrightarrow{\delta(2)} \surd$$

These deadlock transitions are needed to distinguish $a(1) + \delta(2)$ from $a(1) + \delta(3)$. Note that $< a(1) + \delta(1), b >$ does not have a *deadlock* transition at all. *Deadlock* transitions are discussed exhaustively in [Klu91], but they are not important for discussing the silent step. Hence, they will not be mentioned anymore in this paper.

In this transition relation we have *implicit* τ-steps only when they determine a moment of choice. Consider the state $< r \gg p, T >$. Assume that the first moment in time at which $r \gg p$ can do an action is s (e.g. $S(r \gg p) = s$). Furthermore, assume that it can idle till a moment after s (e.g. $U(r \gg p) > s$). Then we say that s is a moment of choice; either the actions with time stamp s are executed or the idling continues and the actions with timestamp s are dropped from the computation. Since there are only finitely many of those moments of choice we have only finitely many τ-steps as well. In Figure 3 the states $< 2 \gg b(3), T >$ and $< 2 \gg (b(3) + \tau(2) \cdot c(3), T >$ may be related by a *timed weak* bisimulation relation. In Section 5 we will give a corresponding semantics where we can use the standard notion of strong bisimulation. The price to pay, however, is that we have to allow infinite many *implicit* τ steps there.

We can prove similarly as in [Klu91]:

Lemma 3.2.2 *Bisimulation equivalence in the alternative operational semantics equals bisimulation equivalence in the original operational semantics.*

$$p \leftrightarrow_{tw} q \quad \Longleftrightarrow \quad p \leftrightarrow_{orig} q$$

Thus we may omit the subscripts of $\leftrightarrow_{tw}$ and $\leftrightarrow_{orig}$. In Section 5 we will prove that bisimulation equivalence is a congruence.

4 The Theory BPA$\rho\delta\tau$

4.1 A Characterizing Law

From the operational semantics we know that a τ-action may be removed if it does not determine a choice. Moreover, this τ-removal can only be applied 'within' a term and not at the level of the root. This is exactly characterized by the τ-law given in Table 4.1. The theory BPA$\rho\delta$ can be found in [BB91] and [Klu91]

TAU1	$t < r < U(X) \ \wedge \ U(Y) \leq r$
$a(t) \cdot (\tau(r) \cdot X + Y) = a(t) \cdot (r \gg X + Y)$	

Table 4: BPA$\rho\delta\tau$ = BPA$\rho\delta$ + TAU1

Lemma 4.1.1 *The axiom TAU1 is sound w.r.t. to bisimulation equivalence.*

Theorem 4.1.2 *Soundness of BPA$\rho\delta\tau$*

$$BPA\rho\delta\tau \ \vdash p = q \quad \Longrightarrow p \leftrightarrow q$$

Proof. A theory is sound w.r.t. to an equivalence if all the axioms are sound and if the equivalence is a congruence w.r.t. to all operators. Since the bisimulation equivalence introduced in this paper identifies more than the one of [Klu91] we may conclude that all the axioms of BPA$\rho\delta$ are still sound. Moreover, in Lemma 4.1.1 we have stated the soundness of the additional τ-law and we will show that bisimulation equivalence is a congruence in Section 5. □

Lemma 4.1.3 *Assume $t < r < min(S(X), S(Y))$ and $U(Z) \leq r$ then*

$$\begin{array}{lll} \tau\text{-}removal & a(t) \cdot \tau(r) \cdot X & = a(t) \cdot X \\ \tau\text{-}swap & a(t) \cdot (\tau(r) \cdot X + Y) & = a(t) \cdot (X + \tau(r) \cdot Y) \\ \tau\text{-}swap & a(t) \cdot (\tau(r) \cdot X + Y + Z) & = a(t) \cdot (X + \tau(r) \cdot Y + Z) \end{array}$$

Proof.

$$\begin{array}{lll} a(t) \cdot \tau(r) \cdot X & = & a(t) \cdot (\tau(r) \cdot X + \delta) \\ & = & a(t) \cdot (X + \delta) \\ & = & a(t) \cdot X \end{array}$$

$$\begin{array}{lll} a(t) \cdot (\tau(r) \cdot X + Y) & = & a(t) \cdot (\tau(r) \cdot X + \tau(r) \cdot Y) \\ & = & a(t) \cdot (X + \tau(r) \cdot Y) \end{array}$$

$$\begin{array}{lll} a(t) \cdot (\tau(r) \cdot X + Y + Z) & = & a(t) \cdot (\tau(r) \cdot X + \tau(r) \cdot Y + Z) \\ & = & a(t) \cdot (X + \tau(r) \cdot Y + Z) \end{array}$$

□

4.2 Completeness

In this Section we prove the completeness of BPA$\rho\delta\tau$, e.g. we have to prove that if two terms are bisimilar then there is a derivation in BPA$\rho\delta\tau$ which proves them equal. We construct for each pair of bisimilar terms another pair of terms by adding τ-actions, such that the resulting pair is also bisimilar in the semantics without closure rules. We only add τ-actions in one term if there is already an associated τ in the other term. Or, put in other words, if implicit idling is matched with explicit idling then the implicit idling is rewritten into an explicit idling. Thus the pair

$$(\; a(1) \cdot b(3) \cdot d(4) \quad , \quad a(1) \cdot \tau(2) \cdot b(3) \cdot (d(4) + d(4)) \;)$$
is rewritten into
$$(\; a(1) \cdot \tau(2) \cdot b(3) \cdot d(4) \quad , \quad a(1) \cdot \tau(2) \cdot b(3) \cdot (d(4) + d(4)) \;)$$

Since we are working in absolute time and since we have timed δ's, we allow terms with a lot of "junk" (redundant parts) in it. A *basic* term is a term without "junk". If we consider a term like $a(2)\cdot b(1)$, then the b can never be executed at 1 after we have executed the a at 2. Thus a *deadlock* will be encountered after executing the a at 2. Hence, we can rewrite the term $a(2) \cdot b(1)$ into the *basic* term $a(2) \cdot \delta$, where the *deadlock* appears explicitly. Similarly we can remove all *redundant* δ's, for example the $\delta(2)$ is *redundant* in the term $a(2) + \delta(2)$.

For the formal definition of *basic* terms and for further details we refer to [Klu91]. The set of *basic* terms is denoted by $\mathcal{B}$. Next, we rewrite all *basic* terms of the form

$$\textstyle\sum_i a_i(r) \cdot p_i + \sum_j b_j(r) + q \qquad \textit{with} \;\; S(q) > r$$
into
$$\textstyle\sum_i a_i(r) \cdot p_i + \sum_j b_j(r) + \tau(r) \cdot q$$

In this way we obtain the set of *ordered* terms which is denoted by $\mathcal{B}^{ord}$.

If p is an *ordered* term starting after s we may write $p \in \mathcal{B}^{ord}(s)$. If we take $\sum_{i\in\emptyset} p_i \equiv \delta$, then every *ordered* term is of the form

$$\sum_i a_i(r) \cdot p_i + \sum_j b_j(r) \quad \text{with } p_i \in \mathcal{B}^{ord}(r)$$

For each $s \in \mathbb{R}^{\geq 0}$ and *timed weak* bisimulation relation R we define a function f_R^s which maps a pair of *ordered* terms onto another pair of *ordered* terms. The construction of $f_R^s(p,q)$ guarantees that

Lemma 4.2.1 *If p,q in $\mathcal{B}^{ord}(s)$ and $(< s \gg p, T >, < s \gg q, T >)$ in R and $f_R^s(p,q) = (p',q')$, then*

- $BPA\rho\delta\tau \;\vdash a(s) \cdot p = a(s) \cdot p' \,, \quad a(s) \cdot q = a(s) \cdot q'$
- $p' \leftrightarrow q'$

Here, $\leftrightarrow$ denotes strong bisimulation in the transition system without *implicit* τ-rule, which is completely characterized by BPA$\rho\delta$. The complexity of a pair of *ordered* terms is the pair of natural numbers $(depth(p) + depth(q)$, number of summands in $(p+q))$, and we assume a lexicographic ordering on pairs of natural numbers.

Definition 4.2.2

$$f_R^s \in \mathcal{B}^{ord}(s) \times \mathcal{B}^{ord}(s) \longrightarrow \mathcal{B}^{ord}(s) \times \mathcal{B}^{ord}(s)$$

We construct $f_R^s(p,q)$ inductively; we assume that we have constructed already the function f_R^t on pairs with smaller complexity for arbitrary t.

Consider (p,q) both in $\mathcal{B}^{ord}(s)$ and a *timed weak* bisimulation relation R containing $(< s \gg p, T >, < s \gg q, T >)$ such that

$$\begin{array}{lcl} p & \simeq & \sum_{j\in J} a_j(t)\cdot p_j + \sum_{j\in J'} a'_j(t) \\ q & \simeq & \sum_{l\in L} b_l(r)\cdot q_l + \sum_{l\in L'} b'_l(r) \end{array}$$

There are two cases, either $J = \emptyset = L$ or $J \neq \emptyset \ \vee\ L \neq \emptyset$. In the first case we simply take $f_R^s(p,q) = (p,q)$. The second case has on its turn two subcases, $t = r$ and $t \neq r$; these subcases are considered below. We assume that $J \neq \emptyset$.

- If $t = r$ then for every j in J $a_j \in A_\tau$ and there is a z_j (with $z_j \equiv q_l$ for some $l \in L$) such that

  $$\begin{array}{ccc} < s \gg p, T > & \stackrel{a_j(t)}{\longrightarrow} & < t \gg p_j, T > \\ R & & R \\ < s \gg q, T > & \stackrel{a_j(t)}{\longrightarrow} & < t \gg z_j, T > \end{array}$$

  By induction we have already constructed $f_R^t(p_j, z_j) = (p'_j, q''_j)$. Similarly for every l we can find a term z'_l obtaining $f_R^t(q_l, z'_l) = (q'_l, p''_l)$. (It is more efficient of course to construct (q'_l, p''_l) only for those $l \in L$ such that $q_l \not\equiv z_j$ for every $j \in J$, but this will not be considered any further).

  Since $(< s \gg p, T >, < s \gg q, T >) \in R$ it is guaranteed that every terminating $a'_j(t)$ step can be matched by some terminating $b'_l(r)$ and vice versa.

  We define

  $$\begin{array}{lcll} f_R^s(p,q) & = & (& \sum_{j\in J} a_j(t)\cdot p'_j + \sum_{l\in L} b_l(t)\cdot p''_k + \sum_{j\in J'} a'_j(t) \quad , \\ & & & \sum_{j\in J} a_j(t)\cdot q''_j + \sum_{l\in L} b_l(t)\cdot q'_l + \sum_{l\in L'} b'_l(t) \quad) \end{array}$$

- If $t \neq r$ then we may assume $t < r$. Then it must be the case that $a_j = \tau$ for all j in J and $J' = \emptyset$. We have for every j that $(< t \gg p_j, T >, < s \gg q, T >)$ in R. Since $s < t$ and $q \in \mathcal{B}^{ord}(t)$ we may extend R such that it remains a *timed weak* bisimulation relation which contains $(< s \gg q, T >, < t \gg q, T >)$. Hence we may extend R further such that it contains $(< t \gg p_j, T >, < t \gg q, T >)$ for each $j \in J$. By induction we have already constructed $f_R^t(p_j, q) = (p'_j, q''_j)$. We define

  $$f_R^s(p,q) \ = \ (\sum_{j\in J} \tau(t)\cdot p'_j, \ \sum_{j\in J} \tau(t)\cdot p''_j\ )$$

Now we are ready to give the completeness proof.

Theorem 4.2.3 *Completeness of BPA$\rho\delta\tau$*

$$p \leftrightarrow q \Longrightarrow BPA\rho\delta\tau \ \vdash p = q$$

Proof. We prove it first for *ordered* terms p and q, assume

$$\begin{array}{lcl} p & \simeq & \sum_{j\in J} a_j(t_j)\cdot p_j + \sum_{j\in J'} a'_j(t'_j) \\ q & \simeq & \sum_{l\in L} b_l(r_l)\cdot q_l + \sum_{l\in L'} b'_l(r'_l) \end{array}$$

We take some *timed weak* bisimulation relation R which contains $(< p, F >, < q, F >)$. From a root state (a state with boolean value F) no *implicit* τ steps have to be considered. Hence, for each j in J there is a l_j in L such that

$$a_j = b_{l_j} \quad \wedge \quad t_j = r_{l_j} \quad \wedge \quad (< t_j \gg p_j, T >, < t_j \gg q_{l_j}, T >) \in R$$

and we take $f_R^{t_j}(p_j, q_{l_j}) = (p'_j, q''_j)$. We do similar for each l in L and its associated index j_l in J. We construct p' and q',

$$\begin{array}{lcl} p' & \simeq & \sum_{j\in J} a_j(t_j)\cdot p'_j + \sum_{l\in L} b_l(r_l)\cdot p''_l + \sum_{j\in J'} a'_j(t'_j) \\ q' & \simeq & \sum_{j\in J} a_j(t_j)\cdot q''_j + \sum_{l\in L} b_l(r_l)\cdot q'_l + \sum_{l\in L'} b'_l(r'_l) \end{array}$$

such that BPA$\rho\delta\tau$ $\vdash p = p', q = q'$. By construction $p' \leftrightarrow q'$. Hence, BPA$\rho\delta$ $\vdash p' = q'$ and BPA$\rho\delta\tau$ $\vdash p = q$ follows immediately.

If we start with *non ordered* terms p and q, with $p \leftrightarrow q$, then we construct *ordered* terms p_o and q_o such that BPA$\rho\delta$ $\vdash p = p_o, q = q_o$. By soundness of BPA$\rho\delta$ we obtain $p \leftrightarrow p_o$ and $q \leftrightarrow q_o$ and by transitivity of $\leftrightarrow$ we get $p_o \leftrightarrow q_o$. Now we have reduced it to the previous case and we conclude BPA$\rho\delta\tau$ $\vdash p_o = q_o$ from which we conclude BPA$\rho\delta\tau$ $\vdash p = q$. □

5 A Third Corresponding Semantics

In the two transition relations of the previous sections we had to keep track of a boolean value in each state to distinguish root states from internal states. In this Section we give another solution, we extend the set of terms $\mathcal{T}$ to $\mathcal{T}^{\gg}$ by adding a new *(absolute) time shift* operator $\gg$, which will be used to encode whether a state is internal or not. We saturate the transition relation with all possible *implicit* τ steps as was the case in the original semantics of Baeten and Bergstra as well. This enables us to deal with strong bisimulation instead of *timed weak* bisimulation.

Furthermore, we define only one relation $\longrightarrow \subset \mathcal{T}^{\gg} \times \mathcal{T}^{\gg}$. We now have $a(r) \xrightarrow{a(r)} \delta$ instead of $a(r) \xrightarrow{a(r)} \surd$ (which abbreviated $(a(r), r) \in Terminate$). By doing so we avoid a lot of rules. The action rules are given in Table 5. Two terms are bisimilar, denoted by $p \leftrightarrow_{\gg} q$, if there is a strong bisimulation relation $R \subset \mathcal{T}^{\gg} \times \mathcal{T}^{\gg}$. This approach only works when there are no occurrences of $\gg$ at the root level. Therefore we have the following equivalence for terms without $\gg$.

Lemma 5.0.4 $p, q \in \mathcal{T}$ $$p \leftrightarrow_{\gg} q \iff p \leftrightarrow q$$

We still have to prove the following Theorem, which can be proven easily for the bisimulation equivalence defined by the transition relation of Table 5.

$$a(r) \xrightarrow{a(r)} \delta \qquad \frac{L(p) < U(p)}{p \xrightarrow{\delta(U(p))} \delta} \qquad \frac{s < r \quad p \xrightarrow{a(r)} p'}{s \gg p \xrightarrow{a(r)} p'}$$

$$\frac{p \xrightarrow{a(r)} \delta}{p \cdot q \xrightarrow{a(r)} r \overline{\gg} q} \qquad \frac{p' \not\equiv \delta \quad p \xrightarrow{a(r)} p'}{p \cdot q \xrightarrow{a(r)} p' \cdot q} \qquad \frac{p \xrightarrow{a(r)} p'}{p + q \xrightarrow{a(r)} p' \,,\; q + p \xrightarrow{a(r)} p'}$$

$$\frac{s \gg p \xrightarrow{b(r)} p'}{s \overline{\gg} p \xrightarrow{b(r)} p'} \qquad \frac{r < s < U(r \gg p)}{r \overline{\gg} p \xrightarrow{\tau(s)} s \overline{\gg} p} \qquad \frac{s \overline{\gg} p \xrightarrow{\tau(t)} p' \quad p' \xrightarrow{a(r)} p''}{s \overline{\gg} p \xrightarrow{a(r)} p''}$$

Table 5: An Operational Semantics without Boolean Value ($a \in A_\tau$, $b \in A_{\delta\tau}$, $r, s > 0$)

Lemma 5.0.5 *Bisimulation Equivalence is a congruence w.r.t. all operators*

Proof. If all action rules of a Transition System Specification are in Groote's *ntyft/ntyxt* format, then bisimulation equivalence is a congruence (see [Gro89]). We have to prove only for the closures rules that they can be written into this format, since in [Klu91] we proved it already for all other action rules of Table 5. The first and the third closure rule are already in the right format and for the second one we may take

$$\frac{s < t \quad r \gg p \xrightarrow{b(t)} p''}{r \overline{\gg} p \xrightarrow{\tau(s)} s \overline{\gg} p} \quad \text{instead of} \quad \frac{r < s < U(r \gg p)}{r \overline{\gg} p \xrightarrow{\tau(s)} s \overline{\gg} p}$$

□

In this paper we will not mention anymore this variant of the semantics, since we do not want to discuss the inclusion of the operator $\overline{\gg}$ in the theory.

6 Symbolic Processes as Timed Processes

In this Section we interpret each symbolic process term as a timed process. We will investigate the resulting subtheory.

6.1 The Interpretation of Symbolic Process Terms as Timed Processes

By using the integral construct of Baeten and Bergstra we can express a process which executes an a somewhere in time by the process term $\int_{v>0} a(v)$. The formal introduction of the integral construct is postponed till the next section. By extending the syntax with the integral construct we obtain BPA$\rho\delta\tau I$. We define a function RT : BPA$\delta\tau \longrightarrow$ BPA$\rho\delta\tau I$, which interprets every symbolic process term as a timed process.

$$\begin{array}{lll} a \in A \quad RT(a) & \stackrel{def}{=} & \int_{v>0} a(v) \cdot \int_{w>0} \tau(w) \\ RT(\tau) & \stackrel{def}{=} & \int_{v>0} \tau(v) \\ RT(\delta) & \stackrel{def}{=} & \int_{v>0} \delta(v) \\ RT(p+q) & \stackrel{def}{=} & RT(p) + RT(q) \\ RT(p \cdot q) & \stackrel{def}{=} & RT(p) \cdot RT(q) \end{array}$$

Originally, Baeten and Bergstra had $RT(a) \stackrel{def}{=} \int_{v>0} a(v)$ (they denote $RT(p)$ by $\underline{p}$). But in this case the first τ-law $X \cdot \tau = X$ ([Mil89]) would not be sound anymore. Since we prefer to maintain this law we define $RT(a) \stackrel{def}{=} \int_{v>0} a(v) \cdot \int_{w>0} \tau(w)$.

The range of the function RT is denoted by RT(BPA$\delta\tau$).

6.2 A Delay Bisimulation Semantics on BPA$\delta\tau$

Here we give a semantics for symbolic processes which corresponds with the semantics of their timed interpretations. In the previous sections we have studied transition relations which where τ-saturated, i.e all possible appropriate τ-steps between internal states were added.

In this Section we will not saturate the transition relation but we move the τ-saturation into the definition of bisimulation. In this way we obtain a notion of delay bisimulation [GW89].

$$a \xrightarrow{a} \surd \qquad \frac{p \xrightarrow{a} \surd}{p+q \xrightarrow{a} \surd} \qquad \frac{p \xrightarrow{a} p'}{p+q \xrightarrow{a} p'}$$

$$\frac{p \xrightarrow{a} \surd}{p \cdot q \xrightarrow{a} q} \qquad \frac{p \xrightarrow{a} p'}{p \cdot q \xrightarrow{a} p' \cdot q}$$

Table 6: Transition System Specification for Symbolic Process Terms ($a \in A_\tau$)

Moreover we want to get rid of this boolean value. In the previous sections the boolean value guaranteed that the closure rules were only applied on internal states, hence from a root only explicit steps were defined. This property will be expressed now by a root condition which is stronger then the usual one ([GW89]).

If there is a path $p_0 \xrightarrow{\tau} p_1 \ldots \xrightarrow{\tau} p_k$ then we may write $p_0 \Longrightarrow p_k$. In this Section we allow ourselves the freedom to consider $\surd$ as a special state.

Definition 6.2.1 *A relation $R \subset$ BPA$\delta\tau \cup \{\surd\} \times$ BPA$\delta\tau \cup \{\surd\}$ is strongly rooted w.r.t. p and q if it obeys the following ($a \in A_\tau$):*

- *R relates p and q with each other and not with other terms.*
- $p \xrightarrow{a} p'$ *implies that there is a* q' *such that* $q \xrightarrow{a} q'$ *and* $(p', q') \in R$.
- $q \xrightarrow{a} q'$ *implies that there is a* p' *such that* $p \xrightarrow{a} p'$ *and* $(q', p') \in R$.

A relation R is *rooted* if it satisfies the first of the conditions above. An example of a relation which is *strongly rooted* is given in Figure 4. In this Figure we can see that the *strongly rooted* requirement corresponds to the requirement that the closure rule is applied on internal states only.

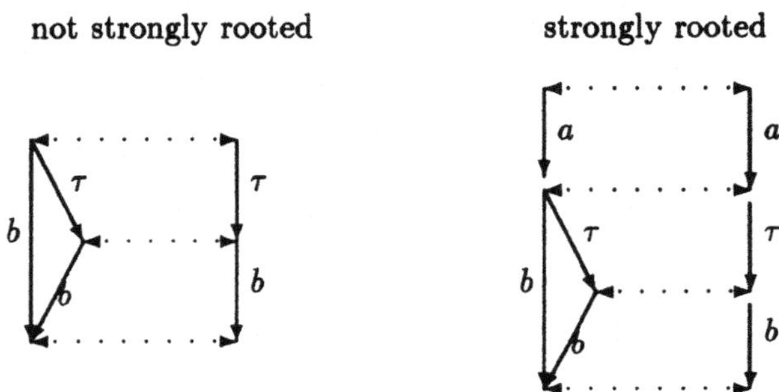

Figure 4: Example of Strongly Rootedness

Definition 6.2.2 *Symbolic Bisimulation or Strongly Rooted Delay Bisimulation*

$$p \underline{\leftrightarrow}_{sym}\, q$$

iff there is a symmetric relation $R \subset \mathrm{BPA}\delta\tau \cup \{\surd\} \times \mathrm{BPA}\delta\tau \cup \{\surd\}$ *which is strongly rooted w.r.t.* p *and* q *such that for every pair* (r, s) *in* R *with* $r \xrightarrow{a} r'$ *either* $a = \tau$ *and* (r', s) *in* R *or* $s \Longrightarrow s'' \xrightarrow{a} s'$ *and* (r', s') *in* R .

In the sequel we will use the definition of rooted Branching Bisimulation ([GW89]) as well.

Definition 6.2.3 *Rooted Branching Bisimulation*

$$p \underline{\leftrightarrow}_{rb}\, q$$

iff there is a bisimulation relation $R \subset \mathrm{BPA}\delta\tau \times \mathrm{BPA}\delta\tau$ *which is rooted w.r.t.* p *and* q *such that for every pair* (r, s) *in* R *with* $r \xrightarrow{a} r'$ *either* $a = \tau$ *and* (r', s) *in* R *or* $s \Longrightarrow s'' \xrightarrow{a} s'$ *and both* (r, s'') *and* (r', s') *in* R.

We have the following Lemma, since strongly rootedness is implied by rooted branching bisimulation.

Lemma 6.2.4 $\quad p \underline{\leftrightarrow}_{rb} q \quad \Longrightarrow \quad p \underline{\leftrightarrow}_{sym} q$

Finally we have the following Theorem which states that the equivalence $\leftrightarrow_{sym}$ is exactly the equivalence which we obtain by interpreting symbolic processes as timed processes. Bisimulation equivalence over BPA$\delta\tau$ is denoted by $\leftrightarrow_{sym}$ and bisimulation equivalence over RT(BPA$\delta\tau$) is denoted by $\leftrightarrow_{time}$.

Theorem 6.2.5 $$p \leftrightarrow_{sym} q \quad \Longleftrightarrow \quad RT(p) \leftrightarrow_{time} RT(q)$$

6.3 Completeness for Strongly Rooted Delay Bisimulation

In this Section we give a complete axiomatization for the equivalence $\leftrightarrow_{sym}$ following the work of Van Glabbeek and Weijland ([GW89]). We take the axioms DEL 1 and 2 from [GW89], where it is proven that these two axioms characterize Branching Bisimulation completely. Furthermore, we take the axiom

$$\tau \cdot Y = \tau \cdot Y + Y\ ,$$

which can be found in [GW89] as well and we require that it is only applied in a context. In this way we obtain

$$\text{DEL3} \quad X \cdot (\tau \cdot Y + Z) = X \cdot (\tau \cdot Y + Y + Z)$$

Since Van Glabbeek and Weijland use a graph model we have to define the following. The set of graphs $\mathcal{G}$ is the set of triples (N, E, r) where N is a set of nodes , $E \subset N \times N$ is a set of edges and $r \in N$ is the root. Moreover, if $g = (N, E, r)$ then $E(g) = E$. A graph g is trivial if $E(g) = \emptyset$. $\mathcal{G}^+$ is the set of non trivial graphs. The graph of a term p is denoted by $[\![p]\!]$, this graph can be seen as that part of the transition relation which is associated with p, where $\surd$ is now considered as a special state.

Definition 6.3.1 *The graph rewriting* $\longrightarrow_\tau$
If a graph g *has a path* $s \xrightarrow{\tau} s' \xrightarrow{a} s''$ *where* s *is not the root of* g *and* g *has no edge* $s \xrightarrow{a} s''$ *then* $s \xrightarrow{a} s''$ *is added.*

Lemma 6.3.2 $$[\![p]\!] \longrightarrow_\tau g \quad \Longrightarrow \quad \exists p' \;\; [\![p']\!] = g \wedge \text{DEL3} \vdash p = p'$$

As in [GW89] we can prove easily

Lemma 6.3.3

DEL1 $\;X \cdot \tau = X$
DEL2 $\;X \cdot (\tau \cdot (Y + Z) + Y) = X \cdot (Y + Z)$
DEL3 $\;X \cdot (\tau \cdot Y + Z) = X \cdot (\tau \cdot Y + Y + Z)$

Table 7: BPA$\delta\tau_{del}$

- *Both $\mathcal{G}$ and $\mathcal{G}^+$ are closed under $\longrightarrow_\tau$.*
- *$\longrightarrow_\tau$ is confluent and terminating.*

Definition 6.3.4 *A graph g is τ-saturated if it can not be reduced any further by $\longrightarrow_\tau$.*

Lemma 6.3.5 *If g and h are τ-saturated graphs then*

$$g \leftrightarrow_{sym} h \iff g \leftrightarrow_{rb} h$$

Proof. Since $\leftrightarrow_{rb}$ is a smaller equivalence than $\leftrightarrow_{sym}$ it is sufficient to prove that $R : g \leftrightarrow_{sym} h$ implies $R : g \leftrightarrow_{rb} h$.

- The roots are related only with each other
- if $R(r,s)$ and $r \xrightarrow{a} r'$ then either
  - $a = \tau$ and $(r', s) \in R$ or
  - $s \Rightarrow s'' \xrightarrow{a} s'$ with $(r', s') \in R$, assume $s = s_0 \xrightarrow{\tau} s_1 \ldots \xrightarrow{\tau} s_k = s''$, since h is τ-*saturated* we have $s_i \xrightarrow{a} s'$ and also $s \xrightarrow{a} s'$. □

Theorem 6.3.6 $$p \leftrightarrow_{sym} q \iff \mathrm{BPA}\delta\tau_{del} \vdash p = q$$

Proof.

- $\Longleftarrow$ The soundness can be seen by investigating the operational semantics.
- $\Longrightarrow$ By construction of the graph model we have $p \leftrightarrow_{sym} q$ iff $[\![p]\!] \leftrightarrow_{sym} [\![q]\!]$. By τ-*saturating* the graphs $[\![p]\!]$ and $[\![q]\!]$ we obtain g and h. By Lemma 6.3.2 we can construct terms p' and q' such that $[\![p']\!] = g$, $[\![q']\!] = h$ and $\mathrm{BPA}\delta\tau_{del} \vdash p = p', q = q'$. By transitivity of $\leftrightarrow_{sym}$ we get $g \leftrightarrow_{sym} h$ and since g and h are τ-*saturated* we obtain $g \leftrightarrow_{rb} g$ and by the completeness result of Van Glabbeek and Weijland we conclude $\mathrm{BPA}\delta\tau_{del} \vdash p' = q'$, from which it follows directly that $\mathrm{BPA}\delta\tau_{del} \vdash p = q$. □

7 Adding Integrals

An *integral* can be considered as a sum over a continuum of alternatives, this notion is introduced in [BB91]. Baeten and Bergstra allow integration over arbitrary subsets of the real numbers and they allow more then one integral behind each other. The idea of *prefixed integration* is that every action has as time stamp a *time variable* v taken from some set $TVar$, and the action is directly preceded by the integral binding this v. Moreover, only *Intervals* are allowed. In [Klu91] a completeness result is given for *prefixed integration*. The term $\int_{v\in<0,1>} a(v)$ denotes the process which executes an action a somewhere between 0 and 1. An *integral* binds a *time variable*, which may occur in the rest of the term, for example the term $\int_{v\in<0,1>} a(v) \cdot \int_{w\in<v+1,v+2>} b(w)$ denotes the process which executes an action a at t where t is within 0 and 1. It waits between 1 and 2 time units after t and executes an action b. Hence, the *bounds* of a interval of an *integral* are (linear) expressions over the real numbers. Let $t \in \mathbb{R}^{\geq 0}, v \in TVar$ then we can define the set *Bounds* as follows:

$$b \in Bounds \quad b := t \mid v \mid b_1 + b_2 \mid b_1 \dot{-} b_2 \mid t \cdot b$$

where $\dot{-}$ denotes the monus operator, i.e $5 \dot{-} 3 = 2$ but $3 \dot{-} 5 = 0$. If $b \in Bounds$ then the set of *time variables* occurring in b is denoted by $tvar(b)$. Now we can construct intervals like $< 1, 9 >$ and $< v + 3, w >$. An interval without free *time variables* can be considered as a connected part of the nonnegative reals. However, we don't want to deal with the complexity of set theory over reals and we want to define intervals containing occurrences of free *time variables.* Hence, every interval is a four tuple, containing two booleans and two reals. The interval $V = (F, 1, 2, T)$ is abbreviated in the sequel by $V =< 1, 2]$, denoting that the lower bound is open and 1, and that the upper bound is closed and 2. If $b \in Bounds$ then $b \in V$ denotes the logical expression of (in)equalities

TAUI1 $V < W < U(X) \wedge U(Y) \leq inf(W)$ $\int_{v \in V} a(v) \cdot ((\int_{w \in W} \tau(w)) \cdot X + Y) = \int_{v \in V} a(v) \cdot (inf(W) \gg X + Y)$
TAUI2 $V < W < U(X + Y) \wedge U(Y) = sup(W)$ $\int_{v \in V} a(v) \cdot ((\int_{w \in W} \tau(w)) \cdot (X + Y) + X) = \int_{v \in V} a(v) \cdot (X + inf(W) \gg Y)$ TAUI3 $V < W < U(X) \wedge U(X) = sup(W)$ $\int_{v \in V} a(v) \cdot ((\int_{w \in W} \tau(w)) \cdot X + Y) = X \cdot ((\int_{w \in W} \tau(w)) \cdot X + inf(W) \gg X + Y)$

Table 8: BPAρI = BPA$\rho\delta_T$ $+ TAUI1 - 3$

$1 < b \leq 2$. Similarly we have $t \in V_1 \cup V_2$, $t < sup(V)$, $V = \emptyset$, $V_1 < V_2$ and $V < t$ as abbreviations for logical expressions over *Bounds*.

We can redefine the set of terms. Let $a \in A_{\delta\tau}$, $V \in Int$, $v \in TVar$, $b \in Bounds$

$$p \in T \quad p := \int_{v \in V} (a(v)) \mid \int_{v \in V} (a(v) \cdot p) \mid p \cdot q \mid p + q \mid r \gg p$$

We abbreviate $\int_{v \in [w,w]} a(v)$ by $a(w)$ and $\delta(0)$ by δ. In this definition the notion of prefixed integration becomes clear; every action has as time stamp a *time variable* v and is directly preceded by its binding integral. Hence, we do not allow a term like $\int_{v \in V} \int_{w \in W} (a(v) \cdot \int_{r \in <v,w>} b(1) \cdot c(r))$. On these terms we have notions as $FV()$ for the set of free *time variables* , α-conversion, and substitution. If a term or interval has no free *time variables,* then it is called *time closed.*

The adaptions of the transition relation as given in Table 3 are given in Table 9. Due to the integral construct there is no more a discrete notion of a moment of choice, hence the closure rule must generate infinitely many τ-steps.

Theorem 7.0.7 *The laws* TAUI1 − 3 *are sound*

$r \in V$	$<\int_{v \in V} a(v), b> \xrightarrow{a(r)} \surd$	instead of	$<a(r), b> \xrightarrow{a(r)} \surd$
$r \in V$	$<\int_{v \in V}(a(v) \cdot p), b> \xrightarrow{a(r)} r \gg p[r/v]$		
$\dfrac{r < s < U(s \gg p)}{<r \gg p, T> \xrightarrow{\tau(s)} <s \gg p, T>}$		instead of	$\dfrac{s = S(r \gg p) < U(s \gg p)}{<r \gg p, T> \xrightarrow{\tau(s)} <s \gg p, T>}$

Table 9: (Additional/Changed) Action Rules for Integral Construct

8 Protocol Verification

Now we are ready to verify a protocol which is time dependent. First we have to state the fact that every time guarded recursive specification has exactly one solution (RSP and RDP). A guarded recursive specification is time guarded if there is a lower bound bound on the time interval between two recursion variable unfoldings. This is only an informal characterization but it is needed to exclude so-called 'Zeno' machines. The proof of this principle and a thorough treatment of time guarded specifications do not fall into the scope of this paper, they will treated in later papers. Next, we have to state an *Unwind Principle* (UP) which allows us to unwind a recursive specification infinitely many times. The dots in the derivation below express that this principle is not provable within the theory BPA$\rho\delta\tau$ in a finite derivation . We take $Y(t)$ such that

$$t \gg Y(t) = Y(t)$$

thus assuming that $Y(t)$ has no parts starting at or before t. We define $X(t)$ as

$$X(t) = \tau(t) \cdot \{Y(t+s) + \tau(t+r_0) \cdot X(t+r_1)\}$$

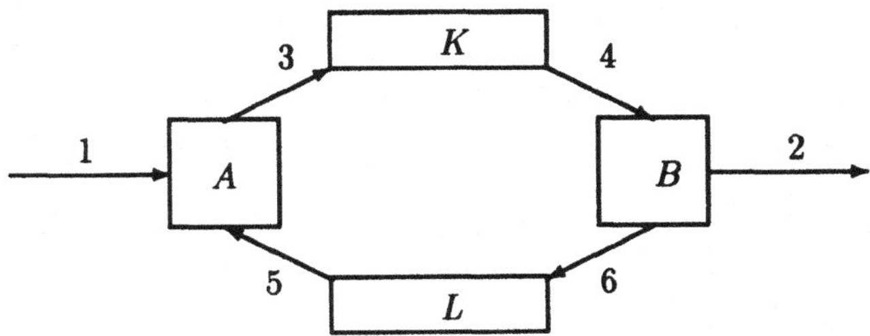

for some $r_0 < r_1$ and $r_0 < s$ then

$$\begin{aligned}
X(t) &= \tau(t)\cdot\{Y(t+s)+\tau(t+r_0)\cdot X(t+r_1)\}\\
&= \tau(t)\cdot\{\tau(t+r_0)\cdot Y(t+s)+X(t+r_1)\}\\
&= \tau(t)\cdot\{\tau(t+r_0)\cdot Y(t+s)+\\
&\qquad \tau(t+r_1)\cdot\{Y(t+s+r_1)+\tau(t+r_0+r_1)\cdot X(t+2\cdot r_1)\}\}\\
&= \tau(t)\cdot\{\tau(t+r_0)\cdot Y(t+s)+\{Y(t+s+r_1)+\tau(t+r_0+r_1)\cdot X(t+2\cdot r_1)\}\}\\
&= \tau(t)\cdot\{\tau(t+r_0)\cdot Y(t+s)+\tau(t+r_0+r_1)\cdot Y(t+s+r_1)+X(t+2\cdot r_1)\}\\
&\cdot\\
&\cdot\\
&\cdot\\
&\overset{UP}{=} \tau(t)\cdot\{\textstyle\sum_{n=0}^{\infty}\tau(t+r_0+n\cdot r_1)\cdot Y(t+s+n\cdot r_1)\}
\end{aligned}$$

We take example 6.15 of [BB91], which is a PAR protocol (Positive Acknowledgement with Retransmission). Some small changes are made. In the example below the set H contains all read and send actions along the internal ports 3,4,5 and 6. The operator δ_H renames every action which occurs in H to δ. It is known as the *encapsulation* operator and it forces actions to communicate, for example if $r_i|s_i = c_i$ then $\delta_{\{r_i,s_i\}}(s_i\|r_i) = c_i$.

8.1 The Specification and the Implementation of the Protocol

First we define the individual components.

$$\begin{aligned}
A &= A(0,0)\\
A(b,t) &= \textstyle\sum_{d\in D}\int_{v>t} r_1(d)(v)\cdot A(b,d,t)\\
A(b,d,t) &= s_3(db)(t+0.001)\cdot\{\textstyle\int_{w\in[t+0.001,t+0.01>} r_5(ack)(w)\cdot A(1-b,w)+\\
&\qquad time_out(t+0.01)\cdot A(b,d,t+0.01)\}
\end{aligned}$$

$$\begin{aligned}
K &= \textstyle\sum_{f\in D\times B}\int_{v>0} r_3(f)(v)\cdot\{s_4(f)(v+0.002)+error_K(v+0.001)\}\cdot K\\
L &= \textstyle\int_{v>0} r_6(ack)(v)\cdot\{s_5(ack)(v+0.002)+error_L(v+0.001)\}\cdot L
\end{aligned}$$

$$\begin{aligned}
B &= B(0)\\
B(b) &= \textstyle\sum_{d\in D}\int_{v>0} r_4(db)(v)\cdot s_2(d)(v+0.001)\cdot B(1-b,v)+\\
&\qquad \textstyle\sum_{d\in D}\int_{v>0} r_4(d(b-1))(v)\cdot B(b,v)\\
B(b,t) &= s_6(ack)(t+0.002)\cdot B(b)
\end{aligned}$$

The implementation of the protocol is the following merge:

$$PAR_{impl} = \delta_H(A \parallel K \parallel L \parallel B)$$

8.2 Expanding the Definitions

We expand the definitions, for each new configuration a new recursion variable is chosen. In this way we obtain the parameterized recursion variables $X_0 - X_4$ and $Y_1 - Y_4$.

$$
\begin{aligned}
PAR_{impl} &= X_0(0,0)\\
X_0(b,t_0) &= \delta_H(A(b,t_0)\|K\|L\|B(b))\\
&= \textstyle\int_{v>t_0} \sum_{d\in D} r_1(d)(v)\cdot X_1(b,d,v)
\end{aligned}
$$

$$
\begin{aligned}
X_1(b,d,t) &= \delta_H\ (\ A(b,d,t)\|\ K\ \|\ L\ \|\ B(b)\ )\\
&= \delta_H\ (\ \underline{s_3(db)(t+0.001)}\cdot\\
&\qquad [\textstyle\int_{w\in[t,t+0.01)} r_5(ack,w)\cdot A(1-b,w)\ +\ time\_out(t+0.01)\cdot A(b,d,t+0.01)]\\
&\qquad \|\ \textstyle\sum_{f\in D\times B}\int_{v>0} \underline{r_3(f)(v)}\cdot[s_4(f)(v+0.002)+error_K(v+0.001)]\cdot K\\
&\qquad \|\ L\\
&\qquad \|\ B(b)\\
&\qquad)\\
&= c_3(\ db)(t+0.001)\ \cdot\ X_2(b,d,t)
\end{aligned}
$$

$$
\begin{aligned}
X_2(b,d,t) &= \delta_H\ (\ [\textstyle\int_{w\in[t,t+0.01)} r_5(ack,w)\cdot A(1-b,w)\ +\ \underline{time\_out(t+0.01)}\cdot A(b,d,t+0.01)]\\
&\qquad \|\ [\underline{s_4(db)(t+0.003)}+\underline{error_K(t+0.002)}]\cdot K\\
&\qquad \|\ L\\
&\qquad \|\ \textstyle\sum_{d\in D}\int_{v>0} \underline{r_4(db)(v)}\cdot \underline{s_2(d)(v+0.001)}\cdot B(1-b,v)\ +\\
&\qquad\quad \textstyle\sum_{d\in D}\int_{v>0} r_4(d(1-b))(v)\cdot B(b,v)\\
&\qquad)\\
&= c_4(\ db)(t+0.003)\cdot s_2(d)(t+0.004)\cdot X_3(b,d,t)\ +\\
&\qquad error_K(t+0.002)\cdot time\_out(t+0.01)\cdot X_1(b,d,t+0.01)
\end{aligned}
$$

$$
\begin{aligned}
X_3(b,d,t) &= \delta_H\ (\ [\textstyle\int_{w\in[t,t+0.01)} r_5(ack,w)\cdot A(1-b,w)\ +\ time\_out(t+0.01)\cdot A(b,d,t+0.01)]\\
&\qquad \|\ K\\
&\qquad \|\ \textstyle\int_{v>0} \underline{r_6(ack)(v)}\ \cdot\ [s_5(ack)(v+0.002)+error_L(v+0.001)]\ \cdot L\\
&\qquad \|\ \underline{s_6(ack)(v)(t+0.005)}\cdot B(1-b)\\
&\qquad)\\
&= c_6(\ ack)(t+0.005)\cdot X_4(b,d,t)
\end{aligned}
$$

$$
\begin{aligned}
X_4(b,d,t) &= \delta_H\ (\ [\textstyle\int_{w\in[t,t+0.01)} \underline{r_5(ack,w)}\cdot A(1-b,w)\ +\ \underline{time\_out(t+0.01)}\cdot A(b,d,t+0.01)]\\
&\qquad \|\ K\\
&\qquad \|\ [\underline{s_5(ack)(t+0.007)}+\underline{error_L(t+0.006)}]\ \cdot L\\
&\qquad \|\ B(1-b)\\
&\qquad)\\
&= c_5(\ ack)(t+0.007)\cdot X_0(1-b,t+0.007)\ +\\
&\qquad error_L(t+0.006)\cdot time\_out(t+0.01)\cdot Y_1(b,d,t+0.01)
\end{aligned}
$$

$$
\begin{aligned}
Y_1(b,d,t) &= \delta_H\ (\ A(b,d,t)\|\ K\ \|\ L\ \|\ B(1-b)\ )\\
&= \delta_H\ (\ \underline{s_3(db)(t+0.001)}\cdot\\
&\qquad [\textstyle\int_{w\in[t,t+0.01)} r_5(ack,w)\cdot A(1-b,w)\ +\ time\_out(t+0.01)\cdot A(b,d,t+0.01)]
\end{aligned}
$$

$$
\begin{aligned}
&\quad \| \ \textstyle\sum_{f\in D\times B}\int_{v>0} \underline{r_3(f)(v)}\cdot[s_4(f)(v+0.002)+error_K(v+0.001)]\cdot K\\
&\quad \| \ L\\
&\quad \| \ B(1-b)\\
&\quad)\\
&= c_3(\ db)(t+0.001)\ \cdot\ Y_2(b,d,t)
\end{aligned}
$$

$$
\begin{aligned}
Y_2(b,d,t) &= \delta_H\ (\ [\textstyle\int_{w\in[t,t+0.01\rangle} r_5(ack,w)\cdot A(1-b,w)\ +\ \underline{time\_out(t+0.01)}\cdot A(b,d,t+0.01)]\\
&\quad \| \ [\underline{s_4(f)(t+0.003)}+\underline{error_K(t+0.002)}]\cdot K\\
&\quad \| \ L\\
&\quad \| \ \textstyle\sum_{d\in D}\int_{v>0}\underline{r_4(d(1-b))(v)}\cdot\underline{s_2(d)(v+0.001)}\cdot B(b,v)+\\
&\quad\quad \textstyle\sum_{d\in D}\int_{v>0} r_4(db))(v)\cdot B(1-b,v)\\
&\quad)\\
&= c_4(\ db)(t+0.003)\cdot Y_3(b,d,t)+\\
&\quad\quad error_K(t+0.002)\cdot time\_out(t+0.01)\cdot Y_1(b,d,t+0.01)
\end{aligned}
$$

$$
\begin{aligned}
Y_3(b,d,t) &= \delta_H\ (\ [\textstyle\int_{w\in[t,t+0.01\rangle} r_5(ack,w)\cdot A(1-b,w)\ +\ time\_out(t+0.01)\cdot A(b,d,t+0.01)]\\
&\quad \| \ K\\
&\quad \| \ \textstyle\int_{v>0}\underline{r_6(ack)(v)}\ \cdot\ [s_5(ack)(v+0.002)+error_L(v+0.001)]\ \cdot L\\
&\quad \| \ \underline{s_6(ack)(v)(t+0.005)}\cdot B(b)\\
&\quad)\\
&= c_6(\ ack)(t+0.005)\cdot Y_4(b,d,t)
\end{aligned}
$$

$$
\begin{aligned}
Y_4(b,d,t) &= \delta_H\ (\ [\textstyle\int_{w\in[t,t+0.01\rangle}\underline{r_5(ack,w)}\cdot A(1-b,w)\ +\ \underline{time\_out(t+0.01)}\cdot A(b,d,t+0.01)]\\
&\quad \| \ K\\
&\quad \| \ [\underline{s_5(ack)(t+0.007)}+\underline{error_L(t+0.006)}]\ \cdot L\\
&\quad \| \ B(b)\\
&\quad)\\
&= c_5(\ ack)(t+0.007)\cdot X_0(1-b,t+0.007)+\\
&\quad\quad error_L(t+0.006)\cdot time\_out(t+0.01)\cdot Y_1(b,d,t+0.01)
\end{aligned}
$$

8.3 Abstracting from Internal Steps

We apply the renaming operator τ_I which renames every atomic action $a(t)$ to $\tau(t)$ except for the actions $r_1(d)(t)$ and $s_2(d)(t)$.

$$
\begin{aligned}
\tau_I(X_0(b,t_0)) &= \textstyle\int_{t>t_0}\sum_{d\in D} r_1(d)(t)\cdot\tau_I(X_1(b,d,t))\\
\tau_I(X_1(b,d,t)) &= \tau(t+0.001)\ \cdot\ \tau_I(X_2(b,d,t))\\
\tau_I(X_2(b,d,t)) &= \tau(t+0.003)\cdot s_2(d)(t+0.004)\cdot\tau_I(X_3(b,d,t))+\\
&\quad \tau(t+0.002)\cdot\tau(t+0.01)\cdot\tau_I(X_1(b,d,t+0.01))\\
\tau_I(X_3(b,d,t)) &= \tau(t+0.005)\cdot\tau_I(X_4(b,d,t))\\
\tau_I(X_4(b,d,t)) &= \tau(t+0.007)\cdot\tau_I(X_0(1-b,t+0.007))+\\
&\quad \tau(t+0.006)\cdot\tau(t+0.01)\cdot\tau_I(Y_1(b,d,t+0.01))
\end{aligned}
$$

$$
\begin{aligned}
\tau_I(Y_1(b,d,t)) &= \tau(t+0.001)\ \cdot\ \tau_I(Y_2(b,d,t))\\
\tau_I(Y_2(b,d,t)) &= \tau(t+0.003)\cdot\tau_I(Y_3(b,d,t))+\\
&\quad \tau(t+0.002)\cdot\tau(t+0.01)\cdot\tau_I(Y_1(b,d,t+0.01))\\
\tau_I(Y_3(b,d,t)) &= \tau(t+0.005)\cdot\tau_I(Y_4(b,d,t))
\end{aligned}
$$

$$
\begin{aligned}
\tau_I(Y_4(b,d,t)) \quad = \quad & \tau(t+0.007)\cdot\tau_I(X_0(1-b,t+0.007))\ + \\
& \tau(t+0.006)\cdot\tau(t+0.01)\cdot\tau_I(Y_1(b,d,t+0.01))
\end{aligned}
$$

Now we can apply the τ-law and its implied identities (such as the τ-swap and the τ-removal).

$$
\begin{aligned}
\tau_I(X_1(b,d,t)) \quad = \quad & \tau(t+0.001)\ \cdot\ \tau_I(X_2(b,d,t)) \\
= \quad & \tau(t+0.001)\ \cdot \\
& \{\ \underline{\tau(t+0.003)}\cdot s_2(d)(t+0.004)\cdot\tau_I(X_3(b,d,t))\ + \\
& \quad \underline{\tau(t+0.002)}\cdot\underline{\tau(t+0.01)}\cdot\tau_I(X_1(b,d,t+0.01))\ \} \\
= \quad & \tau(t+0.001)\ \cdot \\
& \{\ s_2(d)(t+0.004)\cdot\underline{\tau(t+0.005)}\cdot\tau_I(X_4(b,d,t))\ + \\
& \quad \tau(t+0.002)\cdot\tau_I(X_1(b,d,t+0.01))\ \} \\
= \quad & \tau(t+0.001)\ \cdot \\
& \{\ s_2(d)(t+0.004)\cdot \\
& \quad \{\ \underline{\tau(t+0.007)}\cdot\tau_I(X_0(1-b,t+0.007))\ + \\
& \quad\quad \tau(t+0.006)\cdot\underline{\tau(t+0.01)}\cdot\tau_I(Y_1(b,d,t+0.01))\ \}\ + \\
& \quad \tau(t+0.002)\cdot\tau_I(X_1(b,d,t+0.01))\ \} \\
= \quad & \tau(t+0.001)\ \cdot \\
& \{\ s_2(d)(t+0.004)\cdot \\
& \quad \{\ \tau_I(X_0(1-b,t+0.007))\ +\tau(t+0.006)\cdot\tau_I(Y_1(b,d,t+0.01))\ \}\ + \\
& \quad \tau(t+0.002)\cdot\tau_I(X_1(b,d,t+0.01))\ \}
\end{aligned}
$$

$$
\begin{aligned}
\tau_I(Y_1(b,d,t)) \quad = \quad & \tau(t+0.001)\ \cdot\ \tau_I(Y_2(b,d,t)) \\
= \quad & \tau(t+0.001)\ \cdot \\
& \{\ \underline{\tau(t+0.003)}\cdot\tau_I(Y_3(b,d,t))\ + \\
& \quad \tau(t+0.002)\cdot\underline{\tau(t+0.01)}\cdot\tau_I(Y_1(b,d,t+0.01))\ \} \\
= \quad & \tau(t+0.001)\ \cdot \\
& \{\ \underline{\tau(t+0.005)}\cdot\tau_I(Y_4(b,d,t))\ + \\
& \quad \tau(t+0.002)\cdot\tau_I(Y_1(b,d,t+0.01))\ \} \\
= \quad & \tau(t+0.001)\ \cdot \\
& \{\ \{\ \underline{\tau(t+0.007)}\cdot\tau_I(X_0(1-b,t+0.007))\ + \\
& \quad\quad \tau(t+0.006)\cdot\underline{\tau(t+0.01)}\cdot\tau_I(Y_1(b,d,t+0.01))\ \}\ + \\
& \quad \tau(t+0.002)\cdot\tau_I(Y_1(b,d,t+0.01))\ \} \\
= \quad & \tau(t+0.001)\ \cdot \\
& \{\ \tau_I(X_0(1-b,t+0.007))+\tau(t+0.006)\cdot\tau_I(Y_1(b,d,t+0.01))\ + \\
& \quad \underline{\tau(t+0.002)\cdot\tau_I(Y_1(b,d,t+0.01))}\ \} \\
= \quad & \tau(t+0.001)\ \cdot \\
& \{\ \tau_I(X_0(1-b,t+0.007))+\tau(t+0.006)\cdot\tau_I(Y_1(b,d,t+0.01))\ \}
\end{aligned}
$$

Summarizing,

$$
\tau_I(X_0(b,t_0)) \quad = \quad \textstyle\int_{t>t_0}\sum_{d\in D} r_1(d)(t)\cdot\tau_I(X_1(b,d,t))
$$

$$
\begin{aligned}
\tau_I(X_1(b,d,t)) \quad = \quad & \tau(t+0.001)\ \cdot \\
& \{\ s_2(d)(t+0.004)\cdot \\
& \quad \{\ \tau_I(X_0(1-b,t+0.007))\ +\tau(t+0.006)\cdot\tau_I(Y_1(b,d,t+0.01))\ \}\ +
\end{aligned}
$$

$$\tau(t+0.002)\cdot\tau_I(X_1(b,d,t+0.01))\ \}$$

$$\begin{aligned}\tau_I(Y_1(b,d,t)) \quad = \quad & \tau(t+0.001)\cdot \\ & \tau_I(X_0(1-b,t+0.007))+\tau(t+0.006)\cdot\tau_I(Y_1(b,d,t+0.01))\end{aligned}$$

By applying the *Unwind Principle*:

$$\begin{aligned}\tau_I(X_1(b,d,t)) &= \tau(t+0.001)\cdot\textstyle\sum_{n=0}^{\infty}\tau(t+0.002+n\cdot 0.01)\cdot s_2(d)(t+0.004+n\cdot 0.01)\cdot \\ &\quad \{\ \tau_I(X_0(1-b,t+0.007+n\cdot 0.01))+ \\ &\quad\ \ \tau(t+0.006+n\cdot 0.01)\cdot\tau_I(Y_1(b,d,t+(n+1)\cdot 0.01))\ \}\end{aligned}$$

$$\begin{aligned}\tau_I(Y_1(b,d,t)) \quad = \quad & \tau(t+0.001)\cdot\textstyle\sum_{n=0}^{\infty}\tau(t+0.006+n\cdot 0.01) \\ & \tau_I(X_0(1-b,t+0.007+n\cdot 0.01))\end{aligned}$$

Adding together

$$\begin{aligned}\tau_I(X_1(b,d,t)) &= \tau(t+0.001)\cdot\textstyle\sum_{n=0}^{\infty}\tau(t+0.002+n\cdot 0.01)\cdot s_2(d)(t+0.004+n\cdot 0.01)\cdot \\ &\quad \{\ \tau_I(X_0(1-b,t+0.007+n\cdot 0.01))+ \\ &\quad\ \ \{\ \tau(t+0.006+n\cdot 0.01)\cdot \\ &\quad\ \ \ \ \{\textstyle\sum_{n'=0}^{\infty}\tau((t+(n+1)\cdot 0.01)+0.006+n'\cdot 0.01)\cdot \\ &\quad\ \ \ \ \ \ \tau_I(X_0(1-b,((t+(n+1)\cdot 0.01)+0.007+n'\cdot 0.01))\}\ \} \\[1ex] &= \tau(t+0.001)\cdot\textstyle\sum_{n=0}^{\infty}\tau(t+0.002+n\cdot 0.01)\cdot s_2(d)(t+0.004+n\cdot 0.01)\cdot \\ &\quad \{\ \tau(t+0.006+n\cdot 0.01)\ \cdot\ \tau_I(X_0(1-b,t+0.007+n\cdot 0.01))+ \\ &\quad\ \ \{\textstyle\sum_{n'=0}^{\infty}\tau(t+0.006+(n+n'+1)\cdot 0.01)\cdot \\ &\quad\ \ \ \ \tau_I(X_0(1-b,(t+0.007+(n+n'+1)\cdot 0.01))\}\ \} \\[1ex] &= \tau(t+0.001)\cdot\textstyle\sum_{n=0}^{\infty}\tau(t+0.002+n\cdot 0.01)\cdot s_2(d)(t+0.004+n\cdot 0.01)\cdot \\ &\quad \{\textstyle\sum_{n'=0}^{\infty}\tau(t+0.006+(n+n')\cdot 0.01)\cdot \\ &\quad\ \ \tau_I(X_0(1-b,(t+0.007+(n+n')\cdot 0.01))\}\end{aligned}$$

$$\begin{aligned}\tau_I(X_0(b,t_0)) \quad \stackrel{*}{=} \quad & \textstyle\int_{t>t_0}\sum_{d\in D} r_1(d)(t)\cdot \\ & \{\ \textstyle\sum_{n=0}^{\infty}\tau(t+0.002+n\cdot 0.01)\cdot s_2(d)(t+0.004+n\cdot 0.01)\cdot \\ & \quad \{\textstyle\sum_{n'=0}^{\infty}\tau(t+0.006+(n+n')\cdot 0.01)\cdot \\ & \quad\ \ \tau_I(X_0(1-b,(t+0.007+(n+n')\cdot 0.01))\}\ \}\end{aligned}$$

The atomic actions occurring in $\tau_I(X_0(b,t_0))$ are independent of the parameter b, thus with RSP we get:

$$PAR_{impl}(t)=\tau_I(X_0(1,t))=\tau_I(X_0(0,t))$$

The expression on the right hand side of the $\stackrel{*}{=}$ can be considered as the specification of the PAR protocol. However, one can say that it contains too much time information and one would expect a specification which states that sooner or later the incoming datum will be send out at port 2. Hence, one needs a mechanism to abstract from some time information. Moreover, one needs to express a notion of fairness, saying that the datum and the acknowledgement can be lost only a finite amount of times. In the above expression this would mean that the n and n' are finite. One very rough way to obtain this, is to throw away all time information obtaining the (untimed) term:

$$S(b) = \sum_{d \in D} r_1(d) \cdot s_2(d) \cdot S(1-b)$$

9 Conclusions and Further Research

In this report a notion of abstraction is introduced. The adjustment of the model is quite simple and requires the introduction of so-called closure rules. As equivalence we still can use the standard notion of strong bisimulation. The resulting equivalence can be characterized by only one additional τ-law for the calculus without integration.

By interpreting symbolic processes as a special class of timed processes, we obtain a notion of τ equivalence for symbolic processes. The resulting equivalence is delay bisimulation with a strongly rootedness condition.

We can verify a protocol using these laws. To deal with recursion, we need as well the common requirement that every guarded recursive specification has a unique solution (RDP and RSP) and a new principle which we call the *Unwind Principle* (UP).

However, some questions are left open. The completeness proof is given for terms without integration. It is to be expected that the addition of integrals complicates the proof only in a technical way, also because the τ can only be removed if the bounded variable of the associated integral is not used afterwards. But there is a need for techniques dealing with terms with integrals and their transition systems such that these proofs can be done more easily. The statement of the principles RDP, RSP and UP is rather ad hoc and needs further research.

Acknowledgements

The author would like to thank Jos Baeten (Eindhoven Univ. of Technology) for his encouraging comments. Part of the research of this paper was suggested by him. Willem Jan Fokkink (CWI) is thanked for his stylistic advices.

References

[Bae90] J.C.M. Baeten, editor. *Applications of Process Algebra.* Cambridge Tracts in Theoretical Computer Science 17. Cambridge University Press, 1990.

[BB91] J.C.M. Baeten and J.A. Bergstra. Real time process algebra. *Journal of Formal Aspects of Computing Science*, 3(2):142–188, 1991.

[BW90] J.C.M. Baeten and W.P. Weijland. *Process algebra.* Cambridge Tracts in Theoretical Computer Science 18. Cambridge University Press, 1990.

[dR89] W.P. de Roever. Foundations of computer science: Leaving the ivory tower. *Bulletin of the European Association for Theoretical Computer Science*, 44:455–492, 1989.

[Gla87] R.J. van Glabbeek. Bounded nondeterminism and the approximation induction principle in process algebra. In F.J. Brandenburg, G. Vidal-Naquet, and M. Wirsing, editors, *Proceedings STACS 87*, volume 247 of *Lecture Notes in Computer Science*, pages 336–347. Springer-Verlag, 1987.

[Gro89] J.F. Groote. Transition system specifications with negative premises. Report CS-R8950, CWI, Amsterdam, 1989. An extended abstract appeared in J.C.M. Baeten and J.W. Klop, editors, *Proceedings CONCUR 90*, Amsterdam, LNCS 458, pages 332–341. Springer-Verlag, 1990.

[GW89] R.J. van Glabbeek and W.P. Weijland. Branching time and abstraction in bisimulation semantics (extended abstract). In G.X. Ritter, editor, *Information Processing 89*, pages 613–618. North-Holland, 1989.

[Hoa85] C.A.R. Hoare. *Communicating Sequential Processes.* Prentice Hall International, 1985.

[HR90] M. Hennessy and T. Regan. A temporal process algebra. Report 2/90, Computer Science Department, University of Sussex, 1990.

[Klu91] A.S. Klusener. Completeness in realtime process algebra. Report CS-R9106, CWI, Amsterdam, 1991. An extended abstract appeared in J.C.M. Baeten and J.F. Groote, editors, *Proceedings CONCUR 91*, Amsterdam, LNCS 527 , pages 376–392. Springer-Verlag, 1991.

[Mil80] R. Milner. *A Calculus of Communicating Systems*, volume 92 of *Lecture Notes in Computer Science.* Springer-Verlag, 1980.

[Mil89] R. Milner. *Communication and concurrency.* Prentice Hall International, 1989.

[MT90] F. Moller and C. Tofts. A temporal calculus of communicating systems. In J.C.M. Baeten and J.W. Klop, editors, *Proceedings CONCUR 90,* Amsterdam, volume 458 of *Lecture Notes in Computer Science*, pages 401–415. Springer-Verlag, 1990.

[Plo81] G.D. Plotkin. A structural approach to operational semantics. Report DAIMI FN-19, Computer Science Department, Aarhus University, 1981.

[Ree89] M. Reed. A hierarchy of domains for real-time distributed computing. In *Mathematical Foundations of Programming Language Semantics.* Springer-Verlag, 1989.

[RR88] M. Reed and A.W. Roscoe. A timed model for communicating sequential processes. *Theoretical Computer Science*, 58:249–261, 1988.

[Wan90] Y. Wang. Real time behaviour of asynchronous agents. In J.C.M. Baeten and J.W. Klop, editors, *Proceedings CONCUR 90,* Amsterdam, volume 458 of *Lecture Notes in Computer Science*, pages 502–520. Springer-Verlag, 1990.

(Real) Time: A Philosophical Perspective

Ron Koymans
Philips Research Laboratories
P.O.Box 80.000, 5600 JA Eindhoven, The Netherlands
e-mail:koymans@prl.philips.nl

Abstract. We present a perspective on the relationship between time and real-time. This perspective originates from a philosophical viewpoint concerning models of time that does not consider quantitative timing issues such as those relevant for real-time computing. This starting point is then adapted to incorporate real-time features. In doing so we try to combine the views on time and real-time forwarded by mathematical logic and by computer science. To illustrate these issues we use temporal logic, but many of the results presented are independent from a particular language and are also relevant for other (real) time formalisms.

Keywords: time, real-time, temporal logic, models of time, time measurement

Contents

1 Introduction

The topic of the REX '91 Workshop, real-time, has been studied from a theoretical viewpoint mainly in the last decade. In a real-time temporal logic this could be paraphrased by

$$\blacksquare_{<10}\ \textit{Real Time Study}.$$

However, before one should study the more complex issue of real-time it makes sense to study first time proper. In ordinary temporal logic (including past operators) this can be paraphrased by

$$\Box\ (\textit{Real TimeStudy}\ \rightarrow\ \blacklozenge\ \textit{Time Study}).$$

In a sense this paper propagates something like "back to the basics" and intends to create awareness of some fundamental results and issues. Therefore, this is not a technical paper but can be seen as a kind of overview. The motivation for this is that many of the themes considered are not very well-known amongst computer scientists. Although resembling an overview the intention of the paper is not to categorize all the different approaches to (real) time but instead it gives a background in which one can put many approaches in perspective.

The perspective of this paper is more that of a logician than that of a computer scientist although we will try to combine the two views. From this logical perspective it is natural to look at time by means of the logic of time, more familiarly known as temporal logic. Since this paper concentrates on the logical and philosophical aspects of time we will devote almost no consideration to computational models involving time, but mainly look at models of time proper.

The paper is structured as follows. In section 2 we look at possible representations of time, or alternatively, at ways in which time can be structured. This gives rise to a temporal ontology. The corresponding models of time are generally useful and are also relevant outside temporal logic. Since it lays the foundations and is a starting point for the next sections, section 2 is by far the most extensive one of the paper. Section 3 deals with languages for reasoning about some time models treated in section 2, in particular investigating the expressiveness of such languages, that is, their ability to define characteristic properties of time models. Section 4 looks at two topics more relevant to computer science: time measurement and the introduction of states, respectively. Time measurement is directly related to real-time while the introduction of states represents a first step towards computational models. Drawing conclusions is left to the responsibility of the reader.

The material of this paper is influenced by many sources of which we want to mention the reference at the end of the paper in particular, because it contains a very thorough investigation of models and logics of time from a logical and philosophical point of view. In a way this paper starts out from this point of view and extends it to incorporate also real-time issues. For a recent overview on the representation of and the reasoning about time in artificial intelligence, the reader may consult the special issue on Temporal Reasoning of the International Journal of Intelligent Systems (Volume 6, July–August 1991).

2 A Temporal Ontology

Instead of just a few basic choices for models of time, one can actually distinguish a whole spectrum of combination possibilities. To structure this wealth of possibilities we subdivide classes of models along the following four main divisions:

I. Individuals

II. Relations

III. Operations

IV. Conditions.

The choice of individuals relates to the question: what are the basic elements of time? For example, one can view instants or periods to be elementary. The choice of relations relates to the question: what are the elementary relations on time? For example, the 'earlier than' relation seems always a basic relation. The choice of operations relates to the question: how can we construct new time elements from old ones? For example, when one thinks of time elements as days then yesterday provides such an operator. The choice of conditions relates to the question: what is the nature of time? Or in other words, what are the characteristic properties of time, given a certain choice of individuals, relations and operations.

In the next four subsections we treat these four main divisions separately on an informal level based on conceptual ideas. After that we become more technical by formalizing the introduced notions in three more subsections which reflect the fundamental choices for the individuals as treated in the next subsection.

2.1 Temporal Individuals

These are also referred to as "Time Elements".

A further subdivision is in place here:

I.A. Points (Instants)

I.B. Periods (Intervals)

I.C. Events (Occurrences)

- I.C.1. absolute: time precedes events
- I.C.2. relative: events precede time

Comparing points and periods we can remark that points are technically simple while periods are philosophically attractive. For time-continuous models (which play an important role in real-time computing) one can argue, however, that periods encounter additional difficulties such as the problem of determining the position of a moving object.

Events have a standpoint somewhat aside from points and periods because they do not involve proper time elements. That is to say, when events are taken as the primitive elements, time has become a derived notion. This is also the reason for the subdivision of events indicating their relation with time: in the absolute view time 'contains' events while in the relative view events 'constitute' time (as in special relativity theory). The relative view prohibits cyclic time models because each event represents a different time. In the absolute view such cyclic time models could be used to represent periodic events. In subsection 2.4 we will encounter, however, reasons for considering cyclic time models to be unnatural. We nevertheless included events into our considerations because they have distinct philosophical merits, for instance one can take the position that indivisible instants don't exist (since observing anything takes a certain duration) and that periods not related to certain events occurring, are meaningless. Besides, it is often already the case in practice (especially for real-time systems) that special events (e.g. the ticking of a system clock) are used to mimick time.

Traditionally, however, points are seen as the basic time elements from which one can construct periods (as a convex set of points) and one can look upon (occurrences of) events as taking place over periods. The reverse route from events via periods to points is, in principle, possible too. In subsection 2.6 we indicate how periods can be constructed out of points and vice versa.

2.2 Temporal Relations

In this subsection we consider possible relations on time from an intuitive and conceptual point of view.

Two obvious relations independent from the choice of individuals are:

II.A. Equality

II.B. Precedence

Equality is a natural relation in any logical structure and the precedence relation (also referred to as 'earlier than') is the characteristic relation for models of time. Apart from these two relations also the relation of betweenness seems to be natural for points, periods and events. It happens to be the case that this relation of betweenness can already be defined in terms of precedence:

$$Bxyz \;:=\; y < x < z \;\vee\; z < x < y.$$

Here precedence is denoted by $<$ because we will see in subsection 2.4 that the most natural assumption for the precedence relation supposes it to be a (strict) partial order.

As an additional relation for periods we have:

II.C. Inclusion

This relation (also referred to as 'during') is a supplementary natural relation for periods which collapses to equality for points. Other natural relations for periods (overlapping, meeting, starting, ending) are definable in terms of inclusion and precedence, as is shown in subsection 2.6.

Events again give rise to additional relations:

II.D. Simultaneity

II.E. Causality

The relation of simultaneity represents the happening of two events at the same time. For periods this relation collapses to equality (or may be in some cases only to overlapping). The relation of causality represents the dependence of one event on another event and can be considered as a strong form of precedence (one could distinguish this 'causal' precedence from 'incidental' precedence where no causal relation between the two events is supposed). Simultaneity and a characteristic property of causality can be defined in terms of precedence. Furthermore, for events (not for periods) inclusion can also be defined in terms of precedence.

2.3 Temporal Operations

In this subsection we look at several natural operations on time elements to construct other time elements.

For points we consider the following (partial) operation:

III.A. Next Time (Instant)

The next point in time need not exist, so this operation may indeed be partial.

Also for periods we can consider (partial) operations:

III.B. Intersection

III.C. Union

Intersection (also referred to as 'conjunction') may be partial because two periods can have an empty intersection and the 'empty period' need not exist. Union (also referred to as 'disjunction') may be partial because non-convex periods may not be allowed.

For events we do not consider any natural operations since an event usually represents an unseparable atomic entity without direct connections with other events.

2.4 Temporal Conditions

Given a certain choice of individuals, relations and operations we can ask to which natural conditions they are subjected. Or in other words, what are the characteristic properties of time over these individuals, relations and operations?

The following three categories form one of several possible divisions by which we can classify such characteristic properties of time:

IV.A. Order (Precedence)

IV.B. Local Structure

IV.C. Global Structure

The first category is concerned with general assumptions about the ordering on time. The second category deals with the fine structure of time, that is, the relation between 'neighboring' time elements, while the third category treats the coarse structure of time, that is, the relation between arbitrary time elements. These categories are interesting enough to devote separate subsubsections to.

2.4.1 Temporal Order

For this category we can again make a subdivision:

IV.A.1. Strict Partial Order:

- IV.A.1.a. Transitive
- IV.A.1.b. Irreflexive
- IV.A.1.c. Asymmetric

IV.A.2. Linearity:

- IV.A.2.a. Linear
- IV.A.2.b. Left-Linear (Branching Towards Future)
- IV.A.2.c. Right-Linear (Branching Towards Past)

IV.A.3. Directedness (Towards Past and Future)

IV.A.4. Boundedness:

- IV.A.4.a. Unbounded (Towards Past and Future)
- IV.A.4.b. Bounded Towards Past (Beginning)
- IV.A.4.c. Bounded Towards Future (Ending)

Assumption 1 is the standard assumption on time corresponding to the metaphor of the 'River of Time' flowing towards the future. Note that 1.a and 1.b together imply 1.c and that such a strict partial order excludes cyclic time structures (by transitivity we can follow the cycle to return at the original time element which contradicts irreflexivity).

In case that none of the additional assumptions 2.a, 2.b or 2.c is taken assumption 2 just reduces to the standard assumption 1, a (strict) partial order. In computer science the most common (in fact the only one used) form of branching time is 2.b (the idea is that the future is indeterminate relating to the possible evolutions of the modelled system), but it should be remarked that this is based on a model of time corresponding to a tree structure where both points *and paths* are taken into account. It is also worth remarking that the combination of periods as the basic time elements and branching time is technically cumbersome. An interesting possibility which is technically feasible is the combination of linear time with branching events where simultaneity corresponds to the coincidence of the projection of events on the time axis (i.e., assuming a branching structure for events in which the corresponding time elements, obtained by projection, can be linearly ordered).

Assumption 3 amounts to a kind of convergence in a diamond-like fashion (cf. its formulation in subsection 2.5). Concerning assumption 4.b we can remark that it is familiar in computer science as well as in astronomy: in computer science it is derived from the start of operation of the modelled system while in astronomy this assumption is inspired by the well-known Big Bang theory.

2.4.2 Local Temporal Structure

Here we make the following subdivision:

IV.B.1. Discrete

IV.B.2. Dense

IV.B.3. Continuous

Well-known examples of the three categories above are the familiar number systems, for example $\mathbb{N}$ and $\mathbb{Z}$ are discrete, $\mathbb{Q}$ is dense but not continuous and $\mathbb{R}$ is both dense and continuous.

At this point we can illustrate the classification of the structure of time hitherto by the familiar example of classical (Newtonian) physics: its time model is based on points with an ordering that is linear, unbounded and dense.

Stepping from physics to computer science one can claim that the local structure of time is even more fundamental for computer science. We illustrate this by three examples in which this local structure plays an essential role. First there is the important distinction between synchronous and asynchronous sytems. Since synchronous systems operate in a step-wise fashion it is felt that a discrete approach is most suitable in that case. On the other hand, for asynchronous systems events can take place arbitrarily close in time which makes the dense approach more appropriate. A similar phenomenon occurs in the second example, the digital vs. analog dichotomy. This dichotomy is particularly relevant for real-time computing. Since digital systems are discrete by nature and analog systems continuous, it is obvious that a discrete time model is better for digital systems and a dense time model for analog ones (including hybrid systems). The third example concerns the notions of compositionality and refinement. In the process of refinement a discrete time model poses problems because of the possible change of time granularity, for instance when a previously atomic action such as an assignment turns out on a lower level to consist actually of several fetch and store instructions. Also when composing two parallel computations in a discrete time model the resulting merged computation can force such a change of time granularity because now inbetween two events of one component an event of the other component can occur (this is related to the observation above that events may take place arbitrarily close in time in the case of asynchronous sytems). When working with a dense time model these problems with compositionality and refinement disappear at the expense of a more complex mathematical and computational structure.

2.4.3 Global Temporal Structure

Again we make a subdivision:

IV.C.1. Connectedness

IV.C.2. Isotropy

IV.C.3. Homogeneity

IV.C.4. Reflection

Isotropy (also referred to as symmetry) is related to the concept that time is the same in all directions, for instance in a linear structure it is the same when looking to the past as when looking to the future. For example, $\mathbb{N}$ is not isotropic, but $\mathbb{Z}$, $\mathbb{Q}$ and $\mathbb{R}$ are.

A related notion is the third category, homogeneity. It asserts that time is the same everywhere in the sense that any time element can be automorphically mapped onto any other time element. Again $\mathbb{N}$ is not homogeneous while $\mathbb{Z}$, $\mathbb{Q}$ and $\mathbb{R}$ are. Homogeneity is not the same as isotropy, though. For example, the structure $\mathbb{Z} \oplus \mathbb{Z}$ (two consecutive copies of $\mathbb{Z}$) is isotropic but not homogeneous (the 'left zero' and 'right zero' cannot be mapped automorphically onto each other).

The fourth category is reflection which asserts that the parts mirror the whole. Technically this is accomplished by the binary operator $\odot$ which replaces each element of the first structure by a copy of the second structure. Reflection can then be formulated as the isomorphy of a time structure $\mathcal{T}$ with $\mathcal{T} \odot \mathcal{T}$. For example, $\mathbb{Z}$ does not obey reflection while $\mathbb{Q}$ does.

2.5 Point Structures

As we have shown in subsection 2.2, when we consider points to be the basic time elements, we only need a precedence relation. Therefore, a point structure can be represented by

$$(T, <)$$

where T is the set of time points and $<$ is the precedence relation. The list of conditions on the precedence relation given in subsubsection 2.4.1 can be formulated in first-order logic by

TRANS	$\forall xyz\ (x < y < z \ \rightarrow\ x < z)$
IRREF	$\forall x\ \neg\, x < x$
ASYM	$\forall xy\ (x < y \ \rightarrow\ \neg\, y < x)$
LIN	$\forall xy\ (x < y \ \vee\ x = y \ \vee\ y < x)$
L-LIN	$\forall xyz\ ((y < x \ \wedge\ z < x) \ \rightarrow\ (y < z \vee y = z \vee z < y))$
R-LIN	$\forall xyz\ ((x < y \ \wedge\ x < z) \ \rightarrow\ (y < z \vee y = z \vee z < y))$
F-DIR	$\forall xy\ \exists z\ (x < z \ \wedge\ y < z)$
P-DIR	$\forall xy\ \exists z\ (z < x \ \wedge\ z < y)$
P-SUC	$\forall x\ \exists y\ y < x$
F-SUC	$\forall x\ \exists y\ x < y$
P-BOUND	$\exists x\ \neg\, \exists y\ y < x$
F-BOUND	$\exists x\ \neg\, \exists y\ x < y$

Notice that we have split directedness as well as unboundedness (here referred to by SUC for succession) into both the future part and the past part.

Concerning local temporal structure, the three conditions of subsubsection 2.4.2 can be formulated by (the first two in first-order logic, the third one essentially needs second-order logic):

DISC $\forall xy\,(x < y \;\rightarrow\; \exists z\,(x < z \wedge \neg \exists u\; x < u < z)) \;\wedge$
$\quad\forall xy\,(x < y \;\rightarrow\; \exists z\,(z < y \wedge \neg \exists u\; z < u < y))$

DENS $\forall xy\,(x < y \;\rightarrow\; \exists z\; x < z < y)$

CONT $\forall A\,((\forall xy\,((Ax \wedge \neg Ay) \rightarrow x < y) \wedge \exists x\, Ax \wedge \exists x \neg Ax) \;\rightarrow$
$\quad\exists z\,(\forall u\,(z < u \rightarrow \neg Au) \wedge \forall u\,(u < z \rightarrow Au)))$

CONT is a formulation of Dedekind-continuity which can be represented for linear point structures by the picture:

In computer science the two main models of time based on points are linear time (using computation *sequences*) and branching time (using computation *trees*). Both use a discrete model of time. In fact, linear time temporal logic is based on the conditions TRANS, IRREF, LIN, DISC, P-BOUND and F-SUC while branching time temporal logic is based on TRANS, IRREF, L-LIN, DISC, P-BOUND and F-SUC. So, the small difference (on this fundamental level) between linear and branching time is just the assumption of full linearity LIN versus only left-linearity L-LIN. Apart from that, as remarked earlier, branching time temporal logic uses besides points also paths in the computation tree in its semantics. Other point-based models of time such as those underlying partial order temporal logics occur much less frequently in computer science. Outside the domain of temporal logic, the partial order model of time is quite common in computer science with several schools devoted to its study.

Concerning global temporal structure, the four conditions of subsubsection 2.4.3 can be formulated by (all of these need essentially higher-order logic):

CONN $\forall t, t' \in T \;\; \exists < t_1, \ldots, t_k >$
$\quad(t_1 = t \;\wedge\; t_k = t' \;\wedge\; \forall i\,(1 \leq i < k \;\rightarrow\; t_i < t_{i+1} \vee t_{i+1} < t_i))$

ISO $(T, <) \;\simeq\; (T, >)$

HOM Each $t \in T$ can be mapped automorphically onto each other $t' \in T$

REF For $\mathcal{T} = (T, <)$ $\;\mathcal{T} \odot \mathcal{T} \;\simeq\; \mathcal{T}$

Concerning the copy operator $\odot$ it may be interesting to remark that it is not commutative: the structure $\mathbb{Q} \odot \mathbb{Z}$ is discrete but $\mathbb{Z} \odot \mathbb{Q} \simeq \mathbb{Q}$.

We end our account of point structures by giving some interesting subclasses. Interesting because they classify the standard number systems $\mathbb{N}$, $\mathbb{Z}$, $\mathbb{Q}$ and $\mathbb{R}$. First we look at point structures satisfying TRANS, IRREF, LIN, SUC (i.e., both P-SUC and F-SUC) and additionally

- DISC
- DENS
- CONT

Notice first that the combination of LIN and SUC implies DIR (i.e., both F-DIR and P-DIR). The first case (DISC) is satisfied by $\mathbb{Z}$ but also by $\mathbb{Z} \oplus \mathbb{Z}$ and by $\mathbb{Q} \odot \mathbb{Z}$. $\mathbb{Q}$ and $\mathbb{R}$ satisfy the second and third case, respectively. If we want to classify $\mathbb{N}$ we of course should apply to the first case but now with P-SUC exchanged by P-BOUND.

2.6 Period Structures

As we have shown in subsection 2.2, when we consider periods to be the basic time elements, we need apart from the precedence relation also an inclusion relation. Therefore, a period structure can be represented by

$$(I, \sqsubseteq, <)$$

In the case of periods the inclusion relation $\sqsubseteq$ is also referred to by 'during' and the precedence relation $<$ by 'before'. As promised, we now show that the other natural relations for periods of overlapping, meeting, starting and ending are definable in terms of inclusion and precedence:

$$\begin{array}{lcl} iOj & := & \exists k\,(k \sqsubseteq i \ \wedge \ k \sqsubseteq j) \\ iMj & := & i < j \ \wedge \ \neg\, \exists k\,(i < k < j) \\ iSj & := & i \sqsubseteq j \ \wedge \ \neg\, \exists k\,(k \sqsubseteq j \ \wedge \ k < i) \\ iEj & := & i \sqsubseteq j \ \wedge \ \neg\, \exists k\,(k \sqsubseteq j \ \wedge i < k) \end{array}$$

Together with inclusion and precedence these four relations form six basic relations which all have their converses as well (e.g., started by is the converse of starting). When taking into account also the ubiquitous equality relation this makes a grand total of thirteen natural relations for periods. Many interval formalisms used in computer science indeed have these thirteen relations at their basis.

Several interesting conditions for the inclusion relation can be formulated by:

TRANS$_\sqsubseteq$ $\forall ijk\,(i \sqsubseteq j \sqsubseteq k \ \rightarrow \ i \sqsubseteq k)$

REF$_\sqsubseteq$ $\forall i\; i \sqsubseteq i$

ANTIS$_\sqsubseteq$ $\forall ij\,(i \sqsubseteq j \sqsubseteq i \ \rightarrow \ i = j)$

F-DIR$_\sqsubseteq$ $\forall ij\; \exists k\,(i \sqsubseteq k \ \wedge \ j \sqsubseteq k)$

DESC$_\sqsubseteq$ $\forall i\, \forall j \sqsubseteq i\; \exists k \sqsubseteq j\;\, k \neq j$

ATOM$_\sqsubseteq$ $\forall i\; \exists j \sqsubseteq i\; \forall k \sqsubseteq j\;\, k = j$

FOUND$_\sqsubseteq$ $\sqsubseteq$ is well-founded

Transitivity $TRANS_{\sqsubseteq}$, reflexivity $REF_{\sqsubseteq}$ and antisymmetry $ANTIS_{\sqsubseteq}$ make $\sqsubseteq$ a partial order. We can only assume $F\text{-}DIR_{\sqsubseteq}$ because $P\text{-}DIR_{\sqsubseteq}$ is obviously wrong (unless we suppose the existence of the 'empty period' in which case $P\text{-}DIR_{\sqsubseteq}$ can be trivially fulfilled). The last three conditions of the list above deal with local structure and are exclusive: $DESC_{\sqsubseteq}$ formulates 'endless descent', $ATOM_{\sqsubseteq}$ asserts the existence of 'indivisible subperiods' while $FOUND_{\sqsubseteq}$ is even stronger implying both $ATOM_{\sqsubseteq}$ and $ANTIS_{\sqsubseteq}$.

As for conditions on the precedence relations < (cf. the conditions for the ordering in point structures given in subsection 2.5) one can assume $TRANS_<$, $IRREF_<$, $SUC_<$ and $DIR_<$.

Additionally linearity can be replaced by pseudo-linearity:

LIN' $\forall ij\ (i < j\ \vee\ iOj\ \vee\ j < i)$

The assumptions $DISC_<$, $DENS_<$ and $CONT_<$ are problematic for periods, instead one has $DESC_{\sqsubseteq}$, $ATOM_{\sqsubseteq}$ and $FOUND_{\sqsubseteq}$ as defined above. Further reasonable assumptions are $CONN_<$ and $ISO_<$.

Apart from conditions for $\sqsubseteq$ and < separately there is also an interplay between them as formulated by the following 'mixing conditions':

SEP $\forall ij\ (i < j\ \rightarrow\ \neg\, iOj)$

L-MON $\forall ij\ (i < j\ \rightarrow\ \forall k \sqsubseteq i\ \ k < j)$

R-MON $\forall ij\ (i < j\ \rightarrow\ \forall k \sqsubseteq j\ \ i < k)$

CONV $\forall ijk\ (i < j < k\ \rightarrow\ \forall l\,((i \sqsubseteq l\ \wedge\ k \sqsubseteq l)\ \rightarrow\ j \sqsubseteq l))$

The first of these four mixing conditions formulates a kind of separation. The second and third together form monotonicity (MON) consisting of, respectively, left- and right-monotonicity. The fourth one formulates a convexity requirement on periods. All these conditions for periods are not completely independent, for example, MON in combination with $IRREF_<$ implies SEP.

Now that we have defined both points and periods we can ask how we can go from one to the other. Let us start with the direction from points to periods. The following is a standard construction that is also usual in computer science:

$$(T, <)\ \mapsto\ (I, \subseteq, <)\quad \text{where}$$

I is the set of all non-empty convex subsets of $(T, <)$, $\subseteq$ is ordinary set inclusion and < is defined by

$$i < i'\ :=\ \forall t \in i\ \forall t' \in i'\ t < t'$$

($T' \subseteq T$ is convex if and only if $\forall t, t' \in T'\ \forall t'' \in T\ t < t'' < t'\ \Rightarrow\ t'' \in T'$). Assuming the standard assumption for $(T, <)$ that it is a strict partial order (see subsubsection 2.4.1), the so defined period structure satisfies

TRANS, IRREF for <
TRANS, REF, ANTIS, F-DIR, ATOM for $\sqsubseteq$
MON, CONV.

A general problem for periods constructed out of points is the issue of the endpoints:

should periods be open or closed at one or both ends? Taking half-open/half-closed periods seems an unnatural choice. Furthermore, if periods are open at both ends we can get into the trouble of undefinedness inbetween two consecutive periods. On the other hand, if periods are closed at both ends we can get the opposite problem of double definedness at the end, respectively beginning, of two consecutive periods.

The other direction from periods to points is technically much more difficult: this can be done via atoms or via a limiting construction using (downwards converging) filters of periods. However, as already remarked earlier, there is a philosophical question here:

Do points (or point-like periods) *exist* at all?

The reasoning behind this is that points are an abstraction of physical reality because everything has a duration, no matter how small that duration may be. Hence, durationless periods need not exist. On the other hand, mathematical idealizations such as points are often essential for obtaining a simple and elegant theory.

2.7 Event Structures

As we have indicated in subsection 2.2, when we consider events to be the basic time elements, we can do with only the precedence relation. Therefore, an event structure can be represented by

$$(E, <).$$

The characteristic property of causality that there is no effect without a cause can be defined by

$$\forall e \; \exists e' \; e' < e.$$

For the precedence relation we assume that it is a strict partial order (i.e., it is transitive and irreflexive and hence also asymmetric). Then simultaneity can be defined as follows:

$$eSe' \; := \; \neg\, e < e' \;\wedge\; \neg\, e' < e.$$

This definition makes simultaneity reflexive and symmetric. In case $<$ is linear S collapses to equality and becomes an equivalence relation.

From the precedence relation $<$ also the inclusion relation $\sqsubseteq$ is definable:

$$e \sqsubseteq e' \; := \; \forall e'' \; ((e' < e'' \;\rightarrow\; e < e'') \;\wedge\; (e'' < e' \;\rightarrow\; e'' < e)).$$

With this definition $\sqsubseteq$ satisfies TRANS, REF, MON and CONV.

In computer science event structures are well-known, in particular in connection with partial order models of time.

The following construction can be used to transfer events to periods:

$$(E, <) \;\mapsto\; (I, \sqsubseteq, <) \quad \text{where}$$

I is the set of all equivalence classes of mutual inclusion with $\sqsubseteq$ and $<$ defined by taking arbitrary representatives (this is well-defined by TRANS and MON). The resulting period structure satisfies

TRANS, IRREF for $<$
TRANS, REF, ANTIS for $\sqsubseteq$
MON, CONV.

The chain of transformations can be finished by transforming periods into points as before.

3 Temporal Languages

So far our considerations have been quite independent from a particular language and the themes treated are relevant for many theories also those outside the area of temporal logics. In this section we will look at several temporal languages for reasons explained in section 1. First we consider the Priorean language of classical temporal logic (in philosophy better known as tense logic) based on the point structures of subsection 2.5. It uses four unary operators **F**, **P**, **G** and **H** which have the following correspondence with first-order logic:

$$\begin{aligned}\mathbf{F}\,\varphi &\rightleftharpoons \exists t\,(t_0 < t \,\wedge\, \varphi(t))\\ \mathbf{P}\,\varphi &\rightleftharpoons \exists t\,(t < t_0 \,\wedge\, \varphi(t))\\ \mathbf{G}\,\varphi &:= \neg\,\mathbf{F}\neg\,\varphi\\ \mathbf{H}\,\varphi &:= \neg\,\mathbf{P}\neg\,\varphi\end{aligned}$$

where the free variable t_0 denotes the present instant (now). From the list of first-order conditions on the precedence relation given in subsection 2.5 TRANS, L-LIN, R-LIN, SUC and DENS are expressible in the Priorean language while IRREF, ASYM, LIN, DIR, BOUND and DISC are inexpressible. To give 2 examples:

TRANS is expressed by $\mathbf{FF}p \rightarrow \mathbf{F}p$ and
DENS is expressed by $\mathbf{F}p \rightarrow \mathbf{FF}p$.

It is a little bit strange that temporal logic, the logic of time, cannot express about half of the natural characteristic properties one might like time to have. This motivates our next excursion to more expressive temporal logics.

Several alternatives for enriching classical temporal logic in order to obtain a more expressive language have been investigated in recent years. One particularly simple extension is obtained by introducing an additional operator **D** (for difference) having the following correspondence with first-order logic:

$$\mathbf{D}\,\varphi \rightleftharpoons \exists t\ (t \neq t_0 \,\wedge\, \varphi(t))$$

Apart from its dual $\overline{\mathbf{D}}$ several other useful additional operators can be defined from the **D**-operator:

$$\begin{aligned}\overline{\mathbf{D}}\,\varphi &:= \neg\,\mathbf{D}\neg\,\varphi\\ \mathbf{E}\,\varphi &:= \varphi \vee \mathbf{D}\,\varphi\\ \mathbf{A}\,\varphi &:= \neg\,\mathbf{E}\neg\,\varphi\\ \mathbf{U}\,\varphi &:= \mathbf{E}\,(\varphi \wedge \neg\,\mathbf{D}\,\varphi)\end{aligned}$$

E derives from there *exists* a point, **A** from for *all* points and **U** from at a *unique* point. With the **D**-operator all the above conditions become expressible, for example:

IRREF is expressed by $\mathbf{F}p \rightarrow \mathbf{D}p$ and
LIN is expressed by $\mathbf{D}p \rightarrow (\mathbf{P}p \vee \mathbf{F}p)$.

In fact, all universal first-order conditions (and many more) become definable:

Any universal first-order condition on $<$ and $=$ can be written in the form

$$\forall x_1 \ldots \forall x_n\, BOOL(x_i < x_j, x_i = x_j)$$

where $BOOL(\ldots)$ stands for a boolean combination of atomic formulas. Now take as the defining formula in the temporal logic extended with the **D**-operator for such a universal first-order condition:

$$(\mathbf{U}\, p_1 \wedge \ldots \wedge \mathbf{U}\, p_n) \rightarrow BOOL(\mathbf{E}(p_i \wedge \mathbf{F}\, p_j), \mathbf{E}(p_i \wedge p_j)).$$

Notice that the propositions p_i are used to mimic the variables x_i. This is possible because the **U**-operators in the antecedent make the propositions p_i true at a unique point so that the correspondence with the variables can be made one to one.

For the period structures as treated in subsection 2.6 the Priorean language is still usable by interpreting $\varphi(i)$ for a period i as φ being true at i. For point structures the phrase 'φ is true at ...' has an obvious interpretation. For period structures this is not so clear any more: φ is true at i can mean for example that φ is true in the whole period i or alternatively, that φ is true in a part of i. Therefore, it makes sense to introduce operators corresponding to such possible interpretations:

$$\nabla \varphi \rightleftharpoons \forall i(i \sqsubseteq i_0 \rightarrow \varphi(i))$$

$$\Delta \varphi \rightleftharpoons \forall i(i_0 \sqsubseteq i \rightarrow \varphi(i))$$

where i_0 denotes the period where $\nabla \varphi$, respectively $\Delta \varphi$, are evaluated.

Alternatively one may introduce operators that directly correspond to the natural relations for periods as given in subsection 2.6. For instance, the operator $\smile$ can be used to designate the meeting relation M:

$$\smile \varphi \rightleftharpoons \exists i(iMi_0 \wedge \varphi(i)).$$

After defining similar operators for starting and ending and also the converses of meeting, starting and ending, the resulting six operators turn out to be sufficient to characterize all natural relations for periods of subsection 2.6.

4 Turning to Real-Time

In this section we will look at ways to adapt the preceding models of time given in section 2 to incorporate real-time features. The most important addition when switching to real-time is the ability to measure time. In computer science also *computational* models for real-time are important in this respect. Because the traditional computational models are based on states the main question here is how (real) time should be introduced into such state-based models and what the precise relationship between states and time should be like. Since we left from the other end, starting with models of time, we should look how states can be introduced. These two topics, time measurement and the introduction of states, are considered in the two subsections of this section. We will turn back to mainly the conceptual ideas, thereby referring for examples of formalisms working out more of the technical details to several other contributions to the Workshop Proceedings. The results of this section are concrete enough, however, to enable the classification of many real-time formalisms with respect to their treatment of real-time. We leave such a classification of his favourite real-time method to the reader.

4.1 Time Measurement

As the word measurement already indicates, time measurement[1] has to do with a *quantitative* notion of time where, for example, not only the question whether a time element is earlier than another time element can be answered but also the question how much earlier. Several issues can be investigated in the context of time measurement such as:

- notion of time: how should time elements be represented?
  - ⋆ explicitly (in the syntax of the language)
  - ⋆ implicitly (in the semantics of the language)
- notion of measure: how should measure be presented?
  - ⋆ additive (turning the time domain into a group)
  - ⋆ metric (adding a distance function like in topology)
- time reference: how is time measurement calibrated?
  - ⋆ absolute (e.g., 7 June 1991)
  - ⋆ relative (e.g., the last day of the REX '91 Workshop)
- units of time: how is time measurement related to the *real* world?

The notion of time and time reference already play a role in ordinary (qualitative) models of time but the notion of measure and units of time are typical for quantitative models of time. For absolute time reference we gave an example above (7 June 1991) based on points (in this case days) but this can also be nicely illustrated with periods as follows. [1991,6,7] represents the 7th day of the 6th month of the year 1991. This representation gives a natural way of handling subperiods: [1991,6,7] is a subperiod of [1991,6] which again is a subperiod of [1991]; the other way around, [1991,6,7] is a superperiod of [1991,6,7,14] (the 14th hour of ...). An example of a formalism using relative time reference is provided by classical temporal logic because it uses an implicit notion of time based on the current moment of time (now).

In the following we will use the fundamental choice of time elements (points, periods or events) to illustrate these issues. First we deal with time measurement for points. In the explicit approach an additional variable *time* is introduced (which can be used to mimick a system clock) satisfying the following two basic assumptions (formulated in a first-order variant of the Priorean temporal language from section 3):

$$\forall t \ (time = t \ \rightarrow \ \mathbf{G} \ time \geq t)$$
$$\forall t \ \mathbf{F} \ time \geq t.$$

The first assumption is that of monotonicity of the *time* variable while the second one asserts the progress of that variable. Interestingly, relating to a well-known classification of properties in computer science, these two assumptions together enable the reduction of liveness properties to a kind of safety properties. One can object to the explicit approach

[1] A logic dealing with time measurement may be aptly called 'chronologic'.

as being too concrete: time is implicit in classical temporal logic and for time measurement only quantitative elements are additionally required. From the point of view of syntactical abstractness (a language is syntactically abstract when its syntax only mentions elements essential for the abstraction level required) an explicit representation of time itself is undesirable. The implicit approach does conform to syntactical abstractness by only representing quantitative elements (relating to a number of time units) explicitly. One way of doing this is the indexing of temporal operators by such quantitative elements, for example, the operator $\mathbf{G}_3$ addresses all time points 3 time units later than the current moment. Striving for syntactical abstractness makes sense as long as the expressive power of a language conforms to the required needs without falling into unnatural or cumbersome means of expression.

In the additive approach an operation $+$ is added such that $(T, +, 0)$ is a commutative group. The element 0 then represents the current moment (now). If such a special representation of the current moment is not needed, it suffices to use a monoid instead of a group. Apart from addition $+$ often also subtraction $-$ is added. Alternatively, the metric approach introduces a distance function d satisfying at least the usual topological conditions

- $d(t,t') = 0 \Leftrightarrow t = t'$
- $d(t,t') = d(t',t)$
- $d(t,t'') \leq d(t,t') + d(t',t'')$
- $d(t,t') \geq 0$

For branching time the first condition can be relaxed (obtaining a quasi-metric) because simultaneity can lead to different points with distance 0. In the case of linear time the third condition, the triangular inequality, can be strengthened to equality:

$$t < t' < t'' \rightarrow d(t,t'') = d(t,t') + d(t',t'').$$

(This condition is reasonable for all point structures, but in case of linear time any three different points can be arranged as in the antecedent of the above condition.) The additive approach deals with time measurement by interpreting time elements themselves as representing a number of time units. The metric approach on the other hand, measures time by mapping the distance between two points to a structure (the range of d) whose elements represent numbers of time units.

A related question is whether it is possible that

$$range(d) = T?$$

In more general terms: is duration similar to time? A positive answer brings the metric approach quite close to the additive approach. The only difference between the two approaches is then that the metric approach uses a distance function which is total whereas it is not always guaranteed in the additive approach that $+$ satisfies a similar totality property $\forall t \forall t' \exists t''\ t + t'' = t'$ as is exemplified by the structure $\mathbb{Z} \oplus \mathbb{Z}$ with its 'standard' addition. On the other hand, a negative answer to the question above provides more flexibility since it allows different possibilities for measuring time in the form of different choices for the range of d (yielding different representations of time units).

Now we turn to time measurement for periods. In the metric approach the following is possible. First identify certain 'atomic' periods and define their duration by associating a number of time units with them. Then if iMj (i meets j) the duration of the period $i \cup j$ can be defined by

$$duration(i \cup j) = duration(i) + duration(j)$$

where we suppose that

$$\forall k \sqsubseteq i \cup j \ (kOi \vee kOj)$$

in order for this definition to be well-behaved. From this notion of duration a metric can be derived. Alternatively, one can postulate the above equation as a property of *duration* even in the case where no atomic periods exist. By using measure theory it is then possible to define a metric by measuring subsets in a way that is usual in topology. The additive approach is problematic here because it requires the existence of a 0-element.

A possible source of problems in the period approach is the relationship between units of time and subperiods expressed by:

$$i \sqsubseteq j \wedge i \neq j \ \rightarrow \ duration(i) < duration(j).$$

A reasonable solution here is the assumption of atomic periods as already indicated above possibly in combination with the introduction of nested units of time (such as days,hours,minutes,...) like in the example for absolute time reference for periods at the beginning of this subsection.

Finally we look at time measurement for events. For events we can distinguish several possibilities for referencing time:

- absolute time, for example, $e@t$ (e occurs at time t)
- reference event, for example, t after e
- in before/after precedence chain, that is, pure qualitatively (with no measurement at all).

The combination of the implicit with the metric approach seems the most suitable here: the explicit approach is less suited since time is secondary to events and the additive approach has the same problems as for periods (the existence of the 0-element).

4.2 Introducing States

We want to finish our overview with some remarks about computational models, in particular the connection between states and time. The two main possibilities for the relationship between states and time are:

- time is part of the states (e.g. by incorporating timestamps)
- time is an independent axis from the state structure.

In a linear point structure the second possibility is illustrated by the picture

As this picture suggests, states can be interpreted over the time axis and time can be associated to states by means of projection on the time axis. This leaves open the option whether states and time are in a one-to-one correspondence as is the case for the first possibility (time is part of the states): both the case where each time element has an associated state and the case where some time elements have no state associated are possible. The latter case, for example, is useful in the realm of hardware design where — due to stability conditions — a state of a component is only defined during certain periods. Apart from having more options, the second possibility also seems to be more *real*istic since the wall clock progresses independently from system execution. This is especially true for many real-time systems in which the external timing (of e.g. physical and chemical processes) determines the required operation speed of the controlling system and not the other way around.

Another related topic for real-time systems is that they are usually deterministic in order to be able to comply to the promptness requirements. Inspecting the temporal conditions mentioned in subsection 2.4 this would favour linear time models since the added complexity of non-determinism as reasoned with in branching time is not needed in this case. Also timing requirements relating to the interaction between the environment and the system are by nature expressed using a global notion of time. This imposes a total order on time and hence again favours the linear time model. As soon as choices between different possible evolutions of a system are relevant, branching time models should be taken into account.

Reference

Johan van Benthem: *The Logic of Time* (Second Edition), Reidel, Dordrecht, 1991.

Specification and Analysis of Resource-Bound Real-Time Systems*

Richard Gerber
Dept. of Computer Science
University of Maryland
College Park, MD 20742
rich@cs.umd.edu

Insup Lee
Dept. of Computer and Info. Science
University of Pennsylvania
Philadelphia, PA 19104
lee@cis.upenn.edu

Abstract. We describe a layered approach to the specification and verification of real-time systems. Application processes are specified in the CSR application language, which includes high-level language constructs such as timeouts, deadlines, periodic processes, interrupts and exception-handling. Then, a configuration schema is used to map the processes to system resources, and to specify the physical communication links between them. To analyze and execute the entire system, we automatically translate the result of the mapping into the CCSR process algebra. CCSR characterizes CSR's resource-based computation model by a priority-sensitive, operational semantics, which yields a set of equivalence-preserving proof rules. Using this proof system, we perform the algebraic verification of our original real-time system.

Keywords: Real-time, specification, configuration, verification, proof systems, process algebras, programming languages.

Contents

*This research was supported in part by ONR N00014-89-J-1131 and NSF CCR-9014621.

1 Introduction

Once strictly the province of assembly-language programmers, real-time computing has developed into an important area of research. This is a welcome sign, since the practice of building real-time systems is still dominated by the use of arcane and *ad hoc* techniques. As a step toward redressing this problem, there has recently been a spate of progress in the development of real-time formal methods. Much of this work has fallen into the traditional categories of untimed systems – for example, temporal logics (as in [14,1]), assertional methods (as in [16,7]), net-based paradigms (as in [10,3]) and process algebras (as in [15,17]).

In this paper we address the problem of shared resources in real-time systems. As in [9], we model a real-time system not only by its functionality and timing constraints, but also as a collection of one or more shared resources. Each resource is inherently sequential in nature; that is, a resource only has the capacity to execute a solitary event at any time. This constraint quite naturally leads to an interleaving notion of concurrency at the resource level of the system, where we assume that a priority ordering is used to arbitrate between simultaneous resource requests. At the system level, true parallelism occurs when a group of resources are executed simultaneously. In such an environment, various factors can influence the real-time behavior of a system: the number of resources, their timing characteristics, their ordering of priorities, the connectivity between them, and the processes hosted on them.

To study the subtle interplay between these factors, we have developed a two-tiered framework called Communicating Shared Resources (or CSR). At the top layer is the CSR specification language which is used to describe the functional aspects of a real-time system as well as its resource requirements. The specification language consists of an application language and a configuration language. The application language possesses high-level constructs to specify communication primitives, timeouts, delays, interrupts, deadlines, periodic processes and exceptions. The configuration language is used to define the *structure* of the complete system. A configuration schema maps application processes to system resources, specifies the topology of interconnection network, replicates system components and declares priorities. The bottom layer is the Calculus for CSR (or CCSR), which is a process algebra based on a computation model that captures the notions of priority and resource. An automatic translator accepts the application and configuration components of a CSR specification, and then translated them into a CCSR term. The correctness of the CSR specification is verified using the proof system of CCSR.

This paper is organized as follows: In Section 2.1, we present an overview of the CSR Specification Language, with both its syntax and its informal semantics. We proceed to show how a resource-constrained, real-time system can be assembled using a configuration schema. Section 3 is devoted to the CCSR process algebra – its execution model, semantics and the proof system that it yields. In Section 4 we show how a CSR specification and a configuration schema is translated into CCSR, and in Section 5 we show how the CCSR proof rules can then be used to verify that the original CSR program is correct.

2 The CSR Specification Language

A major objective of the CSR paradigm is to facilitate the specification of real-time processes, and then support a static evaluation of various design alternatives. To this end, the CSR paradigm supports the separation of a real-time system's functional specification from its configuration. The functional spcification, which is written in the CSR application language, describes the high-level timing characteristics of a system. The configuration schema, written in the CSR Configuration Language, characterizes the interralationship between these processes; i.e., their resource mappings, their communication links, etc. This separation of concerns more easily lends itself to an evaluation of various system designs. At the CSR application language level, one need only concern oneself with the functionality of each process. The configuration language then gives us the ability to "assemble" the component programs in as intelligent a manner as possible. By experimenting with different process mappings and communication channel connections, one can change the topology of a system without rewriting the actual CSR application specification.

2.1 The Application Language

A CSR application program consists of a collection of processes, each of which contains a declaration section and a CSR statement. The declaration section reserves the ports, local execution events, and free timing parameters that the process will use, while the statement specifies the process' basic control structure. CSR statements include send and receive commands, sequential composition, timeouts, periodic loops, interrupts and exception-handling.

Table 1 shows the syntax of the language; CSR keywords are in boldface, $\langle\ \rangle$ indicates non-terminal symbols, "id" represents an identifier, and "num" denotes a positive integer. We also use | to indicate alternatives and [ ] to indicate optional syntax.

Declarations. Declarations fall into two categories – event declarations and timing declarations. An event declaration reserves identifiers associated either with communication ports or local execution actions. These CSR events are generically called **atoms** as they are used in "atomic" CSR statements: **input** atoms are used in **recv** statements, **output** atoms are used in **send** statements, and **local** atoms are used in **exec** statements.

A timing declaration reserves one or more free *time variables* that may be used in a CSR time-constrained statement such as **wait**, **every** and **scope**. When a time variable appears in such a statement, it becomes the configuration schema's responsibility to bind it to an integer constant. As is shown in Table 1, constants may also be used in these statements.

<table>
<tr><td>⟨program⟩</td><td>::=</td><td>⟨proc⟩ ⟨program⟩ | ⟨proc⟩</td></tr>
<tr><td>⟨proc⟩</td><td>::=</td><td>**process** id ⟨decls⟩ ⟨stmt⟩</td></tr>
<tr><td>⟨decls⟩</td><td>::=</td><td>⟨decl⟩ [⟨decls⟩]</td></tr>
<tr><td>⟨decl⟩</td><td>::=</td><td>**input** ⟨ids⟩ | **output** ⟨ids⟩ | **local** ⟨ids⟩ | **timevar** ⟨ids⟩</td></tr>
<tr><td>⟨ids⟩</td><td>::=</td><td>id [, ⟨ids⟩]</td></tr>
<tr><td>⟨stmt⟩</td><td>::=</td><td>⟨atomic⟩ | **skip** | **wait** ⟨time⟩ | **idle** | **ndet**(⟨atomic⟩,num,num)</td></tr>
<tr><td></td><td>|</td><td>⟨stmt⟩ ; ⟨stmt⟩ | ⟨loop-stat⟩ | ⟨every-stat⟩</td></tr>
<tr><td></td><td>|</td><td>⟨scope-stat⟩ | ⟨interleave-stat⟩</td></tr>
<tr><td>⟨atomic⟩</td><td>::=</td><td>**exec**(id) | **recv**(id) | **send**(id)</td></tr>
<tr><td>⟨loop-stat⟩</td><td>::=</td><td>**loop do** ⟨stmt⟩ **od**</td></tr>
<tr><td>⟨every-stat⟩</td><td>::=</td><td>**every** ⟨time⟩ **do** ⟨stmt⟩ **od**</td></tr>
<tr><td>⟨scope-stat⟩</td><td>::=</td><td>**scope do** ⟨stmt⟩ [⟨triggers⟩] **od**</td></tr>
<tr><td>⟨triggers⟩</td><td>::=</td><td>**interrupt** ⟨atomic⟩ → ⟨stmt⟩ ⟨triggers⟩</td></tr>
<tr><td></td><td>|</td><td>**timeout** ⟨time⟩ → ⟨stmt⟩</td></tr>
<tr><td>⟨interleave-stat⟩</td><td>::=</td><td>**interleave do** ⟨stmt⟩ & ⟨stmt⟩ **od**</td></tr>
<tr><td>⟨time⟩</td><td>::=</td><td>num | id</td></tr>
</table>

Table 1: The CSR Application Language

Statements. An atomic statement – i.e., **send**, **recv** or **exec** – requires one time unit to execute, at which time it terminates. And while it cannot be interrupted *during* execution, it does have the capacity to idle indefinitely *before* execution. There are two reasons for this. First, **recv** and **send** require synchronization with other processes. Second, all three statements must also wait to be scheduled since many processes may be interleaved on the same resource.

The **wait** t statement specifies pure delay for t time units, after which it terminates. (We mandate that t be greater than 0.) The **skip** statement terminates at the first time unit; that is, **skip** is equivalent to **wait** 1. At the other extreme is the **idle** statement, which endlessly idles and never terminates.

The sequential composition of S and T, "S;T", is standard: first S executes until termination, immediately after which T is initiated. For an atomic statement S, **ndet**(S,m,n) executes S between m and n times, where $1 \leq m \leq n$. If m is not equal to n, the exact number of executions is resolved nondeterministically. For example, the statement **ndet**(**send**(ch),3,5) means that **send**(ch) is executed between 3 and 5 times.

There are two kinds of repetitive constructs: **loop** and **every**. The **loop** statement is used for simple, nonterminating loops. For example, **loop do** S **od** endlessly cycles, executing the statement S. On the other hand, the **every** construct denotes a statement with cyclic behavior of a positive periodicity. For example **every 6 do** S **od** has a period of 6 time units; that is, every 6 time units S is reinitiated. There are three possible outcomes of each iteration: (1) S may terminate *exactly* at 6 time units, and then be restarted; (2) S may terminate early, in which case the loop idles for the remainder of the period, and then gets restarted; and (3) S may not terminate within the period, in which case it is aborted, and then restarted.

The **scope** statement allows the specification of interrupts and a deadline associated with a statement. A typical scope statement is as follows: **scope do** S triggers **od**. The body, S, of the scope statement executes, and if and when a triggering condition is raised the execution flow is transferred to its associated exception handler. There are four kinds of trigger guards: send, recv, exec and timeout. We use the following fragment to explain the construct's behavior:

```
scope do
  S
interrupt recv(ch1) → S1
interrupt send(ch2) → S2
interrupt recv(ch1) → S3
interrupt exec(a) → S4
timeout 100 → S5
od
```

Upon the initiation of the scope, the statement S starts executing and the timeout counter – initially set to 100 – starts decrementing upon entering the scope. During the execution of S, the atomic expressions (or "interrupts") are enabled. S is executed until one of the following occurs: (1) S terminates, in which case the timeout and interrupts are disabled, and the entire statement terminates; (2) an interrupt is executed, in which case S is aborted, the timeout and other interrupts are disabled, and the associated handler is then executed; or (3) the timeout occurs, in which case S is aborted, the interrupts are disabled, and the timeout exception handler S5 is initiated.

If there is contention between two interrupts at the same time, the selection is made by the two action's synchronization constraints, by their priority, and as a last resort, nondeterministically. Contention between an interrupt, and an atomic action in S is similarly resolved.

We note that if no **timeout** condition were present, S would not have to terminate within 100 time units; similarly, if there were no interrupts, the only two possibilities would be for S to terminate, or for a timeout exception to be raised.

The CSR paradigm provides two kinds of concurrency: one for processes executing on different resources and another for processes executing on the same resource. As we have stated, it is the responsibility of the configuration schema to define the resource location of each process, and thus, the characteristics of inter-process concurrency. However, we additionally provide the facility for intra-process concurrency, which is defined by the **interleave** statement. For example, the statement, **interleave do** S & T **od**, interleaves the actions of S and T, scheduling them according to their synchronization and priority constraints. The entire statement terminates when both S and T have reached terminating states. We note that one can use the interleave statement to describe a hardware interrupt handling, in which the interrupted statement is resumed after handling the interrupt.

The semantics of the interleave is such that pure idle time is never interleaved with other actions; instead, it is "overlapped." Thus, the fragment

interleave do wait 2 & **recv**(ch1);**recv**(ch2) **od**

is equivalent to "**recv**(ch1);**recv**(ch2)", as the two receives are overlapped with the idles. Thus, **skip** functions as an identity in the **interleave** statement.

```
process S
  local sense, error
  output ch
  timevar t
  every 6 do
    exec(sense);
    scope do idle
    interrupt send(ch) → skip
    timeout t → exec(error) od
  od

process M
  local compute
  input ch
  loop do
    recv(ch); exec(compute); exec(compute)
  od
```

Figure 1: Specification of a Sensor-Monitor System

2.2 A Sensor-Monitor System

Figure 1 displays the two process "S" and "M," where S specifies a sensor process and M specifies the monitor process with which it communicates. We assume that our time granularity is 1 millisecond.

The sensor has a 6 millisecond period, within which it (1) takes a sample reading from the environment, and then (2) attempts to communicate the result to M along channel ch. However, because the environment is subject to very rapid changes, the communication must be made within t milliseconds; otherwise the data becomes worthless. If the communication is successfully accomplished within t milliseconds, S sleeps for the remainder of the period. Otherwise, it records an error.

As for the monitor, its control structure consists solely of an endless loop. During every iteration, the process first waits for S to communicate its data. When the data is received, statistics are computed for 2 milliseconds within a critical section, after which M again waits for communication with S.

2.3 The Configuration Language

The CSR Application Language is designed for the functional description of real-time processes. These individual CSR processes are without "concurrent context"; that is, their relationship to the overall system is left unspecified. This relationship is defined in a *configuration schema* written the CSR configuration language. A system configuration contains the following information: (1) processes are mapped to the system resources; (2) priorities are assigned to the various atoms declared in each process; (3) time variables are bound to integer constants; (4) channels are created by making connections between

⟨sys⟩	::=	⟨config⟩ ⟨sys⟩ | ⟨mainsys⟩
⟨config⟩	::=	**configurator** id ([⟨formals⟩]) ⟨declarations⟩ **end**
⟨formals⟩	::=	⟨formal⟩ [; ⟨formals⟩]
⟨formal⟩	::=	**resource** ⟨ids⟩ | **priority** ⟨ids⟩ | **timeval** ⟨ids⟩
⟨mainsys⟩	::=	**main** ⟨declarations⟩ **end**
⟨declarations⟩	::=	⟨decl⟩ [⟨declarations⟩]
⟨decl⟩	::=	**resource** ⟨ids⟩
	|	**system** id = id ([⟨actuals⟩])
	|	**process** id ⟨attrspec⟩
	|	**assign** ⟨anyids⟩ **on** id
	|	**close** ⟨ids⟩
	|	**connect** ⟨fullids⟩
⟨actuals⟩	::=	⟨value⟩ [, ⟨actuals⟩]
⟨value⟩	::=	num | id
⟨attrspec⟩	::=	⟨attrtype⟩ ⟨attrlist⟩ ⟨attrspec⟩
⟨attrtype⟩	::=	**inport** | **outport** | **local** | **timevar**
⟨attrlist⟩	::=	id (⟨value⟩) [, ⟨attrlist⟩]
⟨ids⟩	::=	id [, ⟨ids⟩]
⟨fullids⟩	::=	fullid [, ⟨fullids⟩]
⟨anyids⟩	::=	anyid [, ⟨anyids⟩]

Table 2: The CSR Configuration Language

the processes' ports; and (5) if we so desire, designated resources are *closed*, meaning that no further processes will be allocated to them.

The configuration language is hierarchical in that a configured system may be an amalgamation of subsystems, which may themselves have subsystems. We also provide for *parameterized configurations*, so that the parent systems may pass both resources and priority assignments to their child subsystems.

Table 2 presents the complete grammar for the Configuration Language. We use the same notational conventions as in the CSR grammar, with the following addition: a "fullid" is an alphanumeric string interspersed with dots, such as "sys.prog.a1", and "anyid" represents either a fullid or an ordinary identifier.

A configuration schema consists of a **main** system (or the root), as well as a (possibly empty) set of configurators for subsystems. Within each component is a set of declarations that define the system characteristics.

We can illustrate the Configuration Language by using it to build a *dual* sensor-monitor system, derived from the sensor and monitor processes in Figure 1. In our new scenario we have two sensors, S1.S and S2.S, each of which with the functionality of our original sensor S. We now bind the S1.S's time variable t to 2 milliseconds, and S2.S's time variable t to 4 milliseconds. Thus S2.S's sampled data has greater temporal persistence than that of S1.S. We also have two monitors M1.M and M2.M, each of which with the functionality of our original monitor M. We use the configuration shown in Figure 3 to "draw" the system layout depicted in Figure 2.

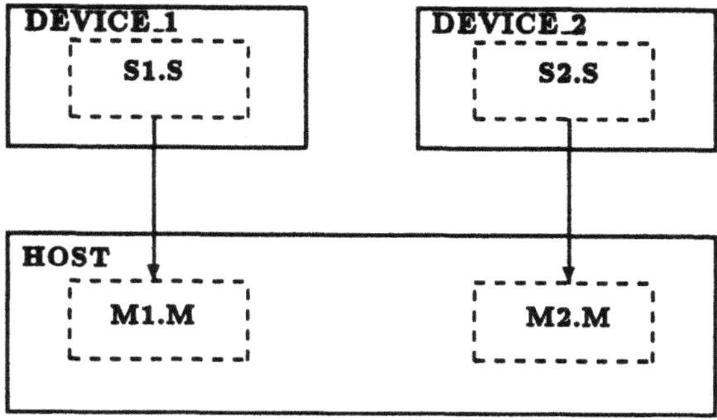

Figure 2: Process to Resource Mapping

Before delving into the functionality of configurators and subsystems, we first consider the basic system-building declarations: **resource**, **process**, **assign**, **close** and **connect**. As we have stated, the resource is the defining aspect of our real-time model, in that a single resource may only execute one atom at a time. Thus the number of resources in a system may significantly alter its runtime behavior. Within a configuration, resources are denoted by the **resource** declaration; e.g., in Figure 3 identifies the three resources, Devicel, Device2 and Host.

Each process used in the system is identified using a **process** declaration, which has the syntax that is quite similar to the header section in a CSR process. That is, it defines the process name, the atoms used within the process and any free time variables that must be bound.

The **assign** declaration is used to map processes onto resources. For example, in Figure 3, processes S1.S and S2.S are mapped to resources Devicel and Device2, respectively, and processes M1.M and M2.M are mapped to resource Host.

In determining the timing behavior of processes on a particular resource, it is useful to know whether the resource is going to host additional processes. The **close** declaration defines that no more processes may be assigned to the named resources. The **close** declaration in Figure 3 denotes that S1.S and S2.S are the *sole* occupants of Devicel and Device2, respectively.

We use **connect** to define connections between atoms; that is, they must execute synchronously when their resources are combined in a system. In Figure 3, the first **connect** declaration specifies that the S1.S and M1.M processes share a point-to-point link. When they execute in parallel, the atoms S1.S.ch and M1.M.ch must always execute simultaneously. We note that the meaning of the **connect** declaration is *transitive*. That is, the following declarations imply that P.a, Q.b, R.c and S.d are all mutually connected:

connect P.a, Q.b
connect R.c, S.d
connect P.a, S.d

Hierarchical, Parameterized Configurations. The Configuration Language supports hierarchical schemas, which can be constructed using the following features:

```
configurator MakeSense(timevar u)
  process S
    local sense(1), error(1)
    outport ch(0)
    timevar t(u)
end

configurator MakeMon(priority chpri)
  process M
    local compute(3)
    inport ch(chpri)
end

main
  resource Device1, Device2, Host
  system S1 = MakeSense(2)
  system S2 = MakeSense(4)
  system M1 = MakeMon(2)
  system M2 = MakeMon(1)
  assign S1.S on Device1
  assign S2.S on Device2
  assign M1.M, M2.M on Host
  close Device1, Device2, Host
  connect S1.S.ch, M1.M.ch
  connect S2.S.ch, M2.M.ch
end
```

Figure 3: Hierarchical Configuration of Sensor-Monitor System

- The **configurator** declaration, which is used to denote configuration "generators"; that is, entities that must be "instantiated" to create a particular configuration.
- The **system** declaration, which "instantiates" a configurator, and thus creates a new subsystem within its scope.

For example, Figure 3 includes a configurator MakeMon. By invoking the configurator twice, the **main** schema creates two "copies" of the system defined in Conf, and in this way we derive the processes M1.M and M2.M. Moreover, M1.M.ch has a priority of 2, and M2.Mon.ch has priority 1.

A configurator may itself make reference to other configurators, which results in a subsystem that owns other subsystems within its scope. The only restriction we make is that no forward references are allowed; this rules out any possibility of "recursive" configurator invocation. Those readers familiar with the ML programming language will note that the relationship between configuration schemas and configurators is similar to that between structures and functors [6].

3 The Calculus for Communicating Shared Resources

In this section we describe the CCSR language and its computation model, developing such notions as resources, priority, synchronization and preemption. We proceed to show that CCSR's semantics gives rise to a set of substitutive proof rules.

3.1 The Computation Model

The basic unit of computation is the *event*, which is used to model both local resource execution as well as inter-resource synchronization. When executed by a resource, each event consumes exactly one time unit. We let Σ represent the universal set of events.

Since a system potentially consists of many resources, multiple events may be observed at any time throughout the course of its execution. We call such observances *actions*, and they are represented by sets in $\mathbf{P}(\Sigma)$. In general, we let the letters a, b and c range over the event set Σ, and the letters A, B and C range over the action set $\mathbf{P}(\Sigma)$.

Termination. The termination event, or "$\surd$", has the unique property that it is not "owned" by any particular resource. Rather, if $\surd \in A$ for some action A, this means that the system executing A is capable of terminating.

Resources and Actions. We consider individual resources to be inherently sequential in nature. That is, at each time unit a resource is capable of executing *at most* a single event. Actions that consist of multiple events must be formed by the synchronous execution of multiple resources. We denote $\mathcal{R}$ to represent the set of resources available to a system, and let i, j, and k range over $\mathcal{R}$. For all i in $\mathcal{R}$ we denote Σ_i as the collection of events exclusively "owned" by resource i:

$$\forall i \in \mathcal{R}, \forall j \in \mathcal{R} . i \neq j, \; \Sigma_i \cap \Sigma_j = \emptyset$$

This type of alphabet partitioning is similar to that found in the I/O Automata model [12], where it is used to define a notion of fairness. However, here it is used to help mandate our resource-induced mutual exclusion condition. The domain of actions executable by any CCSR term, "$\mathcal{D}$", is defined as follows:

$$\mathcal{D} \;=\; \{A \in p(\Sigma) \,|\, \forall i \in \mathcal{R}, \; |A \cap \Sigma_i| \leq 1\}$$

where "$p(\Sigma)$" denotes the set of finite subsets of Σ, and "$|S|$" denotes the cardinality of a finite set "S". For a given action A, we use the notation $\rho(A)$ to represent the resource set that executes events in A: $\rho(A) = \{i \in \mathcal{R} \,|\, \Sigma_i \cap A \neq \emptyset\}$. Note that since for all i, $\surd \notin \Sigma_i$, $\rho(A) = \rho(A - \{\surd\})$.

Priority. At any point in time many events may be competing for the ability to execute on a single resource. We help arbitrate such competition through the use of a priority ordering, $\pi \in \Sigma \rightarrow \boldsymbol{N}$. Using π, we define the preorder "$\leq_p$" that reflects the notion of priority over the domain $\mathcal{D}$. For all $A, B \in \mathcal{D}$, $A \leq_p B$ if and only if for all i in $\rho(A) \cup \rho(B)$,

$$\begin{array}{l} A \cap \Sigma_i = \emptyset \;\vee \\ (\exists a.\; A \cap \Sigma_i = \{a\} \;\wedge\; \pi(a) = 0) \;\vee \\ (\exists a \exists b.\; A \cap \Sigma_i = \{a\} \;\wedge\; B \cap \Sigma_j = \{b\} \;\wedge\; \pi(a) \leq \pi(b)) \end{array}$$

Based on this definition, we use the notation "$A <_p B$" to represent that A has lower priority than B; i.e., $A \leq_p B$ and $B \not\leq_p A$.

Synchronization. In CCSR, the lowest form of communication is accomplished through the simultaneous execution of synchronizing events. The model treats such synchronizing events as being statically "bound" together by the various connections between system resources. To capture this property we make use of what we call *connection sets.* A connection set is a set of events that exhibits the "all or none" property of event synchronization: At time t, if any of the events in a given connection set wish to execute, they all must execute. More formally, a connection set is an equivalence class formed by the equivalence relation "$\bullet\!\!-\!\!\bullet$".

Definition 3.1 $\bullet\!\!-\!\!\bullet \subseteq \Sigma \times \Sigma$ *is an equivalence relation, where* $a \bullet\!\!-\!\!\bullet\, b$ *denotes that* a *is connected to* b. *We use the notation* $connections(a)$ *to represent the equivalence class (or connection set) of* a. □

We say that an action is synchronized with respect to a resource set $I \subseteq \mathcal{R}$ if $sync_{(I)}(A)$ holds, where

$$sync_{(I)}(A) \quad \text{iff} \quad A = (\bigcup_{a \in A} connections(a)) \cap (\bigcup_{i \in I}(\Sigma_i \cup \{\surd\}))$$

That is, if $sync_{(I)}(A)$ holds, A cannot make any additional connections with the resources in I. Also, it is often convenient to be able to decompose an action A into two parts: that which is fully synchronized (or resolved), and that which is not (or still unresolved). To do this, we make use of the following two definitions:

$$\begin{aligned} res(A) &= \bigcup\{B \subseteq A \mid sync_{(\mathcal{R})}(B)\} \\ unres(A) &= A - res(A) \end{aligned}$$

Idle Events. For every $i \in \mathcal{R}$, there is an idle event τ_i^0 in Σ_i such that $\pi(\tau_i^0) = 0$. The way to interpret these events is as follows. A process may idle in two ways – it may either release its processor during the idle time (represented by the execution of no event) or it may hold its processor (represented by the execution of an idle event). We add that such idle events are local with respect to their own resources; that is, they belong to their own connection sets.

3.2 The CCSR Language and its Semantics

The syntax of CCSR resembles, in some respects, that of SCCS [13]. Let $\mathcal{E}$ represent the domain of terms, and let E, F, G and H range over $\mathcal{E}$. Additionally we assume an infinite set of free term variables, FV, with X ranging over FV and $free(E)$ representing the set of free variables in the term E. Let $\mathcal{P}$ represent the domain of closed terms, which we call *agents* or alternatively, *processes*, and let P, Q, R and S range over $\mathcal{P}$. The following grammar defines the terms of CCSR:

$$E \;:=\; NIL \mid A : E \mid E + E \mid E_I \|_J E \mid E \,\Delta_t^B\, (E, E, E) \mid [E]_I \mid fix(X.E) \mid X$$

The semantics of $\mathcal{E}$ is defined by a labeled transition system $\langle \mathcal{E}, \rightarrow, \mathcal{D} \rangle$, which is a relation $\rightarrow \subseteq \mathcal{E} \times \mathcal{D} \times \mathcal{E}$. We denote each member (E, A, F) of "$\rightarrow$" as "$E \xrightarrow{A} F$". We call this transition system *unconstrained*, in that no priority arbitration is made between actions. We then use "$\longrightarrow$" to define a prioritized transition system $\langle \mathcal{E}, \longrightarrow_\pi, \mathcal{D} \rangle$, which is sensitive to preemption. This two-phased approach greatly simplifies the definition of "$\longrightarrow_\pi$"; similar tactics have been used by [2] in their treatment of CCS priority, and by [8] in their semantics for maximum parallelism.

The Unconstrained Transition System, "$\longrightarrow$". Table 3 presents the unconstrained transition system, "$\longrightarrow$". Throughout, we use the following notation. For a given set of resources $I \subseteq \mathcal{R}$, we let Σ_I represent the set $\bigcup_{i \in I} \Sigma_i$. Also, $A * B = (A - \{\surd\}) \cup (B - \{\surd\}) \cup (A \cap B)$; that is, the termination event "$\surd$" is an element of $A * B$ if and only if it is in both A and B.

Inaction. The term NIL executes no action whatsoever, and thus it possesses no transition.

Action. The Action operator, "$A : E$", has the following behavior. At the first time unit, the action A is executed, proceeded by the term E.

Choice. The Choice operator represents selection – either of the terms can be chosen to execute, subject to the constraints of the environment. For example, the term $(A : E) + (B : F)$ may execute A and proceed to E, or it may execute B and proceed to F.

Parallel. The Parallel operator defines the resources that can be used by the two terms, and also forces synchronization between them. Here, $I, J \subseteq \mathcal{R}$ are the resources allotted to E and F, respectively. In the case where $I \cap J \neq \emptyset$, E and F may be able to share certain resources. But as we have stated, such resource-sharing must be interleaved.

The first two conditions define the resources on which the terms E_1 and E_2 may execute, while the third condition stipulates that single resources may not execute more than one event at a time. The final condition defines our notion of inter-resource synchronization; that is, A_1 and A_2 may execute simultaneously if and only if they are connected in the following sense: If some event $a \in A_1$ is connected to an event $b \in \Sigma_J$, then b *must* appear in A_2, and *vice versa*.

Scope. The Scope construct $E \,\Delta_t^B\, (F, G, H)$ binds the term E by a temporal scope [11], and it incorporates both the features of timeouts and interrupts. We call t the *time bound* and B the *termination control*, where $t \in \boldsymbol{N}^+ \cup \{\infty\}$ (i.e., t is either a positive integer or infinity), and $B = \{\surd\}$ or $B = \emptyset$.

The four rules for the Scope operator, correspond to the four actions that may be taken while a term E is bound by a temporal scope: 1) continuing (ScopeC), 2) successfully terminating (ScopeE), 3) timing out with an exception-handler (ScopeT) and 4) being interrupted (ScopeI).

Close. The Close operator assigns terms to occupy *exactly* the resource set denoted by the index I. First, the action A may not utilize *more* than the resources in I; otherwise it is not admitted by the transition system. If the events in A utilize less than the set I, the action is augmented with the "idle" events from each of the unused resources. For example, assume E executes an action A, and that there is some $i \in I$ such that $i \notin \rho(A)$. In $[E]_I$, this gap is filled by including τ_0^i in A. Here we use the notation $\mathcal{T}_J^0$ to represent *all* of the 0-priority events from the resource set J: $\mathcal{T}_J^0 = \{\tau_j^0 \,|\, j \in J\}$.

Recursion. The term $fix(X.P)$ denotes recursion, allowing the specification of infinite behaviors. As an example, consider the term that indefinitely executes the action "A": $fix(X.(A : X))$. By the Action rule, $A : fix(X.(A : X)) \xrightarrow{A} fix(X.(A : X))$, so by the

Action : $A : E \xrightarrow{A} E$

ChoiceL : $\dfrac{E \xrightarrow{A} E'}{E + F \xrightarrow{A} E'}$ **ChoiceR :** $\dfrac{F \xrightarrow{A} F'}{E + F \xrightarrow{A} F'}$

Parallel :

$$\frac{E_1 \xrightarrow{A_1} E_1',\ E_2 \xrightarrow{A_2} E_2'}{E_1\,{}_I\|_J\,E_2 \xrightarrow{A_1 * A_2} E_1'\,{}_I\|_J\,E_2'} \quad \left(\begin{array}{l} \rho(A_1) \subseteq I,\ \rho(A_2) \subseteq J, \\ \rho(A_1) \cap \rho(A_2) = \emptyset,\ sync_{(I \cup J)}(A_1 * A_2) \end{array}\right)$$

ScopeC : $\dfrac{E \xrightarrow{A} E'}{E \,\Delta_t^B\, (F, G, H) \xrightarrow{A} E' \,\Delta_{t-1}^B\, (E, F, G)}$ $(t > 1,\ \surd \notin A)$

ScopeE : $\dfrac{E \xrightarrow{A} E'}{E \,\Delta_t^B\, (F, G, H) \xrightarrow{A * B} F}$ $(t \geq 1,\ \surd \in A)$

ScopeT : $\dfrac{E \xrightarrow{A} E'}{E \,\Delta_t^B\, (F, G, H) \xrightarrow{A} G}$ $(t = 1,\ \surd \notin A)$

ScopeI : $\dfrac{H \xrightarrow{A} H'}{E \,\Delta_t^B\, (F, G, H) \xrightarrow{A} H'}$ $(t \geq 1)$

Close : $\dfrac{E \xrightarrow{A} E'}{[E]_I \xrightarrow{A \cup (\mathcal{T}_I^0 - \mathcal{T}_{\rho(A)}^0)} [E']_I}$ $(\rho(A) \subseteq I)$

Recursion : $\dfrac{E[fix(X.E)/X] \xrightarrow{A} E'}{fix(X.E) \xrightarrow{A} E'}$

Con : $\dfrac{E \xrightarrow{A} E'}{X \xrightarrow{A} E'}$ $(X \stackrel{\text{def}}{=} E)$

Table 3: Unconstrained Transition System

Recursion rule, $fix(X.(A:X)) \xrightarrow{A} fix(X.(A:X))$.
Con. The Constant rule just mandates that if a name "X" is defined to represent the term "E", then X can make the same transitions that E can.

Preemption and the Prioritized Transition System. The prioritized transition system is based on the notion of *preemption*, which unifies CCSR's treatment of synchronization, resource-sharing, and priority. Let "$\prec$", called the *preemption order*, be a transitive, irreflexive, binary relation on actions. Then for two actions A and B, if $A \prec B$, we can say that "A is preempted by B". This means that in all real-time contexts, if a system can choose between executing either A or B, it will execute B.

Definition 3.2 *For all $A \in \mathcal{D}$, $B \in \mathcal{D}$, $A \preceq B$ if and only if*

$$\rho(A) = \rho(B) \wedge unres(A) = unres(B) \wedge res(A) \leq_p res(B)$$

The relation "$\preceq$" defines a preorder over $\mathcal{D}$, and we say $A \prec B$ if $A \preceq B$ and $B \not\preceq A$, i.e., $\rho(A) = \rho(B) \wedge unres(A) = unres(B) \wedge res(A) <_p res(B)$. □

Now we are ready to define the transition system $\langle \mathcal{E}, \rightarrow_\pi, \mathcal{D} \rangle$, grounded in our notion of preemption.

Definition 3.3 *The labeled transition system $\langle \mathcal{E}, \rightarrow_\pi, \mathcal{D} \rangle$ is a relation $\rightarrow_\pi \subseteq \mathcal{E} \times \mathcal{D} \times \mathcal{E}$ and is defined as follows: $(E, A, E') \in \rightarrow_\pi$ (or $E \xrightarrow{A}_\pi E'$) if:*

1. *$E \xrightarrow{A} E'$, and*

2. *For all $A' \in \mathcal{D}$, $E'' \in \mathcal{E}$ such that $E \xrightarrow{A'} E''$, $A \not\prec A'$.* □

Equivalence between processes is based on the concept of *strong bisimulation*, which is defined in the usual sense (see [13]). We denote "$\sim_\pi$" as the largest strong bisimulation over the transition system $\langle \mathcal{E}, \rightarrow_\pi, \mathcal{D} \rangle$, and we call it *prioritized strong equivalence.* The following two theorems state characterize some fundamental properties of CCSR. Theorem 3.1 states that "$\sim_\pi$" forms a congruence over the CCSR operators; that is, whenever two terms are equivalent, all CCSR "contexts" will preserve their equivalence. Theorem 3.2 states that fixpoints exist and are unique. For detailed proofs, refer to [4].

Theorem 3.1 *Prioritized strong equivalence is a congruence with respect to the CCSR operators. That is, for $E, F, G \in \mathcal{E}$, if $E \sim_\pi F$ and $free(G) = \{X\}$, then $G[E/X] \sim_\pi G[F/X]$.*

Theorem 3.2 *For any term E, $fix(X.E)$ is the unique solution to the recursive equation $X \sim_\pi E$.*

Choice(1)	$E + NIL = E$
Choice(2)	$E + E = E$
Choice(3)	$E + F = F + E$
Choice(4)	$(E + F) + G = E + (F + G)$
Choice(5)	$(A : E) + (B : F) = B : F \quad \text{if } A \prec B$
Par(1)	$E_I\|_J NIL = NIL$
Par(2)	$E_I\|_J F = F_J\|_I E$
Par(3)	$(E_I\|_J F)_{(I\cup J)}\|_K G = E_I\|_{(J\cup K)}(F_J\|_K G) \quad \text{if } I \cap J = \emptyset,\ J \cap K = \emptyset,\ I \cap K = \emptyset$
Par(4)	$E_I\|_J(F + G) = (E_I\|_J F) + (E_I\|_J G)$
Par(5)	$(A : X)_I\|_J(B : Y) = \begin{cases} (A * B) : (X_I\|_J Y) & \text{if } \rho(A) \subseteq I,\ \rho(A) \cap \rho(B) = \emptyset, \\ & \quad \rho(B) \subseteq J,\ sync_{(I\cup J)}(A * B) \\ NIL & \text{otherwise} \end{cases}$
Scope(1)	$NIL \,\Delta_t^B\, (F, G, H) = H$
Scope(2)	$(E_1 + E_2) \,\Delta_t^B\, (F, G, H) = (E_1 \,\Delta_t^B\, (F, G, H)) \ + \ (E_2 \,\Delta_t^B\, (F, G, H))$
Scope(3)	$(A : E) \,\Delta_t^B\, (F, G, H) = \begin{cases} (A * B : F) + H & \text{if } \surd \in A \\ (A : (E \,\Delta_{t-1}^B\, (F, G, H))) + H & \text{if } \surd \notin A \text{ and } t > 1 \\ (A : G) + H & \text{otherwise} \end{cases}$
Close(1)	$[NIL]_I = NIL$
Close(2)	$[E + F]_I = [E]_I + [F]_I$
Close(3)	$[A : E]_I = \begin{cases} (A \cup (\mathcal{T}_I^0 - \mathcal{T}_{\rho(A)}^0)) : [E]_I & \text{if } \rho(A) \subseteq I \\ NIL & \text{otherwise} \end{cases}$
Close(4)	$[[E]_I]_J = \begin{cases} [E]_J & \text{if } I \subseteq J \\ NIL & \text{otherwise} \end{cases}$

Table 4: The Axiom System, $\mathcal{A}$

3.3 An Axiomatization of CCSR

The axioms in the CCSR proof system, $\mathcal{A}$, are enumerated in Table 4. In [4] we show that $\mathcal{A}$, (augmented with standard laws for substitution), is sound with respect to prioritized equivalence; further, $\mathcal{A}$ is complete for finite fragments of CCSR. Using the Choice and Parallel laws in $\mathcal{A}$, we can derive an analogue to the Expansion Law from CCS.

Theorem 3.3 (Expansion Law) *Let K and L be finite index sets such that for all $k \in K$, $l \in L$, $A_k : E_k \in \mathcal{E}$ and $B_l : F_l \in \mathcal{E}$. Then*

$$\mathcal{A} \vdash (\sum_{k\in K} A_k : E_k)_I\|_J(\sum_{l\in L} B_l : F_l) \;=\; \sum_{\substack{k\in K,\ l\in L,\\ \rho(A)\subseteq I,\ \rho(A)\cap\rho(B)=\emptyset,\\ \rho(B)\subseteq J,\ sync_{(I\cup J)}(A*B)}} (A_k * B_l) : (E_{k\,I}\|_J F_l)$$

4 Translation of CSR Processes Into CCSR Terms

Using CSR to specify a real-time system is certainly more natural and intuitive affair than using the CCSR process algebra. However, CCSR provides a solid foundation to formally analyze the properties of real-time systems; e.g., it enjoys a well-behaved operational semantics, a rich equational structure and a congruence relation over terms. Our objective in this section is to assign formal meaning to CSR processes by translating them into CCSR terms.

In addition to the standard CCSR notation, we make prolific use of the following derived terms:

$$\begin{aligned} IDLE &\stackrel{\text{def}}{=} \emptyset : IDLE \\ TERM &\stackrel{\text{def}}{=} \{\surd\} : TERM \\ \delta_\infty(a) &\stackrel{\text{def}}{=} (\{a,\surd\} : TERM) \;+\; (\emptyset : \delta_\infty(a)) \\ E \rhd F &\stackrel{\text{def}}{=} E \,\Delta^{\bullet}_{\infty}\, (F, NIL, NIL) \end{aligned}$$

That is, the $IDLE$ process sleeps indefinitely, while $TERM$ is the process that indefinitely signals termination. For some event $a \in \Sigma$, the process "$\delta_\infty(a)$" is an "asynchronizer"; it may indefinitely idle before executing a (the exact time of execution depends on the system's characteristics, such as the priority of a, it's synchronization requirements, etc.). The term $E \rhd F$ (pronounced "E pipe F") executes E until it signals termination, at which time control passes to F. Using the ScopeC and ScopeE rules from Table 3, we can derive the two transition rules for "$\rhd$":

$$\frac{E \xrightarrow{A} E'}{E \rhd F \xrightarrow{A} E' \rhd F}\ (\surd \notin A) \qquad\qquad \frac{E \xrightarrow{A} E'}{E \rhd F \xrightarrow{A-\{\surd\}} F}\ (\surd \in A)$$

4.1 The Translation Approach

Within this section we let S and T range over CSR statements, we let *at* range over atoms, and *act* range over atomic actions (e.g., **send**(*at*) is an atomic action). Now consider the following generic process definition, where *pid* is the process name, ⟨decls⟩ is the declaration section and S is the process body:

process *pid*
⟨decls⟩
S

Throughout we assume that the atoms in the process are consistent, in that no single atom is used for multiple functions (e.g., for both **send** and **exec** atomic actions). That being the case, the function "Tevent" accepts a CSR atomic action and produces an uninterpreted CCSR event:

$$\begin{aligned}\text{Tevent}(\mathbf{send}(at)) &= pid.at\\ \text{Tevent}(\mathbf{recv}(at)) &= pid.at\\ \text{Tevent}(\mathbf{exec}(at)) &= pid.at\end{aligned}$$

Thus all atomic actions are generically mapped to an event that identifies both the process *pid* and the atom name, *at*. Next we define translation function, Tstat, which accepts CSR *statements* within the process *pid*, and produces a CCSR term as its result.

Atomic Statements. Since all atomic statments have the capacity to idle until being scheduled, the "δ_∞" suits our purposes here.

$$\begin{aligned}\text{Tstat}(\mathbf{send}(at)) &= \delta_\infty(\text{Tevent}(\mathbf{send}(at)))\\ \text{Tstat}(\mathbf{recv}(at)) &= \delta_\infty(\text{Tevent}(\mathbf{recv}(at)))\\ \text{Tstat}(\mathbf{exec}(at)) &= \delta_\infty(\text{Tevent}(\mathbf{exec}(at)))\end{aligned}$$

In other words, the translated process may idle before both executing *pid.at* and signaling termination. This is easily illustrated by the transition rules, which yield:

$$\begin{aligned}&\text{Tstat}(\mathbf{recv}(at)) \xrightarrow{\emptyset} \text{Tstat}(\mathbf{recv}(at))\\ &\text{Tstat}(\mathbf{recv}(at)) \xrightarrow{\{pid.at,\surd\}} TERM\end{aligned}$$

Skip and Wait. The CSR statement **wait** t "vamps" for its first $t-1$ time units, and then goes into a terminating state at its tth time unit (**wait** t is defined only for $t \geq 1$).

$$\text{Tstat}(\mathbf{wait}\ t) = \begin{cases} TERM & \text{if } t = 1\\ IDLE\ \Delta^{\bullet}_{t-1}\ (NIL, TERM, NIL) & \text{otherwise}\end{cases}$$

Recall that **skip** is simply syntactic sugar for **wait** 1.

Ndet. The CSR statement **ndet**(act, m, n) nondeterministically executes the atomic action *act* between m and n times, where $1 \leq m \leq n$. Exactly *when* each iteration will execute is, of course, sensitive to the characteristics of the fully configured system. For now we have to retain *all* possible times of execution, which is exactly the purpose of the "δ_∞" operator.

$$\text{Tstat}(\textbf{ndet}(act, m, n)) =$$

$$\begin{cases} \text{Tstat}(act) & \text{if } n = m = 1 \\ \text{Tstat}(act) + (\text{Tstat}(act) \rhd \text{Tstat}(\textbf{ndet}(act, 1, n-1))) & \text{if } m = 1 \text{ and } n \neq 1 \\ \text{Tstat}(act) \rhd \text{Tstat}(\textbf{ndet}(act, m-1, n-1)) & \text{otherwise} \end{cases}$$

Sequential Composition. Our pipe operator was tailor-made to implement CSR's sequential composition. The term Tstat$(S;T)$ executes Tstat(S) until it signals termination; at the very next time unit, Tstat(T) is executed.

$$\text{Tstat}(S;T) = \text{Tstat}(S) \rhd \text{Tstat}(T)$$

Scope. In translating the **scope** statement, we require the use of an auxiliary translation function, Tint, for and any interrupts specified within the scope.

$$\text{Tint}(\textbf{interrupt } act_1 \rightarrow S_1 \ldots \textbf{interrupt } act_n \rightarrow S_n) = \sum_{i=1}^{n} \{\text{Tevent}(act_i)\} : \text{Tstat}(S_i)$$

There are four alternatives for **scope**, corresponding to each of the possible varieties of triggers that bound the scope: (1) no triggers, (2) a timeout trigger, (3) interrupt triggers and (4) both timeout and interrupt triggers.

$$\text{Tstat}(\textbf{scope do } S \textbf{ od}) = \text{Tstat}(S)$$

$$\text{Tstat}(\textbf{scope do } S \textbf{ timeout } t \rightarrow T \textbf{ od}) = \text{Tstat}(S) \,\Delta_t^{\{\surd\}}\, (TERM, \text{Tstat}(T), NIL)$$

$$\text{Tstat}(\textbf{scope do } S \textit{ interrupts } \textbf{od}) = \text{Tstat}(S) \,\Delta_\infty^{\{\surd\}}\, (TERM, NIL, \text{Tint}(interrupts))$$

$$\text{Tstat}(\textbf{scope do } S \textit{ interrupts } \textbf{timeout } t \rightarrow T \textbf{ od}) = \text{Tstat}(S) \,\Delta_t^{\{\surd\}}\, (TERM, \text{Tstat}(T), \text{Tint}(interrupts))$$

Infinite Behaviors – Loop and Every. The CSR **loop** construct endlessly executes its loop body; thus we can use our pipe combinator in conjunction with fixpoint:

$$\text{Tstat}(\textbf{loop do } S \textbf{ od}) = fix(X.\ (\text{Tstat}(S) \rhd X))$$

Recall that the statement **every** t **do** S **od** has a guaranteed period of t time units (where we require that $t \geq 1$). Again the CCSR scope operator is quite helpful in helping us realize the semantics for **every**. First, in creating a scope body of Tstat$(S) \rhd IDLE$, we produce a term that executes Tstat(S), and subsequently idles indefinitely. Thus the body performs all of the work of S, but never signals termination. This allows us to use the timeout argument of the scope operator to repeat the period, as in the following translation:

$$\text{Tstat}(\textbf{every } t \textbf{ do } S \textbf{ od}) = fix(X.\ ((\text{Tstat}(S) \rhd IDLE) \,\Delta_t^{\bullet}\, (NIL, X, NIL)))$$

Interleave. In presenting the formulation for the **interleave** we assume our process is configured on some resource *R.pid*. That is, let *events*(S) be the set of events appearing in the term Tstat(S). Then to translate **interleave do** S & T **od**, we postulate that $\rho(events(\text{Tstat}(S)) \cup events(\text{Tstat}(T))) \subseteq \{R.pid\}$. Thus, the translation of the **interleave** statement is:

$$\text{Tstat}(\textbf{interleave do } S \ \& \ T \textbf{ od}) = \text{Tstat}(S) \ {}_{\{R.pid\}}\|_{\{R.pid\}} \ \text{Tstat}(T)$$

¿From the definition of *sync*, we have that for any event a such that $\rho(\{a\}) = \{R.pid\}$, $sync_{(\{R.pid\})}(\{a\})$ holds, as does $sync_{(\{R.pid\})}(\{a, \surd\})$. And since S and T execute on the same resource, we can derive the following rule for **interleave**:

$$\frac{\text{Tstat}(S) \xrightarrow{A_1} P_1,\ \text{Tstat}(T) \xrightarrow{A_2} P_2}{\text{Tstat}(\textbf{interleave do } S \ \& \ T \textbf{ od}) \xrightarrow{A_1 * A_2} P_1 \, {}_{\{R.pid\}}\|_{\{R.pid\}} \, P_2} \quad (|A_1 * A_2| \leq 1)$$

4.2 Translating the Configuration Schema

The configuration schema is used for two purposes – to determine the characteristics of the action domain, and to fix the final structure of the CCSR system. Each invocation of the **resource** declaration builds up the resource domain, $\mathcal{R}$. The **process** declaration determines the event alphabet, Σ, as well as the priority function π. The **assign** declaration generates the concurrent structure of the final CCSR term, and also determines the resource mapping, ρ. When **connect** is used – as in "**connect** P.a,P.b" – it states that "P.a •—• P.b".

4.3 CCSR Translation of Sensor-Monitor Process Specification

We revisit the sensor-monitor example, and apply our Tstat translation function to the processes in Figure 1 and the configuration in Figure 3. The result is displayed in Table 5; for readability, we have taken the liberty to rewrite fixpoint expressions using equivalent Constant definitions. With the action domain's construction from Table 6, as well as the system's syntax, we may now perform analysis using CCSR's transition system and its proof rules. Indeed, this is precisely what we shall do in Section 5.

5 Using the CCSR Proof Rules

In this section we present a sketch of a correctness proof of the Sensor-Monitor System, as portrayed in Tables 6 and 5. Recall that our safety constraint is as follows: neither Sensor process ever reaches a state in which its *error* event is enabled. We demonstrate this by showing that there is some $System'$ such that $System \sim_\pi System'$, and further,

$$System \stackrel{def}{=} (R\_Device1 \ {}_{\{Device1\}}\|_{\{Device2\}} \ R\_Device2) \ {}_{\{Device1,Device2\}}\|_{\{Host\}} \ R\_Host$$

$$R\_Device1 \stackrel{def}{=} [S1.S]_{\{Device1\}}$$

$$R\_Device2 \stackrel{def}{=} [S2.S]_{\{Device2\}}$$

$$R\_Host \stackrel{def}{=} [M1.M \ {}_{\{Host\}}\|_{\{Host\}} \ M2.M]_{\{Host\}}$$

$$\begin{aligned} S1.S \stackrel{def}{=} & (\delta_\infty(S1.S.sense) \triangleright \\ & \quad (IDLE \, \Delta_2^\bullet \, (NIL, \delta_\infty(S1.S.error), \{S1.S.ch\} : TERM)) \triangleright \\ & IDLE) \, \Delta_6^\bullet \, (NIL, S1.S, NIL) \end{aligned}$$

$$\begin{aligned} S2.S \stackrel{def}{=} & (\delta_\infty(S2.S.sense) \triangleright \\ & \quad (IDLE \, \Delta_4^\bullet \, (NIL, \delta_\infty(S2.S.error), \{S2.S.ch\} : TERM)) \triangleright \\ & IDLE) \, \Delta_6^\bullet \, (NIL, S2.S, NIL) \end{aligned}$$

$$M1.M \stackrel{def}{=} \delta_\infty(M1.M.ch) \triangleright (\delta_\infty(M1.M.compute) \triangleright (\delta_\infty(M1.M.compute) \triangleright M1.M))$$

$$M2.M \stackrel{def}{=} \delta_\infty(M2.M.ch) \triangleright (\delta_\infty(M2.M.compute) \triangleright (\delta_\infty(M2.M.compute) \triangleright M2.M))$$

Table 5: CCSR Sensor-Monitor Process Specification

that neither $S1.S.error$ nor $S2.S.error$ appears in the syntax of $System'$. Specifically,

$$\begin{aligned} System' & \stackrel{def}{=} [\{S1.S.sense, S2.S.sense\} : T]_{\{Device1,Device2,Host\}} \\ T & \stackrel{def}{=} \{S1.S.ch, M1.M.ch\} : \{M1.M.compute\} : \{M1.M.compute\} : \\ & \quad \{S2.S.ch, M2.M.ch\} : \{M2.M.compute\} : \\ & \quad \{S1.S.sense, S2.S.sense, M2.M.compute\} : T \end{aligned}$$

To simplify the proof, we make use of the definitions in Table 7. We refer quite frequently to these terms, and defining them here alleviates the need to repetitively copy them.

Recall that the "$\triangleright$" operator is derived directly from Scope, so there is no formal need to provide separate rewrite rules for it. However, here we present some pertinent equations as a lemma; once we have done so, we no longer have to appeal to its definition in Section 4.

Lemma 5.1 For any CCSR terms $E, F, G \in \mathcal{E}$,

$$\begin{aligned} &\text{Pipe(1)} \quad NIL \triangleright E = NIL \\ &\text{Pipe(2)} \quad (E + F) \triangleright G = (E \triangleright G) + (F \triangleright G) \\ &\text{Pipe(3)} \quad (A : E) \triangleright F = \begin{cases} (A * \emptyset) : F & \text{if } \surd \in A \\ A : (E \triangleright F) & \text{otherwise} \end{cases} \end{aligned}$$

- **Resources:** $Device1$, $Device2$, $Host \in \mathcal{R}$
- **Resource Mapping:**

$$\rho(\{S1.S.sense, S1.S.error, S1.S.ch\}) = \{Device1\}$$
$$\rho(\{S2.S.sense, S2.S.error, S2.S.ch\}) = \{Device2\}$$
$$\rho(\{M1.M.compute, M1.M, ch, M2.M.compute, M2.M.ch\}) = \{Host\}$$

- **Connection Sets:**

$\{S1.S.ch, M1.M.ch\}$, $\{S2.S.ch, M2.M.ch\}$, $\{S1.S.sense\}$, $\{S2.S.sense\}$, $\{S1.S.error\}$, $\{S2.S.error\}$, $\{M1.M.compute\}$, $\{M2.M.compute\}$

- **Priorities:**

$Device1: \ \pi(S1.S.sense) = 1, \ \pi(S1.S.error) = 1, \ \pi(S1.S.ch) = 0$

$Device2: \ \pi(S2.S.sense) = 1, \ \pi(S2.S.error) = 1, \ \pi(S2.S.ch) = 0$

$Host: \ \pi(M1.M.compute) = 3, \pi(M1.M.ch) = 2, \pi(M2.M.compute) = 3, \pi(M2.M.ch) = 1$

Table 6: Resources, Resource Mapping, Connections and Priorities

$$\begin{aligned}
S1.S' &\stackrel{\text{def}}{=} (IDLE \, \Delta^{\bullet}_{2} \, (NIL, \delta_{\infty}(S1.S.error), \{S1.S.ch\} : TERM) \rhd \\
&\qquad IDLE) \, \Delta^{\bullet}_{5} \, (NIL, S1.S, NIL) \\
S1.S'' &\stackrel{\text{def}}{=} (\delta_{\infty}(S1.S.sense) \rhd \\
&\qquad\quad (IDLE \, \Delta^{\bullet}_{2} \, (NIL, \delta_{\infty}(S1.S.error), \{S1.S.ch\} : TERM)) \rhd \\
&\qquad IDLE) \, \Delta^{\bullet}_{5} \, (NIL, S1.S, NIL) \\
S2.S' &\stackrel{\text{def}}{=} (IDLE \, \Delta^{\bullet}_{4} \, (NIL, \delta_{\infty}(S2.S.error), \{S2.S.ch\} : TERM) \rhd \\
&\qquad IDLE) \, \Delta^{\bullet}_{5} \, (NIL, S2.S, NIL) \\
M1.M' &\stackrel{\text{def}}{=} \delta_{\infty}(M1.M.compute) \rhd (\delta_{\infty}(M1.M.compute) \rhd M1.M) \\
M2.M' &\stackrel{\text{def}}{=} \delta_{\infty}(M2.M.compute) \rhd (\delta_{\infty}(M2.M.compute) \rhd M2.M) \\
Sys' &\stackrel{\text{def}}{=} ([S1.S']_{\{Device1\}} \ {}_{\{Device1\}}\|_{\{Device2\}} \ [S2.S']_{\{Device2\}}) \ {}_{\{Device1, Device2\}}\|_{\{Host\}} \ R_Host
\end{aligned}$$

Table 7: Proof Definitions

Proof: Pipe(1) follows directly from the definition of "$\triangleright$", Scope(1). Pipe(2) is just a restatement of Scope(2), while Pipe(3) follows from Scope(3). □

Proof Sketch. By using the definition of "δ_∞," the laws in $\mathcal{A}$ and Lemma 5.1, we can obtain that:

$$(1)\ S1.S = (\{S1.S.sense\} : S1.S') + (\emptyset : S1.S'')$$

Now invoking Close(2) and two applications of Close(3), we arrive at:

$$(2)\quad R\_Device1 \;=\; \{S1.S.sense\} : [S1.S']_{\{Device1\}} + \{\tau^0_{Device1}\} : [S1.S'']_{\{Device1\}}$$

We now have the first opportunity to exploit Choice(5); that is, to prune the proof tree. Note that $\{\tau^0_{Device1}\} \prec \{S1.S.sense\}$, and thus,

$$(3)\quad R\_Device1 \;=\; \{S1.S.sense\} : [S1.S']_{\{Device1\}}$$

Similarly,

$$(4)\quad R\_Device2 \;=\; \{S2.S.sense\} : [S2.S']_{\{Device2\}}$$

Now we turn our attention to the *R_Host* resource. We can use the definition of "δ_∞", Pipe(2), Pipe(3) and finally Theorem 3.3 to derive that:

$$\begin{aligned}(5)\quad & M1.M\,{}_{\{Host\}}\|_{\{Host\}}\,M2.M \\ &= \{M1.M.ch\} : (M1.M'\,{}_{\{Host\}}\|_{\{Host\}}\,M2.M) \\ &+ \{M2.M.ch\} : (M1.M\,{}_{\{Host\}}\|_{\{Host\}}\,M2.M') \\ &+ \emptyset : (M1.M\,{}_{\{Host\}}\|_{\{Host\}}\,M2.M)\end{aligned}$$

Next we apply Close(2) and Close(3) to derive a transformation of *R_Host*. Note that no priority elimination may take place here, since the actions $\{M1.M.ch\}$, $\{M2.M.ch\}$ and $\{\tau^0_{Host}\}$ are mutually uncomparable under "$\prec$."

$$\begin{aligned}(6)\quad R\_Host \;=\;& \{M1.M.ch\} : [M1.M'\,{}_{\{Host\}}\|_{\{Host\}}\,M2.M]_{\{Host\}} \\ +\;& \{M2.M.ch\} : [M1.M\,{}_{\{Host\}}\|_{\{Host\}}\,M2.M']_{\{Host\}} \\ +\;& \{\tau^0_{Host}\} : R\_Host\end{aligned}$$

We may now exploit Theorem 3.3 to arrive the following rewrite for the *System* term.

$$(7)\quad System \;=\; \{S1.S.sense, S2.S.sense, \tau^0_{Host}\} : Sys'$$

Using the Scope, Pipe, Choice and Close laws we have that

$$\begin{aligned}(8)\quad & [S1.S']_{\{Device1\}} \\ &= \{S1.S.ch\} : [IDLE\,\Delta^{\bullet}_4\,(NIL, S1.S, NIL)]_{\{Device1\}} \\ &+ \{\tau^0_{Device1}\} : [((IDLE\,\Delta^{\bullet}_1\,(NIL, \delta_\infty(S1.S.error), \{S1.S.ch\} : TERM)) \\ &\qquad \triangleright IDLE)\,\Delta^{\bullet}_4\,(NIL, S1.S, NIL)]_{\{Device1\}}\end{aligned}$$

And similarly,

$$
\begin{aligned}
(9)\quad & [S2.S']_{\{Device2\}} \\
= \; & \{S2.S.ch\} : [IDLE \,\Delta_4^{\bullet}\, (NIL, S2.S, NIL)]_{\{Device2\}} \\
+ \; & \{\tau^0_{Device2}\} : [((IDLE \,\Delta_3^{\bullet}\, (NIL, \delta_\infty(S2.S.error), \{S2.S.ch\} : TERM)) \\
& \qquad \rhd IDLE) \,\Delta_4^{\bullet}\, (NIL, S2.S, NIL)]_{\{Device2\}}
\end{aligned}
$$

Now we invoke Theorem 3.3 to derive a transformation for Sys', using our results so far.

$$
\begin{aligned}
(10)\quad Sys' = \; & \{S1.S.ch, \tau^0_{Device2}, M1.M.ch\} : \\
& (([IDLE \,\Delta_4^{\bullet}\, (NIL, S1.S, NIL)]_{\{Device1\}} \;{}_{\{Device1\}}\|_{\{Device2\}} \\
& [((IDLE \,\Delta_3^{\bullet}\, (NIL, \delta_\infty(S2.S.error), \{S2.S.ch\} : TERM)) \\
& \quad \rhd IDLE) \,\Delta_4^{\bullet}\, (NIL, S2.S, NIL)]_{\{Device2\}}) \;{}_{\{Device1,Device2\}}\|_{\{Host\}} \\
& [M1.M' \;{}_{\{Host\}}\|_{\{Host\}}\, M2.M]_{\{Host\}}) \\
+ \; & \{\tau^0_{Device1}, S2.S.ch, M2.M.ch\} : \\
& (([((IDLE \,\Delta_1^{\bullet}\, (NIL, \delta_\infty(S1.S.error), \{S1.S.ch\} : TERM)) \\
& \quad \rhd IDLE) \,\Delta_4^{\bullet}\, (NIL, S1.S, NIL)]_{\{Device1\}}) \;{}_{\{Device1\}}\|_{\{Device2\}} \\
& [IDLE \,\Delta_4^{\bullet}\, (NIL, S2.S, NIL)]_{\{Device2\}} \;{}_{\{Device1,Device2\}}\|_{\{Host\}} \\
& [M1.M \;{}_{\{Host\}}\|_{\{Host\}}\, M2.M']_{\{Host\}}) \\
+ \; & \{\tau^0_{Device1}, \tau^0_{Device2}, \tau^0_{Host}\} : \\
& (([((IDLE \,\Delta_1^{\bullet}\, (NIL, \delta_\infty(S1.S.error), \{S1.S.ch\} : TERM)) \\
& \quad \rhd IDLE) \,\Delta_4^{\bullet}\, (NIL, S1.S, NIL)]_{\{Device1\}}) \;{}_{\{Device1\}}\|_{\{Device2\}} \\
& [((IDLE \,\Delta_3^{\bullet}\, (NIL, \delta_\infty(S2.S.error), \{S2.S.ch\} : TERM)) \\
& \quad \rhd IDLE) \,\Delta_4^{\bullet}\, (NIL, S2.S, NIL)]_{\{Device2\}}) \;{}_{\{Device1,Device2\}}\|_{\{Host\}} \\
& Host
\end{aligned}
$$

But we can reduce the term's complexity by using Choice(5), i.e., preemption.

$$
\begin{aligned}
(11)\quad Sys' = \; & \{S1.S.ch, \tau^0_{Device2}, M1.M.ch\} : \\
& (([IDLE \,\Delta_4^{\bullet}\, (NIL, S1.S, NIL)]_{\{Device1\}} \;{}_{\{Device1\}}\|_{\{Device2\}} \\
& [((IDLE \,\Delta_3^{\bullet}\, (NIL, \delta_\infty(S2.S.error), \{S2.S.ch\} : TERM)) \\
& \quad \rhd IDLE) \,\Delta_4^{\bullet}\, (NIL, S2.S, NIL)]_{\{Device2\}}) \;{}_{\{Device1,Device2\}}\|_{\{Host\}} \\
& [M1.M' \;{}_{\{Host\}}\|_{\{Host\}}\, M2.M]_{\{Host\}})
\end{aligned}
$$

There is a leap to the next step, in which the term Sys' is "flattened out." However, the procedure is similar to the previous one in the previous steps, and we omit the details for the sake of brevity.

$$
\begin{aligned}
(12)\quad Sys' = \; & \{S1.S.ch, \tau^0_{Device2}, M1.M.ch\} : \{\tau^0_{Device1}, \tau^0_{Device2}, M1.M.compute\} : \\
& \{\tau^0_{Device1}, \tau^0_{Device2}, M1.M.compute\} : \{\tau^0_{Device1}, S2.S.ch, M2.M.ch\} : \\
& \{\tau^0_{Device1}, \tau^0_{Device2}, M2.M.compute\} : \\
& \{S1.S.sense, S2.S.sense, M2.M.compute\} : Sys'
\end{aligned}
$$

Now, by Close(3) we have that

$$(13)\quad System' \;=\; \{S1.S.sense, S2.S.sense, \tau^0_{Host}\} : [T]_{\{Device1,Device2,Host\}}$$

and thus it remains to be shown that $Sys' \sim_\pi [T]_{\{Device1,Device2,Host\}}$. But by six applications of Close(3), it follows that

$$\begin{aligned}(14)\quad & [T]_{\{Device1,Device2,Host\}} \\ &= \{S1.S.ch, \tau^0_{Device2}, M1.M.ch\} : \{\tau^0_{Device1}, \tau^0_{Device2}, M1.M.compute\} : \\ &\quad \{\tau^0_{Device1}, \tau^0_{Device2}, M1.M.compute\} : \{\tau^0_{Device1}, S2.S.ch, M2.M.ch\} : \\ &\quad \{\tau^0_{Device1}, \tau^0_{Device2}, M2.M.compute\} : \\ &\quad \{S1.S.sense, S2.S.sense, M2.M.compute\} : [T]_{\{Device1,Device2,Host\}}\end{aligned}$$

Now since fixpoints are unique, it follows that $Sys' \sim_\pi [T]_{\{Device1,Device2,Host\}}$, as they solve the same recursive equation. □

The importance of preemption elimination (law Choice(5)) cannot be underestimated here. A simple way to illustrate this is to set $\pi(S1.S.ch)$ to 1, and thus to give $S2.S.ch$ the same priority as that of $S1.S.ch$. In this case, the initial choice between the actions $\{S1.S.ch, \tau^0_{Device2}, M1.M.ch\}$ and $\{\tau^0_{Device1}, S2.S.ch, M2.M.ch\}$ becomes nondeterministic. And if the branch corresponding to $\{\tau^0_{Device1}, S2.S.ch, M2.M.ch\}$ is taken, $M2.M.compute$ will execute for 2 time units, during which time the execution of $M1.M.ch$ will be blocked. But since the deadline for $S1.S.ch$ will have expired, $S1.S.error$ would have been executed. In fact, we can prove that in this case, $System \sim_\pi System''$, where

$$\begin{aligned} System'' &\stackrel{\text{def}}{=} [\{S1.S.sense, S2.S.sense\} : T']_{\{Device1,Device2,Host\}} \\ T' &\stackrel{\text{def}}{=} (\{S1.S.ch, M1.M.ch\} : \{M1.M.compute\} : \{M1.M.compute\} : \\ &\qquad \{S2.S.ch, M2.M.ch\} : \{M2.M.compute\} : \\ &\qquad \{S1.S.sense, S2.S.sense, M2.M.compute\} : T') \\ &\quad + (\{S1.S.ch, M1.M.ch\} : \{M2.M.compute\} : \{M2.M.compute, S1.S.error\} : \\ &\qquad \emptyset : \emptyset : \{S1.S.sense, S2.S.sense, M2.M.compute\} : T')\end{aligned}$$

That is, $S1.S$ may starve completely, and record an error during each period.

6 Conclusion

We have described a two-tiered approach to the specification and verification of real-time systems. The CSR Specification Language is used to design the functionality of a real-time program, and an accompanying configuration schema is then used to specify its structure. To analyze the resulting system, we automatically translate it into a term in the CCSR process algebra.

As we have shown, the CCSR semantics heavily rely on our notions of resource allocation, synchronization and priority. By considering the very subtle interplay between these factors, we have defined a notion of preemption that leads to a congruence relation over the terms. In turn, this result yields a fully substitutive proof system, facilitating the algebraic verification of our original real-time system.

The CSR Specification Language has continually matured since we introduced it in [5], and its expressivity has correspondingly increased. In previous versions, for example, the **scope** construct was allowed only one trigger, which could be either a timeout *or* an interrupt. It is true that scopes could be nested, but nesting alone does not provide for the same expressivity as multiple triggers. Consider, for example, the following fragments $T1$ and $T2$:

$T1$ = **scope do** S **interrupt recv**(ch1) → S1 **timeout** 50 → S2 **od**	$T2$ = **scope do** **scope do** S **interrupt recv**(ch1) → S1 **od** **timeout** 50 → S2 **od**

Certainly $T1$ and $T2$ do not have the same meaning. In $T1$, if **recv**(ch1) is executed, then the timeout is disabled; in $T2$ the timeout remains active even while the exception-handler S1 is being executed. Since many real-time systems have multiple interrupts, it seems that the new **scope** statement is a vast improvement.

Another improvement over the older versions of CSR is the decoupling of the language and configuration issues. In those earlier versions, we did not provide a separate configuration language; instead, we used two parallel operators: "&" denoted interleaving concurrency, while true parallelism was represented by the "||" symbol. Also, connections were declared using global naming conventions; specifically, a unique event "$ch1?$" was forced to synchronize with its counterpart event "$ch1!$". We found these approaches clumsy for several reasons. First, the events "$ch1?$" and "$ch1!$" had unique, system-wide names, which prevented other processes from using different "instances" of them. Second, it enforced one-to-one communication, which precluded broadcasting and other, more sophisticated schemes. But of most importance, by distinguishing at the functional level between the two types of parallelism, we found it difficult to minutely alter the specification without rewriting it completely. For example, suppose we were to determine whether the sensor-monitor system required a dedicated resource for each monitor module. This could quite easily be accomplished within a new configuration schema, while the same functional specification could be used.

Our long-term goal is to develop techniques and tools that can be used to build a real-time system with predictably correct behavior. As a step toward meeting our goal, we have implemented a translator from the CSR specification language to the CCSR process algebra. We are currently investigating the implementation of the CCSR proof system, as well as extending the CSR specification language to support variables and probabilistic timing behavior.

References

[1] R. Alur, C. Courcoubetis, and D. Dill. Model-Checking for Real-Time Systems. In *Proc. of IEEE Symposium on Logic in Computer Science*, 1990.

[2] R. Cleaveland and M. Hennessy. Priorities in Process Algebras. *Information and Computation*, 87:58–77, 1990.

[3] M.K. Franklin and A. Gabrielian. A Transformational Method for Verifying Safety Properties in Real-Time Systems. In *Proc. IEEE Real-Time Systems Symposium*, pages 112–123, December 1989.

[4] R. Gerber. *Communicating Shared Resrouces: A Model for Distributed Real-Time Systems.* PhD thesis, Department of Computer and Information Science, University of Pennsylvania, 1991.

[5] R. Gerber and I. Lee. Communicating Shared Resources: A Model for Distributed Real-Time Systems. In *Proc. 10th IEEE Real-Time Systems Symposium*, 1989.

[6] R. Harper. Introduction to standard ML. Technical Report ECS-LFCS-86-14, Department of Computer Science, University of Edinburgh, The King's Buildings—Edinburgh EH9 3JZ—Scotland, 1986.

[7] J. Hooman. *Specification and Compositional Verification of Real-Time Systems.* PhD thesis, Eindhoven University of Technology, 1991.

[8] C. Huizing, R. Gerth, and W.P. de Roever. Full Abstraction of a Denotational Semantics for Real-time Concurrency. In *Proc.* 14th *ACM Symposium on Principles of Programming Languages*, pages 223–237, 1987.

[9] M. Joseph and A. Goswami. What's 'Real' about Real-time Systems? In *IEEE Real-Time Systems Symposium*, 1988.

[10] J.E. Coolahan Jr. and N. Roussopoulos. Timing Requirements for Time-Driven Systems Using Augmented Petri Nets. *IEEE Trans. Software Eng.*, SE-9(5):603–616, September 1983.

[11] I. Lee and V. Gehlot. Language Constructs for Distributed Real-Time Programming. In *Proc. IEEE Real-Time Systems Symposium*, 1985.

[12] N. Lynch and M. Tuttle. An Introduction to Input/Output Automata. Technical Report MIT/LCS/TM-373, Laboratory for Computer Science, Massachusetts Institute of Technology, 1988.

[13] R. Milner. *Communication and Concurrency.* Prentice-Hall, 1989.

[14] J.S. Ostroff and W.M. Wonham. Modelling, Specifying and Verifying Real-time Embedded Computer Systems. In *Proc. IEEE Real-Time Systems Symposium*, pages 124–132, December 1987.

[15] G.M. Reed and A.W. Roscoe. Metric Spaces as Models for Real-Time Concurrency. In *Proceedings of Math. Found. of Computer Science, LNCS 298*, 1987.

[16] A.C. Shaw. Reasoning About Time in Higher-Level Language Software. *IEEE Transactions on Software Engineering*, 15(7):875–889, 1989.

[17] W. Yi. Ccs + time = an interleaving model for real time systems. In *ICALP*, 1991.

Forward and Backward Simulations for Timing-Based Systems*

Nancy Lynch and Frits Vaandrager
MIT Laboratory for Computer Science
Cambridge, MA 02139, USA

Abstract. A general automaton model for timing-based systems is presented and is used as the context for developing a variety of simulation proof techniques for such systems. As a first step, a comprehensive overview of simulation techniques for simple untimed automata is given. In particular, soundness and completeness results for (1) refinements, (2) forward and backward simulations, (3) forward-backward and backward-forward simulations, and (4) history and prophecy relations are given. History and prophecy relations are new and are abstractions of the history variables of Owicki and Gries and the prophecy variables of Abadi and Lamport, respectively. As a subsequent step, it is shown how most of the results for untimed automata can be carried over to the setting of timed automata. In fact, many of the results for the timed case are obtained as consequences of the analogous results for the untimed case.

Keywords: Simulations, timing-based systems, real-time, timed automata, refinement mappings, forward simulations, backward simulations, forward-backward simulations, backward-forward simulations, history variables, prophecy variables, history relations, prophecy relations.

Contents

---

*This work was supported by ONR contracts N00014-85-K-0168 and N00014-91-J-1988, by NSF grant CCR-8915206, and by DARPA contract N00014-89-J-1988.

1 Introduction

We are currently involved in a project to define a very general formal model for real-time and other timing-based systems. We intend that the model should provide a suitable basis for formal reasoning about timing-based systems, in particular, for verification of their correctness and for analysis of their complexity. It should support many different kinds of correctness proof techniques, including process algebraic and assertional methods. So far, process algebraic and assertional methods have been used primarily to prove properties of untimed (asynchronous) systems; we would also like to use them for timing-based systems. Also, the kinds of properties generally proved using these methods have been "ordinary" safety properties; we would like to use similar methods to also prove timing properties (e.g., upper and lower bounds on time).

In this paper, we describe a candidate for such a model, and use it to express some powerful simulation techniques for proving correctness of timing-based systems. The style of the model we define is *automata-theoretic*, which is the natural style for expressing assertional methods. However, we expect that the model can also serve as a semantic model for interesting algebraic languages, and thus that process algebraic methods can also be employed in the same framework. We define several kinds of simulations including *refinements*, *forward simulations*, *backward simulations*, and hybrid versions that we call *forward-backward* and *backward-forward simulations*. We prove basic results for these kinds of simulations, in particular, soundness and completeness theorems. We also define *history relations* and *prophecy relations*, which are abstract versions of the history and prophecy variables of Abadi and Lamport [1]. We prove theorems describing the properties of these various kinds of simulations and relating the different kinds of simulations to each other.

The goal of extending simulation techniques to timing-based systems is also the motivation for the work of Lynch and Attiya in [19]. That work, however, only explores forward simulations. Also, the model used in [19] has considerably more structure than the very general model proposed here; it is based closely on the *timed automaton* model of Merritt, Modugno and Tuttle [22], which assumes that the system being modeled is describable in terms of a collection of separate tasks, each with associated upper and lower bounds on its speed. This extra structure supports the development of some useful progress measure proof methods, which we do not develop here. On the other hand, the basic theorems about forward simulations that appear in [19] are stated in a setting that has more structure than is really necessary for those theorems. In this paper, we make only those assumptions that are needed for the basic results about simulation proof techniques.

We propose a notion of *timed automaton*, which is just an automaton (or labeled transition system) equipped with some additional structure. Specifically, each state of the automaton has an associated *time*, which indicates the current time. (Thus we use *absolute* time in the sense of [2].) The actions of the automaton are of three kinds: *visible actions*, *time-passage actions*, and a special *internal action* τ. As in many other formalisms for real-time, see for instance [2, 3, 7, 22, 24, 25, 32], all actions except for the time-passage actions are modeled as occurring instantaneously, i.e., they do not change the time component of the state.

To specify times, we use a *dense* time domain, specifically, the nonnegative reals (starting with time 0 in the initial state), and we impose no lower bound on the time between events. This choice distinguishes our work from many others', e.g., [4, 7, 24, 25, 29, 33], in which discrete time values or universal positive lower bounds on step time are used. Use of real-valued time is less restrictive, and we believe that the extra flexibility will be useful in the design and analysis of timing-based distributed algorithms. The penalty we pay for this flexibility is that our automata may admit some "Zeno executions", i.e., infinite executions in which the time component is bounded.

Timed automata are required to satisfy a small set of basic axioms which express natural properties of time. For instance, there is an axiom saying that time-passage actions may not decrease time, and another saying that all the other actions are instantaneous.

Also, time can advance by a particular amount in one time-passage step if and only if it can also advance by the same amount in two steps. (This property is called *continuity* in [32] and, more appropriately, *time additivity* in [26].) We attempt to use as few axioms as possible to obtain the results about simulations. Later, as we try to express different proof methods in terms of this model, we expect to have to add additional requirements to obtain the desired properties. A typical axiom we may have to add at some point is the axiom of *time determinism* [32, 26], which says that if from a given state s there are time-passage actions leading to states s' and s'', which both have the same time, s' and s'' must be equal.

In order to define correctness for timed automata, we require notions of external behavior. We emphasize two notions. First, as the finite behaviors of a timed automaton, we take the *finite timed traces*, each of which consists of a finite sequence of timed external actions together with a final time. Second, as the infinite behaviors, we take the *admissible timed traces*, each of which consists of a sequence of timed external actions that can occur in an execution in which the time grows unboundedly (i.e., a "non-Zeno" infinite execution). In a *feasible* timed automaton, i.e., a timed automaton in which each finite execution can be extended to an execution in which the time is unbounded, the finite timed traces are determined by the admissible ones. For this type of automaton, inclusion of sets of admissible timed traces appears to be a good notion of implementation. One of the main objectives of this paper is to develop proof techniques to show that one automaton implements another in this sense.

Even though our notion of timed automata has less structure than those of [22] and [19], it is closely related to those models. Ours can be regarded as a generalization of the model in [19], in which the notion of separate tasks is removed. (There are some minor distinctions; for instance, we do not include names for internal actions, but label them all by the special symbol τ. This distinction is unimportant in a setting without separate tasks.) On the other hand, the model of [22] includes treatment of fairness and liveness, whereas our model does not. (The model in [22] was originally designed as an extension of the non-timing-based input/output automaton model of [20], which emphasizes the notion of *fair execution*.) The reason we have not equipped our model with facilities for handling fairness and liveness is that we believe that in the setting of timing-based systems, all properties of practical importance can be expressed as safety properties, given the admissibility assumption that time increases without bound. The absence of fairness and liveness considerations in our model seems to remove various technical and philosophical complications, and to lead to simpler and more systematic proof techniques.

The simulations we consider are derived from simulations studied in many places in the research literature. The simplest kind of simulation we consider is a *refinement*, which is a functional simulation similar to those studied in [17] and very similar to a homomorphism between automata in the sense of classical automata theory [6]. A refinement from a timed automaton A to another timed automaton B is a time-preserving function from states of A to states of B such that (a) the image of every start state of A is a start state of B, and (b) every step of A has a corresponding sequence of steps of B that begins and ends with the images of the respective beginning and ending states of the given step, and that has the same visible actions. In the untimed setting, it is well known that the corresponding untimed notion of refinement implies an implementation relation between A and B; we give the analogous soundness result, as well as a partial completeness result, for the timed setting.

We then consider *forward simulations* and *backward simulations*, which are generalizations of refinements that allow a set of states of B to correspond to a single state of A. Forward simulations are similar to the the simulations of [28, 10], the possibilities mappings of [20], the downward simulations of [9, 14, 8], and the forward simulations of [13]. The correspondence conditions (a) and (b) above are generalized so that (a) every start state of A has *some* image that is a start state of B, and (b) every step of A and every state of B corresponding to the *beginning* state of the step yield a corresponding sequence of steps of B ending with the image of the ending state of the given step. The usefulness of such simulations in proving correctness in the untimed setting has been well demonstrated. (See, e.g., [18] for some examples.) Again, we give soundness and partial completeness results for the timed setting. Backward simulations occurred first in [9] under the name of *upward simulations* and were used later in the setting of CSP in [14, 8]. In [21, 12] it is observed that they are closely related to the prophecy variables first defined in [1]. In the case of a backward simulation, conditions (a) and (b) are generalized so that (a) *all* images of every start state of A are start states of B, and (b) every step of A and every state of B corresponding to the *ending* state of the step yield a corresponding sequence of steps of B beginning with the image of the beginning state of the given step. Abadi and Lamport [1] demonstrate the usefulness of prophecy variables (and hence backward simulations) in the untimed setting, with some simple examples. Again, we give soundness and partial completeness results for the timed setting.

We also consider *forward-backward* and *backward-forward simulations*, which are essentially compositions of one forward and one backward simulation, in the two possible orders. The definition of a forward-backward simulation has been inspired by the work of Klarlund and Schneider [15] for the untimed setting (with no internal actions) again, we extend these ideas to the timed setting (with internal actions). The notion of a backward-forward simulation is suggested by symmetry with forward-backward simulations. While some of the results for this case are symmetric with the forward-backward case, others (notably, certain completeness results) do not hold.

We also provide redefinitions of the *history variable* notion of [27] and the *prophecy variable* notions of [1], in terms of timed automata, and prove equivalence results between these explicit definitions and our more abstract simulation definitions.

In order to present our results for timed automata, we find it convenient first to describe corresponding results for the simpler untimed setting. Therefore, we first define a simple untimed automaton model corresponding to the timed automaton model, and explore all the types of simulations described above in terms of this model. The definitions and results for timed automata are given in a subsequent step. The results for the timed setting are completely analogous to those for the untimed setting; in fact, in many cases, our results for the timed setting are derived directly from those for the untimed setting. An advantage of this two-phase approach is that it highlights the adaptability of the various verification techniques from the untimed to the timed setting.

As far as the classification of simulations is concerned, our work is closely related to and extends that of Jonsson [13]. However, whereas we focus on real-time issues, Jonsson addresses fairness instead. Also, Jonsson has more powerful notion of backward simulation, which we prefer not to use since it fails to reduce global reasoning about infinite behaviors to local reasoning about states and actions.

We consider the main contributions of the paper to be the following. First, we give an organized presentation, in terms of a very simple and abstract model, of a wide range of important simulation techniques, together with their basic soundness and completeness properties. We present the various simulation techniques in a "bottom-up" fashion, starting with simple ones such as forward and backward simulations and building up to more complicated simulations such as forward-backward simulations and history relations. We give elegant and short proofs of soundness and completeness results for complicated simulations in terms of soundness and (partial) completeness results for simple simulations. Second, we introduce the notions of a timed automaton and its behavior, and extend existing simulation notions to this new setting. Third, there are several specific new definitions and results, notably: (1) The definition of a notion of composition of forward-backward simulations. This allows us to prove that image-finite forward-backward simulations induce a preorder on the domain of general automata. (2) The introduction of backward-forward simulations. Although these simulations do not lead to a complete proof method, they are sound and possibly useful in practice. They arise naturally as the dual notion of forward-backward simulations. (3) The notions of history and prophecy relations. Fourth and finally, our presentation style, which bases the timed case on the untimed case, explains the connections between these two settings.

In what follows, some of the proofs have been omitted because of length restrictions.

2 Preliminaries

2.1 Sequences

Let K be any set. The sets of finite and infinite sequences of elements of K are denoted by K^* and K^ω, respectively. Concatenation of a finite sequence with a finite or infinite sequence is denoted by juxtaposition; λ denotes the empty sequence and the sequence containing one element $a \in K$ is denoted a. We say that a sequence σ is a *prefix* of a sequence ρ, notation $\sigma \leq \rho$, if either $\sigma = \rho$, or σ is finite and $\rho = \sigma\sigma'$ for some sequence σ'. A set S of sequences is *prefix closed* if, whenever some sequence is in S all its prefixes are also. If σ is a nonempty sequence then *first*(σ) returns the first element of σ, and *tail*(σ) returns σ with its first element removed. Moreover, if σ is finite, then *last*(σ) returns the last element of σ. If σ is a sequence over K and $L \subseteq K$, then $\sigma\lceil L$ denotes the sequence obtained by projecting σ on L. If S is a set of sequences, $S\lceil L$ is defined as $\{\sigma\lceil L \mid \sigma \in S\}$.

2.2 Sets, Relations and Functions

A *relation* over sets X and Y is defined to be any subset of $X \times Y$. If f is a relation over X and Y, then we define the *domain* of f to be *domain*$(f) \triangleq \{x \in X \mid (x, y) \in f \text{ for some } y \in Y\}$, and the *range* of f to be *range*$(f) \triangleq \{y \in Y \mid (x, y) \in f \text{ for some } x \in X\}$. A *total* relation over X and Y is a relation f over X and Y with *domain*$(f) = X$. If X is any set, we let *id*(X) denote the identity relation over X and X, i.e., $\{(x, x) \mid x \in X\}$. We define *composition* of relations in the usual way, i.e., if f and g are relations over X and Y and over Y and Z, respectively, then $g \circ f$ denotes the relation over X and Z consisting of all pairs (x, z) such that there exists $y \in Y$ with $(x, y) \in f$ and $(y, z) \in g$. For all relations f, g and h, $f \circ (g \circ h) = (f \circ g) \circ h$. Also, for $X \supseteq$ *domain*(f) and $Y \supseteq$ *range*(f),

$id(X) \circ f = f \circ id(Y) = f$. If f is a relation over X and Y, then the *inverse* of f, written f^{-1}, is defined to be the relation over Y and X consisting of those pairs (y, x) such that $(x, y) \in f$. Recall that for any pair of relations f and g, $(g \circ f)^{-1} = f^{-1} \circ g^{-1}$. If f is a relation over X and Y, and Z is a set, then $f \lceil Z$ is the relation over $X \cap Z$ and Y given by $f \lceil Z \triangleq f \cap (Z \times Y)$. If f is a relation over X and Y and $x \in X$, we define $f[x] = \{y \in Y \mid (x, y) \in f\}$. We say that a relation f over X and Y is a *function from X to Y*, and write $f : X \to Y$, if $|f[x]| = 1$ for all $x \in X$; in this case, we write $f(x)$ to denote the unique element of $f[x]$. A function c from X to Y is a *choice function* for a relation f over X to Y provided that $c \subseteq f$ (i.e., $c(x) \in f[x]$ for all $x \in X$). If X is a set, $\mathbf{P}(X)$ denotes the powerset of X, i.e., the set of subsets of X, and $\mathbf{PN}(X)$ the set of nonempty subsets of X, i.e., the set $\mathbf{P}(X) - \{\emptyset\}$. We say that a relation f over X and Y is *image-finite* if $f[x]$ is finite for all x in X. If f is a relation over X and $\mathbf{P}(Y)$, then we say that f is *image-2-finite* if every set in the range of f is finite.

2.3 A Basic Graph Lemma

We require the following lemma, a generalization of König's Lemma [16]. If G is a digraph, then a *root* of G is defined to be a node with no incoming edges.

Lemma 2.1 *Let G be an infinite digraph that satisfies the following properties.*

1. *G has finitely many roots.*
2. *Each node of G has finite outdegree.*
3. *Each node of G is reachable from some root of G.*

Then there is an infinite path in G starting from some root.

Proof: The usual proof for König's Lemma extends to this case. ■

3 Untimed Automata and Their Behaviors

This section presents the basic definitions and results for untimed automata.

3.1 Automata

We begin with the definition of an (untimed) automaton. An *automaton* A consists of:

- a set *states*(A) of states,
- a nonempty set *start*(A) $\subseteq$ *states*(A) of start states,
- a set *acts*(A) of actions that includes a special element τ, and
- a set *steps*(A) $\subseteq$ *states*(A) $\times$ *acts*(A) $\times$ *states*(A) of steps.

We let s, s', u, u',.. range over states, and a,.. over actions. We let $ext(A)$, the *external actions*, denote $acts(A) - \{\tau\}$. We call τ the *internal action*. We use the term *event* to refer to an occurrence of an action in a sequence. If σ is a sequence of actions then $\widehat{\sigma}$ is the sequence gained by deleting all τ events from σ. We write $s' \xrightarrow{a}_A s$, or just $s' \xrightarrow{a} s$ if A is clear from the context, as a shorthand for $(s', a, s) \in steps(A)$. In this section as well as the next one, A, B,.. range over automata. Later, however, we will use these symbols to range over timed automata.

An *execution fragment* of A is a finite or infinite alternating sequence $s_0a_1s_1a_2s_2\cdots$ of states and actions of A, beginning with a state, and if it is finite also ending with a state, such that for all i, $s_i \xrightarrow{a_{i+1}} s_{i+1}$. We denote by $frag^*(A)$, $frag^\omega(A)$ and $frag(A)$ the sets of finite, infinite, and all execution fragments of A, respectively. An *execution* of A is an execution fragment that begins with a start state. We denote by $execs^*(A)$, $execs^\omega(A)$ and $execs(A)$ the sets of finite, infinite, and all executions of A, respectively. A state s of A is *reachable* if $s = last(\alpha)$ for some finite execution α of A.

Suppose $\alpha = s_0a_1s_1a_2s_2\cdots$ is an execution fragment of A. Let γ be the sequence consisting of the actions in α: $\gamma = a_1a_2\ldots$. Then $trace(\alpha)$ is defined to be the sequence $\hat{\gamma}$. A finite or infinite sequence β of actions is a *trace* of A if A has an execution α with $\beta = trace(\alpha)$. We write $traces^*(A)$, $traces^\omega(A)$ and $traces(A)$ for the sets of finite, infinite and all traces of A, respectively. These notions induce three *preorders* (i.e., reflexive and transitive relations). For A and B automata, we define $A \leq_{*\mathrm{T}} B \triangleq traces^*(A) \subseteq traces^*(B)$, $A \leq_{\omega\mathrm{T}} B \triangleq traces^\omega(A) \subseteq traces^\omega(B)$, and $A \leq_{\mathrm{T}} B \triangleq traces(A) \subseteq traces(B)$. Recall that the *kernel* of a preorder $\sqsubseteq$ is the equivalence $\equiv$ defined by $x \equiv y \triangleq x \sqsubseteq y \wedge y \sqsubseteq x$. We denote by $\equiv_{*\mathrm{T}}$, $\equiv_{\omega\mathrm{T}}$ and $\equiv_{\mathrm{T}}$, the respective kernels of the preorders $\leq_{*\mathrm{T}}$, $\leq_{\omega\mathrm{T}}$ and $\leq_{\mathrm{T}}$.

Suppose A is an automaton, s' and s are states of A, and β is a finite sequence over $ext(A)$. We say that (s', β, s) is a *move* of A, and write $s' \stackrel{\beta}{\Longrightarrow}_A s$, or just $s' \stackrel{\beta}{\Longrightarrow} s$ when A is clear, if A has a finite execution fragment α with $first(\alpha) = s'$, $trace(\alpha) = \beta$ and $last(\alpha) = s$.

3.2 Restricted Kinds of Automata

Automaton A is *deterministic* if $|start(A)| = 1$, $steps(A)$ contains no τ steps, and for all states s' and all external actions a there is at most one state s such that $s' \xrightarrow{a}_A s$.

A has *finite invisible nondeterminism (fin)* if $start(A)$ is finite, and for any state s' and any finite sequence β over $ext(A)$, there are only finitely many states s such that $s' \stackrel{\beta}{\Longrightarrow}_A s$.

A is a *forest* if for each state of A there is a unique execution that leads to it. Recall that a forest is characterized uniquely by the property that all states of A are reachable, start states have no incoming steps and each of the other states has exactly one incoming step.

The relation $after(A)$ consists of the pairs $(\beta, s) \in (ext(A))^* \times states(A)$ for which there is a finite execution of A with trace β and last state s.

$$after(A) \triangleq \{(\beta, s) \mid \exists \alpha \in execs^*(A) : trace(\alpha) = \beta \text{ and } last(\alpha) = s\}.$$

The relation $past(A) \triangleq after(A)^{-1}$ relates a state s of A to the traces of finite executions of A that lead to s. Also, define $before(A)$ to be the relation that relates a finite sequence

β to those states of A from where an execution with trace β is possible.

$$before(A) \triangleq \{(\beta, s) \mid \exists \alpha \in frag^*(A) : trace(\alpha) = \beta \text{ and } first(\alpha) = s\}.$$

We write $future(A)$ for $before(A)^{-1}$.

Lemma 3.1

1. *If A is deterministic then $after(A)$ is a function from $traces^*(A)$ to $states(A)$.*

2. *If A has fin then $after(A)$ is image-finite.*

3. *If A is a forest then $past(A)$ is a function from $states(A)$ to $traces^*(A)$.*

3.3 Trace Properties

For A an automaton, its *behavior*, $beh(A)$, is defined by $beh(A) \triangleq (ext(A), traces(A))$. In this subsection, we characterize the structures that can be obtained as the behavior $beh(A)$ for some automaton A as *trace properties.*

A *trace property* P is a pair (K, L) with K a set and L a nonempty, prefix closed set of (finite or infinite) sequences over K. We will refer to the constituents of P as $sort(P)$ and $traces(P)$, respectively. Also, we write $traces^*(P) \triangleq K^* \cap L$ and $traces^\omega(P) \triangleq K^\omega \cap L$. For P and Q trace properties, we define $P \leq_{*\mathrm{T}} Q \triangleq traces^*(P) \subseteq traces^*(Q)$, $P \leq_{\omega\mathrm{T}} Q \triangleq traces^\omega(P) \subseteq traces^\omega(Q)$, and $P \leq_{\mathrm{T}} Q \triangleq traces(P) \subseteq traces(Q)$. With $\equiv_{*\mathrm{T}}$, $\equiv_{\omega\mathrm{T}}$ and $\equiv_{\mathrm{T}}$, we denote the kernels of the preorders $\leq_{*\mathrm{T}}$, $\leq_{\omega\mathrm{T}}$ and $\leq_{\mathrm{T}}$, respectively. A trace property P is *limit-closed* if an infinite sequence is in $traces(P)$ whenever all its finite prefixes are.

Lemma 3.2 *Suppose P and Q are trace properties with Q limit-closed. Then $P \leq_{*\mathrm{T}} Q \Leftrightarrow P \leq_{\mathrm{T}} Q$.*

Lemma 3.3

1. *$beh(A)$ is a trace property.*

2. *If A has fin then $beh(A)$ is limit-closed.*

3. *$A \leq_{*\mathrm{T}} B \Leftrightarrow beh(A) \leq_{*\mathrm{T}} beh(B)$, $A \leq_{\omega\mathrm{T}} B \Leftrightarrow beh(A) \leq_{\omega\mathrm{T}} beh(B)$, and $A \leq_{\mathrm{T}} B \Leftrightarrow beh(A) \leq_{\mathrm{T}} beh(B)$.*

Proof: It is easy to see that $beh(A)$ is a trace property.

For Part 2, suppose A has fin. We use Lemma 2.1 to show that $beh(A)$ is limit-closed. Suppose β is an infinite sequence over $ext(A)$ such that all finite prefixes of β are in $traces(A)$. Consider the digraph G whose nodes are pairs (γ, s), where γ is a finite prefix of β and s is a state of A, and where there exists an execution α of A that ends with state s and such that $\gamma = trace(\alpha)$; there is an edge from node (γ', s') to node (γ, s) exactly if γ is of the form $\gamma' a$, where $a \in ext(A)$, and where $s' \overset{a}{\Longrightarrow}_A s$. Then G satisfies the hypotheses of Lemma 2.1, which implies that there is an infinite path in G starting at a root. This corresponds directly to an execution α having $trace(\alpha) = \beta$. Hence, $\beta \in traces(A)$.

Part 3 is immediate from the definitions. ■

Proposition 3.4 *If B has fin then $A \leq_{*\mathrm{T}} B \Leftrightarrow A \leq_{\mathrm{T}} B$.*

Proof: Immediate from Lemmas 3.2 and 3.3. ■

Example 3.1 The automata A and B of Figure 1 illustrate the difference between $\leq_{*\mathrm{T}}$ and $\leq_{\mathrm{T}}$. Note that automaton B does not have fin.

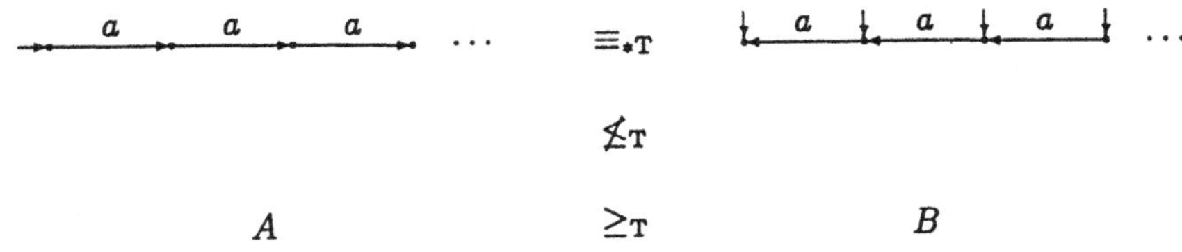

Figure 1: $\leq_{*\mathrm{T}}$ versus $\leq_{\mathrm{T}}$.

We close this subsection with the construction of the *canonical automaton* for a given trace property.

Definition 3.1 For P a trace property, the associated *canonical* automaton $can(P)$ is the structure A given by

- $states(A) = traces^*(P)$,
- $start(A) = \{\lambda\}$,
- $acts(A) = sort(P) \cup \{\tau\}$, and
- for $\beta', \beta \in states(A)$ and $a \in acts(A)$, $\beta' \xrightarrow{a}_A \beta \quad \Leftrightarrow \quad a \in ext(A) \wedge \beta' a = \beta$.

Lemma 3.5

1. *$can(P)$ is a deterministic forest,*
2. *$beh(can(P)) \equiv_{*\mathrm{T}} P$,*
3. *$P \leq_{\mathrm{T}} beh(can(P))$, and*
4. *if P is limit-closed then $beh(can(P)) \equiv_{\mathrm{T}} P$.*

Proof: Parts 1 and 2 follow easily from the definitions. Since $can(P)$ is deterministic it certainly has fin, so it follows by Lemma 3.3 that $beh(can(P))$ is limit-closed. Now 3 and 4 follow by combination of 2 and Lemma 3.2. ■

Lemma 3.6

1. *$can(beh(A))$ is a deterministic forest,*
2. *$can(beh(A)) \equiv_{*\mathrm{T}} A$,*
3. *$A \leq_{\mathrm{T}} can(beh(A))$, and*
4. *if A has fin then $can(beh(A)) \equiv_{\mathrm{T}} A$.*

Proof: By combining Lemmas 3.3 and 3.5. ■

4 Simulations for Untimed Automata

In this section, we develop simulation techniques for untimed automata.

4.1 Refinements

The simplest type of simulation we consider is a *refinement*. A *refinement* from A to B is a function r from states of A to states of B that satisfies the following two conditions:

1. If $s \in start(A)$ then $r(s) \in start(B)$.
2. If $s' \xrightarrow{a}_A s$ then $r(s') \stackrel{\hat{a}}{\Longrightarrow}_B r(s)$.

We write $A \leq_R B$ if there exists a refinement from A to B.

This notion is similar to that of a *homomorphism* in classical automata theory; see for instance Ginzberg [6]. Besides our additional treatment of internal actions, a difference between the two notions is that the classical notion involves a mapping between the action sets of the automata, whereas our refinements do not.

Example 4.1 Figure 2 presents some canonical examples of $\leq_R$.

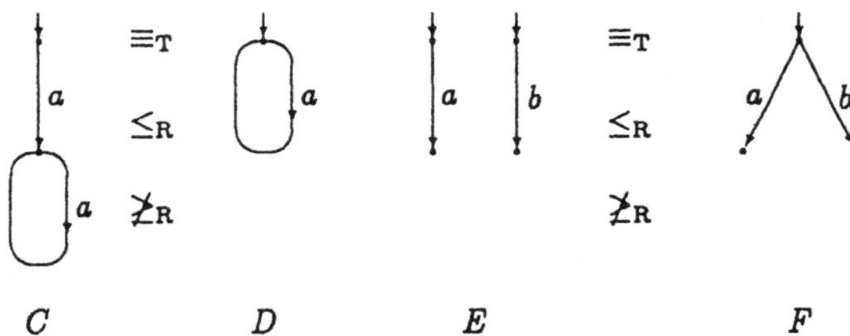

Figure 2: Refinements.

The following technical lemma is a straightforward consequence of the definition of a refinement.

Lemma 4.1 *Suppose r is a refinement from A to B and $s' \stackrel{\beta}{\Longrightarrow}_A s$. Then $r(s') \stackrel{\beta}{\Longrightarrow}_B r(s)$.*

Proposition 4.2 *$\leq_R$ is a preorder (i.e., is transitive and reflexive).*

Proof: The identity function $id(states(A))$ is a refinement from A to itself. This implies that $\leq_R$ is reflexive. Using Lemma 4.1, transitivity follows from the observation that if r is a refinement from A to B and r' is a refinement from B to C, $r' \circ r$ is a refinement from A to C. ∎

Theorem 4.3 *(Soundness of refinements)* $A \leq_R B \Rightarrow A \leq_T B$.

Proof: Suppose $A \leq_R B$. Let r be a refinement from A to B, and let e be a function that maps each move (s', β, s) of B to a finite execution fragment of B from s' to s with trace β. Suppose $\beta \in traces(A)$. Then there exists an execution $\alpha = s_0 a_1 s_1 a_2 s_2 \cdots$ of A with $\beta = trace(\alpha)$. By the first condition in the definition of a refinement, $r(s_0)$ is a start state of B, and by the second condition, $r(s_i) \stackrel{a_{i+1}}{\Longrightarrow}_B r(s_{i+1})$ for all i. For $i \geq 0$, define $\alpha_i = e((r(s_i), \widehat{a_{i+1}}, r(s_{i+1})))$. Next define sequence α' to be the (infinitary) concatenation $\alpha_0 tail(\alpha_1) tail(\alpha_2) \cdots$. By construction, α' is an execution of B with $trace(\alpha') = trace(\alpha) = \beta \in traces(B)$. ■

Theorem 4.4 *(Partial completeness of refinements) Suppose A is a forest, B is deterministic and $A \leq_{*T} B$. Then $A \leq_R B$.*

Proof: The relation $r \triangleq after(B) \circ past(A)$ is a refinement from A to B. ■

4.2 Forward and Backward Simulations

4.2.1 Forward Simulations

A *forward simulation* from A to B is a relation f over $states(A)$ and $states(B)$ that satisfies:

1. If $s \in start(A)$ then $f[s] \cap start(B) \neq \emptyset$.
2. If $s' \stackrel{a}{\longrightarrow}_A s$ and $u' \in f[s']$, then there exists a state $u \in f[s]$ such that $u' \stackrel{\hat{a}}{\Longrightarrow}_B u$.

We write $A \leq_F B$ if there exists a forward simulation from A to B.

Example 4.2 Let C, D, E, F be as in Figure 2. Then $D \leq_F C$ and $F \not\leq_F E$.

Proposition 4.5 $A \leq_R B \Rightarrow A \leq_F B$.

Proof: Any refinement relation is a forward simulation. ■

The following lemma is the analogue for forward simulations of Lemma 4.1.

Lemma 4.6 *Suppose f is a forward simulation from A to B and $s' \stackrel{\beta}{\Longrightarrow}_A s$. If $u' \in f[s']$, then there exists a state $u \in f[s]$ such that $u' \stackrel{\beta}{\Longrightarrow}_B u$.*

Proposition 4.7 *$\leq_F$ is a preorder.*

Proof: For reflexivity, observe that the identity function $id(states(A))$ is a forward simulation from A to itself. For transitivity, use Lemma 4.6 to show that if f and f' are forward simulations from A to B and from B to C, respectively, $f' \circ f$ is a forward simulation from A to C. ■

Theorem 4.8 *(Soundness of forward simulations, [20, 11, 30]) $A \leq_F B \Rightarrow A \leq_T B$.*

Proof: Versions of this proof appears in the cited papers. The proof is similar to that of Theorem 4.3. ■

Theorem 4.9 *(Partial completeness of forward simulations) Suppose B is deterministic and $A \leq_{*T} B$. Then $A \leq_F B$.*

Proof: The relation $f \triangleq after(B) \circ past(A)$ is a forward simulation from A to B. ■

4.2.2 Backward Simulations

In many respects, backward simulations are the dual of forward simulations. Whereas a forward simulation requires that *some* state in the image of each start state should be a start state, a backward simulation requires that *all* states in the image of a start state be start states. Also, a forward simulation requires that forward steps in the source automaton can be simulated from related states in the target automaton, whereas the corresponding condition for a backward simulations requires that backward steps can be simulated. However, the two notions are not completely dual: the definition of a backward simulation contains a nonemptiness condition, and also, in order to imply soundness in general, backward simulations also require a finite image condition. The mismatch is due to the asymmetry in our automata between future and past: from any given state, all the possible histories are finite executions, whereas the possible futures can be infinite.

A *backward simulation* from A to B is a total relation b over $states(A)$ and $states(B)$ that satisfies:

1. If $s \in start(A)$ then $b[s] \subseteq start(B)$.

2. If $s' \xrightarrow{a}_A s$ and $u \in b[s]$, then there exists a state $u' \in b[s']$ such that $u' \stackrel{\hat{a}}{\Longrightarrow}_B u$.

We write $A \leq_{\mathrm{B}} B$ if there exists a backward simulation from A to B, and $A \leq_{\mathrm{iB}} B$ if there exists an image-finite backward simulation from A to B.

Example 4.3 Let A, B be as in Figure 1. Then $A \leq_{\mathrm{B}} B$ but $A \not\leq_{\mathrm{iB}} B$. If C, D, E, F are as in Figure 2, then $D \not\leq_{\mathrm{B}} C$ and $F \leq_{\mathrm{iB}} E$.

Proposition 4.10 $A \leq_{\mathrm{R}} B \Rightarrow A \leq_{\mathrm{iB}} B$.

The following lemma is useful in the proofs of the preorder properties and of soundness.

Lemma 4.11 *Suppose b is a backward simulation from A to B and $s' \stackrel{\beta}{\Longrightarrow}_A s$. If $u \in b[s]$, then there exists a state $u' \in b[s']$ such that $u' \stackrel{\beta}{\Longrightarrow}_B u$.*

Proposition 4.12 *$\leq_{\mathrm{B}}$ and $\leq_{\mathrm{iB}}$ are preorders.*

Proof: The identity function $id(states(A))$ is a backward simulation from A to itself. Using Lemma 4.11 one can easily show that if b is backward simulation from A to B and b' is a backward simulation from B to C, $b' \circ b$ is a backward simulation from A to C. Moreover, if both b and b' are image-finite, then $b' \circ b$ is image-finite too. ■

Theorem 4.13 *(Soundness of backward simulations)*

1. $A \leq_{\mathrm{B}} B \Rightarrow A \leq_{*\mathrm{T}} B$, *and*

2. $A \leq_{\mathrm{iB}} B \Rightarrow A \leq_{\mathrm{T}} B$.

Proof: Suppose b is a backward simulation from A to B and suppose $\beta \in traces^*(A)$. Then there is a move $s' \stackrel{\beta}{\Longrightarrow}_A s$, where s' is a start state of A. Since b is a backward simulation it is a total relation, so there exists a state $u \in b[s]$. By Lemma 4.11, there exists $u' \in b[s']$ with $u' \stackrel{\beta}{\Longrightarrow}_B u$. By the first condition of the definition of a backward simulation, $u' \in start(B)$. Therefore, $\beta \in traces^*(B)$, which shows the first part of the proposition.

For the second part, suppose that b is image-finite. We have already established $A \leq_{*\mathrm{T}} B$, so it is sufficient to show $A \leq_{\omega\mathrm{T}} B$. Suppose that $\beta \in traces^\omega(A)$, and let $\alpha = s_0 a_1 s_1 a_2 \cdots$ be an infinite execution of A with $trace(\alpha) = \beta$.

Consider the digraph G whose nodes are pairs (u, i) such that $(s_i, u) \in b$ and in which there is an edge from (u', i') to (u, i) exactly if $i = i' + 1$ and $u' \stackrel{\widehat{a_i}}{\Longrightarrow}_B u$. Then G satisfies the hypotheses of Lemma 2.1, which implies that there is an infinite path in G starting at a root. This corresponds directly to an execution α' of B having $trace(\alpha') = trace(\alpha) = \beta$. Hence, $\beta \in traces(B)$. ■

In a recent paper, Jonsson [13] considers a weaker image-finiteness condition for backward simulations. Translated into our setting, the key observation of Jonsson is that in order to prove $A \leq_{\mathrm{T}} B$, it is enough to give a backward simulation b from A to B with the property that each infinite execution of A contains infinitely many states s with $b[s]$ finite. We do not explore this extension in this paper, primarily because it lacks a key feature of simulation techniques. Namely, it fails to reduce global reasoning about infinite behaviors to local reasoning about states and actions.

The following partial completeness result slightly generalizes a similar result of Jonsson [12] in that it also alllows for τ-steps in the B automaton.

Theorem 4.14 *(Partial completeness of backward simulations) Suppose A is a forest and $A \leq_{*\mathrm{T}} B$. Then*

1. *$A \leq_{\mathrm{B}} B$, and*

2. *if B has fin then $A \leq_{\mathrm{iB}} B$.*

Proof: We define a relation b over $states(A)$ and $states(B)$. Suppose s is a state of A. Since A is a forest there is a unique trace leading up to s, say β. Now define

$$b[s] = \{u \mid \exists \alpha \in execs^*(B) \colon trace(\alpha) = \beta,\ last(\alpha) = u \wedge [\alpha' < \alpha \Rightarrow trace(\alpha') \neq \beta]\}.$$

By letting $b[s]$ consist only of those states of B which can be reached via a *minimal* execution with trace β, we achieve that, if s is a start state, all the states in $b[s]$ are start states of B. It is also the case that b satisfies the other conditions in the definition of a backward simulation.

Lemma 3.1 implies that b is image-finite if B has fin. ■

Proposition 4.15 *Suppose all states of A are reachable, B has fin and $A \leq_{\mathrm{B}} B$. Then $A \leq_{\mathrm{iB}} B$.*

Proof: Let b be a backward simulation from A to B and let s be a state of A. Since s is reachable we can find a trace $\beta \in past(A)[s]$. From the fact that b is a backward simulation it follows that $b[s] \subseteq after(B)[\beta]$. But since B has fin, $after(B)[\beta]$ is finite by Lemma 3.1. This implies that b is image-finite. ■

Example 4.4 Figure 3 shows that the reachability assumption in Proposition 4.15 is essential. There is a backward simulation from G to H, but even though H is deterministic there is no image-finite backward simulation.

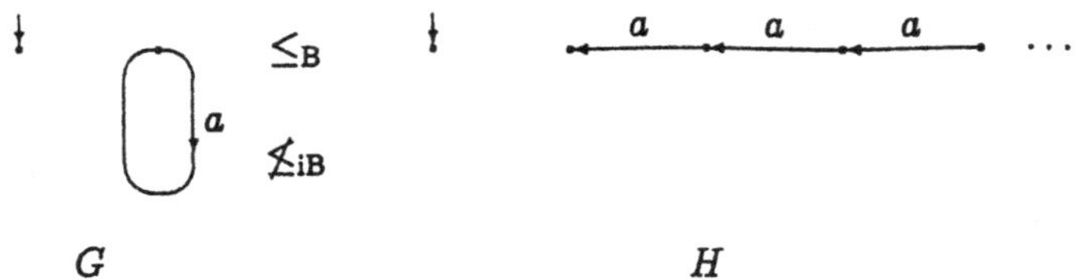

Figure 3: $\leq_{\mathrm{B}}$ and $\leq_{\mathrm{iB}}$ are different, even for automata with fin.

4.2.3 Combined Forward and Backward Simulations

Several authors have observed that forward and backward simulations together give a complete proof method (see [9, 8, 14, 12]): if $A \leq_{*\mathrm{T}} B$ then there exists an intermediate automaton C with a forward simulation from A to C and a backward simulation from C to B. We prove this below.

Theorem 4.16 *(Completeness of forward and backward simulations) If $A \leq_{*\mathrm{T}} B$ then the following are true.*

1. $\exists C : A \leq_{\mathrm{F}} C \leq_{\mathrm{B}} B$.
2. *If B has fin then* $\exists C : A \leq_{\mathrm{F}} C \leq_{\mathrm{iB}} B$.

Proof: Let $C = can(beh(A))$. By Lemma 3.6, C is a deterministic forest and $A \equiv_{*\mathrm{T}} C$. Since C is deterministic, $A \leq_{\mathrm{F}} C$ by Theorem 4.9, and because C is a forest, $C \leq_{\mathrm{B}} B$ follows by Theorem 4.14(1). If B has fin then $C \leq_{\mathrm{iB}} B$ follows by Theorem 4.14(2). ■

4.3 Forward-Backward and Backward-Forward Simulations

4.3.1 Forward-Backward Simulations

Forward-backward simulations were introduced by Klarlund and Schneider [15] who call them *invariants*. They also occur in the work of Jonsson [13] under the name *subset simulations*, and are related to the *failure simulations* of Gerth [5]. Forward-backward simulations combine in a single relation both a forward and a backward simulation. Below we present simple proofs of their soundness and completeness by making this connection explicit.

Formally, a *forward-backward simulation* from A to B is a relation g over $states(A)$ and $\mathrm{PN}(states(B))$ that satisfies:

1. If $s \in start(A)$ then there exists $S \in g[s]$ such that $S \subseteq start(B)$.
2. If $s' \xrightarrow{a}_A s$ and $S' \in g[s']$, then there exists a set $S \in g[s]$ such that for every $u \in S$ there exists $u' \in S'$ with $u' \stackrel{\hat{a}}{\Longrightarrow}_B u$.

We write $A \leq_{\mathrm{FB}} B$ if there exists a forward-backward simulation from A to B, and $A \leq_{\mathrm{iFB}} B$ if there exists an image-2-finite forward-backward simulation from A to B.

The following theorem says that a forward-backward simulation can be obtained by combining a forward and a backward simulation.

Theorem 4.17

1. $A \leq_{\mathrm{F}} C \leq_{\mathrm{B}} B \Rightarrow A \leq_{\mathrm{FB}} B$.

2. $A \leq_{\mathrm{F}} C \leq_{\mathrm{iB}} B \Rightarrow A \leq_{\mathrm{iFB}} B$.

Proof: Suppose f is a forward simulation from A to C, and b is a backward simulation from C to B. Then the relation g over $states(A)$ and $\mathbf{PN}(states(B))$ defined by $g = \{(s, b[u]) \mid (s, u) \in f\}$ is a forward-backward simulation from A to B. If b is image-finite then g is image-2-finite. ■

Proposition 4.18

1. $A \leq_{\mathrm{F}} B \Rightarrow A \leq_{\mathrm{iFB}} B$.

2. $A \leq_{\mathrm{B}} B \Rightarrow A \leq_{\mathrm{FB}} B$.

3. $A \leq_{\mathrm{iB}} B \Rightarrow A \leq_{\mathrm{iFB}} B$.

Proof: Immediate from Theorem 4.17, using that $\leq_{\mathrm{iB}}$ and $\leq_{\mathrm{F}}$ are reflexive. ■

In combination with Theorem 4.17, the following theorem tells us that forward-backward simulations are equivalent to forward simulations followed by backward simulations.

Theorem 4.19

1. $A \leq_{\mathrm{FB}} B \Rightarrow (\exists C : A \leq_{\mathrm{F}} C \leq_{\mathrm{B}} B)$.

2. $A \leq_{\mathrm{iFB}} B \Rightarrow (\exists C : A \leq_{\mathrm{F}} C \leq_{\mathrm{iB}} B)$.

Proof: Let g be a forward-backward simulation from A to B, which is image-2-finite if $A \leq_{\mathrm{iFB}} B$. Define C to be the automaton given by:

- $states(C) = range(g)$,
- $start(C) = range(g) \cap \mathbf{P}(start(B))$,
- $acts(C) = acts(B)$, and
- for $S', S \in states(C)$ and $a \in acts(C)$, $S' \xrightarrow{a}_C S \;\Leftrightarrow\; \forall u \in S \; \exists u' \in S' : u' \stackrel{\hat{a}}{\Longrightarrow}_B u$.

Then g is a forward simulation from A to C. Also, $\{(S, u) \mid S \in states(C)$ and $u \in S\}$ is a backward simulation from C to B, which is image finite if g is image-2-finite. ■

In order to show that $\leq_{\mathrm{FB}}$ and $\leq_{\mathrm{iFB}}$ are preorders, we require a definition of composition for forward-backward simulations, and a transitivity lemma.

Definition 4.1 If g is a relation over X and $\mathbf{PN}(Y)$ and g' is a relation over Y and $\mathbf{PN}(Z)$ then the composition $g' \bullet g$ is a relation over X and $\mathbf{PN}(Z)$ defined as follows.

$$(x, S') \in g' \bullet g \Leftrightarrow \exists S \in g[x], \exists c, \text{ a choice function for } g' \lceil S : S' = \bigcup\{c(y) : y \in S\}.$$

(The nonemptiness assumptions for g and g' immediately imply the nonemptiness assumption for $g' \bullet g$.)

Lemma 4.20 *Suppose g is a forward-backward simulation from A to B, and g' is a forward-backward simulation from B to C. Then $g' \bullet g$ is a forward-backward simulation from A to C. Moreover, if g and g' are image-2-finite then $g' \bullet g$ is also image-2-finite.*

Proof: For Condition 1 of the definition of a forward-backward simulation, suppose $s \in start(A)$. Because g is a forward-backward simulation, there is a set $S \in g[s]$ with $S \subseteq start(B)$. Since g' is a forward-backward simulation, it is possible to find, for each $u \in S$, a set $S_u \in g'[u]$ with $S_u \subseteq start(C)$. Hence all states in the set $S' = \bigcup\{S_u \mid u \in S\}$ are start states of C. Now let c be the function with domain S given by $c(u) = S_u$. Then c is a choice function for $g' \lceil S$. From the definition of $\bullet$ it now follows that $(s, S') \in g' \bullet g$. This shows that $g' \bullet g$ satisfies Condition 1.

Now we show Condition 2 of the definition of a forward-backward simulation. Suppose $s' \xrightarrow{a}_A s$ and $(s', S') \in g' \bullet g$. By definition of $g' \bullet g$, there exist $T' \in g[s']$ and a choice function c' for $g' \lceil T'$ such that $S' = \bigcup\{c'(u') : u' \in T'\}$. Because g is a forward-backward simulation from A to B, there is a set $T \in g[s]$ such that for each $u \in T$ there exists $u' \in T'$ with $u' \stackrel{\hat{a}}{\Longrightarrow}_B u$. Consider any particular $u \in T$. Choose $u' \in T'$ with $u' \stackrel{\hat{a}}{\Longrightarrow}_B u$. Because g' is a forward-backward simulation, there exists a set $S_u \in g'[u]$ such that for every $v \in S_u$ there exists a $v' \in c'(u')$ with $v' \stackrel{\hat{a}}{\Longrightarrow}_C v$. Define a choice function c for $g' \lceil T$ by taking $c(u)$ to be the set S_u.

Now consider the set $S = \bigcup\{c(u) : u \in T\}$. Then $(s, S) \in g' \bullet g$ by definition. By construction, we can find, for each $v \in S$, a state $v' \in S'$ with $v' \stackrel{\hat{a}}{\Longrightarrow}_C v$. Thus S has the required property to show Condition 2.

Finally, it is immediate from the definitions that, if g and g' are image-2 finite, $g' \bullet g$ is also image-2-finite. ■

Proposition 4.21 *$\leq_{\mathrm{FB}}$ and $\leq_{\mathrm{iFB}}$ are preorders.*

Proof: By Lemma 4.20. ■

Theorem 4.22 *(Soundness of forward-backward simulations, [15])*

1. *$A \leq_{\mathrm{FB}} B \Rightarrow A \leq_{*\mathrm{T}} B$, and*
2. *$A \leq_{\mathrm{iFB}} B \Rightarrow A \leq_{\mathrm{T}} B$.*

Proof: For part 1, suppose $A \leq_{\mathrm{FB}} B$. By Theorem 4.19, there exists an automaton C with $A \leq_{\mathrm{F}} C \leq_{\mathrm{B}} B$. By soundness of forward simulations, Theorem 4.8, $A \leq_{\mathrm{T}} C$, and by soundness of backward simulations, Theorem 4.13, $C \leq_{*\mathrm{T}} B$. This implies $A \leq_{*\mathrm{T}} B$. Part 2 is similar. ■

Theorem 4.23 *(Completeness of forward-backward simulations, [15]) Suppose $A \leq_{*\mathrm{T}} B$. Then*

1. *$A \leq_{\mathrm{FB}} B$.*
2. *If B has fin then $A \leq_{\mathrm{iFB}} B$.*

Proof: By Theorem 4.16, there exists an automaton C with $A \leq_{\mathrm{F}} C \leq_{\mathrm{B}} B$. Moreover, if B has fin then $A \leq_{\mathrm{F}} C \leq_{\mathrm{iB}} B$. Then Theorem 4.17 implies the needed conclusions. ■

4.3.2 Backward-Forward Simulations

Having studied forward-backward simulations, we find it natural to define and study a dual notion of backward-formulation simulation.

A *backward-forward simulation* from A to B is a total relation g over $states(A)$ and $\mathbf{P}(states(B))$ that satisfies:

1. If $s \in start(A)$ then, for all $S \in g[s]$, $S \cap start(B) \neq \emptyset$.

2. If $s' \xrightarrow{a}_A s$ and $S \in g[s]$, then there exists a set $S' \in g[s']$ such that for every $u' \in S'$ there exists a $u \in S$ with $u' \overset{\hat{a}}{\Longrightarrow}_B u$.

We write $A \leq_{\mathrm{BF}} B$ if there exists a backward-forward simulation from A to B, and $A \leq_{\mathrm{iBF}} B$ if there exists an image-finite backward-forward simulation from A to B.

As for forward-backward simulations, backward-forward simulations can be characterized as combinations of forward and backward simulations.

Theorem 4.24

1. $A \leq_{\mathrm{B}} C \leq_{\mathrm{F}} B \Rightarrow A \leq_{\mathrm{BF}} B$.

2. $A \leq_{\mathrm{iB}} C \leq_{\mathrm{F}} B \Rightarrow A \leq_{\mathrm{iBF}} B$.

Proposition 4.25

1. $A \leq_{\mathrm{F}} B \Rightarrow A \leq_{\mathrm{iBF}} B$.

2. $A \leq_{\mathrm{B}} B \Rightarrow A \leq_{\mathrm{BF}} B$.

3. $A \leq_{\mathrm{iB}} B \Rightarrow A \leq_{\mathrm{iBF}} B$.

Theorem 4.26

1. $A \leq_{\mathrm{BF}} B \Rightarrow (\exists C : A \leq_{\mathrm{B}} C \leq_{\mathrm{F}} B)$.

2. $A \leq_{\mathrm{iBF}} B \Rightarrow (\exists C : A \leq_{\mathrm{iB}} C \leq_{\mathrm{F}} B)$.

Proof: Let g be a backward-forward simulation from A to B, which is image-finite if $A \leq_{\mathrm{iBF}} B$. Define C to be the automaton given by:

- $states(C) = range(g)$,
- $start(C) = range(g \lceil start(A))$,
- $acts(C) = acts(B)$, and
- for $S', S \in states(C)$ and $a \in acts(C)$, $S' \xrightarrow{a}_C S \quad \Leftrightarrow \quad \forall u' \in S' \; \exists u \in S : u' \overset{\hat{a}}{\Longrightarrow}_B u$.

Then g is a backward simulation from A to C (and image-finiteness carries over). Also, the relation $\{(S, u) \mid S \in states(C) \text{ and } u \in S\}$ is a forward simulation from C to B. ■

In order to show the properties of backward-forward simulations, it is useful to relate them to forward-backward simulations.

Theorem 4.27

1. $A \leq_{\mathrm{BF}} B \Leftrightarrow A \leq_{\mathrm{FB}} B$.

2. $A \leq_{\mathrm{iBF}} B \Rightarrow A \leq_{\mathrm{iFB}} B$.

Proof: For one direction of 1, suppose that $A \leq_{\mathrm{BF}} B$. Then by Theorem 4.26, there exists an automaton C with $A \leq_{\mathrm{B}} C \leq_{\mathrm{F}} B$. By Proposition 4.18, $A \leq_{\mathrm{FB}} C$ and $C \leq_{\mathrm{FB}} B$. Now $A \leq_{\mathrm{FB}} B$ follows by Proposition 4.21. The proof of 2 is similar.

For the other direction of 1, suppose that f is a forward-backward simulation from A to B. Given a state s of A, we define $g[s]$ to be exactly the set of subsets S of $states(B)$ such that S intersects each set in $f[s]$ in at least one element. Then g is a backward-forward simulation. ■

Example 4.5 In general it is not the case that $A \leq_{\mathrm{iFB}} B$ implies $A \leq_{\mathrm{iBF}} B$. A counterexample is presented in Figure 4. The diagram shows two automata I and J. In the diagram a label $> i$ next to an arc means that in fact there are infinitely many steps, labeled $i+1$, $i+2$, $i+3$, etc..

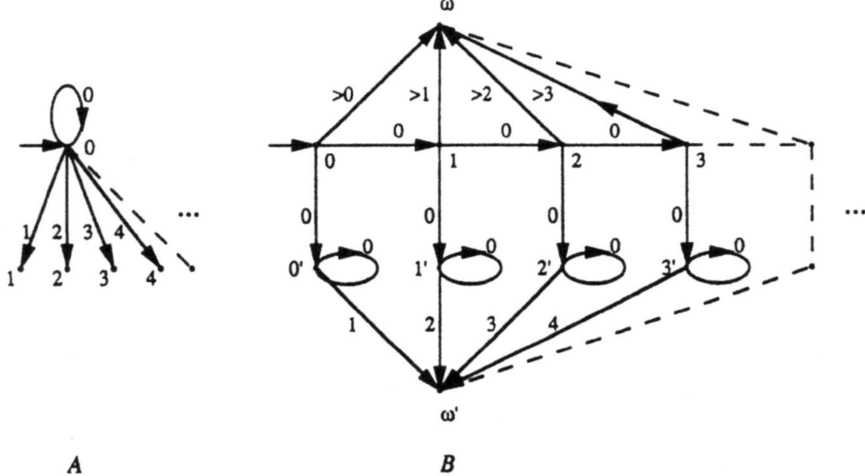

Figure 4: $I \leq_{\mathrm{iFB}} J$ but $I \not\leq_{\mathrm{iBF}} J$.

We claim that the relation g given by

$$\begin{aligned} g[0] &= \{\{0\}, \{0', 1\}, \{0', 1', 2\}, \ldots\} \\ g[n] &= \{\{\omega\}, \{\omega'\}\} \quad \text{for } n > 0 \end{aligned}$$

is an image-finite forward-backward simulation from I to J.

However, there is no image-finite backward-forward simulation from I to J. We see this as follows. Suppose g is an image-finite backward-forward simulation from I to J. In order to prove that this assumption leads to a contradiction, we first establish that $g[0]$ does not contain a finite subset X of N. First note that by the first condition in the definition of a backward-forward simulation, all sets in $g[0]$ are nonempty. The proof proceeds by induction on the maximal element of X. For the induction base, observe that $\{0\} \notin g[0]$, since 0 has an incoming 0-step in I but not in J. For the induction step, suppose that we have established that $g[0]$ contains no finite subset of N with a maximum less than n, and suppose $X \in g[0]$ with X a finite subset of N with maximum n. Using that 0 has an incoming 0-step in I, the second condition in the definition of a backward-forward simulation gives that $g[0]$ contains an element of $g[0]$ which is a subset of N with a maximum less than n. This contradicts the induction hypothesis.

Pick some state $n > 0$ of I and a set $S' \in g[n]$. Since $0 \xrightarrow{n}_I n$, there exists a set $S \in g[0]$ such that every state in S has an outgoing n-step. Then S must be a subset of $\{0, \ldots, n-1, (n-1)'\}$. Since $g[0]$ does not contain the empty set or a finite subset of N, it follows that $(n-1)' \in S$. But since n was chosen arbitrarily (besides being positive) it follows that $g[0]$ has an infinite number of elements. This gives a contradiction with the assumption that g is image-finite.

Proposition 4.28 *$\leq_{\mathrm{BF}}$ is a preorder.*

Proof: Trivially implied by Theorem 4.27 and Proposition 4.21. ■

However, the counterexample of Figure 4 tells us that $\leq_{\mathrm{iBF}}$ is not a preorder in general. If we take the two automata I and J from the example, then we can find an automaton C with $I \leq_{\mathrm{F}} C \leq_{\mathrm{iB}} J$, using Theorem 4.16. By Proposition 4.25, $I \leq_{\mathrm{iBF}} C$ and $C \leq_{\mathrm{iBF}} J$. Hence it cannot be that $\leq_{\mathrm{iBF}}$ is transitive, because this would imply $I \leq_{\mathrm{iBF}} J$.

Soundness and completeness results for backward-forward simulations now follow from those for forward-backward simulations.

Theorem 4.29 *(Soundness of backward-forward simulations)*

1. $A \leq_{\mathrm{BF}} B \Rightarrow A \leq_{*\mathrm{T}} B$.
2. $A \leq_{\mathrm{iBF}} B \Rightarrow A \leq_{\mathrm{T}} B$.

Proof: By Theorems 4.27 and 4.22. ■

Theorem 4.30 *(Completeness of backward-forward simulations)* $A \leq_{*\mathrm{T}} B \Rightarrow A \leq_{\mathrm{BF}} B$.

Proof: By Theorems 4.23 and 4.27. ■

Example 4.5 falsifies the completeness result that one might expect here. That is, Theorem 4.30 does not have a second case saying that if B has fin and $A \leq_{*\mathrm{T}} B$, then $A \leq_{\mathrm{iBF}} B$.

4.4 Auxiliary Variable Constructions

In this subsection, we present two new types of relations, history relations and prophecy relations, which correspond to the notions of history variable and prophecy variable of Abadi and Lamport [1]. We show that there exists a close connection between history relations and forward simulations, and also between prophecy relations and backward simulations. Using these connections together with the earlier results of this section, we can easily derive a completeness theorem for refinements similar to the one of Abadi and Lamport [1]. In fact, in the setting of this paper the combination of history and prophecy relations and refinements gives exactly the same verification power as the combination of forward and backward simulations.

4.4.1 History Relations

A relation h over $states(A)$ and $states(B)$ is a *history relation* from A to B if h is a forward simulation from A to B and h^{-1} is a refinement from B to A. We write $A \leq_H B$ if there exists a history relation from A to B.

We give an example of a history relation, using the construction of the "unfolding" of an automaton; the unfolding of an automaton augments the automaton by remembering information about the past.

Definition 4.2 The *unfolding* of an automaton A, notation $unfold(A)$, is the automaton B defined by

- $states(B) = execs^*(A)$,
- $start(B) =$ the set of finite executions of A that consist of a single start state,
- $acts(B) = acts(A)$, and
- for $\alpha', \alpha \in states(B)$ and $a \in acts(B)$, $\alpha' \xrightarrow{a}_B \alpha \quad \Leftrightarrow \quad \alpha = \alpha' \, a \, last(\alpha)$.

Proposition 4.31 *$unfold(A)$ is a forest and $A \leq_H unfold(A)$.*

Proof: Clearly, $unfold(A)$ is a forest. The function *last* which maps each finite execution of A to its last state is a refinement from $unfold(A)$ to A, and the relation $last^{-1}$ is a forward simulation from A to $unfold(A)$. ∎

Example 4.6 For C, D, E, F as in Example 4.1, $C \not\leq_H D$, $D \leq_H C$, $E \not\leq_H F$ and $F \not\leq_H E$.

Proposition 4.32 *$\leq_H$ is a preorder.*

Proof: Reflexivity is trivial. For transitivity, suppose h is a history relation from A to B and h' is a history relation from B to C. Then h is a forward simulation from A to B and h' is a forward simulation from B to C, so $h' \circ h$ is a forward simulation from A to C, by Proposition 4.7. Also, since h'^{-1} is a refinement from C to B and h^{-1} is a refinement from B to A, $(h' \circ h)^{-1} = h^{-1} \circ h'^{-1}$ is a refinement from C to A by Proposition 4.2. It now follows that $h' \circ h$ is a history relation from A to C. ∎

The notion of a history relation is a new contribution of this paper. It provides a simple and abstract view of the *history variables* of Abadi and Lamport [1]. Translated to the setting of this paper history variables can be simply defined in terms of history relations, as follows.

Definition 4.3 An automaton B is obtained from an automaton A by *adding a history variable* if there exists a set V such that

- $states(B) \subseteq states(A) \times V$, and
- the relation $\{(s,(s,v)) \mid (s,v) \in states(B)\}$ is a history relation from A to B.

Whenever B is obtained from A by adding a history variable, then $A \leq_{\mathrm{H}} B$ by definition. The following proposition states that the converse is also true if one is willing to consider automata up to isomorphism.

Proposition 4.33 *Suppose $A \leq_{\mathrm{H}} B$. Then there exists an automaton C that is isomorphic to B and obtained from A by adding a history variable.*

Proof: Let h be a history relation from A to B. Define automaton C by

- $states(C) = h$,
- $(s,u) \in start(C) \Leftrightarrow u \in start(B)$,
- $acts(C) = acts(B)$, and
- for $(s',u'),(s,u) \in states(C)$ and $a \in acts(C)$, $(s',u') \xrightarrow{a}_C (s,u) \Leftrightarrow u' \xrightarrow{a}_B u$.

Clearly, the projection function π_2 that maps a state (s,u) of C to the state u of B is an isomorphism between C and B.

In order to show that C is obtained from A by adding a history variable, let $states(B)$ play the role of the set V required in the definition of a history variable. It is easy to check that relation $\{(s,(s,v)) \mid (s,v) \in states(C)\}$ is a history relation from A to C. ∎

Proposition 4.33 shows that history relations already capture the essence of history variables. For this reason and also because history relations have nicer theoretical properties, we will state all our results in this subsection in terms of relations, and will not mention the auxiliary variables any further.

Theorem 4.34 *(Soundness of history relations)* $A \leq_{\mathrm{H}} B \Rightarrow A \equiv_{\mathrm{T}} B$.

Proof: Immediate from the soundness of refinements and forward simulations. ∎

In fact, a history relation from A to B is just a functional *bisimulation* between A and B in the sense of Park [28] and Milner [23]. This implies that if there exists a history relation from A to B, both automata are *bisimulation equivalent*. Hence, history relations preserve the behavior of automata in a very strong sense.

Definition 4.4 Suppose k is a relation over $states(A)$ and $states(B)$ satisfying $k \cap (start(A) \times start(B)) \neq \emptyset$. (Typically, k will be a forward or a backward simulation.) The *superposition* $sup(A,B,k)$ of B onto A via k is the automaton C given by

- $states(C) = k$,
- $start(C) = k \cap (start(A) \times start(B))$,
- $acts(C) = acts(A) \cap acts(B)$, and

- for $(s', v'), (s, v) \in states(C)$ and $a \in acts(C)$,

$$(s', v') \xrightarrow{a}_C (s, v) \quad \Leftrightarrow \quad s' \overset{\hat{a}}{\Longrightarrow}_A s \wedge v' \overset{\hat{a}}{\Longrightarrow}_B v.$$

Lemma 4.35 *Suppose f is a forward simulation from A to B. Let $C = sup(A, B, f)$ and let π_1 and π_2 be the projection functions that map states of C to their first and second components, respectively. Then π_1^{-1} is a history relation from A to C and π_2 is a refinement from C to B.*

Theorem 4.36 $A \leq_F B \Leftrightarrow (\exists C : A \leq_H C \leq_R B)$.

Proof: For the implication "$\Rightarrow$", suppose $A \leq_F B$. Let f be a forward simulation from A to B. Take $C = sup(A, B, f)$. The result follows by Lemma 4.35. For the implication "$\Leftarrow$", suppose that $A \leq_H C \leq_R B$. Then $A \leq_F C$ by the definition of history relations, and $C \leq_F B$ because any refinement is a forward simulation. Now $A \leq_F B$ follows by the fact that $\leq_F$ is a preorder. ■

4.4.2 Prophecy Relations

Now we will present prophecy relations and show that they correspond to backward simulations, very similarly to the way in which history relations correspond to forward simulations.

A relation p over $states(A)$ and $states(B)$ is a *prophecy relation* from A to B if p is a backward simulation from A to B and p^{-1} is a refinement from B to A. We write $A \leq_P B$ if there exists a prophecy relation from A to B, and $A \leq_{iP} B$ if there is an image-finite prophecy relation from A to B. We give an example of a prophecy relation, using the construction of the "guess" of an automaton. This construction is a kind of dual to the unfolding construction of the previous subsection in that the states contain information about the future rather than about the past.

Definition 4.5 The *guess* of an automaton A, notation $guess(A)$, is the automaton B defined by

- $states(B) = frag^*(A)$,
- $start(B) = execs^*(A)$,
- $acts(B) = acts(A)$, and
- for $\alpha', \alpha \in states(B)$ and $a \in acts(B)$, $\alpha' \xrightarrow{a}_B \alpha \;\Leftrightarrow\; first(\alpha')\, a\, \alpha = \alpha'$.

Proposition 4.37 $A \leq_P guess(A)$.

Proof: The function $first$ which maps each execution fragment of A to its first state is a refinement from $guess(A)$ to A, and the relation $first^{-1}$ is a backward simulation from A to $guess(A)$. ■

Example 4.7 For the automata of Figure 2 we have $C \not\leq_P D$, $D \not\leq_P C$, $E \not\leq_P F$ and $F \leq_{iP} E$. The difference between $\leq_P$ and $\leq_{iP}$ is illustrated by the automata of Figure 3: $G \leq_P H$ but $G \not\leq_{iP} H$.

Proposition 4.38 *$\leq_P$ and $\leq_{iP}$ are preorders.*

Just as history relations capture the essence of history variables, prophecy relations capture the essence of prophecy variables:

Definition 4.6 An automaton B is obtained from an automaton A by *adding a prophecy variable* if there exists a set V such that

- $states(B) \subseteq states(A) \times V$, and
- the relation $\{(s,(s,v)) \mid (s,v) \in states(B)\}$ is a prophecy relation from A to B.

A prophecy variable is *bounded* if the underlying prophecy relation is image-finite.

Proposition 4.39 *Suppose $A \leq_P B$. Then there exists an automaton C that is isomorphic to B and obtained from A by adding a prophecy variable, which is bounded if $A \leq_{iP} B$.*

Again, we will state all further results in this subsection in terms of relations, and not mention the auxiliary variables any further.

Theorem 4.40 *(Soundness of prophecy relations)*

1. *$A \leq_P B \Rightarrow A \equiv_{*T} B$, and*
2. *$A \leq_{iP} B \Rightarrow A \equiv_T B$.*

Proof: Immediate from the soundness of refinements and backward simulations. ■

Lemma 4.41 *Suppose b is a backward simulation from A to B. Let $C = sup(A,B,b)$ and let π_1 and π_2 be the projection functions that map states of C to their first and second components, respectively. Then π_1^{-1} is a prophecy relation from A to C and π_2 is a refinement from C to B. If b is image-finite then so is π_1^{-1}.*

Theorem 4.42

1. *$A \leq_B B \Leftrightarrow (\exists C : A \leq_P C \leq_R B)$,*
2. *$A \leq_{iB} B \Leftrightarrow (\exists C : A \leq_{iP} C \leq_R B)$.*

Proof: The proof of 1 is analogous to that of Theorem 4.36, using Lemma 4.41. 2 can be proved similarly. ■

We finish this section with versions of the completeness results of [1].

Theorem 4.43 *(Completeness of history relations, prophecy relations and refinements, [1]) Suppose $A \leq_{*T} B$. Then*

1. *$\exists C, D : A \leq_H C \leq_P D \leq_R B$, and*
2. *if B has fin then $\exists C, D : A \leq_H C \leq_{iP} D \leq_R B$.*

Proof: By Theorem 4.16, there exists an automaton E with $A \leq_{F} E \leq_{B} B$. Hence, by Theorem 4.36, there is an automaton C with $A \leq_{H} C \leq_{R} E$. Combining $C \leq_{R} E$ and $E \leq_{B} B$ yields $C \leq_{B} B$. Theorem 4.42 yields an automaton D with $C \leq_{P} D \leq_{R} B$, which proves 1. Now statement 2 is routine. ■

Similarly, we obtain:

Theorem 4.44 $A \leq_{*T} B \Rightarrow \exists C, D : A \leq_{P} C \leq_{H} D \leq_{R} B$.

4.5 Classification of Basic Relations Between Automata

We can summarize the basic implications between the various simulation techniques of this section as follows. Suppose $X, Y \in \{$T, *T, R, F, iB, B, iFB, FB, iBF, BF, H, iP, P$\}$. Then $A \leq_{X} B \Rightarrow A \leq_{Y} B$ for all automata A and B if and only if there is a path from $\leq_{X}$ to $\leq_{Y}$ in Figure 5 consisting of thin lines only. If B has fin, then $A \leq_{X} B \Rightarrow A \leq_{Y} B$ for all automata A and B if and only if there is a path from $\leq_{X}$ to $\leq_{Y}$ consisting of thin lines and thick lines.

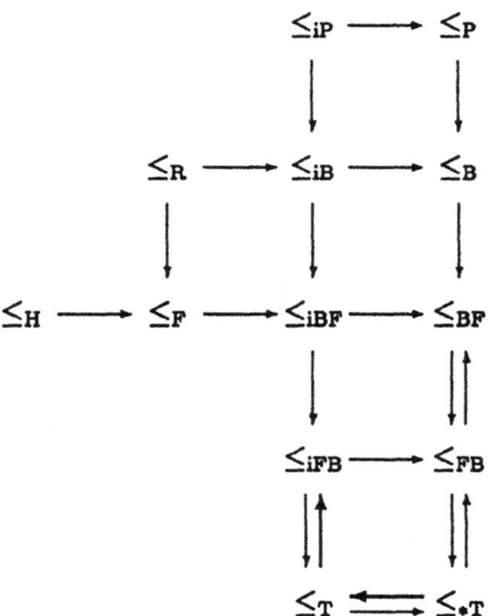

Figure 5: Classification of basic relations between automata.

5 Timed Automata and Their Behaviors

This section presents the basic definitions and results for timed automata. The development is generally parallel to that in Section 3.

5.1 Timed Automata

A *timed automaton* A is an automaton whose set of actions is a superset of $\{\tau\} \cup \mathsf{R}^{\geq 0}$, and whose step relation satisfies a number of axioms that will be presented below. The actions in $\mathsf{R}^{\geq 0}$ are referred to as the *time-passage* actions. (Each action $t \in \mathsf{R}^{\geq 0}$ represents the passage of time exactly up to real time t.) The set of *visible* actions is defined by $vis(A) \triangleq acts(A) - (\{\tau\} \cup \mathsf{R}^{\geq 0})$.

The first axiom a timed automaton A has to satisfy is:

T1 For each state s there is a unique $t \in \mathsf{R}^{\geq 0}$ such that $s \xrightarrow{t} s$.

We call the steps introduced by axiom **T1** *idling* steps. The intended meaning of an idling step $s \xrightarrow{t} s$ is that the current time in state s is t. In this case we write $s.time_A = t$, or $s.time = t$ if A is clear from the context. Instead of the idling steps, we could have included the mapping $.time_A$ as a basic component of a timed automaton. Formally this would have been equivalent, but we prefer the present formulation for technical reasons.

We assume further that a timed automaton A satisfies the following restrictions on individual steps.

S1 If $s \in start(A)$ then $s.time = 0$.

S2 If $s' \xrightarrow{a} s$ and $a \notin \mathsf{R}^{\geq 0}$, then $s'.time = s.time$.

S3 If $s' \xrightarrow{a} s$ and $a \in \mathsf{R}^{\geq 0}$, then $s'.time \leq a = s.time$.

S4 If $s' \xrightarrow{a} s$ and $a = s'.time$, then $s' = s$.

Axiom **S1** says that the time is always 0 in a start state. Axiom **S2** says that non-time-passage actions do not change the time; that is, they occur "instantaneously", at a single point in time. Axiom **S3** says that time-passage actions may not cause the time to decrease; the label of the transition refers to the time in the final state. Axiom **S4** implies that the only time-passage steps that does not cause the time to increase are the idling steps.

We also require that A include a sufficiently rich collection of time-passage steps:

T2 If $s' \xrightarrow{t} s''$ and $s'' \xrightarrow{t'} s$, then $s' \xrightarrow{t'} s$.

T3 If $s' \xrightarrow{t} s$ and $s'.time < t' < t$, then there is an s'' with $s''.time = t'$ such that $s' \xrightarrow{t'} s''$ and $s'' \xrightarrow{t} s$.

Axiom **T2** allows repeated time-passage steps to be combined into one step, and axiom **T3** says that if time can pass to some time t, it can also pass to t in two steps, via any intermediate time t'.

In the rest of this paper, $A, B, \ldots$ will range over *timed* automata.

Suppose α is an execution fragment of A. Then $\alpha.ftime$ denotes the time component of the first state in α, and $\alpha.ltime$ denotes the smallest element of $\mathsf{R}^{\geq 0} \cup \{\infty\}$ larger or equal than (i.e., the supremum of) the time components of all states in α. In particular, if α is an execution, then $\alpha.ftime = 0$, and if α is a finite execution fragment, then $\alpha.ltime = last(\alpha).time$.

5.2 Admissible Executions and Feasibility

Timed automata do not include any features for describing liveness or fairness (such as the class structure of I/O automata). We believe that such features are not so important in the timed setting as they are in the untimed setting. In fact, we think that by simply requiring that time grow unboundedly in infinite executions, we will be able to handle the liveness properties that arise in practice. Thus, in our study of timed automata, we concentrate on the *admissible* executions and execution fragments, i.e., those in which the time components of the states increase without bound. So α is an admissible execution fragment iff $\alpha.ltime = \infty$.

The notion of an admissible execution is more tractable mathematically than the notion of a fair execution in the I/O automaton model; this is because the admissible executions of a timed automaton are exactly the limits of the infinite sequences of finite executions, where each execution in the sequence is a prefix of the next and the time components of the states go to ∞. This characterization permits the reduction of questions about infinite behaviors to questions about finite behaviors. A similar reduction is not possible in untimed models that incorporate fairness.

The idea behind the notion of admissible executions is that time is an independent force, beyond the control of any automaton, which happens to grow unboundedly. We note that, according to our definitions, there are timed automata in which from some (or even all) states no admissible execution fragment is possible. This can either be because from these states onwards time cannot advance at all (that is, a *time deadlock* occurs), or because time can continue advancing, but not beyond a certain point (that is, all executions are so-called *Zeno executions*). The possibility of time deadlocks occurs in several process algebraic models ([2, 7, 24]) but we have no intuition whatsoever about what it means to "stop time". Zeno executions arise due to the inability of automaton models to deal with an infinite amount of activity within a bounded period of time. Some models of real-time computation, for instance the model of real-time CSP [29], exclude Zeno executions altogether. As a result of our attempt to make our results as general as possible, our model does allow for both time deadlocks and Zeno executions. However, in several of our theorems we will require that the automata be *feasible*. A timed automaton A is *feasible* provided that each finite execution is a prefix of some admissible execution. Thus, a feasible timed automaton does not have time deadlocks, but may have Zeno executions.

5.3 Timed Traces

The traces of timed automata do not provide a sufficiently abstract view of their behavior, because they do not reflect the invisible nature of time-passage actions. We illustrate this via the following key example.

Example 5.1 Consider two timed automata, *Idle* and *Idle'*. Automaton *Idle* does nothing except that it lets time pass. Its state set is just $\mathsf{R}^{\geq 0}$, the start state is 0, the set of actions is $\{\tau\} \cup \mathsf{R}^{\geq 0}$, and there is a transition $t' \xrightarrow{t} t$ whenever $t' \leq t$. Automaton *Idle'* is also rather boring: it idles all the time except that it does a τ-step at time 37. In fact, we like to argue that from an observational point of view *Idle'* is just as boring as *Idle* since both automata do not engage in any interaction with their environment at all.

Formally, timed automaton $Idle'$ is defined as follows:

- $states(Idle') = \mathsf{R}^{\geq 0} \times \{\mathsf{T}, \mathsf{F}\}$,
- $start(Idle') = \{(0, \mathsf{T})\}$,
- $acts(Idle') = \{\tau\} \cup \mathsf{R}^{\geq 0}$, and
- $steps(Idle')$ is specified by:

$$(t', b) \xrightarrow{t} (t, b) \qquad \text{if } t' = t \vee (t' < t \wedge (b = \mathsf{T} \Rightarrow t \leq 37))$$

$$(37, \mathsf{T}) \xrightarrow{\tau} (37, \mathsf{F})$$

Although $Idle' \leq_{\mathrm{T}} Idle$, it is not the case that $Idle \leq_{\mathrm{T}} Idle'$. This is because $Idle$ has a trace consisting of 38 only, which $Idle'$ does not have. (Note that $Idle'$ *does* have a trace 37 38.) So if we would use $\leq_{\mathrm{T}}$ as an implementation relation it would not be allowed to implement a specification that only requires an internal (unobservable) step at time 37 by a device that does nothing at all. It is for this reason that we consider $\leq_{\mathrm{T}}$ not to be a good implementation relation.

In this subsection, we define an alternative notion of external behavior for timed automata that does not include explicit individual time-passage actions. We describe the external behavior of timed automata in terms of observations that we call *timed traces*; these contain information about the visible actions that occur, together with their time of occurrence, and also about the final time up to which the observation is made. Along the way to the definition of a *timed trace*, it is helpful to define the basic notion of a *timed sequence pair*.

5.3.1 Timed Sequence Pairs

A *timed sequence* over a given set K is defined to be a (finite or infinite) sequence δ over $K \times \mathsf{R}^{\geq 0}$ in which the time components are nondecreasing, i.e., $t \leq t'$ if (k, t) and (k', t') are consecutive elements in δ. We say that δ is *Zeno* if it is infinite and the limit of the time components is finite.

A *timed sequence pair* over K is a pair $p = (\delta, t)$, where δ is a timed sequence over K and $t \in \mathsf{R}^{\geq 0} \cup \{\infty\}$, such that $t \geq t'$ for all elements (k, t') in δ. We write $p.seq$, and $p.ltime$ for the two respective components of p. We define $p.ftime$ to be equal to the time component of the first pair in $p.seq$ in case $p.seq$ is nonempty, and equal to $p.ltime$ otherwise. We denote by $tsp(K)$ the set of timed sequence pairs over K. We say that a timed sequence pair p is *finite* if both $p.seq$ and $p.ltime$ are finite, and *admissible* if $p.seq$ is not Zeno and $p.ltime = \infty$.

Let p and p' be timed sequence pairs over K such that p is finite and $p.ltime \leq p'.ftime$. Then define $p; p'$ to be the timed sequence pair $(p.seq\ p'.seq, p'.ltime)$. If p and q are timed sequence pairs over a set K, then p is a *prefix* of q, notation $p \leq q$, if either $p = q$, or p is finite and there exists a timed sequence pair p'

Lemma 5.1 *$\leq$ is a partial ordering on timed sequence pairs over K.*

5.3.2 Timed Traces of Timed Automata

Suppose $\alpha = s_0 a_1 s_1 a_2 s_2 \cdots$ is an execution fragment of a timed automaton A. Let γ be the sequence consisting of the actions in α paired with the time of their occurrence:

$$\gamma = (a_1, s_1.time)(a_2, s_2.time)\cdots.$$

Then *t-trace*(α) is defined to be the pair

$$t\text{-}trace(\alpha) \triangleq (\gamma\lceil(vis(A) \times \mathsf{R}^{\geq 0}), \alpha.ltime).$$

So *t-trace*(α) records the occurrences of external actions together with their time of occurrence, and the limit time of the execution fragment. We call *t-trace*(α) the *timed trace of* α. Thus, the timed trace of an execution fragment suppresses both τ and time-passage actions. It is easily checked that *t-trace*(α) is a timed sequence pair over $vis(A)$.

A *timed trace* of A is the timed trace of some finite or admissible execution of A. We write *t-traces*(A) for the set of all timed traces of A, *t-traces*$^*(A)$ for the set of *finite* timed traces, i.e., those that originate from a finite execution of A, and *t-traces*$^\infty(A)$ for the *admissible* timed traces, i.e., those that originate from an admissible execution of A. The following proposition is a direct consequence of the definitions.

Proposition 5.2 *The sets t-traces*$^*(A)$ *and t-traces*$^\infty(A)$ *consist of finite timed sequence pairs and admissible timed sequence pairs over* $vis(A)$*, respectively.*

These notions induce three preorders on timed automata in an obvious way: $A \leq^t_T B \triangleq t\text{-}traces(A) \subseteq t\text{-}traces(B)$, $A \leq^t_{*T} B \triangleq t\text{-}traces^*(A) \subseteq t\text{-}traces^*(B)$, and $A \leq^t_{\infty T} B \triangleq t\text{-}traces^\infty(A) \subseteq t\text{-}traces^\infty(B)$. The kernels of these preorders are denoted by $\equiv^t_T$, $\equiv^t_{*T}$ and $\equiv^t_{\infty T}$, respectively.

Suppose A is a timed automaton, s' and s are states of A, and p is a timed sequence pair over $vis(A)$. Then we say that (s', p, s) is a *t-move* of A, and write $s' \overset{p}{\leadsto}_A s$, or just $s' \overset{p}{\leadsto} s$ when A is clear, if A has a finite execution fragment α with $first(\alpha) = s'$, *t-trace*$(\alpha) = p$ and $last(\alpha) = s$.

Lemma 5.3 *Suppose* $s' \overset{p}{\leadsto}_A s$ *and* $p = q; r$*. Then there exists* s'' *such that* $s' \overset{q}{\leadsto}_A s''$ *and* $s'' \overset{r}{\leadsto}_A s$.

5.3.3 From Traces to Timed Traces

A trace preserves more information about an execution than a timed trace. Below we show how the timed trace of an execution fragment can be reconstructed from its starting time and its trace. This reconstruction will allow us to relate the untimed and the timed trace preorders.

Let K be some set with $\mathsf{R}^{\geq 0} \subseteq K$, and let $\beta = a_1 a_2 a_3 \cdots$ be a sequence over K. We say β is *monotonic* if the time-passage events contained in it increase monotonically, i.e., for all $i < j$, $a_i, a_j \in \mathsf{R}^{\geq 0} \Rightarrow a_i \leq a_j$. Clearly, each trace of a timed automaton A is a monotonic sequence over $ext(A)$.

Let $\beta = a_1 a_2 a_3 \cdots$ be monotonic sequence over K, and let $t \in \mathsf{R}^{\geq 0}$ be less than or equal to all time-passage events in β. We define a timed sequence pair *t-pair*(t, β) in two steps. First, define for $i \in \mathsf{N}$, $t_i \in \mathsf{R}^{\geq 0}$ inductively by: $t_0 \triangleq t$ and if $a_i \in \mathsf{R}^{\geq 0}$ then $t_{i+1} \triangleq a_i$

else $t_{i+1} \triangleq t_i$. Let γ be the sequence $(a_1,t_1)(a_2,t_2)(a_3,t_3)\cdots$, and let t' be the supremum, in $\mathsf{R}^{\geq 0} \cup \{\infty\}$, of all the t_i's. Then

$$\textit{t-pair}(t,\beta) \triangleq (\gamma\lceil((K - \mathsf{R}^{\geq 0}) \times \mathsf{R}^{\geq 0}), t').$$

We write $\textit{t-pair}(\beta)$ for $\textit{t-pair}(0,\beta)$. The following lemma relates the usual notion of trace to the new notion of timed trace.

Lemma 5.4 *Suppose* $\alpha \in \textit{frag}(A)$. *Then* $\textit{t-trace}(\alpha) = \textit{t-pair}(\alpha.\textit{ftime}, \textit{trace}(\alpha))$.

Corollary 5.5 *Suppose* $\beta \in \textit{traces}^*(A)$. *Then* $\textit{t-pair}(\beta) \in \textit{t-traces}^*(A)$.

Lemma 5.6

1. $A \leq_{*\mathrm{T}} B \Rightarrow A \leq^{\mathrm{t}}_{*\mathrm{T}} B$.
2. $A \leq_{\omega\mathrm{T}} B \Rightarrow A \leq^{\mathrm{t}}_{\infty\mathrm{T}} B$.
3. $A \leq_{\mathrm{T}} B \Rightarrow A \leq^{\mathrm{t}}_{\mathrm{T}} B$.

Proof: For 1, suppose that $A \leq_{*\mathrm{T}} B$ and $p \in \textit{t-traces}^*(A)$. Then A has a finite execution α with $p = \textit{t-trace}(\alpha)$. Let $\beta = \textit{trace}(\alpha)$. Then $\beta \in \textit{traces}^*(A)$ and, using $A \leq_{*\mathrm{T}} B$, also $\beta \in \textit{traces}^*(B)$. By Corollary 5.5, $\textit{t-pair}(\beta) \in \textit{t-traces}^*(B)$. But Lemma 5.4 yields $\textit{t-pair}(\beta) = p$. Thus $p \in \textit{t-traces}^*(B)$, and $A \leq^{\mathrm{t}}_{*\mathrm{T}} B$ follows as required.

For 2, suppose that $A \leq_{\omega\mathrm{T}} B$ and $p \in \textit{t-traces}^\infty(A)$. Then there is an admissible execution α of A such that $p = \textit{t-trace}(\alpha)$. Let $\beta = \textit{trace}(\alpha)$. Since $\beta \in \textit{traces}^\omega(A)$ and $A \leq_{\omega\mathrm{T}} B$, also $\beta \in \textit{traces}^\omega(B)$. Thus B has an infinite execution α' with $\textit{trace}(\alpha') = \beta$. Since α is admissible the time-passage actions contained in β grow unboundedly. But since $\textit{trace}(\alpha') = \beta$, this means α' is also admissible. Using Lemma 5.4 we derive:

$$\textit{t-trace}(\alpha) = \textit{t-pair}(\textit{trace}(\alpha)) = \textit{t-pair}(\beta) = \textit{t-pair}(\textit{trace}(\alpha')) = \textit{t-trace}(\alpha').$$

Thus $p = \textit{t-trace}(\alpha') \in \textit{t-traces}^\infty(B)$. It follows that $A \leq^{\mathrm{t}}_{\infty\mathrm{T}} B$.

Finally, 3 follows from the first two parts. ∎

The automata *Idle* and *Idle′* of Example 5.1 illustrate that the reverse implications of the statements in the above lemma are not valid.

5.4 Restricted Kinds of Timed Automata

A has *t-finite invisible nondeterminism (t-fin)* if $\textit{start}(A)$ is finite, and for any state s' and any finite timed sequence pair p over $\textit{vis}(A)$, there are only finitely many states s such that $s' \overset{p}{\rightsquigarrow}_A s$.

Example 5.2 In order to illustrate the difference between fin and t-fin we define a timed automaton *Idle″*. Basically, automaton *Idle″* does nothing except that it lets time pass. However, at one nondeterministically chosen time $t > 0$, *Idle″* makes a τ-step, and then it subsequently remembers t. Formally, *Idle″* is defined as follows:

- $\textit{states}(\textit{Idle}'') = \mathsf{R}^{\geq 0} \times \mathsf{R}^{\geq 0}$,

- $start(Idle'') = \{(0,0)\}$,
- $acts(Idle'') = \{\tau\} \cup \mathsf{R}^{\geq 0}$, and
- $steps(Idle'')$ is specified by:

$$(t'',t) \xrightarrow{t'} (t',t) \quad \text{if } t'' \leq t',$$

$$(t,0) \xrightarrow{\tau} (t,t) \quad \text{if } t > 0.$$

By induction on the length of the sequence of time-passage actions one can easily establish that $Idle''$ has fin. However, $Idle''$ does not have t-fin since for any $t \in \mathsf{R}^{+}$ all the states from the uncountable set $\{(t,t')|0 < t' \leq t\}$ can be reached with timed sequence pair (λ, t) from the initial state.

The requirement that a timed automaton be a forest is not a very interesting one because if a state has one incoming time-passage step from a state with a smaller time component, then it must have an infinite number of them (as a consequence of axiom **T3**) so that the timed automaton cannot be a forest. Now a forest is characterized by the property that for each state there is a unique execution that leads to it. In analogy we will define below the notion of a t-forest. This is a timed automaton with the property that for each state there is an execution that leads to it, which is unique "modulo" axioms **T1**, **T2** and **T3**.

Call a finite execution fragment of A *fat* if it contains no idling steps and no pair of consecutive time-passage steps. Then A is defined to be a *t-forest* if for each state of A there is a unique fat execution that leads to it. The following lemma gives a sufficient condition for a timed automaton to be a t-forest.

Lemma 5.7 *Suppose that all states of A are reachable, the only incoming steps of start states are idling steps, and for every state s, if there are two distinct non-idling steps leading to s, $r \xrightarrow{a} s$ and $r' \xrightarrow{a'} s$, then $a = a' \in \mathsf{R}^{\geq 0}$ and either $r \xrightarrow{t'} r'$ or $r' \xrightarrow{t} r$, where $t = r.time$ and $t' = r'.time$. Then A is a t-forest.*

Proof: Suppose A satisfies the conditions of the lemma. Because all states of A are reachable we know that for each state s there is at least one execution that leads to it. Since we can remove idling steps from an execution, and since by repeated application of axiom **T2** we can contract successive time-passage steps, there is at least one fat execution that leads to s. In order to show uniqueness, suppose that A has two fat executions, α and α' that lead to s. By induction on the sum of the lengths of α and α', using the fact that A is a t-forest, we prove that $\alpha = \alpha'$.

If α consists of state s only, then so does α', and vice versa. We see this as follows. If α consists of s only, then s is a start state. Because A is a t-forest, there are no incoming non-idling steps to s. But since α' contains no idling steps and ends with s, α' must also consist of s only. So if either α or α' contains no steps, then $\alpha = \alpha'$.

Now suppose that $\alpha = \gamma a s$ and $\alpha' = \gamma' a' s$. Let $last(\gamma) = r$, $last(\gamma') = r'$, $r.time = t$ and $r'.time = t'$. If $r = r'$, then $\gamma = \gamma'$ by induction hypothesis, $a = a'$ since A is a t-forest, and hence $\alpha = \alpha'$. So assume that $r \neq r'$. We derive a contradiction. In this case

$r \xrightarrow{a} s$ and $r' \xrightarrow{a'} s$ are two distinct steps ending with s, so since A is a t-forest, it must be that a and a' are both time-passage actions and either $r \xrightarrow{t'} r'$ or $r' \xrightarrow{t} r$. Without loss of generality, we may assume that the former holds.

Now consider the execution $\gamma'' = \gamma t' r'$. Since α is fat, γ'' must be fat too. Thus γ'' and γ' are two fat executions leading to r', and by induction hypothesis we obtain $\gamma'' = \gamma'$. But since γ'' ends with a time-passage step, this means that α' ends with two time-passage steps, which is in contradiction with the fact that this execution is fat.

Thus we have shown that for each state of A there is a unique fat execution that leads to it, which means that A is a t-forest. ■

Suppose A is a timed automaton. In analogy with the untimed case, the relation $\textit{t-after}(A)$ consists of those pairs $(p, s) \in \textit{tsp}(\textit{vis}(A)) \times \textit{states}(A)$ for which there is a finite execution of A with timed trace p and last state s.

$$\textit{t-after}(A) \triangleq \{(p, s) \mid \exists \alpha \in \textit{execs}^*(A) : \textit{t-trace}(\alpha) = p \text{ and } \textit{last}(\alpha) = s\}.$$

The relation $\textit{t-past}(A) \triangleq \textit{t-after}(A)^{-1}$ relates a state s of A to the timed traces of executions that lead to s. Also, define $\textit{t-before}(A)$ to be the relation that relates a timed sequence pair p to those states of A from where an execution with timed trace p is possible.

$$\textit{t-before}(A) \triangleq \{(p, s) \mid \exists \alpha \in \textit{frag}^*(A) : \textit{t-trace}(\alpha) = p \text{ and } \textit{first}(\alpha) = s\}.$$

We write $\textit{t-future}(A)$ for $\textit{t-before}(A)^{-1}$.

Lemma 5.8

1. *If A is deterministic then $\textit{t-after}(A)$ is a function from $\textit{t-traces}^*(A)$ to $\textit{states}(A)$.*

2. *If A has t-fin then $\textit{t-after}(A)$ is image-finite.*

3. *If A is a t-forest then $\textit{t-past}(A)$ is a function from $\textit{states}(A)$ to $\textit{t-traces}^*(A)$.*

Proof: For 1, suppose A is deterministic. By definition, $\textit{t-after}(A)[p]$ contains at least one element for each $p \in \textit{t-traces}^*(A)$. Suppose that for some $p \in \textit{t-traces}^*(A)$, both s and s' are in $\textit{t-after}(A)[p]$. Then A has finite executions α and α' with $\textit{t-trace}(\alpha) = \textit{t-trace}(\alpha') = p$, $\textit{last}(\alpha) = s$ and $\textit{last}(\alpha') = s'$. Without loss of generality we may assume that both α and α' contain no idling steps. Since α and α' have the same timed trace, $s.\textit{time} = s'.\textit{time}$. Since A is deterministic, there are no τ events in either execution.

By induction on the sum of the lengths of α and α' we prove that $s = s'$. If α consists of state s only, then s is the unique start state of A and therefore also the first state of α'. As noted above, α' does not contain τ events. Moreover, α' does not contain any events in $\textit{ext}(A)$ because that would violate the condition that $\textit{t-trace}(\alpha) = \textit{t-trace}(\alpha')$. Thus α' contains no events at all and consists of state s only. But this implies $s = s'$, as required. By a symmetric argument it also follows that $s = s'$ if we start from the assumption that α' consists of s' only.

Now suppose $\alpha = \gamma a s$ and $\alpha' = \gamma' a' s'$, with $\textit{last}(\gamma) = r$ and $\textit{last}(\gamma') = r'$. Let $t = r.\textit{time}$ and $t' = r'.\textit{time}$. Since a and a' are either time-passage actions or visible actions, and α and α' have the same timed trace and end at the same time, it cannot be that one of a and a' is an external action and the other is a time-passage action. In fact, it must be the case that $a = a'$. If $t = t'$, then $\textit{t-trace}(\gamma) = \textit{t-trace}(\gamma')$. This means we can apply the induction hypothesis to obtain $r = r'$. Then in combination with the fact that A is deterministic, this gives $s = s'$. Otherwise, we can assume without loss of generality that $t < t'$. (The other case is symmetric.) In this case, it must be that a and a' are both time-passage actions, and so $t' < s.\textit{time}$. By axiom **T2**, there is an r'' such that $r \xrightarrow{t'} r''$ and $r'' \xrightarrow{s.\textit{time}} s$. Since $\textit{t-trace}(\gamma t' r'') = \textit{t-trace}(\gamma')$, we can apply the induction hypothesis to obtain $r'' = r'$. Now $s = s'$ follows by the fact that A is deterministic.

Parts 2 is immediate from the definitions.

For 3, suppose that A is a t-forest. Because all states of A are reachable we know that for each state s of A, $\textit{t-past}(A)[s]$ contains at least one element. Suppose that both p and p' are in $\textit{t-past}(A)[s]$ for some $s \in \textit{states}(A)$. Then there are finite executions α and α' of A with $\textit{t-trace}(\alpha) = p$, $\textit{t-trace}(\alpha') = p'$ and $\textit{last}(\alpha) = \textit{last}(\alpha') = s$. Without loss of generality we can assume that both α and α' are fat, since we can always remove idling steps, and by repeatedly applying axiom **T1** we can eliminate successive time-passage steps, and this does not influence the timed traces of the executions. But now the assumption that A is a t-forest gives $\alpha = \alpha'$. This immediately implies $p = p'$. ■

5.5 Timed Trace Properties

For each timed automaton A, its *timed behavior*, $\textit{t-beh}(A)$, is defined by $\textit{t-beh}(A) \triangleq (\textit{vis}(A), \textit{t-traces}(A))$. Completely analogous to the way in which we characterized, in Section 3.3, the behaviors of automata in terms of trace properties, we will now characterize the timed behaviors of timed automata in terms of *timed trace properties*.

A set of timed sequence pairs is *prefix closed* if, whenever a timed sequence pair is in the set all its prefixes are also. A *timed trace property* P is a pair (K, L) where K is a set and L is a nonempty, prefix closed set of finite and admissible timed sequence pairs over K. We will refer to the constituents of P as $\textit{sort}(P)$ and $\textit{t-traces}(P)$, respectively. Also, we write $\textit{t-traces}^*(P)$ for the set of finite timed sequence pairs in $\textit{t-traces}(P)$, and $\textit{t-traces}^\infty(P)$ for the set of admissible timed sequence pairs in $\textit{t-traces}(P)$. For P and Q timed trace properties, we define $P \leq^{t}_{*T} Q \triangleq \textit{t-traces}^*(P) \subseteq \textit{t-traces}^*(Q)$, $P \leq^{t}_{\infty T} Q \triangleq \textit{t-traces}^\infty(P) \subseteq \textit{t-traces}^\infty(Q)$, and $P \leq^{t}_{T} Q \triangleq \textit{t-traces}(P) \subseteq \textit{t-traces}(Q)$. The kernels of these preorders are denoted by $\equiv^{t}_{*T}$, $\equiv^{t}_{\infty T}$ and $\equiv^{t}_{T}$, respectively.
P is *limit-closed* if each infinite chain $p_1 \leq p_2 \leq p_3 \leq \cdots$ of elements of $\textit{t-traces}^*(P)$ in which time grows unboundedly has a limit in $\textit{t-traces}^\infty(P)$, i.e., an admissible timed sequence pair p with for all i, $p_i \leq p$.

Lemma 5.9 *Suppose P and Q are timed trace properties with Q limit-closed. Then $P \leq^{t}_{*T} Q \Leftrightarrow P \leq^{t}_{T} Q$.*

A timed trace property P is *feasible* if every element of $\textit{t-traces}^*(P)$ is a prefix of some element of $\textit{t-traces}^\infty(P)$.

Lemma 5.10 *Suppose P and Q are timed trace properties such that P is feasible. Then $P \leq^{t}_{\infty T} Q \Leftrightarrow P \leq^{t}_{T} Q$.*

Lemma 5.11

1. *$\textit{t-beh}(A)$ is a timed trace property.*

2. *If A has t-fin then t-beh(A) is limit-closed.*

3. *If A is feasible then t-beh(A) is feasible.*

4. $A \leq_{\mathrm{T}}^{\mathrm{t}} B \Leftrightarrow$ *t-beh*$(A) \leq_{\mathrm{T}}^{\mathrm{t}}$ *t-beh*(B), $A \leq_{*\mathrm{T}}^{\mathrm{t}} B \Leftrightarrow$ *t-beh*$(A) \leq_{*\mathrm{T}}^{\mathrm{t}}$ *t-beh*(B), *and* $A \leq_{\infty\mathrm{T}}^{\mathrm{t}} B \Leftrightarrow$ *t-beh*$(A) \leq_{\infty\mathrm{T}}^{\mathrm{t}}$ *t-beh*(B).

Proof: We sketch the proof of 2; it is analogous to that of Lemma 3.3. Suppose A has t-fin and $p_1 \leq p_2 \leq \ldots$ is an infinite chain of timed sequence pairs in *t-traces*$^*(A)$ such that the limits of the time components of the p_i's is ∞. Assume without loss of generality that $p_i.ltime < p_{i+1}.ltime$ for all $i \geq 1$. Let p be the limit of the p_i's. We must show that $p \in$ *t-traces*$^\infty(A)$.

We use Lemma 2.1. This time, G is constructed as follows. The nodes are pairs (p_i, s), where p_i is one of the timed sequence pairs in the sequence above, and s is a state of A, such that there exists an execution α of A that ends with state s and such that $p_i =$ *t-trace*(α). There is an edge from node (p_i, s') to node (p_{i+1}, s) exactly if $s' \overset{q}{\rightsquigarrow}_A s$, where $p_{i+1} = p_i; q$. Using Lemma 5.3, it is not difficult to show that G satisfies the hypotheses of Lemma 2.1. Then that lemma implies the existence of an infinite path in G starting at a root; this yields an admissible execution of A having p as its timed trace. ∎

Proposition 5.12

1. *If B has t-fin then* $A \leq_{*\mathrm{T}}^{\mathrm{t}} B \Leftrightarrow A \leq_{\mathrm{T}}^{\mathrm{t}} B$.

2. *If A is feasible then* $A \leq_{\infty\mathrm{T}}^{\mathrm{t}} B \Leftrightarrow A \leq_{\mathrm{T}}^{\mathrm{t}} B$.

Proof: Part 1 follows from Lemmas 5.9 and 5.11. Part 2 is a corollary of Lemmas 5.10 and 5.11. ∎

Example 5.3 We present two timed automata, TA and TB, which are in a sense the timed analogues of the automata A and B of Example 3.1, that illustrate the necessity of the t-fin condition in Proposition 5.12. Automaton TA does an a-action at integer times:

- *states*$(TA) = \mathsf{R}^{\geq 0} \times \mathsf{N}$,
- *start*$(TA) = \{(0,0)\}$,
- *acts*$(TA) = \{\tau, a\} \cup \mathsf{R}^{\geq 0}$, and
- *steps*(TA) is specified by:

$$(t', n) \xrightarrow{t} (t, n) \qquad \text{if } t' = t \vee (t' < t \leq n),$$

$$(t, n) \xrightarrow{a} (t, n+1) \quad \text{if } t = n.$$

Automaton TB also does an a-action at integer times, but only finitely often:

- *states*$(TB) = \mathsf{R}^{\geq 0} \times \mathsf{N} \times \mathsf{N}$,

- *start*$(TB) = \{(0,0,m) \mid m \in \mathsf{N}\}$,
- *acts*$(TB) = \{\tau, a\} \cup \mathsf{R}^{\geq 0}$, and
- *steps*(TB) is specified by:

$$(t', n, m) \xrightarrow{t} (t, n, m) \qquad \text{if } t' = t \vee (t' < t \leq n),$$

$$(t, n, m) \xrightarrow{a} (t, n+1, m) \quad \text{if } t = n < m.$$

One can check that $TA \leq^{\mathrm{t}}_{*\mathrm{T}} TB$ but $TA \not\leq^{\mathrm{t}}_{\mathrm{T}} TB$.

In order to see that the feasibility condition in Proposition 5.12(2) is actually needed, we consider a Zeno machine: a timed automaton *Zeno* with states drawn from the interval $[0,1)$, start state 0, actions from $\mathsf{R}^{\geq 0} \cup \{\tau\}$, and a step $t' \xrightarrow{t} t$ whenever $t' \leq t$. Since *Zeno* has no admissible timed traces, $Zeno \leq^{\mathrm{t}}_{\infty\mathrm{T}} AT$. However, because AT does not allow for initial (nontrivial) time-passage steps, $Zeno \not\leq^{\mathrm{t}}_{\mathrm{T}} AT$.

Definition 5.1 For P a timed trace property, the associated ***canonical timed automaton*** *t-can*(P) is the structure A given by

- *states*(A) = *t-traces*$^*(P)$,
- *start*$(A) = \{(\lambda, 0)\}$,
- *acts*(A) = *sort*$(P) \cup (\{\tau\} \cup \mathsf{R}^{\geq 0})$, and
- *steps*(A) consists of all triples of the form $(\delta', t') \xrightarrow{a}_A (\delta, t)$, where $(\delta, t'), (\delta, t) \in$ *states*(A), $a \in$ *ext*(A), and where the following hold. If $a \in \mathsf{R}^{\geq 0}$ then $t' \leq t$ and $\delta' = \delta$, and if $a \in$ *vis*(A) then $t' = t$ and $\delta'\,(a, t) = \delta$.

(It is not hard to check that *t-can*(P) is indeed a timed automaton).

Lemma 5.13 *Suppose P is a timed trace property. Then*

1. *t-can*(P) *is deterministic and is a t-forest,*
2. *t-beh*$($*t-can*$(P)) \equiv^{\mathrm{t}}_{*\mathrm{T}} P$,
3. $P \leq^{\mathrm{t}}_{\mathrm{T}}$ *t-beh*$($*t-can*$(P))$, *and*
4. *if P is limit-closed then* *t-beh*$($*t-can*$(P)) \equiv^{\mathrm{t}}_{\mathrm{T}} P$.

Proof: 1 and 2 follow easily from the definitions. Since *t-can*(P) has t-fin, it follows by Lemma 5.11 that *t-beh*$($*t-can*$(P))$ is limit-closed. Now 3 and 4 follow by combination of 2 and Lemma 5.9. ■

Lemma 5.14 *Suppose A and B are timed automata. Then*

1. *t-can*$($*t-beh*$(A))$ *is deterministic and is a t-forest,*
2. *t-can*$($*t-beh*$(A)) \equiv^{\mathrm{t}}_{*\mathrm{T}} A$,
3. $A \leq^{\mathrm{t}}_{\mathrm{T}}$ *t-can*$($*t-beh*$(A))$, *and*
4. *if A has t-fin then* *t-can*$($*t-beh*$(A)) \equiv^{\mathrm{t}}_{\mathrm{T}} A$.

Proof: By combining Lemmas 5.11 and 5.13. ■

6 Simulations for Timed Automata

Our aim is to develop proof techniques for showing inclusion between the sets of timed traces of timed automata. In order to do this, we show how this problem can be reduced to the problem of proving inclusion between the sets of traces of certain derived automata. This reduction solves our problem, in a sense, since it allows us to use the various simulation techniques in Section 4 to prove inclusion results for timed automata. The approach is analogous to that followed for Milner's CCS [23] where the problem of deciding weak observation equivalence is reduced to the problem of deciding strong bisimulation. A key role in our reduction is played by the construction of the closure of a timed automaton.

6.1 t-Closed Timed Automata

In the previous section we have shown that for timed automata the traces contain (in general) more information than the timed traces. That is, from the traces of a timed automaton we can retrieve the timed traces (Lemma 5.4), but the reverse is not always possible (Example 5.1). However, there exist certain classes of timed automata for which the traces *can* be retrieved from the timed traces. In this subsection, we will identify one such a class, namely the *t-closed* timed automata.

A timed automaton A is said to be *t-closed* provided that it satisfies the following closure condition:

T4 If $s' \xrightarrow{t} s''$, $s'.time < s''.time$ and $s'' \xrightarrow{\tau} s$, then $s' \xrightarrow{t} s$.

The timed automaton *Idle* of Example 5.1 is t-closed. The timed automata *Idle'* and *Idle''* of Example 5.1 and Example 5.2, respectively, are not t-closed.

In order to show that the (finite) traces of a t-closed timed automaton can be retrieved from its (finite) timed traces, we proceed in two steps. First we define an operation *prune* that associates to each montonic sequence a normal form. We then show (Lemma 6.1) that a sequence is a trace of a t-closed automaton if and only if its normal form is. Next, we define an operation *monot* that takes a timed sequence pair and transforms it into a monotonic sequence in normal form. We show (Lemma 6.2) that *prune* is nothing but the composition of *t-pair*, which takes a trace to a timed trace, and *monot*. In the same lemma we also prove that if p is a timed trace of a t-closed automaton, $monot(p)$ is a trace of that automaton. From these results it follows that $traces^*(A)$ can be retrieved from $t\text{-}traces^*(A)$: $traces^*(A)$ consists of all the monotonic sequences whose normal form equals $monot(p)$ for some timed trace p of A.

Let β be a finite monotonic sequence over some set K, and let $t \in \mathsf{R}^{\geq 0}$ be less than or equal to all time-passage actions in β. Then $prune(t, \beta)$ is the monotonic sequence obtained from β by (1) removing all time-passage events that are either t or preceded (not necessarily directly) by a time-passage event with the same value, and (2) removing all time-passage events that are immediately followed by a time-passage event with a higher value. We write $prune(\beta)$ for $prune(0, \beta)$.

Lemma 6.1 *Suppose A is t-closed, $s', s \in states(A)$, $t = s'.time$, β is a finite monotonic sequence over $ext(A)$ with t less or equal than all time-passage actions in β, and $\beta' = prune(t, \beta)$. Then $s' \overset{\beta}{\Longrightarrow} s$ iff $s' \overset{\beta'}{\Longrightarrow} s$.*

Proof: Suppose $s' \overset{\beta}{\Longrightarrow} s$. Then there exists a finite execution fragment, α, of A with $first(\alpha) = s'$, $trace(\alpha) = \beta$ and $last(\alpha) = s$. Let α_1 be the execution obtained from α by removing all idling steps, and let $trace(\alpha_1) = \beta_1$. By axiom **S4** all instanteneous time-passage steps are idling steps. Using this fact, it is easy to see that the idling steps in α are in one-one correspondence with the time-passage events in β that are either t or preceded by a time-passage event with the same value. This means that β_1 is the sequence obtained from β by applying pruning step (1). Next, let α_2 be the execution fragment obtained from α_1 by eliminating, through application of axiom **T4**, all τ-steps that are immediately preceded by a time-passage step. This transformation does not affect the trace of the execution fragment: $trace(\alpha_2) = \beta_1$. Also both α_1 and α_2 start in s' and end in s. Finally, let α_3 be the execution fragment obtained from α_2 by contracting all successive time-passage steps through application of axiom **T2**. Let $\beta_3 = trace(\alpha_3)$. Since β_3 does not contain successive time-passage steps, it is obtained from β_1 by applying pruning operation (2). Thus in fact we have $\beta_3 = prune(t, \beta) = \beta'$. Since α_3 also leads from s' to s, this implies $s' \overset{\beta'}{\Longrightarrow} s$.

Conversely, suppose $s' \overset{\beta'}{\Longrightarrow} s$. Then there exists a finite execution fragment, α, of A with $first(\alpha) = s'$, $trace(\alpha) = prune(t, \beta)$ and $last(\alpha) = s$. Using axioms **T1** and **T3**, we can simply insert additional time-passage steps in α to obtain another finite execution, α', of A with $first(\alpha') = s'$, $trace(\alpha') = \beta$ and $last(\alpha') = s$. Therefore, $s' \overset{\beta}{\Longrightarrow} s$. ∎

Let $t \in \mathsf{R}^{\geq 0}$ and let $p = ((a_1, t_1) \cdots (a_n, t_n), t_{n+1})$ be a finite timed sequence pair over K with $t \leq p.ftime$. Then the monotonic sequence $monot(t, p)$ is obtained by taking the sequence $t_1 a_1 \cdots t_n a_n t_{n+1}$ and removing from it all t_i events that are either t or preceded by an event t_j that has the same value. We write $monot(p)$ for $monot(0, p)$.

Lemma 6.2

1. *Suppose $t \in \mathsf{R}^{\geq 0}$ and β is a finite monotonic sequence with t less or equal than all time-passage actions in β. Then $prune(t, \beta) = monot(t, t\text{-}pair(t, \beta))$.*

2. *Suppose A is t-closed, $s', s \in states(A)$, $t = s'.time$, p is a finite timed sequence pair over $vis(A)$, and $\beta = monot(t, p)$. Then $s' \overset{p}{\leadsto} s$ implies $s' \overset{\beta}{\Longrightarrow} s$.*

Proof: 1 easily follows from the definitions. For 2, suppose $s' \overset{p}{\leadsto} s$. Then A has an execution fragment α from s' to s with $t\text{-}trace(\alpha) = p$. Let $\beta' = trace(\alpha)$ and $\beta'' = prune(t, \beta')$. Then $s' \overset{\beta''}{\Longrightarrow} s$, by Lemma 6.1. Using 1 and Lemma 5.4, we derive $\beta'' = prune(t, \beta') = monot(t, t\text{-}pair(t, \beta')) = monot(t, p) = \beta$. Thus $s' \overset{\beta}{\Longrightarrow} s$. ∎

Corollary 6.3 *Suppose B is t-closed. Then $A \leq^{t}_{*\mathrm{T}} B \Leftrightarrow A \leq_{*\mathrm{T}} B$.*

Proof: Suppose $A \leq^{t}_{*\mathrm{T}} B$ and $\beta \in traces^*(A)$. By Corollary 5.5, $t\text{-}pair(\beta) \in t\text{-}traces^*(A)$. Using $A \leq^{t}_{*\mathrm{T}} B$, we get $t\text{-}pair(\beta) \in t\text{-}traces^*(B)$. By Lemma 6.2(2), $monot(t\text{-}pair(\beta)) \in traces^*(B)$ and by Lemma 6.2(1), $monot(t\text{-}pair(\beta)) = prune(\beta)$. Now $\beta \in traces^*(B)$ is a consequence of Lemma 6.1. It follows that $A \leq_{*\mathrm{T}} B$.

The converse direction follows from Lemma 5.6. ∎

We also have the following property involving fin.

Lemma 6.4 *Suppose A is t-closed. Then A has t-fin if and only if A has fin.*

Proof: Suppose A does not have fin but does have t-fin. Then A has a state s' and a sequence β such that for infinitely many states s, $s' \stackrel{\beta}{\Longrightarrow} s$. Let $p = \textit{t-pair}(s'.time, \beta)$. Then, by Lemma 5.4, $s' \stackrel{p}{\rightsquigarrow} s$ for infinitely many s. Thus A does not have t-fin, which is a contradiction.

For the other direction, assume that A does not have t-fin but does have fin. Then A has a state s' and a timed sequence pair p such that for infinitely many states s, $s' \stackrel{p}{\rightsquigarrow} s$. Let $\beta = monot(s'.time, p)$. Then it follows by Lemma 6.2(2) that $s' \stackrel{\beta}{\Longrightarrow} s$ for infinitely many s. Thus A does not have fin, which is again a contradiction. ■

6.2 Closure of a Timed Automaton

In this subsection, we give a useful construction to extend an arbitrary timed automaton to a t-closed timed automaton.

Let A be a timed automaton. The *closure* of A, denoted by $cl(A)$, is the structure B which is exactly the same as A, except that the relation $steps(A)$ is augmented by closing it under the closure condition given in **T4** (simultaneously with **T2** to let the result be a timed automaton again).

Lemma 6.5 *$cl(A)$ is a t-closed timed automaton, $cl(cl(A)) = cl(A)$ and $cl(A) \equiv_{\mathrm{T}}^{\mathrm{t}} A$.*

Lemma 6.6

1. *A is deterministic if and only if $cl(A)$ is deterministic.*

2. *A has t-fin if and only if $cl(A)$ has fin.*

Proof: 1 is trivial. Since $cl(A)$ is closed, $cl(A)$ has fin if and only if it has t-fin (Lemma 6.4). But $cl(A)$ has t-fin if and only if A has t-fin, since it is obvious from the definition of the closure operation that $s' \stackrel{p}{\rightsquigarrow}_{cl(A)} s \Leftrightarrow s' \stackrel{p}{\rightsquigarrow}_A s$. ■

The importance of the closure construction is a consequence of the following lemmas.

Lemma 6.7 $A \leq_{*\mathrm{T}}^{\mathrm{t}} B \Leftrightarrow cl(A) \leq_{*\mathrm{T}} cl(B)$.

Proof: By combination of Lemma 6.5 and Corollary 6.3. ■

Lemma 6.8 $cl(A) \leq_{\mathrm{T}} cl(B) \Rightarrow A \leq_{\mathrm{T}}^{\mathrm{t}} B$.

Proof: Suppose $cl(A) \leq_{\mathrm{T}} cl(B)$. Lemma 5.6 implies that $cl(A) \leq_{\mathrm{T}}^{\mathrm{t}} cl(B)$. Then Lemma 6.5 implies that $A \leq_{\mathrm{T}}^{\mathrm{t}} B$. ■

Example 6.1 The reverse implication of Lemma 6.8 does not hold in general. To obtain a counterexample: take B to be a machine, modeled as a timed automaton, which nondeterministically chooses a positive natural number n, then does action a at times $1 - 2^{-1}$, $1 - 2^{-2}$,..., $1 - 2^{-n}$, and then idles for ever. B is a feasible timed automaton with infinite invisible nondeterminism. Let A be the same as B, except that it may also choose ω at the beginning, in which case it subsequently does action a at times $1 - 2^{-1}$,

$1-2^{-2},\ldots,1-2^{-n},\ldots$ Timed automaton A is not feasible because by choosing ω it reaches a state from where only a Zeno execution is possible and no admissible execution. Timed automata A and B have the same timed traces, but $cl(A)$ has an infinite trace $(a,1-2^{-1})$, $(a,1-2^{-2}),\ldots,(a,1-2^{-n}),\ldots$ which $cl(B)$ does not have.

It turns out that we *do* have the reverse of Lemma 6.8 in case B has t-fin.

Lemma 6.9 *Suppose B has t-fin. Then $cl(A) \leq_{\mathrm{T}} cl(B) \Leftrightarrow A \leq^{\mathrm{t}}_{\mathrm{T}} B$.*

Proof: By Lemma 6.6 and Proposition 3.4, $cl(A) \leq_{\mathrm{T}} cl(B)$ iff $cl(A) \leq_{*\mathrm{T}} cl(B)$. By Lemma 6.7, $cl(A) \leq_{*\mathrm{T}} cl(B)$ is in turn equivalent to $A \leq^{\mathrm{t}}_{*\mathrm{T}} B$. Proposition 5.12 gives the equivalence of $A \leq^{\mathrm{t}}_{*\mathrm{T}} B$ and $A \leq^{\mathrm{t}}_{\mathrm{T}} B$. ■

Corollary 6.10 *The following statements are equivalent.*

1. $A \leq^{\mathrm{t}}_{*\mathrm{T}} B$,
2. $cl(A) \leq_{\mathrm{FB}} cl(B)$,
3. $cl(A) \leq_{\mathrm{BF}} cl(B)$.

If B has t-fin then the following statements are equivalent.

1. $A \leq^{\mathrm{t}}_{\mathrm{T}} B$,
2. $cl(A) \leq_{\mathrm{iFB}} cl(B)$.

Proof: The equivalence of the first three statements follows by combining Lemma 6.7 with the soundness and completeness results for $\leq_{\mathrm{FB}}$ and $\leq_{\mathrm{BF}}$ (Theorems 4.22, 4.23, 4.29 and 4.30).

The equivalence of the last two statements follows by combining Lemma 6.9 and Lemma 6.6 with the soundness and completeness result for $\leq_{\mathrm{iFB}}$ (Theorems 4.22 and 4.23). ■

In a sense, we have solved our problem now: we have found a way to prove inclusion of the sets of timed traces of timed automata A and B, under the reasonable assumption that B has t-fin. All we have to do is to establish an image-2-finite forward-backward simulation between two closely related timed automata, $cl(A)$ and $cl(B)$. The timed automata $cl(A)$ and $cl(B)$ are really very similar to A and B: they are the same except for their step relations, which are just a kind of transitive closure of the step relations of A and B. Still, it would be more elegant to define the various simulations directly on the timed automata themselves. This will be done in the next section. A simple lemma will subsequently relate the new simulations to the simulations between the closures of the automata.

6.3 Direct Simulations Between Timed Automata

We require two auxiliary definition. First, if A is a timed automaton, s' and s are states of A, and β is a sequence of elements of $vis(A)$, then we write $s' \overset{\beta}{\hookrightarrow}_A s$, or just $s' \overset{\beta}{\hookrightarrow} s$ when A is clear, if A has a finite execution fragment α with $first(\alpha) = s'$, $trace(\alpha) \lceil vis(A) = \beta$ and $last(\alpha) = s$. Second, if σ is any sequence then $\tilde{\sigma}$ is the sequence obtained by removing all internal and time-passage actions from σ.

Suppose A and B are timed automata. A *timed refinement* from A to B is a function $r : states(A) \rightarrow states(B)$ that satisfies:

1. $r(s).time = s.time$.
2. If $s \in start(A)$ then $r(s) \in start(B)$.
3. If $s' \xrightarrow{a}_A s$ then $r(s') \overset{\tilde{a}}{\hookrightarrow}_B r(s)$.

A *timed forward simulation* from A to B is a relation f over $states(A)$ and $states(B)$ that satisfies:

1. If $u \in f[s]$ then $u.time = s.time$.
2. If $s \in start(A)$ then $f[s] \cap start(B) \neq \emptyset$.
3. If $s' \xrightarrow{a}_A s$ and $u' \in f[s']$, then there exists $u \in f[s]$ such that $u' \overset{\tilde{a}}{\hookrightarrow}_B u$.

A *timed backward simulation* from A to B is a total relation b over $states(A)$ and $states(B)$ that satisfies:

1. If $u \in b[s]$ then $u.time = s.time$.
2. If $s \in start(A)$ then $b[s] \subseteq start(B)$.
3. If $s' \xrightarrow{a}_A s$ and $u \in b[s]$, then there exists $u' \in b[s']$ such that $u' \overset{\tilde{a}}{\hookrightarrow}_B u$.

A *timed forward-backward simulation* from A to B is a relation g over $states(A)$ and $\mathbf{PN}(states(B))$ that satisfies:

1. If u is an element of any set in $g[s]$ then $u.time = s.time$.
2. If $s \in start(A)$ then there exists $S \in g[s]$ such that $S \subseteq start(B)$.
3. If $s' \xrightarrow{a}_A s$ and $S' \in g[s']$, then there exists $S \in g[s]$ such that for every $u \in S$ there exists $u' \in S'$ such that $u' \overset{\tilde{a}}{\hookrightarrow}_B u$.

A *timed backward-forward simulation* from A to B is a total relation g over $states(A)$ and $\mathbf{P}(states(B))$ that satisfies:

1. If u is an element of any set in $g[s]$ then $u.time = s.time$.
2. If $s \in start(A)$ then for all $S \in g[s]$, $S \cap start(B) \neq \emptyset$.
3. If $s' \xrightarrow{a}_A s$ and $S \in g[s]$, then there exists $S' \in g[s']$ such that for every $u' \in S'$ there exists $u \in S$ such that $u' \overset{\tilde{a}}{\hookrightarrow}_B u$.

A relation h over *states*(A) and *states*(B) is a *timed history relation* from A to B if it is a timed forward simulation from A to B and h^{-1} is a timed refinement from B to A.

A relation p over *states*(A) and *states*(B) is a *timed prophecy relation* from A to B if it is a timed backward simulation from A to B and p^{-1} is a timed refinement from B to A.

We write $A \leq_{\mathrm{R}}^{\mathrm{t}} B$, $A \leq_{\mathrm{F}}^{\mathrm{t}} B$, etc. in case there exists a timed refinement, timed forward simulation, etc., from A to B.

6.4 Synchronicity

A new feature in the definitions of the various timed simulations is the requirement that related states have the same time component. In this subsection we explore the consequences of this natural restriction.

Suppose A and B are timed automata. A relation f over *states*(A) and *states*(B) is *synchronous* if for all $(s,u) \in f$, $u.time = s.time$. For each relation f over *states*(A) and *states*(B), we define the subrelation $syn(f)$ to be

$$\{(s,u) \in f \mid u.time = s.time\}.$$

Thus, f is synchronous if and only if $syn(f) = f$.

Similarly, a relation g over *states*(A) and $\mathbf{P}(states(B))$ is *synchronous* if for all $(s,S) \in g$ and all $u \in S$, $u.time = s.time$. For each relation g over *states*(A) and $\mathbf{P}(states(B))$, we define the subrelation $syn1(g)$ to be

$$\{(s,S) \in g \mid \forall u \in S : u.time = s.time\}.$$

Thus, g is synchronous if and only if $syn1(g) = g$.

Also, for each relation g over *states*(A) and $\mathbf{P}(states(B))$, we define the subrelation $syn2(g)$ to be

$$\{(s,S) \mid \exists (s,T) \in g : S = T \cap \{u \mid u.time = s.time\}\}$$

So also g is synchronous if and only if $syn2(g) = g$.

Obviously, all the timed versions of refinements, forward simulations, etc., that we defined above are synchronous. The following observation is more interesting. Note that in the proof below the idling steps play a key role. In fact, the result would not be correct without them.

Lemma 6.11

1. *Any refinement from A to B is synchronous.*

2. *If f is a forward simulation from A to B, then $syn(f)$ is a synchronous forward simulation from A to B.*

3. *Any backward simulation from A to B is synchronous.*

4. *If g is a forward-backward simulation from A to B, then $syn1(g)$ is a synchronous forward-backward simulation from A to B.*

5. *If g is a backward-forward simulation from A to B, then $syn2(g)$ is a synchronous backward-forward simulation from A to B.*

6. *Any history relation from A to B is synchronous.*

7. *Any prophecy relation from A to B is synchronous.*

Proof: For 1, suppose that r is a refinement from A to B and s is a state of A with $s.time_A = t$. By axiom **T1**, $s \xrightarrow{t}_A s$. Thus, since r is a refinement, $r(s) \stackrel{t}{\Longrightarrow}_B r(s)$. From this it folows, by axioms **S2** and **S3**, that $r(s).time = t = s.time$.

For 2, suppose f is a forward simulation from A to B. By the definition of a forward simulation, if $s \in start(A)$, then there is a state $u \in f[s]$ that is in $start(B)$. Axiom **S1** implies that $s.time = u.time = 0$, and thus $u \in syn(f)[s]$.

Now suppose $s' \xrightarrow{a}_A s$ and $u' \in syn(f)[s']$. Then $u'.time = s'.time$. Also, $u' \in f[s']$ and therefore there exists a state $u \in f[s]$ such that $u' \stackrel{\widehat{a}}{\Longrightarrow}_B u$. Then it follows by axioms **S2** and **S3** that $s.time = u.time$. Hence $u \in syn(f)[s]$.

For 3, suppose that b is a backward simulation from A to B, and suppose s is a state of A with $s.time_A = t$. Let $u \in b[s]$. By axiom **T1** $s \xrightarrow{t}_A s$. Thus, since b is a backward simulation there exists $u' \in b[s]$ with $u' \stackrel{t}{\Longrightarrow}_B u$. By axioms **S2** and **S3**, this implies $u.time = t = s.time$.

Parts 4-7 are similar. ∎

6.5 Relating Timed and Untimed Simulations

In Section 6.2, we showed that (under certain finiteness conditions) there is a one-to-one correspondence between inclusion of timed traces on the level of timed automata, and inclusion of traces between the closures of these automata. In this subsection we observe that there is also a strong connection between timed simulations between timed automata, and the same functions viewed as untimed simulations between the closures of these automata. As an immediate consequence of this observation we obtain easy soundness proofs for all the timed simulations of Section 6.3, since soundness of the timed simulations reduces to the soundness of the corresponding untimed simulations. Moreover we obtain "for free" a completeness result for timed forward-backward simulations.

Lemma 6.12 *Suppose $s, s' \in states(A)$ and $a \in acts(A)$ such that if $a \in \mathsf{R}^{\geq 0}$ then $s.time = a$ else $s.time = s'.time$. Then $s' \stackrel{\widetilde{a}}{\hookrightarrow}_A s \Leftrightarrow s' \stackrel{\widehat{a}}{\Longrightarrow}_{cl(A)} s$.*

Proof: Easy from the definitions. ∎

Lemma 6.13 *A synchronous relation is a timed refinement from A to B if and only if it is a refinement from $cl(A)$ to $cl(B)$. Moreover, the above property also holds if both occurrences of the word "refinement" are replaced by "forward simulation", "backward simulation", "forward-backward simulation", "backward-forward simulation", "history relation" or "prophecy relation".*

Proof: Here we prove the case of refinements. The other mappings can be handled similarly.

Suppose r is a timed refinement from A to B. We have to show that r is a refinement from $cl(A)$ to $cl(B)$, and the only thing nontrivial here is to demonstrate that r satsifies the second clause from the definition of a refinement. For this, suppose $s' \xrightarrow{a}_{cl(A)} s$. Then certainly $s' \overset{\hat{a}}{\Longrightarrow}_{cl(A)} s$, and thus, by Lemma 6.12, $s' \overset{\tilde{a}}{\hookrightarrow}_A s$. Since r is a timed refinement, we can use this fact to infer $r(s') \overset{\tilde{a}}{\hookrightarrow}_B r(s)$. Now $r(s') \overset{\hat{a}}{\Longrightarrow}_{cl(B)} r(s)$ follows by another application of Lemma 6.12.

For the other direction, suppose r is a refinement from $cl(A)$ to $cl(B)$. We have to establish that r is a timed refinement from A to B, and for this again the only nontrivial part is the second clause in the definition of a timed refinement. So suppose $s' \overset{\tilde{a}}{\hookrightarrow}_A s$. Since the closure construction only adds transitions, this trivially implies $s' \xrightarrow{a}_{cl(A)} s$. Now we use the fact that r is a refinement from $cl(A)$ to $cl(B)$ to obtain $r(s') \overset{\hat{a}}{\Longrightarrow}_{cl(B)} r(s)$. From this $r(s') \overset{\tilde{a}}{\hookrightarrow}_B r(s)$ follows by Lemma 6.12. ■

Corollary 6.14 *Suppose* $X \in \{R, F, iB, B, iFB, FB, iBF, BF, H, iP, P\}$. *Then* $A \leq^t_X B$ *iff* $cl(A) \leq_X cl(B)$.

Proof: Immediate from Lemmas 6.11 and 6.13. ■

Proposition 6.15 *The relations* $\leq^t_R$, $\leq^t_F$, $\leq^t_B$, $\leq^t_{iB}$, $\leq^t_{FB}$, $\leq^t_{iFB}$, $\leq^t_{BF}$, $\leq^t_H$, $\leq^t_P$ *and* $\leq^t_{iP}$ *are all preorders. (However,* $\leq^t_{iBF}$ *is not a preorder.)*

Proof: By Lemma 6.14, using that the corresponding untimed simulations are preorders. ■

Also the classification of Section 4.5 carries over to the timed setting:

Theorem 6.16 *Suppose* $X, Y \in \{T, *T, R, F, iB, B, iFB, FB, iBF, BF, H, iP, P\}$. *Then* $A \leq^t_X B \Rightarrow A \leq^t_Y B$ *for all timed automata* A *and* B *if and only if there is a path from* $\leq^t_X$ *to* $\leq^t_Y$ *in Figure 6 consisting of thin lines. If* B *has t-fin, then* $A \leq^t_X B \Rightarrow A \leq^t_Y B$ *for all automata* A *and* B *if and only if there is a path from* $\leq^t_X$ *to* $\leq^t_Y$ *consisting of thin lines and thick lines.*

Proof: Note that except for the superscripts t, Figure 6 is the same as Figure 5, which gives an overview of the relationships in the untimed case. Using Corollary 6.14 and Lemmas 6.7 and 6.8, the "thin line" inclusions for the timed case follow from the corresponding inclusions for the untimed case. For the "thick" line inclusions one needs in addition Lemmas 6.6 and 6.9.

In order to show that all the inclusions are strict, one can basically just use the same counterexamples as in the untimed setting. In order to turn the untimed automata into timed automata one only has to attach a 0-loop to each state. Only for establishing the difference between $\leq^t_{*T}$ and $\leq^t_T$ the examples of Section 4 are not adequate, and one has to use Example 5.3 instead. (If A^0 and B^0 denote the timed automata obtained by adding 0-loops to all states of the automata A and B of Example 3.1, respectively, then $A^0 \equiv^t_{*T} B^0$ but, since both timed automata have no admissible traces, also $A^0 \equiv^t_T B^0$.) ■

Here are two more results that carry over because of the correspondence between the timed and the untimed case.

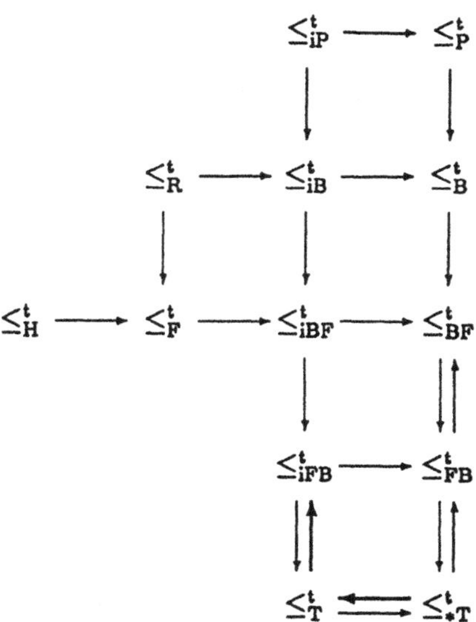

Figure 6: Classification of basic relations between timed automata

Proposition 6.17 *Suppose all states of A are reachable, B has t-fin and $A \leq^t_B B$. Then $A \leq^t_{iB} B$.*

Proof: From the definition of the closure construction it is immediate that all states of $cl(A)$ are reachable. By Lemma 6.6(2), $cl(B)$ has fin, and by Lemma 6.13, $cl(A) \leq_B cl(B)$. Now we can apply Proposition 4.15, the untimed version of the fact we are proving, to obtain $cl(A) \leq_{iB} cl(B)$. By Lemma 6.11 any backward simulation is synchronous, which means that we can apply Lemma 6.13 in the other direction to conclude $A \leq^t_{iB} B$. ■

Theorem 6.18 *(Partial completeness of timed forward simulations) Suppose B is deterministic and $A \leq^t_{*T} B$. Then $A \leq^t_F B$.*

Proof: By Lemma 6.6, $cl(B)$ is deterministic, and by Lemma 6.7, $cl(A) \leq_{*T} cl(B)$. Thus by the partial completeness result for forward simulations (Theorem 4.9), $cl(A) \leq_F cl(B)$. Now Lemmas 6.11 and 6.13 allow us to conclude $A \leq^t_F B$, as required. ■

6.6 Additional Results for Timed Automata

The previous sections show how some simple correspondences cause most of the results for untimed automata to carry over to the timed setting. There are some results about untimed automata that do not carry over because of these correspondences, but are nonetheless true. Firstly, there are the partial completeness results that involve t-forests. These do not carry over since the closure construction does not map t-forests to forests. Secondly, the various results that require the construction of some timed automaton (for instance the timed version of the Abadi-Lamport result) do not carry over via the correspondence. This subsection is devoted to establishing these remaining results in the setting of timed automata.

6.6.1 Partial Completeness Results

Theorem 6.19 *(Partial completeness of timed refinements) Suppose A is a t-forest, B is deterministic and $A \leq^{t}_{*T} B$. Then $A \leq^{t}_{R} B$.*

Proof: Analogous to the proof of Theorem 4.4. If $r \triangleq$ *t-after*$(B) \circ$ *t-past*(A), then r can be shown to be a timed refinement from A to B. The proof uses Lemmas 5.8 and 5.3. ■

Theorem 6.20 *(Partial completeness of timed backward simulations) Suppose A is a t-forest and $A \leq^{t}_{*T} B$. Then*

1. *$A \leq^{t}_{B} B$, and*
2. *if B has t-fin then $A \leq^{t}_{iB} B$.*

6.6.2 Results Involving an Intermediate Timed Automaton

Theorem 6.21 *(Completeness of timed forward and timed backward simulations) Suppose $A \leq^{t}_{*T} B$. Then*

1. *$\exists C : A \leq^{t}_{F} C \leq^{t}_{B} B$, and*
2. *if B has t-fin then $\exists C : A \leq^{t}_{F} C \leq^{t}_{iB} B$.*

Proof: The proof is essentially the same as the proof of Theorem 4.16.

Let $C =$ *t-can*(*t-beh*(A)). By Lemma 5.14, C is a deterministic t-forest and $A \equiv^{t}_{*T} C$. Since C is deterministic, $A \leq^{t}_{F} C$ by partial completeness of timed forward simulations (Theorem 6.18), and because C is a t-forest, $C \leq^{t}_{B} B$ follows by partial completeness of timed backward simulations (Theorem 6.20(1)). Similarly, if B has t-fin then $C \leq^{t}_{iB} B$ follows by Theorem 6.20(2). ■

Definition 6.1 Suppose k is a synchronous relation over *states*(A) and *states*(B) satisfying $k \cap (start(A) \times start(B)) \neq \emptyset$. The *timed superposition t-sup*(A, B, k) of B onto A via k is the timed automaton C given by

- $states(C) = k$,
- $start(C) = k \cap (start(A) \times start(B))$,
- $acts(C) = acts(A) \cap acts(B)$, and
- for $(s', v'), (s, v) \in states(C)$ and $a \in acts(C)$,

$$(s', v') \xrightarrow{a}_{C} (s, v) \quad \Leftrightarrow \quad s' \stackrel{\tilde{a}}{\Longrightarrow}_{A} s \ \wedge\ v' \stackrel{\tilde{a}}{\Longrightarrow}_{B} v \ \wedge\ S_2 \ \wedge\ S_3 \ \wedge\ S_4,$$

where $S_2 \triangleq a \notin \mathsf{R}^{\geq 0} \Rightarrow s'.time = s.time$, $S_3 \triangleq a \in \mathsf{R}^{\geq 0} \Rightarrow s'.time \leq a = s.time$, and $S_4 \triangleq a = s'.time \Rightarrow (s' = s \wedge v' = v)$.

Theorem 6.22 $A \leq^{t}_{F} B \Leftrightarrow (\exists C : A \leq^{t}_{H} C \leq^{t}_{R} B)$.

Proof: Suppose $A \leq^{t}_{F} B$. Let f be a timed forward simulation from A to B, let $C = \textit{t-sup}(A, B, f)$ and let π_1 and π_2 be the projection functions that map states of C to their first and second components, respectively. Then it is easy to check that π_1^{-1} is a timed history relation from A to C and π_2 is a timed refinement from C to B.

The reverse implication also follows via a standard argument. ■

Theorem 6.23

1. $A \leq^{t}_{B} B \Leftrightarrow (\exists C : A \leq^{t}_{P} C \leq^{t}_{R} B)$.
2. $A \leq^{t}_{iB} B \Leftrightarrow (\exists C : A \leq^{t}_{iP} C \leq^{t}_{R} B)$.

Proof: Similar to the proof of Theorem 6.22, using timed backward simulations instead. ■

Theorem 6.24 *(Completeness of timed history/prophecy relations and refinements) If $A \leq^{t}_{*T} B$ then the following are true.*

1. $\exists C, D : A \leq^{t}_{H} C \leq^{t}_{P} D \leq^{t}_{R} B$.
2. *If B has t-fin then* $\exists C, D : A \leq^{t}_{H} C \leq^{t}_{iP} D \leq^{t}_{R} B$.
3. $\exists C, D : A \leq^{t}_{P} C \leq^{t}_{H} D \leq^{t}_{R} B$.

Proof: Completely analogous to the proofs of Theorem 4.43 and Theorem 4.44. ■

6.6.3 Unfold and Guess Constructions

The *timed unfolding* of A, notation *t-unfold*(A), is the timed automaton B defined by

- $\textit{states}(B)$ = the set of fat executions of A,
- $\textit{start}(B)$ = the executions of A that consist of a single start state,
- $\textit{acts}(B) = \textit{acts}(A)$, and
- for $\alpha', \alpha \in \textit{states}(B)$ and $t \in \mathsf{R}^{\geq 0}$,

  $$\alpha' \xrightarrow{t}_B \alpha \;\Leftrightarrow\; \textit{strip-end}(\alpha') = \textit{strip-end}(\alpha) \wedge \textit{last}(\alpha') \xrightarrow{t}_A \textit{last}(\alpha)$$

  and, for $a \in \textit{acts}(B) - \mathsf{R}^{\geq 0}$,

  $$\alpha' \xrightarrow{a}_B \alpha \;\Leftrightarrow\; \alpha = \alpha' \, a \, \textit{last}(\alpha),$$

  where $\textit{strip-end}(\alpha)$ is obtained from α by removing the time-passage step (if present) at the end of α.

(We leave it to the reader to verify that B is a timed automaton.)

Proposition 6.25 *t-unfold(A) is a t-forest and $A \leq^{t}_{H}$ t-unfold(A).*

Proof: From the definitions it easily follows that *t-unfold*(A) is a t-forest. The function *last* which maps each fat execution of A to its last state is a timed refinement from *t-unfold*(A) to A, and the relation $last^{-1}$ is a timed forward simulation from A to *t-unfold*(A). Thus, $last^{-1}$ is a timed history relation from A to *t-unfold*(A). ■

Dual to the timed unfolding is the following timed guess construction. The ***timed guess*** of A, notation *t-guess*(A), is the timed automaton B defined by

- $states(B) =$ the set of fat execution fragments of A,
- $start(B) =$ the set of fat executions of A,
- $acts(B) = acts(A)$, and
- for $\alpha', \alpha \in states(B)$ and $t \in \mathsf{R}^{\geq 0}$,

  $$\alpha' \xrightarrow{t}_B \alpha \quad \Leftrightarrow \quad strip\text{-}begin(\alpha') = strip\text{-}begin(\alpha) \wedge first(\alpha') \xrightarrow{t}_A first(\alpha)$$

  and, for $a \in acts(B) - \mathsf{R}^{\geq 0}$,

  $$\alpha' \xrightarrow{a}_B \alpha \;\Leftrightarrow\; first(\alpha')\, a\, \alpha = \alpha',$$

  where *strip-begin*(α) is obtained from α by removing the time-passage step (if present) at the begin of α.

(Again we leave it to the reader to verify that B is a timed automaton.)

Proposition 6.26 $A \leq_{\mathsf{P}}^{\mathsf{t}}$ *t-guess*(A).

Proof: Similar to the proof of Proposition 6.25. ■

7 Discussion

In this paper, we have presented an automata-theoretic model for timing-based systems, and have used it to develop a variety of proof techniques for such systems. A considerable amount of further work remains to be done.

First, there is a technical issue. Some of the other work on simulations (e.g., [21]) includes reachability restrictions in the step correspondence conditions; we would like theorems justifying the soundness of those simulations in terms of the soundness of our simulations (without reachability hypotheses).

Refinements and forward simulations have already been used extensively and successfully for verifying concurrent algorithms, and backward simulations (in the form of prophecy variables) have also been shown to be of practical value in some cases. Additional work remains to determine the practical utility of the various kinds of simulations studied in this paper, particularly in the case of timing-based systems. This will involve applying the simulation techniques to a wide range of examples. It may also involve development of techniques analogous to the progress measure techniques in [19], based on extra structure to be added to our timed automaton model.

Finally, it remains to carry out process algebraic work using the same timed automaton model. A paper in progress [31] contains the beginning of such work, including definitions of interesting operators on timed automata, and proofs of substitutivity results for the timed trace semantics. However, much remains to be done.

Acknowledgements

We thank Albert Meyer, Jeff Sanders, Roberto Segala, Eugene Stark and George Varghese for their valuable criticism and useful comments. We also thank the organizers of the 1991 REX Workshop for providing the environment for an active research interchange that led to many improvements in our work.

References

[1] M. Abadi and L. Lamport. The existence of refinement mappings. *Theoretical Computer Science*, 2(82):253–284, 1991.

[2] J.C.M. Baeten and J.A. Bergstra. Real time process algebra. *Journal of Formal Aspects of Computing Science*, 3(2):142–188, 1991.

[3] G. Berry and L. Cosserat. The ESTEREL synchronous programming language and its mathematical semantics. In A.W. Roscoe & G. Winskel S.D. Brookes, editor, *Seminar on Concurrency*, volume 197 of *Lecture Notes in Computer Science*, pages 389–448. Springer-Verlag, 1984.

[4] R. Gerber and I. Lee. The formal treatment of priorities in real-time computation. In *Proceedings 6th IEEE Workshop on Real-Time Software and Operating Systems*, 1989.

[5] R. Gerth. Foundations of compositional program refinement (first version). In J.W. de Bakker, W.-P. de Roever, and G. Rozenberg, editors, *REX Workshop on Stepwise Refinement of Distributed Systems: Models, Formalism, Correctness,* Mook, The Netherlands 1989, volume 430 of *Lecture Notes in Computer Science*, pages 777–560. Springer-Verlag, 1990.

[6] A. Ginzburg. *Algebraic Theory of Automata.* Academic Press, New York – London, 1968.

[7] J.F. Groote. Specification and verification of real time systems in ACP. Report CS-R9015, CWI, Amsterdam, 1990. An extended abstract appeared in L. Logrippo, R.L. Probert and H. Ural, editors, *Proceedings* 10th *International Symposium on Protocol Specification, Testing and Verification*, Ottawa, pages 261–274, 1990.

[8] J. He. Process simulation and refinement. *Journal of Formal Aspects of Computing Science*, 1:229–241, 1989.

[9] C.A.R. Hoare, J. He, and J.W. Sanders. Prespecification in data refinement. *Information Processing Letters*, 25:71–76, 1987.

[10] B. Jonsson. *Compositional Verification of Distributed Systems.* PhD thesis, Department of Computer Systems, Uppsala University, 1987. DoCS 87/09.

[11] B. Jonsson. Modular verification of asynchronous networks. In *Proceedings of the* 6th *Annual ACM Symposium on Principles of Distributed Computing,* Vancouver, Canada, pages 152–166, 1987.

[12] B. Jonsson. On decomposing and refining specifications of distributed systems. In J.W. de Bakker, W.-P. de Roever, and G. Rozenberg, editors, *REX Workshop on Stepwise Refinement of Distributed Systems: Models, Formalism, Correctness,* Mook, The Netherlands 1989, volume 430 of *Lecture Notes in Computer Science*, pages 361–387. Springer-Verlag, 1990.

[13] B. Jonsson. Simulations between specifications of distributed systems. In J.C.M. Baeten and J.F. Groote, editors, *Proceedings CONCUR 91,* Amsterdam, volume 527 of *Lecture Notes in Computer Science*, pages 346–360. Springer-Verlag, 1991.

[14] M.B. Josephs. A state-based approach to communicating processes. *Distributed Computing,* 3:9–18, 1988.

[15] N. Klarlund and F.B. Schneider. Verifying safety properties using infinite-state automata. Technical Report 89-1039, Department of Computer Science, Cornell University, Ithaca, New York, 1989.

[16] D.E. Knuth. *Fundamental Algorithms,* volume 1 of *The Art of Computer Programming.* Addison-Wesley, Reading, Massachusetts, 1973. Second edition.

[17] L. Lamport. Specifying concurrent program modules. *ACM Transactions on Programming Languages and Systems,* 5(2):190–222, 1983.

[18] N.A. Lynch. Multivalued possibilities mappings. In J.W. de Bakker, W.-P. de Roever, and G. Rozenberg, editors, *REX Workshop on Stepwise Refinement of Distributed Systems: Models, Formalism, Correctness,* Mook, The Netherlands 1989, volume 430 of *Lecture Notes in Computer Science*, pages 519–543. Springer-Verlag, 1990.

[19] N.A. Lynch and H. Attiya. Using mappings to prove timing properties. In *Proceedings of the* 9th *Annual ACM Symposium on Principles of Distributed Computing,* Quebec, Canada, August 1990. Expanded version: Technical Memo MIT/LCS/TM-412.c, Laboratory for Computer Science, MIT, March 1991. Submitted for publication.

[20] N.A. Lynch and M.R. Tuttle. Hierarchical correctness proofs for distributed algorithms. In *Proceedings of the* 6th *Annual ACM Symposium on Principles of Distributed Computing,* Vancouver, Canada, pages 137–151, August 1987. A full version is available as MIT Technical Report MIT/LCS/TR-387.

[21] M. Merritt. Completeness theorems for automata. In J.W. de Bakker, W.-P. de Roever, and G. Rozenberg, editors, *REX Workshop on Stepwise Refinement of Distributed Systems: Models, Formalism, Correctness,* Mook, The Netherlands 1989, volume 430 of *Lecture Notes in Computer Science*, pages 544–560. Springer-Verlag, 1990.

[22] M. Merritt, F. Modugno, and M. Tuttle. Time constrained automata. In J.C.M. Baeten and J.F. Groote, editors, *Proceedings CONCUR 91,* Amsterdam, volume 527 of *Lecture Notes in Computer Science*, pages 408–423. Springer-Verlag, 1991.

[23] R. Milner. *Communication and Concurrency.* Prentice-Hall International, Englewood Cliffs, 1989.

[24] F. Moller and C. Tofts. A temporal calculus of communicating systems. In J.C.M. Baeten and J.W. Klop, editors, *Proceedings CONCUR 90,* Amsterdam, volume 458 of *Lecture Notes in Computer Science*, pages 401–415. Springer-Verlag, 1990.

[25] X. Nicollin, J.-L. Richier, J. Sifakis, and J. Voiron. ATP: An algebra for timed processes. In M. Broy and C.B. Jones, editors, *Proceedings IFIP TC2 Working Conference on Programming Concepts and Methods,* Sea of Gallilea, Israel, pages 402–429, 1990.

[26] X. Nicollin, J. Sifakis, and S. Yovine. From ATP to timed graphs and hybrid systems, 1991. This volume.

[27] S. Owicki and D. Gries. An axiomatic proof technique for parallel programs. *Acta Informatica*, 6(4):319–340, 1976.

[28] D.M.R. Park. Concurrency and automata on infinite sequences. In P. Deussen, editor, 5th *GI Conference*, volume 104 of *Lecture Notes in Computer Science*, pages 167–183. Springer-Verlag, 1981.

[29] G.M. Reed and A.W. Roscoe. A timed model for communicating sequential processes. *Theoretical Computer Science*, 58:249–261, 1988.

[30] E. W. Stark. Proving entailment between conceptual state specifications. *Theoretical Computer Science*, 56:135–154, 1988.

[31] F.W. Vaandrager and N.A. Lynch. Process algebras for timed automata, 1991. In preparation.

[32] Wang Yi. Real-time behaviour of asynchronous agents. In J.C.M. Baeten and J.W. Klop, editors, *Proceedings CONCUR 90,* Amsterdam, volume 458 of *Lecture Notes in Computer Science*, pages 502–520. Springer-Verlag, 1990.

[33] A. Zwarico. *Timed Acceptance: An Algebra of Time Dependent Computing.* PhD thesis, Department of Computer and Information Science, University of Pennsylvania, 1988.

From Timed to Hybrid Systems *

Oded Maler
INRIA/IRISA[†]

Zohar Manna
Stanford University[‡]and Weizmann Institute of Science[§]

Amir Pnueli
Weizmann Institute of Science[§]

Abstract.

We propose a framework for the formal specification and verification of *timed* and *hybrid* systems. For timed systems we propose a specification language that refers to time only through *age* functions which measure the length of the most recent time interval in which a given formula has been continuously true.

We then consider hybrid systems, which are systems consisting of a non-trivial mixture of discrete and continuous components, such as a digital controller that controls a continuous environment. The proposed framework extends the temporal logic approach which has proven useful for the formal analysis of discrete systems such as reactive programs. The new framework consists of a semantic model for hybrid time, the notion of *phase transition systems*, which extends the formalism of discrete transition systems, an extended version of Statecharts for the specification of hybrid behaviors, and an extended version of temporal logic that enables reasoning about continuous change.

Keywords: Real-time, timed transitions system, hybrid systems, discrete and continuous systems, Statecharts.

Contents

*This research was supported in part by the National Science Foundation under grants CCR-89-11512 and CCR-89-13641, by the Defense Advanced Research Projects Agency under contract NAG2-703, by the United States Air Force Office of Scientific Research under contract AFOSR-90-0057, by the France-Israel project for cooperation in Computer Science, and by the European Community ESPRIT Basic Research Action Project 3096 (SPEC).

[†]INRIA/IRISA, Campus de Beaulieu, Rennes 35042, France

[‡]Department of Computer Science, Stanford University, Stanford, CA 94305

[§]Department of Applied Mathematics, Weizmann Institute, Rehovot, Israel

1 Introduction

This paper concerns the development of formal approaches for the specification, verification, and systematic construction of reliable *reactive* systems. These are systems whose role is to maintain some ongoing interaction with their environment rather than to compute some final result on termination. The correct and reliable construction of reactive programs is particularly challenging. Typical examples of reactive programs are concurrent and real-time programs, embedded systems, communication networks, air-traffic control systems, avionic and process control programs, operating systems, and many others.

There is by now a general agreement that formal specification of reactive systems contributes significantly to a better understanding of the expected functionality of the contemplated system at an early stage, thereby leading to a more reliable and efficient construction of such systems. One of the promising and widely considered approaches to the specification of reactive systems is that of *temporal logic*, which provides a natural and abstract way to describe the behavior of a reactive system.

Traditionally, temporal logic (and similar formalisms) use a *discrete events* approach to model a reactive system. This means that the behavior of a reactive system is described as a sequence of discrete events that cause abrupt changes (taking no time) in the state of the system, separated by intervals in which the system's state remains unchanged. This approach has proven effective for describing the behavior of programs and other digital systems. We refer the reader to [MP81], [Pnu86], [Lam83], and [EC82] for examples of applications of the temporal approach.

The discrete event approach is justified by an assumption that the environment, similar to the system itself, can be faithfully modeled as a digital (discrete) process. This assumption is very useful, since it allows a completely symmetrical treatment of the system and its environment and encourages modular analysis of systems, where what is considered an environment in one stage of the analysis may be considered a component of the system in the next stage.

While this assumption is justified for systems such as communication networks, where all members of the network are computers, there are certainly many important contexts in which modeling the environment as a discrete process greatly distorts reality, and may lead to unreliable conclusions. For example, a control program driving a robot within a maze or controlling a fast train must take into account that the environment with which it interacts follows continuous rules of change.

This paper suggests an extension to the temporal logic framework that will enable it to deal with continuous processes. This extension leads to an integrated approach to *hybrid* systems, i.e., systems consisting of a non-trivial mixture of discrete and continuous components, such as a digital controller that controls a continuous environment, control of process and manufacturing plants, guidance of transport systems, robot planning, and many similar applications. Such an extension may enlarge the domain of systems that yield to formal and rigorous development approaches to include such important practical applications.

Recent Extensions to Real Time

An interesting step towards more realistic modeling and analysis of programs that interact with a continuous environments has been made by various extensions of the temporal framework to deal with *real time* [KKZ87], [RR87], [PH88], [Ost89], [AH89], [NRSV90], [HMP91]. Many other approaches are represented in this volume. It is interesting to note that, while some of these extensions are based on a dense model of time, the general structure of the model is still that of interleaving transitions, each of which causes an abrupt change of state. Some of the models even introduce a special time-passage (a *tick*) transition, which is the only transition causing the clock to progress.

This extension of the methodology allows representation of many additional phenomena in the world of programming [HMP91]. We can now take into consideration the fact that instructions take a nonzero time to complete, and represent the effect of *delay* commands, as well as the phenomena of task scheduling according to time and priorities, and so on.

However, this extension can be characterized as describing the interaction of a digital system with a *single* continuously varying factor — the real time clock. When we have several continuously varying parameters with more complex rules of change, the simple interleaving model is no longer satisfactory.

Extending the Framework

The discrete temporal framework as described, for example, in [MP89] includes the following components:

- An *underlying semantic model*. This captures the notion of a possible behavior of a system. In the case of discrete systems, this will be an infinite sequence of states or events that may occur in a possible run of the system.

- A generic *computational model*. This provides an effective representation of realizable systems. In the discrete case we take a *fair transition system* (a *timed transition system* [HMP91] for the real-time case) and show how concrete programming languages can be mapped onto this generic model. Transition systems provide an abstract representation of reactive programs and systems.

- A *specification language*. In the temporal framework we use temporal logic for specifying properties of reactive programs. In some cases we may use equivalent automata-based formalisms such as Statecharts [Har87] for specifying the detailed behavior of a system.

- A *verification methodology*, providing rules and axioms for formally proving that a proposed system meets its specification.

In the extension of this framework to hybrid systems we propose to extend (or replace) each of the discrete-framework components as follows:

- As an underlying semantic model we take *hybrid traces*, which are a mapping from extended continuous time to system states.
- As a generic computational model we take *phase transition systems* which represent the behavior of a system as a sequence of phases alternating between continuous and discrete changes. A continuous phase takes positive time and allows continuous change of variables governed, for example, by a set of differential equations. The discrete phase consists of a finite number of discrete transitions, each of which causes a (possibly) discontinuous change in the value of the variables.
- We consider two specification formalisms. For describing the detailed behavior of a system, we use an extension of Statecharts in which basic (unstructured) states may be labeled by a set of differential equations, used to describe a continuous change that occurs as long as the system is in that state. For describing properties and requirements of the system, we propose a modest extension of temporal logic, enabling it to refer to continuous change and to time.
- In this preliminary work on hybrid systems, we present only a partial proposal for an appropriate verification methodology, consisting of a rule for safety properties, and leave a more thorough investigation of the subject to subsequent research.

Related Work

The interest in formal treatment of systems that interact with continuous environments is certainly not new. It received a new impetus by the extension of formalisms to deal with real time. Indeed, several papers consider the specification of such systems, some of which are [MSB91], [CHR92], and [HRR91]. While all of these works recommend extensions to the specification language, they do not propose changes to the basic underlying semantic model, considering instead a discrete sequence of points which correspond to the points at which the discrete system samples the continuous environment.

To the best of our knowledge, the paper which comes closest to our semantic model is [San89], which proposes a *piecewise smooth* modeling of physical systems for the purpose of qualitative reasoning about physics.

Our interest in hybrid systems was triggered by a presentation of Fred Schneider at the workshop on real-time and fault tolerant systems held in Warwick in 1988. His approach to the subject is presented in [MSB91]. A closely related study of timed and hybrid systems is presented in [NSY91].

An important motivation for developing this theory came from applications to robotics and to process control and embedded systems.

2 Timed Systems

To deal with reactive systems whose behavior may depend on timing considerations, we present the discrete framework of *timed behaviors*. The notions of *timed trace* and *timed transition system* are taken with some small changes from [HMP91], while the logic MTL (which extends temporal logic by adding time-bounded temporal operators) is taken from [AH90] and is based on [KVdR83].

To model metric time, we assume a totally ordered time domain $\mathbf{T}$ which contains a zero element $0 \in \mathbf{T}$, and a commutative, associative operation $+$, for which 0 is a unique identity element, and such that for every $t_1, t_2 \in \mathbf{T}$,

> $t_1 < t_2$ iff there exists a unique $t \neq 0$ (denoted by $t_2 - t_1$), such that $t_1 + t = t_2$.

We refer to the elements of $\mathbf{T}$ as *time elements* or sometimes as *moments*. In most cases we will take $\mathbf{T}$ to be either the natural numbers N, or the nonnegative real numbers $\mathsf{R}_{\geq 0}$. We extend the domain $\mathbf{T}$ to $\mathbf{T}^{\infty} = \mathbf{T} \cup \{\infty\}$, where it is assumed that $\infty \geq t$ for all $t \in \mathbf{T}^{\infty}$.

With a system to be analyzed we associate

- V : A finite set of *state variables*.
- Σ : A set of *states*. Each state $s \in \Sigma$ is an interpretation of V; that is, it assigns to every variable $x \in V$ a value $s[x]$ in its domain.
- $V_T = V \cup \{T\}$: A finite set of *situation variables*. They are obtained by augmenting V, the set of state variables, with a variable T representing the current time in each situation.
- Σ_T : A set of situations. Every situation $s \in \Sigma_T$ is an interpretation of V_T. In particular, $s[T] \in \mathbf{T}$ is the value of the real-time clock at situation s. We denote by $s[V]$ the *state* corresponding to the situation s. It is obtained by restricting the interpretation s to the state variables V.

Timed Traces

A *progressive time sequence* is an infinite sequence of time elements

$$\theta : \; t_0, t_1, \ldots,$$

where $t_i \in \mathbf{T}$, for each $i = 0, 1, \ldots$, satisfying

- $t_0 = 0$.
- Time does not decrease. That is, for every $i \geq 0$, $t_i \leq t_{i+1}$.
- Time eventually increases beyond any bound. That is, for every time element $t \in \mathbf{T}$, $t_i > t$ for some $i \geq 0$. This is called the *Non-Zeno* requirement in [AL91].

A *timed trace* describing a potential behavior of a timed reactive system is an infinite sequence of situations

$$\sigma : \; s_0, s_1, \ldots,$$

where $s_i \in \Sigma_T$, for each $i = 0, 1, \ldots$. We denote by $t_i = s_i[T]$ the moment at which situation s_i was observed (sampled).

It is required that

- The sequence $t_0, t_1, \ldots$ is a progressive time sequence.
- For every $i \geq 0$, state and time do not change at the same time, i.e., either $s_i[V] = s_{i+1}[V]$ or $t_i = t_{i+1}$. This requirement ensures that each state change is precisely timed.

To illustrate the motivation for the last requirement, assume for a moment that we allow state and time to change in a single step. Then, the following would be an admissible trace

$$\langle x:0\,,T:0\rangle\ ,\ \langle x:1\,,T:1\rangle\ \ldots$$

This trace tells us that x was observed to equal 0 at time 0 while it was observed to equal 1 at time 1. It does not provide answers to the questions of when precisely did x change from 0 to 1 and how long it had been 0 before changing. The second requirement above forces us to choose between several possibilities, such as

$$\langle x:0\,,T:0\rangle\ ,\ \langle x:1\,,T:0\rangle\ ,\ \langle x:1\,,T:1\rangle\ ,\ \ldots,\ \text{or}$$
$$\langle x:0\,,T:0\rangle\ ,\ \langle x:0\,,T:1\rangle\ ,\ \langle x:1\,,T:1\rangle\ ,\ \ldots.$$

Or perhaps even

$$\langle x:0\,,T:0\rangle\ ,\ \langle x:0\,,T:0.5\rangle\ ,\ \langle x:1\,,T:0.5\rangle\ ,\ \langle x:1\,,T:1\rangle\ ,\ \ldots.$$

Timed Transition Systems

A *timed transition system* $S = \langle V, \Theta, \mathcal{T}, l, u\rangle$ consists of the following components:

- State variables V. We denote by Σ the set of all interpretations of V.
- The *initial condition* Θ. A satisfiable assertion that characterizes the states that can appear as initial states in a computation.
- A finite set $\mathcal{T}$ of *transitions*. Every transition $\tau \in \mathcal{T}$ is a function $\tau : \Sigma \mapsto 2^{\Sigma}$, mapping each state $s \in \Sigma$ into a (possibly empty) set of τ-successors $\tau(s) \subseteq \Sigma$.

  A transition τ is *enabled* on s iff $\tau(s) \neq \phi$. Otherwise τ is *disabled* on s.
- A *minimal delay* $l_\tau \in \mathbf{T}$ for every transition $\tau \in \mathcal{T}$.
- A *maximal delay* $u_\tau \in \mathbf{T}^{\infty}$ for every transition $\tau \in \mathcal{T}$. We require that $u_\tau \geq l_\tau$ for all $\tau \in \mathcal{T}$.

Given the state variables V, we can obtain the corresponding set of situation variables $V_T = V \cup \{T\}$, and the set of situations Σ_T interpreting V_T.

With each transition $\tau \in \mathcal{T}$ we associate an assertion $\rho_\tau(V, V')$, called the *transition relation*, which refers to both an unprimed and a primed version of the state variables. The purpose of the transition relation ρ_τ is to express the relation holding between a state s and its τ-successor $s' \in \tau(s)$. We use the unprimed version of variables to refer to values in s, and the primed version to refer to values in s'. For example, the assertion $x' = x + 1$ states that the value of x in s' is greater by 1 than its value in s.

A *computation* of a timed transition system $S = \langle V, \Theta, \mathcal{T}, l, u\rangle$ is a timed trace

$$\sigma :\ s_0, s_1, \ldots,$$

where $s_i \in \Sigma_T$ for each $i = 0, 1, \ldots,$ which satisfies the following requirements:

- *[Initiality]* $s_0 \models \Theta$.
- *[Consecution]* For all $i \geq 0$,
  - Either $t_i = t_{i+1}$ and there is a transition $\tau \in \mathcal{T}$ such that $s_{i+1}[V] \in \tau(s_i[V])$, or
  - $s_i[V] = s_{i+1}[V]$ and $t_i < t_{i+1}$.

  In the first case, we say that τ is *taken* at position i. In the second case, we say that the clock has progressed at position i. Sometimes we refer to the second case by saying that a "tick" step has been taken at position i.
- *[Lower bound]* For every transition $\tau \in \mathcal{T}$ and position $j \geq 0$, if τ is taken at j, there exists a position i, $i \leq j$, such that $t_i + l_\tau \leq t_j$ and τ is enabled on $s_i[V], s_{i+1}[V], \ldots, s_j[V]$ and not taken at any of the positions $i, i+1, \ldots, j-1$. This implies that τ must be continuously enabled for at least l_τ time units before it can be taken.
- *[Upper bound]* For every transition $\tau \in \mathcal{T}$ and position $i \geq 0$, if τ is enabled at position i, there exists a position j, $i \leq j$, such that $t_i + u_\tau \geq t_j$ and

  either τ is not enabled at j,
  or τ is taken at j.

  In other words, τ cannot be continuously enabled for more than u_τ time units without being taken.

As shown in [HMP91], the model of timed transition systems is expressive enough to express most of the features specific to real-time programs such as delays, timeouts, preemption, interrupts and multi-programming scheduling.

Example

Consider the simple timed transitions system given by:

- State Variables $V : \{x, y\}$.
- Initial Condition: $\Theta : (x = 0) \wedge (y = 0)$.
- Transitions: $\mathcal{T} : \{\tau_1, \tau_2\}$ where

τ	ρ_τ	l_τ	u_τ
τ_1	$(y = 0) \wedge (x' = x + 1)$	1	2
τ_2	$(y = 0) \wedge (y' = 1)$	3	3

We present two computations of this timed transitions system. The first computation σ_1 attempts to let x reach its maximal possible value. Therefore, we try to activate τ_1 always at the first possible position and τ_2, which causes both transitions to become disabled, as late as possible.

$$\begin{array}{l}\sigma_1 : \langle x:0, y:0, T:0\rangle \xrightarrow{tick} \langle x:0, y:0, T:1\rangle \xrightarrow{\tau_1} \langle x:1, y:0, T:1\rangle \xrightarrow{tick} \\ \quad \langle x:1, y:0, T:2\rangle \xrightarrow{\tau_1} \langle x:2, y:0, T:2\rangle \xrightarrow{tick} \langle x:2, y:0, T:3\rangle \xrightarrow{\tau_1} \\ \quad \langle x:3, y:0, T:3\rangle \xrightarrow{\tau_2} \langle x:3, y:1, T:3\rangle \xrightarrow{tick} \cdots\end{array}$$

The second computation σ_2 attempts to keep the value of x as low as possible. Consequently, it delays the activation of τ_1 to the latest possible position and tries to activate τ_1 at the earliest possible position.

$$\begin{array}{l}\sigma_2 : \langle x:0, y:0, T:0\rangle \xrightarrow{tick} \langle x:0, y:0, T:2\rangle \xrightarrow{\tau_1} \langle x:1, y:0, T:2\rangle \xrightarrow{tick} \\ \quad \langle x:1, y:0, T:3\rangle \xrightarrow{\tau_2} \langle x:1, y:1, T:3\rangle \xrightarrow{tick} \cdots\end{array}$$ ┘

There are several observations that can be made concerning the computational model of timed transitions systems.

- Computations alternate between *tick* steps that advance the clock and sequences of state-changing transitions that take zero time.
- Transitions *wait* together but *execute* separately in an interleaving manner.

Define $wait(\tau, j)$ to be the largest t such that for some $i \leq j$

- $t = t_j - t_i$,
- τ is enabled on all of $s_i[V], \ldots, s_j[V]$, and
- τ is not taken at any of $i, \ldots, j-1$.

The function $wait(\tau, j)$ measures the length of time that τ has been continuously enabled but not taken up to position j (assuming it is enabled at j).

We say that

τ is *ready* at position j if $wait(\tau, j) \geq l_\tau$, and

τ is *ripe* at position j if $wait(\tau, j) = u_\tau$.

We observe that, in a computation of a timed transition system,

- Time can progress only after all ripe transitions are taken or become disabled.
- When time progresses, it can jump forward only by an amount on which all the enabled transitions agree. That is, it must be such that it will not cause any enabled transition to become "over-ripe."

Not every timed transition system is guaranteed to have computations that satisfy all the requirements given above. For example, a TTS with a single transition τ whose transition relation is $\rho_\tau : (x' = x + 1)$ with lower and upper bounds given by $l_\tau = u_\tau = 0$ does not have a computation. This is because τ is always ripe and does not ever allow time to progress.

Let $\mathcal{T}_0$ be the subset of transitions whose upper bound is 0. A TTS is called *progressive* if there does not exists an infinite sequence of states

$$s_0, s_1, \ldots,$$

such that for every $i = 0, 1, \ldots,$ there exists a $\tau \in \mathcal{T}_0$, such that $s_{i+1} \in \tau(s_i)$. It is not difficult to see that every progressive TTS has at least one computation.

From now on, we restrict our attention to progressive transition systems.

Transitions that belong to $\mathcal{T}_0$ are called *immediate*. Transitions that have a positive upper bound are called *nonimmediate*. The set of all nonimmediate transitions is denoted by $\mathcal{T}_>$.

Specification by Timed Statecharts

A very convenient specification of timed systems can be obtained by extending the visual notation of Statecharts [Har87] by annotating each transition with a pair of numbers $[l, u]$, denoting the lower and upper time bounds of that transition. As an example, we present in Fig. 1 a timed specification of two manufacturing machines which communicate by a conveyer that holds only one item at a time. The conveyer is a mechanical device that travels back and forth between the two machines.

The specification consists of three automata: M_1, M_2, and *Conveyer*, which operate concurrently. These components may represent a first machine that does the initial processing of a part, a second machine which applies more advanced processing to the part, and the conveyer device which moves the part from machine M_1 to machine M_2.

A general label of a transition in this Statechart specification has the form

$$name : e/g!,$$

where *name* is an optional name of the transition (with no semantic meaning), e is a *triggering event* which causes the transition to become enabled, and $g!$ is an optional action which generates the event g when the transition is taken. When the transition has no triggering event, such as transition *good-part* in the diagram, the transition is enabled whenever the state from which it departs (state *Busy* in the diagram) is active.

In addition, each transition is optionally labeled by a pair of real numbers $[l, u]$, which specify the minimal and maximal delays of the transition. Transitions which are not explicitly labeled are considered to be immediate, i.e., to have the time bounds $[0, 0]$. We require that all transitions which have a triggering event be immediate. A transition is called *relevant* if the state from which it departs is currently active. Non-immediate transitions (which have no triggering event) are enabled whenever they are relevant. A transition with a triggering event e is enabled if it is relevant and the event e has just occurred, meaning that time has not progressed since the event was generated. More elaborate trigger conditions such as $put \wedge \neg first$ are allowed. Such a condition is true if the event *put* has been generated since time has last progressed but the event *first* has not been generated since then.

Some states are *compound*. For example, the state encompassing basic states *m2*, @2, and *m1* in the automaton *Conveyer* is compound. It is considered active whenever one of the basic states it contains is active. A transition departing from a compound state

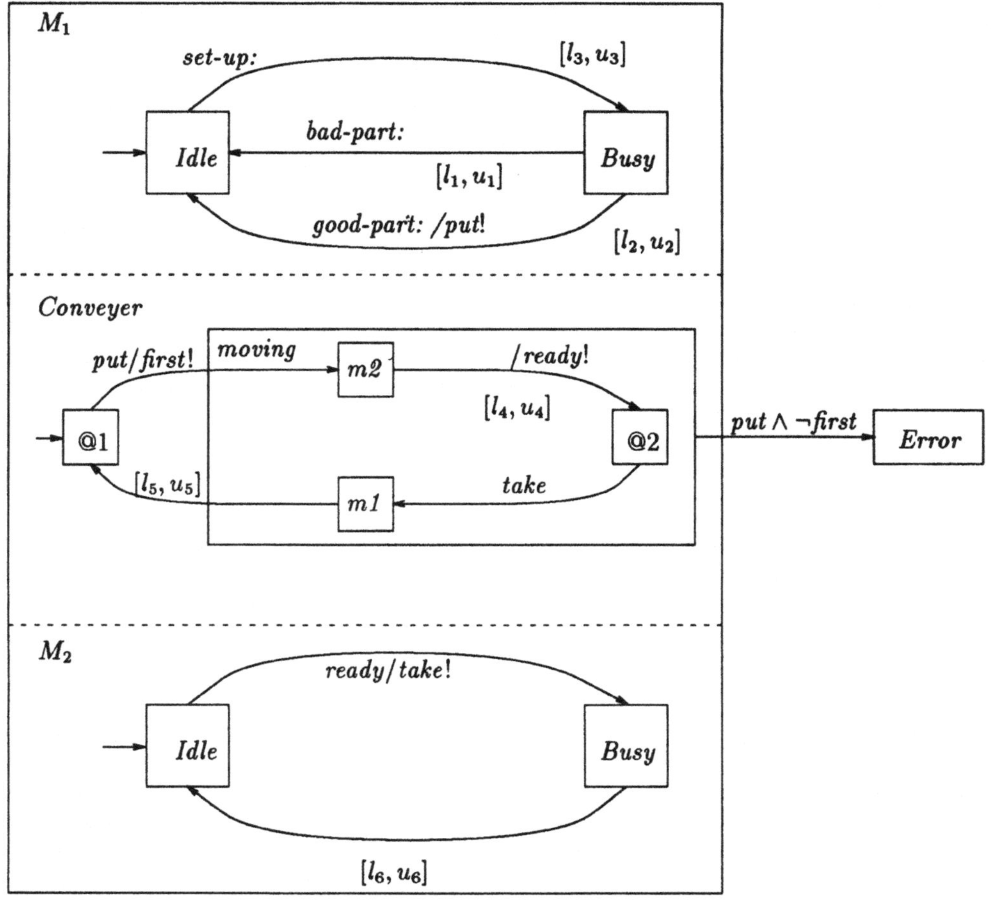

Figure 1: Specification of Two Machines with a Conveyer.

(such as the transition leading into *Error*) is relevant whenever the compound state is active and, when taken, it makes the compound state and all of its substates inactive and activates the state to which the transition leads (*Error* in the example above).

When a transition that generates an event e is taken, one or more immediate transitions that have e as a triggering event and are currently relevant can be taken. This is the mechanism by which the concurrent automata synchronize. For example, if M_1 takes transition *good-part* while *Conveyer* is in state @1, then the transition labeled by *put* can be taken next. Note that, since this transition is immediate and ready (therefore also ripe), it must be taken before time can progress.

Consider for example the transition connecting state *m2* to state @2. Assume that it is taken at position j while, at the same time, machine M_2 is in state *Idle*. On being taken, this transition generates event *ready*. Machine M_2 responds to this generation by taking the transition leading into state *Busy*, generating the event *take*. Since at this point *Conveyer* is at state @2, it can respond immediately by moving to state *m1*. These three transitions must be taken before the clock advances.

Another important element of the behavior of Statecharts is that events that are generated at a certain step persist until time progresses. This allows more than one transition triggered by an event e to respond to e before time progresses.

The given specification describes the following possible scenarios. Both machines start at an idle state. After some time ranging between l_3 and u_3, machine M_1 concludes its set-up procedure and moves to the busy state. While being busy, M_1 may either take time between l_1 and u_1 to produce a bad part, or take time between l_2 and u_2 to produce a good part. In both cases it moves to state *Idle* where it completes another set-up procedure. If a good part is produced, the event *put* is generated, which triggers the transition departing from state @1 in *Conveyer* if it is relevant. This transition represents the initiation of movement of the conveyer between M_1 and M_2. The movement itself may take time between l_4 and u_4 to reach M_2.. Reaching M_2 is represented by the transition connecting to state @2, which also generates the event *ready*. This event is sensed by M_2, which removes the part from the conveyer and starts processing it in its *Busy* state.

If all timings are right, M_1 should never issue the *put* signal when the conveyer is not at state @1. The diagram represents this expectation by having a transition that moves to state *Error* in all other cases.

An interesting analysis question is what the relation between the various time constants should be to ensure that this never happens. Various verification tools, based on algorithms similar to the one proposed in [ACD90], can answer such questions algorithmically.

It is important to note that the semantics of Statecharts presented here is not the standard semantics considered, for example, in [PS91]. The Statecharts presented here are *timed statecharts*, and their behavior is somewhat different than that given by the standard semantics. One of the main differences is that the notions of macro- and micro-steps no longer play such an important role in the semantics. Instead, there is a sequence of steps that can be taken before time progresses. By definition, any signal that is generated at a given time persists as long as time does not progress.

This explains the need for the signal *first*, which is emitted on entry to state *moving*, and whose negation labels the exit to *Error*. The system may enter state *moving* only when it senses the signal *put*. After the transition entering state *moving* is taken, signal *put* is still available. If the transition exiting to *Error* were labeled only by *put*, it would have always been taken following the entry to *moving*. Signal *first*, which is generated by the transition entering *moving*, prevents the error transition from being taken immediately. When time progresses, both *put* and *first* disappear, and the error transition will respond only to a new *put* signal generated at a later time.

For a more detailed description of timed statecharts, the reader is referred to [KP92].

3 Specification and Verification of Timed Transition Systems

To specify properties of timed systems, we use the language of temporal logic with some extensions.

Extensions to the Temporal Language

We assume familiarity with temporal logic and its operators as presented, for example, in [MP91]. The following extensions are introduced.

References to the Next Value

When evaluating a formula at position j of a computation σ, it is often necessary to evaluate terms that appear in atomic formulas. In the standard definition this evaluation is based on the value of the variables in the situation s_j. For a term r, we introduce the notation

$$\bigcirc r,$$

referring to *the next value* of r.

The precise definition uses the notation $val(\sigma, j, r)$ which defines the value of the term r at position j of computation σ.

- For a constant c, $val(\sigma, j, c) = c$, where we use the same notation for a value and its syntactic representation.
- For a variable $x \in V_t$, $val(\sigma, j, x) = s_j[x]$, i.e., the interpretation of x in the situation s_j.
- For a term r, $val(\sigma, j, \bigcirc r) = val(\sigma, j+1, r)$.
- For a function f and terms $r_1, \ldots, r_k$,

$$val(\sigma, j, f(r_1, \ldots, r_k)) \quad = \quad f(val(\sigma, j, r_1), \ldots, val(\sigma, j, r_k))$$

- For a predicate p and terms $r_1, \ldots, r_k$,

$$(\sigma, j) \models p(r_1, \ldots, r_k) \quad \text{iff} \quad p(val(\sigma, j, r_1), \ldots, val(\sigma, j, r_k)) = \text{T}.$$

In [MP91], $\bigcirc r$ is denoted as r^+.

Age of a Formula

To refer to the passage of time, we introduce a temporal function that expresses the age of a formula.

For a formula φ, we introduce the term

$$\Gamma(\varphi),$$

called the *age* of φ. Its intended meaning is that the value of $\Gamma(\varphi)$ at a φ-position j records the time length of the largest interval ending at j in which φ holds continuously. If φ does not hold at j then $\Gamma(\varphi) = 0$ at j. Thus, we define

- $val(\sigma, j, \Gamma(\varphi)) \quad = \quad$ The largest t such that, for some $i \leq j$, $t = t_j - t_i$ and φ holds at all positions $i, \ldots, j$. It is taken to be 0 if φ does not hold at j.

Age functions can be viewed as an alternative and generalization of the delay counters δ_τ introduced in [HMP91], which measure the length of time a transition τ has been continuously enabled and not taken.

A closely related concept is used in [SBM91] to allow assertional reasoning about real-time.

A notion similar to age functions is that of *duration*, proposed in [CHR92] to express properties of continuous systems. One difference between the two notions, is that durations are introduced in the context of interval temporal logic while we use point-based temporal logic. Another difference is that durations measure the *accumulated* time in which a formula was true within an interval, while the age of a formula measures the length of the largest time interval ending in the current position in which the formula held continuously.

Interval-Bounded Operators

Following [HMP91], we introduce for each temporal operator (excluding $\bigcirc$, $\odot$, and the weak previous operator $\widetilde{\odot}$) a bounded version of the operator obtained by subscripting the operator by an interval specification I. An interval specification may have one of the forms

$$[l,u] \quad [l,u) \quad (l,u] \quad (l,u).$$

In the first form, it is required that $l \leq u$, while in the others $l < u$. The semantic meaning of these *bounded operators* is straightforward. For example, $p\mathcal{U}_{(l,u]}q$ holds at position i of a timed trace σ : $(s_0,t_0),(s_1,t_1),\ldots$, iff there exists a j, $i \leq j$, such that $t_i + l < t_j \leq t_i + u$, q holds at j, and for all k, $i \leq k < j$, p holds at k.

We often use abbreviations such as $\Box_{<u}$ and $\Diamond_{\leq u}$ to stand for $\Box_{[0,u)}$ and $\Diamond_{[0,u]}$.

Two Styles of Specification and Verification

We refer to the logic obtained by the described extensions as MTL, standing for *metric temporal logic*. This logic can be used to state both timed and untimed properties of programs or even of detailed specifications. As an example, we will state three properties of the buffer system of Fig. 1. In the formulas describing these properties we use the name of a state as a proposition holding precisely when the state is active.

The first property simply states that the system will never reach state *Error*. This is stated by the untimed formula

$$\varphi_1 \;:\; \Box\neg \mathit{Error}.$$

In order to verify this property, we may want to prove some lemmas that guarantee that state *Error* will never be reached. Obviously, state *Error* can be reached if signal *put* is issued while *Conveyer* is in state *moving*. The following liveness-like property states that *Conveyer* cannot stay in *moving* too long; namely, at most $u_4 + u_5$ time units. This requirement can be expressed by the formula

$$\varphi_2 \;:\; \mathit{moving} \Rightarrow \Diamond_{\leq u_4+u_5}\neg \mathit{moving}.$$

Note that this formula is not always valid, since it depends on the fact that when *Conveyer* generates the signal *ready*, M_2 is in state *Idle* ready to respond to it.

As a last property, consider the formula

$$\varphi_3 \quad : \quad put \Rightarrow \Box_{(0,u_4+u_5]} \neg put.$$

This formula states that any two consecutive *put* signals are separated by a time distance greater than $u_4 + u_5$. This property, together with property φ_2, guarantees the validity of property φ_1.

The Age-based Approach

As explained in [HMP91] and previously in [PH88], there are two different approaches to the specification and verification of timed systems. The *bounded operators* approach expresses the dependency of properties on real time only through the bounded operators introduced above. The preceding formulas illustrate specifications based on this approach, and [HMP91] presents several useful proof rules for establishing properties expressed in this style.

An alternative approach can be described as the *explicit clock* approach. It does not use any bounded operators, but allows instead explicit references to the clock variable T. A possible methodology for explicit clock specification and verification is presented in [HLP90]. The formulas considered there allow arbitrary references to the clock variable T within terms. A brief description of a the explicit clock approach is also included in [HMP91], based on a transformation of a timed transition system into a fair transition system in which the clock variable T is made into a normal state variable, and the *tick* transition made a normal transition equal to the others.

This transformation introduces a special delay variable for each transition, which measures the time the transition has been continuously enabled and not taken. These delay variables are updated by all transitions that may modify the enabling condition or the waiting time of the transition with which they are associated. They are also updated by the *tick* transition.

The bounded operators approach is adequately covered in [HMP91]. In this paper we develop further the explicit clock approach. There are some differences between the presentation of this approach here and its presentation in [HMP91]. The main differences are that instead of introducing explicit delay variables, we work with the temporal function $\Gamma(\varphi)$, and all references to time must be expressed by this function.

We illustrate first the specification style appropriate to this approach. Reconsider the three properties that have been previously specified using the bounded operators approach. Property φ_1 does not use bounded operators, so no changes are necessary. To express property φ_2, stating that *Conveyer* cannot stay in the *moving* state too long, we may use the formula

$$\psi_2 \quad : \quad \Box(\Gamma(moving) \leq u_4 + u_5).$$

This formula states that proposition *moving* cannot hold continuously more than $u_4 + u_5$ at a stretch.

Property φ_3 can be stated without using bounded operators by the formula

$$\psi_3 \quad : \quad \neg put \wedge \bigcirc put \Rightarrow (\Gamma(\neg put) > u_4 + u_5).$$

This formula states that if signal *put* is about to be generated, which means that in the present situation it is still off but in the next situation it will be turned on, then *put* must have been continuously off for a period exceeding $u_4 + u_5$.

Axiomatization of Timed Transitions Systems

There are several ways to construct a proof system that will support proofs of properties of timed transitions systems under the explicit clock approach. Some are based on the translation (or a priori representation) of timed systems into conventional transition systems. Such a translation is described in [HMP91]. A full description of such an approach is presented in [AL91]. See also [SBM91] for a non-temporal proof approach which treats the clock as another state variable.

A certain overhead is associated with the consideration of the clock variable as a regular state variable. As a first step, several auxiliary variables are introduced which measure how long each transition has been continuously enabled. These are called delay variables in the translation of [HMP91]. An alternative but equivalent approach defines instead "deadline" variables which predict when each transition should be next activated. The auxiliary variable associated with a transition τ can be modified by any transition that may cause τ to change its enabling condition. Consequently, each transition relation must be augmented by a clause for each delay variable it may affect.

Another necessary element is the introduction of an explicit *tick* transition that causes time to progress. This transition must update all the delay variables for the transitions that are currently enabled. Furthermore, in order to compute the permissible time step that can be taken, the *tick* transition must make sure that advancing the clock will not cause any transition to be enabled longer than is allowed by its upper bound.

The approach presented here attempts to avoid the introduction of new auxiliary variables. Instead it uses the temporal age function Γ to express the same type of constraints.

We will present a set of axioms that are intended to characterize the set of admissible computations for a given timed transition system, and which will serve as the basis for proving its properties.

Axioms for the Progress of Time

The first set of axioms ensures that the sequence of values $t_0, t_1, \ldots$ forms a progressive time sequence.

$$\begin{aligned} T_{init} &: \ T = 0 \\ T_{\geq} &: \ \Box(\bigcirc T \geq T) \\ T_{\neg Z} &: \ \forall n \Diamond (T \geq n) \\ T_X &: \ (x \neq \bigcirc x) \Rightarrow (T = \bigcirc T) \end{aligned}$$

Axiom T_{init} states that the initial value of T is 0. Axiom $T_{\geq}$ states that time never decreases from one situation to the next. Axiom $T_{\neg Z}$ expresses the *Non-Zeno* requirement by stating that for any natural number n (assuming that the natural numbers are embedded within the time domain $\mathbf{T}$), T eventually grows beyond n. Axiom T_X states that changes of state and changes of time are exclusive. Namely, if some state variable x changes in the current step then the value of T is preserved.

Axioms for Age

This set of axioms deals with the age function Γ. They are stated for an arbitrary formula φ.

$$\begin{array}{rcl} G_{init} & : & \Gamma(\varphi) = 0 \\ G_F & : & \bigcirc\neg\varphi \Rightarrow (\bigcirc\Gamma(\varphi) = 0) \\ G_T & : & \bigcirc\varphi \Rightarrow (\bigcirc\Gamma(\varphi) = \Gamma(\varphi) + (\bigcirc T - T)) \end{array}$$

Axiom G_{init} states that the initial value of all ages is 0. Axioms G_F and G_T describe how the next value of $\Gamma(\varphi)$ is determined. For the case that φ is false in the next situation, G_F states that the next value of $\Gamma(\varphi)$ will be 0. For the case that φ is true in the next situation, G_T states that the next value of $\Gamma(\varphi)$ will be its current value plus the time increment $\bigcirc T - T$, i.e., the amount by which T will increase between the current and the next situation.

Transitions and their Activation

The next set of axioms deals with the effect of the transitions in $\mathcal{T}$ on the computation. We assume that each transition $\tau \in \mathcal{T}$ is associated with a transition relation $\rho_\tau(V, V')$ which expresses the relation between the values of the state variables in the present state (represented by V) and their values in the next state (represented by V').

We define

$$\begin{array}{rcl} \mathit{enabled}(\tau) & : & \exists V'.\rho_\tau(V, V') \\ \mathit{taken}(\tau) & : & \rho_\tau(V, \bigcirc V) \\ \mathit{last\text{-}taken}(\tau) & : & \ominus\, \mathit{taken}(\tau) \\ \mathit{waiting}(\tau) & : & \Gamma(\mathit{enabled}(\tau) \wedge \neg \mathit{last\text{-}taken}(\tau)) \end{array}$$

The formula $\mathit{enabled}(\tau)$ expresses the fact that transition τ is enabled at the current situation. Formula $\mathit{taken}(\tau)$ is true at a position j if the next situation s_{j+1} can be obtained by applying τ to s_j. Note that $\mathit{taken}(\tau)$ may hold at a certain position for more than one transition. Formula $\mathit{last\text{-}taken}(\tau)$ holds at position j if $j > 0$ and τ can account for the passage between s_{j-1} to s_j. The value of function $\mathit{waiting}(\tau)$ at position j is equal to the length of time that τ has been continuously enabled and not taken up to and including position j.

In most of the timed transition systems we consider, all the transitions are *self-disabling*. This means that for every state s and transition τ, $\tau(\tau(s)) = \phi$, i.e., τ cannot be applied twice in succession to any state because it becomes disabled after the first application. For this prevalent situation, $\mathit{enabled}(\tau)$ entails $\neg\mathit{last\text{-}taken}(\tau)$, and we can therefore take $\mathit{waiting}(\tau)$ to be simply $\Gamma(\mathit{enabled}(\tau))$.

The axioms dealing with the requirements of proper initiation and consecution of computations are

$$\begin{array}{rcl} C_{init} & : & \Theta \\ C_{cons} & : & \Box\Big((\bigcirc V = V \wedge \bigcirc T > T) \vee \bigvee\limits_{\tau\in\mathcal{T}} (\mathit{waiting}(\tau) \geq l_\tau \wedge \mathit{taken}(\tau)) \wedge (\bigcirc T = T)\Big) \\ C_{upper} & : & \Box(\mathit{waiting}(\tau) \leq u_\tau) \qquad \text{for every } \tau \in \mathcal{T} \end{array}$$

Axiom C_{init} states that the initial condition Θ holds at position 0 of the computation. Axiom C_{cons} describes what can happen on each step of the computation. One possibility is that all state variables remain the same, which is described by the clause $\bigcirc V = V$, and time increases. Alternately, some transition τ which has been waiting for at least l_τ is taken, while time remains the same. Axiom C_{upper} ensures that all upper bound requirements are respected by requiring that no transition τ ever waits more than u_τ.

Derived Proof Rules

The axioms presented above are adequate for proving properties of timed transition systems expressed by temporal logic formulas that may use the age function $\Gamma(\psi)$ for assertions ψ.

However, for concrete proofs, it is often useful to first derive some auxiliary proof rules that encapsulate common modes of reasoning. Rule INVT is such a rule and is useful for establishing the validity of formulas of the form $\Box q$ where q (and φ appearing in the rule) is an assertion, possibly containing terms of the form $\Gamma(p)$ for assertions p.

INVT
I1. $\varphi \rightarrow q$
I2. $\Theta \rightarrow \varphi$
I3. $(\rho_\tau \wedge \Gamma(enabled(\tau)) \geq l_\tau \wedge T' = T \wedge \varphi) \rightarrow \varphi'$, for every $\tau \in \mathcal{T}$
I4. $$\left(\begin{array}{c} V' = V \wedge T' > T \wedge \varphi \\ \wedge \\ \bigwedge_{\tau \in \mathcal{T}} \Big(enabled(\tau) \rightarrow (\Gamma(enabled(\tau)) + T' - T) \leq u_\tau \Big) \end{array} \right) \rightarrow \varphi'$$
$\Box q$

The rule uses an auxiliary assertion φ which is stronger than q (i.e., implies q) and is shown to be invariant. Premise I1 states that φ implies q. Therefore, if φ is invariant over every computation, so is q. Premise I2 requires that the initial condition Θ implies φ. This establishes that φ holds at position 0 of every computation.

Premises I3 and I4 show that φ is preserved over every possible step in the computation. Premise I3 deals with a step that is caused by taking transition τ. The antecedent of the implication lists the conditions that are necessary for the current and next situation to be τ-related. It uses a primed version of the variables to refer to their values in the next situation and an unprimed version to refer to their values in the current situation. The clause $T' = T$ is derived from axiom T_X, which states that if variables change then time remains constant. The right hand side of I3 contains φ', the primed version of φ. It is obtained by replacing all variables not appearing within a Γ context by their primed version, and replacing the primed version of a Γ expression by

$$\Gamma'(p) = \textbf{if } p' \textbf{ then } \Big(\Gamma(p) + T' - T\Big) \textbf{ else } 0.$$

Assuming no nested Γ expressions, p' is obtained by priming all variables appearing within p.

Premise I4 deals with a step caused by the progress of time. Its antecedent contains the clause $V' = V$, requiring that the state variables retain their values when time progresses. The clause $T' > T$ represents the requirement that time progresses by a positive amount.

In proving the premises' implications, we may use freely primed and unprimed instantiations of the axioms. For example, for a self-disbaling transition τ, we may use the instantiations of C_{upper}

$$\Gamma(enabled(\tau)) \leq u_\tau \quad \text{and} \quad \Gamma'(enabled(\tau)) \leq u_\tau.$$

4 A Verification Example

In this section we demonstrate the style of proofs in the explicit clock approach.

Consider the program presented in Fig. 2.

$$x\text{: } \textbf{integer where } x = 0$$

$$P_1 :: \begin{bmatrix} \ell_0: & \textbf{noncritical} \\ \ell_1: & \textbf{await } x = 0 \\ \ell_2: & x := 1 \\ \ell_3: & \textbf{skip} \\ \ell_4: & \textbf{await } x = 1 \\ \ell_5: & \textbf{critical} \end{bmatrix} \quad \Big\| \quad P_2 :: \begin{bmatrix} m_0: & \textbf{noncritical} \\ m_1: & \textbf{await } x = 0 \\ m_2: & x := 2 \\ m_3: & \textbf{skip} \\ m_4: & \textbf{await } x = 2 \\ m_5: & \textbf{critical} \end{bmatrix}$$

Figure 2: Coordination by Timing.

This program has been suggested by Fred Schneider as a minimal yardstick for assessing the feasibility of proposed proof systems for real time. He attributes it to M. Fischer.

The Associated TTS

As a first step, we should identify the timed transition system associated with this program. For full details of the representation of programs as timed transition systems we refer the reader to [HMP91]. Here we will only provide the details necessary for the treatment of this program.

As state variables we take

$$V \ : \ \{x, \pi\}.$$

These consist of the data variable x and the control variable π ranging over sets of locations. A value $\pi = \{\ell_i, m_j\}$ implies that control of P_1 is currently at location ℓ_i and control of P_2 is currently at m_j.

The initial condition is given by the assertion

$$\Theta \ : \ (x = 0) \wedge (\pi = \{\ell_0, m_0\}),$$

requiring that the initial value of x is 0 and control starts at locations ℓ_0 and m_0.

There is a transition associated with each statement of the program. Let

$$\cdots \lambda : S; \ \mu : \cdots$$

represent any of the statements, where λ and μ stand for the labels appearing before and after the statement. For the case of the **critical** statements which appear last in the program, μ is taken to be empty. With each such statement we associate a transition τ_S, whose transition relation ρ_S is defined according to the type of the statement.

- For S being **noncritical**, **skip**, or **critical**,

  $$\rho_S \; : \; (\lambda \in \pi) \wedge (\pi' = \pi - \{\lambda\} \cup \{\mu\}).$$

  Thus, the enabling condition for these statements is that control is in front of the statement. When taken, control moves to the location following the statement. In this and other transition relations, we follow the convention that variables (such as x) whose primed versions do not appear in the formula are preserved by the transition. That is, for each such variable x the clause $x' = x$ is assumed.

- For S of the form $x := v$,

  $$\rho_S \; : \; (\lambda \in \pi) \wedge (\pi' = \pi - \{\lambda\} \cup \{\mu\}) \wedge (x' = v).$$

- For S of the form **await** $x = v$,

  $$\rho_S \; : \; (\lambda \in \pi) \wedge (x = v) \wedge (\pi' = \pi - \{\lambda\} \cup \{\mu\}).$$

  Thus, for these statements the enabling condition also includes the requirement $x = v$.

The lower and upper bounds associated with the transitions are as follows:

- For the transitions associated with statements **noncritical** and **critical** the bounds are $[0, \infty]$. This means that they may be taken immediately or at any time.

- For all other transitions we assume uniform bounds $[L, U]$, with $0 < L \leq U$.

The Specification and its Proof

Assuming that the time bounds satisfy $2 \cdot L > U$, we are asked to prove mutual exclusion, which can be stated by

$$\psi_0 \; : \; \Box\neg(at\_\ell_5 \wedge at\_m_5).$$

This formula states that there will never be a state in which P_1 is executing at ℓ_5 while P_2 is executing at m_5. The formula uses the control predicates at_ℓ_i and at_m_j which are abbreviations for $\ell_i \in \pi$ and $m_j \in \pi$, respectively.

To apply rule INVT, we identify q as $\neg(at\_\ell_5 \wedge at\_m_5)$. The rule calls for a construction of assertion φ which is stronger than q and is *inductive*, i.e., satisfies premises I2–I4. Usually, q as given is not inductive. Rather than present a complete inductive assertion, we prefer to share with the readers the process by which such an assertion is constructed.

The main heuristic is strengthening a given assertion by adding pre-conditions that must hold if the assertion is in fact invariant. For example, if q is not inductive, there must exist some transition τ such that q is not preserved under τ. Form the assertion

$$p_1 \; : \; \forall V'(\rho_\tau \rightarrow q').$$

Assertion p_1 characterizes precisely the requirement on situation s so that every τ-successor of s will satisfy q. It is also clear that p_1 is not implied by q, so $q \wedge p_1$ is stronger than q. This is because the validity of $q \rightarrow p_1$ is equivalent to the validity of $(\rho_\tau \wedge q) \rightarrow q'$, stating that q is preserved over τ.

Thus, our next candidate for an inductive assertion is $q_1 : q \wedge p_1$. We proceed to check whether q_1 is inductive, and if we find another transition that does not preserve q_1, this gives rise to an even stronger assertion, and so on. Hopefully this process will converge to identify an inductive assertion that implies q.

This incremental strengthening of q is often coupled with additional heuristics that attempt to simplify and generalize the precondition p_1.

In checking for the inductiveness of an assertion, we do not have to check all transitions in great detail. There are certainly transitions that can be discarded after a cursory syntactical examination. These are, for example, all the transitions that do not modify any variable on which the assertion depends. In general, we only should investigate transitions that look as though they may change the value of the assertion from false to true. We refer to such transitions as potentially falsifying or, sometimes, as potentially hazardous.

For assertions that have the form of an implication $p \rightarrow r$, it sufficient to consider transitions that may change p from false to true and those that may change r from true to false.

The two transitions which are potentially hazardous to the validity of q, which can also be written as the implication $at\_\ell_5 \rightarrow \neg at\_m_5$, are m_4 while P_1 is at ℓ_5, and ℓ_4 while P_2 is at m_5. We begin our analysis of the first case. The second case can be handled symmetrically.

The precondition that excludes taking m_4 while P_2 is at ℓ_5 is

$$at\_\ell_5 \wedge at\_m_4 \Rightarrow x \neq 2.$$

Indeed, if we believe q to be invariant, we must also believe (ignoring timing considerations for the moment) that the above formula is invariant. Otherwise, m_4 could be taken and lead to a violation of q.

With some generalization of this formula, we add to our assertion the requirement

$$\varphi_1 \ : \ at\_\ell_5 \Rightarrow x = 1$$

Checking the transitions that may endanger the validity of φ_1, we find m_2 which, when executed, will set x to 2. We therefore add the following requirement that guarantees that m_2 cannot be taken while P_1 is at ℓ_5.

$$\varphi_2 \ : \ at\_\ell_5 \Rightarrow \neg at\_m_2$$

To verify the validity of φ_2, we check all the transitions that may potentially threaten it.

- m_1 while at_ℓ_5.
  To prevent this from occurring, it is sufficient to show that

  $$at\_\ell_5 \wedge at\_m_1 \Rightarrow x \neq 0.$$

  We generalize this to the requirement

  $$\varphi_3 \ : \ at\_\ell_{3..5} \wedge at\_m_{0..2} \Rightarrow x = 1.$$

  By checking all the transitions, we find out that φ_3 is indeed inductive.

- ℓ_4 while at_m_2.
  An intuitive argument showing that this cannot happen is that by the time ℓ_4 is possible (ready), $x = 1$ must have held continuously for at least $2 \cdot L$ time units. However, P_2 cannot wait at m_2 that long without moving on (since $U < 2 \cdot L$).

Formalization of the Time-Dependent Reasoning

Up to this point, the part of the rule we have used and even the recommended heuristic are not influenced by timing considerations. It is only the formalization of the intuitive argument presented above that requires the stronger proof system that takes timing into account.

We start by proving several lemmas.

$$\psi_1 \;:\; \Box(\Gamma(at\_m_2) \leq U)$$

This invariant is an instance of axiom C_{upper} and the fact that m_2 is self-disabling.

The next lemma claims

$$\psi_2 \;:\; at\_m_2 \Rightarrow \Gamma(at\_m_2) \geq \Gamma(x = 1).$$

The potentially endangering transitions are

- m_1: Possible only if $x = 0$, which implies $\Gamma'(x = 1) = 0$.
- m_2: Making $at\_m'_2 = \mathrm{F}$.
- *tick* (passage of time): Clearly if at_m_2 and $\Gamma(at\_m_2) \geq \Gamma(x = 1)$ hold before the tick, then

$$\Gamma'(at\_m_2) \;=\; \Gamma(at\_m_2) + T' - T \;\geq\; \Gamma(x = 1) + T' - T \;\geq\; \Gamma'(x = 1).$$

A final lemma is

$$\psi_3 \;:\; at\_\ell_5 \wedge at\_m_{0..2} \Rightarrow \Gamma(x = 1) \geq 2 \cdot L.$$

This is proven by proving separately

$$at\_\ell_3 \wedge at\_m_{0..2} \Rightarrow \Gamma(x = 1) \geq \Gamma(at\_\ell_3)$$
$$at\_\ell_4 \wedge at\_m_{0..2} \Rightarrow \Gamma(x = 1) \geq L + \Gamma(at\_\ell_4)$$

All these invariants can be proven directly by rule INVT taking φ to be q.

We may assemble now the three lemmas to obtain

$$at\_\ell_5 \wedge at\_m_2 \Rightarrow U \overset{\psi_1}{\geq} \Gamma(at\_m_2) \overset{\psi_2}{\geq} \Gamma(x = 1) \overset{\psi_3}{\geq} 2 \cdot L$$

Since $2 \cdot L > U$, this shows that $at\_\ell_5 \wedge at\_m_2$ is impossible, leading to the validity of φ_2.

5 Hybrid Systems

As a first step in the development of semantics for hybrid systems we discuss the underlying *time model*. From now on, we assume that the time domain $\mathbf{T}$ is $\mathsf{R}_{\geq 0}$, the nonnegative real numbers.

Let $\theta : t_0, t_1, \ldots$ be a progressive time sequence. The *time structure* induced by θ is defined to be the set of pairs

$$\mathsf{T}_\theta \quad : \quad \{\langle i,t\rangle |\quad i=0,1,\ldots, \quad t=t_i \ \vee \ t_i < t < t_{i+1}\}$$

Thus, T_θ consists of all the pairs $\langle i, t_i\rangle$, $i = 0, 1, \ldots$, corresponsing to the elements of θ, as well as the pairs $\langle i, t\rangle$ corresponding to intermediate points $t_i < t < t_{i+1}$.

We refer to the elements of T_θ as *θ-moments*, or simply as *moments* when θ is understood. For each moment $m = \langle i, t\rangle$ we write $time(m)$ for the value t, the time stamp of m. We refer to moments of the form $\langle i, t_i\rangle$ as the *discrete moments* of T_θ, and to moments of the form $\langle i, t\rangle$, where $t_i < t < t_{i+1}$ as the *continuous moments* of T_θ. The set T_θ is ordered by the lexicographic ordering

$$\langle i,t\rangle \prec \langle i',t'\rangle \quad \textit{iff} \quad i < i' \text{ or } (i = i' \text{ and } t < t').$$

We write $m_1 \preceq m_2$ for the case that either $m_1 \prec m_2$ or $m_1 = m_2$. Note that if $\langle i,t\rangle \preceq \langle i',t'\rangle$ then $i \leq i'$ and $t \leq t'$.

The following diagram represents a prefix of a time structure induced by the time sequence θ : 0, 1.5, 1.5, 6, 6, 6, 6, 7, 8, ...

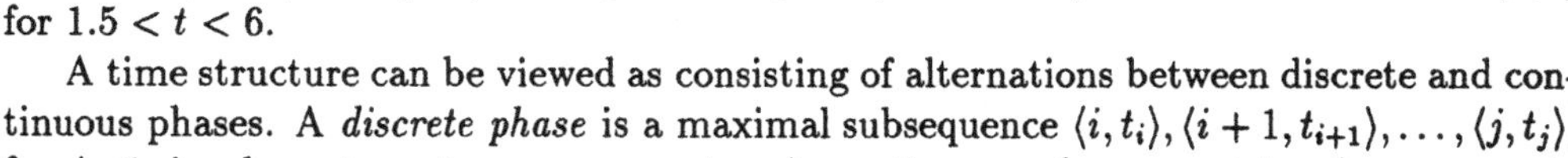

$\langle 0,0\rangle$ $\langle 1,1.5\rangle$ $\langle 2,1.5\rangle$ $\langle 3,6\rangle$ $\langle 4,6\rangle$ $\langle 5,6\rangle$ $\langle 6,6\rangle$

In this diagram, we have only marked the discrete moments, but any two discrete moments with different time stamps are seperated by uncountably many continuous moments. For example, $\langle 2, 1.5\rangle$ and $\langle 3, 6\rangle$ are separated by all (continuous) moments of the form $\langle 2, t\rangle$ for $1.5 < t < 6$.

A time structure can be viewed as consisting of alternations between discrete and continuous phases. A *discrete phase* is a maximal subsequence $\langle i, t_i\rangle, \langle i+1, t_{i+1}\rangle, \ldots, \langle j, t_j\rangle$, for $i \leq j$, where $t_i = t_{i+1} = \cdots = t_j$. A *continuous phase* consists of a nonempty open interval of the form $O_i : \{\langle i,t\rangle \mid t_i < t < t_{i+1}\}$, for $t_i < t_{i+1}$. Sometimes we refer to the closed interval $C_i : \{\langle i, t_i\rangle\} \cup O_i \cup \{\langle i+1, t_{i+1}\rangle\}$ or to the half-open interval $H_i : \{\langle i,t\rangle \mid t_i \leq t < t_{i+1}\}$.

For any closed interval C_i, we denote by $K_i = [t_i, t_{i+1}]$ the set of time values associated with the moments of C_i. A closed interval C_i such that $t_i < t_{i+1} is called a nontrivial interval$.

Hybrid Traces

The state variables of a hybrid system are partitioned into $V = V_c \cup V_d$, where

- V_c is the set of *continuous variables*. These variables are modified by continuous activities in the behavior of a hybrid system.

- V_d is the set of *discrete variables*. These variables are changed by discrete steps.

As before, we define Σ the set of states to consist of all interpretations of V, and Σ_T the set of situations to consist of all interpretations of $V_T = V \cup \{T\}$.

A *hybrid trace* is a pair (θ, σ), where

- θ is a progressive time sequence, and
- $\sigma : \mathsf{T}_\theta \mapsto \Sigma$ is a function assigning a state $\sigma(m) \in \Sigma$ to each *θ-moment* $m \in \mathsf{T}_\theta$. We extend σ to map moments into situations by taking $\sigma(\langle i,t\rangle)[T] = t$.

For ease of notation, we will write $\sigma(i,t)$ for $\sigma(\langle i,t\rangle)$.

Consider a nontrivial closed interval C_i. For each state variable $y \in V$, σ induces a function y_σ from $K_i = [t_i, t_{i+1}]$ to the domain of y, which is defined by

$$y_\sigma(t) = \begin{cases} \sigma(i,t)[y] & \text{for } t_i \le t < t_{i+1} \\ \sigma(i+1, t_{i+1})[y] & \text{for } t = t_{i+1} \end{cases}$$

Thus, the value of y_σ at the left and right boundaries of K_i are taken to be the values of y at the delimiting discrete moments $\langle i, t_i\rangle$ and $\langle i+1, t_{i+1}\rangle$, respectively.

For each variable $y \in V$ and each nontrivial closed interval C_i, it is required that

- If y is a discrete variable then y_σ is a constant function over K_i. This means that discrete variables do not change over continuous phases.
- If y is a continuous variable, then y_σ is a continuous function over K_i. For the end points t_i and t_{i+1} it is only required that y_σ be continuous from the right and from the left, respectively.

Thus, if we consider the time domain depicted above, y_σ should have a right limit at 1.5 which equals the value of y at the state corresponding to the moment $\langle 2, 1.5\rangle$.

A hybrid trace can be described as a continuous activity interspersed with countably many bursts of discrete activity which take zero time.

Phase Transition Systems

The generalization of a timed transition system to the hybrid domain is called a *phase transition system*. Phase transition systems allow an effective description of systems that can generate hybrid traces as previously described.

Before presenting the formal definition, we make the observation that changes in a phase transition system are governed by the dual constructs of *transitions* and *activities*. The table below compares some of the features of these two constructs.

	Transitions	*Activities*
Govern	Discrete Change	Continuous Change
Take	No Time	Positive Time
Execute	By Interleaving	In parallel
Defined by	Transition Relations	Differential Equations

Transitions and activities interact. Transitions start and stop activities and modify the parameters on which the behavior of activities depends. Activities may generate events and conditions that enable or trigger transitions. A typical scenario is that a transition is triggered by the event *becomes*$(x \geq 0)$, which occurs precisely at the moment in which x switches from a negative value to a non-negative one. An immediate transition that depends on this event for its activation will interrupt the continuous change and execute at this precise time point.

A phase transition system Φ consists of $\langle V, \Theta, \mathcal{T}, \mathcal{A}, l, u\rangle$, where

- $V = V_c \cup V_d$ is the set of state variables, partitioned into the continuous variables V_c and the discrete variables V_d.
- Θ is an assertion, characterizing the admissible ***initial states***.
- $\mathcal{T}$ is a finite set of ***transitions***, each transition $\tau \in \mathcal{T}$, mapping each state $s \in \Sigma$ into a set of successors $\tau(s) \subseteq \Sigma$. Each transition τ is associated with a transition relation ρ_τ which characterizes the relation between states and their τ-successors. Transitions are allowed to change the values of continuous variables.
- $\mathcal{A}$ is a finite set of *activities*. Each activity $\alpha \in \mathcal{A}$ is associated with a conditional differential equation of the form

  $$a_\alpha \quad \rightarrow \quad \mathcal{E}_\alpha,$$

  where a_α is a boolean expression over the discrete variables, called the *activation condition*, and $\mathcal{E}_\alpha$ is a differential equation of the form $\dot{y} = r$, where y is a continuous variable and r is a term over V. We say that the activity *constrains the variable* y. It is required that the activation conditions of different activities that constrain the same variable be exclusive.

  An activity α is called *operational* in a state if a_α holds there.
- l is a *lower bound* assigning to each transition τ a minimal delay $l_\tau \in \mathrm{R}_{\geq 0}$.
- u is an *upper bound* assigning to each transition τ a maximal delay $u_\tau \in \mathrm{R}^{\infty}_{\geq 0}$. We require that $u_\tau \geq l_\tau$ for all $\tau \in \mathcal{T}$.

Hybrid Computations

A hybrid trace (θ, σ) is a computation of a phase transition system Φ if it satisfies the following requirements.

- [*Initiality*] $\sigma(0,0) \models \Theta$.
- [*Discrete Consecution*] For each $i \geq 0$ such that $t_i = t_{i+1}$, there exists a $\tau \in \mathcal{T}$, such that

  $$\sigma(i+1, t_{i+1}) \in \tau(\sigma(i, t_i)).$$

  We say that τ *is taken* at $\langle i, t_i\rangle$.

- [*Lower bound*] If τ is taken at $\langle j, t' \rangle$, there exists a moment $\langle i, t \rangle \preceq \langle j, t' \rangle$ such that $t + l_\tau \leq t'$ and τ is enabled on $\sigma(m)$ for all m, $\langle i, t \rangle \preceq m \preceq \langle j, t' \rangle$ and not taken at any m, $\langle i, t \rangle \preceq m \prec \langle j, t' \rangle$.

- [*Upper bound*] If τ is enabled at $\langle i, t \rangle$, there exists a moment $\langle j, t' \rangle \succeq \langle i, t \rangle$ such that $t + u_\tau \geq t'$ and either τ is not enabled at $\langle j, t' \rangle$, or τ is taken at $\langle j, t' \rangle$.

- [*Continuous change*] For every nontrivial closed interval C_i, the functions $y_\sigma(t)$ for each $y \in V_c$ are continuous functions that satisfy *all* the activities $\alpha \in \mathcal{A}$. Note that if a_α is false at a state then activity α is satisfied by any functions. For each discrete variable $y \in V_d$, the function $y_\sigma(t)$ is constant in the interval, implying that discrete variables retain their value throughout the interval. Note that, since activation conditions only depend on discrete variables, an activity is operational at one point in the interval iff it is operational at all points of the interval.

  By default, the function $y_\sigma(t)$, for a continuous variable $y \in V_c$ which is not constrained by any activity that is operational in the interval, is also constant.

Let $\mathcal{T}_0$ denote the set of all *immediate* transitions, i.e., transitions whose upper bound is 0, and $\mathcal{T}_>$ denote the set of transitions whose upper bound is positive. To simplify matters we require that all transitions whose enabling condition depends on continuous variables be immediate. Let $\tau \in \mathcal{T}_0$ be an immediate transition. A careful examination of the *upper bound* requirement shows that τ cannot be enabled at a moment that belongs to a half-open continuous interval, i.e., at a moment $\langle i, t \rangle$, such that $t_i \leq t < t_j$. This is because the only moment $\langle j, t' \rangle \succeq \langle i, t \rangle$ such that $t + u_\tau = t'$ is $\langle j, t' \rangle = \langle i, t \rangle$ $(u_\tau = 0)$ and τ is neither disabled nor taken there.

Example

Consider a phase transition system Φ_1 defined as follows:

The state variables consist of a continuous variable x ranging over the reals, and a discrete variable y ranging over the naturals.

The initial condition is

$$\Theta \ : \ (x = 0) \land (y = 0)$$

There is a single transition τ, with transition relation

$$\rho \ : \ (x = 1) \land (y = 0) \land (y' = 1)$$

The time bounds for τ are $[0, 0]$.
There is a single activity α given by

$$\alpha \ : \ y = 0 \ \rightarrow \ \dot{x} = 1.$$

The computations of this phase transition system are all of the form

$$\langle x:0,\, y:0,\, i:0,\, T:0 \rangle,\ \ \{\langle x:t,\, y:0,\, i:0,\, T:t \rangle \mid 0 < t < 1\},\ \ \langle x:1,\, y:0,\, i:1,\, T:1 \rangle$$
$$\langle x:1,\, y:1,\, i:2,\, T:1 \rangle,\ \ \{\langle x:1,\, y:1,\, i:2,\, T:t \rangle \mid 1 < t < t_3\},\ \ \langle x:1,\, y:1,\, i:3,\, T:t_3$$
$$\{\langle x:1,\, y:1,\, i:3,\, T:t \rangle \mid t_3 < t < t_4\}, \cdots$$

for a progressive time sequence $0 < 1 \le 1 < t_3 < t_4 < \cdots$. The presentation of these computations lists, for each moment $\langle i, t\rangle$, a tuple consisting of $\sigma(i,t)[x]$, $\sigma(i,t)[y]$, i, and t.

All of these computations have a continuous phase in the time interval $[0, 1]$ in which activity α is operational and causes x to rise from 0 to 1 continuously. The phase stops at $t = 1$ because the immediate transition τ becomes enabled. This transition is taken at moment $\langle 1, 1\rangle$, leading to the state $\sigma(2, 1)$ in which $y = 1$. Beyond this moment neither α nor τ can be active, and the only thing that happens is that time progresses. The progress of time is described by an alternation of discrete states and continuous intervals in which all state variables remain constant and the only changing parameter is time itself. ▪

Not every phase transition system has computations. For example, if we replace the transition relation in the preceding example by the relation

$$\rho \ : \ (x > 1) \wedge (y = 0) \wedge (y' = 1),$$

then the resulting phase transition system has no computations. The reason is that while x is increasing uniformly, there is no definite value of T in which the predicate $x > 1$ precisely becomes true. Thus, we cannot let the continuous phase extend beyond 1. On the other hand, if we stop it at 1 then $x = 1$, and τ is not enabled yet.

Consequently, consider an assertion $\varphi(x)$ which depends on a continuous variable x. We say that φ is *sharp* in x if for every t_1 and t_2 and every function $f(t)$ continuous for $t \in [t_1, t_2]$ such that $\varphi(f(t_1))$ is false and $\varphi(f(t_2))$ is true, there exists a t, $t_1 < t \le t_2$ such that $\varphi(f(t))$ is true and for every t', $t_1 \le t' < t$, $\varphi(f(t'))$ is false. This guarantees a definite point at which φ changes from false to true. If all the enabling conditions of every transition are sharp then the problem encountered above is not possible. For the case that φ depends on two or more continuous variables, e.g., on $x_1, x_2, \ldots$, we require that a similar condition holds for every list of continuous functions $f_1(t), f_2(t), \ldots$.

This is not the only obstacle to having a computation. There are other cases when we can obtain a pair (θ, σ) which satisfy all the requirements of a computation except that the elements of θ are bounded by some integer N. This violates the requirement of *Non-Zeno*. Additional conditions may be required to avoid this situation.

An Example of a Hybrid Specification

To give a better picture of how phase transition systems operate, we provide an example of a specification of a hybrid system. The first presentation of the specification uses a Statechart augmented with a notation that annotates some basic states by a set of differential equations. The implied meaning is that, whenever the state is active, the associated differential equations are operational. Thus, activities are associated with annotated *states* of the Statechart while transitions are associated with the *arrows* connecting the states.

The example can be described as follows: at time $T = 0$, a mouse starts running from a certain position on the floor in a straight line towards a hole in the wall, which is at a distance X_0 from the initial position. The mouse runs at a constant velocity V_m. After a delay of Δ time units, a cat is released at the same initial position and chases the mouse at velocity V_c along the same path. Will the cat catch the mouse, or will the mouse find sanctuary while the cat crashes against the wall?

The Statechart in Fig. 3 describes the possible scenarios.

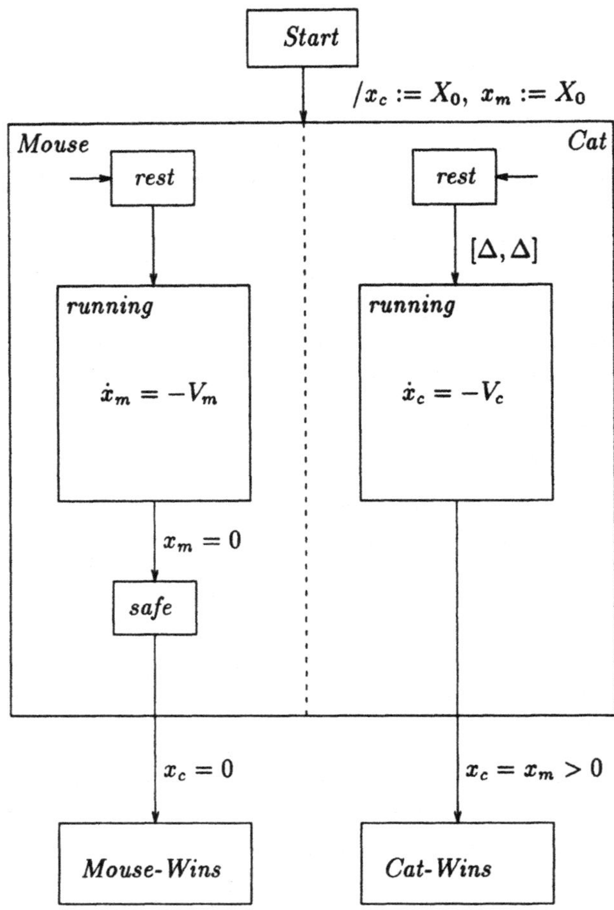

Figure 3: Specification of Cat and Mouse.

The specification (and underlying phase transition system) uses the continuous state variables x_m and x_c, measuring the distance of the mouse and the cat, respectively, from the wall. It refers to the constants X_0, V_m, V_c, and Δ.

A behavior of the system starts by setting the distance variables x_m and x_c to their initial value X_0. Then each of the players begins its local behavior. The mouse proceeds immediately to the state of running, in which his variable x_m changes continuously according to the equation $\dot{x}_m = -V_m$. The cat waits for a delay of Δ before entering its running state. Then there are several possible scenarios. If the event $x_m = 0$ happens first, the mouse reaches sanctuary and moves to state *safe*, where it waits for the cat to reach the wall. As soon as this happens, detectable by the condition $x_c = 0$ becoming true, the system moves to state *Mouse-Wins*. The other possibility is that the event $x_c = x_m > 0$ occurs first, which means that the cat overtook the mouse before the mouse reached sanctuary. In this case they both move to state *Cat-Wins*.

This diagram illustrates the typical interleaving between continuous activities and discrete state changes, which in this example only involves changes of control.

Note that the condition $x_c = x_m > 0$ is not sharp according to our definition. For the current system it is obvious (under the assumption that $\Delta > 0$) that if the condition changes from false to true it always happens at a definite moment. Consequently, in the presented specification, we should not be concerned with the fact that this condition is not sharp. However, an alternative sharp condition that can replace $x_c = x_m > 0$ is

$$(x_c = x_m) \wedge \mathit{Mouse.running}.$$

The idea of using Statecharts with continuous activities associated with certain states (usually basic ones) was already suggested in [Har84]. According to this suggestion, these states are associated with activities that represent physical (and therefore possibly continuous) operations and interactions with the environment.

The Underlying Phase Transition System

Following the graphical representation, we will now identify the phase transition system underlying the picture of Fig. 3.

As state variables we take $V_c = \{x_c, x_m\}$ and $V_d = \{\pi\}$. The variable π is a control variable whose value is a set of basic states of the statechart.

The initial condition is given by

$$\Theta \; : \; \pi = \{\mathit{Start}\}$$

There are several transitions. Following is a list of transitions and the transition relations associated with them. We name transitions according to the states from which they depart.

$$\begin{array}{rcl}
\mathit{Start} & : & (\mathit{Start} \in \pi) \wedge (\pi' = \{\mathit{Mouse.rest},\ \mathit{Cat.rest}\}) \wedge (x'_c = x'_m = X_0) \\
\mathit{Mouse.rest} & : & (\mathit{Mouse.rest} \in \pi) \wedge (\pi' = \pi - \{\mathit{Mouse.rest}\} \cup \{\mathit{Mouse.running}\}) \\
\mathit{Cat.rest} & : & (\mathit{Cat.rest} \in \pi) \wedge (\pi' = \pi - \{\mathit{Cat.rest}\} \cup \{\mathit{Cat.running}\}) \\
\mathit{Mouse.running} & : & (\mathit{Mouse.running} \in \pi) \wedge (x_m = 0) \wedge \\
 & & \qquad (\pi' = \pi - \{\mathit{Mouse.running}\} \cup \{\mathit{Mouse.safe}\}) \\
\mathit{Mouse.safe} & : & (\mathit{Mouse.safe} \in \pi) \wedge (x_c = 0) \wedge (\pi' = \mathit{Mouse\text{-}Wins}) \\
\mathit{Cat.running} & : & (\mathit{Cat.running} \in \pi) \wedge (x_c = x_m > 0) \wedge (\pi' = \mathit{Cat\text{-}Wins})
\end{array}$$

There are two activities α_m and α_c representing the running activities of the two participants. Their equations sets are given by

$$\begin{array}{rcrcl}
\alpha_m & : & (\mathit{Mouse.running} \in \pi) & \rightarrow & \dot{x}_m = -V_m \\
\alpha_c & : & (\mathit{Cat.running} \in \pi) & \rightarrow & \dot{x}_c = -V_c
\end{array}$$

The time bounds for transition *Cat.rest* are $[\Delta, \Delta]$. All other transitions are immediate.

Temporal Specification and Verification

At this preliminary stage of research on hybrid systems, we consider as specification language a minimally extended version of temporal logic. The two main extensions are:

- The underlying time domain are time structures of the form T_θ. Since the basic temporal operators $\mathcal{U}$ and $\mathcal{S}$ are defined on arbitrary totally ordered domains, there is no problem in interpreting them over the hybrid time structures.

  More care is needed to deal with the operators $\bigcirc$ and $\odot$. Some (but not all) moments in T_θ have successors or predecessors. For any pair of moments $\langle i, t_i\rangle$ and $\langle i+1, t_{i+1}\rangle$ such that $t_i = t_{i+1}$, $\langle i+1, t_{i+1}\rangle$ is the successor of $t_i = t_{i+1}$, while $t_i = t_{i+1}$ is the predecessor of $\langle i+1, t_{i+1}\rangle$. We define the formula $\bigcirc p$ (respectively, $\odot p$) to hold at moment $m \in \mathsf{T}_\theta$ if m has a successor (respectively, predecessor) m' and p holds at m'.

- The other extension is allowing references to *age formulas* of the form $\Gamma(p)$. We restrict these reference to formulas p that only refer to discrete variables.

A Rule for Invariance

We propose rule INVH for proving invariance properties of hybrid systems.

INVH

I1. $\varphi \rightarrow q$

I2. $\Theta \rightarrow \varphi$

I3. $(\rho_\tau \wedge \Gamma(enabled(\tau)) \geq l_\tau \wedge T' = T \wedge \varphi) \rightarrow \varphi'$, for every $\tau \in \mathcal{T}$

I4. $$\left(\begin{array}{c} (T = t_1 < T' = t_2) \wedge \varphi \wedge \bigwedge\limits_{\alpha \in J} a_\alpha \wedge \bigwedge\limits_{\alpha \in \mathcal{A}-J} \neg a_\alpha \\ \wedge \\ (V_J = \widehat{V}_J(t_1)) \wedge (V'_J = \widehat{V}_J(t_2)) \wedge (V_{\overline{J}} = V'_{\overline{J}}) \\ \wedge \\ (\forall t \in [t_1, t_2])\widehat{\mathcal{E}}_J(t) \wedge (\forall t \in [t_1, t_2))\Big[\bigwedge\limits_{\tau \in \mathcal{T}_0} \neg \widehat{enabled}(\tau)\Big] \\ \wedge \\ \bigwedge\limits_{\tau \in \mathcal{T}_>} \Big(enabled(\tau) \rightarrow (\Gamma(enabled(\tau)) + t_2 - t_1) \leq u_\tau\Big) \end{array}\right) \rightarrow \varphi' \quad \text{for every } J \subseteq \mathcal{A}$$

$\Box q$

Premise I4 of the rule claims that if there is a continuous phase starting at some moment m and leading to another moment m', then it preserves φ. The premise refers to variables at m in their unprimed version and to variables at m' in their primed version.

The clause $T = t_1 < T' = t_2$ names the time at m as t_1 and the time at m' as t_2. It also states that time has increased between m and m'. The clause φ states that φ holds at m.

Let $J \subseteq \mathcal{A}$ be a subset of activities. The premise considers the case that the set of activities that are operational in the considered phase is J. The conjunction

$$\bigwedge_{\alpha \in J} a_\alpha \ \wedge \ \bigwedge_{\alpha \in \mathcal{A}-J} \neg a_\alpha$$

states that the activation conditions that hold at m correspond precisely to the activities that are in J.

Let $\mathcal{E}_J$ be the set of all equations that appear in $\mathcal{E}_\alpha$ for $\alpha \in J$. We denote by V_J the set of all continuous variables that appear on the left hand side of equations in $\mathcal{E}_J$, and by $V_{\overline{J}}$ the set of all other variables, which includes all discrete variables and some continuous variables that do not appear on the left hand side of equations in $\mathcal{E}_J$.

Clearly, if J is the set of equations that are active in a continuous phase, then the only state variables that can change their values are the variables in V_J, while the variables in $V_{\overline{J}}$ retain their old values. Assume that for each variable $x \in V_J$ there exists a (differentiable) function $\widehat{x}(t)$ defined for $t \in [t_1, t_2]$. The conjunction

$$(V_J = \widehat{V}_J(t_1)) \ \wedge \ (V'_J = \widehat{V}_J(t_2)) \ \wedge \ (V_{\overline{J}} = V'_{\overline{J}})$$

is an abbreviation for

$$\bigwedge_{x \in V_J} (x = \widehat{x}(t_1)) \ \wedge \ \bigwedge_{x \in V_J} (x' = \widehat{x}(t_2)) \ \wedge \ \bigwedge_{x \in V_{\overline{J}}} (x' = x).$$

These clauses state that, for each variable $x \in V_J$, its value at m is equal to the value of the function $\widehat{x}$ at t_1, and the value of x at m' equals the value of $\widehat{x}$ at t_2. Thus, x and $\widehat{x}$ agree on the endpoints of the phase. In addition, the third clause states that variables not in V_J retain their values from m to m'.

The clause $(\forall t \in [t_1, t_2])\widehat{\mathcal{E}}_J(t)$ states that the set of differential equations $\mathcal{E}_J$ holds for $t \in [t_1, t_2]$. This set is obtained by replacing each $x \in V_J$ by the function $\widehat{x}(t)$.

The clause

$$(\forall t \in [t_1, t_2))\Big[\bigwedge_{\tau \in \mathcal{T}_0} \neg \widehat{enabled}(\tau)\Big]$$

states that no immediate transition is enabled at any intermediate moment $m'', m \preceq m'' \prec m'$. The assertion $\widehat{enabled}(\tau)$ is obtained from $enabled(\tau)$ by replacing each variable $x \in V_J$ by $\widehat{x}(t)$.

The clause

$$\bigwedge_{\tau \in \mathcal{T}_>} \Big(enabled(\tau) \ \rightarrow \ (\Gamma(enabled(\tau)) + t_2 - t_1) \leq u_\tau\Big)$$

states that the time step taken in this phase, i.e., $t_2 - t_1$ is such that no enabled transition becomes overripe during the phase.

The primed assertion φ' is obtained by priming all variables in V_J and replacing each occurrence of $\Gamma(p)$ by

$$\Gamma'(p) = \textbf{if } p' \textbf{ then } \Gamma(p) + T' - T \textbf{ else } 0.$$

Example of Verification

Consider the phase transition system Φ_1 presented in the preceding section. We wish to verify that it satisfies the invariant

$$\Box(x \leq 1).$$

We use rule INVH with $q : x \leq 1$. In this case we can take $\varphi = q$, which trivially satisfies premise I1. Premise I2 is similarly obvious since initially $x = 0 \leq 1$. Premise I3 is also immediate since the (only) transition is enabled only when $x = 1$, and it preserves the value of x. It therefore remains to verify premise I4. There are two candidates for the set of operational activities J: ϕ and $\{\alpha\}$. The case $J = \phi$ is trivial since in this case $V_J = \phi$ and therefore $\varphi' = \varphi$.

Let us examine the case $J = \{\alpha\}$. In this case, $V_J = \{x\}$, $V_{\bar{J}} = \phi$, and $\mathcal{E}_J$ contains only $\dot{x} = 1$. Writing I4 with these concrete values we obtain the implication

$$\left(\begin{array}{c} (T = t_1 < T' = t_2) \ \wedge \ (x \leq 1) \ \wedge \ (y = 0) \\ \wedge \\ (x = \widehat{x}(t_1)) \ \wedge \ (x' = \widehat{x}(t_2)) \ \wedge \ (y = y') \\ \wedge \\ (\forall t \in [t_1, t_2])\left[\dot{\widehat{x}}(t) = 1\right] \ \wedge \ (\forall t \in [t_1, t_2))\left[(\widehat{x}(t) \neq 1) \vee (y \neq 0)\right] \end{array}\right) \rightarrow (x' \leq 1)$$

Since $x' = \widehat{x}(t_2)$, we have to show that $\widehat{x}(t_2) \leq 1$. From $x \leq 1$, $x = \widehat{x}(t_1)$, $y = 0$, and the fact that for all $t, t_1 \leq t < t_2$, either $\widehat{x}(t) \neq 1$ or $y \neq 0$, we infer that $\widehat{x}(t_1) < 1$ and that for all $t \in [t_1, t_2)$, $\widehat{x}(t) \neq 1$. Since $\widehat{x}(t)$ is a continuous function for $t \in [t_1, t_2]$, $\widehat{x}(t_2)$ cannot be greater than 1 because, by the intermediate value theorem, there would be a $t \in (t_1, t_2)$ such that $\widehat{x}(t) = 1$, contradicting one of the previous conditions.

Thus $\widehat{x}(t_2)$ and, therefore, x' must be lesser than or equal to 1.

An Invariant for the Cat and Mouse Specification

A more interesting invariant concerns the Cat and Mouse example. Here we may want to determine conditions under which the cat will never catch the mouse. A simple calculation leads to the requirement

$$\frac{X_0}{V_m} < \Delta + \frac{X_0}{V_c} \tag{1}$$

The condition states that the time it takes the mouse to reach the wall is smaller than the time it takes the cat to reach the wall. Since both run at constant speed, this guarantees that they will not meet, except at the wall, the mouse arriving there first.

Assume that condition (1) is given and that $\Delta > 0$). We then would like to establish the invariant

$$Cat.running \wedge (x_c = x_m) \Rightarrow x_m = 0. \tag{2}$$

To prove this invariant we use an auxiliary assertion φ given by a conjunction of the following implications

$$\begin{array}{rcl} Mouse.rest & \rightarrow & x_m = X_0 \\ Mouse.running & \rightarrow & x_m = X_0 - V_m \cdot \Gamma(Mouse.running) \geq 0 \end{array} \tag{3}$$

$$\begin{array}{rcll}
Mouse.safe & \rightarrow & x_m = 0 & (4)\\
Cat.rest & \rightarrow & x_c = X_0 & \\
Cat.running & \rightarrow & x_c = X_0 - V_c \cdot \Gamma(Cat.running) \geq 0 & (5)\\
Cat.rest & \rightarrow & Mouse.rest \vee Mouse.running \vee Mouse.safe & \\
Cat.running & \rightarrow & Mouse.running \vee Mouse.safe & (6)\\
Mouse.rest \wedge Cat.rest & \rightarrow & \Gamma(Mouse.rest) = \Gamma(Cat.rest) = 0 & \\
Mouse.running \wedge Cat.rest & \rightarrow & \Gamma(Mouse.running) = \Gamma(Cat.rest) \leq \Delta & \\
Mouse.running \wedge Cat.running & \rightarrow & \Gamma(Mouse.running) = \Gamma(Cat.running) + \Delta & (7)
\end{array}$$

Assuming that φ has been shown to satisfy premises I2–I4, we will show that it implies $q : (Cat.running \wedge (x_c = x_m)) \rightarrow x_m = 0$. By implication (6), when the cat is running the mouse is either in state *running* or in state *safe*. If it is in state *safe* then, by implication (4), $x_m = 0$. If it is in state *running*, then the assumption $x_c = x_m$ with implications (3), (5), and (7), leads to $V_c \cdot \Gamma(Cat.running) = V_m \cdot (\Gamma(Cat.running) + \Delta)$. From this, we can conclude $V_c > V_m$ and

$$\Gamma(Cat.running) = \frac{V_m \cdot \Delta}{V_c - V_m}.$$

On the other hand, from implication (5) we obtain $X_0 - V_c \cdot \Gamma(Cat.running) \geq 0$ which can be written as

$$\Gamma(Cat.running) \leq \frac{X_0}{V_c}.$$

Comparing the equality and inequality involving $\Gamma(Cat.running)$, we obtain

$$\frac{V_m \cdot \Delta}{V_c - V_m} \leq \frac{X_0}{V_c},$$

which can be rewritten as

$$\frac{X_0}{V_m} \geq \Delta + \frac{X_0}{V_c},$$

contradicting condition (1).

This shows that, under condition (1), if the cat is in state *running* and $x_c = x_m$, then the mouse can only be in state *safe* with $x_m = 0$, implying assertion q.

A more careful analysis shows that the weaker requirement

$$\frac{X_0}{V_m} \leq \Delta + \frac{X_0}{V_c} \tag{8}$$

is already a sufficient condition for the cat not catching up with the mouse except possibly at the wall. A proof of this fact follows similar lines to the proof presented above.

6 Sampling Computations of Hybrid Systems

The notions of hybrid trace and hybrid computation presented in the preceding section are based on extending the discrete sequence structure of timed computations into the dense time structure T_θ. An alternative approach that we will now consider takes a less radical step and bases the description of hybrid behavior on *sequences* of situations, very similar to timed traces.

The Continuous Step

Assume a given phase transition system Φ with state variables $V = V_c \cup V_d$. Consider two situations $s, s' \in \Sigma_T$. We characterize the relation holding between s and s' if they are possible left and right endpoints of a continuous phase in the behavior of Φ. The characterization uses the notation of premise I4 of rule INVH. This notation writes

J	for	a set of activities
$\mathcal{E}_J$	for	the set of differential equations appearing in $\mathcal{E}_\alpha$ for some $\alpha \in J$
V_J	for	the set of (continuous) variables appearing on the left hand side of some equation in $\mathcal{E}_J$
$V_{\overline{J}}$	for	$V - V_J$
$\widehat{x}(t)$	for	a function representing the value of $x \in V_J$ over the continuous phase
$\widehat{V}_J$	for	the set of functions $\widehat{x}(t)$, $x \in J$.

The formula ρ_{cont} expresses the relation holding between the situations at the two endpoints of a continuous phase. It is defined by

$$\rho_{cont}: \quad \exists J, \widehat{V}_J, t_1, t_2 \left(\begin{array}{c} (T = t_1 < T' = t_2) \ \wedge \ \varphi \ \wedge \ \bigwedge_{\alpha \in J} a_\alpha \ \wedge \ \bigwedge_{\alpha \in \mathcal{A}-J} \neg a_\alpha \\ \wedge \\ (V_J = \widehat{V}_J(t_1)) \ \wedge \ (V'_J = \widehat{V}_J(t_2)) \ \wedge \ (V_{\overline{J}} = V'_{\overline{J}}) \\ \wedge \\ (\forall t \in [t_1, t_2])\widehat{\mathcal{E}}_J(t) \ \wedge \ (\forall t \in [t_1, t_2))\Big[\bigwedge_{\tau \in \mathcal{T}_0} \neg \widehat{enabled}(\tau) \Big] \end{array} \right)$$

As usual, unprimed situation variables refer to their values in s while primed variables refer to their values in s'. For detailed explanation of the various clauses appearing in ρ_{cont}, we refer the readers to the explanations following rule INVH. Note that we have omitted the clause

$$\bigwedge_{\tau \in \mathcal{T}_>} \Big(enabled(\tau) \ \rightarrow \ (\Gamma(enabled(\tau)) + t_2 - t_1) \leq u_\tau \Big)$$

from the definition of ρ_{cont}. This is because it will be implied by other requirements.

Sampling Computations

In close analogy with the notion of timed computations, we define a *sampling computation* of a phase transition system Φ to be an infinite sequence of situations

$$\sigma: \ s_0, s_1, \ldots,$$

where $s_i \in \Sigma_T$ for each $i = 0, 1, \ldots$, and the time stamps, $s_0[T], s_1[T], \ldots$ form a progressive time sequence, which satisfies the following requirements:

- [*Initiality*] $s_0 \models \Theta$.
- [*Consecution*] For all $i \geq 0$,

- Either $t_i = t_{i+1}$ and there is a transition $\tau \in \mathcal{T}$ such that $s_{i+1}[V] \in \tau(s_i[V])$, or
- s_i and s_{i+1} jointly satisfy ρ_{cont}.

In the first case, we say that τ is *taken* at position i. The second case is described as a *continuous step* being taken at position i.

- [*Lower bound*] For every transition $\tau \in \mathcal{T}$ and position $j \geq 0$, if τ is taken at j, there exists a position i, $i \leq j$, such that $t_i + l_\tau \leq t_j$ and τ is enabled on $s_i[V], s_{i+1}[V], \ldots, s_j[V]$ and not taken at any of the positions $i, i+1, \ldots, j-1$. This implies that τ must be continuously enabled for at least l_τ time units before it can be taken.

- [*Upper bound*] For every transition $\tau \in \mathcal{T}$ and position $i \geq 0$, if τ is enabled at position i, there exists a position j, $i \leq j$, such that $t_i + u_\tau \geq t_j$ and

  either τ is not enabled at j,
  or τ is taken at j.

  In other words, τ cannot be continuously enabled for more than u_τ time units without being taken.

A temporal axiomatization of sampling computations can be easily obtained by taking all the axioms for timed systems presented in Section 3, except for C_{cons}, which has to be modified. Writing the continuous step relation as $\rho_{cont}(V_T, V_T')$, the axiom for hybrid consecution replacing C_{cons} is given by

$$H_{cons} \quad : \quad \Box\Big[\rho_{cont}(V_T, \bigcirc V_T) \ \vee \ \bigvee_{\tau \in \mathcal{T}} (waiting(\tau) \geq l_\tau \wedge taken(\tau))\Big].$$

This axiom states that, at any position, either a continuous step or a transition is taken.

How Faithful is the Sampling Model?

The main difference between continuous computations based on dense time structures, as presented in the previous section, and the more conservative notion of sampling computations is in the amount of formally visible details given about the change of continuous variables over continuous phases.

Consider two moments $m_i : \langle i, t_i \rangle$ and $m_{i+1} : \langle i+1, t_{i+1} \rangle$ in a computation of a hybrid system, such that $t_i < t_{i+1}$. Obviously there is a continuous phase delineated by m_i and m_{i+1} in which some continuous variables, say $x \in V_c$, change continuously. Continuous computations represent the history of change of x in this phase by recognizing a continuum of intermediate moments $m, m_i \prec m \prec m_{i+1}$, and specifying a state $\sigma(m)$ for each of them. A sampling computation, on the other hand, officially recognizes only the endpoints m_i and m_{i+1} and hides the history of continuous change between them inside the definition of ρ_{cont}.

What are the implications of this difference? One aspect to be considered is the degree of correspondence with our intuition. Clearly, both approaches admit that there is continuous change occurring in the continuous phase. Why not represent it explicitly?

There is, however, another point which we would like to address and clarify. Assume that for a continuous variable x we claim an invariant such as $\square(x \neq 1)$, and that a given computation satisfies this requirement. In the continuous computation case, this implies that x differs from 1 at any time point *including* the continuous phases. On the other hand, if a sampling computation $\sigma : s_0, s_1, \ldots$ is claimed to satisfy $\square(x \neq 1)$, we only know that x differs from 1 at the discrete sampling points but can infer nothing about its value within the continuous phases.

Example

Consider a phase transition system Φ_2 defined as follows:

$V = V_c = \{x\}$
$\Theta : (x = 2)$
Transitions: a single transition τ with $\rho_\tau : (x' = 2)$ and time bounds

$$[l, u] = [1, 1]$$

Activities: a single activity α with conditional equation $\dot{x} = -2$.

This system has the sampling computation

$$\sigma : \langle x:2\,, T:0\rangle \xrightarrow{cont} \langle x:0\,, T:1\rangle \xrightarrow{\tau} \langle x:2\,, T:1\rangle \xrightarrow{cont} \langle x:0\,, T:2\rangle \xrightarrow{\tau} \langle x:2\,, T:2\rangle \xrightarrow{cont} \cdots$$

In each continuous phase x drops continuously from 2 to 0, and therefore, at time points $T = 0.5, 1.5, 2.5, \ldots$ its value is 1. On the other hand, the formula $\square(x \neq 1)$ obviously holds over σ. ▪

However, this problem arises only when we consider formulas that hold over *individual* computations. If we consider specifications not at the level of individual computations but at the system level, and restrict our attention to safety properties, this apparent discrepancy disappears. Namely, if $\square(x \neq 1)$ is claimed to be valid over *all* sampled computations then it is guaranteed that x differs from 1 at all time points, including those falling within continuous phases.

This is because, in taking a continuous step, we do not necessarily have to take the maximal time step possible. The definition allows us to stop at any earlier time point. Thus, while Φ_2 has σ as one of its computations, it also has the computation

$$\sigma' : \langle x:2\,, T:0.0\rangle \xrightarrow{cont} \langle x:1\,, T:0.5\rangle \xrightarrow{cont} \langle x:0\,, T:1.0\rangle \xrightarrow{\tau} \langle x:2\,, T:1.0\rangle \xrightarrow{cont} \langle x:1\,, T:1.5\rangle \xrightarrow{cont} \langle x:0\,, T:2.0\rangle \xrightarrow{\tau} \langle x:2\,, T:2.0\rangle \xrightarrow{cont} \cdots$$

which does not satisfy $\square(x \neq 1)$.

It follows that, at the system level, $\square(x \neq 1)$ is not a valid specification for Φ_2. This observation suggests that the sampling model provides faithful representation of all invariance properties of the form $\square p$, where p is a state formula, that are valid for the hybrid system.

On the other hand, this is not true if we consider other properties. Consider the specification

$$\diamond (x = 1)$$

which states that x eventually equals 1. This formula is valid over all continuous computations of Φ_2 and therefore should be considered a valid property of this system. On the other hand, while it is satisfied by σ', it is not satisfied by σ. This shows that non-invariance properties are not fully captured by the sampling model.

The sampling model has been studied in [MSB91] and recommended by Lamport as a simple way to represent hybrid systems.

References

[ACD90] R. Alur, C. Courcoubetis, and D.L. Dill. Model checking for real-time systems. In *Proceedings of the Fifth Annual Symposium on Logic in Computer Science*, pages 414–425. IEEE Computer Society Press, 1990.

[AH89] R. Alur and T.A. Henzinger. A really temporal logic. In *Proc. 30th IEEE Symp. Found. of Comp. Sci.*, pages 164–169, 1989.

[AH90] R. Alur and T.A. Henzinger. Real-time logics: Complexity and expressiveness. In *Proc. 5th IEEE Symp. Logic in Comp. Sci.*, 1990.

[AL91] M. Abadi and L. Lamport. An old-fashioned recipe for real time. In *Real-Time: Theory in Practice*. Lec. Notes in Comp. Sci., Springer-Verlag, 1991. This volume.

[CHR92] Z. Chaochen, C.A.R Hoare, and A.P. Ravn. A calculus of durations. *Information Processing Letters*, 40(5):269–276, 1992.

[EC82] E.A. Emerson and E.M. Clarke. Using branching time temporal logic to synthesize synchronization skeletons. *Sci. Comp. Prog.*, 2:241–266, 1982.

[Har84] D. Harel. Statecharts: A visual approach to complex systems. Technical report, Dept. of Applied Mathematics, Weizmann Institute of Science CS84-05, 1984.

[Har87] D. Harel. Statecharts: A visual formalism for complex systems. *Sci. Comp. Prog.*, 8:231–274, 1987.

[HLP90] E. Harel, O. Lichtenstein, and A. Pnueli. Explicit clock temporal logic. In *Proc. 5th IEEE Symp. Logic in Comp. Sci.*, pages 402–413, 1990.

[HMP91] T. Henzinger, Z. Manna, and A. Pnueli. Temporal proof methodologies for real-time systems. In *Proc. 18th ACM Symp. Princ. of Prog. Lang.*, pages 353–366, 1991.

[HRR91] K.M. Hansen, A.P. Ravn, and H. Rischel. Specifying and verifying requirements of real-time systems. *Proc. ACM SIGSOFT'91 Conf. on Software for Critical Systems*, 15(5):44–54, 1991.

[KKZ87] R. Koymans, R. Kuiper, and E. Zijlstra. Specifying message passing and real-time systems with real-time temporal logic. In *Esprit 87 Results and Achievements*. North-Holland, 1987.

[KP92] Y. Kesten and A. Pnueli. Timed and hybrid statecharts and their textual representation. In *Formal Techniques in Real-Time and Fault-Tolerant Systems*. Lec. Notes in Comp. Sci., Springer-Verlag, 1992. Proceedings of a Symposium, Nijmegen.

[KVdR83] R. Koymans, J. Vytopyl, and W.-P. de Roever. Real-time programming and asynchronous message passing. In *Proc. 2nd ACM Symp. Princ. of Dist. Comp.*, pages 187–197, 1983.

[Lam83] L. Lamport. What good is temporal logic. In R.E.A. Mason, editor, *Proc. IFIP 9th World Congress*, pages 657–668. North-Holland, 1983.

[MP81] Z. Manna and A. Pnueli. Verification of concurrent programs: The temporal framework. In R.S. Boyer and J.S. Moore, editors, *The Correctness Problem in Computer Science*, pages 215–273. Academic Press, London, 1981.

[MP89] Z. Manna and A. Pnueli. The anchored version of the temporal framework. In J.W. de Bakker, W.-P. de Roever, and G. Rozenberg, editors, *Linear Time, Branching Time and Partial Order in Logics and Models for Concurrency*, pages 201–284. Lec. Notes in Comp. Sci. 354, Springer-Verlag, 1989.

[MP91] Z. Manna and A. Pnueli. *The Temporal Logic of Reactive and Concurrent Systems: Specificaion.* Springer Verlag, New York, 1991.

[MSB91] K. Marzullo, F.B. Schneider, and N. Budhiraja. Derivation of sequential, real-time, process-control programs. Technical report, Cornell University, 1991. To appear in: *Foundations of Real-Time Computing: Formal Specifications and Methods.*

[NRSV90] X. Nicollin, J.-L. Richier, J. Sifakis, and J. Voiron. ATP: an algebra for timed processes. In *Proc. IFIP Working Conference on Formal Description of Programming Concepts, Tiberias, Israel.* North-Holland, 1990.

[NSY91] X. Nicollin, J. Sifakis, and S. Yovine. From ATP to timed graphs and hybrid systems. In *Real-Time: Theory in Practice.* Lec. Notes in Comp. Sci., Springer-Verlag, 1991. This volume.

[Ost89] J.S. Ostroff. *Temporal Logic for Real-Time Systems.* Advanced Software Development Series. Research Studies Press (John Wiley & Sons), Taunton, England, 1989.

[PH88] A. Pnueli and E. Harel. Applications of temporal logic to the specification of real time systems. In M. Joseph, editor, *Formal Techniques in Real-Time and Fault-Tolerant Systems*, pages 84–98. Lec. Notes in Comp. Sci. 331, Springer-Verlag, 1988.

[Pnu86] A. Pnueli. Applications of temporal logic to the specification and verification of reactive systems: A survey of current trends. In J.W. de Bakker, W.-P. de Roever, and G. Rozenberg, editors, *Current Trends in Concurrency*, pages 510–584. Lec. Notes in Comp. Sci. 224, Springer-Verlag, 1986.

[PS91] A. Pnueli and M. Shalev. What is in a step: On the semantics of statecharts. In T. Ito and A. R. Meyer, editors, *Theoretical Aspects of Computer Software*, pages 244–264. Lec. Notes in Comp. Sci. 526, Springer-Verlag, 1991.

[RR87] G.M. Reed and V.W. Roscoe. Metric spaces as models for real-time concurrency. In *Mathematical Foundations of Programming*, pages 331–343. Lec. Notes in Comp. Sci. 298, Springer-Verlag, 1987.

[San89] E. Sandewall. Combining logic and differential equations for describing real-world systems. In R.J. Brachman, H.J. Levesque, and R. Reiter, editors, *Principles of Knowledge Representation and Reasoning*, pages 412–420. Morgan Kaufmann, 1989.

[SBM91] F. B. Schneider, B. Bloom, and K. Marzullo. Putting time into proof outlines. In *Real-Time: Theory in Practice*. Lec. Notes in Comp. Sci., Springer-Verlag, 1991. This volume.

Coping with Implementation Dependencies in Real-Time System Verification

Aloysius K. Mok

Department of Computer Science
University of Texas at Austin
Austin, TX 78712
USA

Abstract

A major difficulty in verifying real-time systems is that behavior involving quantitative timing often depends on assumptions about the execution environment, in particular the availability of resources (e.g., number of CPUs) and the resource sharing policy of the run-time system (e.g., process scheduling algorithm). Thus a proof that a real-time program satisfies its quantitative specification is sensitive to assumptions about implementation dependencies. While these dependencies are in general unavoidable, it is important to isolate them in a proof of correctness so that if the execution environment changes, the impact of a change can be readily identified and understood. In this paper, we discuss a proof method that observes the principle of separation of concerns. This method involves two steps. In the first step, we determine if a timing property can be proved from the system specification, and identify implementation-dependent assumptions, if any, that are required to derive a proof. In the second step, we determine if the system specification and other required implementation dependencies can be enforced by control structures that meet the required timing constraints. The advantage of this method is that implementation dependencies are explicitly identified and are brought in as needed. This separation of concerns is especially important for the maintenance of real-time programs. We show that both steps of this method can be accomplished by making use of the logic RTL (Real Time Logic).

Introduction

Unlike programs used for transaction processing or scientific computation, a real-time program must satisfy not only functional correctness requirements but also timeliness requirements. Real-time correctness may be established by proving the

---

Supported by a research grant from the Office of Naval Research under ONR contract number N00014-89-J-1472.

implication:

$$SP \wedge EA \rightarrow SA$$

where SP is the specification of the program, EA is the set of assumptions (axioms) that captures the behavior of the execution environment, and SA is the safety assertion to be ascertained.

Capturing the behavior of the execution environment (i.e., EA constitutes a model of the environment) is in general an engineering endeavor that often involves implementation details to be abstracted out of high-level programming languages. Indeed, a programmer is supposed not to have to worry about the speed of the underlying hardware or the process scheduling policy of the operating system. Those other details are best left to the electrical engineers who design the hardware or the operating-system specialists who design the run-time resource allocation strategy. Herein lies the difficulty of verifying real-time programs: the programmer must be knowledgeable of the often messy details of the execution environment and more importantly, the programmer must also understand the impact of those details on the timing behavior of the program. For example, a correctness proof may require the establishment of the assertion that the process scheduling policy of the operating system guarantees that the response time to a periodic interrupt does not exceed one millisecond. This may in turn require, in a shared-processor multiprocessing environment, the application of real-time scheduling theory which is a specialty unto itself. It is difficult enough for a programmer to be sufficiently skilled as an applied mathematician to prove the functional correctness of a program. It is certainly beyond most programmers' ability to grasp implementation details and be knowledgeable about diverse areas of expertise such as real-time performance theory in order to engineer reliable real-time systems. Clearly, a discipline of design that observes the principle of separation of concerns is in order.

In this paper, we propose a method for establishing the correctness of real-time programs. Two well-tested ideas are used to achieve a separation of concerns between functional correctness and timeliness. The first idea is that of minimizing the interdependency between functional and timing requirements (an application of information hiding). Technically, the problem is to minimize the dependency on the execution environment by expliciting computing a subset EA' of the environmental assumptions EA that is required to establish the safety assertion SA. That is, we want to formalize the computation of a predicate EA' to establish the implication:

$$SP \wedge EA' \rightarrow SA$$

This is akin to computing the weakest precondition in imperative programming languages, except that the present task has to be performed at the level of specification languages which need not have any particular operational semantics. This is because postponing the computation of EA' until SP is mapped into imperative programs may already bind the implementation to certain execution environments, with a concomitant loss of abstraction.

The second idea is that of providing an interface language that allows the orthogonal specification of functional and timing correctness requirements. For example, we would like to be able to axiomatize the operating system process-scheduling policy apart from the semantics of the programming language which is used to specify the functional behavior of a process. This is to achieve a division of labor so that programmers skilled in proving functional correctness need not understand the details of scheduling theory and vice versa.

The realization of the above two ideas is facilitated by using a formal notation RTL (Real Time Logic) and an annotation system that allows us to "superimpose" timing requirements on top of imperative programming languages. Given the specification of a real-time system, our proof method involves two steps: In the first step, we derive the environmental assumptions (in the form of timing requirements) that are needed to establish the safety assertion to be maintained by the system. In the second step, we establish the compliance of system timing requirements from the first step by either exhibiting a scheduler that satisfies them (scheduler synthesis) or by showing that the given execution environment does not violate them (schedulability analysis).

The thesis of this paper is to argue that the logic RTL is well suited to the application of a design discipline that strives to achieve a separation of concerns between functional and timing correctness. While the logic RTL and its application was first described in [2], we shall give a syntactic extension of RTL to capture implementation dependencies such as process scheduling policies in this paper.

The Logic RTL.

RTL (Real Time Logic) is a multi-sorted first-order logic. A computation in RTL is a sequence of event sets. Time passes between sets of events, and the actual sets of events are instantaneous. In RTL, we reason about individual occurrences of events where an event occurrence marks a point in time which is of significance to the behavior of the system. There is an important distinction between an action and an event in RTL. An action is an activity which requires a non-zero but bounded amount of system resources. However, events serve only as temporal markers. An occurrence of an event defines a time value, namely its time of occurrence, and imposes no requirement on system resources. The execution of an action is represented by two events: one denoting its initiation and the other denoting its completion.

Events have unique names. Two classes of events are of particular interest: (1) start/stop events marking the initiation and completion of an action, and (2) transition events denoting a change in a state variable.

Start and Stop Events: We use the notation $\uparrow$A to represent the event marking the initiation of action A, and $\downarrow$A to denote the event marking the completion of action A. For instance, $\uparrow$REX_TALK and $\downarrow$REX_TALK represent respectively the events corresponding to the start and the stop of action REX_TALK. REX_TALK is the name of the activity of giving a lecture at the REX workshop which is documented by this proceeding respectively.

Transition Events: A state variable may describe a physical aspect or a certain property of a system, e.g., an autopilot switch which is either ON or OFF. The execution of an action may cause the value of one or more state variables to change. A state attribute, S is a predicate which asserts that a state variable takes on a certain value in its domain. For example, S may denote the predicate: the autopilot is ON. The corresponding state variable transition events, represented syntactically by (S:=T) and (S:=F), denote respectively the events that mark the turning on and off of the autopilot switch. Whenever it is unambiguous, we shall use state variable and state attribute interchangeably.

In addition to the above two classes, other classes of events can be specified when modeling a real time system. For instance, in [2], the class of external events was introduced to denote the events that cannot be caused to happen by the computer system but can impact system behavior. We use the notation of any name in capital letters prefixed by the special letter Ω (Omega) to denote an external event. For example, ΩBUTTON1 represents the external event associated with pressing button 1.

The *occurrence relation*, denoted by the letter Θ (Theta), is introduced to capture the notion of real time. The event constants introduced earlier represent the things that can happen in a system. The occurrence relation assigns a time value to each occurrence of an event which happens. Informally, $\Theta(e,i,t)$ denotes that the ith occurrence of an event e happens at time t, where e is an event constant, i is a positive integer term, and t is non-negative integer term. For instance, $\Theta(\downarrow\text{REX\_TALK},1,x)$ denotes that the first occurrence of the event marking the completion of action REX_TALK happens at time x.

In the examples in this paper, we shall use an uninterpreted function instead of a relation to capture the notion of real time. Specifically, we write $@(e,i) = t$ if and only if $\Theta(e,i,t)$ holds. We use the relational notation in defining the formal semantics of RTL because the use of a relation has the advantage of not requiring that all occurrence of an event must happen since an event may occur only a finite number of times or even not at all. This avoids some technicalities that come with the use of a partial function in the functional notation. However, the functional notation is more intuitive and easier to use in manipulating the arithmetic inequalities in proofs.

The notion of an occurrence relation is central to RTL. In particular, a specification of a system and the timing requirements on its behavior are restrictions on the occurrence relation and its arguments.

RTL predicates are formed from the occurrence relation, or from the mathematical relations ($=$, $<$, $\leq$, $>$, $\geq$) and algebraic expressions allowing integer constants, variables, and addition. Multiplication by constants is used as an abbreviation for addition. One further restriction is that time values cannot be added to or compared with occurrence values. RTL formulas are constructed using the occurrence relation, the equality/inequality predicates, universal and existential quantifiers, and the first-order logical connectives ($\neg, \wedge, \vee, \rightarrow$)†.

The Syntax and Semantics of RTL. We begin by introducing the language of Real Time Logic. The formulas of RTL are made up of the following symbols:

- The truth symbols *true* and *false*
- A set of time variable symbols **A**.
- A set of occurrence variable symbols **B**.
- A set of constant symbols **C** including the natural numerals
- A set of event constant symbols **D**
- The function symbol +
- The predicate symbols $<$, $\leq$, $>$, $\geq$, $=$
- The occurrence relation symbol Θ
- The logical connectives $\wedge$, $\vee$, $\neg$ and $\rightarrow$.
- Existential and universal quantifier symbols $\exists$, $\forall$.

The *time terms* of RTL are expressions built up according to the following rules:

- The constant symbols in **C** are time terms.
- The variable symbols in **A** are time terms.
- If t_1 and t_2 are time terms, then the function application

  $$t_1 + t_2$$

  is a time term.

The *occurrence terms* of RTL are expressions built up according to the following rules:

- The constant symbols in **C** are occurrence terms.
- The variable symbols in **B** are occurrence terms.
- If i and j are occurrence terms, then the function application

† The standard precedence order is assumed for these connectives. $\neg$ has the highest precedence, $\wedge$ and $\vee$ the next highest precedence, and $\rightarrow$ the lowest precedence.

$$i + j$$

is an occurrence term.

The *propositions* of RTL are constructed according to the following rules:

- The truth symbols *true* and *false* are propositions.
- If t_1 and t_2 are time terms and ρ is an inequality/equality predicate symbol, then

  $$t_1 \rho t_2$$

  is a proposition.
- If i and j are occurrence terms and ρ is an inequality/equality predicate symbol, then

  $$i \rho j$$

  is a proposition.
- If i is an occurrence term, t is a time term and e is an event constant, then

  $$\Theta(e, i, t)$$

  is a proposition.

The *formulas* of RTL are constructed from the propositions, logical connectives and quantifiers in the usual fashion.

An interpretation for an RTL formula must assign a meaning to each of the free symbols in the formula. It will assign elements from a domain to the constants, functions (over the domain) to the function symbols, and relations (over the domain) to the predicate symbols.

Let **N** be the set of natural numbers, and **E** be a set of events. Usually **D** and **E** are identical, although this is not necessary. An interpretation **I** over the domain $\mathbf{N} \cup \mathbf{E}$ assigns values to each of a set of constant, function, and predicate symbols, as follows:

Each element in the set of constant symbols **C** is assigned an element in **N**, with the numerals being assigned to the corresponding natural numbers. Each element in the set of event constant symbols **D** is assigned a distinct element in **E**. The function symbol '+' is integer addition. The predicate symbols $<$, $\leq$, $>$, $\geq$, and $=$ are assigned the usual equality/inequality binary relations. The predicate symbol Θ is assigned an *occurrence relation.*

Definition: An *occurrence relation* is any relation on the set

$$\mathbf{E} \times \mathbf{Z}^{+} \times \mathbf{N}$$

where **E** is a set of events, $\mathbf{Z}^{+}$ is the set of positive integers, and **N** is the set of natural numbers, such that the following axioms hold:

Monotonicity Axioms: For each event e in the set **D**,

$$\forall i\ \forall t\ \forall t'\ [\ \Theta(e,i,t)\ \wedge\ \Theta(e,i,t')\ ]\ \rightarrow\ t = t'$$
$$\forall i\ \forall t\ [\ \Theta(e,i,t)\ \wedge\ i > 1\ ]\ \rightarrow\ [\ \exists t'\ \Theta(e,i-1,t')\ \wedge\ t' < t\ ]$$

The first axiom requires that at most one time value can be associated with each occurrence *i* of an event *e*, i.e., the same occurrence of an event cannot happen at two distinct times. The second axiom expresses the requirement that if the *i*th occurrence of an event *e* happens, then the previous occurrences of *e* must have happened earlier. This axiom also requires that two distinct occurrences of the same event must happen at different times.

Start/Stop Event Axioms: For each pair of start/stop events in the set **D**,

$$\forall i\ \forall t\ \Theta(\downarrow A,i,t)\ \rightarrow\ [\ \exists t'\ \Theta(\uparrow A,i,t')\ \wedge\ t' < t\ ]$$

where $\uparrow A$ and $\downarrow A$ denote the events marking the start and stop of an action A, respectively. The above axiom requires every occurrence of a stop event to be preceded by a corresponding start event.

Transition Event Axioms: For the transition events in the set **D** corresponding to a state variable S,

$$\begin{aligned}&\Theta((S:=T),1,0)\ \rightarrow\\&(\ \forall i\ \forall t\ \Theta((S:=F),i,t) \rightarrow [\ \exists t'\ \Theta((S:=T),i,t')\ \wedge\ t' < t\ ]\ \wedge\\&\forall i\ \forall t\ \Theta((S:=T),i+1,t) \rightarrow [\ \exists t'\ \Theta((S:=F),i,t')\ \wedge\ t' < t\ ]\ )\end{aligned}$$

$$\begin{aligned}&\Theta((S:=F),1,0)\ \rightarrow\\&(\ \forall i\ \forall t\ \Theta((S:=T),i,t) \rightarrow [\ \exists t'\ \Theta((S:=F),i,t')\ \wedge\ t' < t\ ]\ \wedge\\&\forall i\ \forall t\ \Theta((S:=F),i+1,t) \rightarrow [\ \exists t'\ \Theta((S:=T),i,t')\ \wedge\ t' < t\ ]\ )\end{aligned}$$

The preceding transition event axioms define the order in which two complementary transition events can occur depending on whether S is initially true or false.

The above description constitutes the formal definition of unrestricted RTL. Technically, RTL is a **subset** of Presburger Arithmetic augmented by an uninterpreted relation. The axioms of unrestricted RTL apply to all real-time systems. Depending on the application, RTL may be further restricted by additional axioms or other syntactic constraints.

Derivation of Environmental Assumptions

We now illustrate the first step of our proof method by means of the following example. We first give an informal English specification of the example problem: A telemetry system consists of a sender S and a receiver R and a single-buffer memory between them. This system operates as follows.

• Sender S puts a message in the buffer exactly every P time units.

• Receiver R removes and processes a message from buffer in every period of length P after arrival of message. Processing starts as soon as a message is removed from buffer.

• R takes c_R time units to process each message.

• R's clock and S's clock are not perfectly synchronized. R's clock is at most Θ time units behind. ($\Theta < P$)

A safety assertion for this system is:

• R must remove a message from memory before S puts another one in.

Recall that our goal is to derive a subset of environmental assumptions that is sufficient to ensure that the safety assertion is satisfied by every legal implementation. We shall do this by validating the safety assertion against the system specification (i.e., attempting to derive the safety assertion from the system specification alone). There are three possible outcomes when one attempts to validate a safety assertion against the system specification: (1) The safety assertion is a theorem derivable from the system specification, in which case any correct implementation will be safe. (2) The safety assertion is unsatisfiable with respect to the system specification, in which case every correct implementation will be unsafe. Obviously, the system specification must be revised in this case. (3) The negation of the safety assertion is satisfiable under certain conditions, in which case it is possible to end up with an unsafe implementation, depending on the execution environment. In this case, the system specification may be tightened to restrict the implementation to only those that satisfy the safety assertion. The required restriction is obtained by negating the conditions that may lead to the violation of the safety assertion by a legal implementation. The negation of these conditions constitutes the subset EA' of environmental assumptions that we are looking for.

To validate the safety assertion in the above example, we first express the informal English specification in a set of RTL formulas and then invoke a verifier (a semi-decision procedure) to obtain an answer. We shall use the functional notation of RTL. (Recall that in the functional notation, the term $@(e,i)$ denotes the application of the uninterpreted "@" function to the arguments e, an event and i, an integer which is the instance of the event e. The value of $@(e,i)$ is the time of occurrence of the ith instance of the event *e*.) With this notation, timing constraints can be expressed as restrictions on the @ function. We give below the RTL specification of the telemetry example. The symbols ↑R, ↓R denote respectively the events the Receiver R starting/completing processing a message from the sender S. The symbol ↓*S* denotes the event: the sender S putting a message into the buffer.

• *System specification (SP)*

Sender S: $\forall i \geq 1 \quad @(\downarrow S,i) = (i-1)*P$

Receiver R:
$$\forall i \geq 1 \quad @(\uparrow R,i) \geq (i-1)*P+\Theta \ \wedge$$
$$@(\downarrow R,i) \leq i*P+\Theta \ \wedge$$
$$@(\downarrow S,i) \leq @(\uparrow R,i)$$

$$\forall i \geq 1 \quad @(\downarrow R,i) \geq @(\uparrow R,i)+c_R$$

Receiver's clock skew:
$$\Theta < P$$

• *Safety Assertion (SA)*

$$\forall i \geq 1 \quad @(\uparrow R,i) \leq @(\downarrow S,i+1)$$

With this notation, the objective is to show: $SP \rightarrow SA$. Alternatively, we may show that the formula $SP \wedge \neg SA$ is not satisfiable, where $SA = \forall i \geq 1 \ @(\uparrow R,i) \leq @(\downarrow S,i+1)$ and so $\neg SA = \quad \exists i \geq 1 \ @(\uparrow R,i) > @(\downarrow S,i+1)$. This can be done by first removing the quantifiers and skolemization to obtain:

SP:
$$(1) \quad @(\downarrow S,i) = (i-1)*P$$
$$(2) \quad @(\uparrow R,i) \geq (i-1)*P+\Theta$$
$$(3) \quad @(\downarrow R,i) \leq i*P+\Theta$$
$$(4) \quad @(\downarrow S,i) \leq @(\uparrow R,i)$$
$$(5) \quad @(\downarrow R,i) \geq @(\uparrow R,i)+c_R$$
$$(6) \quad \Theta < P$$

¬SA:
$$(7) \quad @(\uparrow R,I) > @(\downarrow S,I+1)$$

To show that the above inequalities do not admit a solution, we focus on inequalities (1), (3), (5) and (7).

$$@(\downarrow S,i) \;=\; (i\text{-}1) * P \qquad (1)$$
$$@(\downarrow R,i) \le i * P + \Theta \qquad (3)$$
$$@(\downarrow R,i) \ge @(\uparrow R,i) + c_R \qquad (5)$$
$$@(\uparrow R,I) > @(\downarrow S,I+1) \qquad (7)$$

Rewriting the inequalities, we get:

$$@(\downarrow S,i+1) \;=\; i * P \qquad (1)$$
$$i * P + \Theta \ge @(\downarrow R,i) \qquad (3)$$
$$@(\downarrow R,i) \ge @(\uparrow R,i) + c_R \qquad (5)$$
$$@(\uparrow R,I) > @(\downarrow S,I+1) \qquad (7)$$

Finally, we can "chain" the inequalities by observing that the "@" terms on the left and right hand sides cancel each other.

$$@(\downarrow S,I+1) \;=\; I * P \qquad (1)$$
$$I * P + \Theta \ge @(\downarrow R,I) \qquad (3)$$
$$@(\downarrow R,I) \ge @(\uparrow R,I) + c_R \qquad (5)$$
$$@(\uparrow R,I) > @(\downarrow S,I+1) \qquad (7)$$

Obviously, a solution requires: $\Theta > c_R$. This implies that a sufficient condition for validating the system with respect to the safety assertion is to ensure: $\Theta \le c_R$. This is an answer of type case (3) that a verifier may return.

We emphasize that the above analysis is done with the timing specification, not with programs in an imperative language. The result of the analysis is an additional timing obligation EA': $\Theta \le c_R$ that must be satisfied after refinement to programs. It is also important to note that we have not shown that the system specification can be implemented. In fact, no implementation exists if $c_R > P$. All we assert is that if an implementation exists, then it is safe subject to some condition. In general, care must be taken to include the negation of the safety assertion in the set of support in the refutation procedure in order to avoid a schedulability analysis.

In general, the derivation of EA' from SP and SA cannot be completely automated. This is because the logic RTL with no additional application-specific restrictions is undecidable. However, there are semi-decision procedures which seem to be quite practical. In fact, the "chaining" technique shown in the above example makes use of a positive cycle-detection procedure [1] that is ideally suited to reasoning about simple timing inequalities involving two @ terms and a displacement.

An Annotation System for Timing Property Specification

The second step of our proof method is to demonstrate the compliance of the timing requirements in SP and EA' by an implementation. This requires us to relate timing requirements at the specification level to timing constraints on programs. By making use of an annotation system, we can "superimpose" RTL-style timing requirements on top of programs written in block-structured imperative languages. The idea is to introduce *event markers* by means of stylized comments that are placed strategically in the program text. The are two syntactic forms:

--↑NAME

--↓NAME

A event marker can be thought of as a time-keeper of computational activity. If a CPU initiates the execution of a statement which is right below a event marker, say **--↑A** at time *t*, then we say that an instance of the event ↑A occurs at time *t*. Likewise, if a CPU completes the execution of a statement which is right above a event marker, say **--↓A**, at time *t*, then we say that an instance of ↓A occurs at time *t*. This way, the execution of a statement in a program is modelled by an action (a event pair) in RTL. For example, the following programs might correspond to an implementation of the telemetry problem discussed earlier.

EVENT MARKER DEFINITIONS: superimpose event markers on programs.
(Note: "--" starts a comment line.)

```
Task Sender
begin
--↑S
  Send message to Receiver
--↓S
end
```

```
Task Receiver
begin
--↑R
  Buffer and process message from Sender
--↓R
end
```

TIMING CONSTRAINTS: use RTL to specify timing constraints.

Sender S: $\forall i \geq 1 \quad @(\downarrow S,i) = (i-1)*4$

Receiver R: $\forall i \geq 1 \quad @(\uparrow R,i) \geq (i-1)*4 \wedge$
$@(\downarrow R,i) \leq i*4 \wedge$
$@(\uparrow R,i) \leq @(\downarrow S,i)$

More complex timing constraints can be specified quite simply by this annotation system and RTL, as is shown in the following example where we introduce a background task that runs in parallel with the receiver task.

EVENT MARKER DEFINITIONS:

```
Task Receiver
begin
--↑R
  Buffer message from Sender
  Synchronize with Background
--↓SYN_WITH_B
  Process message
--↓R
end
```

```
Task Background
begin
--↑B
  Synchronize with Receiver
--↓SYN_WITH_R
  call Buffer_Manager
--↓B
end
```

```
Procedure Buffer_Manager
--↑M
begin
  Update state information for a size k buffer
end
--↓M
```

TIMING CONSTRAINTS:

- Synchronization between Receiver and Background tasks:
  $\forall i\geq 1\ \ @(\downarrow SYNC\_WITH\_B, i) = @(\downarrow SYNC\_WITH\_R, i)$

- Finite buffer of size *k*:
  $\forall i\geq 1\ \ @(\uparrow M, i+k) \geq @(\downarrow M, i)$

- Mutual exclusion between Receiver and Background tasks:
  $\forall\ i,j\geq 1\ \ @(\uparrow R,i)\geq @(\downarrow B,j)\ \vee\ @(\uparrow B,j)\geq @(\downarrow R,i)$

The annotation system can be used as an interface language between a real-time operating system and the application programs. The timing constraints are then obligations on correct implementations of the real-time operating system. They can also be used as definitions of timing exceptions should an implementation fails to meet a timing constraint at run time. In the next section, we shall show that a syntactic extension of RTL allows us to also specify the behavior of a real-time operating system and other implementation dependencies in a rather compact style.

RTL2

In order to show that an execution environment does indeed satisfy the timing constraints on application programs, we need to capture the notion of the execution of a program on a CPU. While this can be done in RTL, a more compact specification can usually be obtained by introducing another uninterpreted function E(*R*,*t*) which denotes the amount of CPU time allocated to process *R* by time *t*. The axioms restricting E that must apply to every system are:

(P1) $\forall\ t\geq 0\ \ E(R,t+1)-E(R,t)=0 \vee E(R,t+1)-E(R,t)=1$

(P2) $\forall\ t\geq 0\ \ (@(\uparrow R,1)=t \rightarrow E(R,t)=0)$

(P3) $\forall\ i\geq 1, t_1, t_2, t_3 \geq 0$

$$(@(\uparrow R,i)=t_1 \wedge (@(\downarrow R,i)=t_2 \wedge (@(\uparrow R,i+1)=t_3) \rightarrow$$
$$(E(R,t_1+1)-E(R,t_1)>0 \wedge$$
$$E(R,t_2)-E(R,t_1)=c_R \wedge$$
$$E(R,t_3)-E(R,t_2)=0)$$

The axiom (P1) states that the process R must be either executed or not executed in every time unit (time is discrete in our model). The axiom (P2) states that no CPU time has been allocated process R prior to its first execution. The axiom (P3) states that every instance of the execution of process R must start with the allocation of a CPU at the start of the execution, the amount of CPU time allocated must be equal to the computation time c_R of R, and no CPU time is allocated to R between two instances of R.

With the E function, many architectural and implementation dependencies can be stated quite compactly in RTL2. For example, the assertion that *n* homogeneous CPUs are available for allocation is given by:

- CPU availability:

$$\forall\, t \geq 0,\quad E(R,t+1)-E(R,t) + E(B,t+1)-E(B,t) \leq n$$

If the execution of a process is not interruptible, we can assert:

- Non-preemptible execution:

$$\forall\, i \geq 1,\, t \geq 0$$
$$(@(\uparrow R,i)=t \;\rightarrow\; E(R,t+c_R)-E(R,t) = c_R$$

No additional axiom is needed if preemption is allowed.

Suppose a CPU is time-shared by two processes, R and B. Let r_R be the event "process R requests for CPU time". The requirement that an idle processor must be allocated to a ready process is given by the assertion:

- Eager scheduler:

$$\forall\, i \geq 1,\, t \geq 0$$
$$(@(r_R,i) \leq t < @(\downarrow R,i) \wedge E(R,t+1)-E(R,t)=0)$$
$$\rightarrow E(R,t+1)-E(R,t) + E(B,t+1)-E(B,t) = 1$$

Likewise, a scheduling policy may be stated in a general form:

- Scheduling Policy:

$$\forall\, i \geq 1,\, t \geq 0$$
$$(@(r_R,i) \leq t < @(\downarrow R,i) \;\wedge\; \langle R \text{ has priority over } B\rangle$$
$$\rightarrow E(R,t+1)-E(R,t) \geq E(B,t+1)-E(B,t)$$

where <R has priority over B> is:

True (fixed priority scheduler and R has higher priority)

$@(r_R,i)+d_R \leq @(r_B,i)+d_B$ (earliest deadline scheduler)

It should be clear that RTL can also be extended in a similar fashion to express the timing behavior of resources other than a CPU, such as communication links and memory usage. We emphasize, however, that such extensions still fall within the realm of Presburger Arithmetic with uninterpreted functions.

Verification of Timing Constraint Compliance

In general, we can establish the compliance of system timing requirements in an implementation by either exhibiting (and using) a scheduler that satisfies the timing constraints (scheduler synthesis), or by showing that the given execution environment does not violate them (schedulability analysis). In either case, the technical problem concerns the construction of a model for the set of formulas consisting of the timing requirements in the system specification (mapped into timing constraints on programs) and the execution environment (architectural and other implementation restrictions).

Given a set of RTL (RTL2) formulas, the task is to create a mapping of event occurrences to time values such that the @ function may satisfy the restrictions imposed on it by the RTL formulas. However, there are a couple of complications, as explained below.

Each model (schedule) is an infinite table of tuples of the form (e,i,t) where e is the name of an event, i an integer, and t the time of occurrence of the ith instance of e. Since we cannot store an infinite table in practice, a finite representation (e.g., in the form of a "cyclic executive" which repeats a finite list schedule *ad infinitum*) is needed.

The time of occurrence of external events is not assigned by the scheduler. Thus a model (schedule) is conceptually needed for every run of the system, one corresponding to a particular set of occurrence times of external events. This means that we might need to consider a potentially infinite number of models. A finite representation is again needed for the on-line scheduler. A more subtle problem is that even though a finite on-line scheduler may exist, it may depend on knowledge of the arrival times of future requests in order to output a successful schedule. Intuitively, an on-line scheduler is non-clarivoyant if the scheduling decision it makes at every time instance depends only on the arrival time of past requests and *a priori* defined timing parameters. It is not always possible to construct a non-clairvoyant on-line scheduler, as the following example shows. In this example, there are two processes, R and B which are mutually exclusive. R is a periodic process and B is sporadic process (one that may request for service at any time, subject to the constraint that two successive requests must be separated by a specified lower bound) with a deadline. It can be seen from an adversary argument that the scheduling of process B may lead to process R missing its deadline unless the arrival time of R's next request can be predicted.

TIMING CONSTRAINTS OF A PROCESS SYSTEM THAT REQUIRES

CLAIRVOYANT ON-LINE SCHEDULER

(C1) $\forall$ i≥1 $@(\uparrow R,i) \geq 4(i-1) \wedge @(\downarrow R,i) \leq 4i$

(C2) $\forall$ i≥1, $@(\downarrow R,i) \geq @(\uparrow R,i)+2$

(C3) $\forall$ i≥1 $@(\uparrow B,i) \geq @(r_B,i) \wedge @(\downarrow B,i)=@(\uparrow B,i)+1$

(C4) $\forall$ i≥1, $@(r_B,i)+4 \leq @(r_B,i+1)$

(C5) $\forall$ i≥1, j≥1 $@(\uparrow R,i) \geq @(\downarrow B,j) \vee @(\uparrow B,j) \geq @(\downarrow R,i)$

Note that r_B is the event corresponding to a request from B.

Fortunately, we can show that finite representations of non-clairvoyant on-line scheduler do exist for specific types of common timing constraints. The bad news is that model construction methods in logic usually rely on enumeration techniques and are in general far too slow to be practical. A more realistic approach is to divide the synthesis problem into classes of combinatorial optimization problems according to the types of timing constraints involved [4], [5].

Conclusion

In this paper, we discuss a proof method for establishing the correctness of real-time programs by observing the principle of separation of concerns. This method involves two steps. In the first step, we determine if a timing property can be proved from the system specification, and identify implementation-dependent assumptions, if any, that are required to derive a proof. In the second step, we determine if the system specification and other required implementation dependencies can be enforced by control structures that meet the required timing constraints. We have shown that timeliness requirements can be succintly expressed at the system specification level and in application program development by the logic RTL and its syntactic extensions, as can architectural and other resource constraints.

The advantage of this proof method is that implementation dependencies are explicitly identified, and the verification of timeliness is to be done independent of the verification for functional correctness. This separation of concerns is especially important for the maintenance of real-time programs. Indeed, RTL was designed for implementing this "separation of concerns" proof strategy. RTL is especially good for reasoning about timeliness properties which often involve manipulation of arithmetic inequalities. It should be emphasized that RTL is not good (not designed) for reasoning about functional correctness. RTL is not a substitute for the established logics. We believe, however, that the future of practical application of formal methods to large-scale real-time programming hinges on our ability in advancing design disciplines that achieve a separation of concerns. While there are powerful logics that can in principle be applied to solve any problem, one needs to be wary of the Turing tar-pit. Real-time systems often require multiple types of expertise (tools) to build. The real question is how to integrate different expertise (tools) in a proof strategy.

Acknowledgements

This paper derives from some of the work done by the Real-Time Systems Group at the Computer Science Department of the University of Texas at Austin. Past and present members of the RTS Group directly involved in the work reported herein are: Paul Clements, Farnam Jahanian, Douglas Stuart and Farn Wang.

REFERENCES

[1] **F. Jahanian and A. Mok**, "A Graph-Theoretic Approach for Timing Analysis and Its Implementation", *IEEE Transactions on Computers, August 1987.*

[2] **F. Jahanian and A. Mok**, "Safety Analysis of Timing Properties in Real-Time Systems", *IEEE Transactions on Software Engineering, September 1986.*

[3] **F. Jahanian, R. Lee and A. Mok**, "Semantics of Modechart in Real Time Logic", *Proceedings of the 21st Hawaii International Conference on System Science, January 1988.*

[4] **A. Mok**, "Fundamental Design Problems of Distributed Systems for the Hard-Real-Time Environment", *Ph.D Thesis, Department of Electrical Engineering and Computer Science, Massachusetts Institute of Technology, Cambridge, Massachusetts, May, 1983.*

[5] **C. L. Liu and J. W. Layland**, "Scheduling Algorithms for Multiprogramming in a Hard-Real-Time Environment", *JACM, vol. 20, 1973, pp. 46-61.*

Validating Real-Time Systems by Executing Logic Specifications

Angelo Morzenti
Politecnico di Milano, Dipartimento di Elettronica
Piazza Leonardo da Vinci 32, 20133 MILANO, ITALY
Tel. +39-(0)2-23993514; Fax +39-(0)2-23993411;
email: relett01@imipoli.bitnet

Abstract TRIO is a first-order temporal logic language for executable specification of real-time systems. The language is first briefly introduced, with some specification examples and a simple model-theoretic semantics. Algorithms for performing validation activities with reference to finite interpretation domains are illustrated and discussed. With the purpose of providing a consistent meaning to specifications with reference to a variety of temporal structures, both finite and infinite, a model-parametric semantics for the language is provided, and its main properties delineated. Finally, conclusions are drawn and future work is outlined.

Key words software requirements, formal specifications, requirements validation, real-time, first-order logic, temporal logic, model-theoretic semantics

Contents

1. Introduction

Real-time systems are systems whose functionalities are constrained by strict response-time bounds. Very often, such systems may be viewed as embedded computer applications: a computer interacts with an external environment which evolves according to its own logic and interacts with the computer in an unpredictable way, by sending data at a speed that is not under computer control. As [Wir 77] points out, "time" plays a fundamental role in real-time systems, in that their correctness actually does depend on time. If certain events happen too early or too late–where "early" and "late" may be stated precisely in terms of some time scale that depends on the application–the application is incorrect. This constitutes a sharp departure from sequential and concurrent systems, where time affects performance, not correctness.

In a previous paper [GMM 90] we gave a first definition of TRIO, a logic language we developed for specifying real-time systems. The language is presented in section 2 with the purpose of making the present paper self-contained and to provide the reader with a few convincing examples of its practical applicability as a specification language for non-trivial real-time systems. TRIO is one of several extensions of classical temporal logic [Krö 87, Pnu 81] that introduce a quantitative view of time, so that time distances can be measured. The inadequacy of classical temporal logic to the specification of real-time systems stems from the fact that its operators support only a qualitative view of time, thus providing a way to express properties like precedence, eventuality or invariance. The introduction of the next-time operator allows temporal logic to get close to a quantitative view of time: for example, by using it one can state that a given property will hold k time units from the current time instant. The next-time operator, however, is meaningful only with reference to a discrete time domain, like that one used in [Krö 87] to model the execution of synchronous concurrent programs; it cannot deal with dense time structures which are needed to model asynchronous and non-discrete systems.

The work by Bernstein and Harter [B&H 81], based on the linear time temporal logic of [Pnu 81] and [O&L 82], adds a real-time constraint to the operator of temporal implication, thus imposing a maximal or minimal value to the distance in time between related events, and defines an execution model and a proof system for real-time concurrent programs where properties like bounded response time or periodic behavior, besides the usual invariance and eventuality properties, can be proved. Successive work [K&R 85, KKZ 87] extended temporal logic to support specification of real-time systems. The extension adds a numeric parameter to the classical temporal logic operators, to be interpreted as a real-time constraint. For instance, in this logic, the expression $A\ \mathbf{Until}_{<t}B$ requires B to occur within t time units, and A to hold until then.

TRIO, defined in [GMM 89], and Metric Temporal Logic (MTL), defined in [Koy 89], are also extensions of temporal logic. They provide basic operators–*Futr* and *Past*–which state the distance between distinct time instants in a quantitative way. All of the classical temporal logic operators can be derived from Futr and Past by means of first order quantification. TRIO and MTL have similar expressive capabilities; the differences between them derive mainly from the intended use of the specification. In [Koy 89] a sound axiomatization of MTL is defined, with the purpose of providing a deductive verification calculus, while the semantics defined for TRIO in [GMM 90] is model-theoretic, and special care is put in defining conditions under which TRIO formulas can be constructively verified, thus providing a means to validate specifications by executing them, i.e. performing testing and simulation activities. Recent work by Alur and Henzinger [A&H 90] defines a real-time logic, TPTL, where quantification over time is not allowed, thus yielding a decidable language. In our approach we chose not to give up the expressiveness and practical usefulness deriving from temporal quantification, but instead assumed finite domains in order to make satisfiability of formulas and history checking (see sect.3.1) in TRIO decidable problems. Of course this does not provide answers for the corresponding problems in the infinite domain case, which are undecidable in nature, but still provides useful and effective validation methods.

A different approach to extending temporal logic for the specification of real-time systems is taken in Real-Time Temporal Logic (RTTL) [Ost 87, Ost 89]. In this notation, the specification is organized in two layers: an operational part, consisting of an extended state automaton, and a descriptive part, consisting of formulas of classical first order temporal logic. The specification of real-time properties is made possible by introducing a "clock" component in the automaton, i.e. by considering a discrete variable, called *time*, whose value increases monotonically as the system evolves. RTTL possesses a proof system and decision procedures for the finite state cases. However, by using a variable to explicitly represent the absolute time RTTL loses the most valuable advantage of temporal logic–namely, keeping the current absolute time value implicit. RTTL also departs from the original philosophy of temporal logic in that time is considered as a component (albeit distinguished) of the modelled system. This means, for example, that states may change even if the time variable does not change, so that a variable representing a physical quantity might have two distinct values at a given time instant.

The goal of the present research is to provide language support to the formal specification of real-time systems, and design an environment which provides tools for writing and analyzing formal specifications, and thus assess their validity before any development takes place. In particular, such an environment should support the execution of *formal specifications*. The importance of executing formal specifications to validate requirements has been advocated, among others, by [Kem 85]. By executing formal specifications and observing the behavior of the specified system, one can check whether specifications capture the intended functional requirements or not. In other terms, by executing requirements, we perform testing in the early phase of the development process. Although testing cannot prove the absence of errors, it is especially valuable as a mechanism for validating functional requirements.

Thus, a major goal of TRIO is *executability of specifications*. When TRIO specifications are stated, most likely the underlying time structure meant by the specifier corresponds to an infinite domain, such as the set of the reals. An unfortunate consequence is that the properties one might wish to prove to validate specifications are undecidable in the general case. However a system analysis that refers to finite domains can be performed algorithmically by using the classical Tableaux Method [Smu 68], which provides an abstract interpreter of the language. Such analysis increases the confidence in the correcteness of the specification in much the same way as testing a program may increase the confidence in its reliability. As in the case of testing, of course, the inference of the behavior of the system on infinite domains from the analysis performed on finite domains cannot be proven, but is left to the user's responsibility. Abstract algorithms for verifying the satisfiability of a TRIO formula on finite interpretations of a given cardinality, and for checking whether a formula is satisfied in a given finite interpretation are presented and discussed in Section 3.

Unfortunately, the formal semantics we initially defined for TRIO [GMM 89], as for most logic languages, is such that specification formulas may have different validity whenever we change interpretation domains. As a consequence, if we use an interpreter of TRIO to validate specifications on finite execution domains approximating infinite domains, we run into the risk of considering true formulas as false and conversely. Section 4 presents a new semantics of the language which permits to consistently assign a meaning to specification formulas in a parametric way with the cardinality of finite interpretation structures.

2. The TRIO language

TRIO is a first order logical language, augmented with temporal operators that allow the specifier to express properties whose truth value may change over time. The meaning of a TRIO formula is not absolute, but is given with respect to a current time instant which is left implicit in the formula, much in the same way as in classical temporal logic.

2.1 Syntax: the temporal operators

The alphabet of the TRIO language includes sets of names for variables, functions, and predicates, and a fixed set of basic operator symbols. Variables are divided into *time dependent* (TD) variables, whose value may change with time, and *time independent* (TI) variables, whose value is intended to be invariant with time. Every variable name x has an associated *type* or *domain* which is just the set of values the variable may assume. Among the domains there is a distinguished one, required to be numeric in nature, which is called the *Temporal Domain*. Every function name has an associated arity, which is a number $n \geq 0$ (when $n = 0$ the function is called a *constant*), and the indication of a type for every component of the domain and for the range. Similarly, every predicate name is associated with the number and type of its arguments. Like variables, predicates are divided into time dependent and time independent ones: time independent predicates always represent the same relation, while a time dependent predicate corresponds to a possibly distinct relation at every time instant. In principle, functions may also be divided into time independent and time dependent ones: the introduction of this feature would not invalidate any of the results that will be subsequently presented; nevertheless it was avoided for reasons of simplicity and naturalness of the language. The predicates $<$, $\leq$, $=$, and all other usual predicates on numbers, are assumed to be time independent, so that the associated relational operations are applicable to elements of the Temporal Domain. Also, addition and subtraction are assumed to be total functions, with the usual properties, applicable to elements of the temporal domain. Symbols are divided into propositional symbols ($\wedge$ and $\neg$), the quantifier $\forall$, and the temporal operator symbols *Futr* and *Past*.

The syntax of TRIO defines terms in the usual inductive way: every variable is a term, and every n-ary function applied to n terms is a term itself. A *formula* is inductively defined by the following clauses:

1. Every n-ary predicate applied to *n* terms of the appropriate types is a formula (atomic formula).
2. If A and B are formulas, $\neg$A and A$\wedge$B are formulas.
3. If A is a formula and x is a time independent variable, $\forall$xA is a formula.
4. If A is a formula and t is a term of the temporal type, then Futr(A, t) and Past(A, t) are formulas.

The formulas *Futr(A, t)* and *Past(A, t)* intuitively mean that A holds at an instant laying *t* time units in the future (resp. in the past) with respect to the current time value, which is left implicit in the formula.

Abbreviations for the propositional operators $\vee$, $\rightarrow$, true, false, $\leftrightarrow$, and for the derived existential quantifier '$\exists$' are defined as usual. In the following, we assume the usual definitions for the scope of a quantifier, for free and bound occurrence of a (time independent) variable, for substitution A^a_x of term *a* for variable *x* in formula A, and for the closure of a formula–see for instance [Men 63]. In accordance with [And 86], we define universal and existential occurrences of quantifiers. The occurrence of a quantifier[1] in a given TRIO formula is *universal* iff it is in the scope of an even number of negation signs, and *existential* otherwise. Consequently, we say that a (TI) variable is *universally* quantified if it is the argument of a universal occurrence of a quantifier, and is *existentially* quantified otherwise.

A large number of derived temporal operators may be defined by means of quantification over TI variables in the temporal terms of Futr and Past. These derived operators include all the operators of classical linear temporal logic. We mention, among others, the following ones

AlwF(A)	$\stackrel{def}{=}$	$\forall t\,(t > 0 \rightarrow \text{Futr}\,(A, t))$
AlwP(A)	$\stackrel{def}{=}$	$\forall t\,(t > 0 \rightarrow \text{Past}\,(A, t))$
SomF (A)	$\stackrel{def}{=}$	$\neg\,\text{AlwF}\,(\neg A)$
SomP (A)	$\stackrel{def}{=}$	$\neg\,\text{AlwP}\,(\neg A)$
Sometimes (A)	$\stackrel{def}{=}$	$\text{SomP}\,(A) \vee A \vee \text{SomF}\,(A)$
Always (A)	$\stackrel{def}{=}$	$\text{AlwP}\,(A) \wedge A \wedge \text{AlwF}\,(A)$
Lasts (A, t)	$\stackrel{def}{=}$	$\forall t'\,(0 < t' < t \rightarrow \text{Futr}\,(A, t'))$
Lasted (A, t)	$\stackrel{def}{=}$	$\forall t'\,(0 < t' < t \rightarrow \text{Past}\,(A, t'))$
Until (A_1, A_2)	$\stackrel{def}{=}$	$\exists t\,(t > 0 \wedge \text{Futr}\,(A_2, t) \wedge \text{Lasts}\,(A_1, t))$
Since (A_1, A_2)	$\stackrel{def}{=}$	$\exists t\,(t > 0 \wedge \text{Past}\,(A_2, t) \wedge \text{Lasted}\,(A_1, t))$
NextTime (A, t)	$\stackrel{def}{=}$	$\text{Futr}\,(A, t) \wedge \text{Lasts}\,(\neg A, t)$
LastTime (A, t)	$\stackrel{def}{=}$	$\text{Past}\,(A, t) \wedge \text{Lasted}\,(\neg A, t)$
UpToNow (A)	$\stackrel{def}{=}$	$\exists \delta\,(\delta > 0 \wedge \text{Past}\,(A, \delta) \wedge \text{Lasted}\,(A, \delta))$
Becomes (A)	$\stackrel{def}{=}$	$A \wedge \text{UpToNow}\,(\neg A)$

The intuitive meaning of these derived temporal operators stems from that of the basic *Futr* and *Past* temporal operators, according to the kind of quantification they contain. Thus, AlwF(A) means that A will

---

[1] In this definition we assume that formulas are written in the unabbreviated form which contains universal quantifiers only, so that existential quantifications $\exists$xA are rewritten as $\neg\forall$xA.

hold in all future time instants; SomF(A) means that A will hold sometimes in the future; Lasts(A, t) means that A will hold for the next t time units; Until(A_1, A_2) means that A_2 will happen in the future and A_1 will be true until then; NextTime (A, t) means that the first time in the future when A will hold is t time units apart from now. The meaning of the operators AlwP, SomP, Lasted, Since, and LastTime is exactly symmetrical to that of the corresponding operators regarding the future. Sometimes(A) means that there is a time instant–in the past, now, or in the future–where A holds. Always(A) means that A holds in every time instant of the temporal domain. UpToNow (A) means that there is a non-empty time interval ending at the present time, where A has been true. Becomes (A) means that A is true now but did not hold in the most recent time instants.

Example 1. One very simple Real-Time system is a transmission line, which receives messages at one end and transmits them unchanged to the other end with a fixed delay. The time-dependent predicate *in(m)* means that a message *m* has arrived to the enter-end at the current time (left implicit); the predicate *out(m)* means that the same message *m* is emitted at the other end. The TRIO formula

$$\text{in (m)} \rightarrow \text{Futr (out (m), 5)}$$

means that if a message *m* arrives at the current time, then 5 time units later the same message *m* will be emitted, i.e. the message does not get lost. The formula

$$\forall \text{m (out (m)} \rightarrow \text{Past (in (m), 5))}$$

means that no spurious messages are generated.

Example 2. Let *HIGHERLEVEL* and *SAFETYLEVEL* be two significant temperature values for the security of a chemical plant. Let *temp* be a time dependent variable representing the present system temperature. If *lightSignal* and *soundAlarm* are two different alarms in the control system, the formulas

$$\text{lightSignal (ON)} \leftrightarrow \text{temp} \geq \text{HIGHERLEVEL} \quad \text{and}$$
$$\text{soundAlarm (ON)} \leftrightarrow \text{temp} \geq \text{SAFETYLEVEL}$$

mean that the light alarm must be on if and only if the temperature reaches the security level (HIGHERLEVEL), and the sound alarm must be activated if and only if the temperature reaches the SAFETYLEVEL. The reader can note in this example that time is left implicit; and the truth of these formulas change with time because of the presence of time dependent predicates or variables (e.g. *temp*). The indication about a security action to be taken whenever the pressure value exceeds a fixed threshold is expressed by the following formula

$$\text{pressure} \geq \text{VALVETOLERANCE} \rightarrow \text{Futr (Lasts (openGauge, } K_1 \cdot \text{pressure), } K_2 / \text{temp)}$$

This formula specifies that the duration of the gauge opening must be proportional to the pressure, while the activation must be delayed by an interval inversely proportional to the current temperature.

Example 3. As a more complex sample TRIO specification, consider a real-time system composed of an allocator which serves a set of client processes competing for a shared resource. Each process *p* requires the resource by issuing the message *rq(p, δ)*, by which it identifies itself to the allocator and provides a time-out δ for the request to be serviced: if the allocator is able to satisfy p's request within the indicated time-out, then it grants the resource to p by a *gr(p)* signal, otherwise the request must be completely ignored. Once the process has used the resource granted to him by the allocator, it frees it by a *fr* signal. At any time, the allocator will grant the free resource to the least recent pending request. A first, partially formal version of specification is the following

$$\text{Always}\left(\text{grant the resource to process } a \leftrightarrow \left(\begin{array}{c}\text{the resource is free} \wedge \\ \text{there is a valid pending request by } a \wedge \\ \text{there is no other process } a' \text{ with an earlier valid pending request}\end{array}\right)\right)$$

Its refinement yields as the complete specification the TRIO formula:

$$\text{Always}\left(\forall a\left(gr(a) \leftrightarrow \left(\begin{array}{c}\text{Since}_w(\neg\exists b\ gr(b), fr) \wedge \\ \exists t\ \exists\delta \left(\begin{array}{c}\text{Past}(rq(a,\delta), t) \wedge t \le \delta \wedge \text{Lasted}(\neg gr(a), t) \wedge \\ \neg\exists a'\ \exists\delta'\ \exists t'\ (\text{Past}(rq(a',\delta')\ t') \wedge a' \ne a \wedge t' < \delta' \wedge t' > t \wedge \text{Lasted}(\neg gr(a'), t'))\end{array}\right)\end{array}\right)\right)\right).$$

■

TRIO is also well suited for the specification of software and hardware systems. As discussed in [CMS 91], the language allows the description of hierarchical hardware design by describing structural hierarchy and behavioral abstraction, has a wide scope of application, ranging from algorithmic down to gate and circuit level, and permits a natural description of timing aspects such as delay specification, inertial and transport-delay semantics, synchronous and asynchronous systems.

Other examples in the use of TRIO, including the complete specification of a lift system servicing a building of N floors, may be found in [GMM 90]

2.2 A model-theoretic semantics

A straightforward way of defining the semantics of the TRIO language is based on the concept of a temporal structure, from which one can derive the notions of state–an instantaneous assignment of values to time dependent variables and predicates–and of evaluation function, which assigns to every TRIO formula a distinct truth value for every time instant in the temporal domain.

A *temporal structure* is denoted as S = (D, T, G, L), where

- D is a set of types, that is, of variable valuation domains: $D = \{D_1, \ldots D_n\}$. In the following, we will use the notation D(x) to indicate the evaluation domain associated with variable x.
- T is the Temporal Domain. It is assumed to be numeric in nature: it can be, for example, the set **N** of the natural numbers, or the set **Z** of the integers, or the set **R** of the reals, or any subset thereof.
- G is the time independent, or time invariant, part of the structure. G = (ξ, Π, Φ), where
    - ξ is a valuation function defined on a set of time independent variable names, such that, for every variable name x, $\xi(x) \in D_j$, for some $D_j \in D$;

- Π is a valuation function defined on a set of time independent predicate names. If p is the name of an n-ary time independent predicate, Π assigns a relation to it, that is, $\Pi(p) \subseteq D_{p1} \times ... \times D_{pn}$, where $D_{pj} \in D$, for each $j \in [1..n]$;

- Φ is a function defined on a set of function names. If f_j is an n-ary function name, then $\Phi(f_j)$ is a total function of type $D_{ji_1} \times ... \times D_{ji_n} \rightarrow D_{jo}$, with $D_{ji_k} \in D$ for each $k \in [1..n]$, and $D_{jo} \in D$.

- L is the time dependent part of the structure. $L = \{(\eta_i, \Pi_i) \mid i \in T\}$. Every pair (η_i, Π_i) defines a *state* of the temporal structure, which comprises a function η_i defined on a set of time dependent variable names, and a function Π_i defined on a set of time dependent predicate names. For every variable y, $\eta_i(y) \in D_j$, for some $D_j \in D$; if p is the name of an n-ary time dependent predicate name, Π_i assigns a relation to it, that is, $\Pi_i(p) \subseteq D_{p1} \times ... \times D_{pn}$, where $D_{pj} \in D$ for each $j \in [1..n]$.

A temporal structure S = (D, T, G, L) is said to be *adequate* to a TRIO formula if D contains the valuation domains for all the variables occurring in it, and if functions ξ, η_i, Π, Π_i, and Φ, assign values of the appropriate types to all time independent and time dependent variables and predicate names, and to all functions. If S = (D, T, G, L) is a structure adequate to a given TRIO formula F, then it is possible to define an evaluation function assigning a value, at any time instant $i \in T$, to all terms and formulas that can be constructed by using variables, functions, predicates and operators occurring in F. We call such function S_i; its definition for terms is as follows.

$S_i(x) = \xi(x)$ for every time independent variable x;
$S_i(y) = \eta_i(y)$ for every time dependent variable y;
$S_i(f(t_1, ... t_n)) = \Phi(f)(S_i(t_1), ... S_i(t_n))$ for every application of an n-ary function f.

For TRIO formulas, the function S_i yields values belonging to the set {true, false}, and is defined as follows.

$S_i(p(t_1, ...t_n))$ = true iff p is a time independent n-ary predicate and $(S_i(t_1), ... S_i(t_n)) \in \Pi(p)$,
or p is a time dependent n-ary predicate and $(S_i(t_1), ... S_i(t_n)) \in \Pi_i(p)$.

If A and B are formulas, then[2]

$S_i(\neg A)$ = true iff $S_i(A)$ = false;
$S_i(A \wedge B)$ = true iff $S_i(A)$ = true and $S_i(B)$ = true;
$S_i(\forall x A)$ = true iff $S_i(A^a_x)$ = true for every $a \in D(x)$.

Finally, the truth value of a temporal formula is defined according to the following clauses.

---

[2] In the sequel A(x) represents a formula containing a TI variable *x*, correspondingly, A^a_x is the result of substituting a generic value *a* in place of variable *x*.

S_i (Futr (A, t)) = true iff $v = S_i(t)$, $i+v \in T$, and (if $i+v \in T$) $S_{i+v}(A)$ = true;
S_i (Past (A, t)) = true iff $v = S_i(t)$ $i-v \in T$, and (if $i-v \in T$) $S_{i-v}(A)$ = true.

A TRIO formula F is *temporally satisfiable* in a temporal structure S iff S is adequate to it, and there exists a time instant $i \in T$ for which $S_i(F)$ = true. In such a case, we say that the temporal structure constitutes a *model* for F. To state the satisfiability of the TRIO formula F at time instant i of structure S, the abbreviated notation $S,i \models F$ will be used, which is intended to be equivalent to $S_i(F)$=true. A formula F is *temporally valid* in a structure S iff $S_i(F)$ = true for every $i \in T$; it is *valid* iff it is temporally valid in every adequate structure.

3. Algorithms for analyzing specifications

In order to validate requirements expressed as TRIO specifications, one may try to prove the satisfiability of the formula by constructing a model for it. In this view, some parts of the temporal structure to be constructed are assumed to be known–namely the components D, T, Π, and Φ, which describe its static configuration. Given a system specification as a TRIO formula and the static part of a structure adequate to its evaluation, the construction of the remaining parts of the structure determines the dynamic evolution of the modelled system: the events that take place and the values assumed by the relevant quantities.

If the interpretation domains for variables and the temporal domain T are all finite, the satisfiability of a TRIO formula is a decidable problem and effective algorithms to solve it can be defined. In the following, an algorithm will be presented that, under the hypothesis of finite domains, determines the satisfiability of a TRIO formula using a constructive method. Only closed TRIO formulas will be considered, since it is well known that in formulas expressing some kind of property all variables are quantified, although sometimes implicitly. Thus, the precise formulation of the model construction problem for TRIO is as follows: given a closed TRIO formula and the static parts D, T, Π, and Φ, of a structure adequate to it determine whether the formula is satisfiable, at time instant $i \in T$, in a structure with that static part, and construct the remaining parts of the structure (i.e. ξ, η_i, and Π_i).

The principal steps of the decomposition process are schematically depicted in Figure 1; every subformula is associated with a time value *t* that indicates the instant where it is assumed to hold. The decomposition ends when each set of subformulas, called a tableau, contains only literals: every tableau that does not contain any contradiction (i.e. a literal and its negation) provides a compact representation of a model for the original formula, and thus constitutes a constructive proof of its satisfiability.

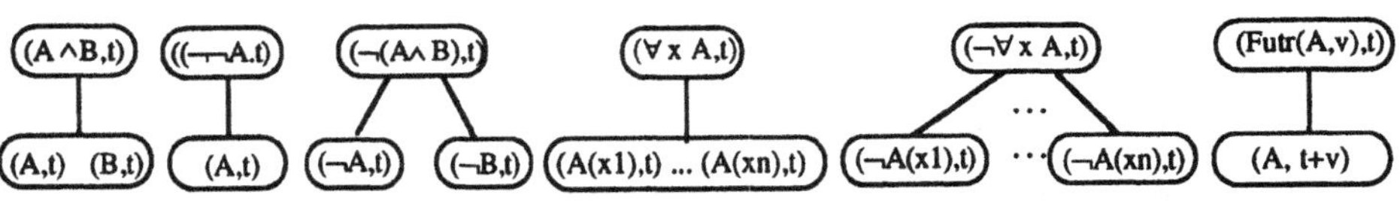

Figure 1. Pictorial description of the decomposition of formulas by the tableaux algorithm.

Tableaux Algorithm for satisfiability

1. Put (F, i) in the root node;
2. repeat until no operation is possible: if a leaf tableau contains a pair (G, i) with G of type
   2.1. $\neg\neg$A: create a son tableau with (A, i) in place of ($\neg\neg$A, i);
   2.2. A$\wedge$B: create a son tableau with (A, i) and (B, i);
   2.3. $\neg$(A$\wedge$B): create two son tableaux with ($\neg$A, i) and ($\neg$B, i);
   2.4. $\forall$xA: create one son tableaux, with |D(x)| pairs of the kind (A_x^a, i), for each distinct $a \in D(x)$;
   2.5. $\neg\forall$xA: create |D(x)| son tableaux, each one containing ($\neg A_x^a$, i) for a distinct a$\in$ D(x);
   2.6. Futr(A, t)
      2.6.1 if term t contains a TD variable *y*: create |D(x)| son tableaux, each one with (Futr(A, t_y^a), i) and an assignment (y, i, a) for a distinct $a \in D(x)$;
      2.6.2. if term t does not contain TD variables: let v = S(t) and k = i + v. If $k \notin T$, (i.e. the referenced time point does not belong to the temporal domain) mark the tableau; otherwise, if $k \in T$, create a son node with (A, k);
   2.7 similarly for $\neg$Futr(A, t);
   2.8 symmetrically for Past;
3. repeat until no operation is possible: if a leaf node contains a pair (L(y), i) with a literal L(y) where a TD variable *y* occurs, then create |*D*(*y*)| son nodes, each containing (L_y^a, i) and (y, i, a), for a different $a \in D(y)$;
4. evaluate all terms contained in literals inside leaf nodes and substitute such terms with their values, so that only ground terms remain;
5. repeat until no operation is possible: if a leaf tableau contains (y, i, a) and (y, i, b) with a $\neq$ b, mark it;
6. repeat until no operation is possible: mark an unmarked tableau if it contains
   6.1. $p(v_1..v_n)$, p being a time independent predicate and $(v_1..v_n) \notin \Pi(p)$, or $\neg p(v_1 .. v_n)$ with $(v_1 .. v_n) \in \Pi(p)$, or
   6.2. both $(q(v_1..v_m), i)$ and $(\neg q(v_1..v_m), i)$, with q a time dependent predicate;
7. repeat until no operation is possible: mark a tableau if all its sons are marked.

The tableaux algorithm for satisfiability succeeds if the construction of the tableaux tree does not mark its root.

A thorough, precise and formal treatment of the computation complexity of the above algorithm is beyond the scope of the present paper, but the foregoing relations should suffice in providing a qualitative characterization of such complexity measure. If we indicate by *N(F)* the number of leaf tableaux constructed by the satisfiability algorithm when starting from a generic TRIO formula *F*, then[3]

[3] In the following relations, t(y) represents a term containing a TD variable *y*; correspondingly, t_y^a is the result of substituting a generic value *a* in place of variable *y*; L represents a literal.

1. $N(A \wedge B) = N(A) \cdot N(B)$
2. $N(\neg(A \wedge B)) = N(\neg A) + N(\neg B)$
3. $N(\neg\neg A) = N(A)$
4. $N(\forall x A(x)) = N(A_x^{a1}) \cdot N(A_x^{a2}) \cdot \ldots \cdot N(A_x^{an}) = O(N(A)^{|D(x)|})$
5. $N(\neg\forall x A(x)) = N(\neg A_x^{a1}) + N(\neg A_x^{a2}) + \ldots + N(\neg A_x^{an}) = O(|D(x)| \cdot N(\neg A_x^{a}))$
6. $N(Futr(A, t(y))) = O(|D(y)| \cdot N(Futr(A, t_y^a)))$
7. $N(L(..t(y)..)) = O(|D(y)| \cdot N(L(..t_y^a..)))$
8. $N(L) = 1$

Relations 6 and 7 above show that a TD variable is equivalent (for what regards the complexity of the computation), to an existentially quantified TI variable. It can be said that an existential quantification results in multiplying the number of leaf tableaux by the cardinality of the domain of the quantified variable, while a universal quantification multiplies such number by itself a number of times equal to the cardinality of the domain D(x) of the quantified variable x. Thus the number of the leaf tableaux is exponential in the number of existential quantifications, with the cardinality of the domains of the quantified TI variables appearing as the base of the exponential, while it is hyperexponential with respect to the number of universal quantifications, with the cardinality of the domain of the quantified variables appearing as the exponent. Such a large complexity derives from the great generality of the satisfiability problem. In fact, if we can decide the satisfiability of a generic formula then we are able to prove the consistency (or inconsistency) of a specification or prove that a property Π is ensured by a specification Σ by showing that the implication $\Sigma \rightarrow \Pi$ is valid (i.e. its negation, $\Sigma \wedge \neg\Pi$, is unsatisfiable).

Executability of TRIO formulas is also provided at lower levels of generality: the tableaux algorithm can be adapted to verify that one given temporal evolution of the system (called a *history*) is compatible with the specification. In the following, this operation will be called history checking. The precise formulation of the history checking problem for TRIO is as follows: given a closed TRIO formula and all parts excepts the variable valuation function ξ of a structure adequate to it, determine whether the formula is true at time instant $i \in T$.

The history checker is implemented through a specialization of the tableaux algorithm, whose principal steps are depicted in Figure 2, where each tableau includes only *one* formula associated with a time instant at which it must be evaluated.

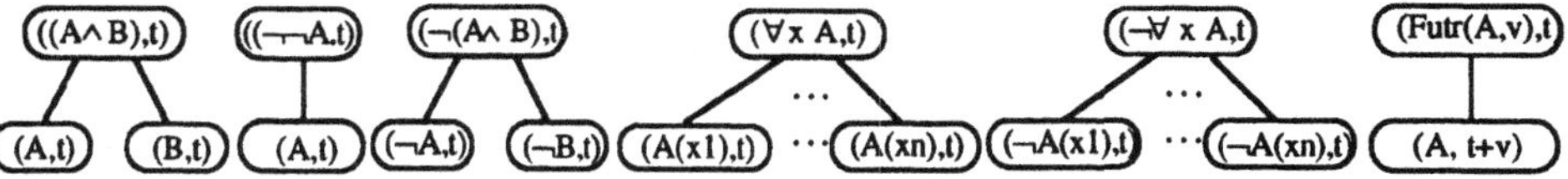

Figure 2. Pictorial description of the decomposition of formulas by the history checker algorithm.

Tableaux Algorithm for history checking

1. Put (F, i) in the root tableau.
2. repeat until no operation is possible: if a leaf tableau contains a pair (G, i) with G of type
   2.1. $\neg\neg A$: create a son tableau with (A, i) in place of ($\neg\neg A$, i);
   2.2. $A \wedge B$: create two son tableaux with (A, i) and (B, i);
   2.3. $\neg(A \wedge B)$: create two son tableaux with ($\neg A$, i) and ($\neg B$, i);
   2.4. $\forall x A$: create $|D(x)|$ son tableaux, each one containing (A^a_x, i) for a distinct $a \in D(x)$;
   2.5. $\neg \forall x A$: create $|D(x)|$ son tableaux, each one containing ($\neg A^a_x$, i) for a distinct $a \in D(x)$;
   2.6. Futr(A, t)
      2.6.1 if term t contains a TD variable y: create *one* son with (Futr(A, $t^{\eta_i(y)}_y$), i), where $\eta_i(y)$ is the value assigned by the history to TD variable *y* at time instant *i*;
      2.6.2. if term t does not contain TD variables: let v = S(t) and k = i + v. If $k \in T$ (i.e. the referenced time point belongs to the temporal domain) then create a son tableau with (A, k); otherwise, if $k \notin T$, mark the tableau;
   2.7 similarly for $\neg$Futr(A, t);
   2.8 symmetrically for Past;
3. repeat until no operation is possible: if a leaf node contains a pair (L(y), i) with a literal L(y) where a TD variable *y* occurs, then create one son tableau containing ($L^{\eta_i(y)}_y$, i);
4. evaluate all terms contained in literals inside leaf nodes and substitute such terms with their values, so that only ground terms remain;
5. repeat until no operation is possible: mark an unmarked tableau if it contains
   5.1. $p(v_1..v_n)$, p being a time independent predicate and $(v_1..v_n) \notin \Pi(p)$, or $\neg p(v_1 .. v_n)$ with $(v_1 .. v_n) \in \Pi(p)$, or
   5.2. ($q(v_1..v_m)$, i) with $(v_1..v_m) \notin \Pi_i(q)$ or ($\neg q(v_1..v_m)$, i) with $(v_1..v_m) \in \Pi_i(q)$, q being a time dependent predicate;
6. repeat until no operation is possible: mark a tableau if all its sons are marked, or if it contains a formula of the type $A \wedge B$ or $\forall x A$ and at least one of its son tableaux is marked.

The algorithm for history checking succeeds (and the structure corresponding to the history is a model for the specification) if the construction of the tableaux tree does not mark its root.

Again, in order to provide a rough estimate of the computational complexity of the algorithm, let us consider the number of leaf nodes in the tree constructed during the execution of the algorithm. Such number, indicated as *N(F)* for a generic formula *F*, satisfies the following relations

1. $N(A \wedge B) = N(A) + N(B) = O\,(2 \cdot N(A))$
2. $N(\neg(A \wedge B)) = N(A) + N(B) = O\,(2 \cdot N(A))$
3. $N(\neg\neg A) = N(A)$
4. $N(\forall x A(x)) = N(\neg \forall x A(x)) = N(A^{a_1}_x) + N(A^{a_2}_x) + \ldots + N(A^{a_n}_x) = O\,(|D(x)| \cdot N(A^a_x))$
5. $N(\text{Futr}\,(A, t)) = N(A)$
6. $N(L) = 1$.

The number of leaf tableaux is exponential with respect to the dimension of the formula, i.e. the number of its quantifications and binary operators. From relations 1 and 2 above it follows that the binary operators give rise to a exponential factor with base 2. For what concerns the exponential factor caused by the quantifications, it should be noted that the cardinality of the domains of the quantified variables appears now as the base of the exponential, not as the exponent like in the more general algorithm for deciding satisfiability of formulas. In other words, for a given formula the complexity of history checking algorithm is a polynomial function of the cardinality of the evaluation domains. This result might be considered discouraging; however it should be pointed out that the dimension of the formula is usually relatively small with respect to the cardinality of the evaluation domains, so that, in the total complexity of checking the specification formula, the exponential factor has a limited influence with respect to the polynomial one.

3.2 The history checker

The previously presented history checking algorithm was the base for the design and implementation of a prototype tool for specification testing. A set of facts representing a possible system evolution is *tested* with reference to a formula describing all the desired system behaviours. A history is represented by a set of time dependent ground predicates, by the predicates invariant on all the temporal domain (time independent predicates) and by the values for the time dependent variables.

The tool provides some facilities to support the user in the most repetitive parts of the testing activity. These facilities provide the opportunity to change the histories, the variable domains and the temporal domain, to re-do the same query with respect to different time instants, to submit new queries with reference to the same history, etc. The histories and the formulas can be edited in a file, from inside or outside the tool. When the history is modified from inside the history checker, the interaction takes place in a facilitated guided way. The foregoing facilities for editing and saving histories allow the user to create a pool of testing histories for a specification. A small language was defined for writing histories on files in human readable format. The user can first edit histories and formulas, then change them interactively by adding or deleting facts, adding new variables or changing their values, or ask new queries in order to perform a more complete test; finally, he or she can save the history and the specification formulas analyzed during an interactive session. Some non-primitive temporal operators, such as Always, Sometimes, AlwF, Since, Until, Lasted, etc, are predefined for a better performance and to facilitate the user's work.

The tool was developed in C under Unix® operating system. Well known data structures were used [AHU 83]: for example the values of a time dependent variable are ordered with respect to the time subintervals in a 2-3-tree, and hash tables are used for the variable and predicate names. In this early version we allow to use subrange of predefined scalar discrete types: no possibility is provided to define enumeration types.

Different data structures were studied for the histories in order to save space and improve the performance of searching algorithms. A computational geometry approach was considered most convenient (see the *Location Point* problem in [P&S 85]). The instances of one predicate are put together with respect to the ranges of their arguments and the time interval. Every predicate defines a hyperspace where each dimension represents an argument range or the temporal domain. Then the instances are represented by hypercubes. In such hypercubes, a point is an instance that is true at the value for the time axis. Time independent predicates are represented as time dependent ones having the same value over all the time interval; in such a case these hypercubes will be as large as the temporal domain for the time axis (i.e. all the time axis range). One possible algorithm is to partition the hyperspace in cells and then to assign each hypercube to the cells that it intersects. This partition allows a direct access to a cell for a given point, and must be defined so that each cell is intersected only by a small number of hypercubes.

Expression trees are used for the expressions as usual, where the internal nodes are operators (+, - , *, /), with the usual precedence. The leaves are constants or variables. These variables are considered time dependent when the expression is evaluated, because all independent ones would be substituted before (remind that the formulas are assumed to be closed). The same holds for the formulas and formula trees.

In Figure 3, we present some performance results, based on the previous allocator example, obtained by running the tool on a DecStation 3100. The response times, measured in seconds, demonstrate the feasibility of the approach. The arrows show the instant where the histories fail to satisfy the formula. In the evaluation we used a temporal domain of cardinality 30 with a maximal possible delay of 10.

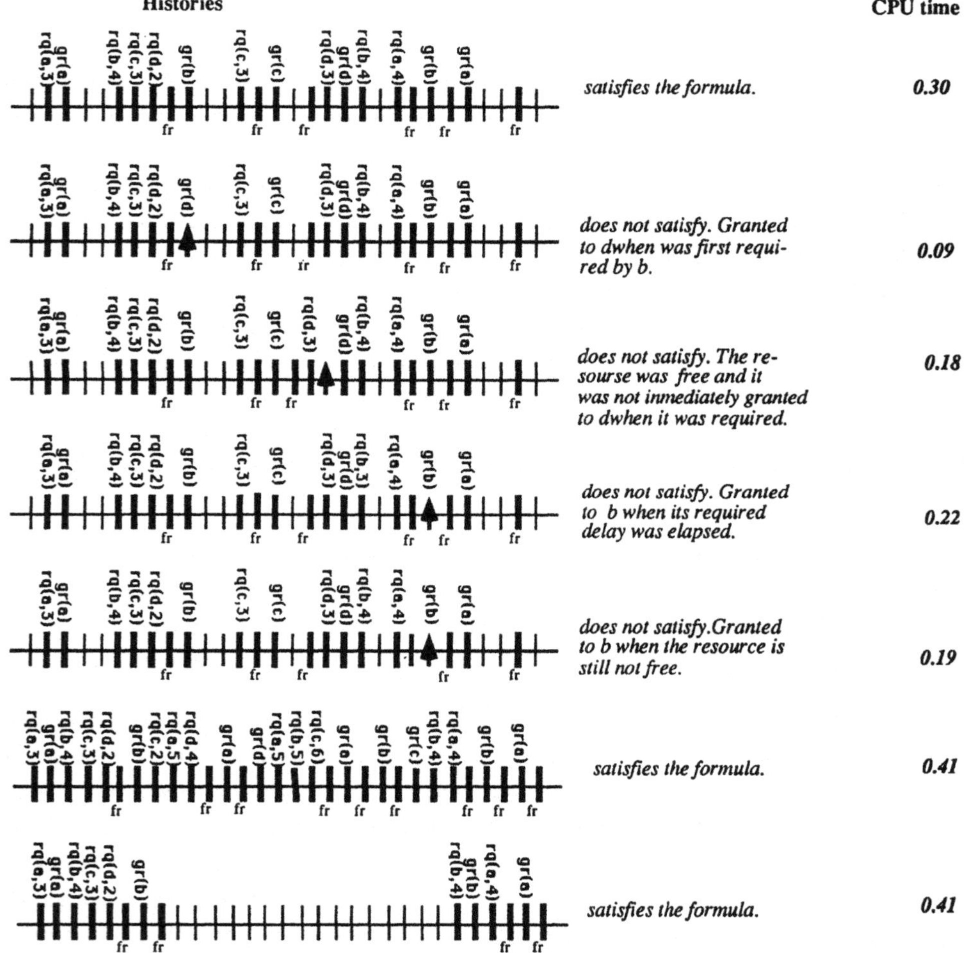

Figure 3. Response time results based on the allocator example.

The history checker program is a recursive implementation of the tableaux-based algorithm, and closely corresponds to the structural induction that constitutes its core part. As a consequence of the sequential implementation, the response times for the "illegal" histories are lower than those for "correct" ones. Whenever the algorithm realizes that the history fails to satisfy the formula, it stops. If not, it continues for all the temporal domain. The number of facts in a history has a small influence in the response times, as is shown by the last two histories.

4. Finite and infinite interpretations: a model-parametric semantics

As illustrated in the preceding section, validation activities in TRIO are not based on deductive proofs but on semantic methods to support testing and simulation, which are implemented in terms of algorithms referring to finite temporal structures, considered as a small *windows* on the infinite or very large history of the system.

When TRIO formulas are interpreted in a finite temporal domain, some functions become partially defined. Consider, as an example, the formula Futr (A, 3) to be evaluated at time instant 8 of a temporal domain that is the integer interval [0..9]. The semantics of TRIO, as stated in Section 2.2, requires evaluating term '3', the argument of the temporal operator Futr, adding its value to the time instant where the evaluation of the formula is performed, and evaluating the other argument A at the time instant thus obtained, 11 in this case. This last evaluation is not possible, since time instant 11 does not belong to the temporal domain; consequently, the time dependent part L of the temporal structure does not provide any value for TD variables and predicates at that time instant, and the evaluation function S_i is not defined. These points are further illustrated in the following example, which specifies a periodic system.

Example 4. The following formula specifies that the event represented by the atomic predicate P, if it ever occurs, then repeats itself every three time units

$$\text{Always}\ (\ P \leftrightarrow \text{Futr}\ (P, 3)\ )$$

Suppose the formula is evaluated at time instant 4 of the temporal domain shown in Figure 4.

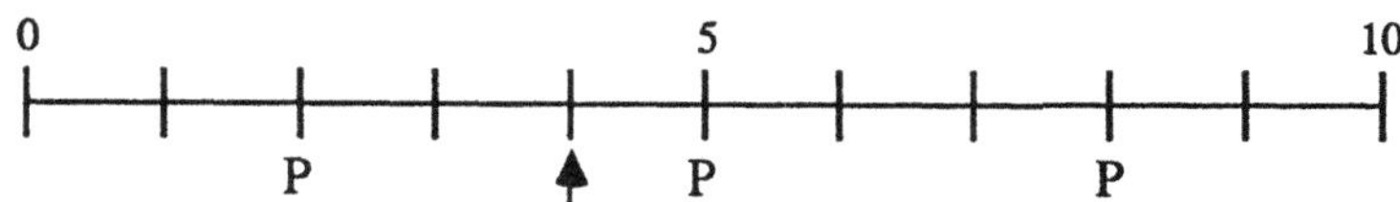

Figure 4. Structure for the evaluation of the TRIO formula: Always (P ↔ Futr (P, 3)). The arrow points to the instant in which the formula is evaluated. P is supposed true at times 2, 5, 8, and false elsewhere.

Intuitively, Figure 4 represents the portion of a possibly infinite behavior that satisfies the specification, but the formula cannot be satisfied in that structure. In fact, under the conventional assumption that everything is false outside the finite temporal domain, the specification requires P to be identically false in [0..10]. Adopting the opposite convention, i.e. everything is *true* outside the temporal domain, would not solve the problem, as the reader can easily verify.

A way to obtain nontrivial models for repetitions of the P event would be to change the specification into

$$\text{Sometimes} (\text{Lasts} (P \leftrightarrow \text{Futr} (P, 3), h))$$

where *h* is a suitable constant related to the cardinality of the temporal domain. The formula requires the implication to be satisfied not at every instant of the temporal domain, but only inside it, excluding "some" values at the borders. However, the solution of changing a specification into another that represents the "same" behaviour, but on a subset of the original temporal structure is unacceptable, because it places on the user of the language (i.e. the specifier of the system) the burden of taking care of the effects of a change of the underlying temporal domain and its cardinality. That is, the specification would need to be changed for any change of the valuation domains.

■

The present approach to model parametric semantics consists of making restrictions on the evaluability of formulas implicit in the definition of the semantics with respect to the chosen domains. For simplicity we restrict our discussion to the restriction of the temporal domain: the problems due to restrictions of the interpretation domains of variables can be dealt with similarly. We define the notion of ***evaluability of a formula*** in a structure adequate to it. If it is not possible to evaluate the formula without any reference to time points external to the temporal domain, the formula is considered to be not evaluable in that temporal structure. In addition, for formulas containing quantifiers, the set of values that can be assigned to the quantified variables does not necessarily coincide with its type, but must be suitably restricted, in order to prevent exiting the temporal domain when evaluating the formula. Thus evaluability of a formula with respect to a structure does not depend just on the types of entities that the structure assigns to the components of the TRIO alphabet–i.e. on the adequacy of the structure–but also on their values.

In order to define the notion of formula evaluability, first we define Touched (F, i, S) as the set of time points touched in the evaluation of the TRIO formula F at instant i, with reference to structure S.

Definition 1. The set Touched (F, i, S) is defined inductively on the structure of formula F by the following clauses:

Touched (A, i, S) = {i}   if A does not contain temporal operators,
Touched (¬A, i, S) = Touched (A, i, S),
Touched (A ∧ B, i, S) = Touched (A, i, S) ∪ Touched (B, i, S),
Touched (Futr (A, t), i, S) = **if** i + S_i (t) ∈ T
  then {i} ∪ Touched (A, i + S_i (t), S)
  else {i, i + S_i (t)},
Touched (Past (A, t), i, S) = **if** i - S_i (t) ∈ T
  then {i} ∪ Touched (A, i - S_i (t), S)
  else {i, i - S_i (t)},

Touched (∀xA, i, S) = Touched (A, i, S).

■

According to the last clause, the presence of quantifications in formula F does not affect the value of Touched (F, i, S): only the ξ component of the temporal structure S affects it.

The definition of Touched allows us to characterize the structures where the evaluation of a formula is possible at a given instant. In order for the evaluation of a formula to be possible in a temporal structure, the evaluation process must not touch points outside the temporal domain, that is, the set of touched points must be a subset of the temporal domain of the structure. We thus define *Evaluable (F, S, i)* as the predicate that establishes whether formula F is evaluable at time instant i of the temporal domain of structure S.

$$\text{Evaluable}(F, i, S) \overset{\text{def}}{=} \text{Touched}(F, i, S) \subseteq T.$$

The meaning of formulas containing temporal operators can be effectively determined, at a given time instant, only if the formula is evaluable, with respect to the structure, at that instant. When the formula is not evaluable, its truth value is conventional, and could indifferently be set to *true* or *false*.

In order to evaluate a formula F containing quantifications of TI variables, it is necessary to determine which set of tuples of values can be substituted for variables quantified in F, thus yielding a formula that is evaluable in S at time instant i. The set of all such values for the quantified TI variables compose what we call the *evaluation domain* Dom (F, i, S) for F at time instant i, with respect to structure S. If $x_1 .. x_q$ are the quantified TI variables of formula F, we define

$$\text{Dom}(F, i, S) \overset{\text{def}}{=} \{(a_1 \dots a_q) \in D(x_1) \times \dots \times D(x_q) \mid \text{Evaluable}(\tilde{F}^{a_1 \dots a_q}_{x_1 \dots x_q}, i, S)\}$$

where $\tilde{F}$ is the *matrix* of the TRIO formula F, defined as the formula deprived of all its quantifications. For a formula F of the type $\forall x A$, we define the *variability domain*, written as Var $(x, \forall x A, i, S)$, as the projection of Dom $(\forall x A, i, S)$ on variable x. Formally, if $x, x_1, .. x_q$ are the quantified variables in $\forall x A$, then

$$\text{Var}(x, \forall x A, i, S) \overset{\text{def}}{=} \{a \in D(x) \mid \exists a_1 \in D(x_1), \dots \exists a_q \in D(x_q): \text{Evaluable}(\tilde{A}^{a\, a_1 \dots a_q}_{x\, x_1 \dots x_q}, i, S)\}$$

We can now provide a formal model parametric semantics for TRIO. The evaluation function S_i for terms and atomic formulas is defined as in Section 2.2. Let F be a non-atomic formula such that Evaluable (F, i, S);

if $F = \neg A$	then $S_i(F) = \text{true}$ iff $S_i(A) = \text{false}$;
if $F = A \wedge B$	then $S_i(F) = \text{true}$ iff $S_i(A) = \text{true}$ and $S_i(B) = \text{true}$;
if F = Futr (A, t)	then $S_i(F) = \text{true}$ iff $v = S_i(t)$ and $S_{i+v}(A) = \text{true}$;
if F = Past (A, t)	then $S_i(F) = \text{true}$ iff $v = S_i(t)$ and $S_{i-v}(A) = \text{true}$;
if $F = \forall x A$	then $S_i(F) = \text{true}$ iff $S_i(A^a_x) = \text{true}$ for all *a* in the set Var $(x, \forall x A, i, S)$.

Notice that all but the last clauses are defined as in Section 2.2. In this model parametric semantics, however, the evaluation is subject to the evaluability of the formula; in particular, since the whole formula is evaluable, the evaluation of subformula A in Futr (A, t) and Past (A, t) is always possible, because time instants i+v and i-v certainly belong to the temporal domain T.

Example 5. Consider the formula presented in Example 4

$$F = \text{Always}\ (\ P \leftrightarrow \text{Futr}\ (P, 3)\ )$$

that could not be meaningfully evaluated in a finite structure, using a semantics that assumes conventional values outside a temporal domain. The formula can be rewritten in unabbreviated form

$$F = (P \leftrightarrow \text{Futr}\ (P, 3)) \wedge \forall s (s>0 \rightarrow \text{Futr}\ (P \leftrightarrow \text{Futr}\ (P, 3), s)) \wedge \forall t\ (t>0 \rightarrow \text{Past}\ (P \leftrightarrow \text{Futr}\ (P, 3), t)).$$

Assuming that variables s and t belong to [1..10], the interpretation of the formula at time instant 4 of the temporal structure of Figure 4, yields the following evaluation domain for the quantified variables

$$\begin{aligned} \text{Dom}\ (F, 4, S) &= \{\ (s, t) \in [1..10]^2 \mid \{4, 7, 4+s, 4+s+3, 4-t, 4-t+3\} \subseteq [0..10]\ \} = \\ &= \{\ (s, t) \in [1..10]^2 \mid 1 \le s \le 3\ \wedge\ 1 \le t \le 4\ \}. \end{aligned}$$

Such evaluation domain is shown in Figure 5. Notice that F is satisfied in the structure, because the evaluation of subformula P ↔ Futr (P, 3) is prevented at time instants that do not belong to the interval [0..7]. ■

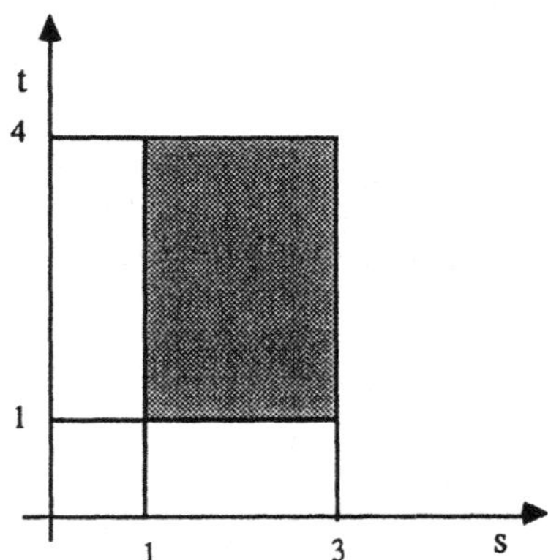

Figure 5. Evaluation domain for quantified variables of formula Always (P ↔ Futr (P, 3)).

The model parametric semantics ensures the usual properties of first order theories. In particular, the propositional equivalences hold, among which De Morgan's laws, the cancellation of double negations, and the temporal *transparency* of negation, namely:

$$\text{Futr}\ (\neg A, t) \equiv \neg\text{Futr}\ (A, t) \quad \text{and} \quad \text{Past}\ (\neg A, t) \equiv \neg\text{Past}\ (A, t).$$

For non atomic formulas the properties stated in the following can be easily proved.

$$\text{Dom}\ (A \wedge B, i, S) = \text{Dom}\ (A, i, S) \times \text{Dom}\ (B, i, S)$$

where × is the Cartesian product operator among sets of tuples.

$$\mathrm{Dom}\ (\forall xA,\ i,\ S) \quad = \bigcup_{a \in \mathrm{Var}(x,\ \forall xA,\ i,\ S)} \{\ a\ \} \times \mathrm{Dom}\ (A_x^a,\ i,\ S)$$

where ∪ is the set union operator among sets of tuples of values.

Concerning the cardinality of the evaluation domains (in case they are finite) the following properties hold.

$$|\ \mathrm{Dom}\ (A \wedge B,\ i,\ S)\ | \ = \ |\ \mathrm{Dom}\ (A,\ i,\ S)\ | \cdot |\ \mathrm{Dom}\ (B,\ i,\ S)\ | \qquad \text{and}$$

$$|\ \mathrm{Dom}\ (\forall xA,\ i,\ S)\ | \quad = \sum_{a \in \mathrm{Var}\ (x,\ \forall xA,\ i,\ S)} |\mathrm{Dom}\ (A_x^a,\ i,\ S)\ |$$

Thus, the model parametric semantics permits to consistently assign a meaning to a formula in any temporal structure where it is evaluable, thus supporting a view of the finite temporal domain of a temporal structure as a small window on a larger, possibly infinite description of the system evolution. Accordingly, it is immediate to introduce the notion of a *restriction* of a structure, which considers only a subset of the set of time points that constitute its temporal domain. It is then useful to state the conditions under which the truth value of a formula in a given structure is preserved in all of its restrictions.

To this purpose we say that a structure $\hat{S} = (\hat{D}, \hat{T}, \hat{G}, \hat{L})$ is a *restriction* of a structure S iff $\hat{T} \subseteq T$, $\hat{D} = D$, $\hat{G} = G$, and $i \in \hat{T}$ implies $\hat{\eta}_i = \eta_i$ and $\hat{\Pi}_i = \Pi_i$.

One might conjecture that, when performing a restriction on a given temporal structure, the truth value of formulas that remain evaluable in the restricted structure remains unchanged, that is, if $\hat{S}$ is a restriction of S, then Evaluable (F, i, S), Evaluable (F, i, $\hat{S}$), and S, i ⊨ F imply $\hat{S}$, i ⊨ F. A simple counterexample shows that this is not the case.

Consider formula F = SomF (P) to be evaluated at time instant i = 7 of the temporal domain of structures S and $\hat{S}$ as shown in Figures 6(a) and 6(b).

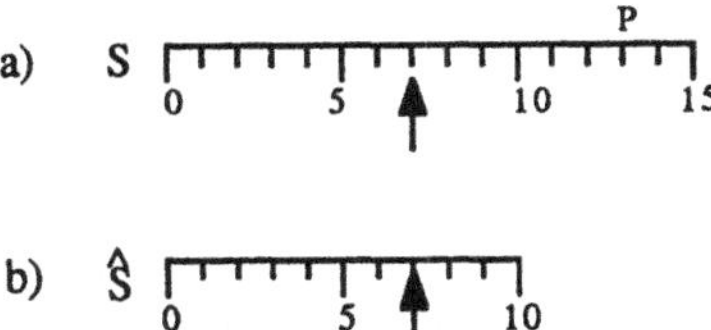

Figure 6. Evaluation of formula SomF (P) in a structure and in its restriction.

In this case, we have S, 7 ⊨ F but $\hat{S}$, 7 ⊭ F. The intuitive explanation of this fact is that formula SomF (P) requires P to take place sometimes in the future. The P event takes place, in structure S, at time instant 13, that does not belong to the temporal domain $\hat{T}$ of the restricted structure $\hat{S}$, where F is thus not verified.

A TRIO formula is said to contain a *temporal quantification* iff a TI quantified variable occurs in a term that is argument of a *Futr* or *Past* operator. The temporal quantification is said to be positive (respectively, negative) in case the variable is positively (respectively negatively) quantified[4]. For example, the formula *Sometimes (P)* contains a negative temporal quantification, whilst formula *Always(P)* contains a positive temporal quantification. The notion of temporal quantification can be used to express precisely the conditions under which truth values of formulas are conserved under the restriction operation on temporal structures. Such conditions are stated by the following two restriction theorems whose proof, not reported here, is included in [MMG 90].

Theorem 1 (First restriction theorem). Let F be a TRIO formula without temporal quantifications, $\hat{S}$ a restriction of structure S, and assume that both Evaluable (F, i, S) and Evaluable (F, i, $\hat{S}$) hold. Then

$$S, i \models F \qquad \text{if and only if} \qquad \hat{S}, i \models F.$$

A further restriction theorem may be proved under the assumption that formulas without negative temporal quantifications do not possess any negation sign between nested positive temporal quantifications.

Theorem 2 (second restriction theorem). Let F be a TRIO formula without negative temporal quantifications, and let $\hat{S}$ be a restriction of structure S, with Evaluable (F, i, S) and Evaluable (F, i, $\hat{S}$); then

$$S, i \models F \qquad \text{implies} \qquad \hat{S}, i \models F.$$

Based on these properties, a variation of the algorithms presented in section 3 for validating specifications can be defined, which refers to the new, model parametric semantics. The version of the history checker which embodies such semantics is currently under implementation.

5. Conclusions and future work

In the present paper a summary of the temporal logic language TRIO for executable specification of real time systems has been provided, together with some non-trivial example of system specification and issues connected to its practical use in the validation of the specified systems, were presented. The discussion was focused on validation activities based on automatic instruments for deciding formula satisfiability in finite interpretation structures, and for verifying whether a completely given interpretation makes the formula satisfied. The intended use of such simulation tools is based on considering a finite (limited and discrete) temporal domain as a window on a possibly infinite behavior of the system: the user can find the "best approximation" in the description of the specified system by changing the width of the window, i.e. the length of the observation interval, or by changing the value of the "temporal quantum" that is, the numerical distance between two adjacent time instants. Since the responsibility of the choice of the temporal domain serving as a satisfactory approximation of the modelled system is ultimately left to the user, this approach does not permit the automatic verification of the specified systems, but provides an effective sup-

---

[4]We remind the reader that TRIO formulas are assumed to be in unabbreviated form.

port for validation activities, which play the same role in specification development as testing does in program development.

The choice of using a first-order logic was motivated by reasons of naturalness, simplicity and compactness of the specifications. The price paid for this choice was the undecidability of formulas in the case of infinite domains and a higher complexity (w.r.t. the dimension of the formulas) in the case of finite domains. On the other hand, it should be pointed out that although "in principle" all finite-state systems may be described using a propositional logic, in practice first-order logic improves the compactness and readability of formulas, most important properties for documents such as specifications, which must be readable and easily manageable by humans in the first place. A support to this view is also provided by the fact that transforming a first-order specification for a finite-state system into an equivalent one in propositional form involves an exponential increase of the size of the specification, and such an increase has an obvious impact on the complexity of the algorithms for analyzing specifications.

An alternative (maybe more traditional) approach in the use of a logic specification would be to define for it a deductive calculus for proving properties of the specified systems starting from their axiomatization in terms of (sets of) formulas of the language. For examples, in [Koy 89] a sound axiomatization for MTL is used to provide proofs of some general temporal properties of real-time systems. An axiomatization for TRIO is now under development, and in order to be practically useful it is supposed satisfy two main requirements. First of all, the calculus must be *simple*, allowing proofs to be compact and, most important, reflect human intuitive reasoning about time: current proof systems are often criticized for being cumbersome and yielding long and complicated proofs. Moreover, the deductive system for TRIO should refer to infinite (temporal) domains and assume total operations on them: in fact the finite case can be effectively dealt with using the semantic methods illustrated in the foregoing paragraphs; this assumption certainly contributes to the simplicity of the axiomatization, since it is often easier to describe infinite objects than finite ones.

TRIO has proved to be a useful specification tool, since it combines the rigor and precision of formal methods with the expressiveness and naturalness of first order and modal logics. However, the use of TRIO for the specification of large and complex systems has shown its major flaw: as originally defined, the language does not support directly and effectively the activity of structuring a large and complex specification into a set of smaller modules, each one corresponding to a well identified, autonomous subpart of the system that is being specified. This is because TRIO specifications are very finely structured: the language does not provide powerful abstraction and classification mechanisms, and lacks an intuitive and expressive graphic notation. In summary, TRIO is best suited to the specification "in the small", that is, to the description of relatively simple systems via formulas of the length of a few lines. However in the description of large and complex systems [CHJ 86], one often needs to structure the specification into modular, independent and reusable parts. In such a case, beyond formality, executability, rigor and absence of ambiguity, other language features become important, such as the ability to structure the specifications into modules, to define naming scopes, to produce specifications by an incremental, top-down process, to attribute a separate level of formality and detail to each portion of the specification [MBM 89]. These issues are similar to those arising in the production of large programs, an activity that is usually called programming-in-the-large [D&K 76]. Hence we may refer to the process of producing specifications of complex systems as specifying-in-the-large.

To support specification in the large, we enriched TRIO with concepts and constructs from object oriented methodology, yielding a language called TRIO+ [M&S 91]. Among the most important features of TRIO+ are the ability to partition the universe of objects into classes, inheritance relations among classes, and mechanisms such as inheritance and genericity to support reuse of specification modules and their top-down, incremental development, an expressive graphic representation of classes in terms of boxes, arrows, and connections to depict class instances and their components, information exchanges and logical equivalences among (parts of) objects. TRIO+ was used successfully in the specification of software/hardware systems of significant architectural complexity, like pondage power stations of ENEL, the Italian electric energy board [M&S 90]. Systems of this kind are highly structured and exhibit quite a complex behavior: they are governed by management programs whose validity lasts several days or weeks, respond with flexible and adaptable actions to a large variety of events coming from the surrounding environment, and include components with intrinsic time constants ranging from several hours (for a water basin) to microseconds (for the electronic circuitry that controls the power distribution).

A further line of research regards the integration of a descriptive formal language like TRIO with more operational, state-based ones, like Petri nets, with the purpose of combining the advantages of the two complementary approaches: immediate, efficient executability of operational languages, and ability to state and prove properties in the descriptive languages. The idea of combining logic-based and state-based formal methods is certainly not new, and several examples are present in the literature: for instance, RTTL [Ost 89] combines explicit-clock temporal logic with time transition models, and all forms of model-checking [ACD 90, CAD 91, AFH 91] ultimately correspond to comparing a temporal-logic specification of a system against its implementation as a state-transition description. Future research will thus be devoted to the integration of TRIO and temporal Petri nets [GMM 91]. The Petri nets model was chosen because it allows the description of nondeterminism and parallelism of real-time systems in an intuitive, graphically evident way. The purpose of the integration is to allow the description of the state of a temporal Petri net and of its transition firings in terms of TRIO time dependent predicates, and express and prove properties of systems specified via Petri nets by means of TRIO formulas and theorems.

Acknowledgements

This paper presented results of the research conducted in the Software Engineering Research Group at Politecnico di Milano, in cooperation with ENEL-CRA and CISE. The author would like to acknowledge the contribution of his colleagues Miguel Felder, Carlo Ghezzi, and Dino Mandrioli, and thank Edoardo Corsetti, Angelo Montanari, and Elena Ratto from CISE, Enrico Crivelli and Roberto Meda from ENEL-CRA for numerous helpful discussions on practical applications of TRIO.

References

[ACD 90] R.Alur, C.Courcoubetis, D.Dill, "Model-Checking for Real-Time Systems", 5th Annual IEEE Symposium on Logic in Computer Science, 1990.

[AFH 91] R.Alur, T.Feder, T.Henzinger, "The Benefits of Relaxing Punctuality", PODC 1991.

[A&H 90] R. Alur, T.A.Henzinger, "Real-Time Logics: complexity and expressiveness", Proc. of the Fifth Annual IEEE Symposium on Logic in Computer Science, 1990.

[AHU 83] A.Aho, J.Hopcroft, J.Ullman, "Data Stractures and Algorithms", Addison Wesley, Reading, MA, 1983.

[And 86] P.B. Andrews, "An introduction to mathematical logic and type theory: to truth through proofs", Academic Press, 1986.

[B&H 81] A.Bernstein, P.K.Harter, "Proving real-time properties of programs with temporal logic", Proc. of the 8th ACM Symposium on Operating Systems, pp.1-11, 1981.

[CAD 91] C.Courcoubetis, R.Alur, D.Dill, "Model-checking dor Probabilistic Real-Time Systems", ICALP '91.

[CHJ 86] B. Cohen, W.T. Harwood, M.I. Jackson, "The Specification of Complex Systems", Addison Wesley Publ. Comp., Reading MA, 1986.

[CMS 91] A. Coen Porisini, A.Morzenti, D. Sciuto, "Specification and Verification of Hardware Systems using the Temporal Logic Language TRIO", "CHDL '91: 10th International Symposium on Hardware Description Languages and their Applications", Marseille, France, 1991.

[D&K 76] F. DeRemer, H. Kron, "Programmaing-in-the-Large Versus Programming-in-the-Small", IEEE Transactions on Software Engineering, SE-2, (June 1976):80-86.

[GMM 89] C.Ghezzi, D.Mandrioli, A.Morzenti, "TRIO, a logic language for executable specifications of real-time systems", 10th French-Tunisian Seminar on Computer Science, Tunis, May 1989.

[GMM 90] C.Ghezzi, D.Mandrioli, A.Morzenti, "TRIO, a Logic Language for Executable Specifications of Real-Time Systems", Journal of Systems and Software, v.12, no.2: May 1990, pp.107-123.

[GMM 91] C.Ghezzi, D.Mandrioli, S.Morasca, M.Pezzè, "A Unified High-Level Petri Net Formalism for Time-Critical Systems", IEEE Transactions on Software Engineering, Vol.17, No.2, February 1991.

[K&R 85] R.Koymans and W.P.de Roever, "Examples of a Real–time Temporal Logic Specification", LNCS 207 Springer Verlag, 1985.

[Kem 85] R.A.Kemmerer, Testing Software Specifications to Detect Design Errors, Transactions on Software Engineering, vol. SE-11, no. 1, Jan 1985.

[KKZ 87] R.Koymans, R.Kuiper, E.Zijlstra, "Specifying message passing and real-time systems with real-time temporal logic", in ESPRIT '87 Achievement and Impact, North Holland, 1987.

[Koy 89] R.Koymans, "Specifying Message Passing and Time-Critical Systems with Temporal Logic", Ph.D. Thesis, Eindhoven University of Technology, 1989.

[Krö 87] F.Kröger, "Temporal Logic of Programs", EATCS Monographs on Theoretical Computer Science, Springer Verlag, 1987.

[M&S 90] A. Morzenti, P. San Pietro, "TRIO+ an Object Oriented Logic Specification Language", ENEL-CRA Research Report, January 1990 (in Italian).

[M&S 91] A.Morzenti, P.San Pietro, "An Object-Oriented Logic Language for Modular System Specification", ECCOP '91, European Conference on Object-Oriented Programming", Lecture Notes in Computer Science, 512, Springer Verlag, 1991.

[MBM 89] A. Mili, N. Boudriga, F. Mili, "Towards structured specifying: theory, practice, applications", Ellis Horwood Ltd., Chichester, England, 1989.

[Men 63] E.Mendelson, "Introduction to mathematical logic", Van Nostrand Reinold Company, New York, 1963.

[MMG 90] A.Morzenti, D.Mandrioli, C.Ghezzi, "A Model-Parametric Real-Time Logic", Report n.90.010, Politecnico di Milano, Dipartimento di Elettronica, 1990.

[O&L 82] S.Owicki and L.Lamport, "Proving Liveness Properties of Concurrent Programs", ACM Transactions on Programming Languages and Systems, vol.4, no.3, July 1982, pp.455-495.

[Ost 87] J.S.Ostroff, "Modelling, Specifying and verifying Real-time Embedded Computer Systems", IEEE Symposium on Real-Time Systems, pp.124-132, IEEE Press, 1987.

[Ost 89] J.S.Ostroff, "Temporal Logic for Real-Time Systems", Advanced Software Development Series. Research Studies Press Limited, England, 1989.

[P&S 85] F.P.Preparata, M.I.Shamos, "Computational Geometry: an Introduction", Springer Verlag, New York, 1985.

[Pnu 81] A.Pnueli, "The temporal semantics of concurrent programs", Theoretical Computer Science 13, North Holland Publishing Company, 1981.

[Smu 68] R.M.Smullian, "First order Logic", Springer Verlag, 1968.

[Wir 77] N.Wirth, "Towards a Discipline in Real-Time Programming", Comm. ACM 20-8, pp.577-583, Aug. 1977.

An Overview and Synthesis on Timed Process Algebras*

Xavier Nicollin Joseph Sifakis

Laboratoire de Génie Informatique
IMAG-Campus B.P. 53X
38041 Grenoble Cedex - FRANCE

Abstract. We present an overview and synthesis of existing results about process algebras for the specification and analysis of timed systems. The motivation is double: present an overview of some relevant and representative approaches and suggest a unifying framework for them.

After presenting fundamental assumptions about timed systems and the nature of abstract time, we propose a general model for them: transition systems whose labels are either elements of a vocabulary of actions or elements of a *time domain*. Many properties of this model are studied concerning their impact on description capabilities and on realisability issues.

An overview of the language features of the process algebras considered is presented, by focusing on constructs used to express time constraints. The presentation is organised as an exercise of building a timed process algebra from a standard process algebra for untimed systems. The overview is completed by a discussion about description capabilities according to semantic and pragmatic criteria.

Keywords: real-time, specification of timed systems, process algebras

Contents

1 Introduction

The paper presents an overview and synthesis of existing results about process algebras for the specification and analysis of timed systems. It has been motivated both by the

*Work supported by the ESPRIT BRA SPEC

drastically increasing number of contributions in the area and by the authors' conviction that most of the existing work admits a unifying common framework. Thus, the motivation is double: first, the presentation of an overview of some relevant and representative approaches in the area and second, the proposal of a framework for these approaches. The paper presents the rather incomplete and eventually biased authors' point of view than a survey of existing work in the area.

Although emphasis is put on algebraic behavioural specification formalisms, we believe that most of the ideas presented here have a more general applicability scope, as they are independent of the features and the nature of the description formalism considered. For instance, general ideas about the nature of time and the underlying model of timed systems may be used when designing logical specification languages; the results on process algebras can be easily transposed on other behavioural specification formalisms like automata, timed graphs, timed transition systems, etc.

A timed system is usually considered to be a system with a global parameter (state variable) called time, used to constrain the occurrences of the actions. Introducing time requires consistent assumptions about its progress with respect to the evolution of the system: correspondence between instants (domain of definition of the time parameter) and action occurrences, duration of the actions.

Most of the existing description formalisms for timed systems adopt implicitly the following view concerning their functioning:

- A timed system is the composition of cooperating sequential components (processes). Each component has a state variable defined on an appropriate time domain D with a binary operation $+$ which has essentially the properties of addition on non negative numbers. A component may modify its state either by executing some (atomic) action or by increasing its time variable (letting time progress).
- System time progresses synchronously in all processes, i.e., from a given global state, time increases by a quantity d if all the components accept to do so.
- An execution sequence is a sequence of two-phase steps: In the first phase φ_1 of a step, components may execute, either independently or in cooperation, a finite though arbitrarily long sequence of actions. In the second phase φ_2, components coordinate to let time progress by some finite or infinite amount. A new step begins when the second phase terminates. Figure 1 illustrates this principle for two interacting processes.

The functioning described combines both synchronous and asynchronous cooperation in two alternating phases: one where all the components agree for the time to progress, and an eventually terminating asynchronous computation phase during which the progress of time is blocked.

Most modes of cooperation of concurrent systems can be obtained by simplifying this functioning scheme. In fact, in the so called asynchronous cooperation only the action execution phase exists. In synchronous languages like Lustre [CHPP87], Esterel [BC85]

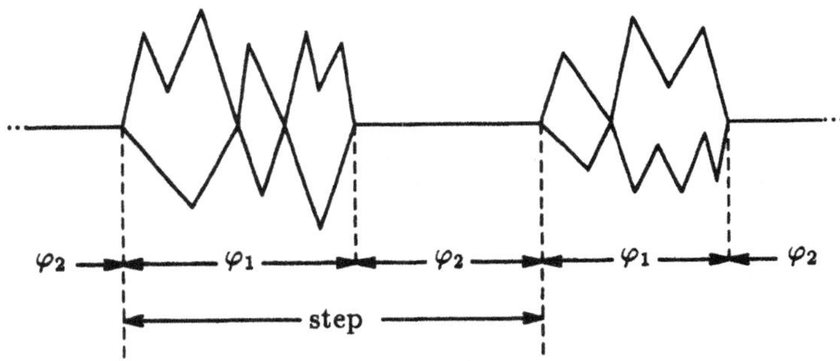

Figure 1: two-phase functioning schema

and the StateCharts [Har87], a step corresponds implicitly to one time unit and only the final state reached at the end of an asynchronous computation phase can be observed. This state is obtained by composing the effects of the actions (microsteps in the current terminology) and its computation raises some well-known causality problems. The so called synchronous cooperation, encountered in process algebras like SCCS [Mil83], CIRCAL [Mil91] and Meije [AB84], corresponds to a particular case of this functioning, where in addition, a process cannot perform more than one action in a step.

Such a mode of two-phase functioning is quite appropriate and natural for modelling reactive systems. For instance, the functioning of hardware and of systems for real-time control ideally follows this principle: a phase of asynchronous evolution is followed by a phase in which conceptually time progresses.

In a recent paper [NSY91], it is proposed a model for hybrid systems which adopts such a two-phase functioning principle. The phase where actions — "instantaneous" discrete changes of the state space — are executed is followed by a phase where state is transformed according to a law depending on time progress.

Considering such a mode of functioning allows to correlate the speeds of a system's components, as the flow of asynchronous computation can be cut by time progress phases in some appropriate manner. Furthermore, it introduces a concept of duration for an execution step and allows to assign durations to sequences of actions.

One might object that this two phase functioning assumption cannot faithfully model real systems where actions always take some non-zero time. In fact, direct consequences of this assumption are the following:

- Atomic actions take no time. This simplifies theoretical development and does not go against generality as non atomic actions can be modelled by sequences of atomic ones. It has been advantageously adopted by programming languages like Esterel [BC85].
- The time considered is *abstract* in the sense that it is used as a parameter to express constraints about instants of occurrences of actions. The implementability of such

constraints taking into account speeds and execution times of processors, is a separate though not independent issue. This distinction between abstract and concrete or physical time is an important one. It allows simplifications that are convenient at conceptual level as it leads to simpler and more tractable models. For instance, the assumption that an action may take zero time, though not realistic for physical time, is quite convenient for abstract time. Of course, such an abstraction should take into account realisability issues by integrating requirements for safe implementations. For instance, eventual termination of the asynchronous computation phase is such a requirement; for a correct implementation it should be possible to determine the clock period as the upper bound of step durations computed so as to take into account execution time of sequences of ideally zero time actions.

It has been often argued that models where any action takes some non zero time — its execution time — allow more faithful descriptions. In fact such an assumption destroys abstractness of time as specifications depend on specific implementation choices. It will be shown that the zero duration assumption for atomic actions is more general and leads to much simpler theories.

The overview is carried out by considering successively the choices for a designer of a timed process algebra, at model level and at language level.

The choice of the model determines the semantics and thus the intrinsic expressivity of a process algebra. As various types of semantics have been used for the algebras considered, we take operational semantics — strong bisimulation semantics — as a basis of the comparison. The reason is that most algebras have been given such semantics or some operational semantics can be deduced in most of cases. In our comparison we take into account features allowing abstraction (silent actions, hiding) only as long as they enhance expressivity.

The languages used for timed process algebras can be viewed as extensions of the languages used for untimed process algebras by adding some specific constructs or by assuming that in some cases prefixing by an action may delay. Some criteria for the comparison of the languages considered are the minimality of the set of the operators and their appropriateness for a natural and direct description.

The paper is organised as follows:

- Section 2 is devoted to the presentation of a general model for timed systems defined for an arbitrary time domain. The model is transition systems labelled with either action names from an arbitrary action alphabet or by elements of an appropriate time domain D. Some general properties of this model are discussed as well as their importance concerning the capability to characterise time constraints of various types.

- In section 3, we present a comparison of the expressive capabilities of the following timed process algebras (presented in alphabetic order):

  - ACP_ρ (Real Time ACP) of J.C.M. Baeten and J.A. Bergstra [BB90,Klu91].

- ATP (Algebra of Timed Processes) of the authors [NRSV90,NS90]. We sometimes make reference to a variant of ATP presented in [NSY91].
- TCSP (Timed CSP) of G.M. Reed and A.W. Roscoe [RR88,DS89,Sch91].
- TeCCS (Temporal CCS, or TCCS) of F. Moller and C. Tofts [MT90].
- TiCCS (Timed CCS, or TCCS) of Wang Yi [Wan90,Wan91].
- TPCCS (Timed Probabilistic CCS) of H. Hansson and B. Jonsson. We focus only on features relative to time.
- TPL (Temporal Process Language) of M. Hennessy and T. Regan [HR90, HR91].
- U-LOTOS (Urgent LOTOS) of T. Bolognesi and F. Lucidi [BL91].

We especially focus on constructs used to describe time constraints and their semantics. The presentation is organised as an exercise for building a timed process algebra from a standard process algebra for untimed systems.

2 The models

In this section, we present a general model for timed systems. We consider labelled transition systems whose states are process expressions, and whose labels are either elements a of a *vocabulary of actions* A or elements d of a *time domain* D. A may contain non-visible (internal) actions denoted by τ; visible actions are denoted by α.

$P \xrightarrow{a} Q$ means that the process P may perform the atomic and timeless action a and then it behaves as Q.

$P \xrightarrow{d} Q$ means that the process P may *idle* for d time units after which it behaves as Q.

Before discussing the properties of such models, we propose a general definition of time domains.

2.1 Time domain

Definition: A *time domain* is a commutative monoid $(D, +, 0)$ satisfying the following requirements.

- $d + d' = d \Leftrightarrow d' = 0$
- the preorder $\leq$ defined by $d \leq d' \Leftrightarrow \exists d'' : d + d'' = d'$ is a total order

The following properties can be easily proved.

- 0 is the least element of D

- for any d, d', if $d \leq d'$, then the element d'' such that $d + d'' = d'$ is unique. It is denoted by $d' - d$

We denote $D - \{0\}$ by D_*. We also write $d < d'$ instead of $d \leq d' \ \wedge \ d \neq d'$.

D is called *dense* if $\forall d, d' \ : \ d < d' \Rightarrow \exists d'' \ : \ d < d'' < d'$

D is called *discrete* if $\forall d \exists d' \ : \ d < d' \ \wedge \ \forall d'' \ : \ d < d'' \Rightarrow d' \leq d''$. Since the order is total, d' is unique and is called the *successor* of d, denoted by $\mathbf{succ}(d)$. An important property of a discrete domain is that for any d, $\mathbf{succ}(d) = d + \mathbf{succ}(0)$. That is, any element of D can be obtained from 0 by adding as many $\mathbf{succ}(0)$ as necessary.

Examples of time domains are $\mathbb{N}$ (discrete), $\mathbb{Q}^+$ and $\mathbb{R}^+$ (dense), or even the singleton $\{0\}$.

In the transition relation defined in the beginning of this section, we do not allow 0 to be a label, that is, labels are elements of $A \cup D_*$.

2.2 The time domain in the algebras considered

TCSP and ACP_ρ are explicitly defined over a dense time domain.

For TiCCS, TeCCS and U-LOTOS, the choice of a discrete or dense time domain is important neither for the syntax nor for the semantics. However, the axiomatisation strongly depends on this choice, especially for that of parallel composition. In TeCCS a complete set of axioms is provided in the discrete case. In [Wan91], Wang explains how an expansion theorem can be given in the dense case. This is possible only if we have a way of recording and use the instant when an action is performed.

TPCCS, TPL and ATP are defined over a discrete time domain. Extending them to a dense time domain requires some modification of the syntax. In [NSY91], a generalisation of ATP, parametrised by an arbitrary time domain, has been proposed.

2.3 Model properties

In this section we give an overview of the most important model properties and their importance for the characterisation of features of timed systems.

2.3.1 Time determinism

It is usually admitted that when a process P is idle (does not perform any action) for some duration d, then the resulting behaviour is completely determined from P and d. In other words, the progress of time should be deterministic. This property, satisfied by the models of all the algebras, we consider, can be expressed by

$$\forall P, P', P'', d \ : \ P \xrightarrow{d} P' \wedge P \xrightarrow{d} P'' \ \Rightarrow P' = P''$$

where $=$ is the syntactic equality.

2.3.2 Time additivity

In order to ensure the soundness of the notion of time, it is usually required that

- a process which can idle for $d + d'$ time units, can idle for d and then for d' time units, and vice-versa
- in both cases, the resulting behaviour is the same

We call this property *time additivity* (*time continuity* in [Wan90]). It is present in all the algebras and it is formally defined by

$$\forall P, P', d, d' \, : \, (\exists P'' \, : \, P \xrightarrow{d} P'' \wedge P'' \xrightarrow{d'} P') \Leftrightarrow P \xrightarrow{d + d'} P'$$

2.3.3 Deadlock-freeness

In untimed systems, a blocked or terminated process is represented by a deadlock in the model, since it cannot perform any action. For timed systems, it is natural to demand that, a terminated process does not block time, because of the strong synchrony hypothesis concerning time progress. If no distinction is made between termination and deadlock, this implies that there is no sink state in the model, which can be written as

$$\forall P \, \exists l \in A \cup D_{*} \, \exists P' \, : \, P \xrightarrow{l} P'$$

In algebras like TeCCS, U-LOTOS and ACP_{ρ}, there exist processes whose models do not satisfy this property, and thus they can block the progress of time Such *time-locks* may be used to detect some timing inconsistencies in specifications.

2.3.4 Action urgency

In all the considered algebras, there are processes which *must* perform an action without letting time pass, that is,

$$\exists P, a, P' \, : \, P \xrightarrow{a} P' \wedge \forall d \, : \, P \stackrel{d}{\not\rightarrow}$$

This defines a notion of urgency for actions, as a process may block the progress of time and enforce the execution of an action before some delay.

However, in TPCCS, TPL, TCSP and TiCCS, urgency is possible — and is enforced — for invisible actions only; this can be expressed by

$$\forall P, P', d, Q : P \xrightarrow{\tau} P' \Rightarrow P \overset{d}{\not\rightarrow} Q$$

This property is called *minimal delay, maximal progress* or *tau-urgency.* In CCS-based algebras, it is strongly related to the communication mechanism. Indeed, a communication in CCS yields a tau action; thus, this property allows to ensure that two processes communicate as soon as they are ready to do so.

In models without the general action urgency, it is not possible, for instance, to characterise the situation where a process sends a message at most 3 time units after it has been requested to do so.

2.3.5 Persistency

In some algebras (TiCCS, U-LOTOS and TCSP), the progress of time cannot suppress the ability to perform an action. This property, called persistency, is expressed by

$$\forall P, Q, P', d, a : P \xrightarrow{a} P' \wedge P \xrightarrow{d} Q \Rightarrow \exists P'' : Q \xrightarrow{a} P''$$

This property is not satisfied by ATP, TPL, TPCCS, TeCCS and ACP_ρ. In the latter two, it is even possible, for instance, to specify a process which may perform an action a at time $\frac{1}{2}$ or an action b at time $\frac{5}{7}$. In TPCCS, TPL and ATP, such a behaviour does not exist. In the generic version of ATP presented in [NSY91], where the time domain may be dense, the models satisfy a weaker requirement than persistency, which we call *interval persistency.* This property asserts that if a process may let time progress, then any action it can perform remains possible during some time interval. This is expressed by

$$\forall P\, \exists d > 0\, \forall d' \in]0, d[, \forall Q, P', a : P \xrightarrow{d'} Q \wedge P \xrightarrow{a} P' \Rightarrow \exists P'' : Q \xrightarrow{a} P''$$

Notice that this property is always true for a discrete time domain. Like ATP, TPL and TPCCS could be easily adapted to a dense domain, in which case their models would also have the interval persistency property.

2.3.6 Finite variability and bounded variability

A process has the *finite variability* (*non-Zenoness, well-timedness*) property if it can perform only finitely many actions in a finite time interval. The only algebra for which every process satisfy this requirement is TCSP. This is achieved by enforcing a *system-delay* between two actions of a sequential process. This assumption seems in fact to be the only solution to ensure finite variability, but it yields a complicated theory, and destroys abstractness of time.

To define formally this property, consider the family of relations $\overset{(a,d)}{\Longrightarrow}$ for $(a, d) \in A \times D_*$ on processes, defined by

$$P \overset{(a,d)}{\Longrightarrow} R \Leftrightarrow P \overset{d}{\longrightarrow} Q \wedge Q \overset{a}{\longrightarrow} R$$

A *time trace* of a process P is a maximal sequence $(a_0, d_0)(a_1, d_1) \ldots (a_i, d_i) \ldots$ such that

$$\exists P_1, P_2, \ldots, P_i, \ldots \; : \; P \overset{(a_0,d_0)}{\Longrightarrow} P_1 \overset{(a_1,d_1)}{\Longrightarrow} P_2 \ldots \overset{(a_i,d_i)}{\Longrightarrow} P_i \ldots$$

We represent by $T(P)$ the set of traces of P.

P satisfies the finite variability property if and only if

$$\forall d \, \forall \sigma = (a_0, d_0)(a_1, d_1) \ldots \in T(P) \; : \\ \left(i < j \leq \text{length}(\sigma) \wedge \sum_{k=i+1}^{j} d_k \leq d \right) \Rightarrow j - i < \infty$$

A stronger requirement should be satisfied by models in order that they represent implementable behaviours — we consider a behaviour to be *implementable* if it can be executed on a processor where the measure of time is provided by a discrete clock. We call this requirement *bounded variability*; it demands that for any duration d, there is an upper bound n of the number of actions performed within any time interval of length d.

This can be stated formally, for a given process P, by

$$\forall d \, \exists n \, \forall \sigma = (a_0, d_0)(a_1, d_1) \ldots \forall i, j \; : \\ \left(i < j \leq \text{length}(\sigma) \wedge \sum_{k=i+1}^{j} d_k \leq d \right) \Rightarrow j - i \leq n$$

This property guarantees implementability in the sense that one can establish a correspondence between model time d and a clock period for safe implementations. From this definition, for model time d one can take a clock period greater than or equal to $n.d_0$ where d_0 is an upper bound of atomic action durations. Bounded variability is satisfied by none of the considered algebras.

2.3.7 Bounded control

If we consider again realisability issues, for the same reasons as above, the set of initial actions of a process should not change too fast in a given time interval.

Given a process P, represent by $init(P)$ the set of the actions it can perform, i.e.,

$$init(P) = \{a \mid \exists P' \; : \; P \overset{a}{\longrightarrow} P'\}$$

A model has the bounded control property if there exists d such that for all states P and P' in the model, if $P \overset{d_1}{\longrightarrow} P'$ and $init(P) \neq init(P')$, then $d_1 \geq d$. In fact, the modification of the initial actions corresponds to a change of the "control state" of the process. Bounded control expresses the fact that for any d, there is a bounded number of such changes in any time interval of duration d, and it means that it is possible to find a clock period which allows to handle these changes.

The bounded control property is satisfied for models defined over a discrete time domain, and for models of TCSP.

2.4 Discussion

An important question is which properties are essential and how their presence or absence influences description capabilities.

Most of the existing work adopt time determinism and additivity. Deadlock-freeness is not in our opinion an essential model property. Time-lock is of course an abnormal situation but in some theories it can correspond to non-realisable specifications.

A property like persistency seems to be a strong requirement which is very often adopted without justification. Saying that time progress does not change system's capabilities to perform actions seems to be counterintuitive as time is often used precisely as a parameter to control action executability (as in timeouts). This property, often combined with urgency with respect to τ only, allows to express the fact that some action *may* be executed during some time interval, but cannot guarantee *obligation* of execution. This corresponds, we believe, to a major distinction concerning description capabilities of formalisms.

Implementability properties prevent from having an unbounded number of state changes within finite time, which is an essential requirement for discrete machines. Both bounded variability and bounded control properties allow to establish a relationship connecting abstract (model) time with a processor's discrete clock period.

In the sequel, we consider models that are time deterministic and additive. As D is usually infinite, the models are generally infinitely branching transition systems. Figure 2 represents the model of the process "P timeout(3) Q" which behaves as P before time 3 or as Q at time 3, for $D = \mathbb{N}$, $D = \{0, 0.5, 1, 1.5, ...\}$ and D dense.

3 The Languages — How to Cook your own Timed Process Algebra

In this section we present an overview of the language features of the process algebras considered. We especially focus on constructs used to describe time constraints, their semantics, and the extension of the semantics of standard operators for timed transitions.

The presentation is organised as an exercise of building a timed process algebra TPA from a standard process algebra for untimed systems. Given such an untimed process algebra UPA we review the different ways of extending it encountered in the literature.

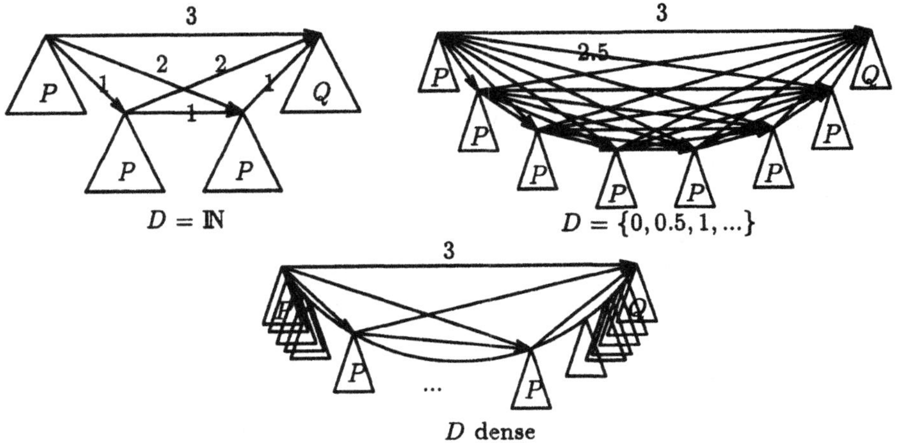

Figure 2

To make the comparison as concrete as possible, we define the meaning of constructs in terms of the common reference model presented in the previous section. The interpretation of the original semantics into this common framework required some simplifications that, we hope, do not bias the comparisons.

3.1 General principles

3.1.1 Process algebra

A process algebra PA is defined as a quadruple $(OP, L, R_L^{OP}, \sim)$ where

- OP is a set of operators defining the language of PA
- L is a set of transition labels
- R_L^{OP} is a set of structural operational semantics rules à la Plotkin [Plo81] associating with a term of PA a transition system labelled on L (a model)
- $\sim \subseteq$ PA $\times$ PA is a behavioural equivalence defined over the models. It it usually required that this equivalence be a congruence, since a compositional semantics is an crucial issue for a language

3.2 Timed process algebra

We consider here an *untimed process algebra* UPA $= (OP, A, R_A^{OP}, \sim)$, where A is a vocabulary of actions and $\sim$ is the strong equivalence relation [Mil80,Mil83].

The *timed process algebra* TPA $= (OP \cup OP', L, R_L^{OP\cup OP'}, \overset{T}{\sim})$ is defined from UPA by adding a set OP' of *time-constraining* operators.

Time-constraining operators are operators which can transform untimed processes into *time-constrained* ones. Examples of such operators are: time-lock constructs, operators which delay the execution of a process, operators which impose some urgency on the execution of a process, timeout operators, watchdog operators.

Processes of TPA are timed systems. Following the ideas in previous section, we decide to represent their models by transition systems labelled on $L = A \cup D_*$. Moreover, we require that the models of processes of TPA be time-deterministic and time-additive.

We choose for the equivalence relation $\overset{T}{\sim}$ the strong equivalence with respect to L-transitions.

In UPA, time progress does not have to be represented in the models, since by definition, it has no influence on the behaviour of an untimed process. In order to embed UPA in TPA, we have to choose the timed model corresponding to an untimed process (its time-equivalent). This must take into account the following requirements.

Semantics conservation: the untimed process and its time-equivalent should have the same behaviour as long as we observe execution of actions only. This imposes that the rules R_A^{OP} of UPA remain valid in TPA, *as far as they are applied on terms of UPA.*

Isomorphism: we also require that for any terms P, Q of UPA $P \sim Q$ if and only if $P \overset{T}{\sim} Q$. This requirement guarantees that the theory of processes of UPA is isomorphic to that of the restriction of TPA to operators of UPA. Thus, any theoretical development in UPA about an untimed process remains valid in TPA, and conversely.

In the sequel we consider a standard process algebra UPA and apply these principles.

3.3 Syntax and semantics of UPA

The language of terms of UPA is described by the following syntax, where Nil is is a constant, a and α are elements of A, $\alpha \neq \tau$, and X is an element of a set of process variables $\mathcal{X}$.

$$P ::= Nil \mid X \mid aP \mid P + Q \mid P \parallel Q \mid P\backslash\alpha \mid \mathbf{rec}X \cdot P$$

All the operators except $\parallel$ are taken from CCS [Mil80]. We choose prefixing instead of sequential composition to simplify the presentation, since it usually yields a simpler theory. The restriction operator $P\backslash\alpha$ prevents P from performing the visible action α.

We do not impose any choice of parallel composition operator, which can be CCS-like, ACP-like (in which case we must define a communication function for actions), or CSP or LOTOS-like (it should then be parametrised by sets of actions).

For such a language, we suppose that a standard operational semantics is defined, in terms of transition systems labelled by element of A (actions), by the following axiom and rules

$$aP \xrightarrow{a} P \qquad \frac{P \xrightarrow{a} P'}{P+Q \xrightarrow{a} P'} \qquad \frac{Q \xrightarrow{a} Q'}{P+Q \xrightarrow{a} Q'}$$

$$\frac{P \xrightarrow{b} P' \,,\, b \neq \alpha}{P\backslash\alpha \xrightarrow{b} P'\backslash\alpha} \qquad \frac{P[(\mathbf{rec}X \cdot P)/X] \xrightarrow{a} P'}{\mathbf{rec}X \cdot P \xrightarrow{a} P'}$$

We do not provide the semantic rules for the parallel composition operator; we only demand that it has an interleaving semantics, as we take the models to be transition systems labelled on A.

3.4 Embedding UPA in a TPA

We first have to define how to add time to an untimed process, taking into account the requirements presented in 3.2.

Isomorphism. A simple answer to the isomorphism requirement is obtained by considering that time progress is possible without effect at any point of the execution of an untimed process. We obtain then the timed model of a term P of UPA by adding loops of the form $P \xrightarrow{d} P$ for any d of D_*. Another possibility is to allow P to idle if and only if it cannot perform any action u of some subset U of *urgent actions* of A. For instance, U may be the subset of internal actions of A. This induces urgency in the models for states with a u among their initial actions. We can express this solution by the rule

$$\frac{\forall u \in U,\ P \stackrel{u}{\not\longrightarrow}}{P \xrightarrow{d} P}$$

The latter principle is implicitly adopted in TiCCS, TPL and TPCCS with $U = \{\tau\}$, whereas the former one is adopted in U-LOTOS, ACP$_\rho$, TeCCS and ATP. We can consider the first solution as a particular case of the second one, with $U = \emptyset$.

In TCSP, the solution adopted (adding a system delay after execution of an action in a sequential process and before each recursive call) does not satisfy the requirement. For instance, the process $\mathbf{rec}X \cdot aX$ is not equivalent to the process $a\,\mathbf{rec}X \cdot aX$ in TCSP while they are equivalent in untimed CSP. Hence, the laws of CSP are no longer valid in TCSP.

Notice that the correspondence between operators of UPA and their equivalent in TPA is not immediate in ACP$_\rho$, TeCCS and ATP.

- In basic ACP_ρ, some of the operators of ACP are not present, but may be derived (for instance the atomic action constants).
- In TeCCS and ATP, the timed process $a\,P$ does not correspond to the untimed process $a\,P$. In fact, the latter corresponds, in TeCCS to $\delta\, a\, P$, and in ATP to $\lfloor a\,P \rfloor^{\omega}$. Similarly, in TeCCS, Nil does not correspond to 0, but to $\delta 0$. The confusion for prefixing may be removed if we denote it differently in the timed algebra.

In the sequel, we consider the general solution to the isomorphism requirement, with a set of urgent actions U.

Semantics conservation. The other requirement demands that the operational semantics rules for time-equivalent of untimed processes of UPA remain valid in TPA. For instance, in TPA, there should be a rule

$$\frac{P, P', Q \in \text{ UPA }, P \xrightarrow{a} P'}{P + Q \xrightarrow{a} P'}$$

Since it is syntactically possible to determine whether a term of TPA is built using operators of UPA only, we can define a predicate InUPA(P), whose value is true if P is in UPA. The rule may then be rewritten in

$$\frac{\text{InUPA}(P), \text{InUPA}(P'), \text{InUPA}(Q),\ P \xrightarrow{a} P'}{P + Q \xrightarrow{a} P'}$$

However, if we want to obtain a compositional semantics of TPA, the premise $P, P', Q \in$ UPA is not enough; it should be replaced by

$$\exists P_1, P_1', Q_1' \ :\ \text{InUPA}(P_1),\ \text{InUPA}(P_1'),\ \text{InUPA}(Q_1),\ P \overset{T}{\sim} P_1,\ P' \overset{T}{\sim} P_1',\ Q \overset{T}{\sim} Q_1$$

This kind of premise is clearly not acceptable in a structural operational semantics rule, since it is not based on a syntactic predicate, but on an semantic one: indeed, it means that we have to decide operationally whether some process of TPA has a model equivalent to a process of UPA.

We have thus to admit that this rule, and all the other rules of R_A^{OP} in UPA, are also valid in TPA.

3.4.1 Timed transitions of UPA operators

Concerning the definition of timed transitions, the semantics of OP in TPA must be defined so that

$$\frac{\forall u \in U,\ P \overset{u}{\not\longrightarrow}}{P \overset{d}{\longrightarrow} P}$$

for any P where only elements of OP occur.

Of course, such a rule should not be applicable to any TPA process. It can be checked that the semantic rules for TPA below satisfy the following properties.

- Their restriction to time-equivalents of UPA gives the same derivations as the above rule,
- They preserve time determinism and additivity,

Moreover, they are perfectly acceptable for TPA processes.

$$Nil \overset{d}{\longrightarrow} Nil \qquad \frac{a \notin U}{aP \overset{d}{\longrightarrow} aP} \qquad \frac{P \overset{d}{\longrightarrow} P'\ ,\ Q \overset{d}{\longrightarrow} Q'}{P+Q \overset{d}{\longrightarrow} P'+Q'}$$

$$\frac{P \overset{d}{\longrightarrow} P',\, Q \overset{d}{\longrightarrow} Q',\, \forall u \in U : \left(P \| Q \overset{u}{\not\longrightarrow}\ \wedge\ \forall d' < d \forall P' : P \| Q \overset{d'}{\longrightarrow} P' \Rightarrow P' \overset{u}{\not\longrightarrow}\right)}{P \parallel Q \overset{d}{\longrightarrow} P' \parallel Q'}$$

$$\frac{P \overset{d}{\longrightarrow} P'}{P\backslash\alpha \overset{d}{\longrightarrow} P'\backslash\alpha} \qquad \frac{P[(\mathbf{rec}X \cdot P)/X] \overset{d}{\longrightarrow} P'}{\mathbf{rec}X \cdot P \overset{d}{\longrightarrow} P'}$$

The rule for parallel composition means that the composition of P and Q can idle for d if both can do so, and moreover, if the composition cannot perform an urgent action before d.

The rules for $+$, $\|$ and restriction apply when the operands of the operators have d-transitions. However, in TPS, there may be processes without such transitions. We have to decide what is the effect of these operators in this case.

- For parallel composition, it is not possible to add a rule without violating the strong synchrony hypothesis.
- In $P\backslash\alpha$, if α is in U and is the only urgent action that P may perform, then the rules for restriction yield a state which is, either a sink state, or a state where non-urgent actions are made urgent. If we do not want such behaviours, we have to add the following rule.

$$\frac{\forall u \in U \, : \, P \stackrel{u}{\longrightarrow} \ \Rightarrow u = \alpha}{P\backslash\alpha \stackrel{d}{\longrightarrow} P\backslash\alpha}$$

- For the alternative choice, we may decide that if P may idle, but not Q, then $P+Q$ may idle, by adding the rule

$$\frac{P \stackrel{d}{\longrightarrow} P' \, , \, Q \stackrel{d}{\not\longrightarrow}}{P+Q \stackrel{d}{\longrightarrow} P'}$$

and its symmetric.

This semantics for $+$ is adopted in ACP$_\rho$. In TeCCS, two alternative choice operators are defined: the *weak choice* operator, for which the latter rules are added, and the *strong choice* one, where they are not. The other algebras propose the strong choice operator (we only consider the external choice of TCSP, which is strong).

3.5 Time-constraining operators

We present time-constraining operators used in the process algebras considered. The aim of the presentation is a classification and comparison without caring about minimality. We also emphasise the effect of the operators on the properties of the models.

3.5.1 Time-lock

It is a constant 0 representing the process performing no transition. It is a basic operator of TeCCS, and it can be derived in U-LOTOS. In ACP$_\rho$, the process $\delta(d)$ is a time-lock at time d.

Naturally, a time-lock process may be present only if the deadlock-freeness property is not required.

3.5.2 Delay operators

Operators for delaying processes are the most common ones in process algebras. Their effect consists in postponing the execution of a process by a parameter d. We can classify them into three groups.

Finite idling is defined with various syntaxes as a basic operator in TiCCS, TeCCS, TPL, U-LOTOS and TCSP. We denote it by a prefixing operator (d). where $d > 0$. $(d)P$ behaves as P after exactly d time units. Its semantics is given by the following rules.

$$\frac{d' < d}{(d)P \xrightarrow{d'} (d - d')P} \qquad (d)P \xrightarrow{d} P$$

Finite idling may be modelised in ATP, TPCCS and ACP$_\rho$, though its definition is not trivial in the latter, especially in the absolute time version.

Time-stamped actions. In ACP$_\rho$, the basic construct of the algebra is obtained by imposing a *time-stamp* to actions. Two versions are presented, with absolute or relative time-stamps. In the absolute case $a(d)$ performs a at time d since the beginning of the process, whereas in the relative case, $a[d]$ performs a d time units after the previous action has been performed. In the latter case, and if we consider it as a prefixing operator, its semantics may be described by

$$\frac{d' \leq d}{a[d] \xrightarrow{d'} a[d - d']P} \qquad a[0]P \xrightarrow{a} P$$

Time-stamped actions induce the general urgency property in the models. It can be modelled only in algebras where this property is allowed. In ACP$_\rho$, due to the choice for the semantics of alternative choice, it suppresses also any kind of persistency in the transition systems.

Unbounded idling is defined in algebras where there may be urgent actions, like TeCCS and ATP. Its purpose is to suppress this urgency. However, it has a different semantics in these two algebras:

- in TeCCS, the unary operator δ has the following semantics:

$$\frac{P \xrightarrow{a} P'}{\delta\, P \xrightarrow{a} P'} \qquad \delta\, P \xrightarrow{d} \delta\, P$$

- in ATP, the operator $\lfloor\,\rfloor^\omega$ has the following semantics:

$$\frac{P \xrightarrow{a} P'}{\lfloor P \rfloor^\omega \xrightarrow{a} \lfloor P' \rfloor^\omega} \qquad \frac{P \xrightarrow{d} P'}{\lfloor P \rfloor^\omega \xrightarrow{d} \lfloor P' \rfloor^\omega} \qquad \frac{\forall d',\ P \stackrel{d'}{\not\longrightarrow}}{\lfloor P \rfloor^\omega \xrightarrow{d} \lfloor P \rfloor^\omega}$$

The difference is that in TeCCS, if P cannot execute immediately an action, then the process $\delta\, P$ may only idle forever, whereas in ATP, the process P is allowed to let time progress.

Such operators are trivially definable in the other algebras, with the restriction that in those where τ is urgent, it is not possible to delay it.

Integral. In ACP$_\rho$, the integral operator $\int_{v\in V} P(v)$ for a process P parametrised by a time variable v behaves as P where v may be replaced by any value of the subset V of D. A simple use of this operator is $\int_{v\in I} a[v]$, where I is an interval. This process may perform an a at any time in I. Thus, it delays the execution of a by some value v in I. It can be described in TeCCS and ATP, provided the interval is right-closed.

Notice that in TiCCS, prefixing $a@v\,P$ is equivalent to an integral, where the interval I is the whole domain. The value v may be used in delay values in P. Such a construct is useful to provide an expansion theorem for parallel composition when the time domain is dense.

3.5.3 Urgency operators

Immediate actions. In TeCCS and ATP, prefixing by an action (aP) impose that this action be performed immediately. To avoid confusion with the prefixing operator of UPA, we denote this urgent prefixing by $\dot{a}P$. Its semantics is given by the unique axiom $\dot{a}P \xrightarrow{a} P$. It is also expressible in the algebras where urgency of actions are allowed, that is in U-LOTOS and ACP$_\rho$, if in the latter we allow the time-stamp 0. Conversely, it has no equivalent in the other algebras considered.

Time-stamped actions (ACP$_\rho$). They have been presented above. They have the double effect of delaying and imposing urgency once the delay has expired. We could call them a *punctuality* feature.

As soon as possible. In U-LOTOS, the primitive operator **asap** enforces the urgency of a set of actions in the whole execution of a process. For sake of simplicity, we only present its semantics in the case where this set of actions is reduced to a singleton.

$$\frac{P \xrightarrow{a'} P'}{\mathbf{asap}_a\,\mathbf{in}\,P \xrightarrow{a'} \mathbf{asap}_a\,\mathbf{in}\,P'} \qquad \frac{P \overset{a}{\not\rightarrow},\ P \xrightarrow{d} P',\ \forall d' < d \forall Q,\ P \xrightarrow{d'} Q \Rightarrow Q \overset{a}{\not\rightarrow}}{\mathbf{asap}_a\,\mathbf{in}\,P \xrightarrow{d} \mathbf{asap}_a\,\mathbf{in}\,P'}$$

The second rule means that the $\mathbf{asap}_a\,\mathbf{in}\,P$ can idle for d if P can do so, and cannot perform an a before d.

This very powerful operator is expressible in ACP$_\rho$, ATP and TeCCS, and clearly not in the other algebras.

3.5.4 Timeout operators

A timeout is an operator with two arguments P and Q and a parameter $d \in D_*$. We call P the body and Q the exception of the timeout.

A timeout for P, Q and d behaves as P if an initial action of P is performed within time d, otherwise it behaves as Q, after time d.

Depending on the interpretation of "initial action" and "within time d", several variants of timeout operators have been proposed.

a) $P \overset{d}{\triangleright} Q$ in ATP$_D$ ([NSY91]) with the following semantics.

$$\frac{P \xrightarrow{a} P'}{P \overset{d}{\triangleright} Q \xrightarrow{a} P'} \qquad \frac{P \xrightarrow{d'} P',\ d' < d}{P \overset{d}{\triangleright} Q \xrightarrow{d'} P' \overset{d-d'}{\triangleright} Q}$$

$$\frac{P \xrightarrow{d} P'}{P \overset{d}{\triangleright} Q \xrightarrow{d} Q} \qquad \frac{P \xrightarrow{d} P',\ Q \xrightarrow{d'} Q'}{P \overset{d}{\triangleright} Q \xrightarrow{d+d'} Q'}$$

The last rule is necessary to preserve time additivity.

With this operator an action that P may perform after some time is also interpreted as an "initial action" of P. "Within time d" is interpreted as "before time d"; we call timeouts with such a interpretation *strong timeouts*.

b) $\lfloor P \rfloor^d(Q)$ in ATP (start-delay operator) with the following semantics.

$$\frac{P \xrightarrow{a} P'}{\lfloor P \rfloor^d(Q) \xrightarrow{a} P'} \qquad \frac{P \xrightarrow{d'} P',\ d' < d}{\lfloor P \rfloor^d(Q) \xrightarrow{d'} \lfloor P' \rfloor^{d-d'}(Q)} \qquad \frac{\forall d'\ P \stackrel{d'}{\not\longrightarrow},\ d'' < d}{\lfloor P \rfloor^d(Q) \xrightarrow{d''} \lfloor P \rfloor^{d-d''}(Q)}$$

$$\lfloor P \rfloor^d(Q) \xrightarrow{d} Q \qquad \frac{Q \xrightarrow{d'} Q'}{\lfloor P \rfloor^d(Q) \xrightarrow{d+d'} Q'}$$

This operator differs from the previous one in that it also allows to postpone the urgent actions P may perform. It is a strong timeout too.

c) $P \triangleright_d Q$ in TPCCS is a strong timeout with a strict interpretation of initial actions:

$$\frac{P \xrightarrow{a} P'}{P \triangleright_d Q \xrightarrow{a} P'} \qquad \frac{d' < d}{P \triangleright_d Q \xrightarrow{d'} P \triangleright_{d-d'} Q}$$

$$P \triangleright_d Q \xrightarrow{d} Q \qquad \frac{Q \xrightarrow{d'} Q'}{P \triangleright_d Q \xrightarrow{d+d'} Q'}$$

d) The timeout of TCSP is a weak one, in the sense that at time d both the body and the exception can be executed; that is, P may start in the interval [0,d], and Q may be chosen at d. The weak timeout preserves persistency in the models. The interpretation of initial actions is the same as in case **a**. In the semantics, an urgent internal action τ is used to enforce a choice between P and Q at time d. The weak timeout can be expressed in terms of the strong one, but the converse is not true.

3.5.5 Watchdog operators

A watchdog is an operator with two arguments P (body) and Q (exception) and a parameter d in D_*.

It behaves as P until time d. At time d, P is "aborted" and Q is started.

Such operators are proposed in ATP (execution delay) and TCSP (time interrupt). As for the timeouts, the watchdog is strong in ATP, and weak in TCSP (in the latter, P may still perform some action at time d, which is not the case in ATP).

In TCSP, if P terminates successfully, the watchdog is cancelled. In ATP, there is no operational notion of termination. However, the watchdog may be cancelled if P performs a special action ξ, called *cancel.* We present hereafter the semantics of the watchdog of ATP.

$$\frac{P \xrightarrow{a} P' \,,\; a \neq \xi}{\lceil P \rceil^d(Q) \xrightarrow{a} \lceil P' \rceil^d(Q)} \qquad \frac{P \xrightarrow{\xi} P'}{\lceil P \rceil^d(Q) \xrightarrow{\tau} P'}$$

$$\frac{P \xrightarrow{d'} P' \,,\; d' < d}{\lceil P \rceil^d(Q) \xrightarrow{d'} \lceil P' \rceil^{d-d'}(Q)} \qquad \frac{P \xrightarrow{d} P'}{\lceil P \rceil^d(Q) \xrightarrow{d} Q} \qquad \frac{P \xrightarrow{d} P' \,,\; Q \xrightarrow{d'} Q'}{\lceil P \rceil^d(Q) \xrightarrow{d+d'} Q'}$$

4 Discussion

The paper is an overview and synthesis of existing results about timed process algebras. It hopefully contributes to the clarification of the following three different problems, designers of timed specification languages should in principle address.

1. What are the underlying principles of functioning of timed systems? In the introduction, we formulate some assumptions about the two-phase mode of functioning and provide pragmatic justifications. This functioning corresponds to some abstraction of the reality which has the advantage of clearly separating the actions from the time progress issue. It is argued that adopting such an "orthogonality" principle between actions and timed transitions is more paying than other approaches

imposing some non-zero durations to actions. In the latter, time is not abstract, i.e., independent of implementation choices.

2. What is a general model for timed systems, and what are its most relevant properties? Following assumptions about the functioning of timed systems, we take as models transition systems whose labels are either elements of an action vocabulary or elements of an appropriately chosen time domain.

   Concerning the properties studied, they can be classified as follows.

   - time determinism and additivity characterise fundamental properties of time.
   - properties characterising the expressivity of the model, like presence of timelocks and the different types of persistency or urgency.
   - realisability properties.

   The choice of a particular class of models should be determined for a given time domain as a compromise between realisability and expressivity.

3. How an untimed specification language can be consistently extended so as to obtain a timed specification language? We suggest a principle which has been more or less followed in several cases of consistent extensions (except for TCSP). Concerning the description capabilities of the language, it is difficult to make a precise comparison due to the differences of the semantic framework adopted. However, an important distinction appears concerning the expression of urgency.

This is a first partial synthesis of results in the area, which hopefully contributes to structuring them and suggests an approach for tackling the problem of introducing time in process algebras.

References

[AB84] D. Austry and G. Boudol. Algèbre de processus et synchronisation. *Theoretical Computer Science*, 30, 1984.

[BB90] J.C.M. Baeten and J.A. Bergstra. *Real Time Process Algebra*. Technical Report CS-R9053, Centre for Mathematics and Computer Science, Amsterdam, the Netherlands, 1990.

[BC85] G. Berry and L. Cosserat. The ESTEREL synchronous programming language and its mathematical semantics. In *LNCS 197: Proceedings CMU Seminar on Concurrency*, Springer-Verlag, 1985.

[BL91] T. Bolognesi and F. Lucidi. LOTOS-like process algebra with urgent or timed interactions. In *Proceedings of REX Workshop "Real-Time: Theory in Practice"*. Mook, the Netherlands, June 1991.

[CHPP87] P. Caspi, N. Halbwachs, D. Pilaud, and J. Plaice. LUSTRE: a declarative language for programming synchronous systems. In *14th Symposium on Principles of Programming Languages*, Munich, January 1987.

[DS89] J. Davies and S. Schneider. *An Introduction to Timed CSP*. Technical Report PRG-75, Oxford University Computing Laboratory, UK, August 1989.

[Har87] D. Harel. StateCharts : a visual approach to complex systems. *Science of Computer Programming*, 8-3:231–275, 1987.

[HR90] M. Hennessy and T. Regan. *A Temporal Process Algebra*. Technical Report 2/90, University of Sussex, UK, April 1990.

[HR91] M. Hennessy and T. Regan. *A Process Algebra for Timed Systems*. Technical Report 5/91, University of Sussex, UK, April 1991.

[Klu91] A.S. Klusener. *Completeness in Real Time Process Algebra*. Technical Report CS-R9106, Centre for Mathematics and Computer Science, Amsterdam, the Netherlands, January 1991.

[Mil80] R. Milner. A Calculus of Communicating Systems. In *LNCS 92*, Springer Verlag, 1980.

[Mil83] R. Milner. Calculi for Synchrony and Asynchrony. *Theoretical Computer Science*, 25, 1983.

[Mil91] G. J. Milne. The Formal Description and Verification of Hardware Timing. *IEEE Transactions on Computers*, 40 (7), July 1991.

[MT90] F. Moller and C. Tofts. A Temporal Calculus of Communicating Processes. In J.C.M. Baeten and J.W. Klop, editors, *LNCS 458. Proceedings of CONCUR '90 (Theories of Concurrency: Unification and Extension), Amsterdam, the Netherlands*, pages 401–415, Springer-Verlag, August 1990.

[NRSV90] X. Nicollin, J.-L. Richier, J. Sifakis, and J. Voiron. ATP: an Algebra for Timed Processes. In *Proceedings of the IFIP TC 2 Working Conference on Programming Concepts and Methods*, Sea of Gallilee, Israel, April 1990.

[NS90] X. Nicollin and J. Sifakis. *The algebra of timed processes ATP: theory and application.* Technical Report RT-C26, LGI-IMAG, Grenoble, France, December 1990.

[NSY91] X. Nicollin, J. Sifakis, and S. Yovine. From ATP to Timed Graphs and Hybrid Systems. In *Proceedings of REX Workshop "Real-Time: Theory in Practice"*. Mook, the Netherlands, June 1991.

[Plo81] G.D. Plotkin. *A Structural Approach to Operational Semantics.* Technical Report DAIMI FN-19, Århus University. Computer Science Department, Århus, Denmark, 1981.

[RR88] G.M. Reed and A.W. Roscoe. A timed model for Communicating Sequential Processes. *Theoretical Computer Science*, 58 (pp 249–261), 1988.

[Sch91] S. Schneider. *An Operational Semantics for Timed CSP*. Programming Research Group, Oxford University, UK, February 1991.

[Wan90] Wang Yi. Real-time behaviour of asynchronous agents. In J.C.M. Baeten and J.W. Klop, editors, *LNCS 458. Proceedings of CONCUR '90 (Theories of Concurrency: Unification and Extension), Amsterdam, the Netherlands*, pages 502–520, Springer-Verlag, August 1990.

[Wan91] Wang Yi. CCS + Time = an Interleaving Model for Real Time Systems. In *Proceedings of ICALP '91, Madrid, Spain*, July 1991.

From ATP to Timed Graphs and Hybrid Systems *

Xavier Nicollin Joseph Sifakis Sergio Yovine

Laboratoire de Génie Informatique
IMAG-Campus B.P. 53X
38041 Grenoble Cedex - FRANCE

Abstract. The paper presents results of ongoing work aiming at the unification of some behavioural description formalisms for timed systems.

We propose for **ATP** a very general semantics in terms of a time domain.

It is then shown how **ATP** can be translated into a variant of timed graphs. This result allows the application of existing model-checking techniques to **ATP**.

Finally, we propose a notion of hybrid systems as a generalisation of timed graphs. Such systems can evolve, either by executing a discrete transition, or by performing some "continuous" transformation.

The formalisms studied admit the same class of models: time deterministic and time continuous, possibly infinitely branching transition systems labelled by actions or durations.

Keywords: real-time, specification of timed systems, process algebra, timed graphs, hybrid systems

Contents

1 Introduction

The paper presents a generic version of the Algebra of Timed Processes **ATP** and its relationships to timed graphs and hybrid systems. The aim of this section is to present

*Work supported by the ESPRIT BRA SPEC

the general framework and assumptions about timed systems that motivated the design choices in **ATP**.

A timed system is usually considered to be a system with a global parameter (state variable) called time, used to constrain the occurrences of the actions. Introducing time requires consistent assumptions about its progress with respect to the evolution of the system: correspondence between instants (domain of definition of the time parameter) and action occurrences, duration of actions...

The model for timed systems used for **ATP** is based on the following principles:

- A timed system is the parallel composition of communicating sequential components (processes). Each component has a state variable defined on an appropriate time domain D with a binary operation $+$ which has essentially the properties of addition on non negative numbers. A component may modify its state either by executing some (atomic) action or by increasing its time variable (letting time progress).
- System time progresses synchronously in all processes, i.e., from a given global state, time increases by a quantity d if all the components accept to do so.
- An execution sequence is a sequence of steps, a step being determined by two successive time evolutions. Within a step, components may execute either independently or in cooperation, a finite though arbitrarily long sequence of actions after which they coordinate to let time progress. This corresponds to the beginning of a new step.

The functioning described combines both synchronous and asynchronous cooperation in two alternating phases: one where all the components agree for the time to progress,, and an eventually terminating asynchronous computation phase during which the progress of time is blocked. Such a mode of two-phase functioning is quite appropriate and natural for modelling reactive systems. For instance, hardware and systems for real-time control function according to this principle. Considering such a mode of functioning, allows to correlate the speeds of a system's components and introduces a concept of duration. Direct consequences of these assumptions are:

- The assumption about atomicity of actions implies that actions take no time. This simplifies theoretical development and does not go against generality as non atomic actions can be modelled by sequences of atomic ones. It has been advantageously adopted by other formalisms like Esterel [BC85].
- The time considered is *abstract* in the sense that it is used as a parameter to express constraints about instants of occurrences of actions. The implementability of such constraints taking into account speeds and execution times of processors, is a separate though not independent issue. This distinction between abstract and concrete or physical time is an important one. It allows simplifications that are convenient at conceptual level as it leads to simpler and more tractable models. For instance, the assumption that an action may take zero time, though not realistic for

physical time, is quite convenient for abstract time. However, such an abstraction can take into account realisability issues: in any correct implementation, the clock period should be taken greater than the longest duration of a step computed so as to take into account execution time of sequences of ideally zero time actions. The assumption about eventual progress of time guarantees that such a bound exists.

Following these ideas, the Algebra of Timed Processes **ATP** has been studied [NRSV90, NS90]. In these papers we considered that the time domain is discrete and this was implemented by assuming that processes can perform, apart from ordinary actions, a special "time action" represented by χ, whose synchronous execution makes time progress by one unit. Apart from standard operators of process algebras like prefixing by an action different from χ, non-deterministic choice and parallel composition, **ATP** has delay constructs allowing to describe timeouts and watchdogs.

This work has been motivated by the study of relationships between **ATP** and timed graphs, a model for the description and analysis of timed systems proposed in [ACD90]. This model is a state-transition graph extended with a mechanism that allows the expression of constraints on the delays between the state transitions. Constraints are expressed as predicates on state variables representing timers. The interesting fact about timed graphs is that there exist model checking methods for temporal logics with quantitative temporal operators which are directly applicable to them.

A main result of the paper is a method for the translation of **ATP** into timed graphs. As the semantics of timed graphs has been defined for dense time domains, we provide a generic definition $\mathbf{ATP}_D$ of **ATP** in terms of an arbitrary time domain D. The proposed translation method allows to obtain from a process of $\mathbf{ATP}_D$ a timed graph whose timers are defined on D. Due to this result, the verification methods applicable to timed graphs can be extended to **ATP**. This work required the definition of a general notion of time domain and the generalisation of well known results about **ATP**.

Another important idea of the paper is the proposition of a general model for hybrid systems as a generalisation of timed graphs. A hybrid system is described as an extended state-transition graph with a set of variables X whose values can be modified as follows:

- Transitions are labelled with guarded commands i.e., pairs $(b(X), X := f(X))$ where $b(X)$ is a condition on X and f is a generalised function. As usually, a transition is enabled for a given configuration of values of the variables X_0 if $b(X_0)$ evaluates to true. The resulting state is obtained by executing the assignment and moving from the current node of the graph to its successor by the transition.

- Nodes are labelled with functions φ representing transformations of the variables in terms of the time t elapsed and of their initial values X_0 when the node is entered. That is, the value of the state variables after sojourn time t at a node is $\varphi(X_0, t)$. The transformation stops when the node is left by executing a transition.

The functioning described is composed as for timed systems of two phases: One where time passes and state transformation follows a law depending on time progress, and another instantaneous where the state is submitted to a "discrete" change. A result of this work is that **ATP**, Timed Graphs and Hybrid Systems can be defined using the same class of models.

The paper is organised as follows:

- Section 2 is devoted to the presentation of the algebra $\mathbf{ATP}_D$. The semantic rules of the operators are parametrised by the time domain D. We present an axiomatisation for sequential processes, and we study the properties of the underlying models.
- In section 3, we define the Action Timed Graphs and their operational semantics in the same class of models as **ATP**. Action timed graph are a variant of the timed graphs proposed in [ACD90] adapted so as to take into account features of **ATP**.
- We present then a method for translating an **ATP** process into an action timed graph with the same time domain, whose model is observationally equivalent to that of the process.
- Finally, in section 5, the issue of hybrid systems is discussed and illustrated by two examples. A definition is proposed, yielding a quite simple operational semantics.

2 $\mathbf{ATP}_D$: ATP for a time domain D

We present here a generic version of the algebra **ATP**, parametrised with an arbitrary time domain. For a complete theory of **ATP**, the reader should refer to [NS90].

The primitive constructs of **ATP** in this paper are different from those presented in [NS90]. We introduce the notion of *delayable action*, and the start-delay operator of [NS90] is replaced by a *timeout* operator. These modifications are motivated by the fact that the timeout operator is much easier to define over timed graphs than the start-delay operator. However, the class of models obtained, in the case where the domain is discrete, is the same.

2.1 Time domains

Definition: A *time domain* is a commutative monoid $(D, 0, +)$ satisfying the following requirements.

- $d + d' = d \Leftrightarrow d' = 0$
- the preorder $\leq$ defined by

  $$d \leq d' \Leftrightarrow (\exists d'')\ d + d'' = d'$$

  is a total, well-founded order.

The following properties can be easily proved.

- 0 is the least element of D
- for any d, d', if $d \leq d'$, then the element d'' such that $d + d'' = d'$ is unique. It is denoted by $d' - d$

We denote $D - \{0\}$ by D_*. We also write $d < d'$ instead of $d \leq d' \ \wedge \ d \neq d'$.

D is called *dense* if $(\forall d, d')\ [d < d' \Rightarrow (\exists d'')\ d < d'' < d']$

D is called *discrete* if $(\forall d)\ (\exists d')\ [d < d' \ \wedge \ (\forall d'')\ d < d'' \Rightarrow d' \leq d'']$. Since the order is total, d' is unique and is called the *successor* of d, denoted by $\mathbf{succ}(d)$. $\mathbf{succ}(0)$ is denoted by χ. An important property of a discrete domain is that for any d, $\mathbf{succ}(d) = d + \mathbf{succ}(0)$. That is, any element of D can be obtained from 0 by adding as many $\mathbf{succ}(0)$ as necessary.

Examples of time domains are $\mathbb{N}$ (discrete), $\mathbb{Q}^+$ and $\mathbb{R}^+$ (dense), or even the singleton $\{0\}$.

2.2 $\mathbf{ASTP}_D$: Sequential ATP

2.2.1 Syntax

Let $\mathcal{A}$ be a vocabulary whose elements, called *actions*, are denoted by possibly indexed lowercase greek letters (except δ). Put

$$\begin{aligned} \dot{\mathcal{A}} &\triangleq \{\dot{\alpha} \mid \alpha \in \mathcal{A}\} \\ \tilde{\mathcal{A}} &\triangleq \{\tilde{\alpha} \mid \alpha \in \mathcal{A}\} \end{aligned}$$

$\dot{\mathcal{A}} \cup \tilde{\mathcal{A}}$ is the set of prefixing operators of the algebra. $\dot{\alpha}$ is called *immediate* action, while $\tilde{\alpha}$ is called *delayable* action. $\underline{\alpha}$ denotes either $\dot{\alpha}$ or $\tilde{\alpha}$.

Let $\mathcal{V}$ be a set of *process variables*, whose elements are denoted by $X, Y, X_1, \ldots$ The syntax of sequential **ATP** with time domain D (noted $\mathbf{ASTP}_D$, or **ASTP** when the time domain is not relevant) is described by the following BNF grammar.

$$\begin{aligned} P ::= \ & \delta \quad \mid \ \underline{\alpha}\, P \quad \mid \ \underline{\alpha}\, X \ \mid \ P \oplus P \\ & P \overset{d}{\rhd} P \ \mid \ P \overset{d}{\rhd} X \ \mid \ \mathbf{rec} X \cdot P \end{aligned}$$

where $d \in D_*$.

In this language, we consider only closed terms.

- δ is a blocked or terminated process.
- $\underline{\alpha}\, P$ is prefixing of P by $\underline{\alpha}$. The process $\dot{\alpha}\, P$ performs the action α immediately, whereas the process $\tilde{\alpha}\, P$ may wait any amount of time before performing α.

- $P \oplus Q$ is the non-deterministic choice between processes P and Q.
- $P \overset{d}{\triangleright} Q$ is a *timeout* construct with delay d. It waits until time d for P to perform an action, in which case it behaves as P. If an action of P is not performed before time d, then it behaves as Q.
- $\mathbf{rec}X \cdot P$ is the classical recursion construct.

When writing processes, we consider that operators have the following decreasing priority: prefixing, timeout, non-deterministic choice, and recursion. Moreover, timeout is considered to be right-associative.

2.2.2 Operational semantics

The operational semantics of $\mathbf{ASTP}_D$ associates labelled transition systems to processes. States are process expressions. Since the time domain is not necessarily $\mathbb{N}$, we cannot use the time action χ, as in [NS90], for temporal transitions. We use, as in [Wan90,MT90], transition systems labelled by $\mathcal{L} = \mathcal{A} \cup D_*$.

The transition relation is then a subset of $\mathbf{ASTP} \times \mathcal{L} \times \mathbf{ASTP}$. It is defined by structural induction, à la Plotkin [Plo81], by the following rules, where $d, d' \in D_*$ and $l \in \mathcal{L}$.

$$\delta \xrightarrow{d} \delta \qquad \frac{P[(\mathbf{rec}X \cdot P)/X] \xrightarrow{l} P'}{\mathbf{rec}X \cdot P \xrightarrow{l} P'}$$

$$\dot{\alpha}\, P \xrightarrow{\alpha} P \qquad \tilde{\alpha}\, P \xrightarrow{\alpha} P \qquad \tilde{\alpha}\, P \xrightarrow{d} \tilde{\alpha}\, P$$

$$\frac{P \xrightarrow{\alpha} P'}{P \oplus Q \xrightarrow{\alpha} P'} \qquad \frac{Q \xrightarrow{\alpha} Q'}{P \oplus Q \xrightarrow{\alpha} Q'} \qquad \frac{P \xrightarrow{d} P',\ Q \xrightarrow{d} Q'}{P \oplus Q \xrightarrow{d} P' \oplus Q'}$$

$$\frac{P \xrightarrow{\alpha} P'}{P \overset{d}{\triangleright} Q \xrightarrow{\alpha} P'} \qquad \frac{P \xrightarrow{d'} P'}{P \overset{d+d'}{\triangleright} Q \xrightarrow{d'} P \overset{d}{\triangleright} Q} \qquad \frac{P \xrightarrow{d} P'}{P \overset{d}{\triangleright} Q \xrightarrow{d} Q} \qquad \frac{P \xrightarrow{d} P',\ Q \xrightarrow{d'} Q'}{P \overset{d}{\triangleright} Q \xrightarrow{d+d'} Q'}$$

Strong equivalence

Transition systems are considered modulo the *strong equivalence* $\sim$, which is the largest binary relation $\mathcal{R}$ on processes such that

$$P \mathcal{R} Q \Rightarrow \begin{cases} \forall l, \forall P', P \xrightarrow{l} P' \Rightarrow \exists Q', Q \xrightarrow{l} Q' \wedge P' \mathcal{R} Q' \\ \forall l, \forall Q', Q \xrightarrow{l} Q' \Rightarrow \exists P', P \xrightarrow{l} P' \wedge P' \mathcal{R} Q' \end{cases}$$

We write $(P)_D$ to denote the model of P in the semantics of $\mathbf{ASTP}_D$.

2.2.3 Properties of the models

The transition relation satisfies the following properties (the terminology used for (2) and (3) is due to Wang [Wan90]).

(1) deadlock-freeness: $(\forall P)(\exists l)(\exists P')\ P \xrightarrow{l} P'$

(2) time determinacy: $(P \xrightarrow{d} P') \wedge (P \xrightarrow{d} P'') \Rightarrow P' = P''$

(3) time continuity: $(P \xrightarrow{d} P') \wedge (P' \xrightarrow{d'} P'') \Leftrightarrow P \xrightarrow{d+d'} P''$

(4) partial persistency: $P \xrightarrow{d} P' \Rightarrow \quad (\exists d' > 0)(\forall \alpha)(\forall P'')(\forall d'' \in]0, d'[)(\exists P_1, P_2)$
$P \xrightarrow{\alpha} P'' \Rightarrow P \xrightarrow{d''} P_1 \xrightarrow{\alpha} P_2$

A process P is said to be *immediate* if it cannot let time progress, i.e., there is no transition $P \xrightarrow{d}$. From property1 follows that an immediate process may perform at least an action α.

The last property asserts that, if a process is not immediate, then any action it can perform immediately remains possible during some non-empty interval (upto d'). Moreover, we have here $P_2 = P''$.

An important property of the models is that, if D' is a time domain such that $D' \subseteq D$, then for all P in $\mathbf{ASTP}_{D'}$, $(P)_{D'}$ can be obtained from $(P)_D$ by restricting its transition relation to $D' \cup \mathcal{A}$. However, even though $D' \subseteq D$, the behaviours described by the same term may be quite different. For instance, take $D' = \mathbb{N}$ and $D = \mathbb{R}^+$, and consider the process

$$P = \tilde{\alpha}\,(\tilde{\beta}\,\dot{\gamma}\,\delta \overset{1}{\rhd} \delta) \overset{1}{\rhd} \delta$$

- In $(P)_{\mathbb{N}}$, α may only be performed before time 1, that is at time 0; then β may also be performed only before time 1, and finally γ is performed immediately after β. So, γ *may only be performed before time 1* (in fact at time 0).

- In $(P)_{\mathbb{R}^+}$, α may be performed before time 1, so it is possible to wait for instance 0.7 time units before executing it. Afterwards, β may be executed until one time unit *after performing* α; hence, β may be performed at time 1.5 for instance. We find then that γ *may be performed at any time before time 2.*

The models are generally infinitely branching transition systems. Moreover the number of states is infinite if the time domain is dense, but it is finite in the discrete case. If D

is discrete, it is possible to build a finite state, finitely branching, transition system, by considering only the transitions labelled by actions or by χ (remember that χ is succ(0)). The time-continuity property is no longer valid, but the definition of strong equivalence and the equivalence classes remain the same in this semantics, which is the one given in [NS90].

For instance, the transition system of the process $\tilde{\alpha}\,\dot{\beta}\,\delta \overset{3}{\rhd} \tilde{\gamma}\,\delta$ in $\mathbf{ASTP}_{\mathbb{N}}$, given in figure 1, may be reduced into the model of figure 2.

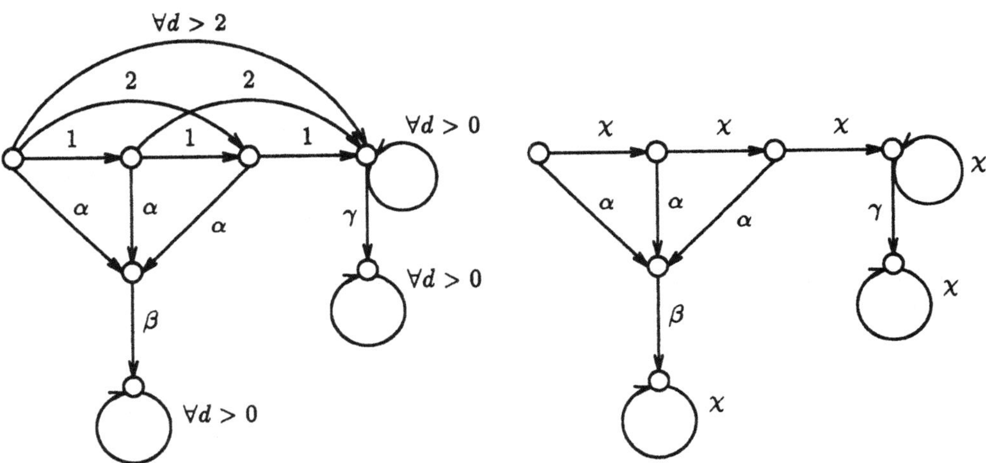

Figure 1: infinitely branching model

Figure 2: finitely branching model

2.2.4 Axiomatisation and canonical form

The following equations, where $d, d' \in D_*$ and $e \in D$, define a sound axiomatisation of **ASTP** for strong equivalence.

$$\begin{array}{lrcl}
[\oplus 1] & P \oplus Q & \equiv & Q \oplus P \\
[\oplus 2] & (P \oplus Q) \oplus R & \equiv & P \oplus (Q \oplus R) \\
[\oplus 3] & P \oplus P & \equiv & P \\
[\oplus 4] & P \oplus \delta & \equiv & P \\
[\oplus 5] & \dot{\alpha}\,P \;\oplus\; \tilde{\beta}\,Q & \equiv & \dot{\alpha}\,P \;\oplus\; \dot{\beta}\,Q \\
[\oplus 6] & \dot{\alpha}\,P \;\oplus\; Q \overset{d}{\rhd} R & \equiv & \dot{\alpha}\,P \;\oplus\; Q \\
[\oplus 7] & P_1 \overset{d}{\rhd} Q_1 \;\oplus\; P_2 \overset{d}{\rhd} Q_2 & \equiv & (P_1 \oplus P_2) \overset{d}{\rhd} (Q_1 \oplus Q_2) \\
[\rhd 1] & \dot{\alpha}\,P \overset{d}{\rhd} Q & \equiv & \dot{\alpha}\,P \\
[\rhd 2] & \tilde{\alpha}\,P \overset{d}{\rhd} \tilde{\alpha}\,P & \equiv & \tilde{\alpha}\,P \\
[\rhd 3] & \delta \overset{d}{\rhd} \delta & \equiv & \delta
\end{array}$$

$$
\begin{array}{ll}
[\,\rhd 4] & (P \overset{d+e}{\rhd} Q) \overset{d}{\rhd} R \;\equiv\; P \overset{d}{\rhd} R \\
[\,\rhd 5] & (P \overset{d}{\rhd} Q) \overset{d+d'}{\rhd} R \;\equiv\; P \overset{d}{\rhd} Q \overset{d'}{\rhd} R \\
[\text{rec1}] & \mathbf{rec}X \cdot P \;\equiv\; P[(\mathbf{rec}X \cdot P)/X] \\
[\text{rec2}] & \text{if } \; P[Q/X] \equiv Q \;\; \text{then} \;\; \mathbf{rec}X \cdot P \equiv Q
\end{array}
$$

Proposition: Any process of **ASTP** is equivalent to a process in one of the following forms.

$$\sum \dot{\alpha}_i\, P_i \qquad \left(\sum \widetilde{\alpha_i}\, P_i\right) \overset{d}{\rhd} P \qquad \delta \overset{d}{\rhd} P$$

□

Moreover, the following result, already presented in [NS90], can be generalised if D is such that $(\forall d, d')\,(\exists n, m \in \mathbb{N})\; nd = md'$, where $nd = \underbrace{d + \ldots + d}_{n \text{ times}}$.

Proposition (canonical form): For any P in $\mathbf{ASTP}_D$, there exist $n \in \mathbb{N}$ and $P_1, \ldots P_n$ in $\mathbf{ASTP}_D$, such that $P \equiv P_1$ and for any i in $[1, n]$,

$$P_i \equiv \sum \dot{\alpha}_j\, P_j \quad \text{or} \quad P_i \equiv \left(\sum \widetilde{\alpha_j}\, P_j\right) \overset{d_i}{\rhd} P_k \quad \text{or} \quad P_i \equiv \delta \overset{d_i}{\rhd} P_k$$

where the j's and k are in $[1, n]$. □

This proposition does not hold if, for instance, $D = \mathbb{R}^+$. Indeed, consider the process $P = Q + R$, where

$$
\begin{aligned}
Q &= \mathbf{rec}X \cdot \tilde{\alpha}\,\delta \overset{1}{\rhd} \delta \overset{1}{\rhd} X \\
R &= \mathbf{rec}Y \cdot \tilde{\beta}\,\delta \overset{\pi}{\rhd} \delta \overset{\pi}{\rhd} Y
\end{aligned}
$$

P may perform α at any instant between $2k$ and $2k+1$, and β at any instant between $2k\pi$ and $(2k+1)\pi$, where $k \in \mathbb{N}$. Following the first proposition, we have

$$P \equiv \left(\tilde{\alpha}\,\delta \oplus \tilde{\beta}\,\delta\right) \overset{1}{\rhd} \left(\delta \overset{1}{\rhd} Q \;\oplus\; \tilde{\beta}\,\delta \overset{\pi-1}{\rhd} \delta \overset{\pi}{\rhd} R\right)$$

but it is not possible to find a *finite* set of equations giving a canonical form of P.

2.3 The algebra $\mathbf{ATP}_D$

2.3.1 Syntax

We present now the algebra $\mathbf{ATP}_D$, by adding three new operators. This presentation in two steps is motivated by the fact that we do not want recursion through these operators. The syntax of $\mathbf{ATP}_D$ is given by

$$
\begin{array}{llll}
P ::= & P \in \mathbf{ASTP}_D & \mid \underline{\alpha} P & \mid P \oplus P \mid P \overset{d}{\triangleright} P \\
& P \parallel P & \mid \partial_H(P) & \mid \lceil P \rceil^d(P)
\end{array}
$$

where $d \in D_*$ and $H \subseteq \mathcal{A}$.

- $P \parallel Q$ is the *parallel composition* operator. It behaves as the parallel composition operator of ACP [BK84,BK86], as far as actions are concerned. Moreover, $P \parallel Q$ may delay for time d iff both P and Q may delay for time d.

  As for ACP, a binary *communication function* $\mid$ is defined over $\mathcal{A}_\perp = \mathcal{A} \cup \{\perp\}$, where $\perp$ is a new symbol not belonging to $\mathcal{A}$. It is such that

$$
\alpha|\beta = \beta|\alpha \qquad \alpha|(\beta|\gamma) = (\alpha|\beta)|\gamma \qquad \alpha|\perp = \perp|\alpha = \perp|\perp = \perp
$$

- $\partial_H(P)$ is the *encapsulation* operator of ACP. It prevents P from performing actions of H.

- $\lceil P \rceil^d(Q)$ is the *execution delay* operator. It behaves as P until time d; at time d, P is "aborted", and Q is started. However, if P performs a special action ξ, called *cancel action*, then the delay is cancelled, and the subsequent behaviour is that of P after ξ. The cancel action is internal, that is, it cannot communicate with any other action. Its effect is restricted to the innermost delay construct only; outside this operator, it is viewed as a τ (internal) action (see [NS90] for more details).

2.3.2 Operational semantics

The semantics of the operators already present in **ASTP** remain the same. For parallel composition, encapsulation and execution delay, the transition relation is given by the following rules.

$$
\frac{P \xrightarrow{\alpha} P'}{P \parallel Q \xrightarrow{\alpha} P' \parallel Q} \qquad \frac{Q \xrightarrow{\alpha} Q'}{P \parallel Q \xrightarrow{\alpha} P \parallel Q'}
$$

$$
\frac{P \xrightarrow{\alpha} P' \,,\, Q \xrightarrow{\beta} Q' \,,\, \alpha|\beta \neq \perp}{P \parallel Q \xrightarrow{\alpha|\beta} P' \parallel Q'} \qquad \frac{P \xrightarrow{d} P' \,,\, Q \xrightarrow{d} Q'}{P \parallel Q \xrightarrow{d} P' \parallel Q'}
$$

$$
\frac{P \xrightarrow{l} P' \,,\, l \notin H}{\partial_H(P) \xrightarrow{l} \partial_H(P')} \qquad \frac{(\forall l \in \mathcal{L} - H)\, P \overset{l}{\not\rightarrow}}{\partial_H(P) \xrightarrow{d} \delta}
$$

$$\frac{P \xrightarrow{\alpha} P' \;,\; \alpha \neq \xi}{\lceil P \rceil^d(Q) \xrightarrow{\alpha} \lceil P' \rceil^d(Q)} \qquad \frac{P \xrightarrow{\xi} P'}{\lceil P \rceil^d(Q) \xrightarrow{\tau} P'}$$

$$\frac{P \xrightarrow{d'} P'}{\lceil P \rceil^{d+d'}(Q) \xrightarrow{d'} \lceil P' \rceil^d(Q)} \qquad \frac{P \xrightarrow{d} P'}{\lceil P \rceil^d(Q) \xrightarrow{d} Q} \qquad \frac{P \xrightarrow{d} P' \;,\; Q \xrightarrow{d'} Q'}{\lceil P \rceil^d(Q) \xrightarrow{d+d'} Q'}$$

The four properties of the models of sequential processes remain valid in **ATP**. However, an important difference is that in the last one (partial persistency), the behaviour subsequent to the action α may depend on the instant when α is performed, as soon as a parallel or execution delay operator is involved. This difference makes impossible the formulation of an expansion theorem for these operators in the case where D is dense. In order to give such a theorem, we need to extend **ATP** by adding time parameters to process, as, for instance, in [Wan91]. However, it is possible to prove that $\mathbf{ATP}_D$ is a conservative extension of $\mathbf{ASTP}_D$ when D is discrete (see [NS90] where this result is proven for $D = \mathbb{N}$).

3 Action Timed Graphs

3.1 Definitions

Let A be an action vocabulary. a denotes an element of A.

A tuple $T = (t_1, ..., t_n)$ of *timers* is a set of variables taking their values in D. We represent by $\mathcal{B}(T)$ the set of the predicates over T, that is, the set of mappings from D^n into $\{\mathtt{tt}, \mathtt{ff}\}$. Furthermore, $\mathcal{F}(T)$ is the set of mappings from D^n into D^n.

An *Action Timed Graph* is a structure $G = (N, T, n_0, \mathbf{div}, \rightarrow)$, where

- N is the finite set of *nodes*
- T is the tuple of *timers*
- $n_0 \in N$ is the *initial node*
- **div** is a mapping from N into $\{\mathtt{tt}, \mathtt{ff}\}$, called the *divergence function*
- $\rightarrow \subseteq N \times A \times \mathcal{B}(T) \times \mathcal{F}(T) \times N$ is the *transition relation*

  We write $n \xrightarrow{a, b, f} n'$ instead of $(n, a, b, f, n') \in \rightarrow$.

For any predicate $b \in \mathcal{B}(T)$, the predicate $\widehat{b}$ is defined by

$$\widehat{b}(T) = (\exists d \in D) \;\; b(T + d)$$

where $T + d = (t_1 + d, ..., t_n + d)$. Notice that $\widehat{b}$ is a predicate meaning "eventually b", i.e., "b is true or will be true in the future".

For instance, if $b = (2 < t_1 \leq t_2) \wedge (t_2 \leq 4)$, then

$$\widehat{b} = (\exists d)\ \ (2 < t_1 + d \leq t_2 + d) \wedge (t_2 + d \leq 4) = t_1 \leq t_2 \leq 4$$

For a node n in N, we define the *enabling condition* of n, $\mathbf{en}(n)$, characterising the values of timers for which a transition can be executed from n:

$$\mathbf{en}(n) \triangleq \bigvee \left\{ b \mid n \xrightarrow{a,b,f} \right\}$$

We also define the *activity condition* of n, $\mathtt{act}(n)$, by

$$\mathtt{act}(n) \triangleq \widehat{\mathbf{en}(n)} \vee \mathtt{div}(n)$$

3.2 Operational semantics of Action Timed Graphs

The timers of an action timed graph are variables which are increased "continuously" and at the same speed. Initially, all the timers have value 0. The nodes represent the control states. From the node n, if the enabling condition b of a transition $n \xrightarrow{a,b,f} n'$ is satisfied by the values of the timers, then the transition *may* be executed. That is, the action a may performed, and the control state becomes n' after modification of the values of the timers according to the function f.

If the divergence condition $\mathtt{div}(n)$ is $\mathtt{tt}$, then it is possible to remain in node n, even though it will nevermore be possible to execute some transition. Conversely, if $\mathtt{div}(n) = \mathtt{ff}$, then the system *must* evolve so as to avoid such a situation. The predicate $\mathtt{act}$ is defined so that the system may remain at node n at the "instant" defined by the value of T only if $\mathtt{act}(n)(T) = \mathtt{tt}$.

Formally, the operational model of an action timed graph is a labelled transition system, where states are pairs (n, T), labels are elements of $(A \cup D_*)$, and the initial state is $(n_0, \vec{0})$, where n_0 is the initial node of the timed graph. The transition relation is defined by the following rules.

$$\frac{n \xrightarrow{a,b,f} n' \ ,\ b(T)}{(n,T) \xrightarrow{a} (n', f(T))} \qquad \frac{\mathtt{act}(n)(T+d)}{(n,T) \xrightarrow{d} (n, T+d)}$$

The first rule asserts that a transition is executable if its enabling predicate evaluates to true. The second one formalises the condition to satisfy for remaining in a node by waiting d time units.

Remark: the divergence condition is not quite necessary for defining timed graphs. In fact, one can consider action timed graphs without divergent nodes. To model then divergence of a node, it is enough to add a transition, labelled by some special internal action τ, whose predicate becomes true only when all the conditions of the other transitions will never more be true. The target of this transition is then a "sink" node, which in fact must also have a transition, consisting in a loop with some predicate which always eventually becomes true. The activity condition of a node n is then defined by $\widehat{\mathbf{en}(n)}$ only, and the semantics rules above remain the same.

4 Translation of ATP into timed graphs

The purpose of this section is to provide a method for translating an **ATP** process into an action timed graph such that the corresponding models are equivalent.

4.1 Translation of ASTP

We first show how a sequential process is translated into a *one-timer relative-time* action timed graph, that is, a timed graph with only one timer which is reset every time an action transition is executed. The reader should convince himself that such a translation is not possible for a process of **ATP**, as soon as the time domain is dense.

The method consists in fact in building the canonical form of the process. Due to the proposition about this form, a sufficient condition for its applicability is that the delay parameters be taken in a subdomain D' of D such that $(\forall d, d' \in D')\,(\exists n, m \in \mathbb{N})\, nd = nd')$.

For technical reasons, the operators $\cdot_{|d}$, where d is an element of D_*, are added to **ASTP**. $P_{|d}$ is called the *time-derivative at* d of P. It is defined only when P may delay upto d, and it behaves as P behaves at time d. Its semantics is quite simple, it is given by the following rule.

$$\frac{P \xrightarrow{d} P' \;,\; P' \xrightarrow{l} P''}{P_{|d} \xrightarrow{l} P''}$$

For technical reasons again, the action vocabulary of the timed graphs we build is $A = \mathcal{A} \cup \{i\}$, where $i \notin \mathcal{A}$. The action i, called *invisible action*, will represent the expirations of timeouts. Using such an action i simplifies considerably the translation.

The nodes of the timed graphs represent elements of **ASTP**, the unique timer is represented by t, and the initial node of the timed graph of P is P.

For P in **ASTP**, we define $S(P)$ as the instant upto which it is possible to stay in node P. For this purpose, ω is added as an upper bound of D, satisfying $\omega - d = \omega$.

$$
\begin{aligned}
S(\delta) &\triangleq \omega \\
S(\dot{\alpha}\, P) &\triangleq 0 \\
S(\tilde{\alpha}\, P) &\triangleq \omega \\
S(P \oplus Q) &\triangleq \min(S(P), S(Q)) \\
S(P \overset{d}{\triangleright} Q) &\triangleq \min(S(P), d) \\
S(P_{|d}) &\triangleq S(P) - d \\
S(\mathbf{rec}X \cdot P) &\triangleq S(P[\mathbf{rec}X \cdot P/X])
\end{aligned}
$$

The divergence in node P is defined by

$$\mathbf{div}(P) \triangleq (S(P) = \omega)$$

For the transition relation, the function f of a transition $P \xrightarrow{a,b,f} Q$ is always the function which resets t to 0; it is omitted here.

The transition relation is given by the following rules. Notice that an expiring timeout is translated into a transition with an invisible action i.

$$\dot{\alpha}\, P \xrightarrow{\alpha, t=0} P \qquad \tilde{\alpha}\, P \xrightarrow{\alpha, 0 \le t} P$$

$$\frac{P \xrightarrow{\alpha, b} P'}{P \oplus Q \xrightarrow{\alpha, b \wedge t \le S(Q)} P'} \qquad \frac{Q \xrightarrow{\alpha, b} Q'}{P \oplus Q \xrightarrow{\alpha, b \wedge t \le S(P)} Q'}$$

$$\frac{P \xrightarrow{i, t=d} P',\ S(Q) > d}{P \oplus Q \xrightarrow{i, t=d} P' \oplus Q_{|d}} \qquad \frac{Q \xrightarrow{i, t=d} Q',\ S(P) > d}{P \oplus Q \xrightarrow{i, t=d} P_{|d} \oplus Q'}$$

$$\frac{P \xrightarrow{i, t=d} P',\ Q \xrightarrow{i, t=d} Q'}{P \oplus Q \xrightarrow{i, t=d} P' \oplus Q'}$$

$$\frac{P \xrightarrow{\alpha, b} P'}{P \overset{d}{\triangleright} Q \xrightarrow{\alpha, b \wedge t < d} P'} \qquad \frac{P \xrightarrow{i, t=d'} P',\ d' < d}{P \overset{d}{\triangleright} Q \xrightarrow{i, t=d'} P' \overset{d-d'}{\triangleright} Q} \qquad \frac{S(P) \ge d}{P \overset{d}{\triangleright} Q \xrightarrow{i, t=d} Q}$$

$$\frac{P \xrightarrow{a, b} P'}{P_{|d} \xrightarrow{a, b[t+d/t]} P'} \qquad \frac{P[\mathbf{rec}X \cdot P/X] \xrightarrow{a, b} P'}{\mathbf{rec}X \cdot P \xrightarrow{a, b} P'}$$

4.2 Translation of ATP

In order to be able to translate **ATP** we present an *algebra of timed graphs*, by defining the operators of **ATP** over the action timed graphs. To obtain the timed graph corresponding to an element P of **ATP**, we proceed then as follows.

- if P is in **ASTP**, then the timed graph is obtained by using the rules above.
- if P in not in **ASTP**, and is in the form $op(P_1, ..., P_n)$, where op is an n-ary operator of **ATP**, then the timed graph of P is obtained by applying the operator op defined below to the timed graphs of $P_1, ..., P_n$.

4.2.1 Operations over action timed graphs

In the sequel, $G_1 = (N_1, T_1, n_1^0, \rightarrow_1, \mathbf{div}_1)$ and $G_2 = (N_2, T_2, n_2^0, \rightarrow_2, \mathbf{div}_2)$ are two timed graphs with the action vocabulary $A = \mathcal{A} \cup \{i\}$, such that $N_1 \cap N_2 = T_1 \cap T_2 = \emptyset$.

The function resetting a set of timers T is denoted by $\mathcal{R}(T)$.

Prefixing
Let α be an element of $\mathcal{A}$. We define $G = \underline{\alpha}\, G_1 = (N, T, n_0, \rightarrow, \mathbf{div})$ as follows.

$$
\begin{aligned}
&N = N_1 \cup \{n_0\} \quad (n_0 \notin N_1)\\
&T = T_1 \cup \{t\} \text{ where } t \text{ may be in } T_1\\
&\text{if } n \in N_1 \text{ then } \mathbf{div}(n) = \mathbf{div}_1(n)\\
&\mathbf{div}(n_0) = \text{ if } \underline{\alpha} = \dot{\alpha} \text{ then } \mathbf{ff} \text{ else } \mathbf{tt}
\end{aligned}
$$

$$
\frac{\underline{\alpha} = \dot{\alpha}}{n_0 \xrightarrow{\alpha, t = 0, \mathcal{R}(T_1)} n_1^0}
\qquad
\frac{\underline{\alpha} = \tilde{\alpha}}{n_0 \xrightarrow{\alpha, t \geq 0, \mathcal{R}(T_1)} n_1^0}
\qquad
\frac{n \in N_1 \,,\ n \xrightarrow{a, R}_1 n'}{n \xrightarrow{a, R} n'}
$$

Non-deterministic choice
$G = G_1 \oplus G_2 = (N, T, n_0, \rightarrow, \mathbf{div})$ is defined as follows.

$$
\begin{aligned}
&N = N_1 \cup N_2 \cup (N_1 \times N_2)\\
&T = T_1 \cup T_2\\
&n_0 = (n_1^0, n_2^0)\\
&\text{if } n \in N_i \text{ then } \mathbf{div}(n) = \mathbf{div}_i(n)\\
&\mathbf{div}(n_1, n_2) = \mathbf{div}_1(n_1) \wedge \mathbf{div}_2(n_2)
\end{aligned}
$$

$$
\frac{n \xrightarrow{a, b, f}_i n'}{n \xrightarrow{a, b, f} n'}
\qquad
\frac{n_1 \xrightarrow{\alpha, b, f}_1 n_1'}{(n_1, n_2) \xrightarrow{\alpha, b \wedge \mathbf{act}(n_2), f} n_1'}
\qquad
\frac{n_2 \xrightarrow{\alpha, b, f}_2 n_2'}{(n_1, n_2) \xrightarrow{\alpha, b \wedge \mathbf{act}(n_1), f} n_2'}
$$

$$\frac{n_1 \xrightarrow{i,b,f}_1 n_1'}{(n_1,n_2) \xrightarrow{i,b \wedge \mathbf{act}(n_2),f} (n_1',n_2)} \qquad \frac{n_2 \xrightarrow{i,b,f}_2 n_2'}{(n_1,n_2) \xrightarrow{i,b \wedge \mathbf{act}(n_1),f} (n_1,n_2')}$$

Timeout

Let d be an element of D_*, and t be a timer not belonging to T_1.
We define $G = G_1 \overset{d}{\triangleright} G_2 = (N, T, n_0, \mathbf{div}, \rightarrow)$ as follows.

$$N = N_1 \cup N_2 \cup (N_1 \times \{n_2^0\})$$
$$T = T_1 \cup T_2 \cup \{t\}$$
$$n_0 = (n_1^0, n_2^0)$$
$$\text{if } n \in N_i \text{ then } \mathbf{div}(n) = \mathbf{div}_i(n)$$
$$\mathbf{div}(n_1, n_2^0) = \mathbf{ff}$$

$$\frac{n \xrightarrow{a,b,f}_i n'}{n \xrightarrow{a,b,f} n'} \qquad (n_1,n_2^0) \xrightarrow{i,(t=d) \wedge \mathbf{act}(n_1),\mathcal{R}(T_2)} n_2^0$$

$$\frac{n_1 \xrightarrow{\alpha,b,f}_1 n_1'}{(n_1,n_2^0) \xrightarrow{\alpha,b \wedge (t<d),f} n_1'} \qquad \frac{n_1 \xrightarrow{i,b,f}_1 n_1'}{(n_1,n_2^0) \xrightarrow{i,b \wedge (t<d),f} (n_1,n_2^0)}$$

Parallel composition

We define $G = G_1 \parallel G_2 = (N, T, n_0, \mathbf{div}, \rightarrow)$ as follows

$$N = N_1 \times N_2$$
$$T = T_1 \cup T_2$$
$$n_0 = (n_1^0, n_2^0)$$
$$\mathbf{div}(n_1,n_2) = \mathbf{div}_1(n_1) \wedge \mathbf{div}_2(n_2)$$

$$\frac{n_1 \xrightarrow{a,b,f}_1 n_1'}{(n_1,n_2) \xrightarrow{a,b \wedge \mathbf{act}(n_2),f} (n_1',n_2)} \qquad \frac{n_2 \xrightarrow{a,b,f}_2 n_2'}{(n_1,n_2) \xrightarrow{a,b \wedge \mathbf{act}(n_1),f} (n_1,n_2')}$$

$$\frac{n_1 \xrightarrow{\alpha_1,b_1,f_1}_1 n_1' \;,\; n_2 \xrightarrow{\alpha_2,b_2,f_2}_2 n_2' \;,\; \alpha_1|\alpha_2 = \alpha \neq \bot}{(n_1,n_2) \xrightarrow{\alpha,b_1 \wedge b_2,f_1 \star f_2} (n_1',n_2')}$$

where $f_1 \star f_2$ denotes the function acting as f_1 on T_1, and as f_2 on T_2.

Encapsulation
Let H be a subset of $\mathcal{A}$. $G = \partial_H(G_1) = (N, T, n_0, \rightarrow, \mathbf{div})$ is defined by

$$\begin{aligned}
&N = N_1 \\
&T = T_1 \\
&n_0 = n_1^0 \\
&\mathbf{div}(n) \;=\; \mathbf{div}_1(n) \vee \left(\left\{a \mid n \xrightarrow{a,b,f}_1 n'\right\} \subseteq H\right) \\
&\rightarrow = \rightarrow_1 \;-\; \{(n,a,b,f,n') | a \in H\}
\end{aligned}$$

Execution delay
Let d be an element of D_*, and t be a timer not belonging to T_1.
We define $G = \lceil G_1 \rceil^d G_2 = (N, T, n_0, \mathbf{div}, \rightarrow)$ as follows.

$$\begin{aligned}
&N = N_1 \cup N_2 \cup (N_1 \times \{n_2^0\}) \\
&T = T_1 \cup T_2 \cup \{t\} \\
&n_0 = (n_1^0, n_2^0) \\
&\text{if } n \in N_i \text{ then } \mathbf{div}(n) = \mathbf{div}_i(n) \\
&\mathbf{div}(n_1, n_2^0) = \mathbf{ff}
\end{aligned}$$

$$\frac{n \xrightarrow{a,b,f}_i n'}{n \xrightarrow{a,b,f} n'} \qquad (n_1, n_2^0) \xrightarrow{i,(t=d) \wedge \mathbf{act}(n_1), \mathcal{R}(T_2)} n_2^0$$

$$\frac{n_1 \xrightarrow{a,b,f}_1 n_1' \;,\; l \neq \xi}{(n_1, n_2^0) \xrightarrow{a, b \wedge (t < d), f} (n_1', n_2^0)} \qquad \frac{n_1 \xrightarrow{\xi,b,f}_1 n_1'}{(n_1, n_2^0) \xrightarrow{\tau, b \wedge (t < d), f} n_1'}$$

4.2.2 Correctness of the translation

The models of an **ATP** process and of the corresponding timed graph are certainly not strongly equivalent, since the latter has transitions labelled by i. However, the following proposition allows to suppress these transitions.

Proposition: Let M be the model of an action timed graph corresponding to a process P. M is *observationally congruent* (with i as the internal action) to a transition system M' without i-transitions. □

If we saturate M' for d-transitions, that is, if we add a transition $q \xrightarrow{d+d'} q''$ for every pair of transitions $q \xrightarrow{d} q'$ and $q' \xrightarrow{d'} q''$, then the resulting transition system is *strongly equivalent* to the model of P.

4.3 Example: the login procedure

To illustrate the translation of an **ATP** process into a timed graph, we present the example of the *login procedure* of [NS90].

To start the procedure, the system sends a login prompt p. After this event, the user has l time units to enter a valid login response v to successfully finish the task and to start a session phase S. When the user supplies an invalid response n, or when time l elapsed, a new login procedure is started. This behaviour can be modelled in **ATP** as follows:

$$L = \dot{p}\left((\tilde{v}\, S \oplus \tilde{n}\, L) \overset{l}{\rhd} L\right)$$

L is a sequential process. Then, it is possible to construct a one-timer relative-time timed graph. Figure 3 shows the timed graph of L. The divergence condition in a node is written inside the node.

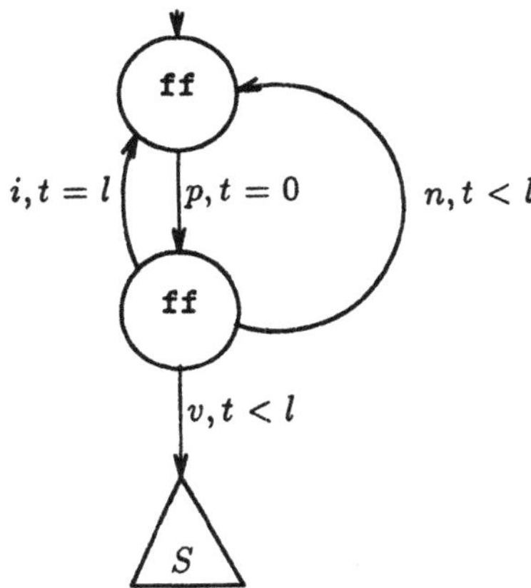

Figure 3: Simple login procedure' timed graph

In addition, the system usually limits the overall duration of the login procedure to a maximum time of d units and forces an exception E to be carried out after that. We can model this process P using the execution delay operator and adding a cancel action ξ in L to quit when a successful response v is provided.

The complete procedure is then described by P, where

$$\begin{aligned} P &= \lceil L \rceil^{d}(E) \\ L &= \dot{p}\left((\tilde{v}\, \dot{\xi}\, S \oplus \tilde{n}\, L) \overset{l}{\rhd} L\right) \end{aligned}$$

Since the whole login procedure P is not a sequential **ATP** process, a one-timer timed graph cannot be constructed for it. Figure 4 shows the timed graph of P in which two timers are used: t_1, with an upper bound d, to limit the overall duration of L, and the timer t of L. Since the function f of a transition is always a resetting of some timers, we write the set of these timers instead of functions. For sake of simplicity, the reset part of a transition is omitted if it is empty.

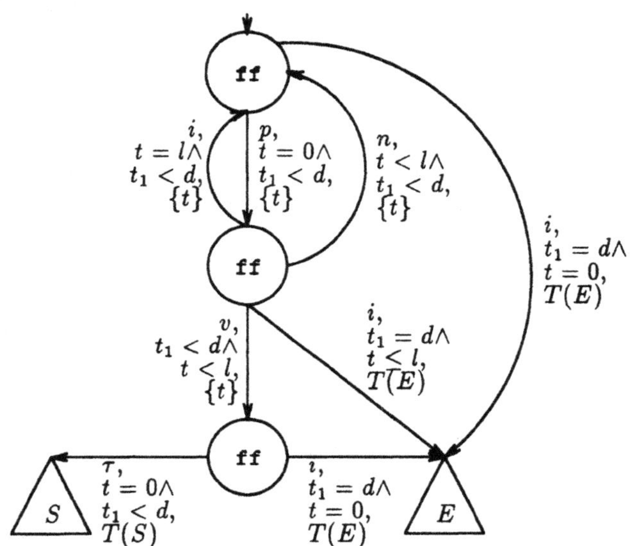

Figure 4: Complete login procedure' timed graph

5 Hybrid Systems

This section presents a model for *hybrid systems*, that is, systems that may evolve

- either by executing transitions, i.e., discrete state changes realised by modification of the state by performing atomic timeless operations
- or by performing some transformation of the state according to a law described as a function of a time parameter.

The model presented here is a straightforward generalisation of Action Timed Graphs obtained by adding to the set of timers T a set of state variables X that do not change linearly with respect to time, but according to an evolution function.

5.1 Definition

A *hybrid system* with action vocabulary A is a structure $(N, T, X, n_0, T_0, X_0, \rightarrow, \varphi)$, where

- N is the set of nodes
- T is a tuple $(t_1, ..., t_m)$ of timers, taking its value in D^m
- X is a tuple $(x_1, ..., x_n)$ of state variables taking its value in some domain D_X
- $n_0 \in N$, $T_0 \in D^m$ and $X_0 \in D_X$ are the initial node, value of T and value of X respectively
- $\rightarrow \subseteq N \times A \times \mathcal{B}(T, X) \times \mathcal{F}(T, X) \times N$ is the transition function. As for timed graphs, we write $n \xrightarrow{a,b,f} n'$ instead of $(n, a, b, f, n') \in \rightarrow$
- $\varphi : (N \times D^m \times D_X \times D) \rightarrow D_X$ is the *evolution function* of the state variables. $\varphi(n, T_1, X_1, d)$ is written $\varphi_n[T_1, X_1](d)$ and is the value of X, d time units after the instant when the timers had value T_1 and the state variables had value X_1. The following requirements should be satisfied by the evolution function.

$$\begin{aligned}\varphi_n[T, X](0) &= X \\ \varphi_n[T, X](d + d') &= \varphi_n[T + d, \varphi_n[T, X](d)](d')\end{aligned}$$

  The first one expresses the fact that the state cannot change within zero duration. The second one ensures that the models satisfy the time-continuity property, as it expresses the fact that the state $<T + d + d', \varphi_n[T, X](d + d')>$, reached from $<T, X>$ within time $d + d'$, is the same as the state reached by transforming successively $<T, X>$ during a time period d to reach a state $<T', X'> = <T + d, \varphi_n[T, X](d)>$, and $<T', X'>$ during a time period of d'.

5.2 Operational semantics

The model of a hybrid system is a labelled transition system where states are pairs (node, values of timers and state variables), and labels are elements of $A \cup D_*$. The transition relation is given by the following rules.

$$\frac{n \xrightarrow{a,b,f} n' \;,\; b(T, X)}{(n, < T, X >) \xrightarrow{a} (n', f(T, X))} \qquad \frac{\exists d' \geq d \;\mathbf{en}(n)(T + d', \varphi_n[T, X](d'))}{(n, < T, X >) \xrightarrow{d} (n, < T + d, \varphi_n[T, X](d) >)}$$

The first rule is the same as the rule specifying discrete transitions of action timed graphs. The second rule says that from a given state $< T, X >$ the state resulting after evolution during d is $< T + d, \varphi_n[T, X](d) >$. The enabling condition allows such an evolution only if at the state reached some transition is eventually enabled.

It is important to notice that hybrid systems have their models in the same class as those of **ATP**. Thus, all the operators of **ATP** can be defined for hybrid systems, in the sense that one can associate a model to any recursion-free expression built from hybrid systems and operators of **ATP**.

5.3 Examples of hybrid systems

5.3.1 A temperature regulator

The temperature θ of a room is controlled by a thermostat commanding a heater. The thermostat is provided with two parameter: θ_m and θ_M which determine the interval in which the temperature of the room is supposed to remain. The thermostat switches ON and OFF a heater, in order to satisfy this requirement. Initially the heater in is ON and the temperature of the room is 0.

Figure 5 describes the hybrid system controlling the room temperature. When the heater is OFF the temperature decreases according to the law $\varphi_{OFF}[\theta](d) = \theta\, e^{-Kd}$. When the heater is ON we take $\varphi_{ON}[\theta](d) = \theta\, e^{-Kd} + \theta_h(1 - e^{-Kd})$ where θ_h is a constant depending on the power of the heater, and K is a constant. No timer is needed, since the function of time describing the evolution of the temperature is inversible.

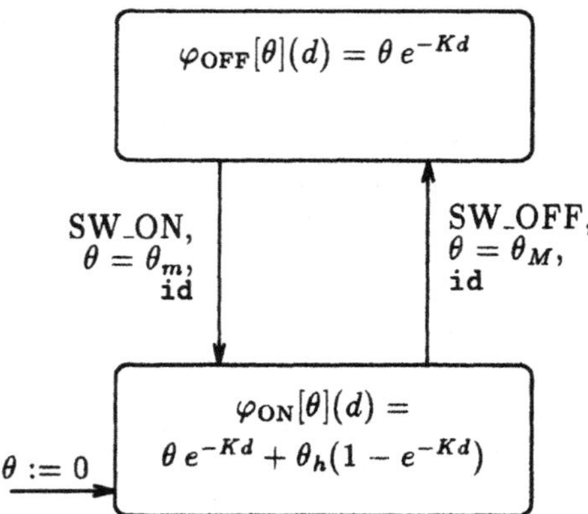

Figure 5: Hybrid system of the temperature regulator

5.3.2 A mobile

We consider the two-dimensional motion of a mobile in a room of width l (figure 6). It is supposed to start from point $(0, h)$, with a horizontal speed v_0.

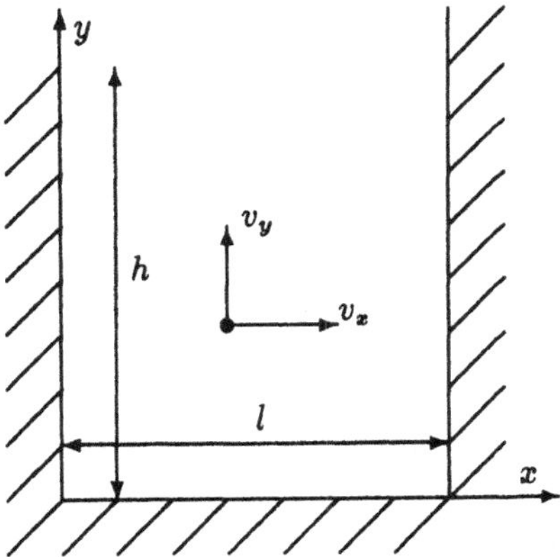

Figure 6: The room

Since the evolutions of x and v_x are independent from those of y and v_y, we can model this motion as the parallel composition of two hybrid systems presented in figure 7 (action names are omitted on the transitions). As in the previous example, the functions of time giving (x, v_x) and (y, v_y) being inversible, we do not need any timer.

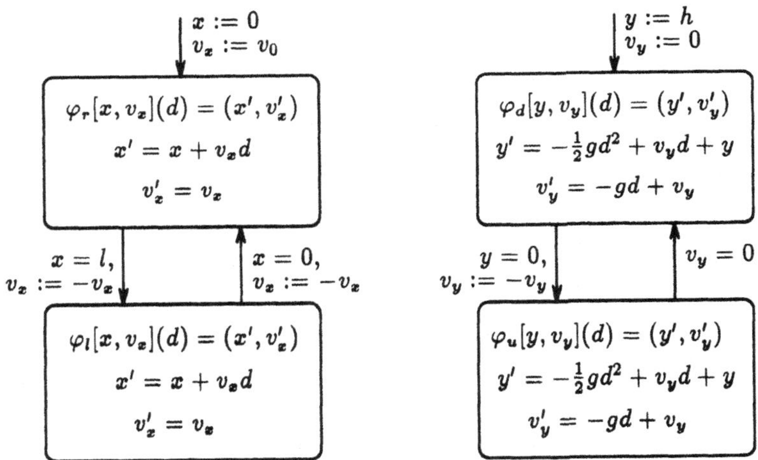

Figure 7: Hybrid systems of the mobile's displacement

6 Conclusion

The paper presents results of ongoing work aiming at the unification of some behavioural description formalisms for timed systems.

- We propose for **ATP** a very general semantics in terms of a time domain. This semantics agrees with the semantics in [NS90] when the time domain is discrete.
- It is shown that **ATP** can be translated into a variant of timed graphs. This result allows the application of existing model-checking techniques to **ATP**.
- Finally, we propose a notion of hybrid systems as a generalisation of timed graphs. Such systems can evolve (modify their state) either by executing a transition (discrete changes) or by performing some "continuous" transformation according to a law described by a function.

The formalisms studied admit the same class of models: time deterministic and time continuous possibly infinitely branching transition systems labelled by actions or durations.

Acknowledgement: This work has been initiated due to fruitful discussions between the authors and C. Courcoubetis when the latter visited IMAG, in September 1990.

References

[ACD90] R. Alur, C. Courcoubetis, and D. Dill. Model-checking for real-time systems. In *Proceedings of the fifth annual IEEE symposium on Logic In Computer Science*, pages 414–425, Philadelphia, PA., June 1990.

[BC85] G. Berry and L. Cosserat. The ESTEREL synchronous programming language and its mathematical semantics. In *LNCS 197: Proceedings CMU Seminar on Concurrency*, Springer-Verlag, 1985.

[BK84] J.A. Bergstra and J.W. Klop. *Algebra of Communicating Processes.* Technical Report CS-R8420, Centre for Mathematics and Computer Science, Amsterdam, the Netherlands, 1984.

[BK86] J.A. Bergstra and J.W. Klop. Process algebra : specification and verification in bisimulation semantics. In M. Hazewinkel, J.K. Lenstra, and L.G.L.T. Meertens, editors, *Proceedings of the CWI Symposium Mathematics and Computer Science II (CWI Monograph 4)*, pages 61–94, North Holland, Amsterdam, 1986.

[MT90] F. Moller and C. Tofts. A Temporal Calculus of Communicating Processes. In J.C.M. Baeten and J.W. Klop, editors, *LNCS 458. Proceedings of CONCUR '90 (Theories of Concurrency: Unification and Extension), Amsterdam, the Netherlands*, pages 401–415, Springer-Verlag, August 1990.

[NRSV90] X. Nicollin, J.-L. Richier, J. Sifakis, and J. Voiron. ATP: an Algebra for Timed Processes. In *Proceedings of the IFIP TC 2 Working Conference on Programming Concepts and Methods*, Sea of Gallilee, Israel, April 1990.

[NS90] X. Nicollin and J. Sifakis. *The algebra of timed processes ATP: theory and application.* Technical Report RT-C26, LGI-IMAG, Grenoble, France, December 1990.

[Plo81] G.D. Plotkin. *A Structural Approach to Operational Semantics.* Technical Report DAIMI FN-19, Århus University. Computer Science Department, Århus, Denmark, 1981.

[Wan90] Wang Yi. Real-time behaviour of asynchronous agents. In J.C.M. Baeten and J.W. Klop, editors, *LNCS 458. Proceedings of CONCUR '90 (Theories of Concurrency: Unification and Extension), Amsterdam, the Netherlands,* pages 502–520, Springer-Verlag, August 1990.

[Wan91] Wang Yi. CCS + Time = an Interleaving Model for Real Time Systems. In *Proceedings of ICALP '91, Madrid, Spain,* July 1991.

Verification of Safety Critical Systems Using TTM/RTTL *

J.S. Ostroff[†]

Abstract. This paper shows how real-time temporal logic can be used for the verification of safety-critical systems. Heuristics are provided that help the designer to construct a proof diagram that either facilitates the presentation of a proof of correctness, or provides a counterexample to indicate the invalidity of the specification that is being checked. The heuristics can be semi-automated using constraint logic programming languages because most of the reasoning does not involve the actual use of temporal logic. The type of reasoning employed in this paper is not limited to finite state systems, but can be used on infinite state systems as well. The heuristics are illustrated using a process control example.

Keywords: Timed Transition Systems, Verification, Real-time Temporal Logic.

Contents

*This work is supported by the Natural Sciences and Engineering Research Council of Canada

†Department of Computer Science, York University, 4700 Keele Street, North York, Ontario, Canada, M3J 1P3. Tel: 416 - 736-5053. Email: jonathan@cs.yorku.ca

1 Introduction

Safety critical systems as found in avionics, robotics, process control, nuclear reactors and traffic systems are difficult to model and verify for correctness. This difficulty is compounded when time constraints on the system behaviour must be satisfied. Since the environment and life itself are often at stake if such systems malfunction, recent research has focussed on providing the designer with formal methods for analyzing these systems.

The TTM/RTTL framework for the verification of safety-critical systems was first introduced in [OW85, Ost86]. Timed Transition Models (TTMs) are used to represent real-time systems, and Real-Time Temporal Logic (RTTL) is the assertion language.

The system under development is usually a set of concurrent processes, perhaps with shared variables or various communication primitives. TTMs present a flexible method for representing such processes, whether these processes are hardware devices (e.g pumps, valves and reactors) or originate as programs in various real-time programming languages, Petri nets, Communicating Sequential Processes or Statecharts. Delays or timeouts are represented by lower and upper time bounds on transitions of TTMs.

Once the system under development is modelled as a suitable TTM, the property that the TTM must satisfy can be written as a formula of RTTL. There is also a sound proof system for checking that the TTM satisfies the required property.

For a complete description of TTMs, the reader is referred to [OW90, Ost90a, Ost90b], and for a complete account of RTTL see [Ost89b]. These references adequately describe the syntax and semantics of the proof system. This paper focuses on the pragmatic issue of how to use the system in practice. Heuristics are presented which help the designer to search for a proof of correctness, or to come up with a counterexample that shows how the system does not satisfy the required property. It is also indicated how the heuristic may be mechanized. Examples are provided that illustrate the use of the heuristics.

The heuristics were presented initially in [Ost86]. In [Ost89b, Ost89a, Ost91a], the use of the constraint logic programming language CLP($\Re$) was discussed for automating proofs in RTTL. More recently the PrologIII language for constraint logic has been used for controller synthesis [Ost91b]. For finite state systems, automated model checking is presented in [Ost90a, Ost92].

2 Summary of the TTM/RTTL framework

2.1 TTMs — Timed Transition Models

State transitions graphs are often used by computing scientists, communication engineers, control theorists and circuit designers to describe physical systems. However, the basic transition as an event leading from one state to the next is much too "low-level" for the adequate representation of programming constructs. Therefore, we generalize transitions by allowing multiple assignments to several variables simultaneously, where these variables may themselves be complex structures. The transitions of TTMs are timed versions of the fair transition systems of Manna and Pnueli [MP83a, Pnu86], and related to the UNITY notion of a transition in the work of Chandy and Misra [CM88].

A TTM M is defined as a 3-tuple $(\mathcal{V}, \Theta, \mathcal{T})$ consisting of a set of variables $\mathcal{V}$, an initial condition Θ, and a finite set of transitions $\mathcal{T}$.

to indicate which variables in the state-assignment are updated on making the transition, i.e. the value of all variables in the successor state-assignment remain the same except for x, y_1, y_2.

A transition τ is *enabled* in a state s (or state-assignment) if it evaluates to true in the state, i.e. $s(e_\tau) = true$, and *disabled* otherwise.

The moment of enablement of τ is called a bound choicepoint. The transition τ remains enabled from the choicepoint until either it is preempted by the occurrence of some other transition that disables τ, or τ must occur between l_τ and u_τ ticks from the choicepoint. When it occurs it instantaneously changes the state as defined by the transformation function.

A trajectory σ of a TTM $M = (\mathcal{V}_M, \Theta_M, \mathcal{T}_M)$ is an infinite sequence of states $s_0 s_1 s_2 \cdots$. Not all trajectories are actual behaviours of a TTM — actual behaviours of a TTM are called its *legal trajectories*. Let state s_i have corresponding state-assignment q_i, and let $s_i(\mathrm{n} = \tau_i) = true$. Then a legal trajectory σ of a TTM M is any trajectory

$$\begin{aligned} \sigma &\stackrel{\text{def}}{=} q_0 \xrightarrow{\tau_0} q_1 \xrightarrow{\tau_1} q_2 \xrightarrow{\tau_2} q_3 \cdots \\ &= s_0 s_1 s_2 s_3 \cdots \end{aligned}$$

satisfying 5 basic requirements: (a) The initial state s_0 must satisfy the initial condition Θ_M, (b) $s_i(e_{\tau_i}) = true$ and $q_{i+1} = h_{\tau_i}(q_i)$ for all i, (c) the *Tick* transition must occur infinitely often, and all bound choicepoints of all transitions τ in σ must satisfy the (d) lower and (e) upper time bound requirements previously described.

Thus, a legal trajectory is a sequence of states whose initial state is in the initial state set, whose successor states are obtained by applying enabled transitions according to the transformation functions, and whose occurrence of transitions in any state must satisfy the bound requirements. Any suffix of a legal trajectory is also a legal trajectory.

The abstract operational semantics of a TTM M is given by the set of all its legal trajectories Σ_M. If the legal trajectories satisfy some specification S of required behaviour then the property S is said to be M-valid.

In [OW90, Ost90a], the parallel composition $M_3 = M_1 \| M_2$ of two TTMs M_1 and M_2 to form a new TTM M_3 is defined. Since the composition M_3 is itself a TTM, the abovementioned trajectory requirements may be used to generate the legal trajectories of M_3. The composed TTM has a variable set which is the union of the component variables set, an initial condition which is the conjunction of the component initial conditions, and a transition set which is the union of the component transition sets (see [OW90, Ost90a] for how to deal with shared or synchronized transitions).

In this paper we will not explore the issue of fairness. However, additional fairness requirements can be added if necessary to ensure that certain sets of transitions that are continuously enabled or infinitely often enabled in the trajectory eventually occur [Ost89b].

2.2 A process control example involving mutual exclusion

A small example is provided in Figure 1 of the kind of problem that the verification procedures of this paper can be applied to. The timed transition model SUD (system under development) consists of the parallel composition of 3 interacting TTMs, i.e. $SUD = SENSOR \| FILTER \| ALARM$.

The variable set $\mathcal{V}$ always has two distinguished variables: t (the current time) and n (the current transition variable).

The transition set $\mathcal{T}$ has a distinguished transition called *Tick*, which is an event corresponding to the tick of a (conceptual) external clock whose current time is represented by the variable t. The clock event *Tick* must occur infinitely often, and it alone changes t by incrementing it by one. All time bounds on transitions are measured with respect to the ticks of the clock. The framework thus uses a linear discrete model of time. Any finite number of transitions can occur between any two ticks of the clock, depending on the transition time bounds.

Each variable $v \in \mathcal{V}$ has an associated range of values $type(v)$, and $\mathcal{R}$ is the disjoint union of all these types. For the time variable, $type(t)$ is usually the non-negative integers union with infinity, and $type(\mathrm{n}) = \mathcal{T}$. The transition variable n is used in RTTL specifications to refer to occurrences of TTM events, thus allowing the logic to directly represent both states and events.

There is at least one activity (or control) variable in the variable set of A TTM. An activity variable x is the point at which a process is currently executing. For example, $(x = red)$ might mean that the traffic light is currently showing red — $red \in type(x)$ is called an *activity*.

There may be zero or more data variables for representing numeric information (such as pressures, temperatures or fluid levels) or other information (such as sets and queues). A data variable may have an infinite set of values in its type — if all the types are finite, then the TTM has a finite state-space.

A state s of a TTM $M = (\mathcal{V}, \Theta, \mathcal{T})$ is a mapping $s: \mathcal{V} \rightarrow \mathcal{R}$ such that $s(v) \in type(v)$ for each $v \in \mathcal{V}$.

Corresponding to each state s there is an associated state-assignment q. The state-assignment q is the restriction of the domain of s to $(\mathcal{V} - \{\mathrm{n}\})$, i.e. the state-assignment is similar to the state but with the transition variable n projected out. Thus if $s = \{(x, red), (t, 10), (\mathrm{n}, Tick)\}$, then the corresponding state-assignment is

$$q = \{(x, red), (t, 10)\}$$

Consider a transition $\tau \in \mathcal{T}$ of a TTM with activity variable x and (e.g. 2) data variables y_1, y_2. When the transition occurs, the variables y_1, y_2 are simultaneously assigned the values of the expressions d_1, d_2 respectively. The transition may be visualized as follows:

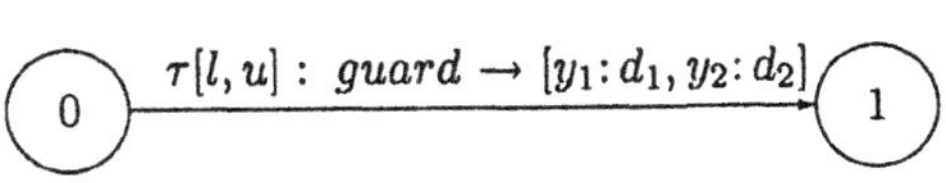

$$0 \xrightarrow{\tau[l,u]\,:\; guard \;\rightarrow\; [y_1: d_1,\, y_2: d_2]} 1$$

Formally, the transition τ is defined by a 4-tuple $(e_\tau, h_\tau, l_\tau, u_\tau)$, where l_τ and u_τ are the lower and upper time bounds[1] respectively with $0 \leq l_\tau \leq u_\tau \leq \infty$. The enabling condition is $e_\tau \stackrel{\text{def}}{=} (x = 0 \wedge guard)$. Where no guard is indicated on the transition graph, the guard is assumed to be *true*. The transformation function is a partial function $h_\tau: \mathcal{Q} \rightarrow \mathcal{Q}$, where $\mathcal{Q}$ is the set of all state-assignments[2]. The function is defined for all state-assignments $q \in \mathcal{Q}$ such that $q(e_\tau) = true$. The transformation function is often denoted by $[x: 1, y_1: d_1, y_2: d_2]$

[1] The bounds may be any integer expression d so long as $s(d) \in type(t)$.

[2] The transformation function may also be a multi-valued function $h_\tau: \mathcal{Q} \rightarrow 2^{\mathcal{Q}}$.

SUD = SENSOR || FILTER || ALARM

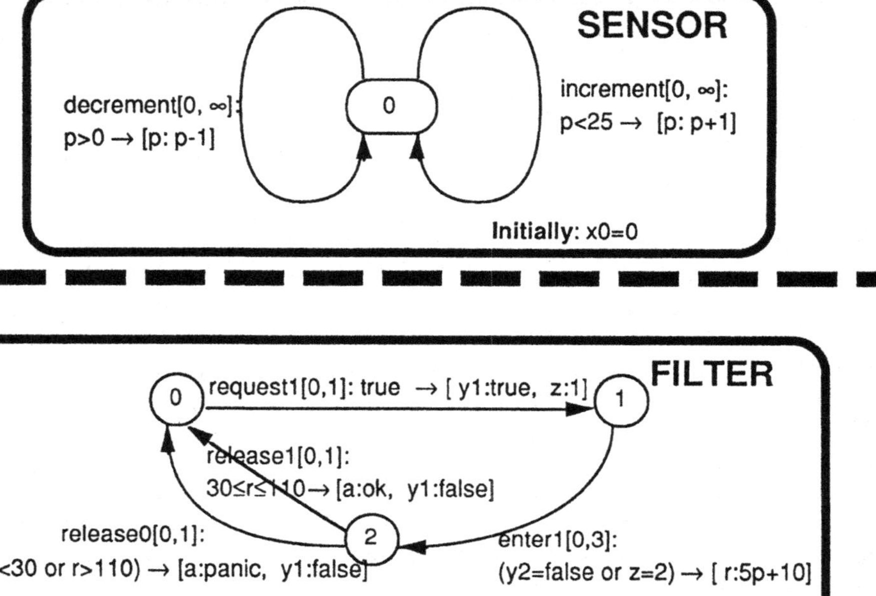

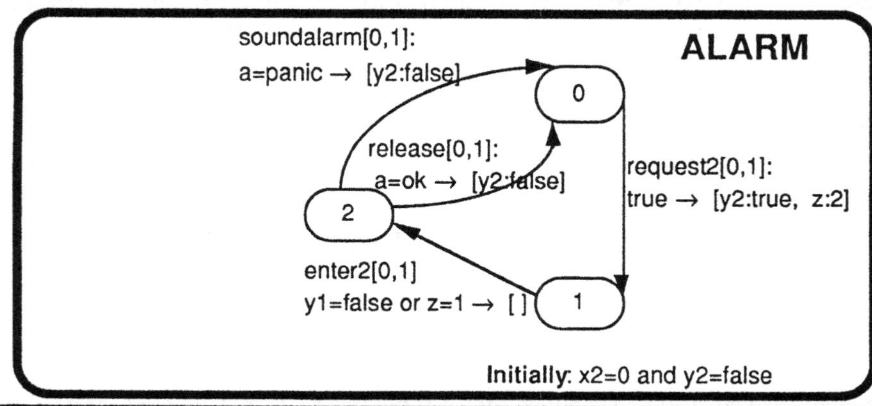

Figure 1: The timed transition model *SUD*.

SENSOR models a pressure sensor in a chemical plant, that measures a pressure p whose normal analog current reading may be anywhere between 4 to 20 milliamps. A reading lower than 4ma may also be detected, although it will never go lower than zero, and a reading of greater than 20ma may also be detected, although it will never exceed 25ma. These abnormal values indicate that there is something wrong either with the sensor reading, or with the chemical plant, and an alarm should be sounded. An analog to digital converter is used to make the pressure readable by the computer — thus $type(p) = \{0, 1, 2, \cdots, 25\}$.

At any moment, the pressure may be incremented or decremented. Thus, the upper time bound is ∞ and the lower time bound 0 for both the *increment* and *decrement* transitions (these events are therefore spontaneous). Because of the constraints on p, the guard of the transition *increment* is $(p < 25)$, and when *increment* occurs, p is increased by one. Similar considerations apply to the *decrement* transition. The initial condition of SENSOR is $\Theta_{SENSOR} \equiv (x_0 = 0)$ (thus the pressure is initially unconstrained). The pressure variable is a "read-only" variable that may be accessed only by the filter TTM.

The purpose of FILTER is to translate milliamp readings into actual pressure values r. Other processes will then use r instead of p for the pressure reading. The conversion equation is $r = 5p + 10$, e.g. if the current p is 4ma. then the pressure is $r = 30$ *psi*. When the transition *enter*1 occurs it reads p and updates the value of r according to the conversion equation. The guard of *enter*1 will be explained later when the need for mutual exclusion of critical regions is discussed.

When FILTER is in activity 2, the transition *release*1 sets an alarm variable a to "ok" if r is within the normal range, or *release*0 sets a to "panic" if p is abnormal. The data variables r and a are read-only shared variables, and can therefore be read by other processes wishing to know what the pressure r in the chemical reactor is, and whether the sensor is working properly or not. To maintain the consistency of a and r with respect to each other, once r is updated by *enter*1 no other process should be allowed to read either r or a, until the filter process returns to activity 0. Activity 2 is thus a critical region, whose operations should not be interrupted by some other process trying to read the data variables r and a.

The ALARM process must continuously check that the pressure reading is within a normal range, and sound an alarm if $(a = \text{panic})$. Similarly, FILTER must continuously scan the digital sensor readout p, compute the actual pressure r and set the alarm variable a to the appropriate value, so that the controlling software's internal model of the pressure (a and r) keeps up with the actual pressure in the plant (i.e. the chemical reactor's pressure p). Errors in safety critical systems are often caused by inconsistency between the controlling software's model of the environment, and the actual state of the environment (the "plant").

We want to prevent any process (e.g. the alarm TTM) from reading the filter's shared data variables a or r when these values are being updated (i.e. when the filter is in its critical region $x_1 = 2$). The alarm process needs to read a when $(x_2 = 2)$, i.e. when the alarm process is in activity 2. A mutual exclusion mechanism without semaphores is thus implemented using the shared variables y_1, y_2, z.

Each process has a variable (y_1 for filter and y_2 for alarm) that expresses its wish to enter its critical region. The variables y_1, y_2 are set to *true* at $(x_1 = 0)$ and $(x_2 = 0)$ respectively, and to *false* at $(x_1 = 2)$ and $(x_2 = 2)$ respectively. In addition, each process leaves a signature in its common variable z, i.e. $(z = 1)$ indicates that filter was the last process to request entry, and $(z = 2)$ indicates that alarm was the last process to request entry. The alarm process enters its critical region $(x_2 = 2)$ via the event *enter2* only if either $y_1 = false$ (i.e. the filter process is not currently in its critical area), or $z = 1$ (i.e. both processes are waiting to enter their respective critical regions, but the alarm process requested entry first). This reasoning also applies to the filter process entering its critical area, and explains the guard and transformation function update of the event *enter1*. Thus both processes will never be in their critical area at the same time. The behaviour of the sensor process is of course unaffected by the other processes — its behaviour affects the filter and alarm processes without itself being affected.

The system under development may be represented by the TTM

$$\begin{aligned} SUD &= SENSOR \| FILTER \| ALARM \\ &= (\mathcal{V}_{SUD},\ \Theta_{SUD},\ \mathcal{T}_{SUD}) \end{aligned}$$

where

$$\begin{aligned} \mathcal{V}_{SUD} &= \{x_0, x_1, x_2, p, r, a, y_1, y_2, z, \mathrm{n}, t\} \\ \Theta_{SUD} &= [(x_0 = 0 = x_1 = x_2) \wedge (a = ok) \wedge (y_1 = false = y_2) \wedge (z = 1)] \end{aligned}$$

and the set of transitions $\mathcal{T}_{SUD}$ is displayed in Table 1.

An initial state of SUD is any state satisfying Θ_{SUD}, e.g.

$$s = \{(x_0, 0), (x_1, 0), (x_2, 0), (p, 4), (r, 30), (a, ok), (y_1, false), (y_2, false), (z, 1), (\mathrm{n}, increment), (t, 0)\}$$

There are an infinite number of such initial states because the time variable t ranges over the natural numbers, and the initial condition imposes no constraints on the initial clock reading. Also, no constraints are imposed on the pressure variable p, and the converted pressure variable r.

The state-assignment q associated with s is given by

$$q = \{(x_0, 0), (x_1, 0), (x_2, 0), (p, 4), (r, 30), (a, ok), (y_1, false), (y_2, false), (z, 1), (t, 0)\}$$

There are also an infinite number of initial state-assignments.

2.3 RTTL — Real-Time Temporal Logic

Real-time temporal logic is based on Manna-Pnueli temporal logic with additional proof rules for real-time properties. However, no new temporal operators over and above the standard ones are needed (thus making the extension from temporal logic to real-time temporal logic straightforward).

A *state-formula* is any first order predicate which does not have any temporal operators. For example, the initial condition Θ_{SUD} is a state-formula, and can thus be evaluated to true or false in a state. If a state-formula φ evaluates to true in a state s, then we write $s(\varphi) = true$. An alternative notation is $\models^{s} \varphi$ — i.e., *s satisfies* φ. Temporal formulas are built up by applying temporal operators to state-formulas.

For simplicity, we use two basic temporal operators $\bigcirc$ (next), and $\mathcal{U}$ (until) from which we can define many other useful operators including: $\Box$ (henceforth), $\Diamond$ (eventually), U

Name	Enabling condition	Transformation	Lower	Upper
decrement	$(x_0 = 0 \wedge p > 0)$	$[p : p - 1]$	0	∞
increment	$(x_0 = 0 \wedge p < 25)$	$[p : p + 1]$	0	∞
request1	$(x_1 = 0)$	$[x_1 : 1,\ y_1 : true,\ z : 1]$	0	1
enter1	$(x_1 = 1 \wedge (y_2 = false \vee z = 2))$	$[x_1 : 2,\ r : 5p + 20]$	0	3
release1	$(x_1 = 2 \wedge 30 \leq r \leq 110)$	$[x_1 : 0,\ a : ok,\ y_1 : false]$	0	1
release0	$(x_1 = 2 \wedge (r < 30 \vee r > 110))$	$[x_1 : 0,\ a : panic,\ y_1 : false]$	0	1
request2	$(x_2 = 0)$	$[x_2 : 1,\ y_2 : true,\ z : 2]$	0	1
enter2	$(x_2 = 1 \wedge (y_1 = false \vee z = 1))$	$[x_2 : 2]$	0	1
release	$(x_2 = 2 \wedge a = ok)$	$[x_2 : 0,\ y_2 : false]$	0	1
soundalarm	$(x_2 = 2 \wedge a = panic)$	$[x_2 : 0,\ y_2 : false]$	0	1
Tick	*true*	$[t : t + 1]$	-	-

Table 1: Transitions of $SUD = SENSOR \| FILTER \| ALARM$

(unless), and $\mathcal{P}$ (precedes). Unlike a state-formula which can be evaluated in a single state, a temporal-formula must be evaluated over a sequence of states (i.e. over a trajectory).

The reader may refer to [Ost90a, OW90, Ost89b] for a complete definition of the satisfaction relation for temporal logic formulas. If w is a state-formula and s_0 the first state of the trajectory σ, then $\models^{\sigma} w$ *iff* $\models^{s_0} w$, i.e. the trajectory σ satisfies the state-formula w iff the formula w evaluates to true in the state s_0. Some examples of the satisfaction relation are:
$\models^{\sigma} \Box w$ *iff* (for all suffixes σ' of σ)$\models^{\sigma'} w$, and
$\models^{\sigma} \Diamond w$ *iff* (for some suffix σ' of σ)$\models^{\sigma'} w$
(where σ is considered a suffix of itself)

Some examples of temporal formulas include:

1. $\Box w$ — henceforth, w is true.
2. $(\mathrm{n} = \tau) \wedge (t = 10) \rightarrow \bigcirc w$ — if τ occurs now at time 10 then in the next state w is true.
3. $w_1 \rightarrow \Diamond w_2$ — if w_1 is now true then eventually w_2 must become true.
4. $w_1 \rightarrow (w_2 \mathcal{U} w_3)$ — if w_1 is now true then eventually w_3 must occur, and until then w_2 remains true.
5. $\Box\Diamond(\mathrm{n} = tick)$ — the clock ticks infinitely often.
6. $w_1 \wedge t = T \rightarrow \Diamond(w_2 \wedge t < T + 4)$ — if w_1 is true at time T then w_2 must happen before the clock reads $T + 4$ (i.e. within 4 clock ticks).

In the last specification, the variable T is a "global" variable that has the same value in every state of a trajectory. In RTTL formulas, quantification is allowed over global variables but not over the "local" variables, i.e. variables in $\mathcal{V}$. Local variables always occur free. Global variables range over fixed data domains (e.g. T ranges over $type(t)$)

and denote elements thereof. Whereas global variables retain the same value in all states of a trajectory, local variables change from state to state.

All formulas with occurrences of global variables are assumed to have their global variables universally quantified. Thus $w_1 \wedge t = T \rightarrow \Diamond(w_2 \wedge t < T + 4)$ actually means

$$\forall T[(w_1 \wedge t = T) \rightarrow \Diamond(w_2 \wedge (t < T + 4))]$$

In the Manna-Pnueli temporal logic proof system there is a rule of inference that states that from any temporal formula w we can deduce $\Box w$. Since the set of legal trajectories of any TTM is suffix closed, this same rule of inference applies to RTTL. Therefore, for example, one may specify either $w_1 \rightarrow \Diamond w_2$ or $\Box(w_1 \rightarrow \Diamond w_2)$ for the eventuality property.

Instead of using the time variable t explicitly in RTTL formulas we may use abbreviations such as:

- $\Diamond_{[l,u]} w$ for $[(t = T) \rightarrow \Diamond(w \wedge (T + l \leq t \leq T + u))]$, i.e. eventually between l and u ticks from now w will become true. The formula $\Diamond_{\leq d} w$ abbreviates $\Diamond_{[0,d]} w$, and $\Diamond_d w$ abbreviates $\Diamond_{[d,d]} w$.
- $w_1 \mathcal{U}_{[l,u]} w_2$ abbreviates $[(t = T) \rightarrow (w_1 \mathcal{U}(w_2 \wedge (T + l \leq t \leq T + u)))]$, i.e. w_2 will become true between l and u ticks from now, and until then w_1 remains true. The formula $(w_1 \mathcal{U}_d w_2)$ abbreviates $(w_1 \mathcal{U}_{[d,d]} w_2)$, and $(w_1 \mathcal{U}_{\leq d} w_2)$ abbreviates $(w_1 \mathcal{U}_{[0,d]} w_2)$.

A variety of real-time properties can be expressed using these abbreviations including:

Exact time: $\Box(w_1 \rightarrow \Diamond_d w_2)$ — every w_1 is followed by a w_2 in exactly d ticks.

Maximum time: $\Box(w_1 \rightarrow \Diamond_{\leq d} w_2)$ — every w_1 must be followed by a w_2 within d ticks.

Minimum time: $\Box(w_1 \rightarrow \neg\Diamond_{\leq d} w_2)$ — w_1 and w_2 are at least d ticks apart.

Periodicity with period d: Let α be an abbreviation for (n = *event*) where *event* is some transition. Then the formula $\Diamond\alpha \wedge \Box[\alpha \rightarrow \bigcirc(\neg\alpha \mathcal{U}_d \alpha]$ specifies that the event occurs regularly with an exact period of d.

Let S be an RTTL specification characterizing the behaviour that a TTM M is required to satisfy. Then S is M-valid iff all legal trajectories of M satisfy S.

2.4 Specifications for the example

The process control example must satisfy the following RTTL specifications:

(S1) Mutual exclusion of critical regions — $\Box\neg(x_1 = 2 \wedge x_2 = 2)$.
The alarm and filter processes must not simultaneously be in their critical regions.

(S2) Accessibility of critical regions — The filter and alarm processes must be guaranteed to access their critical regions within 6 seconds — if not, then the internal model of the data may become inconsistent with the actual plant:

1. $(x_1 = 0) \rightarrow \Diamond_{\leq 6}(x_1 = 2)$.
2. $(x_2 = 0) \rightarrow \Diamond_{\leq 6}(x_2 = 2)$.

(S3) Sound the alarm — *abnormal* $\rightarrow \Diamond_{\leq 10}(\mathbf{n} = soundalarm)$
where *abnormal* $\stackrel{\text{def}}{=} (0 \leq p < 4) \vee (20 < p \leq 25)$. If abnormal pressure is detected then the alarm must sound within 10 ticks from the moment that the abnormality is detected. Note that S3 is actually *SUD*-invalid, as the pressure may return to normal before the alarm can be invoked. There would need to be a minimum delay on the rate of pressure changes for S3 to be valid.

2.5 The RTTL proof system

The RTTL proof system is provided in the appendix. The following conventions will be adopted:

1. The symbols $\psi, \psi_0, \psi_1, \cdots$ or $\phi, \phi_0, \phi_1, \cdots$ or $\varphi, \varphi_0, \varphi_1, \cdots$ will be used for state-formulas (predicates not containing any temporal operators that can be interpreted in a single state), and $w, w_0, w_1, ..$ represent any RTTL formulas (that must be interpreted in trajectories). $T, T_0, T_1, ...$ are global variables with the same type as the clock variable t.

2. For $\tau \in \mathcal{T}$, the assertion $\{\varphi_1\}\tau\{\varphi_2\}$ is an abbreviation for

$$(\mathbf{n} = \tau \wedge \varphi_1) \rightarrow \bigcirc \varphi_2$$

and is read as "τ leads from φ_1 to φ_2" (similar to Manna-Pnueli theory — except that in Manna-Pnueli theory there is no next-transition variable $\mathbf{n}$ to represent events). The state-formula φ_1 is the *source node*, and φ_2 is the *destination node*. Note that the triple $\{\varphi_1\}\tau\{\varphi_2\}$ expresses partial-correctness and not total correctness. Thus *if τ indeed occurs* in φ_1, then in the next state φ_2 holds.

3. If $\mathcal{T}' \subseteq \mathcal{T}$, then $\{\varphi_1\}\mathcal{T}'\{\varphi_2\}$ abbreviates the statement that $\{\varphi_1\}\tau\{\varphi_2\}$ for each $\tau \in \mathcal{T}'$.

4. Let $h = [v_1 \colon a_1, ..., v_n \colon a_n]$ be the transformation function (in state assignment format) of some transition $\tau \in \mathcal{T}$, and let ϕ be any state-formula. Then ϕ^τ stands for $\phi^{v_1,...,v_n}_{a_1,...,a_n}$, i.e. ϕ^τ is the formula obtained from ϕ by simultaneously replacing all free occurrences of v_1 by a_1, v_2 by a_2 and so on. (Care must be taken that illegal capture of variables by quantifiers does not take place.)

The axioms and rules of the RTTL proof system, as well as some derived rules, are presented in the Appendix. The next two sections will illustrate the use of the proof system.

3 Safety Properties

The mutual exclusion specification $\text{S1} \equiv [\Box\neg(x_1 = 2 \wedge x_2 = 2)]$ for the pressure sensor TTM is an example of a *safety* property, i.e. a property that asserts that something should never happen, in this case that a state should never be reached in which both the filter and alarm processes are simultaneously in their critical sections. An assertion that eventually something must happen is called a *liveness* property.

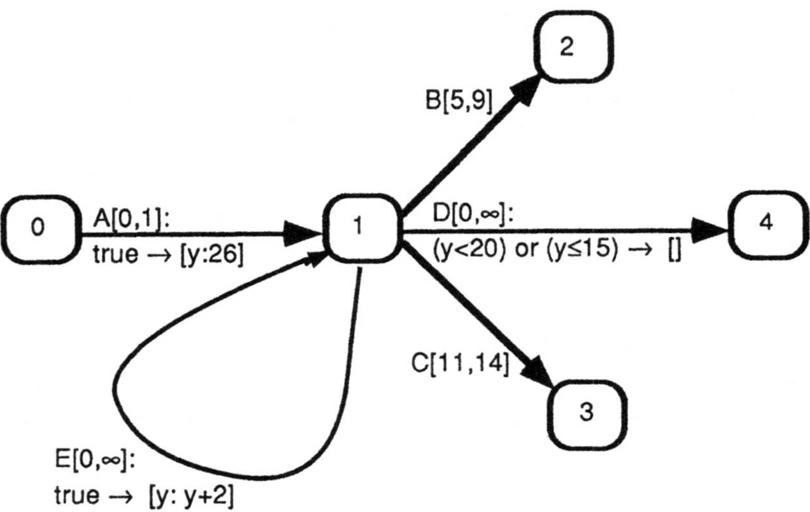

Figure 2: A small TTM

In a non real-time system, safety properties can usually be verified by using the derived proof rule DR5 (or DR5') in the Appendix. However, in a real-time system, DR5 alone is usually not enough to do the job. Additional rules such as RR, RD and RDTT must also be applied to verify the required safety property.

We will illustrate how DR5' is not enough to verify a safety property by using a trivial example. This will also illustrate the style of reasoning employed in TTM/RTTL. In the next section, these techniques will be applied to the pressure sensor example.

An important point to note is that most of the reasoning involves the use of ordinary predicate logic and domain reasoning (e.g. reasoning about arithmetic expressions). The temporal logic component of the reasoning is minimal.

The reasoning usually proceeds as follows. A derived rule appropriate to the form of the specification to be verified is chosen. For example, to prove an invariant safety property such as S1, a combination of DR5' and RDTT (see Appendix) may be used. The premises of the derived rules can usually be proved by an appeal to the transition axiom TA or the derived rule DR1 (which is essentially a corollary of TA) and sentential, predicate and domain reasoning. For this reason also, it is often possible to semi-automate the use of the proof rules, e.g. using constraint logic programming methods [Ost89a, Ost91b, Ost91a], without necessarily having to incorporate a special purpose temporal logic theorem prover.

Consider the infinite state TTM in Figure 2 with activity variable x (with $type(x) = \{0,1,2,3,4\}$) and data variable y (with $type(y) = \{0,1,2,\cdots\}$). In addition to *Tick* there are five transitions A, B, C, D, E with lower and upper time bounds as shown in the square brackets in the Figure. The initial condition is $\Theta \equiv (x = 0 \wedge y \geq 25)$.

Suppose the property $S \stackrel{\text{def}}{=} \Box(x \neq 3 \wedge x \neq 4)$ is to be verified, i.e. the TTM never enters activities 3 or 4. S is obviously true because the upper time bound of B is less than the lower time bound of C; therefore, C never occurs. Also, D never occurs because it is never enabled at activity 1.

The usual way that S would be proved in RTTL is by using a rule such as DR5 (see Appendix). However, at best, DR5 on its own can only prove the weaker property $S' = \Box(x \neq 4)$, but not the stronger property S.

Proof of the weaker property S':

In DR5, set $\psi \stackrel{\text{def}}{=} (y \geq 25 \land x \neq 4)$ and $I \stackrel{\text{def}}{=} (x \neq 4)$. The first two premises of DR5 given by:
(0) $\Theta \rightarrow \psi$, and
(1) $\psi \rightarrow I$
are trivially true by propositional reasoning, and our domain knowledge for *type*(x) that $(x = 0) \rightarrow (x \neq 4)$.

The third premise $\{\psi\}T\{\psi\}$ must now be proved, i.e. we must show that each transition τ leads from ψ to ψ. The derived rule DR1 in the Appendix is useful in this regard. In DR1, set $T' = \{\tau\}$, and $\psi_1 = \psi_2 = \psi$. Then, to show $\{\psi\}\tau\{\psi\}$, it is sufficient to show the truth of
(2) $\psi \land e_\tau \rightarrow \psi^\tau$

Since the transformation function of A has $h_A = [x{:}\,1, y{:}\,26]$ it follows that

$$\begin{aligned} \psi^A &\equiv \psi^{x,y}_{1,26} \\ &\equiv (y \geq 25 \land x \neq 4)^{x,y}_{1,26} \\ &\equiv (26 \geq 25 \land 1 \neq 4) \\ &\equiv \mathit{true} \end{aligned}$$

Therefore, (2) is true for A, and we have by DR1 that
(3) $\{\psi\}A\{\psi\}$

Using similar reasoning we obtain the same result for all the other transitions *Tick*, B, C, D and E. For example, for transition E

$$\begin{aligned} \psi^E &\equiv \psi^{x,y}_{1,y+2} \\ &\equiv (y \geq 25 \land x \neq 4)^{x,y}_{1,y+2} \\ &\equiv (y+2 \geq 25 \land 1 \neq 4) \\ &\equiv y \geq 23 \end{aligned}$$

By a domain axiom for arithmetic and sentential logic $\psi \land e_E \rightarrow \psi^E$ is true, i.e.

$$[(y \geq 25 \land x \neq 4) \land (x = 1)] \rightarrow (y \geq 25)$$

Therefore, (2) above is true for transition E, and hence by DR1 it follows that
(4) $\{\psi\}E\{\psi\}$
The domain axiom is $y \geq 25 \rightarrow y \geq 23$.

For transition D, note that

$$\begin{aligned} \psi^D &\equiv \psi^{x}_{4} \\ &\equiv (y \geq 25 \land x \neq 4)^{x}_{4} \\ &\equiv (y \geq 25 \land 4 \neq 4) \\ &\equiv \mathit{false} \end{aligned}$$

Therefore, we must look at the antecedent of (2) given by $\psi \wedge e_D$.

$$\begin{aligned} \psi \wedge e_D &\equiv [y \geq 25 \wedge x \neq 4] \wedge [(x = 1) \wedge (y < 20 \vee (y \leq 15))] \\ &\equiv \mathit{false} \end{aligned}$$

Therefore, (2) above is true and therefore we have by DR1 that
(5) $\{\psi\}D\{\psi\}$
Using DR1 as in (3), (4) and (5) above we obtain the third premise of DR5 given by
(6) $\{\psi\}\mathcal{T}\{\psi\}$

Hence, by (0),(1),(6) and DR5 we obtain the weaker property S′.

Summarizing the proof of S′:

The above proof of S′ was presented in great detail only to familiarize the reader with the notation and conventions of the proof system. When presenting the proof, only the general outline is written, leaving it up to the reader to check the details. The proof outline is written as follows:

(1)	$\Theta \rightarrow \psi$	SL
(2)	$\psi \rightarrow (x \neq 4)$	SL
(3)	$\{\psi\}\mathcal{T}\{\psi\}$	DR1, SL and DA
(4)	$\square(x \neq 4)$	1,2 3, and DR5

SL stands for sentential (propositional) logic, and DA means that a domain axiom was used. Other abbreviations used are PL for predicate logic and TL for temporal logic.

DR5 is insufficient to prove the stronger property S:

DR5, DR1, SL and DA on their own cannot be used to prove the stronger specification S. To see this, in DR5 set $\psi \stackrel{\text{def}}{=} (y \geq 25 \wedge x \neq 3 \wedge x \neq 4)$ and $I \stackrel{\text{def}}{=} (x \neq 3 \wedge x \neq 4)$. The first two premises of DR5 are true. The third premise of DR5 can be proved, using DR1, for all transitions except C. In the case of C

$$\begin{aligned} \psi^C &\equiv \psi_3^x \\ &\equiv (y \geq 25 \wedge x \neq 3 \wedge x \neq 4)_3^x \\ &\equiv \mathit{false} \end{aligned}$$

Therefore, neither DR1 nor the transition axiom TA can be used to show that C leads from ψ to ψ. This is because DR1 and TA do not take into account timing information carried in the lower and upper time bounds of C and and B; it is these bounds that must be used to obtain the desired result.

The rule RDTT does take into account timing information in the required fashion. It will be shown below in more detail that from RDTT we can obtain the conclusion that $\square(\mathrm{n} \neq C)$, i.e. even though C becomes enabled, it never actually occurs.

Although in this case it is obvious that C never occurs, in general it is not so easy to be certain of such statements. This is because the lower time bound and hence bound choicepoints are involved. A transition such as C may have become enabled earlier than B, in which case the default lower time bound of C has now been decremented, and may no longer exceed the upper time bound of B. The derived rule RDTT is therefore needed to do the proper timing and choicepoint check on C.

Using the result that $\Box(\mathrm{n} \neq C)$ as obtained from RDTT, it follows that

$$\begin{array}{rcl} (\mathrm{n} = C)\wedge\psi & \Rightarrow & (\mathrm{n} = C)\wedge\psi \\ & \Rightarrow & (\mathrm{n} = C)\wedge\psi\wedge\Box(\mathrm{n} \neq C) \\ & \Rightarrow & \mathit{false} \\ & \Rightarrow & \mathit{anything} \\ & \Rightarrow & \bigcirc\psi \end{array}$$

From the above analysis it directly follows that $\{\psi\}C\{\psi\}$ is true. Having proved the truth of $\{\psi\}\mathcal{T}\{\psi\}$ it then follows that S is true.

An important feature of the above proof of S is that standard temporal techniques are used for the most part. The standard techniques themselves require very little temporal reasoning. Mostly sentential, predicate and domain reasoning is used. The real-time part of the proof was only invoked at the point where it was actually needed, viz. to deal with the transition C.

Guesswork is involved in choosing the invariant $\psi = (y \geq 25 \wedge x \neq 3 \wedge x \neq 4)$. This is a standard feature in all program verification involving "do loops". The choice of the right conjunct is obvious as it is just the property S that is to be proved. The choice of the left conjunct $(y \geq 25)$ is more difficult to obtain in the general case, as it involves already knowing something of the behaviour of the TTM.

3.1 The psp-heuristic

In order to (a) guide the proof, (b) help with the choice of the invariant, and (c) help isolate where real-time reasoning must be employed, the following *psp-heuristic* is often useful. The heuristic also introduces the idea of a *proof diagram* which provides the designer with a "high-level" view of the TTM behaviour and the resulting proof of correctness. The proof diagram is similar to a graph of all states reachable from the initial states. However, the nodes are state-formulas representing a possibly infinite set of states rather than individual states. It is therefore possible to have a finite graph representing clustered or lumped behaviours of infinite state TTMs.

The psp-heuristic works together with a modified version of DR5 called DR5' (see Appendix) to prove a property of the form $\Box I$. It is more convenient to use RDTT with DR5' than with DR5. The psp-heuristic is illustrated in the proof diagram of Figure 3.

1. Start with a proof diagram having the single unmarked node φ_0, where φ_0 is a state-formula that satisfies $\Theta \rightarrow \varphi_0$ and $\varphi_0 \rightarrow I$. (For example, $\varphi_0 = \Theta$ is a possible choice.) Repeatedly apply the next step.

2. If φ_i is an unmarked node in the proof diagram, compute all its successor nodes and mark φ_i. Each transition τ must be checked to see if it has a successor node φ_j where $\{\varphi_i\}\tau\{\varphi_j\}$.

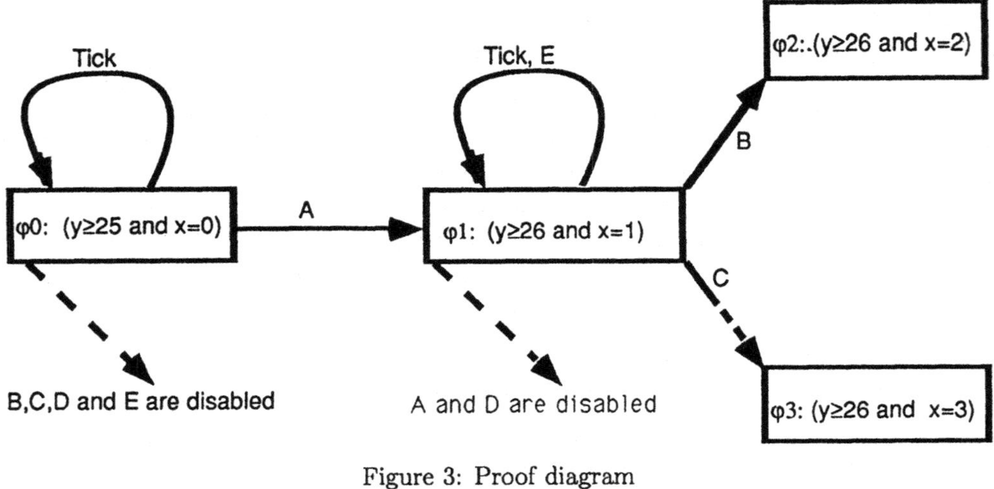

Figure 3: Proof diagram

Not every transition will necessarily lead to a successor node. If (a) τ is disabled at φ_i, i.e $\varphi_i \wedge e_\tau \rightarrow$ *false*, or (b) τ is a selfloop, i.e. $\varphi_i \wedge e_\tau \rightarrow \varphi^\tau$, then τ does not *exit* from φ_i. Transitions that do not exit need not be explored. Note that both (a) and (b) imply that $\{\varphi_i\}\tau\{\varphi_i\}$[3]. Selfloops and transitions disabled at a certain node are not usually shown in the proof diagram.

For each transition τ that exits from φ_i choose the successor to be the strongest postcondition given by $\varphi_j \stackrel{\text{def}}{=} psp(\tau, \varphi_i)$ (see Appendix for the definition of *psp*). It must then be checked, in accordance with the second premise of DR5', that $\varphi_j \rightarrow I$.

A successor node that is at least as strong as an already computed node, need not be explored any further (as it leads back to a node that has already been checked).

3. The heuristic terminates when either all paths lead back to already computed nodes, or there are no more unmarked nodes (all exiting paths have been fully explored).

3.2 Application of heuristic to example

The verification of specification S via the heuristic leads to the the proof diagram in Figure 3. The initial node is chosen as Θ. The only transition that exits from φ_0 is A. The tick transition is a selfloop, and B,C,D and E are all disabled at φ_0.

To obtain the successor φ_1 node so that $\{\varphi_0\}A\{\varphi_1\}$ compute $\varphi_1 \stackrel{\text{def}}{=} psp(A, \varphi_0) \equiv (y = 26 \wedge x = 1)$.

[3]It might seem counterintuitive to the reader that a disabled transition leads from φ_i back to φ_i — how can a disabled transition lead anywhere? Remember, however, that the notation $\{\varphi_i\}\tau\{\varphi_i\}$ denotes only partial correctness, i.e. it does not assert that τ must occur, only what happens if it does occur. Therefore, a disabled transition leads anywhere you like!

In Figure 3, φ_1 has been weakened to $(y \geq 26 \wedge x = 1)$, in order to make the transition E a selfloop at φ_1. Otherwise E would cause the proof diagram to unfold into an infinite sequence of successor nodes containing nodes $(y = 28 \wedge x = 1) \cdots (y = 30 \wedge x = 1) \cdots$ etc. The whole point is to search for nodes that keep the proof diagram finite while satisfying the premises of DR5. Weakening certain nodes may therefore be required to achieve the goal of a finite proof diagram.

The nodes φ_2 and φ_3 can be obtained from their predecessor nodes using the standard *psp* computation, without the need to further weaken the state-formula describing the node.

The psp-procedure breaks down at node φ_1 for transition C leading to φ_3, because it is *not* the case that $\varphi_3 \rightarrow I$. However, by applying RDTT at φ_1 we can show that C will never occur.

In RDTT, set $\tau_u = B$, $\tau_l = C$, $\psi_1 = (x = 0 \wedge \text{n} = A)$ and $\psi_2 = (x = 1)$. The premises of RDTT are then trivially true and hence we have

(1)	$\neg(x = 1) \rightarrow \Box[(x = 1) \rightarrow (\text{n} \neq C)]$	RDTT
(2)	$\Theta \rightarrow \neg(x = 1)$	by propositional reasoning
(3)	$\Box[(x = 1) \rightarrow (\text{n} \neq C)]$	1, 2 and INIT
(4)	$(x = 1) \rightarrow (\text{n} \neq C)$	3 and temporal reasoning
(5)	$(\text{n} = C) \wedge \varphi_1 \rightarrow \mathit{false}$	4 and prop. reasoning
(6)	$\{\varphi_1\} C \{\varphi\}$	5 and prop. reasoning

where $\varphi \equiv (\varphi_0 \vee \varphi_1 \vee \varphi 2)$. Therefore, all the premises of DR5' are true and hence the stronger property S is true.

The above proof for S is usually abbreviated by providing a proof diagram, and pointing out where RDTT had to be applied. The detailed check of all the premises of DR5' can be left to the interested reader.

The property S is obviously true for the trivial example presented. In more complex examples, it is not so easy to see the truth of a safety property. The psp-procedure has been successfully used on more complex examples [Ost89b]. As mentioned previously, it is amenable to automation over those domains successfully treated by constraint logic programming languages (e.g. linear equalities and inequalities over the reals, rationals and integers, trees, lists, booleans, regular expressions and finite sets). A necessary condition for a constraint logic program to work over a certain domain, is that an efficient algorithm exist for checking constraints (state-formulas) over that domain.

It is important to obey certain conventions when presenting proof diagrams. First, if an edge τ is shown leading from a node φ_i to φ_j, then it must be the case that τ exits from φ_i (is not disabled or a selfloop), and that $\{\varphi_i\}\tau\{\varphi_j\}$ is true. Second, all exiting edges must be shown from a node, otherwise a legal path will be overlooked with disastrous consequences.

Obviously, for complicated systems with say 20 or more transitions it becomes an exhausting (although often trivial) task to check all transitions at every node. For this reason, automated techniques have been found very useful.

The next section uses the *pwp-heuristic* to verify a real-time response property. The pwp-heuristic can also be used to verify properties of the form $\Box I$, and it often leads to a much simpler proof than the one presented using the psp-heuristic.

Note that $\Box I \equiv \neg\Diamond\neg I$. To verify the safety property $\Box I$ start from the state-formula $\neg I$ and work backwards using weakest preconditions. First check if there is a transition that leads to $\neg I$ from some node φ in one step. If not, then the safety property is true, i.e. there is no path that will eventually reach the goal node $\neg I$ from the initial condition. If there is such a transition from node φ, then work backwards from that node computing its weakest precondition in turn. The use of this heuristic is explained in more detail in the next section..

4 Real-Time Response

Specifications S2 and S3 for the pressure example SUD involve proving real-time response properties of the form $\phi_1 \rightarrow \Diamond_{\leq d}\phi_3$. Such properties are in essence also safety properties as they state that something should not happen (the clock should not tick more than d ticks before ϕ_3 occurs).

The unbounded property $\phi_1 \rightarrow \Diamond\phi_3$ is a liveness property, but its form is quite similar to real time response properties. The *pwp-heuristic* provided below uses a method that can work on both liveness and real-time response properties.

The property S3 is invalid because of cycles in the proof diagram that prevent the TTM from reaching the goal node ϕ_3. The property S2 is valid because there are no such cycles and every node has a "progress edge" that guarantees movement in the direction of the goal node.

The pwp-heuristic will be illustrated by proving the property S4 given by

$$S4 \stackrel{\text{def}}{=} [(x_1 = 1) \rightarrow \Diamond_{\leq 6}(x_1 = 0)]$$

S4 is SUD-valid, but it can also be used to illustrate the kind of problems that occur when cycles appear in the proof diagram. S2 and S3 can be tackled using the same types of techniques as are shown for S4.

The pwp-heuristic is based on the rules RR and TCHAIN. Temporal logic reasoning had to be used to establish these rules. However, their application via the pwp-heuristic requires very little temporal reasoning; mainly propositional, predicate and domain reasoning is needed.

4.1 The pwp-heuristic

The following steps describe the construction of a proof diagram using the pwp-heuristic to verify the property

$$\phi_1 \rightarrow (\phi_2 \mathcal{U}_{\leq u} \phi_3) \tag{1}$$

(1) Start with a proof diagram consisting of the goal node ψ_0 set to ϕ_3.

(2) (Do Repeatedly) For each node ψ_i in the proof diagram, and for each transition $\tau \in \mathcal{T}$ with finite upper time bound and transformation function as expressed by $h_\tau = [v_1 : a_1, \cdots, v_k : a_k]$, compute a predecessor state formula ψ_j (where $j > i$) as follows:

$$\begin{aligned} \psi_j &\stackrel{\text{def}}{=} pwp(\tau, \psi_i) \\ &\stackrel{\text{def}}{=} [\psi_i]^{v_1,\cdots,v_k}_{a_1,\cdots,a_k} \wedge e_\tau \end{aligned}$$

$pwp(\tau, \psi_i)$ is the partial weakest precondition for τ to reach ψ_i, and the theorem given by $\{pwp(\tau, \psi_i)\}\tau\{\psi_i\}$ holds true (see Appendix). The *pwp* is similar to the weakest precondition of Dijkstra's guarded commands used in the verification of sequential programs [Gri85]. The predecessor state formula ψ_j becomes a new node in the proof diagram (i.e. ψ_j is connected to ψ_i via the edge τ) so long as both of the following conditions hold:

- It is not the case that ψ_j is *false*. If $\psi_j \equiv$ *false* then there is no state in which τ occurs and leads to a state satisfying ψ_i in one step.
- It is not the case that τ is a selfloop. The transition τ is a selfloop if $\psi_j \rightarrow \psi_i$, meaning that all states satisfying ψ_j also satisfy ψ_i. In such a case there is usually no need to create a new node.

(3) For each node ψ_i for $i > 0$, compute all transitions that exit ψ_i (that are not yet indicated in the proof diagram). Each exiting transition must lead to some node ψ_j (which can be computed using partial strongest postconditions) where $j < i$. If $j \not< i$ then there is a cycle in the proof-diagram, which means that there is the possibility of at least one legal trajectory which is not guaranteed to reach the goal node, and the property may therefore not be valid.

Each node ψ_i must have at least one *progress edge*. A progress edge τ of ψ_i is (a) enabled in all states satisfying ψ_i (i.e. $\psi_i \rightarrow e_\tau$), (b) leads to some node ψ_j where $j < i$, and (c) has a finite upper time bound. The progress edge thus forces the TTM to exit the node ψ_i in the direction of the goal ψ_0.

If there is a progress edge at ψ_i, then the premises of RR are satisfied. Let $\phi_{i-1} \stackrel{\text{def}}{=} (\psi_{i-1} \vee \cdots \psi_0)$. BY RR we have $\psi_i \rightarrow (\psi_i \mathcal{U}_{\leq d_i} \phi_{i-1})$, which is a premise of TCHAIN. As this step is repeatedly executed, the premises of TCHAIN are incrementally satisfied.

(4) Steps 2 and 3 are repeated until both

$$\bigvee_{i>0} \psi_i \rightarrow \phi_2$$

and

$$\phi_1 \rightarrow \bigvee_{i\geq 0} \psi_i$$

hold true. There is no guarantee that the above implications will ever hold true.

(5) If the heuristic terminates and there are no cycles in the proof diagram, then by the stopping conditions and TCHAIN the required property (1) is true. The bound u is computed by adding the time bounds of the longest path. Cycles would mean that one of the premises of TCHAIN is not satisfied.

The pwp-heuristic may also be used to verify the weaker property $\phi_1 \rightarrow \Diamond_{\leq u} \phi_3$ by setting $\phi_2 \equiv$ *true*. We will now apply the pwp-heuristic to the verification of the real-time response property S4 given in the beginning of this section.

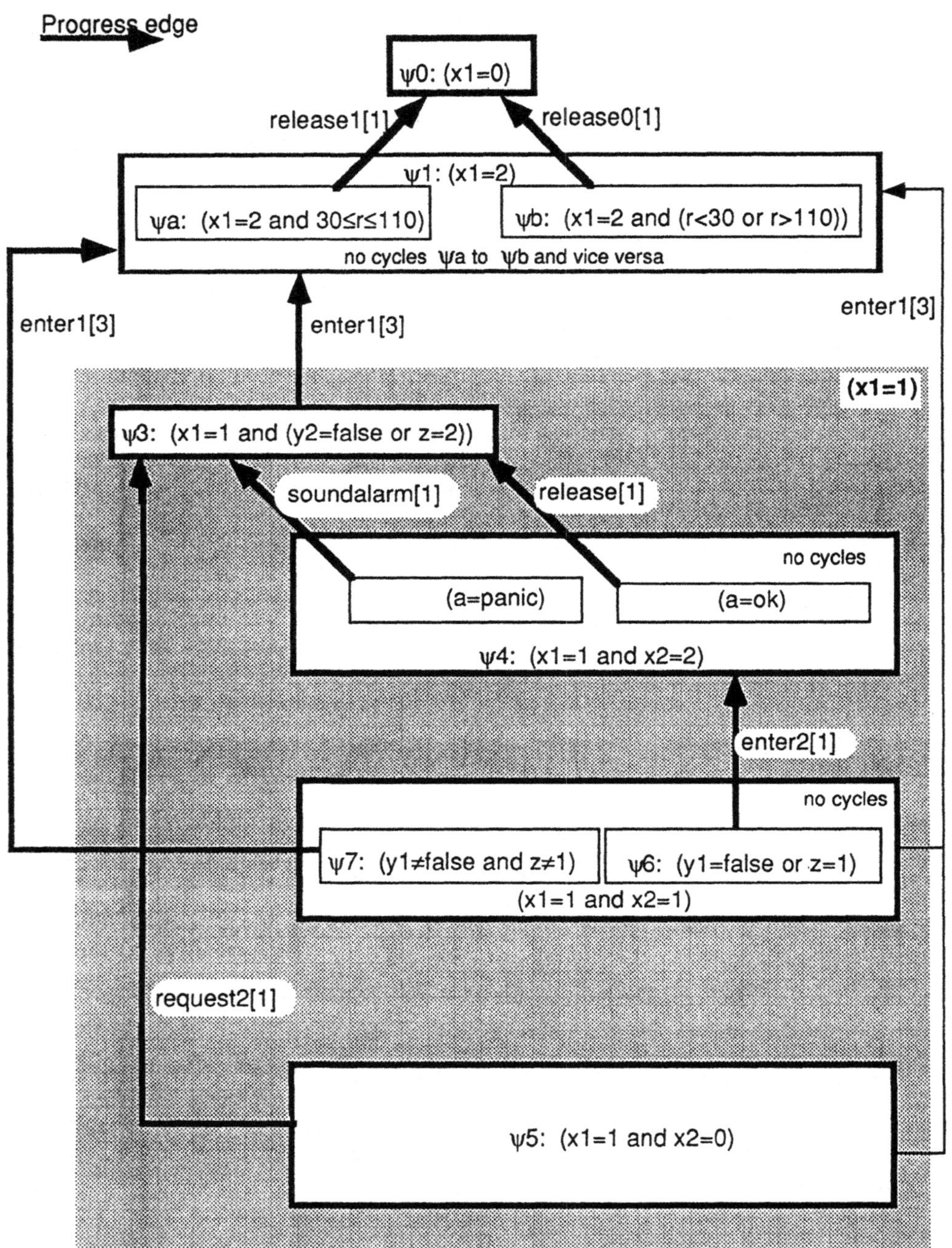

Figure 4: pwp-diagram for SUD.

4.2 Application of heuristic to pressure example

The pwp-heuristic yields the proof-diagram given in Figure 4 for S4. Set the goal node as $\psi_0 \stackrel{\text{def}}{=} (x_1 = 0)$. Using Step 2 to compute the predecececesor nodes ψ_a and ψ_b (e.g. for the transition *release*1) we obtain:

$$\begin{aligned}
\psi_a &= pwp(release1, x_1 = 0) \\
&= (x_1 = 0)^{x_1, a,\ y_1}_{0,\ ok, false} \wedge e_{release1} \\
&= e_{release1} \\
&= (x_1 = 2) \wedge (30 \leq r \leq 110)
\end{aligned}$$

Similarly, $\psi_b = (x_1 = 2) \wedge (r < 30 \vee r > 110)$ as shown in the proof diagram. All other transitions are either selfloops or compute to *false*, and may therefore be ignored.

For ψ_a the only exiting transition is *release*1 which is also a progress edge. Therefore, by RR we have that $\psi_a \rightarrow [\psi_a \mathcal{U}_{\leq 1}(\mathrm{n} = release1)]$. By TA(b) we have that

$$(\mathrm{n} = release1) \rightarrow \bigcirc \psi_0$$

Therefore, by temporal reasoning we have that $\psi_a \rightarrow [\psi_a \mathcal{U}_{\leq 1} \psi_0]$, which is one of the premises in TCHAIN needed to verify S2.

Similarly, for ψ_b and *release*0 we have $\psi_b \rightarrow (\psi_b \mathcal{U}_{\leq 1} \psi_0)$.

We may make a simplification. Set

$$\begin{aligned}
\psi_1 &\stackrel{\text{def}}{=} (\psi_a \vee \psi_b) \\
&\equiv (x_1 = 2)
\end{aligned}$$

By temporal reasoning we then have that $\psi_1 \rightarrow (\psi_1 \mathcal{U}_{\leq 1} \psi_0)$. These simplifications are made wherever possible (e.g. see node ψ_4), and can always be made provided there are no cycles between ψ_a and ψ_b.

In the proof diagram, the grey area represents all states satisfying $(x_1 = 1)$. Any node ψ_i in the grey area characterises a subspace within $(x_1 = 1)$. For example, the complete specification of ψ_6 is given by $\psi_6 \stackrel{\text{def}}{=} [(x_1 = 1 \wedge x_2 = 1) \wedge (y_1 = false \vee z = 1)]$.

Because $type(x_2) = \{0, 1, 2\}$, by domain reasoning we have that

$$[x_1 = 1] \equiv [(x_1 = 1) \wedge (x_2 = 0 \vee x_2 = 1 \vee x_2 = 2)]$$

Therefore, for the nodes ψ_4, ψ_5, ψ_6 and ψ_7 in the grey area we have that

$$\begin{aligned}
(\psi_4 \vee \psi_5 \vee \psi_6 \vee \psi_7) &\equiv (x_1 = 1) \\
&\stackrel{\text{def}}{=} \phi_1
\end{aligned}$$

and we have thus reached the stopping condition of the heuristic.

The node ψ_7 was not computed using the backward mechanism of Step 2. Instead, ψ_7 was obtained by setting $\psi_7 \stackrel{\text{def}}{=} \neg \psi_6$, in order to obtain $(\psi_6 \vee \psi_7) \equiv (x_1 = 1 \wedge x_2 = 1)$, so as to obtain the required stopping condition. All edges exiting from ψ_7 lead in the direction of the goal node, and there is at least one progress edge. Therefore ψ_7 is a valid node in the proof diagram that satisfies the TCHAIN premises.

No path in the proof diagram takes longer than

$$\psi_6 \cdots enter2[1] \cdots soundalarm[1] \cdots enter1[3] release1[1] \cdots \phi_0$$

which takes 6 ticks of the clock. Each node has a progress edge and there are no cycles. Therefore, all the premises of TCHAIN hold true. Hence the the specification S4 is SUD-valid.

It is usually sufficient to present the proof diagram for the response property, and leave it to the reader to check the associated details. The proof diagram is in effect a proof outline.

The transition *enter*1 is shown as exiting from node ψ_6 and leading to node ψ_1. In reality there is no state of a legal trajectory in which *enter*1 and *enter*2 are simultaneously enabled, otherwise the mutual exclusion property S1 would fail to hold. The proof diagram will never omit a behaviour, but it may on occaison (as in this case) show additional behaviours that on subsequent analysis could be eliminated. In the case of S4 it was not necessary to eliminate this additional behaviour as S4 does not depend on mutual exclusion for its proof. In general, however, if S1 has already been proved then it can be used to "prune" the proof diagram, and it may even be necessary to do so in order to obtain the required property.

If the designer had chosen the guards of *release*1 and *release*0 to be $(4 \leq p \leq 20)$ and $(p < 4 \vee p > 20)$ respectively, then there would be a cycle

$$\psi_b \cdots increment \cdots \psi_a \cdots decrement \cdots \psi_b$$

The property S4 would then fail to hold because there is then at least one legal trajectory that does not reach the goal node. The position of the cycle in the proof diagram can be used to "debug" the design by indicating to the designer which guards to choose so as to eliminate the cycle.

In applying the pwp-heuristic to verify that $\phi_1 \rightarrow (\phi_2 \mathcal{U}_{\leq u} \phi_3)$, for some TTM M, it is possible for a situation to arise in which either there are cycles or there are no progress edges, and yet the property is still valid. This happens because the states satisfying ϕ_1 may not be reachable from the initial states. In such a situation, the designer must work backwards from ϕ_1 and check that there is at least one path back to the initial condition. If every path leads backwards to *false* without first passing through the initial condition then the property is M-valid.

Because most of the reasoning involved in computing the proof diagram does not involve the use of temporal logic, the constraint logic theorem prover mentioned in the previous section is effective in this case of real-time properties also, and was used to obtain the proof diagram for this example [Ost91b, Ost91a].

References

[CM88] K.M. Chandy and J. Misra. *Parallel program design.* Addison-Wesley, 1988.

[Gri85] D. Gries. *The Science of Programming.* Springer-Verlag, 1985.

[Kro87] F. Kroger. *Temporal Logics of Programs*, volume 8 of *EATCS Monographs on Theoretical Computer Science.* Springer-Verlag, 1987.

[MP83a] Z. Manna and A. Pnueli. How to cook a temporal proof system for your pet language. In *Proceedings of the Symposium on Principles of Programming Languages*, pages 141–154, Austin, Texas, January 1983.

[MP83b] Z. Manna and A. Pnueli. Verification of concurrent programs: a temporal proof system. Technical report, Dept. of Computer Science, Stanford University, June 1983. See also Foundations of Computer Science IV, Amsterdam, Mathematical Center Tracts, pages 163-225, 1983.

[Ost86] J.S. Ostroff. Real-time computer control of discrete event systems modelled by extended state machines: a temporal logic approach. Technical Report 8618, Systems Control Group, Dept. of Electrical Engineering, University of Toronto, September 1986. revised January 1987.

[Ost89a] J.S. Ostroff. Mechanizing the verification of real-time discrete systems. In *Proceedings of the 15th Symposium on Microprocessing and Microprogramming*. North-Holland, September 1989.

[Ost89b] J.S. Ostroff. *Temporal Logic for Real-Time Systems*. Advanced Software Development Series. Research Studies Press Limited (distributed by John Wiley and Sons), England, 1989.

[Ost90a] J.S. Ostroff. Deciding properties of timed transition models. *IEEE Transactions on Parallel and Distributed Systems*, 1(2):170–183, April 1990.

[Ost90b] J.S. Ostroff. A logic for real-time discrete event processes. *IEEE Control Systems Magzine*, June 1990.

[Ost91a] J.S. Ostroff. Constraint logic programming for reasoning about discrete event processes. *The Journal of Logic Programming*, 1991. (In Press).

[Ost91b] J.S. Ostroff. Systematic development of real-time discrete event systems. In *Proceedings of the ECC91 European Control Conference*, pages 522–533, Paris, France, July 1991. Hermes Press.

[Ost92] J.S. Ostroff. A verifier for real-time properties. *Real-Time Journal*, 1992. (In press).

[OW85] J.S. Ostroff and W.M. Wonham. A temporal logic approach to real time control. In *Proceedings of the 24th IEEE Conference on Decision and Control*, pages 656–657, Florida, December 1985.

[OW90] J.S. Ostroff and W.M. Wonham. A framework for real-time discrete event control. *IEEE Transactions on Automatic Control*, April 1990.

[Pnu86] Amir Pnueli. Applications of temporal logic to the specification and verification of reactive systems: a survey of current trends. In J. de Bakker, W.P de Roever, and G. Rozenburg, editors, *Current trends in concurrency*, LNCS 244. Springer-Verlag, 1986.

A The RTTL proof system

This appendix provides the RTTL proof system taken from [Ost89b]. The proof system is an extension of the Manna-Pnueli proof system [MP83a, MP83b, Kro87] for concurrent programs. The Manna-Pnueli proof system consists of three layers: the general, domain and program layers. This appendix replaces the program layer with a *real-time layer*. We will concentrate on the real-time layer and assume that the reader has access to the axioms and rules of the other layers — a complete account of all the layers is provided in [Ost89b].

A brief summary is presented below of the three layers used in the RTTL proof system. Axiom and rule numbers refer to the numbering system used in [Ost89b].

1. The *general* layer includes the axioms and rules for reasoning about uninterpreted temporal formulas, i.e. formulas that are satisfied in any interpretation. For example, axiom A10 is $(w_1 \mathcal{U} w_2) \rightarrow \Diamond w_2$. Rule R2 (also called $\Box I$) is as follows: from the premise w you can derive $\Box w$. The rule R2 holds for the set of legal trajectories of a TTM because the set of legal trajectories is suffix closed, i.e. all suffixes of legal trajectories are also legal trajectories.

   Whenever this type of reasoning is used in the paper, we will refer to it as *temporal reasoning*. It may use of any of the the axioms A1 to A17, any of the rules R1 to R3, any of the theorems T1 to T78, and any of the derived rules D1 to D37. The general laws of propositional or sentential logic (SL), and the predicate calculus (PL) are included in this layer.

2. The *domain* layer characterizes the properties of the domains (or types) over which the activity and data variables range. The domain part includes:

   - Axiomatic characterizations of integers, sets, lists, trees etc.
   - Induction schemes over well-founded domains so as to do inductive proofs. A typical inductive scheme is $\dfrac{\phi(n+1) \rightarrow \Diamond\phi(n)}{\phi(n) \rightarrow \Diamond\phi(0)}$

   While the general layer allows us to establish the validity of uninterpreted temporal formulas, the combination of general and domain layers extends this ability to deal also with interpreted temporal formulas. Nevertheless, the validity considered is over arbitrary interpreted sequences of states.

   We will not need to do very complicated reasoning about the domains (or types) of TTMs. For example, consider the following property of the clock variable t (where *type*(t) is the natural numbers union with infinity):

   $$(\forall T_1 : t < T_1 \leftrightarrow (\exists T_2 : (t = T_1 - T_2) \wedge (T_2 \neq 0))\ ) \qquad (2)$$

   Clearly (2) is valid for the domain of t.

   Rather than include the Peano axioms for natural numbers, we shall simply introduce properties such as (2) with the justification (DA), which stands for *Domain Axiom*. We always quantify all the free variables of properties introduced with DA.

The constraint logic programming theorem prover referred to in the body of the paper is used to do the above domain reasoning automatically over the types treated by the underlying constraint logic program.

3. The *real-time* layer introduces axioms and rules which restrict the set of trajectories to the set of legal trajectories of a TTM. The real-time layer allows for the establishment of temporal properties that are not valid in arbitrary interpretations, but just over those interpretations associated with the behaviour of the particular TTM under consideration.

   This layer, provided in the rest of this appendix, includes the additional axioms A20 to A22, the rules R4 to R8 and some derived rules, e.g. DR1 to DR10. Some of the axioms and rules have alternative names, e.g. A20 is the transition axiom TA.

A.1 Axioms and Rules of RTTL

The INIT rule follows from the initialization requirement of legal trajectories.

R4 - **INIT** Initialization Rule

$$\frac{\Theta \to \Box w}{\Box w}$$

The transition axiom TA (or Axiom 20) is frequently used to prove the premises of other rules. It follows from the succession requirement of legal trajectories.

(A20) **TA**—Transition Axiom

Let $\tau \in \mathcal{T}$ be any transition with enabling condition e. Let ψ be any state-formula not containing any occurrences of the next-transition variable n. Then

(a) $(\mathrm{n} = \tau) \to e$

(b) $\{\psi^{\tau}\}\tau\{\psi\}$

The real-time clock axiom follows from the ticking requirement of legal trajectories.

(A21) **RT** - Real-time clock axiom

$$\Box\Diamond(\mathrm{n} = tick)$$

The real-time response rule follows from the upper time bound requirement of legal trajectories.

(R6) **RR** - *Rule of real-time Response*

Let $\mathcal{T}$ consist of the disjoint union

$$\{\tau\} \cup \mathcal{T}_{selfloop} \cup \mathcal{T}_{exiting}$$

where τ has enabling condition e and finite upper time bound u. For any φ_1 and $\varphi_2 \overset{\text{def}}{=} \varphi_1 \wedge (\mathrm{n} = \tau \vee \mathrm{n} \in \mathcal{T}_{exiting})$

$$\begin{array}{l} (1)\ \varphi_1 \rightarrow e \\ (2)\ \{\varphi_1\}\mathcal{T}_{selfloop}\{\varphi_1\} \\ \hline \varphi_1 \rightarrow (\varphi_1 \wedge e_\tau)\mathcal{U}_{\leq u}\varphi_2 \end{array}$$

In RR, τ is called a *progress edge* for φ_1 because it guarantees that φ_1 must be exited either via τ, or via an exiting transition.

The delay rule RD follows from the lower time bound requirement of legal trajectories.

(R7) **RD** - *Rule for Delay*

Let $\tau \in \mathcal{T}$ have enabling condition e and lower time bound l. Then, for any φ_0 and φ_1:

$$\begin{array}{l} (1)\ \varphi_0 \rightarrow ((\neg e \vee \mathrm{n} = \tau) \wedge \bigcirc \varphi_1) \\ (2)\ \varphi_1 \rightarrow e \\ \hline \varphi_0 \rightarrow \bigcirc(\mathrm{n} \neq \tau \mathcal{U}_{\geq l} \mathit{true}) \end{array}$$

The hypotheses of RD apply to those states that are choicepoints, and from which the time bounds may thus be measured.

The next rule RDTT is new. RDTT uses the time bounds to deduce that a (possibly enabled) transition τ_l will not occur because there is some other transition τ_u that will always occur first. The transition τ_u is an example of a "progress edge" — progress edges will be explained further in the next section where they are used in forcing certain kinds of behaviour. This rule can be derived from RR and RD.

RDTT — *Rule of Disablement by Time Bounds*

Let τ_l and τ_u be transitions in $\mathcal{T}$ with enabling conditions e_l and e_u (respectively), and τ_l has a lower bound $l > u$ where u is the upper bound of τ_u. Let ψ_1 and ψ_2 be any two inconsistent state-formulas, i.e. $\psi_1 \wedge \psi_2 \rightarrow$ *false*. Then

$$\frac{\begin{array}{l}\{\neg\psi_1 \wedge \neg\psi_2\}\mathcal{T}\{\neg\psi_2\}\\ \psi_1 \rightarrow (\neg e_l \wedge \bigcirc\psi_2)\\ \psi_2 \rightarrow e_u\\ \{\psi_2\}\tau_u\{\neg\psi_2\}\end{array}}{(\neg\psi_2) \rightarrow \Box(\psi_2 \rightarrow \mathrm{n} \neq \tau_l)}$$

A.2 Derived Rules of RTTL

The rules in this section follow from the axioms and rules of RTTL. A typical proof of a derived rule is provided for the first derived rule DR1.

DR1

Let $\mathcal{T}' \subseteq \mathcal{T}$, and let ψ_2 not contain any occurrences of n. Then

$$\frac{\psi_1 \wedge e_\tau \rightarrow \psi_2^\tau \;\text{ for each } \tau \in \mathcal{T}'}{\mathrm{n} \in \mathcal{T}' \rightarrow (\psi_1 \rightarrow \bigcirc\psi_2)}$$

Proof: For any $\tau \in \mathcal{T}'$, we have by hypothesis that

(1)	$\psi_1 \wedge e_\tau \rightarrow \psi_2^\tau$	hypothesis
(2)	$\mathrm{n} = \tau \wedge \psi_1 \wedge e_\tau \rightarrow \mathrm{n} = \tau \wedge \psi_2^\tau$	1,PR
(3)	$\mathrm{n} = \tau \wedge \psi_2^\tau \rightarrow \bigcirc\psi_2$	TA
(4)	$\mathrm{n} = \tau \wedge \psi_1 \wedge e_\tau \rightarrow \bigcirc\psi_2$	2,3,PR
(5)	$\mathrm{n} = \tau \rightarrow e_\tau$	TA
(6)	$\mathrm{n} = \tau \wedge \psi_1 \rightarrow \bigcirc\psi_2$	4,5,PR

Since (6) is true for any $\tau \in \mathcal{T}'$, it therefore follows by propositional reasoning that
(7) $\mathrm{n} \in \mathcal{T}' \rightarrow (\psi_1 \rightarrow \bigcirc\psi_2)$

The conclusion of DR1 contains the *next* temporal operator. The premise, however, requires no temporal reasoning. Thus, the premise should be provable from ordinary predicate calculus (including domain reasoning DA).

The following rule shows how any premise such as $\{\psi_1\}\mathcal{T}\{\psi_2\}$ can be deduced from predicate calculus (and DA).

DR2

Let $\mathcal{T}' \subseteq \mathcal{T}$, and let ψ_2 not contain any occurrence of **n**. Then

$$\frac{\psi_1 \wedge e_\tau \rightarrow \psi_2^\tau \quad \text{for any } \tau \in \mathcal{T}'}{\{\psi_1\}\mathcal{T}'\{\psi_2\}}$$

DR3

Let ψ_1 and ψ_2 be any two state formulas. Then

$$\frac{\{\psi_1\}\mathcal{T}\{\psi_2\}}{\psi_1 \rightarrow \bigcirc\psi_2}$$

The following rule DR4 may be used to verify some invariance properties. In many cases, the rules RR,RD and RDTT must be used in conjunction with DR4.

DR4

Let ψ_1 and ψ_2 be any two state-formulas. Then

$$\frac{\begin{array}{l}\psi_1 \rightarrow \psi_2 \\ \{\psi_1\}\mathcal{T}\{\psi_1\}\end{array}}{\psi_1 \rightarrow \Box\psi_2}$$

The next rule DR5 follows trivially from DR4, INIT and temporal reasoning.

DR5

Let ψ and I be any state-formulas. Then

$$\frac{\begin{array}{l}\Theta \rightarrow \psi \\ \psi \rightarrow I \\ \{\psi\}\mathcal{T}\{\psi\}\end{array}}{\Box I}$$

The next rule DR5' is a variation of DR5

DR5'

Let ψ and I be any state-formulas satisfying $\psi = \psi_1 \vee \psi_2 \vee \cdots \vee \psi_i \vee \cdots \psi_n$. Then

$$\frac{\begin{array}{ll}\Theta \rightarrow \psi & \\ \psi_i \rightarrow I & \text{for each } i \\ \{\psi_i\}\mathcal{T}\{\psi\} & \text{for each } i\end{array}}{\Box I}$$

The rules DR6 and DR7 have to do with proving *unless* and *precedence* properties and are omitted here.

The next rule expresses an intuitively obvious property. If it takes no longer than d_1 ticks to get from a state satisfying w_1 to one satisfying w_2, and from w_2 it takes no longer than d_2 ticks to get to a state satisfying w_3, then it takes no longer than $d_1 + d_2$ to get from w_1 to w_3. The proof is lengthy.

DR8

Let w_1, w_2 and w_3 be any temporal formulas, and let d_1 and d_2 be any constants of $type(t)$. Then

$$\frac{\begin{array}{l} w_1 \rightarrow \Diamond_{\leq d_1} w_2 \\ w_2 \rightarrow \Diamond_{\leq d_2} w_3 \end{array}}{w_1 \rightarrow \Diamond_{\leq d_1 + d_2} w_3}$$

Other more complex properties may be derived using the above type of reasoning. For example, a rule stating that if it takes at least d_1 ticks to get from w_1 to w_2, and at least d_2 ticks to get from w_2 to w_3, then it takes at least $d_1 + d_2$ ticks to go from w_1 to w_3, so long as no trajectory goes through w_3 on the way from w_1 to w_2. This type of rule would use the *until* operator to disallow the occurrence of w_3 on the way from w_1 to w_2.

The following rule comes from Manna-Pnueli theory (where it is often called a CHAIN rule):

DR9 — CHAIN

Let $\psi \stackrel{\text{def}}{=} \psi_0 \vee \ldots \vee \psi_k$, let $\psi_{<i} \stackrel{\text{def}}{=} \psi_{i-1} \vee \ldots \vee \psi_0$, and let $\psi_{1..k} \stackrel{\text{def}}{=} \psi_1 \vee \ldots \vee \psi_k$. Then

$$\frac{\text{For all } i = 1, \ldots, k\text{:} \;\; \psi_i \rightarrow (\psi_i \mathcal{U} \psi_{<i})}{\psi \rightarrow (\psi_{1..k} \mathcal{U} \psi_0)}$$

The rule also implies the weaker consequence $\psi \rightarrow \Diamond\psi_0$.

The rule considers a finite sequence of state-formulas, and assumes that for each state-formula ψ_i, a lemma has already been proved stating that if ψ_i becomes true it remains true until the trajectory reaches a state which satisfies some ψ_j where $j < i$, i.e. ψ_j is of lower rank in the sequence of state-formulas. Usually, each such lemma is proved by one application of JUST (a *justice* rule of Manna-Pnueli logic) or RR. The conclusion of CHAIN states that if any of the ψ_i (where $i = 0...k$) ever holds, then some ψ_j (where $j = 1...k$) will hold until ψ_0 is established.

Using induction on k and reasoning similar to R8 for the base case we obtain:

DR10 — TCHAIN

Let $\psi \stackrel{\text{def}}{=} \psi_0 \vee ... \vee \psi_k$, let $\phi_{i-1} \stackrel{\text{def}}{=} \psi_{i-1} \vee ... \vee \psi_0$, and let $\phi \stackrel{\text{def}}{=} \psi_1 \vee ... \vee \psi_k$. Let $d = d_1 + ... + d_k$. Then

$$\frac{\text{For all } i = 1, \cdots, k\text{:} \quad \psi_i \rightarrow (\psi_i \mathcal{U}_{\leq d_i} \phi_{i-1})}{\psi \rightarrow (\phi \mathcal{U}_{\leq d} \psi_0)}$$

The above rule also implies the weaker consequence $\psi \rightarrow \Diamond_{\leq d}\psi_0$.

TCHAIN is like CHAIN except that each one-step lemma can be proved with a real-time bound, i.e. at each step progress is made towards ψ_0 within some upper time bound. The consequence is that ψ_0 is reached within a time bounded by the sum of all the one-step bounds.

A.3 Partial weakest/strongest preconditions

Definition 1 (partial weakest precondition) *The* partial weakest precondition *of the transition τ with respect to a postcondition ψ (written: $pwp(\tau, \psi)$) is defined as*

$$pwp(\tau, \psi) \stackrel{\text{def}}{=} e_\tau \wedge \psi^\tau$$

where e_τ is the enabling condition of τ.

The partial weakest precondition represents the set of all states, such that τ is enabled, and the occurrence of τ in any one of them will result in the next state satisfying the postcondition ψ. We may therefore think of TA as an extension of the notion of a weakest precondition from a sequential to a distributed environment. Although τ is enabled in a state satisfying $pwp(\tau, \psi)$, there is no guarantee that τ will occur in that state. Thus, weakest preconditions deal with total correctness whereas *partial weakest preconditions* deal only with *partial correctness.*

For example, consider the clock transition

$$\tau = (tick, true, [t : t+1], -, -)$$

Suppose we wish to know what the weakest precondition is to achieve a postcondition ψ given by $(t = 10)$. In other words, what must the clock face read so that on making a transition the time will be 10 ticks? For the *tick* transition we obtain

$$\begin{aligned} pwp(tick, t = 10) &\equiv true \wedge \psi^{t}_{t+1} \\ &\equiv (t = 10)^{t}_{t+1} \\ &\equiv (t+1) = 10 \\ &\equiv (t = 9) \end{aligned}$$

Therefore the partial weakest precondition is that the time should be 9 ticks, as would obviously be expected. The partial weakest precondition thus captures in an intuitively appealing fashion the operational semantic requirement that the transition τ has no global side effects, i.e. τ changes only those variables that are involved in the transition. If we did not use this notation or its equivalent, then we would be forced to add to TA an extra condition stating that there are no unwanted side effects.

Definition 2 (partial strongest postcondition) *Let τ be a transition with transformation function $h = [v_1 : a_1, ..., v_k : a_k]$. The* partial strongest postcondition *of τ leading from φ is defined as*

$$psp(\tau, \varphi) \stackrel{\text{def}}{=} (\exists V_1)...(\exists V_k)(\varphi^{v_1,...,v_k}_{V_1,...,V_k} \wedge v_1 = (a_1)^{v_1,...,v_k}_{V_1,...,V_k} \wedge .... \wedge v_k = (a_k)^{v_1,...,v_k}_{V_1,...,V_k})$$

As an example, for the *tick* transition

$$\begin{aligned} psp(tick, t = 9) &\equiv (\exists T : (t = 9)^{t}_{T} \wedge t = (t+1)^{t}_{T}) \\ &\equiv (\exists T : T = 9 \wedge t = T + 1) \\ &\equiv (t = 10) \end{aligned}$$

as expected.

Part 1 of the following proposition follows directly from TA, and part 2 can be demonstrated in the same fashion as a similar theorem about strongest postconditions in [Gri85]. Any individual application of the proposition can be checked if necessary with TA.

Proposition 1 *For any transition τ and state-formulas φ and ψ*

1. $\{pwp(\tau, \psi)\}\tau\{\psi\}$
2. $\{\varphi\}\tau\{psp(\tau, \varphi)\}$

Predicative Specification of Timed Processes

Michael Schenke*

Universität Oldenburg
Fachbereich Informatik
Ammerländer Heerstr. 114-118
2900 Oldenburg
Germany

Abstract

We present a model for the specification of time restrictions in communicating systems that is based on predicates. The model fits for continuous and discrete time domains, but we fix our attention to the non-negative reals. It is possible to express delays, timed interrupts and the requirement that a process should finish within a given time by means of operators on specifications. Some propositions about such operators are proven. Several examples, how to specify given processes, show the capability of the approach.

1 Introduction

In this paper we present and analyse a simple specification language which reflects those parts of the ProCoS project[1] which deal with the specification of time restrictions in communicating systems.

A timed process engages in certain events in certain moments of time. Mathematically, it is modelled as a set of timed traces, i.e. of finite sequences of time-stamped events. As time domain we consider here the non-negative reals, but our approach would also work for other dense or discrete time domains.

We propose to specify timed processes by a combination of regular expressions over untimed events and time predicates expressing time constraints for the events. Time predicates are drawn from a many-sorted predicate logic with the time domain as one of its sorts. This logic is similar to the first order *real time logic* (RTL) introduced in [JM86]. In their logic one can reason about actions, events (e.g. beginning and end of an action) by state predicates and timing constraints. Their central idea is the introduction of an occurence function that for a given event e and a natural number i delivers the time of the i-th occurence of e. In our formalism it is possible to refer to i-th occurences of elements from *sets* of events. This sometimes yields simpler predicates. The propositions proved here are not mentioned in [JM86], although for accordingly defined operators they are probably true also in original RTL, but the authors' interest is different.

The motivation for combining time predicates with regular expressions comes from ProCoS, where a specification language SL_0 for the specification of untimed communicating processes has been developed. SL_0-specifications roughly consist of a trace part, where regular expressions

*Phone: +49-441-798-3133 E-mail: Schenke@arbi.informatik.uni-oldenburg.de Fax: +49-441-798-2155

[1] ProCoS is an ESPRIT BRA project that covers all steps in the development of provably correct systems from a formal requirements' capture down to the implementation with help of a verified compiler.

state sequencing constraints on communicating channels, and of a state part, where so-called communication assertions describe the value and effect of a communication along these channels. This specification format facilitated the stepwise design of communicating programs from SL_0-specifications. For SL_0 syntax and informal semantics cf. [RS91],[Old91].

Our paper is intended to extend the SL_0-specification format to include continuous real time. For simplicity we ignore here the state part and thus arrive at a specification language, where the trace part of SL_0 is augmented by time predicates.

In a previous paper ([Sch91]) we have presented a purely algebraic approach, how to extend SL_0 by a notion of discrete time similar to [NS90]. During the generalisation of this algebraic approach to continuous time we realised difficulties in developing an expansion theorem and in completeness questions, what seems to be a general problem, as is also pointed out for instance in [NS91] and in [MT90], respectively. This brought us to consider the present abstract description of real time constraints using predicates, what fits together with the fact that SL_0 is provided with a predicative semantics.

Some results from [Sch91] can be confirmed also in the present model, for instance the results on start delay and execution delay operators, can be reformulated and proven much more elegantly. Another major problem in [Sch91], the question, how to put processes in parallel, can be solved here more easily. Also some laws of the ProCoS programming language PL^{time} ([HeJ90]) are proven for the specification language. Some examples demonstrate the usefulness of the approach.

A further comparison with related work can be found in a separate section near the end of the paper.

2 The Time Predicate Model

2.1 Modelling timed processes

In the whole paper let $(a \in) A$ be an alphabet of events and $\overline{R}$ the set of non-negative reals.

Definition: Let $\bot \notin A$.
1. $TimEv =_{df} \{(a,r) \mid a \in A, r \in \overline{R}\} \cup \{\bot\}$, the set of *timed events*.
2. $TimTrac =_{df} \{(a_1,r_1)...(a_m,r_m) \mid m \geq 0,\ a_i \in A, r_i \in \overline{R},\ r_i \leq r_{i+1},\ a_i = a_j \rightarrow r_i \neq r_j\} \cup \{\bot\}$, the set of certain finite sequences of $TimEv$, called *timed traces*.
3. $Proc =_{df} \wp(TimTrac)$, the set of *(timed) processes*.

Mathematically, this definition means that a timed process is modelled as a set of timed traces, i.e. of finite sequences of time-stamped events as in [BB90],[JM86].

Definition:
Let $t = (a,r) \in TimEv$, $tt_1 = (a_1,r_1)...(a_m,r_m)$, $tt_2 = (b_1,s_1)...(b_n,s_n) \in TimTrac$. Then let
1. $ev(t) =_{df} a$, the *event of t*.
2. $tim(t) =_{df} r$, the *time of t* or the *time-stamp of t*.
3. $trac(tt_1) =_{df} a_1...a_m$, the *trace of* tt_1.
4. *Concatenation:* $tt_1.tt_2 =_{df} (a_1,r_1)...(a_m,r_m).(b_1,s_1)...(b_n,s_n)$,
   if $r_i \leq s_j$ and furthermore $a_i = b_j \rightarrow r_i < s_j$, and equal to $\bot$ else.
   $tt_1.\bot =_{df} \bot.tt_1 =_{df} \bot$.

2.2 A predicate logic for timed processes

The logic model we are going to use is a many sorted predicate logic with the following sorts and operator symbols:

A ,the basic alphabet,
R ,the real numbers,
$TimEv$,the set of timed events,
$TimTrac$,the set of timed traces,
$Reg(A)$,the regular expressions over A,
log , the logical values and

$tim : TimEv \rightarrow R,\ ev : TimEv \rightarrow A.$

Letters a, r will appear as constants of sorts A, R. The set of variables contains variables t of sort $TimEv$ and tr of sort $TimTrac$. The syntacs is given by the sets of

$ae ::= a \mid ev(te)$, the set of alphabet expressions,
$re ::= r \mid re_1 + re_2 \mid tim(te)$, the set of real number expressions,
$te ::= (ae, re) \mid t$, the set of timed event expressions,
$tte ::= te \mid tte_1.tte_2 \mid tr$, the set of timed trace expressions,
$reg ::= \varepsilon \mid a \mid reg_1 + reg_2 \mid reg_1.reg_2 \mid (reg_1)^*$, the set of regular expressions,
$le ::= true \mid re_1 = re_2 \mid re_1 < re_2 \mid te \in tte \mid tte \in reg \mid ae_1 = ae_2 \mid \neg le_1 \mid le_1 \wedge le_2 \mid \exists r.le \mid \exists a.le$
, the set of logical expressions.

The *semantics of the logic model* is given in the usual way by means of "environments" ρ, mappings that assign values to free variables in expressions. It is

$\mathcal{I}[\![tte_1.tte_2]\!](\rho) = \mathcal{I}[\![tte_1]\!](\rho).\mathcal{I}[\![tte_2]\!](\rho)$, with the concatenation on $TimTrac$,
$\mathcal{I}[\![te \in tte]\!](\rho) = \exists tr_1, tr_2 : \mathcal{I}[\![tte]\!](\rho) = \mathcal{I}[\![tr_1]\!](\rho).\mathcal{I}[\![te]\!](\rho).\mathcal{I}[\![tr_2]\!](\rho)$,
$\mathcal{I}[\![tte \in reg]\!](\rho) = trac(\mathcal{I}[\![tte]\!](\rho)) \in \mathcal{L}[\![\mathcal{I}[\![reg]\!](\rho)]\!]$.

$\mathcal{L}[\![reg]\!]$ allways means the regular language denoted by reg. All other interpretations are standard or self-explanatory.

Definition: 1. A *time predicate* tp is a logical expression of the form $ev(t) = a \rightarrow le$, where t is a free variable of sort $TimEv$ and le contains at most t as a free variable and a free variable tr of sort $TimTrac$.
2. The satisfaction relation between a timed trace tt and a time predicate $tp(tr, t)$ is defined by

$$tt \vdash tp \longleftrightarrow_{df} \forall te \in tt : tp(tt, te).$$

3. The variables t and tr are dropped henceforth in time predicates.

2.3 Specification language

Time predicates will be used in specifications of the following form

Definition: 1. Given an alphabet A of events, a *specification* is a set $((re_1, G_1), ..., (re_m, G_m), tp_1, ..., tp_n)$ with subsets G_i of A, regular expressions re_i over G_i and time predicates tp_j.
2. The pairs (re_i, G_i) are called *trace assertions*.

3. Let *Spec* denote the set of all specifications.

This is, apart from the time predicates, a simplified form of an SL_0-specification. The trace assertions retain, exactly as in SL_0, the sequencing constraints on communicating channels, whereas the state part, where the value and effect of a communication along these channels is described, has been dropped. The following definition is compatible with the semantics of the untimed version of SL_0, [Old90].

Definition: The *semantics of a specification* is given by $\mathcal{S}[\![((re_1, G_1), ..., (re_m, G_m), tp_1, ..., tp_n)]\!]$ $=_{df} \{tt \in TimTrac \mid \forall i : trac(tt) \downarrow G_i \in \mathcal{L}[\![re_i]\!] \wedge \forall j : tt \vdash tp_j\}$.

Here " $\downarrow G_i$" denotes the projection to G_i.
Note that an assumption of an (arbitrarily small) duration is hidden here:

Example: 1. It is $\mathcal{S}[\![((a^*b, \{a,b\}), ev \in \{a,b\} \rightarrow tim = 0)]\!] = \{(b,0), (a,0).(b,0)\}$.
The result is reasonable, because we do not want to rule out the possibility of a and b happening at the same time. This may occur on a multi-processor. But there is some duration of a and thus at a certain moment at most one a can happen but not more than one, because then synchronisation between them would become necessary.
2. For each $\delta > 0$ it is $\mathcal{S}[\![((a^*b, \{a,b\}), ev \in \{a,b\} \rightarrow tim < \delta)]\!] =$

$$\{(a,t_1)...(a,t_m).(b,t) \mid m \geq 0,\ 0 \leq t_1 < ... < t_m \leq t < \delta\}.$$

The duration of a is arbitrarily small. This means we can also specify *Zeno behaviours*, i.e. the possibility of arbitrarily many events ocurring in finite time. How it is possible to attach explicit durations to the events (and in particular rule out Zeno behaviours, if this is wanted,) will be shown in a later example (sect.3.3).

2.4 Derived operators

In the following we fix up several useful operators.
Operators like $\vee$, $\forall$, $\exists te$, $<$, $>$, $\geq$ are defined as usual or are self-explanatory, as well as $a \in M$ for $M \subseteq A$. Furthermore let

$before(tt, te, te') \Longleftrightarrow \exists tt_1, tt_2 : tt = tt_1.tt_2 \wedge te \in tt_1 \wedge te' \in tt_2$,
stating that te is prior to te' in tt,

$prec_M(tt, te) = te'$, if $te' \in tt \wedge ev(te') \in M \wedge before(tt, te', te)$ $\wedge \forall a \in M\, \forall r : before(tt, (a,r), te) \rightarrow (a,r) = te' \vee before(tt, (a,r), te')$,
$\perp$ else,
chosing the last element of tt with event in M before te,

$exprec_M(tt, te) \Longleftrightarrow \exists te' : te' = prec_M(tt, te) \wedge te' \neq \perp$,
deciding, whether te is preceded by an element from M,

$pos_M(tt, te) =$ 0, if $\neg exprec_M(tt, te) \wedge ev(te) \notin M$,
1, if $\neg exprec_M(tt, te) \wedge ev(te) \in M$,
$pos_M(tt, prec_M(tt, te))$, if $exprec_M(tt, te) \wedge ev(te) \notin M$,
$1 + pos_M(tt, prec_M(tt, te))$, if $exprec_M(tt, te) \wedge ev(te) \in M$,
counting the elements from M in tt not after te (position),

$occtim_M(tt, i) = tim(te)$, for $pos_M(tt, te) = i \wedge ev(te) \in M$,
denoting the time of the i-th occurence of an event from M in tt,

(This is a generalisation of the occurence function in [JM86].)

$succ_M(tt,te) \;=\; te'$, if $te' \in tt \wedge ev(te') \in M \wedge before(tt,te,te')$,
$\wedge \forall a \in M\, \forall r : before(tt,(a,r),te') \rightarrow (a,r) = te \vee before(tt,(a,r),te)$,
$\perp$ else,
denoting the next element from M in tt after te,

$timprec_M(tt,te) = tim(prec_M(tt,te))$, if $exprec_M(tt,te)$,
0 else,

$timsucc_M(tt,te) = tim(succ_M(tt,te))$, if $\exists te' : te' = succ_M(tt,te)$,
∞ else,

$first_M(tt) \;=\; te$, if $ev(te) \in M \wedge pos_M(tt,te) = 1$,
delineating the first event from M in tt,

$timfirst_M(tt) \;=\; tim(first_M(tt))$,

$last_M(tt) \;=\; te$, if $ev(te) \in M \wedge \forall te' : te' \in tt \rightarrow pos_M(tt,te') \leq pos_M(tt,te)$,
delineating the last event from M in tt,

$timlast_M(tt) \;=\; tim(last_M(tt))$,

$isnat(r) \iff r = 1 \vee (r > 1 \wedge isnat(r-1))$,
stating that r is a natural number.

Finally let for tp, possibly with free variables tr and t and for expressions tt and te of sorts $TimTrac$ and $TimEv$, the predicate $tp[tr := tt, t := te]$ be defined as that predicate that derives from tp by replacing tr by tt and t by te. The indices M will be dropped for $M = A$.

3 Examples

In order to illustrate the power of the present model we give some examples, how to specify timed systems.

3.1 Clocks

We shall specify the three clocks that have been described in [BB90].

1.) A clock that, when started at time 0, ticks with absolute precision, whenever one time unit elapses, can be specified by

$$Spec = ((tick^*, \{tick\}), ev = tick \rightarrow isnat(tim)).$$

2.) The second clock allows fluctuations of size δ of the ticks:

$$Spec = ((tick^*, \{tick\}), ev = tick \rightarrow \exists \varepsilon : |\varepsilon| \leq \delta \wedge isnat(tim + \varepsilon)).$$

3.) The third clock cumulates the errors:

$$Spec = ((tick^*, \{tick\}), ev = tick \rightarrow \exists \varepsilon : |\varepsilon| \leq \delta \wedge tim - timprec = 1 + \varepsilon).$$

3.2 Exponential Growth

As an example for exponential growth we shall specify the accumulation of money on an account by a fixed interest rate. Given a certain amount of start capital an event *grow* is assumed to happen, whenever the size of acumulated capital has increased by one unit.

$$Spec_c = ((grow^*, \{grow\}), ev = grow \rightarrow pos_{grow} = c^{tim}).$$

The speed of growth depends on the parameter c, which itself depends on the interest rate.

3.3 Duration of actions

By the semantic definition which interprets events as elements of $TimEv$ it is implicitely stated that actions have an infinitely small duration. Assuming that all processes run on the same processor, it is possible to specify that each action needs a fixed time.
Let $dur : A \rightarrow \overline{R}$ define the duration of an event and $((re_1, G_1), ..., (re_m, G_m), tp_1, ..., tp_n)$ be a specification. For each $a \in A$ then let tp_a be the predicate

$$ev = a \rightarrow timsucc_A - tim \geq dur(a).$$

Then $((re_1, G_1), ..., (re_m, G_m), tp_1, ..., tp_n, tp_a, ...)$, where $tp_a, ...$ stands for all tp_a with $a \in A$, specifies the same process with attributed duration, provided it runs on one processor.

3.4 A login procedure

We present our version of the login procedure from [NS90],[NSY91]:
To start the procedure L, the system sends a login prompt $prompt$. After this event, the user has l time units to enter a valid login response val to successfully finish the task and to start a session phase $Sess$. When the user supplies an invalid response $nonval$, or when time l elapsed, a new login procedure is started.
The first observation is that the untimed behaviour is a solution of

$$L = prompt.(val.Sess + nonval.L + L),$$

of which the minimal solution is

$$L = (prompt.(nonval + \varepsilon))^{*}prompt.val.Sess.$$

We assume that $I =_{df} \{prompt, val, nonval\}$ and the alphabet of events ocurring during the session are disjunct. Then the specification

$$Log = (((prompt.(nonval + \varepsilon))^{*}prompt.val, I)\, TP)$$

specifies the login procedure, where TP consists of the following predicates:

$$\begin{array}{ll}
ev = val & \rightarrow tim - timpred_{prompt} < l, \\
ev = nonval & \rightarrow tim - timpred_{prompt} < l, \\
ev = prompt \wedge pos_{prompt} = 1 & \rightarrow tim = 0, \\
ev = prompt \wedge pos_{prompt} > 1 & \rightarrow tim - timpred_{prompt} < l \wedge pred_I \in \{nonnval, val\} \vee, \\
 & tim - timpred_{prompt} = l \wedge pred_I \in \{prompt, val\} \vee, \\
 & tim - timpred_{prompt} > l \wedge pred_I = val.
\end{array}$$

This example will be extended in the same way as in [NSY91] after the introduction of execution delay operators.

4 Operators on Processes and Specifications

In order to ease the use of the specification language and to show, what can be expressed in the time predicate model, operators for standard situations are introduced.

4.1 Normal Delay

Definition: Let r be a real number and $t \in TimEv$. Then let
$(tim - r)(t) =_{df} tim(t) - r$.

Definition: Let r be a real number (possibly negative), $tt = \{(a_1, r_1)...(a_m, r_m)\} \in TimTrac$, $proc \in Proc$, tp a time predicate and $spec = ((re_1, G_1), ..., (re_m, G_m), tp_1, ..., tp_n) \in Spec$.
The *delay operator* is defined by

1. $\Delta_r(tt) =_{df} \{(a_1, r_1 + r)...(a_m, r_m + r)\}$,
2. $\Delta_r(proc) =_{df} \{\Delta_r(tt) \mid tt \in proc\}$,
3. $\Delta_r(tp) =_{df} tp[tim := tim - r]$,
4. $\Delta_r(spec) =_{df} ((re_1, G_1), ..., (re_m, G_m), \Delta_r(tp_1), ..., \Delta_r(tp_n))$.

Remark: It is $\Delta_r \circ \Delta_s = \Delta_{r+s}$ on all domains.

Lemma: It is $\mathcal{S}[\![\Delta_r(spec)]\!] = \Delta_r(\mathcal{S}[\![spec]\!])$.

The proof is a trival induction on the structure of the time predicates.

The just defined Δ_r can express an exact delay. This can be generalised to

Definition: Let r be a real number (possibly negative), $tt = \{(a_1, r_1)...(a_m, r_m)\} \in TimTrac$, $proc \in Proc$, tp a time predicate and $spec = ((re_1, G_1), ..., (re_m, G_m), tp_1, ..., tp_n) \in Spec$.

1. $\Delta_{\geq r}(tt) =_{df} \{(a_1, r_1 + s)...(a_m, r_m + s) \mid s \geq r\}$,
2. $\Delta_{\geq r}(proc) =_{df} \bigcup_{tt \in proc} \Delta_{\geq r}(tt)$,
3. $\Delta_{\geq r}(tp) =_{df} \exists s : s \geq r \wedge \Delta_s(tp)$,
4. $\Delta_{\geq r}(spec) =_{df} ((re_1, G_1), ..., (re_m, G_m), \Delta_{\geq r}(tp_1), ..., \Delta_{\geq r}(tp_n))$.

Strictly seen, the $\Delta_{\geq r}(tp)$ are no time predicates, since they lack an initial condition on the event. But they can easily be rewritten into a syntactically correct form by the equivalence of the logical formulae $\exists s : a \rightarrow b(s)$ and $a \rightarrow \exists s : b(s)$.

Lemma: It is $\mathcal{S}[\![\Delta_{\geq r}(spec)]\!] = \Delta_{\geq r}(\mathcal{S}[\![spec]\!])$.

Analogously operators like $\Delta_{\leq r}$ or $\Delta_{r \leq s}$ (for intervals) can be defined.

4.2 Alternatives

Definition: Let $proc_1, proc_2 \in Proc$ and
$spec_1 = ((x_1, G), ..., (x_m, G), u_1, ..., u_n)$, $spec_2 = ((y_1, G), ..., (y_k, G), v_1, ..., v_l) \in Spec$.
Then let

1. $proc_1 + proc_2 =_{df} proc_1 \cup proc_2$,
2. $spec_1 + spec_2 =_{df} (..., (x_i + y_j, G), ..., t_{i,j}, ..., w_{i,j}, ...)$,
with $t_{i,j} = trac \in x_i \rightarrow u_j$ and $w_{i,j} = trac \in y_i \rightarrow v_j$.

Again the $t_{i,j}, w_{i,j}$ are no time predicates, since they lack an initial condition on the event. They can be rewritten by the equivalence of the logical formulae $a \rightarrow (b \rightarrow c)$ and $b \rightarrow (a \rightarrow c)$.

Lemma: It is $\mathcal{S}[\![spec_1 + spec_2]\!] = \mathcal{S}[\![spec_1]\!] + \mathcal{S}[\![spec_2]\!]$.

The correctness of the lemma follows from the fact that, as far as the trace assertions are concerned, the left-hand side represents the conjunctive and the right-hand side the disjunctive normalform of the same set of languages. The correctness concerning the time predicates is obvious.

Note that the restriction on the trace assertions to have always the same second component is not as severe as it might seem. This is shown by the following

Lemma: Let $spec = ((re_1, G_1), ..., (re_m, G_m), tp_1, ..., tp_n) \in Spec$ and $a \in A \backslash G_i$ for an i. Then let $\overline{re}_i$ derive from re_i by replacing all events e appearing in re_i by a^*ea^* and let $\overline{spec}$ derive from $spec$ by replacing (re_i, G_i) by $(\overline{re}_i, G_i \cup \{a\})$. Then it is $\mathcal{S}[\![spec]\!] = \mathcal{S}[\![\overline{spec}]\!]$.

The lemma follows immediately from the semantics of specifications.

4.3 Parallelism

One major problem in the discrete case was to define a parallel operator, such that the semantics is the intersection of the operands' semantics, as it is the case in CSP [Hoa85]. This task is solved easily here:

Definition: Let $spec_1 = ((x_1, G_1), ..., (x_m, G_m), u_1, ..., u_n)$, $spec_2 = ((y_1, H_1), ..., (y_k, H_k), v_1, ..., v_l) \in Spec$. Then let $spec_1 \,||\, spec_2 =_{df} ((x_1, G_1), ..., (x_m, G_m), (y_1, H_1), ..., (y_k, H_k), u_1, ..., u_n, v_1, ..., v_l)$.

Lemma: Let $spec_1 = ((x_1, G_1), ..., (x_m, G_m), u_1, ..., u_n)$, $spec_2 = ((y_1, H_1), ..., (y_k, H_k), v_1, ..., v_l) \in Spec$. Then it is $\mathcal{S}[\![spec_1 \,||\, spec_2]\!] = \mathcal{S}[\![spec_1]\!] \cap \mathcal{S}[\![spec_2]\!]$.

For the regular expressions this is clear by definition, for the time predicates it follows from the fact that they contain a premise on the event and the derived operators are defined relative to events.
If, as in the discrete case, the existence of one trace assertion only is required, the methods developed for the untimed case ([RS91]) apply also here because of the strict separation of timed and untimed behaviour.

4.4 Start Delay, Immediate Start

The next we are going to define are analoga of the start delay and execution delay operators that have been repeatedly introduced, cf.[NS90],[HeJ90],[Sch91].

The start delay operators there have the form $\lfloor t \rfloor^n (e)$, where n is a natural number. The intuitive meaning is that $\lfloor t \rfloor^n (e)$ behaves as t, if an initial action of t occurs before the n-th occurrence of the time action. Otherwise it behaves as e (exception) after the n-th occurence of time. In our model we have the following

Definition: Let $\lfloor\rfloor : \overline{R} \times \overline{R} \times Proc \rightarrow Proc$ be defined by
$\lfloor\rfloor(r, s, proc) =_{df} \{\Delta_{-r}(tt) \mid tt \in proc \wedge r \leq timfirst(tt) < s\}$.
It will be written as $\lfloor proc\rfloor_r^s$.

Definition: The *start delay operator* is defined by
$\lfloor\rfloor() : \overline{R} \times \overline{R} \times Proc \times Proc \rightarrow Proc$
$\lfloor\rfloor()(r, s, proc_1, proc_2) =_{df} \lfloor proc_1\rfloor_r^s \cup \Delta_{s-r}(proc_2)$.
It will be written as $\lfloor proc_1\rfloor_r^s(proc_2)$.

The original definition of [NS90] would thus correspond to $\lfloor . \rfloor_0^r(..)$. We also need according operators that work on the syntactical level:

Definition: Let $\lfloor\rfloor : \overline{R} \times \overline{R} \times Spec \rightarrow Spec$ be defined by
$\lfloor\rfloor(r, s, spec) =_{df} \Delta_{-r}(spec')$,
where $spec'$ derives from $spec$ by adding the time predicate

$$ev \in A \rightarrow r \leq timfirst < s.$$

We shall write $\lfloor spec\rfloor_r^s$ for the result of the operator.

Definition: The *start delay operator* is defined by
$\lfloor\rfloor() : \overline{R} \times \overline{R} \times Spec \times Spec \rightarrow Spec$
$\lfloor\rfloor()(r, s, spec_1, spec_2) =_{df} \lfloor spec_1\rfloor_r^s + \Delta_{s-r}(spec_2)$.
It will be written as $\lfloor spec_1\rfloor_r^s(spec_2)$.

Lemma: It is $\mathcal{S}[\lfloor spec\rfloor_r^s] = \lfloor \mathcal{S}[spec]\rfloor_r^s$ and
$\mathcal{S}[\lfloor spec_1\rfloor_r^s(spec_2)] = \lfloor \mathcal{S}[spec_1]\rfloor_r^s(\mathcal{S}[spec_2])$.

The first part follows from the definition and the lemmas on delays. The second part follows from the first and the lemmas on addition and delays of specifications.
In order to model that a given process *proc* should start immediately or within certain time intervals, including upper, excluding lower bounds apply the accordingly defined operators $\lfloor\rfloor_{>r}^{\leq s}$ with appropriate time predicates. For them holds the same lemma.

4.5 Execution Delay , Finish within a Time

In [NS90],[HeJ90],[Sch91] timed interrupts are used to form "Execution Delay Operators", binary operations of the form $\lceil t\rceil^n(e)$, where n is a natural number. The intuitive meaning is that $\lceil t\rceil^n(e)$ for n time units behaves as t and as e after that. In our model it is again possible to define according constructs:

Definition: 1. For $tt \in TimTrac, r \in \overline{R}$ it is $\lceil tt\rceil^r =_{df} tt_1$
with $tt = tt_1.tt_2 \wedge timlast(tt_1) < r \wedge tt_1 \neq \varepsilon \wedge (timfirst(tt_2) \geq r \vee tt_2 = \varepsilon)$.
Else let $\lceil tt\rceil^r =_{df} \perp$.
2. For $proc \in Proc, r \in \overline{R}$ define
$\lceil\rceil : \overline{R} \times Proc \rightarrow Proc$
$\lceil\rceil(r, proc) =_{df} \{\lceil tt\rceil^r \mid tt \in proc, \lceil tt\rceil^r \neq \perp\}$.
This is written as $\lceil proc\rceil^r$.
3. For $proc_1, proc_2 \in Proc, r \in \overline{R}$ let the *execution delay operator* be defined by
$\lceil\rceil() : \overline{R} \times Proc \times Proc \rightarrow Proc$

$\lceil\rceil()(r, proc_1, proc_2) =_{df} \lceil proc_1\rceil^r \cup \Delta_r(proc_2)$.
This will be written as $\lceil proc_1\rceil^r(proc_2)$.

The according operators on specifications are

Definition: Let $\lceil\rceil : \overline{\mathcal{R}} \times Spec \rightarrow Spec$ be defined by
$\lceil\rceil(r, spec) =_{df} spec'$,
where $spec'$ derives from $spec$ by adding the time predicate

$ev \in A \rightarrow tim < r$.

We shall write $\lceil spec\rceil^r$ for the result of the operator.

Definition: The *execution delay operator* is defined by
$\lceil\rceil() : \overline{\mathcal{R}} \times Spec \times Spec \rightarrow Spec$
$\lceil\rceil()(r, spec_1, spec_2) =_{df} \lceil spec_1\rceil^r + \Delta_r(spec_2)$.
It will be written as $\lceil spec_1\rceil^r(spec_2)$.

Lemma: It is $\mathcal{S}[\![\lceil spec\rceil^r]\!] = \lceil\mathcal{S}[\![spec]\!]\rceil^r$ and
$\mathcal{S}[\![\lceil spec_1\rceil^r(spec_2)]\!] = \lceil\mathcal{S}[\![spec_1]\!]\rceil^r(\mathcal{S}[\![spec_2]\!])$.

Again the first part follows from the definitions and the second part from the first and the lemmas on addition and delays of specifications.

Example: Now we are able to extend the specification of the login procedure *Log* from 3.4 along the lines of [NSY91]:
Usual the system limits the overall duration of a login procedure to a maximum time of r units and forces an exception *Exc* to be carried out after that. We can model the whole process *CompLog* using the execution delay operator and interpreting the action *val* additionally as a cancel action in *Log* to quit when a successful response is provided. The complete procedure is described by

$$CompLog = \lceil Log\rceil^r(Exc).$$

□

The operators $\lceil\rceil^r$ are sufficient to specify that a process should stop after an amount of time. In order to specify that a given process *proc* should finish within an amount of time r, i.e. sort out those possible traces whose last time stamp is less than r, apply the following operators :

Definition: For $proc \in Proc, r \in \overline{\mathcal{R}}$ define
$|| : \overline{\mathcal{R}} \times Proc \rightarrow Proc$
$||(r, proc) =_{df} \{tt \mid tt \in proc \wedge timlast(proc) \leq r\}$.
This is written as $|proc|^r$.

Definition: Let $|| : \overline{\mathcal{R}} \times Spec \rightarrow Spec$ be defined by
$||(r, spec) =_{df} spec'$,
where $spec'$ derives from $spec$ by adding the time predicate

$ev \in A \rightarrow timlast \leq r$.

We shall write $|spec|^r$ for the result of the operator.

Again similar operators expressing strict bounds or that processes should last at least some time can be defined. Again the definitions are compatible considering the semantics.

5 Properties of the Operators

The purpose of this section is to prove analoga of the axioms for start delay and execution delay operators from [NS90],[Sch91], what are propositions 1-3 in this context, and some algebraic laws of [HeJ90], what are propositions 2-4, lemmas SD.1, ED.1,2 here. The other algebraic laws of [HeJ90] concerning time are either trivial in our model or not applicable, since the according operators of the programming language are not incorporated into our specification language.
By the compatibility lemmata we can restrict our attention to processes and get the according theorems about specifications for free.

5.1 Start delay

Lemma SD: For $proc, proc_1, proc_2 \in Proc$, $r, s, t \in \overline{R}$ it is
1. $\lfloor proc_1 \cup proc_2 \rfloor_r^s = \lfloor proc_1 \rfloor_r^s \cup \lfloor proc_2 \rfloor_r^s$,
2. $\lfloor proc \rfloor_r^s \cup \Delta_{s-r}(\lfloor proc \rfloor_s^t) = \lfloor proc \rfloor_r^t$,
3. $\lfloor \lfloor proc_1 \rfloor_0^s (proc_2) \rfloor_0^t = \lfloor proc_1 \rfloor_0^t$ for $t \leq s$,
4. $\lfloor \lfloor proc_1 \rfloor_0^s (proc_2) \rfloor_s^t = \lfloor proc_2 \rfloor_s^t$.

Proof: 1. is an immediate consequence of the definition.
2. $\lfloor proc \rfloor_r^s = \{\Delta_{-r}(tt) \mid tt \in proc \wedge r \leq timfirst(tt) < s\}$.
$\Delta_{s-r}(\lfloor proc \rfloor_s^t) = \{\Delta_{s-r}(\Delta_{-s}(tt)) \mid tt \in proc \wedge s \leq timfirst(tt) < t\}$.
Hence $\lfloor proc \rfloor_r^s \cup \Delta_{s-r}(\lfloor proc \rfloor_s^t) =$
$\{\Delta_{-r}(tt) \mid tt \in proc \wedge r \leq timfirst(tt) < s\} \cup \{\Delta_{-r}(tt) \mid tt \in proc \wedge s \leq timfirst(tt) < t\} =$
$\lfloor proc \rfloor_r^t$.
3. and 4. are an immediate consequence of the definition. □

Proposition1: It is $\lfloor proc_1 \rfloor_r^t (proc_2) = \lfloor proc_1 \rfloor_r^s (\lfloor proc_1 \rfloor_s^t (proc_2))$ for $r \leq s \leq t$.

Proof: It is $\lfloor proc_1 \rfloor_r^t (proc_2) = \lfloor proc_1 \rfloor_r^s \cup \Delta_{s-r}(\lfloor proc_1 \rfloor_s^t) \cup \Delta_{t-r}(proc_2) =$
$\lfloor proc_1 \rfloor_r^s \cup \Delta_{s-r}(\lfloor proc_1 \rfloor_s^t \cup \Delta_{t-s}(proc_2)) = \lfloor proc_1 \rfloor_r^s (\lfloor proc_1 \rfloor_s^t (proc_2))$ by part 2 of the lemma. □

Proposition2: It is $\lfloor proc_1 \rfloor_0^s (\lfloor proc_2 \rfloor_s^t (proc_3)) = \lfloor \lfloor proc_1 \rfloor_0^s (proc_2) \rfloor_0^t (proc_3)$.

Proof: It is $\lfloor proc_1 \rfloor_0^s (\lfloor proc_2 \rfloor_s^t (proc_3)) = \lfloor proc_1 \rfloor_0^s \cup \Delta_s(\lfloor proc_2 \rfloor_s^t \cup \Delta_{t-s}(proc_3)) =$
$\lfloor proc_1 \rfloor_0^s \cup \Delta_s(\lfloor proc_2 \rfloor_s^t) \cup \Delta_t(proc_3) =$
$\lfloor \lfloor proc_1 \rfloor_0^s (proc_2) \rfloor_0^s \cup \Delta_s(\lfloor \lfloor proc_1 \rfloor_0^s (proc_2) \rfloor_s^t) \cup \Delta_t(proc_3) = \lfloor \lfloor proc_1 \rfloor_0^s (proc_2) \rfloor_0^t (proc_3)$.
The last equation is due to part 2. the last but one due to parts 3. and 4. of the lemma. □

5.2 Execution delay

Let $s \dot{-} r =_{df} 0$ for $s < r$ and $s - r$ else.
Lemma ED: For $proc, proc_1, proc_2, proc_3 \in Proc$, $r, s \in \overline{R}$ it is
1. $\lceil proc_1 \cup proc_2 \rceil^r = \lceil proc_1 \rceil^r \cup \lceil proc_2 \rceil^r$,
2. $\lceil proc_1 \rceil^r (proc_2 \cup proc_3) = \lceil proc_1 \rceil^r (proc_2) \cup \lceil proc_1 \rceil^r (proc_3)$,
3. $\lceil \lceil proc_1 \rceil^r \rceil^s = \lceil proc_1 \rceil^{min(r,s)}$,

4. $\lceil proc_1 \rceil^0(proc_2) = proc_2$,
5. $\lceil \Delta_r(proc_1) \rceil^s = \Delta_r(\lceil proc_1 \rceil^{s \dot{-} r})$.

Proof: All statements are easy consequences of the definitions.

Proposition3: (Distributivity over start delay) It is
$\lceil \lfloor proc_1 \rfloor_0^s(proc_2) \rceil^t(proc_3) = \lfloor \lceil proc_1 \rceil^t(proc_3) \rfloor_0^s(\lceil proc_2 \rceil^{t-s}(proc_3))$.

Proof: Take $tt \in \lceil \lfloor proc_1 \rfloor_0^s(proc_2) \rceil^t(proc_3)$. Then it is

$$tt \in proc_1 \wedge timfirst(tt) < s \wedge timlast(tt) < t$$
$$\vee\ \exists tt' \in proc_2 : tt = \Delta_s(tt') \wedge timlast(tt) < t$$
$$\vee\ \exists tt" \in proc_3 : tt = \Delta_t(tt").$$

Hence it is $\quad tt \in \lfloor \lceil proc_1 \rceil^t \rfloor_0^s$

$$\vee\ \exists tt' \in \lceil proc_2 \rceil^{t-s} : tt = \Delta_s(tt')$$
$$\vee\ \exists tt" \in proc_3 : tt = \Delta_t(tt") \wedge timfirst(tt) < s$$
$$\vee\ \exists tt" \in proc_3 : tt = \Delta_s(\Delta_{t-s}(tt")).$$

This implies the right hand side. Bounded variables are named equally, if the same timed traces can be taken. The reverse direction is proven the same way. □

Proposition3 encompasses analoga to two axioms in [NS90]. A closer analogon to one of them is the following

Corollary: It is
$\lceil \lfloor proc_1 \rfloor_0^s(proc_2) \rceil^s(proc_3) = \lfloor \lceil proc_1 \rceil^s(proc_3) \rfloor_0^s(proc_3)$.

This is the special case $s = t$.

The next proposition shows how to unnest execution delays and allocate time slices to processes.

Proposition4: For $proc_1, proc_2, proc_3 \in Proc$, $r, s \in \overline{R}$ it is
$\lceil \lceil proc_1 \rceil^r(proc_2) \rceil^s(proc_3) = \lceil proc_1 \rceil^{min(r,s)}(\lceil proc_2 \rceil^{s \dot{-} r}(proc_3))$.

Proof: It is $\lceil \lceil proc_1 \rceil^r(proc_2) \rceil^s(proc_3) = \lceil \lceil proc_1 \rceil^r + \Delta_r(proc_2) \rceil^s + \Delta_s(proc_3) =$
$\lceil \lceil proc_1 \rceil^r \rceil^s + \lceil \Delta_r(proc_2) \rceil^s + \Delta_s(proc_3)$. For $r > s$ this equals $\lceil proc_1 \rceil^s + \Delta_s(proc_3)$,
for $r \leq s$ it is $\lceil proc_1 \rceil^r + \Delta_r(\lceil proc_2 \rceil^{s-r}) + \Delta_r(\Delta_{s-r}(proc_3))$.
In both cases this is equal to $\lceil proc_1 \rceil^{min(r,s)}(\lceil proc_2 \rceil^{s \dot{-} r}(proc_3))$. □

6 Related Work

Apart from [JM86], which has been briefly described and acknowledged already in the introduction as a most similar work, several other papers should be mentioned:

The starting point of the present work was the discrete time calculus [NS90] that has been mentioned several times and adapted to the ProCoS environment in [Sch91].

Their model, a process algebra called ATP, is based on the following principles:
1. The system is the parallel composition of communicating sequential components, all of which may execute a time action. All actions of the system are atomic, i.e.: their beginning and end coincide.
2. Time progresses by synchronous execution of time actions, that is, time actions can be performed only if all components of the system agree to do so.
3. An execution sequence is a sequence of steps, a step being determined by two consecutive ocurrences of time actions. Within a step components may execute a finite though arbitrarily long sequence of asynchronous actions, after which they all synchronously perform a time action, corresponding to progress of time for the system. A component that can perform no asynchronous action can always perform a time action. The synchronous execution of a time action is the beginning of a new step.
In [NSY91] the discrete model has been extended to continuos time domains (and hybrid systems). Also there a distinction between "immediate" and "delayable" actions is introduced, so that it becomes possible to specify upper bounds ("speed ups") on the processes.

A timed process algebra that uses dense time and timed traces is the one of [BB90]. It has also already been mentioned. The characteristica of this approach are atomic actions that take no time and time stamps that are added to them, so that there an absolute time is needed (non-discrete model). The axioms of the underlying process algebra ACP are wrong for a real-time interpretation. These problems of compatibility are overcome by introducing the somewhat complicated notion of so-called multi-actions. Due to the complexity of the new algebra the axioms of the underlying process algebra ACP are not maintained for real-time processes in general. ACP's axioms only hold for a subclass of real-time processes ("symbolic processes").
Differences between the present approach and the ACP-based approach lie (to a minor extent) in another parallel operator and in ACP's necessity of introducing integration as an infinite choice and (more important) in a different way of handling recursion (by an operational semantics and bisimulation). Furthermore no upper bounds are considered, what within ProCoS is desirable.

Closer to the present results are, however, the ideas around *metric temporal logic* as in [KVR83], [KdR85] or [Hoo91]. This is an extension of traditional linear time temporal logic, in which the scope of temporal operators is restricted by extending them with time bounds. In [Hoo91] a proof system is given to decide a satisfaction relation between an OCCAM-like language and an assertion language based on metric temporal logic. The proof system is complete relative to the logic, and it is compositional. So it can also be used for the construction of correct programs, although it seems more suitable for the verification of a given pair of a program and a specification, because the form of the rules support an induction on the structure of the program rather than the structure of the specification. Time is introduced in form of delay statements, as usual in OCCAM. Also here no upper bounds are considered in the programming language. But on the whole it seems very promising to incorporate ideas of [Hoo91] into ProCoS.
[Hoo91] also presents a second formalism that uses correctness formulae based on Hoare triples. These are quadruples, one of whose components containing termination information and a real-time communication interface besides the traditional triples consisting of precondition, program and postcondition.
The models can come quite close to the implementation by the following characteristics:
1. The maximal parellism assumption is dropped. It can be specified which processes share a processor.
2. The execution time of assignments is taken into consideration.

3. The time needed to evaluate Boolean tests is taken into consideration.

An introduction to ideas around timed CSP can be found in [RR88], where a model is presented which shows the following characteristica:
1. The time domaine is continuous (non-negative reals). No lower bounds are observable for the time difference of events from processes operating asynchronously in parallel.
2. Zeno behaviours are excluded by the existence of a system delay constant for the duration of an action or a recursive call.
3. A basis is provided for specification and verification of time critical processes with an adequate treatment of non-determinism that assists in avoidence of deadlock and divergence.
4. No upper bounds are considered.
5. Specification is done by reasoning on the semantic domain without a particular specification language.

References

[BB90] J.C.M.Baeten, J.A.Bergstra. Real time process algebra. Technical Report P8916b, University of Amsterdam, 1990.

[Heh84] E.C.R.Hehner. Predicative Programming. CACM 27 (2), 1984.

[HeJ90] He Jifeng. Specification-Oriented Semantics for ProCoS Programming Language PL^{time}. ProCoS Document PRG/OU HJF 7/1, October 1990.

[Hoa85] C.A.R.Hoare. Communicating Sequential Processes. Prentice Hall, 1985.

[Hoo91] J.J.M.Hooman. Specification and Compositional Verification of Real-Time Systems. Technical University Eindhoven (Diss.).

[JM86] F.Jahanian, A.K.Mok. Safety analysis of timing properties in real-time systems. IEEE Trans. on Software Engineering, SE-12(9), pp.890-904, Sept. 1986.

[KVR83] R.Koymans, J.Vytopyl, W.P.de Roever. Real-time programming and asynchronous message-passing. Proc. of the 2nd ACM symposium on Principals of Distributed Computing, 1983, pp.187-197.

[KdR85] R.Koymans, W.P.de Roever. Examples of a real-time temporal logic specification. The Analysis of Concurrent Systems, LNCS 207 (1985), pp.231-253.

[IN88] INMOS Ltd. occam 2 Reference Manual. Prentice Hall, 1988.

[JORR90] K.M.Jensen, E.-R. Olderog, H.Rischel, S.Rössig. Syntax and informal semantics for the ProCoS specification language level 0. ProCoS Document ID/DTH KMJ 4/2, June 1990.

[MT90] F.Moller, C.Tofts. A temporal calculus of communicating systems. CONCUR 1990, LNCS458.

[NS90] X.Nicollin, J.Sifakis. The Algebra of Timed Processes ATP: Theory and Application. Report RT-C26, Projet SPECTRE, Université de Grenoble.

[NS91] X.Nicollin, J.Sifakis. An Overview and Synthesis on Timed Process Algebras. CAV 1991, Ålborg.

[NSY91] X.Nicollin, J.Sifakis, S.Yovine. From ATP to Timed Graphs and Hybrid Systems. REX 1991 (to appear in Springer Lecture Notes).

[Old90] E.-R. Olderog. Semantics of the ProCoS specification language level 0. ProCoS Document OLD ERO 1/3, June 1990.

[Old91] E.-R. Olderog. Towards a design calculus for communicating programs. CONCUR 1991, LNCS527.

[RR88] G.M.Reed, A.W.Roscoe. A timed model for Communicasting Sequential Processes. Theoretical Computer Science 58, 1988, pp.249-261.

[RS91] S.Rössig, M.Schenke. Specification and stepwise development of communicating systems. VDM 1991 (to appear in Springer Lecture Notes).

[Sch91] M.Schenke. The Bracket Model - a Discrete Model for Timed Processes. ProCoS Document OLD MS 2/2, June 1991.

Putting Time into Proof Outlines

Fred B. Schneider*
Bard Bloom†
Keith Marzullo‡

Department of Computer Science
Cornell University
Ithaca, New York 14853

Abstract. A logic for reasoning about timing properties of concurrent programs is presented. The logic is based on proof outlines and can handle maximal parallelism as well as resource-constrained execution environments. The correctness proof for a mutual exclusion protocol that uses execution timings in a subtle way illustrates the logic in action.

Key words: concurrent program verification, timing properties, safety properties, real-time programming, real-time actions, proof outlines.

Contents

---

*Supported in part by the Office of Naval Research under contract N00014-91-J-1219, the National Science Foundation under Grant No. CCR-8701103, DARPA/NSF Grant No. CCR-9014363, and a grant from IBM Endicott Programming Laboratory.

†Supported in part by NSF grant CCR-9003441.

‡Supported in part by Defense Advanced Research Projects Agency (DoD) under NASA Ames grant number NAG 2-593, and by grants from IBM and Siemens.

1. Introduction

A safety property of a program asserts that some proscribed "bad thing" does not occur during execution. To prove that a program satisfies a safety property, one typically employs an *invariant*, a characterization of current (and possibly past) program states that is not invalidated by execution. If an invariant I holds in the initial state of the program and $I \Rightarrow Q$ is valid for some Q, then $\neg Q$ cannot occur during execution. Thus, to establish that a program satisfies the safety property asserting that $\neg Q$ does not occur, it suffices to find such an invariant I.

Timing properties are safety properties where the "bad thing" involves the time and program state at the instants that various specified control points in a program become active.[1] Timing properties can restrict externally visible events, like inputs and outputs, as well as things that are internal to a program, like the value of a variable or the time that a particular statement starts or finishes. For example, in a process control system, the elapsed time between a stimulus and response must be bounded. This is a timing property where the "bad thing" is defined in terms of the time that passes after one control point becomes active until some other control point does. Timing properties concerning internal events are useful in reasoning about ordinary concurrent programs that exploit knowledge of statement execution times to coordinate processes. One such protocol—for mutual exclusion—is given in section 4.

Because timing properties are safety properties, the invariant-based method outlined above for reasoning about safety properties can be used to reason about timing properties. This means that a programming logic L to verify (ordinary) safety properties can form the basis for a logic L' to verify timing properties. It suffices that in L' we are able to

(1) specify in I and Q information about the times at which events of interest occur and

(2) establish that program execution does not invalidate such an I.

Point (1) means that in defining L', the language of L might have to be extended so that it becomes more expressive. Point (2) means that the inferencing apparatus of L might have to be refined so that I can be proved an invariant for a program whose semantics includes information about execution timings.

This paper describes extensions to a logic of proof outlines [Schneider 92] to enable verification of timing properties for concurrent programs. The approach taken is the one just outlined: we start with a logic for proving ordinary safety properties, augment the language according to (1) and refine the inference rules according to (2). The presentation is organized as follows. In section 2, we describe a logic of proof outlines. Section 3 introduces and axiomatizes a new type of atomic action, called a real-time action. The correctness proof for a mutual exclusion protocol in section 4 illustrates the use of our logic. Related work and some unresolved technical issues are discussed in section 5.

---

[1]Informally, the *active* control points at any instant are determined by the values of the program counters at that instant. See §2 for a more formal definition.

2. Proof Outlines

In order to reason about a program, we must be able to define sets of program states and reason about them. First-order predicate logic is an obvious choice for this task, and we employ the usual correspondence between the formulas of the logic and the programming language of interest—each variable and expression of the programming language is made a term of the logic and each Boolean expression of the programming language is made a predicate of the logic. It will be convenient to assume that predicates and terms are always defined, although the value of a term may be unspecified in some states. For example, we will assume that the term x/y has a value whatever value y has, but that $y*(x/y)$ need not equal x when y is 0 because the value of x/y is unspecified in such states.

Predicates and function symbols for the programming language's data types provide a way to express facts about program variables and expressions. The state of a program, however, also includes information that tells what atomic actions might be executed next. For representing this control information, we will find it convenient to fix some predicate symbols, called *control predicates*, and give axioms to ensure that, as execution proceeds, changes in the values of these correspond to changes to program counters. (An alternative representation would have been to define a "program counter" variable and a data type for the values it can assume.)

2.1. Control Predicates

A program consists of a set of atomic actions, each of which executes as a single indivisible state transformation. The *control points* of the program are defined by these atomic actions. Each atomic action has distinct *entry control points* and *exit control points*. For example, the atomic action that implements **skip** has a single entry control point and a single exit control point; the test for an **if** has one entry control point and one exit control point for each alternative. Execution of an atomic action α can occur only when an entry control point for α is *active*. Among other things, execution causes that active entry control point to become inactive and an exit control point of α to become active.

For each statement or atomic action S, we define the following control predicates:

at(S): an entry control point for S is active.

after(S): an exit control point from S is active.

The various statements in a programming language give rise to axioms relating these control predicates. The axioms formalize how the control predicates for a statement or atomic action S relate to the control predicates for constructs comprising S and constructs containing S, based on the control flow defined by S. For a guarded-command programming language [Dijkstra 75], these axioms are given in Figure 2.1. We use $GEval_{if}(S)$ there to denote the guard evaluation action for an **if** and $GEval_{do}(S)$ to denote the guard evaluation action for a **do**. And, we write $P_1 \oplus P_2 \oplus ... \oplus P_n$ to denote that exactly one of P_1 through P_n holds.

Atomic action: For S a **skip**, guard evaluation action, or assignment:

$\neg(at(S) \wedge after(S))$

Sequential composition: For S the sequential composition $S_1\ S_2$:

(a) $at(S) = at(S_1)$

(b) $after(S) = after(S_2)$

(c) $after(S_1) = at(S_2)$

if *Control Axioms*: For an **if** statement:

S: **if** $B_1 \rightarrow S_1\ [\!]\ B_2 \rightarrow S_2\ [\!]\ \cdots\ [\!]\ B_n \rightarrow S_n$ **fi**

(a) $at(S) = at(GEval_{if}(S))$

(b) $after(S) = (after(S_1) \oplus after(S_2) \oplus \ldots \oplus after(S_n))$

(c) $after(GEval_{if}(S)) = (at(S_1) \oplus at(S_2) \oplus \ldots \oplus at(S_n))$

do *Control Axioms*: For a **do** statement:

S: **do** $B_1 \rightarrow S_1\ [\!]\ B_2 \rightarrow S_2\ [\!]\ \cdots\ [\!]\ B_n \rightarrow S_n$ **od**

(a) $at(GEval_{do}(S)) = (at(S) \oplus after(S_1) \oplus after(S_2) \oplus \ldots \oplus after(S_n))$

(b) $after(GEval_{do}(S)) = (at(S_1) \oplus at(S_2) \oplus \ldots \oplus at(S_n) \oplus after(S))$

cobegin *Control Axioms*: For a **cobegin** statement:

S: **cobegin** $S_1\ //\ S_2\ //\ \cdots\ //\ S_n$ **coend**

(a) $at(S) = (at(S_1) \wedge \ldots \wedge at(S_n))$

(b) $after(S) = (after(S_1) \wedge \ldots \wedge after(S_n))$

Figure 2.1. Control Predicate Axioms

2.2. Syntax and Meaning of Proof Outlines

A *proof outline* $PO(S)$ for a program S is a text in which every atomic action of S is preceded and followed by an *assertion* enclosed in braces ("{" and "}"). Each assertion is a Predicate Logic formula in which

- the free variables are *program variables* (typeset in italics) or *rigid variables*, (typeset in upper-case roman), and
- the predicate symbols are control predicates or the predicates of the programming language's expressions.

Assertions in which all terms are constructed from program variables, rigid variables, and predicates involving those variables are called *primitive assertions*. An example of a proof outline appears in Figure 2.2. In it, x is a program variable and X is a rigid variable. All assertions except the first and last are primitive.

$$
\begin{array}{l}
\{x{=}X \wedge at(S)\} \\
S\text{: } \textbf{if } x{\ge}0 \rightarrow \{x{=}X \wedge x{\ge}0\} \\
\qquad\qquad\qquad S_1\text{: } \textbf{skip} \\
\qquad\qquad\qquad \{x{=}X \wedge x{\ge}0\} \\
\quad [\,]\ x{\le}0 \rightarrow \{x{=}X \wedge x{\le}0\} \\
\qquad\qquad\qquad S_2\text{: } x := -x \\
\qquad\qquad\qquad \{-x{=}X \wedge -x{\le}0\} \\
\quad \textbf{fi} \\
\{x{=}abs(X) \wedge after(S)\}
\end{array}
$$

Figure 2.2. Computing *abs*(x)

The assertion that immediately precedes a statement or atomic action T in a proof outline $PO(S)$ is called the *precondition* of T and is denoted $pre(T)$; the assertion that directly follows T is called the *postcondition* of T and is denoted by $post(T)$. For the proof outline in Figure 2.2, this correspondence is summarized in Figure 2.3. Finally, for a proof outline $PO(S)$, we write $pre(PO(S))$ to denote $pre(S)$, $post(PO(S))$ to denote $post(S)$, and use a *triple*

(2.1) $\{P\}\ PO(S)\ \{Q\}$

to specify the proof outline in which $pre(S)$ is P, $post(S)$ is Q, and all other pre- and postconditions are the same as in $PO(S)$.

A proof outline $PO(S)$ can be regarded as associating an assertion $pre(T)$ with control predicate $at(T)$ and an assertion $post(T)$ with $after(T)$ for each statement T in a program fragment S. Consequently, a proof outline defines a mapping from each control point λ of a program to a set of assertions—those assertions associated with control predicates that are *true* whenever λ is active. In most cases, a control point is mapped to a single assertion. For example, the proof outline

(2.2) $\{P\}\ S_1\ \{Q\}\ S_2\ \{R\}$

maps the entry control point for program $S_1\,S_2$ to the single assertion P. This is because $at(S_1)$ and $at(S_1\,S_2)$ are the only control predicates that are *true* if and only if the entry control point for $S_1\,S_2$ is

Assertion	Assertion Text
$pre(S)$	$x{=}X \wedge at(S)$
$post(S)$	$x{=}abs(X) \wedge after(S)$
$pre(S_1)$	$x{=}X \wedge x{\ge}0$
$post(S_1)$	$x{=}X \wedge x{\ge}0$
$pre(S_2)$	$x{=}X \wedge x{\le}0$
$post(S_2)$	$-x{=}X \wedge -x{\le}0$

Figure 2.3. Assertions in a Proof Outline

active, and (2.2) associates P with both of these control predicates. However, a proof outline can map a given control point to multiple assertions. An example of this appears in Figure 2.2. There, the exit control point for S_1 is mapped to two assertions—$post(S_1)$ and $post(S)$—because whenever the exit control point of S_1 is active both $after(S_1)$ and $after(S)$ are *true*.

The assertions in a proof outline are intended to document what can be expected to hold of the program state as execution proceeds. The proof outline of Figure 2.2, for example, implies that if execution is started at the beginning of S_1 with $x=23$ (a state that satisfies $pre(S_1)$), then if S_1 completes, $post(S_1)$ will be satisfied by the resulting program state, as will $post(S)$. And if execution is started at the beginning of S with $x=\mathrm{X}$, then whatever assertion is next reached—be it $pre(S_1)$ because $\mathrm{X}\geq 0$ or $pre(S_2)$ because $\mathrm{X}\leq 0$—that assertion will hold when reached, and the next assertion will hold when it is reached, and so on.

With this in mind, we define a proof outline $PO(S)$ to be *valid* if it describes a relationship among the program variables and control predicates of S that is invariant and, therefore, not falsified by execution of S. The invariant defined by a proof outline $PO(S)$ is "if a control point λ is active, then all assertions that λ is mapped to by $PO(S)$ are satisfied" and is formalized as the *proof outline invariant* for $PO(S)$:

(2.3) $\quad I_{PO(S)}\colon \bigwedge_{T} ((at(T) \Rightarrow pre(T)) \wedge (after(T) \Rightarrow post(T)))$

For example, the proof outline invariant defined by $PO(S)$ of Figure 2.2 is

$$\begin{array}{lll} & at(S) \Rightarrow (x=\mathrm{X} \wedge at(S)) & \wedge \;\; after(S) \Rightarrow (x=abs(\mathrm{X}) \wedge after(S)) \\ \wedge & at(S_1) \Rightarrow (x=\mathrm{X} \wedge x\geq 0) & \wedge \;\; after(S_1) \Rightarrow (x=\mathrm{X} \wedge x\geq 0) \\ \wedge & at(S_2) \Rightarrow (x=\mathrm{X} \wedge x\leq 0) & \wedge \;\; after(S_2) \Rightarrow (-x=\mathrm{X} \wedge -x\leq 0). \end{array}$$

Equating proof outline validity with invariance of $I_{PO(S)}$ can have disturbing consequences for proof outlines that map a single control point to multiple assertions. The following valid proof outline illustrates this.

(2.4) $\quad \{false\}$
$\quad S\colon$ **if** $true \rightarrow \{false\}\; S'\colon x := 3\; \{x=1\}$ **fi**
$\quad \{x=2\}$

This proof outline maps the exit control point for S' to two assertions, $post(S')$ and $post(S)$. The proof outline is valid because $I_{PO(S)}$

$$\begin{array}{lll} & at(S) \Rightarrow false & \wedge \;\; after(S) \Rightarrow x=2 \\ \wedge & at(S') \Rightarrow false & \wedge \;\; after(S') \Rightarrow x=1 \end{array}$$

is equivalent to *false* (since $after(S')=after(S)$ is valid) and therefore $I_{PO(S)}$ cannot be falsified by execution of any statement. The problem with (2.4) is that $post(S)$, the assertion associated with the exit control point of S, is not implied by $post(S')$, the assertion associated with the exit control point for the last atomic action in S (i.e S'). As a result, what (2.4) really associates with the exit control point for S' (viz. $post(S') \wedge post(S)$) is not accurately characterized by $post(S)$. Given a valid proof outline $PO(S)$, it seems reasonable to expect $post(S)$ to hold whenever an exit control point of S is active. Similarly, $pre(S)$ should be constrained so that if it holds and an entry control point of S is active, then assertions that $PO(S)$ associates with that entry control point also hold. To formalize these constraints, we define a proof outline $PO(S)$ to be *self consistent* if and only if

(2.5) $at(S) \wedge pre(S) \Rightarrow II_{PO(S)}$

(2.6) $after(S) \wedge II_{PO(S)} \Rightarrow post(S)$

where

$$II_{PO(S)}: \bigwedge_{T \neq S}((at(T) \Rightarrow pre(T)) \wedge (after(T) \Rightarrow post(T)))$$

$II_{PO(S)}$ is just $I_{PO(S)}$ with the two conjuncts concerning $pre(S)$ and $post(S)$ (i.e. "$at(S) \Rightarrow pre(S)$" and "$after(S) \Rightarrow post(S)$") omitted.[2] Thus, (2.5) ensures that whenever any entry control point λ for S is active, if $pre(S)$ holds then so does the assertion that $PO(S)$ associates with λ. And (2.6) ensures that whenever any exit control point λ of S is active, if the assertion associated with that control point holds then $post(S)$ will hold as well. Together, (2.5) and (2.6) mean that $pre(S)$ and $post(S)$ constitute a reasonably complete interface to S: provided $pre(S)$ holds when execution of S is started, the assertions of $PO(S)$ will characterize any states that arise as execution proceeds and $post(S)$ will hold if an exit control point for S is ever reached. It should come as no surprise that the proof outline of (2.4) is not self consistent—(2.6) is violated.

The requirements for validity of a proof outline—invariance of $I_{PO(S)}$ and self-consistency—can be formalized in terms of $\mathcal{H}_S^+$-validity of Temporal Logic formulas, where $\mathcal{H}_S^+$ is the set of infinite state sequences that model execution of S started from any program state [Owicki-Lamport 82]. In this formalization, we are able to write $\mathcal{H}_S^+ \models P$ in order to denote that a Predicate Logic formula P is valid because every program state is the first state of some interpretation in $\mathcal{H}_S^+$.

(2.7) **Valid Proof Outline.** A proof outline $PO(S)$ is *valid* if and only if:

Self Consistency: $\mathcal{H}_S^+ \models (at(S) \wedge pre(S) \Rightarrow II_{PO(S)})$

$\mathcal{H}_S^+ \models (after(S) \wedge II_{PO(S)} \Rightarrow post(S))$

Invariance: $\mathcal{H}_S^+ \models (I_{PO(S)} \Rightarrow \Box I_{PO(S)})$ □

Notice that according to Valid Proof Outline (2.7), rigid variables in proof outlines can be used relate the values of program variables from one state to the next. This is because free rigid variables in a temporal logic formula are implicitly universally quantified. Thus, $I_{PO(S)} \Rightarrow \Box I_{PO(S)}$ is $\mathcal{H}_S^+$-valid if and only if for any assignment of values to the proof outline's rigid variables, execution of S

(i) starts in a state that does not satisfy $I_{PO(S)}$ or

(ii) results in a sequence of states that each satisfy $I_{PO(S)}$.

For example, the proof outline of Figure 2.2 is valid and contains a rigid variable X to record the initial value of x. Starting execution in a state where $at(S_2)$ and $x=-23$ holds will satisfy $I_{PO(S)} \Rightarrow \Box I_{PO(S)}$ even if -23 is not assigned to X because then $I_{PO(S)}$ is not satisfied (causing $I_{PO(S)} \Rightarrow \Box I_{PO(S)}$ to be trivially satisfied).

---

[2] *II* is an acronym for *internal invariant*.

2.3. Axiomatization for a Proof Outline Logic

Proof Outline Logic is an extension of Predicate Logic. The language of Predicate Logic is extended with proof outlines for all atomic actions, statements, and programs. The axioms and inference rules of Predicate Logic are extended with axioms and inference rules that allow only valid proof outlines to be proved theorems. In particular, there are some statement-independent inference rules as well as an axiom or inference rule for each type of statement and atomic action.

The statement-independent inference rules for Proof Outline Logic are given in Figure 2.4. Rule of Consequence allows the precondition of a proof outline to be strengthened and the postcondition to be weakened, based on deductions possible in Predicate Logic. Rule of Equivalence allows assertions anywhere in a proof outline to be modified, provided a self consistent proof outline having an equivalent proof outline invariant results. A rigid variable can be renamed or instantiated by using the Rigid Variable Rule; $PO(S)^{\mathrm{X}}_{\mathrm{Exp}}$ in the conclusion of that rule denotes a proof outline in which rigid variable X in every assertion is replaced by Exp, an expression involving constants and rigid variables (only). Finally, the Conjunction and Disjunction Rules allow two proof outlines for the same program to be combined. $PO_A(S) \circledwedge PO_B(S)$ is used to denote the proof outline that associates assertion $A_{cp} \wedge B_{cp}$ with each control predicate cp, where X_{cp} is the assertion that $PO_X(S)$ associates with control predicate cp; $PO_A(S) \circledvee PO_B(S)$ denotes the proof outline that associates $A_{cp} \vee B_{cp}$ with each control predicate cp

Rule of Consequence: $$\frac{P' \Rightarrow P,\ \ \{P\}\ PO(S)\ \{Q\},\ \ Q \Rightarrow Q'}{\{P'\}\ PO(S)\ \{Q'\}}$$

Rule of Equivalence: $$\frac{PO(S),\ \ I_{PO(S)} = I_{PO'(S)},\ \ PO'(S) \text{ self consistent}}{PO'(S)}$$

Rigid Variable Rule: For Exp an expression involving only constants and rigid varibles:

$$\frac{\{P\}\ PO(S)\ \{Q\}}{\{P^{\mathrm{X}}_{\mathrm{Exp}}\}\ PO(S)^{\mathrm{X}}_{\mathrm{Exp}}\ \{Q^{\mathrm{X}}_{\mathrm{Exp}}\}}$$

Conjunction Rule: $$\frac{PO_A(S),\ \ PO_B(S)}{PO_A(S) \circledwedge PO_B(S)}$$

Disjunction Rule: $$\frac{PO_A(S),\ \ PO_B(S)}{PO_A(S) \circledvee PO_B(S)}$$

Figure 2.4. Proof Outline Logic: Statement-independent Rules

We now turn to the axiomatization for a concurrent programming language. The **skip** statement is a single atomic action whose execution has no effect on any program variable.

skip *Axiom*: For a primitive assertion P: $\{P\}$ **skip** $\{P\}$

The assignment statement $x := E$ is also a single atomic action. Its execution involves evaluating E and then storing that value in x.[3]

Assignment Axiom: For a primitive assertion P: $\{P^{\bar{x}}_{\bar{e}}\}\ \bar{x} := \bar{e}\ \{P\}$

Sequential composition of statements is denoted by juxtaposition (without the traditional semicolon separator).

$$\textit{Statement Composition Rule:}\quad \frac{\{P\}\ PO(S_1)\ \{Q\},\ \ \{Q\}\ PO(S_2)\ \{R\}}{\{P\}\ PO(S_1)\ \{Q\}\ PO(S_2)\ \{R\}}$$

An **if** statement consists of an atomic guard evaluation action that selects for execution an alternative whose guard is *true*; if no guard is *true*, then the guard evaluation action blocks. We use the following rule for reasoning about a guard evaluation action.

GEval$_{if}$*(S) Axiom*: For an **if** statement

$$S:\ \textbf{if}\ B_1 \rightarrow S_1\ \ []\ \ B_2 \rightarrow S_2\ \ []\ \ \cdots\ \ []\ \ B_n \rightarrow S_n\ \ \textbf{fi}$$

and a primitive assertion P:

$$\{P\}\ GEval_{if}(S)\ \{P \wedge ((at(S_1) \Rightarrow B_1) \wedge \ldots \wedge (at(S_n) \Rightarrow B_n))\}$$

A proof outline for an **if** is then constructed by combining a proof outline for its guard evaluation action with a proof outline for each alternative.

$$\textbf{if}\ \textit{Rule:}\quad \frac{\begin{array}{l}\text{(a)}\ \{P\}\ GEval_{if}(S)\ \{R\},\\ \text{(b)}\ (R \wedge at(S_1)) \Rightarrow P_1,\ \ \ldots,\ \ (R \wedge at(S_n)) \Rightarrow P_n,\\ \text{(c)}\ \{P_1\}\ PO(S_1)\ \{Q\},\ \ \ldots,\ \ \{P_n\}\ PO(S_n)\ \{Q\},\end{array}}{\begin{array}{l}\{P\}\\ S:\ \textbf{if}\ B_1 \rightarrow \{P_1\}\ PO(S_1)\ \{Q\}\\ \quad\ \ []\ \cdots\\ \quad\ \ []\ B_n \rightarrow \{P_n\}\ PO(S_n)\ \{Q\}\\ \quad\ \ \textbf{fi}\\ \{Q\}\end{array}}$$

Since the guard evaluation action for an **if** blocks when no guard is *true*, we can use an **if** to implement conditional waiting. For example,

[3]For simplicity, we restrict consideration to the case where x is a simple identifier and not an array. See [Gries-Levin 80] for the more general rule.

if $B \rightarrow S$ **fi**

blocks until the program state satisfies B and only then starts executing S.

The guard evaluation action for **do** selects a statement S_i for which corresponding guard B_i holds and if no guard is *true*, then the control point following the **do** becomes active.

GEval$_{do}(S)$ *Axiom*: For a **do** statement

$$S\colon \mathbf{do}\ B_1 \rightarrow S_1 \quad [\,] \quad B_2 \rightarrow S_2 \quad [\,] \quad \cdots \quad [\,] \quad B_n \rightarrow S_n \ \mathbf{od}$$

and a primitive assertion P:

$$\{P\}\ GEval_{do}(S)\ \{P \wedge ((at(S_1) \Rightarrow B_1) \wedge \ \ldots\ \wedge (at(S_n) \Rightarrow B_n) \wedge (after(S) \Rightarrow (\neg B_1 \wedge \ \ldots\ \wedge \neg B_n)))\}$$

The inference rule for **do** is based on a *loop invariant*, an assertion I that holds before and after every iteration of a loop and, therefore, is guaranteed to hold when **do** terminates—no matter how many iterations occur.

do *Rule*:

$$\frac{\begin{array}{l} \text{(a)}\ \{I\}\ GEval_{do}(S)\ \{R\}, \\ \text{(b)}\ (R \wedge at(S_1)) \Rightarrow P_1,\ \ldots,\ (R \wedge at(S_n)) \Rightarrow P_n, \\ \text{(c)}\ \{P_1\}\ PO(S_1)\ \{I\},\ \ldots,\ \{P_n\}\ PO(S_n)\ \{I\} \\ \text{(d)}\ (R \wedge after(S)) \Rightarrow (I \wedge \neg B_1 \wedge \ldots \wedge \neg B_n) \end{array}}{\begin{array}{l} \{I\} \\ S\colon\ \mathbf{do}\ B_1 \rightarrow \{P_1\}\ PO(S_1)\ \{I\} \\ \qquad [\,]\ \cdots \\ \qquad [\,]\ B_n \rightarrow \{P_n\}\ PO(S_n)\ \{I\} \\ \quad \mathbf{od} \\ \{I \wedge \neg B_1 \wedge \ \ldots\ \wedge \neg B_n\} \end{array}}$$

The inference rule for a **cobegin** is based on combining proof outlines for its component processes. An interference-freedom test [Owicki-Gries 76] ensures that execution of an atomic action in one process does not invalidate the proof outline invariant for another. This interference-freedom test is formulated in terms of triples,

$$NI(\alpha, A)\colon\ \{pre(\alpha) \wedge A\}\ \ \alpha\ \ \{A\},$$

that are valid if and only if α does not invalidate assertion A. If no assertion in $PO(S_i)$ is invalidated by an atomic action α then, by definition, $I_{PO(S_i)}$ also cannot be invalidated by α. Therefore, we can prove that a collection of proof outlines $PO(S_1)$, ..., $PO(S_n)$ are *interference free* by establishing:

For all i, j, $1 \le i \le n$, $1 \le j \le n$, $i \ne j$:
  For all atomic actions α in S_i :
    For all assertions A in $PO(S_j)$: $NI(\alpha, A)$ is valid.

The following inference rule determines when a valid proof outline for a **cobegin** will result from combining valid proof outlines for its component processes:

cobegin *Rule*:

$$\frac{\begin{array}{l}\text{(a) } PO(S_1), \ \ldots, \ PO(S_n) \\ \text{(b) } P \Rightarrow pre(PO(S_1)) \wedge \ \ldots \ \wedge pre(PO(S_n)), \\ \text{(c) } post(PO(S_1)) \wedge \ \ldots \ \wedge post(PO(S_n)) \Rightarrow Q, \\ \text{(d) } PO(S_1), \ \ldots, \ PO(S_n) \text{ are interference free.}\end{array}}{\{P\} \ \textbf{cobegin} \ PO(S_1) \ // \ \cdots \ // \ PO(S_n) \ \textbf{coend} \ \{Q\}}$$

Since execution of an atomic action α in one process never interferes with a control predicate *cp* in another, certain interference-freedom triples follow axiomatically.

Process Independence Axiom: For a control predicate *cp* in one process and an atomic action α in another:

$$\{cp=\mathrm{C}\} \ \alpha \ \{cp=\mathrm{C}\}$$

Notice that $NI(\alpha, cp)$ follows directly from this axiom when α and *cp* are from different processes.

2.4. From Proof Outlines to Safety Properties

Theorems of Proof Outline Logic can be used to verify safety properties because of the way proof outline validity is defined. If a proof outline $PO(S)$ is valid then $I_{PO(S)}$ must be an invariant. And, if $I_{PO(S)}$ is an invariant, then according to the method of §1 for proving safety properties we can prove that executions of S starting with $pre(PO(S))$ *true* will satisfy the safety property proscribing $\neg Q$. We simply prove

(2.8) $\quad (cp \wedge A_{cp}) \Rightarrow Q$

for every assertion A_{cp} in $PO(S)$, where A_{cp} is the assertion that $PO(S)$ associates with control predicate *cp*. For example, we prove as follows that for the absolute value program in Figure 2.2, $after(S) \Rightarrow x = abs(\mathrm{X})$ holds during executions started in a state satisfying $at(S) \wedge x = \mathrm{X}$: First, because $post(S) \Rightarrow x = abs(\mathrm{X})$ is valid, for the case where *cp* is $after(S)$, (2.8), which is

$$after(S) \wedge post(S) \Rightarrow (after(S) \Rightarrow x = abs(\mathrm{X})),$$

is valid. Second, for the case where *cp* is not implied by $after(S)$, (2.8) is trivially valid.

3. Real-time Actions

We must know something about the execution times of atomic actions in order to reason about timing properties of programs. Therefore, for each unconditional atomic action[4] α in our programming language, we define corresponding *real-time actions* $\alpha_{[\delta, \varepsilon]}$ where δ and ε are real-valued, non-negative constants. Execution of a real-time action $\alpha_{[\delta, \varepsilon]}$ causes the same indivisible state transformation as α does, but constrains it to occur at some instant between ε and $\varepsilon + \delta$ time units after the entry control point for $\alpha_{[\delta, \varepsilon]}$ becomes active.

[4] An atomic action is *unconditional* if it is executable whenever its entry control point becomes active. In the programming notation of §2.3, **skip**, assignment, and the guard evaluation action for **do** are unconditional. The guard evaluation for **if** is not unconditional.

We have elected to characterize the execution time for a real-time action in terms of two parameters (δ and ε) in order to have flexibility in modeling various execution environments. Parameter ε describes the fixed execution time of the atomic action on a bare machine; δ models execution delays attributable to multiprogramming and other resource contention. A system where each process is assigned its own processor is modeled by choosing 0 for δ; a system where processors are shared is modeled by choosing a value for δ based on the length of time that a runnable process might have to wait for a processor to become available.

3.1. Reasoning About Real-time Actions

Execution of a real-time action $\alpha_{[\delta,\varepsilon]}$ affects the program variables and control predicates in the same ways as the atomic action α from which it was derived. Therefore, we have the following inference rule:

> *Real-time Action Transformation*: For α an unconditional atomic action, P and Q primitive assertions, and $0 \le \delta$ and $0 \le \varepsilon$:
>
> $$\frac{\{P\}\ \alpha\ \{Q\}}{\{P\}\ \alpha_{[\delta,\varepsilon]}\ \{Q\}}$$

To reason about timing properties, additional terms must be added the assertion language. This is because the method of §2.4 for reasoning about safety properties can only be used to prove safety properties for which the negation of the proscribed $\neg Q$ is implied by each of a proof outline's assertions. Timing properties concern the instants at which control predicates become active and so we define a term for each control predicate cp:

$$\uparrow cp \begin{cases} \text{the time that } cp \text{ last became } true \text{ or} \\ -\infty \text{ if } cp \text{ has never been } true \end{cases}$$

We also define a new real-valued term $\mathcal{T}$ to be equal to the current time.

Some additional axioms and inference rule allow us to reason about formulas of our more expressive assertion language. First, the various non-atomic statements of our programming language give rise to axioms based on the way they equate their components' control points. For our programming language, these axioms are given in Figure 3.1. Second, there are some language-independent axioms. In these, cp and cp' can denote any control predicates, including those not associated with entry or exit control points for real-time actions.

(3.1) $\uparrow cp \le \mathcal{T}$

(3.2) $(\uparrow cp = -\infty) \Rightarrow \neg cp$

(3.3) For a real time action $\alpha_{[\delta,\varepsilon]}$ with label S: (a) $at(S) \Rightarrow \uparrow at(S) \le \mathcal{T} \le \uparrow at(S) + \delta + \varepsilon$

(b) $\uparrow at(S) \ne -\infty \Rightarrow \uparrow after(S) \le \uparrow at(S) + \delta + \varepsilon$

Axioms (3.1) and (3.2) follow directly from the definition of $\uparrow cp$. Axiom (3.3) captures that essence of a real-time action—that its entry control point cannot stay active too long. This, in turn, allows us to infer that a control point is not active by using

Sequential Composition Axioms: For S the sequential composition $S_1\ S_2$:

(a) $\uparrow at(S) = \uparrow at(S_1)$

(b) $\uparrow after(S) = \uparrow after(S_2)$

(c) $\uparrow after(S_1) = \uparrow at(S_2)$

if *Axioms*: For an **if** statement:

$$S\text{: } \mathbf{if}\ B_1 \rightarrow S_1\ [\!]\ B_2 \rightarrow S_2\ [\!]\ \cdots\ [\!]\ B_n \rightarrow S_n\ \mathbf{fi}$$

(a) $\uparrow at(S) = \uparrow at(GEval_{if}(S))$

(b) $\uparrow after(S) = \max(\uparrow after(S_1), \uparrow after(S_2), ..., \uparrow after(S_n))$

(c) $\uparrow after(GEval_{if}(S)) = \max(\uparrow at(S_1), \uparrow at(S_2), ...\uparrow at(S_n))$

do *Axioms*: For a **do** statement:

$$S\text{: } \mathbf{do}\ B_1 \rightarrow S_1\ [\!]\ B_2 \rightarrow S_2\ [\!]\ \cdots\ [\!]\ B_n \rightarrow S_n\ \mathbf{od}$$

(a) $\uparrow at(GEval_{do}(S)) = \max(\uparrow at(S), \uparrow after(S_1), \uparrow after(S_2), ..., \uparrow after(S_n))$

(b) $\uparrow after(GEval_{do}(S)) = \max(\uparrow at(S_1), \uparrow at(S_2), ..., \uparrow at(S_n), \uparrow after(S))$

cobegin *Axioms*: For a **cobegin** statement:

$$S\text{: } \mathbf{cobegin}\ S_1\ //\ S_2\ //\ \cdots\ //\ S_n\ \mathbf{coend}$$

(a) $\uparrow at(S) = \uparrow at(S_1) = \cdots = \uparrow at(S_n))$

(b) $\uparrow after(S) = \max(\uparrow after(S_1), ..., \uparrow after(S_n))$

Figure 3.1. $\uparrow cp$ Axioms

(3.4) $\quad \mathcal{T} > \uparrow at(S)+\delta+\varepsilon \ \Rightarrow\ \neg at(S)$

because from (3.3a) we have:

$at(S) \ \Rightarrow\ \uparrow at(S) \le \mathcal{T} \le \uparrow at(S)+\delta+\varepsilon$

= « Predicate Logic»

$at(S) \ \Rightarrow\ ((\uparrow at(S) \le \mathcal{T}) \wedge (\mathcal{T} \le \uparrow at(S)+\delta+\varepsilon)$

= « Predicate Logic»

$((\uparrow at(S) > \mathcal{T}) \vee (\mathcal{T} > \uparrow at(S)+\delta+\varepsilon)) \ \Rightarrow\ \neg at(S)$

= «Axiom (3.1)»

$\mathcal{T} > \uparrow at(S)+\delta+\varepsilon \ \Rightarrow\ \neg at(S)$

The effect on these new terms of executing atomic actions is captured by the following axioms of Proof Outline Logic. First, for any ordinary or real-time atomic action, we have:

$\uparrow cp$ *Invariance*: $\{cp{=}\mathrm{C} \wedge \uparrow cp{=}\mathrm{V}\}\ S: \alpha\ \{(cp \Rightarrow \mathrm{C}) \Rightarrow (\uparrow cp{=}\mathrm{V})\}$

The antecedent in the postcondition is necessary for the case where cp is $after(S)$, since executing S does change the value of $after(S)$.

Next, for any ordinary atomic action:

Action-time Axioms: (a) $\{K \leq \uparrow at(S)\}\ S: \alpha\ \{K \leq \uparrow after(S)\}$

(b) $\{K \leq \mathcal{T}\}\ S: \alpha\ \{K \leq \uparrow after(S)\}$

Action-time Axiom (a) asserts that the exit control point for S becomes active after any of its entry control points last became active. Action-time Axiom (b) asserts that the exit control point of S becomes active later than any time that the entry control point for S was last active.

For a real-time action $\alpha_{[\delta,\,\varepsilon]}$, the following axiom characterizes how execution changes $\mathcal{T}$ and the $\uparrow cp$-terms.

Real-time Action Axiom $\{K \leq \uparrow at(S)\}\ S: \alpha_{[\delta,\,\varepsilon]}\ \{K+\varepsilon \leq \uparrow after(S)\}$

This axiom is analogous to Action-time Axiom (a), except now the postcondition has been strengthened to give a tighter lower bound on when the exit control point for S first becomes active.

Two things that the Real-time Action Axiom does not say are worthy of note. First, this axiom does not bound the interval during which the entry control point for S is active. This is because that bound already can be derived using axiom (3.3a), since $at(S)$ holds whenever the entry control point for S does. Second, one might expect to be able to prove the following triple—its precondition being similar to that of Action-time Axiom (b).

(3.5) $\{K \leq \mathcal{T}\}\ S: \alpha_{[\delta,\,\varepsilon]}\ \{K+\varepsilon \leq \mathcal{T}\}$

Unfortunately, (3.5) is not sound. Execution of S started in a state such that $\uparrow at(\alpha) < K \leq \mathcal{T}$ would satisfy the precondition but might terminate before $K+\varepsilon$. For example, consider an execution of $\alpha_{[0,\,2]}$ that is started at time 0. Thus, at time $\mathcal{T}=1$ the state would satisfy $K \leq \mathcal{T}$ for $K=1$, and so precondition $K \leq \mathcal{T}$ would be satisfied by that state. When execution of $\alpha_{[0,\,2]}$ terminates—2 units after it is started—at time $\mathcal{T}=2$, the postcondition $K+\varepsilon \leq \mathcal{T}$ is $1+2 \leq 2$, which is *false*.

Finally, the following rule allows rigid variables to be instantiated with expressions involving $\uparrow cp$-terms. (Rigid Variable Rule only allows rigid variables to be instantiated by constants, rigid variables, or expressions constructed from these.)

$$\uparrow cp\text{-}Instantiation \quad \frac{\{\uparrow cp = V\}\ \alpha\ \{\uparrow cp = V\},\quad \{P\}\ \alpha\ \{Q\}}{\{P^{X}_{\uparrow cp}\}\ \alpha\ \{Q^{X}_{\uparrow cp}\}}$$

This rule is typically used along with one of the Action-time Axioms or the Real-time Action Axiom. For the case where real-time action α and control predicate cp are in different processes, the first hypothesis of $\uparrow cp$-Instantiation is automatically satisfied, as the following proof of $\{\uparrow cp = V\}\ \alpha\ \{\uparrow cp = V\}$ demonstrates.

Process Independence Axiom:

1. $\{at(\beta) = C\}\ \alpha\ \{at(\beta) = C\}$

$\uparrow cp$ Invariance:

2. $\{at(\beta) = C \wedge \uparrow at(\beta) = V\}\ \alpha\ \{(at(\beta) \Rightarrow C) \Rightarrow (\uparrow at(\beta) = V)\}$

Conjunction Rule with 1 and 2:

3. $\{at(\beta)=C \wedge \uparrow at(\beta)=V\}$ α $\{at(\beta)=C \wedge ((at(\beta) \Rightarrow C) \Rightarrow (\uparrow at(\beta)=V))\}$

4. $at(\beta)=C \wedge ((at(\beta) \Rightarrow C) \Rightarrow (\uparrow at(\beta)=V))$
   $\Rightarrow$ «Predicate Logic»
   $\uparrow at(\beta)=V$

Rule of Consequence with 3 and 4:
5. $\{at(\beta)=C \wedge \uparrow at(\beta)=V\}$ α $\{\uparrow at(\beta)=V\}$

Rigid Variable Rule with 5, replacing C by *true* and then by *false*:
6. $\{at(\beta) \wedge \uparrow at(\beta)=V\}$ α $\{\uparrow at(\beta)=V\}$
7. $\{\neg at(\beta) \wedge \uparrow at(\beta)=V\}$ α $\{\uparrow at(\beta)=V\}$

Disjunction Rule with 6 and 7:
8. $\{(at(\beta) \vee \neg at(\beta)) \wedge \uparrow at(\beta)=V\}$ α $\{\uparrow at(\beta)=V\}$

Equivalence Rule with 8:
9. $\{\uparrow at(\beta)=V\}$ α $\{at(\beta)=V\}$

Thus, we obtain a derived rule of inference:

Derived ↑cp-Instantiation: If atomic action α and control predicate cp are in different processes:

$$\frac{\{P\}\ \alpha\ \{Q\}}{\{P^{V}_{\uparrow cp}\}\ \alpha\ \{Q^{V}_{\uparrow cp}\}}$$

3.2. Interference Freedom Revisited

When the execution times of atomic actions are bounded, certain forms of interference cannot occur. This is illustrated by the proof outline

$\{x=0\}$
cobegin
  $\{x=0\}$ α: $\langle x := x+1\rangle_{[0,2]}$ $\{x=1\}$
//
  $\{x=0\}$ β: $\langle y := x+1\rangle_{[0,1]}$ $\{y=1\}$
coend
$\{x=1 \wedge y=1\}$

which is valid but cannot be derived using the **cobegin** Rule because $PO(\alpha)$ and $PO(\beta)$ are not interference free. In particular, $NI(\alpha, pre(\beta))$ is not valid.

$$\begin{aligned} & NI(\alpha, pre(\beta)) \\ = \ & \{pre(\alpha) \wedge pre(\beta)\}\ \langle x := x+1\rangle_{[0,2]}\ \{pre(\beta)\} \\ = \ & \{x=0\}\ \langle x := x+1\rangle_{[0,2]}\ \{x=0\} \end{aligned}$$

Using operational reasoning, however, it is not difficult to argue that execution of α cannot invalidate $pre(\beta)$ and so $PO(\alpha)$ and $PO(\beta)$ should be considered interference free. This is because according to **cobegin** Axiom (b) in Figure 3.1 both $at(\alpha)$ and $at(\beta)$ become active at the same instant, say time 0. By definition, α completes at time 2, and so x remains 0 until this time. Real-time action β completes at time 1 and, therefore, must find x to be 0. It is simply not possible for α to change the value of x while $at(\beta)$ is active.

Our **cobegin** Rule is based on a form of interference freedom that does not take into account execution-time bounds of real-time actions. In particular, $NI(\alpha, A_{cp})$ does not account for the fact that although A_{cp} might be associated with an active control point cp when α is started, if A is the precondition of a real-time action then we may be able to prove that cp cannot be active when α completes. The remedy is to refine $NI(\alpha, A_{cp})$ taking into account the time bounds for how long an entry control point for a real-time action can remain active. The following triple accomplishes this.

$$NI_{rt}(\alpha, A_{cp})\text{: } \{at(\alpha) \wedge pre(\alpha) \wedge cp \wedge A_{cp}\}\ \ \alpha\ \{cp \Rightarrow A_{cp}\}$$

Returning to the example above, we have:

$$\begin{aligned} & NI_{rt}(\alpha, pre(\beta)) \\ = \ & \{at(\alpha) \wedge pre(\alpha) \wedge at(\beta) \wedge pre(\beta)\}\ \langle x := x+1\rangle_{[0,2]}\ \{at(\beta) \Rightarrow pre(\beta)\} \\ = \ & \{at(\alpha) \wedge at(\beta) \wedge x=0\}\ \langle x := x+1\rangle_{[0,2]}\ \{at(\beta) \Rightarrow x=0\} \end{aligned}$$

And, this obligation can be discharged as follows.

Real-time Action Axiom:
1. $\{K \leq \uparrow at(\alpha)\}\ \ \alpha\text{: } \langle x := x+1\rangle_{[0,2]}\ \ \{K+2 \leq \uparrow after(\alpha)\}$

Derived $\uparrow cp$-Instantiation with 1:
2. $\{\uparrow at(\beta) \leq \uparrow at(\alpha)\}\ \ \alpha\text{: } \langle x := x+1\rangle_{[0,2]}\ \ \{\uparrow at(\beta)+2 \leq \uparrow after(\alpha)\}$

Axiom (3.1):
3. $\uparrow after(\alpha) \leq \mathcal{T}$

Rule of Consequence with 2 and 3:
4. $\{\uparrow at(\beta) \leq \uparrow at(\alpha)\}\ \ \alpha\text{: } \langle x := x+1\rangle_{[0,2]}\ \ \{\uparrow at(\beta)+2 \leq \mathcal{T}\}$

Axiom (3.3a):
5. $at(\beta) \Rightarrow \uparrow at(\beta) \leq \mathcal{T} \leq \uparrow at(\beta)+1$

Predicate Logic:
6. $((\uparrow at(\beta)+2 \leq \mathcal{T})\ \wedge\ (at(\beta) \Rightarrow \uparrow at(\beta) \leq \mathcal{T} \leq \uparrow at(\beta)+1)) \Rightarrow \neg at(\beta)$

Rule of Consequence with 4, 5, and 6:
7. $\{\uparrow at(\beta) \leq \uparrow at(\alpha)\}\ \ \alpha\text{: } \langle x := x+1\rangle_{[0,2]}\ \ \{\neg at(\beta)\}$

Predicate Logic and $\uparrow at(a) = \uparrow at(b)$ from **cobegin** $\uparrow cp$ Axiom (a):
8. $pre(NI_{rt}(\alpha, pre(\beta))) \Rightarrow \uparrow at(\beta) \leq \uparrow at(\alpha)$
9. $\neg at(\beta) \Rightarrow post(NI_{rt}(\alpha, pre(\beta)))$

Rule of Consequence with 7, 8, and 9:
10. $NI_{rt}(\alpha, pre(\beta))$

4. Example: A Mutual Exclusion Protocol

Knowledge of execution times can be exploited to synchronize processes. A mutual exclusion protocol attributed in [Lamport 87] to Mike Fischer illustrates this point. The core of this protocol appears in Figure 4.1. There, c, d, c' and d' are real-time actions. Provided the parameters of these

$x := 0$
cobegin
  b: **if** $x=0$ $\rightarrow$ $c: \langle x := 1 \rangle_{[\delta(c),\, \varepsilon(c)]}$ **fi**
  d: $\langle$**skip**$\rangle_{[\delta(d),\, \varepsilon(d)]}$
  e: **if** $x=1$ $\rightarrow$ f: **skip fi**
  Critical Section 1
//
  b': **if** $x=0$ $\rightarrow$ $c': \langle x := 2 \rangle_{[\delta(c'),\, \varepsilon(c')]}$ **fi**
  d': $\langle$**skip**$\rangle_{[\delta(d'),\, \varepsilon(d')]}$
  e': **if** $x=2$ $\rightarrow$ f': **skip fi**
  Critical Section 2
coend

Figure 4.1. Mutual Exclusion Protocol

real-time actions satisfy

(4.1) $\delta(c')+\varepsilon(c')<\varepsilon(d)$

(4.2) $\delta(c)+\varepsilon(c)<\varepsilon(d')$

this protocol implements mutual exclusion of the marked critical sections.

Mutual exclusion of $after(e)$ and $after(e')$ is a safety property. It can be proved by constructing a valid proof outline in which $post(e) \Rightarrow \neg after(e')$ and $post(e') \Rightarrow \neg after(e)$. A standard approach for this is to construct a valid proof outline in which $\neg(post(e) \wedge post(e'))$ is valid. It is thus impossible for $after(e) \wedge after(e')$ to hold because that would imply $post(e) \wedge post(e')$.

A proof outline for one process is given in Figure 4.2; the proof outline for the other process is

$\{true\}$
b: **if** $x=0$ $\rightarrow$ $\{\uparrow at(c') \leq T\}$
  $c: \langle x := 1 \rangle_{[\delta(c),\, \varepsilon(c)]}$
  $\{x \neq 0 \wedge (at(c') \Rightarrow \uparrow at(c')+\delta(c')+\varepsilon(c')-\varepsilon(d) < \uparrow at(d))\}$
fi $\{x \neq 0 \wedge (at(c') \Rightarrow \uparrow at(c')+\delta(c')+\varepsilon(c')-\varepsilon(d) < \uparrow at(d))\}$
d: $\langle$**skip**$\rangle_{[\delta(d),\, \varepsilon(d)]}$
  $\{x \neq 0 \wedge \neg at(c')\}$
e: **if** $x=1$ $\rightarrow$ $\{x=1 \wedge \neg at(c')\}$
  f: **skip**
  $\{x=1 \wedge \neg at(c')\}$
fi $\{x=1 \wedge \neg at(c')\}$
Critical Section 1

Figure 4.2. Proof Outline for Mutual Exclusion Protocol

symmetric, with "1" everywhere replaced by "2" and the primed labels interchanged with unprimed ones. Notice that $post(e) \Rightarrow x=1$ and $post(e') \Rightarrow x=2$. Thus, the proof outlines satisfy the conditions just outlined for ensuring that states satisfying $after(e) \wedge after(e')$ cannot occur.

It is not difficult to derive the proof outline of Figure 4.2 using the axiomatization of real-time actions given above. The proofs of $\{pre(c)\}\ c\ \{post(c)\}$ and $\{pre(d)\}\ d\ \{post(d)\}$ are the most enlightening, as they expose the role of assumptions (4.1) and (4.2) in the correctness of the protocol. Here is the proof of $\{pre(c)\}\ c\ \{post(c)\}$:

Assignment Axiom:

1. $\{true\}\ c: \langle x := 1\rangle_{[\delta(c),\, \varepsilon(c)]}\ \{x=1\}$

2. $x=1$
   $\Rightarrow$ «Axiom (3.1)»
   $x=1 \wedge \uparrow at(c') \leq \mathcal{T}$
   $\Rightarrow$ «assumption (4.1)»
   $x=1 \wedge \uparrow at(c')+\delta(c')+\varepsilon(c')-\varepsilon(d) < \mathcal{T}$
   $\Rightarrow$ «Predicate Logic»
   $x \neq 0 \wedge \uparrow at(c')+\delta(c')+\varepsilon(c')-\varepsilon(d) < \mathcal{T}$

Rule of Consequence with 1 and 2:

3. $\{true\}\ c: \langle x := 1\rangle_{[\delta(c),\, \varepsilon(c)]}\ \{x \neq 0 \wedge \uparrow at(c')+\delta(c')+\varepsilon(c')-\varepsilon(d) < \mathcal{T}\}$

Action-time Axiom (b):

4. $\{K \leq \mathcal{T}\}\ c: \langle x := 1\rangle_{[\delta(c),\, \varepsilon(c)]}\ \{K \leq \uparrow after(c)\}$

Derived $\uparrow cp$-Instantiation with 4:

5. $\{\uparrow at(c') \leq \mathcal{T}\}\ c: \langle x := 1\rangle_{[\delta(c),\, \varepsilon(c)]}\ \{\uparrow at(c') \leq \uparrow after(c)\}$

Conjunction Rule with 3 and 5:

6. $\{\uparrow at(c') \leq \mathcal{T}\}$
   $c: \langle x := 1\rangle_{[\delta(c),\, \varepsilon(c)]}$
   $\{x \neq 0 \wedge \uparrow at(c')+\delta(c')+\varepsilon(c')-\varepsilon(d) < \mathcal{T} \wedge \uparrow at(c') \leq \uparrow after(c)\}$

7. $\uparrow at(c')+\delta(c')+\varepsilon(c')-\varepsilon(d) < \mathcal{T} \wedge \uparrow at(c') \leq \uparrow after(c)$
   $\Rightarrow$ «assumption (4.1) and $\uparrow after(c) = \uparrow at(d)$»
   $\uparrow at(c')+\delta(c')+\varepsilon(c')-\varepsilon(d) < \uparrow at(d)$
   $\Rightarrow$ «Predicate Logic »
   $at(c') \Rightarrow \uparrow at(c')+\delta(c')+\varepsilon(c')-\varepsilon(d) < \uparrow at(d)$

Rule of Consequence with 6 and 7:

8. $\{\uparrow at(c') \leq \mathcal{T}\}\ c: \langle x := 1\rangle_{[\delta(c),\, \varepsilon(c)]}\ \{x \neq 0 \wedge (at(c') \Rightarrow \uparrow at(c')+\delta(c')+\varepsilon(c')-\varepsilon(d) < \uparrow at(d))\}$

And, here is the proof of $\{pre(d)\}\ d\ \{post(d)\}$.

skip Axiom:

1. $\{x \neq 0\}\ d: \langle \mathbf{skip}\rangle_{[\delta(d),\, \varepsilon(d)]}\ \{x \neq 0\}$

Real-time Action Axiom:

2. $\{K \leq \uparrow at(d)\}\ d: \langle \mathbf{skip}\rangle_{[\delta(d),\, \varepsilon(d)]}\ \{K+\varepsilon(d) \leq \uparrow after(d)\}$

Rigid Variable Rule with 2, instantiating K with $\mathrm{L}+\delta(c')+\varepsilon(c')-\varepsilon(d)+\kappa$ where $0<\kappa$:

3. $\{\mathrm{L}+\delta(c')+\varepsilon(c')-\varepsilon(d)+\kappa\leq\uparrow at(d)\}$
   $d:\langle\mathbf{skip}\rangle_{[\delta(d),\,\varepsilon(d)]}$
   $\{\mathrm{L}+\delta(c')+\varepsilon(c')-\varepsilon(d)+\kappa+\varepsilon(d)\leq\uparrow after(d)\}$

Predicate Logic, since $0<\kappa$:

4. $\mathrm{L}+\delta(c')+\varepsilon(c')-\varepsilon(d)<\uparrow at(d) \Rightarrow \mathrm{L}+\delta(c')+\varepsilon(c')-\varepsilon(d)+\kappa\leq\uparrow at(d)$
5. $\mathrm{L}+\delta(c')+\varepsilon(c')-\varepsilon(d)+\kappa+\varepsilon(d)\leq\uparrow after(d) \Rightarrow \mathrm{L}+\delta(c')+\varepsilon(c')<\uparrow after(d)$

Rule of Consequence with 3, 4, and 5:

6. $\{\mathrm{L}+\delta(c')+\varepsilon(c')-\varepsilon(d)<\uparrow at(d)\}$
   $d:\langle\mathbf{skip}\rangle_{[\delta(d),\,\varepsilon(d)]}$
   $\{\mathrm{L}+\delta(c')+\varepsilon(c')<\uparrow after(d)\}$

Derived $\uparrow cp$-Instantiation, replacing L by $\uparrow at(c')$:

7. $\{\uparrow at(c')+\delta(c')+\varepsilon(c')-\varepsilon(d)<\uparrow at(d)\}$
   $d:\langle\mathbf{skip}\rangle_{[\delta(d),\,\varepsilon(d)]}$
   $\{\uparrow at(c')+\delta(c')+\varepsilon(c')<\uparrow after(d)\}$

8. $\uparrow at(c')+\delta(c')+\varepsilon(c')<\uparrow after(d)$
   $\Rightarrow$ «Axiom (3.1) applied to *after*(d)»
   $\uparrow at(c')+\delta(c')+\varepsilon(c')<\uparrow after(d)\leq\mathcal{T}$
   $\Rightarrow$ «theorem (3.4) applied to *at*(c')»
   $\neg\, at(c')$

Rule of Consequence with 7 and 8:

9. $\{\uparrow at(c')+\delta(c')+\varepsilon(c')-\varepsilon(d)<\uparrow at(d)\}\ d:\langle\mathbf{skip}\rangle_{[\delta(d),\,\varepsilon(d)]}\ \{\neg\, at(c')\}$

Process Independence Axiom:

10. $\{\neg\, at(c')\}\ d:\langle\mathbf{skip}\rangle_{[\delta(d),\,\varepsilon(d)]}\ \{\neg\, at(c')\}$

Disjunction Rule with 9 and 10:

11. $\{at(c')\Rightarrow\uparrow at(c')+\delta(c')+\varepsilon(c')-\varepsilon(d)<\uparrow at(d)\}\ d:\langle\mathbf{skip}\rangle_{[\delta(d),\,\varepsilon(d)]}\ \{\neg\, at(c')\}$

Conjunction Rule with 1 and 11:

12. $\{x\neq 0\wedge(at(c')\Rightarrow\uparrow at(c')+\delta(c')+\varepsilon(c')-\varepsilon(d)<\uparrow at(d))\}$
    $d:\langle\mathbf{skip}\rangle_{[\delta(d),\,\varepsilon(d)]}$
    $\{x\neq 0\wedge\neg\, at(c')\}$

Notice how timing information is used in step 7 to infer that a particular control point cannot be active.

5. Discussion

5.1. Other Work based on Proof Outlines

It is instructive to compare our logic with that of [Shaw 89], another Hoare-style logic [Hoare 69] for reasoning about execution of real-time programs. In [Shaw 89], the passage of time is modeled by augmenting each atomic action with an assignment to an interval-valued variable *RT* so that *RT* contains lower and upper bounds for the program's elapsed execution time. The Statement Composition Rule and the Assignment Axiom are then used to derive rules for reasoning about these augmented atomic actions.[5] Our logic is obtained by augmenting the assertion language (of an underlying logic of proof outlines) with additional terms ($\uparrow cp$ and $\mathcal{T}$) and devising new axioms for reasoning about these terms. We are not able to derive rules for real-time actions by using the original logic because we do not employ assignment statements to model the passage of time.

Although more complex, augmenting the axioms rather than the atomic actions has led us to a more powerful logic. First, having the $\uparrow cp$-terms allows the logic to be more expressive. These terms permit the definition of properties involving historical information—information that is not part of the current state of the program. Timing properties that constrain the elapsed time between events can only be formulated in terms of such historical information. The logic of [Shaw 89] has no way to express historical information and, consequently, can be employed to reason about only certain timing properties.

Second, our axiomatization allows reasoning about programs whose timing behavior is data-dependent. The logic of [Shaw 89] does not permit such reasoning. For example, because of the way statement composition is handled in [Shaw 89], the logic produces overly-conservative intervals for time bounds. This is illustrated by the following program, which takes exactly 10 time units to execute.

$$\textbf{if } B \rightarrow \textbf{skip}_{[0,9]} \;\; [] \;\; \neg B \rightarrow \textbf{skip}_{[0,1]} \textbf{ fi}$$
$$\textbf{if } B \rightarrow \textbf{skip}_{[0,1]} \;\; [] \;\; \neg B \rightarrow \textbf{skip}_{[0,9]} \textbf{ fi}$$

This fact can be proved in our logic; the logic of [Shaw 89] can prove only that execution requires between 2 and 18 time units.

A Hoare-style programming logic for reasoning about real-time is also discussed in [Hooman 91]. That work is largely incomparable to ours. First, the programming language axiomatized in [Hooman 91] is different, having synchronous message-passing and no shared variables. This is symptomatic of a fundamental difference in the two approaches. The emphasis in [Hooman 91] is on the design of compositional proof systems. Shared variables cannot (at present) be handled compositionally and so they are excluded from programs. In contrast, we do not require that our proof system be compositional.[6] Relaxing this compositionality requirement means that it is not difficult to extend our logic for reasoning (non-compositionally) about programs that employ synchronous message-passing or any of the other communication/synchronization mechanisms for which Hoare-style axioms have been proposed.

The types of properties handled in [Hooman 91] is also incomparable to what can be proved using our logic. Timing properties make visible the times at which control points become active through $\uparrow cp$-terms. A compositional proof system cannot include information about control points in its formulas because they betray the internal structure of a component. The logic of [Hooman 91], therefore, may only be concerned with the times at which externally visible events occur: the time of communications events and the time that program execution starts and terminates. This turns out to

---

[5]The idea of augmenting actions with assignment statements in order to reason about the passage of time is discussed in [Haase 81], where it is used to extend Dijkstra's *wp* [Dijkstra 75] for reasoning about elapsed execution time.

[6]The **cobegin** Rule of Proof Outline Logic is not compositional because its interference-freedom test depends on the internal structure of the processes being composed.

allow proofs of certain liveness properties as well as certain safety properties. Our logic cannot be used to prove any liveness properties.

5.2. Incompleteness Concerns

A soundness proof for the logic of this paper will appear elsewhere. The issue of completeness, however, is a bit problematic. The following proof outline illustrates the difficulties. It is valid, but is not provable with our logic.

(5.1) $\{\mathcal{T}=0\}\ a: \mathbf{skip}_{[0,2]}\ \{\mathcal{T}=2\}\ b: \mathbf{skip}_{[0,2]}\ \{\mathcal{T}=4\}$

A related proof outline is provable:

(5.2) $\{0 \le \uparrow at(a) \le \mathcal{T} \le 2\}\ a: \mathbf{skip}_{[0,2]}\ \{2 \le \uparrow at(b) \le \mathcal{T} \le 4\}\ b: \mathbf{skip}_{[0,2]}\ \{4 \le \uparrow after(b) \le \mathcal{T}\}$

Notice that the assertions of (5.2) characterize system states that would exist "during" the execution of *a* and *b*; the assertions of (5.1) do not.

A deficiency in our logic is one explanation for this situation; a deficiency in the definition of proof outline validity is another. Proof outline validity is defined in terms of a set ($\mathcal{H}_S^+$) of infinite state sequences that model execution of *S* started from any program state. This set contains no sequence whose successive states differ only in their values of $\mathcal{T}$, the states that assertions in (5.2) characterize and those in (5.1) do not. Certainly such states exist during program execution; we have simply chosen to define $\mathcal{H}_S^+$ so that states are recorded only when the value of some $\uparrow cp$-term changes. Now consider a set $\mathcal{H}_S^{++}$ that does contain sequences having such *temporal interpolation* states. If we replace $\mathcal{H}_S^+$ in Valid Proof Outline (2.7) by $\mathcal{H}_S^{++}$, then (5.2) remains valid and (5.1) becomes invalid. The incompleteness problem is gone.

There are also other reasons to prefer $\mathcal{H}_S^{++}$ in defining proof outline validity. Invariance under temporal interpolation seems to be the real-time analog of invariance under stuttering, something that is critical when proving that one specification or a program implements another. Unfortunately, the logic of this paper is unsound when $\mathcal{H}_S^{++}$ is used in place of $\mathcal{H}_S^{++}$. The existence of temporal interpolation states causes a new form of interference. This interference is easily dealt with by extending the definition of interference freedom.

Another concern when designing a logic is expressive completeness. Timing properties include many, but not all, safety properties of concern when reasoning about the behavior of real-time programs. This is because the historical information in a timing property is limited to times that control points become active. One might also be concerned with the elapsed time since the program variables last satisfied a given predicate or with satisfying constraints about how the program variables change as a function of time. Both are safety properties but neither is a timing property (according to our definition in §1). In general, safety properties can be partitioned into *invariance properties* and *history properties*. The invariant used in proving an invariance property need only refer to the current state; the invariant used in proving a history property may need to refer to the sequence of states up to the current state. Timing properties are a type of history property.

A version of Proof Outline Logic does exist for reasoning about history properties [Schneider 92]. It extends ordinary Proof Outline Logic by augmenting the assertion language with a "past state" operator and a function-definition facility. In this logic, our $\uparrow cp$-terms can be constructed explicitly; they need not be primitive. And, the more general class of safety properties involving times—be it times that predicates hold or times that control predicates hold—can be handled.

Acknowledgments

We are grateful to Nancy Lynch for pointing out an error in an earlier version of this paper.

References

[Dijkstra 75] Dijkstra, E.W. Guarded commands, nondeterminacy and formal derivation of programs. *CACM 18*, 8 (Aug. 1975), 453-457.

[Gries-Levin 80] Gries, D., and G. Levin. Assignment and procedure call proof rules. *ACM TOPLAS* 2, 4 (Oct. 1980), 564-579.

[Haase 81] Haase, V. Real-time Behavior of Programs. *IEEE Transactions on Software Engineering SE-7*, 5 (Sept. 1981), 494-501.

[Hoare 69] Hoare, C.A.R. An axiomatic basis for computer programming. *CACM 12*, 10 (Oct. 1969), 576-580.

[Hooman 91] Hooman, J. *Specification and Compositional Verification of Real-time Systems*. Ph.D. Thesis. Technische Universiteit Eindhoven. May 1991.

[Lamport 87] Lamport, L. A fast mutual exclusion algorithm. *ACM TOCS 5*, 1 (Feb. 1987), 1-11.

[Owicki-Gries 76] Owicki, S.S., and D. Gries. An axiomatic proof technique for parallel programs I. *Acta Informatica 6*, (1976), 319-340.

[Owicki-Lamport 82] Owicki, S.S., and L. Lamport. Proving liveness properties of concurrent programs. *ACM TOPLAS 4*, 3 (July 1982), 455-495.

[Schneider 92] Schneider, F.B. *On concurrent programming*. In preparation.

[Shaw 89] Shaw, A. Reasoning about time in higher-level language software. *IEEE Transactions on Software Engineering SE-15*, 7 (July 1989), 875-899.

Timed CSP: Theory and Practice

Oxford University Timed CSP Group[1]

Programming Research Group
Oxford University Computing Laboratory
11 Keble Road
Oxford OX1 3QD

Abstract. Over the past five years, G. M. Reed and A. W. Roscoe have directed a large group of research staff and graduate students at Oxford University in a comprehensive study of their theory of Timed CSP. This theory has now matured with associated proof systems, temporal logics, and refinement methods, and it has been employed in several realistic case studies. This paper presents an overview of the Oxford work on Timed CSP.

Keywords: Concurrency, Real-Time CSP, Temporal Logic, Timewise Refinement, Specification and Verification, Robotics, Telephone Switching, Control Software

Contents

[1]The work reported in this paper is due to S.R. Blamey, J. Davies, D.M. Jackson, A. Kay, M.W. Mislove, G.M. Reed, J.N. Reed, A.W. Roscoe, B. Scattergood, S.A. Schneider, R. Stamper, S. Superville, and A. Wallace. [The paper itself was written by Davies, Jackson, the Reeds, Roscoe, and Schneider, who take responsibility for any errors.] This work has been supported by the U.S. Office of Naval Research, Esprit BRA SPEC, Esprit REX, SERC, RSRE, Rolls Royce, BP, and Formal Systems (Europe).

1 Introduction

In [ReR86, ReR87, Ree88, Ree90, ReR91] G. M. Reed and A. W. Roscoe developed a hierarchy of timed and untimed models for CSP. This mathematical hierarchy supports a uniform treatment of concurrent processes at different levels of abstraction: in reasoning about complex systems, we may use the simplest semantic model that is sufficient to express the current requirement, safe in the knowledge that the argument remains valid in the other models of the hierarchy.

The links between the various untimed and timed models in the hierarchy are well-established, and a large group of academic staff, research staff, and graduate students at Oxford under the direction of Reed and Roscoe are exploring the use of this hierarchy in the design and specification of real-time processes. This group includes: J.N. Reed (senior research associate); J. Davies, A. Kay, and S.A. Schneider (research officers); D.M. Jackson, G. Lowe, and B. Scattergood (doctoral students).

Members of the above group have (1) made the explicit addition of channel communication [Sch90]; (2) developed a complete behavioural proof system [DaS89, Sch90, Dav91]; (3) developed a theory of timewise refinement, using relating timed processes to untimed ones in a manner that supports the promotion of correctness results within the hierarchy of semantic models [Sch90, Dav91]; (4) developed a temporal logic consistent with the existing timed semantics [Jac90], and produced a complete temporal logic proof system [Jac91]; (5) constructed an operational semantics for the language [Sch92]; (6) developed a new fixed-point theory based on the operational semantics, and used this fixed-point theory to construct a model based on infinite behaviours, extending Roscoe's work on unbounded nondeterminism in untimed CSP to timed processes [Sch91, MRS91]; (7) constructed the first timed probabilistic model for CSP [Low91]; (8) extended the theory to include an element of broadcast concurrency [Dav91, DJS92].

The theory of Timed CSP has been successfully applied to the usual examples: the alternating bit protocol, a sliding window protocol, and a watchdog timer, see [Ja+90, Sc+90]. More significantly, the theory has been applied by members of this group—and others at Oxford—to the design of control software for aircraft engines [Jac89], to real-time robotics [Sca90, Sta90, Wal91], to the specification of a realistic telephone switching network [KaR90, Su91], and to the verification of a local area network protocol [Dav91].

In this paper, we outline the theory of Timed CSP and examine some common themes from the above applications.

2 The Language of Timed CSP

The language of Timed CSP introduced in [ReR86] is a simple extension of Hoare's Communicating Sequential Processes. The word *process* is used to denote the behaviour pattern of an object, viewed through the occurrence and availability of certain *events*—atomic communications between an object and its environment. Every event is drawn from a universal alphabet of synchronisations Σ. The language of untimed CSP consists of several process constructors, including primitives for parallel composition, nondeterministic choice and hiding.

Note: In this paper, we will present the language of Timed CSP and we will limit our discussion primarily to the Timed Failures Model. We are currently preparing the definitive text on Timed CSP, in which a complete discussion of the language and its hierarchy of semantic models will be given.

2.1 Syntax

In Timed CSP, each of the untimed CSP operators is interpreted in a timed context, and two timing operators are added: delay and timeout. The syntax of *TCSP* terms is given by the following BNF rule:

$$\begin{aligned} P \; ::= \; & STOP \mid SKIP \mid WAIT\, t \mid a \xrightarrow{t} P \mid P\,;P \mid \\ & P \,\Box\, P \mid P \sqcap P \mid P \overset{t}{\rhd} P \mid P\; {}_A\|_A\; P \mid P \,|||\, P \mid \\ & f(P) \mid P \setminus A \mid \mu X \circ F(X) \end{aligned}$$

In the above rule, event a is drawn from the set of all synchronisations Σ, event set A ranges over the set of subsets of Σ, and t is a non-negative real number: we place no lower bound on the interval between consecutive events—this allows us to model asynchronous processes in a satisfactory fashion, without artificial constraints upon the times at which independent events may be observed.

The term *STOP* represents a broken process which will never engage in external communication, corresponding to the undesirable phenomena of deadlock and divergence. The term *SKIP* represents a process which does nothing except terminate immediately. As in untimed CSP, the special event ✓ is used to indicate that a process has terminated. The term *WAIT* t is a delayed form of *SKIP*. It represents a process which does nothing except terminate successfully after time t.

The prefix operator $\rightarrow$ allows us to introduce communication events into the behaviour pattern of a process. In untimed CSP, the term $a \rightarrow P$ models a system which is initially prepared to engage in event a, and then eventually behaves as P. To model real-time systems, we must be able to model constraints upon the time between the observation of an a and the onset of P.

The process $a \xrightarrow{t} P$ will behave as P precisely t time units after the synchronisation a is observed. The relation between prefix and delay is an obvious one:

$$a \xrightarrow{t_1+t_2} P \;\equiv\; a \xrightarrow{t_1} WAIT\; t_2\,;P$$

For example, a process that makes event b available *exactly* four seconds after event a is observed, only to halt two seconds after b is performed, would be written:

$$PROC \;==\; a \xrightarrow{4} b \xrightarrow{2} STOP$$

We consider events to be instantaneous; if the duration of an action is of interest, then that action may be modelled by considering the beginning and the end of the action to be separate events.

The sequential composition operator provides a means of transferring control on termination. In the construct $P\,;Q$, control is passed from P to Q if and when P performs the termination event $\checkmark$. This event is not visible to the environment, and occurs as soon as it becomes available.

Timed CSP provides two forms of choice: external and internal. An external choice $P \Box Q$ may be resolved by the environment. If the environment is prepared to cooperate with P, but not with Q, then the choice behaves as P: the choice is resolved by the first communication. In contrast, the environment has no influence over an internal choice $P \sqcap Q$: the outcome of such a choice is nondeterministic.

The timeout operator $P \overset{t}{\triangleright} Q$ transfers control from P to Q if no communications occur before time t. As above, this time may be any non-negative real number. If an attempt at communication involving P is made at time t precisely, then the outcome will be nondeterministic. If either of the components should terminate, then the entire timeout construct terminates immediately.

In Timed CSP, the parallel combination of two terms P and Q is parametrised by two sets of events. In the construct

$$P \;{}_A\|_B\; Q$$

term P may perform only those events in A, term Q may perform only those events in B, and the two terms must cooperate on events drawn from the intersection of A and B. The asynchronous parallel combinator, $|||$, allows both components to evolve concurrently without interacting.

The hiding operator provides a mechanism for abstraction in Timed CSP. The term $P \backslash A$ behaves as P except that events in A are concealed from the environment. Concealed events no longer require the cooperation of the environment, and so occur as soon as P is ready to perform them. The relabelled term $f(P)$ has a similar control structure to term P, with observable events renamed according to function f.

We use the expression $\mu X \circ F(X)$ to denote the unique fixed point of the semantic domain mapping represented by F. Only recursions that admit such fixed points are allowed.

2.2 The Timed Failures Model TM_F

We will now provide a denotational semantic model to facilitate a formal description of the language, based upon the Timed Failures model presented in [Ree88]. In our model, each piece of process algebra will be associated with a set of observations. Each observation is represented by a pair $(s, \aleph)$. The first component is a timed trace s: a record of timed events observed. The second is a timed refusal $\aleph$: a record of timed events refused.

A timed event is a pair (t, a), where t is a time value and a is a communication event. The domain of time values is defined to be

$$TIME \;==\; [0, \infty)$$

The set of all timed events is thus

$$T\Sigma \;==\; TIME \times \Sigma$$

A timed trace is a chronologically ordered sequence of timed events; the set of all timed traces is given by:

$$T\Sigma^*_{\leqslant} \;==\; \{s \in \text{seq}\, T\Sigma \mid (t,a) \text{ precedes } (t',a') \text{ in } s \Rightarrow t \leqslant t'\}$$

The presence of a timed event (t, a) in a timed trace will correspond to the observation of the synchronisation a at time t.

A timed refusal set is a set of timed events, corresponding to a finite union of refusal tokens. Each token is a Cartesian product set of the form $I \times A$, where I is a half-open time interval and A is a set of events. If we take $TINT$ to be the set of all such intervals, and $RTOK$ to be the set of all refusal tokens, then the set of all timed refusal sets is defined by

$$RSET \;==\; \{\bigcup C \mid C \subseteq_{\text{fin}} RTOK\}$$

where

$$\begin{aligned} TINT \;&==\; \{[b,e) \mid 0 \leqslant b < e < \infty\} \\ RTOK \;&==\; \{I \times A \mid I \in TINT \wedge A \in \mathbb{P}\Sigma\} \end{aligned}$$

The presence of a timed event (t, a) in refusal set $\aleph$ corresponds to the refusal of the process to engage in synchronisation a at time t.

The set of possible observations, or *timed failures*, is given by TF, where

$$TF \;==\; T\Sigma^*_{\leqslant} \times RSET$$

2.3 Notation

We inherit the following operators from [Hoa85]:

$\frown$	concatenation of traces	**in**	contiguous subsequence
$\langle\rangle$	the empty trace	#	length of a sequence
$\leqslant$	trace prefix	$<$	strict trace prefix

The predicate s_1 **in** s_2 holds precisely when trace s_1 is a contiguous subsequence of s_2. If s is a timed trace, then $\#(s)$ returns the number of timed events in that trace.

The *begin* operator returns the time of occurrence of the first event in a timed trace, refusal, or failure:

$$\begin{aligned} begin(s) \;&==\; \min(\{t : TIME \mid \exists\, a : \Sigma \bullet (t,a) \in s\} \cup \{\infty\}) \\ begin(\aleph) \;&==\; \inf(\{t \mid \exists\, a \bullet (t,a) \in \aleph\} \cup \{\infty\}) \\ begin(s,\aleph) \;&==\; \min\{begin(s), begin(\aleph)\} \end{aligned}$$

Similarly, the *end* operator returns the time of occurrence of the last event in a timed trace, refusal, or failure:

$$\begin{aligned} end(s) \;&==\; \max(\{t : TIME \mid \exists\, a : \Sigma \bullet (t,a) \in s\} \cup \{0\}) \\ end(\aleph) \;&==\; \sup(\{t \mid \exists\, a \bullet (t,a) \in \aleph\} \cup \{0\}) \\ end(s,\aleph) \;&==\; \max\{begin(s), begin(\aleph)\} \end{aligned}$$

We define the *during* ($\uparrow$) operator on timed traces and refusals, returning the part of the trace or refusal that lies in a specified time interval:

$$\begin{array}{rcll} \langle\rangle \uparrow I & == & \langle\rangle & \\ (\langle(t,a)\rangle^\frown s) \uparrow I & == & \langle(t,a)\rangle^\frown(s \uparrow I) & \text{if } t \in I \\ & & (s \uparrow I) & \text{otherwise} \\ \aleph \uparrow I & == & \aleph \cap (I \times \Sigma) & \end{array}$$

where I is a set of real numbers. In the case that $I = \{t\}$ for some time t, we may omit the set brackets.

It proves convenient to define a *before* operator on traces and refusals:

$$\begin{array}{rcl} s \upharpoonright t & == & s \uparrow [0,t] \\ \aleph \upharpoonright t & == & \aleph \uparrow [0,t) \end{array}$$

The definition of $\upharpoonright$ on refusal sets differs from that on timed traces. For traces, $s \upharpoonright t$ includes events at t; in the case of refusals, such events are excluded. This choice of definitions is the most convenient for timed failures specifications.

We define an operator to strip the timing information from a timed trace, yielding the corresponding trace of untimed events:

$$\begin{array}{rcl} tstrip(\langle\rangle) & == & \langle\rangle \\ tstrip(\langle(t,a)\rangle^\frown s) & == & \langle a\rangle^\frown tstrip(s) \end{array}$$

Finally, we define an operator that shifts traces, refusals and failures through time:

$$\begin{array}{rcl} \langle\rangle + t & == & \langle\rangle \\ (\langle(t_1,a)\rangle^\frown s) + t & == & (\langle(t_1+t,a)\rangle^\frown(s+t)) \uparrow [0,\infty) \\ \aleph + t & == & \{(t_1+t,a) \mid (t_1,a) \in \aleph\} \uparrow [0,\infty) \\ (s,\aleph) + t & == & (s+t, \aleph+t) \end{array}$$

2.4 The Domain TM_F

We define the Timed Failures model TM_F to be those subsets S of TF which satisfy the following set of healthiness conditions:

1. $(\langle\rangle, \{\}) \in S$
2. $(s^\frown w, \aleph) \in S \Rightarrow (s, \aleph \upharpoonright begin(w)) \in S$
3. $\forall \aleph' : RSET \bullet (s,\aleph) \in S \wedge \aleph' \subseteq \aleph \Rightarrow (s,\aleph') \in S$
4. $\forall t : [0,\infty) \bullet \exists\, n(t) : \mathbb{N} \bullet (s,\aleph) \in S \wedge end(s) \leqslant t \Rightarrow \#(s) \leqslant n(t)$

5. $(s, \aleph) \in S \Rightarrow$
$$\exists \aleph' : RSET \bullet \aleph \subseteq \aleph' \wedge (s, \aleph') \in S \wedge$$
$$\forall (t, a) \in T\Sigma \bullet (t, a) \notin \aleph' \Rightarrow (s \restriction t ^\frown \langle (t, a) \rangle, \aleph' \restriction t) \in S$$
$$\wedge$$
$$((t > 0 \wedge \nexists\, \epsilon > 0 \bullet ((t - \epsilon, t) \times \{a\} \subseteq \aleph')) \Rightarrow (s \restriction t ^\frown \langle (t, a) \rangle, \aleph' \restriction t) \in S)$$

2.5 The Complete Metric on TM_F

We define a distance metric d on TM_F by considering the earliest time after which the elements of two sets may be distinguished.

$$S \restriction t \quad == \quad \{(s, \aleph) \mid (s, \aleph) \in S \wedge end(s, \aleph) \leqslant t\}$$

If S is a element of TM_F then $S \restriction t$ is the set of elements of S which do not extend beyond time t. We may now define the complete metric:

$$d(S, T) \quad == \quad \inf(\{2^{-t} \mid S \restriction t = T \restriction t\} \cup \{1\})$$

2.6 The Semantic Function $\mathcal{F}_T$

We require the following additional operators on traces and refusals:

$$\begin{aligned}
\sigma(s) \quad &== \quad \{a : \Sigma \mid \exists t \bullet (t, a) \text{ in } s\} \\
\sigma(\aleph) \quad &== \quad \{a : \Sigma \mid \exists t \bullet (t, a) \in \aleph\} \\
\aleph \upharpoonleft t \quad &== \quad \aleph \uparrow [t, \infty) \\
\aleph \downharpoonleft A \quad &== \quad \aleph \cap [0, \infty) \times A \\
\langle\rangle \downharpoonleft A \quad &== \quad \langle\rangle \\
(\langle (t, a) \rangle ^\frown s) \downharpoonleft A \quad &== \quad \langle (t, a) \rangle ^\frown (s \downharpoonleft A) \quad \text{if } a \in A \\
& \quad s \downharpoonleft A \quad \text{otherwise}
\end{aligned}$$

The semantic function

$$\mathcal{F}_T : TCSP \rightarrow TM_F$$

is defined by the following set of equations:

$$\begin{aligned}
\mathcal{F}_T[\![STOP]\!] \quad &== \quad \{(\langle\rangle, \aleph) \mid \aleph \in RSET\} \\
\mathcal{F}_T[\![SKIP]\!] \quad &== \quad \{(\langle\rangle, \aleph) \mid \checkmark \notin \sigma(\aleph)\} \\
& \quad \cup \\
& \quad \{(\langle (t, \checkmark) \rangle, \aleph) \mid t \geqslant 0 \wedge \checkmark \notin \sigma(\aleph \uparrow [0, t))\} \\
\mathcal{F}_T[\![WAIT\ t_0]\!] \quad &== \quad \{(\langle\rangle, \aleph) \mid \checkmark \notin \sigma(\aleph \upharpoonleft t_0)\} \\
& \quad \cup \\
& \quad \{(\langle (t, \checkmark) \rangle, \aleph) \mid t \geqslant t_0 \wedge \checkmark \notin \sigma(\aleph \uparrow [t_0, t))\}
\end{aligned}$$

$$
\begin{aligned}
\mathcal{F}_T[\![a \xrightarrow{t_0} P]\!] \;&==\; \{(\langle\rangle, \aleph) \mid a \notin \sigma(\aleph)\} \\
&\quad \cup \\
&\quad \{(\langle(t,a)\rangle^\frown s, \aleph) \mid \; t \geqslant 0 \;\wedge \\
&\qquad a \notin \sigma(\aleph \upharpoonright t) \;\wedge \\
&\qquad begin(s) \geqslant t + t_0 \;\wedge \\
&\qquad (s, \aleph) - (t + t_0) \in \mathcal{F}_T[\![P]\!]\} \\
\mathcal{F}_T[\![P\,;\,Q]\!] \;&==\; \{(s, \aleph) \mid \checkmark \notin \sigma(s) \;\wedge \\
&\qquad (s, \aleph \cup ([0, end(s,\aleph)) \times \{\checkmark\})) \in \mathcal{F}_T[\![P]\!] \\
&\qquad \vee \\
&\qquad s = s_P{}^\frown s_Q \wedge \checkmark \notin \sigma(s_P) \;\wedge \\
&\qquad (s_Q, \aleph) - t \in \mathcal{F}_T[\![Q]\!] \;\wedge \\
&\qquad (s_P{}^\frown\langle(t,\checkmark)\rangle, \aleph \upharpoonright t \cup ([0,t) \times \{\checkmark\})) \in \mathcal{F}_T[\![P]\!]\} \\
\mathcal{F}_T[\![P \sqcap Q]\!] \;&==\; \mathcal{F}_T[\![P]\!] \cup \mathcal{F}_T[\![Q]\!] \\
\mathcal{F}_T[\![P \,\square\, Q]\!] \;&==\; \{(\langle\rangle, \aleph) \mid (\langle\rangle, \aleph) \in \mathcal{F}_T[\![P]\!] \cap \mathcal{F}_T[\![Q]\!]\} \\
&\quad \cup \\
&\quad \{(s, \aleph) \mid s \neq \langle\rangle \wedge (s, \aleph) \in \mathcal{F}_T[\![P]\!] \cup \mathcal{F}_T[\![Q]\!] \\
&\qquad \wedge \\
&\qquad (\langle\rangle, \aleph \upharpoonright begin(s)) \in \mathcal{F}_T[\![P]\!] \cap \mathcal{F}_T[\![Q]\!]\} \\
\mathcal{F}_T[\![f(P)]\!] \;&==\; \{(f(s), \aleph) \mid (s, f^{-1}(\aleph)) \in \mathcal{F}_T[\![P]\!]\} \\
\mathcal{F}_T[\![P \setminus A]\!] \;&==\; \{(s \setminus A, \aleph) \mid (s, \aleph \cup ([0, end(s,\aleph) \times A) \in \mathcal{F}_T[\![P]\!]\} \\
\mathcal{F}_T[\![P \;{}_A\|_B\; Q]\!] \;&==\; \{(s, \aleph_P \cup \aleph_Q \cup \aleph_R) \mid \exists\, s_P, s_Q \bullet \\
&\qquad \sigma(\aleph_P) \subseteq A \wedge \sigma(\aleph_Q) \subseteq B \;\wedge \\
&\qquad \sigma(\aleph_R) \subseteq \Sigma - (A \cup B) \wedge s \in (s_P \;{}_A\|_B\; s_Q) \;\wedge \\
&\qquad (s_P, \aleph_P) \in \mathcal{F}_T[\![P]\!] \wedge (s_Q, \aleph_Q) \in \mathcal{F}_T[\![Q]\!]\;\} \\
\mathcal{F}_T[\![P \,|||\, Q]\!] \;&==\; \{(s, \aleph) \mid \exists\, s_P, s_Q \bullet \;\; s \in s_P \,|||\, s_Q \;\wedge \\
&\qquad (s_P, \aleph) \in \mathcal{F}_T[\![P]\!] \;\wedge \\
&\qquad (s_Q, \aleph) \in \mathcal{F}_T[\![Q]\!]\} \\
\mathcal{F}_T[\![P \overset{t_0}{\rhd} Q]\!] \;&==\; \{(s, \aleph) \mid begin(s) \leqslant t_0 \wedge (s, \aleph) \in \mathcal{F}_T[\![P]\!]\} \\
&\quad \cup \\
&\quad \{(s, \aleph) \mid begin(s) \geqslant t_0 \wedge (\langle\rangle, \aleph \upharpoonright t_0) \in \mathcal{F}_T[\![P]\!] \\
&\qquad \wedge \\
&\qquad (s, \aleph) - t_0 \in \mathcal{F}_T[\![Q]\!]\}
\end{aligned}
$$

$\mathcal{F}_T[\![\mu X \circ F(X)]\!] \;==\;$ the unique fixed point of the mapping corresponding to F on the semantic domain, if this mapping is a contraction mapping under metric d

where the auxiliary functions on timed traces are defined as follows:

$$
s_P \;{}_A\|_B\; s_Q \;==\; \{s \in T\Sigma^*_{\leqslant} \mid s \downharpoonright A = s_P \wedge s \downharpoonright B = s_Q \wedge s \downharpoonright (A \cup B) = s\}
$$

$$s_P \,|||\, s_Q \;==\; \{s : T\Sigma^*_{\leqslant} \mid \forall t : TIME \bullet \forall a : \Sigma \bullet \\ s \uparrow t \downharpoonright \{a\} = s_P \uparrow t \downharpoonright \{a\} \frown s_Q \uparrow t \downharpoonright \{a\}\}$$

2.7 Remarks on Differences with Previous Versions

The Timed Failures Model presented above differs from that originally given in [ReR87, Ree88] in several respects. In particular, there is no constant delay δ required for prefixing or the unwinding of recursions. All time delays are now explicit, and include 0. Recursion is only valid for those recursive functions representing contraction mappings on the complete metric space domain. Note that in [Dav91], Davies shows that valid recursions in the current model can be checked by syntactic analysis alone.

We believe that the current model is more applicable in its greater abstraction. Of course, the original model is now simply one of many possible interpretations.

3 Specification and Verification

A specification of a system is a formal description of its intended behaviour. We say that a program P meets a specification S in a denotational model M if every possible behaviour of P in that model meets the corresponding specification condition. In this case we say that P satisfies S, written P **sat** S. The task of verification is to establish that the specification S is indeed satisfied by process P.

We will describe two styles of specification. The first is mathematical, allowing any predicate S on behaviours as a specification. This approach has the advantage of expressivity, but its generality makes fully formal verification difficult. The second gives a grammar for a temporal logic specification language. This has the advantage of allowing formal verification. It is not so expressive, but nonetheless contains a large class of useful specifications.

Each of these styles of specification has an associated proof system, which reduces the proof that P satisfies S to a number of smaller derivations on the (syntactically simpler) subcomponents of P. Ultimately, the verification task is reduced to tautology checking of statements written in the specification language.

A further method of verification is that of timewise refinement. This approach uses the links between various timed and untimed models for CSP in order to verify specifications in the simpler models, and then translate the result to the more complex model. This may be done in cases where the specification in question is not time-critical, so the additional timing information available in the more complex model is unnecessary for the verification. The higher level of abstraction in the simpler model generally makes reasoning easier.

3.1 Mathematical specification

The satisfaction relation is defined between processes and specifications in the failures model as follows:

$$P \,\mathbf{sat}\, S \;==\; \forall (s, \aleph) \in \mathcal{F}_T[\![P]\!] \bullet S$$

We say that a specification S is satisfiable if there is a process that satisfies it. We identify necessary conditions for a specification to be satisfiable (see [Dav91]); specifications should be checked against these conditions before searching for an implementation:

Lemma 3.1 If S is satisfiable, then $S[(\langle\rangle, \{\})/s, \aleph]$. ♡

Since all processes may exhibit the minimal behaviour, any implementation P may do so; since S must hold for all possible behaviours of P, it must in particular hold for $(\langle\rangle, \{\})$. This condition rules out any requirement that insists that a certain timed event appears in the trace or refusal, without a qualifying assumption.

A more surprising result, which has no analogue in the untimed models, is that a specification may not insist that a certain timed event is absent from the refusal set.

Lemma 3.2 If S is a behavioural specification such that

$$\exists\, e : T\Sigma \bullet S \Rightarrow e \notin \aleph$$

then S is not satisfiable ♡

This result holds because any process may engage in only finitely many copies of any timed event e. Since its environment may always offer more copies of an event than the process is able to perform, the process must refuse another copy of event e if it has already performed as many as possible at the current time. Hence there is always some trace during which the event e may be refused.

As an example of a specification, consider a timed buffer. A t-buffer is a process which, when empty is always prepared to input a message by t, and which when non-empty is always prepared to output the next message within that time. It may be specified as follows:

$$\begin{aligned} BUFF_t \quad == \quad & tstrip(s \downharpoonright OUT) \leqslant tstrip(s \downharpoonright IN) \\ & \wedge \\ & tstrip(s \downharpoonright OUT) = tstrip(s \downharpoonright IN) \Rightarrow IN \cap \sigma(\aleph \upharpoonright end(s) + t) = \{\} \\ & \wedge \\ & tstrip(s \downharpoonright OUT) < tstrip(s \downharpoonright IN) \Rightarrow OUT \not\subseteq \sigma(\aleph \upharpoonright end(s) + t) = \{\} \end{aligned}$$

where M is the set of messages that may be transmitted through the buffer, and

$$\begin{aligned} IN \quad &== \quad \{in.m \mid m \in M\} \\ OUT \quad &== \quad \{out.m \mid m \in M\} \end{aligned}$$

define the event sets corresponding to input messages and output messages, respectively.

A process is t-deadlock-free if it must perform, or at least offer some event over an interval of length t. No execution may exhibit the refusal of the entire set of events over such an interval after the last visible action.

$$DF_t \quad == \quad \forall\, T \bullet T \geqslant end(s) \Rightarrow [T, T + t] \times \Sigma \not\subseteq \aleph$$

Observe that the use of the closed interval $[T, T+t]$ yields the specification that Σ cannot be continuously refused (after the end of the trace) for any length of time strictly greater than t. In order to disallow intervals of length exactly t as well, the half open interval $[T, T + t)$ should be used instead.

Proof System

The semantic function $\mathcal{F}_T$ is directly compositional, in the sense that every behaviour $(s, \aleph)$ of a composite program arises from a combination of a single behaviour from each component program (possibly in more than one way). It is this feature of the semantic function that makes it possible to define a sound and complete proof rule for each TCSP operator. Each rule is complete in the sense that if a specification holds of a composite process built using the corresponding operator, then the rule may be used to deduce this from specifications of the component processes. Since there is one rule for each operator in the syntax, the proof system is complete for all TCSP processes. For example,

STOP

$$\frac{}{STOP \ \mathbf{sat}\ s = \langle\rangle}$$

Prefix

$$\frac{P \ \mathbf{sat}\ S}{\begin{array}{ll} a \xrightarrow{t} P \ \mathbf{sat} & s = \langle\rangle \wedge a \notin \sigma(\aleph) \\ & \vee \\ & s = \langle(t', a)\rangle ^\frown s' \wedge a \notin \sigma(\aleph \upharpoonright t') \wedge begin(s') \geqslant (t' + t) \\ & \qquad\qquad \wedge\ S[(s', \aleph) - (t' + t)/(s, \aleph)] \end{array}}$$

Nondeterministic Choice

$$\frac{\begin{array}{l} P \ \mathbf{sat}\ S \\ Q \ \mathbf{sat}\ T \end{array}}{P \sqcap Q \ \mathbf{sat}\ S \vee T}$$

Parallel

$$\frac{\begin{array}{l} P \ \mathbf{sat}\ S \\ Q \ \mathbf{sat}\ T \end{array}}{P \parallel Q \ \mathbf{sat}\ \exists \aleph_P, \aleph_Q \bullet \aleph = \aleph_P \cup \aleph_Q \wedge S[\aleph_P/\aleph] \wedge T[\aleph_Q/\aleph]}$$

Recursion

$$\frac{X \ \mathbf{sat}\ S \Rightarrow F(X) \ \mathbf{sat}\ S}{\mu X \circ F(X) \ \mathbf{sat}\ S} \quad [\ F \text{ contracting}, S \text{ satisfiable}\ ]$$

The above recursion rule requires first a proof of satisfaction, which can sometimes be nontrivial. In [DaS89], it was shown that this requirement can be relaxed if the natural extension of F to the complete metric space of all subsets of TF preserves satisfaction.

As an illustration of the application of these rules, we prove that the process

$$\mu X \circ in \xrightarrow{1} out \xrightarrow{1} X$$

is *1*-deadlock-free. To do this, we must apply the extended recursion rule. To establish the antecedent to this rule, we use the proof system to prove that the body of the recursion maintains a specification that is at least as strong as the one we wish to establish. In fact we must strengthen the specification, to include the fact that in the initial state, some event is immediately and persistently on offer; thus some event does not appear in the refusal set at all before the first event occurs.

We begin by assuming that X meets the stronger specification:

$$\begin{array}{rrl}
 & X \ \textbf{sat} & DF_1 \wedge (s = \langle\rangle \Rightarrow \sigma(\aleph) \neq \Sigma) \\
\Rightarrow & out \xrightarrow{1} X \ \textbf{sat} & s = \langle\rangle \wedge out \notin \sigma(\aleph) \\
 & & \vee \\
 & & s = \langle(t, out)\rangle^\frown s' \wedge out \notin \sigma(\aleph \upharpoonright t) \wedge begin(s') \geqslant (t+1) \\
 & & \qquad \wedge\ DF_1[(s', \aleph) - (t+1)/(s, \aleph)] \\
 & & \qquad \wedge\ s' - (t+1) = \langle\rangle \Rightarrow \sigma(\aleph - (t+1)) \neq \Sigma \\
 & & \Rightarrow DF_1 \wedge s = \langle\rangle \Rightarrow \sigma(\aleph) \neq \Sigma \\
\Rightarrow & in \xrightarrow{1} out \xrightarrow{1} X \ \textbf{sat} & s = \langle\rangle \wedge in \notin \sigma(\aleph) \\
 & & \vee \\
 & & s = \langle(t, in)\rangle^\frown s' \wedge in \notin \sigma(\aleph \upharpoonright t) \wedge begin(s') \geqslant (t+1) \\
 & & \qquad \wedge\ DF_1[(s', \aleph) - (t+1)/(s, \aleph)] \\
 & & \qquad \wedge\ s' - (t+1) = \langle\rangle \Rightarrow \sigma(\aleph - (t+1)) \neq \Sigma \\
 & & \Rightarrow DF_1 \wedge s = \langle\rangle \Rightarrow \sigma(\aleph) \neq \Sigma
\end{array}$$

Hence the antecedent to the recursion rule holds, so we obtain that

$$\mu X \circ in \xrightarrow{1} out \xrightarrow{1} X \ \textbf{sat}\ DF_1 \wedge s = \langle\rangle \Rightarrow \sigma(\aleph) \neq \Sigma$$

We may weaken the specification to obtain the desired result, that

$$\mu X \circ in \xrightarrow{1} out \xrightarrow{1} X \ \textbf{sat}\ DF_1$$

3.2 Temporal Logic Specifications

The use of a tightly defined logical language for describing specifications has the advantage that verifications may more easily be expressed in terms of a reduced set of manipulations, yielding them more amenable to mechanisation. The restricted syntax also means that common properties of specifications such as safety and liveness may be easily characterised by the form they take.

We use the following language as our temporal logic specification language.

$$p \ ::= \ true \mid A \mid \neg P \mid p \wedge p \mid p\,\mathcal{U}_R\, q$$

The atoms A contain propositions of the form $\mathbb{P}_X$ (some event from the set X is performed) and $\mathbb{O}_X$ (the set X is offered) for each set $X \subseteq \Sigma$. Such atoms may also be labelled to yield other atomic propositions, such as $\mathbb{P}'_X$ and $\mathbb{O}'_X$. In the above syntax, predicate R may take any of the following forms

$$\_ \leqslant T\ ,\ \_ < T\ ,\ \_ = T\ ,\ \_ \geqslant T\ ,\ \_ > T$$

where $T \in \mathbb{R}^+$.

Specifications written in this language are concerned with complete executions of the system, rather than the finite time behaviours used by the denotational models. We will assume the infinite behaviours of the system to be the limits of the finite ones; this assumption is unjustified for processes which have infinite branching nondeterminism (see [Sch91]); such a process may have fewer infinite executions. In the proof system described below, completeness is lost for such processes, though the system remains sound.

We define the infinite failures $\mathcal{I}_T[\![Q]\!]$ of a program Q in terms of its finite failures:

Definition 3.3 The set of infinite failures $\mathcal{I}_T[\![Q]\!]$ of a program Q is given by

$$\mathcal{I}_T[\![Q]\!] \quad = \quad \{(s,\aleph) \mid s \in T\Sigma^*_{\leqslant} \wedge \aleph \subseteq T\Sigma \wedge \forall t < \infty \bullet (s,\aleph) \upharpoonright t \in \mathcal{F}_T[\![Q]\!]\}$$

◇

Infinite failures of the form $(s,\aleph)$ model propositions at times t according to the following definitions:

$$\begin{array}{rcl}
(s,\aleph),t \models \mathbb{P}_X & \Leftrightarrow & (s \uparrow t) \downharpoonright X \neq \langle\rangle \\
(s,\aleph),t \models \mathbb{O}_X & \Leftrightarrow & X \cap \sigma(\aleph \uparrow t) = \{\} \\
(s,\aleph),t \models \neg P & \Leftrightarrow & (s,\aleph),t \not\models P \\
(s,\aleph),t \models P \wedge Q & \Leftrightarrow & (s,\aleph),t \models P \text{ and } (s,\aleph),t \models Q \\
(s,\aleph),t \models P\,\mathcal{U}_R\,Q & == & \exists t_1 \bullet R(t_1 - t) \text{ and } \forall t_2 \bullet t < t_2 < t_1 \Rightarrow (s,\aleph),t_2 \models P \\
& & \text{and } (s,\aleph),t_1 \models P
\end{array}$$

A number of useful abbreviations and derived specification constructs may be defined in terms of these:

$$\begin{array}{rcll}
P\,\mathcal{U}\,Q & == & P\,\mathcal{U}_{<\infty}\,Q & \text{until} \\
P\,\mathcal{W}\,Q & == & (P\,\mathcal{U}\,Q) \vee \mathbf{G}\,(P) & \text{unless} \\
P\,\overline{\mathcal{U}}\,Q & == & (P \wedge P\,\mathcal{U}\,Q) \vee Q & \text{reflexive until} \\
P\,\overline{\mathcal{W}}\,Q & == & (P\,\overline{\mathcal{U}}\,Q) \vee \mathbf{G}\,(P) & \text{reflexive unless} \\
\overline{\mathbf{F}}\,P & == & T\,\overline{\mathcal{U}}\,P & \text{reflexive eventually} \\
\overline{\mathbf{G}}\,P & == & \neg\,\overline{\mathbf{F}}\,\neg P & \text{reflexive always}
\end{array}$$

We then say that P **sat** S if all of P's behaviours at time 0 model the proposition S:

$$P\ \mathbf{sat}\ S \quad == \quad \forall (s,\aleph) \in \mathcal{I}_T[\![P]\!] \bullet (s,\aleph), 0 \models S$$

As an example of a TL specification, consider the requirement that the system should alternate on its performance of *in* and *out* events, starting with *in*. This may be captured in the specification language as follows:

$$\begin{array}{rcll}
\Phi & = & \overline{\mathbf{G}}\,(\mathbb{P}_{in} \Rightarrow (\neg\mathbb{P}_{in})\,\mathcal{W}\,\mathbb{P}_{out}) & (1) \\
& & \wedge\ \overline{\mathbf{G}}\,(\mathbb{P}_{out} \Rightarrow (\neg\mathbb{P}_{out})\,\mathcal{W}\,\mathbb{P}_{in}) & (2) \\
& & \wedge\ (\neg\mathbb{P}_{out})\,\overline{\mathcal{W}}\,\mathbb{P}_{in} & (3)
\end{array}$$

This states (1) that whenever an *in* event is performed, then no further *in* event is performed unless an *out* event occurs; (2) that whenever an *out* event occurs, then no further *out* may be performed unless an *in* event occurs; (3) that *out* may not be performed unless *in* is performed. Since a process satisfies this specification if its behaviours model it at time *0*, condition (3) is the requirement that the first *out* event may not occur before the first *in* event.

Temporal Logic Proof System

The temporal logic proof system consists of a number of rules, one for each TCSP operator. The rules are relatively complete, in the sense that if a TL specification is satisfied by a program, then the rules may be used to reduce the verification to checking a temporal logic tautology. We present few rules here for illustrative purposes; the complete set is presented in [Jac91].

STOP

$$\frac{}{STOP \ \mathbf{sat} \ \forall X \subseteq \Sigma \bullet \overline{\mathbf{G}}(\neg \mathbb{P}_X)}$$

Prefixing

$$\frac{\begin{array}{l} P \ \mathbf{sat} \ p \\ \left.\begin{array}{l} (\mathbb{O}_a \wedge \neg \mathbb{P}_\Sigma) \\ \overline{\mathcal{W}} \\ (\mathbb{P}_a \wedge \neg \mathbb{P}_{\Sigma-\{a\}} \wedge (\neg \mathbb{P}_\Sigma \mathcal{U}_{=t}\, p)) \end{array}\right\} \Rightarrow r \end{array}}{a \xrightarrow{t} P \ \mathbf{sat} \ r}$$

Nondeterministic Choice

$$\frac{\begin{array}{l} P \ \mathbf{sat} \ p \\ Q \ \mathbf{sat} \ q \\ (p \vee q) \Rightarrow r \end{array}}{P \sqcap Q \ \mathbf{sat} \ r}$$

Parallel Composition

$$\frac{\begin{array}{l} P \ \mathbf{sat} \ p \\ Q \ \mathbf{sat} \ q \\ \left.\begin{array}{l} p[\mathbb{O}'/\mathbb{O}_\Sigma] \wedge \\ q[\mathbb{O}''/\mathbb{O}_\Sigma] \wedge \\ \overline{\mathbf{G}}(\mathbb{O} \Leftrightarrow_\Sigma \mathbb{O}' \wedge \mathbb{O}'') \end{array}\right\} \Rightarrow r \end{array}}{P \parallel Q \ \mathbf{sat} \ r}$$

Recursion

$$\frac{X \textbf{ sat } r \Rightarrow F(X) \textbf{ sat } r}{\mu X \circ F(X) \textbf{ sat } r} \quad [\, r \text{ satisfiable, admissible}, F \text{ contracting} \,]$$

A satisfiable predicate r is one for which $\exists P \in TM_F \bullet P \textbf{ sat } r$. An admissible predicate is one which holds for an infinite behaviour $(s, \aleph)$ whenever it holds for all the finite approximations $(s \upharpoonright t, \aleph \upharpoonright t)$. This side condition is needed in the temporal logic proof system because of the use of infinite behaviours in specification. A behaviour upsetting a specification may be absent from every element of a convergent sequence, but present in the limit.

For example, the inadmissible specification $\mathbf{F}\,\mathbb{O}_\Sigma$ is preserved by the function corresponding to $WAIT\ 1\,;X$, but the recursive process $\mu X \circ WAIT\ 1\,;X$ does not satisfy it. Specifications that are built using bounded until operators as the only temporal connective will always be admissible. The issue of admissibility does not arise when only finite behaviours are considered, as in the proof system presented earlier; hence unbounded eventuality cannot even be expressed as a finite behavioural specification.

To illustrate the rules presented above, we perform a simple verification for the specification Φ given above; we prove that $\mu X \circ in \xrightarrow{1} out \xrightarrow{1} X \textbf{ sat } \Phi$. Observe that the specification Φ is admissible: if an infinite behaviour does not model it, then neither does some finite prefix.

$$\begin{array}{lrcl}
 & X & \textbf{sat} & \Phi \\
\Rightarrow & out \xrightarrow{1} X & \textbf{sat} & (\neg \mathbb{P}_{out})\,\overline{\mathcal{W}}\,((\mathbb{P}_{out} \wedge \neg \mathbb{P}_\Sigma)\,\mathcal{U}_{t=1}\,\Phi) \\
 & & & \Rightarrow \left.\begin{array}{l} (\neg \mathbb{P}_{in})\,\overline{\mathcal{W}}\,\mathbb{P}_{out} \\ \wedge\ \overline{\mathbf{G}}(\mathbb{P}_{in} \Rightarrow (\neg \mathbb{P}_{in}\,\mathcal{W}\,\mathbb{P}_{out})) \\ \wedge\ \overline{\mathbf{G}}(\mathbb{P}_{out} \Rightarrow (\neg \mathbb{P}_{out}\,\mathcal{W}\,\mathbb{P}_{in})) \end{array}\right\} = \Phi_1 \\
\Rightarrow & in \xrightarrow{1} out \xrightarrow{1} X & \textbf{sat} & (\neg \mathbb{P}_{in})\,\overline{\mathcal{W}}\,((\mathbb{P}_{in} \wedge \neg \mathbb{P}_\Sigma)\,\mathcal{U}_{t=1}\,\Phi_1) \\
 & & & \Rightarrow \left.\begin{array}{l} (\neg \mathbb{P}_{out})\,\overline{\mathcal{W}}\,\mathbb{P}_{in} \\ \wedge\ \overline{\mathbf{G}}(\mathbb{P}_{out} \Rightarrow (\neg \mathbb{P}_{out}\,\mathcal{W}\,\mathbb{P}_{in})) \\ \wedge\ \overline{\mathbf{G}}(\mathbb{P}_{in} \Rightarrow (\neg \mathbb{P}_{in}\,\mathcal{W}\,\mathbb{P}_{out})) \end{array}\right\} = \Phi
\end{array}$$

Hence the antecedent to the recursion rule holds, so we obtain that

$$\mu X \circ in \xrightarrow{1} out \xrightarrow{1} X \quad \textbf{sat} \quad \Phi$$

3.3 Timewise Refinement

System requirements may often be decomposed into functional and timing aspects. Correct functional behaviour of a composite program may depend upon the logical interaction of its constituents and yet be independent of timing considerations. In such cases, the more abstract nature of the untimed models makes verification of such a program easier than in the timed models, where the increased descriptive power generated by the additional complexity of timed observations has become redundant. Yet the need to consider timing behaviour forces us to complete the analysis of the program in a timed model.

Furthermore, if correctness of timing behaviour rests on functional correctness, then the latter must be established in a timed framework.

Timewise refinement permits correctness-preserving migration between models in the hierarchy. A process in an untimed model is a description of purely functional behaviour; in a timed context, this may be considered as a characterisation of the functional aspects of a process behaviour, with the timing aspects completely unspecified. A correct timed implementation of such a process must be functionally correct with respect to this characterisation, and will in addition provide details of timing behaviour. Such a timed process is said to be a timed refinement of the untimed process.

An ability to link processes throughout the hierarchy permits the use of different models to establish different aspects of a system's correctness. Requirements may be decomposed, and each resulting part may be verified in a different model; timewise refinement allows these separate verifications to be used as a complete verification of the whole system.

The refinements presented here are defined with respect to the timed failures semantics of timed processes. These definitions extend immediately to the timed failures-stability model, since the failures components of the semantics of any TCSP program in the larger model are precisely its semantics in the timed failures model. Hence the results presented also hold for the timed-failures stability model.

Traces refinement

The Traces model M_T for CSP is concerned purely with the order in which events may be performed. Within the context of the hierarchy, it means that a description of a process is concerned purely with permissible sequences of events. This model has abstracted away from all considerations of refusal information, divergence, and timing behaviour. A process in this model may therefore be considered as a specification describing which sequences of events are acceptable; it will be refined by any process in a higher model whose sequences of events do not violate this specification.

We will consider the refinement relation between programs modelled in M_T, and timed programs modelled in the Timed Failures model TM_F. We write $P \sqsubseteq_T Q$ to mean that Q is a (trace) timewise refinement of P. This states that any sequence of events performed by Q must be a possible trace of P. It is defined as follows:

Definition 3.4 The relation $\sqsubseteq_T$ is defined as follows:

$$P \sqsubseteq_T Q \quad = \quad \forall s \in T\Sigma^*_{\leqslant} \bullet s \in \mathit{traces}(\mathcal{F}_T[\![Q]\!]) \Rightarrow \mathit{tstrip}(s) \in \mathcal{T}[\![P]\!]$$

It follows from this definition that if an untimed process meets a specification (with free variable tr ranging over behaviours in the traces model), then a timed process meets a corresponding specification. We obtain the following proof rule:

$$\frac{\begin{array}{l} P \sqsubseteq_T Q \\ P \ \mathbf{sat}\ S \end{array}}{Q \ \mathbf{sat}\ S[\mathit{tstrip}(s)/tr]}$$

The rule is complete: if S is a predicate on tr such that the conclusion holds, then there is a program P which satisfies S and which is refined by Q. If we have a specification on a timed program which is concerned purely with the order in which events can occur, then we may establish correctness by using the Traces model, and translating the correctness result into the timed model.

Refinement of programs

As we would hope, the addition of timing information to a program does not introduce unacceptable functional behaviour, though some acceptable behaviours may no longer be possible because of the additional timing constraints. We may transform an untimed program into a timed one by the addition of times to the event prefix operations, and by the insertion of delays at points throughout the program. Choices may be transformed into timeouts.

We define $\Theta : TCSP \to CSP$ to be the function that removes timing information, so

$$\begin{aligned} \Theta(a \xrightarrow{t} P) &= a \to \Theta(P) \\ \Theta(WAIT\ t) &= SKIP \\ \Theta(P \overset{t}{\rhd} Q) &= \Theta(Q) \sqcap (\Theta(P) \Box \Theta(Q)) \end{aligned}$$

and Θ distributes over the operators of TCSP that also appear in CSP. Then we obtain the welcome result that $\Theta(P) \sqsubseteq_T P$ for all TCSP programs P. Furthermore, the combination of two untimed programs by an operator is refined by the combination of any refinements by the corresponding timed operator; hence each operator preserves refinement.

For example, it is easy to see that

$$\mu X \circ in \to out \to X \quad \textbf{sat} \quad \#(tr \downharpoonright out) \leqslant \#(tr \downharpoonright in)$$

in the traces model M_T. Hence we may deduce as an immediate consequence that

$$\mu X \circ in \xrightarrow{4} out \xrightarrow{7} X \quad \textbf{sat} \quad \#(tstrip(s) \downharpoonright out) \leqslant \#(tstrip(s) \downharpoonright in$$

in the timed failures model TM_F.

Failures refinement

The untimed information that the behaviour (tr, X) is acceptable corresponds in the timed world to the information that a timed version of tr followed by the eventual continuous refusal of the set X is permitted. We need to consider the infinite failures of a process in order to define the $\sqsubseteq_F$ refinement relation, which is concerned with relating untimed and timed processes with respect to the failures of the untimed process.

The relation $\sqsubseteq_F$ is defined by requiring that whenever the timed process may perform a timed trace eventually followed by a continuous refusal of a set X, the untimed process must allow the same sequence of events, followed by the refusal of set X.

Definition 3.5

$$\begin{aligned} P \sqsubseteq_F Q \;=\; & \forall (s, \aleph) \in \mathcal{I}_T[\![Q]\!], t \geqslant 0, X \subseteq \Sigma \bullet \\ & [t, \infty) \times X \subseteq \aleph \Rightarrow (tstrip(s), X) \in \mathcal{F}[\![P]\!] \end{aligned}$$

Observe that any possible trace s of Q must have a corresponding trace of P, since such a trace will always accompany the empty refusal set; thus $(tstrip(s), \{\})$ should be a possible behaviour of P.

The definition of this refinement relation gives rise to the following proof rule:

$$\frac{\begin{array}{l} P \sqsubseteq_F Q \\ P \textbf{ sat } S \end{array}}{Q \textbf{ sat } \forall t, Y \bullet [t, \infty) \times Y \subseteq \aleph \Rightarrow S[(tstrip(s), Y)/(tr, X)]}$$

This rule may be used for example to establish that a timed process is deadlock-free by showing that it refines an untimed deadlock-free process. The untimed specification for deadlock-freedom is $X \neq \Sigma$, that the process may never refuse everything. Hence a refinement of a process satisfying this will have that whenever it refuses $[t, \infty) \times Y$, it cannot be that $Y = \Sigma$; this is the timed characterisation of deadlock-freedom. This will often be useful, since there already exist many techniques for establishing deadlock-freedom in untimed processes. In a similar way, the rule may be used to establish that a refinement of an untimed buffer must be a timed buffer.

We again obtain the result that $\Theta(P) \sqsubseteq_F P$ for all *TCSP* programs P; the introduction of timing constraints into a program maintains correctness with respect to failures specifications. It also follows that timewise refinement is preserved by all of the operators, as long as stability (in TM_{FS}) of processes is maintained.

However, the parallel operator need not preserve refinement for unstable processes. Consider a process that offers the event a during alternate seconds, beginning at time *0*, and another which offers a during alternate seconds, beginning at time *1*. They both refine an untimed process which deterministically offers a, since neither timed process is able to refuse it continuously. The parallel combination of the untimed processes cannot refuse the event a, but the combination of the timed processes that refine them is able to refuse a continuously, and therefore does not refine the untimed parallel combination.

4 Case Studies

This section describes a number of case studies to which Timed CSP has been applied since 1989. They include examples from two main fields: communications, where TCSP has been applied to the real time analysis of protocols and switching systems, and embedded systems such as real-time controllers.

Many of these studies were carried out in collaboration with other groups or companies with experience in the application area. The studies thus served two purposes: they allowed the application community to see how formal techniques in general, and Timed CSP in particular, could be applied to their area of interest, and they allowed the Timed CSP research group to gain knowledge of user requirements, providing a focus for further research and development.

The basic approach adopted in each of these studies was to examine the natural way in which the application is discussed and decomposed by workers within the formalism. Our intention was not to force applications to use a 'Timed CSP development method', but rather to use Timed CSP as a support to the methods which seem natural for a particular application.

One consequence of attempting to relate the formal treatment of each application to the particular structure of that application is that it allows customised formal structures to be built to match the needs of a particular area. These range from simply defining appropriate notations as macros—as for the specifications of the aircraft system, which used predicates defining properties on traces, such as 'alternates' and a 'disables/enables' relation—to the development of application specific proof rules. Some of these may be restricted and specific, such as the rule for adding additional components to a flexible manufacturing system, while others are less so. Examples of general rules which have resulted from these case studies are: the rules for composing constraint-based systems used by the aircraft engine, the rules for establishing correctness of layered network protocols [Dav91], and the rules for a 'rely and guarantee method' applied to a telephone switching network.

In the following sections we describe six case studies:

- a telephone switch—a 'rely and guarantee' method is used for a specification, together with design and proofs of correctness;
- an aircraft engine starter system—timed and untimed models are constructed, and projection of processes between models is used to construct proofs of correctness;
- autonomous guided vehicles—timed failure specifications are given together with a design expressed in the process algebra and outline correctness proofs are discussed;
- an ethernet-like protocol—a Timed CSP analysis of two layers of a local area network protocol, in which each layer provides services to the layer above;
- a laboratory robot—a hierarchical layered approach is demonstrated in a control application;
- a flexible manufacturing system—timed and untimed descriptions of a simple system are analysed using the temporal logic notation.

4.1 A Rely and Guarantee Method Applied to a Telephony Example

In [KR91a, KR91b, KaR90], Kay and Reed present a timed failures specification and a distributed design, also described using the timed failures model for Timed CSP, together with proofs of correctness for a realistically-sized telephone exchange. They use a *rely and guarantee* method for Timed CSP, which can be a key factor in keeping the formalisms to a manageable, meaningful collection. The style of this method is to describe what properties a component guarantees to its environment, *provided* that its environment supplies certain other properties to it. The method has some features in common with earlier work on Timed CSP environmental conditions [Dav91, DJS90] and the rely and guarantee version of VDM [Jon83, Jon91] for shared-variable concurrency.

Standard mechanisms for reasoning about a composition of components P_i are inference rules characterised by the following form, whereby if each P_i guarantees to meet its specification $Guarantee_i$ then one can infer the conjunction of all the $Guarantee_i$:

$$\frac{P_i \ \mathbf{sat}\ Guarantee_i}{\|_i\ P_i\ \mathbf{sat}\ \bigwedge_i\ Guarantee_i}$$

The implementor is obliged to ensure that each P_i unconditionally satisfies $Guarantee_i$ in order for the above rule to be applicable.

Another approach is perhaps more appropriate for highly interdependent systems - that is, for systems for which the desired behaviour of any single component is very much dependent on the desired behaviour of its co-components. A component must guarantee that it will behave in a certain way in order to satisfy its specification. However, the implementor can rely on certain facts about the environment (of cooperating components) in which the component is to be used. Inference rules characterised by the following form are useful for reasoning about such specifications:

$$\frac{P_i \quad \mathbf{sat} \quad Rely_i \Rightarrow Guarantee_i}{\|_i P_i \quad \mathbf{sat} \quad \bigwedge_i\ Guarantee_i} \quad \left[\begin{array}{l}\text{conditions ensuring } Guarantees \\ \text{establish } Relys\end{array}\right]$$

For example, a proof rule for safety properties has the following form (for simplicity we assume only two components):

$$\frac{\begin{array}{l}P \quad \mathbf{sat} \quad S_q \Rightarrow S_p \\ Q \quad \mathbf{sat} \quad S_p \Rightarrow S_q\end{array}}{P \parallel Q \quad \mathbf{sat} \quad S_p \wedge S_q} \quad \left[\begin{array}{l} \qquad S_p(\langle\rangle) \wedge S_q(\langle\rangle) \\ \wedge \ \ \mathbf{prevents}(S_q) \cap \mathbf{prevents}(S_p) = \{\} \end{array}\right]$$

where **prevents** of a safety predicate φ is defined to be those events which can cause φ to become false, that is, thoses events which φ (viewed as a constraint on traces) prevents.

$$a \in \mathbf{prevents}(\varphi) \Leftrightarrow \exists\, s : TRACES, t \geqslant end(s) \bullet \varphi(s) \wedge \neg\, \varphi(s^\frown \mathrm{seq}\,(t, a))$$

We can use the above rule when we want to design a system to meet safety properties S_p and S_q but we do not want (for practicality) to implement S_p and S_q unconditionally for P and Q respectively. Rather the implementor of P can assume S_q, and the implementor of Q can assume S_p, that is implement the pair of weaker constraints $S_p \Rightarrow S_q$ and $S_q \Rightarrow S_p$ with processes P and Q. The apparent circularity (that both S_p and S_q be false) is prevented by the side condition which intuitively ensures that P and Q are initially correct and cannot go wrong simultaneously.

The mode of use of this rule is adopt conventions on input and output whereby the side conditions ensuring that the *guarantees* establish the *relys* are automatically satisfied. For example, if we never place safety conditions on inputs (rather, only on outputs) then it can be shown that the above "**prevents**" side condition is always satisfied for any S_p and S_q and need not be explicitly checked. The additional side condition requiring the predicates to be initially true is usually immediately obvious.

To illustrate, let us assume that a master module sends a client module *request.id* and *abortrequest.id*, and the client responds within time t with an *answer.id* and an *abortdone.id*, respectively. The implementor of the client does not want to guarantee that the client will respond correctly to all *abortrequests*, rather only to those which follow the corresponding *request.id*.

The predicate S_M (for suitably defined **onlyif** to stop errant *abortrequests*):

$$S_M == \mathit{abortrequest.id}\ \mathbf{onlyif}\ \mathit{request.id}$$

is relied upon by the implementor of the client C in order to guarantee the predicate S_C (for suitably defined $\mathbf{stops}_t$ to stop answers going to aborted requests):

$$S_C == \mathit{abortreq.id}\ \mathbf{stops}_t\ \mathit{answer.id}$$

The implementor of the client need only guarantee S_C whilst relying on S_M, and the implementor of the master need only guarantee S_M whilst relying on S_C in order for the parallel system $M \parallel C$ to satisfy $S_M \wedge S_C$. The side conditions of the above inference rule need not be explicitly checked, since each component only makes (safety) guarantees about its own outputs—not inputs. Thus we are able to derive $S_M \wedge S_C$ from $S_M \Rightarrow S_C$ and $S_C \Rightarrow S_M$.

There are analogous rules treating liveness which are inevitably more complex. However, for point-to-point communication systems these rules are applicable whenever components guarantee to poll their inputs in a timely fashion. The proofs of these safety and liveness rules are given in [Kay91].

These rules are the basis for a method which enables one to use properties of a component's environment whilst reasoning about the component in isolation. For the top-level specification of the telephone exchange the concern is with just one component (the system), together with its environment. For the distributed design, there are five interacting components, together with external environment.

The specification for each of these components is given in two parts. Firstly, each component is described in terms of the messages it inputs (from one component) and outputs (to another). These constraints are guarantees which are not specifically relied upon by other components. Secondly, each interface between two components is described in terms of the messages shared by the two components. Each constraint here corresponds to (i) a condition guaranteed by one component, and (ii) the same condition relied upon by the other component. (The design of the telephone exchange has been selectively proved correct with respect to the top-level specification, and implementation of the design into executable code is planned.)

The scope of the specification and design for the telephone exchange encompasses substantial functionality including feature interactions such as caller replacing just as callee receives the ring, and other such race conditions. The method has also been effectively applied to another telephony example characterised by centralised controllers [Su91]. Both case studies indicate that this rely and guarantee approach is very straightforward and intuitive.

There are two major reasons that this method is effective for these applications: (i) the formalisms are manageable, and (ii) the verifier can use strong predicates to prove correctness whilst the implementor can use weaker predicates to produce executable code. In an interface description an individual predicate is only given once, implicitly representing two constraints - one a guarantee and the other a rely. Thus the occurrences of required formal expressions are significantly reduced. Perhaps the most valuable asset of the method is that it bridges a gap which occurs at a design level. Here there is a conflict between strong specifications which facilitate proofs of correctness that the design meets its higher-level specification, and weak specifications which allow efficient and practical implementations but make proofs more difficult. For the design of the telephone exchange the guarantees combine together to imply the top-level specification for the exchange, whilst the relys serve to make more practical implementations for the components.

4.2 Aircraft Engine Starter System

The controllers of gas turbine aircraft engines are complex systems. High reliability operation in real time is obviously essential One function which such systems perform is controlling start sequences. This latter function is included because to start such an engine, it is necessary to control the fuel shut-off valve, starter motor air valve and igniters to a strict sequence, while checking the engine for various failure conditions, a task which would place considerable strain on the pilot. This case study considered the specification of a greatly simplified starter system.

The approach taken was to produce a set of functional requirements which defined the (simplified) behaviour of the system from the actual specifications of a specific engine project. These requirements were formalised as behavioural specifications, which were divided into two groups: the first of which regulated when certain events could occur (safety properties), and a second set which specify when events must be possible (liveness properties). An outline design was then produced which used a *constraint based* structure. A component process was defined for each safety property, which prevented that property being violated.

The control system is then defined to be the concurrent combination of these processes. The verification that such a system meets its safety requirements is simple, requiring only that the enforcing process is correct, but the liveness properties must be verified for every component. In fact, two models of the system were in fact produced. One was a model using Timed Failures specifications and Timed CSP, while a simpler untimed model was created and proved correct using the Failures model of CSP. This allowed many properties of the timed model to be proved by using the timewise refinement techniques described in the previous section.

We will now present some functional requirements typical of the simplified autostart system. The system takes inputs *FuelOn* and *FuelOff*, *AirOn* and *AirOff* from the pilot, and a *run* signal from the engine, and controls two valves: the Starter Air Valve (SAV) which controls the engine starter motor, and the Shut Off Valve (SOV) which can stop any fuel flow to the engine.

1. The SAV should only open when commanded on by the pilot.

2. When the starter is commanded off, but the SAV is open, the system should not refuse to close the valve.

3. If the SAV is open for 180s, the system must not refuse to close it. This ensures that the starter motor does not overheat.

The first item in this list is a safety property. The remaining two are liveness conditions. Global timing requirements define the maximum time allowed for a system to recognise the conditions mentioned in the liveness constraints and act accordingly. We will insist that any required action becomes available in a time T.

We will now consider these properties formalised in the Timed Failures model. The state of devices such as switches and valves depends on which of a pair of events (opening and closing, for example) occurred last. We define abbreviations to describe which states hold at the end of a given trace. The following predicate holds for a trace when it either contains at least one event a, with no subsequent b:

$$s\ \mathit{ENDWITHIN}(a,b) \quad == \quad \begin{array}{l} \lfloor\{a,b\} \neq \langle\rangle \\ \wedge\ \mathit{last}(s \lfloor \{a,b\}) = a \end{array}$$

We can define specific predicates on traces which describe the state of various elements of the system at the end of the trace. *AIRREQD* holds of a trace when the starter system is selected by the pilot at the time corresponding to the end of the current trace:

$$\mathit{AIRREQD}(s) \quad == \quad s\ \mathit{ENDWITHIN}(\mathit{AirOn}, \mathit{AirOff})$$

OPENSAV, *FUELREQD*, *OPENSOV* and *RUNNING* (which holds when the engine is in normal operation at the end of the trace) can be defined similarly. We can also define abbreviations for common specifications. One common form of specification is that the occurrence of one event, c is enabled by another, a, and disabled by a third, b. The following specification describes the case where c is initially disabled:

$$c\ \mathit{BETWEEN}(a,b) \quad == \quad s = u^\frown\langle(t,c)\rangle^\frown v \Rightarrow (u\ \mathit{ENDWITHIN}(a,b))$$

c *OUTSIDE*(b, a) can be defined similarly. The use of parameterised predicates can be considered as a shorthand for substitution.

Using the predicates defined above, our requirements can be described as follows:

- The SAV only opens when it is requested:

$$R_a \quad == \quad \mathit{SAVopen}\ \ \mathit{BETWEEN}\ (\mathit{AirOn}, \mathit{AirOff})$$

- When starter air is turned off by the pilot, the valve should close within T:

$$R_b \quad == \quad \left.\begin{array}{l} \neg\ \mathit{AIRREQD}(s)\ \wedge \\ \mathit{OPENSAV}(s) \end{array}\right\} \Rightarrow \mathit{SAVclose} \not\in \sigma\ (\aleph \upharpoonright (\mathit{end}(s){+}T))$$

- The SAV must also be able to close when the engine reaches idle conditions, or after 3 minutes anyway:

$$R_c \quad == \quad \mathit{OPENSAV}(s) \Rightarrow \mathit{SAVclose} \not\in \sigma\ (\aleph \upharpoonright (\mathit{end}(s){+}180 + T))$$

The implementation strategy used was to produce simple processes corresponding to safety requirements which govern partial correctness, while keeping their actions general enough to satisfy the refusal requirements. The parallel combination of these processes should then meet that overall specification.

The following processes are used to reflect the repeated structure of the specification noted above: The process *DISABLED* prevents c from occurring until an a event has occurred more recently than a b, while *ENABLED* does the reverse (and allows c to occur initially). *DISABLED* corresponds to the *BETWEEN* specification forms, and in fact $DISABLED\ (c, a, b)$ **sat** $c\ \ BETWEEN(a, b)$:

$$\begin{array}{rcl} DISABLED\ (c,a,b) & == & \ (a \rightarrow ENABLED\ (c,a,b)) \\ & & \Box\ (b \rightarrow DISABLED\ (c,a,b)) \\ ENABLED\ (c,a,b) & == & \ (a \rightarrow ENABLED\ (c,a,b)) \\ & & \Box\ (b \rightarrow DISABLED\ (c,a,b)) \\ & & \Box\ (c \rightarrow ENABLED\ (c,a,b)) \end{array}$$

The parameterisation used here is a shorthand for alphabet transformation.

A single process will enforce a single constraint on *SOVopen*,

$$P_a \ == \ DISABLED\ (SAVopen, AirOn, AirOff)$$

Similar processes can be defined for other safety specifications.

To allow *SAVclose* to occur when the relevant conditions are met, two processes can be interleaved, rather than synchronised:

$$\begin{array}{rcl} P_c & == & P_{c1} \ ||| \ P_{c2} \\ P_{c1} & == & ENABLED\ (SAVclose, AirOff, AirOn) \\ P_{c2} & == & \ (SAVopen \rightarrow P_{c3}) \\ & & \Box\ (WAIT\ 180\ ; (SAVclose \rightarrow P_{c3})) \end{array}$$

The controller is then modelled as the interlocked parallel combination of processes enforcing the required safety conditions.

$$CONTROL == (\ldots \underset{\{SAVopen,AirOn,AirOff\}}{\|} P_a) \underset{C}{\|} P_c$$

The correctness of this system can be proved simply by applying the proof system of the previous section, but a simpler method is to project the process algebra into the untimed *CSP* language, and verify the untimed properties relating to ordering of events in a simpler model such as the traces model of *CSP*. This allowed effort to be concentrated on the more complex timing issues of the design. Eventually we hope that mechanical verification of simple untimed properties will be practical in many cases, reducing the burden still further.

To summarise, this study produced timed and untimed versions of real functional requirements and captured them in the language of CSP and Timed CSP behaviour specifications. The use of a constraint based approach to their implementation allowed safety properties to be proven very simply, especially when used in conjunction with projection of processes from the timed to the untimed models. The resulting processes had a form which allowed a simple implementation to be constructed, and in fact a simulation in the occam programming language was produced. The greatest difficulty encountered was the volume and complexity of the correctness proofs, many of which were based largely on simple manipulation of sets and sequences. This observation motivated research into simpler frameworks for verifying properties of *TCSP* processes, and indeed correlates well with a number of the other case studies to be discussed here.

4.3 Autonomous Guided Vehicles

Autonomous Guided Vehicles (AGVs) are mobile robots provided with a variety of sensing equipment, and intended to be able to find their way around an environment, usually in order to locate a target. In addition they may be expected to achieve a task such as acquiring an object, if they are provided with appropriate manipulators.

To cope with these problems many different AGV control systems have been proposed and developed, usually involving a significant degree of parallelism. One common approach is the hierarchical system where higher level control functions pass commands to lower levels which are concerned with more local control. (See section 4.4.2.) An alternative is the "subsumption" architecture which consists of modules each responsible for a specific task-achieving behaviour which may take control by overriding the outputs and inputs of other modules.

This study [Sta90] examined parts of a composite architecture being developed at Oxford University's Robotics Research Group. The AGV is controlled by a land-based computer, which passes sparse points along the intended path to a path-smoothing module in the vehicle. This in turn generates much closer points which are sent to the motor controller at regular intervals. Current work is related to adding an obstacle-avoid mechanism which overrides the normal path-following behaviour if an obstacle is detected by a ring of sonar sensors positioned around the vehicle.

The approach taken in this model was to decompose the system into modules corresponding to the elements of the architecture already proposed by the robotics specialists. The hardware environment is such that these processes could then be run concurrently, allowing the AGV to respond quickly to external stimuli.

As an example, consider the structure shown in Figure 1. The main components have the following functions: The sensors provide data about the vehicle's position and environment. In practice this will include a wide variety of hardware and software. The higher level control system represents the land-based computer system and the on-board path smoothing. It is responsible for accepting high level plans and generating points along the path which the vehicle is required to follow under normal circumstances. These points are produced more or less continually at regular intervals.

The emergency avoid system, however, would normally be in an idle state in which it monitors the vehicle sensors. If a collision appeared imminent, the module switches to an active state and provides points along some alternative same path until the danger of collision has been avoided, then returning to its idle state.

A multiplexor provides a link between the higher level control and the emergency avoid process and directs their output to a buffer. It relays data from the higher level control system to the buffer until a toggle signal is received from the emergency system. It then

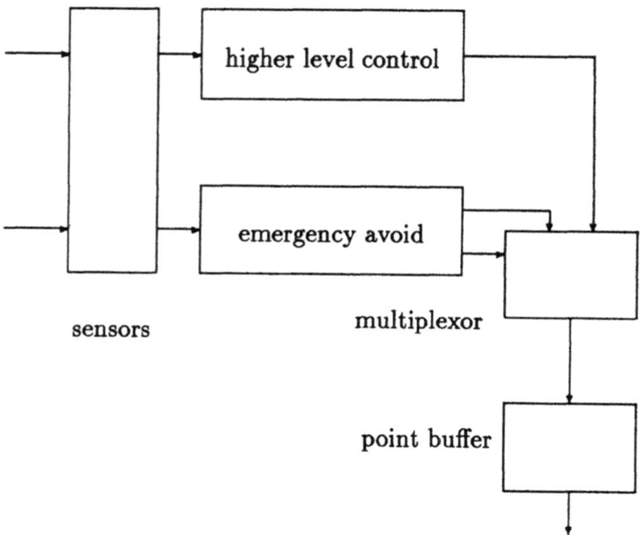

Figure 1: Structure of the AGV model

relays points from the emergency system until another toggle is signalled. In addition, it sends a signal to clear the buffer whenever it changes state.

The buffer itself is a model of the interface to the low level AGV hardware. It is fed with points from the control system, and has points removed from it at regular intervals by the low level control. The receipt of a clear signal resets it to an empty state. This design combines both hierarchical and subsumption styles: in normal operation commands are passed down a hierarchy of controllers, while the emergency system takes effect by overriding the normal hierarchical flow.

The technique adopted was to describe requirements placed on the above components in terms of Timed Failure specifications, to model the behaviour of the systems in the *TCSP* algebra, and to prove that these modules did meet their local requirements. The proof rules relating to parallel composition were then used to demonstrate some simple high level properties of the system. A number of these global properties, however, are best described in terms of the internal state of the system: in Timed CSP, a process and its environment must co-operate on all observable events, so purely internal events cannot be observed by the environment.

To handle this situation, an 'environmental' approach to specification was developed, as described in [DJS90]. Rather than conceal all the communication between the components of the system, these events are left visible, but the system behaviour is only guaranteed when the environment commits to allow such events to happen whenever the system does. Behavioural specifications are written in the form

$$E(s, \aleph) \Rightarrow F(s, \aleph)$$

where $E(s, \aleph)$ gives the assumptions which the system makes about the environment and $F(s, \aleph)$ describes what is required of the process. The 'environmental assumption' required here is that the environment is always willing to observe events in a set A, expressed as

$$\mathrm{act}_{\mathbf{A}}(s, \aleph) \quad == \quad [0, end(s, \aleph)) \times A \subset \aleph$$

Consider the multiplexor. The purpose of this device is to feed points to the point buffer. The source of the points can be either of the two channels in_1, from the emergency avoid system, or in_2 from the higher level control modules. Which of these is used at any one instant is determined by a signal *toggle* activated by the emergency avoid mechanism. The most important requirement is that the multiplexor should behave as a one-place buffer while it is propagating points from one of its input lines. This is a standard and well understood problem. In addition, it must satisfy some conditions on its real-time behaviour. For example following a toggle, a clear signal must be offered to the buffer within M_{clear}.

$$\langle(t, toggle)\rangle \text{ in } s \Rightarrow \quad clear \notin \sigma(\aleph \uparrow [t + M_{clear}, begin(s \upharpoonright t \downharpoonright clear)))$$

Also, following a clear, the multiplexor must be prepared to accept an input or a toggle event within M_{inp}, and the preceding event must have been a toggle

$$\langle(t, clear)\rangle \text{ in } s \Rightarrow \begin{array}{ll} & toggle \notin \sigma(\aleph \uparrow [t + M_{inp}, begin(s \upharpoonright t \downharpoonright toggle))) \\ \wedge & \quad in_1.PT \cap \sigma(\aleph \uparrow [t + M_{inp}, begin(s \upharpoonright t \downharpoonright in_1.PT))) = \{\} \\ & \vee \quad in_2.PT \cap \sigma(\aleph \uparrow [t + M_{inp}, begin(s \upharpoonright t \downharpoonright in_2.PT))) = \{\} \\ \wedge & last(s \uparrow [0, t)) = toggle \end{array}$$

The following Timed CSP process is designed to meet the preceding specification. Using a derived interrupt operator $\underset{toggle}{\nabla}$ to transfer control when an event *toggle* occurs, we can define

$$\begin{array}{lll} M1 & == & (\mu X \circ in_1?x \xrightarrow{M_{prop}} out!x \xrightarrow{M_{rec}} X) \underset{toggle}{\nabla} WAIT\ M_{clear} \,;\, clear \xrightarrow{M_{inp}} M2 \\ M2 & == & (\mu X \circ in_2?x \xrightarrow{M_{prop}} out!x \xrightarrow{M_{rec}} X) \underset{toggle}{\nabla} WAIT\ M_{clear} \,;\, clear \xrightarrow{M_{inp}} M1 \\ MUX & == & M1 \end{array}$$

The full multiplexor is modelled by MUX. In state M1 the multiplexor accepts input from the channel in1, and in state M2 it accepts input from channel in2. We can prove that MUX satisfies the required properties using the proof system described earlier. Other properties, and the other components can be treated in a similar manner.

Having specified the components of the AGV as separate processes, we can investigate the behaviour of them running concurrently and communicating on the appropriate channels. Consider the requirement that the system responds to an emergency input by clearing the point buffer with some time limit M_{resp}. This reduces to local properties on the sensors, the emergency avoid system, and the multiplexor. If the sensor relays its input within some time, say, M_{sens}, and the emergency controller responds within M_{avoid}, the using the property of the multiplexer above, we require that $M_{resp} \geqslant M_{avoid} + M_{sens} + M_{clear}$. The proof can be carried out using the rules for parallelism described in the previous section.

Similar properties can be formalised and proved in a similar manner. These include showing that following a trigger, a point produced by the emergency avoid mechanism will be available from the point buffer within a certain maximum time and that after this event, if the point buffer is not full, then it accepts points at a frequency determined by the rate at which the emergency avoid process calculates path points. These can be extended to make observations about the overall behaviour of the system, for example, to calculate how out-of-date the points coming from the buffer are in normal operation.

One of the major conclusions drawn from this project had also been noticed in the aircraft engine project: the specification notation is, if anything, too flexible, and allows too many ways of asserting the same things. Again some steps were taken to providing some standard predicates relating to offers and the occurrence of internal events. One difference in approach was that the approach taken to finding requirements was to have a specification for each possible event, describing what must occur before, and what may occur and must be offered after, any occurrence of it. It was found that with this method it was easier to be confident that all cases had been covered, than it was if the specifications were divided more conventionally into safety and liveness properties. In the case of the sensors the fact that the behaviour varied on a regular cycle meant that categorising by time was more useful than categorising by event.

The environmental technique proved convenient in talking about the internal behaviour of a system, as well as when dealing with the behaviour of the system as a whole. The proofs turn out to be long-winded if done with anything like formal rigour. A large part of the problem, however, is that specification of timing properties of systems involving concurrency is necessarily complex. Even when proofs of combination properties are not done, process algebra provides a concise but accurate method of representing processes.

4.4 Other Case Studies

4.4.1 A Local Area Network Protocol

A common form of local area network protocol is the *carrier-sense collision detect* protocol, of which the Xerox Ethernet [Xer80] is the best known example. In such a protocol, a number of nodes communicate over a broadcast medium—each is able to receive data transmitted by any other. Each node must wait until local activity on the broadcast medium has ceased before it attempts to transmit a message. If two nodes attempt to transmit within the same time interval, interference will be observed at both nodes. In this case, the nodes will *back off* or delay for some random period before retransmitting.

The protocol specifies interactions on two levels: one relating the physical details of the medium, and one relating the transmission of data packets from one node to another. These correspond to the lowest two levels of the seven layer ISO-OSI protocol model, which defines the function of a physical layer, a data link layer, and a further five layers above, beginning with the network layer. These layers are clients of the layers described by the Ethernet specification: the data link layer provides a virtual communication service for the layers above.

An analysis of the correctness of such a protocol is described in [Dav91]—a far more elegant description that we have space for here. Because the important functions of protocols are specified in terms of layers and the services they provide each other, Davies develops a theory of structured specifications in Timed CSP as a basis for this case study. A typical layer L provides a service to the layer above, described in terms of shared interface A_L. The implementation of L may involve internal communications, and it may rely on the service provided by the layer K below.

If layer K provides a service S_K, and L satisfies a total specification T_L, then the combination of T_L and S_K must be enough to provide the service S_L to the layer above, under the assumption that events outside the interface A_L are to be concealed than L: we use H_L to denote this set of hidden events.

$$T_L \wedge S_K \quad \Rightarrow \quad S_L \mathbin{\backslash\!\backslash} H_L$$

The symbol $\backslash\!\backslash$ corresponds to the assumption that events from H_L are to be concealed. This is the simplest form of environmental assumption.

The data link layer provides a simple service at each node i—messages received on a channel $i.in$ are encapsulated as data frames and transmitted across the network; a status report is returned on channel $i.rep$. Packets received at node i are stripped of framing information, and—if this is their destination—output on channel $i.out$. Given a set $NODE$ of nodes, PKT of packets, and a set REP of report values, the interface between the data link and its client layer is given by

$$\{i.in.p, i.rep.r, i.out.p \mid i \in NODE \wedge p \in PKT \wedge r \in REP\}$$

Some properties relate the service provided at a single node. For example, we may require that the transmitting part of a node alternates between accepting inputs and returning status reports. If IN_i and REP_i are the sets of input and report events at node i, we require

$$\forall i : NODE \bullet 1 \geqslant (\#(s \upharpoonright IN_i) - \#(s \upharpoonright REP_i) + 1) \geqslant 0$$

Other properties relate to the whole network: if $dest(p)$ is the destination node of packet p, a successful transmission at node i should be possibly only if the message is made available for output at the destination node

$$\left.\begin{array}{l} \langle(t, i.rep.success)\rangle \text{ in } s \\ dest(p) = j \\ last(s \upharpoonright IN_i \uparrow [0, t) = (t', i.in.p) \end{array}\right\} \Rightarrow j.out.p \notin \sigma(\aleph \uparrow [t' + t_{max}, begin(s \upharpoonright j.out.p)))$$

where t_{max} is the largest acceptable transmission delay.

Similar specifications can be written for the interface between the physical layer and the data link layer: the layers communicate along channels $i.put$ (transmitted data), $i.cs$ (carrier sense signal), $i.cd$ (collision detect signal) and $i.get$ (received data). The specifications of the components of the data link layer can also be formulated in the same way. In [Dav91], these specifications are presented in a high-level macro language, closer to natural descriptions.

If S_{PL} and S_{DL} denote the service provided by the physical layer and the data link respectively, and T_{DL} denotes the total specification of the data link, then we may use the timed failures proof system to establish that

$$\left.\begin{array}{l} S_{PL}(s \downharpoonright \Sigma_{PL}, \aleph_P) \\ T_{DL}(s \downharpoonright \Sigma_{DL}, \aleph_D) \\ \aleph \downharpoonright A_{PL} = (\aleph_D \cup \aleph_P) \downharpoonright A_{PL} \\ \aleph \setminus A_{PL} = (\aleph_D \cap \aleph_P) \setminus A_{PL} \end{array}\right\} \Rightarrow S_{DL}(s, \aleph) \mathbin{\backslash\!\backslash} H_{DL}$$

The total specification of the data link, together the service provided by the physical layer, is enough to guarantee the service required of the datalink.

We can extend the analysis to model an abstract implementation. For example, the transmission of a packet can be performed by a transmission link manager, *TLM*, defined as follows:

$$\begin{array}{rcl} TLM & == & down?f \xrightarrow{t_3} HOLD_{f,1} \\ HOLD_{f,n} & == & cs \xrightarrow{t_{int}} (SEND_f \underset{cd}{\nabla} HANDLE_{f,n}) \ ; \ TLM \\ SEND_{\langle\rangle} & == & rep!succ \xrightarrow{t_4} SKIP \\ SEND_{\langle x\rangle^\frown s} & == & send! \xrightarrow{t_{bit}} SEND_s \\ HANDLE_{f,n} & == & BACKOFF_n \ ; \ HOLD_{f,n+1} \text{ if } n < 16 \\ HANDLE_{f,16} & == & rep!fail \xrightarrow{t_5} SKIP \end{array}$$

The process *HOLD* corresponds to the state in which the node is waiting to transmit. *SEND* corresponds to bit transmission, and *HANDLE* describes the behaviour following a collision. The random delay is implemented by the *BACKOFF* process.

This case study provides a good illustration of the application of Timed CSP to the analysis of real-time protocols. The abstraction notation for CSP, with a few simple customisations, supports a clear, structured description of a complex protocol.

4.4.2 Laboratory Robot

Another control example is the study of the control of a laboratory robot [Sca90]. This work, carried out in collaboration with BP plc, considered the problem of controlling a cartesian robot used to prepare microscope slides. The control system is responsible for driving the robot to collect samples, mix solutions, place samples on clean slides, transfer slides to dry of a specified period and arrange resulting batches for collection. The parameters of each job, such as number of slides and processing time, are quite varied and the resulting system needs to be flexible.

A hierarchical structure was adopted, based on task structure. This form of architecture is common in robotics applications, as noted above. The higher levels control batch level operations, passing commands down to modules which perform operations on single slides which in turn drive processes which operate single movements or axes of motion. Commands are passed down the hierarchy and status information is passed back when the commands are completed.

The starting point for the study was to build a model of the behaviour of a typical level in terms of Timed CSP. Derived program constructs for building levels were built up, and rules for their proving their correctness were derived. As with the communications protocol example, the correct behaviour of a layer in the system obviously depends on the service provided by lower level layers.

The properties required of the specific system being considered were captured as Timed Failures specifications. The overall form of interface specification was obviously quite simple: after a command *comm* is issued, some status message from the set *STAT* is returned within some time T:

$$\langle (t, comm) \rangle \text{ in } s \Rightarrow STAT \not\subseteq \sigma(\aleph \uparrow [t+T, begin(s \upharpoonright t \downharpoonright STAT)))$$

Overall, this application demonstrated a very simple hierarchal structure which, while being quite common in communication protocols seems less common embedded system applications. This layered approach allowed program constructs to be re-used significantly in the development of this system, and closely relates to a typical systems in which we may well have one microprocessor controlling each axis of a robot, in turn controlled by a local system which guides the whole robot, which itself receives commands from some form of laboratory of plant level scheduling system. Although this higher level scheduling was not studied as part of either this example or the AGV control system case study, it is a task which involves significant communication between parallel modules and many real-time constraints, features which are amenable to analysis in the Timed CSP framework. Our next example study describes an attempt to analyse such a system in this framework, using a temporal logic specification notation to abstract away from some timing detail.

4.4.3 Flexible Manufacturing Systems

A flexible manufacturing system (FMS) is a combination of computer controlled tools, transport devices and controllers which can be used to process mixed batches of jobs of different types. Typical examples are automated machine tool shops in the mechanical engineering industry, where components are moved between stations by AGVs.

In a typical FMS raw parts of various types enter the system at discrete points of time and are processed concurrently, sharing a limited number of resources, such as machines, robots, fixtures and buffers. One major issue which must be addressed is deadlock, but there are also other properties of a manufacturing system which are also of interest, such as the times at which individual jobs start and stop processing, delays during processing, and the length of time that machines stand idle. The study described in [Wal91] considers two models of an FMS: an untimed model used for deadlock analysis, and a timed model which allows calculation of, for example, job completion times.

The FMS model is divided into four types of process: jobs, which represent the sequence of tasks to be performed on some material; machines, which represent the resources to be used; transport devices which represent the constraints on job movement, and a centralised controller.

The first model analysed a simple controller which allocates each job all the machines it needs to complete. Allocation is controlled by semaphores, one for ecah machine. The job processes must satisfy various conditions: it's initial action must be to request a set of resourcesfrom the controller, it must then request an AGV to transfer raw material to the first machine for processing, request transfers to subsequent machines and finally request transfer to the final station and release its resources by sending a message to the controller.

The job communicates with the controller via p and v events which represent the usual semaphore operations. The AGV and jobs are synchronised by commands to the AGV of the form "get job i from machine a, transfer it to machine b". Events of the form *begin* and *end* synchronise the jobs with the machines. The properties of jobs can then be formalised in untimed CSP as predicates on trace refusal pairs. The FMS is represented as the interlocking parallel combination of the jobs, the machines, the AGV and the controller. Deadlock freedom is proved by the usual proof system for behavioural specifications.

The second model considered added timing information to the FMS model: it included the transportation times, the machines processing and resetting times, and the controllers response time. The communications outlined above are not sufficient to encode all the timing information for the model, so the events were changed to pass processing times from the job process to the machines and transport devices.

The process algebra descriptions used in the untimed model can be extended to the timed case:

$$
\begin{aligned}
AGV &= AGV_s \\
AGV_p &= go.(i,a,b,t) \rightarrow MOVE_{p,a} \,;\, done.a \\
&\qquad \rightarrow MOVE_{a,b} \,;\, begin.b!t \rightarrow AGV_b \\
MOVE_{x,y} &== \bigsqcap_{min \leqslant t \leqslant max} WAIT(t-\delta) \,;\, \text{if } x \neq y \\
MOVE_{x,y} &== SKIP \text{if } x = y
\end{aligned}
$$

For simplicity, a simpler timed model was adopted for example analysis. The controller and AGV are replaced by a single scheduler: each job is decomposed into a operations which are placed in order by the scheduler. As an example of the analysis which can be performed, we may then prove a simple inductive property of the system: if an operation is added to the end of a job, and scheduled last, then the completion time is increased by the length of the operation.

The machines will be defined as they are above, except that they will each have a constant processing time p_m, and recovery time r_m. This can easily be extended to the more general variable time in the above model. So we have

$$M_m == begin.m?i \xrightarrow{p_m} done.m!i \xrightarrow{r_m} M_m$$

we assume that the time taken for the recursion is zero, i.e. *begin* will be offered at time r_m after the *done* was performed. We shall need to specify properties of the machines, for example if ever a *begin* and *end* events occur alternately, with a delay corresponding to the processing time between *begin* and *end*. These properties can be captured in temporal logic. First we define a predicate *DONE*. This simply captures the idea that when we offer the event *end.m.j*, no other events are performed until the event is performed, if it is ever performed.

$$DONE_m == ((\mathbb{O}_{end.m!j} \wedge \neg\, \mathbb{P}_{\sigma M_m})\, \overline{\mathcal{W}}\, \mathbb{P}_{end.m!j})$$

This gives the following expression of the property above:

$$P_m \quad == \quad \overline{\mathbf{G}}\,(\mathbb{P}_{begin.m?j} \Rightarrow \neg\, \mathbb{P}_{\sigma M_m}\, \mathcal{U}_{pm}\, DONE_m)$$

We can prove that the machine meets this specification (M_m **sat** P_m) by applying the rules discussed previously. Properties of the scheduler and operations can be captured similarly.

Representing the properties of well defined jobs by predicates $ALLDONE$, ONE_A, and writing $AF[s,t]$ for the specification which asserts that all jobs are complete at some time in the interval $[s,t]$, the proof system allows us to prove the required result: Given system FMS we may add an operation to give a system FMS' which takes between p_a and $p_a + r_a$ longer to complete.

$$\frac{\begin{array}{rcl} FMS & \mathbf{sat} & (\mathrm{act}_\Sigma \Rightarrow AF_{[s,t]}) \wedge ALLDONE \\ \forall j : J & \bullet & J_j \;\mathbf{sat}\; ONE_{\sigma J_j} \\ S_J & \mathbf{sat} & T_J \wedge ONE_{\checkmark} \end{array}}{FMS' \;\mathbf{sat}\;\; \mathrm{act}_\Sigma \Rightarrow AF[s + p_a, t + p_a + r_a]} \quad [\, i \in J\,]$$

where

$$FMS \quad == \quad \left(S_J \;{}_{A_S}\|_{A_J}\; J_J\right) \;{}_{A_S}\|_{A_M} \mathop{|||}_{i \in MACH} M_i$$

$$FMS' \quad == \quad \left(\left(S_J \,;\, OP_{i,a}\right) \;{}_{A_S}\|_{A_J}\; J_{J-\{i\}}\right) \;{}_{A_S}\|_{A_{J_i}} \left(J_i \,;\, OP_{i,a}\right)\Big) \;{}_{A_S}\|_{A_M} \mathop{|||}_{i \in MACH} M_i$$

The following observations were made: CSP can be used to model FMSs in a modular way, and in a manner which should be easily extended to include other aspects not covered here. However, even for simple systems the proofs can become long and involved. Timed CSP is able to model the timing constraints of the simple FMS, although the resulting model is even more complex. Temporal logic provides an a methods of abstracting from some of this detail, but a modular approach to the system design is still highly desirable, using higher level proof rules.

5 Conclusions

We believe that the theory of Timed CSP has now reached maturity; this is demonstrated by the case studies presented in this paper. The strength of the theory lies in its flexibility: a hierarchy of semantic models are available for reasoning at different levels of abstraction, and the methods of reasoning can be tailored to suit application-specific proof theories.

We are now actively engaged in producing two volumes to serve as definitive guides to the theory and application of Timed CSP. If Timed CSP (or any other formal method) is to be used outside the academic community, it is essential that the development process is supported by reliable software tools. The design and development of such tools is currently a major area of research at Oxford.

Acknowledgements

The theory of Timed CSP was inspired by Tony Hoare. Its development has been greatly aided by discussions with Michael Goldsmith and Geraint Jones. Jim Woodcock served as the director of the D.Phil thesis of Jim Davies, and Penny Probert co-directed the M.Sc theses of Scattergood, Stamper, and Wallace.

The foundational work on Timed CSP would not have been possible without the support of R. Grafton and particularly R.F. Wachter at the U.S. Office of Naval Research, and the support of ESPRIT BRA-3096 (SPEC). This research has benefitted considerably from discussions with other participants in the SPEC project.

Finally, we note that the first timed model for Communicating Sequential Processes was constructed in [Jon82], and that a model similar to our Timed Failures Model was constructed independently in [BoG87].

References

[BoG87] A. Boucher and R. Gerth, *A timed model for extended communicating sequential processes*, in *Proceedings of ICALP 87*, LNCS **267**, pp 95–114, Springer 1987.

[Dav91] J. Davies, *Specification and proof in real-time systems*, D.Phil thesis, Programming Research Group Technical Monograph PRG–93, Oxford University 1991.

[DJS90] J. Davies, D.M. Jackson, and S.A. Schneider, *Making things happen in Timed CSP*, Programming Research Group Technical Report TR–2–90, Oxford University 1990.

[DJS92] J. Davies, D.M. Jackson, and S.A. Schneider, *Broadcast communication for real-time processes*, in *Proceedings of the symposium on real-time and fault-tolerant systems, Nijmegen 1992*, to appear in Springer LNCS.

[DaS89] J. Davies and S.A. Schneider, *Factorising proofs in Timed CSP*, in *Proceedings of the fifth workshop on the mathematical foundations of programming language semantics*, LNCS **442**, pp 129–159, Springer 1990.

[DaS90] J. Davies and S.A. Schneider, *An extended syntax for Timed CSP*, Programming Research Group Technical Report TR–4–90, Oxford University 1990.

[DaS91] J. Davies and S.A. Schneider, *Recursion induction for real-time processes*, submitted for publication 1991.

[Hoa85] C.A.R. Hoare, *Communicating Sequential Processes*, Prentice-Hall 1985.

[Jac89] D.M. Jackson, *The specification of aircraft engine control software in Timed CSP*, M.Sc thesis, Oxford University 1989.

[Jac90] D.M. Jackson, *Specifying timed communicating sequential processes using temporal logic*, Programming Research Group Technical Report TR–5–90, Oxford University 1990.

[Jac91] D.M. Jackson, *A temporal logic proof system for Timed CSP*, Programming Research Group Technical Report TR-2-91, Oxford University 1991.

[Ja+90] D.M. Jackson, J. Davies, G.M. Reed, A.W. Roscoe, and S.A. Schneider, *Specifying timed communicating sequential processes in temporal logic*, SPEC report, ESPRIT BRA 3096, 1990.

[Jon82] G. Jones, *A timed model of communicating processes*, D.Phil thesis, Oxford University 1982.

[Jon83] C. Jones, *Tentative steps towards a development method for interfering programs*, ACM Trans Prog Lang **5** 4, pp 596–619, 1982.

[Jon91] C. Jones, *Interference resumed*, Technical Report UMCS–91–5–1, Manchester University 1991; Australian Software Engineering Research 1991, P. Bailes (ed.), Springer 1991.

[Kay91] A. Kay, *A theory of rely and guarantee in Timed CSP*, in preparation 1991.

[KaR90] A. Kay and J.N. Reed, *A Specification of a Telephone Exchange in Timed CSP*, Programming Research Group Technical Report TR–19–90, Oxford University 1990.

[KR91a] A. Kay and J.N. Reed, *Using rely and guarantee in Timed CSP*, Programming Research Group Technical Report TR–11–91, Oxford University 1991.

[KR91b] A. Kay and J.N. Reed, *A rely and guarantee method for Timed CSP*, submitted for publication 1991.

[Low91] G. Lowe, *A probabilistic model of Timed CSP*, D.Phil status transfer thesis, Oxford University, 1991.

[MRS91] M.W. Mislove, A.W. Roscoe, and S.A. Schneider, *Fixed points without completeness*, in preparation 1991.

[Ree88] G.M. Reed, *A uniform mathematical theory for distributed computing*, D.Phil thesis, Oxford University 1988.

[Ree90] G.M. Reed, *A hierarchy of models for real-time distributed computing*, in *Proceedings of the Fifth Workshop on the Mathematical Foundations of Programming Language Semantics*, LNCS **442**, pp 80–128, Springer 1990.

[ReR86] G.M. Reed and A.W. Roscoe, *A timed model for communicating sequential processes*, in *Proceedings of ICALP 86*, LNCS **226**, Springer 1987.

[ReR87] G.M. Reed and A.W. Roscoe, *Metric spaces as models for real-time concurrency*, in *Proceedings of the Third Workshop on the Mathematical Foundations of Programming Language Semantics*, LNCS **298**, pp 331–343, Springer 1987.

[ReR91] G.M. Reed and A.W. Roscoe, *A study of nondeterminism in real-time concurrency*, in *Proceedings of the Second UK–Japan CS Workshop*, LNCS **491**, pp 36–63, Springer 1991.

[Sca90] B. Scattergood, *The description of a laboratory robot in Timed CSP*, M.Sc thesis, Oxford University 1990.

[Sch90] S.A. Schneider, *Correctness and communication of real-time systems*, D.Phil thesis, Oxford University 1990.

[Sch91] S.A. Schneider, *Unbounded non-determinism in Timed CSP*, SPEC report, ESPRIT BRA 3096, 1991.

[Sch92] S.A. Schneider, *An operational semantics for Timed CSP*, in *Proceedings of the Chalmers Workshop on Concurrency*, to appear 1992.

[Sc+90] S.A. Schneider, J. Davies, D.M. Jackson, G.M. Reed, and A.W. Roscoe, *Communication and correctness in Timed CSP*, SPEC report, ESPRIT BRA 3096, 1990.

[Sta90] R. Stamper, *The specification of AGV control software in Timed CSP*, M.Sc thesis, Oxford University 1990.

[Su91] S. Superville, *Specifying complex systems with Timed CSP: a decomposition and specification of a telephone exchange system which has a central controller*, M.Sc thesis, Oxford University 1991.

[Wal91] A.R. Wallace, *A TCSP case study of a flexible manufacturing system*, M.Sc thesis, Oxford University 1990.

[Xer80] The Ethernet Specification, available from the Xerox Corporation, reprinted in ACM *Computer Communication Review*, July 1981.

A Specification of the Cat and Mouse Problem

William G. Wood
Software Engineering Institute
(Sponsored by the U.S. Department of Defense)
Carnegie Mellon University
Pittsburgh, PA 15213

Abstract.

The cat and mouse problem described herein was proposed as a sample real-time pedagogical problem at the REX workshop. It is very simple, and includes some real-time aspects. I decided to specify this particular problem to demonstrate one way of dealing with time in the specification language Z. This paper contains a description of the problem, the Z specification, and a justification for choosing Z as the specification language.

Keywords: Real-time specification, system engineering analysis, formal specification

Contents

1 Introduction

When developing software-intensive systems, there is a significant problem in relating an engineering analysis of the system under design to the resulting software specification for its implementation. This is especially true when the engineering analysis is in continuous time and involves differential equations, and the software specification is in discrete time. The software specification all too often assumes a familiarity with engineering assumptions that is beyond the capabilities of the software engineer, and this can have unpleasant consequences. In practice, this problem is usually resolved in one of two ways. The first way is when the common understanding of the engineering analyst and the software engineer is sufficient to overcome any inconsistencies. The second way is when the engineering analyst develops the software. It would, however, be preferable to have a notation which captures the results of the engineering analysis and leads to the software requirements in a seamless manner and which could be maintained as the system evolves.

This paper documents the capability of the formal specification language Z to capture the results of an engineering analysis of a real-time problem. Since this small pedagogical problem has no equivalent software control process to be executed in real-time, I will not address the extension of using this approach to derive the specification for the software controller.

There have been a number of studies contrasting and comparing various formal methods; these studies discuss and list the properties of formal specification methods. For example, Sannella performed a study comparing specification languages for sequential systems which is reported in [4], and Place et al conducted a survey of formal specification languages for reactive systems, which is reported in [3]. The reasons for choosing Z as the specification language are given in the next section. Later sections specify the problem in Z and describe potential extensions to the specification.

2 Preliminaries

This section describes some of the reasons why the specification language Z [6] was chosen, and outlines the style of specification that is associated with the language. The reasons for choosing the specification language Z are listed below.

- I and some colleagues who could act as reviewers were already familiar with the language.
- The language is *minimalist*. Its basic elements are mathematical sets, predicate logic, and functions, which are embedded in a language with a schema notation that encourages composition. Other useful functions (such as operations on sequences, queues, stacks, and trees) are built into a library.
- The language is state-based. It recognizes that software explicitly captures, records, and updates a system state.
- The language strongly supports the composition of specification components to produce a larger specification.
- There are a number of commercially available tools supporting Z. I used the tool Fuzz, which supports syntax checking, type checking, and document production. The syntax analyzer and type checker operate on the same file as the document production tool.

- There are books specifying the syntax and semantics of the language, [6] and [5], other books containing case studies [1], and many articles describing specifications of systems and software to assist the developer. Training courses are also commercially available.

- There is an obvious style to the development of specifications, and this matches my view of how to engineer a system. This issue is discussed in more detail later.

- There are tools under development to assist the engineer in checking the specification for consistency.

There is a definite style for developing a specification in Z, and I favor refining the specification to develop operational software. A technique for refinement to code is outlined in [6], and an extension to this technique for Ada programming is discussed in [2]. An outline of the Z specification style is given below, and the birthday book example in [6] illustrates this style.

- Specify the essential functionality of the system under development.

- Specify how events and operations change the system state, and cause outputs to occur.

- Specify how to deal with exceptional operating conditions, and how these conditions affect the system state.

- Specify the initialization conditions for a system.

Because of the compositional nature of the language, with some training and practice, one can engineer such a system by first specifying components and then assembling them into larger parts. The example will demonstrate that the documentation trail takes the same approach. The reviewer of the specification is introduced to the system in this manner, and comes to understand how the specification fits together. Informal graphical notations can be used to make the organization of the specification easier to understand.

This is not meant to suggest that the specification emerges smoothly from the mind of the engineer, with no backtracking to correct previously produced components. As in all human endeavor, there is a constant need to re-explore the already created partial specifications, and to rewrite and reorganize them to achieve a more understandable specification.

An additional capability offered by a compositional approach is that it allows for the construction of each schema, the basic structural element, to fit on a viewgraph for presentation purposes.

3 Problem Description and Specification

A cat lies sleeping and a mouse is located between the cat and a mousehole. The problem is one dimensional: the cat, the mouse, and the mousehole are on a straight line, and the cat and mouse must move along the straight line. The initial conditions are given: the cat and mouse each occupy a specific point initially; and the mouse is moving at a given speed for its mousehole at the initial time. The cat wakes up at a later time and chases the mouse at a given speed. The question to be resolved is whether the cat catches the mouse or the mouse is able to reach the mousehole safely. In this statement of the problem, time is treated as a sequence of instances, with each instance being a natural number. The discretization of time has some interesting properties for the problem. There are three possible solutions to the stated problem.

1. The cat catches the mouse.

2. The mouse escapes from the cat.

3. The outcome is indeterminate due to the granularity of time.

The position of the animals is also discrete. This could have been handled in a number of ways. The manner chosen, however, was to require the interval between time instants to be sufficiently large that the mouse's position would always change by at least one unit. Since the only interesting problem is where the cat moves faster than the mouse, this seems like a reasonable position granularity.

The problem is simple, and I could have created a specification in which the time-of-arrival of the cat and the mouse at the mousehole were determined. If the cat arrived earlier than the mouse, then we can safely state that the cat caught the mouse. Conversely, if the mouse's arrival time preceded the cat's arrival time, then the mouse was safe. The granularity of time and space could have been handled by using the speeds of the cat and mouse to calculate the necessary time granularity such that both the cat and mouse moved by at least one unit each time interval. However, I was more interested in demonstrating a general approach to the problem which is relevant to stating more difficult problems. I deliberately overspecied the problem at each stage. For example, in the second stage it is stated that the position of the mouse along the axis decreases with each time interval. This is unnecessary, since the velocity is later stated as being negative, and the granularity of time and position is specified such that this condition must occur. However, when deriving a specification, it is often best to state all that you know at each stage. The stages in the specification are outlined below.

1. The types of variables are introduced as they are used. Hence at the first stage, we define only those types used at that stage, and introduce the other types at the appropriate stage. In this example, the velocities are not used until a later stage, and are introduced at that stage.

2. The method for dealing with time within the specification is introduced. It is treated as a sequence of time instants — partially for convenience, since Z has built-in library functions for sequences, but largely because this is a convenient way to treat time. Some requirements on the intervals between instants will be introduced.

3. The cat and the mouse are introduced as separate entities, with a sufficient number of dynamic properties to understand the discussion of the results in the following stage. The speed of the animals is *deliberately* ignored here, since it is not necessary to use it at this stage in the specification. This is not especially sensible in this specification, but is done because in more complicated specifications it is useful to

postpone complicated dynamics until a later stage. The initial relationship between the positions of the two animals is specified.

4. The conditions for determining the results are given. At the completion of this stage, the problem is specified, with the exception of the dynamics of the animals' movement.

5. The dynamics of animal movement are introduced, using an *integration* operator. This general statement of the problem demonstrates the capability to express such operators in Z. Obviously, such a statement could have been avoided, since, in this case the integration has a closed form solution. However, I kept the statement as general as possible. In a real-world engineering analysis, without a closed form solution, a later schema could elaborate on the integration technique to be used to calculate a numerical solution. I did not take this example to that level of detail.

6. The final stage is to specify how time gets updated. This introduces some restrictions on the updating of time that are necessary to make the specification sensible. A resolution of time granularity and position granularity is included.

3.1 Basic Types and Timing

The first step is to define the basic types to be considered. In this problem, time is considered as a sequence of *instants*. Throughout the remainder of the specification, t designates an instant of time. Time instants of particular significance will use a subscipt : for example the start time of the problem is t_0. The position of the mouse, the cat, and the mousehole along the line each have the type *POS*. The velocities of the cat and the mouse have type *VEL*. *RESULT* describes the status of the outcome and corresponds to the three conditions described above, with the additional condition that insufficient time has passed to determine the results.

$$Instant == \mathbb{N}$$
$$POS == \mathbb{Z}$$
$$Interval == \mathbb{N}$$
$$RESULT ::= mouse\_safe \mid cat\_happy \mid indeterminate \mid unfinished$$

The first schema specifies the way we treat time in the specification as a sequence of instants: this sequence is designated as *Time*. For convenience the position of the mousehole is included in this schema as x_h.

1. The initial time of the problem is designated as t_0 and is the first element of the sequence.

2. Each instant in the sequence must be greater than the instance that preceeds it.

Timing

$t_0 : Instant$
$\delta_t : Interval$
$x_h : POS$
$Time : \operatorname{seq} Instant$

$Time(1) = t_0$
$\forall t : 2 \mathrel{..} \# Time \bullet Time(t-1) < Time(t)$

3.2 Cat and Mouse

The schema *Mouse* specifies the characteristics of the mouse. It uses the schema *Timing* to designate time, and defines a function (x_m) mapping from time into position. This means that $x_m(t)$ designates the position of the mouse at time t. The predicates state the following.

1. The position of the mouse is known only at those instants within the sequence *Time*.
2. As time progresses, the position of the mouse is always decreasing (it is running from a positive position on the line toward its beginning).
3. The mouse can only be registered as having entered the mousehole at the final instant in the sequence. We are not interested in any more time instants beyond this time.

The granularity of the mouse's position, and the use of the "strictly less than" (¡) is based on a later schema, declaring that time updates are only acceptable if the mouse has changed its position by at least one unit of position.

Mouse

Timing
$x_m : Instant \twoheadrightarrow POS$

$\operatorname{dom} x_m = \operatorname{ran} Time$
$\forall t : \operatorname{ran} Time \mid t \neq head(Time)$
$\quad \bullet x_m(t) < x_m(t-1) \land x_h < x_m(t-1)$

The schema *Cat* specifies the characteristics of the cat. It uses the same *Timing* schema to designate time, and defines a function mapping from time to position, such that $x_c(t)$ designates the position of the cat at time t. The time t_c is the time at which the cat starts to chase the mouse. The predicates state the following :

1. The position of the cat is known only at the instances in the timing sequence.
2. The instant the cat starts to move must occur at or after the starting time of the mouse.
3. The cat occupies its initial position until the instant at which it starts to chase the mouse.

4. After the starting instant, the cat's position is always decreasing and can only be registered as being beyond the mousehole at the final instant in the sequence. Position granularity can cause the cat to remain at the same position in the next time instant.

$$
\begin{array}{|l}
\textit{Cat} \\
\hline
\textit{Timing} \\
x_c : \textit{Instant} \twoheadrightarrow \textit{POS} \\
t_c : \textit{Instant} \\
\hline
\mathrm{dom}\, x_c = \mathrm{ran}\ \textit{Time} \\
t_c \geq t_0 \\
\forall t : \mathrm{ran}\ \textit{Time} \mid t \leq t_c \bullet x_c(t) = x_c(t_0) \\
\forall t : \mathrm{ran}\ \textit{Time} \mid t \neq \textit{head}(\textit{Time}) \wedge t > t_c \\
\qquad \bullet\ x_c(t) \leq x_c(t-1) \wedge x_h < x_c(t-1) \\
\hline
\end{array}
$$

The schema Starting _Conditions specifies that the mouse must initially be between the cat and the mousehole.

$$
\begin{array}{|l}
\textit{Starting\_Conditions} \\
\hline
\textit{Mouse};\ \textit{Cat} \\
\hline
x_h < x_m(t_0) < x_c(t_0) \\
\hline
\end{array}
$$

3.3 Specification of Results

This subsection describes how the four possible resolutions are determined.

The mouse is safe if there is a time at which it is beyond the mousehole and it is still ahead of the cat.

$$
\begin{array}{|l}
\textit{Mouse\_Safe} \\
\hline
\textit{Mouse};\ \textit{Cat} \\
\textit{result} : \textit{RESULT} \\
\hline
\exists t : \mathrm{ran}\ \textit{Time} \mid x_m(t) < x_c(t) \wedge x_m(t) \leq x_h \\
\qquad \bullet\ \textit{result} = \textit{mouse\_safe} \\
\hline
\end{array}
$$

The cat is happy if there is an instant at which the mouse has not yet reached the mousehole, but the cat has passed up the mouse, or is occupying the same position.

$$
\begin{array}{|l}
\textit{Cat\_Happy} \\
\hline
\textit{Mouse};\ \textit{Cat} \\
\textit{result} : \textit{RESULT} \\
\hline
x_m(t_0) < x_c(t_0) \\
\exists t : \mathrm{ran}\ \textit{Time} \mid x_m(t) \geq x_c(t) \wedge x_m(t) > x_h \\
\qquad \bullet\ \textit{result} = \textit{cat\_happy} \\
\hline
\end{array}
$$

The result is indeterminate for the given timing sequence if at one instant the mouse was ahead of the cat and had not reached the mousehole, while at the next instant the cat was ahead of the mouse, which was beyond the mousehole.

Indeterminate
Mouse; *Cat*
result : *RESULT*

$\exists\, t : \mathrm{ran}\ Time \mid t \neq head(Time)$
$\quad \wedge\ x_m(t-1) < x_c(t-1) \wedge x_m(t-1) > x_h$
$\quad \wedge\ x_m(t) \geq x_c(t) \wedge x_m(t) < x_h$
$\quad \bullet\ result = indeterminate$

The result is unfinished if at all times the mouse is still between the cat and the mousehole.

Unfinished
Mouse; *Cat*
result : *RESULT*

$\forall\, t : \mathrm{ran}\ Time \mid x_h < x_m(t) < x_c(t)$
$\quad \bullet\ result = unfinished$

The result is the disjunction of the above conditions.

$$Result \mathrel{\widehat{=}} Mouse\_Safe \vee Cat\_Happy \vee Indeterminate \vee Unfinished$$

The above disjunction demonstrates the compositional nature of Z. Each of the relevant conditions are specified separately, and the disjunction of these is the result. This has been done without considering the equations of motion of the animals. At this point in the specification, we have stated all that we need to know about the logic of the problem. The next section describes the movement of the animals.

3.4 Movement

This section specifies the movement of the cat and the mouse. It defines the integration function used to specify the motion of the animals.

$$VEL == \mathbb{Z}$$

$\int_{t_0}^{t} : VEL \times Interval \twoheadrightarrow POS$
$\int_{t_c}^{t} : VEL \times Interval \twoheadrightarrow POS$

The mouse moves with velocity em v_m starting at time t_0. Its position $x_m(t)$ at time t is the integral of its velocity between the initial starting time and the time t, as specified below.

$$
\begin{array}{|l}
\hline
\textit{Mouse\_Motion} \\
\textit{Mouse} \\
v_m : \textit{VEL} \\
d\tau : \textit{Interval} \\
\hline
\delta_t * v_m \geq 1 \\
\forall t : \mathrm{ran}\ \textit{Time} \bullet x_m(t) = x_m(t_0) + \int_{t_0}^{t}(v_m, d\tau) \\
\hline
\end{array}
$$

The cat moves with velocity em v_c. Before it starts at time t_c, the cat remains at its initial position. After its starting time, its position is the integral of its velocity between the initial starting time and the time t, as specified below.

$$
\begin{array}{|l}
\hline
\textit{Cat\_Motion} \\
\textit{Cat} \\
v_c : \textit{VEL} \\
t_c : \textit{Instant} \\
d\tau : \textit{Interval} \\
\hline
\forall t : \mathrm{ran}\ \textit{Time} \mid t \leq t_c \bullet x_c(t) = x_c(t_0) \\
\forall t : \mathrm{ran}\ \textit{Time} \mid t > t_c \\
\quad \bullet x_c(t) = x_c(t_0) + \int_{tc}^{t}(v_c, d\tau) \\
\hline
\end{array}
$$

3.5 Time Updates

Time is treated as a sequence of events and must be updated as the environment dictates. Below is the schema defining the update of the timing sequence. The predicates for allowing a time update are listed below.

1. The input instant cannot have already occurred.
2. The input instant must be greater than the last instant already in the sequence.
3. The result must be unfinished. If the result is finished, we do not want to continue with the game.

The update results in extending the sequence by one element, which is the input instant ($t?$).

$$
\begin{array}{|l}
\hline
\textit{Time\_Update} \\
\textit{Result} \\
\Delta \textit{Timing} \\
t? : \textit{Instant} \\
\hline
t? \notin \mathrm{ran}\ \textit{Time} \wedge t? > \textit{last}(\textit{Time}) + \delta_t \wedge \textit{result} = \textit{unfinished} \\
\textit{Time}' = \textit{Time} \frown \langle t? \rangle \\
\hline
\end{array}
$$

4 Extensions

The problem stated here is very simple. Some obvious extensions could easily be made. The extensions listed below would be simple to handle within Z, but would require a new specification.

1. The mouse and the cat and the mousehole could be treated as two-dimensional shapes. An overlap of the cat and the mouse objects short of the mousehole means that the cat catches the mouse, and an overlap of the mouse and the mousehole means escape. There would still be an indeterminate solution if at one time instant the cat does not overlap with the mouse, or the mouse with the mousehole, but at the next instant the mouse overlaps with the cat and the mousehole.

2. The problem could be extended to be planar (two-dimensional), where the mouse runs directly toward the hole and the cat tries to cut it off. This is a more difficult problem since the cat would have to adjust its direction as it moves and judge its distance from the mouse.

3. A series of *games* are played and the results are recorded. This problem would have to consider that, depending on the timing sequence, the results could differ for the same starting conditions. Some games could be indeterminate, while others with the same initial conditions but different time sequences could have a determinate result. One result of interest would be that if the mouse escapes in one sequence, then there is no time sequence which can result in it's being caught.

4. The stated problem does not concern itself with engineering units for the problem variables. They are implicitly considered to be correct and usable. Good engineering practice would find a way to include these units in the specification. For example, the time instants are in *seconds*, the position variables in *feet*, and the velocities in *feet/second.* In a real problem involving the physical characteristics of a system, it is very important to demonstrate that the units of measurement are consistent.

5. The relationship between time instants and the time interval used in the definition of the integration function is weak. This needs further exploration, which should probably include some idea of how numerical integration techniques could be introduced.

5 Conclusion

The language Z sufficed to yield a good specification of the cat and mouse problem. The obvious inconsistency between the granularity of the sample times and the time at which either the cat catches the mouse or the mouse escapes can be handled in a satisfactory manner. This technique has the virtue of simplicity and conforms to engineering analysis practice. No attempt was made to use the proof rules associated with Z to determine if the schemas are consistent or if specific other characteristics of the problem hold. These proof rules they could be invoked if necessary. The limitations of the problem scope did not allow for an exploration of the issues concerning how an engineering analysis can be coordinated with a design of software.

References

[1] Hayes, Ian, editor. *Specification Case Studies.* Pentice-Hall, Englewood Cliffs, NJ, 1987.

[2] Place, Patrick, Wood, William, Luckham, David C., Mann, Walter, and Sankar, Sriram. Formal development of ada programs using z and anna: A case study. SEI Technical Report CMU/SEI-91-TR-1, Software Engineering Institute, Carnegie Mellon University, Pittsburgh, PA, 1991. ESD-91-TR-1.

[3] Place, Patrick, Wood, William, and Tudball, Mike. Survey of formal specification techniques for reactive systems. SEI Technical Report CMU/SEI-90-TR-5, Software Engineering Institute, Carnegie Mellon University, Pittsburgh, PA, 1990. ESD-TR-90-206.

[4] Sannella, Donald. A survey of formal software development methods. Technical Report ECS-LFCS-88-56, Edinburgh University, 1988.

[5] Spivey, J.M. *Understanding Z,* volume 3 of *Cambridge Tracts in Theoretical Computer Science.* Cambridge Univerity Press, 1988.

[6] Spivey, J.M. *The Z Notation: A Reference Manual.* Prentice-Hall, New York, NY, 1989.

Layering and Action Refinement for Timed Systems

Job Zwiers
University of Twente,
Department of Computer Science,
P.O. Box 217,
7500 AE Enschede,
The Netherlands

Abstract. A separate treatment of time, temporal order and causality is used to explain action refinement for timed systems within a process algebraic setting. Communication closed layers, serializability, the SIMD model of execution, and real-time local clocks are among the phenomena that can be described and explained within the formalism. The relation with L. Lamport's model of Interprocess communication is considered.

Keywords: Action refinement, Serializability, Causality, Real-time

Contents

1 Introduction

Temporal order and causal order are separate notions when non-atomic actions in concurrent systems are concerned. By specifying concurrent systems in a process language where a clear distinction is made between language constructs for specifying causal order and those that specify temporal order, a compositional, algebraic approach can clarify serializability of transactions in distributed databases and communication closed layers as introduced in [EF82]. We present such a process language where sequential composition $P\ ;\ Q$ of processes is distinguished from *layer composition* $P \cdot Q$. The latter operation admits a succinct formulation of the communication closed layers principle from [EF82] as an algebraic law of the form:

$$(P \cdot Q) \parallel (R \cdot S) = (P \parallel R) \cdot (Q \parallel S),$$

provided that a simple syntactic sidecondition is fulfilled, that excludes "communication" between P and S, and between Q and R. This algebraic law can be understood in terms of a causality based model for concurrency. Replacing the causality based layer composition by temporal order based sequential composition, however, would invalidate the above law. Action refinement is another language operator where the distinction between temporal order and causality should be made. We use causality based action refinement as the basis for a definition of system implementation that explains the notion of serializability for atomic transactions. The layer composition operation allows us to view so called *serial* execution of transactions $T_0, T_1, \ldots$ as execution of a system of the form $T_0 \cdot T_1 \cdot \cdots$ rather than as *sequential* execution $T_0\ ;\ T_1\ ;\ \cdots$. Serial execution in this sense is, what is called, *IO-equivalent* to sequential execution, but does nor impose any *temporal* order on the transactions. Consequently we can view *serializable* execution of transactions as action refinement applied to serial execution of transactions as above. Moreover, the algebraic properties of refinement guarantee that the resulting system can also be described as $S_0 \cdot S_1 \cdot \cdots$, where S_i is the implementation for transaction T_i. Since the actions from S_i might (temporally) interleave with actions from S_j, such a simple representation is not possible in terms of sequential composition.

In [Lam86], L. Lamport introduces a similar notion of implementation, also aiming at explaining serializability as serial execution on a high level, followed by implementation of the high level actions. The model in [Lam86] relies on two types of *temporal* order, one of which occurs in our model too and which can be characterized as *total* temporal precedence, denoting that all of the execution of some action a precedes all of the execution of some other action b. The other temporal order, called weak precedence, indicates that some action a "may causally affect" some other action b, in the sense that at least part of the execution of a temporally precedes part of b. Our causal precedence relation is not defined in terms of temporal relationship alone but rather takes the notion of *conflict* between actions into account. Intuitively a conflict between actions a and b exists when the two actions both need access to some common resource, such as a shared variable. As a consequence, knowing the causal order among events that occur in some system execution or "run" as we call it, is (just) sufficient to determine the net overall effect of a run. This is not the case for weak temporal precedence.

Although we have argued that temporal order and causality should be treated separately this does not imply that the two are unrelated altogether. The interaction between the two is made explicit by means of axioms that are related to those in [Lam86]. Moreover, we introduce a process language that allows specification of real-time constraints that induce temporal ordering among events. Indirectly, via the relation between temporal and causal ordering, such timing constraints can also induce causal ordering. Thus, real-time constraints can be used to guarantee *functional correctness*, which is related to causal ordering, of a system. We employ such techniques in an example of a systolic array for sorting, that can be shown correct only under certain real-time assumptions. The algorithm relies on loosely synchronized *local* clocks to enforce certain causal order.

We summarize the contents of the paper. Rather than introducing a complicated process language at once we introduce our final design language DL_4 in a number of successively more complicated languages $DL_0..DL_4$. The first of these, DL_0 explains parallel composition and layer composition for uninterpreted actions, without any further complications. The language DL_1 is just like DL_0 except that we introduce actions in the form of guarded multiple assignments. The important notion of action refinement is introduced in DL_2. The models for DL_0, DL_1 and DL_2 are based on causality alone, i.e. without reliance on temporal order. As a consequence, the partial order models for those languages are in fact isomorphic to multistep and even (not standard) interleaving models for concurrency. The seemingly innocent addition of sequential composition for the language DL_3 does change matters radically. A new model, based on runs of events that are both causally and temporally ordered is introduced. The relation with the model of [Lam86] is discussed in this section. Finally we introduce real-time constraints in language DL_4, together with the example.

2 The DL_0 model

The simplest model does neither include real-time aspects nor action refinement. Moreover we do not interpret atomic actions at this stage. The only assumption that we make is that there is a given, statically determined, *conflict relation*. It is an abstraction of the notion of conflicts between transactions in distributed databases, where two transactions T_0 and T_1 are said to conflict if they access some common part of shared storage. Departing from this intuition we therefore assume that there is a given structure $(\mathcal{A}ct, —)$ consisting of a set of (atomic) actions together with a binary conflict relation "—" which is irreflexive (i.e. not $a — a$ for any $a \in \mathcal{A}ct$) and symmetric (i.e. $a_0 — a_1$ implies $a_1 — a_0$). Conflicts are not required to be transitive which is clear from the underlying intuition concerning database transactions. For if transactions T_0 and T_1 share some storage, say x, and T_1 and T_2 share some storage, say y, then it does not follow that T_0 and T_2 must share common storage too. Based on these actions we introduce our first language DL_0:

$$P \in DL_0,$$

$$P ::= a \mid P \cdot Q \mid P \parallel Q \mid P \,\mathbf{or}\, Q \mid \mathbf{skip} \mid \mathbf{empty}$$

Before discussing the denotational semantics, we provide some intuition for the partial order model, the language operations, and algebraic properties of the language.

A basic assumption is that a (single) computation or *run* of a system can be modeled as a (partially) ordered *set of events* $(E, \longrightarrow)$. A system P as a whole denotes the set $[\![P]\!]$ of all possible runs for that system. Consequently we regard two processes P and Q as equal, denoted by $P = Q$ iff their sets of possible runs are equal, i.e. iff $[\![P]\!] = [\![Q]\!]$. Moreover we define process refinement P *sat* Q as the relation denoting $[\![P]\!] \subseteq [\![Q]\!]$. (Other forms of refinement are considered below) The order "$\longrightarrow$" on the events in a single run indicates the *logical* order, sometimes called causal order, among events that conflict. Our causal order is not required to be transitive, since the conflict relation is not transitive either, but we do require that the transitive closure of "$\longrightarrow$" is a partial order (po). Equivalently one can say that the causal order itself constitutes a directed acyclic graph (dag). For the DL_0 stage, the choice for a non transitive order is just a matter of taste; we could have defined the semantics in terms of the transitive closure of the causal order just as easily. (This is no longer the case when we introduce action refinement.) For events e_0 and e_1, causal ordering $e_0 \longrightarrow e_1$ does not imply that e_0 should precede e_1 in the temporal sense. Rather it denotes that e_0 *effectively* precedes e_1 in the sense that *to determine the net effect of the whole execution* one can *pretend* that all of e_0 preceded all of e_1. This does not exclude a situation where execution of e_0 overlaps in time with execution of e_1. Our requirement that states that conflicting events cannot be unordered is tantamount to saying that execution of events can be regarded as *atomic*, i.e. execution of one event does not interfere with execution of another event.

Next we provide the intuition for the language operations of DL_0. Execution of an action a results in a single event. Therefore, actions are executed atomically. Our semantic domain is such that events, say e_0 and e_1, are ordered if and only if they conflict. Apart from this property, nothing else is required for *parallel composition* $P \parallel Q$ as far as the ordering between P and Q events is concerned. So, the order that necessarily exists between conflicting P and Q events is *nondeterministically* determined. The nondeterministic choices for different pairs of conflicting events are of course subject to the condition that the order must remain acyclic, so certain choices are excluded. Each choice corresponds to a (potential) different net effect of the whole run. Note however that no extra nondeterminism is created by different temporal schedules for causally independent, i.e. non conflicting events, as would be the case for an interleaving model.

For *layer composition* $P \cdot Q$ the situation is the reverse: any P event e_0 logically precedes any Q event e_1 with which it conflicts. This resembles the sequential composition construct, but there is a substantial difference. For sequential composition $P\,;\,Q$ *all* P events should have terminated before *any* Q event can even start. This is not so for layer composition. In the latter case any Q event e must wait only for its causal predecessors, implying that it need not wait for P events that do not conflict with e. Moreover, in the case of sequential composition the ordering between P and Q events is in a *temporal* sense rather than a logical one, excluding any temporal overlap. (Therefore we postpone the inclusion of sequential composition to a later stage, where we introduce a (separate) temporal order among events.)

Nondeterministic choice P **or** Q is a straightforward construct that either executes P or Q.

Finally we have the proces **skip** which performs no action at all, and the **empty** process, which cannot perform any computation at all, not even the computation executed by **skip** which contains no events. Both processes aid in formulating some algebraic properties of DL_0, where they act as a unit element and as a zero element respectively. We provide some algebraic laws, which we claim to be valid for the semantic model that we provide after the following lemma:

Lemma 2.1

Commutativity and Associativity:

$$\begin{array}{rcll} P \parallel Q & = & Q \parallel P & \text{(COM1)} \\ P \textbf{ or } Q & = & Q \textbf{ or } P & \text{(COM2)} \\ P \parallel (Q \parallel R) & = & (P \parallel Q) \parallel R & \text{(ASSOC1)} \\ P \cdot (Q \cdot R) & = & (P \cdot Q) \cdot R & \text{(ASSOC2)} \\ P \textbf{ or } (Q \textbf{ or } R) & = & (P \textbf{ or } Q) \textbf{ or } R & \text{(ASSOC3)} \end{array}$$

Distributivity:

$$\begin{array}{rcll} P \parallel (Q \textbf{ or } R) & = & (P \parallel Q) \textbf{ or } (P \parallel R) & \text{(DIST1)} \\ P \cdot (Q \textbf{ or } R) & = & (P \cdot Q) \textbf{ or } (P \cdot R) & \text{(DIST2)} \\ (P \textbf{ or } Q) \cdot R & = & (P \cdot R) \textbf{ or } (Q \cdot R) & \text{(DIST3)} \end{array}$$

Units and zeros:

$$\begin{array}{lclcll} \textbf{skip} \parallel P & = & P \parallel \textbf{skip} & = & P & \text{(SKIP1)} \\ \textbf{skip} \cdot P & = & P \cdot \textbf{skip} & = & P & \text{(SKIP2)} \\ \textbf{empty or } P & = & P \textbf{ or empty} & = & P & \text{(EMPTY1)} \\ \textbf{empty} \parallel P & = & P \parallel \textbf{empty} & = & \textbf{empty} & \text{(EMPTY2)} \\ \textbf{empty} \cdot P & = & P \cdot \textbf{empty} & = & \textbf{empty} & \text{(EMPTY3)} \end{array}$$

□

More interesting is the relationship between parallel composition and layer composition. We can formulate here a (simple form of) the principle of communication closed layers in the form of an algebraic law. The communication closed layers law (CCL) deviates somewhat from the usual style of algebraic laws in that there is a (syntactic) side condition that should be checked concerning conflicts between processes. Let $act(P)$ denote the (finite) set of actions that (syntactically) occur in a DL_0 process P. We extend the conflict relation on $\mathcal{A}ct$ to sets of $\mathcal{A}ct$ elements as follows: for $X, Y \subseteq \mathcal{A}ct$:

$X — Y$ iff there exist $a \in X$, $b \in Y$ such that $a — b$.

Conflicts between DL_0 processes are then defined thus: $P — Q$ iff $act(P) — act(Q)$. As usual, $P \not— Q$ denotes that $P — Q$ is not the case, i.e. P does not conflict with Q. The CCL laws can now be formulated as follows.

Lemma 2.2
Communication Closed Layers:
Provided that $P \not\to S$, and $Q \not\to R$:

$$\begin{array}{rcll} (P \cdot Q) \parallel (R \cdot S) & = & (P \parallel R) \cdot (Q \parallel S) & \text{(CCL)} \\ (P \cdot Q) \parallel S & = & P \cdot (Q \parallel S) & \text{(CCL-L)} \\ (P \cdot Q) \parallel R & = & (P \parallel R) \cdot Q & \text{(CCL-R)} \\ Q \parallel R & = & Q \cdot R & \text{(Independence)} \end{array}$$

□

The definition of our first model can now be given. We assume a given countable set $\mathcal{E}vent$ of events. For the DL_0 language we moreover assume that there is a given interpretation function $\mathcal{A}$ for actions, mapping from Act to the powerset $\mathcal{P}(\mathcal{E}vent)$. Executing action a will result in a single event e nondeterministically chosen from the set $\mathcal{A}[\![a]\!]$.

The precise structure of events is not the same for all models, but we always rely on a fixed conflict structure $(\mathcal{E}vent, —)$ for events, analogously to the conflict structure $(Act, —)$ for actions. We assume consistency with respect to conflicts between the syntactic (action) level and the semantic (event) level, that is, for any actions a_0, a_1 and events e_0, e_1 such that $e_0 \in \mathcal{A}[\![a_0]\!]$ and $e_1 \in \mathcal{A}[\![a_1]\!]$ we have that $a_0 — a_1$ iff $e_0 — e_1$.
Furthermore we assume that each event e has an attribute $id(e)$ called its identity. An *ordered event set* is then defined as a structure $(E, \longrightarrow)$ where E is a multiset of events, i.e. a subset of $\mathcal{E}vent$ such that all events $e \in E$ have a distinct $id(e)$ attribute, and where $\longrightarrow$ is an order on E such that $(E, \stackrel{+}{\longrightarrow})$ is a partial order. ($\stackrel{+}{\longrightarrow}$ denotes the transitive closure of $\longrightarrow$).

An ordered event set $(E, \longrightarrow)$ is *conflict closed* if for any two $e_0, e_1 \in E$ we have that:

$$e_0 — e_1 \text{ iff } e_0 \longrightarrow e_1 \text{ or } e_1 \longrightarrow e_0.$$

A *run* or *computation* is now defined to be an ordered event set that is conflict closed. The set of all such runs is denoted by $Comp_0$. The semantic domain for DL_0 is the set DS_0 defined as the powerset $\mathcal{P}(Comp_0)$. Finally we define the semantics of the language DL_0 by means of a semantic meaning function of the form

$$[\![\cdot]\!] : DL_0 \rightarrow DS_0.$$

It is defined as usual, by an inductive definition:

Definition 2.3 *Semantics of DL_0*

$$[\![a]\!] = \{(e, \emptyset) \mid e \in \mathcal{A}[\![a]\!]\}$$

$$[\![P \parallel Q]\!] = \{(E_P \cup E_Q, \longrightarrow_P \cup \longrightarrow_Q \cup \longrightarrow_C) \in Comp_0 \mid$$
$$(E_P, \longrightarrow_P) \in [\![P]\!], (E_Q, \longrightarrow_Q) \in [\![Q]\!], E_P \cap E_Q = \emptyset \longrightarrow_C \subseteq (E_P \cup E_Q)^2\}$$

$$
\begin{aligned}
[\![P \cdot Q]\!] &= \{(E_P \cup E_Q, \longrightarrow_P \cup \longrightarrow_Q \cup \longrightarrow_C) \in \mathit{Comp}_0 \mid \\
&\qquad (E_P, \longrightarrow_P) \in [\![P]\!], (E_Q, \longrightarrow_Q) \in [\![Q]\!], \longrightarrow_C \subseteq (E_P \times E_Q)\} \\
[\![P \textbf{ or } Q]\!] &= [\![P]\!] \cup [\![Q]\!] \\
[\![\, \textbf{skip} \,]\!] &= \{(\emptyset, \emptyset)\}
\end{aligned}
$$

(That is, the only run for **skip** has no events, and consequently an empty order.)

$$[\![\, \textbf{empty} \,]\!] = \emptyset$$

(That is, **empty** does not admit any run at all.)
□

Note that in the definition of parallel composition the order "$\longrightarrow_C$" which appears to be a completely arbitrary order on the event set $E_P \cup E_Q$ is in fact constrained by the conflict closedness requirement for Comp_0 runs. Therefore $\longrightarrow_C$ is (nondeterministically) chosen as an augment of the order $\longrightarrow_P \cup \longrightarrow_Q$ such that $(E_P \cup E_Q, \longrightarrow_P \cup \longrightarrow_Q \cup \longrightarrow_C)$ is conflict closed.
For the semantics of layer composition the only difference is the (extra) restriction on $\longrightarrow_C$. For any P events $e_p \in E_P$ that conflicts with some Q event $e_q \in E_Q$, we must have that $e_p \longrightarrow_C e_q$ by the requirement that $(E_P \cup E_Q, \longrightarrow_P \cup \longrightarrow_Q \cup \longrightarrow_C)$ is conflict closed, the restriction that $\longrightarrow_C$ is a relation from E_P to E_Q and the fact that neither $\longrightarrow_P$ nor $\longrightarrow_Q$ does order these two events. So, unlike the parallel composition case, we see that for each pair of runs $(E_P, \longrightarrow_P)$, $(E_Q, \longrightarrow_Q)$ the $\longrightarrow_C$ order is uniquely determined. Note that as a consequence, $[\![P \cdot Q]\!] \subseteq [\![P \parallel Q]\!]$.

3 Shared variables and the DL_1 model

The DL_1 language differs from DL_0 mainly in that we fix a certain interpretation for actions. This is accompanied by the introduction of some new language operations. From now on we assume that processes perform actions a that read and write shared variables $x, y, z, \ldots \in \mathcal{V}ar$, and perform (boolean valued) tests on shared variables. We employ the usual (simultaneous) assignment notation $\mathbf{x} := \mathbf{f}$ where $\mathbf{x}$ and $\mathbf{f}$ are a list of variables and a list of expressions. Such assignments are guarded by means of a boolean expression b which must evaluate to true before executing the assignment. For such actions, that we denote by $b \,\&\, \mathbf{x} := \mathbf{f}$, the evaluation of the guard together with the assignment constitute a single *atomic* action. When the guard b is identically true, we omit it and employ the usual simultaneous assignment notation $\mathbf{x} := \mathbf{f}$. Similarly we regard boolean tests b as degenerate cases where the assignment part has been left out. Such guards can be used to model more conventional constructs. For instance we use

$(b \cdot P)$ **or** $(\neg b \cdot Q)$ as an abbreviation for **if** b **then** P **else** Q **fi**

For an action a of the form $b \,\&\, \mathbf{x} := \mathbf{f}$ the set of variables $\{\mathbf{x}\}$ is called the writeset $W(a)$ of a. Similarly, we define the readset $R(a)$ as the set of variables occurring (free) in b and the expression list $\mathbf{f}$. Finally we define the *base* of a as $\mathit{base}(a) = R(a) \cup W(a)$. Two actions a_0 and a_1 *conflict* if one of them writes a variable x that is read or written by the other one. Formally we define a conflict relation on actions, denoted by $a_0 — a_1$ as follows:

$$a_0 — a_1 \text{ iff } W(a_1) \cap (R(a_0) \cup W(a_0)) \neq \emptyset \text{ or } W(a_0) \cap (R(a_1) \cup W(a_1)) \neq \emptyset$$

The syntax for DL_1 is as follows:

$$P \in DL_1,$$

$$P ::= b \,\&\, \mathbf{x} := \mathbf{f} \quad | \quad P \parallel Q \quad | \quad P \cdot Q \quad | \quad P \;\mathbf{or}\; Q$$

$$| \quad \mathbf{skip} \quad | \quad \mathbf{empty} \quad | \quad P \backslash x \quad | \quad \mathbf{io}(P)$$

There are two new operations, viz. the $\mathbf{io}(P)$ construct, which turns execution of process P into an atomic action, and the *variable hiding construct* $P \backslash x$. $\mathbf{io}(P)$ denotes execution of a single action that captures the net effect of executing P without admitting interference by other events. The $\mathbf{io}(\cdot)$ operation is also called the *contraction* operation, since it contracts complete P runs into single events. Intuitively $\mathbf{io}(P)$ represents the input-output behaviour of a process P if we execute that process in isolation, i.e. without interference from outside. This operation induces an interesting process equivalence, called IO-equivalence, and an associated IO-refinement relation. Such equivalences play an important role in the book by K.R. Apt and E.-R. Olderog [AO].

$$P \overset{IO}{=} Q \text{ iff } \mathbf{io}(P) \;=\; \mathbf{io}(Q),$$

$$P \overset{IO}{sat} Q \text{ iff } \mathbf{io}(P) \; sat \; \mathbf{io}(Q).$$

Specification of what is often called the *functional behaviour* of a process P is really a specification of $\mathbf{io}(P)$, i.e. of the IO-equivalence class of P. The $\mathbf{io}(\cdot)$ operation does (obviously) not distribute though parallel composition. For the case of layer composition we have the following law:

$$P \cdot Q \overset{IO}{=} \mathbf{io}(P) \cdot \mathbf{io}(Q)$$

The intuition here is that although execution of "layer" P might overlap execution of "layer" Q *temporally*, one can pretend that all of P, here represented as an atomic action $\mathbf{io}(P)$, precedes all of Q as far as IO behaviour is concerned.

Next we provide the details for the semantics of DL_1. All that need be done is to define the interpretation of guarded assignments and the meaning of the $\mathbf{io}(\cdot)$ and hiding operations. All other definitions can be taken over from DL_0 provided that we systematically read DS_1 for DS_0 and $Comp_1$ for $Comp_0$. For DL_1 each event $e \in \mathcal{E}vent$ has local initial and final states that are partial functions from variable names $\mathcal{V}ar$ to some appropriate domain of data values $\mathcal{V}al$. We model such partial functions by means of two attributes $Read(e)$ and $Write(e)$, each of which is a set of name-value pairs of the form (x, v) where $x \in \mathcal{V}ar$ and where $v \in \mathcal{V}al$, where for any x there can be at most one value v such that $(x, v) \in Read(e)$, and similarly there can be at most one such pair in $Write(e)$. The sets $R(e)$ and $W(e)$ denote the domains of the initial and final states, that is the sets of variables x for which there is some pair (x, v) in $Read(e)$ or $Write(e)$, respectively. For

$x \in R(e)$ we denote by $\overleftarrow{x}(e)$ the corresponding value in $Read(e)$ and similarly, if $x \in W(e)$ we denote by $x(e)$ the corresponding value in $Write(e)$. For expressions f that have their free variables contained in $R(e)$ we interpret $\overleftarrow{f}(e)$ as the value of the expression f where each free variable x assumes value $\overleftarrow{x}(e)$. Similarly, if the free variables of f are contained in $W(e)$, $f(e)$ denotes the value of f where all free x assume value $x(e)$. Based upon $W(e)$ and $R(e)$ we define *conflict relations* between events along the same lines as above:

$$e_0 — e_1 \text{ iff } W(e_1) \cap (R(e_0) \cup W(e_0)) \neq \emptyset \text{ or } W(e_0) \cap (R(e_1) \cup W(e_1)) \neq \emptyset$$

Finally we give the interpretation of DL_1 actions by fixing the semantic $\mathcal{A}$ function introduced already for DL_0:

$$\begin{aligned} \mathcal{A}[\, b \,\&\, \mathbf{x} := \mathbf{f}\,] \;=\; \{\, e \in \mathcal{E}vent_1 \mid & R(e) = var(b) \cup var(\mathbf{f}),\ W(e) = \{\mathbf{x}\}, \\ & \overleftarrow{b}(e) = true,\ \mathbf{x}(e) = \overleftarrow{\mathbf{f}}(e)\,\} \end{aligned}$$

To define the meaning of the $\mathbf{io}(\cdot)$ operation we define the notion of *state consistency* for runs.

Definition 3.1 *Reads-from relation*

Let $(E, \longrightarrow)$ be a $Comp_1$ run, $e_0, e_1 \in E$. We say that e_1 reads x from e_0 if the following holds:

1. $x \in W(e_0)$,
2. $x \in R(e_1)$,
3. $e_0 \longrightarrow e_1$,
4. There is no $e' \in E$ such that $x \in W(e')$ and $e_0 \longrightarrow e' \longrightarrow e_1$.

Event e is called an *initial read* in $(E, \longrightarrow)$ if:

1. $x \in R(e)$,
2. There is no e' such that e reads x from e'.

□

Definition 3.2 *State consistency*

A $Comp_1$ run $(E, \longrightarrow)$ is x – state consistent if the following conditions hold:

1. For any events $e_0, e_1 \in E$ such that e_1 reads x from e_0 we have that $\overleftarrow{x}(e_1) = x(e_0)$, i.e. the initial state value of x for e_1 equals the final state value of x for e_0.
2. For all initial reads $e_0, e_1, \ldots$ of x in E, if any, the initial state values of x are the same, i.e. $\overleftarrow{x}(e_i) = \overleftarrow{x}(e_j)$ for all relevant e_i, e_j.

The set of all x – state consistent runs is denoted by *State-consistent*(x).

A run is called state consistent if it is x – state consistent for all variables $x \in \mathcal{V}ar$. The set of all state consistent runs is denoted by *State-consistent*
□

State consistency is not a property that holds in general for arbitrary runs of some process P. The simple reason is that P might be composed in parallel with some other process Q. Thus, although for a given P run in isolation it might be the case that some event e_1 reads x from e_0, it is quite possible that after combining with some Q run e_1 actually reads x from e_2, where e_2 is (apparently) some Q event. Such interference is no longer possible for a particular variable x once we *hide* that variable. We define (semantically) hiding as an operation that removes a x related attributes from a run that in the semantics below will be forced to be x – state consistent:

Definition 3.3 *Hiding*

For a run $(E, \longrightarrow)$ we define $(E, \longrightarrow)\backslash x$ as the run that is obtained from $(E, \longrightarrow)$ by removing all occurrences of pairs (x, v) from $Read(e)$ and $Write(e)$ attributes. If this leaves events e with $Read(e) = Write(e) = \emptyset$, the event is removed as a whole. The order on the resulting set of events is the restriction of $\longrightarrow$ to the (uniquely determined) conflict closed order on the remaining events.
□

The hiding operation is extended to sets of runs as usual, by means of pointwise extension. The semantics of the hiding operator from DL_1 is then defined as follows:

$$[\![P\backslash x]\!] = ([\![P]\!] \cap State\text{-}consistent(x))\backslash x$$

A state consistent run $(E, \longrightarrow)$ can be *contracted* into a single event that captures the net effect of that run. We define such contraction formally next:

Definition 3.4 *Contraction*

Let $(E, \longrightarrow)$ be an state consistent run. The contraction $contr((E, \longrightarrow))$ is defined as the set of events e that satisfy the following properties.

1. $R(e) = \bigcup\{R(e') \mid e' \in E\}$,
2. $W(e) = \bigcup\{W(e') \mid e' \in E\}$,
3. For all $x \in R(e)$ the initial state value $\overleftarrow{x}(e)$ is the initial state value $\overleftarrow{x}(e')$ where e' is some (arbitrary) initial read of x in $(E, \longrightarrow)$,
4. For all $x \in W(e)$ the final state value $x(e)$ is the final state value $x(e')$ where e' is the (uniquely determined) $(E, \longrightarrow)$ event that is maximal among the events $e_0, e_1, \ldots$ for which $x \in W(e_i)$, $(i = 0, 1, \ldots)$. Since all our runs are *finite* this final state value is well defined.

Remark. The events in $contr((E, \longrightarrow))$ are uniquely determined except for their (nondeterministically chosen) identity. **(End of remark)**

□

For a set of state consistent runs X we define $contr(X)$ by pointwise extending the contraction operation of above. The semantics for the $\mathbf{io}(\cdot)$ operation can now be given as follows:

$$[\![\mathbf{io}(P)]\!] = contr([\![P]\!] \cap \mathit{State\text{-}consistent})$$

So $[\![\mathbf{io}(P)]\!]$ consists of the contractions of all state consistent P runs.

4 Atomic execution and action refinement in DL_2

Thus far we have relied on a given set of atomic actions $\mathcal{A}ct$, without taking any internal structure of such actions into account. Atomicity of actions should not be understood as "not further decomposable" however. In a language DL_2 we study refinement of atomic actions, and the related notion of atomicity on the level of groups of events. The syntax for the DL_2 language is:

$$P \in DL_2,$$

$$P ::= l : b \& \mathbf{x} := \mathbf{f} \;\mid\; P \parallel Q \;\mid\; P \cdot Q \;\mid\; P \,\mathbf{or}\, Q \;\mid\; \mathbf{skip} \;\mid\; \mathbf{empty}$$
$$\mid\; P \backslash x \;\mid\; \langle l : P \rangle \;\mid\; \mathbf{ref}\; l \;\mathbf{to}\; S \;\mathbf{in}\; P \;\mid\; \mathbf{contr}\; l \;\mathbf{in}\; P$$

Atomic actions for DL_2 are similar to those for DL_1 except that they are *labeled* by means of the l : prefix. The same label can have several occurrences in some process. As an abbreviation we use $b \& \mathbf{x} := \mathbf{f}$ for $nil : b \& \mathbf{x} := \mathbf{f}$, where nil is some fixed label. Labeled actions can be *refined* by means of the *action refinement construct* **ref** l **to** S **in** P, which effectively expands all occurrences of l labeled events to corresponding "atomically executed" S runs. Atomic execution is not the same as executing a single event. Rather it refers to execution that is *IO-equivalent* to execution as a single event. For the refinement construct **ref** l **to** S **in** P we require that within P there are no occurrences of l of the form $\langle l : Q \rangle$ or of the form **ref** l **to** S **in** Q. Such "chunks" as they are sometimes called cannot be refined by means of the refinement construct.
Atomic brackets $\langle l : P \rangle$ serve to indicate that P should execute "atomically". Apart from the fact that it is a useful construct as such, it also allows one to simplify the **ref** l **to** S **in** P construct. For provided that all occurrences of $l : b \& \mathbf{x} := \mathbf{f}$ in P are IO-equivalent to S the refinement boils down to substitution of $\langle l : S \rangle$ for all l labeled actions in P.
The label l within $\langle l : P \rangle$ labels all P events, where again we omit "l :" if it is actually the labeling "nil :". These labeled events are *contracted* into a single (IO-equivalent) event when $\langle l : P \rangle$ occurs within the scope of the **contr** l **in** $\cdots$ construct. The contraction construct is a generalization of the **io**() construct of DL_1. We define the latter as an abbreviation for DL_2:

$$\mathbf{io}(P) = \mathbf{contr}\; nil \;\mathbf{in}\; \langle nil : P \rangle$$

Relying on the **io**() operation we define IO-equivalence and IO-refinement as before. **contr** l **in** $\cdots$ can be seen as a kind of inverse for the **ref** l **to** S **in** P construct. This can be expressed by an algebraic law. Provided that all occurrences of $l : b \& \mathbf{x} := \mathbf{f}$ are IO-equivalent to S we have:

$$\textbf{contr } l \textbf{ in } (\textbf{ ref } l \textbf{ to } S \textbf{ in } P) \; = \; P$$

Reversely, assume that P has only occurences of l in the form of $\langle l : Q \rangle$ that are IO-equivalent to R. Then we can replace Q "chunks" in P by R chunks while preserving IO-equivalence. For in that case we have:

$$\textbf{ref } l \textbf{ to } R \textbf{ in } (\textbf{ contr } l \textbf{ in } P) \overset{IO}{\equiv} P$$

Next we discuss the semantics of refinement in more detail and we provide a revised semantic definition for DL_2. Intuitively, refining action a to some *process* S within the context of a given process P means that occurrences e of a events in P runs $(E, \longrightarrow)$ are replaced by ("expanded to") complete S runs $(E_e, \longrightarrow_e)$. If we denote the resulting run by $(E_r, \longrightarrow_r)$, then the order $\longrightarrow_r$ is determined as follows:

- For two E events e_0, e_1 both unequal to the refined event e the order remains unaffected, i.e. $e_0 \longrightarrow_r e_1$ iff $e_0 \longrightarrow e_1$.
- For two E_e events e_0, e_1 we have a similar situation: $e_0 \longrightarrow_r e_1$ iff $e_0 \longrightarrow_e e_1$.
- For $e_0 \in E$, not equal to e, and $e_1 \in E_e$ we introduce *conflict based order inheritance:* $e_0 \longrightarrow_r e_1$ iff e_0 and e_1 *conflict* and also $e_0 \longrightarrow e$, and $e_1 \longrightarrow_r e_0$ iff e_0 and e_1 *conflict* and also $e \longrightarrow e_0$.

Two remarks should be made here. First of all, although it will be clear that refinement in this sense cannot preserve all relevant properties concerning process behaviour, it seems reasonable that for interpreted actions like those of $DL_1$the *functional behaviour* should be preserved. That is, we expect the refined system to be IO-equivalent to, or at least an IO-implementation of, the original system. Secondly, the *atomicity* of the refined action should be preserved. The latter is, from an intuitive point of view, best understood in an interpreted language like DL_1. Atomicity of a DL_1 event e implies that the (local) state transformation effectuated by e is not interfered by some other event e'. Therefore, *absence of interference* is a property that should be satisfied by any refinement of e too. Now it is well known that simply expanding an event e in some run $(E, \longrightarrow)$ to a (sub) run $(E_e, \longrightarrow_e)$ as described above does result in an overall run where, indeed, E_e is not interfered by E events. However, this property is *not preserved under parallel composition*. One way to circumvent this problem is to use a semantic domain of runs that do not only include events caused by the system under consideration but that also include already, nondeterministical guesses of, events caused by the *environment* of that system. In this approach events are *labeled* as either "P events" (process events) or "E events" (environment events). Then, when some (process) event is expanded to a run $(E_e, \longrightarrow_e)$ as described, there are no events that interfere with this run, neither caused by the process itself, nor caused by the environment. Such an approach has been taken in [JPZ91] In this paper we have taken an alternative approach, where runs do not include environment caused events. To enforce atomicity of a sub run $(E_e, \longrightarrow_e)$ within a run $(E_r, \longrightarrow_r)$ we *label* the E_e events all by a common *atomicity label* α. Moreover, we introduce a domain property for DL_2 computations that implies that the set of α labeled events is *contractable* in the following sense:

Definition 4.1 *Contractability*
Let $(E, \longrightarrow)$ be some run and let C be some subset of E. We call C contractable in $(E, \longrightarrow)$ if for any two events e_0 and e_1 in C and some other E event e that is *not* in C it is not possible that both $e_0 \longrightarrow_r e$ and $e \longrightarrow_r e_1$. □

Intuitively, any event e with properties as indicated would be an *interfering* event for C. If a subset C is contractable there are no such events and consequently we can apply the *contr* operation, introduced for the semantics of the **io**() operation, to C. For the general case, where more than just a single action can be refined, we introduce *weak event congruence* as a means to indicate which groups of events within a given run are to be considered *atomic* in the sense of absence of interference. Atomicity labeling is to be regarded as a representation of event congruence classes, with a unique label for each class.

Definition 4.2 *Weak event congruence*

Let $(E, \longrightarrow)$ be an ordered event set. Let $\simeq$ be an equivalence relation on the set E, with equivalence classes $E_0, E_1, \ldots$. Let $(G, \longrightarrow_G)$ be the corresponding quotient graph where we have an arrow $[E_i] \longrightarrow_G [E_j]$ iff $i \neq j$ and there are events $e_i \in [E_i], e_j \in [E_j]$ such that $e_i \longrightarrow e_j$.

The equivalence $\simeq$ is a *weak congruence* on $(E, \longrightarrow)$ iff the quotient graph $(G, \longrightarrow_G)$ is a dag, i.e. is acyclic. □

We now define the semantic domain $Comp_2$ of runs for DL_2 processes. Essentially we take over the structure of $Comp_1$ for DL_1, except that we introduce two new event attributes $atom(e)(\in Alabel)$ and $label(e)(\in Label)$, where $Alabel$ is a given set of atomicity labels and $Label$ is the set of labels that can occur (syntactically) in DL_2 processes. The two attributes $atom(e)$ and $label(e)$ are defined for each event, where we use the label "*nil*" if no explicit label is specified. For each run $(E, \longrightarrow)$ the atomicity labels $atom(e)$ for $e \in E$ induce an equivalence relation. We require, as a domain property, that for all $Comp_2$ runs this equivalence is actually a weak event congruence. Moreover, we require for each congruence class C of E that $(C, \longrightarrow|C)$ (The restriction of $(E, \longrightarrow)$ to C events) is state consistent in the sense that $(C, \longrightarrow|C) \in$ *State-consistent*.
We extend the definition of *contraction* of runs $contr((E, \longrightarrow))$, introduced for the semantics of DL_1, to the domain $Comp_2$, where we assume that all E events have the same atomicity label and the same label. We define $contr((E, \longrightarrow))$ as a set of events e as before where we add two extra conditions, concerning labeling:

- $atom(e) = atom(e')$ where e' is some (arbitrary) E event,
- $label(e) = label(e')$ where e' is some (arbitrary) E event

Based upon this, we define a more powerful operation $contr(l, (E, \longrightarrow))$, that contracts only the l labeled events within $(E, \longrightarrow)$. Let $(E_l, \longrightarrow_l)$ be the sub run of $(E, \longrightarrow)$ consisting of all l labeled E events together with their induced ordering. Since labels can have several occurences within a process it is possible that not all l labeled events have the same atomicity label. First however consider the simple case where all E_l events do have the same atomicity label, say α. The syntactic constraints on DL_2 guarantee that in this case the sets of α labeled and l labeled events coincide. From State consistency property for the set of all α labeled event it follows that $e_c = contr((E_l, \longrightarrow_l))$ is a properly defined event. Now we define $contr(l, (E, \longrightarrow))$ as the run where $(E_l, \longrightarrow_l)$ is replaced by this e_c event. The details are as follows. We define $contr(l, (E, \longrightarrow))$ as the run

$$((E - E_l) \cup \{e_c\}, \longrightarrow|(E - E_l) \cup \longrightarrow_c),$$

where the order $\longrightarrow_c$ is defined as follows:

- $e \longrightarrow_c e_c$ for $e \in (E - E_l)$ iff there is some $e' \in E_l$ such that $e \longrightarrow e'$, and
- $e_c \longrightarrow_c e$ for $e \in (E - E_l)$ iff there is some $e' \in E_l$ such that $e' \longrightarrow e$

For the general case where not all l labeled events have the same atomicity label α, it is possible to partition these l labeled events into maximal subsets that do have the same atomicity label. $contr(l, (E, \longrightarrow))$ is obtained by applying the construction above to each of these subsets in turn. The domain property requiring that atomicity labels induce a weak congruence guarantees that these successive contractions are possible and moreover that the final resulting run is independent of the order in which subsets are contracted. So in fact, simultaneous refinement of a number of events is equivalent to repeated refinement of single events. As always, we extend the $contr(l, \cdot)$ operation to sets of runs by means of pointwise application.
The semantics for DL_2 is as follows.

Definition 4.3 *Semantics of DL_2*

$$[\![l : b \,\&\, \mathbf{x} := \mathbf{f}]\!] = \{(e, \emptyset) \in Comp_2 \mid e \in \mathcal{A}[\![b \,\&\, \mathbf{x} := \mathbf{f}]\!],\ label(e) = l\}$$

$$[\![P \parallel Q]\!] = \{(E_P \cup E_Q, \longrightarrow_P \cup \longrightarrow_Q \cup \longrightarrow_C) \in Comp_2 \mid (E_P, \longrightarrow_P) \in [\![P]\!],$$

$$(E_Q, \longrightarrow_Q) \in [\![Q]\!],\ E_P \cap E_Q = \emptyset,\ atom(E_P) \cap atom(E_Q) = \emptyset,\ \longrightarrow_C \subseteq (E_P \cup E_Q)^2\}$$

$$[\![P \cdot Q]\!] = \{(E_P \cup E_Q, \longrightarrow_P \cup \longrightarrow_Q \cup \longrightarrow_C) \in Comp_2 \mid (E_P, \longrightarrow_P) \in [\![P]\!],$$

$$(E_Q, \longrightarrow_Q) \in [\![Q]\!],\ E_P \cap E_Q = \emptyset,\ atom(E_P) \cap atom(E_Q) = \emptyset,\ \longrightarrow_C \subseteq (E_P \times E_Q)\}$$

$$[\![P \text{ or } Q]\!] = [\![P]\!] \cup [\![Q]\!]$$

$$[\![\ \mathbf{skip}\ ]\!] = \{(\emptyset, \emptyset)\}$$

$$[\![\ \mathbf{empty}\ ]\!] = \emptyset$$

$$[\![\langle l : P \rangle]\!] = ([\![P]\!] \cap \textit{State-consistent})[atom : \alpha][label : l],$$

where α is some (nondeterministically chosen) atomicity label, i.e. $\alpha \in$ *Alabel*. The set *State-consistent* (introduced already for the semantics of the **io**($\cdot$) operation of DL_0) denotes the set of all interference free runs.

$$[\![\textbf{ref } l \textbf{ to } S \textbf{ in } P]\!] = \text{the largest set } X \text{ such that } contr(l, X) \subseteq [\![P]\!] \text{ and } (X|l) \subseteq [\![\langle l : S$$

where $X|l$ denotes the set of runs obtained by projecting onto l labeled events.

$$[\![\textbf{contr } l \textbf{ in } P]\!] = contr(l, [\![P]\!])$$

□

The definitions for parallel composition and layer composition are almost identical in form to that for DL_0 (and DL_1). Note however that atomicity labels occurring in E_P (denoted by $atom(E_P)$) are kept disjoint from the atomicity labels in E_Q. Moreover, the domain properties for $Comp_2$ ensure that the resulting atomicity labeling for $(E_P \cup E_Q)$ remain a weak event congruence for $(E_P \cup E_Q, \longrightarrow_P \cup \longrightarrow_Q \cup \longrightarrow_C)$.

5 Temporal order, sequential composition and DL_3

Thus far we have dealt with *causal* order of events only. The process languages $DL_0, \ldots, DL_2$ based upon logical event ordering only are perfectly suited for the initial stages of the design of a concurrent system. This is mainly due to the properties of the layer composition operation. This operation, together with parallel composition, allows for an initial design that has the form of *layers* each of which consists of a relatively simple parallel system. During the initial design stages, one is mainly interested in the *functional behaviour* of a system, as opposed to architectural considerations such as the number of parallel processors etc. So for initial design we postulate that IO-equivalence or IO-refinement is an appropriate implementation notion. Layer composition is quite a pleasant operation here, since as far as functional behaviour is concerned it acts much like function composition. This is expressed by the law

$$P \cdot Q \stackrel{IO}{=} \mathbf{io}(P) \cdot \mathbf{io}(Q),$$

or equivalently:

$$\mathbf{io}(P \cdot Q) = \mathbf{io}(\mathbf{io}(P) \cdot \mathbf{io}(Q)).$$

Moreover, layer composition allows for interesting and useful program transformation steps as exemplified by the communication closed layers law and its derivates. Our semantic domain, essentially based on partial orders, is suitable for the semantics of the languages introduced thus far, especially since it allows for elegant definitions of constructs such as action refinement, parallel composition and layer composition. It is interesting to note however that, up to this point, we could have used a *multistep* or *interleaving semantics* that induce the same algebraic laws as our partial order based semantics. This can be explained as follows.

5.1 Multistep and interleaving semantics

Definition 5.1 *Multistep seqences*

- A *multistep sequence* is a sequence $\langle st_0, st_1, \ldots\rangle$ of *steps* st_i, each of which is a countable set of mutually independent, i.e. non conflicting, events. Similar to the domain of runs we assume that each event in a multistep sequence has its own unique identity attribute. For this paper we need only *finite* sequences of *finite* steps. The domain of all such sequences is denoted by $\mathcal{M}step$.
- The *width* of a multistep sequence is the sup of the cardinalities of the steps occurring in that sequence. For finite sequences of finite steps the width is simply the maximum of the step sizes.
- An *interleaving sequence* is a multistep sequence where each step is a singleton. As usual we represent these as sequences of events, rather than as sequences of sets of events. The domain of (finite length) interleaving sequences is denoted by $\mathcal{I}ntl$.

□

Transformation from a run $(E, \longrightarrow)$ to a set of interleaving sequences of events $intl((E, \longrightarrow))$ is straightforward, by (nondeterministically) augmenting the event order $\longrightarrow$ to a total order. For partial orders in general it is possible to reconstruct the order from the set of all its linearizations. The runs for the semantics of $DL_0..DL_2$ however are rather special in that one can reconstruct a run $(E, \longrightarrow)$ from each of its interleaving sequences separately, due to the conflict closedness assumption for runs: two events are ordered if *and only if* they conflict. For an interleaving sequence, or more general for a multistep sequence $\sigma = \langle st_0, st_1, \ldots\rangle$ we define:

$$run(\sigma) = (E_\sigma, \longrightarrow_\sigma), \text{ where}$$

$$E_\sigma = \bigcup_{i=0,\ldots} st_i, \text{ and}$$

$$\text{for } e, e' \in E_\sigma : e \longrightarrow_\sigma e' \text{ iff } e \text{ and } e' \text{ conflict and } e \in st_i, e' \in st_j \text{ for some } i < j$$

We extend this to an operation on sets M of multistep sequences or sets of interleaving sequences I by pointwise application. Note that different sequences can be transformed into the same run. The set of all multistep sequences for runs $(E, \longrightarrow)$ and sets of runs X are defined as follows:

$$mstep((E, \longrightarrow)) \stackrel{\text{def}}{=} \{\sigma \in \mathcal{M}step \mid run(\sigma) = (E, \longrightarrow)\}$$

$$intl((E, \longrightarrow)) \stackrel{\text{def}}{=} \{\sigma \in \mathcal{I}ntl \mid run(\sigma) = (E, \longrightarrow)\}$$

$$mstep(X) \stackrel{\text{def}}{=} \bigcup\{mstep((E, \longrightarrow)) \mid (E, \longrightarrow) \in X\}$$

$$intl(X) \stackrel{\text{def}}{=} \bigcup\{intl((E, \longrightarrow)) \mid (E, \longrightarrow) \in X\}$$

Note that $mstep((E, \longrightarrow))$ and $intl((E, \longrightarrow))$ are never empty. From this and the definitions it follows that $run(mstep((E, \longrightarrow))) = (E, \longrightarrow)$ and $run(intl((E, \longrightarrow))) = (E, \longrightarrow)$. More interesting is that we have similar equalities for sets of runs.

Lemma 5.2

For arbitrary sets of runs X:

$$run(mstep(X)) = X$$

$$run(intl(X)) = X$$

□

Sketch of proof:
From the definitions it is clear that $mstep((E, \longrightarrow)) \cap mstep((E', \longrightarrow')) = \emptyset$ if $(E, \longrightarrow) \neq (E', \longrightarrow')$. From this and the equality $run(mstep((E, \longrightarrow))) = (E, \longrightarrow)$ the result follows easily. The proof for interleaving sequences is similar.
□

The conclusion of this analysis is that for DL_0, DL_1 and DL_2 we can define multistep semantics and interleaving semantics as follows:

$$mstep[\![P]\!] \stackrel{\text{def}}{=} mstep([\![P]\!])$$

$$intl[\![P]\!] \stackrel{\text{def}}{=} intl([\![P]\!])$$

Moreover, these semantics are isomorphic, i.e. for all processes P, Q:

$$[\![P]\!] = [\![Q]\!] \text{ iff } mstep[\![P]\!] = mstep[\![Q]\!] \text{ iff } intl[\![P]\!] = intl[\![Q]\!]$$

We remark that this interleaving semantics does not coincide with "standard" interleaving models for parallelism.

5.2 Temporal order

Causal or logical precedence is suitable for specifying functional behaviour during the first, initial stages of design. It is less suitable when it comes to an implemention of a system on a given architecture that has to satisfy constraints such as a limited number of processors. To satisfy such constraints it is often necessary to schedule independent, i.e. non conflicting events on a single processor. To analyse such scheduling problems within our process language we cannot rely solely on operations such as layer composition that can specify only causal order. Rather we need language operations such as *sequential composition* $P; Q$ in order to indicate that P actions are to be scheduled before Q actions. The general idea is that after one has obtained an intermediate algorithmic solution to a functional specification, program transformation is applied so as to remove layer composition in favor of parallel composition and sequential composition. Such a development strategy allows for in initial design stage developping an intermediate solution from a given (functional) specification that is still largely architecture independent, followed by a more detailed design stage where mapping the intermediate solution onto some particular architecture is the goal. Communication closed layers, right movers and left movers are among the more useful transformation principles that can be used in this second design phase. We make this more concrete in the following example. The example also shows another phenomenon viz. the problems with the analysis of *time complexity* of (parallel) algorithms on the level of causal order.

Example 5.1 Cascade sum on a SIMD architecture

The functional specification. The input to the algorithm is a a sequence of numbers stored in variables $d_1, d_2, \ldots d_N$. The output consists of all prefix sums stored in variables $x_1, x_2, \ldots x_N$, satisfying

$$\bigwedge_{i=1..N} (x_i = \sum_{j=1}^{i} d_j)$$

A functionally correct solution

A naive solution would calculate each of the prefix sums separately, one after another. This would result in a sequential algorithm that takes $O(N^2)$ time to calculate the prefix sums of N numbers. A better (still sequential) solution is to use "recursive doubling" where we use $\log(N)$ phases such that after k iterations each of the variables x_i contains a partial sum as described by the following state predicate:

$$\bigwedge_{i=1..N} (x_i = \sum_{j=i-2^k+1}^{i} d'_j),$$

where $d'_j = d_j$ if $j \geq 1$, else $d'_j = 0$.

We employ the following abbreviations to describe our initial solution:

$$\textbf{for } i \leftarrow [n..m] \textbf{ dopar } P(i) \text{ for: } P(n) \parallel \cdots \parallel P(m)$$

$$\textbf{for } i \leftarrow [n..m] \textbf{ layer } P(i) \text{ for: } P(n) \bullet \cdots \bullet P(m)$$

$$\textbf{for } i \leftarrow [n..m] \textbf{ doseq } P(i) \text{ for: } P(n) ; \cdots ; P(m)$$

The algorithm $Cascade_0$ is:

$$\langle \textbf{ for } k \leftarrow [0..\log(N) - 1] \textbf{ layer}$$

$$\textbf{for } i \leftarrow [N..1] \textbf{ layer } a_i \rangle$$

where action a_i is the assignment $x_i := x_i + x_{i-2^k}$, and where x_{i-2^k} denotes 0 when $i - 2^k < 1$. The atomic brackets around the whole are usually omitted when describing this type of algorithm. For our formal treatment we need them to indicate that we do not intend to execute the program in parallel with some other interfering process. This allows us to show the correctness of the program by one of the classical methods for proving *sequential* programs correct, where we treat layer composition as ordinary sequential composition. This follows from the algebraic law, that will be discussed below, which states that in the absence of interference from outside, layer composition and sequential composition yield IO-equivalent results:

$$\langle P \bullet Q \rangle \overset{IO}{=} \langle P ; Q \rangle$$

We omit the details of this correctness proof; it is a straightforward proof based on the state predicate mentioned above. Rather we prefer to analyse the layer compositions for a given k value. For simplicity we take the first one which is:

$$L_0 \overset{\text{def}}{=} a_N \bullet \ldots \bullet a_2 \bullet a_1$$

where a_i is $x_i := x_i + x_{i-1}$. Note that the order in this sequence is vital, as action a_i conflicts with a_{i+1} for $i = 1..N-1$. What we see here is a chain of conflicting actions of length N, (falsely) suggesting that it takes $O(N)$ time to execute it. This would indeed be the time complexity if we replace the layer compositions by sequential compositions, thus:

$$a_N \,;\, \ldots \,;\, a_2 \,;\, a_1$$

We can do better than this by refining the a_i actions into $(b_i \cdot c_i)\backslash y_i$ where b_i is $y_{i-1} := x_{i-1}$ and c_i is $x_i := x_i + y_{i-1}$. By algebraic laws we then obtain:

$$(b_N \cdot c_N)\backslash y_n \cdot \ldots (b_1 \cdot c_1)\backslash y_1$$

$$= (b_N \cdot c_N \cdot \ldots b_1 \cdot c_1)\backslash y_1, \ldots, y_N$$

The advantage of this decoupling between reading x_{i-1} and reading and writing x_i is that we now can apply the laws for layer composition of independent actions. Note that the only conflicts are between b_i and c_i and between b_i and c_{i-1}. Therefore we can move all b_i actions "to the left", thus obtaining:

$$((b_N \cdot \ldots \cdot b_1) \cdot (c_N \cdot \ldots \cdot c_1))\backslash y_1, \ldots y_N$$

Because the b_i are mutually independent, and similarly for the c_i actions, the latter process is equal to:

$$((b_1 \parallel \cdots \parallel b_N) \cdot (c_1 \parallel \cdots \parallel c_N))\backslash y_1, \ldots, y_N$$

The remaining layer composition can now be replaced by sequential composition. Note that this allows for execution in constant time using $O(N)$ processors. The other layers can be treated similarly. The layer compositions of the "outer loop" in the algorithm above should be eliminated next. Here the architecture of final implementation should be taken into account. If we aim for a *distributed* implementation or an implementation on a MIMD machine, the solution should be of the form:

for $i \leftarrow [1..N]$ **dopar** $P(i)$,

where each $P(i)$ is a seqential process. For the present example we will opt for an implementation on a SIMD machine, which should be of the form:

for $k \leftarrow [1..\#steps]$ **doseq**

for $i \leftarrow [1..N]$ **dopar** $P(i)$

where each $P(i)$ should be a (simple) sequential program.

Remark. The idea of a SIMD machine is that there are a fixed number of processors executing in lockstep the same program text, where the processor index i can occur in the program text. The literature on parallel algorithms usually specify the following program text:

for $k \leftarrow [1..\#steps]$ **doseq** $P(i)$,

together with the remark that these (sequential) programs execute in parallel on a SIMD machine. This is rather misleading, as it suggests that the full program could be understood as follows:

for $i \leftarrow [1..N]$ **dopar**

for $k \leftarrow [1..\#steps]$ **doseq** $P(i)$,

which is incorrect however. **(End of remark)**

Returning to our cascade algorithm, one sees that to obtain a SIMD solution all that remains is to replace the layer compositions from the outer loop by sequential compositions. Thus we obtain our final solution:

$\langle$ **for** $k \leftarrow [0..\log(N)-1]$ **doseq**

(**for** $i \leftarrow [1..N]$ **dopar** $y_i := x_i$;

for $i \leftarrow [1..N]$ **dopar** $x_i := x_i + y_{i-2^k}$

$)\backslash y_1, \ldots, y_N\rangle$

(End of example)

5.3 Sequential composition

We now introduce a process language containing both layer composition and sequential composition. Although syntactically this is only a minor extension the semantic model has to change quite substantial.

$P \in DL_3,$

$P ::= l : b \,\&\, \mathbf{x} := \mathbf{f} \;\mid\; P \parallel Q \;\mid\; P \cdot Q \;\mid\; P\,;Q \;\mid\; P \text{ or } Q$

$\mid\; \textbf{skip} \;\mid\; \textbf{empty} \;\mid\; P\backslash x \;\mid\; \langle l : P\rangle \;\mid\; \textbf{ref } l \textbf{ to } S \textbf{ in } P \;\mid\; \textbf{contr } l \textbf{ in } P$

In [JPZ91] we defined sequential composition of run $(E_P, \longrightarrow_P)$ with run $(E_Q, \longrightarrow_Q)$ as the (disjoint) union of the two runs, with the order augmented such that all E_P events precede all E_Q events. This requires of course that the conflict closedness condition is weakened: two events are ordered if, but not only if, they conflict. The idea is that when $e \longrightarrow e'$ whereas e does not conflict with e' the order indicates temporal order. A major problem with this approach is that temporal order is lost under action refinement. This is due to *conflict based inheritance* of order. On the algebraic level this is exemplified by the fact that in [JPZ91] action refinement does not distribute over sequential composition.
The alternative, explored by for instance [vGG89], is to define action refinement based on *total order inheritance*. Total order inheritance means that whenever we refine some event e_r in some run $(E, \longrightarrow)$, we replace it by some (sub) run $(E_r, \longrightarrow_r)$ and adapt the order "$\longrightarrow'$" on the whole such that for any $e_0 \in E$ and $e_1 \in E_r$ we have that $e_0 \longrightarrow' e_1$ $(e_1 \longrightarrow' e_0)$ iff $e_0 \longrightarrow e_r$ $(e_r \longrightarrow e_0)$. (So, whether e_0 and e_1 conflict or not is not taken into account.) This form of refinement would be fine if all order would be temporal order, but

obviously it does not preserve (minimality of) causal order. As a result, action refinement based on total order inheritance does not distribute over parallel composition or layer composition.
The conclusion drawn from this is that the structure in the form of an ordered set of events is not adequate to model runs. We therefore introduce a new semantic domain where runs are ordered sets of events where a separate order is used to denote *temporal order*. We denote runs by $(E, \longrightarrow, \twoheadrightarrow)$, where E is a set of events, " $\longrightarrow$ " is the logical or causal order, and where " $\twoheadrightarrow$ " denotes the temporal order on events.

Definition 5.3 *Causal-temporal runs*

The semantic domain $\mathcal{C}omp_3$ is defined as the set of runs of the form $(E, \longrightarrow, \twoheadrightarrow)$ where

- E is a finite set of events,
- $\longrightarrow$ is a dag structure on E, i.e. a relation on E such that $(E, \xrightarrow{+})$ is an irreflexive partial order,
- $\twoheadrightarrow$ is an irreflexive partial order on E, i.e. an irreflexive, antisymmetric and transitive relation on E,

such that the following domain properties are satisfied:

1. $(E, \longrightarrow)$ is conflict closed, that is, for all $e, e' \in E$ we have that

   $$e \,\text{—}\, e' \text{ iff } e \longrightarrow e' \vee e' \longrightarrow e.$$

   Here, $e \,\text{—}\, e'$ is a fixed conflict relation on the domain of events $\mathcal{E}vent$, as usual. (That is, "—" is an irreflexive, symmetric relation on $\mathcal{E}vent$.)

2. Causal order and temporal order are consistent in the following sense.
   For all $e, e' \in E$ we have that $e \longrightarrow e'$ implies $\neg(e' \twoheadrightarrow e)$. That is, we cannot have two events e and e' in a single run such that e logically precedes e' while e' temporally precedes e.

3. Causal order and temporal order interact as follows:

   For all $e_0, e_1, e_2, e_3 \in E$:

   $$e_0 \twoheadrightarrow e_1 \longrightarrow e_2 \twoheadrightarrow e_3 \text{ imply that } e_0 \twoheadrightarrow e_3.$$

4. Atomicity labels occurring in E induce an *event congruence* on $(E, \longrightarrow, \twoheadrightarrow)$, as will be explained below.

We denote by $\mathcal{C}lose((E, \longrightarrow, \twoheadrightarrow))$ the structure $(E, \longrightarrow, \twoheadrightarrow \cup \twoheadrightarrow_T)$ where $\twoheadrightarrow_T$ is the unique minimal order on E such that $\twoheadrightarrow \cup \twoheadrightarrow_T$ is transitive and moreover, property (3) is satisfied. (Note that $\mathcal{C}lose((E, \longrightarrow, \twoheadrightarrow))$ need not be a $\mathcal{C}omp_3$ run; in particular properties (1) and (2) need not be satisfied.)
□

The axioms (2) and (3) are similar to those proposed by L. Lamport in [Lam86]. In [ABDM90] similar axioms for what are called interval orders are attributed to Wiener [Wie14]. Below we discuss the relation with [Lam86] Here we would like to explain the necessity of the domain properties. The axioms exclude some, but not all, cycles built up from temporal and causal orderings. An example of a cycle that is not excluded is $e_0 \longrightarrow e_1 \longrightarrow e_2 \longrightarrow\!\!\!\!\!\rightarrow e_0$. It will be clear that an operational model where events are regarded as totally ordered "points" is incompatibele with runs that contain this type of cycles. [Lam86] and [Ang99] describe execution models that associate *real-time intervals* with events. In such models a cycle as above leads to intervals for e_0 and e_2 that each overlap the interval for e_1. Moreover, the interval for e_2 completely precedes the interval for e_0. Next we consider cycles that *are* excluded.

Let

$$\begin{aligned} a &= (x,y) := (0,0), \\ b_0 &= x := 1, \\ b_1 &= y > 0 \,\&\, z := 1, \\ c_0 &= y := 1, \\ c_0 &= x > 0 \,\&\, w := 1, \end{aligned}$$

and let P_C be

$$\langle a \cdot ((b_0 \cdot b_1) \parallel (c_0 \cdot c_1))\rangle.$$

Note that execution of b_1 can only proceed after executing c_0. Similarly, c_1 must wait for action b_0. Note also that b_0 and b_1 are causally independent, and so we have that

$$P_C = \langle a \cdot ((b_1 \cdot b_0) \parallel (c_1 \cdot c_0))\rangle.$$

This equality follows from the algebraic laws provided above. In fact we can rewrite P_C also as

$$\langle a \cdot (b_0 \parallel c_0) \cdot (b_1 \parallel c_1)\rangle,$$

or even as: $(x,y,z,w) := (1,1,1,1)$.

Now assume that we replace layer composition between the b and c actions by sequential composition in the defining term for P_C, thus obtaining

$$P_{seq} = a \cdot ((b_0 \,;\, b_1) \parallel (c_0 \,;\, c_1)).$$

This system is not semantically equal to but nevertheless IO-equivalent to a single atomic action $(x,y,z,w) := (1,1,1,1)$. However, when we now interchange the order of the b and c actions as in

$$P_{dead} = a \cdot ((b_1 \,;\, b_0) \parallel (c_1 \,;\, c_0)),$$

then the resulting sustem P_{dead} is no longer equivalent since it will ***deadlock***. Such a deadlocked situation shows up in the semantics in the form of a cycle of the following form:

$$e_{b_1} \twoheadrightarrow e_{b_0} \longrightarrow e_{c_1} \twoheadrightarrow e_{c_0} \longrightarrow e_{b_1}.$$

By axiom (3) this temporal/causal cycle implies that $e_{b_1} \twoheadrightarrow e_{c_0} \longrightarrow e_{b_1}$ and by axiom (2) such a situation is forbidden, i.e. a run cannot contain a cycle as above. As a result, P_{dead} does not admit any run, and therefore is equal to the process which in this context signals a deadlock.

Remark. For the present semantics we have opted for simply discarding runs containing "deadlock cycles". An alternative would have been not to discard the run as a whole, but rather to replace the events on the deadlock cycle by a special "dead" event δ. This would allow one to distinguish a deadlocked process from the "empty" process and so to avoid equalities such as $Q = Q$ **or** P_{dead}. The only reason for not taking this approach in this paper is that we thus obtain a simpler semantics that allows us to concentrate on action refinement, atomicity and real-time. **(End of remark)**

To define the meaning of action refinement and contraction for DL_3 we must adapt our notion of event congruence so as to take temporal order into account.

Definition 5.4 *Strong event congruence*

Let $(E, \twoheadrightarrow)$ be an event set with a temporal order. Let $\cong$ be an equivalence relation on the set E, with equivalence classes $E_0, E_1, \ldots$. Let $(G, \twoheadrightarrow_G)$ be the corresponding quotient graph where we have an arrow $[E_i] \twoheadrightarrow_G [E_j]$ iff $i \neq j$ and for some events $e_i \in [E_i]$, $e_j \in [E_j]$ it is the case that $e_i \twoheadrightarrow e_j$.

The equivalence $\cong$ is a *strong congruence* on $(E, \twoheadrightarrow)$ iff the quotient graph $(G, \twoheadrightarrow_G)$ is a partial order, and moreover for each equivalence class E_i we have the following *total ordering property:* For any e not contained in E_i, iff $e \twoheadrightarrow e'$ for *any* e' in E_i, then $e \twoheadrightarrow e''$ for *all* e'' in E_i. Similarly, if $e' \twoheadrightarrow e$ for any e' in E_i then for all e'' in E_i we have $e'' \twoheadrightarrow e$.
□

Definition 5.5 *Event congruence*

Let $(E, \longrightarrow, \twoheadrightarrow)$ be a causal-temporal run. An *event congruence* on this run is an equivalence relation on E that induces both a weak congruence on $(E, \longrightarrow)$ and a strong congruence on $(E, \twoheadrightarrow)$.
□

Contraction of complete causal-temporal runs, $contr((E, \longrightarrow, \twoheadrightarrow))$ is simply reduced to $contr((E, \longrightarrow))$ where we employ the contraction operation introduced before. This reduction is possible because adding temporal order to a given causally ordered run does not change the overall IO behaviour of the run. Indeed, temporal order does not appear in for instance the definition of the reads-from relation; the causal order suffices.

We also extend the definition of the more general $contr(l, X)$ operation where X now is a causal-temporal run $(E, \longrightarrow, \twoheadrightarrow)$. As before we may assume, without loss of generality, that the projection of $(E, \longrightarrow, \twoheadrightarrow)$ onto all l labeled events, denoted by $(E_l, \longrightarrow_l, \twoheadrightarrow_l)$, coincides with the set of all α labeled events, where α is some atomicity label. The contraction $contr(l, (E, \longrightarrow, \twoheadrightarrow))$ is defined as the run

$$((E - E_l) \cup \{e_c\}, (\longrightarrow|(E - E_l)) \cup \longrightarrow_c, (\twoheadrightarrow|(E - E_l)) \cup \twoheadrightarrow_c)$$

where

- $e_c \;=\; contr((E_l, \longrightarrow_l))$
- $e \longrightarrow_c e_c$ for $e \in (E - E_l)$ iff there is some $e' \in E_l$ such that $e \longrightarrow e'$,
- $e_c \longrightarrow_c e$ for $e \in (E - E_l)$ iff there is some $e' \in E_l$ such that $e' \longrightarrow e$
- $e \twoheadrightarrow_c e_c$ for $e \in (E - E_l)$ iff for all $e' \in E_l$ it is the case that $e \twoheadrightarrow e'$, and
- $e_c \twoheadrightarrow_c e$ for $e \in (E - E_l)$ iff for all $e' \in E_l$ it is the case that $e' \twoheadrightarrow e$

The fact that atomicity labels induce an event congruence guarantees that for a contracted run as described the resulting atomicity labeling is again a congruence. So we can have repeated contraction applied to some run, where the final result will be independent of the particular order in which different sub runs are contracted.
The semantics for DL_3 is now as follows.

Definition 5.6 *Semantics of DL_3*

$$[\![l : b \,\&\, \mathbf{x} := \mathbf{f}]\!] = \{(e, \emptyset, \emptyset) \in \mathit{Comp}_3 \mid e \in \mathcal{A}[\![b \,\&\, \mathbf{x} := \mathbf{f}]\!],\ \mathit{label}(e) = l\}$$

$$[\![P \parallel Q]\!] = \{\mathit{Close}((E_P \cup E_Q, \longrightarrow_P \cup \longrightarrow_Q \cup \longrightarrow_C, \twoheadrightarrow_P \cup \twoheadrightarrow_Q)) \in \mathit{Comp}_3 \mid$$
$$(E_P, \longrightarrow_P, \twoheadrightarrow_P) \in [\![P]\!],\ (E_Q, \longrightarrow_Q, \twoheadrightarrow_Q) \in [\![Q]\!],\ E_P \cap E_Q = \emptyset,$$
$$\mathit{atom}(E_P) \cap \mathit{atom}(E_Q) = \emptyset,\ \longrightarrow_C \subseteq (E_P \cup E_Q)^2, \}$$

$$[\![P \cdot Q]\!] = \{\mathit{Close}((E_P \cup E_Q, \longrightarrow_P \cup \longrightarrow_Q \cup \longrightarrow_C, \twoheadrightarrow_P \cup \twoheadrightarrow_Q)) \in \mathit{Comp}_3 \mid$$
$$(E_P, \longrightarrow_P, \twoheadrightarrow_P) \in [\![P]\!],\ (E_Q, \longrightarrow_Q, \twoheadrightarrow_Q) \in [\![Q]\!],$$
$$E_P \cap E_Q = \emptyset,\ \mathit{atom}(E_P) \cap \mathit{atom}(E_Q) = \emptyset,\ \longrightarrow_C \subseteq (E_P \times E_Q)\}$$

$$[\![P \,;\, Q]\!] = \{\mathit{Close}((E_P \cup E_Q, \longrightarrow_P \cup \longrightarrow_Q \cup \longrightarrow_C, \twoheadrightarrow_P \cup \twoheadrightarrow_Q \cup (E_P \times E_Q))) \in \mathit{Comp}_3$$
$$(E_P, \longrightarrow_P, \twoheadrightarrow_P) \in [\![P]\!],\ (E_Q, \longrightarrow_Q \twoheadrightarrow_Q) \in [\![Q]\!],$$
$$E_P \cap E_Q = \emptyset,\ \mathit{atom}(E_P) \cap \mathit{atom}(E_Q) = \emptyset,\ \longrightarrow_C \subseteq (E_P \times E_Q)\}$$

$$[\![P \ \mathbf{or}\ Q]\!] = [\![P]\!] \cup [\![Q]\!]$$

$$[\![\ \mathbf{skip}\ ]\!] = \{(\emptyset, \emptyset, \emptyset)\}$$

$$[\![\ \mathbf{empty}\ ]\!] = \emptyset$$

$$[\![\langle l : P \rangle]\!] = ([\![P]\!] \cap \mathit{State\text{-}consistent})[\mathit{atom} : \alpha][\mathit{label} : l],$$

where α is some (nondeterministically chosen) atomicity label, i.e. $\alpha \in \mathit{Alabel}$.

$[\![\ \mathbf{ref}\ l\ \mathbf{to}\ S\ \mathbf{in}\ P]\!] =$ the largest set X such that

- $\mathit{contr}(l, X) \subseteq [\![P]\!]$ and
- for any $\alpha \in \mathit{Alabel}$ such that there are events in X labeled by both l and α we have that

  $$(X|l, \alpha) \subseteq ([\![S]\!] \cap \mathit{State\text{-}consistent})[\mathit{atom} : \alpha][\mathit{label} : l].$$

  where $X|l, \alpha$ denotes the set of runs obtained by projecting onto l and α labeled events.

$$[\![\ \mathbf{contr}\ l\ \mathbf{in}\ P]\!] = \mathit{contr}(l, [\![P]\!])$$

□

5.4 A comparison with related models

In [Lam86], Lamport uses structures, called system executions, of the form $(S, \cdots\!>, \!-\!\!>)$, where S is a set of so-called operation executions $A, B \ldots$. The axioms imposed on *temporal precedence* "$-\!\!>$" and *weak precedence* "$\cdots\!>$" are as follows.

A1 The relation $-\!\!>$ is an irreflexive partial order on E,

A2.1 If $A -\!\!> B$ then $A \cdots\!> B$,

A2.2 If $A -\!\!> B$ then not $B \cdots\!> A$,

A3 If $A -\!\!> B \cdots\!> C$ or $A \cdots\!> B -\!\!> C$ then $A \cdots\!> C$,

A4 If $A -\!\!> B \cdots\!> C -\!\!> D$ then $A -\!\!> D$,

There is also a fifth axiom stating that:

A5 for any A, the set of all B such that not $A -\!\!> B$ is finite.

Since in this paper we deal with finite runs only we do not discuss this axiom any further. Others,[Ang99], have suggested to add the following axioms:

A6 A $\cdots\!>$ A and

A7 If $A \cdots\!> B -\!\!> C \cdots\!> D$ then $A \cdots\!> D$.

Finally there is an independent axiom, which is in general not assumed, called the global-time axiom:

GT $A -\!\!> B$ iff not $B \cdots\!> A$.

Operation executions can be regarded as sets containing atomic events and, recursively, other operation executions. We compare these structures with our runs of the form $(E, \longrightarrow, \longrightarrow\!\!\!\!\!\rightarrow)$. Within our setup, operation executions that are not atomic events themselves could be defined as *arbitrary* sets of events, i.e. without requiring atomic execution of operation executions. Nevertheless, in [Lam86] the aim is to describe implementation of atomic database transactions by means of operation executions, and so the goal is to obtain a system that admits only operation executions that that one can *pretend to be atomic*. Such "atomic" operation executions should be compared to our notion of *contractable* and moreover *state consistent* sets of events.
For operation executions A and B the (strong) precedence relation $A -\!\!> B$ denotes that all elements of A strongly precede those of B. As such we can identify this relation with our temporal order $A \longrightarrow\!\!\!\!\!\rightarrow B$. Note that, although formally speaking we only defined $A \longrightarrow\!\!\!\!\!\rightarrow B$ for the case that A and B are *atomic*, the definition extends to arbitrary operation executions.

Weak precedence, denoted by $A \cdots\!> B$ is more complicated. Informally, $A \cdots\!> B$ can be understood as existence of an event e occurring in A or, recursively in some operation execution of A, and a similar event e' occurring in B, such that $e -\!\!> e'$. Note that weak precedence makes sense even for operation executions that are not atomic. This is not the case for *causal* precedence, as defined in this paper; for a partitioning of some run into non atomic operation executions the induced quotient graph as discussed above would in general not be cycle free! We could relate weak precedence to causal precedence however, by postulating that:

$$e \longrightarrow e' \text{ implies } e \cdots\!> e'.$$

Intuitively, when two events conflict then at least some part of their executions must be temporally disjoint. The postulate above is slightly stronger since it assumes not only that such temporally disjoint fragments can be found but moreover that these fragments are in the form of atomic events on a sufficiently low level. Assuming this postulate our domain property:

$$e_0 \twoheadrightarrow e_1 \longrightarrow e_2 \twoheadrightarrow e_3 \text{ implies } e_0 \twoheadrightarrow e_3$$

follows directly from Lamport's axiom A3. It is interesting to see that a "dual law" of the form

$$e_0 \longrightarrow e_1 \twoheadrightarrow e_2 \longrightarrow e_3 \text{ implies } e_0 \longrightarrow e_3$$

cannot be derived from the postulate and "Angers" axiom A7. In fact the proposed law is not valid for our semantic domain. The same can be said for axioms A2.1, A3 and A6, i.e. it is not the case that for instance $e_0 \twoheadrightarrow e_1$ implies $e_0 \longrightarrow e_1$ or that $e_0 \twoheadrightarrow e_1 \longrightarrow e_2$ implies $e_0 \longrightarrow e_2$.

It will be obvious that the reverse of the postulate does not hold, i.e. weak precedence does not imply any causal relationship. This has important consequences for determining a satisfactory notion of what it means for one system to implement another system. To explain this we consider the notion of a "***higher-level view***" of a system execution as defined in [Lam86]. For most cases of interest a high level view of a run $(S, \cdots\!>, -\!\!>)$ can be regarded as the result of applying an analogon of our contraction operation, defined however on runs that are partitioned into potentially non atomic operation executions. This "contraction" determines weak and strong precedence relations "$\overset{*}{\cdots\!>}$" and "$\overset{*}{-\!\!>}$" on the set H that consists of the equivalence classes of the partitioning by regarding these classes, too, as operation executions, thus defining a run $(H, \overset{*}{\cdots\!>}, \overset{*}{-\!\!>})$, as follows:
If A and B are two equivalence classes of H then

- $A \overset{H}{-\!\!>}$ iff for all elements e of A and all e' of B we have that $e -\!\!> e'$.
- $A \overset{H}{\cdots\!>}$ iff for some elements e of A and e' of B we have that $e -\!\!> e'$.

Lamport now defines the following notion of implementation:
A run $(S, \cdots\!>, -\!\!>)$ implements another run $(H, \overset{H}{\cdots\!>}, \overset{H}{-\!\!>})$ if there is some partitioning of S such that the corresponding contraction of $(S, \cdots\!>, -\!\!>)$ is of the form $(H, \overset{*}{\cdots\!>}, \overset{*}{-\!\!>})$, i.e. results in the same event set H, and moreover, for any operation executions A and B in H, we have that:

$$A \overset{*}{-\!\!>} B \text{ implies that } A \overset{H}{-\!\!>} B \qquad (1)$$

Somewhat unexpected, this definition does not relate weak precedence on the low level ($\overset{*}{\cdots>}$) to weak precedence on the high level ($\overset{H}{\cdots>}$). Moreover, temporal precedence specified on the high level can be ignored when implementing a system, but not vice versa. The intuition behind the idea that high level temporal order should not enforce low level temporal order stems from serializability theory for concurrent databases. Assume that the definition above would require (also) that

$A \overset{H}{-\!\!>} B$ implies that $A \overset{*}{-\!\!>} B$ (2)

This requirement would imply that a high level view of database transactions, in the form of a serial chain $T_0 -\!\!> T_1 -\!\!> T_2 \cdots -\!\!> T_n$, could only be implemented by operation executions $S_1, S_2, \cdots, S_n$ that are executed serially too, i.e. satisfying $S_0 -\!\!> S_1 -\!\!> S_2 \cdots -\!\!> S_n$. The standard definition of *serializable execution*, as opposed to serial execution, allows for partially overlapping execution of the S_i however and so, within the framework of [Lam86], requirement (2) is too strong.

An alternative solution for this problem is possible however within our model based on causality rather than temporal order alone. According to our analysis, the requirement that a high level view of some serializable execution of transactions must be "equivalent" to some serial execution of those transactions should be formulated in terms of causal order among transactions rather than temporal order. So, we take a high level view in the form of a *causal* chain $T_0 \longrightarrow T_1 \longrightarrow \cdots \longrightarrow T_n$. Equivalently, we can express this in our process language as a term of the form:

$T_0 \bullet T_1 \bullet \ldots \bullet T_n.$

On the one hand, the algebraic laws guarantee that this process term is IO-equivalent to a sequential execution of transactions, i.e. an execution with temporally ordered transactions.

$T_0 \,;\, T_1 \,;\, \ldots \,;\, T_n.$

On the other hand, layer composition does not enforce sequential composition but rather allows temporal overlap as long as causal order is preserved. We now formulate our first notion of implementation, that is in terms of causal order only:

Definition 5.7 *Implementation for DL_0, DL_1 and DL_2*

A run $(S, \longrightarrow)$ implements another run $(H, \overset{H}{\longrightarrow})$ if there is some labeling for S that partions S, such that the corresponding contraction $contr(l, (S, \longrightarrow))$ is $(H, \overset{H}{\longrightarrow})$.
□

This implementation relation is exactly the relation that exists between some process term P and a term of the form **ref** l **to** S **in** P. Using the action refinement operation we can describe an implementation of serializable transactions by a process term:

$SR\_Dbase \;=\;$ **ref** T_0 **to** S_0, T_1 **to** $S_1, \ldots, T_n$ **to** S_n **in**

$T_0 \parallel T_1 \parallel \cdots \parallel T_n,$

where $T_0, T_1 \ldots, T_n$ are atomic actions. (The term $T_0 \parallel T_1 \parallel \cdots \parallel T_n$ can also be described as a nondeterministic choice between processes of the form

$$T_{i_0} \cdot T_{i_2}, \cdot \ldots \cdot T_{i_n},$$

where $i_0, i_1, \ldots, i_n$ is some permutation of $0, 1, \ldots, n$. Each of these terms corresponds to a legal execution from a high level view.)

One might think that a similar definition for serializability could be given within the framework of [Lam86] by specifying a high level view of transaction execution as a *weak* precedence chain $T_0 \cdots{>} T_1 \cdots{>} T_2 \cdots{>} \ldots \cdots{>} T_n$. This will not do however, for there is no guarantee whatsoever that such an execution is IO-equivalent to a sequential execution of the transactions.

Our definition above corresponds to the standard notion of serializability taken from the literature on distributed databases as for example in [BHG87]. In [Lam86] this notion is criticized because it allows high level views of transaction execution that pretends that some transaction T_0 precedes another transaction T_1 whereas in "reality", that is, on the implementation level, T_1 temporally completely precedes T_0. Lamport then argues that this situation should be regarded as an incorrect implementation because external observations, such as printing on a terminal, enable one to actually observe certain temporal relations on the implementation level and so to infer precedence relations for the abstract transaction level that actually could *contradict* the high level order that we pretend. This explains Lamports condition for implementation that requires that

$$A \overset{*}{\longrightarrow} B \text{ implies that } A \overset{H}{\longrightarrow} B$$

For if this condition is satisfied it is simply impossible that the high level "pretended" order $\overset{H}{\longrightarrow}$ contradicts the "real" order $\overset{*}{\longrightarrow}$.
This problem with serializability can be dealt with in our model based on the combination of causal and temporal order. Note that we can distinguish between the type of the high level order, which is a *causal* order of transactions, and the observed *temporal* order on the implementation level. External observations regarding temporal relations on the implementation level are interpreted in terms of (extra) temporal order that is imposed on (already causally ordered) events. Whenever such an execution would allow one to infer temporal ordering for the high level view that contradicts certain causal order for that high level view it would not be allowed as a legal implementation. The reason for this is that contracting the execution would yield a high level run where for some events T_i, T_j we would have $T_i \longrightarrow T_j$ and also $T_j \twoheadrightarrow T_i$. Such runs however, are automatically excluded by the domain properties for runs. This motivates our second implementation notion:

Definition 5.8 *Implementation for* DL_3

A run $(S, \longrightarrow, \twoheadrightarrow)$ implements another run $(H, \overset{H}{\longrightarrow}, \overset{H}{\twoheadrightarrow})$ if there is some labeling for S that partions S, such that the corresponding contraction $contr(l, (S, \longrightarrow, \twoheadrightarrow))$ equals the high level run $(H, \overset{H}{\longrightarrow}, \overset{H}{\twoheadrightarrow})$.

A system Q implements another system P if each run of Q implements some run of P. □

A sufficient condition for one system Q to implement another system P is that there is a labeling for Q, resulting in a labeled term Q', such that **contr** l **in** Q' *sat* P.

We remark that our notion of implementation has deliberately not been made as general as possible. For instance one might accept as implementations for some system P all those systems Q that are IO-equivalent to some Q' that implements P according to the definition above. This would for instance allow $a; b$ **or** $b; a$ as an implementation for $a \parallel b$, where a and b are atomic actions. Note that according to both Lamport's definition and our last definition that takes temporal order into account, a nondeterministic interleaving $a ; b$ **or** $b ; a$ does *not* classify as an implementation of $a \parallel b$. (Our definitions do admit $a \cdot b$ **or** $b \cdot a$ as an implementation of $a \parallel b$ however).

Finally we remark that an interesting generalization could be to combine our implementation notion with the idea of abstraction mappings or retrieve functions. In fact one could say that we have defined implementation for a fixed abstraction mapping, where contraction plays the role of abstraction mapping.

6 Time critical systems

Finally we consider systems where temporal relations between events, possibly based on some "real-time" clock, have to be taken into account in order to ensure functional correctness of the system. That is, we are not so much interested in real-time as such, but rather in the interaction between real-time constraints and causal order among events.

To some extent such reasoning can be carried out already within the DL_3 formalism that we discussed before, which does not contain any real-time constructs. This seemingly paradoxical remark can be explained as follows. Proving functional correctness based on real-time properties can often be factorized in two stages:

- First, use real-time based reasoning to infer *temporal* ordering among certain (selected) actions.
- Second, forget about real-time and, based on the axioms that express the relationship between temporal and causal order, infer certain *causal* orderings among actions. The rest of the proof of functional correctness is then carried out on the basis of causality alone.

Now for a limited number of cases, like the SIMD example that we discussed above, it is possible to *directly* translate the relevant real-time constraints into temporal order that moreover can be expressed by means of the sequential composition operator. This proceeds as follows. A concurrent program R, is presented as a process of the form

$$R = P_0 \parallel P_1 \parallel \cdots \parallel P_n,$$

where each of the processes P_i is essentially the same sequential program P of the form $S_0 ; S_2 ; \cdots ; S_m$, where the process index i is allowed to occur in P. The assumption that the program will run on a SIMD ("Single Instruction Multiple Data") machine can be understood as a real-time constraint ensuring that all parallel processes run at the same speed. This latter statement concerning processor speed can be translated however into the assumption that the program is equivalent to a sequential composition of "layers", thus

$$R = L_0 ; L_1 ; \cdots ; L_m,$$

where layer L_j is defined as

$$L_j = S_j^0 \parallel S_j^1 \parallel \cdots \parallel S_j^n$$

Here S_j^i is the S_j component of P, where we have made the occurrences of the processor index i explicit. The layered representation now can be analyzed without concern for processor speed.

Apart from fully synchronized "lockstep" execution models, like the SIMD model, it is usually not possible to express real-time constraints by means of sequential composition. We now consider an extension of DL_3 that admits direct specification of timing constraints. Since we are aiming more at a specification and design language rather than a programming language we have chosen for a language construct that enforces execution of some component within a certain time interval. For a *programming language* this might be considered inappropriate as it is quite possible to specify contradictory timing constraints in this way. (Real-time programming languages often incorporate real-time by means of a "delay" construct, which has the virtue that it cannot compromise implementability.)

An important question for any real-time language is what model of time should be used. Obvious candidates are natural, rational or (really) real numbers. Such models all depart from the assumption that durationless moments are fundamental and that extended periods (intervals) are derived notions. It has been observed however [Rus26] [Kam79] that the reverse is also possible, i.e. one can take "intervals" as primitive notion and define "points" as ideal limits of maximal decreasing sequences of intervals. Note that intervals are only *partially* ordered, as opposed to, for instance, the reals. Therefore we will assume that we have some given *time structure* $(D, <)$ where "$<$" is an irreflexive partial order on D. Interesting examples of time structures include:

1. Intervals of the form $[x, y)$ where $x, y \in R$, and where R denotes the real numbers. The order is of course defined as follows:

   $$[x, y) < [u, v) \text{ iff } y \leq u.$$

2. $(R, <)$ $(R^+, <)$ or $(Q, <)$, or $(N, <)$ etc., where $<$ denotes the standard ordering for real, rational or natural numbers.

3. "Local clock" structures can be obtained from any time structure $(D, <)$ together with a given set of "locations" *Loc*. One simply defines the structure $(Loc \times D, <)$, where "$<$" is defined as follows:

   $$(l_1, d_1) < (l_2, d_2) \text{ iff } l_1 = l_2 \text{ and } d_1 < d_2.$$

4. Loosely synchronized local clocks ("ε synchronized clocks") can be modelled by structures of the form $(Loc \times R, \overset{+}{<})$ where

$$(l_1, t_1) \; < \; (l_2, t_2) \text{ iff } ((l_1 = l_2 \wedge t_1 < t_2) \text{ or } (t_1 + \varepsilon) < t_2),$$

where $\varepsilon \in R^+$ is some fixed positive real indicating the maximal difference that can occur between the readings off different clocks.

5. A variation of loosely synchronized clocks is to assume that (only) clocks that are physically close to each other will be synchronized within a ε margin as described above. This would be the case when some centralized clock periodically broadcasts synchronization signals to all local clocks; clocks that are remote from each other may receive the signal with significantly differing delays. We can model our assumptions as follows. Let ρ denote the distance function for local clocks. We then define time structures of the form $(Loc \times R, <)$ where

$$(l_1, t_1) \; < \; (l_2, t_2) \text{ iff } \rho(l_1, l_2) < \varepsilon_1 \text{ and } t_1 + \varepsilon_2 < t_2.$$

Here, ε_1 and ε_2 are fixed parameters of the model.

6. Departing from the idea that timing is often used to *synchronize* actions in the sense that some action b should not be executed before action a has occurred we can define a rather abstract (degenerated) time structure $(Sig, <)$ as follows.

$$Sig \; = \; \{wait(i), signal(i) \;\; | \;\; i \in N\}$$

and where the order is defined by $signal(i) \; < \; wait(i)$.

We now introduce our last process language DL_4. We assume that there is a given class *Dexp* of *interval expressions* d where d denotes some value in D, where $(D, <)$ is a given time structure. For simplicity we assume that the value of each expression d is statically determined, i.e. there is no dependence on program states, nor can d contain any free variables.

$$P \in DL_4,$$

$$P ::= l : b \& \mathbf{x} := \mathbf{f} \;\; | \;\; P \parallel Q \;\; | \;\; P \cdot Q \;\; | \;\; P \,;\, Q \;\; | \;\; P \textbf{ or } Q$$

$$| \;\; \textbf{skip} \;\; | \;\; \textbf{empty} \;\; | \;\; P \backslash x \;\; | \;\; \langle l : P \rangle$$

$$| \;\; \textbf{ref } l \textbf{ to } S \textbf{ in } P \;\; | \;\; \textbf{contr } l \textbf{ in } P \;\; | \;\; P \textbf{ at } d$$

New in DL_4 is the *process timing* or *scheduling construct* P **at** d. Intuitively this construct enforces execution of all P events within interval d. Moreover, the partial order on intervals induces extra temporal ordering on the events of a system that has several timed components. For instance, in process $(P \textbf{ at } [0:1] \,;\, Q) \parallel (R \cdot S \textbf{ at } [2:3])$ all P events temporally precede all Q events due to the sequential composition operator but also precede temporally all S events due to the timing constructs.

Timing constructs can be *nested*, in which case the outermost timing construct overrules the nested ones. *Refining* a timed action is no problem; all events for the refined action will have the same timing, that is, for **ref** l **to** S **in** $\cdots l : b \& \mathbf{x} := \mathbf{f}$ **at** $d \cdots$ the l labeled events are replaced by executions of $\langle l : S \rangle$ **at** d. Since we do not know how to contract differently timed events into a single one we impose a restriction on occurences of the timing construct inside a construct of the form **contr** l **in** P: Any occurrence of $\langle l : Q \rangle$ in P must either have no timing constructs occurring inside Q or else the whole atomic construct must occur itself inside the scope of a timing construct R **at** d, where R is a component of P. The effect of this somewhat complicated restriction is that either the Q events are not timed at all, or else they all have the same timing.
The semantics for DL_4 can be defined as a simple variation of the DL_3 semantics. We introduce a semantic domain $Comp_4$ of runs which is defined just like $Comp_3$ except that events can have a time attribute $time(e)$. The time attribute is assumed to be partial, that is, either $time(e)$ is not defined for e or else $time(e) \in D$. Moreover, $Comp_4$ runs are required to satisfy the following domain property. For a timed run $(E, \longrightarrow, \twoheadrightarrow)$ and events $e_0, e_1 \in E$ such that $time(e_0)$ and $time(e_1)$ are defined, we have that:

If $time(e_0) < time(e_1)$ then $e_0 \twoheadrightarrow e_1$.

The semantics of the timing construct is then straightforward:

$$[\![P \textbf{ at } d]\!] = [\![P]\!][time : d]$$

That is, the timing construct simply attaches a timestamp, in the form of an "interval" d, to each P event, possibly overruling timestamps attached for timed components of P. The semantics for parallel composition and layer composition must be adapted by taking into account extra temporal order due to timing constructs. We provide the details for parallel composition $P \parallel Q$. If both P and Q contain timed components then this might cause temporal order between P events and Q events, as required by the domain property introduced above for $Comp_4$. Due to transitivity this might cause temporal ordering between other (possibly untimed) events. Therefore we define:

$$\begin{aligned}
[\![P \parallel Q]\!] = \{ & Close((E_P \cup E_Q, \longrightarrow_P \cup \longrightarrow_Q \cup \longrightarrow_C, \twoheadrightarrow_P \cup \twoheadrightarrow_Q \cup \twoheadrightarrow_T)) \in Comp_4 \mid \\
& (E_P, \longrightarrow_P, \twoheadrightarrow_P) \in [\![P]\!], (E_Q, \longrightarrow_Q, \twoheadrightarrow_Q) \in [\![Q]\!], \\
& E_P \cap E_Q = \emptyset, atom(E_P) \cap atom(E_Q) = \emptyset, \longrightarrow_C \subseteq (E_P \cup E_Q)^2 \\
& \text{and where } \twoheadrightarrow_T \subseteq (E_P \cup E_Q)^2 \text{ is such that } e \twoheadrightarrow_T e' \text{ iff } time(e) < time(e') \}
\end{aligned}$$

The semantic definitions for contraction and refinement must be adapted. Due to the language constraints we need define contraction $contr((E, \longrightarrow, \twoheadrightarrow))$ only for the case that all events are either untimed or else they have a uniform timing d. So if $contr((E, \longrightarrow, \twoheadrightarrow))$ is the event e we let $time(e)$ be undefined or $time(e) = d$, whichever does apply. The definitions for general contraction and the semantics of the contraction construct can be taken over from the definition for DL_3. The semantics for refinement is a slight variation of the DL_3 semantics for that construct:

$[\![$ **ref** l **to** S **in** $P]\!]$ = the largest set X such that

- $contr(l, X) \subseteq [\![P]\!]$ and
- for any $\alpha \in Alabel$ such that there are events in X labeled by both l and α we have that

  $$(X|l, \alpha) \subseteq ([\![S]\!] \cap \textit{State-consistent})[atom : \alpha][label : l],$$

  if the events in runs of X are untimed, and

  $$(X|l, \alpha) \subseteq ([\![S]\!] \cap \textit{State-consistent})[atom : \alpha][label : l][time : d],$$

  where d is equal to $time(e)$ for any event e occurring in a run of X, if the events in X runs are timed.

We conclude with an example of a design of a parallel sorting program for an systolic array architecture. We assume that such a systolic array consists of a number of cells that are synchronized by broadcasting clock signals from a centralized clock. It is assumed that for neighbour cells the signal arrives within a reasonably small time interval, so that we can use a time structure as described above as example (5).

systolic_sort $= Cel_0 \parallel Cel_1 \parallel \cdots \parallel Cel_n$,

where Cel_i is as follows:

L_0^i ;

do

$(L_1^i ; L_2^i ; L_3^i ; L_4^i ; L_5^i ; L_6^i)$,

od

and where the components L_j^i are as follows:

$L_0^i = (R_1^i, R_2^i) := (-\infty, -\infty)$

$L_1^i = B^i := (R_1^i > R_2^i)$

$L_2^i =$ **if** B^i **then** $Buf_i := R_1^i$ **else** $Buf_i := R_2^i$ **fi**

$L_3^i =$ **if** B^i **then** $R_1^i := Buf_{i-1}$ **else** $R_2^i := Buf_{i-1}$

$L_4^i = B^i := (R_1^i > R_2^i)$

$L_5^i =$ **if** B^i **then** $Buf_{i-1} := R_1^i$ **else** $Buf_{i-1} := R_2^i$ **fi**

$L_6^i =$ **if** B^i **then** $R_1^i := Buf_i$ **else** $R_2^i := Buf_i$ **fi**

The **do** – **od** construct denotes an infinite loop. Formally speaking we did not introduce loops for our process languages; however, for the present purpose we need to analyse only the body of this loop which is a proper DL_4 process:

$(L_1^i ; L_2^i ; L_3^i ; L_4^i ; L_5^i ; L_6^i)$,

The correctness of this type of sorting networks is well studied, for instance in [Zwi89]. The present version is special since its correctness depends on timing. If we could assume the "lockstep" execution model as introduced above, the correctness of the algorithm could be easily shown, relying on verification techniques for purely sequential programs. For in that case we could describe the system as follows:

L_0 ;

od

$(L_1 \,;\, L_2 \,;\, L_3 \,;\, L_4 \,;\, L_5 \,;\, L_6)$

od

where layer L_j is the following:

$$L_j \;=\; L_j^0 \parallel L_j^1 \parallel \cdots \parallel L_j^n.$$

Note that the processes in the last parallel composition operate on disjoint variables and so are independent. That implies IO-equivalence with layers in the form of sequential processes thus:

$$L_j \;=\; L_j^0 \,;\, L_j^1 \,;\, \cdots \,;\, L_j^n.$$

Next we want to show correctness of the sorting network under a weaker assumption than "lockstep execution", relying only on loosely synchronized clocks for neighbour cells. This assumption is modelled by a time structure of the form $(N \times D, \overset{+}{<})$ where $(D, <)$ is the real-time interval time structure of example (1). A value $(i, [x : y))$ is interpreted as an interval $[x : y)$ on the clock reading for cell i. The order on these local intervals is:

$$(i, [x : y)) \;<\; (j, [u : v)) \text{ iff } (|i - j| = 1 \text{ and } y + \varepsilon \leq u), \text{ or } (i = j \text{ and } y \leq u).$$

We use this time structure as the basis for the following timed version of the loop body for cell i, and their parallel composition:

$TC_i \;=$

L_1^i **at** $(i, [0 : 1]) \cdot$

L_2^i **at** $(i, [1 : 2 - \varepsilon]) \cdot$

L_3^i **at** $(i, [2 : 3]) \cdot$

L_4^i **at** $(i, [3 : 4]) \cdot$

L_5^i **at** $(i, [4 : 5 - \varepsilon]) \cdot$

L_6^i **at** $(i, [5 : 6])$

$TS \;=$

$TC_0 \parallel TC_1 \parallel \cdots \parallel T_n.$

A timing of the form L_1^i **at** $(i, [0:1]$ informally indicates that L_1^i executes within time interval $[0:1]$, as clocked by cell i. Timings as indicated can be achieved in practice by executing one stage as soon as a synchronization signal is received. Moreover, the intervals as indicated can be understood as specifications of the *maximal* execution time for a certain stage. Note that (only) for a few cases we assume that the duration of some stage is sufficiently short that an ε *delay* between execution of two successive stages is *guaranteed*.

Let us compare the parallel composition TS of the TC_i processes with the following layered version:

$$TL =$$

$$(TL_1 \cdot TL_2 \cdot TL_3 \cdot TL_4 \cdot TL_5 \cdot TL_6)$$

where the "timed" layer TL_j is the following:

$$TL_j = TL_j^0 \parallel TL_j^1 \parallel \cdots \parallel TL_j^n.$$

The functional behaviour of this layered version TL is the same as that of the loop body of the "lockstep" program that we discussed above; in fact we do not need the timing to show its correctness. What we claim however is that the TS process is (semantically) equal to the layered version TL, and so, that the functional behaviour of TS is also correct. (Which is what we are aiming at). The equality of TS and TL depends crucially on timing; if we strip off all timing constructs equality does no longer hold and in fact the stripped TS program would be incorrect. Now to prove the equality, we consider the conflicts that are present between actions in different layers. As a representative case we consider the composition $TL_2 \cdot TL_3$. We notice that the conflicts that are relevant here are *local* in the sense that L_2^i conflicts with L_3^i, because of access to the variable R_1^i or R_2^i, and between l_2^i and l_3^{i+1}, because of access to the buffer variable Buf_i. Now, due to our assumptions concerning the synchronization of local clocks we see that L_2^i **at** $(i, [1:2-\varepsilon])$ and L_3^{i+1} **at** $(i+1, [2:3])$ are timewise ordered and thus temporally ordered, that is, we may infer that L_2^i **at** $(i, [1:2-\varepsilon]) \twoheadrightarrow L_3^{i+1}$ **at** $(i+1, [2:3])$. But then the causal order between the two actions must be in the same direction, due to the axioms relating causal and temporal order. The conclusion is that L_2^i **at** $(i, [1:2-\varepsilon])$ and L_3^{i+1} **at** $(i+1, [2:3])$ are causally ordered in TS just as in TL. This concludes our proof.

7 Conclusion

We have discussed the relation and interaction between *time* and *causality* for a sequence of increasingly more powerful languages for the specification and design of concurrent processes. It has been shown how principles such as "layering" can help in the design of processes. Real-time constraints have been introduced as a means to synchronize actions, and to extend the design methodology based on layering to time critical systems where causality alone is not sufficient to explain the correctness of those systems.

References

[ABDM90] U. Abraham, S. Ben-Davis, and M. Magidor. On global-time and inter-process communication. In Thomas, Kwiatkowska, Shields, editors, *Semantics for Concurrency, Leicester 1990*, pages 311–323, 1990.

[Ang99] F.D. Anger. On lamport's interprocess communication model. *ACM TOPLAS*, 11:404–417, 1989.

[BHG87] P.A. Bernstein, V. Hadzilacos, and N. Goodman. *Concurrency Control and Recovery in Database Systems.* Addison-Wesley, 1987.

[EF82] Elrad and N. Francez. Decomposition of distributed programs into communication closed layers. *Science of Computer Programming*, 2, 1982.

[JPZ91] W. Janssen, M. Poel, and J. Zwiers. Action systems and action refinement in the development of parallel systems. In *Proc. of CONCUR '91, Springer LNCS 527*, pages 298–316. Springer-Verlag, 1991.

[Kam79] H. Kamp. Instants, events and temporal discourse. In R. Bauerle at al., editor, *Semantics From Different Points of View*, pages 376–417. Springer, Berlin, 1979.

[Lam86] L. Lamport. On interprocess communication, part I: Basic formalism. *Distributed Computing*, 1:77–101, 1986.

[Rus26] B. Russell. *Our Knowledge of the External World.* Allen & Unwin, London, 1926.

[vGG89] R. J. van Glabbeek and U. Goltz. Equivalence notions for concurrent systems and refinement of actions. Technical Report 366, Arbeitspapiere der GMD, 1989.

[Wie14] N. Wiener. A contribution to the theory of relative position. *Proc. Camb. Philos. Soc.*, 17:441–449, 1914.

[Zwi89] J. Zwiers. *Compositionality, Concurrency and Partial Correctness.* Springer LNCS 321, 1989.

Lecture Notes in Computer Science

For information about Vols. 1–535
please contact your bookseller or Springer-Verlag

Vol. 536: J. E. Tomayko, Software Engineering Education. Proceedings, 1991. VIII, 296 pages. 1991.

Vol. 537: A. J. Menezes, S. A. Vanstone (Eds.), Advances in Cryptology – CRYPTO '90. Proceedings. XIII, 644 pages. 1991.

Vol. 538: M. Kojima, N. Megiddo, T. Noma, A. Yoshise, A Unified Approach to Interior Point Algorithms for Linear Complementarity Problems. VIII, 108 pages. 1991.

Vol. 539: H. F. Mattson, T. Mora, T. R. N. Rao (Eds.), Applied Algebra, Algebraic Algorithms and Error-Correcting Codes. Proceedings, 1991. XI, 489 pages. 1991.

Vol. 540: A. Prieto (Ed.), Artificial Neural Networks. Proceedings, 1991. XIII, 476 pages. 1991.

Vol. 541: P. Barahona, L. Moniz Pereira, A. Porto (Eds.), EPIA '91. Proceedings, 1991. VIII, 292 pages. 1991. (Subseries LNAI).

Vol. 542: Z. W. Ras, M. Zemankova (Eds.), Methodologies for Intelligent Systems. Proceedings, 1991. X, 644 pages. 1991. (Subseries LNAI).

Vol. 543: J. Dix, K. P. Jantke, P. H. Schmitt (Eds.), Nonmonotonic and Inductive Logic. Proceedings, 1990. X, 243 pages. 1991. (Subseries LNAI).

Vol. 544: M. Broy, M. Wirsing (Eds.), Methods of Programming. XII, 268 pages. 1991.

Vol. 545: H. Alblas, B. Melichar (Eds.), Attribute Grammars , Applications and Systems. Proceedings, 1991. IX, 513 pages. 1991.

Vol. 546: O. Herzog, C.-R. Rollinger (Eds.), Text Understanding in LILOG. XI, 738 pages. 1991. (Subseries LNAI).

Vol. 547: D. W. Davies (Ed.), Advances in Cryptology – EUROCRYPT '91. Proceedings, 1991. XII, 556 pages. 1991.

Vol. 548: R. Kruse, P. Siegel (Eds.), Symbolic and Quantitative Approaches to Uncertainty. Proceedings, 1991. XI, 362 pages. 1991.

Vol. 549: E. Ardizzone, S. Gaglio, F. Sorbello (Eds.), Trends in Artificial Intelligence. Proceedings, 1991. XIV, 479 pages. 1991. (Subseries LNAI).

Vol. 550: A. van Lamsweerde, A. Fugetta (Eds.), ESEC '91. Proceedings, 1991. XII, 515 pages. 1991.

Vol. 551:S. Prehn, W. J. Toetenel (Eds.), VDM '91. Formal Software Development Methods. Volume 1. Proceedings, 1991. XIII, 699 pages. 1991.

Vol. 552: S. Prehn, W. J. Toetenel (Eds.), VDM '91. Formal Software Development Methods. Volume 2. Proceedings, 1991. XIV, 430 pages. 1991.

Vol. 553: H. Bieri, H. Noltemeier (Eds.), Computational Geometry - Methods, Algorithms and Applications '91. Proceedings, 1991. VIII, 320 pages. 1991.

Vol. 554: G. Grahne, The Problem of Incomplete Information in Relational Databases. VIII, 156 pages. 1991.

Vol. 555: H. Maurer (Ed.), New Results and New Trends in Computer Science. Proceedings, 1991. VIII, 403 pages. 1991.

Vol. 556: J.-M. Jacquet, Conclog: A Methodological Approach to Concurrent Logic Programming. XII, 781 pages. 1991.

Vol. 557: W. L. Hsu, R. C. T. Lee (Eds.), ISA '91 Algorithms. Proceedings, 1991. X, 396 pages. 1991.

Vol. 558: J. Hooman, Specification and Compositional Verification of Real-Time Systems. VIII, 235 pages. 1991.

Vol. 559: G. Butler, Fundamental Algorithms for Permutation Groups. XII, 238 pages. 1991.

Vol. 560: S. Biswas, K. V. Nori (Eds.), Foundations of Software Technology and Theoretical Computer Science. Proceedings, 1991. X, 420 pages. 1991.

Vol. 561: C. Ding, G. Xiao, W. Shan, The Stability Theory of Stream Ciphers. IX, 187 pages. 1991.

Vol. 562: R. Breu, Algebraic Specification Techniques in Object Oriented Programming Environments. XI, 228 pages. 1991.

Vol. 563: A. Karshmer, J. Nehmer (Eds.), Operating Systems of the 90s and Beyond. Proceedings, 1991. X, 285 pages. 1991.

Vol. 564: I. Herman, The Use of Projective Geometry in Computer Graphics. VIII, 146 pages. 1992.

Vol. 565: J. D. Becker, I. Eisele, F. W. Mündemann (Eds.), Parallelism, Learning, Evolution. Proceedings, 1989. VIII, 525 pages. 1991. (Subseries LNAI).

Vol. 566: C. Delobel, M. Kifer, Y. Masunaga (Eds.), Deductive and Object-Oriented Databases. Proceedings, 1991. XV, 581 pages. 1991.

Vol. 567: H. Boley, M. M. Richter (Eds.), Processing Declarative Kowledge. Proceedings, 1991. XII, 427 pages. 1991. (Subseries LNAI).

Vol. 568: H.-J. Bürckert, A Resolution Principle for a Logic with Restricted Quantifiers. X, 116 pages. 1991. (Subseries LNAI).

Vol. 569: A. Beaumont, G. Gupta (Eds.), Parallel Execution of Logic Programs. Proceedings, 1991. VII, 195 pages. 1991.

Vol. 570: R. Berghammer, G. Schmidt (Eds.), Graph-Theoretic Concepts in Computer Science. Proceedings, 1991. VIII, 253 pages. 1992.

Vol. 571: J. Vytopil (Ed.), Formal Techniques in Real-Time and Fault-Tolerant Systems. Proceedings, 1992. IX, 620 pages. 1991.

Vol. 572: K. U. Schulz (Ed.), Word Equations and Related Topics. Proceedings, 1990. VII, 256 pages. 1992.

Vol. 573: G. Cohen, S. N. Litsyn, A. Lobstein, G. Zémor (Eds.), Algebraic Coding. Proceedings, 1991. X, 158 pages. 1992.

Vol. 574: J. P. Banâtre, D. Le Métayer (Eds.), Research Directions in High-Level Parallel Programming Languages. Proceedings, 1991. VIII, 387 pages. 1992.

Vol. 575: K. G. Larsen, A. Skou (Eds.), Computer Aided Verification. Proceedings, 1991. X, 487 pages. 1992.

Vol. 576: J. Feigenbaum (Ed.), Advances in Cryptology - CRYPTO '91. Proceedings. X, 485 pages. 1992.

Vol. 577: A. Finkel, M. Jantzen (Eds.), STACS 92. Proceedings, 1992. XIV, 621 pages. 1992.

Vol. 578: Th. Beth, M. Frisch, G. J. Simmons (Eds.), Public-Key Cryptography: State of the Art and Future Directions. XI, 97 pages. 1992.

Vol. 579: S. Toueg, P. G. Spirakis, L. Kirousis (Eds.), Distributed Algorithms. Proceedings, 1991. X, 319 pages. 1992.

Vol. 580: A. Pirotte, C. Delobel, G. Gottlob (Eds.), Advances in Database Technology – EDBT '92. Proceedings. XII, 551 pages. 1992.

Vol. 581: J.-C. Raoult (Ed.), CAAP '92. Proceedings. VIII, 361 pages. 1992.

Vol. 582: B. Krieg-Brückner (Ed.), ESOP '92. Proceedings. VIII, 491 pages. 1992.

Vol. 583: I. Simon (Ed.), LATIN '92. Proceedings. IX, 545 pages. 1992.

Vol. 584: R. E. Zippel (Ed.), Computer Algebra and Parallelism. Proceedings, 1990. IX, 114 pages. 1992.

Vol. 585: F. Pichler, R. Moreno Díaz (Eds.), Computer Aided System Theory – EUROCAST '91. Proceedings. X, 761 pages. 1992.

Vol. 586: A. Cheese, Parallel Execution of Parlog. IX, 184 pages. 1992.

Vol. 587: R. Dale, E. Hovy, D. Rösner, O. Stock (Eds.), Aspects of Automated Natural Language Generation. Proceedings, 1992. VIII, 311 pages. 1992. (Subseries LNAI).

Vol. 588: G. Sandini (Ed.), Computer Vision – ECCV '92. Proceedings. XV, 909 pages. 1992.

Vol. 589: U. Banerjee, D. Gelernter, A. Nicolau, D. Padua (Eds.), Languages and Compilers for Parallel Computing. Proceedings, 1991. IX, 419 pages. 1992.

Vol. 590: B. Fronhöfer, G. Wrightson (Eds.), Parallelization in Inference Systems. Proceedings, 1990. VIII, 372 pages. 1992. (Subseries LNAI).

Vol. 591: H. P. Zima (Ed.), Parallel Computation. Proceedings, 1991. IX, 451 pages. 1992.

Vol. 592: A. Voronkov (Ed.), Logic Programming. Proceedings, 1991. IX, 514 pages. 1992. (Subseries LNAI).

Vol. 593: P. Loucopoulos (Ed.), Advanced Information Systems Engineering. Proceedings. XI, 650 pages. 1992.

Vol. 594: B. Monien, Th. Ottmann (Eds.), Data Structures and Efficient Algorithms. VIII, 389 pages. 1992.

Vol. 595: M. Levene, The Nested Universal Relation Database Model. X, 177 pages. 1992.

Vol. 596: L.-H. Eriksson, L. Hallnäs, P. Schroeder-Heister (Eds.), Extensions of Logic Programming. Proceedings, 1991. VII, 369 pages. 1992. (Subseries LNAI).

Vol. 597: H. W. Guesgen, J. Hertzberg, A Perspective of Constraint-Based Reasoning. VIII, 123 pages. 1992. (Subseries LNAI).

Vol. 598: S. Brookes, M. Main, A. Melton, M. Mislove, D. Schmidt (Eds.), Mathematical Foundations of Programming Semantics. Proceedings, 1991. VIII, 506 pages. 1992.

Vol. 599: Th. Wetter, K.-D. Althoff, J. Boose, B. R. Gaines, M. Linster, F. Schmalhofer (Eds.), Current Developments in Knowledge Acquisition - EKAW '92. Proceedings. XIII, 444 pages. 1992. (Subseries LNAI).

Vol. 600: J. W. de Bakker, C. Huizing, W. P. de Roever, G. Rozenberg (Eds.), Real-Time: Theory in Practice. Proceedings, 1991. VIII, 723 pages. 1992.

Vol. 601: D. Dolev, Z. Galil, M. Rodeh (Eds.), Theory of Computing and Systems. Proceedings, 1992. VIII, 220 pages. 1992.

Vol. 602: I. Tomek (Ed.), Computer Assisted Learning. Proceedigs, 1992. X, 615 pages. 1992.

Vol. 603: J. van Katwijk (Ed.), Ada: Moving Towards 2000. Proceedings, 1992. VIII, 324 pages. 1992.

Vol. 604: F. Belli, F.-J. Radermacher (Eds.), Industrial and Engineering Applications of Artificial Intelligence and Expert Systems. Proceedings, 1992. XV, 702 pages. 1992. (Subseries LNAI).

Vol. 605: D. Etiemble, J.-C. Syre (Eds.), PARLE '92. Parallel Architectures and Languages Europe. Proceedings, 1992. XVII, 984 pages. 1992.

Vol. 606: D. E. Knuth, Axioms and Hulls. IX, 109 pages. 1992.

Vol. 607: D. Kapur (Ed.), Automated Deduction – CADE-11. Proceedings, 1992. XV, 793 pages. 1992. (Subseries LNAI).

Vol. 608: C. Frasson, G. Gauthier, G. I. McCalla (Eds.), Intelligent Tutoring Systems. Proceedings, 1992. XIV, 686 pages. 1992.

Vol. 609: G. Rozenberg (Ed.), Advances in Petri Nets 1992. VIII, 472 pages. 1992.

Vol. 610: F. von Martial, Coordinating Plans of Autonomous Agents. XII, 246 pages. 1992. (Subseries LNAI).

Vol. 612: M. Tokoro, O. Nierstrasz, P. Wegner (Eds.), Object-Based Concurrent Computing. Proceedings, 1991. X, 265 pages. 1992.

Vol. 613: J. P. Myers, Jr., M. J. O'Donnell (Eds.), Constructivity in Computer Science. Proceedings, 1991. X, 247 pages. 1992.

Vol. 614: R. G. Herrtwich (Ed.), Network and Operating System Support for Digital Audio and Video. Proceedings, 1991. XII, 403 pages. 1992.

Vol. 615: O. Lehrmann Madsen (Ed.), ECOOP '92. European Conference on Object Oriented Programming. Proceedings. X, 426 pages. 1992.

Vol. 616: K. Jensen (Ed.), Application and Theory of Petri Nets 1992. Proceedings, 1992. VIII, 398 pages. 1992.

Vol. 617: V. Mařík, O. Štěpánková, R. Trappl (Eds.), Advanced Topics in Artificial Intelligence. Proceedings, 1992. IX, 484 pages. 1992. (Subseries LNAI).

Vol. 618: P. M. D. Gray, R. J. Lucas (Eds.), Advanced Database Systems. Proceedings, 1992. X, 260 pages. 1992.

Vol. 620: A. Nerode, M. Taitslin (Eds.), Logical Foundations of Computer Science – Tver '92. Proceedings. IX, 514 pages. 1992.

Vol. 621: O. Nurmi, E. Ukkonen (Eds.), Algorithm Theory – SWAT '92. Proceedings. VIII, 434 pages. 1992.

Vol. 623: W. Kuich (Ed.), Automata, Languages and Programming. Proceedings, 1992. XII, 721 pages. 1992.